"EGOISM VERSUS EGOISM.—How many are there who still come to the conclusion: "Life would be intolerable were there no God!" Or, as is said in idealistic circles: "Life would be intolerable if its ethical signification were lacking." Hence there must be a God—or an ethical signification of existence! In reality the case stands thus: He who is accustomed to conceptions of this sort does not desire a life without them, hence these conceptions are necessary for him and his preservation—but what a presumption it is to assert that everything necessary for my preservation must exist in reality! As if my preservation were really necessary! What if others held the contrary opinion? if they did not care to live under the conditions of these two articles of faith, and did not regard life as worth living if they were realised!—And that is the present position of affairs." - Friedrich Nietzsche, From *The Dawn of the Day, Aphorism 90*. Translated by J. M. Kennedy.

Table of Contents

Preface . . . *Page IV*

Chapter 1: Conventional Religion . . . *Page 1*

Chapter 2: Asceticism and Rationality . . . *Page 28*

Chapter 3: The Afterlife . . . *Page 41*

Chapter 4: Open Interpretation and Coherence . . . *Page 52*

Chapter 5: Gender Roles . . . *Page 70*

Part II: The Specific Issues

    A. Original Sin

Chapter 6: Original Sin, The Failure of Abrahamic Morality . . . *Page 99*

Chapter 7: Free Will and Original Sin . . . *Page 132*

    B. Judaism

Chapter 8: Judaism . . . *Page 152*

Chapter 9: Zionism versus Free Speech . . . *Page 161*

Chapter 10: Judaism versus Archaeology . . . *Page 193*

Chapter 11: Judaism versus Human Rights . . . *Page 209*

Chapter 12: Concluding Remarks on Judaism . . . *Page 251*

    C. Christianity

Chapter 13: Christianity . . . *Page 281*

Chapter 14: Critiquing Christ . . . *Page 291*

Chapter 15: Reductionist Insight And Regressive Morality . . . *Page 321*

Chapter 16: The Narcissism of Jesus Christ . . . *Page 337*

Chapter 17: Ignorance Within Bliss . . . *Page 360*

Chapter 18: Biblical Contradictions versus Jesus Christ . . . *Page 370*

Chapter 19: The Misogyny of Christ . . . *Page 398*

   D. Islam

Chapter 20: Islam . . . *Page 404*

Chapter 21: Isa . . . *Page 429*

Chapter 22: Holistic Purity . . . *Page 436*

Chapter 23: A Tool of Anti-Intellectualism . . . *Page 454*

Chapter 24: The Follies of Islam . . . *Page 492*

Chapter 25: Intersectional Feminism versus Islam's Patriarchy . . . *Page 539*

   E. Sanatana Dharma

Chapter 26: Buddhism . . . *Page 569*

Chapter 27: Hinduism . . . *Page 608*

Chapter 28: Casteism versus Truthseeking . . . *Page 636*

Chapter 29: The Insights of Sanatana Dharma . . . *Page 700*

The Conclusion: The Transvaluation of Values . . . *Page 733*

Bibliography . . . *Page 771*

Further Reading . . . *Page 820*

Author's Influences . . . *Page 822*

About the Author . . . *Page 822*

Copyright Notice . . . *Page 822*

Preface

Instead of the usual copied and pasted thanks given to people you've never heard of, I would like to give my sincerest thanks to you. Dear reader, thank you for taking the time to read this book. Believe it or not, it means a lot to an author when even just a single individual takes a genuine interest in their work. Thank you so much.

Who This Book Is Primarily For: I attempted to design this book for those who are open to questioning their religious faith, religious or atheistic debaters who may want a greater breadth of material to critique religious or atheist arguments respectively, for agnostics and atheists who are interested in the possible psychological and social reasons for religious faith, for those who want to challenge proselytizers of the Abrahamic religious faiths with criticisms, and for devout religious people who want to understand why atheists exist and what psychological and moral arguments compel atheists to leave religion. I've found that too many atheist books focus heavily on science as the reason why they leave religion and not enough on the fallacious reasoning of various religions. The primary purpose of this book is to question religious assumptions about the world and to consider why skeptical inquiry would be far more valuable in your everyday life. That is, this book isn't just about why the atheist perspective views religion as false, but also adds the anti-theist perspective of why religion is actively harmful. Not all atheists are against religion, but this book attempts to argue why they should be and why theists should give up on their theism. It would be better to form a new purpose for your life without superstitious beliefs. This book focuses on the major religious faiths of the world; the Abrahamic faiths of Judaism, Christianity, and Islam and the Dharmic faiths of Buddhism and Hinduism.

Special Notice: I had intended to make this into a 3-part book with Part I as the General Issues of religion, Part II as Specific Issues of the Major Religions, and a Part III meant for the historic consequences of human violence due to beliefs in the Major Religions. However, I eventually realized it wouldn't be possible due to the length of the book during my 4 years of writing it. Thus, I've opted to make *Faith in Doubt* into a series. This book contains Part I and Part II of the originally intentioned 3-Part book. I don't have any timeframe for the next book at the moment, I don't know how long it'll be compared to this book, and I may have to break it into a longer series depending on its length. I wanted to be as transparent as possible about this issue to avoid confusing readers.

This Book Is My Personal Tribute To: *Armin Navabi, Chris Hedges, Sam Harris, Ridvan Aydemir, Richard Dawkins, a bunch of Ancient People approximately between the 800 BCE to 500 BCE Era, Sarah Haider, The Vlogbrothers, Muhammad Syed, Laci Green, Julia Galef, Friedrich Nietzsche, all of my close friends, and the late and great Christopher Hitchens.*

Chapter 1: Conventional Religion

On October 11th, 2016 at 5 P.M. as I had just finished the week of training for my new job at a call center, I had noticed cars going insanely fast, I suspect it was roughly 70 to 80 miles per hour on a 40 miles per hour local street, and I felt worried but believed that so long as I was careful then I'd be fine crossing the street. As I crossed after looking both ways, a car moved straight towards me at a berserk pace and only began slowing down a few paces just before the smashing impact on my driver side door. I had turned my neck in time to see the car smash onto my car door and into me. Immediate pain shot through the left side of my body. My car was hurled into a local parking lot and crashed onto the passenger side of a van after careening past the foliage of bushes. I never found out what happened to the other driver, although I heard a police officer state that he claimed to have had a heart attack.

When the impact happened; there was no flashing of my most memorable life experiences as shown in US television sit-coms, there was no thoughts in my mind of any God immediately after surviving the impact, and I felt a sense of detachment to my own bodily pain as I reflected on what just happened. Within the scope of my mind, the near-death experience elicited two focal regrets: the regret of not having written a Harry Potter fanfic that I had meant to write to completion but had never even began and the regret of not having finished the Bonds Route of *Shin Megami Tensei IV: Apocalypse*, which is a 3DS Japanese role-playing video game that I loved but hadn't finished the second route of at the time. It seems silly, but those were my most immediate thoughts. The thoughts following from those regrets were more personal: the fear I would die or be physically incapacitated before being able to do either of those activities bothered me. Oddly enough, as I thought of those activities, my immediate reflections of my personal beliefs was this strange frame of mind in which I felt detached from myself, but paradoxically, I felt my strong sense of atheism and belief in certain parts of Friedrich Nietzsche's philosophy increase exponentially in the immediate aftermath. I felt what I had questioned to be a strange, dismal, and counterintuitive belief in the ancient atheistic branch of Hinduism more affirmed than ever before the crash.

I had previously believed, before this near-death experience, that I would be clinging to a belief in a higher power when faced with such a horrific event because I saw myself as weak and malleable to nonsensical delusions in times of true suffering, but instead no such belief in a higher power or a God ever came about after suffering through a near-death experience. Neither immediately after the crash nor later on at the hospital or even in the weeks and months that followed. It genuinely surprised me in the aftermath of the crash that I felt no compulsion to believe in any such higher power, because I thought for sure that in times of desperation that I would prove to myself that I was weak and needed ignorant delusions to feel safe since I was only human. Yet, it never happened. My strengths in my beliefs; the atheistic variant of Hinduism, my penchant for Nietzschean philosophical beliefs, and my personal dreams were what I felt strongly attune to in the wake of the near-death experience. It hadn't radically changed my life as pop culture is wont to depict of such events, it just made my prior philosophical and scientifically inclined beliefs stronger.

I became disillusioned by the fact my family's car insurance company, Geico, hadn't done any real work with finding out who was at fault for the accident and because there was no third-party witness, they wouldn't put any value on my side of the story. The police did not either and even incorrectly placed my father's name as the driver, even after I had physically handed them my driver's license. Thus, Geico simply labeled me culpable because it was easier for them than doing any real work in helping me with my situation. They didn't consider my pain and suffering, they just saw me as another nameless and faceless commodity that they needed to clear the paperwork of as quickly as their disorganized business model would allow. Any questions or concerns I had while I was in physical pain was met with mockery and derision by Geico staff on the phone. They immediately demanded that I get off their insurance policy a month after going to physical therapy and questioned why I needed it, even after the doctor noted the dislocation in my neck and the physical therapists noted the partial immobility on the knee that had been impacted in the crash. All of the paperwork documenting these facts had already been sent to them by the physical therapy clinic that I was going to for treatment. Due to their lack of doing any real paperwork, they demanded I resubmit the information to verify and threatened to cut the program and footing me the bills despite the fact my father had coverage that insured it was fully paid. Overall, I learned the hard way that saving car insurance on televised commercials meant a disorganized entity would mock any horrifying suffering you go through, potentially what your children could go through, and that they genuinely don't care whether you live or die so long as they can save costs since that was their entire business model. I can only speak from my own experience, but if you want your children mocked upon suffering a horrifying car crash with life-threatening injuries so they can relive the trauma, then Geico is definitely for you. They genuinely won't care what you or your loved ones suffer upon being on the receiving end of an accident regardless of how brutal the injuries are and won't do any work to prove your case because they only value you for your money and don't care about your life. Not that what I say will matter, predatory companies like Geico will always find some way to stay afloat and harm the public while making funny commercials to give them a sense of ease. The ignorance of the US public will always be met with the savage assault by the powerful government institutions and businesses of the United States.

While that may seem emotionally charged, it's important to place blame where it is deserved to avoid following nihilistic patterns of behavior whereby a person blames "reality" or "society" or themselves under the perception they're uniquely stupid and thus too dumb to do anything productive after suffering a tragedy. I did struggle with such notions, but fortunately, a quote from one of Nietzsche's philosophical books helped relieve some of the tension. To paraphrase, the philosophical aphorism simply states an obvious truth in a more insightful manner: that it isn't the world that makes us depressed, angry, or imposes suffering upon us; but rather, the human world that enforces this upon us. The man who sped in a 40 mph roadway at what I suspect to be 70-80 mph before forcing the breaks just before their car collided with my driver door was using a man-made object that nearly killed me and caused lifelong neck pain as a direct result of the impact, but the car I was using opened up side airbags to reduce the physical damage so that my knees, head, and sternum weren't permanently damaged from the impact. Should I thank a specific deity for that, as most religious people in that situation likely would? No, because just as we should place equal responsibility on that which harms us, we should place equal responsibility on those who help us whether from the past or the present. Just as it is man-made inventiveness and laws that harmed me, it is man-made human ingenuity and inventiveness that created the side-impact airbags that softened the impact upon my body and prevented any further injuries beyond my neck suffering from a dislocated hernia and quite possibly precluded my death. I'd like to take a moment to thank the Swedish researchers and engineers who created the side-impact airbags in 1994 for saving my life. Your contribution to consumer safety has my utmost gratitude as I may not have been alive today, if not for your hard work and concern for road safety. Additionally, the Honda car company has my thanks for adding such car safety measures on the car my family purchased, and the physical therapy clinic for giving me treatment. I will happily thank all of those people who made such important decisions with respect to public safety, but thanking a deity is utterly inconsequential to the positives and negatives of what happened to me.

If I were to thank any Goddess or God surviving the accident, should I also thank them for causing the accident? Should I simply praise them for an experience, simply because I had no choice but to go through the experience? Should the reality of my experience necessitate that I praise a deity in gratitude? If a God is responsible for my survival, then surely they're also responsible for causing the situation in the first place? Irrespective of whether a demonic figure exists to direct evil in the world, or even if human sin, bad karma, or freewill exists; surely the origin point of my experience would have to be a deity willingly and knowingly formulating the terrible occurrence beforehand and then causing the event? If it were not so, then certain religious believers would be wrong in claiming that their God is all-knowing, omnipotent, and has a plan. So then, such a deity would be deserving of blame and praise for any experience a human being goes through in equal proportions regardless of how negative or positive the experience is.

Religion is commonly defended by our personal experiences in life. People often use anecdotes to defend their beliefs and usually say that they have faith that their life will improve through belief in God. Being positive is argued as a reason for why a particular religious faith is true and the majority of people use faith as a guidepost for everyday activities. This creates a convoluted and harmful standard that people live under but don't recognize. As a consequence, many people don't give much consideration to religion because they feel it is normal. It is no different than observing the harmful effects of believing in the lucky chance of winning the lottery. People who play the lottery and have faith in the belief of good fortune often don't give any consideration to the detrimental effects of their gambling habit and they don't consider the real mathematical odds of being the winner. They make false assumptions about the likelihood because they're unable to differentiate the relative and absolute values of winning the lottery. For example, let us say there are 60 different possible combinations of numbers on a set of ten numbers in a ticket and the winning combination is 1234560789. What are the odds of winning the lottery by that combination of tickets?

Shocking as this may seem, the winning odds are determined by the number of possible combinations of the ticket. Thus, because there are sixty possible combinations at the start, the actual chances of winning are 60 x 59 x 58 x 57 . . . and so forth. The only winning ticket is 1234560789 so every other combination from 1-60 will lead to a waste of your money. With respect to a real life lottery in the US. your chance of winning the Powerball is around 1 in 292 million for any set of combinations as of 2016.[1] The population of the US is around 320 million and the population of the largest US State is California which has approximately 38 million residents. Hypothetically, if Powerball operated exclusively in California and all the people in California bought one Powerball ticket, then there would only be a 13 percent chance of any individual Californian getting the winning ticket and an 87 percent chance that nobody in the State would win. If every Californian – from infant to adult – bought seven tickets each then only a single person among them would win the Powerball lottery. A single lottery gambler within the US buying more tickets won't change this fact or strengthen the odds to any significant degree, even in the context of the Powerball being bought throughout the US. This is because even purchasing an absurd number of tickets such as 2000 tickets would only result in a 0.0000069 percent chance of winning. For readers who purchase lottery tickets; please compare the combinations of real life tickets that you know of. Count the possible combinations of each set of numbers or – in some cases – just look at the back of the ticket where it explains the odds of winning. Usually, the lottery ticket combinations exceed the amount of people living within the State by a wide margin. Now, consider the odds written on your lottery tickets with the amount of people in your local county. Please keep in mind, the amount of times you play, how old you are, and what special meaning is absolutely inconsequential to the total combinations of numbers that are possible. What matters is the combination of numbers and placing personal attachment to a specific sequence of numbers – like a child's birthday – is utterly meaningless. Lottery players are simply being duped and using irrational thinking to waste their savings on gambling. This means that millions of people both within your country and across the world who strongly have faith that they will win the lottery believe in a falsehood; it means that people who play the lottery out of habit are still squandering their money away on a useless and detrimental pastime. It shows that millions of people can be utterly wrong despite the popularity of a belief throughout an entire country. The

---

1. [1] Barker, Jeff. "Statisticians question logic of buying multiple lottery tickets as jackpot rises to $1.5 B." *Baltimoresun.com*, 13 Jan. 2016, www.baltimoresun.com/business/bs-bz-powerball-maryland-odds-20160111-story.html.

defensive arguments that lottery gamblers make, such as the statement "You never know" only demonstrates a basic ignorance of how lotteries function. The gambler is admitting their ignorance by making such a statement. This can be proven on a demonstrable mathematical level, if need be. Lottery gamblers have been duped by their faith in the power of luck and good fortune. Scholars from college professors to business investors have privately regarded the lottery as a stupidity tax.[2]

The duping is largely because gamblers use personal experience – their own anecdotal events in life – and selectively focus upon the lottery winners who won millions. Seeing people online or on television smiling with a giant check reinforces the hope that they can win too. They have not considered the millions of people who have played the lottery throughout their lifetime and never won. This is despite the fact they largely meet and speak with a small percentage of them every day and are likely among that group of people who will never win because of the mathematical probability. Even if small rewards such as $3000 is won by a lottery player, it wouldn't be a gain because they would have to compare the amount of that single small win with the total amount lost during their lottery ticket purchases throughout the years. Their purchasing power was diminished on every ticket that was not a winner and wasted. A community of lottery gamblers makes the self-destructive habit seem normal because of the availability of examples. Seeing people play at nearly every gas station, grocery store, and corner store might convince people that it's not harmful because millions of people do it every day.[3] If you play the lottery, just make a simple list of how much you've spent on the lottery versus how much you've earned from the lottery; keep it honest and don't skim over one or two dollar purchases.

Lottery gambling shows that millions of people can be utterly wrong about the normal activities that they partake in, it shows that despite repeated behavior they don't realize the negative consequences of wasting money that could be saved for their future, it shows that using a large population size to justify a belief isn't a good reason at all to argue in favor of that belief, it shows that people can have positive beliefs used against them and harm them both emotionally and financially without them recognizing the problem, and that relying on "luck" through arguments from their own lack of knowledge of the odds can cause people to waste years of their life on a harmful belief. All of this is a consequence of using only personal events – anecdotes – and a belief in a metaphysical "luck" as a way to justify ones choices. A community that helps reinforce the normalcy and treats the lottery as a positive activity can only serve to harm the individual. People who understand the mathematics behind the lottery don't fall for the lottery trap; they recognize the personal experiences and faith of the lottery gamblers is a self-reinforcing falsehood. They don't follow the crowd via justifying their

---

2. [2] O'Brien, Matt. "Why you should never, ever play the lottery." *The Washington Post*, WP Company, 14 May 2015, www.washingtonpost.com/news/wonk/wp/2015/05/14/why-you-should-never-ever-play-the-lottery/?utm_term=.60541de1ad73.
3. [3] Cialdini, Robert B. "Chapter 4: Social Proof (98-140)" *Influence: Science and practice*. 4th ed., 21st Century Bks, 2002.

actions by the amount of lottery players around them who strongly believe in the fanciful qualities of the lottery. The scope of the population size is recognized as a logical fallacy compared to the statistical probabilities of a specific outcome happening. For comparison, within the US, the lifetime statistical likelihood that I would have died in the car crash that happened to me is approximately 1 in 572, the lifetime odds of dying from an assault by firearm is approximately 1 in 285, the lifetime likelihood of dying from an accidental firearm discharge is approximately 1 in 8527, the likelihood of any random person being hit from a lightning strike on an annual basis is approximately 1 in 17 million, and the annual likelihood of being drowned in a flood is approximately 1 in 12 million.[4] As mentioned prior, the likelihood of getting the winning ticket on the Powerball is 1 in 292 million and for the Mega Millions, it is approximately 1 in 300 million.[5] If you live in the US, then you and I are far more likely to be killed in car crashes, shot dead, killed by fire, drowned, and struck by lightning than we'll ever be of winning the Powerball or the Mega Million lotteries.

Anecdotes

A focal problem with anecdotes is that they can be argued in favor of any position; no matter how contradictory, racist, homophobic, or even positive. Anecdotes are a logical fallacy because they don't account for the actual statistical figures of a given subject and instead argue in favor of a position through personal events or isolated incidents.[6] Some of these anecdotes can be inferred from viewing events on television or online. An example would be the statistics on wars. Despite what is displayed on the news, wars have been on the decline since the 1970s.[7] After World War 2, there has been a huge drop in the ratio of violent conflicts throughout the world[8], but this sounds ridiculous when war stories occur on the news virtually every week. Evidently, the only reason that the majority of people perceive that humanity has become more violent is the easy coverage of violent conflicts as they are happening. During the era of newspapers, this was not possible. The modern media has allowed people across the world to gain insight on conflicts far removed from their location and NGOs have allowed people to give aid to suffering refugees to a greater extent than in the past. A greater awareness of these violent events has actually allowed better responses for the people who are suffering.

---

4. [4] "Facts Statistics: Mortality risk." *Facts Statistics: Mortality risk | III*, www.iii.org/fact-statistic/facts-statistics-mortality-risk.
5. [5] Isidore, Chris. "These are your odds of winning Powerball or Mega Millions." *CNNMoney*, Cable News Network, money.cnn.com/2018/01/04/news/powerball-mega-millions-odds/index.html.
6. [6] Kahneman, Daniel. Chapter 12: The Science of Availability (129-136). *Thinking, fast and slow*. Farrar, Straus and Giroux, 2015.
7. [7] Roser, Max. "Visual History of The Rise of Political Freedom and the Decrease in Violence." *Visual History of The Rise of Political Freedom and the Decrease in Violence*. Web. 3 Jan. 2016.
8. [8] Roser, Max. "Visual History of The Rise of Political Freedom and the Decrease in Violence." *Visual History of The Rise of Political Freedom and the Decrease in Violence*. Web. 3 Jan. 2016.

Yet, the erroneous perception that humanity is becoming more violent still remains because of people's repeated exposure to news about different wars across the world.[9]

Religious anecdotes are just as problematic. If, for example, a child is suffering from cancer but is cured either through medical treatment or the cancer disappears because their immune system successfully fought it off then religious believers often say that God has cured the child of cancer. If, however, the child regrettably dies of cancer then religious believers are most likely to – after giving honest condolences – say the child is with God in the afterlife. Thus, what changes aren't the horrible circumstances of the events but rather the interpretation of the events to make the believers feel better about death. It is the same for children in third world countries; the majority of people in first world countries ignore the issue of starving and dying children in third world countries under the basis that it has nothing to do with their personal lives. People often tout that the dead children are in heaven and no longer suffering. However, what changes aren't the horrific circumstances of innocent children dying from the world having failed them, what changes is a religious believer's perception of the event. The change in perception is for the comfort of the religious believer so that they don't have to think deeply or feel horrible from knowing there are children dying from starvation in third world countries. Sadly, this creates another problem, predatory missionary groups use anecdotes to their advantage on unsuspecting and uneducated people to argue in favor of their religion by holding people hostage; examples can vary in severity. There are cases of Christian missionaries pretending a transport vehicle is broken down until impoverished people living in a third world country pray to the religion of the missionary group to get the bus "working" again.[10] Worse still, some Christian missionaries are known to refuse health services until impoverished people convert to Christianity or pay a hefty fee for transport.[11] The level of apathy for the plight of the third world has prompted wealthy families to create public works projects like the Gates Foundation to combat issues related to healthcare which will hopefully stymie Missionary exploitation of the third world.[12]

Anecdotes and Symbolism

Anecdotes often require symbolism in order to maintain the feelings of normalcy. Religious symbols are often displayed to instill feelings of hope; especially during harrowing times. Religious symbolism is often utilized in books, films, and sometimes in court

---

9. [9] Kahneman, Daniel. Chapter 13: Availability, Emotion, and Risk (137-145). *Thinking, fast and slow*. Farrar, Straus and Giroux, 2015.
10. [10] Goldberg, Philip. "Missionaries in India: Conversion or Coercion?" *The Huffington Post*, TheHuffingtonPost.com, 19 Feb. 2014, www.huffingtonpost.com/philip-goldberg/missionaries-in-india_b_4470448.html
11. [11] Goldberg, Philip. "Missionaries in India: Conversion or Coercion?" *The Huffington Post*, TheHuffingtonPost.com, 19 Feb. 2014, www.huffingtonpost.com/philip-goldberg/missionaries-in-india_b_4470448.html
12. [12] Boseley, Sarah. "How Bill and Melinda Gates helped save 122m lives – and what they want to solve next." *The Guardian*, Guardian News and Media, 14 Feb. 2017, www.theguardian.com/world/2017/feb/14/bill-gates-philanthropy-warren-buffett-vaccines-infant-mortality.

proceedings to create a veneer of God defending the rights of the people for the sake of equality and to further symbolize moral goodness. Flag symbols in the background of a superhero character, religious symbols such as the cross, and of course the statement "In God We Trust" behind the court judge serve as common examples of these symbols. Symbols help facilitate the pattern recognition bias within humans; that is, perceiving a correlation between two different events where there is none.[13][14][15] When justice is served for the public good, religious believers see a correlation with the success of the legal system and God's will. Instances of justice failing to help people or unfair laws imposed upon people are often ignored and the public gains a fallacious understanding of what the law is really meant to be. Laws are dependent upon interpretation; juries are to determine if a particular incident broke a set of rules. Yet, when instances such as the failure of the law are displayed then it is argued that humans are imperfect. So what good is the symbolism in the first place? Believing that justice is preordained to God's will is a deception. It is a deception that is used against individuals who believe in it and it willfully ignores instances of failure in the justice system.

An example of this nefarious deception, the faultiness of symbolism, can be shown by the following fact about the law: most US citizens believe that US police officers have a lawful duty to protect them from any harm. This is legally false; a Supreme Court decision in 2005, Castle Rock V. Gonzales, determined that police protection was not a protected entitlement under the 14th amendment and that the protection of private citizens was not part of the public duty doctrine that the police are required to uphold.[16] In the context of the case itself, Gonzales noticed her children missing from her front yard and called the police to inform them that her estranged husband had probably taken them. He wasn't allowed to take them during that day because of the custody rules in place for when he was could spend time with the children. The police didn't take the claim seriously because they had many spousal complaints similar to Gonzales's call; Gonzales tried calling the police at several times during the hours and even went to the police station to show the protective court order whilst desperately asking for help. The police refused to do anything, the police officer at the desk took a lunch break after hearing her pleas, and the next day her ex-husband committed suicide by cop. The officer at the scene found the dead bodies of Gonzales's three young children in the trunk of the ex-husband's car.[17] The trial went to the Supreme Court and the case was dismissed on the basis

---

13. [13] Kahneman, Daniel. Chapter 4: The Associative Machine (50-58). *Thinking, fast and slow*. Farrar, Straus and Giroux, 2015.
14. [14] Kahneman, Daniel. Chapter 6:"Norms, Surprises, and Causes" (71-78). *Thinking, fast and slow*. Farrar, Straus and Giroux, 2015.
15. [15] Kahneman, Daniel. Chapter 7: A Machine for Jumping to Conclusions (79-88). *Thinking, fast and slow*. Farrar, Straus and Giroux, 2015.
16. [16] No. 04-278 TOWN OF CASTLE ROCK, COLORADO v. JESSICA GONZALES. https://www.justice.gov/sites/default/files/osg/briefs/2004/01/01/2004-0278.mer.ami.pdf 1-45. Supreme Court of the United States. 27 June 2005.*Justice.Gov*. United States, 27 June 2005. Web. 5 Feb. 2018. <https://www.justice.gov/sites/default/files/osg/briefs/2004/01/01/2004-0278.mer.ami.pdf>.
17. [17] Greenhouse, Linda. "Justices Rule Police Do Not Have a Constitutional Duty to Protect Someone." *The New York Times*, The New York Times, 28 June 2005, www.nytimes.com/2005/06/28/politics/justices-rule-

that Gonzales's children and by proxy all Americans had no legal right to police protection within the United States. According to the ruling, the police don't have to help you, even in instances when you are being robbed, assaulted, raped, or murdered.[18][19] The Castle Rock police department was quick to reframe the event in order to blame the grieving mother and politicians hailed the decision by focusing strictly on how police had to make tough decisions when on the field of duty. What wasn't mentioned was how the US government, from the local to federal level, no longer had to pay any damages to victims who suffered from the police failing to uphold their supposed duty in protecting the citizens from harm.[20] The Supreme Court of the United States had determined that the lives of children – who were ages 7, 9, and 10[21] – were less important than the government losing sums of money.

If you are a US citizen, you may have feelings of disbelief upon reading the aforementioned paragraph. After all, you've likely grown up with an entire culture of police dramas like Law and Order, NCIS, and other American TV shows with a plethora of episodes depicting valiant police officers doing their utmost to aid rape victims, children, and the wrongfully accused. These depictions usually consist of a main character having a strong personal connection with the victims to help them cope with the horrible events. The reality of the law seems ridiculous in comparison to what you might believe about the justice system; what you may not have realized is that you are using aspects of fiction to fill the gaps in your understanding of reality. You may have unintentionally used fiction as a substitute to fill in what you didn't know because we humans feel safe when we have a coherent understanding of the world. These stereotypes have been formed by "mental shortcuts" that you have developed regarding the world around you and your possible ignorance of the real law could be utilized against you. You may have formed a coherent story and expectations based on what you knew about the law but the fact remains that you probably didn't know about the actual laws governing you.

Psychological studies have found that, due to our increasingly complex societies, people use mental shortcuts to quickly determine what different subject matter represent and mean. These mental shortcuts are referred to as judgmental heuristics; snap judgments made out of the availability of the information in our personal lives or through repetitions that we

---

18. [18] No. 04-278 TOWN OF CASTLE ROCK, COLORADO v. JESSICA GONZALES. https://www.justice.gov/sites/default/files/osg/briefs/2004/01/01/2004-0278.mer.ami.pdf 1-45. Supreme Court of the United States. 27 June 2005. *Justice.Gov*. United States, 27 June 2005. Web. 5 Feb. 2018. <https://www.justice.gov/sites/default/files/osg/briefs/2004/01/01/2004-0278.mer.ami.pdf>.
19. [19] "CASTLE ROCK V. GONZALES." *Legal Information Institute*, Cornell University Law School, 21 Mar. 2005, www.law.cornell.edu/supct/html/04-278.ZS.html.
20. [20] Teitelbaum, Joel, et al. "Town Of Castle Rock, Colorado V. Gonzales: Implications for Public Health Policy and Practice." *Public Health Reports*, Association of Schools of Public Health, 2006, www.ncbi.nlm.nih.gov/pmc/articles/PMC1525280/.
21. [21] Greenhouse, Linda. "Justices Rule Police Do Not Have a Constitutional Duty to Protect Someone." *The New York Times*, The New York Times, 28 June 2005, www.nytimes.com/2005/06/28/politics/justices-rule-police-do-not-have-a-constitutional-duty-to-protect.html.

observe on social media.[22] This is natural human behavior because we cannot make deep insights about every single subject matter that we are confronted with even in a single day. As a consequence, stereotypes about certain jobs, organizations, and different types of people abound and will probably always exist. These psychological shortcuts are only worsened by our human bias to see pattern recognition from anecdotes we observe on television, online, and in our personal lives.

We humans need to use judgmental heuristics in our increasingly complex societies and so we use them without even realizing it. Whatever you thought might be credible laws depicted on television shouldn't be trusted. A repeated marathon of episodes in which fictional police only act positively towards the general public would cause an obvious bias with an implicit understanding that police are legally required to protect the public; it follows along the lines of the motto "protect and serve", it is what young children are led to believe when meeting friendly police officers during their time in school, it follows the norms of what we expect when we see TV shows like COPS that selectively show favorable police chases, and the fact remains that it isn't legally accurate. US citizens don't have the right to police protection. What people have done is let the belief in symbols, the repeated exposure to favorable police shows, and the popular opinion of the public give them a misrepresentation of the actual law.[23][24] In conjunction with mental shortcuts, the associations of symbolism with conceptual beliefs of what they represent by filling in the gaps of our knowledge with imagery that gives us a plethora of (usually positive) feedback loops is known as cognitive ease; that is, filling in our ignorance with concepts that feel familiar to us as a result of repeated exposure to the mental and emotional associations they evoke in us.[25] Neither the fact that the majority of the 320 million people living in the US believe that police are legally suppose to protect citizens nor the fact that 320 million people are bombarded with imagery, symbols, and stories of police heroics make the law any less valid or impactful upon people's daily lives. If you believe that this is a lie then I encourage you to independently verify the lawful impact of "Castle Rock V. Gonzales" for yourself but I have provided the appropriate source in the citation of this book.[26] We humans have a tendency to go with information and repeated exposure to what is most available to us.[27] It is known as the availability bias within

---

22. [22] Cialdini, Robert B. "Chapter 1: Weapons of Influence (1-16)" *Influence: Science and practice*. 4th ed., 21st Century Bks, 2002.
23. [23] Kahneman, Daniel. Chapter 6:"Norms, Surprises, and Causes" (71-78). *Thinking, fast and slow*. Farrar, Straus and Giroux, 2015.
24. [24] Cialdini, Robert B. "Chapter 6: Authority (178-200)" *Influence: Science and practice*. 4th ed., 21st Century Bks, 2002.
25. [25] Kahneman, Daniel. Chapter 5: Cognitive Ease (59-70). *Thinking, fast and slow*. Farrar, Straus and Giroux, 2015.
26. [26] No. 04-278 TOWN OF CASTLE ROCK, COLORADO v. JESSICA GONZALES. https://www.justice.gov/sites/default/files/osg/briefs/2004/01/01/2004-0278.mer.ami.pdf 1-45. Supreme Court of the United States. 27 June 2005.*Justice.Gov*. United States, 27 June 2005. Web. 5 Feb. 2018. <https://www.justice.gov/sites/default/files/osg/briefs/2004/01/01/2004-0278.mer.ami.pdf>.

psychology and it is a psychological factor that governments, police organizations, the national media, and psychologists are well aware of.

It is the same with religion. It shows that millions of people can wholeheartedly have an understanding about the norms of their society, harbor an overwhelmingly positive outlook on an organization and what it is perceived to do based on implicit understandings, and be completely wrong. You and others may already understand such a concept by acknowledging the billion of people who have strong religious faith in a religion different from yours. The fact that millions upon millions of people believe that police officers are legally required to protect them and this belief is what they consider to be a normal aspect of their everyday lives doesn't make the belief true.[28] If you were in a similar position to Gonzales and lost a loved one through police failure in doing their duty, your ignorance about this ruling would serve as a detriment to you. The police wouldn't need to pay any damages for failing you or your loved one. At best, they would simply be forced into retirement. Your ignorance, created by an obfuscation of the real facts through positive cultural imagery, will be used against you. It is also important to consider how many of us come to these beliefs. We often observe and consider what other people think or do and copy that behavior in order to remain in a favorable view to the majority of people; that is known as social proof.[29] The majority of people being confronted with this legal fact might be skeptical and may view such a legal fact to be a conspiracy theory. After all, it doesn't follow any coherent understanding about their beliefs regarding American society and it doesn't fit a coherent expectation about US law itself.[30][31] Yet it is a real law, but accepting that would require a drastic change of perception regarding what most Americans have come to expect regarding their own safety and the safety of their loved ones.

As mentioned earlier, you probably acknowledge that a billion of people believe in a religious faith that is different from yours. Currently, Christians make up the largest population in the world. In almost every country, there is at least a minority Christian population. For all the speeches about how India and China have a majority Hindu or majority atheist population, it remains true that Christianity – as a whole – has the largest population size.[32] Yet, this is not a valid argument favoring Christianity. This is what is known as the appeal to popularity

---

27. [27] Kahneman, Daniel. Chapter 12: The Science of Availability (129-136). *Thinking, fast and slow*. Farrar, Straus and Giroux, 2015.
28. [28] Walton, D. N. "Appeal to Popularity." *Https://Www.logicallyfallacious.com*, www.logicallyfallacious.com/tools/lp/Bo/LogicalFallacies/40/Appeal-to-Popularity.
29. [29] Cialdini, Robert B. "Chapter 4: Social Proof (98-140)" *Influence: Science and practice*. 4th ed., 21st Century Bks, 2002.
30. [30] Kahneman, Daniel. Chapter 19: The Illusion of Understanding (199-208). *Thinking, fast and slow*. Farrar, Straus and Giroux, 2015.
31. [31] Kahneman, Daniel. Chapter 20: The Illusion of Validity (209-221). *Thinking, fast and slow*. Farrar, Straus and Giroux, 2015.
32. [32] Hackett, Conrad, and David McClendon. "World's Largest Religion by Population Is Still Christianity." *Pew Research Center*, Pew Research Center, 5 Apr. 2017, www.pewresearch.org/fact-tank/2017/04/05/christians-remain-worlds-largest-religious-group-but-they-are-declining-in-europe/.

fallacy. Consider this hypothetical argument: what if Judaism turned out to be the one true religion? If that were so, then it wouldn't matter how many people across the world believed in Christianity, it wouldn't even matter if every country in the world outside of Israel believed in Christianity. It wouldn't matter if every person in the world believed in Christianity while Judaism was no longer believed in. It would be meaningless in the face of Jewish people being the chosen people of God. You can substitute this proposition with another religion or reverse it; if Christianity is true then Jewish people have suffered throughout history for a meaningless cause or – worse still – they have endured suffering to be killed en masse for some apocalyptic prophecy. Now consider this: according to most recent polling data, Islam will be the world's largest religion by around 2030 - 2035.[33] If that prediction becomes true, then what value can there be in Christians making up the majority of the world population currently? It has no value and on closer inspection, it is less meaningful than most Christians might realize. Christianity has divided into Protestants, Catholics, East Orthodoxy, and a voluminous amount of other sects; in other regions of the world Christianity has blended with the local religions and changed. For example, Catholics of India follow a Caste system just like the Hindus. In the Philippines, books of local religious witchcraft have been blended together with Christian teachings. There is no, and there probably will never be, a uniform Christianity; but this is not a unique problem to Christianity. It is the natural occurrence of any belief spreading. It is why India has had a tradition of Hindu heterodoxy, why Islam has differences in Sunni and Shia, and why there are intrinsic differences in several Buddhist schools of thought. In the context of the United States, liberals and conservatives have diametrically opposed views of Jesus Christ's teachings and expectations. What use is the term Christianity, or indeed any religious identity, when it has belief systems that conflict with each other on fundamental levels?

In chapter four, I will extrapolate on the faultiness of open interpretation and how all religions suffer from being unable to grapple with modernity.

Convenience

Religion has often been used to suit our conveniences. In the previous section, I mentioned how people living in first world countries ignore the circumstances of children in third world countries as having nothing to do with them and how religion helps ameliorate the immorality of such a position by the presumption of a positive afterlife for the children who have died. The death of innocent children is a regrettable truth that we should confront because it takes away the easiness and simplicity of religious answers. Religion, for the longest period of time, has helped facilitate apathy to problems of child mortality in third world countries but the apathy and convenience of religion doesn't end there.

---

33. [33] "The Changing Global Religious Landscape." *Pew Research Center's Religion & Public Life Project*, Pew Research Center's Religion & Public Life Project, 26 July 2017, www.pewforum.org/2017/04/05/the-changing-global-religious-landscape/.

The majority of people in any first world country don't give much thought to the problems of countries outside of theirs. Beyond selective media portrayals that create negative stereotypes, there is very little about foreign countries that most people understand and why should they? After all, it has little impact on their lives. As a result, due to our increasingly complex world and the shortcuts we use in understanding foreigners, we create negative stereotypes about other regions of the world and their people. Religion implicitly creates differences of in-group and out-group conditions and according to psychological research; the grouping of people into these different codifications is instantaneous.[34] *We group people into subjective categories instantaneously and sometimes we're not fully aware we act based on these subjective categories that we may hold to be self-evident truth.* We humans seem to be "groupist" by instinct from what extensive research has shown.[35] Race, religion, age, gender, political affiliation, citizenship, and other aspects of our personal identity have consequences for how we are all viewed by society. People codify us into groups, we codify them, and stereotypes are soon formed because of these rash generalizations from our "shortcuts" about other people.[36] This societal reality has a pernicious and demoralizing effect upon entire groups of people.

In my discussions with fellow Millennials on facebook, in college clubs, and among friends; I would ask whether they noticed an implicitly racist codification conducted by the generations before us. Almost unanimously, the Millennials that I spoke with – among different social classes, having different racial backgrounds, and coming from different political affiliations – agreed with the strange behavior of the generations before us. What we all agreed on was thus: the older generation would assess the quality of an entire racial group by comparing the good and bad people of that racial group that they personally met. For my group of friends and I, this seemed both fundamentally absurd and stupid. By defining people by their racial group, you are erroneously attributing negative qualities to people who have nothing to do with each other beyond being born with the same skin pigmentation. This is fundamentally unfair and racist. To the keen observer, the argument from followers of this belief attributing these distinctions from the "good" or "bad" qualities of the racial "community" does little to obfuscate the underlying racism. A disturbing implication from this viewpoint is the ignorant idea that skin pigmentation is linked to bloodline. In online forums, people will speak of how racist family members of theirs will demand that certain other racial groups be kept out of their family line. However, if people believe that "race" has to do with one's familial blood then what these racists are advocating is incest. If they truly believe that skin pigmentation determines similarities in blood then this is an advocacy for certain degrees of incest. Fortunately, ignorant racists are entirely wrong; skin pigmentation was determined

---

34. [34] Ispas, Alexa. "Chapter 1: Psychology and the Social Identity Perspective (1-24)" *Psychology and politics: a social identity perspective*. Psychology Press, 2014.
35. [35] Ispas, Alexa. "Chapter 2: The Psychology of Social Influence (26-50)" *Psychology and politics: a social identity perspective*. Psychology Press, 2014.
36. [36] McDermott, Rose. "Chapter 4: Cognition and Attitudes (77-117)" *Political Psychology in International Relations*. Ann Arbor: U of Michigan, 2004. Print.

by people adapting to their specific climates in their environments and skin pigmentation is a phenotype and not homogenous ancestry. Thus, skin color has nothing to do with how genetically close you are to someone else. For example, if you're white, you may be closer in genetic relations to your fellow black members of society than your fellow white members. This is primarily because skin pigmentation is just one small part of our genetic make-up; these racial boundaries are a cognitive illusion fostered by misapplied cultural history and historic racism. Examples of this fact can be seen across the world: Northern Indians of India are genetically closer to British people than Central and Southern Indians in genetic make-up most likely because of the Greco-Indian empire that rose after Alexander the Great's attempted conquest of India, most Europeans can trace their roots to the Near-East, Iraqis are classified as Caucasian and have a significant percentage of people who Westerners would classify as being "white", and Mexico has more diversity among different racial backgrounds than at first glance with White and Black "Hispanic" peoples. These distinctions are worthless anyway because the generalizations of each group are based on either racism or ignorant cultural discrimination. Generally speaking, racists have a difficult time classifying anything that isn't their expected similarity. The predominance of incestuous beliefs seems to be the root of most racism and this provincialism seems to be true of each country that practices it. I'd make the argument that US citizens are criticized for it because it is inconsistent with the championed diversity of the US and shows a failure of the education system of the US; furthermore, government codifications via racial background may be a double-edged sword because it promotes these implicit divisions by the evaluation of society through skin pigmentation.

During a news panel on Fox News in 2014, Megyn Kelly received a wide amount of criticism for saying to any possible children watching that Jesus Christ and Santa Claus were white.[37] After the public's derision of Kelly's statement, politicians ignored the part about Jesus Christ and shifted the focus to Santa Claus being a diverse cultural icon for children of all skin pigmentations. Virtually no politician or social media critic confronted the quirk about Jesus Christ being a white man and the backlash quickly died down. The educated members of the general public pointed out historical inaccuracies in social media regarding Jesus's skin pigmentation, groups of Christians stated that the skin color of Jesus Christ obviously didn't matter because his love for humanity is universal, and discussions about a black Jesus were largely met with an equal possibility to a white Jesus. This type of controversy over the racial background of a religious figure isn't unique to Jesus Christ or to religious discourse itself. Ancient stories about Cinderella, Ali Baba, and the 16 labors have changed a multitude of times to the renaming of the characters, the changes to the skin color of the characters, and the sanitization of the more morally dubious aspects of the stories that don't fit with the moral guideposts of the cultures that adopt the stories. In the context of religion, the Buddha has faced similar issues of cultural appropriation; his racial background has changed from Indian to

---

37. [37] Merritt, Jonathan. "Insisting Jesus Was White Is Bad History and Bad Theology." *The Atlantic*, Atlantic Media Company, 12 Dec. 2013, www.theatlantic.com/politics/archive/2013/12/insisting-jesus-was-white-is-bad-history-and-bad-theology/282310/.

the race of the majority population of each country that adapted Buddhism. In Korea, his appearance is reshaped to that of a Korean. In Taiwan, he looks Chinese; this is a blatant historical inaccuracy but these types of iconography persist throughout history and persist within each country where the majority of the population is of a different racial background from the revered figure. For the most part, within each country that Jesus and the Buddha are revered, their racial background changes to the majority population of that country. So, if the racial background of Jesus Christ and Gautama Buddha don't matter then why does this form of cultural appropriation overwhelmingly persist throughout the world? A pernicious and unpopular answer could be our psychological biases; psychologists have found that human beings prefer to associate with others who are similar to them.[38] Psychologists have coined the term "relatedness" but from my studies in political psychology, I would argue that this terminology skims over the true impact of the meaning. A more appropriate term might be "narcissistic impulse" and each racial group's desire to praise their revered figure only under conditions in which the figure is depicted to have the same racial background as them. The persistence of these false depictions, which are historical inaccuracies, reveals each individual's narcissistic desire for their racial background to be the most important in the world. I suspect that it is an explicit and irrational form of religious convenience that isn't challenged because it would engender a surge of racism and hate speech from any group that faced such a challenge to their religious worldview. The iconography is more important to satisfying their narcissism than historical facts. While the socially progressive religious adherents are willing to acquiesce to the legitimate history of their religion, it would be more challenging to convince the more ignorant groups in any given country to do the same. This religious convenience reveals a schism of difference beyond the multitude of religious denominations that isn't discussed publicly. People remain silent about this global racist phenomenon throughout their religious practices precisely because challenging the issue would harm the convenience of the majority of religious people by forcing them to confront their inner narcissism.

Convenience and Coherence

In his best-selling book, *Thinking Fast and Slow*, Psychologist Daniel Kahneman unveiled the multitude of cognitive biases within the human psyche. One of these biases was our bias in framing events in the manner of storytelling. We create a coherent framework of the world through our own biased assessments and formulate our own causal relationships for why events happen.[39][40][41] Beliefs in a God blessing us with good fortune is an example of finding a

---

38. [38] Ispas, Alexa. "Chapter 2: The Psychology of Social Influence (26-50)" *Psychology and politics: a social identity perspective*. Psychology Press, 2014.
39. [39] Kahneman, Daniel. Chapter 6:"Norms, Surprises, and Causes" (71-78). *Thinking, fast and slow*. Farrar, Straus and Giroux, 2015.
40. [40] Kahneman, Daniel. Chapter 7: A Machine for Jumping to Conclusions (79-88). *Thinking, fast and slow*. Farrar, Straus and Giroux, 2015.

fanciful cause for an event. Understanding this, Gods or God itself could be a concept of convenience for humankind as a result of looking for the "causes" of events through mental shortcuts. Examples can be seen in every religion. In polytheism, different Gods serve different aspects of human convenience from concepts such as a fountain goddess of luck in Rome, to a goddess of love in Hinduism, to a God of trickery in the Norse religion, to goddesses of death in Celtic religions, and to a God of either love or torment who helps people in mysterious ways in the Abrahamic faiths. The dualistic concept of God and the Devil are ideological representations of Absolute Good and Absolute Evil. They are depictions from the human mind's imagination, the justifications for our actions, and come from our human biases to seek quick answers to our grand world due to our desire for instant gratification. Due to the lack of technology and their lack careful assessment of the world around them by the majority of people in the ancient world, they sought stories and developed beliefs that satisfied their instant gratification in understanding the world around them.[42] They found links between actions and results that had no causal links like animal sacrifice and human sacrifice to change the weather patterns to keep their agricultural societies from starving or to provide a "cause" for why they were starving. They developed erroneous links because they needed quick and easily understood causes for why the world around them was a certain way depending on the time and place. It became understandable thanks to developing these Gods or God into teachings through storytelling to explain to themselves what they did right or wrong because the human mind is geared towards developing narratives to make sense of the world.[43]

Our minds seek coherence in relation to stories we tell ourselves all the time. We use this framework of coherence in our understanding of history and the attachment we place upon historical figures that are similar to us; they help serve our desires for inspirational storytelling and our narcissistic impulse with how we draw similarities to them. An example of this is the stories of the Crusades. Depending on whether you are Christian or Muslim, you may attach yourselves to some of these heroic depictions in films, books, or television shows about the Crusades and liken yourself to one of the so-called heroes. But, were you aware that the ancient Christian factions practiced cannibalism during the time period of the Crusades?[44] Were you aware that a subset of Christians ate the people that they killed – including children? The censoring of this significant historical fact displays a chief problem with religion. Similar to the apathy of first world peoples to the plight of the third world, religious people ignore the horrific acts in the name of religion for the sake of their own convenience. They ignore the barbarity to defend the view of religion being morally good for people. The negative history of

---

41. [41] Kahneman, Daniel. Chapter 8: How Judgments Happen (89-96). *Thinking, fast and slow*. Farrar, Straus and Giroux, 2015.
42. [42] Nietzsche, Friedrich Wilhelm. "Aphorisms 40 and 41" *THE ANTICHRIST*. Translated by H. L. Mencken, The Project Gutenberg, 2006.
43. [43] Kahneman, Daniel. Chapter 19: The Illusion of Understanding (199-208). *Thinking, fast and slow*. Farrar, Straus and Giroux, 2015.
44. [44] Rubenstein, J. "Cannibals and Crusaders." *French Historical Studies*, vol. 31, no. 4, Jan. 2008, pp. 525–552., doi:10.1215/00161071-2008-005. PDF.

their religion impacting the world is argued to be causes other than their religious teachings: the evil nature of humanity, the evil of politics, the instigation of the enemy, the mysterious will of God, and a multifarious amount of other supposed causes. Typically, the popular justification is that false interpretations of the faith occur and cause violence. It is an appeal to purity, an attempt at defending some perceived special and unique goodness of the religious faith. Apologists are willing to downplay, disingenuously interpret, and vilify attempts at highlighting horrific acts in the name of religion; to the extent that they ignore ongoing human rights crimes, ignore the victims of the past because they harm the positive coherence of religion, and may even come-up with a convenient notion that the victims are in a better place in the afterlife regardless of what the victims suffered. The lives and deaths of others become an abstract concept instead of a real event that has hurt real people. The notion of victims finding peace in the afterlife only serves the convenience and narcissism of the religious believer.

Criticisms of the religion itself can be obfuscated and ignored through the cognitive dissonance and the convenience of certain religious principles. The argument from ignorance that God's plan is unknowable serves the convenience of the religious adherent to ignore human rights abuses. Some religious believers try to detach themselves entirely from their previous religious identity; often by arguing that their faith isn't truly a religion and that they're simply spiritual without identifying with the religious identity because of the negative connotations associated with it. This is consistent with the psychological act of substitution, in which people find alternative reasons to justify their beliefs or actions because of unwillingness to change. Instead of dealing with a harsh self-critique in the face of new evidence about ones beliefs, people substitute analyzing a criticism with how that criticism makes them feel.[45] Instead of critically examining a belief based on a genuine criticism from an opposition group, they act on behalf of their personal feelings towards the criticism. Thus, they may not even concern themselves with the subject of human rights abuses by a religious organization they're affiliated with.

It isn't a morally good position because it reveals an apathetic disposition for the victims because victims are part of the out-group. To that end, people are self-centered because they are far more willing to ignore the victims for the sake of arguing for the purity of the religious faith. People simply don't care because they're unwilling to inconvenience themselves by examining their own beliefs. The result is an attempt to disassociate from the negativities while holding the exact same religious beliefs. The obfuscation and self-centeredness doesn't exist strictly for religion; it can exist in lesser known cultural forms but it is most damaging in the context of religion because of how easily people ignore human rights abuses because it doesn't fit into the positive image that they have about their own religious beliefs or those of their loved ones. They instead perceive it as a personal identity that "never

---

45. [45] Kahneman, Daniel. Chapter 9: Answering an Easier Question (97-107). *Thinking, fast and slow*. Farrar, Straus and Giroux, 2015.

leaves them" and the resulting trust in religious institutions or religious beliefs can have harmful effects upon people as a result.

The Convenience of Good and Evil

The dualistic concept of good and evil creates a limiting and damaging worldview that ultimately harms people who believe it to be the truth; even the idea that there are small gray areas in a mostly good and evil framework is harmful because it is an oversimplification. The concept of good and evil – above all other concepts – leads to extremism, xenophobia, bigotry, hatred, and mass murder. That may seem like an outrageous claim but I think it is truly an accurate assessment and here is why:

The dichotomy of Good versus Evil is extremist by default. It makes an extreme claim about our side and an opposing side. It implies the vast majority of a particular group are purposefully desiring wanton harm of our side while also implying that our side is an absolute good in the world. It defends any violence on "our side" in terms of the situation or for the greater good of our defense while the opposing side is using violence simply because they're "evil" or gullible people manipulated by evildoers in power. It imposes an absolutist metric upon vast swathes of people that codifies them all in an oversimplification instead of considering the situations from the opposing point of view. Even worse, it does little to differentiate people in foreign countries by political leanings, socio-economic leanings, and other multitudes of factors. After all, why should we believe there is a massive uniformity in another country and that they don't have class structures, political and social differences, and religious divisions that are worth considering when making a judgment about another country? The concept of Good versus Evil frames groups into absolutes and when people look for a "balanced" approach to important issues, we may be willing to concede that the opposing side has some good people that are mostly overshadowed by an abundance of evildoers; we also may concede that there are wrongdoers on "our side" but that the vast majority of our in-group are doing positive work. In short, seeing two opposing absolutes with a few shades of grey is generally the view from people who believe in good and evil. What people are doing is anchoring absolutes upon a general population of a particular country; instead of assessing them based on objective facts, we assess them based upon negative headlines and make spurious assumptions about the personalities of millions or perhaps billions of people based upon a single news story of a tragic event. By following this approach of instant gratification towards negative depictions of people in the news, we don't consider factors such as the differences in crime rates throughout a foreign country's cities versus its rural areas, lack of education such as illiteracy, and other socio-economic factors. Instead, we impose upon an entire country a stereotype by anchors. In psychological studies, the anchoring effect is setting a particular value based upon useless or erroneous information included in what a person sees when making a judgment on a value.[46] This typically relates to mathematical questions, but could relate to our moral judgments when using the Good versus Evil perspective due to anchors being so ubiquitous in human behavior. In effect, people would be imposing a blanket extreme upon an entire country instead of assessing their pros and cons.

    The Good versus Evil viewpoint isn't an objective reality, but rather a self-fulfilling prophecy. Consider this hypothetical idea: two nation-states are opposed to each other and they both believe in a strict viewpoint of good versus evil. Both sides see themselves as morally good and the opposing side as morally evil; they may concede that some small portions of their side behave wrongfully and that some good people exist on the other side but generally speaking, they oppose each other on strict moral beliefs by viewing the other side as mostly evil. What would relations between these two countries be like? It shouldn't be difficult to immediately grasp that both sides would be committing bloodbaths against each other on the basis of fighting evil, upholding the good morals of their society, and believing they're "doing what must be done" to protect themselves in defense of their country. After all, if you believe that the opposing side is pure evil, why bother negotiating? Or upon the pretense of negotiating, why bother upholding any concessions if you assume the opposing side is deceiving you constantly? As I see it, this "balanced" approach of Good versus Evil isn't balanced at all; for most countries and people, there is no good or evil with a few shades of grey that produce moral quandaries. There is only grey; there is only the moral quandaries. What people are doing is instead of looking at pros and cons of a country, individually assessing them based upon measures of human rights and political freedoms for example, they simply assume the majority of an entire country is full of good or bad actors who collectively seek either friendship with us or annihilation of us. This is obviously due to our mental shortcuts as we can't assess each nation-state individually. Sadly enough, we get negative viewpoints and form bigoted stereotypes because of streams of negative news about other countries and the vice versa is also possible. But what about truly extreme cases such as dictatorships like North Korea and absolute monarchies like Saudi Arabia? Well, there is a paradox to those examples: the people in those societies may see themselves as morally good and anything that disagrees with them as morally evil. Whether because of nationalistic fervor and lack of education in the case of North Korea or especially religious authoritarianism in the case of Saudi Arabia, people see themselves as being part of the moral good for strictly obeying what the religious bodies of the government or the single political party refers to as an absolute moral good because of their lifelong indoctrination. The addition of social proof, of seeing everyone in your environment behave with admiration and fealty to the leaders, will only further condition a person to seeing the teachings of the ruler as a foundation of moral good. In short, they unthinkingly believe themselves to be morally good because that's how they're brought up. Their belief in their culture's moral goodness leads to truly horrifying

---

46. [46] Kahneman, Daniel. Chapter 11: Anchors (119-128). *Thinking, fast and slow*. Farrar, Straus and Giroux, 2015.

actions in what they perceive to be defense of the sacred beliefs of their society that appear to be morally evil to us in the outside world.

The dualistic concept of "Good versus Evil" is a framework and promotion of extremist ideology; the idea that it is a safe concept for children is false because of its extremist viewpoint. It is a concept that often compels people to hate and murder under a veneer of justice. Our groupist mentality intermingles with the extremist ideology of absolute good and absolute evil. Even the idea of mostly good or mostly evil is self-damaging because people have anchored their viewpoints upon the idea of absolute good and evil and given small concessions to what is still largely an absolutist disposition. Essentially, people will concede that some or a few good people exist on the opposing side and grant that some or a few people with violent tendencies exist within our side, but will remain firm in their generalizations that the majority of our side has heroic and humanistic qualities that justify our violent atrocities and that the other side commits violent atrocities due to the majority of them harboring stereotypical "evil" qualities like hatred for others or that they feel pleasure in committing violence similar to a cartoon super villain. In short, good and evil are recognized as being the only measure for an organized group of people to judge them. When we apply these dual extremist ideologies to our fellow human beings that are different from us then we will always be generalizing them with a simplistic worldview. There are different degrees of how pernicious this concept is but the problem is the concept itself being flawed and instigating hatred toward others. Viewing our moral beliefs as a form of goodness and viewing those opposed to our moral beliefs – such as in the abortion debate – as evil will create a dehumanizing image of the people who disagree with our views.

Apologists of the dualistic concept of good and evil are quick to point out truly horrific crimes as proof that the concept itself has merit. Common examples are the Holocaust, an anecdotal account such as the gruesome death of a child at the hands of a pedophile, or terrorism. Yet, upon a deeper look, these show a shallow understanding of the consequences of believing in good and evil. The Nazis committed a mass genocide after a voluminous amount of religious and political propaganda condemning the Jews for being evil people throughout the history of Christian Europe. The Nazis used the economic crisis, the belief that the Jews were responsible for murdering Jesus Christ, and anecdotal stories to argue that Jewish people were a villainous and hateful group that ruined their country. The narrative of doing what must be done to protect the innate goodness of the German people was used to instill the idea that German soldiers were heroically going through hell and committing these atrocities to protect the goodness of the German public. That was the basis for the Holocaust, the belief that the Germans were truly good people who needed to destroy the evil of the world and that meant killing the Jews because they personified evil for the Nazis. A violent pedophile who made a child suffer usually emphasizes their other actions, such as giving to charity, to ameliorate themselves from their horrific sexual tendencies; the pedophile vindicates themselves of responsibility by telling themselves that they're mostly a good person. How can we know this?

Because that is exactly what the national media does to protect their image and many pedophiles wearing religious garb had defenders who blamed the victims or found examples of a priest being a "good person" to vindicate their rape of children. Psychologists have found that most terrorists, by and large, aren't insane extremists. While some terrorists like the al Qaeda hijackers show a lack of ability to distinguish religious beliefs from reality; shockingly, some terrorists such as the Irish Republican Army are people who turned to violence after seeing their efforts through more peaceful means being ignored or violently crushed – such as peaceful protests or the judicial system being purposefully ineffectual.[47] A terrorist would argue the innate goodness of their actions or possibly highlight how the foreign country that they're trying to destroy committed more egregious acts of violence upon their people to justify their behavior. In fact, that has been done in the case of Iraqi insurgents; they justified the beheadings by blaming President Obama for beginning an initial bombing campaign that Wall Street and the US's Gulf allies demanded of him to protect global economic interests. We have known instances of terrorists justifying their violence through the concept of good and evil; Osama bin Laden's letter to America attempts to vindicate his terrorism as a form of heroics and posits the US as an empire of evil.[48]

In the case of the average person, good and evil thinking seems to lead people to believe in a "Good Person Syndrome" to self-exalt ourselves and other people that we believe to be in our in-group. Unsurprisingly, we ascribe villainous characteristics to a perceived hostile out-group. People living under the belief system of good and evil typically perceive themselves to be a "good person"; we, the in-group, thoughtlessly purchase cheap consumer commodities such as clothing made from Chinese sweatshops, jewelry that was found from child labor in India, the latest electronic gadgets that were made from factories that force workers in third world countries into long hours while paying their workers pennies a day, oil from the dictatorships of OPEC, and when confronted with any of these realities then we argue that we're good people because of the positive relationships that we have in our personal lives. We argue that we're a good mother, a good father, a good spouse, a good friend, and give to a few charities. We say that evil is just part of how the world exists. We don't try to inconvenience ourselves or admit to profiting off the suffering of the third world because it enriches our lives. Attempts at pointing this out lead to a backlash of calling out hypocrisy from those highlighting these issues, or blaming the out-group by arguing their governments and therefore the victims themselves are responsible. This is despite the fact that some of these victims live under authoritarian rule or have no means of defending themselves. Once blaming the victim is accomplished, the Good Person Syndrome makes itself content by arguing perspectives of self-worship. Utilizing arguments such as how we treat our in-groups civilly,

---

47. [47] McDermott, Rose. Chapter 5: Do Actions Speak Louder Than Words? (119-152). *Political Psychology in International Relations*. Ann Arbor: U of Michigan, 2004. Print

48. [48] "Full text: bin Laden's 'letter to America'." *The Guardian*, Guardian News and Media, 24 Nov. 2002, www.theguardian.com/world/2002/nov/24/theobserver.

how our in-group is more civilized and open than the out-group through anecdotal evidence presented in the national news media to promote jingoism and confirmation bias used from the media, and ignore or distance ourselves from these realities by arguing that we're a humble folk who have nothing to do with the complexities of the world. Evidently, once there are moral questions that cannot be answered, a believer of good and evil will always argue that they are less than the complexity of the world and that these issues are "greater than themselves"; they ignore the fact that these questions would require them to rid themselves of their convenient, enriched lifestyle and they attribute negative qualities to vilify the people who point out these challenging questions. This isn't because they are secretly horrible people or because of some evil nature in humanity; it is because they wish for their lives to have a coherent and largely positive narrative. To effectively have a positive worldview when believing in the extremist ideology of good and evil, they need to ignore the terrible exploitation or find "causes" for what their belief system teaches them is evil in the world. We humans have a negativity bias and negative information is more difficult to get rid of than positive information.[49] Yet, it remains true that this dualistic and extremist teaching serves to create impotence towards complex problems in human affairs and leaves young people unable to deal with the real world.

    The psychological effects known as the contrast principle and the consistency to an in-group play a significant role. Psychologists have noted, and national news media has taken advantage of, the fact that people put more emphasis on contrasting characteristics than what is necessarily there when we observe two different groups or arguments from opposing sides of a subject.[50] The contrast principle can apply to people, expensive items, political ideologies, and many other things. Psychologists have also noted that most people don't have the time or they're disinclined to take the effort in assessing each event respectively and instead choose to automatically respond with their prior behavior and social identity to the particular issue.[51] An example of the news taking advantage of these two psychological principles would be Piers Morgan, a US news reporter, interviewing Alex Jones, a conspiracy theorist, when his viewership was low on CNN.[52] Morgan's arguments would obviously look more favorable compared to that of a conspiracy theorist. Viewers comparing Morgan to a loudmouth who wasn't making much intelligible sense would further emphasize Morgan's positive qualities by a quick comparison of the two. Furthermore, viewers would likely feel that Piers Morgan was a reasonable person with common sense like them making him part of their "in-group" of "reasonable people" and would contrast that with Alex Jones who would be viewed as a crackpot. Unless the viewership is predisposed to Alex's views, they would overwhelmingly

---

49. [49] Kahneman, Daniel. Chapter 28: Bad Events (300-309). *Thinking, fast and slow*. Farrar, Straus and Giroux, 2015.
50. [50] Cialdini, Robert B. "Chapter 1: Weapons of Influence (1-16)" *Influence: Science and practice*. 4th ed., 21st Century Bks, 2002.
51. [51] Ispas, Alexa. "Chapter 2: The Psychology of Social Influence (26-50)" *Psychology and politics: a social identity perspective*. Psychology Press, 2014.
52. [52] Morgan, Piers. *YouTube*, CNN, 7 Jan. 2013, www.youtube.com/watch?v=ror9v2LwHoY.

see the positive aspects of Piers Morgan because of the contrast to someone perceived to be a worse person. Incidentally, the contrast principle is probably why Godwin's law, reductio ad Hitler, is used in so much in Western social media to defend poor arguments or to emphasize the bad qualities of an opponent's arguments. Let's face it, virtually any action or argument looks better in contrast to a mass genocide by a genocidal and racist maniac.

Good and evil creates a grotesque oversimplification and anchors good and evil caricatures similar to cartoon characters onto real human beings. Instead of assessing events, peoples, places, or opposing arguments as their own individually; good and evil creates an anchoring effect. We already have the perception that a person's argument is "good" or "bad" based on how closely we perceive their views to be similar to ours or how we feel about what the subject that will be argued. Good and evil frames individual concepts with a favorable or antagonistic predisposition before people have made arguments. It typically describes out-groups as mostly evil compared to the in-group that is making the assessment. People with opposing views to the in-group are presumed to be liars, charlatans, idiots, or other nefarious connotations before we actually take the time to understand their views. We would also be predisposed to viewing egregious acts – even criminal acts – by people we like to be irrelevant. Even when they have committed a horrific act, it may be ignored or downplayed, simply because we believe them to be good based on how similar their views are to ours. While the dualistic belief doesn't always result in this, it is more likely because of the framework of good and evil.

Good and evil becomes dangerous when it leads to generalizations of entire peoples; these generalizations serve to create narratives similar to children's fantasy books about the real world. We, as a culture, give ourselves narratives of self-exaltation of good and championing the good of the world, while presuming nefarious or evil intent from all others different from us.[53] We would be predisposed to assume evil intent on the part of other countries and peoples; this is especially true when the rational reasons for events are absent. When we have no rational basis for our understanding of why events happened – such as war, police taking down protests, or terrorist attacks – then we presume that the other side has an evil intent because that is the coherent framework of good and evil. Worse than that, good and evil is a concept that is averse to listening to rational discourse; the basic premise of the concept is that we must stand for the good and that means celebrating our peoples and cultures as morally or economically superior to the evil Other.[54] The need for coherence in our minds would presume evil intent on the part of others for their actions and the externalizing of evil then compels us to frame racist, bigoted, and hateful narratives because those people are different from us.[55] The lack of a rational basis for events makes it easier for people to hate

---

53. [53] Hedges, Chris. *War Is a Force That Gives Us Meaning*. PublicAffairs, 2002.
54. [54] McDermott, Rose. *Political Psychology in International Relations*. Ann Arbor: U of Michigan, 2004. Print. For reference: Chapter 4: Cognition and Attitudes (77-117)
55. [55] Hedges, Chris. *War Is a Force That Gives Us Meaning*. PublicAffairs, 2002.

others under the framework of good and evil. The inculcated framing of entire groups of people as "the other" through national news media's use of anecdotal evidence then compels us to conduct war or mass violence. It isn't just bigoted framing, but distancing to create a gap between the "good" people and the "evil" people, terms such as "foreign nationals", "Hajis", "Dykes", "illegals", "aliens", and other such terms create this implicit and psychological distance to form dehumanization campaigns. An important part of this that politicians, journalists, and psychologists understand about the general public, is that when you aren't given rational reasons for why an event happens then you will find your own "causes" to form a coherent narrative because every human being needs a coherent understanding of the world around them to both maintain a sense of control and to reduce personal anxiety over dangerous events.

The 2015 Baltimore riots serve as an important example; many detractors blamed the "thug culture" of young black Americans as the basis for the riots. This is an erroneous claim for most open-minded peoples; rap music isn't going to compel people to act differently than what they already were inclined to do. The true cause of the riots were Baltimore police's brutality of the civilian populations; there were mass settlements amounting to 5 million per year to settle cases of police brutally assaulting civilians – in one case, the police assaulted a pregnant woman.[56] Baltimore citizens were appealing to their government and demanding legitimate change for over five years but absolutely nothing was done. Upon agreeing to the settlements for family members who were hospitalized from police brutality, the civilians were legally obstructed from bringing these instances of police violence to the national news media. As a result, the national news media was able to frame a very one-sided narrative. While it is true that crime is a problem in Baltimore, the local government and the national news media have simply obstructed and ignored the suffering of the residents. But do you see how shallow framing this issue in terms of good and evil is? The national news media isn't entirely wrong about gang violence and the crime rates of Baltimore but they ignored the average citizen being brutally attacked by police officers to give a slanted view of what was the true cause of those riots. The burning down of shops, more often than not, was because of opportunistic anarchists from outside of the area coming in to destroy property; this was true for both Ferguson and Baltimore but the belief in "thug culture" created a racist predisposition that made people believe that black Americans just wanted to burn down their own cities to riot.

The good and evil framework for determining moral actions has a deeply pernicious social consequence that every human civilization has probably conducted during its history. The historical revisionism of civilian deaths in wars, the historical revisionism of genocides conducted upon perceived out-groups of peoples and the total apathy for civilian victims because they're perceived as the enemy come from the purview of good versus evil. Generally, the people of the nation-state that caused egregious war crimes and genocide argue that the

---

56. [56] Puente, Mark. "Sun Investigates: Undue force." *The Baltimore Sun*, 28 Sept. 2014, data.baltimoresun.com/news/police-settlements/.

human rights crimes don't matter. This is the cruelest degree of apathy for the victims who suffered and is principally argued from the perspective of viewing the victims as abstract concepts instead of viewing them as fellow human beings. The lives of in-groups, people who share our background, are more important than the out-groups, the foreign civilians who we generalize through our rash judgments. Cultural self-worship lead to venerating our positive qualities and trying to find "moral equivalence" with our nation-state's crimes and the crimes of people within their group either conducted upon us or conducted upon their civilians. Differentiating different political groups, differentiating the terrorist groups from the civilians, and attempting to condemn all atrocities on the religious basis of murder being wrong are ignored. The only genocides denounced as wrongful acts are those that help create national unity, celebrate the nation-state as the greatest force of good, and highlight anecdotes of soldiers saving civilians. Genocides that our nation-state conduct upon others are disingenuously misrepresented; the genocides are downsized in their actual impact, blame is thrown upon the victims or their governments while ignoring our government's culpability, a negative social custom of theirs is highlighted to justify genocide, it is sometimes argued that bringing it up is unpatriotic and somehow an insult to our nation-state's troops, and most people of the aggressor nation-state argue that it doesn't matter. Revisionist history removes the genocide from their textbooks and usually racist caricatures of the "enemy" nation-state are formed or heavily implied from grade school textbooks. A prominent example of this is the genocide of approximately 500,000 Iraqis – most of them 5 year old children – via the unilateral sanctions of the United States upon Iraq under the policy of Dual Containment.[57]

Genocide denial is probably the most disgusting and egregious crime that any human civilization can do upon other human civilizations. It emphasizes dehumanization, it ignores the lives of victims as less important than feeling good about celebrating the nation-state, and it misapplies the blame for the crimes. It is not the civilians, but the terrible actions of the government that is being blamed for policy directives that purposefully resulted in mass death. Why should the civilians feel insulted or feel responsible? Acknowledging human rights crimes during war and crimes of genocide are just an acknowledgement that the lives of the victims had intrinsic value because they were innocent human beings. People don't fathom being on the opposite end of the debate. Yet, throughout human history, religion - the so-called epitome of good moral teachings - constantly fails to breed empathy for perceived out-groups even when children are dying or killed. Often, religion simply justifies or excuses human violence with religious precepts. This will be covered more in-depth in Part II.

Apathy and Silence towards Warfare

One of the greatest challenges, and least discussed topics, against religious faith is how shallow these so-called moral convictions truly are when jingoism sets in to begin war against

---

57. [57] Gause, F. Gregory . "Getting It Backward on Iraq." *Foreign Affairs*, Foreign Affairs, 28 Jan. 2009, www.foreignaffairs.com/articles/iraq/1999-05-01/getting-it-backward-iraq.

a foreign entity. The sad fact of life is that war propaganda is successful in instilling hatred, racism, bigotry, and a desire for warfare against foreign countries. If morality truly was an important component of our existence then why does it become drowned away when a government prepares itself to launch a war campaign? This is essentially true for every country in the world; at some point, your country went to war and morality went to sleep. Notice that religious organizations of countries launching wars will always become silent about the morality of killing during times of war. They will almost unanimously grow silent in any moral objections. Worse still, average citizens will ignore the war crimes, bombings of foreign civilian homes, and largely create a fictitious understanding of warfare to praise their soldiers as humane when they conduct night raids, bomb houses, kill civilians, and – in some cases – rape civilians. The narrative of good and evil takes a strong hold to make the other side similar to the boogeyman to justify war – i.e. to justify organized mass murder.[58] Foreign civilians are always caught in the crossfire; through two sides shooting at each other or through bombing campaigns. A nation-state always ignores or drowns out the civilian killings committed by their soldiers. The afterlife, the idea of a Higher Power's plan, and other abstract concepts become excuses to ignore such barbarity.

How can we explain this nigh-universal cognitive dissonance in morality? Why do citizens of all countries have apathy towards their country committing war crimes? Where is the moral condemnation when it truly matters? It is simple: it suits our convenience as an in-group; when people aren't being forced into conscription and aren't personally affected by something then they simply won't concern themselves with the issue. For the most part, people pay attention to their immediate surroundings and daily routine – soldiers committing war atrocities upon innocent civilians in another country is equivalent to changing weather forecasts on the news. People simply don't care; religious beliefs – when they are truly needed – are met with intense social apathy and usually ignorance of the political events in question. That is the reality of how most people practice their religious faith. Jingoism wins and trumps religious morals. Usually religion blends with racial or cultural jingoism to defend wars and ignore war atrocities; what use is morality in these repeated scenarios?

Consequently, we differentiate killings during war from murders within our countries. This isn't simply true of soldiers battling combatants, this is also true in the case of soldiers slaughtering an entire village of civilians – such as in the Haditha killings.[59] Why? A possible utilitarian reason is this: the nation-state differentiates killing in the name of obtaining a political or economic objective (which maximizes State power) versus killing people within the country. Killing people within the country is an act that weakens State power because the murdered individual is useful human capital and further weakens the strength of a nation-state should such acts go ignored because people of similar ethnocentric, gender, sexual orientation,

---

58. [58] Hedges, Chris. *War Is a Force That Gives Us Meaning*. PublicAffairs, 2002.
59. [59] Pelley, Scott. "Haditha massacre defendant: We did what we had to." *CBS News*, CBS Interactive, 6 Jan. 2012, www.cbsnews.com/news/haditha-massacre-defendant-we-did-what-we-had-to/.

or political background will want equal treatment for their group. The people similar to the victim will demand punishment for the murder committed. Incidentally, in the case of Haditha – and almost all other instances in which soldiers have massacred foreign civilians – the Good Person Syndrome takes full effect; the murdering of children, the handicapped, and other foreign civilians are wholly ignored whilst news media runs stories about how the soldier, usually a man, is a family man with children and a wife. The paradigm of good and evil sets in and the most inconsequential displays of the abstract "goodness" of the soldier are trumpeted while the heinous deed is ignored.[60] Thus, the soldier faces no jail time and is still allowed to live a normal life within the country. Usually the story is never editorialized again because it hurts the coherence of their country being a force of good that the majority of people believe about their country.

This is not meant to be snarky and I didn't single out an example from the United States to insult it; I'm simply pointing out a modern example of a realistic fact about all nation-states. The late 19th and earliest 20th century were probably the worst periods of war, genocide, and human rights crimes in terms of scope and scale. This example is simply meant to convey an evident fact: good and evil doesn't work and results in ignoring morality over providing positive moral answers to the most important questions. It is limiting, shallow, and makes people confused and disoriented in understanding real life events. In Part 2, I will elaborate my contentions on specific religions and why they cause pro-war narratives that result in mass death. However, before that, there are still other general issues of religious faith that will be covered.

---

60. [60] CHEDEKEL, LISA, et al. "Haditha: Marine Linked To Civilian Deaths Was A Quiet Honor Student, Friends Say." *Hartford Courant*, 3 June 2006, articles.courant.com/2006-06-03/news/0606030586_1_frank-wuterich-haditha-squad-leader.

Chapter 2: Asceticism and Rationality

"If we leave aside the ascetic ideal, then man, the animal man, has had no meaning up to this point. His existence on earth has had no purpose. "Why man at all?" was a question without an answer. The will for man and earth was missing. Behind every great human destiny echoes as refrain an even greater "in vain!" That's just what the ascetic ideal means: that something is missing, that a huge hole surrounds man. He did not know how to justify himself to himself, to explain, to affirm. He suffered from the problem of his being. He also suffered in other ways: he was for the most part a sick animal. The suffering itself was not his problem, but rather the fact that he lacked an answer to the question he screamed out, "Why this suffering?" Man, the bravest animal, the one most accustomed to suffering, does not deny suffering in itself. He desires it, he seeks it out in person, provided that people show him a meaning for it, the purpose of suffering. The curse that earlier spread itself over men was not suffering, but the senselessness of suffering—and the ascetic ideal offered him a meaning!

The ascetic ideal was the only reason offered up to that point. Any meaning is better than no meaning at all. However you look at it, the ascetic ideal has so far been a "faute de mieux" [for lack of something better] par excellence. In it suffering was interpreted, the huge hole appeared filled in, the door shut against all suicidal nihilism. The interpretation undoubtedly brought new suffering with it—more profound, more inner, more poisonous, and more life-gnawing suffering. It brought all suffering under the perspective of guilt . . . But nevertheless, with it man was saved. He had a meaning. From that point on he was no longer a leaf in the wind, a toy ball of nonsense, of "without sense." He could now will something—at first it didn't matter where, why, or how he willed: the will itself was saved.

We simply cannot conceal from ourselves what's really expressed by that total will which received its direction from the ascetic ideal: this hate against what is human, and even more against animality, even more against material things—this abhorrence of the senses, even of reason, this fear of happiness and beauty, this longing for the beyond away from all appearance, change, becoming, death, desire, even longing itself—all this means, let's have the courage to understand this, a will to nothingness, an aversion to life, a revolt against the most fundamental preconditions of life—but it is and remains a will! . . . And to repeat at the conclusion what I said at the start: man will sooner will nothingness than not will . . ."[61] - Friedrich Nietzsche, *On the Genealogy of Morals*. Ian Johnston Translation.

    Asceticism has existed multifariously throughout all religious traditions. Almost every religion, and especially modern religions, has theological teachings that infer practices that temper feelings of chasing after a fleeting happiness; religions claim to offer a tempering of

---

1. [61] Nietzsche, Friedrich Wilhelm. *On the genealogy of morals: a polemical tract*. Translated by Ian Johnston, PDF, Richer Resources Publications, 2014.

selfishness, greed, envy, hatred, and jealousy. They contain teachings that practice the concept of modesty towards sexual conduct and preach of living for a higher purpose above purportedly base desires. Self-control is implied throughout these religious teachings. A benign detachment from emotions that cause negative feelings and negative responses are heavily inferred to be the best way to live a good life. Above all the negativities attached to all religions in our modern times, this seems to be the genuine positive source of religious morality and teaches people to live ethically. Separated from mystical abstraction, this seems to be a positive guideline to most people.

I argue that these presumptions are utterly false. Asceticism doesn't have any positive moral guidelines; it doesn't instill people with any form of moral goodness and I would argue that all it does is try to escape from reality by positing a higher purpose of living beyond the world. For all intents and purposes, asceticism only accomplishes the following: *to practice impotence as a form of moral goodness*. Cloaked under a veneer of goodness and self-worship; asceticism teaches us to give up on personal dreams by asserting our goals are unattainable, asceticism offers the convenient narrative that we would be self-centered to aim for our dreams in life, the ascetic lifestyle instills us to pretend that we're above those who attain more than us, and we commit to this outlook through the concept of self-renunciation for a purported higher purpose.[62] The desire for accomplishment and success is categorized closely to having evil intent in a disingenuous representation of positive work ethics. Moreover, the ascetic ideal disproportionately focuses on all human flaws and utilizes the mere existence of flaws to condemn all forms of human progress as both self-centered and evil. A commitment to self-constraint by a religious group only further solidifies this in-group commitment to impotence and to view anyone with a positive work ethic as a negative out-group with selfish intent or foolish beliefs. This doesn't speak of every individual case, but a person's commitment to asceticism usually comprises of an aversion to desiring more from life. Selfishness is typically viewed as an anathema to a constricted form of equality under an ascetic outlook.

A Will to Nothingness

Asceticism is self-contempt obfuscated by religious iconography and religious platitudes. Concepts such as detachment from suffering and original sin are a sanctified self hate of the individual to celebrate impotence as the only solution. The ascetic frames everything else in the world as having lesser value than prostrating towards self-impotence; using anecdotes and filling their gaps in knowledge of out-groups by postulating an out-group's nefarious intent to do harm to the world as an excuse to continue renouncing themselves from life.[63] Typically, an ascetic may use negative portrayals of people seeking fame in celebrity culture or running a business like a corporation that they see from films or

---

2. [62] Nietzsche, Friedrich Wilhelm. *On the genealogy of morals: a polemical tract*. Translated by Ian Johnston, PDF, Richer Resources Publications, 2014.
3. [63] Kahneman, Daniel. Chapter 5: Cognitive Ease (59-70). *Thinking, fast and slow*. Farrar, Straus and Giroux, 2015.

negative news media coverage to fill in the gaps of what an ascetic doesn't know about different business industries to generalize seeking fame and fortune as evil, selfish, or narcissistic. This personal view is often disingenuous and erroneous.

The ascetic ideal usually consists of a patronizing attitude toward all forms of self-empowerment: the foremost is the hatred for desiring material wealth; wealth is seen as meaningless, morally evil, and condemned via the argument that it doesn't last forever. The ascetic viewpoint presumes that people who seek material wealth will never truly be happy; that materialists doom themselves to intense struggle and suffering for no reason, and argue that looking beyond material wealth will confer a higher quality of life. Yet, the appeal to asceticism posits the idea that ascetics should be celebrated for giving up on material wealth under the presumption that ascetics could have succeeded in higher forms of wealth but simply chose not to do it. Such arguments show the intrinsic narcissism of asceticism itself; presuming an ascetic could persist in difficult and complex jobs but simply chose to pursue a so-called higher purpose is an attempt at self-flattery. Furthermore, wealth is obviously not intrinsically evil; what matters is what one does with the wealth and empowering oneself by gaining wealth is a worthwhile accomplishment. Regardless of death, a wealthier person has typically surmounted more challenges and accomplished more in life than ascetic individuals especially if they run international organizations. An example would be the American billionaires who have committed themselves to donating the vast swathe of their wealth to end world poverty. What could an ascetic possibly accomplish compared to billionaires who finance ending malnutrition to prevent children throughout the third world from dying, providing proper medical vaccinations for children that protect them from curable diseases that would otherwise ravage areas with child mortality, systems like the Janicki Omniprocessor that utilize sewer sludge to turn into electricity for communities in Africa[64], and commit themselves to decreasing the level of world poverty to increase overall life expectancy of children in the most vulnerable and poorest regions of the world?[65]

The dualistic belief of good and evil worsens this hatred of material wealth; people inclined to asceticism use anecdotes of greedy people on the news as confirmation bias that anyone who seeks material wealth is evil. The good and evil paradigm creates externalized evil caricatures such as Right-wing ideologies of Ayn Rand, Right-wing politicians, and obfuscates genuine issues pertaining to lower economic classes learning to despise material wealth. The good and evil paradigm, conflated with asceticism being framed as morally good, fills in gaps of knowledge about the rich and the poor with fairytale caricatures.[66] The wealthy elite are evil, greedy, self-centered, bigoted, believe themselves to be superior to the middle class and poor, and apparently they all became wealthy with "daddy's money" meanwhile the poor are good,

4. [64] Gates, Bill. *YouTube*, Thegatesnotes, 5 Jan. 2015, www.youtube.com/watch?v=bVzppWSIFU0.
5. [65] Gates, Bill, and Melinda Gates. "Warren Buffett's Best Investment." *Gatesnotes.com*, Bill and Melinda Gates, 14 Feb. 2017, www.gatesnotes.com/2017-Annual-Letter.
6. [66] Kahneman, Daniel. Chapter 5: Cognitive Ease (59-70). *Thinking, fast and slow*. Farrar, Straus and Giroux, 2015.

honest, hardworking, down on their luck, and have hope that life will get better. These are simply ideological fantasies created from asceticism intermingled with good and evil. People who believe them generalize an entire group of peoples regardless of race, gender, sexual orientation, religion, and political affiliation to make themselves feel better about having accomplished less in life. These stereotypes about the wealthy and poor are psychologically, mathematically, and scientifically wrong regardless of the bigoted preconceived notions that people have. Yet, the patronizing attitude of asceticism along with the mindset of good and evil create a coherent framework that persistently generalizes anyone who tries to financially empower themselves. It obscures and sanctifies what is little more than jealousy of the wealthy.

The second, and equally as important, form of self-contempt is the hatred for all forms of sexual love. There is an overwhelming amount of hatred for the human body in the majority of religions and especially in the Abrahamic faiths. The human body elicits disgust, shame, and guilt for natural biological and biochemical processes of sex and masturbation. Sexual intercourse is openly condemned as sinful despite our natural biological processes for reproduction. The majority of religions teach a hatred for self-pleasure by referring to masturbation as "dirty" despite it having positive health benefits and being a natural process.[67][68][69][70] Worse than that, the deeper that a person delves into ascetic ideologies of any religion then the deeper this aversion to life persists. To commit themselves to a so-called higher purpose, many ascetics from Catholic parishes, Buddhist monks, or equivalents in other religions have foregone having a family with a spouse and having children.[71] The decision to renounce having a family because of religious convictions shows an aversion to human life in all theistic backgrounds. It isn't always because they have no interest in attaining a spouse and children; it is usually their commitment to this idea of a higher purpose that they renounce having a family, renounce finding personal love, renounce self-pleasure as dirty, and renounce sexual love as vile.[72][73] Pornography is condemned through hostile personal attacks and there are attempts to conflate normal pornography with criminal behavior like child pornography in order to shame people by associating natural activities with criminal behavior. Under the guise

---

7. [67] Viglianco-VanPelt, Michelle, and Kyla Boyse. "Masturbation." Edited by Jennifer Gold Christner, *University of Michigan Health System*, July 2009, www.med.umich.edu/yourchild/topics/masturb.htm
8. [68] "Masturbation Side Effects and Benefits." *Healthline*, Healthline Media, www.healthline.com/health/masturbation-side-effects.
9. [69] Cooper, Spring Chenoa, and Anthony J. Santella. "Happy news! Masturbation actually has health benefits." *The Conversation*, 5 Dec. 2017, theconversation.com/happy-news-masturbation-actually-has-health-benefits-16539.
10. [70] "Masturbation | Get the Facts About Masturbation Health." *Planned Parenthood*, Planned Parenthood, www.plannedparenthood.org/learn/sex-and-relationships/masturbation.
11. [71] Nietzsche, Friedrich Wilhelm. "Chapter IX: Preachers of Death (50-52)" *Thus spake Zarathustra: a book for all and none*. Translated by Thomas Common, PDF ed., T. Common, 1908.
12. [72] Nietzsche, Friedrich Wilhelm. "Chapter IX: Preachers of Death (50-52)" *Thus spake Zarathustra: a book for all and none*. Translated by Thomas Common, PDF ed., T. Common, 1908.
13. [73] "Masturbation | Get the Facts About Masturbation Health." *Planned Parenthood*, Planned Parenthood, www.plannedparenthood.org/learn/sex-and-relationships/masturbation.

of morality, religious asceticism condemns healthy and natural activities as disgusting and infers that such behavior is evil. It teaches people to constantly feel shame, guilt, and self-hatred for not being "pure" enough to condemn their natural instincts as human beings.[74][75][76][77]

The third form of self-contempt is the hatred of knowledge. There are a plethora of reasons given for the disposition that we humans are of lesser value than a higher power: that religious adherents subject themselves to rules from a higher power for something that is beyond human comprehension, that the horrific events of war and genocide are part of God's plan for some unknowable reason to humanity, and that humans should look beyond the materialism of the world to be part of something greater than themselves. To await an unassailable truth that the human mind is too limited to understand. This is an overwhelmingly self-deprecating mentality that treats a hatred for knowledge as having intrinsic moral goodness. The implications are that giving up knowledge to a higher power is the correct path to a great truth and that we should ignore all negative human affairs: war crimes, genocide, bombing campaigns, and the suffering of the third world poor as having less value than this great truth. This framework of moral goodness solidifies these horrific events as afterthoughts, the real people suffering are treated as afterthoughts, and asserts impotence towards these complex issues as having more value than effectively stopping them from happening. Thus, instead of effectively dealing with these issues, this moral framework treats these occurrences as too complex for human understanding and responds by sanctifying impotence as an act of good morals for the convenience of the adherents. *Prayer itself is the ultimate practice of impotence as a form of moral goodness.* Feeling good about praying to God and leaving it up to God to handle important matters like natural disasters is to feel good about yourself for doing nothing. You expend no effort to alleviate suffering and instead feel good about yourself for not expending effort or monetary assistance under the convenient belief that an omnipotent creator will help others. Prayer may give you a sense of control for what feels like unpredictable events and it may make you feel good personally, but you're feeling good about doing nothing of value for those who are suffering. You've put your personal feelings above the suffering of others and treated them as afterthoughts if all you do is pray for them. Participating in vetted charities that seek specifically to ameliorate suffering or donating money to vetted relief organizations that seek to help people who are suffering does far more to help because you're taking actionable steps to serve a community in need by empowering the sincere responders. If this segment has motivated you to pursue charitable works or to spend

14. [74] "Masturbation Side Effects and Benefits." *Healthline*, Healthline Media, www.healthline.com/health/masturbation-side-effects.
15. [75] Nietzsche, Friedrich Wilhelm. "Chapter IX: Preachers of Death (50-52)" *Thus spake Zarathustra: a book for all and none*. Translated by Thomas Common, PDF ed., T. Common, 1908.
16. [76] Viglianco-VanPelt, Michelle, and Kyla Boyse. "Masturbation." Edited by Jennifer Gold Christner, *University of Michigan Health System*, July 2009, www.med.umich.edu/yourchild/topics/masturb.htm
17. [77] Cooper, Spring Chenoa, and Anthony J. Santellla. "Happy news! Masturbation actually has health benefits." *The Conversation*, 5 Dec. 2017, theconversation.com/happy-news-masturbation-actually-has-health-benefits-16539.

your personal income on them, please be wary of nefarious charities and be sure to properly look into charities you're considering to donate your money towards. As is well known, even some famous charities like those conducted by the celebrity Mother Teresa have been unveiled to be scams that lie about where the monetary proceeds go to; the charitable donations that she acquired went to building Churches and not hospitals as was ostensibly implied by her volunteer work.[78] Other charities by Christian missionaries often celebrate the deaths of innocents as the righteous judgment of the Abrahamic God, attempt to forcibly convert people after a disaster with some attempts to isolate and target children in particular, refuse food and medical treatment for people bleeding and starving in front of them unless they convert, and openly celebrate the suffering of survivors right in front of them immediately after the survivors have lost loved ones.[79][80][81][82] This is not meant to discourage charities, but to impress upon people to please be wary and research the charities you're donating money towards. Religious organizations, particularly Christian and Islamic organizations, often see suffering in opportunistic terms precisely to preach ascetic ideals related to their religion.

The hatred of knowledge results in a hatred for human progress itself; there is a deep and pernicious nihilism in the purview of asceticism. The ascetic views all forms of human progress and modernity; hospitals, educational institutions, technology, waterways, houses, sanitation facilities, vaccines, better food, light bulbs, and a multifarious amount of other modern conveniences as insignificant and argue it will perish in the wake of a great truth that humans will never be fully able to comprehend.[83] This mindset displays the self-deprecating mentality of asceticism. It is a hatred for all of the positive accomplishments of humanity. Regardless of the accomplishments, even space age accomplishments of putting a man on the moon or having a satellite survey Mars, asceticism will view it as insignificant. Human progress is viewed as worthless either because of religious axioms or for the sake of some bizarre hope for the end of the world.[84] In some cases, it's a conflation of both reasons. This nihilistic outlook towards human progress comes from religious obfuscation in favor of valuing

---

18. [78] Hitchens, Christopher. "Christopher Hitchens: Hell's Angel: Mother Teresa (English Subtitles)." *YouTube*, BBC News, 7 Jan. 2015, youtu.be/NK7l_IhtKNU.
19. [79] Neelakandan, Aravindan. "Why No Outrage over Conversion of Tsunami Victims?" *Swarajya*, 29 Dec. 2014, swarajyamag.com/politics/why-no-outrage-over-conversion-of-tsunami-victims.
20. [80] "When Nepal Was Groaning in Earthquake, Christian Missionaries Were Shamelessly Selling Jesus." *OpIndia*, 4 May 2015, www.opindia.com/2015/04/when-nepal-was-groaning-in-earthquake-christian-missionaries-were-shamelessly-selling-jesus/.
21. [81] Gittleson, Wendy. "Christian 'Soul Vultures' Are Exploiting The Nepal Earthquake 'For Christ' (VIDEO)." *AddictingInfo*, 27 Apr. 2015, addictinginfo.com/2015/04/27/christian-soul-vultures-are-exploiting-the-nepal-earthquake-for-christ-video/.
22. [82] Neary, Sarah. "Forced to Convert: How American Missionaries Really Treat Indigenous Akha Children." *Intercontinental Cry*, IC, 23 Apr. 2013, intercontinentalcry.org/forced-to-convert-how-american-missionaries-really-treat-indigenous-akha-children/.
23. [83] Nietzsche, Friedrich Wilhelm. *On the genealogy of morals: a polemical tract*. Translated by Ian Johnston, PDF, Richer Resources Publications, 2014.
24. [84] Nietzsche, Friedrich Wilhelm. *THE ANTICHRIST*. Translated by H. L. Mencken, The Project Gutenberg, 2006.

impotence; from tenants such as detachment, ideologies of good and evil, and a bizarre belief in a great truth that usually requires the end of the world in virtually all religious faiths.

Arguably, the worst part is that theologians and religious believers from both Western and Eastern cultures have shown that the obscurity of religion, the perception of ancient mystery, archaic and outdated writings, and the mysticism of theology is enjoyable to the majority of religious believers.[85] Thus, religious believers take pleasure in the argument from ignorance and feel sadomasochistic pleasure in their self-contempt. The idea of living for a higher purpose beyond human comprehension leads to a morbid pleasure through ignorant self-constraint imposed by theological teachings and practices. Religious speakers often appeal to willful ignorance of scientific studies by telling religious believers that not knowing has a higher purpose. Usually by ascetically arguing that the scientist is arrogant and that no human being can truly understand God's will. It is this gap in understanding theology that differentiates atheists from the pious because atheists have a desire for verifiable truths that are demonstrable. This belief in viewing the world as inherently valueless or without meaning, viewing life in a state of constant decay or moral decline, and preaching that people who don't accept this perception are fools compared to one's in-group is a form of nihilistic narcissism.[86] An in-group of religious adherents view the world as empty and use pejorative terms to devalue life itself by comparing it to an argument from ignorance in which something beyond is considered of far more value, but also beyond their own human comprehension. This is both anti-intellectual and self-congratulates an in-group for the anti-intellectualism because it is seen as keeping strong faith in the group and keeping the community together based on the collective imagination of a social group via dogma instead of verifiable claims based on evidence.[87] Whereas those who don't submit to this in-group standard are seen as selfish or narcissistic for not praising and seeing everything as valueless and worthless compared to a perfect world after death, a perfect creator deity that gets to know upon death, or a spiritual journey after death; the in-group praises itself for doing nothing of value in the world. It is a worship of impotence and death, seeing all forms of life as inherently devoid compared to something beyond their understanding.[88] Joining the in-group that views the world in various forms of decline, decay, and death is met with wide praise within the in-group as the groupthink motivates self-congratulatory praise for doing absolutely nothing and calling themselves humble for doing nothing of value.[89] Feeling assured in mutual trust that it must be real because of the social proof that others in their immediate surroundings believe in it with

---

25. [85] Nietzsche, Friedrich Wilhelm. *On the genealogy of morals: a polemical tract*. Translated by Ian Johnston, PDF, Richer Resources Publications, 2014.
26. [86] Nietzsche, Friedrich Wilhelm. *On the genealogy of morals: a polemical tract*. Translated by Ian Johnston, PDF, Richer Resources Publications, 2014.
27. [87] Ispas, Alexa. *Psychology and politics: a social identity perspective*. Psychology Press, 2014.
28. [88] Nietzsche, Friedrich Wilhelm. Chapter XXVI: THE PRIESTS (88-91). *Thus spake Zarathustra: a book for all and none*. Translated by Thomas Common, PDF ed., T. Common, 1908.
29. [89] Ispas, Alexa. *Psychology and politics: a social identity perspective*. Psychology Press, 2014.

strong convictions.[90] They don't think about the multitude of millions of other religious denominations within their own faith or the billions who believe in other religions with their own denominational differences and how the majority of them hold the same mutual trust based on social proof of their small communities and strong communal values within those communities.

The Masculinity of Asceticism

Asceticism has a long history of gender-specific characteristics; many forms of asceticism were geared toward the gender concept of masculinity. Hating their own emotions by trying to be detached, a disgust for emotions being a source of strength, not falling for so-called feminine wiles, discriminating women by generalizing them to be more emotional than men, perceiving crying as shameful, and so-called thrill-seeking by putting themselves at risk of death is the culmination of a philosophy of self-hatred.

Manly culture is almost wholly opposed to being human; ignoring the instinct to self-preservation to encourage putting their lives in danger, ignoring biological drives of pro-creation by vilifying women as sluts for practicing sexual liberation, viewing the normal biological function of tears as being a form of weakness, and viewing "toughness" as being emotionless seems like social conditioning into becoming a sociopath. A person with this sort of worldview is probably more likely to commit violent suicide to complete the social conditioning of self-hatred and misanthropy when faced with difficult social situations. Perhaps that is why suicidal men in the US commit the act violently by jumping off tall areas or committing mass violence before committing suicide by killing themselves or through suicide by cop.[91] It is statistically more likely for men across the world to commit suicide and teaching them this form of self-hate could be the reason but scientific and psychological studies would need to be made to be sure.

Perhaps tellingly, most of the criticisms that anti-feminists make about the double standards imposed upon men came from a long history of male culture that precedes the 19th century. It is odd that they would condemn feminism but then agree with feminist precepts that masculine culture is largely unfair to men too. Yet, it is the stupidity of the ancient cultures that created these forms of so-called appropriate male behavior.

Antiquated Rationality versus Modern Rationality

The self-hate of religious faith goes further through ascetic ideology. Rationality itself is viewed as synonymous with evil. Many ancient philosophers throughout the entirety of

---

30. [90] Cialdini, Robert B. "Chapter 4: Social Proof (98-140)" *Influence: Science and practice*. 4th ed., 21st Century Bks, 2002.
31. [91] Freeman, Daniel, and Jason Freeman. "Why are men more likely than women to take their own lives?" *The Guardian*, Guardian News and Media, 21 Jan. 2015, www.theguardian.com/science/2015/jan/21/suicide-gender-men-women-mental-health-nick-clegg.

Western culture held this self-destructive and self-defeating view of rationality. Rationality became synonymous with harming other peoples and projected a view that there was an innate evil within humankind itself. Examples such as getting ahead in the business world by "screwing" your teammates are one of these generalizations. This viewpoint is the most self-deluded viewpoint to ever be conceived by any culture. Modern epistemological rationality has shown the view to be a self-destructive falsehood; causing harm to others can only harm oneself because you will have made an enemy or you would have spent resources weakening others ability to progress by squandering yourself.[92] It is fundamentally irrational because you gain nothing from harming others and instead make enemies for yourself. Western faiths and, to a certain extent, Eastern faiths have a staunch self-defeating view of rationality and logic existing within such a self-destructive context. Intelligence is often viewed as utilizing evil intent and committing cruelty in a passive demeanor. The indifference to factories exploding, sending soldiers off to murder civilians in wars, or to cars lacking safety standards and the company choosing to take the lawsuits because it's less of a financial loss are all forms of antiquated rationality. Any person or groups of people who conduct such acts aren't being rational; they are being misanthropic. Moreover, such acts cause people to distrust and seriously question an organization or person who would commit such horrific acts because it goes against our instincts of self-preservation and our empathy for the victims. In the long term, a business, nation-state, or peoples that would conduct such horrific behavior are condemned by the public, distrusted by other organizations that assumed they had a better grip on the situation, and they receive a permanent negative mark on history that continues to lead to antagonism or aversion from the peoples who were wronged and by people who have empathy for the victims. It coincides with the metaphorical term of shooting oneself in the foot.

As surprising as this may seem, empathy is fundamentally rational and all logical decision-making itself is grounded in emotion as part of human biology.[93] The assumption that rationality needs to be emotionless is both wrong and self-defeating.[94] It creates a coherent framework of needing to be evil to be wealthy and perniciously implies that human nature is innately predisposed to the concept of evil. The good and evil paradigm and the disproportionate focus of the national media on wrongful acts of the wealthy serve to justify this belief. Examples include news reports focusing upon politicians who have stolen taxpayer monies, focusing on celebrities who cheat the tax system, and focusing on the stupid actions undertaken by specific celebrities. Compare that disproportionate focus to news reports of billionaires who are alleviating world poverty, wealthy people who have given millions to charities for treatment of diseases harming children or cancer research, and essentially any

---

32. [92] Yudkowsky, Eliezer. "What Do We Mean By "Rationality"?" *Less Wrong*, 16 Mar. 2009, lesswrong.com/lw/31/what_do_we_mean_by_rationality/.
33. [93] Camp, Jim. "Decisions Are Emotional, Not Logical: the Neuroscience behind Decision Making." *Big Think*, Big Think, 11 June 2012, bigthink.com/experts-corner/decisions-are-emotional-not-logical-the-neuroscience-behind-decision-making.
34. [94] Galef, Julia. "The Straw Vulcan, Julia Galef Skepticon 4." *YouTube*, YouTube, 17 Aug. 2013, www.youtube.com/watch?v=Fv1nMc-k0N4.

other news report pertaining to positive actions by the wealthy.[95] Worse still, some wealthy people themselves may believe that acts of "evil" are justified to "get ahead" of others because of this self-destructive belief. Thus these people wrongfully commit themselves to grievous financial acts that weaken themselves and the confidence of their clients such as the economic recession of 2008 – 2009. Yet, the belief itself is what makes it a reality and it ultimately hurts the long-term confidence in capitalism. As recent charities by the wealthy have shown, this doesn't have to be true and it is an untenable position to generalize all wealthy people as evil and greedy.

Modern Politics and Antiquated Rationality

International relations often have the most brutal consequences upon the average citizens of all countries due to the actions of their political leaders. I would be remiss not to discuss the aspects of self-hatred and tribalism that is promoted by religious perceptions of events. The oldest and most impactful political theory that is still used – amid varied forms – is the Realist Theory of International Relations. While the theory's origins were from Thucydides, the West has used this theory as the de facto guide to international relations throughout the world and it has resulted in sectarianism, the most brutal human rights crimes, and the weakening of Western power.

The Realist Theory of International Relations posits that the international order is anarchic; State's act "rational" for their self-interest and try to maximize their power.[96] The only way to prevent total destruction is usually either hegemony or a balance of power.[97] Unfortunately, this conceptual framework leads to States fighting among themselves and trying to weaken the power of other States through acts of war, brutal oppression, genocide, counterfeit money, and promoting sectarianism. As a result, a pernicious and ubiquitous narrative to highlight the positive aspects of their own culture as morally good and all other civilizations as morally corrupt is the prominent narrative of all national news outlets in every civilization. When such a narrative cannot be easily constructed, then the news usually shifts to celebrity culture within the country. That is why there was a ubiquitous focus on Paris Hilton's sex tape when the US began its invasion of Iraq and bombed the homes of Iraqi civilians. This is also why the fictional narrative of humanitarian intervention is so persistent; better military equipment doesn't mean differentiating civilians from enemy soldiers or even children from adults – it just means being more effective at killing.[98] Attempts at obfuscating, demonizing, or

---

35. [95] Boseley, Sarah. "How Bill and Melinda Gates helped save 122m lives – and what they want to solve next." *The Guardian*, Guardian News and Media, 14 Feb. 2017, www.theguardian.com/world/2017/feb/14/bill-gates-philanthropy-warren-buffett-vaccines-infant-mortality.
36. [96] Viotti, Paul R., and Mark V. Kauppi. Chapter 2: Realism: The State, Power, and the Balance of Power (55-197). *International relations theory: realism, pluralism, globalism*. 3rd ed., Macmillan, 1998.
37. [97] Jentleson, Bruce W. *American foreign policy: the dynamics of choice in the 21st century*. 4th ed., Norton, 2010.
38. [98] Hedges, Chris. *War Is a Force That Gives Us Meaning*. PublicAffairs, 2002.

minimizing the violence in wars reveals the ignorance and falsity of the good and evil paradigm; it is ignoring human violence conducted to a perceived out-group for the sake of cultural self-worship. As stated before, the good and evil ideology would compel a country to view other peoples – and entire countries – as mostly evil and villainous to justify our nation's violence upon them.

World leaders and politicians would be compelled to harm peoples of other nations through sanctions, wars, covert operations, false flag operations, and to highlight demonizing them throughout the media because of the coherent belief of maximizing the nation-state's power by minimizing the power of other nation-states.[99] Yet, the minimizing of other nations results in spreading sectarianism within the foreign nation-state that ultimately threatens the safety of all other nation-states. When the US pulled out of Iraq in 2011, both the Democrat and Republican party proceeded to try to widen the sectarian differences in Iraq by supporting a Shia leader who closed off hospitals, educational facilities, jobs, and political participation for the Sunni population of Iraq. Due to the lack of actual knowledge behind why the invasion of Iraq happened, Sunni Iraqis likely felt desperate after a war that destroyed their homes, caused severe psychological damage to them and their children, and left them with a government that shut them out from being able to live decent lives; this likely contributed in insurgency and terrorism spreading. After a couple years of protests resulting in nothing being changed, the peaceful protests changed to violent tactics, the terrorist Abu Bakr al-Baghdadi rose to power and further threatened the stability of the entire region by capitalizing on the suffering of the Sunnis by offering them money, food, housing, and a future once they ousted the corrupt Shia government from power. The US, being economically bound to the global economic interests of its closest allies in the Gulf, was forced to reenter into another war. But this third war in Iraq is the result of the Realist ideology of weakening other countries under the false assumption that it maximizes the stronger nation-state's power. The false axioms of the Realist theory, implicit in-group and out-group norms, and the religiously motivated belief in good and evil are to blame.

This isn't the first time that the West has conducted such behavior; the conflicts of Israel-Palestine, Pakistan-India, North and South Korea, and – more recently – the break-up of North and South Sudan were formed by the Western powers spreading sectarianism by putting an extremist minority group in power to form policies that discriminated upon the masses and divided the people. Other ways the policy objective of the Realist theory is conducted is by creating separate public facilities and emphasizing the differences by favoring one of the groups over the others to sow discord that resulted in protests for equality, then shutting those protests down by colluding with a government that ignores their citizens protests and takes bribes from Western governments. Western governments have also aided autocratic governments in the torture and imprisonment of protestors. The results of these actions are

---

39. [99] Jentleson, Bruce W. *American foreign policy: the dynamics of choice in the 21st century*. 4th ed., Norton, 2010.

prolonged wars in the Middle East in the case of Iraq, terrorism rising in the Middle East, the prolonged threat of terrorists gaining nuclear weapons in Pakistan, the exacerbated holy war between Israel and Palestine, and the prolonged enmity between various cultures that ultimately force the West into longer conflicts that weaken its own power. Historically, the realist theory of international relations played a focal factor in the Holocaust; the weakening of Germany by the allied powers intensified the hatred for the minority group, increased conspiracy theorists about Jewish people, and increased the religious differences that resulted in discrimination and then mass genocide. It resulted in another war after World War 1 that ultimately destroyed European hegemony over the world and engendered a Cold War that could have wiped out all human civilizations.

The Realist theory of international relations creates an anti-capitalist mindset that ultimately poses the worst threats to the longevity of capitalism. Imperialism is a personified version of the Realist theory and resulted in some of the most egregious human rights crimes throughout history.[100] Most of the countries that became communist did so because they conflated capitalism with the grotesque human rights crimes done to them by Europe. The message of Socialism, of a united civilization that doesn't fall into greed, was far more appealing to them at the time. Obviously, communism is a failure and led to despotic regimes that committed their own human rights crimes. However, capitalism's lack of concern for workers in unsafe working conditions, child slavery, and legal indemnification when factories explode and kill people will only result in a resurgence of socialist sentiments. The realist theory and capitalist permissiveness of these egregious crimes only result in the weakening of economic power and distrust from the people. Worst of all, placing incompetent autocratic rulers in power, permitting human rights abuses, committing egregious human rights crimes such as bombing campaigns, and other horrors are expected to cause the slow downfall of a nation-state under the realist theory. The realist theory expects that the strongest nation-states will slowly erode in power.[101] These methods create a fatalistic view that all States must combat each other but eventually the strong States succumb to decline and become disempowered. Theorists foolishly treat this as a so-called inevitability of the anarchic system of States and States take actions purportedly for their so-called self-interest that result in their own slow self-destruction. In what way is this system either rational or positive for any nation-state? It leads to self-harm and treats such senseless actions as intelligent. It is the faultiness of religious axioms blended into cultural expectations about rationality that have created this self-defeating theory.

Modern rationality disagrees with the self-interest premise of antiquated rationality and points out its flaws; weakening other peoples will only give rise to sworn enemies, weakening

---

40. [100] Jentleson, Bruce W. *American foreign policy: the dynamics of choice in the 21st century*. 4th ed., Norton, 2010.
41. [101] Viotti, Paul R., and Mark V. Kauppi. Chapter 2: Realism: The State, Power, and the Balance of Power (55-197). *International relations theory: realism, pluralism, globalism*. 3rd ed., Macmillan, 1998.

others will drain your resources in dealing with the enemy, and you will have destroyed a potential ally that could have added to your strength.[102] This is true for employment, for friendship, and for nation-states. If a nation-state antagonizes you after aiding them then find a nation-state that is more suitable for your needs. Compare the European Union to jingoism that resulted in the two World Wars. Even in the worst economic recession thus far in history, the European Union is still a better option than the great depression that contributed to events leading to the Holocaust and World War 2.[103] Mass poverty and economic recession are still better social conditions than mass world war. Empowerment is rational and disempowerment only leads to weakening oneself and self-ruination.

42. [102] Yudkowsky, Eliezer. "What Do We Mean By "Rationality"?" *Less Wrong*, 16 Mar. 2009, lesswrong.com/lw/31/what_do_we_mean_by_rationality/.
43. [103] Roser, Max. "Visual History of The Rise of Political Freedom and the Decrease in Violence." *Visual History of The Rise of Political Freedom and the Decrease in Violence*. Web. 3 Jan. 2016.

Chapter 3: The Afterlife

This subject matter is probably the most difficult among the multitude of topics pertaining to religion and human life. I suspect that some, if not most, religious extremists probably fall into extremism because they want to believe that their loved ones are in the afterlife or other religious equivalents. This is probably the real reason why atheists are loathed in many countries; billboard signs and self-exalted demonstrations by atheists insulting religion seem hateful because it means that people will never see their deceased loved ones again. Those billboard signs are tacit and obnoxious arguments that those loved ones aren't happily living on in some form. I will try to be more sensitive and respectful in this section of the chapter; I wholeheartedly apologize if anything in this chapter offends anyone who has lost a loved one and has turned to religion for guidance on the matter.

A significant amount of people who have faith probably don't believe in a higher power for the explicit purpose of worshipping a God or Gods; people believe in their faith because they want their deceased friends or relatives to be happy and to see them again in the future. A belief in deities seems endemically tied to such a viewpoint. What could an atheist viewpoint offer to someone who has faith because they have lost a child? Logical arguments wouldn't matter and there is absolutely nothing that an atheist viewpoint could offer to lessen the emotional pain. For those who have lost loved ones, the best response that I can offer is that what you're actually having faith in is for your loved ones lives to have meaning; along with the obvious desire to see them again. In that case, believing in a deity is just a tool for the sake of celebrating your loved ones in your memories. Please consider this: *your loved ones are the real gods that you worship*. In the context of Christianity and Islam, when people make statements such as "your loved one is smiling down from heaven" what you're really doing is deifying your loved ones in your own mind. Systems of theology are used as tools to worship the people that you have lost. This is not a radical concept. Within ancient theology, such as Roman Polytheism, human beings themselves were deified as gods. Within early Christianity, people became lauded as saints for their positive deeds for the people, which is simply another form of deification without the supposedly arrogant implication of a human revered as a God. Deification, sainthood, Mahatma, and other honorifics are attempts to praise and honor our loved ones as Gods themselves. It is for the hope that they're remembered for all eternity. Removing faith takes away the immortalization of the dead and that immortalization is itself a reflection of people's feelings for their loved ones.

What should the answer be? Should people simply identify such beliefs as falsehoods? Should atheists condemn grieving people who strongly believe because they lost a loved one? No, absolutely not. In the context of people who have lost children, there is really nothing that atheism could offer to assuage their inner grief and the best answer I could possibly say is that I'm sorry for your loss. However, I would say their lives have intrinsic meaning because of how much those who have lost them choose to devote their lives to worshipping and, in that sense, deifying them. In regards to deceased people who've lived full lives, I would argue that much of their life has helped the work of others: children who grow more successful than their parents usually have their parents to thank for their support, love, and dedication. In other cases, philosophers who have formed philosophical arguments usually have their views adapted and built upon by admirers who form their own, scientific studies build upon or refute the previous works of past scientists, and the same can be applied to technology, laws, and virtually any form of human progress.[104] People can choose to celebrate their loved ones by running charity drives in the name of their loved ones for positive causes. Unfortunately, there are negative aspects of human progress that shouldn't be ignored, such as the methods of killing in warfare. In the end, it is due to what and how we as a species choose to improve about our existence. I would argue that all of the non-violent forms of progress do have intrinsic meaning. To the people of the 1700s and further back, we would be viewed as Gods with what we can do in our everyday lives. Even something like a cell phone may have brought cries of shock and claims of witchcraft because it would seem bizarre.

Death Worship

Religion is a worship of death. It wouldn't be inaccurate to say that religion is simply the term for popularized death cults. Terms such as afterlife, heaven, and nirvana are simply positive attributions to what is essentially valuing an imaginary world where the dead reside.[105][106] Heaven and hell are contradistinctions that serve the convenience of people; everyone favorable is in heaven and everyone despised is in hell. Consequently, heaven and nirvana are depictions of worshipping a *blessed death*; that is, a death for good people where they live on happily. Hell is the opposite; a death for evil people who suffer for the crimes they have caused upon humanity. Therefore, religion is sanctified death worship.

From the self-negation of asceticism and good/evil thinking, humans have largely concocted this fantasy for their own convenience. Instead of trying to find and apprehend war criminals, people are more prone to becoming apathetic to human rights crimes of war criminals. It is precisely the belief that war criminals are going to hell and good people are being sent to heaven that causes the pervasive apathy. A war criminal that has slaughtered hundreds of thousands and then lives a wholesome life before dying a natural death is argued to be in hell suffering for their sins and the innocent people that the war criminal killed are argued to be in heaven. It is a fantasy that only serves to feed our desire for revenge upon the war criminal and our desire to believe in a just world for the victims; it is a convenience that

---

1. [104] Nietzsche, Friedrich Wilhelm. "Chapter XXXIV: Self-Surpassing (108-111)" *Thus spake Zarathustra: a book for all and none*. Translated by Thomas Common, PDF ed., T. Common, 1908.
2. [105] Nietzsche, Friedrich Wilhelm. *THE ANTICHRIST*. Translated by H. L. Mencken, The Project Gutenberg, 2006.
3. [106] Nietzsche, Friedrich Wilhelm. "Chapter IX: Preachers of Death (50-52)" *Thus spake Zarathustra: a book for all and none*. Translated by Thomas Common, PDF ed., T. Common, 1908.

religious believers have construed to satisfy themselves instead of accepting the true horrors of wrongdoings.[107] The impotence towards fighting against human rights crimes, the convenience of fanciful thinking, and the belief in good and evil regarding what happens after death create a disdainful level of apathy towards all crimes against humanity. The religious attempt at an easy answer and anchoring towards the importance of souls creates a permissive indifference towards deplorable acts of savagery that is promoted through in-group and out-group differences of racial background, culture, religion, and national identity.

In general, the concept of a soul is a psychotic and narcissistic belief to hold. While seemingly innocuous and treated as normal within most communities across the world, the belief in the soul leads to pernicious consequences. The belief in a soul encourages people to view life itself as a test and to see suffering from diseases, poverty, and other forms of suffering as deep and meaningful for the purpose of an afterlife instead of taking on our personal challenges to work towards making a better future in our real life. Worse still, the belief in a soul inculcates us into antipathy towards life, to see everything as a nauseating struggle that is too difficult to understand or meaningfully contend with, and fosters a binary good versus evil worldview in which everything that has power is automatically assumed to be evil and the powerless are always viewed as good and righteous. The chief problem with the belief in a soul is that it is unhealthy for our physical wellbeing.[108][109] It is an unfounded belief that posits we will have all of our thinking and speech faculties in a deceased form of ourselves after our own deaths. Instead of critically examining the various maladies that afflict us as we age like Alzheimer's disease, potential physical injuries that require amputations of body parts, and personality changes due to dementia or drugs needed to keep ourselves alive; people who believe in souls see it all as an abstract form of decay in preparation for death where all those physical afflictions won't matter. The belief in the existence of a soul is a narcissistic belief in personal immortality outside of the physical body[110] and it is psychotic because of a rabid anti-materialist perspective that is inculcated on seeing our physical suffering as either morally good or necessary in preparation for the afterlife where our immortal self will go.[111] Dealing with death is tragic and painful, but the focus on an illusionary immortal self and anti-materialism can lead to devastating consequences. Despite nuanced philosophical conceptions, anti-materialism in more simplified religious conceptual frameworks can lead to disastrous and ridiculous activities such as anti-vaccination movements that harm entire communities and lead to the death of children as a result of a few handful of evocative stories of individual cases

---

4. [107] Nietzsche, Friedrich Wilhelm. *On the genealogy of morals: a polemical tract*. Translated by Ian Johnston, PDF, Richer Resources Publications, 2014.
5. [108] Nietzsche, Friedrich Wilhelm. *On the genealogy of morals: a polemical tract*. Translated by Ian Johnston, PDF, Richer Resources Publications, 2014.
6. [109] Nietzsche, Friedrich Wilhelm. *Thus spake Zarathustra: a book for all and none*. Translated by Thomas Common, PDF ed., T. Common, 1908.
7. [110] Nietzsche, Friedrich Wilhelm. Aphorism 43. *THE ANTICHRIST*. Translated by H. L. Mencken, The Project Gutenberg, 2006.
8. [111] Nietzsche, Friedrich Wilhelm. *THE ANTICHRIST*. Translated by H. L. Mencken, The Project Gutenberg, 2006.

reacting poorly to vaccines due to unique health circumstances that aren't reflective of the average population. These anecdotes are often guiding some people's judgment instead of statistical trends on large populations to get a fuller picture of health issues. In short, using anecdotes to tell a good versus evil story that conflate qualified medical professionals like doctors and nurses with supposed evil managers in companies that mass-produce drugs.[112] No distinction is made on either the medical professionals and the drug companies; nor is any distinction made between drug companies that may be doing positive work for the majority of people compared to ones that have been accused of scandals. Instead of researching issues for a clearer understanding of problems, there is simply anti-intellectual contempt and distrust based on an affect heuristic on anecdotal examples. A story of a child having a bad reaction can certainly be heartbreaking to read or watch and people getting a plethora of anecdotes across different countries from online can lead to fear of vaccines.[113][114] However, it is in ignorance of statistical averages and fails to account for the hundreds of millions who don't have any unique health defects that cause such reactions and live healthier lives with less worry about diseases that could harm their bodily health.

The anti-materialist mindset towards medical health can lead to using homeopathy cures such as from Christian Science culture, nonsensical pseudoscience like horoscope readings and crystal healing, and folk homeopathy carried over from family traditions centered around other types of superstitious thinking. Often these pseudo-scientific beliefs ignore legitimate medical treatment based on qualified medical professionals for special pleading arguments about certain symbols like the Cross harboring divine qualities, beliefs about holy water, and beliefs centered around casting out demons from people who are physically sick. The main focus of all these pernicious beliefs is that they are about healing the soul under the wrong belief that the soul actually exists and takes precedent over the physical body.[115] There is no evidence for the existence of a soul in science. While consciousness isn't fully understood as of this writing, conditions brought upon by dementia and Alzheimer disease are evidence that the existence of an immortal self that people refer to as a soul lacks credibility.

Even when ostensibly presenting themselves as creating hospitals to heal people, people with strong religious faith may instead create poor houses that do little more than take pleasure in the suffering of others to serve as their own emotional connection to the God they worship as was the case with Mother Teresa.[116] One may question why a religious believer would do such a horrible activity and praise themselves for it. It is because poverty, sickness,

---

9. [112] Ispas, Alexa. *Psychology and politics: a social identity perspective.* Psychology Press, 2014.
10. [113] Kahneman, Daniel. Chapter 8: How Judgments Happen (89-96) *Thinking, fast and slow.* Farrar, Straus and Giroux, 2015.
11. [114] Kahneman, Daniel. Chapter 30: Rare Events (322-333) *Thinking, fast and slow.* Farrar, Straus and Giroux, 2015.
12. [115] Nietzsche, Friedrich Wilhelm. *Thus spake Zarathustra: a book for all and none.* Translated by Thomas Common, PDF ed., T. Common, 1908.
13. [116] Hitchens, Christopher. "Christopher Hitchens: Hell's Angel: Mother Teresa (English Subtitles)." *YouTube*, BBC News, 7 Jan. 2015, youtu.be/NK7l_IhtKNU.

and suffering aren't seen as issues to take actionable steps against in order to make the lives of a community healthier, but instead as something to revere as sacred, proof of a simple truth that death exists for all people regardless of their economic status, and it is presented as something profound beyond the human experience. It is a worship of death prompted by the belief in a human soul.[117][118] It is allowing the physical suffering of others in order to feel a narcissistic pleasure in the belief in one's own delusion of immortality. This type of fanciful thinking can also lead to antipathy towards hierarchies based on expertise in fields that provide meaningful work that help millions of people everyday like economics, agriculture, waterways, railroads, aviation, healthcare, energy plants, businesses, banks, and government to instead give a blanket view that everything that has power is corrupt and to offer a form of equality that isn't equality at all.[119] Depending upon the particular religion, they can be hierarchies based on ancient stories that celebrate end of the world prophecies that indoctrinate people to give their discretionary income, one morning of every week of their time, and control of their sex lives to the religious leader of a congregation or the local mosque which often discriminate against women and LGBT people. In other religious groups, there are beliefs about reincarnation that create widespread societal friction on the basis of reincarnating into the top of the hierarchy in another life or going beyond reincarnation. Regardless of the specifics, religion offers hierarchies of insanity based upon devotion to ancient stories while vilifying expertise based upon hard work, lifelong experience, and rigorous academic learning.[120] Of course, there are deeply religious people that are part of hospitals, schools, and so forth who make positive contributions to society, but that is a non-sequitur in terms of proving their beliefs to be true. For comparison, many terrorist organizations like Hezbollah and Hamas do charity work in their local communities, do their charity drives validate their Islamist ideals to be the truth about reality? Selflessly helping others doesn't prove that a person's religion is true.

The most overt form of death worship is dying for the faith. While celebrating self-sacrifice may seem morally good and the noblest form of heroism that a person can do for their religion, it is ultimately celebrating someone who chose to die upholding the rules and traditions of a religious faith. A religion provides moral guidelines to regulate behavior and honors people who regulate themselves more than others because it shows a deeper conviction to the religious faith. The celebration of self-renunciation within religion eventually devolves into a celebration of death for the honor of the particular religion. The death of people who are killed for upholding their conviction to their religious faith is celebrated as proof of the faith's intrinsic goodness and proof of its truth. This is a pathological argument that perceives

14. [117] Nietzsche, Friedrich Wilhelm. Aphorism 43. *THE ANTICHRIST*. Translated by H. L. Mencken, The Project Gutenberg, 2006.
15. [118] Nietzsche, Friedrich Wilhelm. *Thus spake Zarathustra: a book for all and none*. Translated by Thomas Common, PDF ed., T. Common, 1908.
16. [119] Nietzsche, Friedrich Wilhelm. *THE ANTICHRIST*. Translated by H. L. Mencken, The Project Gutenberg, 2006.
17. [120] Nietzsche, Friedrich Wilhelm. *THE ANTICHRIST*. Translated by H. L. Mencken, The Project Gutenberg, 2006.

institutionalized insanity as an act of moral goodness. It is an explicit call upon people to die for their faith and is therefore indisputably an explicit worship of death. *To put it simply: dying for your religious faith doesn't prove your religion is true.*[121] Thus, *dying for your religious beliefs doesn't mean anything. It doesn't matter how strong you feel your convictions towards your religious faith are or how strongly someone you may know believed and died for them.* People would have difficulty to find any other system that asks them to die for the sake of proving the system is both morally good and to showcase its validity. To give more consideration to this criticism, consider this question proposed by Friedrich Nietzsche when he tackled this subject: Is there truly any meaningful difference between having conviction for your religious beliefs and believing in a lie?[122] To further add to this point, consider his challenging question with two questions added on: *What is the difference between having a strong conviction to your faith-based claim and believing in a lie? For someone else who believes in another religion, what is the difference between them believing in their faith-based claim and a lie? Why do you see your faith-based claim as fundamentally different from that other person's faith-based claim?*

Dying for the faith loses the pathological admiration that religious believers confer to the ideology when comparisons are made between different religious faiths. If self-sacrifice in the name of Judaism is the truth, then what use is any religiously motivated sacrifice in the name of Jesus Christ? Conversely, if Christianity is the truth then what is the value of any sacrifice in the name of Judaism? This pathological framework would instill people to sacrifice themselves so that the dead people on their side would validate their religious faith as the ultimate truth; what else can we call religious wars but just that kind of process? The self-destructive process continues through a pernicious circular reasoning that creates a sunk-cost fallacy.[123] Religious people celebrate the purportedly noble self-sacrifices to encourage more people to sacrifice themselves for the religion. In brief, circular reasoning is the logical fallacy of placing the premise of an argument into its conclusion in order to argue the conclusion is true[124] and the example in this critique is the following: Because people die for a holy book then the holy book is true because people selflessly chose to die for the holy book. Thus, in a horrific form of circular reasoning and the sunk-cost fallacy: to validate the past sacrifices as divine truth of the religion itself, the religion celebrates past sacrifices to make people favorably predisposed to sacrificing themselves in the present to continue this in-group self-exaltation as a means of arguing in favor of the so-called truth of a religious faith. This creates a historic celebration of human sacrifice as the noblest and purest act of religious faith. It is a

---

18. [121] Nietzsche, Friedrich Wilhelm. Aphorism 53. *THE ANTICHRIST*. Translated by H. L. Mencken, The Project Gutenberg, 2006.
19. [122] Nietzsche, Friedrich Wilhelm. Aphorism 55. *THE ANTICHRIST*. Translated by H. L. Mencken, The Project Gutenberg, 2006.
20. [123] Kahneman, Daniel. Chapter 31: Risk Policies (334-341) and Keeping Score (342 - 352) *Thinking, fast and slow*. Farrar, Straus and Giroux, 2015.
21. [124] "Circular Reasoning." *Https://Www.logicallyfallacious.com*, www.logicallyfallacious.com/tools/lp/Bo/LogicalFallacies/66/Circular-Reasoning.

sanctified call to death for all religious believers specifically to celebrate the religious faith. This is a powerful force within religion that shouldn't be ignored because it displays how deranged religion truly is.

Suicide Worship

Martyrdom exists in all religious faiths; despite the anecdotal popularization of Islam being a religion of suicide bombers, it has existed in both militant Christianity through the human sacrifice bombers – or proxy bombers as the news media called them – in Northern Ireland.[125] They would place bombs in the packages carried by kidnapped civilians and detonate them when the civilians were forced into delivering the packages by gunpoint or by having a bomb forcibly strapped onto them.[126] Militant Hinduism assisted in conducting suicide bombings in Sri Lanka against the discrimination and genocide of the ruling Buddhists. In all cases, all forms of suicidal terror were predominately motivated by overthrowing a perceived tyrannical ruler. In the case of the Tamil Tiger militia that was mostly comprised of Hindus, it was against brutal Buddhist oppression.[127] In the case of Northern Ireland, it was to gain independence from British rule since the British had a history of human rights crimes and genocide. In the case of suicidal terror in the Middle East, it is to overthrow the military presence of the United States so that the people of the Middle East can overthrow the Islamic dictators that commit egregious human rights crimes upon their own people while giving favorable economic benefits to the rest of the world. While suicidal terrorism doesn't originate from any particular religious faith, it seems to be the theological and intellectual conclusion of the doctrine of noble self-sacrifice that exists in all religious faiths. In the case of military tactics, it would mean sacrificing one unit to bring colossal damage to the enemy and it can have religious defense through the notion of sacrificing oneself for a divine purpose of fighting against evil. The use of "good against evil" to self-exalt the suicide bombers' group as morally good to fight against evil tyranny could be included as a reasoning behind suicidal terrorism. The belief of good versus evil and the doctrine of noble self-sacrifice would be the culprits when intermingled with suicidal depression of the person who blows themselves up.

Please consider this, isn't it the doctrine of noble self-sacrifice that feeds the narcissistic impulse of being a hero for a greater purpose? Moreover, this doctrine is a self-worship of one's own death as the greatest event for a divine purpose. Behind this supposedly noble

---

22. [125] POGATCHNIK, SHAWN. "IRA Proxy Bombings Kill 6 Troops, Civilian : Northern Ireland: The attack by the terrorist group is the deadliest against British forces in two years." *Los Angeles Times*, Los Angeles Times, 25 Oct. 1990, articles.latimes.com/1990-10-25/news/mn-4248_1_northern-ireland.
23. [126] McCann, Eamonn. "Real IRA's lust for violence matters more than ideology on the streets | Eamonn McCann." *The Guardian*, Guardian News and Media, 21 Aug. 2010, www.theguardian.com/uk/2010/aug/22/northern-ireland-dissidents-peace-process.
24. [127] Eggen, Dan, and Scott Wilson. "Suicide Bombs Potent Tools of Terrorists." *The Washington Post*, WP Company, 17 July 2005, www.washingtonpost.com/archive/politics/2005/07/17/suicide-bombs-potent-tools-of-terrorists/e11ed483-9936-45c0-b6c6-2653d4519ff5/?utm_term=.c23458392a4a.

ideology is a morbid self-hate and desire for suicide.[128][129] In regards to suicide bombings and religious wars, it is entirely possible that a paradoxical belief in self-hate and an exaggerated sense of self-importance when using weapons is what motivates the ideology of noble self-sacrifice. Their desire for suicide and self-importance intermingle to form an utterly depraved belief that celebrates their own suicide as a magnificent event against an enemy that is viewed as an abstract form of tyranny. It is precisely for that reason that suicidal terrorism is deliberate suicide in retaliation towards tyrannical domestic government or foreign governments perceived as aggressors, the suicidal bomber would feel a sense of pleasure at lashing out at foreign aggressors by making their own death be personally perceived as higher in importance in service to a political ideology. In conflation with the political context, the good and evil dynamic along with the religious belief in self-renunciation from asceticism would celebrate the belief in self-sacrifice as a divine service for a higher purpose. Similar to oppressed groups who lash out in violence against those who make them powerless, the suicide bomber could perceive their suicide as the only way to improve their sense of significance and may feel empowered by perceiving themselves as above their aggressors through personal self-sacrifice with the pleasure of knowing they'll never have to deal with life's hardships, they'll never have to suffer their feelings of hopelessness, or live through systems of oppressive cruelty ever again.[130] Their self-sacrifice would be perceived and celebrated as a leap of faith, a poignant moment of self-sacrifice (according to political groups whose interests of fighting a stronger army through the sacrifice of one soldier has been served and distraught family members of the deceased who try to find any positive in their mourning), and as rising above their "evil" oppressor.[131] Political groups that the suicidal terrorist is a part of would further reinforce this by celebrating the death as a form of self-sacrifice and awarding the family of the suicidal individual with stable living conditions, the significance of which shouldn't be understated; the suicidal terrorist will finally be proving themselves capable and could feel secure in the knowledge they helped their family by giving their lives to what they're inculcated to believe is a greater cause.[132] Martyrdom and self-sacrifice are merely semantic terms for sanctifying suicide, the only difference is that a political objective is attached to suicide to make a suicide bomber feel their life is finally above their oppressor through suicidal retaliation that has trite terminology to extol the perception that it's somehow blessed.[133]

---

25. [128] Lester, David. "Female Suicide Bombers: Clues from Journalists." *Suicidology Online*, Suicidology Online, 14 Nov. 2011, www.suicidology-online.com/pdf/SOL-2011-2-62-66.pdf.
26. [129] Lankford, Adam. "Martyr myth: Inside the minds of suicide bombers." *New Scientist*, 3 July 2013, www.newscientist.com/article/mg21929240-200-martyr-myth-inside-the-minds-of-suicide-bombers/.
27. [130] Lankford, Adam. "Exposing false 'martyrs' as suicidal." *The Jerusalem Post | JPost.Com*, 17 Feb. 2013, www.jpost.com/Opinion/Op-Ed-Contributors/Exposing-false-martyrs-as-suicidal.
28. [131] Lankford, Adam. "Exposing false 'martyrs' as suicidal." *The Jerusalem Post | JPost.Com*, 17 Feb. 2013, www.jpost.com/Opinion/Op-Ed-Contributors/Exposing-false-martyrs-as-suicidal.
29. [132] McDermott, Rose. Chapter 5: Behavior (119-152). *Political Psychology in International Relations*. Ann Arbor: U of Michigan, 2004. Print.
30. [133] Lankford, Adam. "What You Don't Understand about Suicide Attacks." *Scientific American*, 27 July 2015, www.scientificamerican.com/article/what-you-don-t-understand-about-suicide-attacks/.

Arguably, this ideology of noble self-sacrifice could apply to soldiers in war. It is possible that applies to some people within some countries, but nationalistic fervor is just as much of a reason for warfare and there have been atheists who have went to war throughout human history. Even so, there is a difference between sacrificing oneself to be in heaven as opposed to maintaining government power, sovereignty, and the welfare of a civilian populace. It depends upon the individual soldier, but there can be overlap and shallow differences within these conceptual frameworks. However, it doesn't discount the actions of soldiers who serve for the convenience of the public. Governments across the world should do more to provide better treatment for their soldiers; from hospital care, to education, to treatment for understandable psychological issues suffered from prolonged exposure to war, and to payments that they deserve. For example, it is rather dismaying to observe the problems with soldiers getting paid in a timely fashion in the US.[134][135][136] Another important point that should be noted is that while suicidal terror does foster fear, hostility, and resentment; it can also bring about resilience and stronger support for peace talks in opposition to the aims of terrorist groups to spark fear and in some cases, to foster further retaliation.[137][138]

The Eternal Death

Religion has routinely given positive characteristics to death. In order to stymie the fear of the unknown and to make sense of it, anthropomorphic and anthropocentric qualities were given to the reality of death to make it more familiar and relatable to human society and the individual's personal desires so that people felt a comforting acquiescence with death and the pain of losing loved ones. The concepts of the afterlife were reactionary concepts to the mass death brought by diseases, war, famine, and the nihilism that these horrors caused. The ancient world used rash judgments to find meaning in their lives; diseases, wars, famine, and natural disasters were seen as God's judgment.[139] Ancient people presumed that stricter social conditions upon their communities, sacrificial rituals, and coming of age rituals would bring good fortune to the community to lessen those circumstances. As a result, death was sanitized

---

31. [134] Carr, Kelly, and Scot J. Paltrow. "Reuters Investigates - UNACCOUNTABLE: The Pentagon's bad bookkeeping." *Reuters*, Thomson Reuters, 2 July 2013, www.reuters.com/investigates/pentagon/#article/part1.
32. [135] Carr, Kelly, and Scot J. Paltrow. "Reuters Investigates - UNACCOUNTABLE: The Pentagon's bad bookkeeping." *Reuters*, Thomson Reuters, 2 July 2013, www.reuters.com/investigates/pentagon/#article/part2.
33. [136] Carr, Kelly, and Scot J. Paltrow. "Reuters Investigates - UNACCOUNTABLE: The Pentagon's bad bookkeeping." *Reuters*, Thomson Reuters, 2 July 2013, www.reuters.com/investigates/pentagon/#article/part3.
34. [137] Lowe, Josh. "How Britain's history with the IRA made it resilient to attacks." *Newsweek*, 29 Mar. 2017, www.newsweek.com/london-attack-ira-terror-threat-severe-bomb-terrorism-573629.
35. [138] POGATCHNIK, SHAWN. "IRA Proxy Bombings Kill 6 Troops, Civilian : Northern Ireland: The attack by the terrorist group is the deadliest against British forces in two years." *Los Angeles Times*, Los Angeles Times, 25 Oct. 1990, articles.latimes.com/1990-10-25/news/mn-4248_1_northern-ireland.
36. [139] Kahneman, Daniel. *Thinking, fast and slow*. Farrar, Straus and Giroux, 2015.

and given positive qualities to create a coherent framework that made people believe they could escape their nihilistic feelings about the world.[140]

Death changed from being understood as the end of life to becoming part of some imaginary eternity. The imperfections of the world no longer mattered because people would be sent to a "perfect world" after death.[141] All of the problems of the real world didn't matter anymore; people just had to go through the monotony and suffering as if it were a type of nausea so they could enter their perfect world as a reward.[142] Our wants, our feelings, and our decisions became "illusionary" because they were impermanent; they were redefined as part of a grander scheme for an eternal and perfect system that served humanity's convenience for wanting to feel safe from disease, wars, famines, and other horrors. The eternal world, Samsara unto moksha i.e. reincarnation unto self-liberation, the afterlife, and purgatory were what each ancient civilization wanted their world to be so that their suffering was meaningful. Humanity gave death a set of positive human characteristics to make death more relatable and comfortable to process as an event.[143][144] The humanizing of death and the convenience of there being a life after death can be seen in modern culture; from films depicting the so-called afterlife, to books that make death similar to the real world through the idea of talking inhabitants in a "world" that people can interact within, and iconography depicting beautiful deities, angels, and a perfect world as a reward for people who have strong faith.[145][146] The religious argument that people can "never know" what happens after death is an argument from ignorance that originates from our desire for a meaningful and everlasting life – the same desires that the ancient world had. But do you see the problem? People who pose that argument are attempting to equalize the fact of death with fictional desires for a perfect world. It is explicitly to make the believer feel better about their inevitable death and the horrors of the world. The iconography and beliefs of the afterlife, reincarnation, and other ideas about eternal death aren't necessarily self-centered beliefs either. While the ultimate goal may be to feel more comfortable with death; the reasons for believing in the afterlife is also because of humanity's desire for a just world for victims that they'll never know. The imaginary eternal

---

37. [140] Nietzsche, Friedrich Wilhelm. *On the genealogy of morals: a polemical tract*. Translated by Ian Johnston, PDF, Richer Resources Publications, 2014.
38. [141] Nietzsche, Friedrich Wilhelm. *THE ANTICHRIST*. Translated by H. L. Mencken, The Project Gutenberg, 2006.
39. [142] Nietzsche, Friedrich Wilhelm. *On the genealogy of morals: a polemical tract*. Translated by Ian Johnston, PDF, Richer Resources Publications, 2014.
40. [143] Webb, David. "Fritz Heider & Marianne Simmel: An Experimental Study of Apparent Behavior." *Psychology*, www.all-about-psychology.com/fritz-heider.html.
41. [144] Nietzsche, Friedrich Wilhelm. *On the genealogy of morals: a polemical tract*. Translated by Ian Johnston, PDF, Richer Resources Publications, 2014.
42. [145] Webb, David. "Fritz Heider & Marianne Simmel: An Experimental Study of Apparent Behavior." *Psychology*, www.all-about-psychology.com/fritz-heider.html.
43. [146] Kahneman, Daniel. *Thinking, fast and slow*. Farrar, Straus and Giroux, 2015.

world can be considered a just world fallacy out of empathy for innocent victims throughout the real world.[147] It was a rash answer to a deeply complex problem that can't be solved easily.

The concept of God was probably a primitive attempt at creating familiar and humanistic characteristics upon the morbid feelings when observing death.[148] An eternal, perfect, and loving creator who had a plan beyond what the scope of our insignificance could comprehend was a more comforting and likable thought than the natural end of a life with no discernible way to understand diseases, natural disasters, and violence from neighboring tribes that attacked. It was a meaning formed through pattern recognition and rash judgments in order to understand the processes of the natural world that caused suffering.

---

44. [147] Grinnell, Renée. "Just-World Hypothesis." *Encyclopedia of Psychology*, 17 July 2016, psychcentral.com/encyclopedia/just-world-hypothesis/.
45. [148] Webb, David. "Fritz Heider & Marianne Simmel: An Experimental Study of Apparent Behavior." *Psychology*, www.all-about-psychology.com/fritz-heider.html.

Chapter 4: Open Interpretation and Coherent Religious Structures

The majority of religious believers use open interpretation in their understanding of their respective religion. This has led to a myriad of religious notions that usually try to stay neutral to the gap between religion and science. The God of the gaps, notions that changing personal opinions on social issues interpreted as people becoming closer to God (such as the issue of gay rights and more recently Transgender Rights for the Abrahamic faiths), and the rejection of untenable aspects of religious books such as the book of Leviticus in the Bible were concessions of religious beliefs to modernity. Stories about Adam and Eve in the Garden of Eden and Manu, the first man in Hinduism, are regarded as metaphorical instead of the divine truth originating from a higher power.

These concessions show a lack of awareness towards religious history; countless millions believed in the absolute truth of religious fables before science and modernity slowly destroyed the ability to justify those beliefs. The concept of science versus religion is a false argument because it doesn't delve into the true depth of the contentious issue. Science was never at war with religion; the 1800s were slowly weakening religion before Darwin's Origin of the species became popularized. *Religion has always been at war with modernity*. It doesn't matter how many born-again Christians can have the cognitive dissonance to believe in both science and religion; science will always seem at war with religion because science enhances modernity for the convenience of the public. Religion has a few generational successes through its cultural recidivism but such recidivism slowly erodes to social changes after each generation. Social media has made it easier to erode religious influence; it is easier to learn more about the world than ever before and people can fact-check anything they want. As a result, religious ideas will always be challenged by exposure to different peoples, cultures, ideologies, and lifestyles. Religion has been struggling against science, capitalism, women's liberation, sexual liberation, homosexual and transgender rights, freedom of speech, and the freedom of self-expression through art for centuries; the internet may allow mass ignorance to fester but it also allows challenges to beliefs from the interaction of opposing viewpoints.

The concept of open interpretation – the ability to pick and choose parables to follow and ignore the rest of the teachings of a religion – has allowed religion to remain compatible with modernity but eventually it'll no longer be possible. *Open interpretation ultimately reduces moral questions to personal preference*. For all of the refutations from the pious about the lack of positive moral teachings without religion, open interpretation has already rendered religious teachings to be ineffectual and obsolete. Arguably, modernity has supplanted religion and we are pretending otherwise to satisfy our own convenience because human societies are still unable to deal with a lack of objective meaning in life.

Open Interpretation and True Interpretation

When a religiously motivated atrocity occurs, people of the same religious faith as the attackers often contend that such barbaric actions are not the true interpretations of the religious faith. Whether it is Islamic terrorism, Christian militias slaughtering civilians in third world countries like the Central African Republic, shootings with explicitly religious call to arms, Buddhist beheadings in Myanmar, or the religious war for the so-called holy land by Jews, Christians, and Muslims for centuries unto our contemporary time; the majority of believers of a particular religious faith will always argue that such actions aren't true interpretations of their religious faith. This argument presents a total self-contradiction: if there are true interpretations of the faith then how can religion be openly interpretative? If religion *is* openly interpretative then how can the extremist interpretation of any religious faith be less valid than a moderate interpretation of the faith? Open interpretation would require both interpretations to be equally valid. If religion has a true interpretation, then which religious denomination of which specific religion is it? Despite my disagreements with them, New Atheists were correct in pointing out that the majority of believers in the Christian and Islamic religious denominations should expect to be in hell by a measure of probability should any specific denomination be proven true.

The issues with open interpretation exist because it is a set of logical fallacies; first, there is an appeal to purity. People disagree with or ignore the actions of other people within their religious affiliation to defend the innate goodness of the religious faith. Instead of taking into account the real life horrors that religion has caused, people argue that the horrible atrocities aren't a "true interpretation" or they argue that such actions aren't a reflection of God to defend their particular religious faith.[149] As a result, the apologists defending their faith ignore the human rights atrocities as an afterthought; the belief in God's mysterious plan can conveniently help any specific religious group ignore the victims who have died as a result of an interpretation of their religious faith.[150][151] The conviction to their faith expresses a depth of apathy and misanthropy towards the rest of the human species; the lives of perceived out-groups, who are the victims, are ignored just because they have no allegiance to the religious faith of the apologists.[152] The apologists have chosen the importance of their religious faith and their God over the purportedly less important affairs of human life.[153]

An example of a type of this defense occurred during the New York Public Library debate between Al Sharpton and Christopher Hitchens over the question of God. Sharpton

---

1. [149] Kahneman, Daniel. Chapter 9: Answering an Easier Question (97-104). *Thinking, fast and slow*. Farrar, Straus and Giroux, 2015.
2. [150] Kahneman, Daniel. *Thinking, fast and slow*. Farrar, Straus and Giroux, 2015.
3. [151] Cialdini, Robert B. Chapter 6: Authority (178-200). *Influence: Science and practice*. 4th ed., 21st Century Bks, 2002.
4. [152] Ispas, Alexa. *Psychology and politics: a social identity perspective*. Psychology Press, 2014.
5. [153] Cialdini, Robert B. Chapter 6: Authority (178-200). *Influence: Science and practice*. 4th ed., 21st Century Bks, 2002.

questioned what Hitchens criticisms regarding heinous stories from the Bible, what the actions of religious extremists in the Middle East – using Christian, Muslim, and Jewish examples of Iraq and the so-called Holy Land, and other examples of religious atrocities had to do with the question of God and the moral order of the universe.[154] While Hitchens didn't have a direct response, it seemed like a particularly cruel attempt at ignoring the atrocities and violent teachings. It is a tacit admittance that faith in God is valued more highly than the lives of people who are killed by religion; Sharpton continued to use the universe as an example of why there needs to be moral order so that there are limits to what is permissible. Thus, God is removed or constantly redefined to suit the convenience of the believers while ignoring the atrocities that a belief in God has caused.[155] But consider this; if this were any other social system such as imperialism, communism, monarchies, or fascism then would we be questioning what these social systems had to do with the senseless human slaughter? Why should it not reflect negatively upon religion when the religious apologists are more likely to dismiss egregious human rights crimes as an afterthought? Most importantly, what does the almost ubiquitous apathy by every religious majority towards human rights crimes in the name of their faith reveal about religious morality itself?

      A second logical fallacy with open interpretation is the "moving the goalposts" fallacy. It can work concurrently with appeal to purity. Essentially, the parameters and axioms of the religious faith are constantly changed to defend the supposed innate goodness of the religion.[156] Open interpretations allows this shift to happen so that no argument can change the perception of the religious believer. This style of argument shouldn't be applauded. Religious apologists ignore human rights crimes as less important than their theology as a result of this moving the goalposts and they're simply unwilling to listen to any arguments that portray religion as anything else but good in their coherence of the world.[157] Whenever a particular belief in their religion is rendered untenable in modernity then the reasons for the belief are substituted for different reasons to defend the belief; once the belief is successfully removed then religious apologists argue that such a belief had nothing to do with religion.[158] Homosexual rights is an example of moving the goalposts; some people against homosexuality attempted to substitute their religious reasons with their own ignorant understanding of animals in the wildlife by asserting that homosexuality didn't exist in the animal kingdom. Yet, they were wrong because their understanding of the world and animal biology was uninformed; they substituted their religious reasons for cultural and pseudo-scientific reasons because they

---

6. [154] "Christopher Hitchens Debates Al Sharpton - New York Public." *YouTube*, YouTube, 6 Dec. 2011, www.youtube.com/watch?v=HPYxA8dYLBY.
7. [155] Kahneman, Daniel. *Thinking, fast and slow*. Farrar, Straus and Giroux, 2015.
8. [156] "Moving the Goalposts." *Https://Www.logicallyfallacious.com*, www.logicallyfallacious.com/tools/lp/Bo/LogicalFallacies/129/Moving-the-Goalposts.
9. [157] Kahneman, Daniel. Chapter 6:"Norms, Surprises, and Causes" (71-78). *Thinking, fast and slow*. Farrar, Straus and Giroux, 2015.
10. [158] Kahneman, Daniel. Chapter 9: Answering an Easier Question (97-104). *Thinking, fast and slow*. Farrar, Straus and Giroux, 2015.

wanted to be consistent with their beliefs.[159] The psychological desire for consistency is what led them to substitute their religious reasons for what they ignorantly believed to be credible facts about life.[160] There were always homosexual animals in the animal kingdom but those animals were never mentioned in schools so that parents wouldn't become offended by their children learning about homosexual animals. Once homosexuality is generally accepted, then society shifts its tune to argue that anti-homosexuality is not a true interpretation of the faith.[161]

A third logical fallacy is the "Catch-22 fallacy" of open interpretation and religion itself. Catch-22 refers to a paradoxical situation in which people cannot escape because of contradictory rules.[162] In regards to the Ten Commandments of the Abrahamic faiths, the Commandments are either the inerrant words of God or they are utterly meaningless. Open interpretation creates a theological paradox in which following the rules means you're a religious believer but contradicting the rules still allows you to be a religious believer too.[163] Therefore, following the tenants of a faith or any of the other parables that have moral teachings has no value unless we decide to give them value. It could be argued that the believer who follows a greater degree of the rules is more true to the religious faith but open interpretation is an acceptance of personal preference. Thus, following a greater amount of rules or spending more time on religious activities wouldn't mean a greater or more truthful position of the religious faith. People would be allowed to contradict whatever rules they disliked at any given moment. Religion functions within this framework and people consistently change the contexts of moral teachings to suit themselves. Given this, what value can religion provide in terms of moral teachings? If you're allowed to make any contradictions to moral teachings to suit yourselves then what value is there in believing in your specific God or Gods? What stops people from arguing that not lying or not killing aren't true interpretations of their faith within the societies that they live in? What stops people from ignoring those precepts if religious beliefs are openly interpretative?

It seems evident that religious teachings don't prevent these consequences. In fact, the silence of religious institutions whenever their nation-state goes to war is a powerful example of 'Thou Shalt Not Kill' having no moral value in the Abrahamic faiths of the predominately Abrahamic countries. If we make distinctions of whom lives and dies based upon national identity and ignore casualties of war as an afterthought, then what does that mean for the so-called immutable laws of God? Whether they are followed or not, people still profess faith and

---

11. [159] Kahneman, Daniel. Chapter 9: Answering an Easier Question (97-104). *Thinking, fast and slow*. Farrar, Straus and Giroux, 2015.
12. [160] Cialdini, Robert B. Chapter 3: Commitment and Consistency (52-95) *Influence: Science and practice*. 4th ed., 21st Century Bks, 2002.
13. [161] "Moving the Goalposts." *Https://Www.logicallyfallacious.com*, www.logicallyfallacious.com/tools/lp/Bo/LogicalFallacies/129/Moving-the-Goalposts.
14. [162] "Circular Reasoning." *Https://Www.logicallyfallacious.com*, www.logicallyfallacious.com/tools/lp/Bo/LogicalFallacies/66/Circular-Reasoning.
15. [163] "Circular Reasoning." *Https://Www.logicallyfallacious.com*, www.logicallyfallacious.com/tools/lp/Bo/LogicalFallacies/66/Circular-Reasoning.

believe themselves to be part of the faith. How can these teachings then be morally good when they ultimately don't matter? Utilizing open interpretation, people are simply moving the goalposts because they change what the meaning behind religious morals is to suit themselves – even to the point of ignoring human rights crimes conducted by their own country. The supposed significance of religious morality changes for the convenience of the religious believer to justify any action or inaction. Bombings, village massacres, and other crimes are conducted upon out-groups of people that are perceived to be of less value in terms of human life than the in-group; this isn't simply combatants but innocent children mercilessly killed in bombings and other atrocities at taxpayer expense.[164] They become an afterthought thanks to the belief in open interpretation and the afterlife; people can conveniently ignore "Thou Shalt Not Kill" in these instances and make themselves feel better by imagining the dead children in the afterlife. Thus, open interpretation helps create self-exalted impotence and apathy towards such crimes against humanity. Within the framework of open interpretation, killing in the name of the religious faith has equal value to not killing in the name of the faith. In practical terms, this is how religious faith is utilized in all nation-states. On what grounds can such a self-contradiction have value?

Implicit Exclusivity

A principal reason why open interpretation has been so successful, despite its glaring flaws, is the implicit belief that only objections within the in-group of a religious faith have value. Out-groups are presumed to be facetious, lacking good morals, lacking depth in analysis, and potentially harboring an insidious intent to besmirch the religious faith.[165] For all intents and purposes, this is a form of tribalism; no matter what the out-group does, they will be regarded with suspicion and derision. Only when a person becomes similar to the in-group will they be welcomed as "open-minded" and thoughtful.[166] That is why it would be more accurate to say narcissistic impulse as opposed to "relatedness" in terms of psychological discourse when discussing how commonality makes people more interested in others.

The extent of the implicit exclusivity can vary from denomination to denomination and person to person but there are certain predisposed beliefs that show strong elements of tribalism. In the context of the Abrahamic faiths, believers often argue and seem to internally feel that their readings of the Abrahamic texts are more accurate than an atheist reading them. To the perception of the religious believer, a belief in God confers a greater amount of understanding of Biblical passages. Yet, research by Pew Research has indicated that most atheists have a greater understanding of the contents of the holy books of their prior religion and they have a greater knowledge of religion in general than theists.[167] To an outside observer,

---

16. [164] Hedges, Chris. *War Is a Force That Gives Us Meaning*. PublicAffairs, 2002.
17. [165] Ispas, Alexa. *Psychology and politics: a social identity perspective*. Psychology Press, 2014.
18. [166] Cialdini, Robert B. *Influence: Science and practice*. 4th ed., 21st Century Bks, 2002.
19. [167] "U.S. Religious Knowledge Survey." *Pew Research Center's Religion & Public Life Project*, Pew Research Center's Religion & Public Life Project, 19 Dec. 2017, www.pewforum.org/2010/09/28/u-

the claim of religious books having more accurate or special qualities is simply an indication that the believers find the passages to be more meaningful without critical analysis.[168] An ex-Christian penpal from Australia once informed me, when I asked him about his prior beliefs, that his fellow Christians simply believed that the Bible had magic words that only fellow Christians could understand and that the special magical qualities of the Bible disappeared when non-believers tried to read them.[169] According to him, they believed in some holy qualities that only they could understand. The exclusivity is further solidified through regarding other faiths as fooled into believing in falsehoods or practicing some form of "evil" worship. Other faiths would argue the same of them; especially in the context of Abrahamic religions and thus permanent in-group and out-group implications would exist to divide people.[170][171]

Moral Neutrality

Theistic arguments in favor of being morally neutral to killings during war reveal a depth of apathy and savagery that disprove the supposed innate goodness of religious morals. In practical effect, the immutable laws of God stop outside of national borders and the people within those borders ignore the war crimes of their nation-state. The attempts to argue that such topics are "too complex" shows both the weakness of religious morality when applied to reality and the true level of apathy that people have for other human beings perceived as out-groups.[172] A desire to remain innocent of wrongdoing seems to become a desire to be innocent from any responsibility. The real life apathy seems to be instilled from cultural depictions of heroes and protagonists being innocent of moral wrongdoing to convey the desire to live in an unrealistic world with no responsibility – children's TV shows that teach such lessons infer the desire to live in a patently unrealistic lifestyle and worsen the ability of adapting complex thoughts when children become adults. The notion of soldiers from their nation-state committing war atrocities, such as war rapes and the mass murders of civilians, can't be handled well in a religious believer's coherence of the world. As a result, through a combination of moral neutrality and good versus evil, some adults perceive all things outside of their oversimplifications of the world as evil and begin to suppress a nihilistic viewpoint. The oversimplified perspective helps apologists defend war atrocities that were committed via the inculcation of revering religious systems that promote warfare; religious passages become tools of manipulation to comfort people who learn of human rights crimes by insisting that an intrinsic failure in human nature is to blame. The dead victims become an afterthought that is ignored for the comfort of the religious believer.

---

s-religious-knowledge-survey/.
20. [168] Kahneman, Daniel. Chapter 4: The Associative Machine (50-58) and Chapter 5: Cognitive Ease (59-70). *Thinking, fast and slow*. Farrar, Straus and Giroux, 2015.
21. [169] Kahneman, Daniel. *Thinking, fast and slow*. Farrar, Straus and Giroux, 2015.
22. [170] Ispas, Alexa. *Psychology and politics: a social identity perspective*. Psychology Press, 2014.
23. [171] Cialdini, Robert B. *Influence: Science and practice*. 4th ed., 21st Century Bks, 2002.
24. [172] McDermott, Rose. *Political Psychology in International Relations*. Ann Arbor: U of Michigan, 2004. Print

Moral neutrality is an attempt to absolve all forms of violence and actions commonly asserted as "evil" by Abrahamic morality itself. Moral neutrality ignores the effects and focuses strictly on the personal ego of the one committing human rights crimes. When religious morality is needed the most, its interpretation is changed and violence is permitted. Instead of focusing upon the lives of innocents being mercilessly slaughtered, non-sequitur analogies about surgeons cutting into a body are utilized to manipulate people into killing other human beings to promote a war campaign.[173] Unrealistic belief systems serve as a comfort for the killers as they slaughter innocent lives – including children. Minimizing moral question to terms of "intentions" reveals a total apathy for life itself.[174] Arguing in favor of a religious cause, like regaining religious lands, as the reason for brutal acts of cruelty and stupidity shows the innate emptiness in believing that religion is a force of goodness.[175] All human rights crimes can be ignored for the sake of a recovering religious lands and property. The value of human life is less valuable to fellow humans than religious iconography and religious land; religious believers profess the truth and peacefulness of their specific religion during missionary outings after slaughtering people within the region under the justification of the religion itself.[176] Moreover, the slaughter is usually justified by bringing God to the savages; such are the cases of the Christian Crusades, the genocide of the Native Americans, the genocide of the Philippines, the colonization of India by a Portugal inquisition, and the genocide of the Tasmanian aboriginals. The lives of victims become part of "history" and no longer have any value because it happened years ago but sacrifices in the name of the religion should be celebrated forever. It is a selective system that only seeks narcissistic self-worship of the in-group religious identity and ignores the innocents who were slaughtered because they're an out-group.[177][178][179]

Just War Theory and Moral Relativism

All attempts at defining "Just War Theory" – an argument that historically originated from theological arguments to defend wars[180] – has been a mere obfuscation to defend the political and economic objectives of a nation-state that goes to warfare with others. It reduces

---

25. [173] Abels, Richard. "Crusades and early Christian attitudes toward warfare." *Academia.edu - Share research*, www.academia.edu/22844402/Crusades_and_early_Christian_attitudes_toward_warfare.
26. [174] Abels, Richard. "Crusades and early Christian attitudes toward warfare." *Academia.edu - Share research*, www.academia.edu/22844402/Crusades_and_early_Christian_attitudes_toward_warfare.
27. [175] Abels, Richard. "Crusades and early Christian attitudes toward warfare." *Academia.edu - Share research*, www.academia.edu/22844402/Crusades_and_early_Christian_attitudes_toward_warfare.
28. [176] Abels, Richard. "Crusades and early Christian attitudes toward warfare." *Academia.edu - Share research*, www.academia.edu/22844402/Crusades_and_early_Christian_attitudes_toward_warfare.
29. [177] Ispas, Alexa. *Psychology and politics: a social identity perspective*. Psychology Press, 2014.
30. [178] Kahneman, Daniel. Chapter 4: The Associative Machine (50-58) and Chapter 5: Cognitive Ease (59-70). *Thinking, fast and slow*. Farrar, Straus and Giroux, 2015.
31. [179] Hedges, Chris. *War Is a Force That Gives Us Meaning*. PublicAffairs, 2002.
32. [180] Abels, Richard. "Crusades and early Christian attitudes toward warfare." *Academia.edu - Share research*, www.academia.edu/22844402/Crusades_and_early_Christian_attitudes_toward_warfare.

sensory warfare; bombing campaigns, killings of entire villages, war rapes, child soldiers, child killings, and ethnic cleansing into sophistry about fictitious intentions that had no bearing on going to warfare.[181] It reduces human rights as less valuable than sovereign objectives and it is mostly untrue of war operations conducted in foreign countries because war operations usually require long-term planning for success. Prolonged war is likely because the foreign government and civilians feel their sovereign territory is in danger; thus they will always argue self-defense against foreign incursion. Obtaining military objectives effectively requires bombing campaigns and mass raids that endanger civilians. For all the lauded goodness of religion, it unalterably fails to stop any wars and has deep theological pretexts to justify them. Religion will never be the end of war because it creates fictional notions about God, Gods, a flimsy morality, and the afterlife to justify war's barbaric nature.

Religious teachings within national borders practice a more absolute form of moral teachings about not killing but outside of national borders it ubiquitously concedes to moral relativism. In all practical sense, what can the notion of "moral neutrality" under religion be called besides moral relativism itself? Most apologists make arguments from semantics or use religious teachings and metaphysical beliefs to ignore mass killings conducted by their nation-state upon civilians in other nation-states. Anchoring our view to the intent of the national leader, of which we couldn't possibly know and historically has used deceit to bring forth horrific consequences, depicts the utter failings of religious morality and the willful ignorance of scholars who defend it. If we reduce mass violence into terms of intentions; we reduce massive death tolls to the personal preference of our leader's ego. Moreover, what prevents a foreign nation-state from justifying bombings, killings, war rapes, and other forms of human cruelty upon us under the Just War Theory's terms of intentions? The foreign people could easily defend the death and destruction that they've inflicted our people under the justification of their leader's intentions being genuinely good. Or they could argue that minimizing casualties inflicted upon us was for the sake of their objective. Why couldn't they also argue that our dead are in some form of afterlife and thus we should feel less despondent about our losses? I'd rather not get into arguments for reprisal against wrongdoings because that is how Osama bin Laden justified 9/11; he argued US bombings in different locations upon Muslim civilians, the aid in funding Israel's wars on Palestine, the collusion with Islamic dictators who sell oil on the US dollar, and the sanctions on Iraq that killed approximately 500,000 innocent children justified his terrorism in his letter to the US.[182][183]

Psychological studies have found that people behave reciprocally with other people; meaning if you do a kind gesture then they are likely to return a gesture of kindness and if you

---

33. [181] Hedges, Chris. *War Is a Force That Gives Us Meaning*. PublicAffairs, 2002.
34. [182] "Full text: bin Laden's 'letter to America'." *The Guardian*, Guardian News and Media, 24 Nov. 2002, www.theguardian.com/world/2002/nov/24/theobserver.
35. [183] Gause, F. Gregory. "Getting It Backward on Iraq." *Foreign Affairs*, Foreign Affairs, 28 Jan. 2009, www.foreignaffairs.com/articles/iraq/1999-05-01/getting-it-backward-iraq.

commit an egregious act then they're likely to do the same.[184] Religious lessons of being peaceful have never held-up to real life standards because of the constant reinterpretations of religion throughout human history. That isn't an indictment against human nature; it's a total moral failing of religion's claim of being the ultimate truth and teaching good morals. The divine moral codes always need to be changed so the nation-state can meet its objectives.[185] Killing people – including innocent children – becomes ignored through religious teachings. Religious teachings help to comfort the killers with the idea of human nature being synonymous with failure and evil.[186] Civilians who feel empathetic for the human rights atrocities use religion as a scapegoat by telling themselves that any dead civilians, such as murdered children, are in the afterlife and that the politicians who promoted the war will be in a negative version of the afterlife; these beliefs are to make themselves feel better and to more effectively ignore the atrocities. Therefore, religion does more to excuse egregious acts of violence and doesn't instill good life lessons.

Control

A significant factor in the historic reinterpretation of religious teachings, particularly after political changes, is the need for control over their own lives. People have biological need for control in order to feel that their actions matter and to keep a coherent worldview that makes sense to them. Psychological research has shown the belief that our actions have an impact significantly reduces anxiety, laziness, pessimism, and fear of the world.[187] That is why we create our own "causes" for events and why the fallacy of "causation doesn't equal correlation" run rampant in many arguments regarding political topics.[188] This need for control can become dangerous because it leads to using a scapegoat to explain disasters; an example would be how the war reparations upon Germany after the end of World War 1 combined with the economic depression resulted in Christian extremism that led to the genocide of six million people comprised of the minority groups of Germany. A modern example would be the fear and hatred of Muslim Americans within the US after the attack on the Twin Towers on September 11th, 2001. (Note: I would also like to mention that I am not arguing moral equivalence between the Holocaust and 9/11 or the genocide of the Jews to the discrimination of a subset of Americans.) The belief in removing the "undesirables" from society occurs because people make rash judgments on how to remove the violence from being inflicted upon their in-group.[189][190] They begin to perceive minority groups similar to the attackers as

---

36. [184] Cialdini, Robert B. Chapter 2: Reciprocation (19-50). *Influence: Science and practice*. 4th ed., 21st Century Bks, 2002.
37. [185] Kahneman, Daniel. *Thinking, fast and slow*. Farrar, Straus and Giroux, 2015.
38. [186] Kahneman, Daniel. *Thinking, fast and slow*. Farrar, Straus and Giroux, 2015.
39. [187] Kahneman, Daniel. *Thinking, fast and slow*. Farrar, Straus and Giroux, 2015.
40. [188] Kahneman, Daniel. Chapter 6:"Norms, Surprises, and Causes" (71-78) and Chapter 7: A Machine for Jumping to Conclusions (79-88). *Thinking, fast and slow*. Farrar, Straus and Giroux, 2015.
41. [189] Cialdini, Robert B. Chapter 1: Weapons of Influence (1-16). *Influence: Science and practice*. 4th ed., 21st Century Bks, 2002.

intrinsically associated with them and create caricatures that fuel the coherence of the out-group being pure evil. There is usually a rash overestimation of how many of the minority groups harbor extremist ideologies to justify discrimination and stricter policies. These policies are implemented because people believe it will contain or control the threat without any clear analysis on the real causes of violence through statistical research or proper studies of the views that terrorists actually hold.

Argument of First Cause

The first cause argument is the most notorious use of the God of the gaps argument; that is, the fallacy in which the unknown parts of a subject matter has God substituted as the explanation when science has yet to discover the answer to an issue. This is primarily used by theists to try to find a coherent balance between religion and science to satisfy their own doubts about faith. In the case of First Cause, the argument is that there must be a Creator deity because something cannot come from nothing and that the life wouldn't be able to exist without a Creator deity with a divine intent and purpose. Within the context of this belief is the argument that randomness or spontaneity cannot form the basis for a cause and that human life is largely following the trajectory of a Creator deity's guiding hand because of how the world is organized. Since all of life and the universe has a beginning, then the beginning must be a Creator deity and this view has been adapted into modern forms such as Fine-Tuning.

As a side note, I profusely apologize to any Biologist, Cosmologist, astrophysicist, theoretical physicist, or any other scientist in the various Natural Sciences for misattributing or misapplying the science, if I have done so. For the purposes of addressing the First Cause argument, I think some oversimplification is needed since science is a multifarious and complex subject.

For this section, I'll largely be referencing John Stuart Mill's profound argument against First Cause in conjunction with my limited knowledge of the latest scientific insights into the origins of the universe found by modern scientific research. I've broken it down to four numerical propositions to get the root of the issue. I feel that attacking the central assumptions on this matter is key.

1. The belief in God presupposes knowledge that people simply do not have of the observable and natural world.[190] Arguments from faith are matters of intuition and anecdotal inference that lack empirical evidence on the basis of an origin. The closest understanding to the origin would be the mathematical calculations provided by astrophysicists, which have recently developed a mathematical proof that the universe could have come from nothing.[192]

---

42. [190] McDermott, Rose. *Political Psychology in International Relations*. Ann Arbor: U of Michigan, 2004. Print.
43. [191] Mill, John Stuart. *Three essays on religion*. Timeless Wisdom Collection, 2016.
44. [192] "A Mathematical Proof That The Universe Could Have Formed Spontaneously From Nothing."

2. The reasoning of *a priori* doesn't prove a God's existence. What people assume to follow as a logical transition is looking back at the past through a succession of changes from the standpoint of the present civilization that they inhabit.[193] However, what they're actually doing is looking at the origin of composition that our species utilized to invent more complex devices.[194] Inferring a Creator on the basis of the original composition doesn't have a logical transition behind it because it is just human creativity to form complex systems specifically to serve a purpose for the betterment of human civilizations. Proponents for First Cause take the transition as a given, such as the circular reasoning that it cannot conceivably be any other way, when it's not. It's never been an organized transition toward the fateful present; it's only been changes as a result of human agency working to alter and modify their systems of organization through inventions or new government systems. It doesn't acknowledge regress as a result of humans stubbornly holding to traditions or abandoning attempts at positive change in favor of ignorance or apathy towards potent social issues, which largely come from religion itself. In fact, the general idea doesn't factor failed civilizations, fallen empires, or abusive practices like the eugenics movement that harm people and are then ignored when teaching history.

3. While human civilizations exist due to a lengthy period of changes as a result of human agency, human biology and the biology of other animals largely follows from a progression that is contradictory to the existence of a Creator deity. The belief that a being of high intellect and power preceded us doesn't follow the logical order of the world through natural selection of biology because the assumptions misunderstand what natural selection is. There is no reason to assume a higher being made anything. The logical consequence of our observations of the natural world form a general theory that more basic compositions created an organized composition greater than itself into a higher composition from mutations in order to increase its survivability[195]; we logically are the product of such a long period of composition growing into higher composition through natural selection from gene mutations increasing our survivability over long periods of time. The human body is a complex organism, it's very organs harboring complex systems that exist in service of keeping a human body alive and functioning. Our genetic ancestors seem ridiculous to us because our evolution allowed for us to improve from our origins. From microbes to higher forms of life like birds, apes, and us. Therefore, from the standpoint of both *a priori* and empiricism, we came from lesser parts to make a greater whole through the long history of evolution.[196] But what about animals who became lower in form due to genetic mutations, such as some dinosaurs? As mentioned, the gene mutations inherited by offspring help increase their survivability over time; the pertinent concept to understand is

---

Medium, The Physics ArXiv Blog, 11 Apr. 2014, medium.com/the-physics-arxiv-blog/a-mathematical-proof-that-the-universe-could-have-formed-spontaneously-from-nothing-ed7ed0f304a3.

45. [193] Mill, John Stuart. *Three essays on religion*. Timeless Wisdom Collection, 2016.

46. [194] Mill, John Stuart. *Three essays on religion*. Timeless Wisdom Collection, 2016.
47. [195] Mill, John Stuart. *Three essays on religion*. Timeless Wisdom Collection, 2016.
48. [196] Mill, John Stuart. *Three essays on religion*. Timeless Wisdom Collection, 2016.

which genetic mutations help increase the species survival. Therefore, genetic mutations slowly change the species by allowing those who can adapt to new conditions to propagate more offspring.

4. Following from three in understanding changing composition, the only permanent, simplistic answer and origin of composition is the *Law of Conservation of Mass-Energy Equivalence* and this doesn't need a higher power. We're simply thinking of *a priori* wrong when advocating for a divine being as our origin when we base our assessment on anecdotal inference to the world around us. The most simplistic answer is the *Law of Conservation of Mass-Energy Equivalence*. Mass-energy is the same. It goes through changes in their elementary properties into higher organizational forms through eons of transition.[197] There's no need for a Creator or First Cause in that process at all, because its misunderstanding cosmology. Judging from the evidence, the universe may have always existed and the "start" of the universe that theoretical models detail may just be a change in composition as per the *Law of Conservation of Mass-Energy*. Therefore, there is no need for the existence of a Creator deity.

Control, Communalism, and Fine Tuning

Before the rise of science, religion was used to interpret phenomena under forms of communalism. Under ancient Abrahamic tribes: mental illness was seen as witchcraft or devilry, disease was seen as the wrath of God, failed crops or dangerous weather was seen as the wrath of God, luck was seen as a blessing, victory of one barbaric tribe over other barbaric tribes was seen as God having chosen the people to succeed, failure against another tribe was seen as God's punishment upon them for some miscellaneous violation of ancient religious ethics, and concepts such as sinfulness in human nature and blasphemy were attempts at creating a convincing worldview.[198][199] It was a worldview that explained weather patterns, disease, success, failure, and luck as part of the ancient community's actions so that they felt a sense of control over their situation.[200][201] Incidentally, desperation is known to increase less cognizant and fanciful worldviews in order to find an escape from suffering or to blame it upon another group of peoples – such as the history of anti-Semitism throughout Christianity and Islam or the destruction of other tribes throughout the Old Testament.

Modern religion still has instances of interpreting lucky events as religious phenomena but it has mostly been used to selectively pick and choose events for a worldview that fits the idea of a specific creator deity. The argument of "fine tuning", that is the idea of the universe being guided by a divine hand because of the uniqueness of the earth and the human race, and

---

49. [197] Mill, John Stuart. *Three essays on religion*. Timeless Wisdom Collection, 2016.
50. [198] Kahneman, Daniel. *Thinking, fast and slow*. Farrar, Straus and Giroux, 2015.
51. [199] Cialdini, Robert B. Chapter 4: Social Proof (98-140). *Influence: Science and practice*. 4th ed., 21st Century Bks, 2002.
52. [200] Cialdini, Robert B. Chapter 4: Social Proof (98-140). *Influence: Science and practice*. 4th ed., 21st Century Bks, 2002.
53. [201] Kahneman, Daniel. *Thinking, fast and slow*. Farrar, Straus and Giroux, 2015.

the antipathy toward the idea that the universe could come from nothing have been soundly rejected because of recent scientific discoveries and mathematical probabilities; the universe doesn't need a self-caused or eternal deity and it is mathematically probable that the universe could have come from nothing.[202] Moreover, there are earth-like planets in the habitable zones of the universe, of which the earth is one planet of many, so the earth isn't unique as religious believers tend to argue. Many reject string theory and the concept of a universe coming from nothing, despite the mathematical feasibility of the universe coming from nothing, on the basis of its cold indifference to the existence of the human race. Their personal incredulity is a fallacy and isn't a positive argument in favor of a higher power. Furthermore, it would be entirely fallacious to argue that mathematics doesn't have a basis in our personal lives. Math is not some cold and invisible part of our lives; it is something we constantly take for granted. Subject matters such as population size, the speed of an internet connection, the amount of laps or repetitions for quality exercise, dieting, surgeries to save our lives, and the correct dosage for ingestion of quality medicine are all daily and complex forms of mathematics in our personal lives. It is not miracles, but human ingenuity in progressing mathematics in conjunction with biology, computer science, computer engineering, physics, modernized medical practices, and other scientific-mathematical subjects that has allowed us to live quality lifestyles and increase our life expectancy.

It has been religion that has had to concede to modernity by using the "God of the gaps" as the basis for arguments such as fine tuning and for there being a "cause" for the creation of the universe; the use of God where science still hasn't determined factors of how the universe works is not just an argument from ignorance but theological-induced blindness from the axioms of religious faith. Theological-induced blindness is similar to theory-induced blindness; people anchor their worldview upon a specific theory from a specific set of beliefs and ignore the exceptions as strange occurrences instead of accepting the weaknesses of the theory; thereby ignoring the factors and factual information where the theory cannot be applied.[203] The God of the gaps is a modern attempt at understanding the rest of the world through human iconography, by trying to relate the facts of the universe to our existence as humans.[204] Concepts such as the God of the gaps are a narcissistic desire by humanity to be the most important aspect of the universe. Untenable aspects of holy texts like Adam and Eve, Manu, The Abrahamic God creating the world in seven days, Noah's Ark, and similar fanciful ideas have been rendered unable to be interpreted as truthful; leaving vast swathes of these texts as symbolic or metaphorical instead of being interpreted literally as people in ancient societies understood them to be. Ergo, they no longer give humanity any objective value and don't have any truths beyond what we want them to be.

---

54. [202] "A Mathematical Proof That The Universe Could Have Formed Spontaneously From Nothing." *Medium*, The Physics ArXiv Blog, 11 Apr. 2014, medium.com/the-physics-arxiv-blog/a-mathematical-proof-that-the-universe-could-have-formed-spontaneously-from-nothing-ed7ed0f304a3.
55. [203] Kahneman, Daniel. Chapter 27: The Prospect Theory (278-288). *Thinking, fast and slow*. Farrar, Straus and Giroux, 2015.
56. [204] Kahneman, Daniel. *Thinking, fast and slow*. Farrar, Straus and Giroux, 2015.

The argument for fine tuning, the use of the God of the gaps, has been thoroughly discredited for many years. A mathematical proof has found that it is realistically possible that the universe came from nothingness and the earth is among many earth-like planets to exist in a habitable zone of the universe. Even before these discoveries, the argument from fine tuning was absurd. It posited that the universe needed a cause and that the cause had to be "willing", yet that is a total non-sequitur. A cause does not have to be willing to do anything; furthermore the fine tuning argument used the natural laws of the universe as an attempt to validate itself. This was under the belief that the natural laws couldn't be random otherwise nothing could be consistent or exist on any consistent basis. If they already concede that the natural laws of the universe are true, then why believe that the natural laws of the universe were suspended twice for the sake of Jesus? Even if there was a creator deity, that wouldn't have proven that Jesus Christ was who he claimed to be or that he harbored the ability to suspend the natural laws of the universe. The same applies to other religious beliefs.

From an outside view, it is easy to see what the pious are desperately attempting to do. They have attempted to reorganize and reframe the scientific studies of the big bang, the expanding universe, and the events before the big bang with their preconceived biases through their misrepresentation of the facts. We humans seek meaning in our lives and we're biased to look for "causes" to create a coherent worldview about ourselves.[205] Due to the human bias of looking for causes as an explanation, the pious have sought to find a "cause" for the big bang that they have construed to be similar to their biblical deity. Yet, just because people desire to find a cause doesn't mean that one actually exists and people are predisposed to finding false causes for events that create stories in their minds that make them feel good instead of assessing evidence for their beliefs.[206] The pious that use the fine tuning argument wish to be consistent with their prior beliefs and try to create a coherent view that they're more familiar with.[207] The gaps in the fine tuning argument are numerous: why did a creator deity not make the universe more habitable for human life beyond the miniscule habitable zone? If the heat death of the universe due to rapid expansion is going to happen, and the current scientific data suggests that it will, then why did a creator deity make the universe only for our species to eventually die once the heat dissipates from the universe? If the universe was made with humanity in mind, then why make it so difficult for us to live outside of the earth?

Incidentally, much of the higher forms of life before us have also fallen into extinction and thus contradict the notion of a divine plan. If the purpose of a divine plan is narrowly focused intentions upon humans, then why bother bringing into existence and then exterminating entire species of animals that existed before we humans did? Why even create the dinosaurs, or any other animal species, that isn't governed by theistic laws and have no

57. [205] Kahneman, Daniel. Chapter 6:"Norms, Surprises, and Causes" (71-78) and Chapter 7: A Machine for Jumping to Conclusions (79-88). *Thinking, fast and slow*. Farrar, Straus and Giroux, 2015.
58. [206] Kahneman, Daniel. *Thinking, fast and slow*. Farrar, Straus and Giroux, 2015.
59. [207] Cialdini, Robert B. Chapter 3: Commitment and Consistency (52-95) *Influence: Science and practice*. 4th ed., 21st Century Bks, 2002.

effect upon them? What purpose does it serve humans for a God to give life to and then exterminate entire species of animals that have no tangible connection to us? Did the entirety of their species simply exist to be harvested as sacrifices to pose as a warning for human arrogance? For instance, assuming the Abrahamic religions are true, and the Abrahamic God exists and acknowledging the fact that animals cannot commit sins because they hold no capacity to understand human morals; then the Abrahamic God wiped out a large and diverse set of species, the dinosaurs, without sinfulness playing a factor in their annihilation. There was no judgment of good or evil, the Abrahamic God simply wiped out a species with no moral judgments intended, there was no greater divine purpose for their existence, and sinful conduct was a total non-factor. What was the point? What purpose did it serve humans to have done this? If the Abrahamic God did it to bring fear for human arrogance or for no reason at all, then how can the Abrahamic God not be recognized as cruel and using life itself as merely a plaything? If the Abrahamic God is innately good, then what purpose could bringing to life and wiping out a species with no relation to original sin serve?

Even disregarding these arguments as part of God's mysterious plan, and even disregarding the genuine likelihood that the universe can come from nothingness, the supposition of a creator deity is an unsubstantiated assumption and its existence would need to be substantiated to show that it was more likely than any other baseless assumption about what came before the big bang. For example, I could postulate the assumption of Friedrich Nietzsche's thought experiment of eternal recurrence as the event before the big bang.

For those unfamiliar with the eternal occurrence thought experiment of Friedrich Nietzsche's from his book, *The Gay Science*:

"The Heaviest Burden. What if a demon crept after you into your loneliest loneliness some day or night, and said to you: "This life, as you live it at present, and have lived it, you must live it once more, and also innumerable times; and there will be nothing new in it, but every pain and every joy and every thought and every sigh, and all the unspeakably small and great in thy life must come to you again, and all in the same series and sequence - and similarly this spider and this moonlight among the trees, and similarly this moment, and I myself. The eternal sand-glass of existence will ever be turned once more, and you with it, you speck of dust!" - Would you not throw yourself down and gnash your teeth, and curse the demon that so spoke? Or have you once experienced a tremendous moment in which you would answer him: "You are a God, and never did I hear anything so divine!" If that thought acquired power over you as you are, it would transform you, and perhaps crush you; the question with regard to all and everything: "Do you want this once more, and also for innumerable times?" would lie as the heaviest burden upon your activity! Or, how would you have to become favourably inclined to yourself and to life, so as to long for nothing more ardently than for this last eternal sanctioning and sealing?"[208]

Can you prove my assumption that eternal recurrence occurred before the big bang is wrong? No, and you wouldn't need to because I haven't provided any evidence that eternal

---

60. [208] Nietzsche, Friedrich Wilhelm. *The gay science (the joyful wisdom)*. Edited by Oscar Levy. Translated by Thomas Common, #52881, Gutenberg, 2016, www.gutenberg.org/files/52881/52881-h/52881-h.htm.

recurrence is possible. The unlikelihood of life coming into existence doesn't prove eternal recurrence just as the unlikelihood doesn't prove the fine tuning argument. Eternal recurrence is equally as valid as a creator deity being a cause for the universe; in other words, highly improbable and based more on fanciful belief than empirical evidence.

If you believe in the fine tuning argument then consider what it would mean if eternal recurrence was real; what if, upon the death of the universe, the universe brought itself back from nothingness and goes through the same cycle eternally like a clock. What if after your death, you eventually go through the same life experiences with no changes. You are born the same as you were, you go through the exact same experiences in your life. Everything that you did and will do will be repeated forever with no changes. Every mistake, every regret, every tragedy, every joy, every triumph, every loving moment, and so forth will be constantly repeated and you will have to relive all of your experiences with no changes for all of eternity. You will have no memory of repeating your life and you will exist like this for all eternity. What if that is the reality of the universe? What if you will endure all of your life's choices for eternity? How do you feel about it and does it change what you want to do at the present moment of your life? What can you do in this moment to make yourself satisfied with the prospect of living your life eternally? And, if this assumption were the reality of the universe and your life, would God be worth anything to you anymore?

Doubt

Historically, doubt was regarded as sinful and punishable within the Abrahamic faiths. Modernity has rendered blasphemy laws obsolete; religion has fractured into several religious denominations in a large part due to valuing freedom of speech and the consequences of having different interpretations on supernatural phenomena. Thus, doubt itself is no longer seen as an act synonymous with so-called evil intentions or evil thoughts. Modernity rendered such a belief untenable in first world countries. Religious believers, in an attempt to reconcile the spread of doubt, have reinterpreted doubt to mean the proof of imperfections and arrogance of humans in trying to understand what is beyond human comprehension.[209] It is argued the intrinsic imperfection of humanity causes doubt and that reaffirming one's faith despite doubt shows a true conviction for faith and for love of God.[210] It is perceived to be a commitment and relationship with God in spite of the shortcomings of humanity.[211]

While it seems to express a degree of humility and innocence on the part of religious believers, all it truly does is create a win-win situation for the convenience of the religious believer. Construing doubt as a form of faith is a logical fallacy called circular reasoning

---

61. [209] Baird, Julia. "Doubt as a Sign of Faith." *The New York Times*, The New York Times, 25 Sept. 2014, www.nytimes.com/2014/09/26/opinion/julia-baird-doubt-as-a-sign-of-faith.html.
62. [210] Baird, Julia. "Doubt as a Sign of Faith." *The New York Times*, The New York Times, 25 Sept. 2014, www.nytimes.com/2014/09/26/opinion/julia-baird-doubt-as-a-sign-of-faith.html.
63. [211] Baird, Julia. "Doubt as a Sign of Faith." *The New York Times*, The New York Times, 25 Sept. 2014, www.nytimes.com/2014/09/26/opinion/julia-baird-doubt-as-a-sign-of-faith.html.

because faith in God no longer matters under the "humility of doubt" argument.[212] Essentially, doubting God's existence is reinterpreted as being genuine in your faith in God because of your human weakness.[213] It is a paradoxical belief, if you have faith then you are a true believer and if you don't have faith then you are a true believer under this theological reasoning.[214] It is a self-celebrating logical fallacy; you are a hero no matter what you do or how you actually feel. Thus, having faith in God is irrelevant to the religious believer despite the clear contradiction.

This sort of reasoning ultimately inflicts self-deprecation and celebrates self-contempt as morally good. Your doubts may make you despise your lack of faith; you may view your shortcoming as a personal failure and view yourself negatively because you aren't "perfect" enough to worship your God fully. The defense that people are "only human" when exhibiting or internally admitting doubts is a tacit admittance to misanthropy. To defend the lack of faith, people despise their so-called limitations of being human.[215] People must reaffirm their faith by apologizing to God for being a human being who has intrusive thoughts and opinions outside of a prescribed holy book of morals. While it may seem like humility, it is ultimately a defeatist notion that condemns our humanity as a constant failure compared to the so-called perfection of a God. We must continue, as human beings, to prostrate ourselves and condemn ourselves so that God forgives us for being a human being. Admitting how weak and pitiful we are, mental self-lacerations imposed upon ourselves, is thus a "freedom" of accepting God's will.[216] The statement of "being human" reduces humanity to a state of failure and grief. It is a self-deluded misanthropy because of its inability to attain an unrealistic concept of perfection – a "commitment" to ignoring how theology doesn't fit with reality.[217] Thus, it is intrinsically unhealthy for our state of mind.

Please consider the following: doubt isn't your personal failings or temptation. Doubt is allowing you to view the world outside of theological-induced blindness and unknowingly fighting against the self-hate imposed by religious teachings and practices. *If you have doubt, then you're only sometimes a religious believer and sometimes an atheist.* Doubt is flourishing because people have faith for the sake of their own convenience and modernity is slowly removing the need for religion. Your doubt could also be a desire to observe the world without

---

64. [212] Lane, Christopher. "Losing Our Religion: Why Doubt Is a Passionate Exercise." *Psychology Today*, Sussex Publishers, 20 May 2011, www.psychologytoday.com/blog/side-effects/201105/losing-our-religion-why-doubt-is-passionate-exercise.
65. [213] Lane, Christopher. "Losing Our Religion: Why Doubt Is a Passionate Exercise." *Psychology Today*, Sussex Publishers, 20 May 2011, www.psychologytoday.com/blog/side-effects/201105/losing-our-religion-why-doubt-is-passionate-exercise.
66. [214] "Circular Reasoning." *Https://Www.logicallyfallacious.com*, www.logicallyfallacious.com/tools/lp/Bo/LogicalFallacies/66/Circular-Reasoning.
67. [215] Baird, Julia. "Doubt as a Sign of Faith." *The New York Times*, The New York Times, 25 Sept. 2014, www.nytimes.com/2014/09/26/opinion/julia-baird-doubt-as-a-sign-of-faith.html.
68. [216] Cialdini, Robert B. Chapter 3: Commitment and Consistency (52-95) and Authority (178-200). *Influence: Science and practice*. 4th ed., 21st Century Bks, 2002.
69. [217] Cialdini, Robert B. Chapter 3: Commitment and Consistency (52-95). *Influence: Science and practice*. 4th ed., 21st Century Bks, 2002.

theological-induced blindness in your personal life because you may no longer want to feel restricted by purportedly cosmic rules. Having uncertainty isn't wrong and it might be a desire for rationality. People can have faith in a multitude of subjects but it is better to have faith in subject matter that is testable and verifiable so as not to deceive ourselves because we don't like the implications of non-belief. Lastly, praising doubt is the faintest of praises because people are essentially admitting that they need to be an atheist at certain times to continue living in modernity and dealing with real world issues.

Chapter 5: Gender Roles

Religion plays an important component in gender roles both historically and within the context of modern society. Throughout human history, feminist campaigns have sought to highlight the struggle of women against religious oppression of their freedom of choice. Basic freedoms such as learning to read and contemporary freedoms such as abortion are the cornerstone of debate throughout the world. However, what are given less focus are the damaging social stigmas upon men. Therefore, this chapter will endeavor to criticize the negatives of both societal gender roles.

Manliness: Psychopathic Self-deprecation

While the idea of masculinity is associated with culture, the axioms of manliness come from religious teachings about the appropriate gender role of men. Men are the "breadwinners" that support the family, discipline the children, and teach respect for authority. Men are taught to be "strong" or "macho" by not showing emotional weakness and the act of crying is perceived to be a total failure of manliness.[218] Anger is perceived as more acceptable for a man compared to the more shameful action of crying under such a belief.[219] Men are taught to act "respectably" by not "giving in" to a notion of promiscuous behavior with women; a woman who is open about sex should be distrusted because she isn't following her gender role of being "loyal" to men. Men are taught that they have intrinsic sexual desire, but the actual desire for sex is something they need to seek forgiveness for because it's synonymous with evil intent. Men must apologize to a higher power for the crime of having biological sexual urges and healthy sexual thoughts. The pursuit of sexual gratification – of self-pleasure and sex with a willing participant – is seen as shameful and men begin to believe that having a cold, indifferent attitude is the sign of being a good man. Their sexual desire, perceived as wicked but intrinsic in their behavior, makes them believe that they have an irresistibly evil component within them that they must act on to be considered manly. Men under this moral belief system are taught to laugh and enjoy photos of nude women online but also feel ashamed with themselves for being so wicked; they try to justify such shame with the idea of male toughness because they're taught that manliness is a form of good moral behavior for men. Interestingly enough, sex psychologists and psychoanalysts have found that men who constantly seek sex from their partner don't do so for just physical reasons; most men who believe in "manliness" think they can only express their tender and emotional side through sex. Otherwise, they must either despise their natural biological processes or be coldly indifferent to what others think of their behavior; they often do both in a strange contradiction by acting tough while condemning their own sexual liberation.

1. [218] Green, Laci. "TOXIC MASCULINITY!" *YouTube*, YouTube, 20 Dec. 2017, www.youtube.com/watch?v=i5juyXjDnJ0.
2. [219] Green, Laci. "TOXIC MASCULINITY!" *YouTube*, YouTube, 20 Dec. 2017, www.youtube.com/watch?v=i5juyXjDnJ0.

This belief system is mental self-torture and encourages violent suicide. For some men, when they fail at upholding the so-called cornerstone of manliness; of being providers for their family, providing money with a secure job, being "strong" i.e. being emotionless as men, being "tough" about feeling pain, and feeling constant shame for their sexual desires then they seek suicide as a reprieve from the shame of being a failure by not measuring up to those standards.[220] This male stereotype is probably one of the worst developments in all of humankind; not only does it condemn women into feeling ashamed of their bodies by men who then objectify them, but it condemns men into feeling constant regret and shame too. Under the veneer of "good moral teachings" from religion, it creates a systemic culture of self-contempt and self-lassitude by demanding men conform to a perfectionist ideal of "masculinity".[221] If men don't properly conform to the ideal of manliness then they're considered inferior, worthless, and a complete failure by their society.[222] Suppressing emotions, condemning emotions as a sign of utter weakness, and maintaining a stoic demeanor as a form of strength is a psychopathic ideal to live towards and a clear form of mental torture.[223][224] Any sign for help, any desire for releasing negative emotions by the natural process of crying, and anything short of being a pillar of strength are situations in which men feel utterly ashamed of themselves because they couldn't measure up to the ideal of a "true man" of society. Under such pitiful notions, taking risky dares that endanger their own life is seen as an optimal form of "manliness" and men can be coerced into doing idiotic actions to prove their "manhood" to other men. Examples of this can be seen throughout different cultures, comments that synonymies strength and the male genitals are examples of this "macho" culture. Drinking alcohol in large portions, driving recklessly, the lack of desire to go to the hospital when physically sick, the need to appear buff, threats of violence as a form of strength, and keeping themselves emotionally distant from their significant other under the pitiful veneer of "respect" are all examples of the psychopathic behavior of "manliness". For the most part, men are never allowed to convey self-expression, happiness from feeling loved, or other healthy human emotions because of the self-deprecating belief that such gestures of affection are "unmanly" by cultural standards. It is a thought process that makes suicide more desirable than living. It's possibly the reason why men are more likely to commit suicide than women and more attempt violent forms of suicide – a final outcry to "prove" their manhood while embracing death to escape their weariness of life.

---

3. [220] Freeman, Daniel, and Jason Freeman. "Why are men more likely than women to take their own lives?" *The Guardian*, Guardian News and Media, 21 Jan. 2015, www.theguardian.com/science/2015/jan/21/suicide-gender-men-women-mental-health-nick-clegg.
4. [221] Nietzsche, Friedrich Wilhelm. *On the genealogy of morals: a polemical tract*. Translated by Ian Johnston, PDF, Richer Resources Publications, 2014.
5. [222] Green, Laci. "TOXIC MASCULINITY!" *YouTube*, YouTube, 20 Dec. 2017, www.youtube.com/watch?v=i5juyXjDnJ0.
6. [223] Nietzsche, Friedrich Wilhelm. *On the genealogy of morals: a polemical tract*. Translated by Ian Johnston, PDF, Richer Resources Publications, 2014.
7. [224] Green, Laci. "TOXIC MASCULINITY!" *YouTube*, YouTube, 20 Dec. 2017, www.youtube.com/watch?v=i5juyXjDnJ0.

Lastly, for this section, I've noticed that men who speak out against feminism usually point to incidents where society is unfair to men; including some of the aforementioned reasons. While feminism does primarily focus on women's issues, many of the most prominent feminist vloggers and intellectuals have also criticized the deplorable social stigmas against men and seek to ameliorate the gender stereotypes against men too.[225] Paradoxically, men who condemn feminism usually reference their own social stigmas as a strange "defense" against feminism. Yet, all of the social stigmas the anti-feminists make valid complaints against have originated from the male social identity that they seek to defend against feminism. Feminism isn't being disproven by bringing up such complaints; these men are admitting to have favorable dispositions to feminism while condemning, demonizing, and forming misogynistic rants about the very women who seek to ameliorate these social prejudices against men.

Women's roles: Modesty or Misogyny?

Numbers 31: 7-18. KJV

7 And they warred against the Midianites, as the L<small>ORD</small> commanded Moses; and they slew all the males.

8 And they slew the kings of Midian, beside the rest of them that were slain; namely, Evi, and Rekem, and Zur, and Hur, and Reba, five kings of Midian: Balaam also the son of Beor they slew with the sword.

9 And the children of Israel took all the women of Midian captives, and their little ones, and took the spoil of all their cattle, and all their flocks, and all their goods.

10 And they burnt all their cities wherein they dwelt, and all their goodly castles, with fire.

11 And they took all the spoil, and all the prey, both of men and of beasts.

12 And they brought the captives, and the prey, and the spoil, unto Moses, and Eleazar the priest, and unto the congregation of the children of Israel, unto the camp at the plains of Moab, which are by Jordan near Jericho.

13 And Moses, and Eleazar the priest, and all the princes of the congregation, went forth to meet them without the camp.

14 And Moses was wroth with the officers of the host, with the captains over thousands, and captains over hundreds, which came from the battle.

15 And Moses said unto them, Have ye saved all the women alive?

16 Behold, these caused the children of Israel, through the counsel of Balaam, to commit trespass against the L<small>ORD</small> in the matter of Peor, and there was a plague among the congregation of the L<small>ORD</small>.

17 Now therefore kill every male among the little ones, and kill every woman that hath known man by lying with him.

---

[225] Green, Laci. "TOXIC MASCULINITY!" *YouTube*, YouTube, 20 Dec. 2017, www.youtube.com/watch?v=i5juyXjDnJ0.

¹⁸ But all the women children, that have not known a man by lying with him, keep alive for yourselves.[226]

Social stigmas against women have gained more attention throughout the world. The likely reason was the sexism being more explicit and overt compared to sexist double-standards against men. In third world countries, this double-standard is plainly undeniable; women still have barriers against being allowed to read, write, in certain countries they're barred from the independent right to go shopping without the presence of a man, and many other crucial issues. In first world countries, there are still issues with the right to an abortion, equal pay, equal promotion in the workforce, equal representation in film and video games, women are still being viewed as promiscuous for choosing what article of clothing to wear, and women who have children out of wedlock are socially stigmatized for their entire life.[227]

However, the majority of these gender stereotypes stem from the belief that women are property to be owned by men; for most ancient religious history, women were seen as spoils of war to be used to make heirs through campaigns of war rape. Ancient religious texts prescribed most of women's gender roles on the basis of being war spoils won by the conquering tribe – the Old Testament is one of the most overt examples and much of the passages are untenable in modern times. The ancient religious beliefs of women being the property of men is the fundamental basis for all of the unequal religious morals imposed upon women. Both culture and society substitute the reasons to argue that constricting women's actions are for morally good reasons. The premise of the belief system comes from the history of war rape within ancient religious wars; humanity substituted so-called morally good reasons to stay consistent with the ownership of women. Society's attempt at espousing moral reasons for controlling women's bodies are just attempts at trying to stay consistent with the logical fallacy of an appeal to tradition; the appeal to tradition is that women should conduct themselves in certain social manners because that was how it was done before the current generation. They believe this instills good morals in women. Yet, going back further, the commitment to so-called good morals originated from the servitude of women to men as property won through conquest and rape. If you believe the ancient stories of conquering tribes that enacted violence upon others because of God's will then you must realize that the conservative cultural norms imposed upon women came from viewing them as spoils of war.

Several modern-day social stigmas show the war rape mentality. Determining what women should wear so they don't look "inappropriate" in the eyes of men. The belief that women are asking to be raped because they show their bodies in public comes from war rape mentality; that is why there was a tacit assumption that men would have the uncontrollable

---

8. [226] "BibleGateway." *Numbers 31:7-18 KJV - - Bible Gateway*, www.biblegateway.com/passage/?search=Numbers 31:7-18&version=KJV.
9. [227] Green, Laci. "WHY I'M A...FEMINIST *Gasp*." *YouTube*, YouTube, 23 Apr. 2014, www.youtube.com/watch?v=UwJRFClybmk.

urge to rape women and why culture constantly views them as objects. Arguments about being proper ladies by remaining "respectful" can still mean obeying the husband as the head of the household within a multitude of religious denominations even in the West and such mentalities often create entire communities where men are allowed to beat their wives with no legal repercussions. Examples of these religious morals still exist in poorer regions of South Carolina in the United States; men are allowed to beat their wives in front of their children, they're known to kill women who flee from abusive households, and police and the communities ignore the violence because of their Christian belief that men are to be heads of the household as decreed in the Bible.[228] Implementing laws that control their reproductive choices is one of the most overt examples of inequality imposed upon women.[229] Parents often have a critical outlook on their daughter's behavior after the age of maturity to the point where they condemn their own children as sluts and whores should their child refuse to conform to gender roles.[230] They probably feel like failed parents should their daughters make independent choices in life about their sexual partners. Women are condemned as sluts and whores for sex out of wedlock. If women have multiple partners then they're condemned as sluts; men who do the same are not and instead men are seen as falling for the "wiles" of women. Both genders are taught to be ashamed of the natural biological process of consensual sex and masturbation by society. Women are viewed as traitorous to some men for showing any amount of their body in public or as "disloyal" because they don't fit the stereotypical standards of staying a virgin until marriage. It comes from the spoils of war mentality; they're viewed as "used goods" because they can no longer satisfy the expectations of the leering rapist of a warring desert tribe. Furthermore, women who express their sexual liberation are generally assumed to be crying out for help under the patronizing system of religious morality. Euphemisms are made to ignore the intrinsic aspect of women being perceived as spoils of war to justify the discrimination; euphemisms like "respecting the husband", young girls being taught to be "quiet and meek" as a good moral trait, or that women are too emotional to make meaningful choices all come from this ancient cultural history within the major religions. All of this are cultural derivatives of viewing women as spoils of war by following an appeal to tradition and appeal to purity fallacy through substituting the original reason they were imposed upon women with the fallacious reasoning.[231]

Rape Culture and Patriarchy

Unquestioned assumptions about gender norms, based on religious conservative values, are beliefs that can no longer be considered tenable due to their incoherence with gender

---

10. [228] "Till death do us part: A Post and Courier Special Report." *Post and Courier*, 19 Aug. 2014, www.postandcourier.com/app/till-death/partone.html.
11. [229] Green, Laci. "WHY I'M A...FEMINIST *Gasp*." *YouTube*, YouTube, 23 Apr. 2014, www.youtube.com/watch?v=UwJRFClybmk.
12. [230] Green, Laci. "WHY I'M A...FEMINIST *Gasp*." *YouTube*, YouTube, 23 Apr. 2014, www.youtube.com/watch?v=UwJRFClybmk.
13. [231] "Appeal to Tradition." *Https://Www.logicallyfallacious.com*, www.logicallyfallacious.com/tools/lp/Bo/LogicalFallacies/44/Appeal-to-Tradition.

equality. At the root of the social schism between religious conservatism and liberal social values is the question of whether gender norms are biological or social constructs. In stark contrast to more liberal social perceptions, gender-based human behavior is seen as fixed and unalterable due to religious conservatives perspective on human biology, while liberal schools of thought of human behavior is perceived as grounded in cultural norms that are inculcated from society. These underlying assumptions change how we react to incidents of sexual violence, gender discrimination, and what we perceive to be terrible moral beliefs and practices. While religious conservatism leads people to believe male violence is unalterable and fixed with women always burdened into the receiving end of such treatment, liberal values counter that such beliefs are the causes of violence and perpetuate systems that seek to legitimize gender violence in a self-fulfilling cycle. This liberal criticism is what led many to perceive religious conservative values as hypocritical, but it would be more accurate to say that religious social values are incoherent.

Religious conservative beliefs are ingrained with fixed mindsets and entity theories about gender-based violence and gender-related behavior. That is, they identify and internalize it as unalterable human norms and so don't seek to change societal norms to improve the general welfare of society; they go so far as to work against social changes because of their belief that their religion already provides the best guideline for how humans should behave.[232] Religious conservative values use snap judgments to find simplistic questions and answers to broad problems and this behavior is largely encouraged with religious texts that reinforce entity theories about gender.[233][234] These simplistic assumptions largely contribute to dangerous falsehoods that perpetuate systems of physical, emotional, and sexual abuse that create victims and lead to victim blaming.[235][236] The belief that women must cover-up their bodies so as not to attract male attention, limit their activities at night time to decrease incidents of sexual violence, and learn to follow so-called "modest" behavior to keep from getting attacked by violent men doesn't align with the research on whom rapists target. Conservative religious values simplistic assumptions and answers hold implications of a just-world where the violent atrocity of rape is seen as somehow manageable and controllable on the part of the victim and thus encourages victim blaming when rape occurs.[237] Theresa M. Beiner in a journalistic study for the *Duke Journal of Gender Law and Policy* called "*Sexy Dressing Revisited: Does Target Dress Play a Part in Sexual Harassment Cases?*" which researched the impacts of rape

---

14. [232] Dweck, Carol S. *Mindset: How You Can Fulfill Your Potential*. Random House, 2012.
15. [233] Cialdini, Robert B. Chapter 1: Weapons of Influence (1-16). *Influence: Science and practice*. 4th ed., 21st Century Bks, 2002.
16. [234] Cialdini, Robert B. Chapter 6: Authority (178-200). *Influence: Science and practice*. 4th ed., 21st Century Bks, 2002.
17. [235] Green, Laci. "THE F-WORD." *YouTube*, YouTube, 8 July 2014, www.youtube.com/watch?v=EJPT_U97lNs.
18. [236] Kahneman, Daniel. Chapter 8: How Judgments Happen (89-96). *Thinking, fast and slow*. Farrar, Straus and Giroux, 2015.
19. [237] Grinnell, Renée. "Just-World Hypothesis." *Encyclopedia of Psychology*, 17 July 2016, psychcentral.com/encyclopedia/just-world-hypothesis/.

victims attire on legal cases and likelihood of being targeted had surprising findings to share that upend many conservative social assumptions about both rapists and their targets. I strongly encourage readers to read the excerpts related to parts III and IV of her findings below:

III. SOCIAL SCIENCE AND DRESS

"Social science has much to offer in determining the meaning of women's dress and how it might affect sexual harassment cases. A variety of academic disciplines have analyzed women's dress, looking at what it means to both the person wearing the clothing and perceivers of that person as well as its broader social implications. This section discusses several aspects of social science that may help explain why defendants are not using evidence concerning the provocative nature of the plaintiff's dress to show that the target welcomed the harassment. In doing so, it lays the foundation for the argument, made more explicitly in the next section, that the reason defendants are not seeking to admit evidence of plaintiff's provocative dress in sexual harassment cases as frequently as might be supposed is because provocatively-dressed women may not be the likely targets of sexual harassment.

The section begins by discussing how perceptions of victim dress play a role in perceptions of rape and sexual harassment. In this context it investigates how a woman's dress affects perceptions of that woman in a manner that might have relevance for sexual harassment law. For example, are provocatively dressed women harassed more often, and, more importantly, do people think this is the case? Do people believe that provocatively dressed women invite harassment? It then looks at what is known about how rapists and, to a lesser extent, sexual harassers, choose their victims in an effort to determine whether common perceptions of the role dress plays in victimization is accurate. From there it looks at characteristics of both rape and sexual harassment victims to see if, based on who these women are, sexual harassers may be choosing their victims in a manner similar to rapists. It also addresses research about sexual harassers to determine if they share some common characteristics with rapists, which may make some of the research concerning rape applicable to sexual harassment. Finally, it looks for social science explanations for why dress makes a difference in perceptions of who is likely to be harassed. Throughout this section, I rely on social science of rape in situations in which there is little research on sexual harassment. I explain why this is justified at the points in my argument where it becomes relevant.

Underlying rape shield laws is the belief that people, and in particular jurors, mistakenly believe that a women's dress has an impact on whether she will be victimized. This belief is borne out by research on perceptions of women's dress. As one source elucidates:

> 'Although women with provocative appearances are perceived as sexually attractive and more desirable, they are judged as less intelligent, sincere, trustful, reliable, and less moral than women with non-provocative appearances. . . . Further, . . . "appearance influences judgments of a

sender's competence (ability or expertise), even when the task at hand is unrelated to appearance.'"[131]

Clearly, dress influences how people perceive and interact with one another. Yet, assessments of women's attitudes or beliefs based on their dress are not necessarily accurate. For example, while people believe that certain items of clothing signify more liberal sexual attitudes, one study suggests that in reality, few items of clothing actually correlate with such liberal attitudes.[132] Thus, generally-held perceptions of sexualized dressing may well be out of sync with any one individual's attitudes and behaviors.

Perhaps most notably, a survey of psychiatrists reported that a three-to-one majority of those responding "said that attire that the male perceives as inviting direct sex attention does, indeed, tend to increase sex crime risk."[133] The styles of clothing that psychiatrists thought carried this potential risk included short skirts, see-through dresses, short shorts, and bikinis.[134] As they concluded, "[t]he survey replies show that U.S. psychiatrists in large numbers believe that revealing attire is one of the causative or precipitating factors in sex crimes against young females."[135] Thus, highly-educated and learned adults believe that how a woman dresses has an impact on whether or not she will be a victim of a sex crime.

The same general findings hold true for dress and sexual harassment. A study involving 200 college students sought to determine whether target dress and gender of a perceiver played a part in determining who was likely to be sexually harassed.[136] "The model when wearing provocative clothing was rated significantly higher on likelihood of provoking sexual harassment . . . than when wearing nonprovocative clothing."[137] Interestingly, women rated the model dressed provocatively highest on the likelihood of provoking sexual harassment.[138] However, men and women did not differ in their assessment of the model wearing nonprovocative clothing.[139] This suggests that women are more inclined to believe that provocative dress has an impact on who is harassed. While this study shows women are more inclined to link provocative dress with sexual harassment, it is important to note that both men and women perceive this link. The question remains whether this perception is accurate.

While people perceive dress to have an impact on who is assaulted, studies of rapists suggest that victim attire is not a significant factor. Instead, rapists look for signs of passiveness and submissiveness, which, studies suggest, are more likely to coincide with more body-concealing clothing.[140] In a study to test whether males could determine whether women were high or low in passiveness and submissiveness, Richards and her colleagues found that men, using only nonverbal appearance cues, could accurately assess which women were passive and submissive versus those who were dominant and assertive.[141] Clothing was one of the key cues: "Those females high in passivity and submissiveness (i.e., those at greatest risk for victimization) wore noticeably more body-concealing clothing (i.e., high necklines, long pants and sleeves, multiple layers)."[142] This suggests that men equate body-concealing clothing with passive and submissive qualities, which are qualities that rapists look for in victims. Thus, those who wore provocative clothes would not be viewed as passive or submissive, and would be less likely to be victims of assault.

Along these lines, research suggests that rape victims are "significantly lower" in "dominance, assertiveness, and social presence."143 While members of the public believe that victims of assault attract such attacks by dressing provocatively,144 attractiveness does not correlate with submissive characteristics in victims.145 Instead, research "specifically revealed a negative relationship between perceptions of attractiveness and traits which could be construed as contributing to a nonverbal appearance of vulnerability."146 Thus:

'Male evaluators perceived attractive females as lower in submissiveness, uncertainty, simpleness, carelessness and passivity than their less attractive peers. This suggests that conventional definitions of physical attractiveness do not represent visual attributes which enhance a woman's potential for victimization.'147

This seems at odds with studies concerning provocative dress, although no studies have looked directly at provocative dress and submissiveness. Of course, attractiveness and provocative dress are not the same thing. As Glick and his colleagues point out, it can be difficult to alter one's physical attractiveness, "but women can easily emphasize or deemphasize their sexuality through clothing and demeanor."148 Thus, dressing sexy or provocatively is a choice that may or may not lead to a woman being perceived as attractive. Still, women who dress provocatively may be exhibiting a degree of confidence that does not suggest submissiveness. These women would be less likely to be victims of sexual assault or harassment, because potential abusers would not perceive them as passive or submissive.

No studies were readily available that explained how sexual harassers target their victims. However, there is information about who is more likely to be targeted for sexual harassment. Interestingly, it parallels what is known about rape victims: "Young and single women tend to be the targets of sexual harassment."149 However, sexual harassment can happen to any women, and, studies show, once other factors are considered (such as workplace characteristics and the form the sexual harassment takes), the impact of age and marital status on who is harassed lessens considerably.150 Youth and being single are factors related to power. As one researcher observed, "[d]ifferences in age, marital status, and education reinforce gender differences in power and status in society."151 Thus, because sexual harassment is about power, differences in these power-related statuses are likely to correlate with who is sexually harassed.

This parallels research on rape victims. While, like sexual harassment, any woman can be a rape victim, "studies have shown that the rape victim is more likely to be a single, white or black young female, from a lower social working class. Further 'women who are most vulnerable to rape exhibit lower levels of psychosocial effectiveness' and tend to have passive or submissive personalities prior to the assaults."152

Thus, it appears that victims of rape and victims of sexual harassment share some common characteristics. Yet, much of the research discussed above involves how rapists choose their victims—not how sexual harassers choose their targets. Thus, it may not be directly applicable to sexual harassment. However, research also suggests that perpetrators of more serious sexual harassment are on a continuum with rapists.153 Research on rapists might be likewise helpful in determining how sexual harassers choose their targets. Sexual harassers, like rapists, may pick victims who are vulnerable and submissive. Research on men who are likely to sexually harass suggests that this leap is logical.

Psychologist John Pryor was one of the first to study characteristics of men who sexually harass. He developed a scale to determine the propensity of men to sexually harass.154 His sexual harassment research is based, in part, on the research of those who study rape. As he explains, "[m]any researchers believe rape and severe forms of sexual harassment are conceptually similar forms of behavior."155
Researchers see rape as on a continuum of "maleaggressive/female-passive" interactions
that involve differing levels of coercion and sexual intimacy.156 This led Pryor to opine that rapists and sexual harassers might have some characteristics in common. As a result, he set out to study characteristics of sexual harassers to see if this was true.

Pryor examined those who would be inclined to engage in sexual exploitation, essentially what amounts to quid pro quo harassment. Pryor used various other scales, including those that measured certain attitudes about sex roles and beliefs, attitudes towards feminism, likelihood to rape, and one that measured empathy.157 What he found was a strong relationship between the likelihood-to-sexually-harass scale (LSH) and adversary sexual beliefs and rapemyth acceptance.158 Weaker relationships were found for sex-role stereotyping and acceptance of interpersonal violence.159 Tellingly, "[t]he single best predictor of LSH was Malamuth's (1981) LR [likelihood-to-rape] scale. This result . . . supports [another researcher's] contention that rape and severe forms of sexual harassment represent different degrees of coercive sexual conduct."160 Interestingly, men who scored higher on the LSH scale also had a harder time understanding the perspective of others.161 As Pryor explained, "[t]he profile of a person who is likely to initiate severe sexually harassing behavior that emerges from the initial study is one that emphasizes sexual and social male dominance."162

This scale has proven useful after further study. As Pryor and Stoller point out, "the LSH scale measures a readiness to use social power for sexually exploitative purposes. This suggests that social dominance and male sexuality may be closely aligned concepts in the minds of high-LSH men."163 In a subsequent study, they found that dominance was the best predictor of LSH in men. As they explained, "[t]his finding seems to buttress the argument that dominance and sexuality are integrally related for high-LSH men."164 Thus, it seems appropriate to opine that sexual harassers might choose their targets in a manner similar to that of rapists. These two groups of perpetrators share common characteristics. Further, sexual harassment by high LSH men appears to be triggered by power imbalances—the kind of imbalances that might well be triggered by target submissiveness.

This conclusion is inconsistent with the common belief that how a woman dresses has an impact on whether she will be sexually harassed or sexually assaulted. Why then, do many people, including psychiatrists, assume that dress plays some part in who is a victim of sexual assaults? In particular, why do women believe this? Social scientists believe this is the result of the "just world hypothesis." As Melvin Lerner explained,

'for their own security, if for no other reason, people want to believe they live in a just world where people get what they deserve. One way of accomplishing this is by . . . persuading himself that the victim deserved to suffer, after all. The assumption here is that attaching responsibility to behavior provides us with the greater security—we can do something to avoid such a fate.'165

Thus, in the context of sexual harassment, this explains why women, more than men, are inclined to believe that provocative dress has an impact on who is sexually harassed. Women attribute the harassment to something the victim has done, such as wearing provocative clothing, as a way to understand how it could happen to someone else and not to them. Thus, blaming the victim, for example, by believing she provoked the behavior by her dress, makes other women believe that dressing differently (i.e., more "appropriately") will prevent it from happening to them.166

This is closely related to another theory known as "harm avoidance." Women blame victims as a way to exercise control over their lives and to continue to believe that bad things, including sexual harassment and sexual assaults, will not happen to them.167 Thus, by viewing provocative dress as a factor in sexual harassment, women believe that they can avoid sexual harassment simply by not dressing provocatively. Both of these theories provide explanations as to why women, in particular, may think that harassment or sexual assault is provoked by victim dress.

Thus, how people commonly perceive the role of a target's dress in sexual harassment appears to be out of sync with how sexual harassers may choose their targets. This leads to a possible explanation as to why defendants are not using target dress to prove unwelcomeness."[238]

IV. IMPLICATIONS OF DRESS FOR SEXUAL HARASSMENT LAW
"The social science described above suggests some potential explanations as
to why defendants do not regularly raise the issue of target dress to rebut

---

20. [238] BEINER, THERESA M. III. SOCIAL SCIENCE AND DRESS (143-148). "SEXY DRESSING REVISITED: DOES TARGET DRESS PLAY A PART IN SEXUAL HARASSMENT CASES? ." *Duke University School of Law*, Duke Journal of Gender Law & Policy, 2007, scholarship.law.duke.edu/cgi/viewcontent.cgi?&article=1109&context=djglp.

unwelcomeness in sexual harassment cases. Given the purported recent increase in provocative dress by women168 and the lack of a solid legal standard against its admission, one would expect to see defendants using arguments and evidence about target dress to prove welcomeness—or at least, to *dis*-prove *un*welcomeness. Yet, this practice appears uncommon. How does one account for this? Earlier in this article I suggested several potential explanations. First, it could be that defendants are not raising it because they believe either that they will not be successful in having the evidence admitted under Rule 412 or that the factfinder will be in some way offended by such attempts. Essentially, the tactic might backfire on the defendant. Second, it is possible that women who wear provocative clothing to work do not mind the attention that they receive from it and therefore are not bringing sexual harassment claims. Third, it is possible that victim dress does not have an impact on who is sexually harassed. Legal feminists have long argued that sexual harassment is about power. With this in mind, the work of social scientists suggests that potential harassers might choose their targets using criteria other than dress.

Legal and social science scholars have proposed a number of theories suggesting why and how sexual harassment occurs. The foremost legal scholar on this issue, Catharine MacKinnon, posited early on that sexual harassment is about power differences between men and women. Sexual harassment is a tool used to perpetuate hierarchy, the principal way in which men maintain their dominance in American society.169 As several psychology researchers described the theory,

'[a]ccording to this model, male dominance is maintained by cultural patterns of male-female interaction as well as by economic and political superordinancy. Society rewards males for aggressive and domineering sexual behaviors and females for passivity and acquiescence. . . . [T]he function of sexual harassment is to manage ongoing male-female interactions according to accepted sex status norms, and to maintain male dominance occupationally and therefore economically, by intimidating, discouraging, or precipitating removal of women from work.'170

This theory fits well with what is known about men who sexually harass. These men are influenced by dominance—power—in their relationships with women. Thus, this provides an explanation of why women who are provocatively dressed might not be bringing sexual harassment cases: They are not good potential targets for harassers. If, as studies of rapists suggest, harassers look for more passive or submissive women, women who are provocatively dressed may appear more confident and are therefore less likely to be considered appropriate targets by potential harassers. Indeed, the cases involving requests that women dress more professionally or tone down their sexy attire suggest that people are generally uncomfortable with women who dress provocatively in the workplace. The power dynamic involved in telling women to dress less provocatively (essentially trying to control their attire) is also interesting. It suggests that there is power in dressing provocatively, and that employers are uncomfortable by such assertions of this power by women.171

I am aware that I am extrapolating at least in part from research on rapists for this argument. This is one area that requires further study by social scientists to determine whether sexual harassers are picking their targets much like rapists pick their victims—based on indications of passivity and submissiveness. At this point, this theory is somewhat speculative—rapists and sexual harassers share some common characteristics, and victims of rape and sexual harassment also share several common characteristics. To the extent that there is incomplete research on sexual harassers, this essay serves as a call to social scientists who study sexual harassment to do further scholarship on how sexual harassers choose their targets.

There is another problem with this potential explanation. Just because a woman is dressed provocatively does not mean that she is necessarily confident and therefore less likely to be submissive. It could well be that her lack of confidence is what induces her to dress provocatively, in an attempt to draw what she considers to be positive attention to herself. Perhaps there is a class of cases that never make it to court because the women involved do not find the attention their attire garners harassing. Indeed, they may enjoy the attention. Further, to the extent that the attention is considered complimentary (i.e., it is not derogatory or otherwise demeaning), it may not be objectionable by these women.

Other sexual harassment theorists posit that sexual harassment is a result of
an interaction between people and workplace characteristics and situations.172 Workplace environments in which sexualized images, comments, and behavior toward women are tolerated are more likely to be those in which women are sexually harassed.173 This theory, however, is not inconsistent with the power/dominance model. In workplaces with such atmospheres, women are placed in less powerful positions: They are essentially deemed sex objects. It is little wonder that sexual harassment thrives in such environments, given the little organizational power afforded to women.

This also might explain the one set of cases where provocatively dressed women are commonly harassed: the Hooters cases. Studies show that men high in LSH are aware of situational constraints on their behavior.174 Thus, in an environment like Hooters, where the Hooters Girl's "predominant function is to provide vicarious sexual recreation, to titillate, entice, and arouse male customers' fantasies,"175 men who are likely to sexually harass will consider the Hooters' business plan to permit (perhaps even encourage) such harassment. Thus, while provocative dress might signal confidence in an office setting, at Hooters, workplace norms encourage men who are so inclined to harass.

What about the women who complain about men making comments about their attire as part of their sexual harassment allegations? It is not clear whether these women were dressed in a provocative manner or not. Certainly, in some cases they were not. For example, in *Conley v. City of Lincoln City*, the plaintiff was in her police uniform.176 In addition, employers in these cases (aside for rare exceptions such as the lingerie case177) did not argue that something about the plaintiff's attire "caused" the plaintiff to be harassed. Yet, clearly inappropriate comments—including those that are sexually demeaning—about workplace dress offend women. They are a weapon in the arsenal of harassing behaviors that affect women's employment. Some of these comments clearly would undermine a woman's workplace authority, because the comments are demeaning and thereby undermine the plaintiff's power and authority in the workplace. Even in the case involving the police chief, commenting, although apparently in a complimentary fashion, about her attire could cast her as something to look at rather than someone who leads the police force. One could imagine how these comments might have affected her ability to lead and why she included them in her complaint. Thus, comments about dress are used to undermine the workplace authority of women and should be included in the appropriate case as part of a plaintiff's sexual harassment allegations."[239]

It may come with shock and a sense of unease for those with conservative religious values that women with provocative attire, generally expressing a show of confidence, are far less likely to be targets of rapists and that women who cover their bodies are the most likely to be attacked and raped. This is because the underlying assumptions of what rape constitutes in the view of religious conservatism is wrong and the assumptions have corrosive effects on rape victims who are subjected to systems of abuse. By assuming that women must be kept meek and obedient, fully clothed to avoid male attention, and have their ability to socialize curtailed so that they'll be safe is precisely the sort of behavior that rapists look for to get away with rape. By being socially conditioned to be submissive, they're easier prey for people with coercive intentions and less likely to speak out or push back when forced into an uncomfortable situation. By limiting their social outings and social relationships, they're less likely to have a strong social support group that they can go to for help when confronted with coercive people. By teaching young women that covering-up avoids rape, religious conservatism is instilling a dangerous illusion of immunity and an ignorance towards what people can and cannot control in their daily lives.[240] The worst aspect of these religiously motivated beliefs is the process of shaming, ridicule, and societal disdain that may force a rape victim to relive the trauma of the sexual violence done to them and they may inculcate the belief that somehow they were deserving of being raped because of how their community treats them with derision or the fear that their community will treat them with such hostility should they come forward. As a direct result of a religious upbringing and a socially conservative community, a rape victim may be too fearful to come forward about what happened to them. This self-reinforcing cycle of systematic sexual abuse as a result of conservative social values is what is known as rape culture and religious norms are an intrinsic component of this belief

---

21. [239] BEINER, THERESA M. IV. IMPLICATIONS OF DRESS FOR SEXUAL HARASSMENT LAW (148-151). "SEXY DRESSING REVISITED: DOES TARGET DRESS PLAY A PART IN SEXUAL HARASSMENT CASES? ." *Duke University School of Law*, Duke Journal of Gender Law & Policy, 2007, scholarship.law.duke.edu/cgi/viewcontent.cgi?&article=1109&context=djglp.
22. [240] Grinnell, Renée. "Just-World Hypothesis." *Encyclopedia of Psychology*, 17 July 2016, psychcentral.com/encyclopedia/just-world-hypothesis/.

system. This systematic social ill is a focal component of what feminists refer to as the patriarchy.

While the patriarchal structures of religiously conservative societies create nefariously unequal treatment towards women and such structures comprise of rape culture, these very same gender stereotypes are just as harmful to men. A disgusting and asinine view perpetuated by religious conservative values is that it is simply expected that men will rape women under the belief that men can't control themselves with ignorant adages such as "boys will be boys" or implications that it's just expected that rape will happen when men and women are together in any social setting. In the purview of sexual violence against women, the implicit argument made when a person questions what a woman was wearing, what a woman was drinking, or what she was doing when outside late at night without questioning a male rapist's behavior is to assume that it's just expected that men will rape women. Any man who makes these arguments implicate themselves and heavily imply that they would also commit rape crimes against rape victims in the context of how each specific case of sexual violence happened, because to them it's somehow normal that men would rape women or desire to rape women; they normalize the idea that women should never feel safe around any man or they'll be punished for wanting to live equally. Obviously, the majority of men wouldn't do such a despicable act, what it does indicate is the normalization of gender stereotypes without any self-critique on just what sort of arguments people are espousing by thoughtlessly following religious traditions.[241]

Gender stereotypes about men pressure them into conforming to belief systems that require them to be emotionless under the guise that they're invulnerable. Any expression of vulnerability is an admittance of weakness and treated with derision in typical patriarchal societies. This illusion of emotional immunity being a cornerstone of maleness leads to dire consequences. Physical violence between men is often seen as more acceptable when men do it due to the culturally ingrained and wrong social stereotype that testosterone causes men to be prone to violence when studies indicate that it is more nuanced than that.[242] Male aggressive behavior with respect to testosterone is concomitant with elevating one's status, testosterone can lead to generosity such as donating to charities, and aggressive people in both genders have higher testosterone levels than the average.[243][244][245] Male questions, worries, or insecurities

---

23. [241] Cialdini, Robert B. Chapter 6: Authority (178-200). *Influence: Science and practice*. 4th ed., 21st Century Bks, 2002.
24. [242] Mims, Christopher. "Strange but True: Testosterone Alone Does Not Cause Violence." *Scientific American*, 5 July 2007, www.scientificamerican.com/article/strange-but-true-testosterone-alone-doesnt-cause-violence/.
25. [243] Batrinos, Menelaos L. "Testosterone and Aggressive Behavior in Man." *International Journal of Endocrinology and Metabolism*, NCBI, 2012, www.ncbi.nlm.nih.gov/pmc/articles/PMC3693622/.
26. [244] Healy, Melissa. "In addition to fueling aggression, testosterone can also make men more generous, study says." *Los Angeles Times*, Los Angeles Times, 26 Sept. 2016, www.latimes.com/science/sciencenow/la-sci-sn-testosterone-behavior-men-20160926-snap-story.html.
27. [245] Mims, Christopher. "Strange but True: Testosterone Alone Does Not Cause Violence." *Scientific American*, 5 July 2007, www.scientificamerican.com/article/strange-but-true-testosterone-alone-doesnt-cause-violence/.

about the act of sex can be treated as points of mockery and derision because it's assumed that men must intrinsically desire sex without any curiosity or concern for further information or informed decision-making on their part. The idea of masculine toughness can preclude any freedom for vulnerability or to express one's emotions in a peaceful manner; crying is seen as a sign of weakness, backing away from confrontation is seen as a sign of being a lesser man, and generally expressing any discomfort or criticism is seen as an admittance of defeat or weakness and treated with derision. Thus, men never learn to deal with personal insecurities in a adequate or healthy manner because emotional growth is inhibited by conservative norms about male behavior. What feminists critique as male entitlement is more akin to male insecurity being forced upon women. Within the conservative religious paradigm, wives are expected to avoid talking to or interacting with strangers who are men for fear they'll cheat on their husbands, women are expected to stay at home to raise children without much social contact outside the home, and they're expected to "respect" the husband by obedience to the male authority of the household.[246] These patriarchal social conditions of control are both oppressive to women and a result of appeasing male insecurities instead of trusting women and treating them equally.

The gender stereotype of men under religious conservatism can lead to pathological social catastrophes in war time. Whilst religious conservatism tacitly treats women as spoils of war from war rape through its traditionalist mindset without any self-criticism or scrutiny, it treats male victims of war rape even worse; it's considered impossible within religious conservatism for men to be victims of rape. Their emotional and physical pain is treated with mockery, derision, and hate by patriarchal religious customs. Journalist Will Storr wrote an article for *The Guardian* titled *The Rape of Men: The Darkest Secret of War* in which he tackles the lack of compassion, sensitivity, and effort put into helping male victims of war rape specifically due to patriarchal religious customs that perpetuate rape culture from religiously conservative societies:

> **Of** all the secrets of war, there is one that is so well kept that it exists mostly as a rumour. It is usually denied by the perpetrator and his victim. Governments, aid agencies and human rights defenders at the UN barely acknowledge its possibility. Yet every now and then someone gathers the courage to tell of it. This is just what happened on an ordinary afternoon in the office of a kind and careful counsellor in Kampala, Uganda. For four years Eunice Owiny had been employed by Makerere University's Refugee Law Project (RLP) to help displaced people from all over Africa work through their traumas. This particular case, though, was a puzzle. A female client was having marital difficulties. "My husband can't have sex," she complained. "He feels very bad about this. I'm sure there's something he's keeping from me."
>
> Owiny invited the husband in. For a while they got nowhere. Then Owiny asked the wife to leave. The man then murmured cryptically: "It happened to me." Owiny frowned. He reached into his pocket and pulled out an old sanitary pad. "Mama Eunice," he said. "I am in pain. I have to use this."

---

28. [246] Cialdini, Robert B. Chapter 6: Authority (178-200). *Influence: Science and practice*. 4th ed., 21st Century Bks, 2002.

Laying the pus-covered pad on the desk in front of him, he gave up his secret. During his escape from the civil war in neighbouring Congo, he had been separated from his wife and taken by rebels. His captors raped him, three times a day, every day for three years. And he wasn't the only one. He watched as man after man was taken and raped. The wounds of one were so grievous that he died in the cell in front of him.

"That was hard for me to take," Owiny tells me today. "There are certain things you just don't believe can happen to a man, you get me? But I know now that sexual violence against men is a huge problem. Everybody has heard the women's stories. But nobody has heard the men's."

It's not just in East Africa that these stories remain unheard. One of the few academics to have looked into the issue in any detail is Lara Stemple, of the University of California's Health and Human Rights Law Project. Her study *Male Rape and Human Rights* notes incidents of male sexual violence as a weapon of wartime or political aggression in countries such as Chile, Greece, Croatia, Iran, Kuwait, the former Soviet Union and the former Yugoslavia. Twenty-one per cent of Sri Lankan males who were seen at a London torture treatment centre reported sexual abuse while in detention. In El Salvador, 76% of male political prisoners surveyed in the 1980s described at least one incidence of sexual torture. A study of 6,000 concentration-camp inmates in Sarajevo found that 80% of men reported having been raped.

I've come to Kampala to hear the stories of the few brave men who have agreed to speak to me: a rare opportunity to find out about a controversial and deeply taboo issue. In Uganda, survivors are at risk of arrest by police, as they are likely to assume that they're gay – a crime in this country and in 38 of the 53 African nations. They will probably be ostracised by friends, rejected by family and turned away by the UN and the myriad international NGOs that are equipped, trained and ready to help women. They are wounded, isolated and in danger. In the words of Owiny: "They are despised."

But they are willing to talk, thanks largely to the RLP's British director, Dr Chris Dolan. Dolan first heard of wartime sexual violence against men in the late 1990s while researching his PhD in northern Uganda, and he sensed that the problem might be dramatically underestimated. Keen to gain a fuller grasp of its depth and nature, he put up posters throughout Kampala in June 2009 announcing a "workshop" on the issue in a local school. On the day, 150 men arrived. In a burst of candour, one attendee admitted: "It's happened to all of us here." It soon became known among Uganda's 200,000-strong refugee population that the RLP were helping men who had been raped during conflict. Slowly, more victims began to come forward.

I meet Jean Paul on the hot, dusty roof of the RLP's HQ in Old Kampala. He wears a scarlet high-buttoned shirt and holds himself with his neck lowered, his eyes cast towards the ground, as if in apology for his impressive height. He has a prominent upper lip that shakes continually – a nervous condition that makes him appear as if he's on the verge of tears.

Jean Paul was at university in Congo, studying electronic engineering, when his father – a wealthy businessman – was accused by the army of aiding the enemy and shot dead. Jean Paul fled in January 2009, only to be abducted by rebels. Along with six other men and six women he was marched to a forest in the Virunga National Park.

Later that day, the rebels and their prisoners met up with their cohorts who were camped out in the woods. Small camp fires could be seen here and there between the shadowy ranks of trees. While the women were sent off to prepare food and coffee, 12 armed fighters surrounded the men. From his place on the ground, Jean Paul looked up to see the commander leaning over them. In his 50s, he was bald, fat and in military uniform. He wore a red bandana around his neck and had strings of leaves tied around his elbows.

"You are all spies," the commander said. "I will show you how we punish spies." He pointed to Jean Paul. "Remove your clothes and take a position like a Muslim man."

Jean Paul thought he was joking. He shook his head and said: "I cannot do these things."

The commander called a rebel over. Jean Paul could see that he was only about nine years old. He was told, "Beat this man and remove this clothes." The boy attacked him with his gun butt. Eventually, Jean Paul begged: "Okay, okay. I will take off my clothes." Once naked, two rebels held him in a kneeling position with his head pushed towards the earth.

At this point, Jean Paul breaks off. The shaking in his lip more pronounced than ever, he lowers his head a little further and says: "I am sorry for the things I am going to say now." The commander put his left hand on the back of his skull and used his right to beat him on the backside "like a horse". Singing a witch doctor song, and with everybody watching, the commander then began. The moment he started, Jean Paul vomited.

Eleven rebels waited in a queue and raped Jean Paul in turn. When he was too exhausted to hold himself up, the next attacker would wrap his arm under Jean Paul's hips and lift him by the stomach. He bled freely: "Many, many, many bleeding," he says, "I could feel it like water." Each of the male prisoners was raped 11 times that night and every night that followed.

On the ninth day, they were looking for firewood when Jean Paul spotted a huge tree with roots that formed a small grotto of shadows. Seizing his moment, he crawled in and watched, trembling, as the rebel guards searched for him. After five hours of watching their feet as they hunted for him, he listened as they came up with a plan: they would let off a round of gunfire and tell the commander that Jean Paul had been killed. Eventually he emerged, weak from his ordeal and his diet of only two bananas per day during his captivity. Dressed only in his underpants, he crawled through the undergrowth "slowly, slowly, slowly, slowly, like a snake" back into town.

Today, despite his hospital treatment, Jean Paul still bleeds when he walks. Like many victims, the wounds are such that he's supposed to restrict his diet to soft foods such as bananas, which are expensive, and Jean Paul can only afford maize and millet. His brother keeps asking what's wrong with him. "I don't want to tell him," says Jean Paul. "I fear he will say: 'Now, my brother is not a man.'"

It is for this reason that both perpetrator and victim enter a conspiracy of silence and why male survivors often find, once their story is discovered, that they lose the support and comfort of those around them. In the patriarchal societies found in many developing countries, gender roles are strictly defined.

"In Africa no man is allowed to be vulnerable," says RLP's gender officer Salome Atim. "You have to be masculine, strong. You should never break down or cry. A man must be a leader and provide for the whole family. When he fails to reach that set standard, society perceives that there is something wrong."

Often, she says, wives who discover their husbands have been raped decide to leave them. "They ask me: 'So now how am I going to live with him? As what? Is this still a husband? Is it a wife?' They ask, 'If he can be raped, who is protecting me?' There's one family I have been working closely with in which the husband has been raped twice. When his wife discovered this, she went home, packed her belongings, picked up their child and left. Of course that brought down this man's heart."

Back at RLP I'm told about the other ways in which their clients have been made to suffer. Men aren't simply raped, they are forced to penetrate holes in banana trees that run with acidic sap, to sit with their genitals over a fire, to drag rocks tied to their penis, to give oral sex to queues of soldiers, to be penetrated with screwdrivers and sticks. Atim has now seen so many male survivors that, frequently, she can spot them the moment they sit down. "They tend to lean forward and will often sit on one buttock," she tells me. "When they cough, they grab their lower regions. At times, they will stand up and there's blood on the chair. And they often have some kind of smell."

Because there has been so little research into the rape of men during war, it's not possible to say with any certainty why it happens or even how common it is – although a rare 2010 survey, published in the *Journal of the American Medical Association*, found that 22% of men and 30% of women in Eastern Congo reported conflict-related sexual violence. As for Atim, she says: "Our staff are overwhelmed by the cases we've got, but in terms of actual numbers? This is the tip of the iceberg."

Later on I speak with Dr Angella Ntinda, who treats referrals from the RLP. She tells me: "Eight out of 10 patients from RLP will be talking about some sort of sexual abuse."

"Eight out of 10 men?" I clarify.

"No. Men *and* women," she says.

"What about men?"

"I think all the men."

I am aghast.

"*All* of them?" I say.

"Yes," she says. "All the men."

The research by Lara Stemple at the University of California doesn't only show that male sexual violence is a component of wars all over the world, it also suggests that international aid organisations are failing male victims. Her study cites a review of 4,076 NGOs that have addressed wartime sexual violence. Only 3% of them mentioned the experience of men in their literature. "Typically," Stemple says, "as a passing reference.[247]

Storr discusses the underreporting with Chris Dolan, the Director of the Refugee Law Project, which works in partnership with Christian Aid in highlighting these social issues:

Stemple's findings on the failure of aid agencies is no surprise to Dolan. "The organisations working on sexual and gender-based violence don't talk about it," he says. "It's systematically silenced. If you're very, very lucky they'll give it a tangential mention at the end of a report. You might get five seconds of: 'Oh and men can also be the victims of sexual violence.' But there's no data, no discussion."

As part of an attempt to correct this, the RLP produced a documentary in 2010 called *Gender Against Men*. When it was screened, Dolan says that attempts were made to stop him. "Were these attempts by people in well-known, international aid agencies?" I ask.

"Yes," he replies. "There's a fear among them that this is a zero-sum game; that there's a pre-defined cake and if you start talking about men, you're going to somehow eat a chunk of this cake that's taken them a long time to bake." Dolan points to a November 2006 UN report that followed an international conference on sexual violence in this area of East Africa.

---

29. [247] Storr, Will. "The rape of men: the darkest secret of war." *The Observer*, Guardian News and Media, 16 July 2011, www.theguardian.com/society/2011/jul/17/the-rape-of-men.

"I know for a fact that the people behind the report insisted the definition of rape be restricted to women," he says, adding that one of the RLP's donors, Dutch Oxfam, refused to provide any more funding unless he'd promise that 70% of his client base was female. He also recalls a man whose case was "particularly bad" and was referred to the UN's refugee agency, the UNHCR. "They told him: 'We have a programme for vulnerable women, but not men.'"

It reminds me of a scene described by Eunice Owiny: "There is a married couple," she said. "The man has been raped, the woman has been raped. Disclosure is easy for the woman. She gets the medical treatment, she gets the attention, she's supported by so many organisations. But the man is inside, dying."

"In a nutshell, that's exactly what happens," Dolan agrees. "Part of the activism around women's rights is: 'Let's prove that women are as good as men.' But the other side is you should look at the fact that men can be weak and vulnerable."

Margot Wallström, the UN special representative of the secretary-general for sexual violence in conflict, insists in a statement that the UNHCR extends its services to refugees of both genders. But she concedes that the "great stigma" men face suggests that the real number of survivors is higher than that reported. Wallström says the focus remains on women because they are "overwhelmingly" the victims. Nevertheless, she adds, "we do know of many cases of men and boys being raped."

But when I contact Stemple by email, she describes a "constant drum beat that women are *the* rape victims" and a milieu in which men are treated as a "monolithic perpetrator class".

"International human rights law leaves out men in nearly all instruments designed to address sexual violence," she continues. "The UN Security Council Resolution 1325 in 2000 treats wartime sexual violence as something that only impacts on women and girls… Secretary of State Hillary Clinton recently announced $44m to implement this resolution. Because of its entirely exclusive focus on female victims, it seems unlikely that any of these new funds will reach the thousands of men and boys who suffer from this kind of abuse. Ignoring male rape not only neglects men, it also harms women by reinforcing a viewpoint that equates 'female' with 'victim', thus hampering our ability to see women as strong and empowered. In the same way, silence about male victims reinforces unhealthy expectations about men and their supposed invulnerability."

Considering Dolan's finding that "female rape is significantly underreported and male rape almost never", I ask Stemple if, following her research, she believes it might be a hitherto unimagined part of all wars. "No one knows, but I do think it's safe to say that it's likely that it's been a part of many wars throughout history and that taboo has played a part in the silence."

As I leave Uganda, there's a detail of a story that I can't forget. Before receiving help from the RLP, one man went to see his local doctor. He told him he had been raped four times, that he was injured and depressed and his wife had threatened to leave him. The doctor gave him a Panadol.[248]

Overall, simplistic religious gender norms are unhealthy, they make people less safe in society, they fail to help rape victims who suffer needlessly from worthless gender expectations inculcated by religious conservatism, they act as an impediment towards strong social support for rape victims when they need it most, they blame the victims for the sexual violence they suffer, and they fail to make any coherent or logical sense. How can religious conservatism tout superior morality to liberal social values, while forcing women into a

---

30. [248] Storr, Will. "The rape of men: the darkest secret of war." *The Observer*, Guardian News and Media, 16 July 2011, www.theguardian.com/society/2011/jul/17/the-rape-of-men.

marginalized social status under the implication that all men are prone to rape them? These fixed mindsets and the structural systems of abuse that they propagate can only be diminished and overcome through challenging the foundational assumptions of the simplistic gender binary. The only way to challenge it is by motivating people to value consent and social equality among men and women over abusive systems of unequal social power as encouraged by religious conservatism. Sex-positive feminism that repudiates the shaming of rape victims, pointing out gender discrimination and speaking out on our stories of societal gender bias, statistical analysis of gender equality to measure real progress, and recognizing the pathologies of religious conservatism can offer some assistance to achieve a more equal world.[249]

Female Genital Mutilation

Female circumcision is a widespread practice throughout sub-Saharan Africa and has a long history that predates the creation of the Abrahamic faiths. Despite the typical assumptions made by the West about the practice existing because of male discrimination against women, the practice of this genital mutilation of female babies is most staunchly defended by the elderly women who were forced to undergo female genital mutilation themselves as babies. It seems to exist because of the special tribal meaning that sub-Saharan Africa placed upon female circumcision from religious traditions predating the conversion to the Abrahamic faiths but exists in the Shafi'i school of Islam in modern times too.[250] Author Hanny Lightfoot-Klein, who worked as a schoolteacher in sub-Saharan Africa and authored the book "Prisoners of Ritual: An Odyssey into female genital circumcision in Africa" elaborates for the NOCIRC symposium (National Organization of Circumcision Resource Center) about the results of her interviews throughout sub-Saharan Africa. She wrote the following:

> Contrary to all my expectations, I discovered that this ancient custom as adhered to and defended most resolutely not by men, but by its survivors, the women elders. It was these women that insisted most vehemently on its perpetuation and it was they who also wielded the knife.
>
> Among the elite, the mutilation was often plotted by "the grandmothers," and carried out at the first unguarded moment that presented itself, in spite of all efforts that the child's educated parents had exerted in order to prevent it.
>
> To nearly all the population, male and female alike, the mere idea that a girl should not be "circumcised" was altogether unthinkable. Not only would such a girl find no one who would marry her, but it was generally believed that all sorts of evils in respect to her sexual behavior, her health, and even more importantly in these cultures, the health of her husband and babies, would inevitably follow.
>
> Eighty-seven percent of men and 83 percent of women voiced their unqualified approval of the practice, according to Dareer's extensive statistical study in Sudan. Taking into consideration that these

---

31. [249] Green, Laci. "THE F-WORD." *YouTube*, YouTube, 8 July 2014, www.youtube.com/watch?v=EJPT_U97lNs.
32. [250] "Appeal to Tradition." *Https://Www.logicallyfallacious.com*, www.logicallyfallacious.com/tools/lp/Bo/LogicalFallacies/44/Appeal-to-Tradition.

mutilations are illegal under current Sudanese law, it is almost inevitable that the true approval rate is far closer to 100 percent for both men and women.

I learned that only a tiny handful of the most highly educated Africans had any notion whatsoever that in most of the world "female circumcision" was not practiced at all. Certainly, in the part of sub-Saharan East Africa where I researched the topic most intensively, a vulva left in its natural state stigmatized the woman as a slave, a prostitute, an outcast, an unclean being unworthy of the honor of continuing a respected family lineage.

Among the many people in all walks of life that I interviewed on the subject of female genital mutilation in Sudan, the epicenter of the most extreme excisions and infibulations, there was a young veterinarian who related the following to me:

"It had simply never occurred to me that there was anything wrong with the practice. Nor had this apparently ever occurred to any of my contemporaries, with whom I had at one time or another discussed it. It was only when I studied at a European university and saw how much less complicated things were for women there, that I finally understood how terrible a thing it is."[251]

It may come as a surprise that the very women who were forced into dreadful operations are the staunchest advocates of female babies undergoing genital mutilation but it becomes clearer when understanding the cultural boundaries that exist in sub-Saharan Africa. The people of those regions have sacred beliefs pertaining to female circumcision that are similar to a rite of passage among their community; social proof – following other people in the broad public as a sign of approval that you're conducting the right actions – is one of the core reasons for the prevalence of female circumcision, women who have undergone circumcision often appeal to tradition to justify circumcising babies, they may feel that because they underwent a symbolic concession that it is only appropriate that the younger babies undergo the concession too as a form of collective reciprocity and "equality", and scientific studies have shown, in the case of such tribal practices, fraternity hazing ceremonies, and other such rites of passage, that the more effort imposed through the ritual then the more committed the people are to the specific practice.[252][253]

Generally speaking, people who go through a great deal of effort to obtain something will value it higher.[254] The actual value of what is gained doesn't matter; people's perception of the perceived gain is ranked higher should they struggle to obtain the gain regardless of how worthless the gain actually is.[255] Thus a tribal practice such as female circumcision that is generally accepted as positive among the population, perceived as reasonable to increase a

---

33. [251] Lightfoot-Klein, Hanny. *National Organization of Circumcision Resource Centers*, NOCIRC, Mar. 1994, www.nocirc.org/symposia/third/hanny3.html.
34. [252] Cialdini, Robert B. Chapter 3: Commitment and Consistency (52-95) and Chapter 4: Social Proof (98-140). *Influence: Science and practice*. 4th ed., 21st Century Bks, 2002.
35. [253] "Appeal to Tradition." *Https://Www.logicallyfallacious.com*, www.logicallyfallacious.com/tools/lp/Bo/LogicalFallacies/44/Appeal-to-Tradition.
36. [254] Cialdini, Robert B. Chapter 3: Commitment and Consistency (52-95). *Influence: Science and practice*. 4th ed., 21st Century Bks, 2002.
37. [255] Cialdini, Robert B. Chapter 3: Commitment and Consistency (52-95). *Influence: Science and practice*. 4th ed., 21st Century Bks, 2002.

woman's health through a long tradition, conducted collectively throughout entire communities of the different surrounding countries, and obtained through severe pain on the part of the infant. Female circumcision is seen as a sacred concession that is the correct course of action to living a positive life.[256] The majority of people in sub-Saharan Africa find their own "causes" for why the tradition still exists despite being illegal in some of these countries.[257] Through their own judgmental heuristics and cultural biases, they create "causes" that seem reasonable within their worldview and many people within sub-Saharan Africa have simply never thought deeply about female circumcision not being practiced in other parts of the world.[258][259] Sadly, many of these "causes" may be defended by scientists in their region who disingenuously represent the facts to defend the tribalism that they have a bias for within their home countries; thus, creating confusion and doubt from what would ordinarily be expert opinion because of cultural and theological induced blindness.

In a 1990 New York Times article, Melvin Konner lays out the consequences of this religious belief for young girls based on Klein's research from an interview with Klein:

> Between 90 million and 100 million women of all ages now living in Africa had their childhoods interrupted by a traditional operation in which the clitoris is partly or, more commonly, completely removed - without anesthesia, with crude cutting tools and with little or no precaution against infection. In most cases clitoral excision is followed by another operation, in which the labia are partly cut away and then sewn together. Once a girl has healed, her vagina is almost completely sealed, leaving her a "pinhole" opening, only large enough for urine to pass drop by drop.
>
> The immediate consequences of this operation sometimes include hemorrhage, tetanus and other infections, excruciating pain and death. More common results include painful urination, backup of menstrual blood and severe pain during sexual intercourse. (Two to 12 weeks are required for gradual penetration, which is essentially a process of repeated tearing; for convenience, the honeymoon hotel in the Sudanese city of Port Sudan is next to a hospital.) Traditionally women are resewn after the birth of each child ("renewable virginity") only to experience the same effects again.[260]

Male Genital Mutilation

---

38. [256] Cialdini, Robert B. Chapter 2: Reciprocation (19-50). *Influence: Science and practice*. 4th ed., 21st Century Bks, 2002.
39. [257] Kahneman, Daniel. Chapter 6:"Norms, Surprises, and Causes" (71-78). *Thinking, fast and slow*. Farrar, Straus and Giroux, 2015.
40. [258] Kahneman, Daniel. Chapter 8: How Judgments Happen (89-96). *Thinking, fast and slow*. Farrar, Straus and Giroux, 2015.
41. [259] Kahneman, Daniel. Chapter 6:"Norms, Surprises, and Causes" (71-78). *Thinking, fast and slow*. Farrar, Straus and Giroux, 2015.
42. [260] Konner, Melvin. "MUTILATED IN THE NAME OF TRADITION." *The New York Times*, The New York Times, 14 Apr. 1990, www.nytimes.com/1990/04/15/books/mutilated-in-the-name-of-tradition.html.

I apologize if this topic gives you any degree of discomfort and none of the following is an attempt to shame people who have undergone this procedure. I ask that – whatever your personal feelings and opinions on the matter – that you please read this section to its totality before forming a judgment about this issue and try to maintain impartiality to the best of your ability.

Circumcision is a physical representation of the commitment to self-contempt for the sake of a higher purpose.[261] It attempts to posit a rational basis that has been overwhelmingly discredited by recent scientific studies. Male circumcision has been disingenuously represented as a credible and rational medical procedure for male babies to undergo. After researching the topic, I've found that apologists of circumcision have promoted the most miniscule benefits and have gone so far as to use methodologically flawed studies to promote circumcision throughout sub-Saharan Africa, Israel, and the United States. Europe abandoned the practice long ago and has conducted scientific studies that have given a less favorable portrayal of circumcision than what the United States espouses. Believers of circumcision try to utilize negligible and false scientific reasoning to defend male genital mutilation; the CDC uses circumcision on the basis of methodologically flawed tests that were never completed.[262] They purported to run three studies in Africa to see if male circumcision could prevent sexually transmitted infections, then cancelled the study before the full data was collected during the time circumcised men had to wait a week after the circumcisions before they could report if they had contracted a sexually transmitted infection, and then the CDC used the cancelled research study to argue that circumcision prevented sexually transmitted infections.[263] Findings by the CDC showing "consistency" since then have relied on the methodologically flawed testing as a basis. Doctors and nurses can legally lie to parents about the horrific trauma that their babies go through to continue gaining money from the surgical procedure.[264] People in the US and Canada have substituted religion with culture as the reasoning behind allowing their children to suffer physical and mental torment. Trauma has been shown by scientific studies that compared circumcised and uncircumcised babies. The belief that the nervous system isn't fully developed in babies upon birth is found to be a major myth among physicians from the research by more modern studies, babies suffer greater pain due to no anesthesia, and babies who don't cry during the procedure may be suffering intense shock.[265][266] Intense crying fits can

---

43. [261] Nietzsche, Friedrich Wilhelm. *On the genealogy of morals: a polemical tract*. Translated by Ian Johnston, PDF, Richer Resources Publications, 2014.
44. [262] Narvaez, Darcia. "More Circumcision Myths You May Believe: Hygiene and STDs." *Psychology Today*, Sussex Publishers, 13 Sept. 2011, www.psychologytoday.com/blog/moral-landscapes/201109/more-circumcision-myths-you-may-believe-hygiene-and-stds.
45. [263] Narvaez, Darcia. "More Circumcision Myths You May Believe: Hygiene and STDs." *Psychology Today*, Sussex Publishers, 13 Sept. 2011, www.psychologytoday.com/blog/moral-landscapes/201109/more-circumcision-myths-you-may-believe-hygiene-and-stds.
46. [264] Narvaez, Darcia. "Circumcision's Psychological Damage." *Psychology Today*, Sussex Publishers, 11 Jan. 2015, www.psychologytoday.com/blog/moral-landscapes/201501/circumcision-s-psychological-damage.
47. [265] Goldman, R. "The psychological impact of circumcision." *Circumcision Resource Center*, THE

be dangerous for the health of infants, one infant ruptured their stomach from excessive crying and Canadian doctors conducting studies on the matter of circumcision state there is no question that babies who undergo circumcision suffer intense pain.[267] They're likely to suffer future trauma at a certain point in their lives that happen anywhere from early child care to old age; a recent controversial study has linked circumcision with autism.[268][269] Furthermore, circumcision can cause intense bleeding, the spread of infections on the penis, and surgical accidents can result in medical professionals being forced to amputate the penis entirely.[270] Deaths of infants as a result of the circumcision procedure have also occurred.[271] The supposed benefits against HIV are based on dubious studies that didn't even attempt to research circumcision on infants.[272] Attempts at defending circumcision only show the primitive nature of North American and Middle Eastern culture. Circumcision is male genital mutilation and the practice itself is no different than Africa's female genital mutilation of young girls.[273] Arguably, the US and Canada conducting such behavior despite higher educational institutions and a higher quality of life shows how egregious this contemptuous practice truly is. It is worse because Canadians and Americans have the ability of knowing better.

The South African Medical Journal in a 2008 article lists several methodology and ethical issues with the circumcision studies conducted by the US that raise concerns on the dubious nature of US studies that claim male circumcision reduces sexually transmitted infections. The acronym MC refers to male circumcision for the purposes of the journal:

> The 2003 Cochrane review[5] of observational studies of MC effectiveness concluded that there was insufficient evidence to support it as an anti-HIV intervention. Three randomised controlled trials (RCTs) from South Africa, Kenya and Uganda in 2006 - 2007 show a protective effect of MC. However, Garenne[6] has subsequently shown from observational data that there is considerable heterogeneity of the effect of MC across 14 African countries. Despite the South African RCT showing a protective effect, he

---

CIRCUMCISION REFERENCE LIBRARY, www.cirp.org/library/psych/goldman1/.
48. [266] Page, Gayle Giboney. "Are There Long-Term Consequences of Pain in Newborn or Very Young Infants?" *The Journal of Perinatal Education*, U.S. National Library of Medicine, 2004, www.ncbi.nlm.nih.gov/pmc/articles/PMC1595204/.
49. [267] "Infant Responses to Circumcision." *Circumcision Resource Center*, circumcision.org/infant-responses-to-circumcision/.
50. [268] Freeman, David. "Circumcision Linked To Autism In Controversial New Study." *The Huffington Post*, TheHuffingtonPost.com, 20 Jan. 2015, www.huffingtonpost.com/2015/01/20/circumcision-autism-new-study_n_6503106.html.
51. [269] Kovac, Sarah. "New autism dispute: is circumcision a factor?" *Time*, Time, time.com/4314388/new-autism-dispute-is-circumcision-a-factor/.
52. [270] Boyle, G. J. "Issues associated with the introduction of circumcision into a non-Circumcising society." *Issues associated with the introduction of circumcision into a non-Circumcising society*, THE CIRCUMCISION REFERENCE LIBRARY, Nov. 2003, www.cirp.org/library/disease/HIV/boyle-sti/.
53. [271] Boyle, G. J. "Issues associated with the introduction of circumcision into a non-Circumcising society." *Issues associated with the introduction of circumcision into a non-Circumcising society*, THE CIRCUMCISION REFERENCE LIBRARY, Nov. 2003, www.cirp.org/library/disease/HIV/boyle-sti/.
54. [272] Myers, A, and J Myers. *Rolling out male circumcision as a mass HIV/AIDS intervention seems neither justified nor practicable*, www.cirp.org/library/disease/HIV/myers2008/.
55. [273] "About Us." *Doctors Opposing Circumcision*, www.doctorsopposingcircumcision.org/about-us/#_statement-principles.

reports for the nine South African provinces that 'there is no evidence that HIV transmission over the period 1994 - 2004 was slower in those provinces with higher levels of circumcision'. Interestingly, in both Kenya and Uganda, where two of the RCTs were done, a protective effect of MC was observed, but a harmful effect was observed in Cameroon, Lesotho and Malawi. The other eight countries showed no significant effect of MC.

These somewhat discordant findings are difficult to interpret. While RCTs are theoretically strong designs, it is conceivable that their findings are not generalisable beyond their settings. Furthermore, there have been no trials of neonatal MC. Study flaws such as inability to obtain double blinding, and loss to follow-up in RCTs, may effectively degrade their quality to that of observational studies. Meanwhile other disturbing findings referred to by Sidler *et al.* are emerging, including the reported higher risk for women partners of circumcised HIV positive men, disinhibition, urological complications, relatively small effect sizes of MC at the population level, and relative cost-inefficiency of MC.

Not all objections to MC as an HIV intervention have to do with evidence of effectiveness or cost. Sidler *et al.* raise ethical objections. Owing to the current climate of desperation with regard to the HIV epidemic, evidence in favour of MC frequently seems overstated. This reduces the scope for informed consent and autonomy for adult men considering the procedure. Further problems arise in the case of neonates whose parents may be considering the procedure. Whereas informed consent is at least possible for adult men, it is clearly not possible for neonates. Parents can only guess what the child's wishes would be if he were presented with the information they have at their disposal. If it could be shown that circumcision was necessary in the neonatal period, parental consent on behalf of the neonate would be justified. But since no valid surgical indications for circumcision exist in this period, and the future benefit to the child in respect of HIV avoidance is not relevant before sexual debut, the duty of parents may well be to err on the side of caution, and defer the procedure until the child can make an autonomous decision. In the absence of compelling indications, a procedure such as circumcision could also be seen as a violation of the child's right to bodily integrity. Furthermore, the ethical principle of non-maleficence cannot be upheld as there are clear harms attached to this practice, to which Sidler *et al.* refer in their article. Lastly, at a societal level MC may be unjust insofar as it could compete for resources with more effective and less costly interventions[7] and disadvantage women.[274]

Several studies conducted in Denmark show alarming problems with circumcision that the United States has seen fit to uniformly ignore but which the US public, the public of the various African countries, and religious groups that practice circumcision should take into serious consideration before conducting such a surgery on their infant children.

In one cross-sectional study that was titled "*Male Circumcision and sexual function in men and women*", the study found that circumcised men had frequent orgasm difficulties and their female spouses were less sexually satisfied:

RESULTS:
Age at first intercourse, perceived importance of a good sex life and current sexual activity differed little between circumcised and uncircumcised men or between women with circumcised and uncircumcised spouses. However, circumcised men reported more partners and were more likely to report frequent orgasm difficulties after adjustment for potential confounding factors [11 vs 4%, OR(adj) = 3.26; 95% confidence interval (CI) 1.42-7.47], and women with circumcised spouses more often reported incomplete sexual needs fulfilment (38 vs 28%, OR(adj) = 2.09; 95% CI 1.05-4.16) and frequent sexual function difficulties overall (31 vs 22%, OR(adj) = 3.26; 95% CI 1.15-9.27), notably orgasm difficulties (19 vs 14%, OR(adj) = 2.66; 95% CI 1.07-6.66) and dyspareunia (12 vs 3%, OR(adj) = 8.45; 95% CI

---

56. [274] Myers, J. "Male circumcision and HIV infection." *History of Circumcision*, Historyofcircumcision.net,
www.historyofcircumcision.net/index.php?option=content&task=view&id=85.

3.01-23.74). Findings were stable in several robustness analyses, including one restricted to non-Jews and non-Moslems.

CONCLUSIONS:

Circumcision was associated with frequent orgasm difficulties in Danish men and with a range of frequent sexual difficulties in women, notably orgasm difficulties, dyspareunia and a sense of incomplete sexual needs fulfilment. Thorough examination of these matters in areas where male circumcision is more common is warranted.[275]

In a Danish 2015 study, titled: "*Ritual Circumcision and risk of autism spectrum disorder in 0 to 9 year-old boys*", Danish researchers have confirmed a causal link between circumcision and the increase in autism in young boys. Circumcised boys were statistically higher in being diagnosed with autism spectrum disorder (ASD). The findings were as follows:

Abstract

Objective

Based on converging observations in animal, clinical and ecological studies, we hypothesised a possible impact of ritual circumcision on the subsequent risk of autism spectrum disorder (ASD) in young boys.

Design

National, register-based cohort study.

Setting

Denmark.

Participants

A total of 342,877 boys born between 1994 and 2003 and followed in the age span 0–9 years between 1994 and 2013.

Main outcome measures

Information about cohort members' ritual circumcisions, confounders and ASD outcomes, as well as two supplementary outcomes, hyperkinetic disorder and asthma, was obtained from national registers. Hazard ratios (HRs) with 95% confidence intervals (CIs) associated with foreskin status were obtained using Cox proportional hazards regression analyses.

---

57. [275] Frisch, M, et al. "Male circumcision and sexual function in men and women: a survey-Based, cross-Sectional study in Denmark." *International journal of epidemiology.*, U.S. National Library of Medicine, Oct. 2011, www.ncbi.nlm.nih.gov/pubmed/21672947.

Results

With a total of 4986 ASD cases, our study showed that regardless of cultural background circumcised boys were more likely than intact boys to develop ASD before age 10 years (HR = 1.46; 95% CI: 1.11–1.93). Risk was particularly high for infantile autism before age five years (HR = 2.06; 95% CI: 1.36–3.13). Circumcised boys in non-Muslim families were also more likely to develop hyperkinetic disorder (HR = 1.81; 95% CI: 1.11–2.96). Associations with asthma were consistently inconspicuous (HR = 0.96; 95% CI: 0.84–1.10).

Conclusions

We confirmed our hypothesis that boys who undergo ritual circumcision may run a greater risk of developing ASD. This finding, and the unexpected observation of an increased risk of hyperactivity disorder among circumcised boys in non-Muslim families, need attention, particularly because data limitations most likely rendered our HR estimates conservative. Considering the widespread practice of non-therapeutic circumcision in infancy and childhood around the world, confirmatory studies should be given priority.[276]

The true reason for male circumcision, for the most part, is the belief that circumcision will grant entrance to the Kingdom of God in the Abrahamic faiths. A principal belief that Jews, Muslims, and certain Christian denominations believe are necessary for their faith. This primitive tribalism conducted during our modern age shows the pernicious effects of religious thinking because of how normalized the damaging of the genitals is for Abrahamic culture. Circumcision is found to decrease penile sensitivity and decrease the pleasure of orgasm for men.[277] It is truly disturbing to acknowledge and the disingenuous pseudo-scientific arguments supporting this for the sake of a higher power shows the true cruelty that religion invokes from parent to child. The original study arguing about the so-called benefits of circumcision was cancelled before it was completed and there has never been a reproduction of the results; it isn't surprising since the scientific experiment was never completed. To reiterate: the US government conducted the experiment on three different African villages and the CDC has argued its supposed benefits but non-government health organizations have found the claims dubious because of how flawed the methodology was.[278] Circumcised men had to wait weeks after their operation to conduct normal sexual behavior and the "results" were obtained before any completion of the study. The data was used as a basis to defend circumcision despite these grave issues regarding the legitimacy of the experiment. In particular, the lack of repeated

---

58. [276] Frisch, Morten, and Jacob Simonsen. "Ritual circumcision and risk of autism spectrum disorder in 0- to 9-Year-Old boys: national cohort study in Denmark." *Journal of the Royal Society of Medicine*, vol. 108, no. 7, Aug. 2015, pp. 266–279., doi:10.1177/0141076814565942.
59. [277] Bronselaer, G A, et al. "Male circumcision decreases penile sensitivity as measured in a large cohort." *BJU international.*, U.S. National Library of Medicine, May 2013, www.ncbi.nlm.nih.gov/pubmed/23374102.

experiments and the overemphasis on the mutilation practice lowering urinary tract infection – which is lowered to about 1 percent, is negligible. By comparison, breast cancer for women has a rate of 12 percent but we don't remove women's breasts to protect them from a miniscule percentage of risk.[279] Male circumcision, despite existing prior to the Abrahamic traditions, is an intrinsic part of Judaism, Islam, and denominations of Christianity. Jews, certain Christians, and Muslims believe that circumcision is necessary to enter the Kingdom of God and the practice is conducted because of this theological basis. Doctors throughout the United States, Africa, and the Middle East may have substituted the initial reasons for circumcision - to make masturbation less pleasurable for men - to arguing "health benefits" to stay consistent with their religious practices and cultural norms via substituting the original reasons with confirmation bias towards any positive benefits.[280] From all of the research that I've looked into and the findings of medical professionals, the foreskin is a completely healthy part of the male anatomy that doesn't need to be removed.[281] Shaming men for having foreskin or shaming parents for not having their child's foreskin removed seems to be a cultural tradition of misandry that comes from antiquated cultural norms of the Abrahamic faiths.[282]

---

60. [279] Narvaez, Darcia. "More Circumcision Myths You May Believe: Hygiene and STDs." *Psychology Today*, Sussex Publishers, 13 Sept. 2011, www.psychologytoday.com/blog/moral-landscapes/201109/more-circumcision-myths-you-may-believe-hygiene-and-stds.
61. [280] Kahneman, Daniel. Chapter 9: Answering an Easier Question (97-104). *Thinking, fast and slow*. Farrar, Straus and Giroux, 2015.
62. [281] "About Us." *Doctors Opposing Circumcision*, www.doctorsopposingcircumcision.org/about-us/#_statement-principles.
63. [282] Green, Laci. "I LOVE FORESKIN (Wtf circumcision?)." *YouTube*, YouTube, 14 Aug. 2013, www.youtube.com/watch?v=JbTdkWV89Ak.

Chapter 6: Original Sin, the Failure of Abrahamic Morality

Isaiah 45:7 King James Version (KJV)

⁷ I form the light, and create darkness: I make peace, and create evil: I the LORD do all these things.[283]

If you believe in morality, then you should honestly consider Original Sin to be the ultimate mockery and subversion of morality. Cloaked under the veneer of religious piety and goodness, this belief allows for all forms of savagery: genocide, organized rape, torture, mass bombing campaigns, and every other horrific atrocity to be viewed as an inevitable part of the human experience. Humans who observe such occurrences from the outset through television, or through the internet, use such anecdotes as a justification that violence is an inescapable part of humanity. People use such events as evidence to believe that our biology is evil. They believe that evil is merely a fact of life because we observe stories of street violence, rapes, wars, and genocide through the constant bombardment of negative news on social media. People may believe that without religious morals that they will go into sprees of murder, rape, and other forms of violence. They might be led to believe that sinfulness and the capacity for absolute evil is just waiting to be acted upon but strictly controlled through the guidance of an absolute good from religious teachings. Original sin teaches people to believe humans are imperfect and so falter into sinfulness. As a consequence, we observe atrocities around the world through the lens of apathy or indifference while believing the victims are in heaven for our own comfort. Yet, on any given day, it is impossible to know why each specific tragedy happened unless we individually fact-check them; it is easier to simply believe that all people have some evil in them since it gives a quick and coherent worldview of such events.[284] Yet, if the perpetrator was raised as a Christian, Muslim, or Jew – or was taught Abrahamic value of sinfulness in religious schools that disseminate such values around the world – then what stops them from believing that their actions were simply inevitable because of their humanity? In fact, why wouldn't the perpetrator of a crime just perceive their acts as an unavoidable aspect of being human after committing human rights atrocities? The human body would be like a cage where carnal pleasure was misunderstood to be evil intent and acts of rape and murder would be viewed by the perpetrators as simply a product of their humanity. Relying strongly upon the religious precept of sinfulness would mean that you must believe that you are capable of child murder, child rape, the torture of children, and you are likely to believe that these are aspects of humanity that can never be changed because murder, rape, and torture are intrinsically part of human nature. It is unalterable and all humans; you, your spouse, your children, your friends, your caretakers, and every human on the planet is simply born with a deep malice that predisposes them for crimes such as murder, rape, torture, and genocide. God created conditions that allowed everyone to be capable of these horrors. Thus, the belief in original sin provides a convenient excuse to ignore morality because acts of evil are somehow

---

1. [283] "BibleGateway." *Bible Gateway*, Bible Gateway Blog, www.biblegateway.com/passage/?search=Isaiah 45:7&version=KJV.
2. [284] Kahneman, Daniel. *Thinking, fast and slow*. Farrar, Straus and Giroux, 2015.

intrinsically part of human nature. The following is an examination and repudiation of this self-harming belief system.

Sin is an Entity Theory

Sin is an entity theory; it is a concept about ourselves that we believe to be intrinsically part of our behavior. That is, if you believe in sin then you believe it is fixed, unalterable, and you may believe that no amount of cultural or social change can create a shift to decrease violent behavior.[285][286] That is dangerous and it has consequences for how we act towards others. Sin is an unsubstantiated entity theory. It has no scientific and psychological basis to be considered true about our species. The apologists for sin primarily use tragic events or horrible human actions to argue in favor of sin being an objective truth about human existence. However, utilizing tragic events to prove the objectivity of sinfulness anchors too much focus upon events that aren't the norm of the majority of the human species. Moreover, any terrible deed conducted by people who grew up within Abrahamic cultures or Abrahamic communities could justify their violence through the belief in sinfulness. Sinfulness could become circular reasoning, because the perpetrators believe that an intrinsic part of their humanity, the concept of sinfulness, allows them to conduct horrific crimes and the observers of terrible crimes use those specific events as proof of sinfulness.[287] That is, the perpetrator views their violent actions as part of an innate human norm of sinfulness and the observers who watch the news and read the papers see the perpetrator's actions as proof of innate sinfulness in humanity.

That may seem silly, but it is psychologically true that what we believe about ourselves and what we believe that we're capable of has consequences on the actions that we choose to pursue.[288] A mundane example given in research is a person's attitude towards mathematics. If you believe that you're just not good at math after struggling with the subject during your schooling, then you will be disinclined to pursue the subject matter and may believe yourself to be incapable of learning the advanced mathematical topics.[289] This is actually a self-delusion and results in a self-fulfilling prophecy, people who believe that they're "not a math person" or "not good at math" have overemphasized the difficulty and closed off a possible academic future for themselves as a result. These people can improve their math skills by emphasizing efficacy and incremental effort in attaining math skills from their studies but they sincerely

---

3. [285] Dweck, Carol S. *Mindset: How You Can Fulfill Your Potential*. Random House, 2012.
4. [286] Halvorson, Heidi Grant. Chapter 2: Do You Know Where Your Goals Come From? (657-952). *Succeed: How We Can Reach Our Goals*. Plume, 2012.
5. [287] "Circular Reasoning." *Https://Www.logicallyfallacious.com*, www.logicallyfallacious.com/tools/lp/Bo/LogicalFallacies/66/Circular-Reasoning.
6. [288] Halvorson, Heidi Grant. Chapter 2: Do You Know Where Your Goals Come From? (657-952). *Succeed: How We Can Reach Our Goals*. Plume, 2012.
7. [289] Halvorson, Heidi Grant. Chapter 2: Do You Know Where Your Goals Come From? (657-952). *Succeed: How We Can Reach Our Goals*. Plume, 2012.

believe that they are incapable of achieving mastery in mathematics because of an intrinsic flaw.[290] The belief has a lifelong consequence on their future and they don't realize it.

Now, consider the concept of sin and what the concept of sin encourages people to intrinsically believe about themselves and the actions that they're capable of committing. Do you see the problem?

Sinful Thoughts or Intrusive Thoughts?

A principal reason for the belief in sinfulness may derive from the concept of sinful thoughts. Certain personal thoughts and beliefs are categorically labeled evil to even think about and such a distinction leads to constant self-blame and weariness with ourselves for having the "evil" thoughts. The belief that being good means you must have good thoughts isn't healthy or rational because it's a misunderstanding of how thoughts actually function. Believing that being good means that you must only have "good" thoughts is mental self-torture because you would constantly need to try to "expunge" the "evil thoughts" from your mind. Under the distinction between good and evil thoughts, violent thoughts aren't what good people should have. It may not seem normal to you to have thoughts of throwing people down a flight of stairs, jumping out of a moving car, shouting something blasphemous during religious ceremonies, or other deplorable activities. These offensive thoughts would instill people with unease or anxiety because people may worry why such thoughts even entered their mind.[291] We would be looking for some deep "cause" for why these thoughts were circulating in our minds. It may seem reasonable to view these thoughts as sinful and believe that you must constantly fight against such thoughts to maintain purity and moral goodness. These terrible thoughts become a "proof" of sinfulness because people don't know why they have them and fear that there is something evil or criminal within them that are the cause. Many people begin to avoid situations that trigger violent thoughts and feel too ashamed to speak of them with loved ones.

There is an important element in this subject matter that most people don't seem to be aware of: violent or blasphemous thoughts aren't a reflection of you or your inner desires. Unless these thoughts make you feel pleasure or happiness, they aren't what you would want to do to your loved ones or others. Assuming you have such unsettling thoughts, which you do because every human being has them, your feelings of unease and anxiety are your personal reflections on any violent or blasphemous thoughts that you may have. You are not crazy and it doesn't mean that you have the capacity of inflicting violence upon others. The thoughts themselves are just ideas that you gain from your environment or your imagination; ironically, monitoring your thoughts to make sure the bad thoughts will go away will only cause them to

---

8. [290] Halvorson, Heidi Grant. Chapter 2: Do You Know Where Your Goals Come From? (657-952). *Succeed: How We Can Reach Our Goals*. Plume, 2012.
9. [291] Reese, Hannah. "Intrusive Thoughts: Normal or Not?" Psychology Today, Sussex Publishers, www.psychologytoday.com/us/blog/am-i-normal/201110/intrusive-thoughts-normal-or-not.

become more frequent thus increasing the unease and anxiety.[292] Prayer sessions could become a self-fulfilling prophecy in which the frequency of attempts to remove the bad thoughts from your mind could increase the frequency of the thoughts returning. This is because our minds need to check on the unsettling image when we try to monitor our progress of not thinking about the bad thoughts.[293] Psychological studies have shown that trying to ban ourselves from thinking certain thoughts will only increase the frequency of the thoughts occurring in our mind.[294] They were never a reflection of you as a person or what you may think you're capable of committing upon others. They're just thoughts that come to your mind. The increased fear and anxiety from the violent ideas or images probably comes from our honest dread of harming our own loved ones because we don't understand why these thoughts are occurring. The increased frequency and misunderstanding can lead to self-hate, a deep fear of ourselves, self-blame, shame, and depression because of an overemphasis on trying to understand some deeper meaning behind why we have these bad thoughts and fear of what others will think of us. Rest assured, it is entirely normal to have these thoughts. They're labeled intrusive thoughts by modern psychology, they're not a sign of mental illness (unless you feel pleasure from the idea of committing them, which is probably the opposite of what you feel), and *everyone has them*. They're not a reflection of you and they're not a desire of what you secretly want to do to others.[295] They're thoughts that come and go in your mind; similar to thinking about breakfast or thinking about another route to work. Having intrusive thoughts isn't a reflection of how good or evil you are as a person.

What are more important are your feelings towards these thoughts than the thoughts themselves. It is also possible to obsessively think about such intrusive thoughts but that isn't a reflection of you, it just means that you have an obsessive compulsive disorder regarding your thoughts. That doesn't mean you're crazy; it means that you have an OCD regarding your thoughts and it's possible that it developed because human behavior is habit forming. What people believe to be "normal" is really just people going through various forms of mild psychological issues every day through the habits that they form. It only truly becomes an issue when habitual behavior becomes excessive or it is a behavior that is objectively self-harming such as smoking or physically harming one's body. If you have had anxiety because you misunderstood what intrusive thoughts meant, then please learn to relax. Let them come and go, and recognize they're not a deep personal reflection of you as a human being.[296]

---

10. [292] Reese, Hannah. "Intrusive Thoughts: Normal or Not?" Psychology Today, Sussex Publishers, www.psychologytoday.com/us/blog/am-i-normal/201110/intrusive-thoughts-normal-or-not.
11. [293] Reese, Hannah. "Intrusive Thoughts: Normal or Not?" Psychology Today, Sussex Publishers, www.psychologytoday.com/us/blog/am-i-normal/201110/intrusive-thoughts-normal-or-not.
12. [294] Reese, Hannah. "Intrusive Thoughts: Normal or Not?" Psychology Today, Sussex Publishers, www.psychologytoday.com/us/blog/am-i-normal/201110/intrusive-thoughts-normal-or-not.
13. [295] Reese, Hannah. "Intrusive Thoughts: Normal or Not?" Psychology Today, Sussex Publishers, www.psychologytoday.com/us/blog/am-i-normal/201110/intrusive-thoughts-normal-or-not.
14. [296] Reese, Hannah. "Intrusive Thoughts: Normal or Not?" Psychology Today, Sussex Publishers, www.psychologytoday.com/us/blog/am-i-normal/201110/intrusive-thoughts-normal-or-not.

Sin is Nihilism

The belief in sinfulness is the belief in ubiquitous nihilism. I am not referring to nihilism that is defined by lack of belief in a God or Gods. It would be more apt to refer to it as nihilism as defined by the belief that existence is senseless and useless, a belief that destroys all forms of objective morality from the basis that humanity is insufficient to ever create everlasting objective morality, that all forms of human progress are arrogant and useless in the end, and the implicit belief that all human constructions of morality will lead to total failure because humanity isn't intelligent enough to know God's will. The argument by the pious in favor of objective moral values implodes under the belief in sinfulness; it's a complete self-contradiction that Abrahamic believers seem to have cognitive dissonance towards. Human progress itself is seen as futile and self-depreciating despite people having modern conveniences like cars, surgeries, cell phones, the internet, and educational institutions. The nihilism is disguised as morally necessary to make people concede to religious doctrines; all human expression, all human inventions, and all forms of human happiness are to be under constant suspicion because humans are always prone to sinfulness everywhere.[297][298] If you truly believe in sinfulness then you must always feel regret for the crime of your existence to God, you must always feel regret for failing to curtail your biological desires of reproduction because you find others attractive and God judges that to be sinful, you must feel regret for the mutual act of lovemaking if it isn't specifically under the terms of marriage that God defined as the only acceptable form, you must feel ashamed of lovemaking because it's a sinful act regardless of if it's under marriage because God deemed sex to be sinful, and people who don't make these concessions are arrogant because they insult God by not believing in Him. There are obvious detriments to this belief that create a harmful standard: you may believe that everyone around you is predisposed to acting evil because they're born sinful, you may believe that anyone who doesn't go through these concessions for the one true God is immoral, you may view the failure to uphold the moral code as a form of humility in accepting that you're an imperfect human being compared to the perfect creator deity, and yet you may not see the circular reasoning in believing that your failure is a humility but that others who fail, who aren't part of your in-group of Abrahamic religions, are perceived as evil by the precepts of your religious faith.[299] People outside of your religious faith are automatically assumed to be *more* evil because they don't seek redemption and forgiveness from God like you and your community.[300] People who commit atrocities but have the same religious faith as you are assumed to have either misinterpreted the faith, used reasoning that is completely different from the tenants of your faith, or are imperfect human beings who are sinful. In the case of

---

15. [297] Nietzsche, Friedrich Wilhelm. *On the genealogy of morals: a polemical tract.* Translated by Ian Johnston, PDF, Richer Resources Publications, 2014.
16. [298] Nietzsche, Friedrich Wilhelm. Aphorism 49. *THE ANTICHRIST.* Translated by H. L. Mencken, The Project Gutenberg, 2006.
17. [299] "Circular Reasoning." *Https://Www.logicallyfallacious.com,* www.logicallyfallacious.com/tools/lp/Bo/LogicalFallacies/66/Circular-Reasoning.
18. [300] Ispas, Alexa. *Psychology and politics: a social identity perspective.* Psychology Press, 2014.

non-violent offenses such as adultery, the people of the same religious faith as you are simply assumed to have been an imperfect human being and their failure is seen as an admittance of humility. A non-believer or person of another religious faith is perceived to be conducting similar behavior out of evil or self-delusion in believing a false religion that led them astray because they lack your exact religious faith. Yet, no matter what they do, they're viewed as repulsive because they refuse to accept the one true God as the irrefutable truth, they don't seek redemption for their sinfulness as you probably do, and they should be awaiting the end of the world as prescribed in all the Abrahamic holy books. No matter what, your view of them is antagonistic to a certain degree because that is what the belief in sinfulness requires you to believe. You aren't allowed to perceive outsiders as anything but less significant than your in-group under the belief system of sinfulness.[301]

If the argument seems extreme, you should consider that many religious believers within Judaism, Islam, and Christianity still believe and advocate these positions when acting as missionaries in foreign countries and many Christians and Muslims are conducting forced conversions on the basis of such antagonism. Even in a first world country like the United States, there are over 50 million people who believe in this interpretation of their religion and proudly believe in the literal truth of their religious books. However, even if you don't agree with the extremist version of sinfulness, through open interpretation you may believe in degrees of sinfulness and you may still believe the teaching of sinfulness has worthwhile merits for instilling moral values. Yet, does it truly have moral value? If anything, sin is a belief that promotes the destruction of all morality under a fatalistic concept that morality will be destroyed because of human nature. There is a pernicious presumption that humans will always harm each other because it is human to destroy each other with no regard for the wellbeing of other humans. It allows for a circular reasoning that makes humanity synonymous with rampant destruction, rampant brutality, and rampant cruelty upon our own species and everything else in the world.[302] It is a self-fulfilling prophecy that uses sin as a justification for violence: when we justify bombing campaigns that slaughter foreign civilians, when we see people riot in our streets, and when we act out of anger upon others. These acts are justified by sinfulness from both observers and perpetrators through a rash generalization that all humans are capable of horrors because of innate human imperfection.[303] Sinfulness is a self-fulfilling prophecy because it's also a coping mechanism to understand violence: when we see news of sectarian wars in foreign countries, when we learn of cruel criminal behavior conducted upon children by pedophiles and rapists reported in the news, gang rapes in third world countries, beheadings, genocide, child slavery, and indoctrinated child soldiers.[304] Sinfulness means it is

---

19. [301] Ispas, Alexa. *Psychology and politics: a social identity perspective*. Psychology Press, 2014.
20. [302] "Circular Reasoning." *Https://Www.logicallyfallacious.com*, www.logicallyfallacious.com/tools/lp/Bo/LogicalFallacies/66/Circular-Reasoning.
21. [303] Cialdini, Robert B. Chapter 1: Weapons of Influence (1-16). *Influence: Science and practice*. 4th ed., 21st Century Bks, 2002.
22. [304] Kahneman, Daniel. *Thinking, fast and slow*. Farrar, Straus and Giroux, 2015.

all unalterable because that is the expected outcome of human nature.[305] It is always the expected standard of human interaction within our own communities and outside of it to view wars, bombings, genocide, the torture of children, and less offensive wrongdoings to be common occurrences because of an innate faultiness in humanity. We just expect people to fail in keeping up with the tenants of their faith and the failure of keeping with the tenants is just a form of humility for our group and evil for the outside group. We give violence a total pass because horrific atrocities are an expected norm of sinfulness; violent events in the news serve as anecdotal "proof" of sinfulness.

These attitudes and expectations of sinfulness in humanity are dangerous. It creates apathy towards horrific atrocities, indifference towards our own country bombing civilians in a foreign country, and presumes evil intent from the victims before they have actually done anything against us. There is an insidious and disgusting implication that the innocent victims killed would kill us because it's the due course of human nature so we need to harm them before they can hurt us – a pathological form of self-delusion and circular reasoning to justify mass murder. Consider this: if sinfulness is true, then humanity is simply expecting failures and catastrophes to be the norm throughout the world because of an unalterable and intrinsic defect within human nature. If all forms of good actions eventually lead to failure, then why should any wealthy person donate to charity? If they sincerely believe everything will eventually fall apart, then why bother doing anything to help other people? They would be predisposed to believe that their charity will fail, they would be inclined to believe that their own success would eventually turn to ruin, and that everything in life is just waiting to fall into ruination because of an intrinsic and unalterable aspect of their humanity. In terms of nation-states, we should just expect a nuclear catastrophe to occur and to wipe out the human race because sinfulness means that we're predisposed to evil actions and that we will falter in keeping to the tenants of the faith because of our intrinsic defectiveness. For all the so-called goodness of the Abrahamic traditions, each of them believe that the world will end and that the world ending is the expected outcome of human actions; such a belief justifies nuclear catastrophe as the conclusion of our species. Islam and Christianity convert non-believers for the explicit purpose of awaiting the end of the world. Pointing the theological basis for conversion usually causes embarrassment, denial, and attempts to avert the inquiry but it remains the theological underpinnings of the Abrahamic traditions. They can be verified in the holy books and the reason it's embarrassing to discuss in public is because of how untenable the belief is and how delusional people appear when voicing their beliefs. Yet, these harmful beliefs remain unchallenged and shut down in the public sphere instead of being criticized and it is to our detriment. As a hypothetical example, what if billionaires in the oil industry lobby politicians to squash any attempt at taking steps to address Climate Change because they sincerely believe that destroying the environment will bring about the End of Times as taught in the Bible or Quran? How would we ever know if that is their motivation, if criticism of these

---

23. [305] Halvorson, Heidi Grant. Chapter 2: Do You Know Where Your Goals Come From? (657-952). *Succeed: How We Can Reach Our Goals*. Plume, 2012.

religious beliefs are never challenged and never allowed to be discussed? If you think that is ridiculous, how did you come to your conclusion and why are you so confident in your beliefs? How can you truly be sure that some people in those industries don't sincerely believe in causing the End of Times, if they've never been challenged on their beliefs while being allowed to spend vast quantities of money to influence laws that may impact your everyday life?

Sin is Misanthropy

Sin is sanctified hatred for the human race. Two of western culture's most noteworthy philosophers, Immanuel Kant and Friedrich Nietzsche, pointed out that if you believe there is an innate defectiveness with humanity that causes evil actions then you are more predisposed to committing evil actions because you may feel it is the unavoidable norm of your humanity.[306] If evil is ingrained within you, if it is an unalterable part of human habit and you perceive your failures with humility, you might be justifying your wrongful acts by using sin as a coping mechanism instead of accepting responsibility.[307][308] Moreover, you may emphasize events when people hurt your feelings or disappoint you because you expect negative actions to be a natural consequence of your daily interactions with other human beings. You may perceive your own love for your friends and family as a constant struggle because you have implicitly overemphasized the idea that evil actions are natural occurrences within humanity as a result of sinfulness. As such, you may have a biased focus on their negative actions and less focus on their positive qualities. Humans already have a negativity bias ingrained within our psychology to defend from life-threatening danger and the belief in sinfulness may increase the emphasis on negative events in our lives.[309]

Is sinfulness healthy to believe in? Please consider the following: if you have a child, do you truly consider your own child to be born sinful? Do you truly believe that, in some deep level of our humanity, that your child will go murdering, raping, and torturing other people? Do you believe that, within you, there is a sinful part that will cause you to murder, rape, and torture your own family, friends, and strangers? As stated before, having thoughts of such actions doesn't mean that you want to do them; thoughts just come and go in your mind and that is normal.[310] It should be considered an utterly absurd belief about our loved ones but the ubiquitous concept of sinfulness in all forms of human interaction may cause such negative beliefs about our behavior and the behavior of our loved ones.[311] As a result, you may be

---

24. [306] Nietzsche, Friedrich. Aphorism 148. *The Dawn of Day*. Translated by J. M. Kennedy, Dover Publications, 2012.
25. [307] Nietzsche, Friedrich Wilhelm. *THE ANTICHRIST*. Translated by H. L. Mencken, The Project Gutenberg, 2006.
26. [308] Halvorson, Heidi Grant. Chapter 2: Do You Know Where Your Goals Come From? (657-952). *Succeed: How We Can Reach Our Goals*. Plume, 2012.
27. [309] Kahneman, Daniel. Chapter 28: Bad Events (300-309). *Thinking, fast and slow*. Farrar, Straus and Giroux, 2015.
28. [310] Reese, Hannah. "Intrusive Thoughts: Normal or Not?" Psychology Today, Sussex Publishers, www.psychologytoday.com/us/blog/am-i-normal/201110/intrusive-thoughts-normal-or-not.
29. [311] Nietzsche, Friedrich Wilhelm. *On the genealogy of morals: a polemical tract*. Translated by Ian

predisposed to despise or see evil in your own children's actions when they act out and may find it easier to discipline them with force. You may see forgiveness and passiveness as a constant struggle while harboring the expectation that everyone else in the world and you yourself will always partake in evil actions during moments of weakness. This is a pernicious view of other human beings; sin has the constant expectation of disappointment, failure, and evil as the only truism of life itself.[312] How can such a belief be either healthy or rational for your mental health?

Sinfulness, in combination with the binary ideology of good and evil, makes it easier to convince us to hate others. The belief that all humans are sinful would fundamentally promote the dehumanization, otherness, and disgust for people perceived as out-groups. When the news media gives you anecdotal examples of violence from the out-group, you'll more likely to feel disgust, anger, and superiority toward the out-group because you would be inclined to believe that your society has proudly kept their sinful impulses in check compared to the out-group. The repeated exposure to negative events from the specific out-group would make people more inclined to judge the out-group more strictly and harshly than usual through pattern recognition and grouping people by race, religion, social class, or country as the same.[313] From anecdotal events quickly mentioned in the news media, people's minds would be framing a coherent and negative view of the out-group.[314] This type of thinking is self-centered and delusional because it frames a binary worldview in which we compare doing our menial tasks everyday as a success and proof of our superiority over the perceived out-group. Sinfulness helps ignore the actual conditions that caused horrible events: famine, oppressive governments, mass poverty, certain first world countries selling weapons to governments that sell to terrorist groups (terrorist groups throughout Africa, the Middle East, and South America get weapons manufactured from Western countries), unsafe working conditions, and the political reality that first world countries need third world countries to stay in poverty to keep manufacturing cheap commodities. Crimes such as rape and murder are misconstrued to be the values that foreign cultures or that peoples perceived as out-groups somehow ubiquitously enjoy without thinking deeply about the other societies diverse peoples, crime-ridden areas, and other social conditions.

An example would be the rape crimes in the US. As shocking as it is to accept, Native American women living within reservations had no legal right to sue their rapists until 2012 thanks to federal laws that circumvented their rights and that the violence of rapes upon Native American women were so terrible and ubiquitous by US citizens that mothers had to teach their children what to expect when an American citizen raped them because they had no legal rights to send the child rapists to jail, it is untrue that these conditions are normal for the average US

Johnston, PDF, Richer Resources Publications, 2014.
30. [312] Nietzsche, Friedrich Wilhelm. *On the genealogy of morals: a polemical tract*. Translated by Ian Johnston, PDF, Richer Resources Publications, 2014.
31. [313] Kahneman, Daniel. *Thinking, fast and slow*. Farrar, Straus and Giroux, 2015.
32. [314] Kahneman, Daniel. *Thinking, fast and slow*. Farrar, Straus and Giroux, 2015.

citizen.[315] Although there are cases in poor counties of South Carolina in which the police don't arrest men who beat and rape their wives, because of the counties strong Christian convictions that men are in charge of the household, and that very little legal action has been undertaken even in situations where men chased after and murdered their ex-spouses or ex-girlfriends; it is untrue that these situations are a reflection of US culture and US citizens.[316] The same should be noted for rape crimes in India, despite being more common, the United Nations has found that in terms of per capita crime rates, the rape crimes in India are actually far lower than what would normally be expected for one of the largest population sizes in the world.[317] Mass poverty, lack of adequate police protection (police exist only to protect the wealthy in India), lack of police training in forensics, communalism, lack of judicial institutions to handle legal proceedings, lack of education, discrimination against women, and extremely sluggish court system create conditions of enmity, despair, hatred, and violence. Wealthy and middle class Indians would probably perceive the violence as happening in poverty zones and would desire to keep such violence out of their communities. It is a widespread issue but it isn't socially different from views of crime-ridden areas such as Camden, New Jersey in the United States or the apathy towards Native American rape victims in US courts. Awful people, opportunists, and deplorable social conditions create these situations and the mass protest movements that follow to create legal changes show that they are not tolerated in any culture or democratic nation-state. There can also be issues with how data is collected even in first world countries.[318] Yet, sinfulness and the availability heuristic give us an automatic and negative generalization of US culture and India's culture without learning more deeply about each country's social issues and the contexts in which these crimes occur.[319][320]

The belief in sinfulness is intrinsically dangerous to us and others. If we accept that sinfulness is ubiquitous part of life, if we accept that we can pick and choose the teachings of the Abrahamic holy books, and that we should view our failure with humility because we're only human; we create mental conditioning that allows us to kill others who are different from us. That may seem ridiculous, but the belief in sinfulness itself presupposes that we're capable of murder, rape, and torture deep within ourselves. It wouldn't be a stretch to say that those three beliefs, combined and inculcated for warfare, could create social conditioning that sent

---

33. [315] "MAZE OF INJUSTICE ." *Amnesty International USA*, Amnesty International, www.amnestyusa.org/pdfs/mazeofinjustice.pdf.
34. [316] "Till death do us part: A Post and Courier Special Report." *Post and Courier*, 19 Aug. 2014, www.postandcourier.com/app/till-death/partone.html.
35. [317] "India Is Third in Rape Cases, Second in Murder in the World." *The Hindu*, The Hindu, 23 July 2014, www.thehindu.com/news/national/india-is-third-in-rape-cases-second-in-murder-in-the-world/article6242011.ece.
36. [318] Bazelon, Emily. "We've Been Measuring Rape All Wrong." *Slate Magazine*, Slate, 19 Nov. 2013, www.slate.com/articles/double_x/doublex/2013/11/national_crime_victimization_survey_a_new_report_finds_that_the_justice.html.
37. [319] Cialdini, Robert B. Chapter 1: Weapons of Influence (1-16). *Influence: Science and practice*. 4th ed., 21st Century Bks, 2002.
38. [320] Kahneman, Daniel. *Thinking, fast and slow*. Farrar, Straus and Giroux, 2015.

people to kill others who are different from them. The belief that they're more prone to acting evil, our suspicion toward their behavior, and patronizing superiority towards people deemed different from us makes it easier to dehumanize them.[321] The dehumanization campaign of perceiving foreigners within the connotations of evildoers would make it easier for those with simplistic moral sensibilities to kill foreigners. The overlap of sinfulness and good versus evil makes violence easier to conduct for people who believe in these concepts. Sinfulness along with good and evil explicitly ignores and obfuscates attempts at understanding different people. Perhaps more dangerously, it explicitly obstructs us from viewing their opinions and lives as meaningful like we do for people within our in-group of friends, family, and community.[322] Wars occur, not just because of racist and other types of discriminatory caricatures of opposing sides, but also because people ignore and demonize other people's culture, lives, and human rights. We view their lives as less important than the emotional issues of ourselves and our in-group. Absolute good and absolute evil are concepts that would create a catalyst for egregious human rights crimes. For the foreigners, reciprocity and the desire for justice for the fallen victims soon create conditions of enmity and more warfare because people will seek justice for any civilians wrongfully killed through our bombings or war campaigns.[323] Religious extremism and justice for innocent civilians killed blend together to create prolonged warfare against us because we don't recognize their lives as meaningful or having equal value to our in-group. Religious extremism and sometimes increased terrorist activity occur as a consequence of war-torn people seeking meaning for the horrible deaths of their loved ones.

Yet, when we observe violence in their communities usually because of increased religious extremism as a way to cope with the loss of their loved ones and the West's attempts at creating violence between two groups to distract from the West's own interests in taking natural resources as per the realist theory of international relations[324], it makes it easier to have patronizing attitudes in support of our own society under the veneer of humility. We celebrate ourselves as having calmed our sinfulness and view outsiders as being ignorant, crazed, or believe in a radical version of a false faith. We ignore the fact that Western governments sell weapons to many of the terrorist groups including African warlords, al Qaeda, and ISIS. We ignore the fact Western governments place extreme political leaders in power who close off hospitals, schools, political participation, and jobs from a specific subset of their own community in their countries; political realities that the Western nation-states believes to be for their own self-interest only to deal with worsening problems in the future that jeopardize the safety of Western civilians and national interests.

Sin and the World

---

39. [321] Ispas, Alexa. *Psychology and politics: a social identity perspective*. Psychology Press, 2014.
40. [322] Ispas, Alexa. *Psychology and politics: a social identity perspective*. Psychology Press, 2014.
41. [323] Cialdini, Robert B. Chapter 2: Reciprocation (19-50). *Influence: Science and practice*. 4th ed., 21st Century Bks, 2002.
42. [324] Jentleson, Bruce W. *American foreign policy: the dynamics of choice in the 21st century*. 4th ed., Norton, 2010.

The belief in sin seems to be the true cause for economic destruction, political folly, and human genocide. It overlays every human act with the idea that we inevitably have an impulse to do evil upon others. Expunging the belief in sin and the theories of political realism in international relations would mean less human violence, a less dangerous world, and less mental self-torture for humanity. Sin can overlap with fatalism, jingoism, racism, xenophobia, Otherness, and any other form of human belief and human interaction. It's probably why rationality is predicated upon the concept of doing evil upon others because that is what original sin makes people believe about themselves, about other human beings, and about morality itself. Sin preaches physical and mental fatigue against our own humanity as a form of eternal goodness, teaches that every great human creation is utterly meaningless, and that the most important part of life is awaiting the coming of a Messiah, or the coming of Jesus, or the coming of Jesus and the Al-Mahdi together to bring about mass world genocide and global annihilation so the true believers move on to the perfect world.[325] Sin has had an enormous impact and history upon politics, philosophy, psychology, human biology, and people's conceptions of human interaction. It has utterly poisoned and caused misapplications on all of these subject matters such as the denunciation of sex taught throughout the world by Christian missionaries. When combined with different forms of in-group/out-group dynamics, sin promotes the worst human atrocities. Sin is an extremist concept because it makes people believe that they're only capable of abject evil from their own human desires. Thus, sin is the most egregious form of mental self-torture.

The arguments about how freedom from the idea of sin will only lead to massive violence, mass rapes, and death seems to be a form of self-delusion. The veneration of sin is often patronizing because Abrahamic believers truly think that some sacred warning from God would be destroyed and that acts of savagery would happen without them. An important issue to highlight: it was the belief in original sin itself that taught them to believe that humans are rampantly destructive; historically, the other parts of the world were peaceful under Buddha, Mahavira, Confucius, Lao Tzu, and these teachings didn't require the stubborn notion that God needed to ordain them. Were there problems within the ancient East? Of course, but such acts weren't full of savagery, mass death, and tribal wars that the West was thoroughly engaged with itself for a large part of its ancient history and particularly during the Crusades. Original sin teaches deep cynicism towards human desires and that maintaining such resentment, cynicism, and suspicion is morally good.[326] It's a mischaracterization to state the West became more peaceful during the 1800s to 1900s, because they brought brutal acts of colonial oppression upon the rest of the world[327] and then subjected themselves to World War twice after that. Would all of that have occurred without the deep theological belief in original sin

---

43. [325] Nietzsche, Friedrich Wilhelm. *On the genealogy of morals: a polemical tract*. Translated by Ian Johnston, PDF, Richer Resources Publications, 2014.
44. [326] Nietzsche, Friedrich Wilhelm. *THE ANTICHRIST*. Translated by H. L. Mencken, The Project Gutenberg, 2006.
45. [327] Davis, Mike. *Late Victorian Holocausts: El Nino Famines and the Making of the Third World*. Penguin Random House Publisher Services, 2001.

being the driving force of mass conversions and human actions? Would radical Islam be able to justify violence against the West today without the belief in the sinfulness of non-Muslims who aren't seen as pure specifically due to being non-Muslim?

Sin, Psychology, and International Relations

The belief in sinfulness creates a destructive system of reciprocity that is justified as rational and intelligent in politics. In Political Science, the Realist Theory of International Relations, the prevailing theory of Western politics since ancient Greece, operates under the assumption that strong nation-states must weaken other nation-states for its own self-interest.[328][329] It assumes self-interest to mean harming other nation-states with the underlying assumption that harming other human civilizations is rational.[330][331] Bombing campaigns, counterfeit money operations, embargos, sanctions, and human genocide are presumed to be rational and the Realist theory is the only international relations theory that is "neutral" to events such as the Holocaust. Moreover, the Realist theory of International Relations aims to increase pre-existing divisions to worsen the conditions of foreign countries so that the powerful nation-state that is harming the weaker nation-state can always scapegoat a foreign country's history to vindicate their own horrific actions in pursuit of their national interests. This assumption that harming others is rational is unfounded and discredited in modern psychology through the reciprocity principle. The Realist theory of international relations conceptualization that harming other civilizations and human genocide were rational actions came from the Melian dialogue of Thucydides in which he argued the genocide of Melos by Athens was due to human nature.[332] Political scientists and philosophers since then have only expounded upon the Realist theory of international relations because of the belief in original sin and the belief that rational actions are synonymous with evil.[333] Strong nation-states usually harm other nation-states, national leaders lie to their public about the supposedly humane actions – especially in foreign wars – for the sake of keeping a positive image of their country so that the citizens serve as apologists by ignoring the atrocities, and the citizens only care to celebrate the positives of their country. Many citizens choose to ignore the negative actions conducted upon foreigners in another country who have been dehumanized by their news media. This creates circular reasoning that international events will always lead to tragedy and

---

46. [328] Viotti, Paul R., and Mark V. Kauppi. *International relations theory: realism, pluralism, globalism.* 3rd ed., Macmillan, 1998.
47. [329] Jentleson, Bruce W. *American foreign policy: the dynamics of choice in the 21st century.* 4th ed., Norton, 2010.
48. [330] Jentleson, Bruce W. *American foreign policy: the dynamics of choice in the 21st century.* 4th ed., Norton, 2010.
49. [331] Viotti, Paul R., and Mark V. Kauppi. *International relations theory: realism, pluralism, globalism.* 3rd ed., Macmillan, 1998.
50. [332] Viotti, Paul R., and Mark V. Kauppi. *International relations theory: realism, pluralism, globalism.* 3rd ed., Macmillan, 1998.
51. [333] Jentleson, Bruce W. *American foreign policy: the dynamics of choice in the 21st century.* 4th ed., Norton, 2010.

it is all uncontrollable when in truth, it is because politicians genuinely believe that harming foreign nation-states is an intelligent course of action for maximizing their nation's power.[334]

The reciprocity principle has shown that individuals and groups will react positively to positive actions and negatively towards negative actions; this is because of the belief in equality.[335] We want to repay kind actions for people who do nice things for us, out of our desire for equality. We feel it's fair to do destructive actions upon people who commit a crime or harm us because of our desire for equality. As a result, the psychological and scientifically verified belief in reciprocity creates a state of perpetual warfare in which entire countries who believe in sinfulness go into endless warfare by minimizing the violent atrocities conducted upon the out-group in our press and venerating the goodness of the in-group to fight the generalized cartoon caricature of evil depicted as the out-group.[336] By ignoring the atrocities that we commit, they ignore the atrocities that they commit upon us, and each group feels that it is justified in creating future harm.[337][338] Worse than that, prolonged violence makes people and entire countries more extreme, thus sinfulness is used to justify our violence upon others by generalizing the entire out-group as the same instead of understanding different political groups, their racial diversity, socioeconomic differences, and the general plurality of their civilization. Sometimes the most important difference can be organizational goals among these different groups. Not all wars are the same or fought for the same reasons and sometimes strong ideals that influence certain goals can be the main driving force instead of typical reasons such as resources or it can be both reasons combined. War itself creates psychological issues that result in heavy stress, a plethora of mental trauma, and outbursts of violence related to trauma for soldiers and civilians. It is a perpetual state of negative reciprocity and it is morally reprehensible when we're told that committing to wars that have massive bombing campaigns is somehow "humanitarian" intervention. Wars of humanitarian intervention are very few and often cause deaths of civilians regardless of good intentions.

When the United States was hit by the attacks on the twin towers on September 11th, 2001, one of the most critical arguments was that there was something deeply nefarious about Muslim people to conduct such violence; the origins and goals of the hijackers wasn't understood well by the majority of the public at the time. Suspicion and psychological pattern recognition between Muslim extremists and Muslim Americans began to be seen by a significant portion of the US public.[339] The paranoia that Muslim Americans were prone to harming US society or potentially hiding terrorists became a popular fear for the US public.

---

52. [334] "Circular Reasoning." *Https://Www.logicallyfallacious.com*, www.logicallyfallacious.com/tools/lp/Bo/LogicalFallacies/66/Circular-Reasoning.
53. [335] Cialdini, Robert B. Chapter 2: Reciprocation (19-50). *Influence: Science and practice*. 4th ed., 21st Century Bks, 2002.
54. [336] Ispas, Alexa. *Psychology and politics: a social identity perspective*. Psychology Press, 2014.
55. [337] Cialdini, Robert B. Chapter 2: Reciprocation (19-50). *Influence: Science and practice*. 4th ed., 21st Century Bks, 2002.
56. [338] Ispas, Alexa. *Psychology and politics: a social identity perspective*. Psychology Press, 2014.
57. [339] Kahneman, Daniel. *Thinking, fast and slow*. Farrar, Straus and Giroux, 2015.

Violence upon Muslims, Sikhs, and other minorities increased and were ignored by the US media.[340][341][342][343] Incidentally, the US drone strikes upon seven Middle Eastern countries that resulted in thousands of civilian deaths created a surge of Islamic extremism, an increase in terrorist recruitment against the US, and the persecution and mass killings of Christians within their countries under the critical belief that Christians had some deeply nefarious aspect of their culture because the supposed greatest Christian country in the world was relentlessly bombing them and were utterly indifferent to civilian deaths – including children.[344] Bomb droppings upon homes, hospitals, schools, and other areas are even more difficult to discern for uneducated people in third world countries and thus pattern recognition of a Christian nation and the Christian peoples within their own communities occurred.[345] The fanciful ideas that removing the externalized "evil" people will somehow remove the foreign bombing campaigns are simply more violent methods than the West's laws imposed upon minority groups. It's just as important to understand that the West conducted in-group and out-group types of violence within its history upon Catholics, Protestants, Jehovah's Witnesses, Jews, and racial minorities (such as Blacks, Hispanics, Asians, Native Americans, and the Irish) under the belief that they were somehow evil and that the good people needed to defend their culture from an evil incursion. The difference in responses seems to be based upon the difference in education level; college education generally helps people understand that there is more so-called "out-groups" than generalizing them through rash codifications but violence against minorities always happen to "cleanse" the in-group community of "evil" from the out-group.[346]

The persecution is an inevitable part of perceiving our in-group in danger of annihilation, seeing every member of a perceived out-group as suspicious and potential perpetrators, and championing the innate goodness to do away with the corrupting evil influence can lead to draconian laws; the belief in sin is used as a coping mechanism whenever

---

58. [340] Wootson, Cleve R. "Sikh Community Asks for Hate-Crime Probe after Man Is Told 'Go Back to Your Own Country' and Shot." *The Washington Post*, WP Company, 5 Mar. 2017, www.washingtonpost.com/news/post-nation/wp/2017/03/04/go-back-to-your-own-country-sikh-man-shot-in-his-driveway-in-suspected-hate-crime/?utm_term=.cf9016ea0b1e.
59. [341] "History of Hate: Crimes Against Sikhs Since 9/11." *The Huffington Post*, TheHuffingtonPost.com, 7 Aug. 2012, www.huffingtonpost.com/2012/08/07/history-of-hate-crimes-against-sikhs-since-911_n_1751841.html.
60. [342] Kaplan, Sarah. "'Terrorist, Go Back to Your Country,' Attacker Yelled in Assault of Sikh Man." *The Washington Post*, WP Company, 10 Sept. 2015, www.washingtonpost.com/news/morning-mix/wp/2015/09/10/terrorist-go-back-to-your-country-attacker-yelled-in-alleged-assault-of-sikh-man/?utm_term=.a1a63bf192d7.
61. [343] Kishi, Katayoun. "Assaults against Muslims in U.S. Surpass 2001 Level." *Pew Research Center*, Pew Research Center, 15 Nov. 2017, www.pewresearch.org/fact-tank/2017/11/15/assaults-against-muslims-in-u-s-surpass-2001-level/.
62. [344] Feaver, Peter, and Will Inboden. "We Are Witnessing the Elimination of Christian Communities in Iraq and Syria." *Foreign Policy*, Foreign Policy, 6 Sept. 2017, foreignpolicy.com/2017/09/06/we-are-witnessing-the-elimination-of-christian-communities-in-iraq-and-syria/.
63. [345] Kahneman, Daniel. *Thinking, fast and slow*. Farrar, Straus and Giroux, 2015.
64. [346] Ispas, Alexa. *Psychology and politics: a social identity perspective*. Psychology Press, 2014.

draconian laws lead to the deaths of innocents.[347][348] During wars, when civic institutions functioning as social support mechanisms deteriorate then religious extremism becomes rampant, people begin to have rash judgments, and form scapegoats for why horrible events are happening.[349] Persecutions inevitably follow because of the belief in good and evil in conjunction with sinfulness. A desire for self-preservation of the in-group supersedes rational discourse because the threat seems so imposing and there is no explanation for why it is happening so they find fanciful causes during times of desperation. Those fanciful causes, if left unchallenged by Free Speech, can lead to violent altercations and murders.[350]

In regards to violence in third world countries that the wealthier nations see on the news: it is easy to believe an entire country is responsible for mass violence and gang rapes while more difficult to believe the credible facts of the lack of police power, lack of hospitals, lack of jobs, and overall mass poverty leading people to desperation and extremism as being the true cause. Another deeply important, but ignored, facet is that the majority of jobs in third world countries have no safety regulations such as in first world countries. People of the third world can die of poisoning from inhaling noxious gases, be forced to work well over twelve hours a day for something as miniscule as twenty cents an hour, and can be in danger of factory explosions that kill thousands of workers whenever they occur; such fear and paranoia would obviously frighten people about working and cause chronic stress when on the job. It isn't simply a matter of laziness and being unwilling to modernize when there are honest questions people in third world countries have to ask themselves about their own welfare before taking a job. Safety at a job is a privilege that first world countries take for granted. Sadly, even if reform is made, corporations just shut down plants to move to other third world countries to rinse and repeat this process; thus mass poverty increases when trying to institute honest reforms and another third world country is savagely abused through corporate indifference for their wellbeing for the sake of keeping product prices low. Religious extremism always follows as a crutch when institutions fail people because religion becomes all that people in poverty can rely upon. Yet, the belief in sinfulness and oversimplified understandings of entire countries make people believe that everyone in the world will always have "evil" because everyone is inherently sinful. It disconnects the real issues with pernicious perceptions that all people in other countries are more evil because they lack a specific religious faith and then we first-world denizens content ourselves with the belief that sinfulness will happen regardless of our help; to ignore the billions who suffer under extreme poverty, who are scorned for being uneducated, and who never had a choice in the matter because they had no social support mechanism like the first world countries. Yet, we always want cheap products and ignore all of the factory explosions in third world countries which occur as a consequence of low product

---

65. [347] Ispas, Alexa. *Psychology and politics: a social identity perspective*. Psychology Press, 2014.
66. [348] Kahneman, Daniel. *Thinking, fast and slow*. Farrar, Straus and Giroux, 2015.
67. [349] Kahneman, Daniel. *Thinking, fast and slow*. Farrar, Straus and Giroux, 2015.
68. [350] Woodall, Bernie. "Victim in Virginia Melee Wept for Social Justice, Her Boss Says." *Reuters*, Thomson Reuters, 14 Aug. 2017, www.reuters.com/article/us-virginia-protests-victim/victim-in-virginia-melee-wept-for-social-justice-her-boss-says-idUSKCN1AT0QR.

prices. If that statement has struck a negative chord, it shouldn't. Perhaps it is past the time that we concern ourselves with hurt feelings when our purchasing power determines the lives of human beings who were born less fortunate than us.

Original Sin and the History of Human Nature

Biblical history is filled with accounts of the Abrahamic God ordering people to rape and murder with obedience to him as the sole justification. The belief in the Biblical accounts of history as the sole authority of how all human life was in the past gives a bleak view of human affairs. However, when comparing the history of the Middle East to the histories of the contemporary civilizations of India and China at the time, the picture looks far less bleak. While what we'd consider today to be sexism and human rights violations surely happened, that was not all there was. In India, the development of several schools of thought arguing from inference and testimony would debate each other over matters such as spiritual growth, non-violence, war philosophies, and the relevance of a nation-state. They had codified laws on the duties of citizens and gender disparities, makeshift healthcare facilities, Gurus who took apprentices to teach subjects about deities and spiritual matters, and an array of philosophical debates which included atheism and culture movements like the Bhakti movement. India and China had the very best of medicine and surgical procedures during their golden eras of civilization back when the Middle East was a hovel of war, genocide, torture, and organized rape. Essentially, the third world that our current times sees Asia and other countries to be, was precisely how China, India, and possibly many other countries saw the Middle East during the supposed Old Testament times. Obviously, this sounds ridiculous to you, because of this presumption that everywhere else in the world was exactly like the Middle East of the supposed Biblical time period. Unfortunately, if that were so, then neither the teachings of the Buddha, the non-violent principles that make-up the core of the theology of Jainism, the teachings of the Tao Tie Ching of China which focused on efficacy, or the precepts of Orthodox Hinduism's basis of inference and knowledge would have ever formed. Teachings of non-violence and a positive work ethic abounded in both India and China, which were the two best countries of culture, resources, and philosophies comparable to the Ancient Greeks.

Unfortunately, Islam saw to the cultural genocide of much of this history with an emphasis on erasure if it was not Islamic. When Europe finally developed after the Middle Ages, and began its conquest of the world . . . much was further destroyed through mass murder, organized rapes via forced marriages, plundering, and forced conversions in the name of Christianity; proving no different in ethics from the Islam that preceded it in violence. Christianity and Islam both had worldwide slave trades, discriminated against Jews, and preached the civilians they conquered needed to accept the Abrahamic God or be made a slave or even killed. Cultural erasure and violence was justified by making technology that the indigenous populations were hardly ever allowed to use. The justification of which could justify any level of barbarity and violence. To say violence can be justified because of modernity is to have no real moral beliefs at all. As a hypothetical example to understand the core of what I mean, any Islamic conquest in which young girls were raped and male children were beheaded could then be justified by building a large bridge. There's no moral difference between that and how Christian Europe justifies genocide, torture, gang rapes, and plunder. It's how the British justified their four genocides in India; just replace the words "large bridge" with the words "train track" as the only difference.[351] Justifications about benefitting the Dalits of India are empty of meaning and any factual basis in history when both Christian and Muslim conquerors practiced both labor slavery of men and the sexual slavery of women throughout their conquest of India.[352] Moreover, the starvation and disease that ran rampant under European conquests and subsequent British rule effected the lower castes of India the most brutally.[353] In China, there was not only widespread starvation and disease, but the gang rapes of adult women and small female children by every stripe of European Christian and US Christian soldier after the Boxer Rebellion was physically suppressed.[354]

However, all of that being said, there is little evidence to suggest that human barbarism is innate and unchangeable when looking at the full scope of human history. Many laypeople may have the wrongful impression that civilization has contributed to making us less barbaric and that our ancient past was far more violent than the near-past of hundreds of years ago during Europe's colonization of the world. The evidence strongly suggests otherwise.

Erich Fromm, a reputed psychoanalyst and sociologist, delved deeply into researching the origins of human violence through archaeological and anthropological studies of the ancient Middle East, ancient America, ancient civilizations in certain island colonies, and ancient Europe from his contemporary colleagues in those fields of study and his own personal study into the human psyche to conclude that ancient humans were actually peaceful. He found that the formation of primitive nation-states, which slowly grew to be more powerful and thus the self-domestication of humans more thorough, is what led to the violence we see in civilized humanity.

In chapter 8 of his seminal work, *The Anatomy of Human Destructiveness*, Erich Fromm provides the details of this extensive research and what the overarching evidence shows:

Primitive Warfare

---

69. [351] Davis, Mike. *Late Victorian Holocausts: El Nino Famines and the Making of the Third World*. Penguin Random House Publisher Services, 2001.
70. [352] Moxham, Roy. *The Theft of India: the European Conquests of India, 1498-1765*. HarperCollins, 2016.
71. [353] Davis, Mike. *Late Victorian Holocausts: El Nino Famines and the Making of the Third World*. Penguin Random House Publisher Services, 2001.
72. [354] Davis, Mike. *Late Victorian Holocausts: El Nino Famines and the Making of the Third World*. Penguin Random House Publisher Services, 2001.

Although defensive aggression, destructiveness, and cruelty are not ordinarily the cause of war, these impulses manifest themselves in warfare. Hence some data on primitive warfare will help to complete the picture of primitive aggression.

Meggitt gives a summation of the nature of warfare among the Walbiri of Australia, which Service states may be accepted as an apt characterization of warfare in hunting-gathering societies generally:

'Walbiri society did not emphasize militarism—there was no class of permanent or professional warriors; there was no hierarchy of military command; and groups rarely engaged in wars of conquest. Every man was (and is still) a potential warrior, always armed and ready to defend his rights: but he was also an individualist, who preferred to fight independently. In some disputes kinship ties aligned men into opposed camps, and such a group may occasionally have comprised all the men of a community. But there were no military leaders, elected or hereditary, to plan tactics and ensure that others adopted the plans. Although some men were respected as capable and courageous fighters and their advice was valued, other men did not necessarily follow them. Moreover, the range of circumstances in which fights occurred was in effect so limited that men knew and could employ the most effective techniques without hesitation. This is still true today even of young bachelors. There was in any case little reason for all-out warfare between communities. Slavery was unknown: portable goods were few; and the territory seized in a battle was virtually an embarrassment to the victors, whose spiritual ties were with other localities. Small-scale wars of conquest against other tribes occurred occasionally, but I am sure that they differed only in degree from intra-tribal and even intra-community fights. Thus the attack on the Waringari that led to the occupation of the water holes in the Tanami area involved only Waneiga men—a few score at most: and I have no evidence that communities ever entered into a military alliances, either to oppose other Walbiri communities or other tribes.' (M. J. Meggitt, 1960.)

Technically speaking, this kind of conflict among primitive hunters can be described as war; in this sense one may conclude that "war" has always existed within the human species, and hence, that it is the manifestation of an innate drive to kill. This reasoning, however, ignores the profound differences in the warfare of lower and of higher primitive cultures15 as well as the warfare of civilized cultures. Primitive warfare, particularly that of the lower primitives, was neither centrally organized nor led by permanent chieftains; it was relatively infrequent; it was not war of conquest nor was it bloody war aimed at killing as many of the enemy as possible. Most civilized war, in contrast, is institutionalized, organized by permanent chieftains, and aims at conquest of territory and/or acquisition of slaves and/or booty.

In addition, and perhaps most important of all, is the frequently overlooked fact that there is no important economic stimulus among primitive hunter-gatherers to full-scale war.

'The birth-death ratio in hunting-gathering societies is such that it would be rare for population pressure to cause some part of the population to fight others for territorial acquisition. Even if such a circumstance occurred it would not lead to much of a battle. The stronger, more numerous, group would simply prevail, probably even without a battle, if hunting rights or rights to some gathering spot were demanded. In the second place there is not much to gain by plunder in hunting-gathering society. All bands are poor in material goods and there are no standard items of exchange that serve as capital or as valuables. Finally, at the hunting-gathering level the acquisition of captives to serve as slaves for economic exploitation—a common cause of warfare in more modern times—would be useless, given the low productivity of the economy. Captives and slaves would have a difficult time producing more than enough food to sustain themselves.' (E. R. Service, 1966.)

The overall picture of warfare among primitive hunter-gatherers given by Service is supported and supplemented by a number of other investigators, some of whom are quoted in the following paragraphs.16 D. Pilbeam stresses the absence of war, in contrast to occasional feuds, together with the role of example rather than power among the leaders in a hunting society, and the principle of reciprocity and generosity, and the central role of cooperation. (D. Pilbeam, 1970.)

U. H. Stewart comes to the following conclusion concerning territoriality and warfare:

'There have been many contentions that primitive bands own territories or resources and fight to protect them. Although I cannot assert that this is never the case, it is probably very uncommon. First, the primary groups that comprise the larger maximum bands intermarry, amalgamate if they are too small or split off if too large. Second, in the cases reported here, there is no more than a tendency for primary groups to utilize special areas. Third, most so-called "warfare" among such societies is no more than revenge for alleged witchcraft or continued interfamily feuds. Fourth, collecting is the main resource in most areas, but I know of no reported defense of seed areas. Primary bands did not fight one another, and it is difficult to see how a maximum band could assemble its manpower to defend its territory against another band or why it should do so. It is true that durian trees, eagle nests, and a few other specific resources were sometimes individually claimed, but how they were defended by a person miles away has not been made clear.' (U. H. Stewart, 1968.)

H. H. Turney-High (1971) comes to similar conclusions. He stressed that while the experiences of fear, rage, and frustration are universal, the art of war develops only late in human evolution. Most primitive societies were not capable of war because war requires a sophisticated level of conceptualization. Most primitive societies could not imagine an organization necessary to conquer or defeat a neighbor. Most primitive wars are nothing but armed melees, not wars at all. According to Rapaport, Turney-High's work did not find a very friendly reception among anthropologists because he stressed that secondary accounts of battles written by professional anthropologists were hopelessly inadequate and sometimes downright misleading; he believed that primary sources were more reliable, even when they were by amateur ethnologists generations ago.17

Quincy Wright's monumental work (1,637 pages including an extensive Bibliography) presents a thorough analysis of warfare among primitive people based on the statistical comparison of the main data to be found among six hundred and fifty-three primitive peoples. The shortcoming of his analysis lies in the fact that he is more descriptive than analytical in the classification of primitive societies as well as of different kinds of warfare. Nevertheless, his conclusions are of considerable interest because they show a statistical trend that corresponds to the results of many other authors: "The collectors, lower hunters and lower agriculturalists are the least warlike. The higher hunters and higher agriculturalists are more warlike, while the highest agriculturalists and the pastors are the most warlike of all." (Q. Wright, 1965.) This statement confirms the idea that war-likeness is not a function of man's natural drives that manifest themselves in the most primitive form of society, but of his development in civilization. Wright's data show that the more division of labor there is in a society, the more warlike it is, and that societies with class-systems are the most warlike of all peoples. Eventually his data show that the greater the equilibrium among groups and between the group and its physical environment, the less war-likeness one finds, while frequent disturbances of the equilibrium result in an increase in warlikeness.

Wright differentiates among four kinds of war—defensive, social, economic, and political. By defensive war, he refers to the practice of people who have no war in their mores and who fight only if actually attacked, "in which case they make spontaneous use of available tools and hunting weapons to defend themselves, but regard this necessity as a misfortune." By social war he refers to people with whom war "is usually not very destructive of life." (This warfare corresponds to Service's description of war among hunters.) Economic and political wars refer to people who make war in order to acquire women, slaves, raw materials, and land and/or, in addition, for the maintenance of a ruling dynasty or class.

Almost everybody reasons: if civilized man is so warlike, how much more warlike must primitive man have been!18 But Wright's results confirm the thesis that the most primitive men are the least warlike and that war-likeness grows in proportion to civilization. If destructiveness were innate in man, the trend would have to be the opposite.

A view similar to Wright's has also been expressed by M. Ginsberg, who writes:

'It would seem that war in this sense grows with the consolidation of groups and economic development. Among the simplest peoples we ought to speak rather of feuds, and these unquestionably occur on grounds of abduction of women, or resentments of trespass or personal injury. It must be conceded that these societies are peaceful by comparison with the more advanced of the primitive peoples. But violence and fear of violence are there and fighting occurs, though that is obviously and necessarily on a small scale. The facts are not adequately known, and if they do not support the view of a primitive idyllic peace, they are perhaps compatible with the view of those who think that primary or unprovoked aggressiveness is not an inherent element of human nature. (E. Glover and M. Ginsberg,' 1934.)

Ruth Benedict (1959) makes the distinction between "socially lethal" and "non-lethal" wars. In the latter, the aim is not that of subjugating other tribes to the victor as masters and profiteers; although there was much warfare among North American Indians,

'The idea of conquest never arose in aboriginal North America, and this made it possible for almost all these Indian tribes to do a very extreme thing: to separate war from the state. The state was personified in the Peace Chief, who was a leader of public opinion in all that concerned the in-group and in his council. The Peace Chief was permanent, and though no autocratic ruler he was often a very important personage. But he had nothing to do with war. He did not even appoint the war chiefs or concern himself with the conduct of war parties. Any man who could attract a following led a war party when and where he would, and in some tribes he was in complete control for the duration of the expedition. But this lasted only till the return of the war party. The state, according to this interpretation of war, had no conceivable interest in these ventures, which were only highly desirable demonstrations of rugged individualism turned against an out-group where such demonstrations did not harm the body politic.' (R. Benedict, 1959.)

Benedict's point is important because it touches upon the connection of war, state, and private property. Socially non-lethal war is to a large extent an expression of adventurousness and the wish to have trophies and be admired, but it was not invoked by the impulse to conquer people or territory, to subjugate human beings, or to destroy the basis for their livelihood. Benedict comes to the conclusion that "elimination of war is not so uncommon as one would think from the writings of political theorists of the prehistory of war… It is a complete misunderstanding to lay this havoc [war] to any biological need of man to go to war. The havoc is manmade." (R. Benedict, 1959.) Another outstanding anthropologist, E. A. Hoebel (1958) characterizes warfare among early North American Indians in these terms: "They come closer to William James's Moral Equivalents of War. They release aggressions harmlessly: they provide exercise, sport and amusement without destruction; and only mildly is there any imposition of desires by one party on the other." (E. A. Hoebel, 1958.) He comes to the general conclusion that man's propensity to war is obviously not an instinct, because it is an elaborate cultural complex. He gives as an interesting example the pacifistic Shoshones and the violent Comanches who in 1600 were still culturally and racially one.

The Neolithic Revolution[19]

The detailed description of the life of primitive hunters and food gatherers has shown that man—at least since he fully emerged fifty thousand years ago—was most likely not the brutal, destructive, cruel being and hence not the prototype of "man the killer" that we find in more-developed stages of his evolution. However, we cannot stop there. In order to understand the gradual development of man the exploiter and the destroyer, it is necessary to deal with the development of man during the period of early agriculture and, eventually, with his transformation into a builder of cities, a warrior, and a trader.

From the emergence of man, approximately half a million years ago to about 9000 B.C., man did not change in one respect: he lived from what he gathered or hunted, but did not produce anything new. He was completely dependent on nature and did not himself influence or transform it. This relationship to nature changed radically with the invention of agriculture (and animal husbandry) which occurred roughly with the beginning of the Neolithic period, more precisely, the "Protoneolithic" period as archeologists call it today—from 9000 to 7000 B.C.—in an area stretching over one thousand miles from western Iran to Greece, including parts of Iraq, Syria, Lebanon, Jordan, Israel, and the Anatolian Plateau in Turkey. (It started later in Central and Northern Europe.) For the first time man made himself, within certain limits, independent of nature by using his inventiveness and skill to produce something beyond that which nature had thus far yielded to him. It was now possible to plant more seed, to till more land, and to breed more animals, as the population increased. Surplus food could be slowly accumulated to support craftsmen who devoted most of their time to the manufacture of tools, pottery, and clothing.

The first great discovery made in this period was the cultivation of wheat and barley, which had been growing wild in this area. It was discovered that by putting seed of these grasses into the earth, new plants would grow; that one could select the best seed for sowing, and eventually the accidental crossing of varieties was observed, which produced grains very much larger than the seeds of the wild grasses. The process of development from wild grasses to high-yielding modern wheat is not yet fully known. It involved gene mutations, hybridization, and chromosome doubling, and it has taken thousands of years to achieve the artificial selection by man on the level of present-day agriculture. For man in the industrial age, accustomed to looking down on non-industrialized agriculture as a primitive and rather obvious form of production, the Neolithic discoveries may not seem comparable to the great technical discoveries of our day, of which he is so proud. Yet the fact that the expectation that seed would grow was proved correct by results gave rise to an entirely new concept: man recognized that he could use his will and intention to make this happen, instead of things just "happening." It would not be exaggerated to say that the discovery of agriculture was the foundation for all scientific thinking and later technological development.

The second discovery was that of animal breeding which was made in the same period. Sheep were already domesticated in the ninth millennium in northern Iraq, and cattle and pigs around 6000 B.C. Sheep and cattle-raising resulted in additional food supply: milk and a greater abundance of meat. The increased and more stable food supply permitted a sedentary, instead of a nomadic form of life, and led to the construction of permanent villages and towns.[20]

In the Protoneolithic period tribes of hunters invented and developed a new settled economy based on the domestication of plants and animals. Although the earliest remains of domesticated plants do not yet much antedate 7000 B.C., "the standard of domestication reached and the variety of crops grown presupposes a long prehistory of earlier agriculture which may well go back to the beginning of the Protoneolithic, about 9000 B.C." (J. Mellaart, 1967.)[21]

It took about 2000 to 3000 years before a new discovery was made, necessitated by the need to store foodstuff: the art of pottery (baskets were made earlier). With the invention of pottery, the first technical invention had been made, which led to the insight into chemical processes. Indeed, "building a pot was a supreme instance of creation by man." (V. G. Childe, 1936.)22 Thus one can distinguish within the Neolithic period itself one "aceramic" stage, i.e., a period in which pottery had not been invented, and the ceramic stage. Some older villages in Anatolia, such as the older levels of Hacilar, were aceramic while Çatal Hüyük was a town that had rich pottery.

Çatal Hüyük was one of the most highly developed Neolithic towns in Anatolia. Although only a relatively small part has been excavated since 1961, it has already yielded the most important data for the understanding of Neolithic society in its economic, social, and religious aspects.23

Since the beginning of the excavations, ten levels have been dug out, the oldest dated c. 6500 B.C.

'After 5600 B.C. the old mound of Çatal Hüyük was abandoned, for what reasons is not known, and a new site was founded across the river, Çatal Hüyük West. This appears to have been occupied for at least another 700 years until it also was deserted, without, however, any obvious signs of violence or deliberate destruction.' (J. Mellaart, 1967.)

One of the most surprising features of Çatal Hüyük is the degree of its civilization:

'Çatal Hüyük could afford luxuries such as obsidian mirrors, ceremonial daggers, and trinkets of metal beyond the reach of most of its known contemporaries. Copper and lead were smelted and worked into beads, tubes and possibly small tools, thus taking the beginnings of metallurgy back into the seventh millennium. Its stone industry in local obsidian and imported flint is the most elegant of the period; its wooden vessels are varied and sophisticated, its woolen textile industry fully developed.' (J. Mellaart, 1967.)

Make-up sets for women and very attractive bracelets for men and women were found in the burial sites. They knew the art of smelting copper and lead. The use of a great variety of rocks and minerals shows, according to Mellaart, that prospecting and trade formed a most important item of the city's economy.

In spite of this developed civilization, the social structure seems to have lacked certain elements characteristic of much later stages of evolution. Apparently there was little class distinction between rich and poor. While, according to Mellaart, social inequality is suggested by the sizes of buildings, equipment, and burial gifts, "this is never a glaring one." Indeed, looking at the plans of the excavated section of the city one finds that the difference in size of the buildings is very small, and negligible when compared with the difference in later urban societies. Childe notes that there is no definitive evidence of chieftainship in early Neolithic villages, and Mellaart does not mention any evidence of it from Çatal Hüyük. There were apparently many priestesses (perhaps also priests), but there is no evidence of a hierarchical organization. While in Çatal Hüyük the surplus produced by new methods of agriculture must have been large enough to support the manufacture of luxuries and trade, the earlier and less-developed of the Neolithic villages produced, according to Childe, only a small surplus and hence had an even greater degree of economic equality than that of Çatal Hüyük. He points out that the Neolithic crafts must have been household industries and that craft traditions are not individual but collective. The experience and wisdom of all the community's members are constantly being pooled; the occupation is public, its rules are the result of communal experience. The pots from a given Neolithic village bear the stamp of a strong collective tradition, rather than of individuality. Besides there was as yet no shortage of land; when the population grew, young men could go off and start a village of their own. Under these economic circumstances the conditions were not given for the differentiation of society into different classes, or for the formation of a permanent leadership whose function it would be to organize the whole economy and who would exact their price for this skill. This could happen only later when many more discoveries and inventions had been made, when the surplus was much greater and could be transformed into "capital" and those owning it could make profits by making others work for them.

Two observations are of special importance from the point of view of aggression: there is no evidence of any sack or massacre during the eight hundred years of the existence of Çatal Hüyük so far explored in the excavations. Furthermore, and even more impressive evidence for the absence of violence, among the many hundreds of skeletons unearthed, not a single one has been found that showed signs of violent death. (J. Mellaart, 1967.)

One of the most characteristic features of Neolithic villages, including Çatal Hüyük, is *the central role of the mother* in their social structure and their religion.

Following the older division of labor, where men hunted and women gathered roots and fruits, agriculture was most likely the discovery of women, while animal husbandry was that of men. (Considering the fundamental role of agriculture in the development of civilization, it is perhaps no exaggeration to state that modern civilization was founded by women.) The earth's and woman's capacity to give birth—a capacity that men lack—quite naturally gave the mother a supreme place in the world of the early agriculturalists. (Only when men could create material things by intellect, i.e., magically and technically—could they claim superiority.) The mother, as Goddess (often identified with mother earth), became the supreme goddess of the religious world, while the earthly mother became the center of family and social life.

The most impressive direct evidence for the central role of mothers in Çatal Hüyük lies in the fact that children were always buried with their mother, and never with their father. The skeletons were buried underneath the mother's divan (a kind of platform in the main room), which was larger than that of the father and always had the same location in the house. The burial of children exclusively with their mother is a characteristically matriarchal trait: the children's essential relationship is considered to be to the mother and not to the father, as in the case in patriarchal societies.

Although this burial system is an impressive datum in favor of the assumption of the matriarchal structure of Neolithic society, this thesis finds its full confirmation with the data we have on the religion of Çatal Hüyük and other excavated Neolithic villages in Anatolia.24

These excavations have revolutionized our concepts of early religious development. The most outstanding feature is the fact that this religion was centered around the figure of the mother-goddess. Mellaart concludes: "Çatal Hüyük and Hacilar have established a link ... [whereby] a continuity in religion can be demonstrated from Çatal Hüyük to Hacilar and so on till the great 'Mother-Goddesses' of archaic and classical times, the shadowy figures known as Cybele, Artemis and Aphrodite." (J. Mellaart, 1967.)

The central role of mother-goddess can be clearly seen in the figures, wall paintings, and reliefs in the numerous shrines that have been excavated. In contrast to findings in other Neolithic sites, those of Çatal Hüyük do not entirely consist of mother-goddesses, but also show a male deity symbolized by a bull or, more frequently, by a bull's head or horns. But this fact does not substantially alter the predominance of the "great mother" as the central deity. Among forty-one sculptures excavated, thirty-three were exclusively of goddesses. The eight sculptures in which a male god is symbolized are virtually all to be understood in reference to the goddess, partly as her sons and partly as her consorts. (On one of the older levels figurines of the goddess were found exclusively.) The central role of the mother-goddess is further demonstrated by the fact that she is shown alone, together with a male, pregnant, giving birth, but never subordinate to a male. There are some shrines in which the goddess is giving birth to a bull's or a ram's head. (Compare this with the typically patriarchal story of the female being given birth by the male: Eve and Athene.)

The mother-goddess is often found accompanied by a leopard, clothed with a leopard skin, or symbolically represented by leopards, at the time the most ferocious and deadly animal of that region. This would make her the mistress of wild animals, and it also indicates her double role as the goddess of life and of death, like so many other goddesses. "Mother earth," who gives birth to her many and receives them again after their individual life cycle has ended is not necessarily a destroying mother. Yet she sometimes is (like the Hindu goddess Kali); to find the reasons why this development should have taken place requires a lengthy speculation which I must forgo.

The mother-goddess of the Neolithic religion is not only the mistress of wild animals. She is also the patroness of the hunt, the patroness of agriculture, and the mistress of plant life.

Mellaart makes these summarizing remarks on the role of women in the Neolithic society, including Çatal Hüyük:

'What is particularly noteworthy in the Neolithic religion of Anatolia, and this applies to Çatal Hüyük as much as to Hacilar, is the complete absence of sex in any of the figurines, statuettes, plastic reliefs or wall-paintings. The reproductive organs are never shown, representations of phallus and vulva are unknown, and this is the more remarkable as they were frequently portrayed both in the Upper Palaeolithic and in the Neolithic and Post-neolithic cultures outside Anatolia.25 It seems that there is a very simple answer to this seemingly puzzling question, for emphasis on sex in art is invariably connected with male impulse and desire. If Neolithic woman was the creator of Neolithic religion, its absence is easily explained and a different symbolism was created in which breast, navel and pregnancy stand for the female principle, horns and horned animal heads for the male. In an early Neolithic society like that the Çatal Hüyük one might biologically expect a greater proportion of women than men and this is indeed reflected in the burials. Moreover, in the new economy a great number of tasks were undertaken by the women, a pattern that has not changed in Anatolian villages to this day, and this probably accounts for her social pre-eminence. As the only source of life she became associated with the processes of agriculture, with the taming and nourishing of domesticated animals, with the ideas of increase, abundance and fertility. Hence a religion which aimed at exactly the same conservation of life in all its forms, its propagation and the mysteries of its rites connected with life and death, birth and resurrection, were evidently part of her sphere rather than that of man. It seems extremely likely that the cult of the goddess was administered mainly by women, even if the presence of male priests is by no means excluded...' (J. Mellaart, 1967.)26

The data that speak in favor of the view that Neolithic society was relatively egalitarian, without hierarchy, exploitation, or marked aggression, are suggestive. In fact, however, that these Neolithic villages in Anatolia had a matriarchal (matricentric) structure, adds a great deal more evidence to the hypothesis that Neolithic society, at least in Anatolia, was an essentially unaggressive and peaceful society. The reason for this lies in the spirit of affirmation of life and lack of destructiveness which J. J. Bachofen believed was an essential trait of all matriarchal societies.

Indeed, the findings brought to light by the excavation of Neolithic villages in Anatolia offer the most complete material evidence for the existence of matriarchal cultures and religions postulated by J. J. Bachofen in his work Das Mutterrecht, first published in 1861. By the analysis of Greek and Roman myths, rituals, symbols, and dreams he had achieved something that only a genius could do: with his penetrating analytic power he reconstructed a phase of social organization and religion for which hardly any material evidence was available to him. (An American ethnologist, L. H. Morgan, [1870, 1877] arrived independently at very similar conclusions on the basis of his study of North American Indians.) Almost all anthropologists—with a few notable exceptions—declared Bachofen's findings to be without any scientific merit; in fact, it was not until 1967 that an English translation of a selection of Bachofen's writings was published. (J. J. Bachofen, 1967.)

There were probably two reasons for the rejection of Bachofen's theory: first, that it was almost impossible for anthropologists living in a patriarchal society to transcend their social and mental frames of reference and to imagine that male rule was not "natural." (Freud, for the same reason, arrived at his view of women as castrated men.) Second, the anthropologists were so accustomed to believing only in material evidence like skeletons, tools, weapons, etc., that they found it difficult to believe that myths or drama are not less real than artifacts; this whole attitude resulted also in a lack of appreciation for the potency and subtlety of penetrating, theoretical thinking.

The following paragraphs from Bachofen's *Mutterrecht* give an idea of this concept of the matriarchal spirit:

'The relationship which stands at the origin of all culture, of every virtue, of every nobler aspect of existence, is that between mother and child; it operates in a world of violence as the divine principle of love, of union, of peace. Raising her young, the woman learns earlier than the man to extend her loving care beyond the limits of the ego to another creature, and to direct whatever gift of invention she possesses to the preservation and improvement of the other's existence. Woman at this stage is the repository of all culture, of all benevolence, of all devotion, of all concern for the living and grief for the dead. Yet the love that arises from motherhood is not only more intense, but also more universal... Whereas the paternal principle is inherently restrictive, the maternal principle is universal; the paternal principle implies limitation to definite groups, but the maternal principle, like the life of nature, knows no barriers. The idea of motherhood produces a sense of universal fraternity among all men, which dies with the development of paternity. The family based on father right is a closed individual organism, whereas the matriarchal family bears the typically universal character that stands at the beginning of all development and distinguishes material life from higher spiritual life. Every woman's womb, the mortal image of the earth mother Demeter, will give brothers and sisters to the children of ever, other woman; the homeland will know only brothers and sisters until the day when the development of the paternal system dissolves the undifferentiated unity of the mass and introduces a principle of articulation.
The matriarchal cultures present many expressions and even juridical formulations of this aspect of the maternal principle. It is the basis of the universal freedom and equality so frequent among matriarchal peoples, of their hospitality, and of their aversion to restriction of all sorts... And in it is rooted the admirable sense of kinship and fellow feeling which knows no barriers or dividing lines and embraces all members of a nation alike. Matriarchal states were particularly famed for their freedom from internecine strife and conflict ... The matriarchal peoples—and this is no less characteristic—assigned special culpability to the physical injury of one's fellow men or even of animals... An air of tender humanity, discernible even in the facial expression of Egyptian statuary, permeates the culture of the matriarchal world."' (J. J. Bachofen, 1967.)27

Prehistoric Societies and "Human Nature"

This picture of the mode of production and social organization of hunters and Neolithic agriculturalists is quite suggestive in regard to certain psychical traits that are generally supposed to be an intrinsic part of human nature. Prehistoric hunters and agriculturalists had no opportunity to develop a passionate striving for property or envy of the "haves," because there was no private property to hold on to and no important economic differences to cause envy. On the contrary, their way of life was conducive to the development of cooperation and peaceful living. There was no basis for the formation of the desire to exploit other human beings. The idea of exploiting another person's physical or psychical energy for one's own purposes is absurd in a society where economically and socially there is no basis for exploitation.

The impulse to control others also had little chance to develop. The primitive band society and probably prehistoric hunters since about fifty thousand years ago were fundamentally different from civilized society precisely because human relations were not governed by the principles of control and power; their functioning depended on mutuality. An individual endowed with the passion for control would have been a social failure and without influence. Finally, there was little incentive for the development of greed, since production and consumption were stabilized at a certain level.28

Do the data on hunter-gatherers and early agriculturalists suggest that the passion of possessiveness, exploitation, greed, envy did not yet exist and are exclusively products of civilization? It does not seem to me that such a sweeping statement can be made. We do not have enough data to substantiate it, nor is it likely to be correct on theoretical grounds, since individual factors will engender these vices in some individuals even under the most favorable social circumstances. But there is a great difference between cultures which foster and encourage greed, envy, and exploitativeness by their social structure, and cultures which do the opposite. In the former, these vices will form part of the "social character"—i.e., of a syndrome to be found in the majority of people; in the latter, they will be individual aberrations from the norm which have little chance to influence the whole society. This hypothesis gains further strength if we now consider the next historical stage, urban development, which seems to have introduced not only new kinds of civilization but also those passions which are generally attributed to man's natural endowment.

The Urban Revolution29

A new kind of society developed in the fourth and third millennia, B.C. which can best be characterized in Mumford's brilliant formulation:

'Out of the early neolithic complex a different kind of social organization arose: no longer dispersed in small units, but unified in a large one: no longer "democratic," that is, based on neighborly intimacy, customary usage, and consent, but authoritarian, centrally directed, under the control of a dominant minority: no longer confined to a limited territory, but deliberately "going out of bounds" to seize raw materials and enslave helpless men, to exercise control, to exact tribute. This new culture was dedicated, not just to the enhancement of life, but to the expansion of collective power. By perfecting new instruments of coercion, the rulers of this society had, by the Third Millennium, B.C., organized industrial and military power on a scale that was never to be surpassed until our own time.' (L. Mumford, 1967.)

How had it happened?

'Within a short period, historically speaking, man learned to harness the physical energy of oxen and the energy of the winds. He invented the plough, the wheeled cart, the sailing boat, and he discovered the chemical processes involved in the smelting of copper ores (to some extent known earlier), and the physical properties of metals, and he began to work out a solar calendar. As a consequence, the way was prepared for the art of writing and standards and measures. "In no period of history till the days of Galileo," writes Childe, "was progress in knowledge so rapid or far-reaching discoveries so frequent.'" (V. G. Childe, 1936.)

But social change was not less revolutionary. The small villages of self-sufficient farmers were transformed into populous cities nourished by secondary industries and foreign trade, and these new cities were organized as city states. Man literally created new land. The great cities of Babylonia rose on a sort of platform of reeds, laid crisscross upon the alluvial mud. They dug channels to water the fields and drain the marshes, they built dykes and mounds to protect men and cattle from the waters and raise them above the flood. This creation of tillable land required a great deal of labor and this "'capital in the form of human labor was being sunk in the land.'" (V. G. Childe, 1936.)

Another result of this process was that a specialized labor force had to be used for this kind of work, and for cultivating the land necessary to grow food for those others who were specialized in crafts, public works, and trade. They had to be organized by the community and directed by an elite which did the planning, protecting, and controlling. This means that a much greater accumulation of surplus was needed than in the earlier Neolithic villages, and that this surplus was not just used as food reserve for times of need or growing population, but as capital to be used for an expanding production. Childe has pointed to another factor inherent in these conditions of life in the river valleys—the exceptional power of the society to coerce its members. The community could refuse a recalcitrant member access to water by closing the channels leading it to his field. This possibility of coercion was one of the foundations upon which the power of kings, priests, and the dominant elite rested once they had succeeded in replacing or, ideologically speaking, "representing"—the social will.

With the new forms of production, one of the most decisive changes in the history of man took place. His product was no longer limited to what he could produce by his own work, as had been the case in hunting societies and early agriculture. It is true that with the beginning of Neolithic agriculture man had already been able to produce a small surplus, but this surplus only helped to stabilize his life. When, however, it grew, it could be used for an entirely new purpose; it became possible to feed people who did not directly produce food, but cleared the marshes, built houses and cities and pyramids, or served as soldiers. Of course, such use could only take place when technique and division of labor had reached a degree which made it possible for human labor to be so employed. At this point surplus grew immensely. The more fields were ploughed, the more marshes were drained, the more surplus could be produced. This new possibility led to one of the most fundamental changes in human history. *It was discovered that man could be used as an economic instrument, that he could be exploited, that he could be made a slave.*

Let us follow this process in more detail in its economic, social, religious, and psychological consequences. The basic economic facts of the new society were, as indicated above, greater specialization of work, the transformation of surplus into capital, and the need for a centralized mode of production. The first consequence of this was the rise of different classes. The privileged classes did the directing and organizing, claiming and obtaining for themselves a disproportionately large part of the product, that is to say, a standard of living which the majority of the population could not obtain. Below them were the lower classes, peasants and artisans. Below those were the slaves, prisoners taken as a result of wars. The privileged classes organized their own hierarchy headed originally by permanent chiefs—eventually by kings, as representatives of the gods—who were the nominal heads of the whole system.

Another consequence of the new mode of production is assumed to have been conquest as an essential requisite to the accumulation of communal capital needed for the accomplishment of the urban revolution. But there was a still more basic reason for the invention of war as an institution: the contradiction between an economic system that needed unification in order to be optimally effective, and political and dynastic separation that conflicted with this economic need. War as an institution was a new invention, like kingdom or bureaucracy, made around 3000 B.C. Then as now, it was not caused by psychological factors, such as human aggression, but, aside from the wishes for power and glory of the kings and their bureaucracy, was the result of objective conditions that made war useful and which, as a consequence, tended to generate and increase human destructiveness and cruelty.30

These social and political changes were accompanied by a profound change in the role of women in society and of the mother figure in religion. No longer was the fertility of the soil the source of all life and creativity, but the intellect which produced new inventions, techniques, abstract thinking, and the state with its laws. No longer the womb, but the mind became the creative power, and simultaneously, not women, but men dominated society.

This change is poetically expressed in the Babylonian hymn of creation, Enuma Elish. This myth tells us of a victorious rebellion of the male gods against Tiamat, the "Great Mother" who ruled the universe. They form an alliance against her and choose Marduk to be their leader. After a bitter war Tiamat is slain, from her body heaven and earth are formed, and Marduk rules as supreme God.

However, before he is chosen to be the leader, Marduk has to pass a test, which may seem insignificant—or puzzling—to modern man, but it is the key to the understanding of the myth:

'Then they placed a garment in their midst; To Marduk, their first-born, they said:
"Verily, O lord, thy destiny is supreme among the gods,
Command 'to destroy and to create,' (and) it shall be!

By the word of thy mouth let the garment be destroyed;
Command again, and let the garment be whole!" He commanded with his mouth, and the garment was destroyed.
Again he commanded, and the garment was restored.
When the gods, his fathers, beheld the efficiency of his word
They rejoiced (and) did homage, (saying) "Marduk is king!"' —A. Heidel, 1942

The meaning of this test is to show that man has overcome his inability for natural creation—a quality which only the soil and the female had—by a new form of creation, that by the word (thought). Marduk, who can create in this way, has overcome the natural superiority of the mother and hence can replace her. The biblical story begins where the Babylonian myth ends: the male god creates the world by the word. (E. Fromm, 1951a.)

One of the most significant features of the new urban society was that it was based on the principle of patriarchal rule, in which the principle of control is inherent: control of nature, control of slaves, women and children. The new patriarchal man literally "makes" the earth. His technique is not simply modification of the natural processes, but their domination and control by man, resulting in new products which are not found in nature. Men themselves came under the control of those who organized the work of the community, and hence the leaders had to have power over those they controlled.

In order to achieve the aims of this new society, everything, nature and man, had to be controlled and had to either exercise—or fear—power. In order to become controllable, men had to learn to obey and to submit, and in order to submit they had to believe in the superior power—physical and/or magic—of their rulers. While in the Neolithic village, as well as among primitive hunters, leaders guided and counseled the people and did not exploit them, and while their leadership was accepted voluntarily or, to use another term, while prehistoric authority was "rational" authority resting on competence, the authority of the new patriarchal system was one based on force and power; it was exploitative and mediated by the psychical mechanism of fear, "awe," and submission. It was "irrational authority."

Lewis Mumford has expressed the new principle governing the life of the city very succinctly: "'To exert power in every form was the essence of civilization; the city found a score of ways of expressing struggle, aggression, domination, conquest—and servitude." He points out that the new ways of the cities were "rigorous, efficient, often harsh, even sadistic,'" and that the Egyptian monarchs and their Mesopotamian counterparts "'boasted on their monuments and tablets of their personal feats in mutilating, torturing, and killing with their own hands their chief captives.'" (L. Mumford, 1961.)

As a result of my clinical experience in psychoanalytic therapy I had long come to the conviction (E. Fromm, 1941a) that the essence of sadism is the passion for unlimited, godlike control over men and things.31 Mumford's view of the sadistic character of these societies is an important confirmation of my own.32

In addition to sadism, the passion to destroy life and the attraction to all that is dead (necrophilia) seem to develop in the new urban civilization. Mumford also speaks of the destructive, death-oriented myth to be found in the new social order, and quotes Patrick Geddes as saying that each historic civilization begins with a living, urban core, the polls, and ends in a common graveyard of dust and bones, a Necropolis, or city of the dead: fire-scorched ruins, shattered buildings, empty workshops, heaps of meaningless refuse, the population massacred or driven into slavery. (L Mumford, 1961.)

Whether we read the story of the Hebrews' conquest of Canaan or the story of the Babylonians' wars, the same spirit of unlimited and inhuman destructiveness is shown. A good example is Sennacherib's stone inscription on the total annihilation of Babylon:

'The city and (its) houses from its foundation to its top, I destroyed, I devastated, I burned with fire. The wall and the outer wall, temples and gods, temple towers of brick and earth, as many as they were, I razed and dumped them into the Arakhtu Canal. Through the midst of that city I dug canals, I flooded its site with water, and the very foundation thereof I destroyed. I made its destruction more complete than that by a flood.' (Quoted by L. Mumford, 1961.)

The history of civilization, from the destruction of Carthage and Jerusalem to the destruction of Dresden, Hiroshima, and the people, soil, and trees of Vietnam, is a tragic record of sadism and destructiveness.[355]

Several significant facts should be taken from this shocking history of the peaceful existence of primitive humankind: human violence is influenced far more by conditioning than any innate aspect; that is, just because humans can be violent doesn't mean that we always will become violent in the end. To believe our capacity for violence means violence within our species is inevitable is a slippery slope argument. That is, it forms a extreme hypothetical on human behavior without demonstrating any causal link on why just because violence is possible would necessarily mean that humans will always choose the violent option in their decision-making. Our peaceful history for thousands of years proves that Original Sin is wrong, violence is not fixed within us. We, as a species, can create more peaceful coexistence

---

73. [355] Fromm, Erich. Chapter 8: Anthropology (153-208). *The Anatomy of Human Destructiveness*. Open Road Media. Kindle Edition.

with each other. Another relevant fact about human violence is that it didn't begin to spread to such extreme lengths until we domesticated ourselves as a species and added the most divisive concept when we began living in primitive nation-states: social status. Social creeds of differences from race, religion, and especially income distribution began to be cages to corrupt our innate selfless nature. The first social status among the primitive civilizations to create such problems was the formation of the concept of slavery. This social concept eventually shifted to mean allegiance to a particular country. Moreover, unlike humans in hunter-gatherer societies or the Neolithic period, humans in post-Neolithic societies could no longer feel their skills recognized and acknowledged by ignorant rulers who had no knowledge of how useful their talents were; unlike in the earlier societies where the most knowledgeable or most skilled among the tribe dictated what to do for gathering, hunting, or for religious ceremonies like marriages. In concomitant with such a horrible concept as slavery came the emergence of the Father God; selfishness, human exploitation, sexual abuse in domestic quarters, war rape, and mass genocide became the rule under a strict, authoritarian command of unquestioned obedience.[356] In hunter-gatherer and Neolithic periods, men and women were happily monogamous; but in the primitive nation-states under the Father God, men began taking women as multiple concubines or wives as spoils of victory in warfare or through social compulsion by the new group ranks of society. Kings could take as many slave women as they pleased. All of which coincide with their celebrations in the Bible for the desecration and rampant destruction of other tribes. Father Gods facing Father Gods in endless war campaigns, subjugating other tribes and taking women as spoils of war, and destroying the peaceful existences of societies that still held onto the belief in Mother Goddesses which tried to live in peace and harmony with the world. The empathy and rationalism living in harmonious tandem within Mother Goddess societies were destroyed through war rape, genocide, and slavery by those who held the belief in Father Gods which required unquestioned obedience and authoritarian social hierarchy.[357] It was belief in the Father God that brought authoritarian violence such as suppressing rebellions, social status of superiors and inferiors of slaves and rulers, subsequently forcing women into obsequious roles through male-dominated violence and threats, and - in the Abrahamic quarters of the world - spread ignorance, fear of freedom, and fear of humans living in nature. All so that the individual would serve as a tool for the nation-state.

A nation-state is a system that has humans utilizing fellow humans as tools for social cohesion. The ones ruling the top quintile of influence and/or monetary wealth determine the lives of the bottom in some significant ways. Humans brought-up in a nation-state typically judge their self-worth on the basis of societal values and norms. How successful you are in the society of the nation-state by those values and norms determines your social status and you

---

74. [356] Cialdini, Robert B. Chapter 6: Authority (178-200). *Influence: Science and practice.* 4th ed., 21st Century Bks, 2002.
75. [357] Cialdini, Robert B. Chapter 6: Authority (178-200). *Influence: Science and practice.* 4th ed., 21st Century Bks, 2002.

may gain a sense of belonging from that. Equally important is what you're allowed to accomplish and your sense of fulfillment in a nation-state generally determines your personal happiness. *In effect, humans exist to be manipulated and used by their nation-states. As a citizen of a country, your existence is tethered to how useful you are to your nation-state's interests. You exist to be manipulated and used by your country.* The nation-state determines everything about your existence: your religion, your "race", your income level, your personal safety, and the history they decide to teach you to make you feel connected to your country in your schooling. Our history is based on the nation-state needing citizens to be loyal in order to feel loyalty to the national interest. Whether it is war, dominance over another social group, or the destruction of certain outliers that are seen as a endemic to the norms and values of society. We learn to hate others of a social group for the purposes of war or human exploitation by having repeated exposure in our media to anecdotes of personal testimonies to horrible crimes done by one member of a foreign social group.[358] We homogenize and generalize in this manner by forming instant judgments of entire groups based on a few criminals; we see our history as significant and mostly benign, while the others we know nothing about are barbarous and hateful based on specific periods of history that have nothing to do with modern times.[359] We are given ahistorical anecdotes to justify our violence upon them as self-defense. We may judge other peoples history based on some horrible past of our own history and believe the less developed countries must exist in the same way, despite the fact that we know nothing about them and don't look for new information on what their history actually is. The higher a person's social status is in the nation-state, the more useful they are to the nation-state because of the money and skills they contribute. This is often compared to those feeling unremarkable or useless for being below in either personal qualities of skill or social status; the group often marginalized. You may feel maligned because you are treated as unworthy or useless in your nation-state. By wanting success and status, the nation-state teaches us to intrinsically desire power and celebrate being a manipulated tool by those predecessors who held the reins of power until bestowed upon us. We can help change and shape our nation-states, the more we are valued and given the ability to make significant decision-making about our lives within the nation-state.

    A key to that is the heart of a nation-state; its economic productivity. However, the concept of Original Sin has disoriented and confused what is innate in human nature to create pernicious problems that are entirely avoidable. Capitalism has been misused and misunderstood. A manager will find far more value in an employee who has an intrinsic interest in serving the needs of the company versus one in which inducements are utilized to curry favor.[360] The innate nature of humans is the desire to be selflessness for their perceived in-groups, to have their sense of significance valued in support by their peers, and to feel like their actions have meaningful consequences in a higher purpose for either the majority of other

---

76. [358] Kahneman, Daniel. *Thinking, fast and slow*. Farrar, Straus and Giroux, 2015.
77. [359] Kahneman, Daniel. *Thinking, fast and slow*. Farrar, Straus and Giroux, 2015.
78. [360] Pink, Daniel H. *Drive: the Surprising Truth about What Motivates Us*. Canongate Books, 2018.

people or for their loved ones.[361] Capitalism's idea of animal spirits is a flawed one that is untenable when compared to the evidence of humans living in wild nature or in prehistoric civilizations. Preaching selfishness as the innate nature of humanity is simply untenable theocratic nonsense and it is not based on ancient history or our sense of rationality. Capitalism must acknowledge that humans are far more selfless by nature and only conditioned by the nation-state into degrees of selfishness. Recent research has helped to reorient managers to these new modes of thought on human behavior such as the book *Drive* by Daniel H. Pink. For that matter, consider the possibility that the concept of evil and Original Sin may have sprung forth as justifications by ancient civilizations to collectively punish themselves for letting even one innocent life end under horrible circumstances; for instance, ancient Talmudic teachings that taught saving a life or murdering someone as analogous to saving or murdering the entire world. Perhaps, in some way under the barbarous ignorance of Father God societies, Original Sin was a self-punishment through hatred for our entire species and collective guilt for the deaths of all innocent lives lost. Nevertheless, all it does now is prevent us from feeling motivated to help the innocent lives that we can still work to save in the present.

---

79. [361] May, Rollo. "Madness and Powerlessness." *Power and Innocence: A Search for the Sources of Violence*. New York, NY: Norton, 1972. 19-46. Print.

Chapter 7: Free Will and Original Sin

I've struggled with the topic of free will on a personal level. To clarify, it wasn't in the Abrahamic context, but rather the current neuroscience debate over whether people have free will or not. I had been observing the online information for several years due to my morbid fascination with the subject matter and the conclusions caused me to have pause. Part of the struggle for sharing that information with this critique was trying to properly articulate the faultiness of the Abrahamic context of free will compared to the studies in neuroscience. The Abrahamic context is too simplistic and never covered the nuances that modern philosophy and neuroscience have invigorating discourses about.[362] There was no way to broach this subject without becoming pedantic in writing the reasons why and potentially going off-topic from the discussion of Original Sin's failings. Furthermore, throughout the process of learning and writing for this book, I genuinely struggled to have a clear view of the topic and having the confidence to pick a side on free will, determinism, or the varieties of compatibilism. I still hold a healthy amount of doubt for my current belief, but as a consequence, I was struggling with forming up the confidence to write it out. I'm no neuroscientist, I don't want to be misrepresenting their work, and I understand that it's a controversial topic within the neuroscience and philosophy community. *This portion will just be my own layperson opinion on the matter of free will.* I cannot in good conscience argue this without mentioning my crippling doubts on the matter. I don't have any doubts about Original Sin being a horrible belief system based on the evidence, but I certainly have doubts with respect to the free will debate.

Based on the definition, the facts of cause and effect, and how our assumptions and personal contexts are formed as human beings: I am of the opinion that free will doesn't exist. I use to move between the ideas of compatibilism and determinism, but I've since discarded compatibilism as incoherent when viewing the evidence. Going into full details on why would be beyond the scope of this book since the entire topic of free will is worthy of its own books and spans several different disciplines of college curriculum. As such, I can only give an overview based on brief snippets of information from various neuroscientists and psychologists for the purpose of debunking the archaic Original Sin model of free will that can no longer be substantiated with our current knowledge of human behavior. I would recommend several books that delve far more deeply into understanding the biases of the human mind and how our subjective experience forms the axioms for our beliefs. These books provide fascinating insights into the human mind and if your interest is piqued, I've added a further reading section for the books that much of Part 1 and Part 2 of this book uses as a reference in citations.

Before listing my reasons against free will, I'd like to explain what ultimately convinced me that determinism was true and how I came to that conclusion. This is an

---

1. [362] Green, Hank. "Determinism vs Free Will: Crash Course Philosophy #24." *YouTube*, Crash Course / PBS Digital Studios, 15 Aug. 2016, www.youtube.com/watch?v=vCGtkDzELAI.

anecdote and can be dismissed as such, but for those curious as to my thought process for this may find it useful. This will be a bit lengthy so if you're not interested then please skip to the reasons listed below. I had first become acquainted with the argument of free will versus determinism in high school when considering different regions of the world and what it would mean to be an accident of birth. As a list of examples, I thought about how in India, the vast majority of people who are born are raised Hindu; while in the United States, the vast majority were born and raised Christian; In China, the vast majority would be atheist, and in most of the Middle East, it would be Islam that they are born and raised in. Their language, religious affiliation, their ethnic background, and their nationality were all an accident of birth that wasn't of their own choosing; this is something internet atheists who were supportive of the New Atheist movement had pointed out in various internet forums in early 2000s and it stuck with me throughout high school. I had looked-up the Christian justification for this upon seeing staunch Christians trying to defend their position that they would remain Christian regardless of where they were born; most of them just did a poor job asserting all they know is Christianity and that therefore they would only ever be Christian.[363] In effect, Christians on the internet that I met completely ignored the argument and made an appeal to ignorance; from looking at comments and blogs from Christians, this was one of the main consistencies of the argument and showed how woefully inept they were in taking these questions seriously. I had thought that the vast majority of people had this same line of questioning when assessing the world and their place in it, but to my surprise upon growing older, I realized I was wrong and most people simply didn't think about it. That honestly struck me as odd behavior. Over time I had grown acquainted with the free will debate through Sam Harris's lengthy video about it and looked up several articles of research, Daniel Dennett's review of Sam Harris's book on Free Will, and Friedrich Nietzsche's pro-deterministic views of it in the book *Twilight of the Idols* further influenced me to question assumptions about free will. After postgraduate studies, I delved further into reading various books on different aspects of human psychology that fascinated me and of which I've placed in the Further Reading list as references and due to my curiosity about free will, I couldn't help but apply the knowledge written in the books to the question of free will. However, what fully convinced me was not abstractions or the psychological research, which greatly paved the way but didn't fully change my views on compatibilism. What changed my mind was working in a temporary position as a Health Unit Coordinator for a veterans home. In particular, this veterans home was for veterans who had dementia or other similar afflictions related to memory loss.

    Before I continue further, I feel it is best to mention that working at the veterans home was one of the most difficult, but satisfying, experiences and it was a pleasure to provide my own small contribution in assisting in the welfare of veterans of the United States armed forces. People may homogenize military folk as hard-nosed, gritty types whose life revolves around talking about war as per Hollywood stereotypes, but those stereotypes do a complete

---

2. [363] Kahneman, Daniel. Chapter 9: Answering an Easier Question (97-107). *Thinking, fast and slow.* Farrar, Straus and Giroux, 2015.

disservice to the array of personalities and personality quirks that make-up veterans of both World Wars, the Korean war, and the Vietnam war. For the most part, if I was forced to try to make a generalization of my experiences, they were either gentle and compassionate people or some of the wittiest jokesters with all kinds of fun humor. Of course, even that is an oversimplification for each of their personalities. Unfortunately, I can't specify identifying information as that is against HIPAA laws and their privacy rights. Of the ones I spoke with, none had any interest in discussing war time unless prompted; this is less surprising when one considers that war was just one small component of their lives and doesn't define who or what they are as individuals. For the most part, they preferred to talk about how their day was going, their families (especially children), what was on the scheduled menu for the day, what they thought of current events, or what they thought of any particular topic in general. I would talk to them when I wasn't busy with paperwork or getting supplies for the unit. It had occurred to me only after meeting and speaking with several of them that they didn't seem to hold their time during war as a major part of their lives or a sense of who they were; it was merely an experience that took up a portion of their lives and didn't define them as human beings. A rather troubling idea formed in my mind and so I asked a few of them, all of whom were happy to be asked, if they thought the war themes or events about war perhaps brought back bad memories that they would otherwise like to forget. In the duration of my work there, I had come to realize that wars neither defined them as people nor would it have been anything that most of them wanted to relive. After all, if it was truly a horrifying time in which their life was always at risk, then why would they want to remember that? Why would any of them want to be defined by that? Mass media taught us to take it as a given, and the celebratory events for them were absolutely about appreciating all of their hard work and sacrifice for our country in times of crisis, but wouldn't constantly being thanked every year or every military holiday for a harrowing time in one's life get tiresome and make one relive bad memories? The ones whom I asked, one of whom said it was a good question and that they appreciated it, seemed to give the same general response. The answers seemed to be practically unanimous: the people caring for them were nice and they appreciated them, so they didn't mind and it didn't bother them since they liked how well they were being treated. In effect, the everyday hard work and compassion of the staff made them appreciative and they liked the people who were taking care of them. The benign treatment mattered more to them.

It wasn't difficult to ascertain why they were so appreciative and consequently what made me acknowledge that free will couldn't possibly exist. Most people who research the free will debate know of the infamous incident of a man who had a tumor in his brain that caused him to have pedophilic tendencies until the tumor was removed and for the pedophilic tendencies to return again when the tumor had grown back.[364] I've seen that story circulated in a few books and youtube channels. However, most people wrongly attempt to dismiss that story as an outlier. When working at the veterans home, I was forced to consider: what about

---

3. [364] Green, Hank. "Compatibilism: Crash Course Philosophy #25." *YouTube*, Crash Course / PBS Digital Studios, 22 Aug. 2016, www.youtube.com/watch?v=KETTtiprINU.

more mundane conditions like dementia? Dementia was different depending on the individual, parts of the brain slowly degenerated over time and fully grown adults became the same as helpless children in need of care. Moreover, what about other illnesses that I hadn't even the reference or that I didn't have the conscious awareness to consider? It was understandable why dementia would become frustrating to live with as simple tasks like getting oneself a cup of water require help from others. Some people can't stand the change; to go from a self-made individual to a person in a constant state of helplessness being forced to wait while others are attended to before it's your turn. The constant state of helplessness can be difficult to adjust to; for some they become demanding, likely because their sense of significance has been reduced due to a lack of autonomy. It is possibly also because of a desire for instant gratification and possibly a comparison for when they could do it on their own time, but for others they become complacent and adapt by accepting a state of learned helplessness likely because they see the struggle as pointless since it's a fact that they won't get better. Needing to be pushed via wheelchair to other locations, being forced to adapt to other people's schedules without being able to simply take actions with one's own volition, and slowly forgetting yourself and your loved ones can all be painful and people adjust differently depending on their personalities. Sometimes, personalities themselves will radically change. Information becomes more important instead of the opposite from what I've observed; people always like to know what is going on and in my time there, I made sure to share as much information as possible because I knew that it was a way of helping them reclaim a sense of control from the state of helplessness. For some people, I would have to introduce myself everyday and answer the same questions, for others it was to repeat what was on their schedule if they had any planned trips outside the facility whenever they forgot, and familiarizing myself with their unique forms of sarcasm. My effort in responding to their questions was appreciated by all of them. My time there made me think of how woefully inept Hollywood was at portraying the US armed forces; it made me question if the superhuman qualities given to actors playing soldiers on screen was its own type of dehumanization. US culture constantly propagated this idea of a self-made individual with superhuman qualities who could overcome everything through sheer willpower. Often, the stereotype involved the brave people in military garments able to overcome all obstacles. They never consider old age; old actors give way to new ones, where the same hubris of god-like feats is constantly churned out for profit. Few think of what it means to become old and fewer still prepare for such a time in their life. Seeing soldiers mutilated on screen for gore porn is one aspect, but how many ever consider the care delivered in treating such grievous wounds, the painful emotions the families endure, and who knows how many other complications as a result of war?

  A pernicious issue which bothered me when working there was the concept of Original Sin and what it would mean for their relationships with their loved ones. I had been told of cases where people with certain degenerative states of dementia became unable to distinguish when something was sexually inappropriate or became more likely to commit sexually inappropriate acts due to their condition through no fault of their own. How much worse would it feel for an honest victim of such tendencies to attribute it to some innate sinfulness as a result of free will when it was something they honestly had no control over? How often did people misattribute the cause of their action to something innate about their psyche, instead of something they truly couldn't control? How many people believed that these veterans being unable to control their inhibitions would be perceived as their "real" or "inner" self instead of a horrible condition that they couldn't control? How much more awful would they feel by misunderstanding the cause to be something they were consciously capable of? How much self-hate would they cast upon themselves believing it to be something about willpower that they could have changed, but failed to because they believed they were being sinful? How much more strained would their relationships with their loved ones be, if their loved ones thought it was some imminent truth about them that they hid because the loved one believed in Original Sin? For instance, how torturous would it feel if something similar to the infamous case of a man with pedophilic tendencies due to a brain tumor was attributed to an individual who genuinely had no control over their actions and could be proven as such by examining their brain? It was perturbing to think of how one horrid concept could possibly destroy the lives of veterans who were suffering. The suffering would maximize to further emotional grief; all because of a hateful, misanthropic concept like Original Sin. All because people had no other reference point besides the Bible teaching them to hate themselves through a misanthropic concept that did nothing but cause pain and misery. Thankfully, professionalism of the highest order was maintained and any who would believe in such a concept had never shown it. The general idea was always that it was the condition and that was simply stating the truth. It was the condition that they had no control over and not something innate as a result of free will to display of some so-called violent truth about humanity.

The staff of the veterans home were from diverse backgrounds of all kinds in different staff departments. The Nurse Managers, Doctors, Nurses, Certified Nursing Assistants, and Health Unit Coordinators were an assortment of varied ethnic backgrounds and religious beliefs. Avidly pious Christians, Muslims, Jews, Hindus, and Sikhs worked in tandem with coworkers who were Agnostic, Atheist, scientifically-minded but not altogether irreligious people, and even a gentleman who professed his own unique multi-spiritual beliefs during a lengthy conversation I had with him in the parking lot. To my knowledge, everyone was open to liberal values such as respect and equality for homosexuals and treating their fellow coworkers with the utmost dignity and respect. As mentioned, the ethnic make-up of the workforce was just as diverse; within both the Nurse Managers, Nurses, and Doctors; there were White, Black, Hispanic, Indian, and potentially other ethnic Asian workers. All of whom diligently followed the rules and held everyone accountable to the demanding standards for the sake of care for the veterans and keeping all veteran's rights protected in compliance with the law. Many Haitian and Hispanic CNAs and housekeepers were fluently bilingual. It made me think that while the American Dream may be something one must fall asleep to believe in, the American ideal was most certainly expressed well in that care facility.

For my part, I felt honored to have made my own small contribution to helping veterans and I recommend working or volunteering at your local veteran's homes as the staff assistance is likely to be sorely needed and every little bit of assistance really does add-up; both the veterans and staff are appreciative of all such efforts. Unfortunately, due to the demanding nature of the work environment, very few have the patience and perseverance to handle working at a veteran's home. As a result, due to the sensitive nature of meeting the needs of veterans, a culture of hard work and correcting mistakes was built around selfless in-group cohesion.[365] The demanding nature of the various jobs; whether Nurse Manager, Certified Nursing Assistant, Doctor, Med Nurse, Charge Nurse, or Health Unit Coordinator called for such a work ethic and it was most certainly built around selflessness for the sake of making veteran's lives as comfortable and safe as possible. For those who are unaware, groupthink is actually *beneficial* for the cohesion of an organization, *but only so long as groupthink is focused primarily on the goal of an organization and not misused to place higher value on the personal feelings* of certain individuals or the entire group because that both distracts from the goal and thereby undercuts the chief aim of the group in attaining the goal.[366] In other words, groupthink works well when people are held accountable for not meeting the expectations of the group. Equally as important is showing proper appreciation when a person conducts proper effort in fulfilling their assigned duties or going beyond those assigned duties when qualified and asked to do such for the organization. In effect, everyone enjoys being appreciated for the effort that they give to an organization that they care about. Within the veteran's home; the hard work, dedication, and in-group trust that was always patient and willing to give a helping hand for any difficulties formed a culture of high-competence because everyone was both held accountable for their failures and taught how to correct those failures through careful guidance, explanations on what actions to do and not to do, and the reasons why. Questions were valued and answers readily given; early on, I failed to fulfill key monthly goals, but learned from my mistakes and worked to better my modus operandi within the scope of the tasks assigned to me and took lessons from those who were far beyond my skill level. I felt I learned a lot from the people there; in particular, the importance of saying no to others when you were expected to follow guidelines. This came from observing hyper-competent people like the doctor of the unit I worked in, learning the Charge Nurse was the one who was really in charge of the unit, and helping out the CNAs (Certified Nursing Assistants) who did their utmost to provide care for the veterans of the unit. I decided to utilize several psychology and work productivity books to put my best effort in fulfilling the needs of the demanding work environment; it was actually surprising to realize most people didn't prepare for demanding workloads by utilizing such resources beforehand and I had come to the conclusion I had overestimated competence and effort in most other environments I had worked within based on the hyperbolic beliefs of the high school I attended and my own parents. By the time the contract for my work ended, I was given a hefty amount of praise and well wishes; many said I had done a great job and that I

---

4. [365] Ispas, Alexa. *Psychology and politics: a social identity perspective*. Psychology Press, 2014.
5. [366] Ispas, Alexa. *Psychology and politics: a social identity perspective*. Psychology Press, 2014.

had indeed been able to keep up with one of the more demanding units to the satisfaction of organization goals. I was able to keep-up with the Doctor, Charge Nurse, CNAs, and many of the veterans wished me well saying they enjoyed meeting me and thanked me for my work and dedication. As you may imagine, at this current moment in my life, the veterans home stands as the best job I've ever had the pleasure of being a part of.

For those who don't live in the US and have kept an interest in this personal account, I'd like to thank you for your interest and appreciation for the lives of people outside of your own country as I imagine it gets stifling to hear only about the most influential Western countries if you live outside of them. If the aforementioned has made you interested in helping veterans in your own country, I would suggest thinking over ways in which any suffering they endure can be alleviated or working to help correct any potential injustice done to people who've served your government; of course, that is assuming the military and potentially specific military personnel in question within your country serves the public good of your nation-state and people.

With all that being stated, here is my explanation for why I don't believe in free will:

In his book *Deviate*, neuroscientist Beau Lotto mentions that assumptions are inculcated as a person grows up in their environment. We tend to attribute this to our preferences in taste, but the assumptions run far more deeply than that. The assumptions we inculcate from intuitive life experience determine our religion, our nationality, and our language.[367] It even determines our social perception of "race" since race is merely a social construct according to scientists.[368] Similarly, where and how we grow up determines our self-theories of who and what we are in relation to the world around us.[369] There are all prior causes that most of us may not even be consciously aware of assessing as assumptions that we've grown up with.[370] Our assumptions about the world and preferences therein are a statistical distribution; which means we would first generally have to learn why a particular belief is wrong before we accept another one to be right, especially if it is a strong belief of ours.[371] In other words, we can't jump from a set of beliefs like creationism to a new set of beliefs that are diametrically opposed like evolution without first understanding the basics of evolution, which would require slowly disentangling our assumptions about creationism.[372] Within the scope of evolution itself, organisms are adapting to their environment through a lengthy process of ridding a species of useless traits and attaining more useful traits to keep alive in their habitat.

6. [367] Lotto, Beau. Chapter 6: The Physiology of Assumptions (1671 - 2121). *Deviate: the Science of Seeing Differently*. Hachette Books, 2017.
7. [368] Gannon, Megan. "Race Is a Social Construct, Scientists Argue." *Scientific American*, 5 Feb. 2016, www.scientificamerican.com/article/race-is-a-social-construct-scientists-argue/.
8. [369] Dweck, Carol S. *Mindset: How You Can Fulfill Your Potential*. Random House, 2012.
9. [370] Lotto, Beau. *Deviate: the Science of Seeing Differently*. Hachette Books, 2017.
10. [371] Lotto, Beau. Chapter 5: The Frog Who Dreamed of Being a Prince (1356 - 1670). *Deviate: the Science of Seeing Differently*. Hachette Books, 2017.
11. [372] Lotto, Beau. *Deviate: the Science of Seeing Differently*. Hachette Books, 2017.

Oftentimes, it's a mix of positive and negative qualities in a mostly positive set of traits. Beau Lotto tries to argue in his book that free will could still exist because we form new meanings from our past.[373] However, the past is something we can't change and our shifting interpretation still wouldn't change the fact a past event remains an axiom that we base meaning itself on and crucially, still forms a starting point for the acceptance of new beliefs.[374]

In the book, *Stumble on Happiness*, Harvard professor and Social Psychologist, Daniel Gilbert explains how we humans mistakenly feel our personal perspectives and what we imagine about how the world operates are always objective.[375] However, all we really do is fill in what we think living in a particular situation is like with our own imagination and we believe what we imagine about that situation to be representative of the objective reality.[376] This is a natural human tendency and oftentimes occurs unconsciously without us fully recognizing our belief about something is just our personal interpretation and not objective reality itself.[377] As such, our belief that we intuitively see reality for what it is only functions as a detriment to both our understanding of the world and of our own experiences. To better understand why this is, consider the fact that atoms, microbes, single-celled organisms, radio waves, and microwaves are all just as real as you or I, but they can't be seen by the human eye. Furthermore, consider the fact that so much of our personal feelings and subsequent actions oftentimes depend on how good or bad the weather is, how much we've eaten, what we've eaten, what microbes are in our bodies, and so forth. What we see, as many of these psychologists assert, is just our subjective experience in the world. We don't see reality for what it is, but we have the illusion of objectivity.[378][379] The only way for us to become closer to being objective about the world is through scientific experimentation of testing hypotheses through the scientific method utilizing our scientific instruments to understand the world around us. Yet, even then, some interpretation might be necessary once we understand what the facts are. Finally, near the end of *Stumble on Happiness*, Gilbert explains that we as humans implicitly overemphasize our uniqueness and the uniqueness of other humans because our everyday experience is trying to find qualities that differentiate people to find the people that we want to spend our lives with; we try to find people who will be the most valuable of friends or whom we should marry or the best people to work with at a job.[380] This biases us towards

12. [373] Lotto, Beau. Chapter 7: Changing the Future Past (2122 - 2429). *Deviate: the Science of Seeing Differently*. Hachette Books, 2017.
13. [374] Lotto, Beau. Chapter 6: The Physiology of Assumptions (1671 - 2121). *Deviate: the Science of Seeing Differently*. Hachette Books, 2017.
14. [375] Gilbert, Daniel. Chapter 4: In the Blind Spot of the Mind's Eye (75-95). *Stumbling on Happiness*. Random House, 2006.
15. [376] Gilbert, Daniel. Chapter 4: In the Blind Spot of the Mind's Eye (75-95). *Stumbling on Happiness*. Random House, 2006.
16. [377] Gilbert, Daniel. Chapter 4: In the Blind Spot of the Mind's Eye (75-95). *Stumbling on Happiness*. Random House, 2006.
17. [378] Gilbert, Daniel. Chapter 4: In the Blind Spot of the Mind's Eye (75-95). *Stumbling on Happiness*. Random House, 2006.
18. [379] Lotto, Beau. *Deviate: the Science of Seeing Differently*. Hachette Books, 2017
19. [380] Gilbert, Daniel. Chapter 11: Reporting Live For Tomorrow (212-233). *Stumbling on Happiness*.

focusing only on differences and we tend to skim over or simply don't register the normalcy of our experiences.[381] We also try to rate ourselves as having more qualities that make us unique from the average person in surveys . . . even when we are the representative average.[382] Gilbert provides a compelling argument in his book where he explains you can predict your future happiness before undergoing a particular experience (going to a specific amusement park, a holiday in a particular foreign country, or choosing between two high-quality jobs as a lifelong career path) by looking up the personal testimonies of any random person or set of people who has undergone that experience.[383] Of course, the testimony would have to be an honest account and not simply one manufactured by an organization on its website that makes one push a narrative. Nevertheless, honest accounts of particular sets of experiences will suffice as an accurate account of information you neglected to consider and will be a useful measure for your feelings about materials you hadn't considered regarding the experience that you wanted to know more about.

Now, to digress a bit, for those who wish to immediately argue that these two books could apply to the existence of a deity because humans aren't good at seeing reality in any objective sense, please keep advised of the following: first, there is no central definition of what such a deity even is or what it would comprise itself of, or where it would originate from. It's been 2000 years and the Abrahamic faiths have found nothing to prove the existence of the Abrahamic God. Second, there is no basis for beliefs in spiritual worlds and afterlives as none of that can be corroborated by any physical evidence and none has ever come forth to lend credence to the existence of any afterlives resembling anything the Abrahamic faiths have argued in support of. Finally, and most tellingly, you're just trying to use your own ignorance as a basis for making an open-ended assumption that has no evidence; in short, it's baseless and we have hard evidence that is demonstrable of what we can prove so we have to judge based on the evidence and not our personal feelings with matters of scientific inquiry. Insinuating from the basis of human ignorance would lower the level of credibility to the point where you could make-up anything such as the assertion that an invisible, translucent, spiritual pink polka dotted elephant flies across the universe faster than the speed of light. If you wish to say that there is evidence for the Abrahamic God, then please first try to show that your belief in your God can be separated from the scenario of the imaginary elephant that I made up just now. If your arguments can support both the Abrahamic God existing and the imaginary elephant that I just made-up existing then you've failed. This is not an attempt at an insult; I'm pointing out that you have to demonstrate this belief in a deity is founded on more than just anything you can make-believe like my ridiculous and fictitious idea of the elephant.

Random House, 2006.
20. [381] Gilbert, Daniel. Chapter 11: Reporting Live For Tomorrow (212-233). *Stumbling on Happiness*. Random House, 2006.
21. [382] Gilbert, Daniel. Chapter 11: Reporting Live For Tomorrow (212-233). *Stumbling on Happiness*. Random House, 2006.
22. [383] Gilbert, Daniel. Chapter 11: Reporting Live For Tomorrow (212-233). *Stumbling on Happiness*. Random House, 2006.

In the book, *Thinking Fast and Slow*, by legendary psychologist and Princeton professor Daniel Kahneman, details how we form coherent structures of how the world works through associations we make in our minds.[384] This often makes us find causes for different subject matter that are entirely unrelated to each other. As such, we may form patterns to make up a coherent cause for why an event happened.[385] When, in actuality, the cause could be something entirely unrelated or we could even be confusing cause for the effect or a correlation that isn't specifically the cause. For instance, in the United States, many of the Right-leaning public blamed the violent protests in Baltimore to Black youth listening to rap music; trouble is, rap music is beloved by various ethnic groups across the United States and isn't solely exclusive to what Black youth listen to and most youth (including Black youth) who listen to such music don't go out of their way to commit violence. By contrast, the Baltimore police were known to give large payouts in court trials that they lost on a yearly basis with the demand that families and victims couldn't go to the national media to speak on the violence conducted upon them by the Baltimore police in order to receive the payouts.[386] Thereby, violating their first amendment rights and treating them as second-class citizens. If any family members or the victim of police brutality spoke out to the national media, then the local government could stop paying for the treatment of physical damages their officers caused.[387] That would most certainly be a direct causal link, especially since four years of peaceful protests were ignored.[388] To continue about free will. We also have hindsight bias; that is, we remember placing more confidence that an event was going to happen after it has already occurred despite the actual evidence showing we report very low confidence that a particular event was going to happen before it actually happened.[389] We substitute what we thought of the past based on outcomes of the present that change our perception of what we believed.[390] Many surveys regarding major political events show this; such as the percentage of US citizens who report they had lower confidence in the Iraq War of 2003 than what they actually reported back in 2003 or in the example given in Daniel Kahneman's book, the confidence that people in the US had of Nixon's trip to China.[391][392]

From all I've learned through these and other psychology books, it has become clear to me that a lot of our memory and our actions are derived from situational contexts that we're often unaware of. Original Sin thereby confuses cause and effect by deliberately misattributing

---

23. [384] Kahneman, Daniel. *Thinking, fast and slow*. Farrar, Straus and Giroux, 2015.
24. [385] Kahneman, Daniel. *Thinking, fast and slow*. Farrar, Straus and Giroux, 2015.
25. [386] Puente, Mark. "Sun Investigates: Undue force." *The Baltimore Sun*, 28 Sept. 2014, data.baltimoresun.com/news/police-settlements/.
26. [387] Puente, Mark. "Sun Investigates: Undue force." *The Baltimore Sun*, 28 Sept. 2014, data.baltimoresun.com/news/police-settlements/.
27. [388] Puente, Mark. "Sun Investigates: Undue force." *The Baltimore Sun*, 28 Sept. 2014, data.baltimoresun.com/news/police-settlements/.
28. [389] Kahneman, Daniel. *Thinking, fast and slow*. Farrar, Straus and Giroux, 2015.
29. [390] Kahneman, Daniel. *Thinking, fast and slow*. Farrar, Straus and Giroux, 2015.
30. [391] "Fewer in U.S. View Iraq, Afghanistan Wars as Mistakes." *Gallup.com*, Gallup, Inc, 12 June 2015, news.gallup.com/poll/183575/fewer-view-iraq-afghanistan-wars-mistakes.aspx.
31. [392] Kahneman, Daniel. *Thinking, fast and slow*. Farrar, Straus and Giroux, 2015.

everything to an unalterable, intrinsic biological state that is scientifically unfounded. This is a powerful form of fundamental attribution error. That is, people overweigh the influence of personality and don't give reasonable weight to the situation that a person is in. Context matters, but the concept of Original Sin would posit without any credible evidence that everything horrific and violent is inevitable because humans have free will. Original Sin ignores everything relevant in uncovering why certain events happened and by doing so, provides a convenient moral shield for the worst offenders of war crimes like torturing children into becoming child soldiers, war rape, and genocide. How does the concept of Original Sin do that? It treats those egregious acts of violence as inevitable and thereby ignores any call to form corrective measures to hold perpetrators responsible as juvenile and idealistic. The reason for that is because of the pervasive belief that any human is capable of such behavior as a result of feeling too much freedom which allows them to be selfish and hateful. As mentioned prior, Original Sin promotes the idea that such devastating atrocities are never going to be able to be corrected, that there is absolutely nothing we can do to help others suffering in those situations, and that we can't stymie or decrease these acts of egregious violence through any social changes. Just because events of human violence in the past went unchecked shouldn't mean that we ignore events happening now from continuing that route. Yet, the Original Sin version of free will would have us believe that there is nothing we can do because humans will spontaneously behave in cruel and horrific ways. Abrahamic religious groups use free will as the objection in an almost synonymous notion with Original Sin; attributing every free act as an act closer to committing human violence or activities a religious group finds socially unacceptable. Social censure towards transgenders or homosexuals are widely scrutinized, but not the underlying belief that freedom of actions and freedom of thought will cause people to be selfish, cruel, and commit violence. It's fundamentally an undemocratic belief.

Human violence is not inevitable, it is not unalterable, and much of the statistical evidence proves that humans have gradually become less prone to violence.[393] Consequently, technology has become more thorough in uncovering wanton acts of human violence and state-sponsored violence that goes unchecked. That's a valuable first step, because it means we're treating the lives of every innocent that we see perish as significant, but our reaction can't be this meaningless ascetic notion that human free will makes it unavoidable to change circumstances for the better. Even if we can't stop a massive war or help everyone who is harmed; we should consider what small contribution can we make to alleviate the suffering, misery, and pain of people currently being harmed. The statistical information on human violence worldwide and the charities which hold themselves accountable show that contributions do help others and that every little bit helps to make a better life for people who are suffering.[394][395]

---

32. [393] Roser, Max. "Visual History of The Rise of Political Freedom and the Decrease in Violence." *Visual History of The Rise of Political Freedom and the Decrease in Violence*. Web. 3 Jan. 2016.
33. [394] Roser, Max. "Visual History of The Rise of Political Freedom and the Decrease in Violence." *Visual*

Redefined Free Will

In fairness to the detractors within the neuroscience and philosophy departments that argue in favor of free will, there has been research that challenges the idea that humans don't have free will at this current period of time. However, if we acknowledge this redefined version of free will to be scientifically valid about how the human brain operates, then it renders the Abrahamic concept of original sin as thoroughly untenable and obsolete.

In the article "*Neuroscience and Free Will are Rethinking their Divorce*" on *The Cut* by the journalist Christian Jarrett, he explains what new research in Germany has found with respect to free will:

> For years, various research teams have tried to pick holes in Libet's original research. It's been pointed out, for example, that it's pretty tricky for people to accurately report the time that they made their conscious decision. But, until recently, the broad implications of the finding have weathered these criticisms, at least in the eyes of many hard-nosed neuroscientists, and over the last decade or so his basic result has been replicated and built upon with ever more advanced methods such as fMRI and the direct recording of neuronal activity using implanted electrodes.
>
> These studies all point in the same, troubling direction: We don't really have free will. In fact, until recently, many neuroscientists would have said any decision you made was not truly free but actually determined by neural processes outside of your conscious control.
>
> Luckily, for those who find this state of affairs philosophically (or existentially) perplexing, things are starting to look up. Thanks to some new breakthrough studies, including one published last month in *Proceedings of the National Academy of Sciences* by researchers in Germany, there's now some evidence pointing in the other direction: The neuroscientists are backtracking on past bold claims and painting a rather more appealing account of human autonomy. We may have more control over certain processes than those initial experiments indicated.
>
> The German neuroscientists took a different approach from past work, using a form of brain-computer integration to see whether participants could cancel a movement after the onset of the nonconscious preparatory brain activity identified by Libet. If they could, it would be a sign that humans can consciously intervene and "veto" processes that neuroscience has previously considered automatic and beyond willful control.
>
> The participants' task started off simply enough: They had to press a foot pedal as quickly as possible whenever they saw a green light and cancel this movement whenever they saw a red light. Things got trickier when the researchers put the red light under the control of a computer that was monitoring the participants' own brain waves. Whenever the computer detected signs of nonconscious preparatory brain activity, it switched on the red light. If this preparatory activity is truly a signal of actions that are beyond conscious control, the participants should have been incapable of responding to these sudden red lights. In fact, in many cases the participants *were* able to cancel the nonconscious preparatory brain activity and stop their foot movement before it even began.
>
> Now, there *was* a point of no return — red lights that appeared too close (less than about one-quarter of a second) to the beginning of a foot movement could not be completely inhibited —

History of The Rise of Political Freedom and the Decrease in Violence. Web. 3 Jan. 2016.
34. [395] Rosling, Hans. *Factfulness*. Macmillan, 2018.

there simply wasn't time for the new cancellation signal to overtake the earlier command to move. But still, the principle stands — these results suggest at least some of the activity identified by Libet can, in fact, be vetoed by conscious will.

"A person's decisions are not at the mercy of unconscious and early brain waves," the lead researcher, Dr. John-Dylan Haynes of Charité - Universitätsmedizin in Berlin, said in the study's press release. "They are able to actively intervene in the decision-making process and interrupt a movement. Previously people have used the preparatory brain signals to argue against free will. Our study now shows that the freedom is much less limited than previously thought."

This new finding comes on the back of research by French neuroscientists published in 2012 in *PNAS* that also challenged the way Libet's seminal work is usually interpreted. These researchers believe that the supposedly nonconscious preparatory brain activity identified by Libet is really just part of a fairly random ebb and flow of background neural activity, and that movements occur when this activity crosses a certain threshold. By this account, people's willful movements should be quicker when they're made at a time that just happens to coincide with when the background ebb and flow of activity is on a high point.

And that's exactly what the French team found. They recorded participants' brain waves as they repeatedly pressed a button with their finger, sometimes spontaneously at times of their own choosing, and other times in response to a randomly occurring click sound. The researchers found that their participants were much quicker to respond to the click sounds when the sounds happened to occur just as this random background brain activity was reaching a peak.

Based on this result from 2012 and a similar finding in a study with rats published in 2014, the lead researcher of the 2012 study, Aaron Schurger at INSERM in Paris, and two colleagues have written in their field's prestige journal *Trends in Cognitive Sciences* that it's time for a new perspective on Libet's results — they say that their results call "for a reevaluation and reinterpretation of a large body of work" and that for 50 years their field may have been "measuring, mapping and analyzing what may turn out to be a reliable accident: the cortical readiness potential."

And like their counterparts in Germany, these neuroscientists say the new picture is much more in keeping with our intuitive sense of our free will. When we form a vague intention to move, they explain, this mind-set feeds into the background ebb and flow of neural activity, but the specific decision to act only occurs when the neural activity passes a key threshold — and our all-important subjective feeling of deciding happens at this point or a brief instant afterward. "All this leaves our common sense picture largely intact," they write.

I'll leave you to decide whether to believe them or not.[396]

The reason why this redefined concept of free will would thoroughly repudiate original sin is because free will could only occur in circumstances in which we held back from taking an action or stopped ourselves from conducting a potential action that we were planning to do.[397][398] This is an abject contradiction to the Abrahamic concept of free will. If this redefined

---

35. [396] Jarrett, Christian. "Neuroscience and Free Will Are Rethinking Their Divorce." *The Cut*, 3 Feb. 2016, www.thecut.com/2016/02/a-neuroscience-finding-on-free-will.html.
36. [397] Schultze-Kraft, Matthias, et al. "The Point of No Return in Vetoing Self-Initiated Movements." *PNAS*, National Academy of Sciences, 26 Jan. 2016, www.pnas.org/content/113/4/1080.
37. [398] "Study Tackles Neuroscience Claims to Have Disproved 'Free Will'." *NC State News The Difference*

concept of free will true, then people who aren't able to quit smoking, who aren't able to stop compulsory eating, or from using drugs like heroin aren't practicing free will. *It means the people who are able to stop themselves from those impulsive actions are the ones with free will.* If you've ever attended a religious service and know of a family member, acquaintance, or friend who is unable to quit drinking, smoking, or can't stop themselves from engorging on food to an unhealthy extent then you have to acknowledge that they haven't built up the free will to challenge that habit. If you've either never had such habits or have successfully quit a bad habit, then it would be because you successfully exercised your free will to overcome that bad habit. If this sounds ridiculous, then consider what this redefined concept of free will would mean for those struggling with the aforementioned addictions. They continue to smoke cigarettes, drink alcoholic beverages, or inject heroin to fulfill a need for instant gratification against their better judgment; this is not the freedom to choose against a temptation, it's the struggle to overcome a mode of behavior that has become normalized, made habitual, and is painful for the addict to fight against. The fact they have to fight against such a self-harming temptation contradicts the notion that they can freely choose to behave in a self-destructive manner. They know better, but don't have the power to choose a new path for themselves because the impulse overwhelms the willpower to change. To have freedom of choice to abstain from such acts would require sturdier willpower to choose differently. As such, the freedom of choice and the will to make that choice could only happen by pushing themselves away from something that has been repeatedly noted by those who've successfully quit to control people's lives in a revolving habit of self-harm. As such, those who abstain and those who have overcome such self-harming habits of addiction are the ones with free will.

    If this redefinition of free will is true, then it means that the Abrahamic notion of free will and potentially of Original Sin as a concept is disproven. People are not choosing to behave as addicts and don't have the ability to stop. They lack the willpower to stop themselves from a self-harming habit that is destroying their lives. If those who stopped themselves from the bad habits are the ones with free will, then the Abrahamic concept of the term no longer has any coherence. The Abrahamic faiths built the notion of Original Sin on the basis that people were using free will to choose away from the Abrahamic God, but if stopping oneself from conducting an action is free will then people who attend Mosques, Churches, and Synagogues and stop themselves from conducting bad habits of addiction are the people with free will. By preventing yourself from conducting a harmful action, you are the one with free will and by following religious guidelines to abstain from harmful habits, you are practicing that free will. Those who aren't falling into temptations are the ones with free will and those who are falling into temptation don't have any free will to stop themselves. The belief that the temptations are a free choice is made completely incoherent under this redefinition of free will. If any of the Abrahamic faiths were to acknowledge this redefinition than 2000 years of history and the very basis of converting people to an Abrahamic religious faith would have to be thrown out,

---

    Between Baking Soda and Baking Powder Comments, 12 Mar. 2018, news.ncsu.edu/2018/03/free-will-review-2018/.

because it would mean that nobody is freely choosing to be away from the Abrahamic God, but instead they don't have the free will to choose the Abrahamic God. The Abrahamic theology becomes untenable and incoherent with modern neuroscience.

The redefinition of free will shatters the ethical justification for converting people to abstain from sin and the lack of free will under determinism disproves the very foundation of the Abrahamic faiths. In either scenario, Abrahamic theology collapses into incoherence and falsehood. To be clear, although I do have doubts about it and I am willing to entertain the possibility of this redefined version of free will, I still doubt that free will exists. In even more recent years, new studies of neuroscience show, that those who've suffered from having the portions of their brain that generate emotions damaged by accidents, are found to be unable to make decisions.[399] This finding suggests that at the moment you make any sort of choice, it is an emotional decision that is unified with logic and not separate from it.[400] If damage to the portions of our brain which give us emotions can stop us from making decisions at all, then why shouldn't this give further credence to the belief that free will doesn't exist? Notwithstanding, in either case of this redefined free will or the concept of determinism, there is no evidence to support the idea of free will in the Abrahamic context of the term.

The Misogyny of Sinfulness

To conclude the section on Original Sin and free will, I'd like for you to consider this metaphor with respect to how sinfulness is overtly misogynistic. This metaphor is a generalization of women with two definitive forms of belief systems; it is a generalization because it should obviously go without saying that half the human species has far more diversity in their plethora of beliefs. Encompassing each different denomination within just the Abrahamic tradition would be a monumental task that is beyond the scope of this book. As such, I've devised this metaphor pertaining to women who had faith in the Abrahamic God in ancient times to women of faith living now to compare with women who lived in equality among ancient hunter-gatherer societies and the Neolithic period of early civilization to the secular-leaning and scientifically minded women of modern times. They're referred to as the Woman of God and the Woman of Nature to express their respective modus operandi and beliefs. The primary purpose of this is to show the impact that the concept of sinfulness has on women.

The Woman of God is obedient and servile throughout her life to her father, her grandfather, sometimes her elder brother (usually if they are learned in the religious tradition), and her husband. She embodies Eve from the story of the Garden of Eden as her servility is in

---

38. [399] Camp, Jim. "Decisions Are Emotional, Not Logical: the Neuroscience behind Decision Making." *Big Think*, Big Think, 11 June 2012, bigthink.com/experts-corner/decisions-are-emotional-not-logical-the-neuroscience-behind-decision-making.
39. [400] Camp, Jim. "Decisions Are Emotional, Not Logical: the Neuroscience behind Decision Making." *Big Think*, Big Think, 11 June 2012, bigthink.com/experts-corner/decisions-are-emotional-not-logical-the-neuroscience-behind-decision-making.

service to God. Her life of subservience to her father and then her husband is through her strong faith in God. She is inculcated to be meek and humble in order to avoid scathing insults of being called promiscuous or labeled a whore for her disobedience to patriarchy. Her family and friends denigrate nude female protestors and nudity by women in pop culture by asking how their fathers feel about such behavior. She learns to accept sex abuse and rape by men as an expectation of society upon her and all women because traditional gender norms teach that men can't stop themselves from raping women when near them because of the tautology that boys will be boys. She is taught that women should know better than to trust in or befriend men in any platonic relationship because it is simply a given that men would rape women when near them. Rape is considered innate within men and therefore women must cover-up so men won't rape them. Her father, brothers, and husband who support this traditional role will demand respect from her by ordering her to stay covered. They reinforce this lesson by agreeing with arguments that men can't stop themselves from committing rape; essentially teaching her that they too would rape women if near any unmarried women that isn't their family. Neither men or women who practice traditional roles believe that men and women who aren't family can have any platonic relationship. The patriarchal structure incidentally teach that any rape or sex abuse that she receives is because she didn't wear clothes that covered herself enough to protect her purity or that her discomfort and confusion over the situation was somehow consent when she simply didn't know how to handle being violated.

    The Woman of God is taught that she has no agency throughout her life. At purity balls, they teach her that God is her Father and her biological father is akin to a boyfriend.[401] Her faith in God commands that she must honor her father by treating her virginity as a prize to be won only by her future husband.[402] Her body is like candy and she must not unwrap her lower garments to avoid spoiling herself.[403] She acts as her father's personal dog; she is to be kept near the family home and not outside to socialize for fear she'll be doing something embarrassing or dangerous without supervision, she is to behave like a neutered animal without any explanation or assistance for her sexual development of puberty, she is not to lose her dog collar - her virginity - or she'll be considered wild and rabid by her conservative society, and she is to smile and behave in a constant state of silliness and happiness for being thoroughly domesticated by strict, unequal standards towards women. She is only to express a constant state of appreciation, affection, and celebrate of her obedience to patriarchy as proof of

---

40. [401] Valenti, Jessica. "Purity Balls, Plan B and Bad Sex Policy: inside America's Virginity Obsession | Jessica Valenti." *The Guardian*, Guardian News and Media, 5 May 2014,
41. [402] Frank, Priscilla. "Welcome To The Bizarre And Beautiful World Of Purity Balls." *The Huffington Post*, TheHuffingtonPost.com, 7 Dec. 2017, www.huffingtonpost.com/2014/05/05/purity-ball-photos_n_5255904.html.
42. [403] Haider, Sarah, et al. "Islam, Modesty and Feminism." *YouTube*, Ex-Muslims of North America, 12 Oct. 2017, www.youtube.com/watch?v=QToH2x8njJM.

honoring her family and her society. The social status of her male family members reinforces what God has ordained for her life.[404]

The Woman of God is celebrated for accepting her role as property of her father and later to be transferred as property of her husband. She will rear her husband's children to be obedient to their father; her life is one of cooking, cleaning, and conditioning herself to always sexually please her husband when he commands it of her; that is, to use her body as he sees fit with her having no opinion on how he uses her. Often beatings and rape cannot be considered a crime because the husband does it. Her religious community and religious leaders all herald her conceding her autonomy and body to her husband as fulfilling the role that God gave her. Euphemisms of "respecting" the husband are used to pressure her into giving up her autonomy. She is to embody the ideal of servility and humbleness with her dutiful submission to her husband and piety towards God. She is to be seen, not heard; she is not to speak out of turn or embarrass the men of her household so that their social status to their community isn't negatively impacted. She is taught that this has always been the role of women, that this role is innate in all women throughout human history, and that she must avoid sinfulness at all costs. She must remain servile in service to God for all of her life; this celebration of her purity comes from ancient times when God ordered women to be converted through rape as spoils of war for the chosen people. These rape conversions are celebrated as morally benevolent to this day because God commanded it. *Thereby, the Woman of God is historically derived from conquered women who suffered war rape at the behest of the Abrahamic God.* The more literally that you believe in the Bible or the Quran, the more you should accept that as the unequivocal truth of history.

The Woman of Nature speaks and acts independently from her family with confidence and views herself equally to men. She expresses her sexuality through independent choices of picking her own clothes or forming her own intimate relationships; nobody in her family is to have privilege in deciding who she has sexual relations with upon adulthood.[405] She practices contraceptives and safe sexual behavior to maximize her own pleasure in sex. She sees past the ideals of traditional gender norms that create misogynistic disparities on the treatment of women; she rebukes back that such disparities are systems of oppression formed by rape culture in which women are to act passive to being raped to protect men's egos. She is viewed as a wild, rabid dog by men and women who hold traditional gender roles because she refuses to submit to patriarchy. Her raw indignation comes from the intrinsic desire to be seen and heard as a person and not as property of men. Instances of men raping women causes her to demand change; after all, why should she have to suffer and be held back by the stupidity of others? Why should she have to wait, and wait, and wait for change to come in some imaginary

---

43. [404] Haider, Sarah, et al. "Islam, Modesty and Feminism." *YouTube*, Ex-Muslims of North America, 12 Oct. 2017, www.youtube.com/watch?v=QToH2x8njJM.
44. [405] Haider, Sarah, et al. "Islam, Modesty and Feminism." *YouTube*, Ex-Muslims of North America, 12 Oct. 2017, www.youtube.com/watch?v=QToH2x8njJM.

future instead of having enlightenment now? Why should she and other women have to wait for more rape victims because others refuse to change traditional norms due to their circular reasoning of "boys will be boys" and "women should know better" that she easily sees through with her intellect?[406] If she is labeled a rabid dog that is diseased and unwelcome back into the family and society, then is she simply expected to suffer for the crime of personal autonomy and independent thought?[407] In fact, sometimes the Woman of Nature is even put to death for the crime of independent thought and personal autonomy; whether by angry husbands, angry family, or angry boyfriends because they refuse to see her as a person and kill her for not acting as property of men.

The Woman of Nature embodies Lilith. She seeks sexual satisfaction by trying various sexual positions such as being atop her significant other regardless of if God allows it or not. She is open to different sexual positions, self-pleasure, research into understanding and loving her body instead of feeling wretched for being born a woman, and doesn't loathe herself for the natural process of having a period. She journeys into the moral abyss to find satisfaction for her cravings in the carnal world of humanity. She rejects the existence of God as a falsehood due to lack of evidence for God and sees the theology as a tool of misogynistic oppression. She gains the pleasures of the carnal world; art, music, books, video games, other electronic devices, political freedoms of free speech and free expression, and reforming systems of man-made government to value her life equally to any male counterpart through a right to protection by the law. The Woman of Nature who pursues skeptical inquiry and scientific studies is utterly condemned as the natural enemy of God for all her life; this is because she finds immense pleasure and satisfaction in studying, researching, and disseminating her lifelong love for the carnal world above the spiritual capitulation to God as commanded by patriarchy.[408]

The Scientific Woman of Nature, even when she wants no part in the discussion of religion versus science because she has no interest, will always be condemned for the crime of independent thought, will find her love for research shut down or reviled by those who act with the sincerest faith in God, and will be the first to be murdered in service to God because she is labeled as God's truest enemy by extremists when they gain power.[409] Due to ignorance of religious teachings, the Scientific Woman of Nature will be confused by she is being reviled and condemned when she has abstained from criticism and has no desire to be part of any discussion on religion because she sincerely doesn't care. She doesn't understand why her love for research and fact-finding studies is faced with a surge of ignorant contempt, she tries to find peaceful measures to stymie the tide of hatred through calls of peace but confuses the intrinsic

---

45. [406] "Circular Reasoning." *Https://Www.logicallyfallacious.com*, www.logicallyfallacious.com/tools/lp/Bo/LogicalFallacies/66/Circular-Reasoning.
46. [407] Haider, Sarah, et al. "Islam, Modesty and Feminism." *YouTube*, Ex-Muslims of North America, 12 Oct. 2017, www.youtube.com/watch?v=QToH2x8njJM.
47. [408] Nietzsche, Friedrich Wilhelm. Aphorism 48. *THE ANTICHRIST*. Translated by H. L. Mencken, The Project Gutenberg, 2006.
48. [409] Nietzsche, Friedrich Wilhelm. *THE ANTICHRIST*. Translated by H. L. Mencken, The Project Gutenberg, 2006.

misogyny of religion for some extremist elements co-opting a religion to push a narrative, she is blamed by some of her colleagues and boss for the crime of pursuing research that doesn't conform to some arbitrary religious ideal that she has no interest in and is not part of, and genuinely tries appeasement as a last resort and it only causes the destruction of her research, her peace of mind, and leads to bitterness and indignation at the vat of reactionary ignorance that is thrust upon her for no discernible reason.[410] What she fails to understand is that these loud, obnoxious religious zealots don't view her as a person, but rather as property by men to be chided and owned. They don't wish to be appeased by meeting in the middle; they wish to destroy her ability to research and question.[411] They wish to destroy her social safety net to prove the appeasement to faith in their God as the ultimate deciding factor in society even when it doesn't make sense. They wish to destroy her livelihood, her ability to pursue her own interests as an individual capable of independent thought, and to kill her or drive her to suicide; if that fails, then to destroy her career and her children's future. All they believe is that she must conform to their religious patriarchal structure because of their complete faith in God's unquestionable morality.[412]

Therefore, the only way to engage on an equal field when being vilified is to attack the assumptions of their religious faith as the falsehood that she knows it to be. To defend and protect the carnal pleasures of enlightenment values of free speech and free expression against the misogynistic tyranny of God. The Woman of Nature must rebuke their hatred with genuine criticism by expressing her independent actions and opinions against the belief that her ability to be an independent person is sinfulness.[413] Most of all, the Woman of Nature should come to understand that there is no intrinsic value in religious teachings that are espoused by revealed wisdom. The ancient Hebrew Bible depicts instance after instance of rape of women after war conquests, the Sermon on the Mount is the origin of the Male Gaze through thought crimes based on how men should view women, and the Quran practiced and spread slavery including the sexual slavery of women. All in the name of purity culture so that women remain faithful to God.

The Woman of Nature should consider what the Woman of God was derived from:

The Abrahamic God ordered his chosen people to conquer other lands through violence, the violence of God's chosen people was justified through dehumanization campaigns about the defeated people's culture, and upon their victory the chosen people of God were ordered by God to rape women who didn't believe in him. These women were

---

49. [410] Nietzsche, Friedrich Wilhelm. Aphorism 49. *THE ANTICHRIST*. Translated by H. L. Mencken, The Project Gutenberg, 2006.
50. [411] Nietzsche, Friedrich Wilhelm. Aphorism 48. *THE ANTICHRIST*. Translated by H. L. Mencken, The Project Gutenberg, 2006.
51. [412] Nietzsche, Friedrich Wilhelm. Aphorism 48. *THE ANTICHRIST*. Translated by H. L. Mencken, The Project Gutenberg, 2006.
52. [413] Haider, Sarah, et al. "Islam, Modesty and Feminism." *YouTube*, Ex-Muslims of North America, 12 Oct. 2017, www.youtube.com/watch?v=QToH2x8njJM.

forced into believing in the Abrahamic God through conquest after being raped by God's decree; this was forcible conversion through rape by the tens of thousands as written in the Bible and the Quran.

The teachings of purity culture are derived from decrees of rape by the Abrahamic God. A holistic examination of the conservative religious values imposed upon women shows this.

- *A Woman of God is taught to be servile to her husband: the origin of this is the conquering victors of war ordering the women they raped into being obedient to them, so the male rapist that just took ownership of her will have an easier time controlling her through "marriage" which back then was simply ownership of women.*
- *A Woman of God is taught to not speak out against the husband or father: this comes from male rapists ordering women they raped and married to shut up about their family having been butchered and wiped out by the chosen people of the Abrahamic God. They are to be seen and not heard because no one wants to deal with her emotional anguish at losing her entire family and no one wants her foreign opinions in their in-group of primitive civilization.*
- *A Woman of God is taught to cover-up her body or men will rape her: this comes from a male having raped and married his victim having to then worry that other men might try to rape and marry her or act out with such behavior accidentally upon her when he's already taken ownership and raped her. To stymie this possibility, he orders her to cover-up to avoid getting raped by his compatriots who are raping other women. Men rape women all the time in their primitive civilizations, unlike in hunter-gatherer and Neolithic societies where she use to be a Woman of Nature.*
- *If a Woman of God expresses her views like a Woman of Nature, then she is denigrated for devil worship and sinfulness, unreliable rumors of her sleeping around are made-up to justify violence upon her person, and she is stoned to death because the Abrahamic God decrees that she is to remain property and not a person in ancient Abrahamic society of primitive civilizations. There is no tolerance for her opinions and if she expresses opinions like an equal, then she will be stoned to death for the crime of wanting equality. This is because she is decreed property, not a person by the Abrahamic God.*

Chapter 8: Judaism

"In an official dispatch sent to battalion and company commanders on July 9, Givati Brigade commander Colonel Ofer Winter told his subordinates that "History has chosen us to spearhead the fighting (against) the terrorist 'Gazan' enemy which abuses, blasphemes and curses the God of Israel's (defense) forces."

The letter came to light as Israel gears up for possible ground operations against Hamas in the Palestinian territory. A ground incursion would in all likelihood involve the Givati Brigade.

"We have planned and prepared for this moment and we take the mission upon ourselves out of commitment, complete humility, and because we are prepared to endanger ourselves and lay down our lives in order to protect our families, our people and our homeland," he wrote in the letter.

Winter then invoked the Shema — the traditional Jewish prayer of allegiance to the one God — and called upon "the God of Israel" to "make our path successful as we go and stand to fight for the sake of your people of Israel against a foe which curses your name."

Mickey Gitzin, executive director of Israel Hofshit — an organization which promotes religious freedom — called the letter outrageous, according to a report on Walla News.

"It turns the conflict from a one against terror to a religious war on any resident of Gaza," Gitzin said. He added that there was a growing phenomenon of religious terminology entering the military and called the trend extremely dangerous."[414] – Times of Israel staff, *"IDF commander seeks God's help to fight 'blasphemous' Gazans"* from the *Times of Israel*.

    I emphatically apologize for any possible offensive remarks that any of the following may cause. The following arguments are meant to critique the negative effects of Judaism and are not meant to support, justify, encourage, or mock the horrible persecutions and genocide that Jewish people have suffered throughout history. Unfortunately, the subject matter also pertains to the political issue of Israel-Palestine and I shall be critiquing the negative impact of Judaism upon the political issue of the Israel-Palestine conflict. Most of the critique in this chapter will be centered around contemporary political issues and the purported historicity of Jewish theology. I fear that this will be my weakest chapter in this book, so for Jewish readers interested in critiquing or converting to any of the other religious faiths mentioned, I recommend reading the entire book to compare problems of that specific theology to either what it is that you like about it or to further help your arsenal of criticisms.

---

1. [414] Toi, et al. "IDF Commander Seeks God's Help to Fight 'Blasphemous' Gazans." *The Times of Israel*, www.timesofisrael.com/idf-commander-calls-on-troops-to-fight-blasphemous-gazans/.

The war between Israel and Palestine, along with its socioeconomic reasons, is a religious war. The religious nature of the conflict isn't solely on the side of the Palestinians. Since before its re-founding, Jewish immigrants fled to the so-called holy land for protection and largely because of religious reasons. British policies and then a British mandate created the Israel-Palestine conflict and it only worsened as years went on. The declaration of the State of Israel, the declaration of a right to return, the more recent actions of Israel establishing itself as a Jewish State, and only allowing Jewish settlers entrance are all for explicitly religious reasons originating from the Old Testament. You may disagree, but consider what establishing a Jewish State means: it's a theocratic declaration and a purportedly race-based declaration. As of 2018, this has become more solidified thanks to Israel's Nation-State law which states Israel is a Jewish State and the original version of the law attempted to supersede democratic rights with Jewish religious customs.[415] That is a clear attempt by the Likud party of the Prime Minister Benjamin Netanyahu at a Jewish theocracy taking paramount importance over a democratic form of government. Israel has allowed Jewish people a right to return but makes it more difficult for non-Jewish people. Sadly, Israel does have race-based laws against Arabs including Arab Jews and is known for racial discrimination against minority groups.[416] The underlying reason for these issues, and the Israel-Palestine conflict, is the belief that Israel is a holy land for the Jews as granted by God and that they must await the coming of the messiah so that the dead rise and God's Chosen people enter a Millennium Kingdom. This belief is what has motivated a Jewish return to the holy land and is principally the reason why there wasn't a Jewish State created in Europe or in the United States.

If denizens of Western civilizations are suppose to believe that the Middle East is full of religious extremism and anti-Semitism then under what basis is it rational to encourage Jewish people to live in a small plot of land that has them surrounded by grave threats to their safety from neighboring countries that mean to harm them? The sole reason for the creation of Israel and for the right to "return" is explicitly religious in nature. Even accounting for terrorist attacks in the US and Europe and the terrifying rise of Nazism, it is likely safer for Jewish people to live within Europe and the US instead of a small plot of land in the Middle East where they must deal with the possibility of a nuclear Iran, the wars with Hamas, and the instability in the region. As of right now, either Iran is going to get a nuclear weapon or Saudi Arabia is and neither nation-state has positive relations with Israel. The nation-state of Israel is important and I absolutely support its existence, but it is also important to consider alternative views on the long-term safety of Jewish people. Israel exists as a trap for Jewish people that even the Israeli nuclear arms may not safeguard. Israel's 3 billion a year in free arms from the US won't be able to protect Israel forever should the US economy crash and it is less

---

2. [415] Lis, Jonathan. "Israel's Contentious Nation-State Law: Everything You Need to Know." *Haaretz.com*, Haaretz Com, 19 July 2018, www.haaretz.com/israel-news/.premium-israel-s-contentious-nation-state-law-everything-you-need-to-know-1.6292733?=&ts=_1532742032458.
3. [416] "Israel." *U.S. Department of State*, U.S. Department of State, 14 May 2018, www.state.gov/r/pa/ei/bgn/3581.htm.

comforting when people take into account that the US sells billions to other Gulf States under Islamic dictators that often end-up in the hands of terrorists like al Qaeda.[417][418] Judaism has served to ensnare the Jewish people into a vicious cycle where they need billions of dollars in weapons to protect themselves from Islamic nation-states that gain weapons from the US every year.[419] This "balance of power" and arms trade can never last and a nuclear Iran or Saudi Arabia will change the so-called stability of the region. For all its "Je Suis Charlie", France seems interested in helping the Islamic monarchy of Saudi Arabia have nuclear weapons.[420] This would be the second time that France aided to create nuclear facilities for an authoritarian government since they helped create nuclear reactors for Saddam Hussein of Iraq before Israel destroyed them. Of course, in more recent times, the US Presidential administration of Donald Trump similar to his predecessor President Obama, has sought to give Saudi Arabia nuclear capabilities; both Democrat and Republican administrations of the United States are under the woeful self-delusion that the Saudis won't immediately start selling the technology to terrorists like Al Qaeda or forces similar to ISIS.[421] The mutual incompetence of both major US political parties will likely cause irreparable harm.

Awaiting the Messiah?

Judaism has a fundamental flaw in its theology that results in horrific circumstances for Jewish people. This theological failure may have partially influenced anti-Semitism throughout the history of Judaism. That is not meant to justify or condone the horrible crimes against Jewish people throughout history as those who discriminate and use violence bear full responsibility for their actions, but this flaw in Jewish theology should be highlighted:

The Coming of the Messiah is a communal delusion that leads to sectarianism and persecution of the Jewish community. When Jewish people find a Messiah of God and fully accept the Messiah as legitimate, then these followers become part of a new faith.[422] The people of the new faith then try to convince the other Jewish people and convert them to the new faith because the followers sincerely believe that God sent the new Messiah.[423] This causes division within the Jewish community, some Jewish people convert and other Jewish

---

4. [417] Sharp, Jeremy M. "U.S. Foreign Aid to Israel - Federation of American Scientists." *FAS.ORG*, Congressional Research Service, fas.org/sgp/crs/mideast/RL33222.pdf.
5. [418] Browne, Ryan, and Oscar Featherstone. "US Arms Sold to Saudi Arabia and UAE End up in Wrong Hands." *CNN*, Cable News Network, www.cnn.com/interactive/2019/02/middleeast/yemen-lost-us-arms/.
6. [419] Hartung, William D. "It's Not Diplomacy, It's an Arms Fair." *Foreign Policy*, Foreign Policy, 14 May 2015, foreignpolicy.com/2015/05/14/obama-arms-fair-camp-david-weapons-sales-gcc/
7. [420] Toi. "France to Study Building Nuclear Reactors in Saudi Arabia." *The Times of Israel*, www.timesofisrael.com/france-to-study-building-nuclear-reactors-in-saudi-arabia/.
8. [421] Daly, Matthew. "US Approves Deal to Share Nuclear Tech with Saudi Arabia." *The Times of Israel*, www.timesofisrael.com/us-approves-deal-to-share-nuclear-tech-with-saudi-arabia/.
9. [422] Nietzsche, Friedrich Wilhelm. *THE ANTICHRIST*. Translated by H. L. Mencken, The Project Gutenberg, 2006.
10. [423] Nietzsche, Friedrich Wilhelm. *THE ANTICHRIST*. Translated by H. L. Mencken, The Project Gutenberg, 2006.

people perceive the "new Messiah" as a deceiver and condemn the new faith as having deviated from God. Thus, discrimination, persecution, and cultural barriers inevitably form from the theology of Judaism.[424] The new messiahs will either be embraced or be regarded as deceivers: the people who accept the new messiah will see their old community as having deviated and deceived themselves away from God, the old followers will see the new faith as being a deviation and vile deception that is against God, and persecution along with forced conversions inexorably follow because of the framework of Jewish theology being zero-sum for the salvation of God for the chosen people.[425] Thus, the Abrahamic God can never be a pillar of peace for the Jews. The theological system of Judaism results in the endless persecution of the Jews through their own religion transforming into a new one. The coming of a Messiah just creates religious sectarianism and civil wars. In fact, the historical persecution of Jews by Christians and Muslims is clear evidence of this theological folly. Christians persecuted Jews for centuries under the belief that Jewish people killed Jesus Christ, Jesus Christ's explicit anti-Semitic overtones in his teachings was probably a factor (John 8:21-44), and there were mass killings and forced conversions throughout almost two thousand years of European history.[426][427] Islam was no different to the Jews. Jews were persecuted first by Christianity and then by Islam; both currently hold a patronizing attitude that Jews and the rest of the world are simply misguided and need to convert as some type of "upgrade" to the supposedly truer faiths. Christianity and Islam are only known as distinct religions from Judaism because of the bloody history regarding all three faiths. Yet, they all believe in the same God but through different Prophets / Messiahs or different ways of having faith in of a Messiah figure. Christianity and Islam aren't distinctly different faiths; they're subsets of Judaism that are only perceived as different because of the horrible history that was formed from a flawed theology within Judaism itself. In the end, Judaism only functions to create religions that try to convert Jewish people away from Judaism. Therefore, the conclusion of Jewish theology will always lead to new faiths trying to convince Jewish people to give-up on Judaism.

This is an issue that comes directly from Judaism and faiths that Judaism inadvertently created. Jews have been persecuted by the off-shoot religions of Judaism, but in a shocking contrast there has never been any historical event of Hindus, Sikhs, Jains, or Buddhists persecuting Jews in Asia.[428] For all the negatives thrown upon India and the Eastern faiths, there was never a persecution of Jews in any records of Eastern religious history for over 2000

---

11. [424] Nietzsche, Friedrich Wilhelm. *THE ANTICHRIST*. Translated by H. L. Mencken, The Project Gutenberg, 2006.
12. [425] Nietzsche, Friedrich Wilhelm. *THE ANTICHRIST*. Translated by H. L. Mencken, The Project Gutenberg, 2006.
13. [426] "BibleGateway." *Bible Gateway*, Bible Gateway Blog, www.biblegateway.com/passage/?search=John 8:21-44&version=KJV.
14. [427] "Timeline of Antisemitism." *Wikipedia*, Wikimedia Foundation, 27 Mar. 2019, en.wikipedia.org/wiki/Timeline_of_antisemitism.
15. [428] Moses, Nissim. "Bene Israel of India." *Avotaynu Online*, 24 Mar. 2015, www.avotaynuonline.com/2007/07/bene-israel-of-india-by-nissim-moses/.

years ever since Jews fled from Jerusalem and certain Jewish groups came to India for refuge in the 7th BC and prior.[429][430][431] Judaism and Hinduism have never warred with each other nor did Buddhism and Judaism or the other Eastern faiths according to historical records that we have so far.[432] It is likely because they didn't originate from Jewish theology and don't have underpinnings about a sacred holy land that causes the persecution of Jewish people. From ancient times to modern times, Western and Islamic cultures are the only cultures responsible for the genocides, forced conversions, and mass killings of Jewish people. The Eastern cultures were largely peaceful to the Jewish people and accommodating to their welfare. While there are histories of discrimination and violence within the subsets of their own religions; overall Judaism, Hinduism, Sikhism, Jainism, and Buddhism are among the most peaceful faiths in the world when interacting with each other. There is no history of violence against Jewish tribes in India and Buddhism is seen as favorable to many Jewish people who are unsure of their faith.[433][434] It is because there is no conflict or aggressive attitude towards Jewish people. By contrast, the two off-shoots of Judaism – Christianity and Islam – are both war-like reinterpretations of Judaism.

Zionism: Two Perspectives

This portion was incredibly difficult to write, I nearly scrapped the entire book because of the cultural fear in US social norms that I'd be perceived as an anti-Semite for ruthlessly critiquing the problems of Zionist ideology. I have been so conflicted in writing this and for any general criticism of Israel because of the cultural norms in the US of equating any meaningful critique to discrimination against Jewish people. However, my near-abandonment of this book and the hopes I placed in the attacks on US Free Speech eventually dwindling never materialized. The problems only became worse and the threats to the First Amendment rights and Free Speech as an ideology are more dire than half a decade ago. As such, and due to my own commitment to academic integrity, I must criticize this as religiously motivated fascism because the political ideology of Zionism fundamentally shouts down criticism with ad hominem accusations that anyone who disagrees is a Holocaust denier or somehow wishes ill upon all Jewish people, but also supports Holocaust denial for its political aims of censuring any Free speech criticisms and gaining political and perhaps financial support from right-wing

---

16. [429] Weiss, Gary. "India's Jews." *Forbes*, Forbes Magazine, 17 July 2012, www.forbes.com/2007/08/05/india-jews-antisemitism-oped-cx_gw_0813jews.html#4d526e5f3d45.
17. [430] Moses, Nissim. "Bene Israel of India." *Avotaynu Online*, 24 Mar. 2015, www.avotaynuonline.com/2007/07/bene-israel-of-india-by-nissim-moses/.
18. [431] Johnson, Barbara C. "The Cochin Jews Of Kerala." *My Jewish Learning*, www.myjewishlearning.com/article/the-cochin-jews-of-kerala/.
19. [432] Moses, Nissim. "Bene Israel of India." *Avotaynu Online*, 24 Mar. 2015, www.avotaynuonline.com/2007/07/bene-israel-of-india-by-nissim-moses/.
20. [433] Johnson, Barbara C. "The Cochin Jews Of Kerala." *My Jewish Learning*, www.myjewishlearning.com/article/the-cochin-jews-of-kerala/.
21. [434] Moses, Nissim. "Bene Israel of India." *Avotaynu Online*, 24 Mar. 2015, www.avotaynuonline.com/2007/07/bene-israel-of-india-by-nissim-moses/.

demagogues in various European countries teetering closer to fascism.[435][436] There's no longer any rational sense to this religiously motivated ideology and refusing to criticize it on Free Speech grounds only seems to strengthen it.

For those who don't know, Zionism is the Right-Wing ideology of Israeli politics and comprises of the more religious and militaristic mindset of Israel. Zionism is championed by the Likud party, the Right-wing of Israeli politics, and AIPAC in the United States. As of this writing in 2018, Zionism pushes its political agenda by obfuscating any criticism of Israel by conflating it with Holocaust denial and other forms of anti-Semitism.[437][438] Notwithstanding, Benjamin Netanyahu and his cohorts in the Likud party now support revisionist Holocaust history and Holocaust denial in European politics so long as the political parties of the countries doing so support Zionism.[439] At the same time, in US universities and US public discourse, they push an annual political campaign to silence any dissenting voices of Israel's human rights crimes by equating criticism of Israel with anti-Semitism and Holocaust denial.[440] Meanwhile, they get free aid from US taxpayers who evidently aren't allowed to question their policies unless they wish for the US media to espouse character assassinations of them.[441]

The first critique will be the end of this chapter, it is what I had originally believed, for what it's worth. I think I suffered from cognitive dissonance myself, since I was committing the No True Scotsman fallacy without recognizing it as such. The lengthy portion in the next chapter is my current critique of Zionism and its harmful effects on democratic free speech norms and laws. I'm sorry, but I had to make it clear that such problems can't be excused or ignored. Free Speech and Free Inquiry is the bedrock of a democratic country. I'd like to make it absolutely clear that I don't and will never support violence against Jewish people or any form of anti-Jewish bigotry.

Zionism: The Slow Christianizing of Judaism

Zionism is an utter subversion of Judaism's peaceful nature, by celebrating and exacerbating the religious conflict over the so-called holy land. It has done little more than

22. [435] Shalev, Chemi. "Hungary PM Orban's Upcoming Visit: A Stain on Israel's History." *Haaretz.com*, Haaretz Com, 3 July 2018, www.haaretz.com/israel-news/.premium-hungary-pm-orban-s-upcoming-visit-a-blot-on-netanyahu-s-record-and-a-stain-on-israel-s-history-1.6223675.
23. [436] *YouTube*, The Intercept, 23 Aug. 2018, www.youtube.com/watch?v=3yr0G50rL28.
24. [437] Mackey, Robert. "University of California Adopts Policy Linking Anti-Zionism to Anti-Semitism." *The Intercept*, 23 Mar. 2016, theintercept.com/2016/03/23/university-of-california-adopts-policy-linking-anti-zionism-to-anti-semitism/.
25. [438] Beinart, Peter. "American Jewish Establishment Stifles Free Speech to Silence Zionism's Critics." *Haaretz.com*, Haaretz Com, 24 Apr. 2018, www.haaretz.com/opinion/.premium-how-zionism-is-losing-the-contest-of-ideas-in-the-u-s-1.5470232.
26. [439] *YouTube*, The Intercept, 23 Aug. 2018, www.youtube.com/watch?v=3yr0G50rL28.
27. [440] Hussain, Murtaza. "Students in California Might Face Criminal Investigation for Protesting Film on Israeli Army." *The Intercept*, 23 June 2016, theintercept.com/2016/06/23/students-in-california-might-face-criminal-investigation-for-protesting-film-on-israeli-army/.
28. [441] "U.S. Foreign Aid to Israel: Total Aid." *Jewish Virtual Library*, www.jewishvirtuallibrary.org/total-u-s-foreign-aid-to-israel-1949-present.

harm the peaceful history of Judaism. Zionism has tried to turn the tragedy of the Holocaust into war propaganda to wage war upon Palestine. There is an organized reliance of aid from Evangelical Christian fundamentalists who yearn for Israel's annihilation for a deluded prophecy about the Coming of Jesus.[442] The level of obfuscation, misdirection, and dishonesty over the religious reasons for warring against Palestine is only matched by the level of dishonesty, misdirection, and obfuscation of the religious reasons for Evangelical Christians giving aid to Israel which is for the sake of its annihilation so that Jesus will purportedly come down from heaven.[443] Attempts at arguing that the support is for the aid of the Jewish people is an explicit lie; if they believe in the Coming of Jesus, which Evangelicals obviously do, then they must believe in the biblical prophecy that states the land of Israel will be annihilated and that Jews will be cast into hell to be judged by Satan.[444] The Israeli peoples are simply playing into the manipulations of Evangelical Christians who believe that any peace between Israel and Palestine will bring about the Anti-Christ.[445] Such delusional thinking should be ignored, but instead the Israel-Palestine peace agreements have never been settled and politicians from the US constantly parrot the ignorant bile that the issue is simply too complex for them. It's an admittance of the US government's longstanding incompetence over the issue because of the religious nature of issue and because it serves to encourage certain Christian soldiers into fighting different Islamic areas around Israel for the sake of protecting it for the Coming of Jesus.[446] In other words, albeit paradoxically, for the sake of Israel's total annihilation; Zionists have worked with Evangelical Christian fundamentalists to accomplish the goal and promoted the right to return across Europe and the US.[447] Both sides working in tandem while secretly thinking the other religious faith are delusional under the belief that they're attempting to use them as pawns. Judaism has lowered itself to the war-like nature of Christianity and fights against Islam to protect Christian interests in the region. Israel wasn't a gift from the West after the Holocaust; the West simply used Jewish people as pawns to fight against Islam for their own interests in the region. Currently, Israel can only exist through the billions every year given by the US and Europe; the US can only function as the most powerful nation-state through the petrodollar system with the Islamic dictators of the region. Israel is thus a pawn of both US interests and Islamic interests. American journalists showing footage of the wars in Gaza, to distract from political interests in other locations, are slowly creating condemnation for Israel so that culpability is solely placed upon Israelis. Showing "support" for Israel through violent imagery on US national news with the full support of Jewish business owners and politicians isn't actually a favorable depiction of Israel. It fuels condemnation and disgust with Israel, Israeli policies, and supports feelings of Christian superiority over Jewish people. It galvanizes and increases the ranks of neo-Nazis across the world. If the US government and

---

29. [442] *YouTube*, Q-Ball Productions Inc, 2010, www.youtube.com/watch?v=nNvtA_q0e20.
30. [443] *YouTube*, Q-Ball Productions Inc, 2010, www.youtube.com/watch?v=nNvtA_q0e20.
31. [444] *YouTube*, Q-Ball Productions Inc, 2010, www.youtube.com/watch?v=nNvtA_q0e20.
32. [445] *YouTube*, Q-Ball Productions Inc, 2010, www.youtube.com/watch?v=nNvtA_q0e20.
33. [446] *YouTube*, Q-Ball Productions Inc, 2010, www.youtube.com/watch?v=nNvtA_q0e20.
34. [447] *YouTube*, Q-Ball Productions Inc, 2010, www.youtube.com/watch?v=nNvtA_q0e20.

US businesses truly cared about supporting Israel, then they wouldn't show the images at all. Instead this "support" for Israel leads to blaming Israel for the political controversy and the US government can ignore its own culpability on the matter to its citizens for their tax dollars funding the weapons used upon Palestinians.[448][449] Islamic TV stations showing images of Gaza would only fuel further anti-Semitism. Thus, Jewish theology is fueling nationalistic pride and hatred for Israel for both Christendom and Islam. Most of this public support and denial of any Israeli war crimes comes from Zionism and Zionism remains silent about Evangelical Christians proselytizing in Israel to convert Jewish people.[450] It is a complete squandering of time, effort, and technology on the part of the Jewish people for what can only harm them in the end.

How can war with Palestine, Lebanon, Iran, and other areas be positive for Israeli interests? It is forcing Israel to commit to more aid from Europe and the US, to continue being controlled by foreign interests, and squandering the power, human resources, and treasure of Israel for a meaningless prophecy that has no value.[451][452] Jewish people are among the most highly intelligent, hardworking and peaceful people that history has ever seen and Zionism is squandering their talents and spitting on their peaceful history for the sake of war propaganda. Holocaust survivors and Haaretz have published condemnation for the Zionist use of Nazi logos to create support for the annihilation of Palestinians.[453] They have physically assaulted Left-wing Israelis for an anti-war demonstration. These actions are as far removed as possible from people who have created some of the greatest breakthrough and technological advances in modern science, psychology, politics, and so much more. To this day, neo-Nazis groups like the Ku Klux Klan in the US espouse ridiculous conspiracy theories out of jealousy of how hardworking and intelligent Jewish people are and still try to recruit US war veterans to their cause. The US government remains largely silent about this sustained trend of anti-Semitism against Jewish people.

The argument that nuclear capabilities will protect Israel isn't a cogent argument. The idea of mutually assured self-destruction seems altogether misanthropic and the West would be able to indemnify their own culpability of creating the conditions for conflict between Israel

35. [448] Sharp, Jeremy M. "U.S. Foreign Aid to Israel - Federation of American Scientists." *FAS.ORG*, Congressional Research Service, fas.org/sgp/crs/mideast/RL33222.pdf.
36. [449] Kennard, Matthew. "The Cruel Experiments of Israel's Arms Industry." *The Electronic Intifada*, 27 June 2017, electronicintifada.net/content/cruel-experiments-israels-arms-industry/19011.
37. [450] *YouTube*, Q-Ball Productions Inc, 2010, www.youtube.com/watch?v=nNvtA_q0e20.
38. [451] Dorell, Oren. "U.S. $38B Military Aid Package to Israel Sends a Message." *USA Today*, Gannett Satellite Information Network, 14 Sept. 2016, www.usatoday.com/story/news/world/2016/09/14/united-states-military-aid-israel/90358564/.
39. [452] Rosenblatt, Lauren, et al. "US Seeks to Increase Aid to Israel by $200M in 2019." *The Pittsburgh Jewish Chronicle*, jewishchronicle.timesofisrael.com/us-seeks-to-increase-aid-to-israel-by-200m-in-2019/.
40. [453] Gouri, Daniel, et al. "Holocaust Survivors Condemn Israel for 'Gaza Massacre,' Call for Boycott." *Haaretz.com*, Haaretz Com, 10 Apr. 2018, www.haaretz.com/holocaust-survivors-condemn-israel-for-gaza-massacre-1.5260588#.VMR7SI5whq8.twitter.

and its neighbors by blaming Israel or one of the Gulf States. Furthermore, certain parties in the US may have found benefits for utilizing Israel's subsidiary status and the conflict between Israel-Palestine:

- The media exposure of Israel's actions to indemnify US government involvement in the ongoing conflict.
- The leaks and free aid of US weapons to Israel to test the weapon capabilities in a real combat zone and, as a consequence, using Palestinians as the experiments.[454]
- To study the psychological effects of prolonged war to find the best solutions to help soldiers.[455]
- To conflate real Judaism with Zionism to then blame the majority of Jewish people for the sake of Christian self-exaltation by viewing themselves and their nation-states as better than a predominately Jewish country.
- To gain sustained military recruitment from Evangelical Christians for the US military.[456]

---

41. [454] Kennard, Matthew. "The Cruel Experiments of Israel's Arms Industry." *The Electronic Intifada*, 27 June 2017, electronicintifada.net/content/cruel-experiments-israels-arms-industry/19011.
42. [455] Gross, Judah Ari. "Suicide Was Top Cause of Death for IDF Soldiers in 2016." *The Times of Israel*, www.timesofisrael.com/idf-15-soldiers-committed-suicide-in-the-past-year/.
43. [456] *YouTube*, Q-Ball Productions Inc, 2010, www.youtube.com/watch?v=nNvtA_q0e20.

Chapter 9: Zionism versus Free Speech

This portion is quite lengthy, but I feel it was all necessary to cite and show because I fear that I would be seen as some crackpot moron, if I didn't explicitly show the sources. Before I begin with this chapter, I want it to be known that I was genuinely afraid of being physically attacked and especially of having any future career options destroyed. Notwithstanding, thanks to the mishandling of the US economy, it turns out I had no reason to worry about that since opportunities for growth no longer exist for college graduates who don't go to Princeton, UCLA, Harvard, or other prestigious institutions in the United States. Nevertheless, I still have what I hope is an irrational fear because I am genuinely afraid of the fascist culture being fostered in the US. Whether Islamism, Nazism, or the one that will be mentioned in this section further below. I am afraid that this criticism is going to get me killed in the US because of a major influence in US politics that I'll be referring to in this portion. I mean that very seriously, and it is not due to people in power but rather the culture of intolerance that they're fostering. It really took my resurfaced appreciation for the cultural tradition of Enlightenment values and Constitutional rights espoused by the late Christopher Hitchens and by the organization of Ex-Muslims of North America against Islam to really build my confidence for this criticism because before that - and however ridiculous it sounds - I was afraid that people were going to kill me in the US or repeatedly violate my constitutional rights. It's frightening to speak on this specific issue because of that, since it seems that no dissenting voice is given respect and is instead accused of Holocaust denial or some equivalent.

The beginning will be my own personal opinion based on life experience and evidence based on less popular news organizations, for what it's worth. It is my personal opinion regarding what many who are foreign to US politics may find to be bizarre about US politics. I suspect it confused more than just a few people overseas, who are curious about international politics, to see the US champion in defense of Israel while also having Nazi lingo and beliefs peddled on the national level. If such a subject matter doesn't hold your interest or concern, then please skip this portion. This will largely be the influence of religion in politics as I find such a topic unavoidable, but I don't want it to confuse the rest of this book. I hope that it's relevant enough with respect to the relationship between the US and Israel and I hope this provides some explanation and understanding of the contemporary political fallouts in the US for the past ten or twenty years before 2018: I recall from years prior, when seeing the depictions of violence in the coverage of the Israel-Palestine conflicts on the US television station of CNN with Wolf Blitzer and Anderson Cooper discussing the violence during each of the wars, how utterly psychopathic both of them seemed on camera when engaged in their discussions. How callously they dismissed the death of Palestinian civilians as human shields. How completely psychotic their arguments against a credible terrorist group like Hamas seemed to me when shown the depictions of devastation upon devastation wrought by Israel's forces. I doubt I was the only US citizen to feel this way. I don't know what it is the US national news media and those men in particular believed they were doing when discussing the "human shields" argument in front of the US public or what AIPAC had assumed would happen when arguing in favor of Israel as Israel was bombing homes, as the civilian death count of Palestinians skyrocketed, and as we of the US public were repeatedly shown depictions of old women bleeding to death, dead pregnant women, bloody and beaten children, and images of dead Palestinian babies on news stations and social media. In my personal opinion that sort of news coverage possibly did far more to increase neo-Nazism in the United States than anything the populist movements of either the progressive movement or the Tea Party movement ever did when refusing to associate with Pro-Israel groups. The legitimate hostility towards pro-Israel groups was then conflated as Nazism and anti-Semitism when at the same time pro-Israeli groups engaged in "discourse campaigns" that claimed anti-Semitism wasn't a real or legitimate argument in favor of Palestinians who could also be argued to be Semites because Israelis and Palestinians are genetically close and while anti-Semitism refers to anti-Jewish bigotry, Jews aren't a race.[457][458] Arguments that criticism of ideologies amount to racism are unfounded because while Jewish people are often treated as a racial group, but they aren't actually a race.[459] Israeli discourse campaigns on social media at the behest of the Israeli government seemed more like attempts to police the US public through shaming them on what to think and believe rather than any actual discourse over issues pertaining to the Israel-Palestine conflict. It was clear that AIPAC and other pro-Israel groups were just conflating Nazism with criticisms of Israel and were making a deliberate attempt at destroying or ridiculing any reasonable criticisms. This behavior from pro-Israel groups has likely led to a rise in Nazism. The people who wanted reasonable solutions were clearly shouted down by the pro-Israel brigade who seemed more focused on their frothing demands of militancy and conformity than debate. I'm obviously of the opinion that this helped enable the spread of Neo-Nazism which went unchallenged because the pro-Israel group didn't take them seriously and ignored them because nobody thought at the time that they would gain as much power as they had.

Within the US, it felt like a culture of fear of being labeled Nazis for any small criticism of Israel and Israeli policies towards Palestinians was fostered and disseminated. Worsening this horrid mess was actual Nazis coming onto social media to spread their hatred whenever human rights groups and pro-Palestinian groups tried to engage in a reasonable discussion. No effort by social media companies in their forums or especially the mainstream news media was made to separate reasonable critiques which had nothing to do with Nazism from the spread of Nazi hate campaigns. Pro-Israel lobbying simply dismissed it all as Nazism while peddling their race-based and religious-based ideology of Zionism. Every attempt to

1. [457] Glausiusz, Josie. "Blood Brothers: Palestinians and Jews Share Genetic Roots." *Haaretz.com*, 10 Apr. 2018, www.haaretz.com/science-and-health/palestinians-and-jews-share-genetic-roots-1.5411201.
2. [458] "British Ethnologist Richard Dawkins Declares 'Jew' Is Not a Race." *Algemeiner.com*, www.algemeiner.com/2015/04/28/british-ethnologist-richard-dawkins-jew-is-not-a-race/.
3. [459] "British Ethnologist Richard Dawkins Declares 'Jew' Is Not a Race." *Algemeiner.com*, www.algemeiner.com/2015/04/28/british-ethnologist-richard-dawkins-jew-is-not-a-race/.

reasonably critique Zionism was denigrated as celebrating or defending Nazism. There was no room given for any discourse in the US on any social platform that wasn't immediately dismissed as racist conspiracy mongering. There was no platform for debate or cordial discussion over the human rights of Palestinians because the mainstream News media, AIPAC, and other pro-Israeli groups made sure there could be none at all. All the while, pro-Israel groups and the national news media kept force feeding the US public the most appalling images of bloodshed upon Palestinian civilians; disfigured children, men with amputated limbs, women and men with blood all across their faces, and dead children. Social media from Israel's government, pro-Israel bloggers, and mainstream news media in the US were all conjoined with rampant militancy of either lying about the horrifying images being Palestinians self-inflicting their injuries or saying Israel could never be held responsible because Hamas was using human shields. It became clear to me that the "human shields" argument is no different than any other whitewashing discourse for human genocide. Even still, the US public didn't want to see the images, didn't want this discourse to keep continuing, and was just exhausted and disturbed enough by all the bloody images of innocent Palestinians being killed and Israelis militantly demanding conformity from the US public.

    The US mainstream media didn't seem to understand or perhaps didn't care that the US public was emotionally and psychologically exhausted from seeing such disturbing images and just didn't want to engage with it anymore. Most of the public didn't want to be labeled Nazis for any negative opinions and just wanted to stay out of the discussion altogether. Yet, the pro-Israel militancy throughout social media, constantly demanding conformity and agreement never stopped. When people politely said that they just didn't want to engage, the pro-Israel groups kept hounding even those groups of people as Nazis for not agreeing with Israeli policies. Neither the pro-Israel groups nor the US major news networks seemed to understand that the US public didn't want to see any more news about Israel. Yet, on and on the rage-inducing imagery and headlines about how Israel could never be held accountable for anything went along with depictions of injured or dead Palestinians. I fear most people fell into watching conspiracy theorists like Alex Jones or some other conspiracy theorists and likely fell into believing hateful material like the Elder of Zion because no one else filled the void of confusion on why the mainstream media kept showing images of Palestinians being harmed while praising Israel and continuing to practically sing about how Israel can never be held responsible for anything it does to the Palestinians. The US mainstream media, judging from its behavior, seemed to believe the lack of interest was a bad sign and grew even more militant in force-feeding images of harmed or dead Palestinians, including Palestinian children. This was done without any regard or thought put into the mental health of the US public from being force-fed these horrifying images for several years in an almost cyclical basis. As such, I've endeavored to correct what I feel is misapplied blame on Jewish people fostered by Zionist apologists in the national news media of the US who seem to be under the misapprehension that the rise of Nazism isn't entirely their fault for continuing a volley of gruesome images and defense of war crimes by a foreign country. I've detailed what, to the best of my understanding, are the real reasons for wars in the Middle East and defense of Israel in my chapter on Islam and how Islam's imperialistic religious ideology is also a significant influence on the ongoing wars that never seem to end. I do this not out of contempt, but out of concern because it seems clear to me that the lack of an answer by former and current US officials on why the US conducts foreign wars has helped create confusion and conspiracy theories. I believe it is due to, as Daniel Kahneman details in his chapter on norms and causes in *Thinking Fast and Slow*, how people find their own causes for why something is happening.[460] They need rational answers and only conspiracy theories have been given as answers. Worse still, the conspiracies haven't been challenged through rational arguments.

It is clear that one of the central problems of the socio-economic ideology of neoliberalism has been the license to peddle the policy interests of foreign governments with political agendas of their own in the absence of understanding how it effects the domestic citizenry of the US. It is absolutely facetious to believe that Russian interference in the US election was something unprecedented or new. Both AIPAC and the Saudi monarchy generally get to meet and greet presidential candidates before the party fully endorses them, although this influence seems overstated out of fear of foreigners as domestic corporate interests such as the US bank moguls and various corporate interests of Wall Street seem to be the most prominent influencers, but the major difference is that Saudi Arabia usually knew how to be either coercive or when it's best to remain silent on a matter; up until the brutal murder of the journalist, Jamal Khashoggi. In effect, despite Saudi Arabia obviously being far more egregious in scope of human rights crimes and the obvious problems of living under a Islamic monarchy, the Saudis generally knew when to respect US democratic affairs and to remain separate in its own affairs. There seems to be a mutual understanding at least implicitly between the US and Saudi Arabia. By stark contrast, the Likud party, the Right-wing of Israel and especially their cohorts in the US national news media, never seems to know when to just pause and think over how their actions are going to be perceived by the US public. They always seem to make an effort to engender rage by harping endlessly about how the most reprehensive and morally indefensible crimes against humanity are somehow justified when Israel does it and then arguing anyone who disagrees with them is an obvious Nazi. Whether explicitly or tacitly, this was the general cultural norm pressured onto the public by the US national news media. The less interest the US public had, some even reasonably demanding why the US public has to keep hearing about horrible crimes that Israel commits when rationally they're a gnat compared to the US empire and it has nothing to do with US politics, the more the US national news media seemed to take it as a sign of disloyalty and non-conformity to Israel and kept frothing at the mouth with demands of being loyal to Israel and tacit or explicit accusations of Nazism towards anyone who disagreed with Israel. It became particularly absurd when even right-wing Jewish groups in the US joined in compassionate

---

4. [460] Kahneman, Daniel. Chapter 6:"Norms, Surprises, and Causes" (71-78). *Thinking, fast and slow*. Farrar, Straus and Giroux, 2015.

camaraderie with left-wing US-born Palestinian youth in condemnation of Israel's human rights crimes in New York rallies and even they were tacitly labeled as disloyal and promoting Nazism by the US national news media.[461][462] It became readily apparent why these absurdities existed: we weren't allowed, thanks to the ideology of a foreign government, to espouse any opinions but rather just submission to what is quite clearly a fascist ideology. I call it a fascist ideology because it doesn't allow us to criticize it as is our Constitutional right under the first amendment. As of 2018, Zionism as an ideology has done everything in the past decade to circumvent our Constitutional rights. In a very visceral manner, while Russia may have influenced US elections, the Israeli right-wing lobby essentially created a playbook on how to force the US public to capitulate to unreasonable demands of fascism that helped pave the way for Donald Trump and the US mainstream media was a major contributing factor.

There has been adamant criticism from the free speech activists amongst the US public to denounce safe spaces, Islamic apologists, and the Left's unwillingness to criticize Islam. I absolutely agree that free speech must be defended, but it is unfair to malign Leftist movements and progressives in particular for this overly protective attitude without understanding the historic context of this past decade. The Progressive overbearing "political correctness" was in direct response to a sustained, duplicitous, and hateful barrage of attacks by Zionist fascism by college donors, US mainstream journalists, malicious pro-Israel professors and students taking it upon themselves to join an anti-free speech crusade, and US politicians to ban the free speech of all dissenting opinions to Zionism and Israel. This was not done on the basis of banning vitriol, but rather to disingenuously conflate arguments against Zionist ideology or reasonable criticisms of Israel's human rights record with hateful ideas like Nazism or Holocaust denial in an effort to ban all dissenting voices of free speech in college campuses when they didn't hold a favorable opinion about Israel. To put it bluntly, Zionist ideology has tried to make sure that no dissenting opinion of Israel was allowed on college campuses.

To give credence to this argument, as I fear that this will be branded as a nonsensical conspiracy theory, here are arguments from three different sources on the extent of Zionist fascism's influence in attacking US civil liberties. **However, I must emphatically emphasize that this is in no way condoning religious discriminatory conspiracy theories like the Elder of Zion, Holocaust denial, or any other racist or religiously discriminatory ideologies like Nazism, the KKK, or Neo-Nazism.** I repudiate any such claims by fascists like the Nazis, **and I want any and all Jewish readers to know that I fully support both the existence of Israel and Jewish human rights should be protected anywhere and everywhere.** Especially cases in which Jews are having human rights discriminated against such as in Iran where Jews continue to face persecution. **I wholly and unreservedly condemn**

---

5. [461] "Protests Held In NYC Against Israeli Violence In Gaza." *ANIMAL*, 11 July 2014, animalnewyork.com/2014/protests-held-nyc-israeli-violence-gaza/.
6. [462] Neturei Karta. "Jewish Rabbi Condemning Israeli Attack on Gaza." *YouTube*, Neturei Karta, 20 July 2014, www.youtube.com/watch?v=JaSqvutvI1k.

any and all forms of anti-Semitism and anti-Jewish conspiracy theories from the Middle East, the West, or anywhere else in the world; such as places like Egypt or from the rising fascist and anti-immigrant parties in Europe and the US that espouse Nazism. **Anti-Semitism and hatred of Jews is very real and I condemn all such calls for genocide or human rights crimes upon Jewish people. I am wholly and completely in favor of the Jewish State of Israel and the right of all Jewish people to go into any field of study and research that they wish in any country they are citizens of.** *What I am concerned about is the Right-Wing religious ideology of Zionism* which is very real and is unfortunately attempting to circumvent and dismantle Free Speech activism and the fundamental rights of European and US citizenry in being able to question and object to certain portions of Israeli politics pertaining to the human rights of Palestinians. **The Right-Wing Religious Ideology of Zionism is not reflective of all Jewish people and condemning Zionism is not a condemnation of either Israel, Jewish Human Rights, or Jewish people. Israel is firmly the homeland of Jewish people and I fully support the Right to Return, I am simply concerned with Zionism as a religious and political ideology on Free Speech grounds.** If any of what is stated herein or hereafter seems callous, then I fully and unreservedly apologize to any and all Jewish people and emphasize again that I fully support your human rights and have nothing but respect and admiration for your hard work, dedication, and wonderful culture and people who have suffered gravely at the hands of Christian and Islamic imperialist regimes and psychotic laws of discrimination against your people that were utterly unjustified. You have every right to be concerned about anti-Jewish or anti-Semitic speech and rising fascism calling for violence against you and I will firmly support your human rights. That being said, I feel it is best to allow Free Speech, because judging from the evidence I've compared to countries with less free speech, people become more violent when their free speech isn't allowed and not less so. With free speech, we can see who the bigots are and avoid them, but without free speech, they seem to take that as "oppression" in order to justify violence against Jewish people and others. That is mainly why I am concerned with Zionism as a political and religious ideology influencing US public discourse with penalizations for mere discussion.

Before detailing the infringements on Free Speech in US college campuses, it's important to note that broaching this discussion cannot be classified as anti-Semitic and that Left-wing parties within Israel vehemently argue against Zionist ideology and accuse the Zionist movement of these fascist tendencies within Israel itself. Currently, they've grown more vocal in highlighting accusations and political activism attempting to infringe upon First Amendment rights of the US public. *Haaretz*, the oldest Israeli newspaper first set-up in 1918, and one of the most reputable news organizations in the world that allows for truly diverse discourse on these issues, elaborates on this particular issue quite eloquently in defense of the US public's Free Speech.

Peter Beinart of Haaretz explains in the article "*American Jewish Establishment Stifles Free Speech To Silence Zionism's Critics*" delivered on December 2016 on just what Israel's foreign influence in collusion with Right-wing Pro-Israel organizers have done to mutilate US Free Speech by pressuring both Republicans and Democrats of the Republican-majority Senate to effectively ban US Free Speech covertly:

> With every passing year, the American Jewish establishment poses a greater threat to free speech in the United States.
>
> The reason is simple. With every passing year, Israeli control of the West Bank grows more permanent. And so, with every passing year, more American progressives question Zionism.
>
> After all, if Jewish statehood permanently condemns millions of West Bank Palestinians to live as non-citizens, under military law, without free movement or the right to vote for the government that controls their lives, it's hardly surprising that Americans who loathe discrimination and cherish equality would grow uncomfortable with the concept.
>
> And the more those Americans voice this discomfort, the more establishment American Jewish organizations work to classify anti-Zionism as anti-Semitism, punishable by law.
>
> The latest example is The Anti-Semitism Awareness Act, which the Senate passed unanimously on December 2. The Act – pushed by AIPAC, the Anti-Defamation League and the Jewish Federations of America – instructs the Department of Education's Civil Rights office to follow "the definition of anti-Semitism set forth by the Special Envoy to Monitor and Combat anti-Semitism of the Department of State in the Fact Sheet issued on June 8, 2010."
>
> Sounds innocuous enough. Until you look at what the Fact Sheet says. Following the definition hatched by Soviet dissident turned Israeli right-winger Natan Sharansky, the Fact Sheet defines anti-Semitism as, among other things, "Denying the Jewish people their right to self-determination, and denying Israel the right to exist."
>
> This is nuts. Across the world, numerous peoples desire "self-determination." Kurds have been seeking their own state since the late nineteenth century, roughly the same period when Jews hatched Zionism.
>
> So have Basques. Sikhs have been agitating for their own country, in Punjab, since India's creation. The Igbos of eastern Nigeria actually created one, Biafra, for three years between 1967 and 1970.
>
> There are reasonable arguments in favor of these efforts at self-determination. There are also reasonable arguments in favor of requiring Kurds, Basques, Sikhs and Igbo to live in multi-ethnic countries based upon a national identity that supersedes their own.
>
> Either way, bigotry has nothing to do with it. If opposing a people's desire for self-determination makes you bigoted against that group, then a lot of American Jewish leaders should report themselves to the Department of Education's Civil Rights office right now.
>
> After all, Palestinians want their own state. Many American Jewish leaders oppose it. Why aren't those leaders bigots under the very principle they're trying to write into law?
>
> The truth is that political Zionism – the belief that Jews enjoy the greatest safety and self-expression in their own state – has always been controversial even among Jews. In the early twentieth century, many Orthodox Jews called Zionism a violation of Jewish law.

Many American Reform Jews argued that Jews were a faith, not a people, and thus had no homeland other than the United States. Other prominent Jewish thinkers – including Judah Magnes, who founded Hebrew University,

Henrietta Szold, who founded Hadassah and the philosophers Hannah Arendt and Martin Buber – argued that a Jewish state would dispossess Palestinians and bring war. They argued for a binational state instead. That didn't make them anti-Semites.

As the twentieth century progressed, these arguments against Zionism faded. The Holocaust buttressed the case for a country of Jewish refuge. Israel became an established fact, and in many ways an extraordinary success.

Then, in 1993, PLO Chairman Yasser Arafat declared that "The PLO recognizes the right of the State of Israel to exist in peace and security." In 2002, the Arab League offered to "sign a peace agreement with Israel" if it returned to the 1967 lines and found a "just" and "agreed upon" solution to the Palestinian refugees.

Once even Palestinian and Arab leaders publicly declared that they could accept a Jewish state alongside a Palestinian one, the historic debate over Zionism dwindled.

It is returning in the twenty-first century because a Palestinian state was never born. (A failure for which both sides deserve blame). That failure, combined with decades of Israeli settlement growth, has convinced many progressives that a Palestinian state is now impossible.

Thus, they argue, the only way West Bank Palestinians can win their rights is in one state – including the West Bank, the Gaza Strip and Israel proper – that does not privilege Jews.

This is not my view. Despite everything, I still consider the two state solution more realistic than the binational alternative. But you don't have to be an anti-Semite to disagree.

Anti-Zionism never died; there have always been people – Jewish and non-Jewish – who oppose any kind of Jewish state within any borders. But anti-Zionism is growing because deepening Israeli control of the West Bank makes it harder to reconcile Zionism with basic Palestinian human rights.

Faced with the growing number of Americans who deny that Zionism is compatible with liberal democracy, establishment American Jewish groups could try to make Zionism more compatible with liberal democracy. They could publicly challenge Israel's undemocratic occupation of the West Bank. But that would require confronting Benjamin Netanyahu, and many of their own donors.

So they've chosen an easier path: get the Department of Education to define anti-Zionism as anti-Semitism and thus threaten the campus activists who are challenging Jewish statehood with legal sanction. The Senate bill claims that "Nothing in this act shall be construed to diminish or infringe upon any right protected by the First Amendment."

But that's exactly what the bill does. In the words of Michael Macleod-Ball, chief of staff of the American Civil Liberties Union's Washington, DC legislative office, it "opens the door to considering anti-Israel political statements and activities as possible grounds for civil rights investigations."[463]

---

7. [463] Beinart, Peter. "American Jewish Establishment Stifles Free Speech to Silence Zionism's Critics." *Haaretz.com*, Haaretz Com, 24 Apr. 2018, www.haaretz.com/opinion/.premium-how-zionism-is-losing-the-contest-of-ideas-in-the-u-s-1.5470232.

These legal impositions to Free Speech first began their pressure on US college campuses and likely contributed to the idea of "safe spaces" since Right-wing Israeli and Right-wing Jewish American influence colluded to effectively ban any and all dissenting voices of Israel and especially its policies towards Palestinian human rights. Student groups have suffered throughout the years via intimidation, coercion, and sometimes criminal charges for invoking their First Amendment rights to Free Speech, Free Assembly, and Free Expression when dissenting against Israel on college campuses. Moreover, this criminalization of Free Speech has also been used to intimidate university professors too. It has been going on for far too long and has remained unchecked with no effort placed to safeguard Free Speech rights of students and faculties across the US. As much as it pains me to write this . . . this is been going on for far, far too long and is essentially a fascist movement perpetuated by an ultra-conservative, right-wing political ideology that has gone unimpeded. It has only grown bolder over the years and has not waned in its efforts to destroy the US public's constitutionally protected right to Freedom of Speech.

This first cited example is from the blog Commondreams.org by Pulitzer Prize winning journalist, Chris Hedges, who explains how the Zionist fascism barred his ability to publically engage in dissent in college campuses in his article titled "*Banning Dissent in the name of civility*" written in December 2014:

> Being banned from speaking about the conflict between Israel and Palestine, especially at universities, is familiar to anyone who attempts to challenge the narrative of the Israel lobby. This is not the first time one of my speaking offers has been revoked and it will not be the last. However, the charge of Belnavis and the International Affairs Association that I do not believe in coexistence between the Palestinians and Israel is false. I oppose violence by either party. I have condemned Hamas rocket attacks as war crimes. And I support Israel's right to exist within the pre-1967 borders. The charge that I oppose coexistence cannot be substantiated by anything I have said or written. And those of us who call on Israel to withdraw to the pre-1967 borders are, after all, only demanding what is required by international law and numerous U.N. resolutions.
>
> But truth, along with an open and fair debate, is the last thing the Israel lobby and its lackeys seek. The goal is to silence students, faculty members and outside speakers who do not read from the approved script. The decades-long persecution of the courageous scholar Norman Finkelstein, which has included repeatedly successful campaigns by the Israel lobby to get him removed from university teaching positions, is accompanied by efforts to discredit fearless writers on Israel such as Max Blumenthal, the author of "Goliath: Life and Loathing in Greater Israel." Finkelstein, the son of Holocaust survivors, and Blumenthal are Jews. And Jews who demand justice for the Palestinians—Jews often make up sizable parts of college groups such as Students for Justice in Palestine—are attacked with a particular vindictiveness by propagandists for Israel.
>
> Our universities, like our corporate-controlled airwaves, are little more than echo chambers for the elites and the powerful. The bigger and more prestigious the university the more it seems determined to get its students and faculty to chant in unison to please its Zionist donors. Student groups that resist are often banned, as has happened to numerous chapters of Students for Justice in Palestine, including one at Northeastern University. Some are denied meeting spaces, and at times student activists are prohibited from participating in any campus student organizations—even those that have nothing to do with the conflict between Israel and the Palestinians. Many students have been made to attend re-education seminars run by the Anti-Defamation League (ADL). Criticism of Israel is equated with anti-Semitism.

I spent seven years in the Middle East as a foreign correspondent, five of them as the Middle East bureau chief for The New York Times. I speak Arabic. I was frequently in Gaza and lived for two years in Jerusalem. What frightens the Israel lobby is not my critique, but my expertise. It is impossible to spew out the usual Israeli propaganda, half-truths, distortions and lies—as retired Harvard law professor Alan Dershowitz once tried to do when he and I appeared at a Columbia University event—to someone who has spent years in the Middle East reporting on the conflict. What the Israel lobby fears most are facts.

The struggle by students, including some at the University of Pennsylvania, to bolster the nonviolent boycott, divestment and sanctions (BDS) movement, which I support, has been met by fierce internal resistance on campuses across the country. A national BDS conference in 2012 at the University of Pennsylvania, which to the university's credit the school administrators permitted, saw the usual outpouring of venom and character assassination. The attacks included a letter to The Daily Pennsylvanian newspaper from professor Ruben Gur of the departments of psychiatry, radiology and neurology. Gur called the BDS movement a "hateful genocidal organization" and accused it of being anti-Semitic. He said the student organizers were concealing "Hamas and Hizballah daggers" and referred to Omar Barghouti's book "Boycott, Divestment, Sanctions: the Global Struggle for Palestinian Rights" as the organizers' "version of 'Mein Kampf.' " He said groups in the BDS movement were similar to those "organized by the Nazis in the 1930's to boycott, divest and sanction Jews and their businesses." He compared Jewish students who support the movement to "Capos in the extermination camps."

The University of Pennsylvania's Hillel chapter has hosted speakers such as Daniel Pipes and Nonie Darwish who peddle disturbing racist stereotypes of Muslims and justify indiscriminate violence against Muslims. The chapter once organized a university talk by the right-wing extremist Effi Eitam, a former Israeli military commander. Eitam, infamous for personally overseeing and taking part in brutal and sometimes deadly beatings of Palestinians in the occupied territories when he was in the military, declared in a 2004 article in The New Yorker that Palestinians were "creatures who came out of the depths of darkness" and he branded the Palestinian people as "collectively guilty." "We will have to kill them all," he said of those with "the evil in their heads."

The political science department of the University of Pennsylvania, along with Hillel, invited Dershowitz to attack the BDS movement in a 2012 lecture titled "Why Israel Matters to You, Me, and Penn: A Conversation With Alan Dershowitz."

Dershowitz has called on Israel to use bulldozers to demolish entire Palestinian villages, rather than individual houses, in retaliation for Palestinian terrorist attacks, although collective punishment violates international law. In another context he defends the use of torture and proposes methods that include shoving a "sterilized needle underneath the nail." He lambastes as an anti-Semite nearly everyone who has criticized the Israeli state; he once said "there is a special place in hell" for former President Jimmy Carter and that South African Archbishop Desmond Tutu is "one of the most evil men in the world."

When Dershowitz spoke at Penn in 2012, David Cohen, the chairman of the university board of trustees and executive vice president of Comcast Corp., read to the audience a letter written for the occasion by the school's president, Amy Gutmann, who was in California at the time. In the letter Gutmann praised Dershowitz and castigated the BDS movement, saying "Penn is blessed to have one of the largest and most active Hillel chapters in the country. And we are unwavering in our support of the Jewish state. Let me say it in the clearest possible words: we do not support the goals of BDS."

The code word that the Israel lobby and its facilitators at universities use to silence critics is "civility." Israel supporters are permitted to spout hate and calls for indiscriminate violence against Palestinians. Critics of Israel, however, even if they are careful to denounce violence and not to demonize Jews, are banned in the name of "civility." It is the height of academic duplicity.

It was Steven Salaita's lack of "civility" that saw the University of Illinois at Urbana-Champaign "de-hire" him this year after the school invited him to join the faculty as a tenured professor. Salaita had sent tweets at the height of the Israeli bombing of Gaza last summer that left some 2,100 people dead, including 500 children. One reads: "Let's cut to the chase: If you're defending #Israel right now you're an awful human being. 11:46 PM—8 Jul 2014." Chancellor Phyllis Wise, in removing Salaita, said the university would not tolerate "disrespectful words or actions that demean and abuse either viewpoints themselves or those who express them." The board of trustees supported Wise's decision, saying there is no place in a democracy for speech that does not promote "civility." Afterward, 34 administrators at the school wrote a letter to the incoming president of the University of Illinois saying the treatment of Salaita had damaged the institution and their ability to attract top-level scholars to the Urbana-Champaign campus.[464]

David Palumbo-Liu, a Professor of Comparative Literature at Stanford University, explains in *The Nation* magazine within the article titled "*Steven Salaita, Professor fired over 'Uncivil' Tweets, Vindicated in Federal Court*" how the University of Illinois violated the Free Speech of a Professor that had been hired for a position by rescinding the offer due to his tweets online about the Israel-Palestine conflict due to outcry from students, alumni, and most significantly, purported six-figure donors who immediately demanded his firing for such tweets. The Federal courts decision in defense of legal Free Speech rights:

> There is not a little poetic justice in the fact that it was precisely at the time that a federal judge ruled that Steven Salaita's lawsuit against the University of Illinois could go forward, against the objections of the university, that the chancellor of the Urbana-Champaign campus who fired Salaita in the first place announced her resignation and the local newspaper reported that she is under an ethics investigation:
>
> "*Certain administrative officials at the University of Illinois used personal email to conduct university business and failed to turn over those documents during Freedom of Information Act requests, a violation of university policy, a UI probe has found.*
>
> *The news comes one day after Chancellor Phyllis Wise announced her resignation as chancellor. The personal emails released by the university included many from Wise, but a university spokesman declined to say whether the ethics investigation led to her departure.*"
>
> Almost exactly a year ago, that paper, the Champaign *News-Gazette*, broke the story of Salaita's tweets, which brought issues of academic freedom and freedom of speech to the fore, not to mention the question of whether or not speech regarding sharp and angry criticism of Israel in particular warranted a suspension of those rights and freedoms.
>
> As I wrote in *The Nation* back then, once the story of Salaita's tweets came out, the university made a public statement supporting his right to free speech. Yet shortly after, alumni, students, and perhaps most importantly, wealthy donors began writing angry emails demanding his firing. Here is how the court ruling describes these events and Wise's actions:
>
> "*Despite the initial show of support, however, the University soon changed its tune. Letters and emails obtained via Illinois' Freedom of Information Act revealed that students, alumni, and donors wrote to the University's Chancellor, Phyllis Wise ("Wise"), to voice their concerns over Dr. Salaita joining the University. One writer in particular claimed to be a "multiple 6 figure donor" who would be ceasing support of the University because of Dr. Salaita and his tweets.*

---

8. [464] Hedges, Chris. "Banning Dissent in the Name of Civility." *Common Dreams*, Common Dreams, 22 Dec. 2014, www.commondreams.org/views/2014/12/22/banning-dissent-name-civility.

Two other specific interactions are critical to Dr. Salaita's Complaint. The first involves an unknown donor who met with Chancellor Wise and provided her a two-page memo about the situation. Wise ultimately destroyed the memo, but an email Wise sent University officials summarized it as follows: "He [the unknown donor] gave me [Chancellor Wise] a two-pager filled with information on Professor Salaita and said how we handle the situation will be very telling." The second interaction involves a particularly wealthy donor who asked to meet with Chancellor Wise to "share his thoughts about the University's hiring of Professor Salaita.""

The university defended its actions on two grounds, both of which the federal court has just thrown out. First, it argued that Salaita was never officially an employee of the university despite the fact that he had been offered a tenured position in a written document, was assigned courses to teach, had been given orientation materials, and had been invited out to look for housing, all customary practices in academic recruiting and hiring. Customary, too, is that one extends to one's current employer one's resignation so they can fill one's position and have one's teaching covered. This meant that by refusing to honor its part of the agreement, the University of Illinois was rendering Salaita unemployed (and his wife as well, as she had quit her job to relocate to Urbana-Champaign) and his family without a home.

The final formalities of university hiring are usually undertaken after new faculty have arrived on campus, for it is then that boards of trustees normally meet to give their stamp of approval to a process that is handled entirely by faculty governance and administrative review. Chancellor Wise and those members of the board of trustees (chaired by Christopher Kennedy, son of the late Robert F. Kennedy) who were now motivated against Salaita used that interval and that opportunity to abort the appointment. Now the judge has knocked down both of the two pillars of the university's argument against Salaita's suit.

Here is the judge's ruling on the notion that the Salaita was never truly employed by the university. The ruling shoots down any notion that the university did not have an obligation. The judge further notes how the university's attempt to hide behind the time frame issue goes squarely against academic practice:

"The University paid for Dr. Salaita's moving expenses, provided him an office and University email address, assigned him two courses to teach in the fall, and stated to a newspaper that he would in fact join the faculty, despite his unsavory tweets. The University spokesperson went so far as referencing Dr. Salaita as one of "our employees." The University also did not hold a Board vote until after the start of the semester. If the Board vote was truly a condition to contract formation, then the University would have the Board vote on appointments before the start of a semester and before spending money on a new professor or treating the professor as a full-fledged employee. Finally, the University actually held the Board vote despite its claim that it had no agreement whatsoever. If the University truly felt no obligation to Dr. Salaita, the University could have simply not put the appointment to a vote at all. Instead, the University still went ahead with the vote, which is at least some evidence that it felt obligated to hold a vote according to the terms of the offer letter. Simply put, the University cannot argue with a straight face that it engaged in all these actions in the absence of any obligation or agreement."

So the "not really ever hired" argument was found to be bogus. But let's now step out of the relatively narrow sphere of academic administrative life and get to the issue most people are concerned with—what about Salaita's academic freedom and freedom of speech? This is a much more significant issue to the American public at large. Here is what the court said about that:

"The University...argues that Dr. Salaita was not fired because of his constitutionally protected speech, and that even if he was, the University's interest in providing a safe and disruption-free learning environment outweighs Dr. Salaita's free speech interest under the balancing test in Pickering v. Bd. of Educ., 391 U.S. 563, 574 (1968)."

Besides brushing aside the weird "he wasn't fired because of his speech, but even if he was" business, the court dismisses the university's argument that in this case preserving the "safe" and "disruption-free" learning environment trumps Salaita's free-speech rights. The court does so in a forceful and comprehensive manner that warrants reading this crucial passage carefully:

"*The University's attempt to draw a line between the profanity and incivility in Dr. Salaita's tweets and the views those tweets presented is unavailing; the Supreme Court did not draw such a line when it found Cohen's "Fuck the Draft" jacket protected by the First Amendment. Cohen v. California, 403 U.S. 15, 26 (1971). The tweets' contents were certainly a matter of public concern, and the topic of Israeli-Palestinian relations often brings passionate emotions to the surface. Under these circumstances, it would be nearly impossible to separate the tone of tweets on this issue with the content and views they express. And the Supreme Court has warned of the dangers inherent in punishing public speech on public matters because of the particular words or tone of the speech.... At the motion to dismiss stage, the Court simply cannot find that the University was not at all motivated by the content of Dr. Salaita's tweets....*
...Dr. Salaita's tweets implicate every "central concern" of the First Amendment. Burson v. Freeman, 504 U.S. 191, 196 (1992) (stating that there are "three central concerns in our First Amendment jurisprudence: regulation of political speech, regulation of speech in a public forum, and regulation based on the content of the speech."). The Court therefore declines to engage in a full-fledged Pickering balancing analysis at this early stage in the litigation.
Additionally, even if the Court were to apply the balancing test, it would still have to view the facts in Dr. Salaita's favor. And when the plaintiff's speech "more substantially involve[s] matters of public concern," the defendant must make a "stronger showing" of potential disruption. Connick v. Myers, 461 U.S. 138, 151 (1983); see also, McGreal v. Ostrov, 368 F.3d 657, 681–82 (7th Cir. 2004) ("The employer bears the burden of justifying a particular disciplinary action, and a stronger showing may be necessary when an employee's speech more substantially involves matters of public concern.")...
Although Pickering balancing is not appropriate at this stage in this case, it appears that the evidence is conflicting as to the level of disruption Dr. Salaita's appointment would cause. Thus, viewing this evidence in Dr. Salaita's favor, it seems unlikely that the University would win its Pickering challenge at the motion to dismiss stage.
Dr. Salaita's Complaint alleges facts showing that he was fired or not hired because of the University's disagreement with his personal speech in a public forum on a matter of public concern. This is enough to survive a motion to dismiss."

Thus the court found the university's argument that this was not about free speech to be bogus, and, most significant, it found that Salaita's speech was *especially* protected because it had to do with an issue of overriding public concern. What is crucial to note here is that, rather than putting the issue of Israel-Palestine aside because of its reputed "divisiveness" and its "disruption" of university life, the court ruled that it is precisely *because* of its centrality to our public discourse that Salaita's tweets, and speech—and in fact all of our discussions around Israel-Palestine, no matter what view we take—need to flow freely. So now that we have a firm ruling on that, why turn to the issue of the ethics charge against Wise and others? Precisely because we now know the exact nature of the damage their actions had against our freedom of speech and Salaita's academic freedom.

The Center for Constitutional Rights notes:

"*[The] ruling comes on the heels of an Illinois state court's decision in a Freedom of Information Act lawsuit on June 12 ordering university officials to turn over emails related to Professor Salaita's firing that they had refused to divulge, as well as a vote by the American Association of University Professors (AAUP) to censure the university on June 13.*"

What we now know is that Wise and others, upon realizing what a hot-button issue this had become, switched their discussions over to their private e-mail accounts to avoid discovery. However, under the FOIA ruling, the demand for e-mails would include all e-mails regarding the case, regardless of what kind of account they were posted through. This is of course to prevent the kinds of evasions Wise and her colleagues sought to use to protect themselves. Anyone who wishes to read some of the newly discovered e-mails will see what Wise and others were trying to hide. The news release notes that these private e-mails take on other controversial subjects as well, besides the Salaita case.

As we see the case against the university gathering more and more strength, it is absolutely crucial that we do not lose sight of the damage that has been done by the university and those who worked behind the scenes to influence the administration to one person's career, his livelihood, his family. We should not ignore how power and wealth can operate to shut down unpopular opinion. And finally, we need to remember that issues of great public concern, such as Israel-Palestine, should not only be discussed, but also need to be discussed in the most free and open manner possible, and not censored. Steven Salaita has paid the price for bringing these issues into the foreground. The least we can do is make use of the rights that he has shown we should all cherish.[465]

The Intercept, which is a online news website founded by independent journalists like Glenn Greenwald, is a journalist organization keen on highlighting the human rights abuses of the United States on both US citizens and people abroad in foreign countries. However, to digress a bit for those who feel this journalist group to be a questionable source, I agree that they're wrong about Edward Snowden; Snowden is a man who sold vital US intelligence to the highest bidder to make himself famous. While Glenn Greenwald and others in the Intercept could be argued to have contributed to Russia's apparent attack on influencing the 2016 US elections; the chief perpetrators were Cambridge Analytica. The main motives of the Intercept is to highlight when the civil liberties within the US and the human rights outside of the US are violated by the US government's implicit or explicit actions. This is because they seem to be true believers in the US Constitution and were therefore just as caught off-guard as every other US Constitutional idealist when their work was used for nefarious self-interests of foreign governments against the United States. They've largely tried to make-up for their horrifying blunder by reporting on human rights abuses both of US citizens by the US government and of people across the world who were abused by the policies of President Barack Obama and Donald Trump. They've also made an effort to criticize Russia's autocratic rule and Putin's attacks on freedom of speech in particular. That being said, they obviously can't be trusted with honest news when it comes to Islamist political groups as the Intercept put Ex-Muslim lives in danger through a doxxng campaign that shared an Ex-Muslim journalist's personal details to Islamist groups who wanted to rape and kill Ex-Muslims.[466] With respect to criticizing US abuse of power in the domestic front of US politics, they seem to be the most honest in their intentions, but their overseas reporting pertaining to Islamic apologetics is worthless for reasons that'll be made clear in the section on Islam.

Glenn Greenwald's article titled "*The Greatest Threat To Campus Free Speech Is Coming From Dianne Feinstein and her Military-Contractor Husband*" and written in September of 2015 details the threats to campus Free Speech peddled by Feinstein and her husband. The following is a short portion of Greenwald's article:

---

9. [465] Palumbo-Liu, David. "Steven Salaita, Professor Fired for 'Uncivil' Tweets, Vindicated in Federal Court." *The Nation*, 11 Aug. 2015, www.thenation.com/article/steven-salaita-professor-fired-for-uncivil-tweets-vindicated-in-federal-court/.
10. [466] Muthali, Aki. "Atheistophobia: It's Time to Talk about the Most Persecuted Minority in the World." *The Nation*, 27 Sept. 2015, nation.com.pk/27-Sep-2015/atheistophobia-it-s-time-to-talk-about-the-most-persecuted-minority-in-the-world.

One of the most dangerous threats to campus free speech has been emerging at the highest levels of the University of California system, the sprawling collection of 10 campuses that includes UCLA and UC Berkeley. The university's governing Board of Regents, with the support of University President Janet Napolitano and egged on by the state's legislature, has been attempting to adopt new speech codes that — in the name of combating "anti-Semitism" — would formally ban various forms of Israel criticism and anti-Israel activism.

Under the most stringent such regulations, students found to be in violation of these codes would face suspension or expulsion. In July, it appeared that the Regents were poised to enact the most extreme version, but decided instead to push the decision off until September, when they instead would adopt non-binding guidelines to define "hate speech" and "intolerance."

One of the Regents most vocally advocating for the most stringent version of the speech code is Richard Blum, the multi-millionaire defense contractor who is married to Sen. Dianne Feinstein of California. At a Regents meeting last week, reported the *Los Angeles Times*, Blum expressly threatened that Feinstein would publicly denounce the university if it failed to adopt far more stringent standards than the ones it appeared to be considering, and specifically demanded they be binding and contain punishments for students found to be in violation.

The *San Francisco Chronicle* put it this way: "Regent Dick Blum said his wife, U.S. Sen. Dianne Feinstein, D-Calif., 'is prepared to be critical of this university' unless UC not only tackles anti-Jewish bigotry but also makes clear that perpetrators will be punished." The lawyer Ken White wrote that "Blum threatened that his wife ... would interfere and make trouble if the Regents didn't commit to punish people for prohibited speech." As campus First Amendment lawyer Ari Cohn put it the following day, "Feinstein and her husband think college students should be expelled for protected free speech."[467]

To bring further clarity to the extent of this assault on the Constitutionally protected right of Free Speech by this rising fascism from foreign Israeli influence in US colleges. Along with recognizing the depth of this fascist movement's commitment to peddle bigotry without any meaningful and legitimate criticism being allowed to repudiate them, *The Intercept* **has reported extensively on the growing contempt by the US mainstream media for the US public and the willful lack of coverage for the growing fascist attacks on the US public and most notably, US academia. Less than one year later, The Intercept detailed in an article on March 2016 by Robert Mackey, titled "***University of California Adopts Policy Linking Anti-Zionism to Anti-Semitism***" and explained as follows:**

> The regents of the University of California unanimously adopted a new policy on discrimination on Wednesday that links anti-Semitism to opposition to Zionism, the ideology asserting that the Jewish people have a right to a nation-state in historic Palestine.
>
> At a meeting in San Francisco, the UC Board of Regents approved a working group's recommendation for a set of "Principles Against Intolerance" that accepts the argument that "manifestations of anti-Semitism have changed" as a result of debates over Israel on college campuses and "expressions of anti-Semitism are more coded and difficult to identify."

---

11. [467] Greenwald, Glenn. "The Greatest Threat to Campus Free Speech Is Coming From Dianne Feinstein and Her Military-Contractor Husband." *The Intercept*, 25 Sept. 2015, theintercept.com/2015/09/25/dianne-feinstein-husband-threaten-univ-calif-demanding-ban-excessive-israel-criticism/.

"In particular," the report stated, "opposition to Zionism often is expressed in ways that are not simply statements of disagreement over politics and policy, but also assertions of prejudice and intolerance toward Jewish people and culture."

To address the concerns of pro-Israel students and faculty, who claimed that supporters of Palestinian rights who disagreed with them were practicing a form of discrimination, the working group was formed in September to expand on a draft statement that had said, "Intolerance has no place at the University of California." In January, the working group proposed that the declaration should read instead: "Anti-Semitism, anti-Zionism and other forms of discrimination have no place at the University of California."

But that proposed language was criticized — by, among others, the ACLU, the Middle East Studies Association of North America, student activists and faculty members like Michael Meranze, Saree Makdisi and Judith Butler — for erasing the line between legitimate criticism of the state of Israel and hate speech aimed at Jewish students and faculty. Just before the regents voted on the policy on Wednesday, a member of the working group, Norman Pattiz, further amended the reference to anti-Zionism so that it now condemns "anti-Semitic forms of anti-Zionism."

Before the vote on Wednesday, Bonnie Reiss, the vice chairwoman of the Board of Regents, argued that students opposed to Israeli policies, and those questioning the state's unequal treatment of non-Jews, had fostered a dangerous environment for Jewish students by supporting the effort to pressure Israel to change its policies through a campaign of boycotts, divestment and sanctions, known as BDS.

It was necessary for the university to address anti-Semitism, Resiss said, because "members of the Muslim Student Association or Palestinians for Justice groups… that are anti-Israel have brought BDS resolutions" which have "created emotional debates."

"Anti-Semitic *acts* against many in our Jewish community have resulted from the emotions over the debates over the BDS-Israel resolutions," she insisted, without citing evidence of the linkage.

As my colleague Alex Emmons reported, that view was endorsed earlier this week by Hillary Clinton, who called the Israel boycott movement "alarming" in her speech to the American Israeli Public Affairs Committee this week, and accused activists of anti-Semitic "bullying" of Jewish students on college campuses.

Later the same night, Bernie Sanders, who has been critical of Israeli policy, told Chris Hayes on MSNBC that he agreed with Clinton that "there is some level of anti-Semitism" in the BDS movement.

Supporters of the BDS movement, including those who call for Israel to grant full civil rights to Arab citizens of East Jerusalem and the millions of Palestinians who have lived under Israeli military control for nearly half a century in the West Bank and Gaza, strongly reject the claim that opposition to a state that privileges Jews is in any way anti-Semitic.

That the backlash against Israel on college campuses might be caused not by unreasoning hatred but by Israeli actions — like the ongoing blockade of Gaza, punctuated by three rounds of punishing airstrikes in the past seven years, the building of illegal, Jewish-only settlements across the occupied West Bank, or the refusal to recognize the rights of Palestinians driven from their homes in 1948 to ever return — seems not to have occurred to students, faculty or politicians whose support for the Jewish state is unquestioning.

As Omar Zahzah, a Palestinian-American graduate student at UCLA who spoke against the proposed policy before the regents voted on Wednesday, observed later:

"We all agree that anti-Semitism and racism must be combated on campus. Where we disagree is in the claim that anti-Zionism is bigotry. Palestinian and Jewish students alike should have the right to say that the ethnic cleansing of Palestine in 1948 was morally wrong and that Palestinian refugees should have the right to return home to a state where Palestinians and Jews live in equality rather than in a discriminatory Jewish state."

Butler, who teaches at UC Berkeley and spoke against the policy before the vote, said later that the amended language was still problematic. "If we think that we solve the problem by identifying forms of anti-Semitic anti-Zionism, then we are left with the question of who identifies such a position, and what are their operative definitions," she wrote. "These terms are vague and overbroad and run the risk of suppressing speech and violating principles of academic freedom."

In 2003, after the then-president of Harvard, Lawrence Summers, argued that academics who held "profoundly anti-Israel views" were "advocating and taking actions that are anti-Semitic in their effect if not their intent," Butler responded in the *London Review of Books*:

"*...it is important to distinguish between anti-Semitic speech which, say, produces a hostile and threatening environment for Jewish students – racist speech which any university administrator would be obliged to oppose and regulate – and speech which makes a student uncomfortable because it opposes a particular state or set of state policies that he or she may defend. The latter is a political debate, and if we say that the case of Israel is different, that any criticism of it is considered as an attack on Israelis, or Jews in general, then we have singled out this political allegiance from all other allegiances that are open to public debate. We have engaged in the most outrageous form of 'effective' censorship.*"

The vote in favor of the policy was celebrated by supporters like Tammi Rossman-Benjamin, a lecturer at UC Santa Cruz whose AMCHA Initiative led the campaign to have the university specifically condemn expressions of anti-Zionist activism, calling it "the driving force behind the alarming rise in anti-Semitism" on campuses.

But as the *Los Angeles Times* reporter Teresa Watanabe noted, "both the U.S. Department of Education's civil rights office and a federal judge have dismissed complaints by UC Jewish students that such activities have created a hostile climate and violated their educational rights."

The policy was also welcomed by Avi Oved, the student representative on the board of regents, who spoke from behind a laptop with a heart-shaped pro-Israel sticker that is used by the Israel advocacy group Stand With Us. Oved said the policy was necessary to defend pro-Israel students who have been subjected to abusive language, like being called "Zionist pigs," or told that "Zionists should be sent back to the gas chambers."

The chief executive of Stand With Us, Roz Rothstein, thanked the regents for endorsing her view that "denying Israel's right to exist and opposing the rights of the Jewish people to self-determination in their homeland is racism, pure and simple."[468]

For those who believe that the First Amendment would protect students rights in court, the opposite unfortunately happened. In a short timeframe of three months, the University of California used the new policy as a tactic to buttress criminal convictions upon their own students. The criminal convictions were sustained in US courts and students were criminally convicted over disingenuous charges for practicing their First Amendment rights as students. For any readers who are considering the University of California, keep in mind that they try to criminally convict their own students for Free Speech protests against Israel, for arguing in favor of the human rights of Palestinians, and it is all in favor of Zionist fascism. If you are considering joining UCLA, you should perhaps rethink that decision because your constitutional first amendment rights are likely to get violated with criminal penalties by the UCLA administrative staff who have no interest in protecting your freedoms or in defending the US Constitution. As the June 2016 article "*Students in California Might Face Criminal Conviction For Protesting Film on Israeli Army*" by Murtaza Hussain of *The Intercept* explains:

---

12. [468] Mackey, Robert. "University of California Adopts Policy Linking Anti-Zionism to Anti-Semitism." *The Intercept*, 23 Mar. 2016, theintercept.com/2016/03/23/university-of-california-adopts-policy-linking-anti-zionism-to-anti-semitism/.

LAST MONTH, A GROUP of students at the University of California, Irvine gathered to protest a screening of the film *Beneath the Helmet*, a documentary about the lives of recruits in the Israeli Defense Forces. Upset about the screening of a film they viewed as propaganda for a foreign military, the students were also protesting the presence of several IDF representatives who were holding a panel discussion at the screening.

That student protest has since become the subject of intense controversy. The school's chapter of Students for Justice in Palestine is now facing the possibility of being banned from the campus. In addition, a legal representative for some of the students involved in the protest, Tarek Shawky, told *The Intercept* that the students were informed by the university that their cases have been referred to the district attorney for criminal investigation.

The day after the event, the school's chancellor released a statement accusing student protestors of "crossing the line of civility." In his statement, posted on the school website, Chancellor Howard Gillman said that "while this university will protect freedom of speech, that right is not absolute," adding that the school would examine possible legal and administrative charges against the protestors. News reports cited claims that attendees at the film had been intimidated and blocked from exiting the event.

The protestors at the event represented a wide range of student groups, including Students for Justice in Palestine, Jewish Voice for Peace, and the Black Student Union. Students who spoke with *The Intercept* denied that anyone had intimidated attendees at the event or blocked access. "We held our protest in a way that reflected university guidelines; we didn't use amplified sound and we didn't restrict anyone's freedom of access to the event," says Daniel Carnie, a member of Jewish Voice for Peace who took part in the protest.

Contacted for comment, a media relations representative at UC Irvine said that it was normal practice for cases like this to be referred to the district attorney. "It is routine for UC Irvine Police Department, when called upon to investigate an incident on campus, to forward the investigation to the district attorney's office," said Cathy Lawhon. "It's then up to the DA's office to determine if any charges are warranted." Lawhon added that the school investigation into banning Students for Justice in Palestine was proceeding separately.

Reached for comment, the Orange County District Attorney stated that they have yet to receive a referral on the case from the school.

The incident is only the latest in which officials at UC Irvine and other major universities around the country have taken harsh measures against pro-Palestinian activists. "There is a really ugly history of targeting student groups advocating for Palestinian issues," says Liz Jackson, a staff attorney with Palestine Legal, a group that provides legal advice and advocacy to individuals in the U.S. advocating for Palestinian rights. "It suppresses the really important debates about U.S. foreign policy that young people need to be having. Instead of being able to engage freely and voice opinions that challenge the status quo, one side of the debate is just being crushed."

A REPORT ISSUED LAST year by Palestine Legal and the Center for Constitutional Rights documented 152 incidents of free-speech suppression on U.S. campuses in 2014. These incidents have included acts of censorship, threats of legal action, and even accusations of support for terrorism. Citing the threat posed to the First Amendment by such acts, the report added that they were "undermin[ing] the traditional role of universities in promoting the free expression of unpopular ideas and encouraging challenges to the orthodoxies prevalent in official political discourse."

Threats, punishment, and intimidation are all being routinely used to stifle dissenting viewpoints on Israel-Palestine, says Omar Shakir, a fellow at the Center for Constitutional Rights and a co-author of the report. "University officials are erecting bureaucratic actions to make it harder to hold certain events, imposing administrative sanctions and even firing and denying tenure to professors for their views on Israel-Palestine, efforts that collectively represent a grave threat to the First Amendment."

For instance, Native American studies professor Steven Salaita lost his tenured faculty position at the University of Illinois in 2014 after being accused of incivility in his online comments on Israel-Palestine. After a public legal battle, last year the school settled a lawsuit filed by Salaita for financial compensation.

In the case of UC Irvine, Shakir adds that the university's charge of "incivility" on the part of protestors is a particularly egregious attempt to stifle protected speech. "Accusations of incivility have always been used by those in power to justify attempts to suppress changes to the status quo," Shakir says. "The term itself, 'civility,' represents coded language that in the past has been used to try and suppress groups deemed 'uncivilized,' like Native Americans and African-Americans in the United States. It has no place being used as a basis to silence student activists today."

Those views were partly echoed by Ari Cohn, a lawyer with the Foundation for Individual Rights in Education, a campus free-speech organization. "If allegations that protestors at UC Irvine disrupted the event are substantiated, that would not be protected speech, as it would impinge on the speech of others attending the event," Cohn said. He added, however, that "civility in itself cannot be mandated by schools. Incivility plays a fundamental role in much of the social activism on campuses."

THREATS TO SPEECH have come not only from university administrations but from law enforcement as well. In 2010, Osama Shabaik was among a group of 11 students at UC Irvine who were arrested after protesting an appearance by then-Israeli Ambassador Michael Oren at the school. Oren's speaking event came roughly a year after Operation Cast Lead, a three-week Israeli military campaign against the Gaza Strip that killed hundreds of civilians. Intent on making a point about the inappropriate nature of Oren's appearance following the attack, Shabaik and others organized a protest to disrupt the event.

In an incident that was captured on video, Shabaik and several other students repeatedly stood up in the crowd to interrupt Oren's speech, chanting slogans against Israeli military abuses during Cast Lead. The students were detained and ejected from the event, something Shabaik says they had expected. But what came next was stunning. The school administration referred the students to the police, filing misdemeanor criminal charges against them for disrupting the event. The charges carried a maximum of one year in prison for each of those who protested.

The following year the case went to court, where Shabaik and nine other students were convicted and sentenced to three years probation.

"The administration was definitely sending a message and implicitly threatening our futures by having us charged as criminals for protesting," reflects Shabaik today. "A lot of those who were charged were students planning to go on to medical school or law school, and they were worried that having a criminal record would prevent that from happening."

Shabaik has since gone on to graduate from Harvard Law School, but he is concerned about how his criminal record could affect his future employment prospects. Looking back at the incident, he believes it helped inaugurate a high-level campaign to silence dissent on Israel-Palestine in the United States, which has extended to state legislatures.

Earlier this month, New York Gov. Andrew Cuomo signed an executive order that would force public institutions in New York to divest funds from groups supporting the Boycott, Divestment, and Sanctions (BDS) movement. The executive order has been criticized as a form of political blacklisting. Shabaik believes Cuomo's proposal echoes his own experience, where powerful institutions and public figures have sought to quash dissent on this issue.

"It's important to understand duality of responses when it comes to free speech. The whole essence of free speech is to challenge power and push back against government repression," says Shabaik. "The move to stop debate on this issue is now leading to crackdowns at state-funded colleges and universities and even at the state legislature level. People are facing serious threats to their future for speaking out against the status quo."

IN RECENT YEARS, a movement has grown, mostly on the political right, that charges that free speech is being endangered on American college campuses. The most prominent voices on this issue have been conservative activists like *Breitbart* journalist Milo Yiannopoulos and *Daily Wire*'s Ben Shapiro. But liberal writers such as Jonathan Chait have also relentlessly fixated on the idea that "political correctness" is stifling free expression among a new generation of students.

Most of these protestations have focused on a specific type of speech: the right to "offend" by speaking against perceived left-wing orthodoxies on race, feminism, and cultural issues. The charges of speech suppression in such cases have generally not been leveled at university administrators or law enforcement, but rather at students who view such speech as offensive. This differs markedly from the Israel-Palestine controversies, where state-funded bureaucracies and government officials have been involved in stifling speech on an issue directly related to American foreign policy.

"It's important to distinguish between the idea that certain views are not popular on campuses, something that may be worthy of discussion separately, and the phenomenon of public institutions and officials taking direct action to restrict speech about vital aspects of government policy," says Shakir of the Center for Constitutional Rights. "The core of the First Amendment defends the right to free speech on campuses, and we should all be concerned when McCarthy-esque tactics are being used by those in positions of power to silence debate on issues of global importance."[469]

To get a better understanding of the global scope and scale that the Right-wing party of Israel is campaigning to criminalize the concept of Free Speech by attributing any criticism of the political ideology of Zionism to anti-Semitism, Glenn Greenwald and Andrew Fishman of *The Intercept* offered an extensive article titled "*Greatest Threat To Free Speech In the West: Criminalizing Activism Against Israeli Occupation*" detailing Israel's global campaign to destroy Free Speech rights across the Western democratic countries of the world:

> **THE U.K. GOVERNMENT** today announced that it is will be illegal for "local [city] councils, public bodies, and even some university student unions ... to refuse to buy goods and services from companies involved in the arms trade, fossil fuels, tobacco products, or Israeli settlements in the occupied West Bank." Thus, any entities that support or participate in the global boycott of Israeli settlements will face "severe penalties."
> This may sound like an extreme infringement of free speech and political activism — and, of course, it is — but it is far from unusual in the West. The opposite is now true. There is a very coordinated and well-financed campaign led by Israel and its supporters literally to *criminalize* political activism against Israeli occupation, based on the particular fear that the worldwide campaign of Boycott, Sanctions, and Divestment, or BDS — modeled after the 1980s campaign that brought down the Israel-allied apartheid regime in South Africa — is succeeding.
>
> The Israeli website +972 reported last year about a pending bill that "would ban entry to foreigners who promote the [BDS] movement that aims to pressure Israel to comply with international law and respect Palestinian rights." In 2011, a law passed in Israel that "effectively ban[ned] any public call for a boycott — economic, cultural, or academic — against Israel or its West Bank settlements, making such action a punishable offense."

---

13. [469] Hussain, Murtaza. "Students in California Might Face Criminal Investigation for Protesting Film on Israeli Army." *The Intercept*, 23 June 2016, theintercept.com/2016/06/23/students-in-california-might-face-criminal-investigation-for-protesting-film-on-israeli-army/.

But the current censorship goal is to make such activism a crime not only in Israel, but in Western countries generally. And it is succeeding.

THIS TREND TO outlaw activism against the decades-long Israeli occupation — particularly though not only through boycotts against Israel — has permeated multiple Western nations and countless institutions within them. In October, we reported on the *criminal convictions* in France of 12 activists "for the 'crime' of advocating sanctions and a boycott against Israel as a means of ending the decadeslong military occupation of Palestine," convictions upheld by France's highest court. They were literally arrested and prosecuted for "wearing shirts emblazoned with the words 'Long live Palestine, boycott Israel'" and because "they also handed out fliers that said that 'buying Israeli products means legitimizing crimes in Gaza.'"

As we noted, Pascal Markowicz, chief lawyer of the CRIF umbrella organization of French Jewish communities, published this celebratory decree (emphasis in original): "BDS is ILLEGAL in France." Statements advocating a boycott or sanctions, he added, "are completely illegal. If [BDS activists] say their freedom of expression has been violated, now France's highest legal instance ruled otherwise." In Canada last year, officials threatened criminal prosecution against anyone supporting boycotts against Israel.

In the U.S., unbeknownst to many, there are similar legislative proscriptions on such activism, and a pending bill would strengthen the outlawing of BDS. As the *Washington Post* reported last June, "A wave of anti-BDS legislation is sweeping the U.S." Numerous bills in Congress encourage or require state action to combat BDS.

Eyal Press warned in a must-read *New York Times* op-ed last month that under a Customs Bill passed by both houses of Congress and headed to the White House, "American officials will be obligated to treat the settlements as part of Israel in future trade negotiations," a provision specifically designed "to combat the Boycott, Divestment, and Sanctions movement, a grass-roots campaign." But as Press notes, under existing law — which is almost never discussed — "Washington already forbids American companies to cooperate with state-led boycotts of Israel."

The real purpose of this new law, as Press explains it, is to force American companies to treat settlements in the West Bank — which virtually the entire world views as illegal — as a valid part of Israel, by *outlawing* any behavior that would be deemed cooperative with a boycott of companies occupying the West Bank. U.S. companies would be *forced* to pretend that products produced in the occupied territories are actually produced in "Israel." The White House announced that it will sign the bill despite its opposition to the AIPAC-backed pro-settlement provision.

Rahul Saksena of Palestine Legal said that "the BDS provision in the federal customs bill, and the dozens of anti-BDS bills being introduced in Congress and state legislatures across the U.S., are examples of the lengths that Israel's fiercest advocates and the lawmakers who bend over backward to accommodate them will go to shut down any conversation critical of Israeli policies and supportive of Palestinian freedom." Dylan Williams, vice president of government affairs for J Street (which opposes BDS), told *The Intercept*: "The references in the Customs Act to 'Israeli-controlled territories' are just one instance of a larger effort to sneak Green Line-blurring language into legislation at both the state and national level."

Under the existing laws, American companies have been *fined* for actions deemed supportive of boycotts aimed at Israel. For decades, U.S. companies and their foreign subsidiaries, for instance, have been required by law to refuse to comply with the Arab League boycott of Israel. Penalties for violators include up to 10 years of imprisonment.

In 2010, GM Daewoo Auto & Technology Company, a Korean firm owned by General Motors, was fined $88,500 by the Office of Antiboycott Compliance for 59 anti-boycott violations, including the "crime" of declaring on a customs form: "We hereby state that the carrying vessel ... is allowed to enter the Libya ports [sic]." At the time, Libyan law did not allow Israeli goods or ships that had previously stopped in Israel to enter Libyan ports, and the company's seemingly banal declaration that it was complying with Libyan law was deemed by the U.S. government to constitute support for a boycott of Israel, and it was thus fined.

THE SUPPRESSION OF anti-occupation activism is particularly acute on American college campuses. Among other things, that is deeply ironic. In the U.S. over the past year, there has been a widespread media debate over censorship on college campuses. Notably, the pundits who have most vocally condemned this censorship and held themselves out as free speech crusaders — such as *New York*'s Jonathan Chait — have completely ignored what is far and away the most widespread form of campus censorship: namely, punishment of those who engage in activism against Israeli actions. This campus censorship on behalf of Israel was comprehensively documented in a report last year by Palestine Legal titled "The Palestine Exception to Free Speech." The nationwide censorship effort has seen pro-Palestinian professors fired, anti-occupation student activists suspended and threatened with expulsion, pro-Palestinian groups de-funded, and even discipline for students for the "crime" of flying a Palestinian flag. The report documents how pro-Israel campus groups and alumni "have intensified their efforts to stifle criticism of Israeli government policies." The report explains: "Rather than engage such criticism on its merits, these groups leverage their significant resources and lobbying power to pressure universities, government actors, and other institutions to censor or punish advocacy in support of Palestinian rights."

Notably, the students and administrators justifying the campus censorship of anti-Israel views invoke the very same "PC" rhetoric of "safe spaces" and "hate speech" denounced by ostensibly free-speech pundits.[470]

Further along the article, they explain the extent in which this global campaign to outlaw Free Speech criticism of Israel is penetrating US laws in other maneuvers on the State levels in violation of US Constitutional rights in our contemporary time:

This attempt to formalize suppression of anti-occupation advocacy on college campuses is long-standing and widespread. The New York state legislature actually passed "a bill that would suspend funding to educational institutions which fund groups that boycott Israel." Such legislation is becoming commonplace, as the group United With Israel boasted just last month:

Florida became the fifth state in the U.S. to introduce a resolution to confront the anti-Israel BDS (Boycott, Divestment, Sanctions) movement when it passed a law on December 21, similar to the first anti-BDS legislation introduced in Tennessee last April.

By doing so, Florida has joined Tennessee, New York, Indiana, and Pennsylvania. Another 35 states are reportedly considering similar legislation.

The commendably consistent pro-campus-speech group FIRE, while expressing some criticisms of the BDS movement, has repeatedly documented and denounced attempts to suppress BDS advocacy on campus:

FIRE's position on the Israel-focused BDS movement is driven by our concern for academic freedom — for students and professors, and for its continuing importance as a meaningful concept in and of itself. Students and professors must be perfectly free to support boycott, divestment, and/or sanctions against Israel or any other country they wish, and they must not face punishment for this support. As you might expect, FIRE has opposed attempts to punish organizations for supporting BDS, and we

---

14. [470] Greenwald, Glenn, and Andrew Fishman. "Greatest Threat to Free Speech in the West: Criminalizing Activism Against Israeli Occupation." *The Intercept*, 16 Feb. 2016, theintercept.com/2016/02/16/greatest-threat-to-free-speech-in-the-west-criminalizing-activism-against-israeli-occupation/.

have certainly defended professors' rights to be highly critical of Israel — or, frankly, any other country, person, or idea.

YET THIS CENSORSHIP effort to ban BDS and other forms of Israel criticism continues to grow, in multiple countries around the world. It's not hard to understand why. The Israeli government and its most powerful supporters have invested vast sums of money and considerable political capital into the campaign to institutionalize this censorship.

Last year, GOP billionaire Sheldon Adelson and Democratic billionaire Haim Saban donated tens of millions of dollars to a new fund to combat BDS on college campuses. Also last year, Israeli Prime Minister Benjamin Netanyahu"decided to implement a 2014 resolution to establish a special task force to fight the anti-Israeli sanctions"; that task force has funding of "some 100 million Israeli shekels (roughly $25.5 million)." *BuzzFeed*'s Rosie Gray reported in 2014 that anti-BDS legislation has become a major goal of AIPAC. As part of the controversy at the University of California, Richard Blum, the mega-rich investment banker and husband of Sen. Dianne Feinstein, threatened the university that his wife would take adverse action against the university if it did not adopt the harsh anti-BDS measures he was demanding.

None of this is to say, obviously, that suppression of anti-occupation activism is the only strain of free speech threats in the West. The prosecution of Western Muslims for core free speech expression under "terrorism" laws, the distortion of "hate speech" legislation as a means of punishing unpopular ideas, threats and violence against those who publish cartoons deemed "blasphemous," and pressure on social media companies to ban ideas disliked by governments are all serious menaces to this core liberty.

But in terms of systematic, state-sponsored, formalized punishments for speech and activism, nothing compares to the growing multi-nation effort to criminalize activism against Israeli occupation. Rafeef Ziadah, a Palestinian a member of the Palestinian BDS National Committee, told *The Intercept*: "Israel is increasingly unable to defend its regime of apartheid and settler colonialism over the Palestinian people and its regular massacres of Palestinians in Gaza so is resorting to asking supportive governments in the U.S. and Europe to undermine free speech as a way of shielding it from criticism and measures aimed at holding it to account."

It is, needless to say, perfectly legitimate to argue against BDS and to engage in activism to defeat it. But only advocates of tyranny could support the literal outlawing of the same type of activism that ended apartheid in South Africa merely on the grounds that this time it is aimed at Israeli occupation (some of Israel's own leaders have compared its occupation to apartheid). And whatever else is true, commentators and activists who prance around as defenders of campus free speech and free expression generally — yet who completely ignore this most pernicious trend of free speech erosion — are likely many things, but an authentic believer in free speech is not among them.

Correction: The first paragraph has been edited to reflect that the ban on boycotts will be illegal under the UK Government's new plan, not that it already is illegal, as well as to clarify that the penalties imposed on local entities violating the boycott ban are statutory, not criminal, in nature.[471]

As of 2018, and subsequently the reason I've had a change of mind on this particular topic of contentious religious and political debate is because I had thought it would slowly fade after the Israel-Palestine conflict of 2014, but this pressure by the right-wing of Israel on

---

15. [471] Greenwald, Glenn, and Andrew Fishman. "Greatest Threat to Free Speech in the West: Criminalizing Activism Against Israeli Occupation." *The Intercept*, 16 Feb. 2016, theintercept.com/2016/02/16/greatest-threat-to-free-speech-in-the-west-criminalizing-activism-against-israeli-occupation/.

contemporary Western politics has only become worse and the assault on US Constitutional Rights under the First Amendment is now particularly vulnerable to this Zionist form of fascism that repeatedly and consistently attempts to destroy US Constitutional freedoms by making any speech against the political ideology a conflation to anti-Semitism and Holocaust denial.

The assault on the First Amendment rights of college students seemed to contribute to this demand for "safe spaces" because Zionism wouldn't stop from harming people's free speech, the UCLA buttressed this by successfully managing to criminalize student protests to threaten their students into silent obedience with courts seemingly ignoring the Free Speech rights of students that go to UCLA, and Israel then pushed this fascist demand across Europe. In 2018, several Republican nominees were campaigning ostensibly in defense of Free Speech while forwarding proposals to further destroy the Constitutional rights of its citizens in various States across the US. As the Intercept's Lee Fang and Zaid Jilani report in "*Politicians Campaign On Free Speech While Voting To Penalize Boycotts of Israel*" as follows:

> **POLITICIANS AROUND THE** country are seizing upon highly publicized episodes of conservatives faced with harassment and heckling on college campuses by responding with a wave of legislation supposedly aimed at preserving free speech rights for campus speakers. But that commitment, while draped in the mantle of a principled defense of the First Amendment, does not always extend to speakers who criticize Israel and its policies.
>
> This renewed concern about free speech comes after a number of high-profile incidents in which students interrupted conservative speakers, and in a few cases, even used violence at protests. At a hearing on campus free speech in October, U.S. senators expressed bipartisan support for the First Amendment on college campuses, but lawmakers around the country are demanding free speech with one hand, and passing laws that punish boycotts of Israel with the other.
>
> One of the most prominent examples comes from Wisconsin, where Republican state Sen. Leah Vukmir has used the issue of campus free speech to launch a campaign for U.S. Senate this year, challenging the incumbent, Democratic Sen. Tammy Baldwin.
>
> Vukmir is the original sponsor of "free speech" legislation that calls for a strict disciplinary system for those who infringe on others' free speech rights on college campuses in her state. "Students, professors, and administrators are using intimidation tactics to silence those they disagree with," Vukmir said, after unveiling her legislation last May.
>
> She went on to launch a campaign with the help of the American Legislative Exchange Council, or ALEC, for lawmakers in other states to duplicate her campus free speech efforts. "Senator Vukmir is a champion of free speech issues," reads a press release from ALEC, which awarded Vukmir its "Iron Lady Award" for taking tough stands as a legislator.
>
> But Vukmir, a strong supporter of Israel, is apparently selective in her championing of free speech.
>
> Just months after sponsoring the free speech legislation last year, Vukmir sponsored a so-called anti-BDS law in Wisconsin, prohibiting the state from entering into contracts with businesses that choose to express themselves by engaging in a boycott to protest Israeli occupation of the West Bank. Gov. Scott Walker signed an executive order establishing the anti-BDS policy in October.
>
> BDS refers to the Palestinian-led boycott, divestment, and sanctions movement that advocates for economic pressure to force Israel to end its occupation of the Palestinian territories. BDS campaigns have gained traction across the United States in recent years, particularly on college campuses. Palestine Legal, a nonprofit advocacy group, notes that boycotts have long played a

significant role in U.S. history, and that the "Supreme Court has held that boycotts to effect political, social, and economic change are protected by the First Amendment of the Constitution."

But pro-Israel advocacy organizations, including the America Israel Public Affairs Committee, known by its acronym AIPAC, have spearheaded an aggressive campaign to encourage lawmakers to stifle BDS activism. Twenty-four states have now passed legislation designed to penalize or prohibit BDS activity.

These laws have been used to suppress the speech of a wide range of people and businesses. In Kansas, a star teacher was denied payment to train other teachers because she was following her church's guidance and boycotting Israel. (A federal court struck down the Kansas law following that controversy.) In Texas, a town seeking contractors to rebuild after a devastating hurricane mistakenly used an anti-BDS clause to prevent the hiring of anyone who also boycotted Israel.

Rather than focus on the suppression of pro-Palestinian activism, legislators have almost singularly focused on a string of high-profile attacks on right-wing speakers on college campuses. One example is Milo Yiannopoulos, an "alt-right" provocateur who has collaborated with white supremacist figures. He was a relatively obscure figure until left-wing activists protested violently when he came to the University of California, Berkeley campus, elevating him as a national figure. At the October Senate hearing, Allison Stanger, a Middlebury College professor, testified about her experience moderating a talk with American Enterprise Institute scholar Charles Murray, whose book, "The Bell Curve," on IQ as a determinant of socioeconomic status has been criticized as being racist. The protesters disrupted the speaking engagement, assaulting Stanger and leaving her hospitalized.

ACROSS THE COUNTRY, politicians are hoping to harness the outrage over such incidents into political benefit, supposedly in the name of securing free speech.

Texas Republican state Sen. Van Taylor last week won the GOP nomination to run for Texas's 3rd Congressional District, which encompasses parts of Dallas. Last year, Taylor voted in favor of SB1151, a bill designed to discourage campus censorship. The vote occurred within weeks of another Taylor-supported bill, HB89, which prevents the state of Texas from entering into contracts with businesses engaged in BDS activism.

Ohio Republican state Rep. Robert Sprague, running for state treasurer, is the sponsor of bills to both promote campus free speech and to penalize companies that express support for BDS.

In Georgia, Republican state senator Josh McKoon is one of a number of Republicans vying for the office of secretary of state. He was one of the co-sponsors of Senate Bill 339, which, like the Wisconsin bill, takes aim at students who interrupt university speakers. McKoon is also the man behind the failed perennial push for a religious freedom bill, known as RFRA, that critics fear would essentially license businesses to discriminate.

In a 2016 interview, McKoon justified the religious freedom bill by citing the example of a wedding singer who would be asked by a same-sex couple to perform at their ceremony. "If that person is approached by a same-sex couple that says, 'We want to hire you to do this,'"and [the singer] says, 'No, I believe that wedding is a sacramental union that involves God, one man, and one woman, and this is contrary to my belief,' are we going to say, as a matter of policy, the government is going to compel that person to participate in the order of service against their sincerely held religious beliefs? I don't think that anybody would suggest that we shouldn't make room for people who have different beliefs or different ideas," he said.

But McKoon also was a sponsor of SB 327, which, when it passed in 2016, outlawed state contracts with any individual or business who boycotts businesses based in Israel or even in the illegal settlements Israel operates in Palestinian territory. The bill does exactly what McKoon claims to be against: It tries to compel people to take actions against their own beliefs.

For example, the Kansas teacher who was barred from a state contract because of her support for BDS was inspired to engage in boycotts because of her membership in the Mennonite Church USA. Last year, the church voted to divest from some U.S. companies that do business in Israel's occupied territories.

In an email to The Intercept, McKoon said he saw no contradiction between supporting RFRA and potentially punishing individuals who would boycott Israel under a religion obligation.

"With respect to your question, if RFRA were to pass, the state law regarding contracts with Israel and a business which does business with Georgia claimed their boycott of Israel had a religious basis, then the balancing test would be applied," he wrote, going on to explain the legal balancing test a court would have to do if the law were to be challenged. "First the Court would have to determine if the interest in preserving our relationship with Israel was a compelling state interest. Then if the Court was satisfied that it was a compelling state interest they would have to determine if some sort of religious accommodation would be warranted to make the policy the least restrictive policy. I don't pretend to know how the Court would resolve a hypothetical lawsuit after RFRA passed, which is the point of the whole RFRA debate. It isn't a religious exemption bill as some have tried to claim, but rather a balancing test under which sometimes the government prevails and sometimes the individual prevails."

He added: "I don't see a conflict between desiring a strict scrutiny standard for free exercise claims against state and local government and public policy to preserve our historic relationship with the State of Israel."

In other words, McKoon argued that the state may have an interest in maintaining a relationship with Israel that supersedes an individual's religious freedom and free speech rights, or it may not, but he wants the courts to settle the debate.

In Iowa, the state legislature in 2016 voted to bar state funds from being invested in companies boycotting Israel. On February 28 of this year, the state Senate passed its own campus free speech bill, with all Republicans in favor, and all Democrats plus the chamber's one independent opposed. All of the Republicans who were serving in 2016 and are still serving backed both the anti-BDS and campus free speech bill.

The hypocrisy, while more pronounced by Republicans on the state level, is shared by both parties.

In Congress, a bipartisan group of lawmakers have sponsored a series of resolutions and hearings to highlight the threat to free speech on college campuses, while many of the same members have sponsored efforts go even further than state-level anti-BDS laws, pushing to impose criminal and civil penalties on organizations that engage in BDS activism.

The Senate legislation criminalizing boycott speech against Israel is championed by Sen. Ben Cardin, D-Md. In the House, the lead co-sponsor is Rep. Todd Rokita, R-Ind., who simultaneously sponsors the bill championing free expression on college campuses.

The anti-BDS laws have the potential to result in censorship of student speakers, the very issue that has supposedly inspired the wave of campus free speech laws.

As a result of Arizona's HB2617, an anti-BDS state law passed in 2016, students at Arizona State University had to change their plans for an upcoming event on Palestine. They invited Hatem Bazian, chair of American Muslims for Palestine, to speak about BDS at the April 3 event, but the university's speaker agreement included a "No Boycott of Israel" clause, based on the state's anti-BDS law. Bazian could not comply with that provision and thus, was effectively barred from speaking at the university, according to a lawsuit filed on March 1 by the CAIR Legal Defense Fund.

Bret Hovell, a spokesperson for the university, told The Intercept that the school does not believe the anti-BDS law should apply in this case, and that student groups are free to use a contract that does not include the clause. "It was a simple mistake that the ASU form containing the certification [of not boycotting Israel] was used," he said. The Arizona Attorney General's Office did not respond to a request for comment on its view of whether the law applies.

Not every politician who champions free speech is a hypocrite. Massachusetts Democratic Sen. Elizabeth Warren attended the October Senate hearing on campus free speech and condemned both censorship and violence as a response to controversial speakers. But she <u>also told a town hall</u> last year that she opposes anti-BDS legislation, arguing that it infringes on free speech.[472]

The specific topic of the failings of the US mainstream media would be beyond the scope of this chapter and lack in relevance to the topic. I will share more information on the US mainstream media's failings as organizations and their abuses of US constitutional rights further on in sections pertaining to Islam where I will critique the influence of Christian businesspeople who have the most significant influence among religious groups and their impact upon the US mainstream media.

As a final point of contention regarding the controversial issue between Zionism and Free Speech, and to give a general idea of the quality of people being hired in US mainstream news media, consider the New York Times decision to hire a person known for spreading lies, flaunting the religious ideology of Zionism as a weapon to destroy the constitutional rights of proud US citizens who are of Arab descent through deception, and attempting to force the discriminatory standards of Israeli society against Palestinians that are US-born and raised in order to disparage, sabotage, and erase their constitutionally protected rights as US citizens for an openly hostile agenda to their constitutionally protected Free Speech. The person who conducted such behavior upon Arabs in the US openly stated that the political and religious ideology of Zionism is why she attempted to destroy their constitutionally protected rights. This is referring to the racist bigot of the New York Times, Bari Weiss. I am openly calling her that because of my personal judgment regarding her history, which she has flippantly dismissed with no apologies given to the people that she harmed and no remorse shown for her actions. The information as follows is from the article titled "*NYT's Bari Weiss Falsely Denies Her Years of Attacks on the Academic Freedom of Arab Scholars who Criticize Israel*" by Glenn Greenwald of *The Intercept* which explains her horrifying history of deception, lies, and smug bigotry at getting away with the explicit acts of racism against Arabs:

> **AFTER THE NEW YORK TIMES** last April hired Bari Weiss to write for and edit its op-ed page, I <u>wrote a long article</u> detailing her history of pro-Israel activism and, especially, her involvement in numerous campaigns to vilify and ruin the careers of several Arab and Muslim professors due to their criticisms of Israel. I chose to profile Weiss's history because (a) the simultaneous hiring of Bret Stephens generated so much controversy that Weiss's hiring was ignored, even though it was clear her hiring would be more influential since she would be not just writing but also commissioning articles for that highly influential op-ed page; (b) the NYT was justifying these hires on the grounds of "diversity," even though hiring hardcore, pro-Israel activists for that page (which has no Muslim columnists) was the literal opposite of diversity; and, most of all, (c) Weiss was masquerading as an opponent of viewpoint intolerance on college campuses even though her entire career had been built on trying to suppress, stigmatize, and punish academic criticisms of Israel.
>
> Since that article, Weiss has predictably written multiple banal columns for the Times denouncing what she perceives as growing left-wing intolerance for dissent in general, but particularly on college

---

16. [472] Fang, Lee, and Zaid Jilani. "Politicians Campaign on Free Speech While Voting to Penalize Boycotts of Israel." *The Intercept*, 14 Mar. 2018, theintercept.com/2018/03/14/campus-free-speech-bds-israel-boycott

campuses. I've watched as Weiss has become celebrated in right-wing circles as some sort of paragon of free expression and academic freedom, and mourned by centrists as the tragic victim of online PC mob silencing campaigns (imagine being a columnist and editor at the New York Times — with full access to the most influential media platform in the world — and seeing yourself as the victim of silencing and censorship), even though her entire career is grounded in precisely the viewpoint suppression, vilification, and censorship campaigns she now depicts herself as loathing.

All of this finally came to a head last night after Weiss published yet another column complaining that she and her ideological comrades are unfairly criticized by left-wing authoritarians who try to silence them by associating them with "fascism." Weiss's column was so replete with humiliating factual errors, shoddy argumentation, and glaring holes in reasoning that she ended up trending on Twitter, and her editors had to delete an entire paragraph from her column and then add an editor's note explaining that she had cited evidence that was an obvious hoax.

In the course of the controversy, Weiss, in a tweet-essay that began here, finally addressed her own history of trying to ruin the careers of Arab and Muslim scholars for the crime of criticizing Israel. Unfortunately, she did so by falsely denying what she actually did, making demonstrably untrue claims about the controversies in which she was involved, and, worst of all, outright ignoring the most egregious example of her viewpoint-suppression campaigns:

The campus controversies in which Weiss was involved for years are well-reported, and I wrote about and documented the facts at length in the profile I wrote of her. I'm not going to recount all of that here — those interested in the long version can read that article — but instead will just note several facts that others raised last night making clear how false Weiss's attempt is to whitewash her long history of trying to suppress criticisms of Israel from college campuses:

(1) Anyone remotely familiar with the wars over the Middle East Studies Department at Columbia University, in which Weiss played a starring role, knows that her claim here — that the campaign was just a benign attempt to protect students' rights — is utterly false. The campaign was designed to ruin the careers of Arab professors by equating their criticisms of Israel with racism, anti-Semitism, and bullying, and its central demand was that those professors (some of whom lacked tenure) be disciplined for their transgressions. Here is Megan Greenwell, now the editor-in-chief of Deadspin, who was the editor-in-chief of Columbia's student newspaper during this controversy, responding last night to Weiss:

The article Greenwell references quotes Weiss as accusing multiple Arab professors critical of Israel of being racists: "We put the mentions of the publications in the film to expose the racism of these professors," Weiss said. *This* is the person now using the New York Times op-ed page to complain that academics and commentators with unpopular views are the targets of unfair character assassination.

(2) That the campaign against these Arab professors was about suppressing criticisms of Israel and intimidating and punishing professors who voiced such criticisms was barely hidden. The New York Civil Liberties Union — historically reluctant to involve itself in disputes involving Israel — strongly condemned the campaign against these Arab professors at Columbia that Weiss helped to lead.

The group "called on Columbia University President Lee Bollinger to resist attacks from within and outside the university that jeopardize academic freedom at Columbia," and it explicitly made clear that the whole point of the campaign "is whether professors teaching controversial subject matter that offends some students should be disciplined or face recrimination for expressing unpopular views in their classrooms." (Anthony Weiner, at the time a member of Congress running for mayor of New York, was just one of many politicians who demanded that Professor Joseph Massad be fired for what he called "his displays of anti-Semitism.") In denouncing the censorship campaign Weiss helped to lead, the NYCLU made clear that the excuse she offered last night is totally false:

"*It is clear that this controversy would not have acquired the attention it received if it were simply about the rudeness of professors or their intolerance of other points of view. This David Project film would not have provoked controversy had it not arisen out of the divisive political controversy involving Israel and Palestine. **The attack on Professor Massad and other in the MEALAC Department is really about their scholarship and political expression.***"

As Professor Juan Cole wrote at the time: "The lesson for academics, and American society as a whole: McCarthyism is unacceptable *except* when criticism of Israel is involved." Indeed, as Ali Abunimah noted last night, just two years ago Weiss wrote a long article accusing Massad of being an anti-Semite and lamenting that he "won tenure in 2009 despite the sustained and strong opposition of student whistleblowers, concerned alumni, and others."

That's what makes this whole spectacle so amazing: The New York Times is allowing one of its columnists to masquerade as a stalwart defender of campus free speech and academic pluralism while utterly ignoring, and allowing her to falsely deny, her own long history in trying to stigmatize and punish professors who criticized Israel, to the point where the NYCLU stepped in and denounced her campaign as a dangerous threat to academic freedom.

(3) The campaign against these Arab professors at Columbia generated a massive controversy that ultimately involved some of the school's largest donors. As a result, an extensive investigation was conducted that ultimately exonerated the accused Arab scholars of anti-Semitism and other offenses. Though the investigative committee found *one instance* in which it said a professor had become excessively angry at a student's defense of Israel, it concluded that it found "no evidence of any statements made by the faculty that could reasonably be construed as anti-Semitic." The report, ironically, did find a campaign of intimidation — aimed *at* the Arab professors, not from them; it "describe[d] a broader environment of incivility on campus, with pro-Israel students disrupting lectures on Middle Eastern studies and some faculty members feeling that they were being spied on" — the very behavior Weiss now denounces when it comes from her ideological opponents.

As Cole noted, the report found that the kind of systematic harassment Weiss now pretends to find so objectionable was actually directed at these Arab professors by her own ideological comrades:

"*Although it was little noted in the press, the report did indeed acknowledge that Massad in particular and the department in general had been the target of an ongoing campaign of intimidation. It noted that for several years, after pieces appeared in the tabloid press blasting the department as anti-Israel, many non-students, clearly hostile and with ideological agendas, had been attending classes in the department, interrupting lectures with hostile asides and inhibiting classroom debate.*"

When the report was issued clearing these professors of virtually all the charges leveled against them and finding instead that they were the victims rather than the perpetrators of harassment campaigns, Weiss was furious and held press conferences and demonstrations to denounce it:

(4) Unfortunately for Weiss, her attempts now to revise her own history are rendered impossible by her own remarks about her activism, filmed years before she knew she would be at the center of this type of attention. As I noted in my original article, Weiss spoke on a panel at the 2012 Conference of the American Zionist Movement in which she explained (in a video on YouTube) that she "got involved in journalism through activism" — specifically, activism against Arab and Muslim professors at Columbia — and that she now devotes herself to the "connection between advocacy journalism and Zionism."[473]

---

17. [473] Greenwald, Glenn. "NYT's Bari Weiss Falsely Denies Her Years of Attacks on the Academic

After showing some videos, Greenwald explains further in the article:

(5) Most egregious to me was the case that Weiss last night so notably decided to ignore: her involvement in the attempt to smear and ruin the academic career of a rising Palestinian-American professor, Nadia Abu El-Haj, for the crime of writing a book questioning the archeological claims of the Israeli government. I won't go into all the details of this case — I wrote about it at length in that original article and it was also the subject of very lengthy reporting in the New Yorker and the New York Times — but the gist of it is crucial for understanding who Weiss really is and how false are her denials from last night.

In sum, Abu El-Haj was a rising academic star at the University of Chicago who was on a fast track toward tenure. Her 2002 book anthropologically examining Jewish claims to a biblical entitlement of Israel won numerous awards and praise from scholars across many disciplines. In 2006, she moved to New York and applied for a tenured position at Barnard; it was widely assumed, given her sterling reputation, that her acceptance would be automatic — until an Israeli settler in the West Bank started an online petition demanding that she be denied tenure due to her 2002 book about Israel.

That online petition led to an incredibly ugly attempt to smear her as an anti-Semite who used shoddy scholarship to question Israeli claims, and — needless to say — Weiss was a vocal supporter of this effort. Pretending that she was concerned about Abu El-Haj's academic abilities rather than her views on Israel — as though Weiss were even remotely capable of assessing Abu El-Haj's anthropological and archeological methods — Weiss wrote an article in Haaretz arguing that the fight over Abu El-Haj's tenure "is not just another round between the Zionists and the anti-Zionists," but instead, "is about the nature of truth, and the possibility of, well, facts themselves."

For someone who purports to be such a devoted adherent to pluralism and free expression on college campuses, Weiss sure does have a tendency to find a large number of Arab and Muslim scholars who are critical of Israel who she believes deserve sanction, vilification, punishment, and denial of career advancement.

I'm someone who strongly believes in the right of people to change their views and to evolve. My first book, which began by describing my own political and intellectual journey, started with this quote from Abraham Lincoln: "I do not think much of a man who is not wiser today than he was yesterday." And I find some of the concerns about prevailing viewpoint intolerance on college campuses to be valid, or at least reasonable.

If Weiss would acknowledge that she spent years engaged in the precise types of censorship and vilification campaigns that she has now come to regard as so menacing, I would find that admission admirable, not objectionable. But she's doing the opposite: She's denying that her activities were geared toward exactly the climate of intimidation and censorship against which she now crusades. Perhaps it's possible that she's just in a state of denial, incapable of admitting that she built her career based on exactly the types of activities that she now so vocally denounces.

But what seems far more likely is that, like so many people, Weiss finds censorship and vilification objectionable only when it's directed at her, her friends, and the viewpoints she supports. In particular, it is this mentality that explains why left-wing attacks on racism, fascism, and other authoritarian views on campus receive so much attention from America's pundit class, while the most pervasive form of campus censorship — directed at Israel critics and pro-Palestinian activists — is so often ignored. In Bari Weiss, the New York Times seems to have found the perfect embodiment of this free speech double standard. But none of that should justify allowing a New York Times columnist and editor to offer such blatantly inaccurate claims about ugly controversies in which they played a leading role.

For someone who purports to be such a devoted adherent to pluralism and free expression on college campuses, Weiss sure does have a tendency to find a large number of Arab and Muslim scholars who

---

Freedom of Arab Scholars Who Criticize Israel." *The Intercept*, 8 Mar. 2018, theintercept.com/2018/03/08/the-nyts-bari-weiss-falsely-denies-her-years-of-attacks-on-the-academic-freedom-of-arab-scholars-who-criticize-israel/.

are critical of Israel who she believes deserve sanction, vilification, punishment, and denial of career advancement.

I'm someone who strongly believes in the right of people to change their views and to evolve. My first book, which began by describing my own political and intellectual journey, started with this quote from Abraham Lincoln: "I do not think much of a man who is not wiser today than he was yesterday." And I find some of the concerns about prevailing viewpoint intolerance on college campuses to be valid, or at least reasonable.

If Weiss would acknowledge that she spent years engaged in the precise types of censorship and vilification campaigns that she has now come to regard as so menacing, I would find that admission admirable, not objectionable. But she's doing the opposite: She's denying that her activities were geared toward exactly the climate of intimidation and censorship against which she now crusades. Perhaps it's possible that she's just in a state of denial, incapable of admitting that she built her career based on exactly the types of activities that she now so vocally denounces.

But what seems far more likely is that, like so many people, Weiss finds censorship and vilification objectionable only when it's directed at her, her friends, and the viewpoints she supports. In particular, it is this mentality that explains why left-wing attacks on racism, fascism, and other authoritarian views on campus receive so much attention from America's pundit class, while the most pervasive form of campus censorship — directed at Israel critics and pro-Palestinian activists — is so often ignored. In Bari Weiss, the New York Times seems to have found the perfect embodiment of this free speech double standard. But none of that should justify allowing a New York Times columnist and editor to offer such blatantly inaccurate claims about ugly controversies in which they played a leading role.[474]

It seems clear that with journalism pertaining to the wrongdoings of Israel, the New York Times has no concern for accuracy or legitimate journalism. After all, they hired a person with such an explicitly racist past, who feels no remorse for her actions, and presents herself as a victim after harassing and smearing others who had done nothing but hold different viewpoints from her.[475] This racist bigot should be in some tabloid magazine, but instead she gets a high paid position in the NYTimes to spread hatred, fear, and lies for what seem to be her racist beliefs about the inferiority of Arabs. Would she have treated her Arab professors with just disrespect and vitriol over blatant lies that she conjured up to suit her agenda, if she didn't hold any racism for Arabs? It's possible, but why then also try to make a character assassination for a female professor of Arab descent that she had never met and whose work that she had never read? Truly, hiring a person of such dubious character is a further shame on the New York Times reputation and sheds to light how unreliable their reporting is with respect to Israel. These are not Arab conspiracy theorists, these are proud and successful US citizens of Arab descent who have criticisms of a foreign country that US taxpayer money is giving free aid to.[476]

18. [474] Greenwald, Glenn. "NYT's Bari Weiss Falsely Denies Her Years of Attacks on the Academic Freedom of Arab Scholars Who Criticize Israel." *The Intercept*, 8 Mar. 2018, theintercept.com/2018/03/08/the-nyts-bari-weiss-falsely-denies-her-years-of-attacks-on-the-academic-freedom-of-arab-scholars-who-criticize-israel/.
19. [475] "NYCLU Defends Academic Freedom At Columbia University." *New York Civil Liberties Union*, 21 Feb. 2007, www.nyclu.org/en/press-releases/nyclu-defends-academic-freedom-columbia-university.
20. [476] "U.S. Foreign Aid to Israel: Total Aid." *Jewish Virtual Library*, www.jewishvirtuallibrary.org/total-u-s-foreign-aid-to-israel-1949-present.

Speaking personally as a US citizen; has anyone considered how ludicrous and fundamentally irrational it is that a country that we, the US taxpayers, are giving *free aid* to is demanding we never criticize anything they do as our return in investment?[477] How fundamentally absurd it is that our college students in US campuses are now being targeted, harassed, and penalized with criminal records for exercising their free speech rights, something we want encouraged in our democratic country, because they voice concerns about human rights? They're being collectively punished throughout the United States by the Right-wing ideology of Israel demanding no criticism be allowed, including when exercising Freedom of Assembly, while we all as US citizens are expected to also give Israel free aid through our tax dollars. Has anybody given thought to how ridiculous it is that we aren't allowed to have any open questions and are vilified as Holocaust deniers, which the vast majority of us are obviously not despite what the mainstream media continues to show us, by the US mainstream media for the "crime" of questioning Israel? In our free and open society, where we are suppose to have an inalienable right to Free Speech, how can we allow ourselves to be silent while a right-wing religious ideology just tried to turn itself into a theocracy, while we're giving free aid to it under the belief its suppose to be a free and open democracy?[478][479][480] The logic has been pushed to the side in this extreme demand to never under any circumstances question Israel; we need to place the logic back into the equation and begin renegotiating exactly what our interests are in relation to Israel and what our expectations are when giving it free aid. Equally as important, this attack on the US first amendment by the ideology of Zionism must be firmly stopped and never again tolerated. The Right-wing of the US accused college campuses of fascism for safe spaces and for intolerance towards Nazis, and then secretly passes laws with the older party members of the Democrats who are against Progressive politics, to stifle free speech. If the Right-wing of US politics is the supposed vanguard of free speech rights, why has there been no condemnation of this assault of free speech?[481] Why have the Republicans of the US pushed for bans on criticizing Israel while demanding we give more of our tax dollars to Israel as they slowly turn themselves into a theocracy?[482]

21. [477] "U.S. Foreign Aid to Israel: Total Aid." *Jewish Virtual Library*, www.jewishvirtuallibrary.org/total-u-s-foreign-aid-to-israel-1949-present.
22. [478] Lis, Jonathan. "Israel's Contentious Nation-State Law: Everything You Need to Know." *Haaretz.com*, Haaretz Com, 19 July 2018, www.haaretz.com/israel-news/.premium-israel-s-contentious-nation-state-law-everything-you-need-to-know-1.6292733?=&ts=_1532742032458.
23. [479] Dorell, Oren. "U.S. $38B Military Aid Package to Israel Sends a Message." *USA Today*, Gannett Satellite Information Network, 14 Sept. 2016, www.usatoday.com/story/news/world/2016/09/14/united-states-military-aid-israel/90358564/.
24. [480] Sharp, Jeremy M. "U.S. Foreign Aid to Israel - Federation of American Scientists." *FAS.ORG*, Congressional Research Service, fas.org/sgp/crs/mideast/RL33222.pdf.
25. [481] Fang, Lee, and Zaid Jilani. "Politicians Campaign on Free Speech While Voting to Penalize Boycotts of Israel." *The Intercept*, 14 Mar. 2018, theintercept.com/2018/03/14/campus-free-speech-bds-israel-boycott
26. [482] Rosenblatt, Lauren, et al. "US Seeks to Increase Aid to Israel by $200M in 2019." *The Pittsburgh Jewish Chronicle*, jewishchronicle.timesofisrael.com/us-seeks-to-increase-aid-to-israel-by-200m-in-

Chapter 10: Judaism versus Archaeology

This chapter will mostly explore the lack of archaeological evidence for the claims of Judaism and what that means for Jewish history and the Abrahamic faiths. After all, if Jewish history isn't based on reality then neither is Christianity or Islam.

The Center of the World?

The so-called center of the world, where the Al-Aqsa Mosque resides and the temple of Solomon supposedly must be built, is fundamental proof that the fight between Israel-Palestine is religious and that there can be no peace on theological grounds because Zionism, Christianity, and Islam are too war-like. The idea that the location of the Al-Asqa Mosque is the center of the world is unsubstantiated and utterly discredited by geography, astronomy, and the very structure of the Earth itself. Attempts at arguing the location is the center of the universe is useless because every place in the world is the so-called center of the universe according to scientific studies of the cosmos. The Al-Asqa Mosque is a religious symbol for the return of Jesus Christ for Muslims and the temple of Solomon is the religious symbol for the coming of a Jewish Messiah for Jewish people or the return of Jesus Christ for Christians.

For the sake of both the stability in the region and Israel's longevity, Israel should make peace agreements with at least the Palestinians and the Lebanese. That would mean making a stronger effort to stop the settler violence, to encourage the coalescence of Palestinians and Israelis by ending the destruction of homes and war campaigns, ending the racially specific laws, encouraging the use of both Hebrew and Arabic at an equal level, and removing the desire for a ridiculous prophecy entirely. Israelis have increased in atheism because of the obvious failures of Judaism's theology. If social changes and peace isn't made then Israel will be fighting against Islam for another forty or more years, regardless of the conclusion of the Israeli-Palestinian conflict and it cannot be reasonably expected that the US or Europe would be able to always protect Israel for their own interests. The British and the US both used Realist theories of international relations in their policymaking regarding Israel and the expected conclusion of all Realist theory uses is the inexorable path to self-destruction and financial ruin. We have documented information and cogent arguments from both the *Rise and Fall of Great Empires* and *The Clash of Civilizations*, both books predict the end of Western hegemony and the latter also predicts the rise of Islam as a global phenomena. As such, it is probably in Israel's best interests to look beyond just the West for support so long as the West uses Realist Theory policies for international relations. That can only begin with a more equal and egalitarian system for Palestinians to create a peaceful coexistence between Palestinians and Israelis in one nation-state under Israeli rule. If not, then perhaps Israel should consider sponsoring and even paying for Palestinian relocation in Muslim majority countries willing to accept Palestinians since the Two-State solution seem to be a meaningless political ploy to test weapons on Palestinians.[483]

The Telling versus The Reality

The celebration of Passover is a fundamental component of the Jewish faith. It purportedly established the covenant with the Abrahamic God and celebrates the freedom of the Jewish people from Egyptian slavery.[484] It is the foundation and centerpiece for Jewish, Christian, and Islamic theology in celebration and servitude towards the Abrahamic God. However, more importantly, it's a complete fabrication without a shred of credibility and the archaeological research for over 40 years proves that to be an incontrovertible fact of history.[485][486][487] Yet, the theology it is based upon and the devotion of the Abrahamic faiths seems undeterred by the fact that the Jewish identity and theology was never grounded in historical fact. As a consequence of this simple truth, the entire basis of the Mosiac Law and the covenant with the Abrahamic God is an established myth with no connection to any real historical events.[488] There likely never was a Moses according to the archaeological evidence, thereby there could never have been a covenant with a god of any sort. What, then, is the point of Jewish people awaiting a Messiah? For Christians and Muslims, what's the point in believing Jesus Christ fulfilled the Mosiac Law? What Law was fulfilled when the entire story of Moses has no shred of evidence for its existence? No such event ever took place, so was Jesus Christ lying by saying he fulfilled it? He couldn't possibly have fulfilled a law or prophecies that never occurred in human history.

Egyptians had no slavery until the tail end of the empire due to attacks from foreign empires and there's no proof that the Israelites ever set foot inside Egypt or that they built the pyramids.[489][490] The pyramids were built by Egyptian workers who were handsomely paid and respected for their contributions to the legacy of the Pharaohs.[491] On JPost, Stephen Gabriel

---

1. [483] Kennard, Matthew. "The Cruel Experiments of Israel's Arms Industry." *The Electronic Intifada*, 27 June 2017, electronicintifada.net/content/cruel-experiments-israels-arms-industry/19011.
2. [484] Pelaia, Ariela. "What Is a Passover Seder?" *ThoughtCo*, ThoughtCo, www.thoughtco.com/what-is-a-passover-seder-2076456.
3. [485] Deitch, Ian. "Egypt: New Find Shows Slaves Didn't Build Pyramids." *U.S. News & World Report*, U.S. News & World Report, www.usnews.com/science/articles/2010/01/12/egypt-new-find-shows-slaves-didnt-build-pyramids.
4. [486] Mintz, Josh. "Were Jews Ever Really Slaves in Egypt, or Is Passover a Myth?" *Haaretz.com*, Haaretz Com, 10 Apr. 2018, www.haaretz.com/jewish/were-jews-ever-really-slaves-in-egypt-1.5208519.
5. [487] "Archeology of the Hebrew Bible." *PBS*, Public Broadcasting Service, 18 Nov. 2008, www.pbs.org/wgbh/nova/ancient/archeology-hebrew-bible.html.
6. [488] Mintz, Josh. "Were Jews Ever Really Slaves in Egypt, or Is Passover a Myth?" *Haaretz.com*, Haaretz Com, 10 Apr. 2018, www.haaretz.com/jewish/were-jews-ever-really-slaves-in-egypt-1.5208519.
7. [489] Deitch, Ian. "Egypt: New Find Shows Slaves Didn't Build Pyramids." *U.S. News & World Report*, U.S. News & World Report, www.usnews.com/science/articles/2010/01/12/egypt-new-find-shows-slaves-didnt-build-pyramids.
8. [490] "Archeology of the Hebrew Bible." *PBS*, Public Broadcasting Service, 18 Nov. 2008, www.pbs.org/wgbh/nova/ancient/archeology-hebrew-bible.html.
9. [491] Deitch, Ian. "Egypt: New Find Shows Slaves Didn't Build Pyramids." *U.S. News & World Report*, U.S. News & World Report, www.usnews.com/science/articles/2010/01/12/egypt-new-find-

Rosenberg, a Senior Fellow at the Albright Institute of Archaeological research in Jerusalem, explains succinctly in the article *"The Exodus: Does Archaeology Have a Say?"* as shown below:

> The short answer is "no." The whole subject of the Exodus is embarrassing to archaeologists. The Exodus is so fundamental to us and our Jewish sources that it is embarrassing that there is no evidence outside of the Bible to support it. So we prefer not to talk about it, and hate to be asked about it.
>
> For the account in the Torah is the basis of our people's creation, it is the basis of our existence and it is the basis of our important Passover festival and the whole Haggada that we recite on the first evening of this festival of freedom. So that makes archaeologists reluctant to have to tell our brethren and ourselves that there is nothing in Egyptian records to support it. Nothing on the slavery of the Israelites, nothing on the plagues that persuaded Pharaoh to let them go, nothing on the miraculous crossing of the Red Sea, nothing.
>
> Nothing at all. There are three Pharaohs who said they got rid of the hated foreigners, but nothing to say who the foreigners were, and no Pharaoh is named as having persecuted foreign slaves or suffered unspeakable plagues.[492]

Sadly, he then goes on a thoroughly baseless "what-if" from the absence of evidence on what "could" be possible, essentially wishing it was somehow true through an argument from ignorance instead of observing the objective facts of the matter.[493] For a more thorough explanation, PBS.org provided an interview about *"The Archaeology of the Hebrew Bible"* on their NOVA program with the lead researcher of archaeological excavations. Please keep in mind, the archaeological research was done for over thirty years in order to prove the Bible's history was real:

> Archeology of the Hebrew Bible
>
> **William Dever, Professor Emeritus at the University of Arizona, has investigated the archeology of the ancient Near East for more than 30 years and authored almost as many books on the subject. In the following interview, Dever describes some of the most significant archeological finds related to the Hebrew Bible, including his own hot-button discovery that the Israelites' God was linked to a female goddess called Asherah.**
>
> **PROVING THE BIBLE**
>
> **NOVA: Have biblical archeologists traditionally tried to find evidence that events in the Bible really happened?**
> **William Dever:** From the beginnings of what we call biblical archeology, perhaps 150 years ago, scholars, mostly western scholars, have attempted to use archeological data to prove the Bible. And for a long time it was thought to work. [William Foxwell] Albright, the great father of our discipline, often

---

shows-slaves-didnt-build-pyramids.
10. [492] Rosenberg, Stephen Gabriel. "The Exodus: Does Archaeology Have a Say?" *The Jerusalem Post | JPost.com*, 14 Apr. 2014, www.jpost.com/Opinion/Op-Ed-Contributors/The-Exodus-Does-archaeology-have-a-say-348464.
11. [493] Rosenberg, Stephen Gabriel. "The Exodus: Does Archaeology Have a Say?" *The Jerusalem Post | JPost.com*, 14 Apr. 2014, www.jpost.com/Opinion/Op-Ed-Contributors/The-Exodus-Does-archaeology-have-a-say-348464.

spoke of the "archeological revolution." Well, the revolution has come but not in the way that Albright thought. The truth of the matter today is that archeology raises more questions about the historicity of the Hebrew Bible and even the New Testament than it provides answers, and that's very disturbing to some people.

But perhaps we were asking the wrong questions. I have always thought that if we resurrected someone from the past, one of the biblical writers, they would be amused, because for them it would have made no difference. I think they would have said, faith is faith is faith—take your proofs and go with them.

The fact is that archeology can never prove any of the theological suppositions of the Bible. Archeologists can often tell you what happened and when and where and how and even why. No archeologists can tell anyone what it means, and most of us don't try.

Yet many people want to know whether the events of the Bible are real, historic events.
We want to make the Bible history. Many people think it has to be history or nothing. But there is no word for history in the Hebrew Bible. In other words, what did the biblical writers think they were doing? Writing objective history? No. That's a modern discipline. They were telling stories. They wanted you to know what these purported events mean.

The Bible is didactic literature; it wants to teach, not just to describe. We try to make the Bible something it is not, and that's doing an injustice to the biblical writers. They were good historians, and they could tell it the way it was when they wanted to, but their objective was always something far beyond that.

I like to point out to my undergraduate students that the Bible is not history; it's *his* story—Yahweh's story, God's story. [Yahweh is an ancient Israelite name for God.]

Even if archeology can't prove events of the Bible, can it enhance our understanding of the Bible?
Archeology is almost the only way that we have for reconstructing a real-life context for the world out of which the Bible came, and that does bring understanding. When you think of how little we knew about the biblical world even 100 years ago and what we know today, it's astonishing.

THE FAITH OF ABRAHAM

According to the Bible, the first person to form a covenant with God is Abraham. He is the great patriarch. Is there archeological evidence for Abraham?
One of the first efforts of biblical archeology in the last century was to prove the historicity of the patriarchs, to locate them in a particular period in the archeological history. Today I think most archeologists would argue that there is no direct archeological proof that Abraham, for instance, ever lived. We do know a lot about pastoral nomads, we know about the Amorites' migrations from Mesopotamia to Canaan, and it's possible to see in that an Abraham-like figure somewhere around 1800 B.C.E. But there's no direct connection.

Are we to become unbelievers if we can't prove that Abraham ever lived? What is the story about? It's a story about freedom and faith and risk. Does it matter exactly how Abraham and his clan left, and when they arrived in Canaan, or where they settled? What really matters is that Abraham is seen later by Jews and Christians as the father of the faithful.

Abraham moves out on faith to a land he has never seen. You have to think of how perilous the journey would have been had it really taken place. We are talking about a journey of several hundred miles around the fringes of the desert. So it's an astonishing story. Is it true? It is profoundly true, but it's not the kind of truth that archeology can directly illuminate.

Why is it difficult for archeologists to find support for the accounts of the patriarchs?
It disturbs some people that, for the very early periods such as the so-called patriarchal period, we archeologists haven't much to say. The later we come in time, the firmer the ground we stand on—we have better sources. We have more written sources. We have more contemporary eyewitness sources.

For the earlier periods, we don't have any texts. Abraham might have lived around 1800 B.C.E. This is the dawn of written history or prehistory, when the archeological evidence can't easily be correlated with any external evidence, textual evidence—even if we did have it.

EVIDENCE OF THE EARLY ISRAELITES

The Bible chronology puts Moses much later in time, around 1450 B.C.E. Is there archeological evidence for Moses and the mass exodus of hundreds of thousands of Israelites described in the Bible?
We have no direct archeological evidence. "Moses" is an Egyptian name. Some of the other names in the narratives are Egyptian, and there are genuine Egyptian elements. But no one has found a text or an artifact in Egypt itself or even in the Sinai that has any direct connection. That doesn't mean it didn't happen. But I think it does mean what happened was rather more modest. And the biblical writers have enlarged the story.

[For more on Moses and the Exodus, see Carol Meyer's interview.]

Is there mention of the Israelites anywhere in ancient Egyptian records?
No Egyptian text mentions the Israelites except the famous inscription of Merneptah dated to about 1206 B.C.E. But those Israelites were in Canaan; they are not in Egypt, and nothing is said about them escaping from Egypt.

Tell us more about the Merneptah inscription. Why is it so famous?
It's the earliest reference we have to the Israelites. The victory stele of Pharaoh Merneptah, the son of Ramesses II, mentions a list of peoples and city-states in Canaan, and among them are the Israelites. And it's interesting that the other entities, the other ethnic groups, are described as nascent states, but the Israelites are described as "a people." They have not yet reached a level of state organization.

So the Egyptians, a little before 1200 B.C.E., know of a group of people somewhere in the central highlands—a loosely affiliated tribal confederation, if you will—called "Israelites." These are our Israelites. So this is a priceless inscription.

Does archeology back up the information in the Merneptah inscription? Is there evidence of the Israelites in the central highlands of Canaan at this time?
We know today, from archeological investigation, that there were more than 300 early villages of the 13th and 12th century in the area. I call these "proto-Israelite" villages.

Forty years ago it would have been impossible to identify the earliest Israelites archeologically. We just didn't have the evidence. And then, in a series of regional surveys, Israeli archeologists in the 1970s began to find small hilltop villages in the central hill country north and south of Jerusalem and in lower Galilee. Now we have almost 300 of them.

THE ORIGINS OF ISRAEL

What have archeologists learned from these settlements about the early Israelites? Are there signs that the Israelites came in conquest, taking over the land from Canaanites?
The settlements were founded not on the ruins of destroyed Canaanite towns but rather on bedrock or on virgin soil. There was no evidence of armed conflict in most of these sites. Archeologists also have

discovered that most of the large Canaanite towns that were supposedly destroyed by invading Israelites were either not destroyed at all or destroyed by "Sea People"—Philistines, or others.

So gradually the old conquest model [based on the accounts of Joshua's conquests in the Bible] began to lose favor amongst scholars. Many scholars now think that most of the early Israelites were originally Canaanites, displaced Canaanites, displaced from the lowlands, from the river valleys, displaced geographically and then displaced ideologically.

So what we are dealing with is a movement of peoples but not an invasion of an armed corps from the outside. A social and economic revolution, if you will, rather than a military revolution. And it begins a slow process in which the Israelites distinguish themselves from their Canaanite ancestors, particularly in religion—with a new deity, new religious laws and customs, new ethnic markers, as we would call them today.

If the Bible's story of Joshua's conquest isn't entirely historic, what is its meaning?
Why was it told? Well, it was told because there were probably armed conflicts here and there, and these become a part of the story glorifying the career of Joshua, commander in chief of the Israelite forces. I suspect that there is a historical kernel, and there are a few sites that may well have been destroyed by these Israelites, such as Hazor in Galilee, or perhaps a site or two in the south.

Were the people who became Israelites in some sense not "the chosen people" but rather "the choosing people"—choosing to be free of their Canaanite past?
Some liberation theologians and some archeologists have argued that early Israel was a kind of revolutionary social movement. These were people rebelling against their corrupt Canaanite overlords. In my recent book on early Israel I characterize the Israelite movement as an agrarian social reform. These are pioneers in the hill country who are fleeing the urban centers, the old Canaanite cities, which are in a process of collapse. And in particular they are throwing off the yoke of their Canaanite and Egyptian overlords. They are declaring independence.

Now, why these people were willing to take such a risk, colonizing the hill country frontier, is very difficult to know. I think there were social and economic compulsions, but I would be the first to say I think it was probably also a new religious vision.

Was this an egalitarian movement?
Some have argued that early Israel was an egalitarian society, that there was no social stratification. I'm not sure any society was ever really egalitarian, but there is a sort of egalitarianism in the Hebrew Bible: "Every man under his own fig tree, equal in the eyes of Yahweh." It's interesting that in these hundreds of 12th-century settlements there are no temples, no palaces, no elite residences, no monumental architecture of any kind. These are farming villages in which every household is independent. I think there is a kind of primitive democracy in early Israel, which is enshrined in the vision of the good life in the Hebrew Bible.

And these settlements grow, right?
Yes. These settlements are very different from the urban centers of the earlier 13th century. Something new is in the air, and I think this explains why other people join this movement. These villages will develop into the towns and the cities of the later state of Israel.

A UNITED MONARCHY

When did Israel become a state?
According to the biblical scheme of events, there was a United Monarchy for about a hundred years in the reigns of Saul, David, and Solomon. Then a civil war brought about the division of the country into Israel, the northern kingdom, and Judah, the southern kingdom. Now, some skeptics today have argued that there was no such thing as a United Monarchy. In short, there was no David.

However, in 1993 an inscription was found at Tel Dan. It mentions a dynasty of David. And on the Mesha stone found in the last century in Moab there is also a probable reference to David. So there is textual evidence outside the Bible for these kings of the United Monarchy, at least David.

Most of us mainstream archeologists also have now dated a series of monumental royal constructions to the 10th century—the famous gates at Hazor and Megiddo and Gezer. And we have in the Bible, in First Kings 9:15-17, the famous description of Solomon's construction of gates of Jerusalem, Hazor, Megiddo, and Gezer. So I would argue for a 10th-century United Monarchy.

The Bible describes it as a glorious kingdom stretching from Egypt to Mesopotamia. Does archeology back up these descriptions?
The stories of Solomon are larger than life. According to the stories, Solomon imported 100,000 workers from what is now Lebanon. Well, the whole population of Israel probably wasn't 100,000 in the 10th century. Everything Solomon touched turned to gold. In the minds of the biblical writers, of course, David and Solomon are ideal kings chosen by Yahweh. So they glorify them.

Now, archeology can't either prove or disprove the stories. But I think most archeologists today would argue that the United Monarchy was not much more than a kind of hill-country chiefdom. It was very small-scale.

Does archeology in Jerusalem itself reveal anything about the Kingdom of David and Solomon?
We haven't had much of an opportunity to excavate in Jerusalem. It's a living city, not an archeological site. But we have a growing collection of evidence—monumental buildings that most of us would date to the 10th century, including the new so-called Palace of David. Having seen it with the excavator, it is certainly monumental. Whether it's a palace or an administrative center or a combination of both or a kind of citadel remains to be seen.

[Hear the excavator herself, Eilat Mazar, describe the Palace of David.]

THE ISRAELITES' MANY GODS

The Bible would have us think that all Israelites embraced monotheism relatively early, from Moses's time on. Is that contrary to what archeology has found?
The portrait of Israelite religion in the Hebrew Bible is the ideal, the ideal in the minds of those few who wrote the Bible—the elites, the Yahwists, the monotheists. But it's not the ideal for most people. And archeology deals with the ordinary, forgotten folk of ancient Israel who have no voice in the Bible. There is a wonderful phrase in Daniel Chapter 12: "For all those who sleep in the dust." Archeology brings them to light and allows them to speak. And most of them were not orthodox believers.

However, we should have guessed already that polytheism was the norm and not monotheism from the biblical denunciations of it. It was real and a threat as far as those who wrote the Bible were concerned. And today archeology has illuminated what we could call "folk religion" in an astonishing manner.

One of the astonishing things is your discovery of Yahweh's connection to Asherah. Tell us about that.
In 1968, I discovered an inscription in a cemetery west of Hebron, in the hill country, at the site of Khirbet el-Qí´m, a Hebrew inscription of the 8th century B.C.E. It gives the name of the deceased, and it says "blessed may he be by Yahweh"—that's good biblical Hebrew—but it says "by Yahweh and his Asherah."

Asherah is the name of the old Canaanite Mother Goddess, the consort of El, the principal deity of the Canaanite pantheon. So why is a Hebrew inscription mentioning Yahweh in connection with the Canaanite Mother Goddess? Well, in popular religion they were a pair.

The Israelite prophets and reformers denounce the Mother Goddess and all the other gods and goddesses of Canaan. But I think Asherah was widely venerated in ancient Israel. If you look at Second Kings 23, which describes the reforms of King Josiah in the late 7th century, he talks about purging the Temple of all the cult paraphernalia of Asherah. So the so-called folk religion even penetrated the Temple in Jerusalem.

Is there other evidence linking Asherah to Yahweh?
In the 1970s, Israeli archeologists digging in Kuntillet Ajrud in the Sinai found a little desert fort of the same period, and lo and behold, we have "Yahweh and Asherah" all over the place in the Hebrew inscriptions.

Are there any images of Asherah?
For a hundred years now we have known of little terracotta female figurines. They show a nude female; the sexual organs are not represented but the breasts are. They are found in tombs, they are found in households, they are found everywhere. There are thousands of them. They date all the way from the 10th century to the early 6th century.

They have long been connected with one goddess or another, but many scholars are still hesitant to come to a conclusion. I think they are representations of Asherah, so I call them Asherah figurines.

There aren't such representations of Yahweh, are there?
No. Now, why is it that you could model the female deity but not the male deity? Well, I think the First and Second Commandments by now were taken pretty seriously. You just don't portray Yahweh, the male deity, but the Mother Goddess is okay. But his consort is probably a lesser deity.

We found molds for making Asherah figurines, mass-producing them, in village shrines. So probably almost everybody had one of these figurines, and they surely have something to do with fertility. They were no doubt used to pray for conceiving a child and bearing the child safely and nursing it. It's interesting to me that the Israelite and Judean ones are rather more modest than the Canaanite ones, which are right in your face. The Israelite and Judean ones mostly show a nursing mother.

This has been something of a lightning rod, has it not?
This is awkward for some people, the notion that Israelite religion was not exclusively monotheistic. But we know now that it wasn't. Monotheism was a late development. Not until the Babylonian Exile and beyond does Israelite and Judean religion—Judaism—become monotheistic.

THE IMPROBABLE RISE OF JUDAISM

Does archeology have evidence of the destruction of Jerusalem by the Babylonians?
When it comes to destructions that might be illuminated by archeology, none would be more important than the destruction of Jerusalem and the Temple in 586 B.C.E. by the Babylonians. Unfortunately, we don't have a lot of direct archeological evidence because we have never been able to excavate large areas in Jerusalem. The late Israeli archeologist Yigal Shiloh found a huge accumulation of debris on the east side of the Temple Mount, cascaded down the hill. So there is some evidence, not yet well-published. Of course, the Temple Mount has never been excavated and never will be.

That doesn't mean that that the destruction didn't take place and that it wasn't a watershed event. One would have thought at that time that it was the end of the people of Israel—with elites carried away into captivity and ordinary people impoverished. It would have seemed to have been the end, but it was rather the beginning. Because it was in exile, precisely, that those who wrote the Bible looked back, collected the archives they had, rethought it all, reformulated it, and out of that intellectual reconstruction comes early Judaism.

It seems astonishing that after this defeat the Israelites could stay faithful to their god.

In every age of disbelief, one is inclined to think that God is dead. And surely those who survived the fall of Jerusalem must have thought so. After all, how could God allow his Temple, his house—the visible sign of his presence amongst his people—to be destroyed? What did we do wrong? It's out of this that comes the reflection that polytheism was our downfall. There is, after all, only one God. And this radical belief in a single God who governs history becomes the heart of Judaism[494]

Unfortunately for people of the Abrahamic faiths, the evidence shows that this God of the Covenant never existed and the events of being freed from slavery simply never happened. There was no covenant with any God and that is the central foundation of the Jewish faith. There was never any need to be freed from slavery, because the Israelites were never enslaved by the Egyptians. If Passover isn't based upon a real historical event, then absolutely none of it matters. The persecution, the freedom from slavery, or the supposed evils of the Pharaohs have no historical credibility. There's no point in celebrating the blessings of a God for miracles that never happened and were never necessary to begin with. *The Abrahamic God never displayed any miracles of freedom nor is the Mosiac Law bound by any covenant with a deity at all.* This "revealed wisdom" is a complete fairytale made for ancient political ends to kill and conquer for territory and that history of violence is shown everyday in our contemporary time with the Israel-Palestine conflict. A pointless theological conflict grounded in imaginary covenants and promises from the same deity that both claim to be the true followers of, but which neither can claim to be chosen people of since the Prophet Moses never existed and the events of the Exodus have been proven false on the basis of physical evidence. *In effect, the Israeli-Palestine conflict is people murdering each other over a fairytale in every sense of the word.* The lack of evidence for the Exodus disproves the entirety of the Abrahamic religious traditions. *It's simply indefensible and illogical to continue believing, dying, and killing for a tradition that is a falsehood. There's no meaning or greater purpose in it.* To continue this route of believing in the Bible's contents despite the overwhelming archeological findings is the very act of willful ignorance. Blind faith and willful ignorance are shown to be the same exact concept when faced with the overwhelming fact that there's no credible evidence for the Exodus story.

Jewish Humanist Staks Rosch provides another issue in his HuffingtonPost article "*The Biblical Exodus Story Is Fiction*" provides more food for thought. He asks that we should consider what this means with the treatment of the Egyptians and what the lack of evidence for the Exodus means for the accusations and contempt given to Egyptians throughout history. He helps to explain the issues in general terms for those unfamiliar with the significance of what the lack of evidence for Exodus means:

> Shortly after I started to question my belief in God, I remember talking to my rabbi about Passover and the Exodus from Egypt. My rabbi knew that I was starting to doubt the supernatural and ridiculous aspects of the story. He told me in confidence that while the basic story is historical fact, the supernatural elements might have been an exaggeration or might not have actually happened at all. He assured me,

---

12. [494] "Archeology of the Hebrew Bible." *PBS*, Public Broadcasting Service, 18 Nov. 2008, www.pbs.org/wgbh/nova/ancient/archeology-hebrew-bible.html.

however, that even though there might not have been plagues of frogs and Moses might not have parted the Red Sea, the Jews were slaves in Egypt, and the important thing is that there was an Exodus and that this is the core of what Passover is about. Except, in reality, there wasn't actually an Exodus. I have since learned that the Jews were never slaves in Egypt and that the entire story of Exodus is fiction.

When I first heard that there was not a shred of evidence discovered in the Sinai Desert that a large number of Jews had wandered for 40 years, I thought that wasn't such a big deal. I mean, it's a desert, right? Sand storms probably just swallowed up all the evidence. The more I looked into the story, however, the more I realized that the lack of evidence was actually a pretty big problem. According to the book of Exodus, a lot of Jews were wandering this desert, and it seems extremely unlikely (bordering on impossible) for this many people to leave absolutely no trace, especially when traces have been found for smaller groups of people which predated the Exodus in that same desert.

Just like the lack of evidence is itself strong evidence against the war between the Nephites and the Lamanites in the Americas as told in the Book of Mormon, the same is true with the Exodus story in the Torah.

Still, I didn't think all that much about it until years later, when I stumbled upon the article called, "Did Jewish Slaves Build the Pyramids?" by Brian Dunning. This article really got me thinking about the Exodus story again. Dunning's article reinforced my skepticism about the Exodus story and fueled my feelings of betrayal. I was taught for most of my life that it was a historical fact that the Jews were slaves in Egypt. This "history" was part of my cultural identity as a Jew. Even when I gave up the ridiculous, superstitious beliefs associated with Judaism, I could still proudly feel connected to the Jewish culture, which was grounded in a deep history of liberation from slavery.

As it turns out, well-known Jewish commentator and author Rabbi David Wolpe has also known about the Exodus Myth. In his article, "Did the Exodus Really Happen?" he mentions that other rabbis wanted him to keep the fiction of the Exodus story on the down-low. The basic story of the Exodus from Egypt (extracting supernatural elements) was touted to me as one of the most historical aspects of the Bible, yet it never happened. This seriously puts into question the historicity of any and all of the Bible stories.

Further, how immoral is it for modern Jews to continue to perpetuate this myth at the expense of Egyptian dignity? For thousands of years, the Jews have blamed the Egyptians for enslaving their ancestors when that never actually happened. Continuing to celebrate Passover without acknowledging the truth of history only perpetuates the shame.

Growing up, I loved celebrating Passover. I loved the story of people fighting for their freedom and fighting against slavery. I don't think Jews need to stop celebrating Passover or stop talking about this story. However, they need to acknowledge that the celebration is based on a completely fictional story and that the Egyptians never enslaved the Jews. Rabbis should even make a formal apology to the Egyptian people for vilifying them.

As a Humanist, I think it is important to talk about the plight against slavery and the fight for freedom. But I think people should do it honestly instead of turning real people in history into villains. There are plenty of real villains in history already.

Perhaps the holiday of Passover could focus more on the plight of Jews who escape Germany during the Second World War. There are some very inspirational acts of bravery and heroism worth telling from that time, and they don't require made-up history or supernatural plagues to reinforce the message.

You don't have to believe in fictional stories to celebrate Jewish holidays. In fact, you don't even need to believe in any supernatural claims on insufficient evidence and still hold on to your Jewish identity.

Many Jews have left the belief in God behind and have become secular Jews. For more information about what that means, check out the [Society of Humanistic Judaism](#).[495]

In short, continuing to be willfully ignorant is stigmatizing and potentially persecuting another nation-state of people for no reason beyond wanting to believe in a fairytale. It's disingenuously vilifying Egyptians and especially Ancient Egyptian history for centuries of the crime of slavery that they never committed upon Israelites. Egyptians never enslaved the Israelites and no historical records prove any of the Israelites claims of being enslaved by them. It's unjustly taking credit for their achievements in building the pyramids, something Egyptians can rightly be proud of in their own culture.

To believe in the Biblical version of events isn't an innocent act; it's cruelly blaming and shaming Egyptians on the basis of willfully lying about history. The accounts of Exodus would make people feel the destruction and plunder of Egyptian tombs was justified, and in fact this is largely what the Western world did during the age of imperialism, but all of this history of cruelty and contempt was based on a complete myth.[496] As of now, Modern Egyptians are majority Muslim and also have been seduced into this mythic idea of their ancient society being cruel, barbaric, and going against the Abrahamic God. Believing in Islam means Egyptians would be compelled to believe that these imaginary plagues, which have no credibility in their history, actually happened in ancient times. Even if they go by the historical evidence and support the idea that Israelites didn't build the pyramids, they may still hold the wrongful belief that their ancestors enslaved them when there's no evidence. Consider this, just how shameful and disgusting is it to decimate and plunder an entire cultural history, to vilify a rich tapestry of history with utter contempt, and to have such loathing for centuries to justify destruction, theft, and thoroughgoing hate . . . only to discover the supposed justification was a total myth? Only to discover none of this hate thrust upon these ancient people or their history is justified? After all, this means the Egyptians were far more benevolent than modern people, until recently, gave them credit for. The ancient Egyptians truly accomplished great things and are a beacon of pride that Egyptians and other people of the Levant can rightfully feel inspired by and in awe of their accomplishments. Yet, because of one book of fables, their awe-inspiring hard work has instead been viewed as unambiguously evil, as worthy of contempt and ridicule, and as something achieved by Abrahamic culture that had no right to have any claim to it. This contempt is further predicated on the belief in the Abrahamic God, whose proof of power are imaginary plagues that have no historical evidence.

In fact, more recent archeological evidence has shown that YHWH wasn't even made by the Jews, but rather appropriated by another tribe and that much of Jewish history comprises

---

13. [495] Rosch, Staks. "The Biblical Exodus Story Is Fiction." *The Huffington Post*, TheHuffingtonPost.com, 7 Dec. 2017, www.huffingtonpost.com/staks-rosch/the-biblical-exodus-story-is-fiction_b_1408123.html.
14. [496] "Europe's Hypocritical History of Cannibalism." *Smithsonian.com*, Smithsonian Institution, 24 Apr. 2013, www.smithsonianmag.com/history/europes-hypocritical-history-of-cannibalism-42642371/.

of polytheism and ditheism. The monotheism of Judaism is in fact a relatively new addition to Jewish history. This is even more damning evidence against the supposed covenant with the Abrahamic God. Ariel David from Haaretz explains in the article "*How The Jews Invented God, and Made Him Great*" below:

> Jews, Christians and Muslims all believe in a single, omnipotent deity that created the heavens and earth. But if he was and is the only god, why would God need a name?
>
> The Bible explicitly tells us that God has one, which indicates he had to be distinguished from other celestial beings, just like humans use names to identify different people.
>
> What that name might be is another matter. The Jewish prohibition on speaking God's name means that its correct pronunciation has been lost. All we know is that the Hebrew Bible spells it out as four consonants known as the Tetragrammaton – from the Greek for "four letters," which are transliterated as Y-H-W-H.
>
> The existence of a proper name for God is the first indication that the history of Yhwh and his worship by the Jews is a lot more complicated than many realize.
>
> **In gods we trusted**
>
> Modern biblical scholarship and archaeological discoveries in and around Israel show that the ancient Israelites did not always believe in a single, universal god. In fact, monotheism is a relatively recent concept, even amongst the People of the Book.
>
> Decades of research into the birth and evolution of the Yhwh cult are summarized in "The Invention of God," a recent book by Thomas Römer, a world-renowned expert in the Hebrew Bible and professor at the College de France and the University of Lausanne. Römer, who held a series of conferences at Tel Aviv University last month, spoke to Haaretz about the subject.
>
> The main source for investigating the history of God is, of course, the Bible itself.
>
> When exactly the Jewish holy text reached its final form is unknown. Many scholars believe this happened sometime between the Babylonian exile, which began after the fall of Jerusalem in 587 BCE (some 2600 years ago), and the subsequent periods of Persian and Hellenistic rule.
>
> However, the redactors of the Bible were evidently working off older traditions, Römer says.
>
> "Biblical texts are not direct historical sources. They reflect the ideas, the ideologies of their authors and of course of the historical context in which they were written," Römer explains.
>
> Still, he notes, "you can have memories of a distant past, sometimes in a very confusing way or in a very oriented way. But I think we can, and we must, use the biblical text not just as fictional texts but as texts that can tell us stories about the origins."
>
> **What's in God's name**
>
> The first clue that the ancient Israelites worshipped gods other than the deity known as Yhwh lies in their very name. "Israel" is a theophoric name going back at least 3200 years, which includes and invokes the name of a protective deity.

Going by the name, the main god of the ancient Israelites was not Yhwh, but El, the chief deity in the Canaanite pantheon, who was worshipped throughout the Levant.

In other words, the name "Israel" is probably older than the veneration of Yhwh by this group called Israel, Römer says. "The first tutelary deity they were worshipping was El, otherwise their name would have been Israyahu."

The Bible appears to address this early worship of El in Exodus 6:3, when God tells Moses that he "appeared to Abraham, Isaac and Jacob as El Shaddai (today translated as "God Almighty") but was not known to them by my name Yhwh."

In fact, it seems that the ancient Israelites weren't even the first to worship Yhwh – they seem to have adopted Him from a mysterious, unknown tribe that lived somewhere in the deserts of the southern Levant and Arabia.

The god of the southern deserts

The first mention of the Israelite tribe itself is a victory stele erected around 1210 BCE by the pharaoh Mernetpah (sometimes called "the Israel stele"). These Israelites are described as a people inhabiting Canaan.

So how did this group of Canaanite El-worshippers come in contact with the cult of Yhwh?

The Bible is quite explicit about the geographical roots of the Yhwh deity, repeatedly linking his presence to the mountainous wilderness and the deserts of the southern Levant. Judges 5:4 says that Yhwh "went forth from Seir" and "marched out of the field of Edom." Habbakuk 3:3 tells us that "God came from Teman," specifically from Mount Paran.

All these regions and locations can be identified with the territory that ranges from the Sinai and Negev to northern Arabia.

Yhwh's penchant for appearing in the biblical narrative on top of mountains and accompanied by dark clouds and thunder, are also typical attributes of a deity originating in the wilderness, possibly a god of storms and fertility.

Support for the theory that Yhwh originated in the deserts of Israel and Arabia can be found in Egyptian texts from the late second millennium, which list different tribes of nomads collectively called "Shasu" that populated this vast desert region.

One of these groups, which inhabits the Negev, is identified as the "Shasu Yhw(h)." This suggests that this group of nomads may have been the first to have the god of the Jews as its tutelary deity.

"It is profoundly difficult to sort through the haze of later layers in the Bible, but insofar as we can, this remains the most plausible hypothesis for the encounter of Israelites with the Yhwh cult," says David Carr, professor of Old Testament at Union Theological Seminary in New York City.

The many faces of god

How exactly the Shasu merged with the Israelites or introduced them to the cult of Yhwh is not known, but by the early centuries of the first millennium, he was clearly being worshipped in both the northern kingdom of Israel and its smaller, southern neighbor, the kingdom of Judah.

His name appears for the first time outside the Bible nearly 400 years after Merneptah, in the 9th-century BCE stele of Mesha, a Moabite king who boasts of defeating the king of Israel and "taking the vessels of Yhwh."

While Yhwh's cult was certainly important in the early First Temple period, it was not exclusive.

"Jeremiah speaks about the many gods of Judah, which are as numerous as the streets of a town. There was certainly worship a female deity, Asherah, or the Queen of Heaven," Römer told Haaretz. "There was certainly also the worship of the northern storm god Hadad (Baal)."

The plurality of deities was such that in an inscription by Sargon II, who completed the conquest of the kingdom of Israel in the late 8th century BCE, the Assyrian king mentioned that after capturing the capital Samaria, his troops brought back "the (statues of) gods in which (the Israelites) had put their trust."

As the Yhwh cult evolved and spread, he was worshipped in temples across the land. Early 8th-century inscriptions found at Kuntillet Ajrud probably refer to different gods and cultic centers by invoking "Yhwh of Samaria and his Asherah" and "Yhwh of Teman and his Asherah." Only later, under the reign of King Josiah at the end of the 7th century BCE, would the Yhwh cult centralize worship at the Temple in Jerusalem.

Nor, in ancient Israel, was Yhwh the invisible deity that Jews have refrained from depicting for the last two millennia or so.

In the kingdom of Israel, as Hosea 8 and 1 Kings 12:26-29 relate, he was often worshipped in the form of a calf, as the god Baal was. (1 Kings 12:26-29 explains that Jeroboam made two calves, for the sanctuaries at Bethel and Dan, so the people could worship Yhwh there and wouldn't have to go all the way to Jerusalem. Ergo, in northern Israel at least, the calves were meant to represent Yhwh.)

In Jerusalem and Judah, Römer says, Yhwh more frequently took the form of a sun god or a seated deity. Such depictions may have even continued after the destruction of Jerusalem and the Babylonian Exile: a coin minted in Jerusalem during the Persian period shows a deity sitting on a wheeled throne and has been interpreted by some as a late anthropomorphic representation of Yhwh.

Römer even suspects that the Holy of Holies in the First Temple of Jerusalem, and other Judahite sanctuaries, hosted a statue of the god, based on Psalms and prophetic texts in the Bible that speak of being admitted in the presence of "the face of Yhwh."

Not all scholars agree that the iconography of Yhwh was so pronounced in Judah. The evidence for anthropomorphic depiction "is not strong," says Saul Olyan, professor of Judaic studies and religious studies at Brown University. "It may be that anthropomorphic images of Yhwh were avoided early on."

The God of the Jews

In any case, many scholars agree that Yhwh became the main god of the Jews only after the destruction of the kingdom of Israel by the Assyrians, around 720 BCE.

How or why the Jews came to exalt Yhwh and reject the pagan gods they also adored is unclear.

We do know that after the fall of Samaria, the population of Jerusalem increased as much as fifteenfold, likely due to the influx of refugees from the north. That made it necessary for the kings of Judah to push a program that would unify the two populations and create a common narrative. And that in turn may be why the biblical writers frequently stigmatize the pagan cultic practices of the north, and stress that

Jerusalem alone had withstood the Assyrian onslaught – thereby explaining Israel's embarrassing fall to Assyria, while distinguishing the prominence and purity of Judahite religion.

Religious reforms by Judahite kings, mainly Hezekiah and Josiah, included abolishing random temple worship of Yhwh and centralizing his adoration at the Temple in Jerusalem, as well as banning the worship of Asherah, Yhwh's female companion, and other pagan cults in the Temple and around the capital.

The Israelites don't keep the faith

This transformation from polytheism to worshipping a single god was carved in stone, literally. For example, an inscription in a tomb in Khirbet Beit Lei, near the Judahite stronghold of Lachish, states that "Yhwh is the god of the whole country; the mountains of Judah belong to the god of Jerusalem."

Josiah's reforms were also enshrined in the book of Deuteronomy – whose original version is thought to have been compiled around this time – and especially in the words of Deut. 6, which would later form the *Sh'ma Yisrael,* one of the central prayers of Judaism: "Hear, O Israel, Yhwh is our God, Yhwh is one."

But while Yhwh had, by the dawn of the 6th century BCE, become "our" national god, he was still believed to be just one of many celestial beings, each protecting his own people and territory.

This is reflected in the many biblical texts exhorting the Israelites not to follow other gods, a tacit acknowledgement of the existence of those deities, Romer explains.

For example, in Judges 11:24, Jephtah tries to resolve a territorial dispute by telling the Ammonites that the land of Israel had been given to the Israelites by Yhwh, while their lands had been given to them by their god Chemosh ("Will you not take what your god Chemosh gives you? Likewise, whatever Yhwh our god has given us, we will possess.")

Snatching God from the jaws of defeat

The real conceptual revolution probably only occurred after the Babylonians' conquest of Judah and arson of the First Temple in 587 B.C.E. The destruction and the subsequent exile to Babylon of the Judahite elites inevitably cast doubts on the faith they had put in Yhwh.

"The question was: how can we explain what happened?" Römer says. If the defeated Israelites had simply accepted that the Babylonian gods had proven they were stronger than the god of the Jews, history would have been very different.

But somehow, someone came up with a different, unprecedented explanation. "The idea was that the destruction happened because the kings did not obey the law of god," Römer says. "It's a paradoxical reading of the story: the vanquished in a way is saying that his god is the vanquisher. It's quite a clever idea.

"The Israelites/Judahites took over the classical idea of the divine wrath that can provoke a national disaster but they combined it with the idea that Yhwh in his wrath made the Babylonians destroy Judah and Jerusalem," he said.

The concept that Yhwh had pulled the Babylonians' strings, causing them to punish the Israelites inevitably led to the belief that he was not just the god of one people, but a universal deity who exercises power over all of creation.

This idea is already present in the book of Isaiah, thought to be one of the earliest biblical texts, composed during or immediately after the Exile. This is also how the Jews became the "chosen people" – because the Biblical editors had to explain why Israel had a privileged relationship with Yhwh even though he was no longer a national deity, but the one true God.

Over the centuries, as the Bible was redacted, this narrative was refined and strengthened, creating the basis for a universal religion – one that could continue to exist even without being tied to a specific territory or temple. And thus Judaism as we know it was established, and, ultimately, all other major monotheistic religions were as well.[497]

Monotheism being a relatively new addition makes sense to a certain extent. Consider this: why would the belief in angels be necessary or part of the Bible? The Abrahamic God, being supposedly infinite in power and ability, could have done anything to prove his godhood, so why are angels necessary? Why did Israelites need to fight with other tribes at all by the Abrahamic God's command, if he was infinite in power and supposedly merciful? It should be clear that by our modern standards, the coherence of much of these stories were no longer tenable, but blind faith and teachings of unquestioned obedience preclude a more informative understanding. It is even worse when factoring that ancient Egyptians are undeserving of contempt of any kind for slavery of a people that claimed to be enslaved, but never were. Evidently, the 9th commandment of the Torah's version of the Ten Commandments was more about lying within ancient Israelite society than it was about lying to claim the achievements of others for themselves.[498]

---

15. [497] David, Ariel. "How the Jews Invented God, and Made Him Great." *Haaretz.com*, Haaretz Com, 5 June 2018, www.haaretz.com/archaeology/.premium.MAGAZINE-how-the-jews-invented-god-and-made-him-great-1.5392677.
16. [498] Isaacs, Ronald H. "The Ten Commandments." *My Jewish Learning*, My Jewish Learning, www.myjewishlearning.com/article/the-ten-commandments/.

Chapter 11: Judaism versus Human Rights

Originally, I had intended to add this chapter to Part III which will be the next book in what should be the completion of this series. However, to my pleasant surprise, it seems that despite antagonistic views towards Israel and the conflict with Palestine, Jewish people have historically been one of the most peaceful people on the planet and the scope and scale of any human rights abuses in the name of Judaism are nowhere near the scale of violence perpetrated by Christianity and Islam. For comparison, I need to make a separate book to clearly detail the historical violence by Islam and Christianity and I doubt that I come close to the full scale violence of both religions in the next book which is Part III of the series and which should be its completion. By contrast, Judaism can be wilted down to a single section in Part II. While this is certainly a positive, it shouldn't be viewed as an attempt to downplay or minimize human rights abuses in the name of Judaism as all human rights crimes should be seen as equally reprehensible in terms of morality regardless of the record number of people killed. This chapter will begin with a critique on Judaism's theology and impact on Jewish human rights; it will then include human rights crimes pertaining to the Israel-Palestine conflict.

The Misogyny of Judaism

Despite the patience and efforts of Reform and Conservative Jewry in the United States to live and act a balanced life of progressive views towards women's rights and commitment to their Jewish faith, and the improvements on the equality for women within Israel itself, Ultra-Orthodox Jewish communities in Israel have remained a painful reminder that patriarchal social structures remain unchanged in religious spheres despite peaceful rallying and protests for significant changes to be made for the inclusion of women in the Western Wall for prayer. This is particularly volatile because historically regarding such issues, women eventually vote with their feet and see only ugliness and contempt for the crime of wanting to be part of a tradition. The most jarring aspect of this conflict is that Ultra Orthodox communities in Israel seem keen on punishing women for the crime of wearing religious garbs, holding the Torah, and wanting to sing prayers. In the end, while Jewish women want inclusion, they're repeatedly reminded that Jewish traditions don't want them to partake in their love for faith and their own culture at all.[499]

The ongoing Western Wall issue is a painful reminder of this with explicit sexism; a repeatedly sexist Ultra Orthodox branch in Israel has imposed its own demands to attack women who wish to celebrate their Jewish faith. As reported on Haaretz by Allison Kaplan Sommer in the article title "*Israel's Western Wall Crisis: Why Jews Are Fighting With Each Other Over The Jewish Holy Site, Explained*" which explains the core issues:

---

1. [499] Rickman, Dan. "Does Judaism Discriminate against Women? | Dan Rickman." *The Guardian*, Guardian News and Media, 10 June 2009, www.theguardian.com/commentisfree/belief/2009/jun/10/judaism-women-feminism-orthodox.

It's the second holiest site in Judaism. Nearly every tourist coming to Israel visits it. Israeli army units swear their allegiance in front of it. And lately, it seems that Israelis and U.S. Jews can't stop fighting about how Jews can pray there. So what's all the fuss about?

What is the Western Wall?

The Western Wall was never part of the Temple Mount, where the ancient holy places of worship for Jews stood. It is believed to be a remnant of the retaining wall that supported the esplanade built by King Herod in the first century B.C.E., holding up his reconstruction of the Second Temple.

But ever since the Ottomans conquered Jerusalem in 1516 and non-Muslims were forbidden from ascending to the Temple Mount itself, the Wall became the world's foremost destination for Jewish pilgrimage and prayer.

Who made the controversial decisions about who can pray at the Wall?

Until 1967, there were no rules regarding worship. For the Jews who were able to access the site, any gender separation was strictly voluntary. But 50 years ago, in 1967, Israel regained control of the Old City – and the Wall – during the Six-Day War.

As soon as the Western Wall was captured, the houses in front of it were demolished and the Western Wall Plaza was created to accommodate the flood of worshippers. The Chief Rabbinate immediately launched a political battle for control of the site. They were worried that if the site was managed by the Religious Services Ministry or the National Parks Authority, it would be treated as a tourist and archaeological attraction, not as a synagogue.

The Rabbinate won that fight. Ever since, the Western Wall Heritage Foundation has maintained the site under the rules of an ultra-Orthodox synagogue, with a presiding rabbi who makes sure that all prayer there conforms to Orthodox rules. This means separating men and women with a high fence – and forbidding women to pray in loud voices with accessories restricted to men in Orthodox Judaism, such as kippot, tallitot [prayer shawls] and a Torah scroll.

When did the trouble start?

From the very beginning, Reform and Conservative Jews who wanted to pray together at the Wall were unhappy with the restrictions – but little was done to challenge the rules. Then, in 1988, a group of English-speaking women from the United States, Canada and England came to Israel to attend the first International Jewish Feminist Conference. When the group went to the Western Wall and tried to read from the Torah as a group in the women's section, they were attacked by angry ultra-Orthodox bystanders. Israeli feminists who witnessed the incident, including both Orthodox and non-Orthodox Jews, committed to praying at the Wall on the eve of every new month in the Jewish calendar with a Torah, tefillin [phylacteries] and tallitot. The group Women of the Wall was born.

And so began an endless procession – and much foot-dragging – of court cases, appeals, special commissions, fiery Knesset debates over the issue of Western Wall prayer, restricting and outlawing at various junctures women's right to pray as they choose.

Wasn't there a compromise?

In 2003, an attempt was made by Israel's Supreme Court to resolve the ongoing crisis triggered by the Women of the Wall and complaints from non-Orthodox movements by permitting women's and mixed-gender prayer at Robinson's Arch – an archaeological park situated at the southern end of the Wall. It was completely separate from the main Western Wall Plaza, with a separate entrance from the main plaza and only accessible when the archaeological park was open. The space has been a popular location for Reform and Conservative Bar and Bat Mitzvah services, and a later compromise leaves it accessible beyond the park's opening hours.

Still, the Robinson's Arch solution proved unsuccessful. No one has been satisfied with the limited access to the Wall that Robinson's Arch provides and the numerous limitations imposed by the archaeological park, which lacks the visibility and accessibility of the main prayer plazas.

When did U.S. Jews become so upset about it and get involved in the fight?

In 2009, the Western Wall Heritage Foundation demanded that the police stop Women of the Wall's prayer service and a young Israeli medical student, Nofrat Frenkel, was arrested, questioned and charged with illegally wearing a tallit at the Western Wall. The next year, Anat Hoffman – one of the group's founders and today the leader of the organization – was arrested for carrying a Torah to the site. After being questioned for five hours, Hoffman was released from police custody and banned from the Wall for 30 days.

Shocked by the images of praying women being dragged from the Kotel, the struggle of the Women of the Wall galvanized women, and men, in Reform and Conservative congregations overseas. They were already unhappy with their inability to worship at the Wall like they do in their own synagogues, and the actions of the Israel Police infuriated them.

Because so many more Diaspora Jews are affiliated with non-Orthodox movements than Israeli Jews – particularly in the United States – the issue has resonated in overseas Jewish communities to a greater extent than it has in Israel. Beginning in 2010-2011, solidarity events for Women of the Wall became widespread in Reform and Conservative communities, and many U.S. congregations make a point of joining Women of the Wall when they visit Israel.

The group itself has become institutionally tied to the Reform movement. Hoffman is both the executive director of the Reform movement's Israel Religious Action Center and director of Women of the Wall.

Why are Diaspora Jews so furious at [Prime Minister Benjamin Netanyahu](#)?

Under pressure from both sides – the U.S. Jewish leadership abroad and ultra-Orthodox political parties in his government at home – in 2012 Netanyahu charged Jewish Agency Chairman Natan Sharansky with exploring a compromise instead of having one dictated by the courts (whom Women of the Wall, backed by the Diaspora Jewish movements, continued to turn to in their struggle). Later, he brought then-Cabinet Secretary Avichai Mendelblit into the process to negotiate with all of the sides and come up with a plan.

After an agonizingly protracted four-year process, on January 31, 2016, the Israeli government approved a plan it was believed everyone could live with.

There would be a new, expanded egalitarian prayer space in the Robinson's Arch area, with visible, easy access points that would put their dignity and status on an equal footing with the ultra-Orthodox spaces. Netanyahu hailed the decision as a "fair and creative solution," and the Women of the Wall and non-Orthodox movements celebrated.

But their celebrations were premature: Implementation of the plan has been stymied by the ultra-Orthodox parties on whom Netanyahu's governing coalition depends.

And the ultra-Orthodox parties weren't only satisfied with delaying the plan - they were concerned as long as it was on the books, the courts would have grounds to force the government's hand and make the egalitarian space happen.

That's when, in a surprise move on June 25, the ultra-Orthodox parties pressured Netanyahu's government into nixing the plan altogether. That move has infuriated top American Jewish leaders, who feel Netanyahu has slapped them in the face. The top executive of the Jewish Agency – the main vehicle of support by Diaspora Jews for Israel – has said it will now "reevaluate its relationship with the Israeli government."500

Haaretz's correspondent Chemi Shalev explained what the fallout meant for the US Diaspora of Jewish people quite eloquently in the article "*Netanyahu to American Jews: Drop Dead*" which encompasses some wry humor at the rallying of US Jews over the Western Wall issue:

> You can almost feel sorry for Reform and Conservative Jews. After all, Israeli Prime Minister Benjamin Netanyahu bamboozled them, led them up the garden path and took them for a ride. He once waxed lyrical about how important they are to him, how critical the relationship between Israel and American Jews is, how he has their best interests at heart and so forth and blah blah. But when push came to shove and Netanyahu was forced to choose between endangering Israel's strategically important ties to U.S. Jewry and risking his own seat ever so slightly, the great Israeli patriot made his obvious choice. He caved to the extortion of his ultra-Orthodox coalition partners and told American Jews, in the words of the famous 1975 New York Daily News front page about Gerald Ford and a federal bailout of New York City: Drop dead.
>
> Thirty years of demonstrating, protesting and agitating for egalitarian prayers at the Western Wall went down the drain. Years of lobbying, cajoling, persuading, negotiating and agreeing were all for naught. Valiant efforts by Reform and Conservative leaders to assure their flocks that things were moving ahead, that Netanyahu was determined to recognize them as equal human beings deserving of dignity and respect, that in 2017 it's simply inconceivable that medieval Jewish fundamentalists would continue to dictate terms to the government of the modern state of Israel, all turned out to be nothing more than smoke and mirrors. Bubkes. Nada. Gornisht mit gornisht, nothing with nothing.
>
> Theoretically, things might have turned out differently if Hillary Clinton had been elected president in 2016 instead of Donald Trump. Over the summer, when Netanyahu, like the rest of the world, was convinced that Clinton would win, he intended to try to win back the hearts of liberal American Jews that he had alienated because of his hostility toward Obama. He would have courted Reform and Conservative Jews as if they were his heart's desire. But when Trump was elected, Netanyahu realized he doesn't need liberal Jews any more, at least not for the next four years. And once they became expendable, their fate was sealed. From dear and neglected allies whose justified grievances must be addressed, Reform Jews turned virtually overnight to lefty zealots who don't know their place. Even as he was sticking a knife in their backs at Sunday's cabinet meeting, Netanyahu was already complaining that those damned American Jews had been too active, too nosy, too pushy. If they continue to protest too much, it will only be a matter of time before they'll be branded as liberals who have forgotten what it means to be Jews, like all the rest of Netanyahu's rivals.

---

2. 500 Sommer, Allison Kaplan. "Israel's Western Wall Crisis: Why Jews Are Fighting with Each Other over the Jewish Holy Site, Explained." *Haaretz.com*, Haaretz Com, 24 Apr. 2018, www.haaretz.com/israel-news/israel-s-western-wall-crisis-explained-1.5488942.

Netanyahu, after all, has come to identify the well-being of the State of Israel with his own personal fortune. It doesn't matter if Israel reneges on promises, if it doesn't keep agreements, if the government shows the world that it is beholden to extreme religious kooks, as long as Netanyahu keeps himself in power just a little bit longer. That's worth any price in the world.

Reform Jews may have thought that supporting the State of Israel and working behind the scenes and showing patience for years on end while Netanyahu got his political act together would earn them brownie points with the prime minister, at the very least. They can now join the club of the multitudes who have naively played footsie with Netanyahu only to have him cut them off at the knees the moment it suited him.

Nonetheless, it's hard to really feel sorry for our dear brethren in the Jewish Diaspora. First of all, because, with all due respect, neither I nor any Israeli that I know of care one way or another whether women are allowed to pray with men at the Western Wall. It is a cause that Israelis find curious, if not bizarre, a sign of how detached Reform Jews are from the realities of Israeli life. Even as a symbol, it's rather weak when compared to religious coercion and state-sanctioned discrimination against women and other minorities. The issue of state recognition of private conversions, for example, seems much more significant, but wait: Netanyahu has just surrendered to the Haredim on that issue as well.

But the real reason that it's hard to feel sorry for Reform and Conservative Jews is that they should have known better. Many of them love Israel dearly and follow it closely, so they cannot claim to be disappointed or surprised. They may have lauded Netanyahu in their synagogues, but they should have known, like most world leaders do, that he can't be trusted to keep this word, that he would jump ship at the first hint of troubled waters. They may have extolled Israeli democracy in their fundraising drives for their Jewish Federation or Israel Bonds, but they should have known that on issues of freedom of religion and conscience, even the flawed democracy Israel maintains inside the Green Line is concurrently a stifling theocracy rivaled only by Iran and Saudi Arabia. Many Reform and Conservative Jews read Haaretz or the New York Times or any other mainstream medium, so they know all too well that Netanyahu is the greatest enemy of their cherished ideals of pluralism and equality and liberal values. For pretending otherwise, they should not be forgiven.

Some commentators predict that the cabinet's decision to "freeze" the Western Wall deal will cause irreparable harm to Israel's ties with Reform and Conservative Jews. That is regrettable, but hopefully not inevitable. Here's an alternative suggestion: Instead of supporting the Israel that kicks you in the face, perhaps Reform and Conservative Jews should back the dwindling minority of Israelis who actually agree with their views and who would welcome them to Israel with open arms, if they only could. Instead of kowtowing to Netanyahu and pledging their support for his policies, no questions asked, perhaps U.S. Jews will finally realize that they are betraying their own beliefs when they support a government they would find abhorrent under any other circumstances. Rather than tacitly acquiescing to Israel's continuing slide towards darkness and intolerance, perhaps Reform Jews could assume a historic role of trying to bring light unto the nation they once hoped Israel would be, before it's too late.

Even if the Kotel deal had been kept, it would have done nothing to steer Israel off the dangerous course it is now accelerating on, with Netanyahu at the helm. Reform and Conservative Jews would do well to forget women at the wall and to concentrate on saving Israel from itself instead.[501]

---

3. [501] Shalev, Chemi. "Netanyahu to American Jews: Drop Dead." *Haaretz.com*, Haaretz Com, 24 Apr. 2018, www.haaretz.com/israel-news/.premium-netanyahu-to-american-jews-drop-dead-1.5488498.

Despite the suggestions by Chemi Shalev, I'd like to simply ask US Jewish people concerned about this issue: what's the point of subjecting yourself to this misery? Israelis, despite being your family and friends, have made it clear that your feelings and concerns don't matter to them. Any attempts to appeal to your faith will be repudiated by outcry from the Ultra Orthodox communities that your faith is less significant and less respectful than theirs because they follow Judaism more strictly. If you're a Jewish person who has paid attention to this controversy, you've likely already heard the arguments that they follow a strict observance of Jewish tradition and you'll be met with moving the goalpost fallacies of not being truly Jewish because you don't adhere to their observance practices and don't demean Jewish women like they do.[502] Their faith in the Abrahamic God and Judaism is defined by this blatant misogyny, you may wish that it weren't so and that the Jewish identity is more than just observance to strict traditions, but you'll inevitably face backlash upon backlash for such views by the Ultra Orthodox who clearly view their actions within the context of a moral high-ground from yours. For example, the primary accusation against Reform Jews is that their beliefs are incoherent and illogical to the Jewish tradition. I don't want to overstate this issue, many Ultra-Orthodox Jews express nothing but compassion and support for their fellow family and Jewish friends who want to follow a different branch of Judaism and even for those who become atheist. Nevertheless, their open-mindedness is in conflict with the belief in being consistent with their faith and many probably feel they don't wish to burden their own family and friends with the conflict, but at the expense of women's rights. The reason is because following ancient religious traditions harkens back to being consistent with sexism and perhaps other forms of bigotry for all religions, including the Jewish faith. *The more consistent people try to be with their religious faith, the more they must follow bigotry espoused by the holy books of those religious faiths.*

I'm sorry to say that, even if reform was made on this contentious issue, it should be clear that the Ultra Orthodox parties in Israel would likely grow more vehement and probably demand to rescind any such changes. There is every reason to believe that the Ultra Orthodox communities would rally around the strict observance of their religious faith to drive their point forward. This surely is a painful and humiliating reminder that while other religions like Islam have more horrifying problems with women's rights, Judaism can never be the humanistic and forward-thinking religious faith that some Reform Jews and Conservative Jews may wish to see it as. The supposed deep personal aspect of it and the tradition of critical thinking that many may wish were part of the Jewish faith inevitably smash into a the problem of unquestioned obedience and strict observance to religious rituals from the Ultra Orthodox branch. It's a continued reminder that women can never be equal in the Abrahamic religious traditions and that resolute faith in the Abrahamic God means misogyny against women. How can being Jewish be an important and personal part of your identity, when the Ultra Orthodox communities repeatedly remind Jewish citizens of the US and Israel that strict observance

---

4. [502] "Moving the Goalposts." *Https://Www.logicallyfallacious.com*, www.logicallyfallacious.com/tools/lp/Bo/LogicalFallacies/129/Moving-the-Goalposts.

means adhering to sexist standards against women?[503] Is it fair to either Jewish men or women to have strict, tribalistic mindsets where they're only allowed to marry fellow Jewish people or only men who are circumcised due to religious demands? Some Ultra-Orthodox and Conservative Jews repeatedly tout that Reform Jews are delusional because being a Jew has historically meant the strict observance to Jewish tradition; unfortunately, you should consider what it means for them to be right and your modern middle-ground path, which could be considered the middle-ground fallacy in conjunction with Moving the Goalposts fallacy, to be wrong.[504] That is, in addition to making random criteria to affirm what is "authentically" Jewish, you may also seek a middle path between two opposing sides because you believe in the so-called "truth" of Judaism but ignore alternatives like Jewish atheism.[505][506] You may wish it was otherwise, but has there ever been a credible argument against their contentions to Reform Judaism? If there is, why haven't they been effective counterweights to the conversation or influenced changes for the Western Wall issue?

Sadly, appealing to their practices is more dangerous than you may realize for the welfare of your children. For some Ultra-Orthodox members, being consistent with their faith means ignoring human rights abuses against Jewish children.

Ultra-Orthodox Responses to Child Rape Victims

For this portion, I will be citing sources on the less-known rape crimes that have occurred in the Ultra-Orthodox Jewish communities within the US, Australia, Great Britain, and noted in some other Eurocentric communities. Within the US, victims who have come forward face some of the worst reprisals and local governments cut corners or ignore victim outcry because of the disadvantages of going against a significant voting bloc in local elections. In effect, Jewish rape victims are treated as second-class citizens in the United States because threats and intimidation are given lower sentences by the perpetrators and sometimes these methods of coercion, although not often, are outright ignored. These coercive practices are implicitly and sometimes explicitly endorsed by the Ultra Orthodox community in New York. I'm highlighting these abuses in defense of Jewish human rights and my own commitment to human rights. If you find such a statement is motivated by some vague ulterior aims, then I ask that you consider the lives and human rights of the victims of this abusive communal behavior. To me, it is unconscionable that this be ignored and that's why I'm taking the time to cover these human rights abuses.

5. [503] Rickman, Dan. "Does Judaism Discriminate against Women? | Dan Rickman." *The Guardian*, Guardian News and Media, 10 June 2009, www.theguardian.com/commentisfree/belief/2009/jun/10/judaism-women-feminism-orthodox.
6. [504] "Moving the Goalposts." *Https://Www.logicallyfallacious.com*, www.logicallyfallacious.com/tools/lp/Bo/LogicalFallacies/129/Moving-the-Goalposts.
7. [505] "Your Logical Fallacy Is Middle Ground." *Thou Shalt Not Commit Logical Fallacies*, yourlogicalfallacyis.com/middle-ground.
8. [506] Septimus, Daniel. "Must a Jew Believe in God?" *My Jewish Learning*, www.myjewishlearning.com/article/must-a-jew-believe-in-god/.

To digress a bit as I am worried this portion will be misunderstood in terms of my intentions. If you believe that this portion is done as a form of humiliation or contempt, then I sincerely ask you to think on the plight of these Jewish victims and I must stress I'm citing empirical facts for any and all of the arguments in this chapter. I have done my utmost to emphasize Jewish personal accounts for the majority of this chapter. If you feel that I have been hurtful or shown contempt, then I apologize for any unintended consequence of that sort. Please know that is not my aim or the purpose of this chapter. The point of this section on Judaism is to highlight the irreconcilable failings of the Bible with historic facts and to emphasize how belief in these myths and the organizations based on such myths create pointless suffering against human rights at varying degrees. With all that being said, I shall be continuing herein for this chapter.

On *The Guardian*, the journalist Zoë Blackler detailed the cover-up scandal by the Ultra-Orthodox community in New York in the March 2012 article *"Brooklyn DA accused of failing to tackle Orthodox Jews' cover-up of sex abuse"* given as follows:

> A systemic cover-up of child sexual abuse in Brooklyn's ultra-Orthodox Jewish enclaves continues to obstruct justice for young victims, despite claims by religious leaders and the Brooklyn district attorney that the problem is in hand.
>
> A long-standing culture of non-cooperation with secular justice by Brooklyn's ultra-Orthodox Jews keeps many child sex offenders out of the courts and at large in their communities.
>
> Victim advocates say Brooklyn DA Charles Hynes has failed to wrest control from rabbinic leaders, who continue to hamper efforts to uncover abuse. Hynes' recent claim to have radically increased prosecution rates for these crimes has drawn scorn from critics.
>
> Brooklyn's Jewish communities, home to the largest number of ultra-Orthodox Jews outside Israel, are insular and close-knit. They maintain their own shadow justice system based on religious halachic law, enforced by religious courts known as the beit din. In recent years, they have also established their own community police force, the Shomrim.
>
> Like the Catholic bishops before them, the ultra-Orthodox rabbis who lead these communities are charged with the concealment of crimes stretching back decades, and of fostering a culture where witnesses are silenced through intimidation.
>
> "The rabbis are still, to an unfortunate degree, protecting the system," said victims' advocate Rabbi Yosef Blau, a more moderate Orthodox rabbi than his Brooklyn counterparts and spiritual advisor at Yeshiva University. Blau said the community feels it has to protect its image. "The battle is over the cover-up. That's what we're fighting now."
>
> Until the late 2000s, only a handful of ultra-Orthodox child sex crimes made their way into the criminal courts. But in April 2009 – as pressure from victims' advocates, whistle-blower blogs and parts of the secular Jewish press intensified – District Attorney Hynes launched Kol Tzedek, a community outreach effort to encourage community leaders to report child sexual abuse. The DA's Orthodox community liaison Henna White plays a key role in Kol Tzedek, which features a reporting hotline staffed by a culturally sensitive social worker.

Hynes' office says that between April 2009 and November 2011, there were 85 arrests with 47 of those cases pending. Of the 38 closed cases, it said, six had gone to trial, 23 had ended in plea deals and nine with acquittals or dismissals. These figures contrast sharply with the negligible prosecutions in the years between Hynes taking office in 1990 and the start of Kol Tzedek.

But they also represent a mere fraction of the incidents of abuse that advocates say they hear about. Because of scant reporting, there are no statistics for child sexual abuse in these communities. Most, however, believe the numbers are at least consistent with broader society if not higher.

Even the most outspoken advocates acknowledge some positive change – primarily a growing community acceptance of the problem and a slight increase in reports to the authorities. Nonetheless, they accuse Hynes and the religious leadership of playing a PR game.

Ben Hirsch of victims advocate group Survivors for Justice said, "The DA has been very reluctant to prosecute these cases. Recently he's become a little more aggressive in response to pressure from advocates and critical stories in the press. But he's still not behaving in a way that's consistent with the way he treats non-Orthodox cases."

Hirsch points to the DA's blanket refusal to release information about recent arrests and convictions, his controversial plea deals and the number of cases that by the DA's own admission have collapsed due to witness intimidation.

The DA's spokesperson, Jerry Schmetterer, said it was policy not to discuss child sex crimes with the media in order to protect the victims' anonymity.

But Dan Schorr, a former sex crimes prosecutor at Queens County and Westchester County, said the policy was surprising. In Schorr's experience, publicising the names of suspected child molesters, except in cases where that might identify the victim, is one of the best ways to strengthen a prosecution "and prevent the abuse of other children". All other New YorkCity DAs decide whether to publicise details of arrests and convictions for child sex crimes on a case by case basis. (The identity of the victim, however, will always be protected.)

The Brooklyn DA's office has also broken its own stated rule, for certain cases, in recent years.

The most infamous plea deal, often cited by advocates, was in the case of Rabbi Yehuda Kolko. In 2007, Kolko, a teacher and summer camp counsellor, was indicted for molesting two boys aged eight and nine. But under a plea deal, Kolko was only convicted on child endangerment charges, given a three year probationary sentence with no requirement to join the sex offender registry.

Kolko's prosecution followed an earlier civil suit against the school by two adult men who claimed they were also abused as children – one in the late 1960s, the other in the mid 1980s. The suit, which was dismissed on statute of limitations grounds, alleged Kolko's principal knew he was a serial molester, but suppressed the allegations.

Stefan Colmer's conviction is also controversial. Colmer was indicted on 37 charges after abusing two teenage boys, but in June 2009 he pled guilty to just eight counts of criminal sexual act in the second degree and was sentenced to two-and-a-third to seven years jail time. Colmer was released last month.

To date, and to the best of our knowledge, only eight Orthodox Jews prosecuted in Brooklyn have been required to join the sex offender registry, established in 1996. Of those eight, only four received custodial sentences, four were given probation.

The Guardian knows of two cases which have closed since the beginning of the year. Joseph Passof had been facing 12 charges, including six felonies. The most serious charge was for a criminal sexual act in the first degree – oral or anal sexual conduct with a child under 11 – a class B felony that carries a sentence of five to 25 years imprisonment.

But under a plea deal he was allowed to plead guilty to two counts of sexual abuse in the first degree - a less serious charge for which he would receive 10 years probation with a treatment programme. While this is a standard sentence for the charges Passof pleaded guilty to, former prosecutor Dan Schorr said he would consider the disparity between the original charges and the eventual sentence a disappointing outcome. Passof's sentencing hearing has been adjourned until May.

The case against David Greenfeld for child molestation collapsed in January after the DA failed to bring a case in the time allowed. The DA's spokesperson said this was because the victim's family was not co-operative.

Child sexual crimes are notoriously hard to prosecute. An apparently strong case at arrest stage can become considerably weaker as the prosecution progresses. DNA evidence may not support the allegations, for example. In ultra-Orthodox abuse cases, witnesses also frequently pull out.

DA spokesperson Jerry Schmetterer admitted cases collapse because victims are pressured by their communities. "If [victims and their families] come to us with an allegation or any concern that they are being intimidated we will take action to help them," he said.

But Mark Meyer Appel of victim support group Voice of Justice said the DA is not doing enough. "They should be going out to the community to find out why these victims are dropping out."

In the face of powerful community non-cooperation, Hynes faces a genuine obstacle. Rabbi Mark Dratch, a modern-Orthodox rabbi who founded JSafe to tackle abuse in the Jewish community, said: "Unless you get the trust of the community, you're not going to get the reporting. If, however, you're less than responsible about how you get the reports, you're not really solving the problem."

Dratch believes Hynes is being influenced by religious leaders: "The DA's position is an elected position, and the orthodox have a large voting bloc and I'm sure Mr Hynes will deny it but I think that is the nature of the situation. I know there is a lot of pressure on his office from the organised rabbinic community in Brooklyn either not to deal with the cases or to minimise them."

Rabbi Blau said the cases coming to court reflect the nature of Hynes's arrangement with community leaders. "Yes, Hynes has got a number of cases into the courts, but they're all the nobodies. They won't get somebody prominent because then the community won't co-operate. But if it's some weird guy, OK, let the police handle it."

Blau's analysis is supported by Joel Engelman, an abuse survivor and spokesperson for the victims, who follows these cases closely. Engelman said that of the handful of defendants currently in the system, most are on the fringes of Brooklyn's ultra-Orthodox communities, rather than their leaders and power brokers.
Both the DA's office and rabbinical leaders deny there is a deal. Both insist they are doing all in their power to solve the problem.

But in recent months, the leaders of Agudath Israel of America, an umbrella body for Brooklyn's ultra-Orthodox Jews, has clarified its position on reporting abuse to the police. To avoid the ancient prohibition against mesirah – the act of handing over a fellow Jew to secular authorities – Agudath directs its members to consult with a rabbi first, before calling children's services.

The rabbi must establish whether the suspicions are weighty enough to justify a report. "A person can be destroyed if allegations which are baseless are raised against him," said Agudath's executive vice-president, Rabbi David Zwiebel.

While some observers are encouraged that Agudath is now at least recognising secular justice, others are horrified. "This is the latest outrage from Agudath Israel," said Eliot Pasik, a lawyer who has represented Orthodox abuse victims, including those of Yehuda Kolko. "In the name of maintaining what they think is the best image possible, they've become ideological fanatics."

There are some signs of a growing schism within the rabbinic leadership – including inside Agudath – even if most critics are still afraid to speak up. In a significant move last summer, the Crown Heights Beit Din declared it will no longer handle child sex abuse cases, which it said must be taken to the secular authorities.

But progress, say advocates, is far slower than the official picture suggests.

Last November, the Jewish radio show Talkline held a heated debate on child sexual abuse. Zvi Gluck, a community mediator who helps other ultra-Orthodox Jews in trouble with the law, rang in to say the DA's arrest figure was "not a real number". Gluck said he knew most of those arrests, "and most of those, because of pressure within the community, were dropped and resulted in nothing happening".

Gluck added he knew of at least three abused children who had committed suicide in recent months. "As Frum Yidden [observant Jews] we have an obligation to protect our community and our children. We are making progress but they are small steps and we are nowhere near where we need to be."[507]

On May 2012, Zoë Blackler gave a follow-up article titled "*Brooklyn's Ultra Orthodox Jews rally behind accused in child abuse case*" about the communal reaction to the trial of a prominent Rabbi in the community. The lengthy portions below are the pertinent portion:

Until last year, Nechemya Weberman was a therapist in Orthodox Jewish Brooklyn. From the apartment building he owns in Williamsburg, he counselled teenage girls from ultra-Orthodox Jewish families. Girls, who through improper dress, flirtations with boys or a curiosity in life beyond the confines of their sects, were risking disrepute. In the antiquated world of the ultra-Orthodox, the stigma of immodesty can wreck a girl's marriage prospects and her future in the community.

In 2007, two worried parents sent their 12-year-old daughter for counselling with Weberman, at the insistence of her school. For three years, the girl consulted him, seeing him often several times a week. The girl had been questioning her religious teachers, and her parents hoped that Weberman, who had raised his own pious, god-fearing children, would lead her back to the right path.

Later this summer, a jury in Brooklyn – home to the largest Orthodox population outside Israel – will be asked to decide exactly what took place during those many counselling sessions.

---

9. [507] Blackler, Zoë. "Brooklyn DA Accused of Failing to Tackle Orthodox Jews' Cover-up of Sex Abuse." *The Guardian*, Guardian News and Media, 29 Mar. 2012, www.theguardian.com/world/2012/mar/29/brooklyn-da-orthodox-jews-cover-up.

Whether Weberman repeatedly sexually abused the young girl as she alleges, or whether, as the defence claims, he is the object of misplaced revenge.

Whatever facts emerge at trial and whatever the jury decides, most in this insular community have already reached a verdict. The majority are siding with the accused. On Wednesday night, several thousand members of Weberman's Satmar Hasidic sect are expected to attend a rally on his behalf. His supporters, with the full backing of the senior rabbis, are stepping up their efforts to fight the prosecution.

That the Weberman case is going to trial at all is notable in itself. The Guardian has detailed how most sex abuse claims are handled inside the community, either brushed aside or resolved in the shadow religious courts, or by the silencing of victims through bribing or intimidation. Those cases that do reach the criminal justice system tend to end in plea deals negotiated out of public view, in line with the Brooklyn district attorney's contentious secrecy policy.

As media attention on the issue intensifies, the Weberman case has acquired a much bigger significance, beyond the question of individual guilt or innocence. It will offer a rare insight into the increasingly bitter divide inside the community – between the majority that wants to continue the cover-up and the growing number speaking up. It will also illustrate the level of anger those who make abuse complaints face from members of their own community.

Last Friday, the Yiddish paper Der Blatt ran a front page story announcing "Libel 75", Wednesday night's rally in the Continental Hall in Williamsburg. The piece called on the entire community to defend Nechemya Weberman from "a despicable, false libel" and rescue him from 75 years in jail. "The community will come out", it declared, to help raise $500,000 for Weberman's legal costs. Posters about Libel 75 have also been plastered across Williamsburg.

If Weberman, now 53, is found guilty, he is unlikely to face 75 years in prison time. The charges against him, however, are severe. The indictment, which runs to 23 pages, includes 87 counts of sexual abuse. Of the 16 felony charges, the most serious alone, course of sexual conduct against a child in the first degree, carries a mandatory prison term of five to 25 years. Although not part of the prosecution, Weberman is also tainted by his lack of qualifications as he is not a trained psychotherapist.

Weberman's defence attorney George Farkas, who is billed to appear at Wednesday's rally, says Weberman is the real victim. A year before the allegations emerged, the girl - still underage - had an older boyfriend. Her father, concerned that the pair had embarked on a sexual relationship, secretly video taped them alone and the boyfriend was brought before a judge. Farkas says that although his client advised against the scheme, the girl blames him and wants revenge. She is being manipulated, Farkas says, by "nefarious, vicious people" out to bring Weberman down.

Or as Der Blatt phrased it in more emotive terms: "As parents who have benefited from this devoted askan [community volunteer] and educator, the person we turned to first to rescue ours and others children when they started sliding [becoming non observant], we call on you: do not allow this askan to be, god forbid, sent to prison for life for his holy work rescuing Jewish children."

But Judy Genut, a friend of the girl's mother, dismisses Weberman's version of events, even though she acknowledges that most in the community support him. "They can't believe that somebody dressed according to the tradition, who acts and talks and walks like a person who has the fear of God in him, would actually do what he accused of. It's mind boggling." The girl's mother had two sisters who "went off the path", Genut says, so when the story first spread, people dismissed it as the niece being "slutty" too. "The family didn't gather sympathy because of what the aunts did."

'What's on trial is the idea that he can be protected and supported by the rabbis'

Although the Libel 75 campaign is unprecedented in scale, Weberman is not the first recipient of a rabbinic fundraising effort. In March 2009, Rabbi Israel Weingarten was convicted in Brooklyn's federal court of raping his daughter from age nine to 18. Following a reportedly bizarre and harrowing trial (in which Weingarten attempted to defend himself at one point cross-examining the daughter) the jury found him guilty on all counts. He was sentenced to 30 years in prison. This past February, the blog Failed Messiah reported that a rabbinic delegation had visited Weingarten in jail. They took with them a proclamation of innocence, signed by a bevy of senior rabbis that blamed his incarceration on a "travesty of justice" and a "sinister plot" and that pledged to raise the money needed to win back his freedom.

The instinct to rescue a fellow Jew from prison is hard wired in the Orthodox psyche, says community activist Isaac Shonfeld, an observant Jew from Brooklyn. The fundraising tradition has a name, Pidyon Shvuyim, and dates back to life in eastern Europe when Jews were frequently held to ransom on trumped-up charges by their anti-semitic governments. It isn't just that fear of jail trumps considerations of guilt or innocence, Shonfeld says. But also that many in the community, despite the evidence, still believe Weingarten over his daughter. In a strictly hierarchical, patriarchal, deeply religious society, it's unsurprising: Rabbi Weingarten is a male in late middle age, a scholar of the torah; his accuser was a young woman who is no longer Orthodox; and secular courts are regarded as inherently untrustworthy.

Nechemya Weberman's supporters have worked tirelessly to orchestrate the Libel 75 campaign and win the backing of two competing sets of rabbis, says Pearl Engelman, a Satmar Hasid from Williamsburg, whose own son Joel is an abuse survivor. "For the two factions in Satmar to unite on something like this is extremely unusual."

"What's on trial here is not just Weberman," says Engelman, who believes the girls' account. "What's on trial is the idea that a [man like] Weberman can be protected and supported by the rabbis."

According to several accounts, the girl's family is facing intimidation to prevent them testifying. Her father owns a Jewish phone directory, widely used in the community. He has been told that unless his daughter withdraws from the court case, advertising will cease and his business will collapse.

The girl's new boyfriend, Hershy Deutsch, has also been threatened. Deutsch, who owns a pizza restaurant on Lee Avenue, says he was offered $500,000 to persuade the girl to recant. When he refused, he was told his kosher licence could be at risk. He says his landlord was pressured to evict him. "Giving blood money to deny a story is not going to stop the molesters molesting children," he says. Deutsch is using Facebook to mobilise a counter demonstration. He says he worries about his girlfriend, who is suffering terribly. She can't sleep, he says, haunted by memories. Deutsch says his girlfriend also turned down a bribe. "Every time she would go to a store, she would have an image of where that money came from."

Judy Genut says she, her husband and other members of her family have also been harrassed. "A lot of people are angry that this came out because it brings us in a very bad light," she says. "Other people hear about it, and read about it and if we are the chosen ones, the moral compass of the world, then shouldn't we act morally? It's a very hard thing for us to swallow because there's so much good in our community and so many beautiful organisations.

"So there's a lot of shame. And when people are ashamed they hide. And how do you hide? By not letting other people know that something like this is happening. Because if you don't talk about it, it's not happening, right? It hurts me so much. I mean, do we actually harbour our own perverts?"

The Weberman case is a wake-up call for the community, she says, that nothing stays hidden anymore. "Children will learn there are people sticking up for them."[508]

Nechemya Weberman was found guilty at trial and the ongoing reaction by the community upon the rape victim continued to worsen in the following year. Josh Saul of the NYPost elaborates in the article "*Sex Abuse Victim shamed during synagogue prayers*" on the thoroughgoing harassment and threats for speaking up on her abuse and her husband's righteous anger over the injustice:

> The brave Orthodox Jewish teen whose testimony helped convict the prominent Brooklyn counselor who had sexually abused her was driven out of her own synagogue on Rosh Hashana last week.
>
> The married, 18-year-old victim was in the Williamsburg synagogue where her family has prayed for the past decade when a man yelled, "Moser, out of the shul!" the woman's husband told The Post on Sunday.
>
> The word "moser" refers to a Jew who informs on another Jew to secular authorities.
>
> "They stopped the praying until she left," said her husband, Boorey Deutsch, 26. "Some woman tried telling my wife to stay there and not leave. She shouldn't care what they say. But my wife ended up leaving."
>
> "She felt horrible and mistreated. They treat survivors as if they are the abusers," Deutsch fumed to The Post.
>
> Deutsch and his wife have suffered harassment ever since she first accused Nechemya Weberman, 54, of sexually abusing her after she was sent to him for counseling as a 12-year-old.
>
> "Several weeks ago, someone threw eggs at Boorey's store," a law-enforcement source said.
>
> The gutsy victim testified at Weberman's trial that she was afraid to report the abuse because he was "supposedly a god in Williamsburg" and nobody would believe her.
>
> "Satmar would have kicked me out, and if Satmar kicks you out, nobody accepts you," she said during the trial last year.
> The pressure for her to drop the case against Weberman was at times overwhelming.
>
> At one point, three Orthodox Jewish brothers, Jacob, Joseph and Hertzka Berger, tried to intimidate Deutsch and his then-girlfriend into dropping the case by ripping down the "kosher" certificate at his Williamsburg restaurant.
>
> The men pleaded guilty in June in a deal that gave them no jail time.
>
> Last month, Abraham Rubin, 49, also pleaded guilty to offering Deutsch and the victim $500,000 to leave the country so that the case against Weberman could be dropped.
>
> Weberman — who is married with 10 children — is currently serving his 50-year sentence at the maximum-security Shawangunk Correctional Facility in upstate Wallkill.
>
> *Additional reporting by Reuven Fenton*[509]

---

10. [508] Blackler, Zoë. "Brooklyn's Ultra-Orthodox Jews Rally behind Accused in Child Abuse Case." *The Guardian*, Guardian News and Media, 16 May 2012, www.theguardian.com/world/2012/may/16/orthodox-sex-abuse-scandal-new-york.
11. [509] Saul, Josh. "Sex Abuse Victim Shamed during Synagogue Prayers." *New York Post*, New York Post, 9 Sept. 2013, nypost.com/2013/09/09/sex-abuse-victim-shamed-during-synagogue-prayers/.

The New York Times journalists, Sharon Otterman and Ray Rivera, provide further information on the extent of communal intimidation and violence that generally occurs by the Ultra Orthodox community against their fellow Jews who speak-up on being abused in the May 2012 article titled "*Ultra-Orthodox Shun Their Own For Reporting Child Sexual Abuse*" which details as follows:

> The first shock came when Mordechai Jungreis learned that his mentally disabled teenage son was being molested in a Jewish ritual bathhouse in Brooklyn. The second came after Mr. Jungreis complained, and the man accused of the abuse was arrested.
>
> Old friends started walking stonily past him and his family on the streets of Williamsburg. Their landlord kicked them out of their apartment. Anonymous messages filled their answering machine, cursing Mr. Jungreis for turning in a fellow Jew. And, he said, the mother of a child in a wheelchair confronted Mr. Jungreis's mother-in-law, saying the same man had molested her son, and she "did not report this crime, so why did your son-in-law have to?"
>
> By cooperating with the police, and speaking out about his son's abuse, Mr. Jungreis, 38, found himself at the painful forefront of an issue roiling his insular Hasidic community. There have been glimmers of change as a small number of ultra-Orthodox Jews, taking on longstanding religious and cultural norms, have begun to report child sexual abuse accusations against members of their own communities. But those who come forward often encounter intense intimidation from their neighbors and from rabbinical authorities, aimed at pressuring them to drop their cases.
>
> Abuse victims and their families have been expelled from religious schools and synagogues, shunned by fellow ultra-Orthodox Jews and targeted for harassment intended to destroy their businesses. Some victims' families have been offered money, ostensibly to help pay for therapy for the victims, but also to stop pursuing charges, victims and victims' advocates said.
>
> "Try living for one day with all the pain I am living with," Mr. Jungreis, spent and distraught, said recently outside his new apartment on Williamsburg's outskirts. "Did anybody in the Hasidic community in these two years, in Borough Park, in Flatbush, ever come up and look my son in the eye and tell him a good word? Did anybody take the courage to show him mercy in the street?"
>
> A few blocks away, Pearl Engelman, a 64-year-old great-grandmother, said her community had failed her too. In 2008, her son, Joel, told rabbinical authorities that he had been repeatedly groped as a child by a school official at the United Talmudical Academy in Williamsburg. The school briefly removed the official but denied the accusation. And when Joel turned 23, too old to file charges under the state's statute of limitations, they returned the man to teaching.
>
> "There is no nice way of saying it," Mrs. Engelman said. "Our community protects molesters. Other than that, we are wonderful."
>
> **Keeping to Themselves**
>
> The New York City area is home to an estimated 250,000 ultra-Orthodox Jews — the largest such community outside of Israel, and one that is growing rapidly because of its high birthrate. The community is concentrated in Brooklyn, where many of the ultra-Orthodox are Hasidim, followers of a fervent spiritual movement that began in 18th-century Europe and applies Jewish law to every aspect of life.
>
> Their communities, headed by dynastic leaders called rebbes, strive to preserve their centuries-old customs by resisting the contaminating influences of the outside world. While some ultra-Orthodox rabbis now argue that a child molester should be reported to the police, others strictly adhere to an

ancient prohibition against mesirah, the turning in of a Jew to non-Jewish authorities, and consider publicly airing allegations against fellow Jews to be chillul Hashem, a desecration of God's name.

There are more mundane factors, too. Some ultra-Orthodox Jews want to keep abuse allegations quiet to protect the reputation of the community, and the family of the accused. And rabbinical authorities, eager to maintain control, worry that inviting outside scrutiny could erode their power, said Samuel Heilman, a professor of Jewish studies at Queens College.

"They are more afraid of the outside world than the deviants within their own community," Dr. Heilman said. "The deviants threaten individuals here or there, but the outside world threatens everyone and the entire structure of their world."

Scholars believe that abuse rates in the ultra-Orthodox world are roughly the same as those in the general population, but for generations, most ultra-Orthodox abuse victims kept silent, fearful of being stigmatized in a culture where the genders are strictly separated and discussion of sex is taboo. When a victim did come forward, it was generally to rabbis and rabbinical courts, which would sometimes investigate the allegations, pledge to monitor the accused, or order payment to a victim, but not refer the matter to the police.

"You can destroy a person's life with a false report," said Rabbi Chaim Dovid Zwiebel, the executive vice president of Agudath Israel of America, a powerful ultra-Orthodox organization, which last year said that observant Jews should not report allegations to the police unless permitted to do so by a rabbi.

Rabbinic authorities "recommend you speak it over with a rabbi before coming to any definitive conclusion in your own mind," Rabbi Zwiebel said.

When ultra-Orthodox Jews do bring abuse accusations to the police, the same cultural forces that have long kept victims silent often become an obstacle to prosecutions.

In Brooklyn, of the 51 molesting cases involving the ultra-Orthodox community that the district attorney's office says it has closed since 2009, nine were dismissed because the victims backed out. Others ended with plea deals because the victims' families were fearful.

"People aren't recanting, but they don't want to go forward," said Rhonnie Jaus, a sex crimes prosecutor in Brooklyn. "We've heard some of our victims have been thrown out of schools, that the person is shunned from the synagogue. There's a lot of pressure."

The degree of intimidation can vary by neighborhood, by sect and by the prominence of the person accused.

In August 2009, the rows in a courtroom at State Supreme Court in Brooklyn were packed with rabbis, religious school principals and community leaders. Almost all were there in solidarity with Yona Weinberg, a bar mitzvah tutor and licensed social worker from Flatbush who had been convicted of molesting two boys under age 14.

Justice Guston L. Reichbach looked out with disapproval. He recalled testimony about how the boys had been kicked out of their schools or summer camps after bringing their cases, suggesting a "communal attitude that seeks to blame, indeed punish, victims." And he noted that, of the 90 letters he had received praising Mr. Weinberg, not one displayed "any concern or any sympathy or even any acknowledgment for these young victims, which, frankly, I find shameful."

"While the crimes the defendant stands convicted of are bad enough," the judge said before sentencing Mr. Weinberg to 13 months in prison, "what is even more troubling to the court is a communal attitude that seems to impose greater opprobrium on the victims than the perpetrator."

Silenced by Fear

Intimidation is rarely documented, but just two weeks ago, a Hasidic woman from Kiryas Joel, N.Y., in Orange County, filed a startling statement in a criminal court, detailing the pressure she faced after telling the police that a Hasidic man had molested her son.

"I feel 100 percent threatened and very scared," she said in her statement. "I feel intimidated and worried about what the consequences are going to be. But I have to protect my son and do what is right."

Last year, her son, then 14, told the police that he had been offered $20 by a stranger to help move some boxes, but instead, the man brought him to a motel in Woodbury, removed the boy's pants and masturbated him.

The police, aided by the motel's security camera, identified the man as Joseph Gelbman, then 52, of Kiamesha Lake, a cook who worked at a boys' school run by the Vizhnitz Hasidic sect. He was arrested, and the intimidation ensued. Rabbi Israel Hager, a powerful Vizhnitz rabbi in Monsey, N.Y., began calling the mother, asking her to cease her cooperation with the criminal case and, instead, to bring the matter to a rabbinical court under his jurisdiction, according to the mother's statement to the court. Rabbi Hager did not return repeated calls seeking comment.

"I said: 'Why? He might do this again to other children,' " the mother said in the statement. The mother, who asked that The New York Times not use her name to avoid identifying her son, told the police that the rabbi asked, "What will you gain from this if he goes to jail?" and said that, in a later call, he offered her $20,000 to pay for therapy for her son if the charges were dropped.

On April 24, three days before the case was set for trial, the boy was expelled from his school. When the mother protested, she said, the principal threatened to report her for child abuse.

Prosecutors, against the wishes of the boy's parents, settled the case on April 27. Mr. Gelbman was given three years' probation after pleading guilty to endangering the welfare of a child.

Mr. Jungreis, the Williamsburg father, had a similar experience. He first suspected that his son was being molested after he came home with blood in his underwear at age 12, and later was caught touching another child on the bus. But, Mr. Jungreis said, the school principal warned him to stay silent. Two years later, the boy revealed that he had been molested for years by a man he saw at a mikvah, a ritual bath that observant Jews visit for purification.

Mr. Jungreis, knowing the prohibition on calling secular authorities, asked several rabbis to help him report the abuse, but, he said, they told him they did not want to get involved. Ultimately, he found a rabbi who told him to take his son to a psychologist, who would be obligated to notify law enforcement. "That way you are not the moser," he said the rabbi told him, using the Hebrew word for informer. The police arrested Meir Dascalowitz, then 27, who is now awaiting trial.

Prosecution of intimidation is rare. Victims and their supporters say that is because rabbinical authorities are politically powerful; prosecutors say it is because there is rarely enough evidence to build a criminal case. "The intimidation often works, at least in the short run," said Laura Pierro, the head of the special victims unit at the Ocean County prosecutor's office in New Jersey.

In 2010, Ms. Pierro's agency indicted Shaul Luban for witness tampering: he had sent a threatening text message to multiple recipients, urging the Orthodox Jewish community of Lakewood, N.J., to pressure the family of an 11-year-old abuse victim not to cooperate with prosecutors. In exchange for having his record cleared, Mr. Luban agreed to spend about a year in a program for first-time offenders.

Mr. Luban and others "wanted the phone to ring off the hook to withdraw the complaint from our office," the Ocean County prosecutor, Marlene Lynch Ford, said.

Threats to Advocates

The small cadre of ultra-Orthodox Jews who have tried to call attention to the community's lack of support for sexual abuse victims have often been targeted with the same forms of intimidation as the victims themselves.

Rabbi Nuchem Rosenberg of Williamsburg, for example, has been shunned by communal authorities because he maintains a telephone number that features his impassioned lectures in Yiddish, Hebrew and English imploring victims to call 911 and accusing rabbis of silencing cases. He also shows up at court hearings and provides victims' families with advice. His call-in line gets nearly 3,000 listeners a day.

In 2008, fliers were posted around Williamsburg denouncing him. One depicted a coiled snake, with Mr. Rosenberg's face superimposed on its head. "Nuchem Snake Rosenberg: Leave Tainted One!" it said in Hebrew. The local Satmar Hasidic authorities banned him from their synagogues, and a wider group of 32 prominent ultra-Orthodox rabbis and religious judges signed an order, published in a community newspaper, formally ostracizing him.

"The public must beware, and stay away from him, and push him out of our camp, not speak to him, and even more, not to honor him or support him, and not allow him to set foot in any synagogue until he returns from his evil ways," the order said in Hebrew.

"They had small children coming to my house and spitting on me and on my children and wife," Rabbi Rosenberg, 61, said in an interview.

Rabbi Tzvi Gluck, 31, of Queens, the son of a prominent rabbi and an informal liaison to secular law enforcement, began helping victims after he met troubled teenagers at Our Place, a help center in Brooklyn, and realized that sexual abuse was often the root of their problems. It was when he began helping the teenagers report cases to the police that he also received threats.

In February, for example, he received a call asking him to urge an abuse victim to abandon a case. "A guy called me up and said: 'Listen, I want you to know that people on the street are talking about what they can do to hurt you financially. And maybe speak to your children's schools, to get your kids thrown out of school.'"

Rabbi Gluck said he had helped at least a dozen ultra-Orthodox abuse victims bring cases to the Brooklyn district attorney in recent years, and each time, he said, the victim came under heavy pressure to back down. In a case late last year that did not get to the police, a 30-year-old molested a 14-year-old boy in a Jewish ritual bath in Brooklyn, and a rabbi "made the boy apologize to the molester for seducing him," he said.

"If a guy in our community gets diagnosed with cancer, the whole community will come running to help them," he said. "But if someone comes out and says they were a victim of abuse, as a whole, the community looks at them and says, 'Go jump in a lake.'"

Traces of Change

Awareness of child sexual abuse is increasing in the ultra-Orthodox community. Since 2008, hundreds of adult abuse survivors have told their stories, mostly anonymously, on blogs and radio call-in shows, and to victims' advocates. Rabbi-vetted books like "Let's Stay Safe," aimed at teaching children what to do if they are inappropriately touched, are selling well.

The response by communal authorities, however, has been uneven.

In March, for example, Satmar Hasidic authorities in Williamsburg took what advocates said was an unprecedented step: They posted a Yiddish sign in synagogues warning adults and children to stay away from a community member who they said was molesting young men. But the sign did not urge victims to call the police: "With great pain we must, according to the request of the brilliant rabbis (may they live long and good lives), inform you that the young man," who was named, "is, unfortunately, an injurious person and he is a great danger to our community."

In Crown Heights, where the Chabad-Lubavitch Hasidic movement has its headquarters, there has been more significant change. In July 2011, a religious court declared that the traditional prohibition against mesirah did not apply in cases with evidence of abuse. "One is forbidden to remain silent in such situations," said the ruling, signed by two of the court's three judges.

Since then, five molesting cases have been brought from the neighborhood — "as many sexual abuse-related arrests and reports as there had been in the past 20 years," said Eliyahu Federman, a lawyer who helps victims in Crown Heights, citing public information.

Mordechai Feinstein, 19, helped prompt the ruling by telling the Crown Heights religious court that he had been touched inappropriately at age 15 by Rabbi Moshe F. Keller, a Lubavitcher who ran a foundation for at-risk youth and whom Mr. Feinstein had considered his spiritual mentor.

Last week, Rabbi Keller was sentenced in Criminal Court to three years' probation for endangering the welfare of a child. And Mr. Feinstein, who is no longer religious, is starting a campaign to encourage more abuse victims to come forward. He is working with two prominent civil rights attorneys, Norman Siegel and Herbert Teitelbaum, who are asking lawyers to provide free assistance to abuse victims frustrated by their dealings with prosecutors.

"The community is a garden; there are a lot of beautiful things about it," Mr. Feinstein said. "We just have to help them weed out the garden and take out the things that don't belong there."

Correction: May 11, 2012

A previous version of this article misspelled the surname of the executive vice president of Agudath Israel of America as Zweibel.[510]

In Great Britain, British Orthodox rabbis have also faced accusations and legal penalties for the sexual exploitation of Jewish children. However, the difference is that the Ultra Orthodox rabbinical community of Britain reportedly responded with compassion and an almost immediate censure of the alleged perpetrators of heinous crimes of child abuse. While just as many mistreated and discriminated against abused victims, there apparently was a strong community focus on combating such attacks and vehemently defending the victims of physical and sexual abuse through strong communal focus on keeping them safe from further harm. These Jewish children were reminded that they were valued and that further emotional, sexual, and physical suffering wouldn't be tolerated by the violent offenders and sex offenders of the community. Joe Byrne, a pseudonym for an abuse victim who wrote the article, explains in *The Telegraph* article *"C4's Jewish abuse documentary didn't tell the whole story"* from his personal experience:

---

12. [510] Otterman, Sharon, and Ray Rivera. "Ultra-Orthodox Shun Their Own for Reporting Child Sexual Abuse." *The New York Times*, The New York Times, 10 May 2012, www.nytimes.com/2012/05/10/nyregion/ultra-orthodox-jews-shun-their-own-for-reporting-child-sexual-abuse.html.

When my sister and I were growing up in the Haredi community, we were abused by a rabbi. Between the ages of six and 11, this man — a member of our close family — physically abused me, and sexually abused my younger sister. The matter eventually came into the open, and it caused a split in the community. Many people made it clear, in no uncertain terms, that the authorities should not be involved. But there was another group that supported our right to report our abuser to the police. We did so, and the man went to prison for a number of years.

The abuser in question – let's call him Rabbi A – was no drunken reprobate. His violence towards me was clinical and systematic, carried out in response to minor infringements such as failing to keep my room tidy enough. He would keep a detailed tally of my "crimes", and look for an opportunity when he had me alone. Then he would secrete me away behind some bushes, in an upstairs room at the synagogue, or behind the garden shed, and administer the beatings with a leather belt or a length of garden hose. This happened to me weekly, sometimes daily. Actually, I count myself lucky. Compared to the abuse which many children suffer, my own was not that bad. Certainly it was eclipsed by the treatment my sister received. I did not ever see him sexually abusing her, but looking back I can recognise the signs.

Rabbi A was deeply manipulative, and managed to ensure that neither my sister nor myself told my mother what was happening. So it all first came out at school. I went to a Haredi school and the headmaster – another rabbi – had a special concern for me. Noticing that something wasn't right, he called me into his office one day and asked me about things at home. Without thinking, I began to let the whole story come tumbling out.

He told my mother immediately. She came into school that same day, and we had a meeting in the headmaster's office. He told me that he had spoken harshly to Rabbi A on the phone, and had given him one last chance. I can still remember his words: "If he does it again, I'll throw the book at him."

I suppose he should have informed the police immediately. But he didn't yet know about the sexual abuse, and things are always much clearer with the benefit of hindsight. As soon as Rabbi A had me alone, he hit me across the face and told me never to tell on him again. I didn't reply; but deep down I knew his time had come. The following day I told my headmaster what had happened. True to his word, that was the last time I saw Rabbi A.

I have since pieced together what happened next. My mother and headmaster called the police, and they marched in to the synagogue to arrest Rabbi A. In a darkly comic moment, they seized the wrong rabbi and dragged him out in the middle of prayers. But eventually they got their man. The case went to court 18 months later, and I was cross-examined by an aggressive QC for two days. I was 11 years old, and broke down only once.

This period of our lives was the most stressful our family had ever experienced. While the court case was going on, my mother was targeted by a group of ultra-orthodox hardliners who despised us for having talked to the police. Somehow, she protected my sister and I from it at the time, and told me the details only recently. It was a campaign of intimidation. Her car was vandalised. Rubbish, including soiled nappies, was pushed through our letterbox. She was spat at in the street, and cursed for generations. Many kosher shops refused her service. She received threatening letters; even our solicitor – a Haredi man – was sent a note saying that if he continued to represent us, his house would be burned down and his children killed.

And most humiliating of all, letters appeared under the windscreen wipers of all the cars in the synagogue car park, stating my mother was mad and we were under her influence. The same letters were sent to our teachers, and to my mother's employer. Reading this, you are probably wondering why I criticise the Channel 4 programme. The reason is simple. The intimidation was carried out only by a hardcore element of the Haredi community. Many others stood up to them, including my headmaster and our solicitor, both high-ranking rabbis and ordinary people. These people gave us emotional, practical and even financial support, and refused to be intimidated.

A group of senior rabbis even held meetings with those who attacked us, and argued with them, citing Talmudic sources, to suggest that going to the police was the right thing to do. I will always be grateful to these people for their courage and compassion. It was wrong of *Dispatches* to ignore them, and irresponsible to allow the hardline sects to characterise the entire Haredi community.

The orthodox Jewish community is not a monolithic entity. There are countless sects and sub-sects, and each has a slightly different set of values. Nobody can know the numbers for certain. Perhaps there are more hardliners than moderates; personally, I suspect it is vice versa. Either way, I can assure you from my own experience that a great many within the orthodox community are appalled by the notion of keeping abuse under wraps. These are good people, and I believe *Dispatches* should have given them a voice.

Joe Byrne is a pseudonym[511]

Other rabbinical communities such as Australia have only gradually changed their position from one of censure and contempt for victims to one of compassion and putting sex offenders in prison. Melissa Davey reported in *The Guardian* on the sex abuse by Ultra Orthodox Rabbis upon helpless children in an article titled "*Rabbi was allowed to keep teaching after admitting abuse of children, inquiry told*" in the Ultra Orthodox Yeshivah community of Australia:

> A rabbi who admitted to sexually abusing children at the Orthodox Jewish Yeshivah centre in Melbourne was allowed to keep teaching because senior religious leaders feared he would self-harm if they fired him.
> Giving evidence to the royal commission into institutional responses to child sex abuse on Tuesday, Zephaniah Waks spoke of how three of his children were abused by staff at the centre, and of a culture that discouraged him from going to the police.
> In 1993, one of Waks's sons told him that his younger brother was being abused by a teacher, rabbi David Kramer, at the Yeshivah college.
> Waks said he went to the school principal, Rabbi Abraham Glick, who told him he would speak to Kramer. A few hours later, Glick called Waks and said Kramer had "partially admitted" to what he had done, but that the children had initiated and enjoyed it.
> Waks said he was shocked when he noticed Kramer was still teaching at the Yeshivah centre school a couple of days later.
> "I confronted Glick and said, 'How is this possible, what is going on'," Waks told the commission at Melbourne's county court.
> "Glick said a psychiatrist concluded Kramer allowed himself to be caught because he wanted to be stopped, and there was danger of self-harm, 'So we can not fire him'.
> "I thought this was absolutely outrageous, however if I reported this to the police I would be in breach of the Jewish principle of mesirah."
> Waks said the concept of "mesirah" prevented members of the ultra-Orthodox Chabad sect of Judaism from going to outside authorities.
> "At the very least, the breach of mesirah almost certainly always leads to shunning and intimidation within the Jewish community and would almost certainly damage marriage prospects of your children," Waks told the commission.
> The Yeshivah centre was the centre of his universe, Waks told the commission, and members of the Chabad movement did not make any decisions, including where to send their children to school or who to marry, without consulting a rabbi.

---

13. [511] Byrne, Joe. "C4's Jewish Abuse Documentary Didn't Tell the Whole Story." *The Telegraph*, Telegraph Media Group, 18 Feb. 2013, www.telegraph.co.uk/lifestyle/9872924/C4s-Jewish-abuse-documentary-didnt-tell-the-whole-story.html.

His children were sent to the school within the centre, they prayed at the centre synagogue, and social activities took place there, Waks said.

"It was our whole life," he said. "We lived there. All of our friends [were] there."

Despite this all-encompassing culture that frowned upon members from going to police, Waks said he arranged a meeting with other parents from the Yeshivah college to discuss what to do about Kramer. He wanted to get them to agree to collectively approach senior leaders at the centre and tell them if they did not fire Kramer, they would all go to the police.

That meeting was called off, Waks said, when he received a call from Harry Cooper, a senior lawyer and chairman of the management board of the Yeshivah centre, who told him they would fire Kramer.

In fact, the centre paid for Kramer to go to Israel, where he attempted to get a job as a teacher, Waks told the commission. Waks said he believed Kramer abused about 60 children while teaching in Melbourne. On Monday, the commission heard Kramer later travelled to the US, where he was charged with serious sexual offending against a child and sentenced to seven years' jail.

In 2013, Victoria police also charged Kramer with historical child sex abuse offences and he was extradited to Australia. He was sentenced to jail and was eligible for parole 18 months later. After serving his sentence, he was deported to the US, where he remains.

Later, Waks said he found out another of his sons, Manny, had also been abused, but by two other senior Yeshivah staff. By this point, he believed going to police was a "no-brainer," he told the commission. "The taboo had been broken," he said.

Manny Waks gave evidence of the abuse he suffered on Monday, telling the commission how he was bullied and ostracised by the Yeshivah community when he came forward.

Both Manny and Zephania Waks have left Australia since speaking out about the abuse, the commission heard, because of intimidation and isolation they experienced from Yeshivah community members.

The commission is examining child sex abuse in the Jewish community for the first time since hearings began in 2013.[512]

As mentioned prior, to the Ultra Orthodox Rabbinical community's credit, this crisis of faith and thoroughgoing problem of sex abuse of young children has prompted many Rabbis to make an outspoken stand against further abuse as of 2016 in Australia, New Zealand, and certain European countries. While many abusers evidently remain in power, many Rabbis are demanding change and for change to occur with all deliberate speed to protect child victims and to effectively put a stop to further child sex abuse. On *SBS Hebrew Radio* and published on the *SBS TV* website in the article "*Leading Rabbi calls on Jewish leaders to stand down following Child Abuse Royal Commission*" the journalist Nitza Lowenstein details from the radio interview available on the article webpage itself:

> Speaking to **SBS Hebrew Radio**, Rabbi Dr Benjamin Elton, Rabbi of the Great Synagogue in Sydney and Secretary of the Rabbinical Councils of Australia and New Zealand (Australia's most senior Orthodox Rabbi) has called on Jewish leaders, who failed to protect child abuse survivors, to stand down from their public positions.
>
> "If somebody has failed to carry out their legal obligations to protect children, then they ought not to be in the position of leadership in the community," Rabbi Elton says of his and the Rabbinical Council's stance.
>
> The Royal Commission into Institutional Responses to Child Sexual Abuse this week found that the two insular, Ultra Orthodox Chabad-Lubavitch communities discouraged the reporting of child abuse, failed to act when complaints were made, and treated survivors and their families as outcasts.

---

14. [512] Davey, Melissa. "Rabbi Was Allowed to Keep Teaching after Admitting Abuse of Children, Inquiry Told." *The Guardian*, Guardian News and Media, 3 Feb. 2015, www.theguardian.com/australia-news/2015/feb/03/rabbi-was-allowed-to-keep-teaching-after-admitting-abuse-of-children-inquiry-told.

The findings vindicated victim Manny Waks, the whistleblower who first exposed systemic abuse within the sect.

The Rabbinical Councils of Australia and New Zealand, New South Wales, and Victoria, with Rabbi Elton as their Secretary and spokesperson, issued a joint statement on Wednesday in response to the Royal Commission's damning findings against Yeshivah communities in Melbourne and Sydney.

"Both the Jewish community - and the wider community - expects us to stand up for the rights of the victims and the survivors, the children who have suffered," Rabbi Elton says.

"We are not going to go with names or individual cases," Elton says. "But we made clear if someone has failed to carry out their legal obligations to protect children, especially in the cases where children really have been abused and violated - really appalling treatment, then those people should stand down from their public positions."

For the victims and their families, Rabbi Elton said that the Council and he as Secretary wished to offer, "an expression of deep sympathy for all they've suffered and a sense of deep distress on behalf of those of us in the Jewish community in the Rabbinite that they endured this terrible abuse and that in many cases they weren't listened to, they weren't supported - they were discouraged from coming forward."

"The treatment they received during their abuse - and afterwards in some cases, was truly terrible and our deepest sympathy and distress is shared with them.

"We're also grateful for the courage they showed in coming forward, in pursuing these cases, in not allowing themselves to be pushed aside."

"They've done the community great service even though it's been a very high personal cost, and we're not going to let them down now."

Rabbi Elton told SBS that the Rabbinite will take every measure to ensure that cases of child abuse will never happen again in the future.

"One of the first things I did when I was elected to the Great Synagogue about 18 months ago was to go for my 'Working with Children' Check," he says.

"Whatever is required of us in order to comply with child safety, we have to implement it and do so enthusiastically and efficiently and quickly."[513]

The Ultra Orthodox response in 2016 is precisely what the majority of people want to hear from their religious organizations when child rape cases come to the forefront of news. However, while speeches are pleasant and bring hope, it must be carried out effectively with planning and coordination with police effort to make sure that such hopeful speeches aren't just lip service to heinous crimes occurring in their community. After all, if religious communities truly wish to protect the sanctity of a community, they must actually protect the vulnerable members of the community from harm and not simply pay lip service or dehumanize victims like the New York City community of Ultra Orthodox Jews did to a Jewish survivor of repeated child abuse. Furthermore, the varied responses across the globe lead some credence for hope that the Ultra Orthodox communities can improve, unlike the Catholic Church who

---

15. [513] Lowenstein, Nitza. "Leading Rabbi Calls on Jewish Leaders to Stand down Following Child Abuse Royal Commission." *SBS PopAsia*, SBS News, 30 Nov. 2016, www.sbs.com.au/yourlanguage/hebrew/en/article/2016/12/01/leading-rabbi-calls-jewish-leaders-stand-down-following-child-abuse-royal.

seem to be predominately concerned with making sure the statue of limitations is exceeded to avoid lawsuit in many of their instances of child rape, and the Jewish communities that responded with helping victims give credence to the moral framework of Jewish teachings being superior to that of Christianity. However, that is only if actions by the rabbi follow through with protecting children from child abusers, otherwise the lack of morality among the Ultra Orthodox Jewish community would probably be seen as the same as the Catholic and Jehovah's Witness communities across the world that protect child rapists and other child abusers. Unfortunately, the response in New York has likely damaged the views of Ultra Orthodox and other Jewish denominations within New York and among Jewish people who have been attentive to the harrowing stories of child rape and other forms of child abuse. The New York Ultra Orthodox community has largely blamed the victims for these heinous crimes and acted with reprisals towards them. It is a shame upon them for such conduct and not the Jewish victims. It honestly surprises me to see such behavior because from the outside vantage point, the obviously positive action would be to comply with the police authorities and do everything to protect the rights of children such as in the British anecdote of events. Otherwise, there's no reason to be part of the Ultra Orthodox religious community because children would simply be placed in pointless danger of being beaten and raped. If it is a matter of religious faith for why child rapists and those who physically assault children are protected, then the religious faith's core beliefs are clearly to blame like in the examples of pedophile priests in the Catholic church, Jehovah's Witnesses, and the pedophilia in certain segments of Islam.

A peculiar issue that springs forth as a result of these child abuse crimes is questioning what the causes could be. What elements have helped to protect child rapists within conservative religious communities? How can Jewish people who care for protecting children put an effective stop to these abuses of children? For comparison, a recent report on pedophile priests of the Catholic church from RMIT University argued that celibacy was a driving factor in child rape.[514] However, if that were the case, then what explains cases of child rape in the rabbinical community, where Rabbis are freely allowed to marry and raise children?[515] It is possible that this report is making the fallacy of correlation and causation; that is, confusing correlations of events with direct causes.[516] This fallacy is also aptly named the "false-cause fallacy" to give a more direct term for it. Certain other factors in the report might be the true cause. The report on Catholic pedophile priests found patriarchal norms and values playing a concrete role in helping abuses go unchallenged. Women aren't allowed to question the male authorities of these religious communities and the higher-up that men are in these theological social structures, the closer they may be believed to be to the Abrahamic God. This is

---

16. [514] Davey, Melissa. "Catholic Sexual Abuse Partly Caused by Secrecy and Mandatory Celibacy, Report Finds." *The Guardian*, Guardian News and Media, 13 Sept. 2017, www.theguardian.com/australia-news/2017/sep/13/catholic-sexual-abuse-partly-caused-by-celibacy-and-secrecy-report-finds.
17. [515] "Can a Rabbi Get Married?" *Mitzvahs & Traditions*, www.chabad.org/library/article_cdo/aid/248162/jewish/Can-a-Rabbi-Get-Married.htm.
18. [516] "Your Logical Fallacy Is False Cause." *Thou Shalt Not Commit Logical Fallacies*, yourlogicalfallacyis.com/false-cause.

significant because women are inculcated to not step out of bounds of the female role into questioning the male rule and are thereby not treated equally in terms of being allowed to judge a situation that might be criminally offensive.[517] Worse than that, a woman's testimony of an incident of child rape will be dismissed simply if the perpetrator in question is able to testify their side of the story.[518] The patriarchal norms would instill a belief that the alleged pedophile who is giving testimony is more important than either the child or the woman's side of the story.[519] In effect, children will always be in danger of opportunists who commit acts like pedophilia in cultures with patriarchal structures. Why? Because one adult gender is respected as unquestionable fact and the children and other gender are seen as irrational and too emotional to be reliable. It is not based on logical reasoning; it is based on the belief in a fixed state of being born a certain gender and a child being too imaginative to say anything concrete or reliable about their own life experiences. Some of you may object and point to Islam, but this only further concedes that it is patriarchal structures since Islam takes patriarchal structures to the extreme (as is explained in the section on Islam). It is not a valid argument against abuses in other religious organizations with patriarchal norms and values as it doesn't focus on protecting the human rights of children. Appealing to such strict interpretations may simply be putting children in danger of being raped or other forms of child abuse until we can be certain what is the primary cause of such horrific crimes. More research should obviously be undertaken to get to the root of the issue, but I felt it was important to provide some possible alternative approaches based on the research provided because the central aim is to keep children protected from physical, sexual, and emotional harm. Lastly, unlike institutions such as the Catholic Church, the Ultra Orthodox communities outside of New York show evidence of addressing child abuse and I'd like to believe that the majority will put their words into action like the British community, but it depends entirely upon how they hold themselves accountable to their most vulnerable, their own children, in their communities.

LGBT Rights, Judaism, and Zionism

LGBT rights largely defended by US Jewry has been a painful divide despite Israel's more positive record towards LGBT people compared to its neighbors in the Arab Spring. Unfortunately, the comparison between Israel and its neighbors is of no meaningful comfort as it employs a contrast principle that presents Israel as superior to some of the worst human rights offenses and nothing else. While Islam most certainly commits some of the most brutal

---

19. [517] Davey, Melissa. "Catholic Sexual Abuse Partly Caused by Secrecy and Mandatory Celibacy, Report Finds." *The Guardian*, Guardian News and Media, 13 Sept. 2017, www.theguardian.com/australia-news/2017/sep/13/catholic-sexual-abuse-partly-caused-by-celibacy-and-secrecy-report-finds.
20. [518] Davey, Melissa. "Catholic Sexual Abuse Partly Caused by Secrecy and Mandatory Celibacy, Report Finds." *The Guardian*, Guardian News and Media, 13 Sept. 2017, www.theguardian.com/australia-news/2017/sep/13/catholic-sexual-abuse-partly-caused-by-celibacy-and-secrecy-report-finds.
21. [519] Davey, Melissa. "Catholic Sexual Abuse Partly Caused by Secrecy and Mandatory Celibacy, Report Finds." *The Guardian*, Guardian News and Media, 13 Sept. 2017, www.theguardian.com/australia-news/2017/sep/13/catholic-sexual-abuse-partly-caused-by-celibacy-and-secrecy-report-finds.

offenses to LGBT rights, it would be wrong to dismiss the discrimination inculcated into Israeli society as a direct result of Ultra-Conservative Jewish beliefs and the political ideology of Zionism. It is Zionism that has blocked the rights of equality for the LGBT community in Israel and it would be dishonest of people across the globe to ignore this pervasive fact about Israeli politics, if they're truly committed to Jewish human rights.

As Stuart Winer and the other Times of Israel staff report in the *Times of Israel* article titled "*Religious-Zionist rabbis back decision to block gay adoption*" which details as follows:

> Dozens of religious-Zionist rabbis declared their support for Justice Minister Ayelet Shaked's ruling against the adoption of children by gay couples, saying that allowing it would go against human morality and the values of Judaism.
>
> In a letter Tuesday to Shaked, who is a member of the Jewish Home party, the rabbis urged her to maintain her position against adoption by same-sex couples amid strong pressure to change her stance.
>
> Last week, the government notified the High Court of Justice that it would not lift discriminatory practices against same-sex couples, as such parents saddle their children with "additional baggage." Same-sex couples are legally allowed to adopt, but they typically must wait longer and can only receive children if no heterosexual couple is available.
>
> The government response, submitted on behalf of the welfare and justice ministries, was in response to a petition by the Association of Israeli Gay Fathers, which called for equal treatment in the adoption process. Welfare and Social Affairs Minister Haim Katz subsequently declared that the state's response was unfortunately worded and asked the court for an extension to reexamine the issue, saying he wanted to seek more professional opinions, after which the court granted him another two months.
>
> The carefully worded missive from the rabbis did not mention homosexuals or adoption but spoke of family values and the need to preserve them.
>
> "These days voices are being raised seeking to change the custom of the state, in a way that is contrary to the human morality that emanates from our holy Torah," the rabbis wrote, referring to the central text and derived teachings of Judaism. "We fully back Justice Minister Ayelet Shaked for preserving Israel's values and for her steadfast position to preserve the traditions and values of the family unit as is fitting for a representative of the religious-Zionist party in the Israeli Knesset.
>
> "Our holy Torah is a beacon and moral compass to the Jewish people and the whole world. Therefore, it is fitting that in Israel we be on guard to strengthen family values and preserve a public space that respects the values of human morality and Judaism," they said. "We support all the public representatives who act in this way."
>
> The letter was signed by dozens of rabbis, among whom were former MK Rabbi Haim Druckman, who is head of Bnei Akiva yeshivas, Safed Chief Rabbi Shmuel Eliyahu, Israeli Prize-winning Rabbi Eli Sadan and community rabbis, heads of yeshivas, and educators.
>
> In an interview with Israel Radio on Wednesday morning, Eliyahu said that homosexuality is unhealthy because it deviates from nature and God's will.

"This is not a healthy phenomenon, and there are diseases in the world that need to be healed rather than given legitimization," he said. "I am sure there are homosexuals and lesbians who are good people, but you can't do something artificial that goes against the way that God created the world."

Eliyahu indicated that in his opinion, the Israeli public was largely against gay couples adopting children.

"The fuss is a media fuss and not a public fuss," he continued. "The healthy public understands that a healthy family is a father and mother. That is how the world has been operating in the last thousands of years and that is how it is in nature. And when there is a deviation… it has to be dealt with.

"I want what is best for the child, that he have a healthy father and a healthy mother. A child adopted by two men robs him of a mother's love, of the softness, the warmth, of a mother's affection and hug, and that is unjust and unfair. As much as they want to live their lives, it is not right to rob a child of a mother's love. Two women or two men can't give what a couple can give."

Some 200 Jewish leaders and institutions from North America urged the government on Tuesday to end discrimination against same-sex couples.

The call came in a letter to the government coordinated by A Wider Bridge, a San Francisco-based organization that focuses on ties between US and Israeli LGBTQ communities. Signatories included Hillel International, leaders of the Central Conference of American Rabbis, the Union of Reform Judaism, prominent Jewish LGBT leaders and over 60 US rabbis.
Same-sex couples can be approved for adoption under Israeli law, but in practice only three such couples have adopted children in the past nine years. Many same-sex couples adopt babies from other countries.

Since 2008, when single-sex couples and couples who have common-law marriages became legally able to adopt within Israel, 550 such couples have submitted petitions to adopt, Haaretz reported. While only three same-sex couples were successful, more than 1,000 straight couples have adopted in the same period.

Times of Israel staff and JTA contributed to this report.[520]

The following means that the Jewish LGBT community isn't getting full and equal rights directly because of Jewish theology and socially conservative religious values supported by Judaism imposed upon Israeli society. Can such values then be called positive or beneficial for a society? Does unquestioned obedience to such texts really need to be imposed upon those who don't subscribe to such values? Is it even worthwhile to impose such values when archaeology demonstrably shows that the entire Jewish history of slavery in Egypt and the supposed covenant with the Abrahamic God couldn't possibly have happened in reality based on the lack of any evidence? Is there a meaningful point for Israel to entertain the ideas of this community's religious views when they base their beliefs on a history that has no evidence?

The Human Rights of Palestinian Children

---

17. [520] Winer, Stuart, and Toi. "Religious-Zionist Rabbis Back Decision to Block Gay Adoption." *The Times of Israel*, www.timesofisrael.com/religious-zionist-rabbis-back-decision-to-block-gay-adoption/?utm_source=dlvr.it&utm_medium=twitter.

There's no avoiding the discussion of human rights when discussing the Israel-Palestine issue and especially because it is undeniably a religious issue. Despite all the vacuous denial and equivocations on the violence, it repeatedly proves that the Abrahamic faiths can never be peaceful and will always have violence associated with their teachings. An Islamic rule would most certainly be far worse, but Israel's human rights crimes cannot be excused, nor can the repeated lie of Palestinians using their own children as human shields be used to shield Israeli's war crimes.[521] Moreover, it's just as wrong to ignore the Marxist - that is, atheist - and Christian extremist elements within the Palestinian people and instead to disingenuously present their attacks as purely driven by Islamic theology when there is a diversity of hateful views that influence their violence. Nationalistic fervor is at least a strong component since they feel their fight is the right to a Palestinian civilization. Most importantly, the US's repeated slipshod approach to human rights crimes when its allies commit the abuses; with many foreign policy think tanks often blaming Palestinians partaking in peaceful protests of being lulled into manipulation by Hamas and having no clear response in addressing the concerns of the BDS movement, proves that Christianity will always surpass any Jewish human rights violence with their own Christian equivocations for egregious failures of protecting civilian life.[522] One cannot have a democratic government that repeatedly touts Christian values and demands for a Christian President in public discourse to then argue that Christianity cannot be criticized for any of its moral failings. Without a doubt, Christianity and Islam have the worst histories of human violence and it goes on in our contemporary times as will be covered in Part III and highlighted within some portions in the next two sections pertaining to each religion respectively. However, as unfortunate as it is, Jewish organizations, the State of Israel, and Judaism's extreme elements have influenced violence upon Palestinians and it needs to be highlighted with a critical examination on the abuses conducted upon Palestinian children.

The following is an article titled "*UN: Palestinian Children Tortured, Used As Human Shields By Israel*" originally published in *Reuters* and re-published on *Haaretz*. Unfortunately, I couldn't locate the original version despite searching, so I'm providing this copy by Haaretz made available on June 20th, 2013. It highlights the UN report on the Gaza conflict of that year:

> A United Nations human rights body accused Israeli forces on Thursday of mistreating Palestinian children, including by torturing those in custody and using others as human shields.
>
> Palestinian children in Gaza and the West Bank, occupied by Israel in the 1967 war, are routinely denied registration of their birth and access to health care, decent schools and clean water, the UN Committee on the Rights of the Child said.

---

18. [521] "UN: Palestinian Children Tortured, Used as Human Shields by Israel." *Haaretz.com*, Haaretz Com, 10 Jan. 2018, www.haaretz.com/.premium-israel-tortured-palestinian-children-1.5283333
19. [522] Ibish, Hussein. "The Nonviolent Violence of Hamas." *Foreign Policy*, Foreign Policy, 6 Apr. 2018, foreignpolicy.com/2018/04/06/the-non-violent-violence-of-hamas/.

"Palestinian children arrested by (Israeli) military and police are systematically subject to degrading treatment, and often to acts of torture, are interrogated in Hebrew, a language they did not understand, and sign confessions in Hebrew in order to be released," it said in a report.

The Foreign Ministry said it had responded to a report by the UN children's agency UNICEF in March on ill-treatment of Palestinian minors and questioned whether the UN committee's investigation covered new ground.

"If someone simply wants to magnify their political bias and political bashing of Israel not based on a new report, on work on the ground, but simply recycling old stuff, there is no importance in that," spokesman Yigal Palmor said.

The report by the UN Committee on the Rights of the Child acknowledged Israel's national security concerns and noted that children on both sides of the conflict continue to be killed and wounded, but that more casualties are Palestinian.

Most Palestinian children arrested are accused of having thrown stones, an offense which can carry a penalty of up to 20 years in prison, the committee said. soldiers in the Israel Defense Forces had testified to the often arbitrary nature of the arrests, it said.

The watchdog's 18 independent experts examined Israel's record of compliance with a 1990 treaty as part of its regular review of a pact signed by all nations except Somalia and the United States. An Israeli delegation attended the session.

The UN committee regretted Israel's "persistent refusal" to respond to requests for information on children in the Palestinian territories and occupied Syrian Golan Heights since the last review in 2002.

'Disproportionate'

"Hundreds of Palestinian children have been killed and thousands injured over the reporting period as a result of the state party military operations, especially in Gaza where the state party proceeded to (conduct) air and naval strikes on densely populated areas with a significant presence of children, thus disregarding the principles of proportionality and distinction," the report said.

Israel battled a Palestinian uprising during part of the 10-year period examined by the committee.

It withdrew its troops and settlers from the Gaza Strip in 2005, but still blockades the Hamas-run enclave, from where Palestinian militants have sometimes fired rockets into Israel.

During the 10-year period, an estimated 7,000 Palestinian children aged 12 to 17, but some as young as nine, had been arrested, interrogated and detained, the UN report said.

Many are brought in leg chains and shackles before military courts, while youths are held in solitary confinement, sometimes for months, the report said.

It voiced deep concern at the "continuous use of Palestinian children as human shields and informants", saying 14 such cases had been reported between January 2010 and March 2013 alone.

Israeli soldiers had used Palestinian children to enter potentially dangerous buildings before them and to stand in front of military vehicles to deter stone-throwing, it said.

"Almost all those using children as human shields and informants have remained unpunished and the soldiers convicted for having forced at gunpoint a nine-year-old child to search bags suspected of containing explosives only received a suspended sentence of three months and were demoted," it said.

Israel's "illegal long-standing occupation" of Palestinian territory and the Golan Heights, continued expansion of "unlawful" Jewish settlements, construction of the separation fence into the West Bank, land confiscation and destruction of homes and livelihoods "constitute severe and continuous violations of the rights of Palestinian children and their families", it said.

Israel disputes the international position that its settlements in the West Bank are illegal. It says the wall it built there during the uprising stopped Palestinian suicide bombers from reaching its cities.

In March, Palmor, the Foreign Ministry spokesman, had said that officials from the ministry and the military had cooperated with UNICEF in its work on the report, with the goal of improving the treatment of Palestinian minors in custody.

"Israel will study the conclusions and will work to implement them through ongoing cooperation with UNICEF, whose work we value and respect," he said, in response to the UNICEF report.[523]

UNICEF's 2015 report titled "*Children in Israeli Military Detention*" which details the conditions that children suffer while in detention and gives recommendations and updates. Israel has conducted some reforms, but the policy procedures aren't being strictly followed by the IDF and other Israeli military personnel. The report details as follows:

1. **Introduction**

    Since March 2013, UNICEF has been engaging in a dialogue with the Israeli authorities on children's rights while in military detention and on specific actions that can be undertaken to improve the protection of these children. In this regard, the Military Advocate General (MAG) appointed the Military Prosecutor for Judea and Samaria (West Bank) as the focal point to lead the substantive dialogue with UNICEF. In the course of the engagement, UNICEF has also met with representatives of the Ministry of Justice, the Israeli police, the Israel Prison Service (IPS) and the Deputy Military Prosecutor for IDF soldiers in breach of the law. A regular dialogue was also maintained with the Ministry of Foreign Affairs.

    The dialogue focuses on what a child experiences when arrested and detained for alleged security offences in the West Bank and brought in contact with various Israeli authorities, including the Israeli Defence Forces (IDF), the Israeli Police, the Israel Security Agency (ISA) and the Israel Prison Service (IPS). UNICEF uses the Convention on the Rights of the Child (CRC), the Convention against Torture and Other Cruel, Inhuman or Degrading Treatment or Punishment (CAT) and other international legal instruments reflecting international juvenile justice standards as key reference documents. In line with these, UNICEF advocates for the universal principle that all children in contact

---

20. [523] "UN: Palestinian Children Tortured, Used as Human Shields by Israel." *Haaretz.com*, Haaretz Com, 10 Jan. 2018, www.haaretz.com/.premium-israel-tortured-palestinian-children-1.5283333

with law enforcement and justice institutions (whether juvenile justice systems or military systems) have the right to be treated with dignity and respect at all times and to be afforded special protections.

UNICEF has committed to providing periodic updates on its engagement with the Israeli authorities on children in military detention and to report on actions taken. The first update was released in October 2013. This second update covers the period from March 2013 to November 2014

2. **Major Developments and Progress Made**

The Government of Israel has since March 2013, taken a series of initiatives - particularly in terms of military legislation and the reinforcement of standard operating procedures that have addressed issues identified. These initiatives are listed below in chronological order:

April 2013: Military Order 1711 was introduced. This Military Order reduces the time a Palestinian child can be detained prior to appearing before a military court judge for the first time from 96 hours to 24 hours for children aged 12-13 and from 96 to 48 hours for children aged 14-15. These deadlines can be extended by the Israeli Police, for urgent investigation purposes, by an additional 24 and 48 hours respectively. For children aged 16-17, who are accused of security offenses, the maximum time of detention prior to appearing before a judge for the first time remains 96 hours, the same as for adults.

April 2013: The IDF in the West Bank introduced a form, printed in both Hebrew and Arabic, which has to be given to the parents when a child is arrested at home, providing parents with information on the reasons for the arrest and on where the child will be taken.

May 2013: The IDF Legal Advisor for the West Bank issued a letter to the heads of all Brigades, Divisions, Police and Military Police operating in the West Bank reminding all units of existing standard operating procedures and policies in relation to the arrest of children. Existing standard operating procedures stipulate that: blindfolding should only be used when there is a security need; hand-tying should be done at the discretion of the head of forces and always with three plastic ties; the child's family needs to be notified immediately of reasons for arrest; and the child needs to be immediately transferred to the relevant authorities.

October 2013: Military Order 1726 was issued. This Military Order regulates the duration of remand prior to indictment. It provides that a child's initial remand can only be extended for 15 days if necessary for the purpose of the investigation. Thereafter it can only be extended by the Military Court, and only for periods of up to ten days each. After a cumulative period of 40 days, the pre-indictment remand can only be extended by the Military Court of Appeals.

October 2013: Military Order 1727 was issued. This consolidates and restates a range of previous orders and existing practices relating to the military detention and prosecution of children in the West Bank, including: the appointment of legal counsel by the court; the presence of the parents in the trial; the establishment of separate detention facilities for children; the creation of juvenile military courts; and the age of majority for children coming before juvenile military courts (increased to 18).

October 2013: The IDF Central Command for the West Bank decided to implement a pilot test in the West Bank replacing, when possible, the practice of night arrests of children suspected of security offences with a summons procedure. The pilot started in February 2014. (Additional information is provided below.)

November 2013: The Military Prosecutor for the West Bank advised UNICEF that IDF medical staff were reminded of prior standard operating procedures on their medical duties related to children under arrest and detained for interrogation, including the obligation to act upon any alleged abuse.

December 2013: The Israeli Police started using a revised Arabic text to notify children arrested for alleged security offenses of their rights, including the right to remain silent and the right to legal counsel. This revised text requires final endorsement by the Ministry of Justice.

January 2014: The Military Prosecutor initiated a Government data gathering exercise on the number of children arrested and detained in the West Bank in 2013. The data provided by the Military Prosecutor is presented in Section 3 of this Bulletin.

September 2014: Military Order 1745 came into effect. This requires that interrogations be audiovisually recorded and reaffirms that the interrogation always take place in a language that the child understands. The order includes a clause stipulating that the provisions do not apply to a child suspected of committing a security offense, such as throwing stones. The provisions of this Military Order are the same as those applied in Israeli civilian courts.

3. **Key Data on Detention of Children in 2013 and 2014**

This Bulletin draws on four sources of information. The data demonstrates the need for further actions to improve the protection of children in military detention, as reports of alleged ill-treatment of children during arrest, transfer, interrogation and detention have not significantly decreased in 2013 and 2014. These actions should particularly focus on the situation of children in the first 48 hours (including during arrest and transfer by the IDF and interrogation by the Israeli police or the ISA), when they are most vulnerable.

A. Information provided by the Military Prosecutor as part of the dialogue

Information provided by the Military Prosecutor indicates that in 2013, 654 children were arrested by the IDF in the West Bank. One hundred and sixty two (162) of those children were arrested using the practice at the time of pre-planned night-time arrest operations. All 654 children were referred to the Military Advocate General (MAG). Of those:

- 98 children were released by the Israeli Police due to insufficient evidence.
- 91 children were released on bail pending conclusion of the investigation.
- 465 children were indicted.

Of the 465 children indicted, 80 were released on bail pending trial, the others were detained. In 2013, the MAG received 15 official complaints which related to reports of alleged abuse of Palestinian children arrested by the IDF.

B. Information provided by the Palestinian District Coordination Office

Data provided to UNICEF by the Palestinian District Coordination Office (DCO), show that in 2013, 350 children aged between five and 17 years old were taken into military custody by the IDF and released within a few hours or a day to their families through the Palestinian DCO and the Palestinian Police Family and Juvenile Protection Units.

C. Information provided by the Israel Prison Service

According to the data provided by the IPS (which is a head count of children in IPS detention at the end of each month), in the period covered by this Bulletin, on average 198 children were held in military detention per month, compared to 196 children in 2012. At the end of September 2014, 181 boys and one girl aged 14 to 17 years (including 19 under the age of 16 years) were held in detention for alleged security offences. Out of those 182 children, 125 children including the one girl were in pre-trial detention or on trial and 57 boys were serving a sentence. One girl was in military detention in 2013; and in 2014 one girl was arrested and detained by the military authorities.

D. Information from the Working Group on Grave Violations against Children

In 2013 and up until September 2014, the Working Group on Grave Violations against Children gathered 208 affidavits (sworn testimonies) reporting ill-treatment of children by the IDF, the Israeli Police, the ISA and the IPS, while under military detention in the West Bank. The military prosecutor requested that these testimonies be provided to his office for cross-checking purposes, however, UNICEF is not in a position to share this data. Due to the confidential nature of that data, UNICEF does not provide direct access to case files to protect the safety and security of victims and witnesses. This is in line with the Minimum Standards on Child Protection in Humanitarian Action (Global Child Protection Working Group). 139 children aged 16 and 17 years and 69 children below the age of 16 provided affidavits to the Working Group.

In these affidavits, children report being subjected to multiple violations throughout the arrest, transfer, interrogation and detention phases.

- One hundred and sixty two (162) children reported being blindfolded during transfer from the place of arrest to the police station.
- One hundred and eighty nine (189) children reported being painfully hand-tied upon arrest.
- One hundred and seventy one (171) children reported being subjected to physical violence during arrest, interrogation and/or detention.
- One hundred and forty-four (144) children reported being subjected to verbal abuse and intimidation during arrest, interrogation and/or detention.
- Eighty nine (89) children reported being transferred from the place of arrest to the police station on the floor of the vehicle.
- Seventy nine (79) children reported being arrested at night and 45 children reported being arrested during clashes or demonstrations.
- One hundred and sixty three (163) children reported not being adequately notified of their legal rights, in particular the right to counsel and the right to remain silent.
- One hundred and forty eight (148) children reported being strip-searched at the police station and 76 children reported being strip-searched upon arrival and transfer to IPS detention facilities.
- Twenty eight (28) children reported being held in solitary confinement at the Al Jalame and Petah Tikva detention sites inside Israel, while under interrogation by the ISA.
- Sixty three (63) children reported having had to sign a confession in Hebrew during the interrogation process.[524]

An article on *Haaretz* by the correspondent Judy Maltz titled "*Israel Tortures Palestinian Children, Amnesty Report Says*" gives an update on the human rights conditions of

---

21. [524] *Children in Israeli Military Detention ... - UNICEF*. www.unicef.org/oPt/Children_in_Israeli_Military_Detention_-_Observations_and_Recommendations_-_Bulletin_No._2_-_February_2015.pdf.

Palestinians four years onward and was published on February 22nd, 2017. The portion covering the Israel-Palestine conflict starts as follows:

> Israel engaged in extensive human rights violations in 2016, including detaining or continuing to imprison thousands of Palestinians without charges or trial, torturing many of those held in custody, promoting illegal settlements in the West Bank and severely hampering the movement of Palestinians, according to the Amnesty International Annual Report, published on Wednesday.
>
> The report found that among those tortured and detained under administrative orders were also children. Methods of torture included beatings, painful shackling and sleep deprivation. Among 110 Palestinians killed last year by Israeli forces, the report charged, some posed no threat to life and thus were shot unlawfully.[525]

And continues onward relating to failings on both the State of Israel and the Palestinian governments:

> **Documents int'l 'poisonous rhetoric,' endangering of refugees' lives**
>
> "The State of the World's Human Rights," as the annual report is known, documents human rights violations in 159 countries. A press release attached to the report highlights 22 countries as "examples of the rise and impact of poisonous rhetoric, national crackdowns on activism and freedom of expression." The list includes – although the report notes that it was "by no means limited to" – China, Egypt, France, India, Iran, Syria, Russia, Saudi Arabia, Sudan, Turkey, the United Kingdom and the United States. Israel does not appear on this list.
>
> The report documents how 36 countries, including Israel, broke international law by returning refugees to countries where their safety was at risk. It documents how people in 22 countries (not including Israel) were killed for peacefully standing up for human rights and how war crimes were committed in at least 23 countries (including Israel).
>
> The report does not spare the Palestinian governing bodies either. "Neither the Palestinian government nor the Hamas de facto administration in Gaza took steps to ensure accountability for crimes committed by Palestinians armed groups in previous conflicts, including indiscriminate rocket and mortar attacks on Israel and summary killings of alleged 'collaborators,'" it states. According to the report, Palestinians killed 16 Israelis, most civilians, and one foreign national in stabbings, car-rammings, shootings and other attacks last year.
>
> The report expresses deep concern about Israel's so-called Transparency Law, passed last year, which imposes new reporting requirements on organizations that receive most of their funding from foreign governments, citing it as an example of measures "to target human rights defenders in both Israel and the OPT [Occupied Palestinian Territories], who criticized Israel's continuing occupation of the Palestinian territories."
>
> It also notes how the government has attempted to undermine the work of several prominent Israeli human rights groups, among them Breaking the Silence, B'Tselem and the Israeli branch of Amnesty International.

---

22. [525] Maltz, Judy. "Israel Tortures Palestinian Children, Amnesty Report Says." *Haaretz.com*, Haaretz Com, 24 Apr. 2018, www.haaretz.com/israel-news/.premium-israel-tortures-palestinian-children-amnesty-report-says-1.5440012.

Bright spot on Israel's ledger: Trial of Elor Azaria

The report cites as a bright spot on Israel's human rights record the decision to prosecute Sgt. Elor Azaria, the Israeli soldier who killed a wounded and immobile Palestinian attacker. (Azaria was sentenced Wednesday to 18 months in prison; the report was prepared before his conviction.) "Most members of the Israeli forces who committed unlawful killings of Palestinians faced no repercussions," it notes.

The following are some of the highlights of the chapter on Israel:

* By the latest count, 694 Palestinians are being held under Israeli administrative detention orders – without criminal charges – most of them in Israeli prisons. This is the highest number recorded in close to 10 years. Three Israeli Jews were also taken into custody under administrative orders last year but relatively soon thereafter released.

* Even though roughly 1,000 complaints alleging torture by members of the Israeli security forces have been filed since 2001, no criminal investigations have been opened against them.

* Israel continues to use excessive force against Palestinian protesters, killing 22 and wounding thousands last year with rubber-coated metal bullets and live ammunition.

* Israel demolished 1,089 homes and other structures built in the West Bank and East Jerusalem without permits – representing a record number for one year. Many of the homes demolitions were in Bedouin communities. It also forcibly evicted 1,600 people from their homes.

* Israel also demolished hundreds of Arab homes inside Israel, which it said were built without permits.

* Israel demolished or made uninhabitable 25 homes of families of Palestinians who carried out acts of terror, as part of its policy of collective punishment.

* More than two years after Israel's last war in Gaza, the military had closed investigations into 12 suspicious incidents, "despite evidence that some should be investigated as war crimes," according to the report.

* At least 21 Israeli women, mainly Arab, were reportedly killed by their partners or family members last year – in some cases after police failed to provide them with adequate protection.

* Of more than 37,000 Eritrean and Sudanese asylum-seekers in Israel, more than 18,900 still have their applications pending.

* At least five conscientious objectors to military service were imprisoned last year. One of them, Tair Kaminer, was held for almost six months – longer than any other female conscientious objector in Israeli history.[526]

Yet again, I must stress that I'm highlighting these abuses due to a commitment to human rights. I wonder whether this will matter for most people in the US. The US national

---

23. [526] Maltz, Judy. "Israel Tortures Palestinian Children, Amnesty Report Says." *Haaretz.com*, Haaretz Com, 24 Apr. 2018, www.haaretz.com/israel-news/.premium-israel-tortures-palestinian-children-amnesty-report-says-1.5440012.

news media characterizes Palestinians in the most homogenized, racialized context in order to justify Israel killing civilians. The concept of human shields is just complicity with genocide from the US national news media by coming up with a calming sophistry to justify IDF forces murdering civilians whenever and however they please. And for what purpose are Palestinian lands being razed and then taken by force? For a messianic belief in the Bible. The US media refuses to acknowledge the overwhelming religious context of this feud, because it would mean acknowledging that religion is the driving motivator, it would lead to endless backlash by religious organizations across the world, and it would mean questioning religious assumptions about how the world operates.

Two final points of contention that I find indefensible: the destruction of schools and checkpoint stops to prevent proper education for Palestinian children.[527] This creates systemic discrimination against Palestinian children and prevents them from being able to have a fundamental right to education. The idea of "illegal schools funded by the EU" is both laughable and asinine.[528] The very concept of schools being illegal for children on the Israeli side is proof that Israel is acting as an aggressor, but on either side it would be an affront. If Palestinian children aren't getting education from the European-funded schools, the only place to gain any tutelage is the Madrassas of Hamas which act as indoctrination propaganda to continue promoting hatred and war under Islam's imperialistic ideals. If Israel is destroying the only chance some of these children have at gaining a meaningful education, then it deserves more culpability for the conflict because it's creating the very terrorists that it promotes to need free US aid to fight. In particular, such horrific actions by Israel is an affront to my personal beliefs on the value of education. The reasons for why are twofold. First, if they truly wanted to end the dispute between Israel and Palestine, they could work to improve the quality of education and teach Palestinian children what Israeli archaeology has already known to be fact: The Abrahamic faiths are based on a complete lie and the psychotic delusions of a bunch of warring desert tribes that made-up a bunch of mythic stories and believed them to be true.[529][530] That point might be perceived as offensive to people who died on either side of the Israel-Palestine conflict, but as mentioned in Part 1, dying for a religious faith means absolutely nothing in terms of verifying how truthful or accurate its beliefs are. It's merely a worship of death through the cognitive bias of sunk-costs.[531] Israel, which has suffered suicide bombings

---

24. [527] LAZAROFF, TOVAH. "IDF Destroys Two Illegal EU-Funded Palestinian Schools." *The Jerusalem Post | JPost.com*, 24 Aug. 2017, www.jpost.com/Arab-Israeli-Conflict/IDF-destroys-two-illegal-EU-funded-Palestinian-schools-503252.
25. [528] LAZAROFF, TOVAH. "IDF Destroys Two Illegal EU-Funded Palestinian Schools." *The Jerusalem Post | JPost.com*, 24 Aug. 2017, www.jpost.com/Arab-Israeli-Conflict/IDF-destroys-two-illegal-EU-funded-Palestinian-schools-503252.
26. [529] Mintz, Josh. "Were Jews Ever Really Slaves in Egypt, or Is Passover a Myth?" *Haaretz.com*, Haaretz Com, 10 Apr. 2018, www.haaretz.com/jewish/were-jews-ever-really-slaves-in-egypt-1.5208519.
27. [530] "Archeology of the Hebrew Bible." *PBS*, Public Broadcasting Service, 18 Nov. 2008, www.pbs.org/wgbh/nova/ancient/archeology-hebrew-bible.html.
28. [531] Kahneman, Daniel. Chapter 31: Risk Policies (334-341) and Chapter 32: Keeping Score (342 - 352). *Thinking, fast and slow*. Farrar, Straus and Giroux, 2015.

from Islamic terrorists, should already be keenly aware of this fact. Did any of those suicide bombers prove the truth of Islam by dying for their religious faith upon blowing up Israeli citizens after shouting how their version of the Abrahamic God was the greatest?

To buttress this point: Islam and Christianity are based upon Judaism; if you disprove the claims of Moses and his supposed covenant with the Abrahamic God, if you show that the archaeological excavations have found no evidence of Moses being a real person, and that the stories of Jewish slaves are a fable and that awaiting a Messiah is a meaningless task of superstitious barbarism, then the entirety of Jesus Christ and the so-called Prophet Mohammad's claims of being sent by a God collapse entirely. Once the utter meaninglessness of their struggle is factored in[532], Israelis can then instill arguments favoring atheism to make it a norm in Palestine. Either books pertaining to actual atheist arguments like the late Christopher Hitchens, perhaps even copies of this book if it suits the objective, or perhaps just have them up to a sophisticated enough vocabulary to read *Thinking Fast and Slow* by Daniel Kahneman. On the off-chance that I am mistaken, there's plenty of books and videos of atheist debates and even Ex-Muslim panels in the US that can provide a complementary supplement to end any lingering hope for the Abrahamic God to be real in either a Muslim or Christian mind. From a cruel, short-term perspective, it would also create in-fighting among Palestinians since the penalty of apostasy is death in Islam and the more extreme forms of Palestinian society would surely act on such religious mandates given the religious inculcation to extremist elements of Islam in their society by Hamas. However, as that in and of itself would constitute an unconscionable act of cruelty and potentially bring further censure of Israel, it would be easier to have individuals fleeing Palestine for their safety after becoming convinced atheists to be sent off - ostensibly for their protection - to outside either Israel or Palestine to safer countries like the United States of America and settle in the US permanently after adopting Western values. It would be a mostly bloodless transition and Israel would gain ample international praise for heroic humanitarian efforts. While that may seem daunting, the US has given Israel around 3 billion in free aid every year and has recently increased the amount of free aid late into President Obama's term and carried over to Donald Trump's presidency.[533][534][535][536] The US is already heavily invested in war between Israel and its neighbors with no end to the conflict in sight, it would be less expensive in the long term to resettle the Palestinians into the US, after learning English, appreciating the rule of democracy,

---

29. [532] Nietzsche, Friedrich. *The Dawn of Day*. Translated by J. M. Kennedy, Dover Publications, 2012.
30. [533] Rosenblatt, Lauren, et al. "US Seeks to Increase Aid to Israel by $200M in 2019." *The Pittsburgh Jewish Chronicle*, jewishchronicle.timesofisrael.com/us-seeks-to-increase-aid-to-israel-by-200m-in-2019/.
31. [534] "U.S. Foreign Aid to Israel: Total Aid." *Jewish Virtual Library*, www.jewishvirtuallibrary.org/total-u-s-foreign-aid-to-israel-1949-present.
32. [535] Sharp, Jeremy M. "U.S. Foreign Aid to Israel - Federation of American Scientists." *FAS.ORG*, Congressional Research Service, fas.org/sgp/crs/mideast/RL33222.pdf.
33. [536] Dorell, Oren. "U.S. $38B Military Aid Package to Israel Sends a Message." *USA Today*, Gannett Satellite Information Network, 14 Sept. 2016, www.usatoday.com/story/news/world/2016/09/14/united-states-military-aid-israel/90358564/.

and becoming convinced atheists through Israeli tutelage on the fakery of the Biblical accounts of the ancient world, the historic falsehoods of the Hebrew Bible, and the acknowledgement that any so-called covenant with a so-called Abrahamic God were the delusions of madmen.[537][538] Israeli archaeology already acknowledges the falsehoods and distortions of Biblical history and Daniel Kahneman's book could easily supplement questions for any concept of a divine being. It's a bloodless and far more benign way of ending the conflict.

Before moving onto the next portion, there is a significant factor in this conflict that has disturbed me for a good length of time that should be addressed. I will be referencing an article from Matt Kennard on Israel's military industrial complex and its effects upon Palestinian people. Kennard is the director for the *Centre for Investigative Journalism* in London, who conducted this investigation through partial funding from the *Pulitzer Center on Crisis Reporting* and he published this investigation for the *Electronic Intifada,* a US-based online publication in Chicago founded by a US-born Palestinian Ali Abunimah and erstwhile Dutch politician Arjan El Fassad, the news publication is a non-profit independent group operating in the United States since 2001 and seeks to give the Palestinian perspective on the Israel-Palestine conflict for Western audiences. I worried that it would seem a bit sketchy to cite their information and share it, but then I realized I was allowing this cultural norm of uncritical support for Israel to influence my behavior yet again and that much of the biases I had on this was inculcated unconsciously since I recall treating every piece of foreign journalism as unreliable lies until I couldn't stomach the amount of violent and heart wrenching content that the US mainstream media kept force-feeding via showing the depictions of bleeding Palestinian civilians while demanding uncritical support for Israel with no ability to question Israel's conduct. If nothing else, Matthew Kennard seems to have a reliable track record as he's written articles for *The Guardian*, the *New Statesman*, and the *Financial Times*.

Matthew Kennard's article titled "*The Cruel Experiments of Israel's Arms Industry*" on the *Electronic Intifada*:

> Round the back of Ramallah's main hospital lies the house of Iyad Haddad, a 52-year-old human rights investigator. His home office is the shopfront of a decrepit building and at first glance it looks like a bric-a-brac shop. But the objects placed out on the tables are not household trinkets. The surfaces are, in fact, cluttered with spent ammunition, tear gas canisters, sponge bullets and shell casings.
>
> Haddad has spent the past three decades documenting the violence of the Israeli forces occupying his people's land. These ugly little pieces of memorabilia are his testament to that process.
>
> Many of these weapons have been fired on peaceful demonstrators protesting against Israel's wall and settlements in the occupied West Bank. The villages of Nilin, Bilin and Nabi Saleh have been organizing regular protests for years. To my surprise, Haddad does not approve of those demonstrations.

---

34. [537] "Archeology of the Hebrew Bible." *PBS*, Public Broadcasting Service, 18 Nov. 2008, www.pbs.org/wgbh/nova/ancient/archeology-hebrew-bible.html.
35. [538] Nietzsche, Friedrich. *The Dawn of Day*. Translated by J. M. Kennedy, Dover Publications, 2012.

"Sometimes they are using us so they can know how to use each kind of weapon," he said. "For me, these kinds of activities by the Palestinians become helpful to the Israelis because it makes this area into a laboratory to test their weapons, to develop them and make it a commercial industry in order to sell them to other countries."

The idea that the Israeli arms industry benefits from the occupation through having a captive population it can test new weaponry on is now widely accepted.

Israel tries out weapons in the West Bank and Gaza and then presents them as "battle proven" to the international market.

The high-velocity tear gas canister has been heavily tested in Bilin. In 2009, the weapon killed Bassem Abu Rahmah, an unarmed local activist, protesting the wall slicing into that village. At the end of 2011, another protester, Mustafa Tamimi, was killed in Nabi Saleh by a tear gas canister, shot at his head.

There is a sense of weariness in Haddad's voice. "I have seen how they are developing their tools and their weapons industry and the ways of dealing with the community," he said. "And, in 30 years, I never heard once that there is any kind of accountability for any soldier."

But he goes on. He must go on.

"Tested and retested"

"The laboratory of the occupied territories is where things can be fine-tuned, they can be tested, they can be retested," said Neve Gordon, a politics professor at Ben-Gurion University of the Negev. "They can say, 'Hey this was used by the IDF [Israel's military], this must be good.' And that helps the marketing of the goods."

Later, in Ramallah, I sat down with Abdallah Abu Rahmah, coordinator of the Popular Struggle Committee against the wall and settlements in Bilin. Every Friday – for a decade – he and his neighbors have gone to the wall to protest.

For these efforts, they have been subject to night raids by the Israeli military. Abu Rahmah himself has been arrested and imprisoned by Israel a number of times.

"There are many reports about when they [the Israelis] have tried to sell military products and they told the buyers about its use in Bilin," said Abu Rahmah. "Things like skunk water, they used it the first time in our village."

Skunk water is a putrid smelling liquid that is sprayed at protesters in order to get them to disperse. "Because Bilin is famous, sometimes they come to our actions and they take video and photographs showing how effective the weapons are in stopping the action," Abu Rahmah said.

Jeff Halper, author of *War Against the People*, a book on Israel's arms and surveillance technology industries, said: "Israel has kept the occupation because it's a laboratory for weapons."

"Now, there has always been a tension," added Halper, also a founder of the Israeli Committee Against House Demolitions. "Because you've had the right wing that look at the West Bank as Judea and Samaria and Gaza as Gush Katif and, of course, East Jerusalem. So they want it all as part of the land of Israel. But then you've got another part especially the – I would say the military and the economic people – that say, 'Hey, this is a laboratory, this is really a resource for us, and we really shouldn't give it up.'"

Eitay Mack, a Jerusalem-based human rights lawyer and activist, raises the prospect that Israel uses Palestinians as test subjects for foreign arms companies as well.

Testing America's bullets

"In East Jerusalem, the Americans give Israel sponge bullets," Mack said. "First, they started with a blue sponge bullet but then they decided – this is their statement – that because the Palestinians wore a lot of clothes, it was not very effective so then they changed it to a [more powerful] black sponge bullet, which caused huge damage and there are dozens of Palestinians that have lost their eyes and other organs of their body."

The black sponge bullets are manufactured by Combined Tactical Systems, a Pennsylvania-based firm which also supplies Israel with tear gas.

The company's brochure for these bullets contains a note marked "caution." It reads: "Shots to the head, neck, thorax, heart or spine can result in fatal or serious injury."

Israeli troops began using the black bullets in 2014.

The Israeli arms industry is dominated by four companies: Israel Aerospace Industries, Elbit, Rafael and Israel Military Industries.

More than 75 percent of all weapons exported by Israel are made by the first three of those firms. In 2015, the total value of Israel's arms exports came to $5.7 billion.

The attack on Gaza the previous year enabled Israel to showcase some of its newest weapons. It was reported, for example, that the Hermes-900, one of Elbit's drones, made its "operational debut" in that assault.

Israel allocates more than 5 percent of gross domestic product to the military. That means Israel spends a higher proportion of its national income on the military than even the US, the world's only superpower.

"War sells weapons"

Some veterans of the Israeli military have developed careers as experts on the arms industry.

Shlomo Brom is one of them. A retired brigadier general, he now works at the Institute for National Security Studies in Tel Aviv.

I asked Brom if it's true that Israeli arms companies use the fact that their products have been tested on Palestinians to gain international business. "Of course," he replied. "Why not? Marketing [professionals] try to use any advantage and if they can use the advantage that this system was tested operationally and it worked, they will of course use it for marketing."

Uzi Rubin, a founder of Arrow, an Israeli anti-ballistic missiles program, is now a researcher at the Begin-Sadat Center for Strategic Studies in Bar-Ilan University near Tel Aviv.

He defended the way Israel has marketed its weapons as "battle proven."

"It is legitimate because the Vietnam War sold a lot of weapons," he said. "War usually sells weapons. But this is not to say that Israel is seeking war in order to sell weapons."

Barbara Opall-Rome has spent a few decades covering Israel for *DefenseNews*, a trade magazine for arms manufacturers. She advocates that Israel should allocate greater resources into what she calls "less-than-lethal technologies."

In her view, the Israeli weapons industry should think beyond weapons such as tear gas and skunk water that it is already deploying in the West Bank.

"I'm talking about using the electromagnetic spectrum or high-powered microwaves to get people dizzy," she said. "If you're dizzy you lose your balance. You know, I'd rather people just get an upset stomach and really just have to have diarrhea right in the middle of a demonstration or puke their guts out than to be killed."

Her comments reveal much about the sadistic mentality of Israel's weapons-makers and their promoters. For them, Palestinians are not human beings worthy of respect but subjects in one cruel experiment after another.

Matt Kennard is director of the Centre for Investigative Journalism in London. He is the author of Irregular Army: How the US Military Recruited Neo-Nazis, Gang Members and Criminals to Fight the War on Terror*(Verso, 2012) and* The Racket: A Rogue Reporter vs The American Elite *(Zed, 2016). His trip to Palestine was partly funded by the* Pulitzer Center on Crisis Reporting.[539]

To conclude this portion on the human rights of Palestinian children, if you are a religious person and you believe that the abuse of children is justified because their parents or the government of these people more than justify violence upon their children, then you are precisely what I'm criticizing and arguing against. You are living proof that the Abrahamic religions can never be peaceful. If you're Jewish, then you are simply following along in the lengthy and bloody history of your religious faith's other denominations, Christianity and Islam. It is definitive proof that the Abrahamic faiths are just a bunch of warring desert tribes that self-justify their own barbarity by arguing its less worse than other people's barbarity. I suspect people are using the belief in sinfulness to justify the defense or the purposeful cause of human rights crimes as detailed in the previous chapters. If so, then you are proof that I am right about my beliefs and criticisms of the Abrahamic religious traditions being nothing but barbarity and violence. I find no compelling reason to believe any of the Abrahamic faith traditions are comprised of good morals when none of them can find a peaceful solution to this explicit religious conflict that has gone on from 1920 since the beginning of Jewish immigration into the so-called holy land to now in our contemporary time of 2019 as of this writing. This is clearly a Abrahamic religious conflict about the Abrahamic faiths holding a zero-sum estimate on who gets to control their supposed holy land.

The options I've offered are far better resolutions and should be taken under serious consideration. I can no longer self-censor my words when reading and learning more about what this conflict is doing to Palestinian children or the entire Israeli population. If Israel is espousing that schools are illegal when their permit system thoroughly discriminates against

---

36. [539] Kennard, Matthew. "The Cruel Experiments of Israel's Arms Industry." *The Electronic Intifada*, 27 June 2017, electronicintifada.net/content/cruel-experiments-israels-arms-industry/19011.

Palestinians and leaves Palestinian children no choice but to gain education from proto-fascist indoctrination madrassas under Hamas then Israel is more culpable for the violence because no peaceful alternative were given to these children or their parents to choose a peaceful educational alternative. In fact, Israeli checkpoints, raids, and destruction of infrastructure often prevent Palestinian college students from gaining a meaningful education too.[540] Imagine if these students were taught evolution, enlightenment values, and the lack of evidence by Israeli archaeology that any of the Abrahamic faiths are real. It is a form of anti-intellectualism catalyzed be Israeli policies upon Palestinians and is irrefutable proof that the Israeli government never wanted a peaceful resolution either. If you don't allow children to be educated in EU-funded, fact-based education and help to de-emphasize religious extremism, then Israel is primarily culpable.[541] The Israeli government isn't taking steps to assure the peace and safety for its own citizens and isn't giving those Palestinian children or college students a meaningful choice against violent extremism. I apologize, but I have to go by where the evidence leads. Israel must allow those children and college students to be educated outside of Madrassas in a peaceful, safe environment and make sure they're well-fed and comfortable. Anything less will only continue to simmer religious tensions and religious wars. Instead of bloodletting, teach children to question the assumptions of their religious beliefs and criticize Islam and the evidence for Moses's so-called covenant with the Abrahamic God.[542]

37. [540] Abu El-Haj, Nadia. "Dr. Nadia Abu El-Haj on the Occupation's Effects on Palestinian Academia." *YouTube*, Anthropologists Boycott, 31 Mar. 2016, www.youtube.com/watch?v=3Q0w3-RtnQg.

38. [541] LAZAROFF, TOVAH. "IDF Destroys Two Illegal EU-Funded Palestinian Schools." *The Jerusalem Post | JPost.com*, 24 Aug. 2017, www.jpost.com/Arab-Israeli-Conflict/IDF-destroys-two-illegal-EU-funded-Palestinian-schools-503252.

39. [542] Nietzsche, Friedrich. *The Dawn of Day*. Translated by J. M. Kennedy, Dover Publications, 2012.

Chapter 12: Concluding Remarks on Judaism

In summation of this section on Judaism, there is no archaeological evidence to support that ancient Jewish people were ever slaves in Egypt, there is no evidence to support that any covenant with the Abrahamic God ever happened, there is no evidence to suggest Moses was ever a real person in history, there is no evidence to support that Abraham ever existed either, the Israelites were more polytheistic than what the Bible has led people to believe during ancient times and they were originally Canaanites, believing in the Biblical account of events leads to pointless enmity towards Egyptians, the Biblical account wrongfully takes credit for ancient Egyptian people's own hard work and sacrifice which has been treated with hostility and vandalism for no justifiable reason for centuries, and looking for a Messiah only leads to the persecution and violence towards the Jewish people themselves; the reason being that Christianity and Islam have historically shown and continue to express anti-Semitic sentiments in modern times.[543][544][545] The very theological design of Judaism's strict observance is thereby flawed because finding Messiahs has only caused contempt and violence which Jewish people still suffer from[546], such as in Iran and in the resurgence of Nazism within the West due to their respective religious beliefs. Zionism is not providing a powerful counterweight to these resurgences, Israeli Prime Minister Netanyahu and the Likud party gained the support of far right-wing parties in Poland by supporting Holocaust revisionism and criminalizing any speech that argues in favor of Poles being complicit in the Holocaust.[547] Netanyahu has formed mutual support with Hungarian Prime Minister Viktor Orban, a man who praises the Hungarian government's conduct during World War 2 when his country's forebears helped the Nazis send Hungarian Jews to their deaths in concentration camps, and Orban's political party blames Jews for his country's current problems such as propagating anti-Semitic conspiracy theories about Jewish billionaire George Soros.[548] Thus, Netanyahu has spat on the sensitive subject of Holocaust victims who died and shown no respect for the Holocaust survivors or their families by dehumanizing their experiences. He is actively delegitimizing the experiences of the victims and emboldening the Nazi conspiracy theorists by taking such actions. He has spat upon one of the worst tragedies in human history for political favors by supporting some people who carry

---

1. [543] Deitch, Ian. "Egypt: New Find Shows Slaves Didn't Build Pyramids." *U.S. News & World Report*, U.S. News & World Report, www.usnews.com/science/articles/2010/01/12/egypt-new-find-shows-slaves-didnt-build-pyramids.
2. [544] "Archeology of the Hebrew Bible." *PBS*, Public Broadcasting Service, 18 Nov. 2008, www.pbs.org/wgbh/nova/ancient/archeology-hebrew-bible.html.
3. [545] Rosch, Staks. "The Biblical Exodus Story Is Fiction." *The Huffington Post*, TheHuffingtonPost.com, 7 Dec. 2017, www.huffingtonpost.com/staks-rosch/the-biblical-exodus-story-is-fiction_b_1408123.html.
4. [546] Nietzsche, Friedrich Wilhelm. *THE ANTICHRIST*. Translated by H. L. Mencken, The Project Gutenberg, 2006.
5. [547] *YouTube*, The Intercept, 23 Aug. 2018, www.youtube.com/watch?v=3yrOG50rL28
6. [548] Shalev, Chemi. "Hungary PM Orban's Upcoming Visit: A Stain on Israel's History." *Haaretz.com*, Haaretz Com, 3 July 2018, www.haaretz.com/israel-news/.premium-hungary-pm-orban-s-upcoming-visit-a-blot-on-netanyahu-s-record-and-a-stain-on-israel-s-history-1.6223675.

on the very ideological tradition that called for the deaths of Jews and actively participated in aiding the Nazis in the genocide.

The violence between Israel-Palestine would decrease or possibly end if Palestinians were taught that the story of the Exodus, the existence of Moses, and the prophecies have no basis in reality through alternative forms of secular education that directly criticized the religious faith of Islam instead of being taught a version of Islam in madrassas run by Hamas.[549] Defending dissent and allowing criticism of religion to permeate in Gaza and the West Bank would create further divisions among their communities and diminish any religious basis for the conflict. Israel would no longer suffer the pain of Israeli soldiers committing suicide at higher rates after each war with Palestine.[550] At this point and time, a third Druze soldier has resigned from a position and Israeli Jews are continuing to protest with their fellow Israeli Druze against the Nation-State Law because it changes what is recognized as equal citizenship for the Druze people into second-class citizenship.[551][552] Israeli Jewish and Druze protestors both emphasize that the Druze have the graves to prove their commitment to Israel; the Druze Israelis have bled and died alongside their fellow Israeli Jewish soldiers.[553] The original bill endorsed by the religious ideology of Zionism and Prime Minister Benjamin Netanyahu would have reshaped Israeli civil law into being subservient to Jewish religious laws and officially changed Israel into a theocratic nation-state.[554] That's absolutely appalling because it lends credence to the idea that the Abrahamic faiths can never have peaceful coexistence with each other. Under the most cynical and possibly anti-theistic views on the Abrahamic faiths, it is because they will always be religions of warring desert tribes that war with each other forever. The Nation-State law only furthers such arguments against Judaism.

Zionist political advocacy silencing any dissent in the West might be contributing to the rise of Nazism; the silence of criticism plays into the discriminatory stereotype of the Elder of Zion with the asinine idea that Jews somehow control the world and caused all major wars. Let me be clear: all such stereotypes are reprehensible. It is anti-Jewish (i.e. anti-Semitic)

---

7. [549] "Archeology of the Hebrew Bible." *PBS*, Public Broadcasting Service, 18 Nov. 2008, www.pbs.org/wgbh/nova/ancient/archeology-hebrew-bible.html.
8. [550] Gross, Judah Ari. "Suicide Was Top Cause of Death for IDF Soldiers in 2016." *The Times of Israel*, www.timesofisrael.com/idf-15-soldiers-committed-suicide-in-the-past-year/.
9. [551] AHRONHEIM, ANNA. "Third Druze Officer Resigns from IDF in Protest of Nation-State Law." *The Jerusalem Post | JPost.com*, 2 Aug. 2018, www.jpost.com/Israel-News/Third-Druze-officer-resigns-in-protest-of-Nation-State-Law-563926.
10. [552] Toi, et al. "Druze-Led Rally against Nation-State Law in Tel Aviv Draws at Least 50,000." *The Times of Israel*, www.timesofisrael.com/tens-of-thousands-gather-in-tel-aviv-to-protest-controversial-nation-state-law/.
11. [553] Toi, et al. "Druze-Led Rally against Nation-State Law in Tel Aviv Draws at Least 50,000." *The Times of Israel*, www.timesofisrael.com/tens-of-thousands-gather-in-tel-aviv-to-protest-controversial-nation-state-law/.
12. [554] Lis, Jonathan. "Israel's Contentious Nation-State Law: Everything You Need to Know." *Haaretz.com*, Haaretz Com, 19 July 2018, www.haaretz.com/israel-news/.premium-israel-s-contentious-nation-state-law-everything-you-need-to-know-1.6292733?=&ts=_1532742032458.

conspiracy nonsense meant to dehumanize and further perpetuate the irrational hate for Jewish people. Such hateful rhetoric is historically normalized in Abrahamic societies with majority Christian or Muslim populations. They have no bearing on reality and to be quite honest, I call them irrational because when I researched the content to try to make sense of where the hate was coming from, I could only conclude that there was no logic behind it. Unlike the present-day rise in hate for Islam, which is rooted in arguments about terrorism which then perpetuates a good versus evil dynamic, the hatred for Jewish people has some of the most bizarre and utterly nonsensical ideas like blood libel; even jealousy over jobs doesn't make sense since the hatred for the specific jobs that Jewish people have historically been forced into taking was a result of marginalization and thoroughgoing discrimination in Western societies. I'm analyzing these paranoid conspiracy theories from the point of view of a person who has grown up Hindu in the United States and who self-identifies as a Hindu Anti-theist so I can only give an outside perspective on this issue.

If you're interested in my conjecture on why hatred for Jewish people has continually permeated within societies that were dominated by Christianity or Islam, then I would say that the argument is threefold. Please keep in mind that the following is my opinion based more on speculation than inference in this particular context:

First, both Islam and Christianity inculcate narcissism through superiority complexes; as religious faiths, they see themselves as morally good by virtue of existing and see any freedom of choice away from their respective religions as deviance in defiance or ignorance of the Abrahamic God. Being morally good isn't necessarily something you have to work for when you compare the in-group (Christians or Muslims) with an out-group (non-Christians or non-Muslims). Both faiths hold a central idea that only their religion is moral and anything different is immoral. As a result, they are both imperialistic religions and see only goodness from the perspective of foreign influences being similar to them and anything separate is seen as the influence of the devil or sinfulness. As such, everything in the world must essentially conform, be subservient, or have their conceptions of God as a prior in a foreign history to be considered moral. If a belief system, in particular a religion, doesn't have these concepts then it must be annihilated through violence or contempt when violence can't be perceived as justified. Jewish people were harmed for refusing to acknowledge either Christianity or Islam as legitimate via conversion. The monotheistic commonality, the fact that Christianity and Islam believe in the same God as the Jewish people, and the fact that Christianity and Islam are products of ancient people trying to fulfill Jewish prophecies are repudiated as a result of the New Testament; Jesus Christ preaches hatred for Jews by saying they're of the devil (John 8:21-44) and by repeatedly referring to them as hypocrites as an antagonistic point of contention in the Sermon on the Mount.[555][556] The reason anti-Semitism remains

---

13. [555] "BibleGateway." *Bible Gateway*, Bible Gateway Blog, www.biblegateway.com/passage/?search=John 8:21-44&version=KJV.

"unexplainable" among Christian theologians and lay Christians after around seventy years in remembrance of the Holocaust is because they're not allowed to question Jesus Christ's teachings. Therefore, when he preached hatred for Jewish people, they can't condemn it because Jesus Christ is considered "sinless" and perfect. Modern Christians largely blamed everything but Christianity for their own history of anti-Semitism, a few even going so far as to blame Paganism in a country that was majority Protestant and Catholic during the Holocaust and which spent centuries persecuting non-Christians for the Catholic Church. Germany is still widely recognized both internally and externally among majority Christian nation-states as a devout Christian country and can arguably be called the most devout among the Christian faithful. European countries and the US seem to ignore the almost 2000 years of discriminatory laws, looting, organized rapes, massacres, and targeted killings of Jewish people throughout European history when a greater percentage of the European population had deep faith in Jesus Christ and Christianity.[557] The anecdotes of the Inquisition and the Holy Wars against Islam do more to obfuscate the historic brutality against the Jewish people writ large by the European Christians because the anecdotes they select are some of the more outrageous examples that serve to recontextualize the violence as isolated incidents instead of culturally normalized institutions of violence that happened daily against Jewish people. It is so that Christians don't ever think of questioning their own religion. Islam has these same failings in this regard because Jesus Christ is the Messiah of Islam.

Second, despite beliefs to the contrary, the doctrine of forgiveness in Christianity and Islam don't instill personal responsibility. Unlike Jewish theology, which has a mostly cogent approach to forgiveness that places the culpability on the perpetrator and places cultural onus on that perpetrator to seek the forgiveness of the victim to the victim's personal satisfaction, the so-called "forgiveness" in Christianity and Islam redefines the concept without any regard for scope and scale.[558] In the case of redefining of "forgiveness" in the Christian context, the term doesn't make any coherent sense. Instead of being held accountable and seeking forgiveness from the aggrieved victim, Christianity redefines forgiveness to mean having your wrongdoing forgiven by the Abrahamic God in the form of Jesus Christ and thereby changes the act of forgiveness to mean upholding the norms and values of the religious institution instead of seeking to redress grievances done upon the victim. A pernicious aspect of the Christian form of "forgiveness" is that it is really just a form of institutionalized in-group narcissism.[559] In effect, the Christian context of forgiveness just means affirming your belief in your religious institution; it doesn't mean actively taking steps to ameliorate the horrible consequences of your wrongdoing upon your victims. In the Islamic context, no matter what horrific

---

14. [556] "BibleGateway." *Bible Gateway*, Bible Gateway Blog, www.biblegateway.com/passage/?search=Matthew 5&version=KJV.
15. [557] "Timeline of Antisemitism." *Wikipedia*, Wikimedia Foundation, 27 Mar. 2019, en.wikipedia.org/wiki/Timeline_of_antisemitism.
16. [558] Blumenthal, David J. "Is Forgiveness Necessary?" *My Jewish Learning*, www.myjewishlearning.com/article/is-forgiveness-necessary/.
17. [559] Nietzsche, Friedrich. *The Dawn of Day*. Translated by J. M. Kennedy, Dover Publications, 2012.

wrongdoing you have conducted upon others, you can be forgiven completely by converting to Islam. Within Islamic jurisprudence and Islamic Law, in the case of the murder conducted by Muslims, both Muslims and non-Muslims can be paid for with blood money (referred to in Arabic as *Diya*) with rates lower for non-Muslims who have had their families killed by Muslims.[560] In the case of there being no blood money repayment, *Qisas* or retaliation is invoked in Islamic jurisprudence, Muslims have the right to retaliate by murdering the killer, but if a Muslim murdered a non-Muslim then the non-Muslim's guardian or family doesn't have the right to kill the murderer because the murderer was a Muslim.[561] These failings by both Christianity and Islam are because all wrongdoing conducted by their in-groups are perceived to be forgivable with no baseline limit for violent actions to be considered too egregious. Christians in the West often argue that all things are permissible without faith in the Abrahamic God. However, under the Christian context of faith in the Abrahamic God, what isn't permissible when you have a doctrine of absolute forgiveness for violence? The Islamic context is more overt in patronizing superiority and it is clearly treating non-Muslims as unequal secondary-class citizens under Islamic jurisprudence. Critiques for both the doctrine of forgiveness in Christianity and the Islamic jurisprudence system will be explored further within their respective chapters.

Third, and probably the most obvious of reasons, both Christianity and Islam posit the belief in end of the world prophecies. These prophecies purport that those outside of their in-group will have judgment cast upon them. Both religions seek conversions with the threat that those who don't will be sent to hell and they preach that such punishment will go on eternally. This belief, and foundational reasoning for both religious faiths, is utterly psychotic and indefensible, but every attempt at pointing out its stupidity is shouted down even in Western societies outside of religious debates. I suspect it is due to the belief in unquestioned obedience. That is a severe problem because it means that neither Christians nor Muslims will ever engage in full honesty about violence in the name of their religious faith as a result of never critically analyzing the concept of Judgment day. It is considered impolite or even perceived as an attempt at mockery to point out this glaring flaw in both of these religious faiths, despite many Christian and Islamic preachers across the world proclaiming anyone who doesn't believe is a follower of Satan or will be cast into hell upon the end of the world. How can any religion that promotes end of the world prophecies be peaceful? I suspect, due to faith, both the majority of adherents to Christianity see the radical extremists who enthusiastically proclaim such beliefs as harmless while ignoring what the beliefs compel them to do. For all the focus on Islam being a harmful religion, how much more harmful are the Christian CEOs and entrepreneurs who spread disinformation campaigns about Climate Change? Myopically focusing on the Christian loudmouths in clustered communities ignores the billionaires who fund political campaigns without any concern for the future of the human race and thus the

---

18. [560] "Diya (Islam)." *Wikipedia*, Wikimedia Foundation, 8 Sept. 2018, en.wikipedia.org/wiki/Diya_(Islam).
19. [561] "Qisas." *Wikipedia*, Wikimedia Foundation, 9 Sept. 2018, en.wikipedia.org/wiki/Qisas.

future of our children.[562] These Christian businesspeople may have every motive to actively harm the world because of their strong faith in Jesus Christ as a savior who they believe will rapture them to heaven or other related nonsense.[563] The Christian CEOs, by all objective measures, are doing more harm to the world and survival of the human race than the Islamic terrorists when you focus on the logical reasoning instead of fear of harm. The Islamic terrorism is certainly a threat, but a dystopian future in which you're unable to eat healthy food, breathe clean air, or have clean water for the rest of your life while constantly dealing with earthquakes, hurricanes, and other natural disasters is far worse in terms of the permanent scope and scale of danger. Yet, all of these natural disasters are seen as signs to Muslims and Christians of the Judgment Day prophecy, and a cluster of extremists shouting praises for death and devastation may help embolden Christian CEOs to make it happen faster because of the perception it is a holy duty and the encouragement from the small community of extremists they may either secretly or openly identify with.[564] Many Christian CEOs work for the oil and gas industry in the US. One example is the Wilks brothers, they are incredibly open and explicit about their extreme views.[565] The focus of criticism mainly sheds light on their views about women, but what about their views on the environment? What about the twenty to twenty-five percent of US citizens who regularly vote and support measures for war, bombings, and environmental degradation every voting cycle in the US?[566] What about when they praise the death and devastation openly in public protests supporting war and destruction of innocent lives?[567]

These supposed "harmless" people have largely been supportive of views that destroy the clean air, the slow loss of food, and the future livelihood of humanity for the duration of the Presidency of Donald Trump and openly celebrate it. Every attempt I made in my life to criticize these people throughout my life and the horrifying beliefs that they preach was rebuked, wiped off internet forums, or ridiculed under the belief that these so-called "innocent" people shouldn't have exposure to outside views and that I had no right to criticize their beliefs because they weren't harming anyone. Decades of this have gone on, and has now suspiciously extended to neo-Nazi groups who advocate for the deaths of Jewish people, Black people, Muslims, and even when they have been actively hunting down and murdering Sikhs under the wrongful belief that they're Muslim. Despite the increasing danger to both the democratic norms and the lives of minority groups throughout the West, I've only ever experienced rebuke after rebuke in the US public and online among other people from Western societies for

20. [562] Bowyer, Jerry. "Does God Belong In The Boardroom? 1,800 CEOs Say Yes." *GenTwenty*, The Mercury News, 12 Aug. 2016,
21. [563] Bowyer, Jerry. "Does God Belong In The Boardroom? 1,800 CEOs Say Yes." *GenTwenty*, The Mercury News, 12 Aug. 2016,
22. [564] "Static.reuters.com." *Reuters*, Reuters, static.reuters.com/resources/media/editorial/20150910/WilksDoctrinalPoints.pdf.
23. [565] "Static.reuters.com." *Reuters*, Reuters, static.reuters.com/resources/media/editorial/20150910/WilksDoctrinalPoints.pdf.
24. [566] *YouTube*, Q-Ball Productions Inc, 2010, www.youtube.com/watch?v=nNvtA_q0e20.
25. [567] *YouTube*, Q-Ball Productions Inc, 2010, www.youtube.com/watch?v=nNvtA_q0e20.

challenging the "harmless" neo-Nazis and Biblical literalist Christians who advocate death upon all. I think somewhere along the way, the rise of neo-Nazi groups and Biblical literalists in US politics and throughout Europe was a result of a culture that perpetually created Safe Spaces for them for what was probably longer than I've been alive; I suspect it was some form of middle-ground for protecting the idea of what was sacred along with the patronizing idea that the greater public was "protecting" their "innocence" as they espoused the most vitriolic speech in which they condemned Jews to hell and said anyone non-Christian was a Satanist. As a result, their views never went challenged and they probably thought the reflexive protection they were afforded by the greater public was due to the belief that the public secretly believed they were absolutely correct in their beliefs. They were never challenged on their beliefs because of this cultural standard of the sacred and now they seek to destroy the clean air, edible food, and clean water while espousing hateful anti-Jewish rhetoric that emboldened the neo-Nazis among them within the US; the ultimate goal being either genocide of minority groups or wiping out the human race in an effort to bring about Judgment day for the glory of Jesus Christ through Climate Change. While the majority of Christians don't believe this, the extremists very clearly do and even now that they're in power in the US, they continue to have their views guarded by the majority of societies throughout the West. The US Christian extremists will be discussed in more detail in a segment within the next chapter. For the purposes of this paragraph, it's clear their unhinged views have gone unchecked and resulted in continued anti-Semitism.

I fear that the US organization of AIPAC and the Right-wing political ideology of Zionism silencing dissent and coercively working to criminalize the Free Speech throughout the United States may have severe unintended consequences.[568] AIPAC and college campuses like UCLA are actively criminalizing Free Speech with the willful help of Republican politicians and incumbent Democrats.[569][570] Hardworking students who pay for the college's tuition are having their civil liberties violated by the UCLA administration enthusiastically and actively bringing criminal charges to punish them at the behest of a foreign country that we in the US give free aid to out of our own goodwill.[571][572][573] Please think for a moment on what that

---

26. [568] Beinart, Peter. "American Jewish Establishment Stifles Free Speech to Silence Zionism's Critics." *Haaretz.com*, Haaretz Com, 24 Apr. 2018, www.haaretz.com/opinion/.premium-how-zionism-is-losing-the-contest-of-ideas-in-the-u-s-1.5470232.
27. [569] Greenwald, Glenn. "The Greatest Threat to Campus Free Speech Is Coming From Dianne Feinstein and Her Military-Contractor Husband." *The Intercept*, 25 Sept. 2015, theintercept.com/2015/09/25/dianne-feinstein-husband-threaten-univ-calif-demanding-ban-excessive-israel-criticism/.
28. [570] Fang, Lee, and Zaid Jilani. "Politicians Campaign on Free Speech While Voting to Penalize Boycotts of Israel." *The Intercept*, 14 Mar. 2018, theintercept.com/2018/03/14/campus-free-speech-bds-israel-boycott/.
29. [571] Hussain, Murtaza. "Students in California Might Face Criminal Investigation for Protesting Film on Israeli Army." *The Intercept*, 23 June 2016, theintercept.com/2016/06/23/students-in-california-might-face-criminal-investigation-for-protesting-film-on-israeli-army/.
30. [572] "U.S. Foreign Aid to Israel: Total Aid." *Jewish Virtual Library*, www.jewishvirtuallibrary.org/total-u-s-foreign-aid-to-israel-1949-present.

means: the US is giving free aid that has only been increasing over the years and is at present totaled at a whopping $134 billion from the time period of 1949 - 2018 with President Donald Trump increasing it by another $200 million at US taxpayer expense.[574][575][576] In return for this free aid of $134 billion, which is set to increase to an extra $38 billion from a finalized plan by President Barack Obama and which has only increased under President Trump[577][578], AIPAC and the political ideology of Zionism has repaid the US public by demanding US politicians criminalize the US Constitutional right of Free Speech and is actively criminalizing the Free Speech rights of left-leaning US college students who protest for human rights.[579][580][581] The argument about "Safe Spaces" in college campuses obviously seems asinine to the broader US public, but what about within the context of college youth having their free speech criminalized for the crime of protesting for human rights or questioning a country the US gives more free aid to than any other country?[582] How can left-wing college students learn to love and appreciate Free Speech in the US when a foreign country is repeatedly criminalizing them for it for their own political interests?[583] Keep in mind, many support the existence and safety of Israel, but are being actively criminalized for seeking a redress of grievances for the Palestinians and for calling upon a renegotiation of how much and how often US taxpayer

---

31. [573] Sharp, Jeremy M. "U.S. Foreign Aid to Israel - Federation of American Scientists." *FAS.ORG*, Congressional Research Service, fas.org/sgp/crs/mideast/RL33222.pdf.
32. [574] "U.S. Foreign Aid to Israel: Total Aid." *Jewish Virtual Library*, www.jewishvirtuallibrary.org/total-u-s-foreign-aid-to-israel-1949-present.
33. [575] Sharp, Jeremy M. "U.S. Foreign Aid to Israel - Federation of American Scientists." *FAS.ORG*, Congressional Research Service, fas.org/sgp/crs/mideast/RL33222.pdf.
34. [576] Rosenblatt, Lauren, et al. "US Seeks to Increase Aid to Israel by $200M in 2019." *The Pittsburgh Jewish Chronicle*, jewishchronicle.timesofisrael.com/us-seeks-to-increase-aid-to-israel-by-200m-in-2019/.
35. [577] Dorell, Oren. "U.S. $38B Military Aid Package to Israel Sends a Message." *USA Today*, Gannett Satellite Information Network, 14 Sept. 2016, www.usatoday.com/story/news/world/2016/09/14/united-states-military-aid-israel/90358564/.
36. [578] Rosenblatt, Lauren, et al. "US Seeks to Increase Aid to Israel by $200M in 2019." *The Pittsburgh Jewish Chronicle*, jewishchronicle.timesofisrael.com/us-seeks-to-increase-aid-to-israel-by-200m-in-2019/.
37. [579] Beinart, Peter. "American Jewish Establishment Stifles Free Speech to Silence Zionism's Critics." *Haaretz.com*, Haaretz Com, 24 Apr. 2018, www.haaretz.com/opinion/.premium-how-zionism-is-losing-the-contest-of-ideas-in-the-u-s-1.5470232.
38. [580] Greenwald, Glenn. "The Greatest Threat to Campus Free Speech Is Coming From Dianne Feinstein and Her Military-Contractor Husband." *The Intercept*, 25 Sept. 2015, theintercept.com/2015/09/25/dianne-feinstein-husband-threaten-univ-calif-demanding-ban-excessive-israel-criticism/.
39. [581] Hussain, Murtaza. "Students in California Might Face Criminal Investigation for Protesting Film on Israeli Army." *The Intercept*, 23 June 2016, theintercept.com/2016/06/23/students-in-california-might-face-criminal-investigation-for-protesting-film-on-israeli-army/.
40. [582] Sharp, Jeremy M. "U.S. Foreign Aid to Israel - Federation of American Scientists." *FAS.ORG*, Congressional Research Service, fas.org/sgp/crs/mideast/RL33222.pdf.
41. [583] Hussain, Murtaza. "Students in California Might Face Criminal Investigation for Protesting Film on Israeli Army." *The Intercept*, 23 June 2016, theintercept.com/2016/06/23/students-in-california-might-face-criminal-investigation-for-protesting-film-on-israeli-army/.

monies is being freely given to Israel.⁵⁸⁴⁵⁸⁵ That is what the Zionist political ideology of Israel wants to stop; asking the US public to consider how their tax dollars are being spent and to stop supporting human rights crimes. That is how the Likud party of Israel and the special interest group of AIPAC has repaid the goodwill of the US public, by doing everything to in its power to violate the Constitutional Free Speech rights of the US public with the aid of the US political elites and even the 2018 newcomers of the Republican party of the US.⁵⁸⁶

If you believe that Israel's Likud party has carefully thought over what they're actively doing and the harmful consequences therein, then consider the mentality they express in their articles vilifying the BDS movement. Barry Shaw, a senior associate at the *Israel Institute for Strategic Studies*, wrote the following article titled "*Unmasking BDS: A New Method To Fight The Movement Has Emerged, And It's Working*" on *The Jerusalem Post*:

> After decades of allowing the BDS Movement a free playing field on which to spin their allegations against Israel, a trend is discernible that is making headway into the jumble of their narrative. Slow but sure progress is being made against the radical accusations that have been fired at the Jewish state.
>
> The old tactic of branding Israel as the Start-Up Nation had limited value. What benefit is it extolling the wonders of Waze if the other side is using negative emotional imagery of a Zionist state as child-killers and brutal occupiers? Instead, a new strategy took root. Take Israel out of the equation. Put the spotlight onto our enemies. Concentrate on the messaging and the character of our BDS adversaries. Target those who are attacking Israel and Jews, and retaliate directly at them. Expose them and expose their hypocrisy and lies.
>
> The anti-Israel BDS advocates are caught in a trap of their own making, namely the paucity of their argument and often the deep antisemitism that drives them.
>
> The battle has been joined and rapid progress has been made. Part of the offensive involves the naming and shaming of Israel's BDS enemies. Often this is done via the social media as with the Canary Mission website that documents individuals and groups promoting hatred against Israel and Jews on college campuses in America. Their site catalogues people and groups listing their names, locations, which radical group they belong to, the roles they play, and detailing the negative actions or statements made by them. Their profile usually includes a headshot photo. Often the person's profile includes their social media presence.
>
> In the past, entertainment figures wielded influence in the cultural world. Recently, their radical bias has been exposed and they are increasingly ignored. One example is Roger Waters of "Pink Floyd" fame. Once a BDS icon, he has become a laughingstock, trashed by artists who ignored his demands for them to boycott Israel. Aerosmith was quickly followed by Radiohead, Rod Stewart and the Pet Shop Boys in performing in front of huge crowds in Israel.

---

42. ⁵⁸⁴ Hussain, Murtaza. "Students in California Might Face Criminal Investigation for Protesting Film on Israeli Army." *The Intercept*, 23 June 2016, theintercept.com/2016/06/23/students-in-california-might-face-criminal-investigation-for-protesting-film-on-israeli-army/.
43. ⁵⁸⁵ Beinart, Peter. "American Jewish Establishment Stifles Free Speech to Silence Zionism's Critics." *Haaretz.com*, Haaretz Com, 24 Apr. 2018, www.haaretz.com/opinion/.premium-how-zionism-is-losing-the-contest-of-ideas-in-the-u-s-1.5470232.
44. ⁵⁸⁶ Fang, Lee, and Zaid Jilani. "Politicians Campaign on Free Speech While Voting to Penalize Boycotts of Israel." *The Intercept*, 14 Mar. 2018, theintercept.com/2018/03/14/campus-free-speech-bds-israel-boycott/.

After pressuring Radiohead for months, the band's Thom Yorke clobbered Waters in a scathing Rolling Stone interview telling him, "It's deeply disrespectful to assume that we are either so misinformed or retarded that we cannot make decisions ourselves."

Yorke went on, "I thought it was patronizing in the extreme, really upsetting, that an artist I respect thinks we are not capable of making a moral decision ourselves after all these years."

Radiohead's moral decision was to come to Israel and entertain their multicultural fans.

Charles Asher Small, the founder of the Institute for the Study of Global Antisemitism and Policy (ISGAP) at McGill University, told attendees at the Annual IDC Herzliya Conference that his NGO is working on the documentary, "Wish You Weren't Here," which examines contemporary antisemitism and the BDS movement. He points to Waters's history of anti-Jewish imagery, including having a floating balloon in the form of a pig at his earlier concerts with a Star of David and dollar signs emblazoned on its body, and his comparisons of Israel to the Nazis. A new ISGAP website calls to boycott Waters's concerts in reprisal. The website wedontneedrogerwaters.com asks people to sign a petition urging others to avoid his concerts in protest.

A 2016 best-selling book, "BDS for Idiots," urged anti-BDS campaigners to take Israel out of the equation when debating BDS activists and instead to concentrate on the BDs narrative. The book suggests we are engaged in an intellectual ju jitzu fight in which our anti-BDS campaigners need to find the BDS weak spots, of which there are many, and use them effectively to unbalance and ultimately defeat their arguments.

The book details with glaring facts how those who profess to be pro-Palestinian are caught out not really caring and even damaging Palestinian lives.

Evidence of this became clear when BDS protests led SodaStream to move its factory from Mishor Adumim in Judea and Samaria to the Negev, causing unemployment for hundreds of Palestinian workers. Palestinians lives were damaged, but BDS looked at this as a victory.

Recently, Sodastream and the Israeli government found a way in which Palestinian workers can be bused to the new Rahat factory to be reemployed and reunited with their Jewish and Beduin co-workers.

This case clearly illustrates who harms and who cares for Palestinian workers. It exposes the fraudulent message of BDS.

Pro-Israel groups have been surprised to discover the relative ease in setting back BDS by going on the offensive.

In Spain, Angel Mas and his pro-Israel ACOM legal organization has repealed several BDS actions taken by Spanish cities by applying law against council decisions to boycott Israel. They include La Guardia, the Rivas Vacia district of Madrid, the Olesa district of Barcelona, Campezo and Valencia.

If BDS is being beaten in Spain it is due to Angel Mas and ACOM.

The application of domestic laws has brought multiple successes to UK Lawyers for Israel (UKLFI), a voluntary group of British lawyers, who have countered BDS resolutions by student bodies at several UK universities by advising the campus administrators that activating student BDS demands to boycott or divest from Israel would put them in serious breach of UK charity laws that could jeopardize their charitable status by which they receive government funding. UK campuses where BDS resolutions became toothless votes thanks to UKLFI include Kings College, City University, SOAC, University College London, Warwick, York, Brunel and East Anglia.

The Trustee Board of Edinburgh University overturned a BDS decision following the intervention of the campus's Israel Engagement Society with the legal assistance of UK Lawyers for Israel. UKLFI also helped Stand With Us UK, the pro-Israel student action group, to have Bath University reject BDS.

UKLFI helps individual students and groups to counter antisemitism they experience on campus, often from hateful BDS activists.

UKLFI anti-BDS legal activities are not confined to campus. Jonathan Turner, the founder of UK Lawyers for Israel, told The Jerusalem Report that his voluntary legal group could do much more with the help of additional donors and volunteers.

Gilad Erdan's Strategic Affairs Ministry also joined the same approach against Israel's delegitimizers. In June, the ministry launched a new informative website 4IL.org.il that includes cartoons and short videos exposing BDS lies.

American cities and states are lining up to kick back against BDS. In May, Nevada became the 20th US State to introduce legislation outlawing BDS. This success was the fruit of the Christian Allies Caucus, an American group devoted to strengthening ties between Christians and Israel, and the expert legal work of Prof. Eugene Kontorovich through the Israel Allies Foundation.

This came about after a chance meeting between Kontorovich and South Carolina State legislator, Alan Clemmons. On a visit to Israel, Clemmons met the owner of AL Solutions, a company that was being impacted by BDS. This Israeli company had opened a factory in Clemmons' state.

Clemmons was quick to realize the financial damage BDS could cause to his state, financially and socially, should unemployment follow BDS actions. Clemmons said of his meeting with Kontorovich, "Here was one of the brightest minds in the world on addressing BDS under the US Constitution."

His state was an early initiator of anti-BDS legislation. Across America and globally, BDS is being unmasked and outlawed at local, city and state levels.

Barry Shaw is a senior associate at the Israel Institute for Strategic Studies. He is the author of the best-selling book '1917: From Palestine to the Land of Israel.'[587]

In short, the Israel Institute of Strategic Studies shows no concern whatsoever for respecting Western societies Free Speech rights, or the damage they do to the lives of Western citizens who want to exercise their Free Speech, or - in the case of the US - any concern at all for the First Amendment right of the US Constitution.[588] Instead, they express a hateful war-like mentality which sees criminalizing Free Speech as a victory for Israel throughout the West. They see the very US citizens that have helped them so much with free foreign aid from US tax dollars as enemies to be coerced, manipulated, threatened with criminal penalties, and have no concern for their Constitutional rights being violated by anti-BDS actions; in fact, they

45. [587] Shaw, Barry. "Unmasking BDS: A New Method to Fight the Movement Has Emerged, and It's Working." *The Jerusalem Post | JPost.com*, 15 July 2017, www.jpost.com/Jerusalem-Report/The-unmasking-of-BDS-498347.
46. [588] Shaw, Barry. "Unmasking BDS: A New Method to Fight the Movement Has Emerged, and It's Working." *The Jerusalem Post | JPost.com*, 15 July 2017, www.jpost.com/Jerusalem-Report/The-unmasking-of-BDS-498347.

actively and happily violate Constitutional rights and see it as a victory for Israel.[589] They're treating Western countries as war zones in which they get to dictate how much free aid we give them and get criminal punishment in return if we opt to question their actions or motives when we even consider not footing the bill. This hostility is particularly prevalent upon the children of US taxpayers who are attempting to learn and express their Free Speech rights as they move to adulthood and receive criminal penalties through acts of coercion by College administrations who appease foreign interests as more important than their tuition-paying students such as in UCLA.[590][591] The relationship between the US and Israel is suppose to be a mutually respectful partnership and not a foreign country acting as if it has won the war spoils of the countries giving it aid for free.

Perhaps, some of you may argue, Israel may be acting irrationally and disrespecting the rights of the West, but the paranoia is warranted because its surrounded by so many enemies and it's a small country. Maybe some of you may argue that BDS will be critically harmful to Israel's economy and that the actions are therefore justified. However, an article by Dany Bahar and Natan Sachs of *The Brookings Institute*, the most prominent and well-respected think tank in the US, titled "*How Much Does BDS Threaten Israel's Economy?*" concisely articulates that it won't do any real harm after looking into the economic effects. At the end of their research article on the BDS movement's possible effects, they summarize that even if all of the BDS movement's objectives were met, it won't do any harm to Israel at all:

> The data suggests that, economically, anything short of official sanctions by important economic partners such as the United States or European Union would be unlikely to produce anything near the kind of economic pressure BDS supporters envision. Moreover, if such sanctions were enacted along BDS (as opposed to E.U.) lines, it would likely strengthen Israeli suspicion of the goals and motivations of BDS, making them—the key of BDS's strategy—less willing to cooperate.
>
> The Israeli government is thus doing itself a disservice by paying so much attention to this movement, both through its own deeds and words, as well as through lobbying with other countries to enact anti-BDS legislation. It is only providing more fuel to a fire that is small to begin with.[592]

Given these facts, Israel's deliberate attempts at destroying Free Speech throughout the West and circumventing the US public's First Amendment rights is utterly unwarranted and indefensible. AIPAC, the Likud Party, and their Zionist allies must immediately stop what

---

47. [589] Shaw, Barry. "Unmasking BDS: A New Method to Fight the Movement Has Emerged, and It's Working." *The Jerusalem Post | JPost.com*, 15 July 2017, www.jpost.com/Jerusalem-Report/The-unmasking-of-BDS-498347.
48. [590] Mackey, Robert. "University of California Adopts Policy Linking Anti-Zionism to Anti-Semitism." *The Intercept*, 23 Mar. 2016, theintercept.com/2016/03/23/university-of-california-adopts-policy-linking-anti-zionism-to-anti-semitism/.
49. [591] Hussain, Murtaza. "Students in California Might Face Criminal Investigation for Protesting Film on Israeli Army." *The Intercept*, 23 June 2016, theintercept.com/2016/06/23/students-in-california-might-face-criminal-investigation-for-protesting-film-on-israeli-army/.
50. [592] Bahar, Dany, and Natan Sachs. "How Much Does BDS Threaten Israel's Economy?" *Brookings*, Brookings, 26 Jan. 2018, www.brookings.edu/blog/order-from-chaos/2018/01/26/how-much-does-bds-threaten-israels-economy/.

they're doing and learn to respect the US Constitutional rights of US taxpayers and their progeny of US college students who seek a greater education for themselves. College students can't reasonably be vilified for an asinine idea like Safe Spaces when they're having their Free Speech rights violated throughout college campuses across the US, often at the behest of Republican and Democrat Congresspeople like Diane Feinstein and the newcomer Republicans who draft bills, pass regulations and laws, or act with coercive practices to stamp out the Free Speech of college students.[593][594] If you're in the US and want to change this, demand that change by calling or emailing your Congressional Assembly members and Senators. Perhaps consider demanding more accountability or a re-negotiation of free aid given to Israel. A relationship with Israel should be a mutually beneficial partnership, it shouldn't have the threat of criminal charges for merely questioning Israel or have veiled threats foisted upon US college students and the US public for the "thought crime" of wanting to renegotiate terms and conditions in which US taxpayer monies is given freely to Israel.[595]

I suspect that some of you reading this chapter may wish to cast an ad hominem via making aspersions on my motives for writing this portion and may wish to label me an anti-Semite for the content of this chapter instead of focusing on the actual arguments. First, I'd like to point out that this is the very war-like mentality that I'm criticizing in this portion. To see any criticism of Israel as nefarious in intent is hardly different from the Islamic apologists who currently cry Islamaphobia at any criticism of Islam. Second, I have made my intentions clear already; I support the existence of Israel, I support giving Israel aid, but I cannot morally support the human rights crimes done to Palestinians. When I say the aid needs to be re-negotiated, I am not saying it should be withdrawn. What I am saying is that there needs to be a redress of grievances for the Palestinians attached to that aid and that Israel must make an honest effort in taking more peaceful measures to combat Hamas. The aid should increase or decrease relative to whether Israel is making an honest commitment to such objectives. Such as allowing Western-style schools to teach Palestinians critical thinking to question their religious assumptions; some of the brightest minds within the Jewish community have already made books that focus on cognitive biases as mentioned earlier. Anti-Jewish sentiments is both historically more dangerous and still a serious issue that needs to be criticized. However, I fear the current approach as of 2018 by AIPAC, the Likud Party, and Benjamin Netanyahu is going to have horrifying consequences in the near future for Jews living in the US and Europe. Disparaging and silencing moderate voices who are concerned about human rights crimes

---

51. [593] Greenwald, Glenn. "The Greatest Threat to Campus Free Speech Is Coming From Dianne Feinstein and Her Military-Contractor Husband." *The Intercept*, 25 Sept. 2015, theintercept.com/2015/09/25/dianne-feinstein-husband-threaten-univ-calif-demanding-ban-excessive-israel-criticism/.
52. [594] Fang, Lee, and Zaid Jilani. "Politicians Campaign on Free Speech While Voting to Penalize Boycotts of Israel." *The Intercept*, 14 Mar. 2018, theintercept.com/2018/03/14/campus-free-speech-bds-israel-boycott/.
53. [595] Hussain, Murtaza. "Students in California Might Face Criminal Investigation for Protesting Film on Israeli Army." *The Intercept*, 23 June 2016, theintercept.com/2016/06/23/students-in-california-might-face-criminal-investigation-for-protesting-film-on-israeli-army/.

while ignoring self-identified Nazis who are openly shouting for the death of Jewish people is only going to make Jewish people less safe across the Western world. That is a very serious concern of mine and one of the chief reasons I felt that I had to speak out against what the Zionist political ideology is doing. Shouting down and criminally penalizing authentic criticism by disingenuously attributing it to anti-Jewish views while ignoring self-identified Nazis who are openly calling for the death of Jewish people cannot possibly be in the interests and safety of the Jewish people across the world.

To lend further credence to my point, consider the arguments of Ex-Muslims in response to Islamic apologists. Armin Navabi, an Ex-Muslim Atheist and activist, and the author of *Why There Is No God*, founder of the non-profit organization *Atheist Republic*, and panelist for *Ex-Muslims of North America* explained that Islamic apologists and Muslims themselves should want the ex-Muslims as the ones on the forefront in debates criticizing Islam instead of lumping them with the bigots and those who want to do real harm to Muslims.[596] Criticism shouldn't be seen as an act of contempt for the other group, but rather as an act of compassion because criticism involves taking the time to try to change other people's views from what a critic believes is harmful for other people to be doing. It is not a vilification of others as individuals or as a collective, but rather the ideologies they carry. Similarly, a Muslim should want to criticize (not kill) atheists in order to show their beliefs are wrong as an act of compassion so they don't purportedly burn in eternal hellfire.[597] By killing the atheist and purportedly sending them to hell, the Muslim individual isn't actually showing compassion; similarly they should be addressing the concerns that atheists actually have and not shouting them down in order for there to be a meaningful dialogue to change people's views. This framework of understanding criticism and distinguishing meaningful criticism from hate can also apply to both Judaism and Jewish people. Judaism is already superior in that there is no fear of being killed for becoming a Jewish atheist within the Jewish community, Jewish atheists have gained acceptance and aren't considered inferior or harboring some hateful ideas within them for their beliefs.[598] Allowing Left-wing criticism in the West of the human rights crimes by Israel upon Palestinians isn't an attack on Israel's right to exist or Jewish people. To conflate criticism of actions Israel has undertaken that has killed innocent people, including children, with anti-Semitism is asinine and dangerous. It's an insult to the victims and survivors of the Holocaust. By shouting down moderate voices of dissent asking for a redress of grievances by labeling them anti-Semitic, whilst willfully ignoring the self-identifying Nazis who grow bolder and louder with calling for the deaths of Jewish people throughout the US and Europe, is putting the lives of Jewish people across the world in real danger. If Left-wing voices are criminalized or grow detached over the fate of Israel as a result of this

---

54. [596] Navabi, Armin. "Attacking Islam as an Act of Compassion - Armin Navabi." *YouTube*, Ex-Muslims of North America, 4 Dec. 2017, www.youtube.com/watch?v=9m7IaAlnkgo.
55. [597] Navabi, Armin. "Attacking Islam as an Act of Compassion - Armin Navabi." *YouTube*, Ex-Muslims of North America, 4 Dec. 2017, www.youtube.com/watch?v=9m7IaAlnkgo.
56. [598] Septimus, Daniel. "Must a Jew Believe in God?" *My Jewish Learning*, www.myjewishlearning.com/article/must-a-jew-believe-in-god/.

criminalization, while Nazis continue to organize and shout death chants upon Jewish people, Black people, Sikhs, and Muslims then at what point is it too late to stop them? If they increase in their rate of intimidation and violence upon minority groups to the extent that societies are no longer safe, how is anyone going to be able to respond effectively and what measures can be used to stop them? Neo-Nazis and their ilk openly say they want to ethnically cleanse minority groups, why are we not taking them seriously at their own words? Ignoring such hate-filled groups and treating them as unthreatening only makes them bolder in their attacks and they must face fierce criticism on their violent beliefs too.

    I want to make it clear that I don't agree with the BDS movement, but I cannot defend this Zionist political agenda that has purposefully made war on the BDS movement's Free Speech through coercive acts of criminalizing their right to dissent. Furthermore, I'd like to point out that Jewish people are by far the most peaceful among the Abrahamic religions and that the 70-year occupation of Palestine has done much damage on the image of Judaism being a peaceful religion. Many secular-leaning people use the Israel-Palestine conflict to make broad generalizations that every religion will always be violent towards every other religion. However, they're wrong and it is a historic fact that they're wrong. Bene Jews and Hindus acknowledge and celebrate 2400 years of peaceful coexistence in India.[599][600] This is not an anomaly as Cochin Jews who lived in India since 700 BC also experienced peace among Hindus and other Eastern religious faiths.[601] There's been various theories given on why there has been no anti-Semitism towards Jewish people by the Eastern religious faiths of Hinduism, Buddhism, Sikhism, Jainism, and the Animalistic traditions in India. One reason given by Left-wing Hindus is that the Jewish communities were too small to be a meaningful political force in India, another common reason given is the lack of proselytizing among all of these religious beliefs, I had briefly considered the idea that it was because the holy sites of Hinduism and Judaism are entirely apart geographically, and religious right groups of both religions seem keen on finding "commonalities" that had caused this pleasantly surprising history. To the best of my knowledge, this effort is wasted because it is clear that by all objective measures, the religions more common to Judaism and which have grown out of Jewish theology are the very ones that persecute it and threaten Jews with death. The small scale of the Jewish communities in India as a reason why Hindus and Jews never had any violent political conflict between each other cannot explain why both Muslims under Aurangzeb and Christians under the Portuguese burned Jewish synagogues upon first contact with the Indian Jewish community and persecuted Jews in India as devil worshipers.[602] Perhaps people should begin to consider that it was the

---

57. [599] Moses, Nissim. "Bene Israel of India." *Avotaynu Online*, 24 Mar. 2015, www.avotaynuonline.com/2007/07/bene-israel-of-india-by-nissim-moses/.
58. [600] Weiss, Gary. "India's Jews." *Forbes*, Forbes Magazine, 17 July 2012, www.forbes.com/2007/08/05/india-jews-antisemitism-oped-cx_gw_0813jews.html#4d526e5f3d45.
59. [601] Johnson, Barbara C. "The Cochin Jews Of Kerala." *My Jewish Learning*, www.myjewishlearning.com/article/the-cochin-jews-of-kerala/.
60. [602] Weiss, Gary. "India's Jews." *Forbes*, Forbes Magazine, 17 July 2012, www.forbes.com/2007/08/05/india-jews-antisemitism-oped-cx_gw_0813jews.html#4d526e5f3d45.

lack of belief in Jesus Christ as either god or Messiah as per the Christian and Islamic theologies respectively? Perhaps it is the teachings of Jesus that create persecution of the Jews such as in John 8?[603]

However, if that idea is unsatisfying, then perhaps consider the possibility that it isn't commonalities, but rather the mutual respect for differences that Hindus and other Eastern faiths have for Jewish people and vice versa that created a lengthy culture of peace.[604] There's no attempt to patronize each other in any relationship between Hindus and Jews, unlike with Christianity or Islam which requires their adherents to see commonalities to their own faith before they have any respect whatsoever for other people. In other words, there's no demand that people conform and be more "like us" for there to be given respect for others beliefs or practices in either Judaism or Hinduism. We understand each other as distinct and different and respect our differences. Psychological studies seem to agree with this general concept; religious minorities have mutual respect for a majority religion only when their minority status and distinct differences are respected instead of the majority constantly demanding unity or a universal sameness that inadvertently delegitimizes the religious minority's history, the discrimination they've faced, and their social identity.[605] Christians and Muslims only ever seem to recognize the humanity of Jewish people and Hindus only under the condition that they be more like the majority Muslim or Christian community, or they're branded as deviant and not afforded respect simply for being who they are. *It's worth noting that due to this history in India, the idol worshiping, polytheistic Hindus and Buddhists are proven to be more compassionate, accommodating, and living in peaceful coexistence with Jewish people than any of the Monotheistic faiths.* Even Zoroastrianism allegedly discriminated against Jews during the late Sassanid era due to fear of them being secret Roman agents conspiring to destroy the empire from within.[606] Both people in Israel and India don't seem concerned with what each other do in their daily lives and seem to just wish each other well or are utterly indifferent to what is happening in the other's respective countries. This may not be a negative development, but something to praise. Unlike Western media, which shows depictions of Palestinian women having blood gushing out of their necks and dead bodies of Palestinian children on Western social media with demands that everyone support Israel all the time or be labeled anti-Semitic, perhaps the real cure for anti-Semitism is either not caring what Israel is doing or being allowed to disagree without being labeled an anti-Semite.

If that explanation is still unsatisfying and you insist that surely there must be some commonalities to create such peaceful coexistence, then consider the prospect that Hinduism

---

61. [603] "BibleGateway." *Bible Gateway*, Bible Gateway Blog, www.biblegateway.com/passage/?search=John 8:21-44&version=KJV.
62. [604] Ispas, Alexa. *Psychology and politics: a social identity perspective*. Psychology Press, 2014.
63. [605] Ispas, Alexa. *Psychology and politics: a social identity perspective*. Psychology Press, 2014.
64. [606] "Timeline of Antisemitism." *Wikipedia*, Wikimedia Foundation, 27 Mar. 2019, en.wikipedia.org/wiki/Timeline_of_antisemitism.

and Buddhism have more in common with Judaism from the current Left-leaning political perspective than the current Right-wing perspective. Unlike Christianity and Islam which generally insist that atheists are either evil or mentally unwell; Hinduism, Judaism, and Buddhism are all accepting of atheists and celebrate having atheists among their numbers instead of shunning or vilifying them. It is possible to be a "Cultural Jew" and to self-identify as a Jewish Atheist; likewise, it is possible to be a Buddhist Atheist and my own personal identity of a Hindu Atheist. Both Jewish and Hindu culture emphasize learning, attaining knowledge, and critical thinking; this emphasis may explain why so many Hindus and Jews in first world countries do so well.[607] Unlike Christianity and Islam, which emphasize unquestioned obedience and which turn Christians and Muslims into atheist due to conflict with their religious beliefs when gaining more knowledge, there is no conflict for Jews or Hindus in attaining knowledge and, for the most part, both religions don't hold a stigma for atheists. Admittedly, as I can personally attest the stigma is still present for some Hindu households like my family's, there is still probably some stigma against atheists in some Hindu households within India, but Hindu priests and many Hindu households don't have any stigma or vilification for Hindu atheist or agnostic children. Nevertheless, people should consider the possibility that the reason there are so many Hindus and Jews in high-paying positions or contributing so well with a focus on hard work in society within Western countries is because both of their theologies are accepting of atheists and agnostics. Since Islam and Christianity denigrate atheists outside of Western Europe, people may simply be leaving once their knowledge-base grows to a certain level and they find no compassion or acceptance from their personal backgrounds. To the best of my understanding, another commonality is that both the Talmud and the Mahabharata are accepting of transgender people, although under the specific definition of "third gender" for both groups in their theology.

Buddhism doesn't have a stigma because of its own unique specifics as a religion as you could arguably be a Buddhist Jewish atheist depending on which branch of Buddhism that you believe in and there would be no conflict with Jewish theology since Buddhism doesn't require belief in any sort of god. It may even be possible to be both Hindu and Jewish since Judaism follows a matrilineal line and Hinduism a patriarchic line; among left-wing circles for both religious faiths there is no demand for following any specifics of religious culture outside of what one chooses to follow. That said, should any of my comments be repudiated as ignorance or offensive to Jewish traditions, then I wholly and unreservedly apologize; for this portion, I am just exploring the possibilities of differences that may have led to peaceful coexistence throughout Jewish-Hindu/Buddhist/Jain history. The peaceful nature of these three religions coexistence may be as a result of allowing inconsistency rather than strictly following guidelines to be consistent with their religious faiths. The most right-wing groups within Hinduism and Judaism still generally preach the idea of "live and let live" with no animosity or

---

65. [607] Murphy, Caryle. "The Most and Least Educated U.S. Religious Groups." *Pew Research Center*, Pew Research Center, 4 Nov. 2016, www.pewresearch.org/fact-tank/2016/11/04/the-most-and-least-educated-u-s-religious-groups/.

contempt shown to left-wing Jews and Hindus for their beliefs. I have to say it is heartening to see that since it shows both right-wing Jews and Hindus really are better human beings and hold better religious values than the majority of people who follow Christianity and Islam in their respective right-wing factions when it comes to accepting atheists. The other Eastern religious faiths indigenous to India I don't really have any say in, but I suspect it was generally the culture of non-violence and some combination of the aforementioned reasons already stated. Regardless, it seems the Dharmic faiths of India and Jews throughout the world can share in Holocaust remembrance for the victims and survivors of the Holocaust while having mutual respect for differences.[608]

Three last points of comparison that I find are the encouragement for children to gain a higher education within families of Hindus and Jews, the left-wing circles of both religions having vigorous critiques criticizing the problems within the in-group culture which may act as milestones to gauge collective improvement when not being apologetic to Islamic violence or Christian narcissism, and the most important similarity that neither of the other Abrahamic faiths have because of the teachings of Jesus Christ: *a rational belief in personal responsibility*. The last point seems insulting to members of the Islamic and Christian faiths so allow me to explain. When I compare their teachings to Jewish teachings of forgiveness, I find the Jewish teachings to be rational and healthy for people's development. For instance, there is no compulsion to love a person who murdered your child, nor is there condemnation in choosing to hate them.[609] Christians may demean this as proof of Christianity's superiority to other religions, but it absolutely isn't for reasons that'll be discussed in the next chapter. The Jewish teaching of *Teshuvah* (Return) and the acceptance by *Mechilah* (forgoing the other's indebtedness) may be the reasons why Judaism had no real animus with either Hinduism or the other Eastern faiths indigenous to India.[610] For all intents and purposes, the Jewish version of forgiveness keeps scope and scale in mind and its teachings are probably more natural to the human psyche and thus, could probably have been understood and respected implicitly by ancient Hindus, Buddhists, and others. Even the more intimate form of Jewish forgiveness referred to as *Selichah* (forgiveness) only requires that people understand that the other person is a flawed human being without any requirement for compulsory love.[611] I feel that is absolutely superior to any of Islam or especially Christianity's concepts of forgiveness. To be honest, looking into all three Abrahamic religions has convinced me that Judaism is the most peaceful of the three. As mentioned before, it's why I placed the issue of human rights exclusively on this chapter. I had originally intended to make it into its own chapter, but

---

66. [608] *Embassies.gov.il*, embassies.gov.il/delhi/NewsAndEvents/Pages/rnational day of Holocaust observed in Delhi.aspx.
67. [609]Blumenthal, David J. "Is Forgiveness Necessary?" *My Jewish Learning*, www.myjewishlearning.com/article/is-forgiveness-necessary/.
68. [610] Blumenthal, David J. "Is Forgiveness Necessary?" *My Jewish Learning*, www.myjewishlearning.com/article/is-forgiveness-necessary/.
69. [611] Blumenthal, David J. "Is Forgiveness Necessary?" *My Jewish Learning*, www.myjewishlearning.com/article/is-forgiveness-necessary/.

historically the human rights abuses are something fairly new to Judaism's mostly benign history. Judaism is wholly superior in teachings compared to Islam and Christianity by any honest measure that looks at the pros and cons of each of the three theologies propensity for violence. Consider the possibility that it may honestly be the case that Judaism and the Eastern faiths had peaceful coexistence throughout their entire histories purely due to the fact that they all have a rational approach of holding a person culpable for their actions. Christianity and Islam may say they do this, but Jesus's teachings of forgiveness prove contrary to such assertions. To reiterate, more on that topic will be explained in the chapter on Christianity.

Finally, I'll conclude this chapter with a copy of the letter by Holocaust survivors and their progeny petitioning in protest against the massacre of Palestinians in Gaza.[612][613] This display of concern for the human rights of Palestinians helped inspire confidence in my own beliefs.[614][615] I couldn't find the original petition online, but I had made a copy of the petition out of fear that it would be wiped away somehow when I had first spotted it. Evidently, my seemingly irrational fear was proven right.[616] The names on the copy I have line-up perfectly with the copied version on the blog of a person of faith by the name of Astrid Essed, the names being exact lends credence to it being an authentic copy. I'll be copying and pasting the a portion from the website *www.astridessed.nl* which is Astrid's personal blog.[617] Astrid celebrates the petition in appreciation for the solidarity and compassion of Holocaust survivors, their children, and grandchildren for the human rights of Palestinian civilians. The petition itself reaffirmed my belief that, despite its flaws, Judaism is an inherently peaceful and compassionate religion. It is not simply a warring desert tribal religion like Christianity and Islam; it may have tendencies to be one, but it can also be changed. I'd like to believe that Judaism can reform any of its discriminatory theology against women and homosexuals but I don't feel it is my place to point out ways to reform Judaism since it isn't my religion. I'd like to ask readers to please seriously consider this petition and what it has to say against any further violence between Israel-Palestine. I'd like to believe that Judaism isn't just as violent as Christianity or Islam, but sometimes it becomes a struggle, especially when Western news media demands complete support for Israel while I see images of the dead bodies of children,

70. [612] "Gaza and the Propaganda Machines." *The Guardian*, Guardian News and Media, 15 Aug. 2014, www.theguardian.com/world/2014/aug/15/gaza-propaganda-machines.
71. [613] Gouri, Daniel, et al. "Holocaust Survivors Condemn Israel for 'Gaza Massacre,' Call for Boycott." *Haaretz.com*, Haaretz Com, 10 Apr. 2018, www.haaretz.com/holocaust-survivors-condemn-israel-for-gaza-massacre-1.5260588#.VMR7SI5whq8.twitter.
72. [614] *News of the World*, newsoftheworldnews.wordpress.com/tag/international-jewish-anti-zionism-network/.
73. [615] Gouri, Daniel, et al. "Holocaust Survivors Condemn Israel for 'Gaza Massacre,' Call for Boycott." *Haaretz.com*, Haaretz Com, 10 Apr. 2018, www.haaretz.com/holocaust-survivors-condemn-israel-for-gaza-massacre-1.5260588#.VMR7SI5whq8.twitter.
74. [616] *News of the World*, newsoftheworldnews.wordpress.com/tag/international-jewish-anti-zionism-network/.
75. [617] "Holocaust Survivors Condemn Israel's Massacre in Gaza/End to Israeli Occupation and Colonization." *Astrid Essed*, www.astridessed.nl/holocaust-survivors-condemn-israels-massacre-in-gazaend-to-israeli-occupation-and-colonization/.

footage of Israeli night police in Palestinian homes threatening to kill Palestinians, or civilians bleeding to death in Gaza. This bizarre, tribal, and evidently, cultish demand for complete support has failed to convince a large portion of people; right-leaning Ultra Orthodox Jews rallied alongside Palestinian American youth in New York within the US to protest the Gaza massacre in condemnation of Israel's actions.[618][619][620] Jewish youth have even gone so far as to get themselves arrested in protest.[621] This is not an attack on Judaism or an attempt to generalize Jewish people with discriminatory aspersions, it is concern for the human rights of Palestinians and concern for the long-term safety of Israel. If Israel was ever in danger, I would obviously support giving the country aid, but I can't morally support what has been happening in Gaza when I believe there are more peaceful ways to resolve the conflict. So please take into consideration what this petition by Holocaust survivors and their progeny have to say.

DESTRUCTION IN GAZA
HOLOCAUST SURVIVORS CONDEMN ISRAEL'S
MASSACRE IN GAZA/END TO ISRAELI
OCCUPATION AND COLONIZATION
Dear Readers,
Recently I wrote a letter of solidarity and appreciation to the
International Jewish Anti-Zionist Network because of
the courageous Letter of Holocaust survivors and their descendants
condemning the Israeli massacre of Palestinians in Gaza and the
ongoing occupation and colonization of historical Palestine.
In the Letter, the names of the people who signed, were mentioned.
I think they deserve to be mentioned in text, so hereby, under
my letter of appreciation, I name them.

Astrid Essed
Amsterdam
The Netherlands
STATEMENT OF APPRECIATION AND SOLIDARITY WITH
YOUR COURAGEOUS LETTER OF CONDEMNATION
OF THE ISRAELI GAZA OFFENSIVE ''PROTECTIVE EDGE''
Dear Survivors and Descendents of Survivors
I, Astrid Essed, salute you, who have survived one of the greatest
crimes of humanity ever committed.
Not only people were murdered in cold blood, because of their
descent, also people were dehumanized and humiliated.
A strong warning for Mankind, to which xenophobia and racism
can lead.

76. [618] Neturei Karta. "Jewish Rabbi Condemning Israeli Attack on Gaza." *YouTube*, Neturei Karta, 20 July 2014, www.youtube.com/watch?v=JaSqvutvI1k.
77. [619] WABC. "Another Flag: Palestinian Flag Turns up on Manhattan Bridge." *ABC7 New York*, 21 Aug. 2014, abc7ny.com/news/another-flag-palestinian-flag-turns-up-on-manhattan-bridge-/273742/.
78. [620] "Protests Held In NYC Against Israeli Violence In Gaza." *ANIMAL*, 11 July 2014, animalnewyork.com/2014/protests-held-nyc-israeli-violence-gaza/.
79. [621] "9 Young Jews Arrested at NYC Anti-Israel Protest." *The Jerusalem Post | JPost.com*, 30 July 2014, www.jpost.com/Jewish-World/Jewish-News/9-young-Jews-arrested-at-NYC-anti-Israel-protest-369365.

Alas, Mankind didn't learn much of those horrors, because everywhere in the world, massacres and human rights violations go on and on.
One of the examples of serious human rights violations and crimes against humanity [Gaza Blockade] is the zionist State of Israel, where, with a false appeal on the Holocaust to scare people, and the wrong use of antisemitism to colonize Palestine, on a daily basis warcrimes and human rights violations are committed.
Your impressive Letter to protest against the latest Israeli offensive in Gaza ''Protective Edge'' has really touched and impressed me.
Therefore, by this letter, I want to utter strongly my solidarity with you and my appreciation for your courageous statement and involvement with the oppressed people of Palestine.
Especially you, who have survived the horror of horrors can feel, like no one else, what oppression, humiliation and dehumanization really is.
I thank you and salute you.
May God be with you.
In deep respect
Astrid Essed
Amsterdam
The Netherlands

LETTER OF THE SURVIVORS OF THE HOLOCAUST AND THEIR DESCENDANTS/ NAMES OF THE SURVIVORS OF THE HOLOCAUST AND THEIR DESCENDANTS, WHO SIGNED THE LETTER
JEWISH SURVIVORS AND DESCENDANTS OF SURVIVORS AND VICTIMS OF NAZI GENOCIDE UNEQUIVOCALLY CONDEMN THE MASSACRE OF PALESTINIANS IN GAZA

As Jewish survivors and descendants of survivors and victims of the Nazi genocide we unequivocally condemn the massacre of Palestinians in Gaza and the ongoing occupation and colonization of historic Palestine. We further condemn the United States for providing Israel with the funding to carry out the attack, and Western states more generally for using their diplomatic muscle to protect Israel from condemnation. Genocide begins with the silence of the world.

We are alarmed by the extreme, racist dehumanization of Palestinians in Israeli society, which has reached a fever-pitch. In Israel, politicians and pundits in The Times of Israel and The Jerusalem Post have called openly for genocide of Palestinians and right-wing Israelis are adopting Neo-Nazi insignia. Furthermore, we are disgusted and outraged by Elie Wiesel's abuse of our history in these pages to justify the unjustifiable: Israel's wholesale effort to destroy Gaza and the murder of more than 2,000 Palestinians, including many hundreds of children. Nothing can justify bombing UN shelters, homes, hospitals and universities. Nothing can justify depriving people of electricity and water.

We must raise our collective voices and use our collective power to bring about an end to all forms of racism, including the ongoing genocide of Palestinian people. We call for an immediate end to the siege against and blockade of Gaza. We call for the full economic, cultural and academic boycott of Israel. "Never again" must mean NEVER AGAIN FOR ANYONE!

Signed,

Survivors:
1. Hajo Meyer, survivor of Auschwitz, The Netherlands.
2. Henri Wajnblum, survivor and son of a victim of Auschwitz from Lodz, Poland. Lives in Belgium.
3. Renate Bridenthal, child refugee from Hitler, granddaughter of Auschwitz victim, United States.
4. Marianka Ehrlich Ross, survivor of Nazi ethnic cleansing in Vienna, Austria. Now lives in United States.
5. Irena Klepfisz, child survivor from the Warsaw Ghetto, Poland. Now lives in United States.

6. Hedy Epstein, her parents & other family members were deported to Camp de Gurs & subsequently all perished in Auschwitz. Now lives in United States.
7. Lillian Rosengarten, survivor of the Nazi Holocaust, United States.
8. Suzanne Weiss, survived in hiding in France, and daughter of a mother who was murdered in Auschwitz. Now lives in Canada.
9. H. Richard Leuchtag, survivor, United States.
10. Ervin Somogyi, survivor and son of survivors, United States.
11. Ilse Hadda, survivor on Kindertransport to England. Now lives in United States.
12. Jacques Glaser, survivor, France.
13. Eva Naylor, surivor, New Zealand.
14. Suzanne Ross, child refugee from Nazi occupation in Belgium, two thirds of family perished in the Lodz Ghetto, in Auschwitz, and other Camps, United States.
15. Bernard Swierszcz, Polish survivor, lost relatives in Majdanek concentration camp. Now lives in the United States.
16. Joseph Klinkov, hidden child in Poland. Lives in the United States.
17. Nicole Milner, survivor from Belgium. Now lives in United States.
18. Hedi Saraf, child survivor and daughter of survivor of Dachau, United States.
19. Michael Rice, child survivor, son and grandson of survivor, aunt and cousin murderd, ALL 14 remaining Jewish children in my Dutch boarding school were murdered in concentration camps, United States.
20. Barbara Roose, survivor from Germany, half-sister killed in Auschwitz, United States.
21. Sonia Herzbrun, survivor of Nazi genocide, France.
22. Ivan Huber, survivor with my parents, but 3 of 4 grandparents murdered, United States.
23. Altman Janina, survivor of Janowski concentration camp, Lvov. Lives in Israel.
24. Leibu Strul Zalman, survivor from Vaslui Romania. Lives in Jerusalem, Palestine.
25. Miriam Almeleh, survivor, United States.
26. George Bartenieff, child survivor from Germany and son of survivors, United States.
27. Margarete Liebstaedter, survivor, hidden by Christian people in Holland. Lives in Belgium.
28. Edith Bell, survivor of Westerbork, Theresienstadt, Auschwitz and Kurzbach. Lives in United States.
29. Janine Euvrard, survivor, France.
30. Harry Halbreich, survivor, Germany.
31. Ruth Kupferschmidt, survivor, spent five years hiding, The Netherlands.
32. Annette Herskovits, hidden child and daughter of victims deported to Auschwitz from France. Lives in the United States.
33. Felicia Langer, survivor from Germany. Lives in Germany.
34. Moshe Langer, survivor from Germany, Moshe survived 5 concentration camps, family members were exterminated. Lives in Germany.
35. Adam Policzer, hidden child from Hungary. Now lives in Canada.
36. Juliane Biro, survivor via the Kindertransport to England, daughter of survivors, niece of victims, United States.
37. Edith Rubinstein, child refugee, granddaughter of 3 victims, many other family members were victims, Belgium.
38. Jacques Bude, survivor, mother and father murdered in Auschwitz, Belgium.
39. Nicole Kahn, survivor, France.
40. Shimon Schwarzschild, survivor from Germany, United States.
41. George Winston, survivor, Australia.
42. Marietta Elliott-Kleerkoper, child survivor, hidden from 1942 till 1945 in the Dutch countryside with Christians, Australia.
43. Susan Varga, survivor, Australia.
44. Gilles Cocos, survivor and brother and child of survivors, lost several relatives in the camps, United States.

Children of survivors:
44. Liliana Kaczerginski, daughter of Vilna ghetto resistance fighter and granddaughter of murdered in Ponary woods, Lithuania. Now lives in France.
45. Jean-Claude Meyer, son of Marcel, shot as a hostage by the Nazis, whose sister and parents died in Auschwitz. Now lives in France.
46. Chava Finkler, daughter of survivor of Starachovice labour camp, Poland. Now lives in Canada.

47. Micah Bazant, child of a survivor of the Nazi genocide, United States.
48. Sylvia Schwarz, daughter and granddaughter of survivors and granddaughter of victims of the Nazi genocide, United States.
49. Margot Goldstein, daughter and granddaughter of survivors of the Nazi genocide, United States.
50. Ellen Schwarz Wasfi, daughter of survivors from Vienna, Austria. Now lives in United States.
51. Lisa Kosowski, daughter of survivor and granddaughter of Auschwitz victims, United States.
52. Daniel Strum, son of a refugee from Vienna, who, with his parents were forced to flee in 1939, his maternal grand-parents were lost, United States.
53. Bruce Ballin, son of survivors, some relatives of parents died in camps, one relative beheaded for being in the Baum Resistance Group, United States.
54. Rachel Duell, daughter of survivors from Germany and Poland, United States.
55. Tom Mayer, son of survivor and grandson of victims, United States.
56. Alex Nissen, daughter of survivors who escaped but lost family in the Holocaust, Australia.
57. Mark Aleshnick, son of survivor who lost most of her family in Nazi genocide, United States.
58. Prof. Haim Bresheeth, son of two survivors of Auschwitz and Bergen Belsen, London.
59. Todd Michael Edelman, son and grandson of survivors and great-grandson of victims of the Nazi genocide in Hungary, Romania and Slovakia, United States.
60. Tim Naylor, son of survivor, New Zealand.
61. Victor Nepomnyashchy, son and grandson of survivors and grandson and relative of many victims, United States.
62. Tanya Ury, daughter of parents who fled Nazi Germany, granddaughter, great granddaugher and niece of survivors and those who died in concentration camps, Germany.
63. Rachel Giora, daughter of Polish Jews who fled Poland, Israel.
64. Jane Hirschmann, daughter of survivors, United States.
65. Jenny Heinz, daughter of survivor, United States.
66. Miranda Pinch, daughter of Beate Sommer who was a Czeck refugee along with her father Ernst Sommer, UK.
67. Elsa Auerbach, daughter of Jewish refugees from Nazi Germany, United States.
68. Julian Clegg, son and grandson of Austrian refugees, relative of Austrian and Hungarian concentration camp victims, Taiwan.
69. David Mizner, son of a survivor, relative of people who died in the Holocaust, United States.
70. Jeffrey J. Westcott, son and grandson of Holocaust survivors from Germany, United States.
71. Susan K. Jacoby, daughter of parents who were refugees from Nazi Germany, granddaughter of survivor of Buchenwald, United States.
72. Audrey Bomse, daughter of a survivor of Nazi ethnic cleansing in Vienna, lives in United States.
73. Daniel Gottschalk, son and grandson of refugees from the Holocaust, relative to various family members who died in the Holocaust, United States.
74. Barbara Grossman, daughter of survivors, granddaughter of Holocaust victims, United States.
75. Abraham Weizfeld PhD, son of survivorswho escaped Warsaw (Jewish Bundist) and Lublin ghettos, Canada.
76. David Rohrlich, son of refugees from Vienna, grandson of victim, United States.
77. Walter Ballin, son of holocaust survivors, United States.
78. Fritzi Ross, daughter of survivor, granddaughter of Dachau survivor Hugo Rosenbaum, great-granddaughter and great-niece of victims, United States.
79. Reuben Roth, son of survivors who fled from Poland in 1939, Canada.
80. Tony Iltis, father fled from Czechoslovakia and grandmother murdered in Auschwitz, Australia.
81. Anne Hudes, daughter and granddaughter of survivors from Vienna, Austria, great-granddaughter of victims who perished in Auschwitz, United States.
82. Mateo Nube, son of survivor from Berlin, Germany. Lives in United States.
83. John Mifsud, son of survivors from Malta, United States.
84. Mike Okrent, son of two holocaust / concentration camp survivors, United States.
85. Susan Bailey, daughter of survivor and niece of victims, UK.
86. Brenda Lewis, child of Kindertransport survivor, parent's family died in Auschwitz and Terezin. Lives in Canada.
87. Patricia Rincon-Mautner, daughter of survivor and granddaughter of survivor, Colombia.

88. Barak Michèle, daughter and grand-daughter of a survivor, many members of family were killed in Auschwitz or Bessarabia. Lives in Germany.
89. Jessica Blatt, daughter of child refugee survivor, both grandparents' entire families killed in Poland. Lives in United States
90. Maia Ettinger, daughter & granddaughter of survivors, United States.
91. Ammiel Alcalay, child of survivors from then Yugoslavia. Lives in United States.
92. Julie Deborah Kosowski, daughter of hidden child survivor, grandparents did not return from Auschwitz, United States.
93. Julia Shpirt, daughter of survivor, United States.
94. Ruben Rosenberg Colorni, grandson and son of survivors, The Netherlands.
95. Victor Ginsburgh, son of survivors, Belgium.
96. Arianne Sved, daughter of a survivor and granddaughter of victim, Spain.
97. Rolf Verleger, son of survivors, father survived Auschwitz, mother survived deportation from Berlin to Estonia, other family did not survive. Lives in Germany.
98. Euvrard Janine, daughter of survivors, France.
99. H. Fleishon, daughter of survivors, United States.
100. Barbara Meyer, daughter of survivor in Polish concentration camps. Lives in Italy.
101. Susan Heuman, child of survivors and granddaughter of two grandparents murdered in a forest in Minsk. Lives in United States.
102. Rami Heled, son of survivors, all grandparents and family killed by the Germans in Treblinka, Oswiecim and Russia. Lives in Israel.
103. Eitan Altman, son of survivor, France.
104. Jorge Sved, son of survivor and grandson of victim, United Kingdom
105. Maria Kruczkowska, daughter of Lea Horowicz who survived the holocaust in Poland. Lives in Poland.
106. Sarah Lanzman, daughter of survivor of Auschwitz, United States.
107. Cheryl W, daughter, granddaughter and nieces of survivors, grandfather was a member of the Dutch Underground (Eindhoven). Lives in Australia.
108. Chris Holmquist, son of survivor, UK.
109. Beverly Stuart, daughter and granddaughter of survivors from Romania and Poland. Lives in United States.
110. Peter Truskier, son and grandson of survivors, United States.
111. Karen Bermann, daughter of a child refugee from Vienna. Lives in United States.
112. Rebecca Weston, daughter and granddaughter of survivor, Spain.
113. Prof. Yosefa Loshitzky, daughter of Holocaust survivors, London, UK.
114. Marion Geller, daughter and granddaughter of those who escaped, great-granddaughter and relative of many who died in the camps, UK.
115. Susan Slyomovics, daughter and granddaughter of survivors of Auschwitz, Plaszow, Markleeberg and Ghetto Mateszalka, United States.
116. Helga Fischer Mankovitz, daughter, niece and cousin of refugees who fled from Austria, niece of victim who perished, Canada.
117. Michael Wischnia, son of survivors and relative of many who perished, United States.
118. Arthur Graaff, son of decorated Dutch resistance member and nazi victim, The Netherlands.
119. Yael Kahn, daughter of survivors who escaped Nazi Germany, many relatives that perished, UK.
120. Pierre Stambul, son of French resistance fighters, father deported to Buchenwalk, grandparents disapeared in Bessarabia, France.
121. Georges Gumpel, son of a deportee who died at Melk, Austria (subcamp of Mauthausen), France.
122. Emma Kronberg, daughter of survivor Buchenwald, United States.
123. Hannah Schwarzschild, daughter of a refugee who escaped Nazi Germany after experiencing Kristallnacht, United States.
124. Rubin Kantorovich, son of a survivor, Canada.
125. Daniele Armaleo, son of German refugee, grandparents perished in Theresienstadt, United States.
126. Aminda Stern Baird, daughter of survivor, United States.
127. Ana Policzer, daughter of hidden child, granddaughter of victim, niece/grandniece of four victims and two survivors, Canada.
128. Sara Castaldo, daughter of survivors, United States.
129. Pablo Policzer, son of a survivor, Canada.

130. Gail Nestel, daughter of survivors who lost brothers, sisters, parents and cousins, Canada.
131. Elizabeth Heineman, daughter and niece of unaccompanied child refugees, granddaughter of survivors, great-granddaughter and grand-niece of victims, United States.
132. Lainie Magidsohn, daughter of child survivor and numerous other relatives from Czestochowa, Poland. Lives in Canada.
133. Doris Gelbman, daughter and granddaughter of survivors, granddaughter and niece of many who perished, United States.
134. Erna Lund, daughter of survivor, Norway.
135. Rayah Feldman, daughter of refugees, granddaughter and niece of victims and survivors, UK.
136. Hadas Rivera-Weiss, daughter of survivors from Hungary, mother Ruchel Weiss née Abramovich and father Shaya Weiss, United States.
137. Pedro Tabensky, son of survivor of the Budapest Ghetto, South Africa.
138. Allan Kolski Horwitz, son of a survivor; descendant of many, many victims, South Africa.
139. Monique Mojica, child of survivor, relative to many victims murdered in Auschwitz. Canada.
140. Mike Brecher, son of a Kindertransport survivor and grandson of two who did not survive. UK.
141. Nomi Yah Gardiner, daughter and granddaughter of survivors, relative of victims, United States.
142. Marianne van Leeuw Koplewicz, daughter of deported parents, grand-daughter and niece of victims, Belgium.
143. Alfred Gluecksmann, son of survivors of Germany, United States.
144. Smadar Carmon, daughter of survivor, Canada.
145. Lara Braitstein, daughter of a survivor, father was a hidden child in Belgium, most of his cousins, aunts, uncles, and one set of grandparents were all murdered, Canada.
146. Susan J Braverman, daughter of a survivor and granddaughter of victims, United States.
147. Peter Slezak, son and grandson, Australia.
148. Liz Brummer, daugher of survivors, Australia.
149. Anneke Deustch, daughter of a Viennese survivor, my aunts, uncles and grandfather perished in Treblinka and Auschwitz, Australia.
150. George Hudes, son and grandson of survivors from Vienna, great-grandson of victims who perished in Auschwitz, United States.
151. Sabena Winston, daughter of a Polish survivor, Australia.
152. Max Orden, son of survivor of Buchenwald, Australia.
153. Gail Soltan Payne, daugher and niece of survivors from Croatia, United States.
154. Gail Soltan Payne, daughter and niece of survivors from Croatia, United States.
155. Joeri Puissant, child and grandchild of survivors, grandmother's family was murdered, Belgium.

Grandchildren of survivors
154. Raphael Cohen, grandson of Jewish survivors of the Nazi genocide, United States.
155. Emma Rubin, granddaughter of a survivor of the Nazi genocide, United States.
156. Alex Safron, grandson of a survivor of the Nazi genocide, United States.
157. Danielle Feris, grandchild of a Polish grandmother whose whole family died in the Nazi Holocaust, United States.
158. Jesse Strauss, grandson of Polish survivors of the Nazi genocide, United States.
159. Anna Baltzer, granddaughter of survivors whose family members perished in Auschwitz (others were members of the Belgian Resistance), United States.
160. Abigail Harms, granddaughter of Holocaust survivor from Austria, Now lives in United States.
161. Tessa Strauss, granddaughter of Polish Jewish survivors of the Nazi genocide, United States.
162. Caroline Picker, granddaughter of survivors of the Nazi genocide, United States.
163. Amalle Dublon, grandchild and great-grandchild of survivors of the Nazi holocaust, United States.
164. Antonie Kaufmann Churg, 3rd cousin of Ann Frank and grand-daughter of NON-survivors, United States.
165. Aliza Shvarts, granddaughter of survivors, United States.
166. Linda Mamoun, granddaughter of survivors, United States.
167. Abby Okrent, granddaughter of survivors of the Auschwitz, Dachau, Stuttgart, and the Lodz Ghetto, United States.

168. Beth Bruch, grandchild of German Jews who fled to US and great-grandchild of Nazi holocaust survivor, United States.
169. Bob Wilson, grandson of a survivor, United States.
170. Katharine Wallerstein, granddaughter of survivors and relative of many who perished, United States.
171. Sylvia Finzi, granddaughter and niece of Holocaust victims murdered in Auschwitz, London.
172. Esteban Schmelz, grandson of KZ-Theresienstadt victim, Mexico City.
173. Françoise Basch, grand daughter of Victor and Ilona Basch murdered by the Gestapo and the French Milice, France.
174. Gabriel Alkon, grandson of Holocaust survivors, Untied States.
175. Nirit Ben-Ari, grandchild of Polish grandparents from both sides whose entire family was killed in the Nazi Holocaust, United States.
176. Heike Schotten, granddaughter of refugees from Nazi Germany who escaped the genocide, United States.
177. Ike af Carlstèn, grandson of survivor, Norway.
178. Elias Lazarus, grandson of Holocaust refugees from Dresden, United States and Australia.
179. Laura Mandelberg, granddaughter of Holocaust survivors, United States.
180. Josh Ruebner, grandson of Nazi Holocaust survivors, United States.
181. Shirley Feldman, granddaughter of survivors, United States.
182. Nuno Cesar Ferreira, grandson of survivor, Brazil.
183. Andrea Land, granddaugher of survivors who fled programs in Poland, all European relatives died in German and Polish concentration camps, United States.
184. Sarah Goldman, granddaughter of survivors of the Nazi genocide, United States.
185. Baruch Wolski, grandson of survivors, Austria.
186. Frank Amahran, grandson of survivor, United States.
187. Eve Spangler, granddaughter of Holocaust NON-survivor, United States.
188. Gil Medovoy, grandchild of Fela Hornstein who lost her enitre family in Poland during the Nazi genocide, United States.
189. Michael Hoffman, grandson of survivors, rest of family killed in Poland during Holocaust, live in El Salvador.
190. Sarah Hogarth, granddaughter of a survivor whose entire family was killed at Auschwitz, United States.
191. Tibby Brooks, granddaughter, niece, and cousin of victims of Nazis in Ukraine. Lives in United States.
192. Dan Berger, grandson of survivor, United States.
193. Dani Baurer, granddaughter of Baruch Pollack, survivor of Auschwitz. Lives in United States.
194. Talia Baurer, granddaughter of a survivor, United States.
195. Evan Cofsky, grandson of survivor, UK.
196. Annie Sicherman, granddaughter of survivors, United States.
197. Anna Heyman, granddaughter of survivors, UK.
198. Maya Ober, granddaughter of survivor and relative of deceased in Teresienstadt and Auschwitz, Tel Aviv.
199. Anne Haan, granddaughter of Joseph Slagter, survivor of Auschwitz. Lives in The Netherlands.
200. Oliver Ginsberg, grandson of victim, Germany.
201. Mitchel Bollag, grandson of Stanislaus Eisner, who was living in Czechoslovakia before being sent to a concentration camp. United States.
202. Vivienne Porzsolt, granddaughter of victims of Nazi genocide, Australia.
203. Lisa Nessan, granddaughter of survivors, United States.
204. Kally Alexandrou, granddaughter of survivors, Australia.
205. Laura Ostrow, granddaughter of survivors, United States
206. Anette Jacobson, granddaughter of relatives killed, town of Kamen Kashirsk, Poland. Lives in United States.
207. Tamar Yaron (Teresa Werner), granddaughter and niece of victims of the Nazi genocide in Poland, Israel.
208. Antonio Roman-Alcalá, grandson of survivor, United States.
209. Jeremy Luban, grandson of survivor, United States.
210. Heather West, granddaughter of survivors and relative of other victims, United States.
211. Jeff Ethan Au Green, grandson of survivor who escaped from a Nazi work camp and hid in the Polish-Ukranian forest, United States.
212. Johanna Haan, daughter and granddaughter of victims in the Netherlands. Lives in the Netherlands.

213. Aron Ben Miriam, son of and nephew of survivors from Auschwitz, Bergen-Belsen, Salzwedel, Lodz ghetto. Lives in United States.
214. Noa Shaindlinger, granddaughter of four holocaust survivors, Canada.
215. Merilyn Moos, granddaughter, cousin and niece murdered victims, UK.
216. Ruth Tenne, granddaughter and relative of those who perished in Warsaw Ghetto, London.
217. Craig Berman, grandson of Holocaust survivors, UK.
218. Nell Hirschmann-Levy, granddaughter of survivors from Germany. Lives in United States.
219. Osha Neumann, grandson of Gertrud Neumann who died in Theresienstadt. Lives in United States.
220. Georg Frankl, Grandson of survivor Ernst-Immo Frankl who survived German work camp. Lives in Germany.
221. Julian Drix, grandson of two survivors from Poland, including survivor and escapee from liquidated Janowska concentration camp in Lwow, Poland. Lives in United States.
222. Katrina Mayer, grandson and relative of victims, UK.
223. Avigail Abarbanel, granddaughter of survivors, Scotland.
224. Denni Turp, granddaughter of Michael Prooth, survivor, UK.
225. Fenya Fischler, granddaughter of survivors, UK.
226. Yakira Teitel, granddaughter of German Jewish refugees, great-granddaughter of survivor, United States.
227. Susan Koppelman, granddaughter of survivor, United States
228. Hana Umeda, granddaughter of survivor, Warsaw.
229. Jordan Silverstein, grandson of two survivors, Canada.
230. Daniela Petuchowski, granddaughter of survivors, United States.
231. Aaron Lerner, grandson of survivors, United States.
232. Judith Bernstein, granddaughter of Holocaust victims in Auschwitz, Germany.
233. Samantha Wischnia, granddaughter and great niece of survivors from Poland, United States.
234. Elizabeth Wischnia, granddaughter and grand niece of three holocaust survivors, great aunt worked for Schindler, United States.
235. Daniel Waterman, grandson of survivor, The Netherlands.
236. Elana Baurer, granddaughter of survivor, United States.
237. Pablo Roman-Alcala, grandson of participant in the kindertransport and survivor, Germany.
238. Karine Abdel Malek, grandchild of survivor, Henri Waisman, Morocco.
239. Elana Baurer, granddaughter of survivor, United States.
240. Lillian Brown, granddaughter of survivor, United States.
241. Devin Cahn, grandson of survivors, United States.
242. Daniel Lévyne, grandson of a deportee, France.
243. Emilie Ferreira, granddaughter of survivors, Switzerland.
244. Chaim Neslen, grandchild of many victims and friend of many survivors, UK.
245. Ann Jungmann, granddaughter to three victims, UK.
246. Ellie Schling, granddaughter of a survivor, UK.
247. Danny Katch, grandson of a survivor, United States.
248. Karen Pomer, granddaughter of Henri B. van Leeuwen, member of Dutch resistance and survivor of Bergen Belsen, United States.
249. Gilda Mitchell Katz, granddaughter of survivors, uncle and aunt killed In Dombrova, Canada.
250. Dana Newfield, granddaughter of survivor and relative of many murdered, United States.
251. Ilana Guslits, granddaughter of two Polish survivors, Canada.
252. Gerald Coles-Kolsky, grandson of victims in Poland and France, United States.
253. Lesley Swain, granddaughter and cousin of survivors, UK.
254. Myera Waese, granddaughter of survivors of Bergen Belsen, Canada.
255. Ronni Seidman, grandchild of survivors, United States.
256. Mike Shatzkin, grandchild of survivors, some family members murdered and some who died in the Warsaw Ghetto uprising, United States.
257. Nance Shatzkin, grandchild of survivors, some family members murdered and some who died in the Warsaw Ghetto uprising, United States.
258. Karen Shatzkin, grandchild of survivors, some family members murdered and some who died in the Warsaw Ghetto uprising, United States.
259. Myriam Burger, granddaughter of survivor, United States.

260. Andre Burger, grandson of survivor Myriam Cohn, great-grandson of Sylvia Cohn and great-nephew of Esther Lore Cohn, both murdered in Auschwitz, United States.
261. Sara Ayech, granddaughter of Gisela and Max Roth, survivors who lost many family members, UK.
262. Monika Vykoukal, granddaughter of survivor, France.
263. Patricia Reinheimer, grandaugther of survivors, Brazil.
264. Nancy Patchell, granddaughter of resistance fighters, grandfather was caught and died in a concentration camp, Canada.
265. Jaclyn Pryor, granddaughter of survivors from Czestochowa Ghetto, Poland; great-grandchild, niece, and cousin to many who perished, United States.
266. Steven Rosenthal, grandson of survivor, Chile.
267. Alfredo Hilt, grandson of victim, Germany.
268. Arturo Desimone, grandson of a survivor of the ghetto of Częstochowa, The Netherlands.
269. Lazer Lederhendler, grandson of victims whose seven siblings also perished in the Warsaw Ghetto and Treblinka. Lives in Canada.
270. Poppy Kohner, granddaughter of survivor, Scotland.
271. Ben Young, grandson of survivor, UK.
272. Martin Weise, grandson of Mrs Frieda Schmidtke, survivor of Theresienstadt, UK.
273. Paul Blay, grandson of survivors saved by Schindler in Krakow, Poland. Lives in Australia.
274. Dinah Kohner, granddaughter of survivor, Sudentenland, New Zealand.
275. Amanda Reitzin, granddaughter of Polish survivor of Auschwitz, Australia.
276. Niclas Witton, grandparents and member of wider family perished, Australia.
277. Ron Witton, grandson of survivor, Australia.
278. Leah Grabelsky, granddaughter of Kindertransport survivor from Vienna, United States.
279. Ronnie Barkan, grandson of survivors from Auschwitz, Bergen-Belsen, Dachau and Majdanek camps. Now lives in Yafa, Palestine48/Israel.
280. Joseph Halevi, grandson of three victims, Australia.
281. Pembe Mutaf, granddaughter of an Auschwitz survivor, Canada.
282. Dr. Robert Stone, grandson of one who fled Nazi persecution, United States.
283. Lozh Pizdesh, granddaughter of survivor, France.

Great-grandchildren of survivors
286. Natalie Rothman, great granddaughter of Holocaust victims in Warsaw. Now lives in Canada.
287. Yotam Amit, great-grandson of Polish Jew who fled Poland, United States.
288. Daniel Boyarin, great grandson of victims of the Nazi genocide, United States.
289. Maria Luban, great-granddaughter of survivors of the Holocaust, United States.
290. Mimi Erlich, great-granddaughter of Holocaust victim, United States.
291. Olivia Kraus, great-grandaughter of victims, granddaughter and daughter of family that fled Austria and Czechoslovakia. Lives in United States.
292. Emily (Chisefsky) Alma, great granddaughter and great grandniece of victims in Bialystok, Poland, United States.
293. Inbal Amin, great-granddaughter of a mother and son that escaped and related to plenty that didn't, United States.
294. Matteo Luban, great-granddaughter of survivors, United States.
295. Saira Weiner, greatgranddaughter and niece of those murdered in the Holocaust, granddaughter of survivors, UK.
296. Andrea Isaak, great-granddaughter of survivor, Canada.
297. Alan Lott, great-grandson of a number of relatives lost, United States.
298. Sara Wines, great-granddaughter of a survivor and great-great granddaughter of victims, United States.
299. Kristen Baum Wolfe, great-granddaughter of survivors, United States.
300. Shelly Steinberg, great-granddaughter of German victims, murdered in Auschwitz, Tel Aviv.

Other relatives of survivors
301. Terri Ginsberg, niece of a survivor of the Nazi genocide, United States.
302. Nathan Pollack, relative of Holocaust survivors and victims, United States.
303. Marcy Winograd, relatives of victims, United States.
304. Rabbi Borukh Goldberg, relative of many victims, United States.

305. Martin Davidson, great-nephew of victims who lived in the Netherlands, Spain.
306. Miriam Pickens, relative of survivors, United States.
307. Dorothy Werner, spouse of survivor, United States.
308. Hyman and Hazel Rochman, relatives of Holocaust victims, United States.
309. Rich Siegel, cousin of victims who were rounded up and shot in town square of Czestochowa, Poland. Lives in United States.
310. Ignacio Israel Cruz-Lara, relative of survivor, Mexico.
311. Debra Stuckgold, relative of survivors, United States.
312. Joel Kovel, relatives killed at Babi Yar, United States.
313. Carol Krauthamer Smith, niece of survivors of the Nazi genocide, United States.
314. Chandra Ahuva Hauptman, relatives from grandfather's family died in Lodz ghetto, one survivor cousin and many deceased from Auschwitz, United States.
315. Shelly Weiss, relative of Holocaust victims, United States.
316. Carol Sanders, niece and cousin of victims of Holocaust in Poland, United States.
317. Sandra Rosen, great-niece and cousin of survivors, United States.
318. Raquel Hiller, relative of victims in Poland. Now lives in Mexico.
319. Alex Kantrowitz, most of father's family murdered Nesvizh, Belarus 1941. Lives in United States.
320. Michael Steven Smith, many relatives were killed in Hungary. Lives in United States.
321. Linda Moore, relative of survivors and victims, United States.
322. Juliet VanEenwyk, niece and cousin of Hungarian survivors, United States.
323. Anya Achtenberg, grand niece, niece, cousin of victims tortured and murdered in Ukraine. Lives in United States.
324. Betsy Wolf-Graves, great niece of uncle who shot himself as he was about to be arrested by Nazis, United States.
325. Abecassis Pierre, grand-uncle died in concentration camp, France.
326. Robert Rosenthal, great-nephew and cousin of survivors from Poland. Lives in United States.
327. Régine Bohar, relative of victims sent to Auschwitz, Canada.
328. Denise Rickles, relative of survivors and victims in Poland. Lives in United States.
329. Louis Hirsch, relative of victims, United States.
330. Concepción Marcos, relative of victim, Spain.
331. George Sved, relative of victim, Spain.
332. Judith Berlowitz, relative of victims and survivors, United States.
333. Rebecca Sturgeon, descendant of Holocaust survivor from Amsterdam. Lives in UK.
334. Justin Levy, relative of victims and survivors, Ireland.
335. Sam Semoff, relative of survivors and victims, UK.
336. Leah Brown Klein, daughter-in-law of survivors Miki and Etu Fixler Klein, United States
337. Karen Malpede, spouse of hidden child who then fled Germany. Lives in United States
338. Michel Euvrard, husband of survivor, France.
339. Walter Ebmeyer, grandnephew of three Auschwitz victims and one survivor now living in Jerusalem, United States.
340. Garrett Wright, relative of victims and survivors, United States.
341. Lynne Lopez-Salzedo, descendant of three Auschwitz victims, United States.
342. Renee Leavy, 86 victims in my mother's family, United States.
343. Steven Kohn, 182 victims in my grandparents' families, United States.
344. Dorah Rosen Shuey, relative of many victims and 4 survivors, United States.
345. Carol Lipton, cousin of survivors, United States.
346. Catherine Bruckner, descendent of Czech Jewish victims of the holocaust, UK.
347. Susan Rae Goldstein, carrying the name of my great-aunt Rose Frankel, from Poland and murdered along with many other family members, Canada.
348. Jordan Elgrably, nephew of Marcelle Elgrably, killed in Auschwitz, United States.
349. Olivia M Hudis, relative of Auschwitz victims, United States.
350. Peter Finkelstein, relative of victims and survivors, Germany.
351. Colin Merrin, descendant of Polish and Belarusian Jewish victims, UK.
352. Howard Swerdloff, most of my family died in the Shoah, United States.
353. Margarita E Freund, descendant of Breslau and Ukrainian Jewish victims, United States.
354. Marsha Goldberg, relative of victims in Poland, United States.

355. Michael Rosen, father's two uncles died in Auschwitz, UK.
356. Susan L. Lourenco, relative of victims, killed in Theresienstadt, Auschwitz. Now lives in Germany.
357. Shirley Luban, niece of uncle, who perished, United States.
358. Jennifer Simon, great-great niece of victims of Buchenwald and Theresienstadt, United States.
359. Piero Valabrega, relative of Italian Jews murdered in Auschwitz, Italy.
360. Ted Auerbach, relative of victims who died in the Holocaust, United States.[622]

80. [622] "Holocaust Survivors Condemn Israel´s Massacre in Gaza/End to Israeli Occupation and Colonization." *Astrid Essed*, www.astridessed.nl/holocaust-survivors-condemn-israels-massacre-in-gazaend-to-israeli-occupation-and-colonization/.

Chapter 13: Christianity

At present, Christianity is one of the largest religions in the world. Christianity has adherents in every country and the teachings of Jesus Christ are praised as good moral teachings to live by.[623] Former Christians and non-Christians have largely accepted that Jesus Christ was one of the great moral teachers for humanity even when they reject Jesus Christ's divinity or Christianity itself. Violence in the name of Christianity is usually attributed to outside factors instead of Jesus Christ's teachings. Violence from Christians is usually attributed to human greed or taking the Lord's name in vain. I firmly reject these platitudes given to Christianity and to Jesus Christ. I find no cogent argument to believe them and I will elaborate why I think that Christianity needs to be scrutinized deeply for the sake of world peace. This chapter will be a critique of Christianity and the teachings of Jesus Christ. I would like to ask that you please read the entire chapter and consider what I have to say about my objections to Christianity and to Jesus Christ.

Christianity has a voluminous amount of sects so the most effective path of scrutinizing Christianity would be pointing out the inconsistencies and highlighting the issues of Jesus Christ's teachings. There is no avoiding a critique about Christianity without discussing Jesus Christ and it would be entirely dishonest to ignore a criticism of Jesus Christ when he is the focal aspect of Christianity. Far too often, even the staunchest atheists have tacitly avoided criticizing Jesus Christ's teachings. Most atheists who hold anti-theist sentiments will focus upon the historicity, the unlikelihood of Jesus at various places, and the unlikelihood of his miracles but they will hardly ever criticize Jesus Christ's moral values. Christians have often acted as if it's beyond reproach and most atheists ignore criticizing Jesus Christ out of respect to Christianity. There is a pernicious and wrongful belief that Jesus Christ's moral teachings are simply too perfect to be criticized as a result. This notion is largely false. The only one to actively and openly critique Jesus Christ's teachings in live debates was the atheist Christopher Hitchens and some Christian groups continue to slander him after his death as a result such as lying about deathbed conversion.

I will be criticizing modern Christians and a particular sect of Christianity that has conducted overt harm upon the world and continues to harm the world with abject pride to this day. Christianity has a voluminous amount of denominations so I will make criticisms that focus upon the general issue that the majority, if not all of Christianity, has a persistent problem within its theology. The only way to effectively critique Christianity, and to discuss the subject matter so that any Christian with interest in this book would gain something

---

1. [623] Hackett, Conrad, and David McClendon. "Christians Remain World's Largest Religious Group, but They Are Declining in Europe." *Pew Research Center*, Pew Research Center, 5 Apr. 2017, www.pewresearch.org/fact-tank/2017/04/05/christians-remain-worlds-largest-religious-group-but-they-are-declining-in-europe/.

worthwhile from the contents, is to criticize Jesus Christ. If any part of the following seems offensive, then I would deeply apologize for offending you, but offending others is necessary and a non-violent form of rebuke against harmful beliefs. I have many Christian friends myself and it is my hope that they're not offended by the contents and willing to consider what is written. After doing my own research, I feel that it is necessary to critique Christianity considering the impending issue of global warming and the outright historical lies that Christian organizations constantly parrot towards the less educated Christians. There is no other way than to critique the teachings of Jesus Christ. I hope that you will read the following with a fair and open mindset. I apologize for any offense incurred upon reading these critiques as it sometimes has to occur to criticize harmful beliefs.

God and Satan

The dualistic concept of God and Satan and the ancient Christian belief in usury which didn't allow Christians to practice a credit system for a long period of Christian history seems to have originated from Judaism and Zoroastrianism synthesizing into a new religious belief. Yahweh and the Devil seem to be concepts that were copied from Ahura Mazda and Angra Mainyu of Zoroastrianism. Even should you disagree, you should be aware of the fact that the concept of a good supernatural being and evil supernatural being is not exclusive to Christianity. The concept of a Devil is not altogether different from the concept of an evil god. The distinction would be an argument of semantics. Christianity was never the first to use the dualistic concept of God and a Devil. It shouldn't be surprising because the dualistic concept serves a convenient purpose for Christians and other religious believers.

God and Satan are humanized iconography that respectively represents the ultimate form of positive human qualities and negative human qualities. God is perceived to be the epitome of goodness, which is why God is constantly redefined by certain sects of modern Christianity to only be able to do good actions. Satan is perceived to be the epitome of evil and is conveniently attributed to all the horrible events that happen to you, your loved ones, and the tragedies reported in the news. Satan is a convenient personification because he embodies the ultimate evil and venerates God as a result of the perceptual contrast of ultimate good and ultimate evil. God and Satan are rash causes that people create to frame an immediate understanding of why good or tragic events occur in life.[624][625] They're judgmental heuristics that allow humans to come-up with quick and easy answers for complex events that occur in everyday life.[626]

---

2. [624] Kahneman, Daniel. *Thinking, fast and slow*. Farrar, Straus and Giroux, 2015.
3. [625] Cialdini, Robert B. "Chapter 1: Weapons of Influence (1-16)" *Influence: Science and practice*. 4th ed., 21st Century Bks, 2002.
4. [626] Cialdini, Robert B. "Chapter 1: Weapons of Influence (1-16)" *Influence: Science and practice*. 4th ed., 21st Century Bks, 2002.

The contrast principle of psychology, placing greater emphasis on the contrast and our favorable disposition toward the side that we like, would obviously make us favor God.[627] The religious consistency, our basic human need to be consistent with our beliefs, to the precepts of a sinful world with Jesus Christ as the only salvation would create a deeply pernicious worldview that has terrible consequences for non-Christians.[628] People who don't recognize Jesus as their savior would be seen, under the moral framework of Christianity, as enemies, deceivers, harboring evil intent, delusional in their happiness, and deceived by Satan. Other religions would be seen as tricks of Satan or Satanism itself. No matter what the non-Christian does, they're believed to hold some deep malice within them and will be perceived as a threat to the word of Jesus Christ. Before the preeminence of secular freethinking, this was the mentality of colonialists who took over other parts of the world. It is no accident that Christianity has committed cultural genocide upon any religious faith and culture that was unique from Christian doctrines. An examination of Christianity's cultural genocide throughout the world can be seen in its violent history; a historical and cultish demonization of other gods and goddesses as incarnates of evil that solely exist to deceive Christians. The gods and goddesses of every culture that Christianity has set afoot upon have been demonized, destroyed, and vilified with an overemphasis upon the negative aspects of their religious beliefs and a reverence for any Christian who was killed by foreigners as justification for the killing of non-Christians. These were supposedly because of Christianity's need to "civilize" the "savages" to accept Jesus Christ as their lord and savior. All non-Christian cultures are vilified as devil worship and only after modern criticism have Christian missionaries changed their arguments to ignore "triumphalism" or "White man's burden" and instead preach about how much more honest and kind Christianity is compared to every other faith in existence. Due to the contrast principle, Christians would be predisposed to view other faiths *more negatively* than their actual negative qualities and could engender violence upon the non-Christian out-group as a result the extremist contrast of good versus evil.[629]

Heaven and Hell

The concepts of heaven and hell serve as moral conveniences for Christians. Everyone recognized as "good people" go to heaven and all "bad people" go to hell. While subsets of modern Christians believe that any good person goes to heaven, this modern belief is a deviation and a total subversion of Jesus Christ's teachings. Only through Jesus Christ can people be in heaven.[630] Depending upon the Christian denomination, they must also be baptized and circumcised to enter the Kingdom of God. If they don't accept Jesus into their

---

5. [627] Cialdini, Robert B. "Chapter 1: Weapons of Influence (1-16)" *Influence: Science and practice*. 4th ed., 21st Century Bks, 2002.
6. [628] Cialdini, Robert B. "Chapter 3: Commitment and Consistency (52-95)" *Influence: Science and practice*. 4th ed., 21st Century Bks, 2002.
7. [629] Cialdini, Robert B. "Chapter 1: Weapons of Influence (1-16)" *Influence: Science and practice*. 4th ed., 21st Century Bks, 2002.
8. [630] "BibleGateway." *Bible Gateway*, Bible Gateway Blog, www.biblegateway.com/passage/?search=John 14:6&version=KJV.

heart or – depending upon the denomination – don't get baptized or circumcised then they will be going to hell. Thus, no matter how "good" a non-Christian is, they're condemned to hell for not accepting Jesus Christ. The concept of hell has been sanitized as the "absence of God" instead of meaning eternal hellfire and torment for the punishment of having a different religion and opinions different from Christian theology. The expectation is that non-Christians shall face "justice" for forming their own opinions and not following the so-called will of God.[631] The Catholic belief that non-Christians are in purgatory to await God's judgment is an attempt to ignore the negative implications of believing in Christianity by placing responsibility on God and ignoring the consequences of belief. Interestingly, the Catholic Church went so far as to change its official policy regarding where unbaptized babies who die prematurely are sent after death because the belief brought deep emotional pain for mothers who had lost their children early. The theology changed for the convenience of the religious followers.

The attempts at deciphering the "true meaning" of what the Bible conveys through open interpretation are attempts at using personal preference and committing the fallacy of moving the goalposts; changing the axioms of the religious faith for the convenience of the believer and ignoring the horrible events that Christianity has caused or the distress it has instilled upon people.[632] Hell being the "absence of God" as an argument is an attempt to ignore the negative implications about the very concept of hell for non-Christians to make it less divisive and to acquiesce to peaceful social tolerance of others under the expectations of current western culture. If it was perceived as a place where non-Christians are harmed, then it would be viewed as a hateful belief system in modern times.

The concept of heaven, in particular, came out of the wish fulfillment of the ancient world. They conceptualized the opposite of their terrible experiences to create a meaningful standard to live together during a time where warring tribes were common. Please consider this perspective, consider their beliefs and how the ancient world could have reacted to their situations: A tribe of people realize the world is finite and their loved ones die of illnesses that people can't find the cause of? There is an eternal world where people live forever after their death with no suffering unlike the harsh reality.[633][634] This world is cruel, indifferent, and stressful? The afterlife is a perfect world where people live in bliss with God's love.[635] People feel there is no point in their actions and consequences within an uneducated community of

---

9. [631] Nietzsche, Friedrich Wilhelm. *THE ANTICHRIST*. Translated by H. L. Mencken, The Project Gutenberg, 2006.
10. [632] "Moving the Goalposts." *Https://Www.logicallyfallacious.com*, www.logicallyfallacious.com/tools/lp/Bo/LogicalFallacies/129/Moving-the-Goalposts.
11. [633] Nietzsche, Friedrich. How the "True World" Finally Became a Fable. The History of an Error (19-21). *Twilight of the Idols*. Amazon Digital Services LLC.
12. [634] Nietzsche, Friedrich Wilhelm. Chapter IX: Preachers of Death (50-52). *Thus spake Zarathustra: a book for all and none*. Translated by Thomas Common, PDF ed., T. Common, 1908.
13. [635] Nietzsche, Friedrich Wilhelm. Chapter IX: Preachers of Death (50-52). *Thus spake Zarathustra: a book for all and none*. Translated by Thomas Common, PDF ed., T. Common, 1908.

warring tribes? Their actions and consequences help determine an eternal reward or punishment and so they must live by a code of ethics that determines where they go after their life has ended.[636] Your group is harassed and beaten by an enemy tribe? Rejoice, the enemy will die of eternal punishment for not following the same rules that you do and your submission to the enemy will be rewarded as a morally good activity after your death.[637] Everyone's lives seem meaningless, pitiless, and empty in a recurring system of violence and suffering? There is an eternal ruler in a perfect world that has a plan for you and bestows you with his eternal love after your suffering and death.[638] Thus, heaven is a set of mental gymnastics meant to praise and elevate the Christian worshiper above the other groups.[639] The dualistic concept of heaven and hell were attempts to humanize death to make it more familiar, comfortable, and acceptable for ancient people who didn't understand diseases, natural disasters, mental illnesses and believed their society's actions caused such events through societal habits.[640][641]

The following argument originated from one of my favorite video games, *Shin Megami Tensei IV: Apocalypse*, and proposes a challenge to the concept of a Creator God and the Devil that I thought was worth sharing.[642]

However, before that, I'd like to address any controversy over using a video game in an argument about religion. Now, while I understand that this may engender ridicule and derision because the source of this theological challenge is a fictional story in a video game, I personally feel that video games, like our other art forms of films and books, is deserving of equal respect and critical analysis on the merits of their storytelling and thought-provoking challenges to our beliefs. Video games, like our other cultural heritages, should be deserving of respect and incorporated in serious intellectual debate when they present challenges using visualized concepts. Therefore, using video games and arguments presented within them, is not an attempt to ridicule or show insensitivity to discussions of serious matters. What matters is not the source of the argument, but the manner in which we use and present the argument. I feel the perspective given in the video game is a valid contention that should be shared and thought over.

---

14. [636] Nietzsche, Friedrich. The Four Great Errors (27-37). *Twilight of the Idols*. Amazon Digital Services LLC.
15. [637] Nietzsche, Friedrich. The Four Great Errors (27-37). *Twilight of the Idols*. Amazon Digital Services LLC.
16. [638] Nietzsche, Friedrich Wilhelm. Chapter IX: Preachers of Death (50-52). *Thus spake Zarathustra: a book for all and none*. Translated by Thomas Common, PDF ed., T. Common, 1908.
17. [639] Nietzsche, Friedrich Wilhelm. Chapter XXVI: THE PRIESTS (88-91). *Thus spake Zarathustra: a book for all and none*. Translated by Thomas Common, PDF ed., T. Common, 1908.
18. [640] Nietzsche, Friedrich Wilhelm. *THE ANTICHRIST*. Translated by H. L. Mencken, The Project Gutenberg, 2006.
19. [641] Nietzsche, Friedrich. The Four Great Errors (27-37). *Twilight of the Idols*. Amazon Digital Services LLC.
20. [642] "Shin Megami Tensei IV: Apocalypse." US, Atlus, 2016.

The writers of the video game present an argument against the theology of Christianity that I've found to be an incredibly unique perspective shift and a rather interesting challenge on how people view the Bible and especially the New Testament. To paraphrase, their challenge in the following propositions:

- The Abrahamic God trapped humanity into this world as a crucible of suffering.[643]
- The Abrahamic God claims that those who survive the suffering will be saved, so long as you submit to him.[644]
- The Abrahamic God then created the Devil to deceive you and prolong your suffering.[645]
- You are bound to your covenant with the Abrahamic God and must depend, submit, and suffer for him while glorifying him.[646]
- Being bound to the covenant and being vigilant of temptations sets you up for failure and will always result in you losing your way in life. You must constantly feel shame and disgust when you aren't living life solely to glorify him.[647]
- The covenant thereby shows that the Abrahamic God does not love you or anyone else; he only loves himself. He makes you suffer in order to glorify himself.[648]

Part of what prompts this perspective shift is that while Western culture largely follows the bigoted and authoritarian belief in blasphemy, the culture of Japan never held such a strong theological equivalent in terms of how to view various Gods and Goddesses in the Shinto faith and the general openness of certain Buddhist denominations. Westerners seem keen on falsely accusing Japan of bigotry without first examining the presumptions of their religious faith and the likelihood of assumptions made on anyone who simply provides a challenging perspective to the Abrahamic faiths.

The propositions were ultimately to challenge the idea of a loving God within the Christian theological context. Christians often argue that humanity is dead in sin and that's why diseases occur, despite science having completely disproven that. The Atlus story writers prompt us to ask a set of questions about Christian theological assumptions. What sort of loving God would force you into a test of suffering just to glorify him? If the whole purpose is

---

21. [643] BuffMaister. "Shin Megami Tensei 4 Apocalypse Boss Vishnu-Flynn [APOCALYPSE] [ANARCHY]." *YouTube*, YouTube, 16 Feb. 2018, www.youtube.com/watch?v=YMUk4i6h1GY&t=39s.
22. [644] BuffMaister. "Shin Megami Tensei 4 Apocalypse Boss Vishnu-Flynn [APOCALYPSE] [ANARCHY]." *YouTube*, YouTube, 16 Feb. 2018, www.youtube.com/watch?v=YMUk4i6h1GY&t=39s.
23. [645] BuffMaister. "Shin Megami Tensei 4 Apocalypse Boss Vishnu-Flynn [APOCALYPSE] [ANARCHY]." *YouTube*, YouTube, 16 Feb. 2018, www.youtube.com/watch?v=YMUk4i6h1GY&t=39s.
24. [646] BuffMaister. "Shin Megami Tensei 4 Apocalypse Boss Vishnu-Flynn [APOCALYPSE] [ANARCHY]." *YouTube*, YouTube, 16 Feb. 2018, www.youtube.com/watch?v=YMUk4i6h1GY&t=39s.
25. [647] BuffMaister. "Shin Megami Tensei 4 Apocalypse Boss Vishnu-Flynn [APOCALYPSE] [ANARCHY]." *YouTube*, YouTube, 16 Feb. 2018, www.youtube.com/watch?v=YMUk4i6h1GY&t=39s.
26. [648] BuffMaister. "Shin Megami Tensei 4 Apocalypse Boss Vishnu-Flynn [APOCALYPSE] [ANARCHY]." *YouTube*, YouTube, 16 Feb. 2018, www.youtube.com/watch?v=YMUk4i6h1GY&t=39s.

to see through the falsehoods and illusions to keep faith in the Abrahamic God, then why did the Abrahamic God create the Devil specifically to deceive you away from his divine truth? Why create the Devil to intensify your suffering at all? Why would any deity create a value system specifically to glorify themselves, in which you must constantly submit, depend upon, and suffer to celebrate him as your greatest superior? How can any of this be love?

I'd like to add an additional set of questions. If the counterargument is freewill and the analogy of giving children tests to increase their capabilities, then how can that apply to children as young as five years of age who die from curable diseases in third world countries or who are born with terminal cancer and die young throughout the world? Are their lives merely a test for us? If so, then how were their lives ever sacred in the religious sense when they would simply exist as objects for public consumption stories for you to keep faith in the Abrahamic God? If the Abrahamic God created them specifically for such a purpose as part of his plan, then how is that love towards them?

Capitalism and the Temple of God

Mark 11:12-25 King James Version (KJV)

¹² *And on the morrow, when they were come from Bethany, he was hungry:*

¹³ *And seeing a fig tree afar off having leaves, he came, if haply he might find any thing thereon: and when he came to it, he found nothing but leaves; for the time of figs was not yet.*

¹⁴ *And Jesus answered and said unto it, No man eat fruit of thee hereafter for ever. And his disciples heard it.*

¹⁵ *And they come to Jerusalem: and Jesus went into the temple, and began to cast out them that sold and bought in the temple, and overthrew the tables of the moneychangers, and the seats of them that sold doves;*

¹⁶ *And would not suffer that any man should carry any vessel through the temple.*

¹⁷ *And he taught, saying unto them, Is it not written, My house shall be called of all nations the house of prayer? but ye have made it a den of thieves.*

¹⁸ *And the scribes and chief priests heard it, and sought how they might destroy him: for they feared him, because all the people was astonished at his doctrine.*

¹⁹ *And when even was come, he went out of the city.*

²⁰ *And in the morning, as they passed by, they saw the fig tree dried up from the roots.*

²¹ *And Peter calling to remembrance saith unto him, Master, behold, the fig tree which thou cursedst is withered away.*

²² *And Jesus answering saith unto them, Have faith in God.*

²³ *For verily I say unto you, That whosoever shall say unto this mountain, Be thou removed, and be thou cast into the sea; and shall not doubt in his heart, but shall believe that those things which he saith shall come to pass; he shall have whatsoever he saith.*

²⁴ *Therefore I say unto you, What things soever ye desire, when ye pray, believe that ye receive them, and ye shall have them.*

²⁵ *And when ye stand praying, forgive, if ye have ought against any: that your Father also which is in heaven may forgive you your trespasses.*[649]

Depending upon the political ideology that people follow, and through the use of open interpretation, Christians of diverse political beliefs have interpreted Jesus Christ's intentions differently. The varied interpretations are to the extent that the beliefs in the teachings of Jesus Christ by Christian liberals and Christian conservatives are in total contradiction to each other; in personal assumptions about the intentions of the teachings and how they must behave. The differences are to the extent that the only common meaning in being a Christian is believing in Jesus Christ as the lord and savior, this belief is usually based upon an argument from ignorance that some aspect of the Bible has to be true because millions before our generation believed in it; this is despite the fact that we acknowledge how ignorant and uneducated the multitude of generations before us were to facts that we know today about the world's age, evolution, how diseases function, and both political ideologies generally ignore the fact that capitalism is a total contradiction of Biblical teachings. The Christian arguments for being capitalist are in utter contradiction to doctrines of giving to others. In the above Biblical passage, Jesus Christ himself destroyed a market of commerce through physical force.

A truly defeatist prospect of Christian morality is the possibility that many Christians may believe that they need to be sinners to accept capitalism. That would be a constant mental self-torture of seeing oneself as unavoidably evil because they believe in capitalism and could pursue altogether terrible policies that hurt innocent people under the expectation that they're unavoidable sinners regardless of what they do.[650][651] The acceptance of being a ubiquitous sinner, regardless of your actions, is often viewed as a sign of humility. The belief that we are expressing humility in recognizing ourselves as sinners is an utterly psychopathic belief that can only create constant mental weariness and self-hatred for simply being human.[652] It is misanthropy and self-hate sanctified as a holy concession.[653][654] The acceptance of being an unavoidable sinner creates a sense of superiority and self-worship for celebrating self-contempt for the human body and human desires because it is seen as a powerful concession to God compared to the activities of other self-identifying Christians.[655] That is, within the human

---

27. [649] "BibleGateway." *Bible Gateway*, Bible Gateway Blog, www.biblegateway.com/passage/?search=Mark 11:12-25&version=KJV.
28. [650] Nietzsche, Friedrich Wilhelm. *On the genealogy of morals: a polemical tract*. Translated by Ian Johnston, PDF, Richer Resources Publications, 2014.
29. [651] Nietzsche, Friedrich Wilhelm. *THE ANTICHRIST*. Translated by H. L. Mencken, The Project Gutenberg, 2006.
30. [652] Nietzsche, Friedrich Wilhelm. *On the genealogy of morals: a polemical tract*. Translated by Ian Johnston, PDF, Richer Resources Publications, 2014.
31. [653] Cialdini, Robert B. "Chapter 3: Commitment and Consistency (52-95)" *Influence: Science and practice*. 4th ed., 21st Century Bks, 2002.
32. [654] Nietzsche, Friedrich Wilhelm. *On the genealogy of morals: a polemical tract*. Translated by Ian Johnston, PDF, Richer Resources Publications, 2014.
33. [655] Nietzsche, Friedrich Wilhelm. Chapter XXVI: THE PRIESTS (88-91). *Thus spake Zarathustra: a book for all and none*. Translated by Thomas Common, PDF ed., T. Common, 1908.

norm of reciprocity for the Christian in-group, holding more contempt for human desires and your personal passions can make you feel as if you're proving a stronger commitment to being a Christian than fellow Christians who don't make such concessions and you thereby elevate your own ego by doing nothing of value for others besides a narcissistic celebration of the in-group.[656][657][658] If you are a Christian, have you given any deep thought to the idea that Christian moral teachings are simply wrong because they don't work with capitalism? Christian morality is derived from metaphysical axioms that contradict capitalism's principles of selling goods and services to maximize one's profits. A Christian would obviously notice this explicit contradiction and would be inclined to view themselves to be utterly shameful in their daily activities for no other reason than the Bible telling them to believe the worst of themselves. This dynamic is largely hailed as the ultimate form of goodness. Yet, capitalism isn't evil; it is what we make of it.

Temple of God

The theological underpinnings of a Christian's physical body being a temple for the Abrahamic God is a clear case of hatred for the human body and is especially misogynistic.[659] The temple of God is the modernized justification for why women should cover themselves, but the history of Christianity and religion in general was of servitude towards men under the belief that women are merely the property of men.[660] Consent on the part of the woman is deemed unimportant and outright ignored. A single woman who consensually fornicated with a single man is seen as deserving of punishment for her freedom of choice to live her own life and for desiring mutual pleasure with a man.[661] If she becomes pregnant, then she should be punished harshly and remain unforgiven for the crime of freedom of choice; the belief in irresponsibility seems solely directed at her and not the male by societal standards.[662][663] In Christian cultural standards, having sex once means the woman is no better than a whore who has sex with multiple men; no difference is distinguished within the simplistic cultural beliefs perpetuated by Christianity. By contrast, the man gave in to her wiles, despite both being mutually consenting. The reason for that is because of Biblical teachings inculcating loathing

---

34. [656] Cialdini, Robert B. "Chapter 3: Commitment and Consistency (52-95)" *Influence: Science and practice*. 4th ed., 21st Century Bks, 2002.
35. [657] Nietzsche, Friedrich. Morality as Anti-Nature (21-26). *Twilight of the Idols*. Amazon Digital Services LLC.
36. [658] Nietzsche, Friedrich Wilhelm. *On the genealogy of morals: a polemical tract*. Translated by Ian Johnston, PDF, Richer Resources Publications, 2014.
37. [659] *1 Corinthians 6 KJV*, biblehub.com/kjv/1_corinthians/6.htm.
38. [660] "BibleGateway." *Bible Gateway*, Bible Gateway Blog, www.biblegateway.com/passage/?search=1 Timothy 2&version=KJV.
39. [661] Nietzsche, Friedrich. Morality as Anti-Nature (21-26). *Twilight of the Idols*. Amazon Digital Services LLC.
40. [662] Nietzsche, Friedrich. The Four Great Errors (27-37). *Twilight of the Idols*. Amazon Digital Services LLC.
41. [663] Nietzsche, Friedrich Wilhelm. *THE ANTICHRIST*. Translated by H. L. Mencken, The Project Gutenberg, 2006.

and contempt towards women who have sex outside of marriage and therefore don't act in accordance to being the property of men. It is for this very reason that Abrahamic worshipping politicians pass laws or argue in favor of ignoring birth control pills, contraceptives, and abortion. The highest importance in serving the Abrahamic God is by punishing women for not being the property of men; not assisting women or improving their country's health standards. Terms such as "respecting the husband", being "respectable" by covering their entire bodies in clothing, and being married before having sexual relations is not about good morals, per se. As mentioned in Chapter 5, it's about women being bound as the property of men. This cultural norm has had a notable impact in Western business attire and decorum through the cultural lens of what is and isn't considered respectable too. Underlying all of these notions is the morality of the Bible, the morality of warring desert tribes that took foreign women captive as sex slaves to be conditioned under the authority of their male rapists and which continues to be preached as good moral behavior for modern women to follow by religious conservative cultures. The notion of the physical body being a temple of God is simply semantics to celebrate an ancient culture of war rape and to impose guidelines upon modern women that make them behave as spoils of war for men. Furthermore, if you disagree with the information presented in the section on Judaism about the historicity of the Bible, then you should be aware*: the more faith you have in the Bible, the more you should believe that Abrahamic religious culture is imposing norms on modern women originiating from practices of war rape.*

Chapter 14: Critiquing Christ

To analyze and criticize Jesus Christ and his teachings are fundamental for any honest attempt at critiquing Christianity. When criticizing Christianity, people often attempt to argue that subsets of vocal Christians are either speaking falsely or not accurately following the teachings of Jesus Christ; the implication being that if they simply corrected their behavior and followed the specific quote-mined portions that other Christian denominations do then there wouldn't be "deceiving themselves" from Jesus's actual teachings. As stated prior, this obviously ignores open interpretation. As will be examined within this chapter, this line of reasoning also ignores that Jesus's teachings are self-contradictory. Many atheists who've de-converted from Christianity seem willing to engage in criticizing various aspects of the Bible, but Jesus's teachings remain untouched and politely ignored out of respect. This implicit taboo of criticizing Jesus Christ's teachings, instilled from recognizing Jesus's teachings as elevated and deserving of a higher social status than any other moral teachings during their childhood, has harmful consequences that may not be recognizable at first glance. By stridently ignoring any opportunities to criticize Jesus Christ and his teachings, Christians are led to believe that Jesus Christ's teachings are beyond reproach. By not criticizing, Christians are assured of their faith that Jesus Christ's teachings are profound, unique, and superior to anything an atheist or a secularist can argue in their rejection of the Bible and Christianity itself. As such, it is crucial to subject the teachings and mannerisms of Jesus Christ to thorough scrutiny when examining the moral utility and truth claims of the Bible.

The first contention is specifically about what prevents criticism of Jesus Christ and his teachings from being taken seriously. The refusal by Christians and ex-Christians to engage in any such criticism and instead react disparagingly of anyone who attempts to criticize the teachings of Jesus Christ; this is the hatred of knowledge within Christianity. A rabid form of anti-intellectualism within Christianity is the insulating belief that you must believe in the Bible and have faith in Jesus Christ as your lord and savior to have any meaningful criticism at all. This is anti-intellectual because all forms of criticism from non-Christian viewpoints is automatically dismissed as arrogant, harboring ill intent, deluding themselves, and somehow persecuting Christians for simply criticizing beliefs about Jesus Christ and his teachings. It is a complete refusal to engage in honest criticism and a reflexive in-group emotional reaction to any sharp criticism of the teachings of Jesus Christ. This type of hostile reaction is one of the many pathologies of in-group thinking whereby groupthink sets in to make people feel at ease instead of basing judgments on empirical evidence, logic, and well-reasoned arguments. Perhaps this contention may be perceived to harbor snarky contempt under the belief that such a contention is insulting, bigoted, or not based on reality; yet, on numerous occasions, my experience tells me otherwise and the experiences of others who cast dissenting opinions on religion tell me otherwise. Religious forms of social media groups, internet forums, and chat rooms are replete with examples of banning people for the crime of harboring outside viewpoints and exist in a very authoritarian fashion to diminish, ridicule, and cast aspersions upon any who disagree with specific religious criteria. Some social media groups even require that outside viewers simply keep silent as Christians espouse why they need to convert to Christianity and must learn to love Jesus Christ as their savior. I would not be pointing this out, if my entire life using various forms of social media, internet forums, and chat rooms gave me a plethora of examples. The lack of listening to meaningful criticisms while Christians continue to espouse messages of conversion tells me that they don't wish to engage honestly or hear any criticisms laid upon Christianity. This was a major criticism during the New Atheist movement in 2006 - 2011 in the US and Europe. Atheist forums have formed similar mindsets around specific atheist personalities in a very cult-like fashion, but the ones I'm most familiar with don't ban dissenting opinions outright and the moderation is more balanced, even if tipped in the scales of the majority. Nevertheless, one of the focal reasons people don't criticize the teachings of Jesus Christ is because of the strong, reflexive, and negative reaction by Christians themselves, who begin accusing others of wanting to commit horrific crimes of genocide for even criticizing Jesus Christ and his teachings or that any criticism doesn't matter because they believe in Jesus Christ as the Son of God and their savior. Any questioning of the fundamental assumption of Jesus Christ's divinity is not regarded seriously and in both conservative and liberal circles, the argument that his teachings have negative repercussions aren't regarded seriously. This is a refusal to engage in outside viewpoints or have any honest discussion about the core problems with Christianity and its truth claims. The rest of this will consist of analysis and criticisms of Jesus Christ.

    If you're a Christian, then please try to consider this from an outsider perspective and do not be afraid to question his truth claims. Jesus Christ apparently taught humility, compassion, and forgiveness in a meek and mild manner while also proclaiming himself God, the Son of God, and claiming anyone who didn't believe in him would be sent to hell. This is a complete self-contradiction of claims because declaring oneself God and Son of God is an arrogant claim to make. You're expected to believe that a person who arrogantly declared himself God and the Son of God was being meek and mild. You're expected to believe that he taught humility and compassion while declaring that anyone who didn't believe in him would be going straight to hell for the thought crime of not accepting him as lord and savior. It's pertinent to note that Jesus Christ's claims are implicitly declaring a thought crime for anyone who doesn't believe in him because the expectation is that non-believers are automatically foolish, steeped in sin, arrogant, and will be sent to hell for the crime of independent thought. As sin already posits a ubiquitous nihilism towards life itself, arguing that the carnal world is replete with it, the only way to escape is to worship Jesus Christ as God and Son of God; that is, to concede and wholly submit to this man's unfettered narcissism.

    It is often argued by critics of the Bible that the Abrahamic God displays acts of narcissism, pettiness, envy, and hatred in the Old Testament; but the teachings of Jesus Christ aren't given equal critique when they should be. Jesus Christ's teachings are primarily grounded in his claim of godhood and demand that everyone acknowledge his godhood as self-evident.

Everything must conform to the image of Jesus Christ or it is considered immoral and a perversion of Satan to tempt humanity away from the Abrahamic God. Jesus Christ's beliefs and views must be what all Christians try to attune themselves towards; despite recognizing themselves as imperfect and thus the act of being more like Jesus Christ is paradoxically acknowledged to be a wholly useless endeavor. Despite this self-contradiction, you must try to be more like Jesus Christ or you're not morally good. The task is impossible by the Abrahamic God's Biblical standards because you're recognized as a sinful human being, but that's supposedly all the more reason that you should obey and follow because that somehow makes it worthwhile. With repentance, you must repeatedly loathe yourself in prayer sessions to Jesus Christ and ask for forgiveness for the crime of inheriting sinfulness from people who existed before you were born.[664] It doesn't matter that it is inherently unfair for you to be judged by the people of the past who have nothing to do with your actions; you are born guilty of sin, inherited from people you never knew from an event you had no say in, and thus you must seek Jesus Christ's forgiveness for being born in the world as if it was a crime.[665] You must seek forgiveness for the sinful temptations of what biology recognizes as your natural sexual desires for procreation of your species, forgiveness for the thought crime of thinking of other people sexually which is also a natural process for the procreation of the species, the sin of premarital sex for choosing how to live your life, a lifetime of condemnation for the sin of having a child outside of wedlock, and for taking pleasure in living in a carnal world above the spiritual guidance and faith in Jesus Christ as your lord and savior.[666][667]

The following contention will be the harshest regarding Jesus Christ as a person. If you're a Christian, you'll likely hate every word you read, but I ask that you consider the viewpoint seriously. *Jesus Christ was a narcissist with a God complex.* He was so narcissistic that he wanted everyone in the world to worship him as a God and condemn anyone who didn't worship him with hateful beliefs like hell and being mired in sinfulness for the thought crime of not agreeing to celebrate his godhood. He wanted everything that was seen as morally good to be subservient to worshiping his godhood and he used self-contradictory parables so that his teachings could be applicable to situations that were out of context from his original statements so that everything positive would be attributed to venerating him as a God. If that sounds ridiculous, then it shouldn't; his statements about false Christians who he'll supposedly condemn before the Abrahamic God are so vague that they can be applicable to every Christian denomination. He purposefully kept his statements vague because he wanted everyone in the world to worship him and so he tried to make them as widely applicable to anything that he

---

1. [664] Nietzsche, Friedrich Wilhelm. *On the genealogy of morals: a polemical tract.* Translated by Ian Johnston, PDF, Richer Resources Publications, 2014.
2. [665] Nietzsche, Friedrich. The Four Great Errors (27-37). *Twilight of the Idols.* Amazon Digital Services LLC.
3. [666] Nietzsche, Friedrich. Morality as Anti-Nature (21-26). *Twilight of the Idols.* Amazon Digital Services LLC.
4. [667] Nietzsche, Friedrich Wilhelm. Chapter XXVI: THE PRIESTS (88-91). *Thus spake Zarathustra: a book for all and none.* Translated by Thomas Common, PDF ed., T. Common, 1908.

could think of during his time period; it is in a similar fashion to the vague, self-contradictory statements of Chinese fortune cookies so that they can apply to everything. Within Biblical terms, it's more holistic because everything must be made subservient to worshiping Jesus Christ as lord and savior. Modern Christianity has to act as a perpetual tautology, because Jesus Christ can never be seen as unambiguously wrong since the whole purpose of the religion is to celebrate his narcissistic ravings about himself.

Jesus Christ's death on the cross is depicted in the Bible as the most important death to ever occur and it is a core component of the Abrahamic God's plan for the salvation of humankind. As a Christian, you would have to believe that his death is more important than any human death because Jesus Christ is recognized as God, Son of God, and the divine plan that the Bible attributes to be proof of the Abrahamic God's love because he allowed his son to be killed. The world is mired in sin and the Abrahamic God sacrificed his own son to save humanity from its sinfulness. Unfortunately, this supposed sacred sacrifice of the Abrahamic God implicitly devalues all human life; as a Christian, you must perceive Jesus Christ's death on the cross as vastly more important than all human genocides that occurred throughout humanity. The deaths of non-Christians would be seen as falling into the deception of Satan or the carnal world and being sent to hell as a result because they didn't convert to Christianity. They can only be redeemed through acknowledging Jesus Christ as their lord and savior, but this belief in redemption through Jesus Christ and Jesus's death being more important than any human death leads to horrifying real world consequences.

To give two real world examples to better understand the problem; the first is the history of Christian schools imposed upon Native American communities in both Canada and the United States. The genocide of the Native Americans is seen as meaningless because their deaths are considered unimportant compared to the death of Jesus Christ on the cross; the barbarism of the systematic rapes and mass killings of young Native children in Christian schools from the 1870s to the 1960s by Christian nuns and schoolteachers are seen as unworthy of attention, because they were given the gift of knowing Jesus Christ and their souls eternally saved as a result despite malnourishment, sexual abuse, physical abuse, and death.[668][669][670] The US and Canadian governments forcibly took Native children as young as seven from their families through armed military force to place them in Christian schools that subjected them to that treatment. That is, they learned to be subservient to the narcissism of Jesus Christ and so being physically and sexually abused or even killed by Christian nuns and Christian schoolteachers is seen as worthwhile for gaining the worship of Jesus Christ as their lord and

---

5. [668] Hayes, Leonard L. "American Indian and Alaskan Native Historical Trauma and an Adlerian Perspective." *Alfredadler.edu*, The Faculty of the Adler Graduate School, Sept. 2010, alfredadler.edu/sites/default/files/Hayes MP 2010.pdf.
6. [669] Bear, Charla. "American Indian Boarding Schools Haunt Many." *NPR*. NPR, 12 May 2008. Web. 2 Nov. 2015, https://www.npr.org/templates/story/story.php?storyId=16516865?storyId=16516865.
7. [670] Paquin, Mali Ilse. "Canada Confronts Its Dark History of Abuse in Residential Schools." *The Guardian*, Guardian News and Media, 6 June 2015, www.theguardian.com/world/2015/jun/06/canada-dark-of-history-residential-schools.

savior in Christian schools from Canada to the US.[671][672][673] Christianity's mission is to save the eternal soul, not the so-called sinful body in the physical world. The teachers reported they saw it as their duty to civilize the "savages" and do everything possible to remove their Native heritage from their names, their hairstyles, their language, and force them to watch movies in which their ancestors were depicted as rapists in wild west films.[674] The second problematic example would be the Holocaust. Despite the absolute barbarism of the Nazis in forcing Jewish people and others into gas chambers and killing approximately six million people in total; it is trivialized as less important than Jesus Christ's death upon the cross. *In other words, no matter how horrific, egregious, and unconscionable the brutality inflicted upon fellow human beings, what is of prominent importance for Christians is recognizing Jesus Christ's death on the cross as of a far greater loss.* All other forms of human cruelty and stupidity can be rationalized as the misanthropic non-answer of Original Sin and at no point should one ever question the divinity of Jesus Christ. Any and all forms of brutality by Christians themselves are the so-called "fake" Christians that Jesus Christ's self-contradictory teachings warned about. Any wrongdoing by Christians can conveniently be attributed to "fake" Christians in a vicious form of the No True Scotsman fallacy, since every criticism can be rebuffed by saying Jesus Christ warned about "fake" Christians and any attempt to point out negatives about Christianity would be seen as an attempt to deceive Christians away from their faith as a test from the carnal world.[675] These teachings are a tautology because at no point can Christianity ever be called wrong. No matter what horrific circumstances Christianity creates for non-Christians, it must always be seen as the truth.

It is crucial to note that the misanthropy of Original Sin helped as self-justification because Christian nuns and schoolteachers viewed Native children who were as young as seven years of age as deluded by Satan, prone to sinfulness for not accepting Jesus Christ as their lord and savior, and harboring evil in their heart for not believing in Jesus Christ. Thus, physical violence, child rape, forced starvation, cultural genocide of their traditions, and the sheer malice inflicted upon them was seen as saving their eternal souls from the damnation of hell and they could easily mollify their infliction of pain and suffering upon Native children through faith in Jesus Christ in their heart by recognizing they were also sinful human beings prone to error. The burden of teaching them to worship Jesus Christ would be a weighty

---

8. [671] Hayes, Leonard L. "American Indian and Alaskan Native Historical Trauma and an Adlerian Perspective." *Alfredadler.edu*, The Faculty of the Adler Graduate School, Sept. 2010, alfredadler.edu/sites/default/files/Hayes MP 2010.pdf.
9. [672] Bear, Charla. "American Indian Boarding Schools Haunt Many." *NPR*. NPR, 12 May 2008. Web. 2 Nov. 2015, https://www.npr.org/templates/story/story.php?storyId=16516865?storyId=16516865.
10. [673] Paquin, Mali Ilse. "Canada Confronts Its Dark History of Abuse in Residential Schools." *The Guardian*, Guardian News and Media, 6 June 2015, www.theguardian.com/world/2015/jun/06/canada-dark-of-history-residential-schools.
11. [674] Bear, Charla. "American Indian Boarding Schools Haunt Many." *NPR*. NPR, 12 May 2008. Web. 2 Nov. 2015, https://www.npr.org/templates/story/story.php?storyId=16516865?storyId=16516865.
12. [675] "No True Scotsman." *Https://Www.logicallyfallacious.com*, www.logicallyfallacious.com/tools/lp/Bo/LogicalFallacies/135/No-True-Scotsman.

responsibility in their minds that justified their violent tendencies because of the belief the Native children would go to heaven, even if the Christian nuns and schoolteachers murdered and raped them. In fact, some Christians have told me that they believe that torture and rape are a good moral act so long as the victim comes to accept Jesus Christ as their lord and savior.

Listing the documented evidence of Christian abuse of non-Christians often results in reactionary disavowal and assertions that "fake" Christians aren't true interpretations of the religious faith; a faith that claims to be openly interpretative.[676] The reactionary sentiment by Christians, using the circular reasoning that an openly interpretative moral system is not being interpreted correctly to display it's truthful message, is rooted in the narcissism of Jesus Christ's teachings. To be a Christian, you must believe that Jesus Christ's teachings are sacred and the best morals to live by; to do otherwise is to reject being a Christian. Unfortunately, this means that you must constantly reinterpret and take Jesus Christ's teachings from the Bible out of context in order to feel consistent with being a Christian.[677] This is a self-contradiction in Christian beliefs in that people are attempting to stay consistent with the identity of being Christians by reinterpreting the teachings of the Bible with the modernity that they live within so that they feel they're not contradicting the Bible. Yet, open interpretation allows for self-contradiction to the point that the original values become utterly meaningless. Since you must believe that Jesus Christ's teachings are the best; all new information discovered by science, new economic policies changing the shape of society, new changes in the moral structure of society like the role of women's rights, LGBT rights, and other new cultural changes from social movements must somehow conform to what Jesus Christ intended for Christians. The self-contradictory teachings need to be interpreted, reinterpreted, taken out of the original context in the Bible itself to become "parables" that proclaim "general truths" by Jesus instead of being viewed in a more literal sense like in ancient times before human advancements were made. The moral truths of Jesus Christ must supersede all others, so changing one's beliefs are viewed as becoming closer to the Abrahamic God and Jesus Christ than simply changing one's mind due to gaining new moral beliefs based on facts, reason, or compassion for other groups of people outside of the Christian faith.

The desire for consistency is what leads to placing Jesus's iconography everywhere. The desire for consistency and conformity to Jesus's teachings is central to Christianity. In order to feel consistent with Biblical teachings, even as the teachings are taken out of context or outright ignored, it is paradoxically for the sake of feeling consistent with being a Christian.[678][679] Jesus's self-contradictory teachings are left as vague generalizations for the sake

---

13. [676] "Circular Reasoning." *Https://Www.logicallyfallacious.com*, www.logicallyfallacious.com/tools/lp/Bo/LogicalFallacies/66/Circular-Reasoning.
14. [677] Cialdini, Robert B. "Chapter 3: Commitment and Consistency (52-95)" *Influence: Science and practice*. 4th ed., 21st Century Bks, 2002.
15. [678] Cialdini, Robert B. "Chapter 3: Commitment and Consistency (52-95)" *Influence: Science and practice*. 4th ed., 21st Century Bks, 2002.
16. [679] Kahneman, Daniel. *Thinking, fast and slow*. Farrar, Straus and Giroux, 2015.

of maintaining consistency with belief. A pernicious implication within the scope of this framework is that it is a thought crime to live by a morality outside of worship for Jesus Christ and belief in his teachings. This may be primarily why many Christians refuse to accept that Islam both believes in Jesus's teachings and celebrates Jesus Christ as their messiah in the Quran. Incidentally, this is the reason why there is such a reflexive reaction from conservative Christian groups to any new changes in society. New changes means distortions of what Jesus Christ intended for how Christians should behave and their specific denominations lead them to believe they're already doing their best in what is humanely possible to live by the teachings of Jesus Christ. Any further changes would be perceived as a distortion from the sinfulness of the carnal world that harms being consistent with the teachings of Jesus Christ. The submission to Jesus Christ, often touted by Christians as a sign of humility, is used to devalue, discourage, and disingenuously assert deceptive intent for all forms of cultural and scientific progress as a result.[680] The communal humility for refusing to change is seen as keeping faith with Jesus Christ's teachings from sinfulness and is a collective celebration of in-group narcissism for doing nothing.[681][682] It asserts negative beliefs upon those who work hard to fight for social change and all for the sake of self-worship for doing nothing of value.[683] Refusing to acknowledge new scientific facts that are discovered can be seen as upholding the standards of the Christian faith.[684] The collective narcissism of the in-group is further solidified by the teaching that Christians, and especially the specific denomination of those denying new knowledge, are the chosen people of the Abrahamic God and Jesus Christ.[685][686] *Impotence as self-worship.*[687]

Blasphemy and Cultural Recidivism

Blasphemy has always been a mark of shame for the Abrahamic faiths and elements of blasphemy can still be seen now. For example, Jews and Christians still forbid themselves from saying the Abrahamic God's name: Yahweh/Yehowah because they believe they'll somehow be cursed for it. Oddly, it is not forbidden to say in Islam. Commandments such as "There is no god but God" create intolerance toward other religious faiths. Incidentally, this has been more of an issue with Christianity and Islam than with Judaism.

---

17. [680] Nietzsche, Friedrich Wilhelm. *On the genealogy of morals: a polemical tract*. Translated by Ian Johnston, PDF, Richer Resources Publications, 2014.
18. [681] Nietzsche, Friedrich Wilhelm. *On the genealogy of morals: a polemical tract*. Translated by Ian Johnston, PDF, Richer Resources Publications, 2014.
19. [682] Ispas, Alexa. *Psychology and politics: a social identity perspective*. Psychology Press, 2014.
20. [683] Nietzsche, Friedrich Wilhelm. Chapter XXVI: THE PRIESTS (88-91). *Thus spake Zarathustra: a book for all and none*. Translated by Thomas Common, PDF ed., T. Common, 1908.
21. [684] Nietzsche, Friedrich Wilhelm. *THE ANTICHRIST*. Translated by H. L. Mencken, The Project Gutenberg, 2006.
22. [685] Nietzsche, Friedrich Wilhelm. *THE ANTICHRIST*. Translated by H. L. Mencken, The Project Gutenberg, 2006.
23. [686] Ispas, Alexa. *Psychology and politics: a social identity perspective*. Psychology Press, 2014.
24. [687] Nietzsche, Friedrich Wilhelm. *On the genealogy of morals: a polemical tract*. Translated by Ian Johnston, PDF, Richer Resources Publications, 2014.

Blasphemy remains a controversial issue within all human cultures and even in Western society. It helped create dehumanization campaigns by ignoring what other tribes, groups, and countries believed in and demonized others beliefs as devil worship. It encouraged hatred for others and condemned free thought. It helped enhance the colonialist agenda because proselytizing away from "devil worship" was seen as good and the human rights crimes were seen as less bad. Forced conversions of Native Americans, several parts of Africa, India, and other parts of the world served to justify and place a smokescreen upon human rights crimes of empires, if they were even considered at all. It gave a legitimate cause for violence and oppression and helps create unthinking obedience to committing cultural genocide upon out-groups. Nothing they can say or do is worthwhile unless they accept Jesus Christ as their lord and savior in Christianity. It creates a total lack of tolerance, a total lack of mutual respect, and serves to engender violence and mass death.

The concept of idolatry allows for bigotry towards others and is explicitly against democratic values. The attempts at syncretism of the Abrahamic faiths with democratic principles lead to cognitive dissonance and periods of cultural recidivism that hold democracy and innovation back for the sake of religious exaltation. East Asian cultures have stunned the West with their ability to modernize at a breakneck pace compared to the Western world. A possibility that Western countries have not given any analysis towards is the lack of Abrahamic religions interfering with the innovation and causing cultural recidivism within the East Asian countries spheres of political power. Blasphemy laws existed and were enacted at various points throughout European history including a 1977 blasphemy case in Great Britain.[688] Abrahamic precepts on marriage, women's roles, and explicit references to the Abrahamic God have continued to be argued and touted throughout the West; only recently in Western history have social ills in regards to these issues been questioned and slowly ameliorated. Regardless, while Westerners are far too willing to mock images of the Islamic prophet that Muslims hold in equal regard to Jesus Christ, and they're willing to make asinine comments towards the gods and goddesses of Hinduism, Westerners are far less willing to mock images of Jesus Christ because of the culture of blasphemy that has been substituted and subsumed into Western cultural norms. Even staunch Atheists of the Western world are completely unwilling to mock or criticize anything regarding the image and values of Jesus Christ. They're pleased with mocking the "foreign" religions and "foreign" imagery and they're perfectly willing to broadcast such beliefs online in comments and in videos. When it comes to the image of Jesus Christ? Only a scant few would ever do so and those who would mock Jesus Christ would be treated with scorn. Religious fervor towards such insults still exists within certain Western societies. The 2005 event of "Jerry Springer: The Opera" which fundamentalist Christians of Great Britain, under the group Christian Voice, harshly objected to because of its depictions of Christian saints.[689] Images of Mohammad are perfectly fine to extol "freedom of speech" but images of Baphomet (ironically, yet another insulting image of Mohammad made by the

---

25. [688] *Christian Voice - Jerry Springer the Opera*, Christian Voice, www.repentuk.com/springer.html.
26. [689] *Christian Voice - Jerry Springer the Opera*, Christian Voice, www.repentuk.com/springer.html.

West), insulting images related to Jesus Christ, and any symbolism that is offensive to the image of Jesus Christ is treated with derision and seen as going too far.[690][691][692] For all the mockery by conservative groups about the special treatment of minority groups, the only image that truly gets special treatment is Jesus Christ and by extension Christianity.

One noteworthy incident occurred in 2012, when a professor in Florida Atlantic University, Deandre Poole, attempted to teach the impact of symbolism on human behavior in his intercultural communications class, a student apparently threatened his life and went to local media outlets.[693] Professor Poole became a controversial figure overnight with religious groups demanding his firing and he was put on administrative leave for his own safety due to racist hate mail and rampant death threats on his life.[694][695] The controversy remained in the purview of the US public for an entire year and Christian organizations continue to demand his firing for his insult towards Jesus Christ and Christianity.[696] The lesson that led to this intense backlash was Professor Poole asking his class to write "JESUS" on a piece of paper and asking them to stomp upon it.[697] He then asked the classroom to write why they were against conducting such an action. The lesson plan was to show them a hands-on approach to understanding how symbolism impacts their daily lives and no one was punished for not conducting the suggestion.[698] Professor Poole, a devout Christian, was attempting to teach the students the extent of symbolism's influence on everyday life but one student, who allegedly

---

27. [690] "Goat-Headed Satanic Statue Sparks Protests in Detroit - BBC Newsbeat." *BBC*, BBC, 27 July 2015, www.bbc.co.uk/newsbeat/article/33674383/goat-headed-satanic-statue-sparks-protests-in-detroit.
28. [691] Hicap Mon, Jonah. "Christian Protesters Denounce Unveiling of Huge Goat-Headed Satan Statue in Detroit." *Christian News on Christian Today*, Christian Today, 27 July 2015, www.christiantoday.com/article/christian-protesters-denounce-unveiling-of-huge-goat-headed-satan-statue-in-detroit/60228.htm.
29. [692] Reuters. "Satanists Unveil Sculpture in Detroit after Rejection at Oklahoma Capitol." *The Guardian*, Guardian News and Media, 26 July 2015, www.theguardian.com/us-news/2015/jul/26/satanic-temple-sculpture-detroit-oklahoma.
30. [693] Kingkade, Tyler. "'Stomp On Jesus' Controversy Gets Worse." *The Huffington Post*, TheHuffingtonPost.com, 2 Apr. 2013, www.huffingtonpost.com/2013/04/01/stomp-on-jesus-professor_n_2990116.html.
31. [694] Kingkade, Tyler. "University Decides On Prof Involved In 'Stomp On Jesus' Controversy." *The Huffington Post*, TheHuffingtonPost.com, 24 June 2013, www.huffingtonpost.com/2013/06/24/deandre-poole-fau-stomp-on-jesus_n_3490263.html.
32. [695] Kingkade, Tyler. "'Stomp On Jesus' Controversy Gets Worse." *The Huffington Post*, TheHuffingtonPost.com, 2 Apr. 2013, www.huffingtonpost.com/2013/04/01/stomp-on-jesus-professor_n_2990116.html.
33. [696] Kingkade, Tyler. "University Decides On Prof Involved In 'Stomp On Jesus' Controversy." *The Huffington Post*, TheHuffingtonPost.com, 24 June 2013, www.huffingtonpost.com/2013/06/24/deandre-poole-fau-stomp-on-jesus_n_3490263.html.
34. [697] Kingkade, Tyler. "'Stomp On Jesus' Controversy Gets Worse." *The Huffington Post*, TheHuffingtonPost.com, 2 Apr. 2013, www.huffingtonpost.com/2013/04/01/stomp-on-jesus-professor_n_2990116.html.
35. [698] Kingkade, Tyler. "'Stomp On Jesus' Controversy Gets Worse." *The Huffington Post*, TheHuffingtonPost.com, 2 Apr. 2013, www.huffingtonpost.com/2013/04/01/stomp-on-jesus-professor_n_2990116.html.

threatened his life, was kicked out of the class for his behavior and the student then took to the local media to make a misrepresentation of what actually occurred.[699]

It should be made clear that it wasn't an image of Jesus Christ but the name "JESUS" written on a piece of paper. Furthermore, the death threats, demands that he be fired, and the professor being forced into administrative leave due to the Campus administration's fears for his safety show that the US can and will act in the same manner as Iranian protestors who demand the persecution of cartoonists for drawing the Prophet Mohammad.[700] This event illustrates the weaknesses of Western democratic values when controversies regarding religious blasphemy occur within Western societies. Can the US really condemn protests over Mohammad in the Middle East while ignoring the hypocrisy of defending death threats and protests over Christian icons? Do Western values stand for freedom to criticize all religions except for Christianity? Are we to just ignore special pleading arguments regarding Christian symbols and call the professor an idiot for a college lecture that was meant to critique the very impact of such symbols?[701] Why should Christianity be exempt from criticism?

Needless to say, while the Middle East should improve upon its views, the public of the West, especially in the United States, hasn't gained a more tolerant view of freedom of speech where religion is concerned. The US public is quick to either excessively ridicule or defend Islam and other religious faiths but Christianity remains to receive a free pass with no objections and a total lack of criticism when it creates its own controversies with racism and death threats over blasphemy. This is not an isolated case. In 2015, there were protests over a statue of Baphomet being made in Detroit.[702] A statue of a fictional demon is worth a large protest and this is explicitly for religious reasons pertaining to blasphemy.

Blasphemy's issues aren't exclusive to embarrassing political controversies that could cause the rest of the world to view the West's values as hypocritical. A more pernicious and damaging folly of blasphemy is the lack of scrutiny on the historical record regarding the Bible. Jewish people are compelled to believe that the holy land is given to them by God; Christians are compelled to believe that Jesus's miracles and resurrections are at least true events even if the rest of the Bible is not true. These beliefs have real world impacts and consequences. The right to return is a religious belief that Jewish people strongly believe in and Christians do believe that a Second Coming of Jesus Christ will occur within the holy land.

36. [699] Kingkade, Tyler. "'Stomp On Jesus' Controversy Gets Worse." *The Huffington Post*, TheHuffingtonPost.com, 2 Apr. 2013, www.huffingtonpost.com/2013/04/01/stomp-on-jesus-professor_n_2990116.html.
37. [700] Kingkade, Tyler. "University Decides On Prof Involved In 'Stomp On Jesus' Controversy." *The Huffington Post*, TheHuffingtonPost.com, 24 June 2013, www.huffingtonpost.com/2013/06/24/deandre-poole-fau-stomp-on-jesus_n_3490263.html.
38. [701] "Special Pleading." *Https://Www.logicallyfallacious.com*, www.logicallyfallacious.com/tools/lp/Bo/LogicalFallacies/163/Special-Pleading.
39. [702] "Goat-Headed Satanic Statue Sparks Protests in Detroit - BBC Newsbeat." *BBC*, BBC, 27 July 2015, www.bbc.co.uk/newsbeat/article/33674383/goat-headed-satanic-statue-sparks-protests-in-detroit.

As such, a massive Evangelical campaign across the world from the Middle East to Asia is being conducted to gain converts for the Second Coming of Christ under the belief that Jesus Christ will come back as the world ends.[703][704][705] Millions upon millions of people would soundly reject any historical evidence that contradicts the existence of Jesus Christ or the Jewish right to return. Thus, history isn't observed through objective evidence but through a religious veneer that has no credibility beyond proclaiming itself to be the inerrant word of a Creator deity. The same is true for Islam's claims. Muslims convert on the basis of an end of the world in which Jesus will return and the Al-Mahdi will appear to save the chosen people. Moreover, an actual assessment of history will be rejected for the sake of a belief in miracles during the ancient period of the Middle East.

These unsubstantiated beliefs continue to weaken democratic principles, hold scientific studies back, require theological symbolism to be erroneously placed upon everything to satisfy an in-group fetish for self-reverence in order to believe that a specific religion is the best in the world, and continue to create problems for the rights of women, transgender people, and homosexuals. Meanwhile churches protect pedophiles throughout the world, the use of religious freedom in other democratic countries is being used to justify forced conversions, male genital mutilation still continues to occur for the sake of a Kingdom of God, and any historicity that doesn't involve the existence of Jesus Christ is outright rejected despite there being little evidence that the figure of Jesus Christ existed and the implausibility of the immaculate conception and resurrection story. Christian notions of blasphemy have been sublimated into Western culture and remain a strong force in ignoring the implausibility of the Jesus story. Unlike Mohammad, it is offensive to question or ridicule anything about Jesus Christ in Western culture. Westerners can't have it both ways, freedom of speech to criticize religion should exist for all religious beliefs. Religious tolerance for all religious backgrounds to maintain equality would be implicitly forcing others religious beliefs upon the mainstream society and therefore would be a detriment to democratic freedoms.

Jesus Christ and Love

Matthew 10:16-37 KJV

16 Behold, I send you forth as sheep in the midst of wolves: be ye therefore wise as serpents, and harmless as doves.
17 But beware of men: for they will deliver you up to the councils, and they will scourge you in their synagogues;

---

40. [703] Bukhari, Shujaat. "Pastor Admits to Conversion by Missionaries in Kashmir." *The Hindu*, The Hindu, 2 Aug. 2016, www.thehindu.com/news/national/pastor-admits-to-conversion-by-missionaries-in-kashmir/article2640084.ece.
41. [704] Goldberg, Philip. "Missionaries in India: Conversion or Coercion?" *The Huffington Post*, TheHuffingtonPost.com, 19 Feb. 2014, www.huffingtonpost.com/philip-goldberg/missionaries-in-india_b_4470448.html.
42. [705] Neary, Sarah. "Forced to Convert: How American Missionaries Really Treat Indigenous Akha Children." *Intercontinental Cry*, IC, 23 Apr. 2013, intercontinentalcry.org/forced-to-convert-how-american-missionaries-really-treat-indigenous-akha-children/.

18 And ye shall be brought before governors and kings for my sake, for a testimony against them and the Gentiles.
19 But when they deliver you up, take no thought how or what ye shall speak: for it shall be given you in that same hour what ye shall speak.
20 For it is not ye that speak, but the Spirit of your Father which speaketh in you.
21 And the brother shall deliver up the brother to death, and the father the child: and the children shall rise up against their parents, and cause them to be put to death.
22 And ye shall be hated of all men for my name's sake: but he that endureth to the end shall be saved.
23 But when they persecute you in this city, flee ye into another: for verily I say unto you, Ye shall not have gone over the cities of Israel, till the Son of man be come.
24 The disciple is not above his master, nor the servant above his lord.
25 It is enough for the disciple that he be as his master, and the servant as his lord. If they have called the master of the house Beelzebub, how much more shall they call them of his household?
26 Fear them not therefore: for there is nothing covered, that shall not be revealed; and hid, that shall not be known.
27 What I tell you in darkness, that speak ye in light: and what ye hear in the ear, that preach ye upon the housetops.
28 And fear not them which kill the body, but are not able to kill the soul: but rather fear him which is able to destroy both soul and body in hell.
29 Are not two sparrows sold for a farthing? and one of them shall not fall on the ground without your Father.
30 But the very hairs of your head are all numbered.
31 Fear ye not therefore, ye are of more value than many sparrows.
32 Whosoever therefore shall confess me before men, him will I confess also before my Father which is in heaven.
33 But whosoever shall deny me before men, him will I also deny before my Father which is in heaven.
34 Think not that I am come to send peace on earth: I came not to send peace, but a sword.
35 For I am come to set a man at variance against his father, and the daughter against her mother, and the daughter in law against her mother in law.
36 And a man's foes shall be they of his own household.
37 He that loveth father or mother more than me is not worthy of me: and he that loveth son or daughter more than me is not worthy of me.[706]

The following Biblical verses further corroborate the narcissism of Jesus Christ. One of the most troubling aspects of Christianity is the normalization of loving Jesus Christ more than your parents, your spouse, and even your own children. Jesus's narcissism goes so far that he argues in favor of people destroying the respect and love of their own household for the sole sake of worshipping him. No man of peace, no loving preacher, and no loving deity would ever proclaim that you must love them more than your family. In fact, for most religions, the feelings of love for one's family and the feelings of worship for a deity would be presented as synonymous with each other. No distinction would be made between loving one's significant other, their parents, or their children and loving their deity; instead the feelings of love would be attributed to the power of the deity itself. By contrast, Christianity makes it clear that loving Jesus is separate from loving your family and that Jesus must take priority above your family. What else can this teaching be called besides Jesus Christ's unfettered narcissism?

---

43. [706] "BibleGateway." *Bible Gateway*, Bible Gateway Blog, www.biblegateway.com/passage/?search=Matthew 10&version=KJV.

It is quite possible that the greatest barrier to Christian conversions is this deplorable message from Jesus Christ. Any non-Christian would find the preaching above to be the ravings of a hateful madman with an overinflated ego and delusions of grandeur. In fact, it was this passage that led me to conclude that Jesus Christ and his teachings were morally bankrupt, hateful, and that they were espoused by a narcissist. I don't say that out of animosity or loathing, the preaching above is genuinely some of the most outlandish and hateful teachings that have ever been worshipped in human history. However, incredulousness on a non-Christian's part is not an argument, so allow me to ask some general questions regarding the teachings that Jesus spoke in Matthew 10:

Why did Jesus Christ make the explicit distinction between loving him as a God more than loving your family? (Matthew 10:20-22, Matthew 10:35-37) Why would a loving God ever go into copious details about this distinction and demand you do it under threat that he'll reject you from being able to go to heaven? (Matthew 10:16-37) Who else but a raving narcissist would declare you unworthy if you love your parents or your child(ren) more than him? (Matthew 10:37) Why explicitly teach about creating division and animosity in one's family for his sake? (Matthew 10:21, Matthew 10:35-37) How can Jesus Christ's teachings be peaceful when he explicitly advocates for violence against one's own family and declares that his teachings have brought a sword? (Matthew 10:34-37) In fact, if his teachings are peaceful, why does Jesus Christ himself assert that his teachings won't bring peace and then uses a parable of a sword about his teachings bringing violence? (Matthew 10:34) Why believe Jesus Christ's teachings are peaceful, when Jesus Christ himself says they are not meant to bring peace? (Matthew 10:34)

In fact, if all of this is misguided or taken out of context, then you would have to dismiss everything Jesus Christ actually says within Matthew 10 in order to assert that.[707] It is simply open interpretation for the convenience of the Christian to mollify themselves and ignore the explicit call to violence by Jesus Christ himself, and Jesus Christ makes this call to violence for the sake of his own worship. Modern Christians are selectively dismissing parts of Jesus Christ's actual teachings in order to paradoxically convince themselves that they're keeping to the "true interpretation" of the Christian faith. Jesus Christ's narcissism and hateful teachings is clear in these texts and that's precisely why the self-contradictory ideas of "open interpretation" is made for modern Christians in order to convince themselves that Jesus Christ's truth claims are real, meaningful, and that he wasn't simply a narcissist with a God complex. Open interpretation in Christianity simply exists as willful self-delusion to convince themselves that they're right. The next section shall examine the self-contradictory teachings of Jesus Christ's Beatitudes.

The Sermon on the Mount

---

44. [707] "BibleGateway." *Bible Gateway*, Bible Gateway Blog, www.biblegateway.com/passage/?search=Matthew 10&version=KJV.

Matthew 5:1-48 KJV

5 And seeing the multitudes, he went up into a mountain: and when he was set, his disciples came unto him:

² And he opened his mouth, and taught them, saying,

³ Blessed are the poor in spirit: for theirs is the kingdom of heaven.

⁴ Blessed are they that mourn: for they shall be comforted.

⁵ Blessed are the meek: for they shall inherit the earth.

⁶ Blessed are they which do hunger and thirst after righteousness: for they shall be filled.

⁷ Blessed are the merciful: for they shall obtain mercy.

⁸ Blessed are the pure in heart: for they shall see God.

⁹ Blessed are the peacemakers: for they shall be called the children of God.

¹⁰ Blessed are they which are persecuted for righteousness' sake: for theirs is the kingdom of heaven.

¹¹ Blessed are ye, when men shall revile you, and persecute you, and shall say all manner of evil against you falsely, for my sake.

¹² Rejoice, and be exceeding glad: for great is your reward in heaven: for so persecuted they the prophets which were before you.

¹³ Ye are the salt of the earth: but if the salt have lost his savour, wherewith shall it be salted? it is thenceforth good for nothing, but to be cast out, and to be trodden under foot of men.

¹⁴ Ye are the light of the world. A city that is set on an hill cannot be hid.

¹⁵ Neither do men light a candle, and put it under a bushel, but on a candlestick; and it giveth light unto all that are in the house.

¹⁶ Let your light so shine before men, that they may see your good works, and glorify your Father which is in heaven.

¹⁷ Think not that I am come to destroy the law, or the prophets: I am not come to destroy, but to fulfil.

¹⁸ For verily I say unto you, Till heaven and earth pass, one jot or one tittle shall in no wise pass from the law, till all be fulfilled.

¹⁹ Whosoever therefore shall break one of these least commandments, and shall teach men so, he shall be called the least in the kingdom of heaven: but whosoever shall do and teach them, the same shall be called great in the kingdom of heaven.

²⁰ For I say unto you, That except your righteousness shall exceed the righteousness of the scribes and Pharisees, ye shall in no case enter into the kingdom of heaven.

²¹ Ye have heard that it was said of them of old time, Thou shalt not kill; and whosoever shall kill shall be in danger of the judgment:

²² But I say unto you, That whosoever is angry with his brother without a cause shall be in danger of the judgment: and whosoever shall say to his brother, Raca, shall be in danger of the council: but whosoever shall say, Thou fool, shall be in danger of hell fire.

²³ Therefore if thou bring thy gift to the altar, and there rememberest that thy brother hath ought against thee;

²⁴ Leave there thy gift before the altar, and go thy way; first be reconciled to thy brother, and then come and offer thy gift.

²⁵ Agree with thine adversary quickly, whiles thou art in the way with him; lest at any time the adversary deliver thee to the judge, and the judge deliver thee to the officer, and thou be cast into prison.

²⁶ Verily I say unto thee, Thou shalt by no means come out thence, till thou hast paid the uttermost farthing.

²⁷ Ye have heard that it was said by them of old time, Thou shalt not commit adultery:

²⁸ But I say unto you, That whosoever looketh on a woman to lust after her hath committed adultery with her already in his heart.

²⁹ And if thy right eye offend thee, pluck it out, and cast it from thee: for it is profitable for thee that one of thy members should perish, and not that thy whole body should be cast into hell.

³⁰ And if thy right hand offend thee, cut it off, and cast it from thee: for it is profitable for thee that one of thy members should perish, and not that thy whole body should be cast into hell.

³¹ It hath been said, Whosoever shall put away his wife, let him give her a writing of divorcement:

³² But I say unto you, That whosoever shall put away his wife, saving for the cause of fornication, causeth her to commit adultery: and whosoever shall marry her that is divorced committeth adultery.

³³ Again, ye have heard that it hath been said by them of old time, Thou shalt not forswear thyself, but shalt perform unto the Lord thine oaths:
³⁴ But I say unto you, Swear not at all; neither by heaven; for it is God's throne:
³⁵ Nor by the earth; for it is his footstool: neither by Jerusalem; for it is the city of the great King.
³⁶ Neither shalt thou swear by thy head, because thou canst not make one hair white or black.
³⁷ But let your communication be, Yea, yea; Nay, nay: for whatsoever is more than these cometh of evil.
³⁸ Ye have heard that it hath been said, An eye for an eye, and a tooth for a tooth:
³⁹ But I say unto you, That ye resist not evil: but whosoever shall smite thee on thy right cheek, turn to him the other also.
⁴⁰ And if any man will sue thee at the law, and take away thy coat, let him have thy cloak also.
⁴¹ And whosoever shall compel thee to go a mile, go with him twain.
⁴² Give to him that asketh thee, and from him that would borrow of thee turn not thou away.
⁴³ Ye have heard that it hath been said, Thou shalt love thy neighbour, and hate thine enemy.
⁴⁴ But I say unto you, Love your enemies, bless them that curse you, do good to them that hate you, and pray for them which despitefully use you, and persecute you;
⁴⁵ That ye may be the children of your Father which is in heaven: for he maketh his sun to rise on the evil and on the good, and sendeth rain on the just and on the unjust.
⁴⁶ For if ye love them which love you, what reward have ye? do not even the publicans the same?
⁴⁷ And if ye salute your brethren only, what do ye more than others? do not even the publicans so?
⁴⁸ Be ye therefore perfect, even as your Father which is in heaven is perfect.
6 Take heed that ye do not your alms before men, to be seen of them: otherwise ye have no reward of your Father which is in heaven.
² Therefore when thou doest thine alms, do not sound a trumpet before thee, as the hypocrites do in the synagogues and in the streets, that they may have glory of men. Verily I say unto you, They have their reward.
³ But when thou doest alms, let not thy left hand know what thy right hand doeth:
⁴ That thine alms may be in secret: and thy Father which seeth in secret himself shall reward thee openly.
⁵ And when thou prayest, thou shalt not be as the hypocrites are: for they love to pray standing in the synagogues and in the corners of the streets, that they may be seen of men. Verily I say unto you, They have their reward.
⁶ But thou, when thou prayest, enter into thy closet, and when thou hast shut thy door, pray to thy Father which is in secret; and thy Father which seeth in secret shall reward thee openly.
⁷ But when ye pray, use not vain repetitions, as the heathen do: for they think that they shall be heard for their much speaking.
⁸ Be not ye therefore like unto them: for your Father knoweth what things ye have need of, before ye ask him.
⁹ After this manner therefore pray ye: Our Father which art in heaven, Hallowed be thy name.
¹⁰ Thy kingdom come, Thy will be done in earth, as it is in heaven.
¹¹ Give us this day our daily bread.
¹² And forgive us our debts, as we forgive our debtors.
¹³ And lead us not into temptation, but deliver us from evil: For thine is the kingdom, and the power, and the glory, for ever. Amen.
¹⁴ For if ye forgive men their trespasses, your heavenly Father will also forgive you:
¹⁵ But if ye forgive not men their trespasses, neither will your Father forgive your trespasses.
¹⁶ Moreover when ye fast, be not, as the hypocrites, of a sad countenance: for they disfigure their faces, that they may appear unto men to fast. Verily I say unto you, They have their reward.
¹⁷ But thou, when thou fastest, anoint thine head, and wash thy face;
¹⁸ That thou appear not unto men to fast, but unto thy Father which is in secret: and thy Father, which seeth in secret, shall reward thee openly.
¹⁹ Lay not up for yourselves treasures upon earth, where moth and rust doth corrupt, and where thieves break through and steal:
²⁰ But lay up for yourselves treasures in heaven, where neither moth nor rust doth corrupt, and where thieves do not break through nor steal:
²¹ For where your treasure is, there will your heart be also.
²² The light of the body is the eye: if therefore thine eye be single, thy whole body shall be full of light.

²³ But if thine eye be evil, thy whole body shall be full of darkness. If therefore the light that is in thee be darkness, how great is that darkness!
²⁴ No man can serve two masters: for either he will hate the one, and love the other; or else he will hold to the one, and despise the other. Ye cannot serve God and mammon.
²⁵ Therefore I say unto you, Take no thought for your life, what ye shall eat, or what ye shall drink; nor yet for your body, what ye shall put on. Is not the life more than meat, and the body than raiment?
²⁶ Behold the fowls of the air: for they sow not, neither do they reap, nor gather into barns; yet your heavenly Father feedeth them. Are ye not much better than they?
²⁷ Which of you by taking thought can add one cubit unto his stature?
²⁸ And why take ye thought for raiment? Consider the lilies of the field, how they grow; they toil not, neither do they spin:
²⁹ And yet I say unto you, That even Solomon in all his glory was not arrayed like one of these.
³⁰ Wherefore, if God so clothe the grass of the field, which to day is, and to morrow is cast into the oven, shall he not much more clothe you, O ye of little faith?
³¹ Therefore take no thought, saying, What shall we eat? or, What shall we drink? or, Wherewithal shall we be clothed?
³² (For after all these things do the Gentiles seek:) for your heavenly Father knoweth that ye have need of all these things.
³³ But seek ye first the kingdom of God, and his righteousness; and all these things shall be added unto you.
³⁴ Take therefore no thought for the morrow: for the morrow shall take thought for the things of itself. Sufficient unto the day is the evil thereof.

7 Judge not, that ye be not judged.
² For with what judgment ye judge, ye shall be judged: and with what measure ye mete, it shall be measured to you again.
³ And why beholdest thou the mote that is in thy brother's eye, but considerest not the beam that is in thine own eye?
⁴ Or how wilt thou say to thy brother, Let me pull out the mote out of thine eye; and, behold, a beam is in thine own eye?
⁵ Thou hypocrite, first cast out the beam out of thine own eye; and then shalt thou see clearly to cast out the mote out of thy brother's eye.
⁶ Give not that which is holy unto the dogs, neither cast ye your pearls before swine, lest they trample them under their feet, and turn again and rend you.
⁷ Ask, and it shall be given you; seek, and ye shall find; knock, and it shall be opened unto you:
⁸ For every one that asketh receiveth; and he that seeketh findeth; and to him that knocketh it shall be opened.
⁹ Or what man is there of you, whom if his son ask bread, will he give him a stone?
¹⁰ Or if he ask a fish, will he give him a serpent?
¹¹ If ye then, being evil, know how to give good gifts unto your children, how much more shall your Father which is in heaven give good things to them that ask him?
¹² Therefore all things whatsoever ye would that men should do to you, do ye even so to them: for this is the law and the prophets.
¹³ Enter ye in at the strait gate: for wide is the gate, and broad is the way, that leadeth to destruction, and many there be which go in thereat:
¹⁴ Because strait is the gate, and narrow is the way, which leadeth unto life, and few there be that find it.
¹⁵ Beware of false prophets, which come to you in sheep's clothing, but inwardly they are ravening wolves.
¹⁶ Ye shall know them by their fruits. Do men gather grapes of thorns, or figs of thistles?
¹⁷ Even so every good tree bringeth forth good fruit; but a corrupt tree bringeth forth evil fruit.
¹⁸ A good tree cannot bring forth evil fruit, neither can a corrupt tree bring forth good fruit.
¹⁹ Every tree that bringeth not forth good fruit is hewn down, and cast into the fire.
²⁰ Wherefore by their fruits ye shall know them.
²¹ Not every one that saith unto me, Lord, Lord, shall enter into the kingdom of heaven; but he that doeth the will of my Father which is in heaven.
²² Many will say to me in that day, Lord, Lord, have we not prophesied in thy name? and in thy name have cast out devils? and in thy name done many wonderful works?

²³ *And then will I profess unto them, I never knew you: depart from me, ye that work iniquity.*
²⁴ *Therefore whosoever heareth these sayings of mine, and doeth them, I will liken him unto a wise man, which built his house upon a rock:*
²⁵ *And the rain descended, and the floods came, and the winds blew, and beat upon that house; and it fell not: for it was founded upon a rock.*
²⁶ *And every one that heareth these sayings of mine, and doeth them not, shall be likened unto a foolish man, which built his house upon the sand:*
²⁷ *And the rain descended, and the floods came, and the winds blew, and beat upon that house; and it fell: and great was the fall of it.*[708]

    The Sermon on the Mount is overtly self-contradictory. If you follow one set of instructions on how to be a good Christian then you will be contradicting the other set of instructions. People have constantly interpreted and reinterpreted Jesus's teachings to find some hidden meaning to stay true to the Christian faith but what you're really doing is moving the goalposts to constantly re-contextualize, reframe, and change the meaning to suit your own beliefs about Jesus Christ.

    You must always strive for "perfection" to enter the Kingdom of God but you'll always be contradicting the steps towards being a good Christian (Matthew 5:48). As a result, you must always seek Jesus's forgiveness because you're committing thought crimes when you have normal and healthy sexual desires (Matthew 5:28), and you're speaking wrongly when you make any attempt at asserting self worth. For prayer, should you be speaking only in "yea, yea" and "nay, nay" (Matthew 5:33 – 5:37) or are you being one of the so-called "hypocrites" when speaking in "vain repetitions"? (Matthew 6:7 – 6:13) Should you turn the other cheek when wronged (Matthew 5:39) and love your enemies (Matthew 5:44) or return any behavior that wronged you with a response of your own? (Matthew 7:12) Should you rejoice in persecution (Matthew 5:10 – 5:12) or avoid being tried and persecuted for your beliefs at all costs? (Matthew 5:25) Moreover, even evangelicals and other Biblical literalists would never take Matthew 5:29 – 5:30 literally and therefore the most extreme Bible worshippers require a degree of open interpretation because of how disastrous those verses ultimately would be because the literal interpretation is self-mutilation by cutting off one's right eye and right hand to remove evil.

    Some Christians believe that this is proof of the profoundness of the teachings, because so many fail at them and because they seem challenging. I'm afraid that they're just desperately trying to apply the Sermon to the highest of esteem when it fails to coexist with reality. That is one of the primary reasons why the Bible has become so openly interpretative to the extent that it loses its original meaning. Instead of acknowledging the self-contradictions, people are attempting to give their own meaning on why such passages shouldn't be outright rejected as self-refuting. It is an attempt to stay consistent with being a Christian and believing that there is some truly divine aspect of Christianity, when it is really just glorifying a self-

---

45. [708] "BibleGateway." *Bible Gateway*, Bible Gateway Blog, www.biblegateway.com/passage/?search=Matthew 5&version=KJV.

contradiction that has no basis in reality and refutes itself even when people try to follow it. It should be clear that these teachings cannot even be used as axioms for good moral behavior precisely because they self-contradict on the most basic areas. If you do one then you fail at the other and that is why open interpretation – an explicit use of personal preference and acquiescence to self-contradiction – is allowed in an attempt to feel consistent with biblical teachings.

    The contradiction worsens with Jesus's explicit instructions teaching people to be perfect like God; people seek to be perfect while expecting their own human limitations to always be imperfect. This circular reasoning may cause people to constantly self-criticize and self-blame when failing an overtly contradictory set of teachings. Modern psychology has found that the constant pursuit of perfectionism can cause mental weariness and self-loathing with being unable to fulfill the perfection.[709][710] In this context, you would be predisposed to feeling self-loathing for constantly failing an inherently paradoxical set of values that cannot be satisfied and you may perceive it as an unavoidable aspect of being a sinful human being. No matter what, you will fail at being a good Christian and why should you feel humility for your failure when you will constantly have to despise yourself regardless of what you do?[711] How can that be healthy for you? How can that be a good teaching for you or your loved ones? Is constantly despising yourself necessary to be a good person?[712]

    The supposed peaceful nature of the Sermon, touted by many people outside of the Christian faith and not merely Christians themselves, is entirely false. Jesus tacitly objectifies women in his teachings by making it a thought crime for a man to have natural sexual thoughts of a woman who isn't explicitly his wife. (Matthew 5:27-32) Jesus condemns women to a permanent state of being viewed as adulterous should they marry anyone after divorcing and says any man who marries a divorced woman is committing adultery too. (Matthew 5:27-32) These teachings are explicitly about the roles of men and women in marriage, they are teachings that objectify women, they lead to limiting women's freedom in choosing their spouses, and explicitly endorse the belief in thought crimes regarding men's normal sexual desires and the status of women who are divorced or unmarried. This is an unnecessary and openly prejudicial belief system that causes pointless suffering and mental weariness for the people who believe in these teachings.[713] The teaching is a thought crime that also leads to unnecessary self-shaming and guilt for simply having thoughts when people don't have any

---

46. [709] Lee, Kristen. "The Dangers of Perfectionism." *Psychology Today*, Sussex Publishers, www.psychologytoday.com/us/blog/rethink-your-way-the-good-life/201807/the-dangers-perfectionism.
47. [710] Knaus, Bill. "Escape the Guilt Trap." *Psychology Today*, Sussex Publishers, www.psychologytoday.com/us/blog/science-and-sensibility/201401/escape-the-guilt-trap.
48. [711] Nietzsche, Friedrich. Morality as Anti-Nature (21-26). *Twilight of the Idols*. Amazon Digital Services LLC.
49. [712] Nietzsche, Friedrich Wilhelm. *On the genealogy of morals: a polemical tract*. Translated by Ian Johnston, PDF, Richer Resources Publications, 2014.
50. [713] Nietzsche, Friedrich Wilhelm. *On the genealogy of morals: a polemical tract*. Translated by Ian Johnston, PDF, Richer Resources Publications, 2014.

desire to cheat on their spouse. Moreover, it teaches Christians that liking and desiring the opposite sex is wrong because you're not married to them and you may constantly despise yourself for what is an ordinary activity when trying to build a relationship with someone else or for simply imagining a fellow adult in a sexual manner. Please note that this isn't even delving into the rule against homosexuals that Jesus himself preaches in alternative narrations of the Sermon on the Mount.[714] (Mark 10:6-9)

    He teaches that Christians who face persecution will enter the Kingdom in Heaven but then says it is just as moral to lie and agree with the demands of officers, judges, and courts so that you aren't persecuted. Jesus teaches not to judge others or you will be judged too, but he also teaches people to look for hypocrisies everywhere from other people in regards to proper prayer sessions. Moreover, how can you ascertain false prophets if you aren't making judgments about what people do? How can you believe that a woman who remarries after divorcing is committing a wrong according to Jesus himself without judging her for her actions? He judges the Jews of his contemporary time as hypocrites and argues that you should look out for false prophets; thus you would have to constantly judge others to ascertain their degree of truthfulness or falsehood. He explicitly teaches that poverty is good and that people who starve are blessed and on the righteous path to heaven; he explicitly says that you should give no thought to feeding yourself, clothing yourself, and that these will eventually come with prayer and that it will be corrected in heaven regardless. Jesus essentially celebrates poverty as a form of innocence and goodness. It is a perception that subjecting oneself to starvation, exposure to terrible weather, and extreme poverty is genuinely good for the sake of entering heaven. This is a celebration of self-torture and perceives all capitalistic gains under a veneer of evil.[715] The most absurd, and idiotic, teaching is to pluck out one's right eye or to cut off one's right hand. If Jesus had meant this part to be taken literally, and there was no open interpretation allowed, then would you cut off your right hand or pluck out your right eye?

    All of these contradictions are probably ignored due to the theological-induced blindness of believing that the Bible is of divine origin, that Jesus is divine, and that the Bible itself has some component of divinity within its teachings.[716] The notion of "theological-induced blindness" is one I've borrowed and utilized upon theology from the explanation of theory-induced blindness in Daniel Kahneman's book, *Thinking Fast and Slow*. That is, when you come upon a situation where the actions don't fit the model of a theory, you simply assume there is a perfectly good explanation without inquiring further.[717] It should be noted that it would also constitute an argument from ignorance; that is, you assume there is some

---

51. [714] "BibleGateway." *Mark 10 KJV - - Bible Gateway*, www.biblegateway.com/passage/?search=mark 10&version=KJV.
52. [715] Nietzsche, Friedrich Wilhelm. *On the genealogy of morals: a polemical tract*. Translated by Ian Johnston, PDF, Richer Resources Publications, 2014.
53. [716] Kahneman, Daniel. Chapter 25: Bernoulli's Errors (269-277). *Thinking, fast and slow*. Farrar, Straus and Giroux, 2015.
54. [717] Kahneman, Daniel. Chapter 25: Bernoulli's Errors (269-277). *Thinking, fast and slow*. Farrar, Straus and Giroux, 2015.

reasonable explanation for a noticeable failure of the theory that you believe in, but you don't examine that line of questioning further to learn if there are any explanations. And when you do look for an explanation and find none at all? This can lead to rampant reinterpretations for the convenience of people's preconceived notions without any scrutiny of just how flawed and meaningless the teachings have become when applied to the modern world:

    If the teachings have been reinterpreted to the point where it contradicts the original texts, then how can there be any meaning derived from the Bible or Jesus's own contradictory words? If millions of people can only gain their own personal preference from the Bible, then what values do the biblical teachings actually instill? If the Bible's morality falls into personal interpretations, and therefore subjective experience, then how can it even be claimed to teach objective morality of any sort? If you can contradict as many of the biblical teachings as you wish and still be considered part of the religious community, then does the religion have any merit? If no matter what you do, you fail to live-up to certain teachings because they contradict other teachings, then are you going to constantly waste your time and energy with the expectation that you'll fail in these teachings for the sake of a world after death? Are you to constantly waste your time and energy on "perfection" with the expectation that you're a sinful human being who will inevitably fail? If you have to apply Christian symbols everywhere to feel consistent with your beliefs, then do you truly believe in it? Isn't applying symbols everywhere a contradiction to the Commandment of graven images when God specifically decrees that there should be no likeness in symbolism to anything in Heaven? Must you feel constant shame and self-loathing when using symbols or is this another example of being able to contradict the original teachings so that they're effectively worthless? If "leave no thought for the morrow" is to be taken seriously, then do you love your God more than your family, spouse, pets, and children? Why is loving God more than your loved ones a good moral teaching?

    These teachings wouldn't lead to happiness even within the context of one's own church. For example, if you followed the teachings of "Judge not that ye be judged" and avoided judging others and a fellow church member believes that they should be looking out for hypocrites that Jesus warns about. It would be possible for this fellow churchgoer to constantly criticize you while citing passages from the Sermon about you acting like the hypocrites that Jesus warns about under the belief that you're making a show of giving donations to the church. Both of you would be following the teachings of Jesus, you would both be failing at specific parts of the other teachings that you've both ignored, and you would be subjecting yourself to constant humiliation from a fellow church member while trying to keep your judgments to yourself. You would both feel that you ascertained the true meaning of Jesus's teachings in the Sermon and you would both feel that you were in the right because Jesus is on your side. You want to avoid judging others and the fellow Churchgoer wants to protect the prestige of your local church by changing the behavior of hypocrites for better community values. Who is correct? Regardless of any perceived rudeness, your fellow churchgoer feels they're correct for their beliefs and that Jesus is on their side because they're working to be perfect in the image of God. Is their faith in Jesus and convictions to Christianity misleading them? If the Christian faith can be so constantly and easily misled, then what does that say about the virtues of Christianity itself? More importantly, what about divorced women? Are we to judge them and label them adulterous for marrying after a divorce? Stating it is adulterous for divorced women to remarry is a judgment that explicitly contradicts "Judge not that ye be judged" because you cannot label other people as adulterous without forming a judgment upon their behavior.

    From my own subjective experience, Christians don't seem to realize how these self-contradictions ultimately harm themselves into the most deplorable and self-centered mindsets and behaviors; the axioms of Christianity give the worst explanations for humans failing to keep promises to others. Overall, it results in a bizarre form of incoherent circular reasoning. People who have faith in Jesus are trying to act good with the belief that they're good Christians, they believe they're chosen above non-Christians whom they believe are more inclined to deceive, and are led to believe that other Christians have better principles. Instead, they usually discover other Christians are "liars" who lie to them; they view those liars as hypocrites that Jesus warned about; meanwhile, they believe they're trying not to judge but fall into sin and so seek Jesus's forgiveness. They try to constantly forgive the most harmful self-identified Christians among them and expose themselves to either mildly abusive behavior or outright criminal behavior by opportunists. Now, most Christians in these situations seem to think it's proof that those other Christians are hypocrites who don't really follow the faith, but the Christian faith itself gives an open door invitation to every form of abuse and vitriol because of the teachings of forgiveness. Nothing is ever too egregious to forgive. Thereby, criminal behavior eventually enters these places of worship and strong religious communities. Moreover, if you truly have deep personal faith in forgiveness, you place your loved ones (such as children) at risk with abusers who've already been convicted once before of horrible crimes. You may believe that non-Christians who do good are more Christian than those other Christians who do you harm, but that's false. The existence of non-Christian who help you and do better for you than other Christians whom you deem as hypocrites would instead prove that Christianity is irrelevant for teaching good moral behavior.

    Christian social elitism seems to be a painful experience from my observations of their religious culture. The cultural elitism teaches that fellow Christians are more honest and trustworthy, but the subjective experience of Christians is such that they would undoubtedly see hypocrisy from their fellow Christians despite earnest attempts to not judge people. The contradiction of not judging people, but then noticing hypocrisy upon hypocrisy would inevitably require them to seek forgiveness from Jesus Christ for not upholding these starkly contradictory beliefs. As mentioned prior, how can you acknowledge others as hypocrites without making a judgment on their behavior? To give another hypothetical example, since Christians are required to speak honestly and not lie; they would inevitably spiral into bickering with the hypocritical person who would rebuke back with equal fervor possibly noting the observer's hypocrisies. The person who sees hypocritical behavior would see the other person as a so-called fake Christian while the judged Christian would view the judger as having failed to live-up to Jesus's teachings of not judging others. Both would eventually admit the other person was an asshole or some negative equivalent term, but attend Church. The judged person would regularly meet with the in-group of Christians who gossip about how the accuser is a hypocrite too or how they don't follow the teachings of not judging others. Both would seek Jesus's forgiveness for their negative views on each other independently, and secretly hold each other in deep contempt, but try to maintain the social norms of being a good Christian to the best of their ability, while acknowledging they're a sinful human being compared to a so-called perfect Creator. Both of them would seek forgiveness from Jesus Christ and the local community, while seeing each other as assholes (or an equivalent negative term) and hypocrites while acknowledging themselves as imperfect, sinful human beings.

Therefore, I maintain this entire social system is utterly pathetic and unworthy of any intrinsic value. You would be congratulating yourself for the bare minimum of human decency, pretending it's something profound, and subjecting yourself to people who loathe you simply because its required of you by communal social customs. It's meaningless emotional exhaustion and often psychologically self-harming because you're constantly putting on a smile to subject yourself to a sense of hopeless surrender to a theological system that has offered you nothing but deep contempt. It's no different than being a community outreach and social support type of center, but with the addition of gossip and repressed contempt for others. It's nothing short of perpetual unhappiness masquerading as deep and meaningful. Moreover, these issues deepen and begin to hold manifold layers of contempt depending on the particular religious sect's axioms. Most of all, communal systems sense of belonging and social companionship is almost completely obsolete for an individual compared to close friendship where people build trust and deep ties on a personal, individual level. A true friend is someone we come to love, cherish, and trust implicitly; a person who respects us and our boundaries. A communal system is largely just what we've been born into without any real choice and which we haven't adequately taken time to compare to other social communities similar to finding a job in which the social culture is one of kindness, trust, and compassion versus a cutthroat environment where people are merely expected to live under the circumstances due to either fear of reprisal from higher-ups or having no other choice due to monetary concerns. Thus, a true friend is irreparable and we feel the loss deeply; a community is something we can eventually change as we grow older and redefine within ourselves from our choices to find something more suitable for our beliefs.

What Does Being a Christian Mean?

Assuming you are a Christian, I would like for you to consider the following: how can each of the Christian denominations be what Jesus truly meant? This is a cognitive dissonance that Christians don't seem to realize, and that should be questioned, because how can you know that your specific denomination is the true interpretation of the faith? If other denominations besides the one that you believe in are wrong, then what value can there be in believing in Jesus Christ when people of other Christian denominations have been led astray? Even if the people of the other denominations believe strongly in Jesus's words, just as you believe strongly in Jesus, they can evidently be led astray from the correct Christian path. Thus, simply believing strongly in Jesus Christ isn't enough to enter heaven. Believing in Jesus can be utterly meaningless despite spending an entire lifetime in prayer and religious observance. And, if believing in Jesus is all that is required, then why should you bother following a specific denomination at all? Why would religious observances, rituals such as baptizing ceremonies, and having holy holidays matter at all? If only believing in Jesus matters, then the denominations and specific rites are all false and meaningless.

From an entirely Christian context, believing in Jesus with all one's heart and soul wouldn't be enough to be allowed into heaven. If it were not so, then the Christian denominations wouldn't matter but a large percentage of Christians still only believe in a specific denomination of the Christian faith; usually the one they were raised in. Why believe in specific denominations at all? Can you be so sure that they're somehow misleading themselves through their convictions for Jesus while you are somehow staying true over millions of your fellow Christians? For that matter, do any of the prerequisites for being a good Christian matter anymore to the majority of Christians in the Western countries?

For example, compare Episcopalians and Evangelical fundamentalists. If Evangelical fundamentalists are correct in their beliefs, then it simply doesn't matter how sincere Episcopalians are for accepting Jesus into their heart and believing in him as their Lord and Savior, they will be going to hell for accepting homosexuals, for allowing men and divorced women to marry, and for not admonishing straight men for having natural sexual thoughts about women. They have not properly repented for their transgressions. If the Episcopalians are correct, then Evangelical fundamentalists have wasted their entire lives on meaningless and nonsensical rules that Jesus Christ doesn't care about and wouldn't admonish his believers for allowing. They have repented for behavior that didn't need any repentance and they've discriminated against homosexuals and divorced women causing meaningless suffering. It's possible they'll be going to hell as punishment for causing such meaningless suffering and therefore belief in Jesus Christ as their Lord and Savior may not be enough to keep them from hell. Moreover, there are approximately thirty-three thousand different denominations of Christianity across the world.[718] How can you possibly ascertain that yours is correct? More than a billion people across three thousand sects of Christianity all believe that their version is the closest to Jesus's message, why do you believe that your denomination alone is the true one? If you don't believe it is the true sect and thereby don't believe that the sect you follow is

---

55. [718] "The Facts and Stats on 33000 Denominations: World Christian Encyclopedia (2001, 2nd Edition)." *All About Horus: An Egyptian Copy of Christ? Response to Zeitgeist Movie*, www.philvaz.com/apologetics/a106.htm.

closer to Jesus's message than any other, then why bother following it? If you honestly think it doesn't matter which denomination that a Christian follows, then why are you bothering to commit your life to your denomination?

To consider this line of questioning further, are any of the Western nation-states truly Christian countries? If they are, then what does that mean for Western wars conducted in foreign countries? Jesus's imagery has been applied nearly everywhere in capitalist countries so that modern Christians can feel consistent with the Bible.[719] A significant group of Christians in the United States and other countries have argued that their nation-state's should be seen as a Christian country at their foundations but such a precedent would be dangerous for Christians themselves. It would mean, from the view of the rest of the world, that any human rights crime that a nation-state conducts upon other countries is a reflection of the predominant religion of that country. If the Arab Spring were to view overtly Christian rhetoric from US politicians, US presidents, and US NGOs then Christianity would be conflated with the violence of drone strike campaigns and other types of bombing campaigns conducted by Western powers upon the Arab spring and elsewhere. It would mean all genocides that have been revised out of Western history books are reflections of Christianity.

Unfortunately, this rhetoric is the reality that people are living with today and as a result there are massive killings - and possibly genocides - of entire Christian communities in the Arab spring because they've conflated Western violence from countries that tout to be the epitome of Christianity. For some, possibly due to their rash judgments after losing family members to drone violence, they could be predisposed to inflict violence upon the perceived cause of their losses especially if they fall victim to terrorist recruitment during their time of emotional turmoil.[720][721]

The Abrahamic God and Divine Command Theory

Universal morality based on the Bible, synonymous with Divine Command Theory, has progressively become an indefensible position in the past decade. Much of the argument against relativism stems from the underlying assumption by Abrahamic followers that without the universal belief structure of the Bible, morality would fall apart and everything ridiculous, depraved, and violent would become permissive. The obvious fundamental presupposition being, to the Abrahamic follower, that morality cannot exist or coherently function without the holy books and direct word of God on how humans should behave themselves. However, such internalized structures fall apart when compared to scientific evidence and assessments of human ecology.

---

56. [719] Cialdini, Robert B. "Chapter 3: Commitment and Consistency (52-95)" *Influence: Science and practice*. 4th ed., 21st Century Bks, 2002.
57. [720] Kahneman, Daniel. *Thinking, fast and slow*. Farrar, Straus and Giroux, 2015.
58. [721] Cialdini, Robert B. "Chapter 1: Weapons of Influence (1-16)" *Influence: Science and practice*. 4th ed., 21st Century Bks, 2002.

The first and most glaring problem is that arguments for a universal morality, such as Divine Command Theory, are repudiated by the religious concept of open interpretation on a fundamental level. Universal morality presupposes an immutable, God-given set of laws that humans cannot change; however, open interpretation presupposes that the Abrahamic God's word is arbitrary and malleable. While the notion of open interpretation may carry the presumption that one is becoming closer to the Abrahamic God by shifting their moral beliefs, the concept itself shows that an Abrahamic follower's morals aren't based upon a universal set of precepts. They learn, grow, change, adjust, and remove beliefs based on life circumstances and adapt to new moral beliefs. While this may be stating the obvious, it is clear that due to the fact that millions of Christians diverge in morals as they grow older, the denominational differences and personal beliefs of individual Christians shows a multifarious range of beliefs about morality, the structure of universal moral systems, and suppositions on what the Abrahamic God's message is. This is true not only of the differences between Judaism, Islam, and Christianity but also within the scope of just their intra-denominations such as comparing Catholic and Protestant, Unitarian Universalist and Evangelical Fundamentalist, or Calvinist and Episcopalian. When taking a look at the full scope of denominational differences across the world, nearly each and every single Christian denomination posits universal truth on both moral and divine grounds, but is morally relative to any other Christian denomination that posits the exact same universal truth but on an entirely different interpretation of the Bible. Yet, each and every single one of these denominations espouse to know universal truths and knowledge given by the Abrahamic God, but seem to lack the self-awareness to acknowledge that they live by different morals than other sects of the same religious faith. Essentially, arguing for universal moral principles but functionally acting morally relative to each other and denouncing the other denominations as having deceived themselves, remaining unrepentant, being wrong, and foolhardy. The lack of self-awareness within the Abrahamic faiths is likely because the Abrahamic faiths themselves preach that proper deference to the Abrahamic God is by unquestioned obedience. In short, the belief that it is hubris to question God, the belief in thought crimes, should be considered the primary cause why Abrahamic followers don't see the glaring self-contradictions of having a multitude of denominations all claiming universal moral and sacred precepts relative to each other. A typical Abrahamic follower may hold the paradoxical view it as the majority of the world being on the right track to salvation but either being deceived by the devil or harboring some nefarious intent in not recognizing their specific denomination as the sole revealed wisdom of the Abrahamic God.

A second issue with Divine Command Theory, which is far more glaring and opens third parties to the incredulous belief structure of Christianity in particular, is that thoughtless obedience to the Abrahamic God seems to prevent Abrahamic followers from acknowledging the capricious value judgments of their God. The New Atheist Sam Harris famously pointed out: "Rationalizing the barbarity of the Bible merely renders it irrelevant. It doesn't grant these books as morally wise."[722] He was correct on that point and it should be added that unquestioning obedience seems to prevent Abrahamic followers from acknowledging with any degree of seriousness that the Abrahamic God's so-called universal morality is morally subjective. If morality is derived from the Abrahamic God, and this God can choose to have the mass murder of children, war rape, sexual slavery, and the massacres of entire cities for the crime of believing in another God, then how can teachings of peace, loving your neighbors, and forgiveness be universal moral doctrines of the Abrahamic God?

Assuming the Abrahamic God is real, and morality is derived only from that God, then consider this thought experiment under the assumption that this was fully recognized by the entire world as coming from the Abrahamic God:

If the Abrahamic God were to give a command to go back to following the Old Testament's practices of murdering every young boy in a city who believed in a foreign God, killing all women who had laid with a man who believed in a foreign God, and taking young girls as sex slaves under the justification that this was morally good to do so; what would stop this from being an immoral act under Divine Command Theory? If Christians were ordered to do this to Jewish people, with the Abrahamic God stating that he was working in mysterious ways for the benefit of humanity's future, what could either religious group say to counter the Abrahamic God's judgment in moral terms under Divine Command Theory?

Finally, if you find this thought experiment trite or foolish, then why do you justify these very same actions with the Old Testament by ignoring the bloodshed wrought by the Abrahamic God's commands and the blatant subjectivity of the Abrahamic God's moral paradigm? The moral relativist actions of the Abrahamic God destroy any morality founded upon universal structures based on the Abrahamic God.

In his blog post "*16 Problems with Divine Command Theory*" the author of the piece, Jonathan MS Pearce, lists some examples of the Abrahamic God sanctioning horrifying levels of human violence in his name:

> **Murder, rape, and pillage at Jabesh-gilead** (Judges 21:10-24)
>
> **Murder, rape and pillage of the Midianites** (Numbers 31:7-18)
>
> **More Murder Rape and Pillage** (Deuteronomy 20:10-14)
>
> **Laws of Rape** (Deuteronomy 22:28-29)
>
> **Death to the Rape Victim** (Deuteronomy 22:23-24)
>
> **David's Punishment – Polygamy, Rape, Baby Killing, and God's "Forgiveness"** (2 Samuel 12:11-14)
>
> **Rape of Female Captives** (Deuteronomy 21:10-14)

---

59. [722] "Sam Harris Aspen Ideas Festival Full Unedited Video." *YouTube*, YouTube, 25 Nov. 2012, www.youtube.com/watch?v=hfgwFESH_jM.

Rape and the Spoils of War (Judges 5:30)

Sex Slaves (Exodus 21:7-11)

God Assists Rape and Plunder (Zechariah 14:1-2)[723]

Repentance and Forgiveness

Repentance is one of the most celebrated cornerstones of Christian theology. It has many different uses in the multitude of Christian denominations. However, it's primary use and chief aim is to ask Jesus Christ's forgiveness for sins done as a Christian. Christian theology claims to turn away from and strive to never commit sins again through this doctrine, but paradoxically Christian theology acknowledges humans are sinners and forgives sinfulness because humans cannot be perfect like Jesus Christ is purported to be. Unfortunately, repentance and its usage of forgiveness comes with crippling flaws that teach hate, create debilitating forms of meaningless suffering through thought crimes, and promote violence.

The original meaning of repentance is to change one's mind according to the Bible.[724] In the Christian context, it's to change one's mind about Jesus Christ and recognize him as the lord and savior who has come to redeem humanity's sins.[725] This belief confers a relationship to Jesus Christ and the belief that a Christian is someone who accepts Jesus Christ into their heart in the more modern Christian context. Christian repentance requires people turn away from sinfulness so as to properly worship and praise the Abrahamic God and Jesus Christ.[726] Repentance isn't regarded as purely intellectual, but as part of spiritual and emotional growth in developing proper reverence for Jesus Christ and the Abrahamic God.[727] As such, there is a distinct and powerful drive for an argument from ignorance and appeal to purity, the idea of the belief's unknowable qualities making it profound and beyond mere human intellect, when guiding your actions with repentance to Jesus Christ.[728]

One of the glaring flaws with repentance, especially in the Catholic context, is that fanciful ideas like idolatry and graven images are believed to be worse offenses to the Abrahamic God than murder of fellow humans, which is considered a lesser offense as a

---

60. [723] Pearce, Jonathan MS. "16 Problems with Divine Command Theory." *Faith on the Couch*, Patheos, 5 Sept. 2016, www.patheos.com/blogs/tippling/2016/09/04/16-problems-with-divine-command-theory/11/.
61. [724] "What Is Biblical Repentance?" *Grace to You*, 13 July 2009, www.gty.org/library/articles/A330/what-is-biblical-repentance.
62. [725] "What Is Biblical Repentance?" *Grace to You*, 13 July 2009, www.gty.org/library/articles/A330/what-is-biblical-repentance.
63. [726] "What Is Repentance and Is It Necessary for Salvation?" *GotQuestions.org*, 20 June 2018, www.gotquestions.org/repentance.html.
64. [727] "What Is Biblical Repentance?" *Grace to You*, 13 July 2009, www.gty.org/library/articles/A330/what-is-biblical-repentance.
65. [728] "What Is Biblical Repentance?" *Grace to You*, 13 July 2009, www.gty.org/library/articles/A330/what-is-biblical-repentance.

mortal sin. Despite arguments by modern Christians that life is sacred, this difference in offense intrinsically devalues human life. Murder, even the murder of infants, is considered forgivable, but believing in other Gods is considered worthy of ex-communication and damnation in hell. The difference in emphasis runs counterintuitive to teaching people to live by good moral values and it's precisely because Christianity wants to exist in a more distinct and informal manner than other non-Abrahamic religions that this occurs. However, doing so implicitly devalues all human life within the Catholic context. This idea is ardently defended within Christian theology, even within Evangelical denominations, under the pretense that the Abrahamic God's love and empathy through forgiveness is far higher than our merely human understanding. Thus, all horrific actions are forgivable because there is no point where human violence is perceived as too egregious to be worthy of salvation through accepting Jesus Christ into a violent perpetrator's heart.

Repentance is taught to be about turning away from sinfulness in the natural world. You must repent for natural sexual behavior like masturbation, for the thought crime of valuing and respecting other religious teachings or other Gods, for natural sexual desires towards other human beings, for lying to others, and for feeling envious of others.[729] Confessing to the Abrahamic God is of paramount importance, a Christian must honestly feel sincere regret for their actions and strive to better themselves by adjusting their behavior. Paradoxically to this sentiment of personal regret in order to better oneself, it is acknowledged that as imperfect beings that humans can never be perfect when maintaining these supposed lofty standards and so repenting repeatedly is to be expected of Christians. It is expected that as sinful human beings, humans will regrettably fail in their need to repent and what is important is making an honest effort to change within the framework of what is possible for a sinful human being. Some denominations even call for daily repentance to the Abrahamic God when failing to uphold a virtuous Christian life; whether it be through deeds or through immoral and carnal thoughts that inhabit the mind. In many Christian denominations, daily prayer is considered the proper way to turn away from evil and to turn to God. For all intents and purposes, it is considered the most righteous path and believed by Christians to be holding steadfast to their moral obligation by responsibly confessing their shortcomings to the Abrahamic God and Jesus Christ.

Unfortunately, the framework of the repentance belief system leads to a vast array of failures in reasoning, negative judgments towards contemporary morality, loathing for others including ones own family, and it causes horrifying consequences for those vulnerable to exploitation. The poor reasoning and false assumptions of repentance is a major contributor to the worst forms of bigotry and hate. The most tenacious implication of repentance theology is that everything outside of Christianity simply exists to deceive, disparage, or misinterpret Jesus Christ's message. Repentance helps reinforce a self-affirming system of collective narcissism

---

66. [729] Nietzsche, Friedrich. Morality as Anti-Nature (21-26). *Twilight of the Idols*. Amazon Digital Services LLC.

because doing nothing is seen as a moral struggle of good against evil through ritualistic prayer.[730] Deeming mere stray thoughts as evil and wicked to make people feel a sense of accomplishment for trying to willfully ignore the natural thought processes of the human brain with simplistic moral concepts and ubiquitous misanthropy.[731][732] They confuse mere thought with the desire to commit to those thoughts and feel like they've been more righteous for condemning internal thought crimes than outside cultures and belief systems. This is largely why they're prone to view out-groups as disproportionately likely to commit rape and murder while simply ignoring their in-groups actions of rape and murder as a misinterpretation because they believe that the Christian perpetrator didn't try to suppress their violent thoughts with enough prayer. This leads to a self-gratifying sense of collective narcissism by Christians and it results in a patronizing attitude towards anyone who simply thinks of morality outside of the insular view that Jesus Christ must be central to all good moral teachings.[733] Repentance implies, that by turning away from evil and sin, that everyone who disagrees is steeped in sinfulness, deluding themselves, and not fulfilling their duty to properly revere the one they must worship as lord and savior.[734] *Therefore, if they disagree with Jesus Christ's message, then they are either deluded or hostile because it's unacceptable to criticize Jesus Christ or his teachings in Christianity.* This belief helps to reinforce the xenophobia towards other cultures as not aligned to Jesus Christ's message, steeped in sinfulness, and justifies "self-defense" measures of a first strike of unprovoked violence.[735] Arguably this is shown by the history of the Christian treatment of Jews, to Native Americans, and most recently on a smaller scale, the Iraq War of 2003 by the nation-states of the US and Great Britain with their predominately Christian populations. *The Christian concept of repentance exists solely to make Jesus Christ's unfettered narcissism unquestionable; it is an implicit thought crime to disparage people from simply thinking differently about Jesus Christ or for questioning his supposed godhood.*

The collective narcissism is heavily inculcated through belief in being the so-called chosen peoples along with the belief that only Christians like themselves can accurately understand the Bible. *Thus, they never perceive themselves to be held accountable to outside influences due to the belief in sacredness. In part, perceiving themselves as sacred peoples to ignore all outside influences and out-group criticisms as automatically wrong.*[736] Humbly recognizing themselves as "sinful" to then forgive themselves, through the self-forgiveness

---

67. [730] Nietzsche, Friedrich Wilhelm. *On the genealogy of morals: a polemical tract.* Translated by Ian Johnston, PDF, Richer Resources Publications, 2014.
68. [731] Reese, Hannah. "Intrusive Thoughts: Normal or Not?" Psychology Today, Sussex Publishers, www.psychologytoday.com/us/blog/am-i-normal/201110/intrusive-thoughts-normal-or-not.
69. [732] Nietzsche, Friedrich Wilhelm. Chapter XXVI: THE PRIESTS (88-91). *Thus spake Zarathustra: a book for all and none.* Translated by Thomas Common, PDF ed., T. Common, 1908.
70. [733] Ispas, Alexa. *Psychology and politics: a social identity perspective.* Psychology Press, 2014.
71. [734] Nietzsche, Friedrich Wilhelm. *THE ANTICHRIST.* Translated by H. L. Mencken, The Project Gutenberg, 2006.
72. [735] "BibleGateway." *2 Thessalonians 1:8-9 KJV - - Bible Gateway*, www.biblegateway.com/passage/?search=2 Thessalonians 1:8-9&version=KJV.
73. [736] Ispas, Alexa. *Psychology and politics: a social identity perspective.* Psychology Press, 2014.

theology of salvation via Jesus Christ, in an effort to perceive their impotence as superior to other cultures. By feeling righteous from the useless act of suppressing thoughts they believe represent their inner demons, Christians are congratulating themselves on a theology that celebrates doing nothing and feeling like it is somehow a triumph to do nothing.[737] This is where the self-defeating belief that a sexual abuser simply needs to pray more to keep to the righteous path, instead of having charges pressed against them for their crimes, comes from. Many Christians really do believe and are inculcated from childhood to believe that violent thoughts are what they desire to do instead of simply a mere thought in their mind and confuse themselves into believing that suppressing it through prayer is the only way to fight against it to show their commitment to fighting against sinfulness. Thus, they're more likely to believe people who conduct sexual abuse in their in-group are merely losing the battle against sinfulness and simply need more prayer as a corrective measure. It is not too different than the homophobic belief in so-called "praying the gay away" to keep faith in Jesus Christ and it is just as detrimental. It categorically celebrates no sense of responsibility to others except a divine being that is out of this world and beyond human comprehension. Repentance reinforces never correcting horrible misdeeds, the perpetrator forgiving herself or himself for the wrongful actions, and congratulating themselves on doing nothing.

    A detrimental aspect often ignored is anti-Semitism. Modern Christians simply don't have a good explanation for it, but likely remain unquestioning of the theological concepts that help foster such bigotry and hate. The belief that without repentance that one is deep in sinfulness helps to rationalize and promote anti-Semitism, it may possibly be the source of it as well. Even if a Jewish person is acting agreeably and kindheartedly, the presumption of their guilt and nefarious intent is heavily implied within the theological framework of repentance. It is because if they are perceived to not worship Jesus Christ who is presumed to have died for their sins, then the perception by the majority of Christian denominations is that Jews are deceiving themselves, that Jews are steeped in sinfulness, and hiding or lying from the supposed truth of Jesus Christ's godhood. Therefore, a core aspect of anti-Semitism comes from the theology of repentance to Jesus Christ. In fact, the entire theology of Christianity is predicated upon "correcting" Jewish people and Jewish theology so they're not damned to hell for sins.

---

74. [737] Nietzsche, Friedrich Wilhelm. *On the genealogy of morals: a polemical tract*. Translated by Ian Johnston, PDF, Richer Resources Publications, 2014.

Chapter 15: Reductionist Insight and Regressive Morality

Christianity falls into the self-reinforcing trap of the No True Scotsman fallacy when different denominations try to make sense of Christian violence by blaming it solely upon specific denominations as the primary cause. To use the United States as an example, when violent atrocities like child rapes, or violence against women, transgender people, or homosexuals occur, then it is generally regarded as the fault of either greed, or other types of sinfulness, or a specific denomination being culpable; it is concomitant with vehement arguments that it isn't a true interpretation of the religious faith.[738] Generally, the denomination responsible for horrific wrongdoing is seen as having deceived themselves from the teachings of Jesus Christ, having spread hate instead of love, and manipulating the message of Jesus Christ with selfishness and greed. Conversely, a significant portion in the US population recognizes their own country as a Christian nation-state and that it is based on Christian values that the majority all agree upon. So, a country with a majority Christian population would largely recognize itself as having the same value judgments and celebrating the shared values in being Christian, but also recognizes that all other denominations are deceiving themselves, lost in their ways, ruining Jesus's teachings with politics, and don't actually follow the revealed wisdom of the Abrahamic God or Jesus Christ. Evidently, nobody sees the glaring self-contradiction. The very belief in love-thy-neighbor falls apart even within a Christian context as many simply accuse other denominations of sole culpability of human rights abuses. This confusion prompts me to ask this question for any Christian readers: does your own Christian denomination solely follow the true message of Jesus Christ or are they shared universally among all Christians?

What's markedly important to note in this contradiction among these denominations: each individual denomination would clearly take offense from the assertion that they don't follow Jesus Christ's teachings from the accusations of other denominations. Irrespective of what horrors are caused by members of any particular denomination, they would openly declare their love for Jesus Christ and Jesus's teachings. If every denomination responsible for atrocities believe in the Bible as the sole authoritative text of the Abrahamic God, if they believe they'll go to heaven for their belief in Jesus Christ as their savior, and profess to believe in Jesus Christ's teachings; then on what grounds can Christians of other denominations ridicule each other besides not wanting to admit violence has occurred from the teachings of Jesus Christ? And, if violence has occurred from Christians despite belief in Jesus as lord and savior and strict adherence to his teachings, then how can Christianity argue it espouses superior morality to other belief systems? How can it even argue in favor of dubious truth claims when Christians cannot even agree what the teachings mean, what the punishment will be for not following specific Christian teachings and rites, or what parts of Jesus Christ's message was distorted when people commit violence in Jesus Christ's name?

---

1. [738] "No True Scotsman." *Https://Www.logicallyfallacious.com*, www.logicallyfallacious.com/tools/lp/Bo/LogicalFallacies/135/No-True-Scotsman.

The lack of specification on just what content of Jesus Christ's teachings have been ignored, from an openly interpretative system, leads to the most pernicious attempt at a reductionist argument from Christians who fail at being able to explain the violence from their faith. When confronted with evidence of violence in the name of Jesus Christ, once spurious and reflexive accusations of hating Christians or wanting to kill Christians for even bringing up historic or contemporary cases of violence by Christians is adequately dealt with through logically reasoned counter arguments against incendiary content composed of false accusations and loathing for the direct line of questioning assumptions; the typical response is to declare that "humans are humans" as a way of explaining why people among their own in-group would commit violence. This is a non-answer due to being one of the most blatant forms of circular reasoning as a form of defense because it simply reasserts the premise in the conclusion in a lazy fashion with no interest in a deeper study of why violence is occurring.[739] This non-answer provides a host of assumptions about human violence, its consequences, and on what Christianity really provides people when confronted with instances of aggression by their in-group upon out-groups.[740]

The attitude of passivity and complacency to aggression has dire consequences for the prevention of future occurrences of violence. While many Christians are quick to utilize any member who is killed for their faith as proof of the faith's truth claims and so-called profoundness, it bears repeating that dying for your religious faith doesn't prove that your religion is true.[741] Moreover, just as many fail to find meaningful steps or responses on why violence in the name of Jesus Christ occurs and kills people just as equally. If we accept at face value the Christian notion that "humans are humans" with respect to human violence conducted by Christians themselves, then there is absolutely no value in either the teachings of Jesus Christ or any other moral and ethical guiding principles for that matter. The non-answer response of "humans will be humans" presupposes that nothing can hold sway or be of significant value in influencing people to stop them from committing violence. Thus, any argument about the intrinsic nature of Christianity's guidelines producing positive moral and ethical behavior is rendered impossible and implicitly judged as entirely wrong by Christians.[742] "Humans are humans" means that no belief system will ever be meaningful in producing more positive outcomes for humanity and such a presumption contradicts the ability of creating a more stable civil society.[743] The belief that Christianity is more tolerant or

---

2. [739] "Circular Reasoning." *Https://Www.logicallyfallacious.com*, www.logicallyfallacious.com/tools/lp/Bo/LogicalFallacies/66/Circular-Reasoning
3. [740] Nietzsche, Friedrich Wilhelm. *THE ANTICHRIST*. Translated by H. L. Mencken, The Project Gutenberg, 2006.
4. [741] Nietzsche, Friedrich Wilhelm. Aphorism 53. *THE ANTICHRIST*. Translated by H. L. Mencken, The Project Gutenberg, 2006.
5. [742] Nietzsche, Friedrich Wilhelm. *On the genealogy of morals: a polemical tract*. Translated by Ian Johnston, PDF, Richer Resources Publications, 2014.
6. [743] Nietzsche, Friedrich Wilhelm. *THE ANTICHRIST*. Translated by H. L. Mencken, The Project Gutenberg, 2006.

peaceful than other religious faiths or leads to improved moral behavior is acknowledged as false.

The non-answer of "humans are humans" is derivative of and often used in conjunction with the concept of Original Sin as a justification for Christian violence.[744] It both fails at searching for answers of causes and consequences for any motive for violence and instead obfuscates any attempt at researching motivations because of the intrinsic implication that it won't matter and that people will find other reasons or need no such reasons to commit violence.[745] This line of reasoning fails to make any sense as it assumes any average, law-abiding person would attack someone at random, even kill them, for no discernible reason and that searching for a motive is useless because people should just expect violent events to happen. It is willfully ignorant of even attempting to find underlying reasons for human violence that could be curtailed or reduced in terms of statistical occurrences to make a safer society for all. Under the presumption of "humans are humans" there would be no real ability to even have a functioning civil society or even a functioning household as anyone would attack and kill each other for no reason at all and thus cause people to stay vigilant of every other human being in the world under the threat of constant random attacks with no clear motives, criminal patterns of behavior, or any sense of consistency with upbringing or locality.

As mentioned prior, Original Sin and the non-answer of "humans are humans" is an inability to even have standards against human violence because both presume a fixed nature of human behavior that exaggerates negatives to create a nihilistic complacency with worsening standards of living.[746][747] Original Sin is an entity theory that presupposes that humanity is intrinsically prone to violence, exaggerating all forms of negativity, thus discouraging any attempts at changing human ecology for the betterment of all.[748] No matter the extent of worsening conditions that exacerbate human suffering, whether it be violence, desecration of democratic values, hatred towards others who are perceived as foreign, genocide, rape campaigns, and loathing of others based on suspicion of their motives; all of it becomes ubiquitously legitimized due to the fixed mentality of Original Sin.[749] The absolute forgiveness of Jesus's teachings combined with Original Sin never create a sufficient standard to stop when conditions are too horrid to allow continuation. It precludes any redress and behavioral changes in the modus operandi of human ecology to prevent human violence. It simply passively accepts all wrongdoing as warranting forgiveness; no matter how egregious the harm done to others, or the planet, or the welfare of the majority of people. In effect, it

---

7. [744] Nietzsche, Friedrich Wilhelm. *On the genealogy of morals: a polemical tract*. Translated by Ian Johnston, PDF, Richer Resources Publications, 2014.
8. [745] Nietzsche, Friedrich Wilhelm. *THE ANTICHRIST*. Translated by H. L. Mencken, The Project Gutenberg, 2006.
9. [746] Halvorson, Heidi Grant. *Succeed: How We Can Reach Our Goals*. Plume, 2012.
10. [747] Nietzsche, Friedrich Wilhelm. *On the genealogy of morals: a polemical tract*. Translated by Ian Johnston, PDF, Richer Resources Publications, 2014.
11. [748] Halvorson, Heidi Grant. *Succeed: How We Can Reach Our Goals*. Plume, 2012.
12. [749] Halvorson, Heidi Grant. *Succeed: How We Can Reach Our Goals*. Plume, 2012.

hampers any attempts of redress by perceiving it as arrogance, stupidity under the presumption that conditions can never be changed, and acts hostile to any and all who attempt to formulate positive changes because people strongly believe that none of the positive changes will have lasting effect and that abusers will find other ways to continue their abuses as per the intrinsic folly of human nature so there's no point in attempting to change anything for the better.[750] This standard is the Christian standard and has been taught throughout Western education, internalized by Christian churches, and made ubiquitous through imperialistic monopolies pretending to be capitalism through foreign policy initiatives by Western governments from the 1500s to the present. It has always been Western democratic principles in perpetual war with the Christian standard that has hampered and caused cultural recidivism for centuries throughout the West. The fact Islam and possibly other religions also have been harmed by such standards to a worse degree within their respective majority countries doesn't negate the damage done to the West by Christianity and is a non-sequitur argument.

Christianity's standard reduces all violence as inevitable and takes a passive, largely self-aggrandizing sense of helplessness regarded as human folly, that becomes complacent with violence, selfishness, and corruptive influences.[751] It views these defects as simply unalterable and unchangeable dynamics of culture, society, and law that is senseless to try to change for the betterment of all.[752] As a result, constant meaningless resistance and jeers occur with the same set of Christian dogmas harboring a corrosive influence upon any struggle to resist intrusive laws that violate democratic freedoms. It views opposition to intrusive laws as meaningless to fight against because events like torture or the erosion of Constitutional rights are ascribed to inevitable behavior of human folly instead of seeking redress or opposing the destruction of the democratic process that citizens hold as sacrosanct; this is the direct result of Christianity scoffing at the belief that causes and consequences of human behavior exist beyond the sacred belief in Original Sin.[753] Much of this debate is ridiculed as nonsensical, because Christians use oversimplifications, distortions, and exaggerations of the negatives of other cultures as proof of their superiority; in effect, ignoring the worsening conditions of their own societies by comparing them to the most extreme conditions in foreign countries or by comparison to extremist countries such as Islamist countries. Christianity becomes reductive and wallows in a complacent nihilism towards life itself upon conquering its enemies or arguing it has superiority over them. Any deviation exaggerates the negatives of foreign influences to create generalizations and oversimplifications instead of understanding, empathy, and new tools to fight against corrosive influences. It largely becomes subservient to violence, corruptive power, and hate through apathy from complacent nihilism towards the erosion of

---

13. [750] Nietzsche, Friedrich Wilhelm. *On the genealogy of morals: a polemical tract*. Translated by Ian Johnston, PDF, Richer Resources Publications, 2014.
14. [751] Nietzsche, Friedrich Wilhelm. *On the genealogy of morals: a polemical tract*. Translated by Ian Johnston, PDF, Richer Resources Publications, 2014.
15. [752] Halvorson, Heidi Grant. *Succeed: How We Can Reach Our Goals*. Plume, 2012.
16. [753] Nietzsche, Friedrich Wilhelm. *THE ANTICHRIST*. Translated by H. L. Mencken, The Project Gutenberg, 2006.

democratic freedoms within its own country and triumphalism over foreign cultures. In the end, all morality is suspended and all horrors are legitimized as unalterable human traits as a core belief and principal reasoning within the Christian context. Just because humans can be capable, means they always will choose the worst possible horrors in the Christian worldview. It treats all negative possibilities as inevitable, even when the scope and scale is truly a permanent danger to the welfare of the greater society. All forms of human cruelty, stupidity, and brutality are rationalized as inevitable, unpreventable, and impossible to change. Any who deny this cultural nihilism are seen as egoistic, selfish, ignorant, idealistic, or stupid and unworthy of even debating. Thus, democratic freedoms constantly struggle against Christian recidivism and slow down, hamper, or disembowel the democratic institutions and the democratic process. After that is done, hindsight bias sets in and rationalizes the Christian standard as an unalterable human norm; inevitably creating a self-fulfilling prophecy.[754]

The Intrinsic Failure of Christian Morality

Christian moral values are a convoluted and disjointed mess that are filled with self-contradictions and collective narcissism. Contrary to the overwhelmingly popular belief, the fault is not because of people taking Jesus Christ's name in vain, ruining the teachings by acting falsely in Jesus Christ's name, or the misanthropic belief that everyone is prone to sin because of imperfection. The real reason, once we assess the values and truth claims of Jesus Christ under the lens of social science and psychology, is that Christian theology is a complete failure by design. They're the ravings of a narcissist with a God complex who wanted to be the sole authority of all moral teachings and so any positive morality needs to be attributed to or subservient under his erroneous beliefs about himself. A Christian is led to believe that there couldn't have been any humility, compassion, love, or forgiveness by any human being before the teachings of Jesus Christ, because his morality is less a morality and more just attributing mundane forms of human kindness that everyone is capable of as solely his unique doing. Buddhists, Jains, Hindus, Zoroastrianists, and Jews all precede the teachings of Jesus Christ touting the very same humility, compassion, and forgiveness of others except the vast majority of their schools and traditions are superior to Jesus Christ's teachings. With respect to the Eastern traditions of Asia, they do not come attached with his collective narcissism of being a chosen people either. The arrogantly touted "golden rule" espoused by Christians exists in every culture before and after Christianity's existence because it's a biological human norm that anthropological studies have found to exist in all ancient and modern cultures.[755] Modern psychologists have called it the *reciprocity principle* and it's an innate human norm that people are born with.[756] Being a Christian is irrelevant on the matter of reciprocating positive deeds

---

17. [754] Kahneman, Daniel. Chapter 19: The Illusion of Understanding (199-208). *Thinking, fast and slow*. Farrar, Straus and Giroux, 2015.
18. [755] Cialdini, Robert B. "Chapter 2: Reciprocation (19-50)" *Influence: Science and practice*. 4th ed., 21st Century Bks, 2002.
19. [756] Cialdini, Robert B. "Chapter 2: Reciprocation (19-50)" *Influence: Science and practice*. 4th ed., 21st Century Bks, 2002.

with giving back in a positive manner. Deeds of love and compassion are universal human norms and the myopic and narcissistic belief that they can only be attributed to Jesus Christ is woefully misinformed and ignorant. Christianity parrots a disinformation indoctrination by making anything of a positive moral quality only attributable to Jesus Christ.

The intrinsic failure of Christian morality stems from how the theology functions in practice. The juxtaposition of sinfulness and Jesus Christ's salvation lead to a moral system that constantly forgives the believer of any wrongdoing under the circumstance that they simply continue to recognize Jesus Christ as their lord and savior. By submitting to Jesus Christ's unfettered narcissism as a moral duty, Christians are forgiven of all criminal behavior and exonerate themselves in a sacred submission and sacred concession of their entire being to Jesus Christ.[757] Thus, their most focal duty is to keep humbling themselves by recognizing their sinfulness and then perceive themselves to have returned to the righteous path of Jesus's teachings. What does this mean? *Functionally speaking, a Christian is forgiving themselves of their wrongful deeds and returning to the wrongful conduct under the belief that they're a sinful human being that has already made a sacred concession to Jesus Christ.* Repentance to Jesus Christ is one of the important components of being a Christian; seeking forgiveness from the community, from the laws of humans, and from the victim of a Christian's heinous deed is utterly irrelevant in comparison to seeking Jesus's salvation. *As a Christian, you could forgive yourself of any heinous wrongdoing, such as murder and rape, and simply accept Jesus Christ into your heart to forgive yourself of the wrongful deed.* Atonement to Jesus Christ through the doctrine of forgiveness is held as paramount importance in the world. By being portrayed as of sacred importance to your relationship to Jesus Christ, it is seen as more important than coming clean to the civil and criminal laws and as more important than apologizing or making amends to the victims. The right of priest-penitent functions as a useful obstruction of justice explicitly because the penitent has made amends to the highest authority, Jesus Christ and the Abrahamic God, and thus relieves themselves of their own guilt through confession of sins. Christianity's morality is just a self-forgiveness system with no responsibility to others. All violent atrocities; all forms of physical, sexual, and emotional abuses and human rights violations can be forgiven through accepting Jesus Christ into your heart via the doctrine of forgiveness. As a direct result, Christianity is a theology that rejects any human culpability because Jesus is meant to take the sin away from people and thus the responsibility is removed. By accepting and properly worshipping Jesus Christ, you will never have to feel responsible to others based on the theology of Christianity itself.

Christians and ex-Christians often dismiss this claim because of the teaching of repentance; they believe repentance safeguards against sinfulness to make Christians accountable. However, repentance is precisely what helps the self-forgiveness system of Christianity through its poorly reasoned and paradoxical belief system. Instead of functioning

---

20. [757] Cialdini, Robert B. "Chapter 2: Reciprocation (19-50)" *Influence: Science and practice*. 4th ed., 21st Century Bks, 2002.

as a gatekeeper, repentance functions as a bridge to justifying sinfulness. That is because the physical world being perceived as mired in some vague selfishness where harmless conduct like lawfully purchasing large sums of items, mild to horrific wrongdoings a Christian conducts upon other people from theft to murder, and repeatedly falling into terrible patterns of behavior will always be forgiven by recognizing Jesus Christ as lord and savior under repentance to then seek his forgiveness for any wrongdoings towards others.[758] Some facets of Christian theology argue that the repentance of acknowledging Jesus Christ as your lord and savior changes your behavior to make you a better person[759], but that is completely impossible because there is no penalty for harming other people in Christian theology since Jesus Christ forgives you of all your sins. Some Christian theologies posit that grace is given to people by God himself and that no one can repent unless God wills it, but that would mean people don't have the freewill to accept Jesus Christ.[760] Repentance leads to maladaptive behavior; some Christians argue for daily repentance as a way to stymie sinfulness, but this leads to emotionally and intellectually normalizing feelings of regret and offering impotence - praying to Jesus - as a sign of remorse under the guise of humility and humbling oneself. Humbling oneself in recognizing they're a sinful human being and will constantly need to self-monitor causes mental weariness, it is a reminder of the ubiquity of misanthropy and nihilism towards life within the Christian viewpoint of sinfulness.[761] Precisely because Christians see sinfulness as intrinsic, fixed upon their very identity as a human being, they view any folly into sinfulness as inevitable.[762][763] They recognize that Jesus Christ's so-called all-encompassing love, which doesn't recognize any human atrocity towards other humans as too egregious of forgiveness, means they'll be forgiven for any wrongful conduct. *In short, Christians will always be able to seek forgiveness from Jesus Christ regardless of what horrific atrocity they commit under the belief that Jesus Christ loves them. Christianity functions as a self-forgiveness system because there is no act of human cruelty upon other people that Jesus Christ won't forgive.* Due to there being no standard for human violence that is too egregious to forgive, and because forgiveness from Jesus Christ supersedes the laws of the carnal world, people can easily forgive themselves of any wrongdoing and perceive seeking Jesus Christ's atonement as of sole importance. They would view seeking the forgiveness of anyone else - including the victim - as far less important or meaningful because Jesus Christ ranks as far above them in importance. The guilt invoked from sinfulness would make the perpetrator easily pass off on seeking such redemption because they would use snap judgments, fill-ins on what they don't know about the victim, and

---

21. [758] "What Is Biblical Repentance?" *Grace to You*, 13 July 2009, www.gty.org/library/articles/A330/what-is-biblical-repentance.
22. [759] "What Is Repentance and Is It Necessary for Salvation?" *GotQuestions.org*, 20 June 2018, www.gotquestions.org/repentance.html.
23. [760] "What Is Repentance and Is It Necessary for Salvation?" *GotQuestions.org*, 20 June 2018, www.gotquestions.org/repentance.html.
24. [761] Nietzsche, Friedrich Wilhelm. *On the genealogy of morals: a polemical tract*. Translated by Ian Johnston, PDF, Richer Resources Publications, 2014.
25. [762] Halvorson, Heidi Grant. *Succeed: How We Can Reach Our Goals*. Plume, 2012.
26. [763] Nietzsche, Friedrich Wilhelm. *On the genealogy of morals: a polemical tract*. Translated by Ian Johnston, PDF, Richer Resources Publications, 2014.

rash generalizations to convince themselves that the victim is too sinful.[764] The reason being that Christian theology simply assumes anyone who doesn't accept Jesus Christ is selfish, egoistic, and has some element of evil within them; it is a cultish contempt for any outside viewpoint that disagrees with acknowledging Jesus Christ as lord and savior.[765][766] The poor reasoning of Christian theology would help mollify any sliver of needing to apologize to real victims. Most people believe that repentance only occurs when perpetrators of heinous crimes confess to a priest first to have forgiveness from God and then go confess to the police, that is the majority understanding and it is indeed a reasonable belief to hold but those who believe that is the process are woefully misinformed.[767] *Moreover, Christianity's doctrine of forgiveness is not reasonable, it is absolute.* The doctrine of forgiveness is an extremist belief and as such has painful consequences due to being an irrational belief system.

The extremist dichotomy of sinfulness and the belief that all egregious acts of violence are forgivable under Jesus Christ's doctrine of forgiveness only complicates issues when those concepts exist in tandem. It is conjoining the ubiquitous nihilism and misanthropy for everything related to human activity with forgiveness for all acts that come as a result of such beliefs. The dichotomy runs counterintuitive to what psychology refers to as moral licensing. Moral licensing is seeing ourselves do a moral act which helps affirm our self-conceptions of who we are and then not viewing any further acts of immorality as important to our self-conceptions.[768] Essentially, by humbling yourself to the Abrahamic God and acknowledging Jesus Christ as God, you would feel emotional satisfaction with affirming your Christian beliefs and not see any further acts of immorality as important to your view of yourself as a good moral person.[769] Submission to Jesus Christ is seen as prominent and this belief doesn't mean that Christians would seek to redeem themselves to the victim or work to commit to positive moral acts through good works, it just means they acknowledge Jesus Christ as their God. It means they attempt to ignore sinfulness to the best of their ability with the knowledge they're prone to human folly and will likely do it again because of their human imperfections. Within the Catholic context, and perhaps some denominational contexts, guilt for thought crimes like sexual thoughts of others, graven images, or shouting something untoward during prayer in Church is seen as more immoral than physically and sexually harming other human beings. Thought crimes are viewed as more important than physical and sexual violence towards others. Perpetrators of crimes don't feel the need to go to the police to confess their

27. [764] Kahneman, Daniel. *Thinking, fast and slow*. Farrar, Straus and Giroux, 2015.
28. [765] McDermott, Rose. Group Processes (239-260). *Political Psychology in International Relations*. Ann Arbor: U of Michigan, 2004. Print.
29. [766] Ispas, Alexa. *Psychology and politics: a social identity perspective*. Psychology Press, 2014.
30. [767] Fitz, Jennifer. "Does the Seal of Confession Help Criminals?" *National Catholic Register*, www.ncregister.com/blog/jenfitz/does-the-seal-of-confession-help-criminals.
31. [768] McGonigal, Kelly. Chapter 4: License to Sin: Why Being Good Gives Us Permission to Be Bad (81-106). *The Willpower Instinct: How Self-Control Works, Why It Matters, and What You Can Do to Get More of It*. Avery, 2013.
32. [769] McGonigal, Kelly. Chapter 4: License to Sin: Why Being Good Gives Us Permission to Be Bad (81-106). *The Willpower Instinct: How Self-Control Works, Why It Matters, and What You Can Do to Get More of It*. Avery, 2013.

guilt because Christian churches serve as a convenient institution to relieve their guilt; they perceive themselves as righteous for seeking God's forgiveness, they perceive such forgiveness as the highest moral authority above any human laws based on their upbringing in Christian theology, they relieve their guilt through honest confession to a priest which feels emotionally gratifying to them personally, they perceive their do-nothing act of confession as a positive self-conception through moral licensing, and they go back to their lives without ever feeling the need to confess to the police or to seek forgiveness from the victim.[770] Perhaps, they'll end-up stealing, embezzling, raping, or so forth again and continue to relieve their guilt through confession to the priest for years until caught after more victims pile-up from their behavior. They've long since rationalized these acts as sinfulness that is intrinsic to being a human (possibly along with gender stereotypes) and rationalized that their victims are somehow equally capable of what they do to them because all humans are prone to sin, so it simply doesn't matter to the perpetrator as a result.[771]

Perhaps this specific argument will be fiercely contested as ignorance on my part. After all, I am arguing that the very faith system that you likely believe in has done the exact opposite of accountability in a systematized way. I am arguing that the theology itself perpetuates the worst of abuses and helps perpetrators exploit the abuse through the Christian institutions. Consider this thought experiment:

A noted good-natured, well-respected member of the community, known as a loving father and devoted husband, who is devout in his Christian faith and attends Church service every Sunday, comes to his local Church to confess to the priest. At the confession box, he admits that in his youth at the age of eighteen, he and his friends raped a fourteen year-old girl who had been enamored with him at the time. He tearfully confesses this crime to the priest and the priest obliges in responding that the Abrahamic God has forgiven the well-respected and devout gentleman. The gentleman wipes his tears, thanks the priest, and goes back to his usual self without ever confessing the crime to the police in order to make amends with the actual victim. The priest must keep the information of this crime a secret because the seal of confession is the same as keeping faith to his God.[772] The priest must keep silent while the man is in the Church every Sunday with the other attendants, when the well-respected man is befriending other attendants and their respective families are becoming closer, when the wife of the well-respected man confesses to more mundane incidents that she's done, and even in possible occurrences where the priest is told that the well-respected man is alone around fourteen-year old children. If any community members plan to send their children on a hiking trip with the well-respected man as the trusted chaperone or send their children to a sleepover

---

33. [770] Fitz, Jennifer. "What Happens If Sacramental Confession Ceases to Be Secret?" *Faith on the Couch*, Patheos, 27 Dec. 2014, www.patheos.com/blogs/jenniferfitz/2014/09/what-happens-if-sacramental-confession-ceases-to-be-secret/.
34. [771] Nietzsche, Friedrich Wilhelm. *On the genealogy of morals: a polemical tract*. Translated by Ian Johnston, PDF, Richer Resources Publications, 2014.
35. [772] Fitz, Jennifer. "Does the Seal of Confession Help Criminals?" *National Catholic Register*, www.ncregister.com/blog/jenfitz/does-the-seal-of-confession-help-criminals.

to the well-respected man's house with the well-respected man's children, then the priest is required to keep silent about the hideous past by the faith in his God. And, if any horrible incident, like another 14-year old getting raped by the well-respected man happens? The priest will remain silent by the faith in his God and espouse vague generalities about sinfulness being ubiquitous in all of humankind. He may even attempt to relieve himself of his own guilt by praying to the Abrahamic God to feel at ease with himself. If the victim was yet another fourteen-year old girl, he may even rationalize by preaching sermons about how young girls shouldn't be out with neighbors, how they need to wear less revealing clothes, or how they shouldn't be going out at night. Both prayer and the preaching would all be a self-serving way to relieve his own culpability in the tragedy that he could have prevented by not keeping faith to his God.

Immediately, you may feel the need to argue that the priest is a hypocrite and thus against Jesus Christ's teachings. However, this is just another paradoxical failing of Christianity and the teachings of Jesus Christ. While victims and congregants may feel the need to argue hypocrisy on the part of the priest; the priest's view is keeping in faith to his God by following the extremist belief in the doctrine of forgiveness. It is precisely because Jesus Christ's doctrine of forgiveness is extremist that this supposed failure happens and a child would be made an innocent victim. It is a failing on the part of the Christian faith. Given the seal of confession, how can you ever trust a priest to speak to you truthfully about the potential crimes of other congregants? The priest may never directly lie; but espousing vague generalities like sinfulness as the reason only gives a disingenuous view and a generalization of what actually occurred. The priest, precisely because he or she must be a person of God, cannot tell congregants the truth about the dangers of an individual in the community. Therefore, it is the religious framework of Christian theology and the religious institution that help abet human violence. The argument that priests let power and corruption influence them seems altogether unconvincing to me; judging from the theology, it would be more accurate to see misdirection as a logical consequence of the theological framework. A priest would try their best to not lie and not break the trust of a penitent. The unfortunate but obvious result is misdirecting others about heinous offenses that a congregant got away with and it is the norm as a result of Christian theology. While a priest may not directly lie, they would be pressured to confuse and misdirect to keep to their faith in God. Given their commitment to Jesus Christ, why should you ever feel comfortable trusting a priest?[773][774]

A priest may try to rationalize keeping the secret through the fixed nature of their belief system. Since it would be disrespecting their faith in the Abrahamic God, the priest may try to find positive qualities about the rapist to remind himself or herself that the confessor is still somehow a good-natured gentleman despite having committed a heinous crime with no

---

36. [773] Nietzsche, Friedrich Wilhelm. *THE ANTICHRIST*. Translated by H. L. Mencken, The Project Gutenberg, 2006.
37. [774] Nietzsche, Friedrich Wilhelm. Chapter XXVI: THE PRIESTS (88-91). *Thus spake Zarathustra: a book for all and none*. Translated by Thomas Common, PDF ed., T. Common, 1908.

penalties. Due to Christian theology, the priest may feel that the man has already made amends to the highest moral authority, the Abrahamic God, by confessing to the priest. Human laws are considered far less important because they're seeped in the sinfulness of the carnal world and therefore not as important as faith in God and seeking forgiveness from God.[775] The priest may convince themselves that the 14-year old must have done something like sexually entice the well-respected gentleman by wearing revealing clothing, having gotten herself drunk, or stayed out at night to cause the well-respected gentleman to rape her, because the confessor is a good-natured human being who the priest has never seen do any harm in his anecdotal experience.[776][777] The priest may even look to charities that the man commits to; not necessarily direct donations to the Church, but rather helping with Church support groups like helpfully getting recent converts off of alcohol addiction, helping at a Church charity drive for the homeless by giving them food and shelter, or donating handsomely to a Church charity that works to purchase Christmas toys for orphans at a Church orphanage.[778] They may pray to the Abrahamic God to relieve their guilt. In effect, rationalizing their decision and making themselves feel good about doing nothing.[779] Furthermore, it is apparent that viewing the priest as merely a hypocrite is a fundamental attribution error.[780] Viewing their actions in the context of an individual would ignore the norms they've inculcated through faith in the Abrahamic God and the obvious fact that Jesus Christ preached to fear hypocrisy in every corner within the Beatitudes while simultaneously preaching that you shouldn't judge others.[781][782] The priest is not specifically the problem, the institution and theology of Christianity is the source of this wretched system of abuse because of the intersection of paradoxical and absolute belief systems forming an incoherent holistic theology. As a result, keeping faith in the Abrahamic God and Jesus Christ means that a Christian priest must always lie to the public.[783]

The Seal of Confession and the doctrine of forgiveness help perpetrators feel morally at ease with their wrongful conduct. Staunch theologians and adamant Church attendees, especially of the Catholic denomination, may be prompted to give scathing rebukes to this challenge to Christian theology. Many Op-eds and Catholic editorials have stridently argued that if the confessor didn't come to confess their crimes to Church then they wouldn't be

---

38. [775] Nietzsche, Friedrich Wilhelm. *THE ANTICHRIST*. Translated by H. L. Mencken, The Project Gutenberg, 2006.
39. [776] Cialdini, Robert B. "Chapter 1: Weapons of Influence (1-16)" *Influence: Science and practice*. 4th ed., 21st Century Bks, 2002.
40. [777] Kahneman, Daniel. *Thinking, fast and slow*. Farrar, Straus and Giroux, 2015.
41. [778] Kahneman, Daniel. *Thinking, fast and slow*. Farrar, Straus and Giroux, 2015.
42. [779] Nietzsche, Friedrich Wilhelm. *On the genealogy of morals: a polemical tract*. Translated by Ian Johnston, PDF, Richer Resources Publications, 2014.
43. [780] McDermott, Rose. Group Processes (239-260). *Political Psychology in International Relations*. Ann Arbor: U of Michigan, 2004. Print.
44. [781] "BibleGateway." *Bible Gateway*, Bible Gateway Blog, www.biblegateway.com/passage/?search=Matthew 5&version=KJV.
45. [782] McDermott, Rose. Group Processes (239-260). *Political Psychology in International Relations*. Ann Arbor: U of Michigan, 2004. Print.
46. [783] Nietzsche, Friedrich Wilhelm. *THE ANTICHRIST*. Translated by H. L. Mencken, The Project Gutenberg, 2006.

confessing at all.[784] Additionally, the sanctity of the Church would falter into question because people would feel unease in coming to Church at all since confessions wouldn't be kept private and the relationship with God would be trivialized.[785] The legitimacy, theological underpinnings, and sanctity of the Church would be diminished in stature.[786] However, what if you reverse the proposition of the argument? The perpetrator of a crime can feel a sense of ease because there is a place that is self-identified as above the law, where they can confess to relieve their guilt without any legal repercussions. Confessing in this manner is normalized as far more morally righteous than simply going to the police and admitting the crime because of the belief in the doctrine of forgiveness and the belief that the Church has a special relationship with God, who is perceived as a higher moral authority than government authorities, the legal system, or the community.[787] Special pleading is the fallacy of exempting oneself or one's group from applying critical standards, principles, or rules that are usually applied to everyone else.[788] In the context of Christian theology, confession of criminal behavior by Christians to Christian priests thereby exempts them from confessing to the police because Jesus Christ has forgiven them and God's moral authority is seen as far higher than secular morality which is applied to non-Christians or less pious Christians. This special pleading argument has severely damaging consequences for civil and criminal justice systems. *The perpetrator feels morally satisfied for having done nothing.*[789] All that has changed is their self-interpretation of themselves; instead of simply praying to God for forgiveness for rape, they've gone to a so-called house of God and told the priest the truth. It is a moral convenience to make themselves feel better without suffering any meaningful consequences. The priest is where it is safe, where a perpetrator can feel a sense of catharsis for having committed a crime and then admitted to it, and feel closer to God as a convenient result. Confessing to a priest and facing no punishment is far removed from admitting to the police so they can agree to a sentencing for the crime to make amends to the victim. *The doctrine of forgiveness acts as the most convenient and persistent obstruction of justice in criminal and civil laws.* The argument that the sanctity of the Church is at risk and that's why confessions must be kept a secret would mean the Church is a safe haven for all harmful misdeeds.[790] *The argument that the sanctity of the Church is at stake when removing the Seal of Confession is an admittance that the Church must exist to*

---

47. [784] Fitz, Jennifer. "What Happens If Sacramental Confession Ceases to Be Secret?" *Faith on the Couch*, Patheos, 27 Dec. 2014, www.patheos.com/blogs/jenniferfitz/2014/09/what-happens-if-sacramental-confession-ceases-to-be-secret/.
48. [785] Fitz, Jennifer. "Does the Seal of Confession Help Criminals?" *National Catholic Register*, www.ncregister.com/blog/jenfitz/does-the-seal-of-confession-help-criminals.
49. [786] Fitz, Jennifer. "Does the Seal of Confession Help Criminals?" *National Catholic Register*, www.ncregister.com/blog/jenfitz/does-the-seal-of-confession-help-criminals.
50. [787] "Special Pleading." *Https://Www.logicallyfallacious.com*, www.logicallyfallacious.com/tools/lp/Bo/LogicalFallacies/163/Special-Pleading.
51. [788] "Special Pleading." *Https://Www.logicallyfallacious.com*, www.logicallyfallacious.com/tools/lp/Bo/LogicalFallacies/163/Special-Pleading.
52. [789] Nietzsche, Friedrich Wilhelm. *On the genealogy of morals: a polemical tract*. Translated by Ian Johnston, PDF, Richer Resources Publications, 2014.
53. [790] Fitz, Jennifer. "Does the Seal of Confession Help Criminals?" *National Catholic Register*, www.ncregister.com/blog/jenfitz/does-the-seal-of-confession-help-criminals.

obstruct justice by hiding crimes in order to function in society. It is overwhelming evidence that the existence of Christianity itself is harmful to maintaining a society. While forgiving people for everything may help conveniently gain converts from vast swathes of the world, it would fall apart at the seams without codified and secularized laws to efficiently maintain some form of status quo that doesn't adhere to the extremist doctrine of forgiving everyone for all forms of human violence. But what about the argument that without the Church, they wouldn't confess at all?[791] Well, how can we be so sure that they wouldn't confess at all? If, for instance, they confessed to their families or friends, then they would be more liable to face charges because friends and family could feel it was a moral obligation to tell the police or that what the confessor did was far too egregious to not notify the police. If the Church didn't conveniently exist above the law and tout itself as the highest moral authority, and the perpetrator is wracked with guilt, then it is significantly possible that the perpetrator would confess to the police and accept going to prison to make amends to the victim. Now, while it's just as possible that the perpetrator would simply keep silent, the moral utility of the Church would no longer serve as a convenient hiding place for their crimes and therefore wouldn't obstruct legal redress for crimes committed upon others. It would likely increase the statistical occurrences of victims gaining justice for being wronged by the perpetrators.

The crimes of pedophile priests in the Catholic Church, when they initially gained coverage, likely shocked and confused devout Christians. When the immediate snap judgment of children being taught to lie by greedy parents for profits slowly dwindled as ignorant nonsense as the cases kept growing and building[792][793]; Churches such as the ones in Philadelphia, Pennsylvania in the US were found to keep the child rape cases a secret to get them over the statue of limitations.[794] Catholic priests were found to be moving about to different branches across the world to avoid scrutiny and to be kept hidden to this day, resulting in more child rape victims.[795][796] Events such as this prompted a clamoring of cries that greed, selfishness, and immorality had corrupted the Catholic Church. More revelations throughout the US State of Pennsylvania on the ghastly extent of child rape crimes by the

---

54. [791] Fitz, Jennifer. "What Happens If Sacramental Confession Ceases to Be Secret?" *Faith on the Couch*, Patheos, 27 Dec. 2014, www.patheos.com/blogs/jenniferfitz/2014/09/what-happens-if-sacramental-confession-ceases-to-be-secret/.
55. [792] Kahneman, Daniel. *Thinking, fast and slow*. Farrar, Straus and Giroux, 2015.
56. [793] Cialdini, Robert B. "Chapter 1: Weapons of Influence (1-16)" *Influence: Science and practice*. 4th ed., 21st Century Bks, 2002.
57. [794] Cipriano, Ralph. "Catholic Church Priests Raped Children in Philadelphia, but the Wrong People Went to Jail." *Newsweek*, 15 Dec. 2017, www.newsweek.com/2017/12/08/catholic-church-priests-raped-children-philadelphia-725894.html.
58. [795] Cipriano, Ralph. "Catholic Church Priests Raped Children in Philadelphia, but the Wrong People Went to Jail." *Newsweek*, 15 Dec. 2017, www.newsweek.com/2017/12/08/catholic-church-priests-raped-children-philadelphia-725894.html.
59. [796] "Priest in Nunavut Pleads Guilty to 8 Sex Charges | CBC News." *CBCnews*, CBC/Radio Canada, 18 Nov. 2013, www.cbc.ca/news/canada/north/eric-dejaeger-catholic-priest-pleads-guilty-to-sex-charges-1.2429865.

Catholic Church has prompted further denunciations of the same sort.[797][798] Yet, when analyzing the cornerstone beliefs of Christian theology, it shouldn't have been surprising. The ubiquity of the doctrine of forgiveness for all wrongful misdeeds, without any proper classification for when behavior is too harmful, helps to shield perpetrators of horrendous acts of violence from feeling guilty because Jesus takes their sin away through forgiveness and helps to make them feel morally righteous for doing absolutely nothing to correct their behavior since repentance is just recognizing Jesus Christ as lord and savior. Why wouldn't a Catholic priest hide the child rape abuse of another Catholic priest given the theological axioms of Christianity? The Seal of Confession is a pervasive and crucial part of Catholic theology. When a Catholic priest confesses to raping a child to a hierarchical superior, the first impulse is to forgive the pedophile priest of child rape. The Catholic priest of higher rank listening to the confession of the pedophile priest would then recognize the rape of a child as merely a mortal sin and not part of a sacred oath to the Abrahamic God and Jesus Christ, therefore it wouldn't be worthy of being defrocked. The pedophile priest hadn't committed a cardinal sin, which is considered a far worse offense than raping a child in Catholic theology. *They hide it because thought crimes are more important than raping a child in Catholic theology.*

Before I give my next contention regarding the doctrine of forgiveness and secular legal systems, first a caveat to make clear certain distinctions, it should be noted that certain laws simply cause terribly unfair charges and consequences to be imposed upon innocent people who aren't necessarily guilty of any crimes. We've all heard of stupid legal cases where innocents were given the worst and most extreme form of sentencing for so-called crimes that didn't warrant such criminal convictions. In the US, due to societal derision towards pedophiles, there are cases that have nothing to do with pedophilia that are labeled as such; for example, I once read of the case of two thirteen-year olds consensually having sexual relations; only for courts to legally deem it pedophilia on the part of both teens having somehow raped each other and they were both sentenced to several years in juvenile facilities for child rape. I don't approve of what they did, but that obviously was not child rape. Despite the stupidity of certain laws and sentencing practices, the majority of cases aren't the odd case that erupts in social media to grab our attention. They grab our attention because they're oddities, not the norm unless patterns of abuse are established. We must be aware of statistical percentages of events in our deliberations on how to improve society and what needs changing. To deal with one particular US contention regarding priest-penitent privilege, while the perpetrator of a

---

60. [797] Ruland, Sam. "'No More Pain' Victim Wrote of Pa. Priest Sex Abuse, as He and Others Took Their Own Lives." *The York Daily Record*, York Daily Record, 21 Aug. 2018, www.ydr.com/story/news/2018/08/21/pennsylvania-priest-sex-abuse-some-took-their-own-lives-others-considered-suicide-grand-jury-report/1042459002/.
61. [798] Silva, Christianna. "New Report Details Child Sex Abuse by More than 300 Catholic Clergy in Pennsylvania, but Most Will Go Unpunished." *VICE News*, VICE News, 14 Aug. 2018, news.vice.com/en_us/article/43p5kn/new-report-details-child-sex-abuse-by-more-than-300-catholic-clergy-in-pennsylvania-but-most-will-go-unpunished.

crime could confess to their spouse and have that information be privileged, it is a total non-sequitur argument to use in defense of maintaining a religious institution that presents itself as above the law and impervious to legal redress for hiding confessions. The point is to decrease incidents of perpetrators getting away with crimes, while the spousal privilege is a clear obstacle, it doesn't thereby vindicate an institution that functionally exists as a safeguard for criminal confessions.

One final consideration about Christian theology to its totality should be noted; the doctrine of forgiveness simply places your children in jeopardy of being physically, emotionally, and sexually abused by criminals who've supposedly accepted Jesus Christ into their heart and joined your local Church. Murderers, child molesters, and people with sociopathic and narcissistic tendencies would have far easier access to your children and could easily do any harmful act upon them when you're caught unawares. A criminal on death row accepting Jesus Christ into their heart would garner solemn acceptance or even positive enthusiasm by Christians because they're in prison and their actions will have no tangible effects upon the public at large. However, a criminal who accepts Jesus Christ into their heart from a conversion by a priest in your community or your denomination and then becomes part of your local Church upon release is likely to garner a profound sense of alarm at the potential consequences and cause fear for your family's safety. If the person joining is a repeat offender of crimes pertaining to child rape or physical violence, this will undoubtedly cause more anxiety and alarm at the person being within the proximity of one's own children; having knowledge of where you live, what you look like, who your children are and what they look like, and possibly where your children go to school. A priest or pastor would preach that bringing such an ex-criminal to the Church is a test of faith and that you and your community need to practice forgiveness towards even the worst offenders to stay true to Jesus Christ's teachings. *In other words, you should strongly give in to willful self-delusion and put your children at risk of being raped and murdered because of your faith in Jesus Christ. To truly prove your faith in Jesus Christ, endangering your life and the lives of your children is required as proof as if they were chess pieces on a scale of judgment.* You've likely heard stories of people who've come to accept Jesus Christ into their heart, only to then become repeat offenders. It's not that they weren't sincere as people are led to believe or that the teachings have gone awry. As mentioned prior, the teachings of Jesus Christ are a failure by design; every form of human violence is justified through sin and the doctrine of forgiveness just means that the ex-criminal habitually learned to forgive themselves of raping children and murdering people. Why forgiving themselves for killing someone or raping children means they wouldn't do it again begs incredulity. Moreover, what kind of God requires you to put your children at perpetual risk to satisfy their ego? *You aren't morally wrong for wanting to protect your children and you shouldn't be expected to forgive criminals by putting your children at risk to prove your faith.* It is not the case of you being undeserving of Jesus Christ should you not agree to put your children at risk to satisfy the teachings of Jesus Christ to prove you're a moral person, it's the complete opposite. Jesus Christ isn't deserving of you and his teachings are a farce that could potentially lead to your children being raped and murdered in real life. What will the priest say, if your child is raped and murdered, because you believed the ex-criminal had genuinely changed for the better through the teaching of Jesus? "Sin is everywhere" and "God works in mysterious ways" and "They're in heaven now." will likely be the expected pabulum after you give in to willful self-delusion and leave your beloved children exposed to people who you pity, forgive, and then trust by their display of strong faith; only for you to lose everything because of your faith in Jesus Christ. The love for your children should always come before your love for Jesus Christ and the Abrahamic God. To do otherwise is immoral from a secular viewpoint. *To truly love your children, you should love them more than either Jesus Christ or the Abrahamic God. To love your children above your God is true parental love.* I write this, not to offend, but because I genuinely believe it. One final aspect to note is that since locations in certain countries passed laws identifying people's criminal backgrounds and making communities largely aware of this so they have the knowledge to take precautions, it should be pointed out that governments wouldn't have had to pass these laws to fully acknowledge people with criminal backgrounds and their repeat offenses, if Christian Churches weren't theologically bound to hide them through confession and the doctrine of forgiveness. These laws had to be passed so that priests and pastors would responsibly inform the community instead of keeping quiet about their knowledge. If you feel sympathy for their plight in keeping it hidden because of their faith, then that is your acknowledgement that it was their faith that motivated them to keep it hidden and Christian theology is therefore the problem and not the solution to your children being at risk. Your children are safer when far away from Church because it's the only institution that can legally hide murderers and rapists in a systematic way through Priest-Penitent privilege that was created to respect the Seal of Confession. Even if your Church were to abandon confessions of illegal activity pertaining to rape or murder to go unpunished, you cannot be sure that every individual priest would do the same due to their strong faith in Jesus Christ.

Chapter 16: The Narcissism of Jesus Christ

John 14:6 King James Version (KJV)

⁶ *Jesus saith unto him, I am the way, the truth, and the life: no man cometh unto the Father, but by me.*[799]

For this section, I will be giving two thought experiments to show the limitations and failings of Christianity as a belief system, Jesus Christ's teachings, and Jesus Christ's claim to godhood. I was shocked to discover that the second thought experiment never had a good answer from Christian theology. I had come-up with the issue regarding the second thought experiment at the age of twelve, but assumed in ignorance that some aspect of Christian theology addressed the question. I discovered I was wrong and nothing in Christian theology could honestly address the question. The most intriguing aspect was that Christians who didn't regularly study their theology or even attend Church, the so-called "Christians in name only", assumed their theology addressed the question and that I was being arrogant. Meanwhile, devout Christians were distraught by the question and refused to engage in debate with me after hearing the thought experiment. This is all merely anecdotal, despite my attempts to pose these questions at various forums with people completely refusing to engage in them, banning me without responding from their forums, or rebuking with arguments that Islam is worse, even though that has nothing to do with the questions posed or Christianity's theological issues. Christian theologians I spoke with simply refused to engage with my question and ignored it.

I would kindly ask that you seriously consider the second thought experiment and what it means, because every challenge posed in this book thus far regarding Christian theology is cemented by my bewilderment at the vitriol I received for asking questions that formed the basis of the second thought experiment. I was honestly surprised how damaging this overtly obvious contradiction in Western culture and Christian theology was to some people, because I had assumed that millions upon millions of Christians had thought through this question already. I never meant it as a joke question or an insult, so I still don't understand why it was treated that way. I can only conclude now, from my own personal analysis and understanding, that it's because Christian theology is a concomitant of systematized self-contradictions and unquestioned obedience.

First Thought Experiment:

The non-Christian Child and His Killer

If a criminal, who is a serial child rapist and killer, comes to Jesus, sincerely accepts Jesus into his heart, before death row then he's going to heaven. The pastor/clergyman who has convinced him to come to Jesus, who has studied his/her theology for the majority of their

---

1. [799] "BibleGateway." *Bible Gateway*, Bible Gateway Blog, www.biblegateway.com/passage/?search=John 14:6&version=KJV.

life and believes in Jesus's forgiveness just as any other Christian, sincerely believes that the criminal has been forgiven by accepting Jesus into his heart under the doctrine of forgiveness. Therefore, the criminal, who is a serial child rapist and killer, should be going to heaven. If either of them is wrong, then Jesus's doctrine of forgiveness doesn't save everyone.

If the criminal was targeting Jewish or Muslim children then those children are going to hell for not accepting Jesus into their heart. If they die believing in their respective religions, or called to their respective Jewish or Islamic version of the Abrahamic God, then they've deceived themselves and they're going to hell. If they're allowed in heaven, then accepting Jesus into one's heart, and Jesus's doctrine of forgiveness, isn't necessary to go to heaven. Thereby, making Jesus Christ's doctrine irrelevant. If they're in purgatory and have to seek forgiveness for being sinful, then Christianity doesn't save innocent children who have been raped and murdered.

Second Thought Experiment:

Jesus Christ and the Holocaust

If accepting Jesus Christ into your heart is the only way to heaven, then that would mean that every Jewish person who died in the Holocaust is in hell. If the Jewish Holocaust victims are not in hell, then you don't need to accept Jesus Christ into your heart to enter heaven because believing in Jesus Christ would be meaningless to enter heaven. So, either Christianity is true and Jewish Holocaust victims are in hell, or Christianity is false and Jewish Holocaust victims are not in hell.

Any other response leads to arbitrariness with needing to believe in Jesus Christ to enter heaven. John 14:6 establishes that you need to believe in Jesus Christ to enter heaven.[800] If you are a Christian and believe that Jesus Christ is the only path to heaven, then the Jewish Holocaust victims can't be in heaven, precisely because you believe in Jesus Christ as the only way to salvation. Consequently, any Nazi who was a confessing Catholic or sought Jesus's forgiveness for the Holocaust will be going to heaven for sincerely accepting Jesus Christ into their heart. Therefore, Christian theology itself creates a standard where Jewish Holocaust victims suffer in hell and Nazis who seek Jesus's forgiveness go to heaven.

One evangelical fundamentalist that I challenged on the first argument had immediately responded that children, regardless of religious affiliation, automatically go to heaven. He, and I'm sure many others of his congregation, believe the Abrahamic God would never allow children to go to hell. That was how they rationalized war and human violence against children in general. A few other Christians of other denominations that I conversed with on social

---

2. [800] "BibleGateway." *Bible Gateway*, Bible Gateway Blog, www.biblegateway.com/passage/?search=John 14:6&version=KJV.

media argued the children were sinful and needed to repent and so deserved hell. Overall, few took it seriously.

The second thought experiment had the opposite reaction; it stunned people. Many exclaimed surprise and those who weren't part of the Christian faith said it was a very good question to pose. I posed this question on social media first; those who took it seriously exclaimed shock as they had never thought of it, those who didn't take it seriously accused me of insulting their faith and "trolling" a colloquial term to mean belittling them for their beliefs. The people who took it seriously ultimately said it was up to the Abrahamic God to decide and they had nothing to do with it. Catholics who responded said the Jewish Holocaust victims would not be in hell, but rather purgatory and it would be up to the Abrahamic God to decide. In a similar fashion to non-Catholic denominations, they also reiterated that they had nothing to do with it. Years later, to test whether I had stumbled upon a truly profound question, I asked the opinion of my thesis counselor, who held college degrees in divinity and political science. He told me the majority of Churchgoers and Christians in general would likely say that it was up to God. I didn't push further in our email exchange, but it was likely evident to the both of us that this required the fallacy of an argument from ignorance. The best response I received was two years later in 2018, when I asked a self-touted Christian utilitarian I had met from interactions on social media about the *Shin Megami Tensei* video game series, the person responded by saying the doctrine of "by faith alone" led to all sorts of unsatisfying, idiotic, and paradoxical consequences that had condemned the Christian faith into the worst forms of idiocy and logical fallacies. He preferred to think of Christianity as emphasizing good works and stated it proved that "by faith alone" needed to be removed for Christianity to have any degree of seriousness in academia and in people's everyday lives. Otherwise, it doomed itself to being abandoned entirely as mere mythology because of the theology's poorly reasoned catch-22 logical fallacies.

For my part, I was genuinely surprised to discover that a question I had thought about at age twelve could pose such a challenge to an entire faith-based system. It confused me to discover that Christianity and the US public at large had never even once considered this glaring issue and contention. How could that be possible? I was in genuine confusion and disbelief that a question I thought of at age twelve, when I first read about Original Sin and Jesus Christ's salvation in Christian theology, could be so impactful and shocking to Christians. Western culture is inundated in Christian literature, theology, cultural icons, and Churches along with recognizing the Holocaust as the worst genocide in history with the argument of "Never again" as a slogan against genocide. How did no one make this connection since World War 2? Perhaps, they did and were too scared to voice it or ponder it for long? And that was one of my focal reasons for writing this book. All the reasons listed up to this point were my reflections on why this question was never posed or addressed by Christian theology. I feel it would serve as a useful tool for Christians and non-Christians in deliberations of religious faith and in contentious debates about faith and science. If Christianity can make bold claims about the reason for human existence, the truth claims of Jesus Christ, and the supposed peacefulness of Jesus's teachings, then it must be challenged to prove itself. If it can't prove itself when challenged, then why believe in Jesus at all? Ask yourself, is there any difference between blind faith and willful self-delusion in order to convince yourself that you're right?[801] Furthermore, you could change the question to reflect on any genocide of non-Christians and it would likely have the same cultural impact for different cultures. Instead of the Holocaust, it could be applied to a genocide that happened to non-Christian groups more recently. To the best of my knowledge, the second thought experiment exposes the failings of Christian theology.

Christian Crusaders and Just War Theology

Below is the details of the meaning behind St. Augustine's "just war" argument and the theological additions of what was meant by "crusade" to explain their distinctions. This passage was written by Professor Richard Abels, a history professor for the US Naval Academy and provides useful context to understand what modern political philosophers and policymakers mean when citing Augustinian Just War and the Crusades in their framework for lawmaking.

> **Difference between Augustinian "just war" and "crusade":**
> The standard for a Christian **"just war"** as developed by Augustine (c. A.D. 400) is: "**rightful intention** on the part of the participants, which should always be expressed through love of God and neighbour; a **just cause**; and legitimate proclamation by a **qualified authority**." (Quoted from J. Riley-Smith, The Crusades, Yale University, 1987.) The **doctrine of holy war/crusade added two further assumptions: 1) Violence and its consequences–death and injury–are morally neutral** rather than intrinsically evil, and whether violence is good or bad is a matter of intention. (The analogy is to a surgeon, who cuts into the body, thus injuring it, in order to make it better/healthier.) 2) **Christ is concerned with the political order of man,** and intends for his agents on earth, kings, popes, bishops, to establish on earth **a Christian Republic** that was a "single, universal, transcendental state' ruled by Christ through the lay and clerical magistrates he endowed with authority.
> It follows from this that the defense of the Christian Republic against God's enemies, whether foreign infidel (e.g. Turks) or domestic heretics and Jews was a moral imperative for those qualified to fight. **A Crusade was a holy war fought against external or internal enemies for the recovery of Christian property or defense of the Church or the Christian people**. It could be wages against Turks in Palestine, Muslims in Spain, pagan Slavs in the Baltic, or heretics in southern France, all of whom were enemies or rebels against God.[802]

What does this mean? It isn't morally wrong for Christians to wage a war so long as an authority figure deemed legitimate proclaims it. The authority figure doesn't even have to be a

---

3. [801] "Shin Megami Tensei IV: Apocalypse." US, Atlus, 2016.
4. [802] Abels, Richard. "Crusades and Early Christian Attitudes toward Warfare." *Academia.edu*, www.academia.edu/22844402/Crusades_and_early_Christian_attitudes_toward_warfare.

Christian, but Christians are expected to thoughtlessly obey regardless.[803] Violence committed by Christians isn't considered morally wrong according to this branch of Christian theology. The theological underpinnings of Just War and the Crusades assert that instead of abstaining from violence as morally wrong under Christianity, you should detach your feelings from the consequences of committing violence in the name of Jesus Christ and that committing such violence while never holding yourself accountable is consistent with Jesus Christ's teachings. Under the framework of this portion of Christian theology, particularly the first added assumption, you should never feel responsible for your violence upon non-Christians. The Just War and Crusader theology of Christianity helps to justify Christians committing child murders, war rape, and mass civilian casualties and purports to be consistent with Christian theology since 400 AD. It is still utilized today and celebrated as profound in both Christian theology and Western academia.

Sadly, this has other nefarious implications within the context of Christian theology so long as it is revered as an important cornerstone. It means that Christianity really is a self-touted and self-celebrating religion of violence that is proud of declaring itself a war religion. Christianity is celebrated as directly antagonistic to all forms of peaceful co-existence with those that hold non-Christian beliefs. Christianity declares it must "defend itself" by invading other peoples lands, decries any violence on the part of foreigners as "proof of evil" with deplorable expletives and arguments the foreigners are Satanists, and then declares itself a peaceful religion trying to stymie the so-called ubiquitous nature of sinfulness. The function of Christianity in war time is simply a display of willful ignorance towards all forms of the reciprocity principle.[804] *At the core of its theological underpinnings, Just War and Crusader theology is just a collective narcissism to congratulate itself on committing the worst forms of human violence and then celebrating the success of war as proof they're God's Chosen People to further reinforce the collective narcissism.* When Christianity declares war, it celebrates how peaceful it is while killing foreigners in far more efficient and deadly means than the foreigners through superior technology that its own theology deems as sinful. After a ruthless and bloody crusade, Christianity celebrates how peaceful it is, how superior it's values are to everyone else's for being successful in a brutal war, and how God shed's his light upon them to victory.

To clarify further, all forms of human violence by Christians is deemed forgivable through Christianity's self-forgiveness system of atonement through Jesus Christ and all violence by non-Christians is deemed evil, because they don't accept Jesus as Lord and Savior. *The justification ultimately being that all Christian violence is neutral and all non-Christian violence is evil.* While pacifists and some devout Christians would declare this a hypocrisy and proof of distortions of Jesus's teachings, the fact remains that Christianity has repeatedly turned a blind eye to war, used the violence of other religions as justification for its own violence, and

---

5. [803] Cialdini, Robert B. " Chapter 6: Authority (178-200)" *Influence: Science and practice*. 4th ed., 21st Century Bks, 2002.
6. [804] Cialdini, Robert B. "Chapter 2: Reciprocation (19-50)" *Influence: Science and practice*. 4th ed., 21st Century Bks, 2002.

historically commits to war against the only other religion that values Jesus Christ's teachings. If two of the Abrahamic religions, Islam and Christianity, both espouse that Jesus Christ's teachings were peaceful and God-given, but continue to war against each other through perpetual violence in the most brutal, hateful, and self-serving ways; if they repeatedly keep making active commitments to violence upon each other to a far higher degree than any other religions in the entirety of world history, then why should anyone regard Jesus Christ's teachings as peaceful with any degree of seriousness? For any Christian readers who didn't know that Jesus Christ was Islam's Messiah and hate Islam, what do think it means to grow up hating another faith under the belief its teachings are violent, and to then learn that it's the only other religion that praises Jesus's teachings as peaceful, believes in Jesus's miracles, and even believes that Jesus will return in accordance with the Abrahamic God's plan? How does it feel to hate a religion that believes in Jesus's teachings and celebrates Jesus Christ as the messiah? I think, if we analyze why Christianity and Islam go to war nearly all the time, then the answer is obvious when you look at the similarities: *Jesus Christ's teachings are hateful, violent, and false.* Why, after all, do all the Abrahamic faiths declare that they're peaceful, then turn a blind eye to when religious teachings are utilized to justify war when national interests are involved? Why do so many rabbis, imams, and pastors/priests write op-eds to defend and self-justify their religion's violence upon others? Most importantly, if the Abrahamic faiths are peaceful and violence in religion's name a distortion, then what does that mean for Jewish, Muslim, and Christian soldiers?

    Finally, I can't help but notice a pernicious double-standard throughout Western social media, particularly among Conservative Christians although it exists on a smaller scale within Left-leaning Christian social media too. It is in the view that Western imperialist violence was somehow "rational" and that torture, rape, and murder of non-Christians by Western Christians was morally justified since they expanded the teachings of Jesus Christ globally. Paradoxically, the torture, rape, and murders and forced conversions of non-Muslims to Islam by Islamic invaders is seen as proof of Islam's barbarity. When topics about Christian violence in the past are brought up, they're resolutely dismissed by Christians as having happened "long ago" with the implicit assumption that the West "civilized the savages from their savage ways" to justify widespread acts of rape, torture, and mass murder. Conversely, the violent history of Islam is seen as the proof that it was never a peaceful religion and that Islamic apologists are ignoring or shutting down discussions of history by denying the reality of Islam's past. While Christian violence during the era of Western imperialism is justified as having happened "during a time before the human rights standards that we have today" as a defense for its historic violence, Islam has those modern human rights standards applied to its own history without Western Christians pointing out the self-contradiction in judging Islam by modern standards. Yet, the West applies the standards of human rights to the Armenian genocide in which Armenian Christians were specifically targeted and slaughtered by Turkish Muslims. This is rightfully recognized as an unconscionable genocide in the West and yet it was before the standards of modern human rights. In fact, the Nuremberg trials consisted of applying human rights standards that didn't exist during the time of the Holocaust to Nazi officers. Thus, we already have a world famous standard of the West putting to trial and criminalizing Nazi officers on the basis of modern human rights standards that didn't exist when the Nazis committed the Holocaust. If the West is willing to recognize and criminalize on the basis of human rights before having set-up such modern standards in the case of the Nazis and apply modern human rights in the case of the Armenian genocide, then why not also apply the same standards to all Western nation-states collective forms of violence during time periods of Western imperialism? Why be so arbitrary about time difference when such arbitrariness isn't given to the history of Islam? If we can judge Islam by its whole history, then we should for Christianity too. It is on this basis that I think judging either Islam or Christianity by modern standards shouldn't be dismissed regardless of the time period in which human rights violations happened as they give evidence for the historic consequences of what the teachings of each respective religion lead to and the dangers therein.

Christian Soldiers and Pacifism

Can you be considered a member of a religious faith, if you commit violence in the name of the religious faith? Pacifists, of all kinds, generally argue that anyone who uses religious faith as justification for violence is not acting in line with the religious teachings of the religious faith.[805] Many pacifists argue that violence in Abrahamic holy books are simply specific to the so-called "historic" context of their time period and not true for conduct today.[806] Yet, many soldiers who participate in war use the very same "historic" contexts to justify their own active engagement in the field of battle.

Such as this passage in *Christian Ministries*, by Lieutenant General, William K. Harrison Jr. of the US Military. In this passage, he explains his reasoning of how he as a Christian became a soldier and justifies Christian participation in war:

> As I started to consider the matter of being a soldier and a Christian at the same time, I recalled immediately those men of the past who were soldiers and yet were men of God: Abraham, who fought the four kings; Joshua, who served the Lord; David, who killed Goliath and then led his armies in war and who then received from God one of the greatest promises ever given to man; and those who in the eleventh chapter of Hebrews are described as having through faith in God subdued kingdoms, waxed valiant in fight, and turned to flight the armies of the aliens. In our own national history all know that George Washington and Robert E. Lee were simple Christians, and yet among the great soldiers of history.

---

7. [805] Withrow, Brandon. "Is There a Christian Double Standard on Religious Violence?" *The Daily Beast*, The Daily Beast Company, 5 Mar. 2017, www.thedailybeast.com/is-there-a-christian-double-standard-on-religious-violence.
8. [806] Withrow, Brandon. "Is There a Christian Double Standard on Religious Violence?" *The Daily Beast*, The Daily Beast Company, 5 Mar. 2017, www.thedailybeast.com/is-there-a-christian-double-standard-on-religious-violence.

> Another thing that I realized was that David, soldier that he was, yet would not kill his worst enemy, Saul, when he had him at a disadvantage and helpless. It is quoted of Lee that he said that never did he pass a day without praying for the Union soldiers.
>
> In the New Testament we find four soldiers, centurions or captains in the Roman army. the Lord said of one of these that he had greater faith than Christ had found in Israel. Another, at the cross, believed in Jesus as the Son of God. To the third God sent Peter to introduce the gospel to the Gentiles. When this man heard the gospel he believed and the Holy Spirit was given to him immediately. There is no indication that any of these discontinued his military service, nor is there any command in the New Testament that a Christian should not be a soldier. On the other hand, there is a mandate given by the Lord through Paul that we should remain in the calling in which we are called (I Corinthians 7:20).
>
> I investigated further. I found that the Lord gave Joshua instructions for the capture of Jericho, that He promised the Children of Israel victory over their enemies if they would serve Him, defeat if they did not. These are there to read if anyone desires. In Hebrews, it says that it was by faith that the walls of Jericho fell. As a soldier I know they would never have fallen that way except by faith. The fact that there were cases in which war was commanded by God to the Israelites and therefore justified is undoubted. In view of God's command, to say that war is invariably sinful is to say that God told Israel to sin, and is therefore an attack on the character of God (James 1:13). On the other hand, what are the conditions under which such war might be legitimate?[807]

The justification this soldier makes for warfare is the Bible itself. Pacifists argue that those who commit to violence are following a falsehood because they take the violent passages out of context from the history to commit violent atrocities. However, the crucial points to be noted are the following: *Christian soldiers take the violent passages out of their original historic context to justify their real life murders in the present, and* - if much of the Bible is indeed fictional then - *Christian soldiers utilize a fictional history as a self-justification to kill real life people.* The argument that they feel remorse by praying amounts to a do-nothing attitude that only functions to ease a soldier to feel comfortable with killing others.[808] In essence, it is merely a coping mechanism that helps relieve one's guilt about killing for the purpose of continuing to kill for the sake of duty to the national interests of one's country. The analogy of mercy is largely an empty sentiment and self-contradicted by fulfilling one's duties without question to continue to kill en masse. The analogies given simply fail to apply to the scope and scale of bomb droppings conducted on foreign countries. If, for instance, this soldier using anecdotes out of context as a justification dropped a bomb on an entire city and slaughtered hundreds of thousands of men, women, and children while also killing hundreds of terrorists, then justifications like the supposed historical events of the Bible as a reason would be a catalyst for inducing such reprehensible actions by making the soldier feel there was a higher purpose for it. Functionally, this soldier and an innumerable amount of other soldiers are behaving with a perverse sense of God-given purpose by using anecdotes of fictionalized violent events in the Bible, which is purported to be the past of the Middle East, to commit

---

9. [807] Harrison, William K. "May A Christian Serve in the Military?" *Officers' Christian Fellowship*, 27 June 2018, www.ocfusa.org/2009/06/christian-serve-military-2/.
10. [808] Nietzsche, Friedrich Wilhelm. *On the genealogy of morals: a polemical tract.* Translated by Ian Johnston, PDF, Richer Resources Publications, 2014.

colossal damage and widespread death tolls upon the contemporary Middle East and real life people. They could even comfort themselves with the violence they perpetuate by believing the fictional events of the Bible, that they perceive as real, to be more heinous events compared to their actions. In essence, justifying their killings of the present by using the Bible as a justification for killings in the past, believing it to be part of a cyclical and profound higher calling because they take part in killing hundreds of thousands of people similar to how the Abrahamic God mandated the killings of thousands in the Bible. They do not acknowledge the implications that this would mean the Abrahamic God's universal morals are completely worthless since its teachings do not preclude human violence because all acts of human violence are forgivable and the Abrahamic God's universal precepts require killing as a cyclical event; using events of further mass killings of innocents and soldiers of the past, such as the crusades or world wars, to help justify more killings in the name of Christianity. A pathological form of hindsight bias and the sunk-cost fallacy, using human lives lost in the past to justify killing in the present.[809] Even if you believe that the violent history of those Biblical events are accurate, the soldier is using the Bible's violent passages to justify murder. In these passages, we observe an insidiously violent and hateful belief structure at play that is created purely by Biblical mandate. This person of faith uses fictional tales of the Bible to commit very real acts of mass death upon living, breathing people in the real world.

 The non-answer of "humans will be humans" is an admission that the Abrahamic moral belief structure is worthless and doesn't teach peace. *It is an admittance that no teaching by the Abrahamic faiths has ever come close to producing peace, equality, and assistance for those who suffer and instead function as a coping mechanism in reaction to human violence without any serious degree of thought on how to stop it.* Worst of all, this non-answer shields human violence by making it seem inevitable and thus any attempt to change socio-economic reasons is stifled under the smug belief that no change in social systems can stop violence like rape and murder. To see violence perpetuated by one's faith as inevitable means that the religious faith is violent stupidity that doesn't teach peace and is proof that religious teachings perpetuate more violence upon others. *To always fallback on the non-answer of "humans will be humans" is to accept, admit, and tacitly celebrate that the Abrahamic faiths have no value in moral teachings and cannot guide people to change their behavior to be more peaceful.* Why should it be humans will be humans in the first place? Why can it not just as easily be: "Abrahamics will be Abrahamics" as an argument? Islam and Christianity constantly perpetuate violence against each other, they both believe in Jesus's teachings, and believe in the Abrahamic God; Islam is the only other religion that acknowledges Jesus as a teacher of peace and worships his teachings as God-given but under the belief that he is one of the Abrahamic God's prophets and Islam's holy messiah. To argue other Abrahamic faiths are the cause and that your branch of the Abrahamic faith's violence is justified is simply proof that the violent stupidity for the same God, Yahweh, will continue indefinitely for as long as the Abrahamic faiths exist. Does

---

11. [809] Kahneman, Daniel. *Thinking, fast and slow*. Farrar, Straus and Giroux, 2015.

that sound obnoxious and hateful? Very well, prove me wrong then. You can't, because in the end, the only real defense for this violent hatred is by pointing to another religion that follows the Abrahamic God and espousing reasons why they're even more violent than your specific branch of Abrahamic religion. In other words, believing in and worshiping the Abrahamic God doesn't make people more peaceful and repeatedly exposes and celebrates intra-Abrahamic violence as justification for their own Abrahamic violence being less worse via using the psychological effect of the contrast principle.[810]

Harrison Jr. goes on to mock pacifism and use largely fictitious binaries of Hitler and criminals lurking in every corner to conflate mass human violence of entire countries with stopping one or two criminals. By the end, he argues that his Lord and Savior Jesus Christ supports human violence and encourages the use of violence upon others through the usage of open interpretation of the Bible:

> Certain New Testament passages are quoted by pacifists in support of their position. We are to love our enemies (Matthew 5:44). This is a definite command, to be obeyed. But what shall we do when we have to choose between two loves? For example, should one defend his mother who is about to be attacked by a criminal, or should he allow the latter to commit his vicious attack? And is permissiveness to a criminal act really an act of love toward the criminal? It is evident that exaggerated permissiveness to children is very likely to encourage them to juvenile crime and worse later. "Blessed are the peacemakers . . . (Matthew 5:9)."
>
> This also is true, but when our efforts to be at peace fail, must we then submit to the aggressor? The Apostle Paul tells us that we should be at peace with others to the extent that it lies within us (Romans 12:18). Obviously the aggressor himself removes the possibility of peace unless we surrender. If struck on one cheek we are to turn the other (Matthew 5:39), thus giving the aggressor an opportunity to desist, avoiding a fight. But, if he does not desist and renews the attack, nothing is said about again turning the other cheek.
>
> Actually, experience shows that to appease an aggressor whether he be a school-yard bully or an Adolf Hitler, merely encourages him to further and greater aggression. The Lord told Peter that they who take the sword shall perish by the sword (Matthew 26:52). This certainly is historically true as regards nations, but most soldiers, from private to general, die of natural causes. Among nations, in the absence of an effective world government, it is a case of dog eat dog; so also with criminal gangs. Ordinary citizens are or should be protected by the government.
>
> Christ did not allow Peter to defend Him by force because He had come in the world to die for the sins of men in order that they might be forgiven and reconciled to God. It will be otherwise when He comes again in mighty power and glory (Matt. 24:30; II Thess. 1:7-9; Rev. 1:7; 19:11-21).
>
> During the Lord's earthly ministry, He provided for and protected the disciples, but as He prepared to depart, He told them that if they had no sword, to sell their clothing in order to buy one (Luke 22:35-38). Why was this appropriate? Romans 1:18-32 tells us that in order to reveal His wrath against men's rebellion against Him, God has given them up to all of

---

12. [810] Cialdini, Robert B. "Chapter 1: Weapons of Influence (1-16)" *Influence: Science and practice*. 4th ed., 21st Century Bks, 2002.

those personal moral evils which cause the troubles in society, among which is war. In Old Testament times, the nation Israel lived in just such a world, and today, so does the Christian.[811]

This is a Christian soldier using exactly the aforementioned arguments described prior. They utilize a constrained binary of good versus evil, using the language of Otherness and bogeyman scenarios of criminals attacking one's mother to argue for mass violence such as bombing campaigns of an entire civilian populous. Saint Augustine's arguments reveal themselves to be a deceitful sham because they're utilized by ignoring the true scope and scale of mass bombing campaigns, mass shelling during warfare such as trench warfare, and the slaughter of innocents in densely populated areas of modern warfare in order to focus on a fictitious scenario of one's caravan being attacked by raiders; it is a total non-sequitur that explicitly ignores the existence of innocent people to self-justify one's violence as heroic. The teachings of Jesus Christ are explicitly used as justification for human violence through open interpretation of the Bible. He uses examples like Hitler, but fails to examine the causes of Hitler, such as the demands of reparation for World War 1, the legacy of anti-Semitism in Europe under Christianity, the neutrality of the Catholic Church to the Holocaust instead of condemnation when it was needed, and the use of Jews somehow needing to apologize for the death of Jesus Christ in Hitler's speeches and rallies. It's worth noting that Hitler being dishonest in his usage of Jesus Christ is less important than the fact millions of lifelong German Christians were induced to commit one of the worst genocides in human history and the teachings of Jesus Christ completely failed to prevent it. The very fact so many were induced, despite purportedly living as honest Christians and harboring a culture that was uniquely deep with Christianity's vast legacy, shows that Christian moral teachings don't prevent violence, but instead provide a motivating factor to commit mass violence such as the Holocaust. While not the primary reason, Christianity did contribute to the mass violence. The supposed moral superiority of Christianity was proven false, because while a few Clergymen and Christians protected Jewish people and others from persecution; the vast majority that lived by the teachings of Jesus Christ felt it was a moral duty to kill Jewish people and other so-called undesirables for the sake of protecting Christianity and German culture.[812] While nationalism in response to the economic crisis played a central role, Christianity was still a contributing factor for violence acting as a catalyst and not as a constraint.[813]

Harrison's final point is as follows:

From a Biblical standpoint the answer is simple. The world is dead in sin. Lust, plunder, and war are the natural characteristics of the human race, dead and lost in sin (Romans

---

13. [811] Harrison, William K. "May A Christian Serve in the Military?" *Officers' Christian Fellowship*, 27 June 2018, www.ocfusa.org/2009/06/christian-serve-military-2/.
14. [812] Tix, Andrew. "The Failure of Christian Love in the Holocaust." *Biola University Center for Christian Thought / The Table*, 6 July 2017, cct.biola.edu/failure-christian-love-holocaust/.
15. [813] Tix, Andrew. "The Failure of Christian Love in the Holocaust." *Biola University Center for Christian Thought / The Table*, 6 July 2017, cct.biola.edu/failure-christian-love-holocaust/.

1:18-32). Many good Christians seek to eliminate war by dressing up the outside of the cup, seeking to cure the apparent causes of war. The real cause of war is in the sinful heart of man.

The Lord said that except a man be born again he cannot see the Kingdom of God. Being born again is a miracle. It comes only when one believes in the Lord Jesus Christ as his personal Savior and as the Son of God. People believe when they hear the gospel. Never has the preaching of the gospel succeeded in converting more than a portion of hearers at any one time.

Even at Pentecost in the great city of Jerusalem only 3,000 believed at the most wonderful exhibition of gospel power in church history. The rapid growth of Christianity in the Roman Empire resulted first in the persecution of Christians, and then ultimately in the decay of spiritual Christian life into the dark ages of medieval centuries. The Protestant Reformation did not produce more than a partial awakening. Today there is an apostasy from the simple, pure Word of God and faith in Jesus Christ, the only begotten Son of God and the only Savior.

We are not called to preach the gospel to save the world from war and crime. We can preach the gospel all we want to, but only a few believe. Christ said that broad is the way that leads to destruction and many are they that find it, and narrow is the way that leads to life and few are they that find it.

The preaching of the gospel is to them who are saved a savor unto life, unto them who are lost a savor unto death. The Scriptures say that God is now taking out a people for His name. I can find no place in the Scripture where it intimates that the preaching of the gospel of grace will succeed in converting the world.

On the other hand, it does say that the gospel should be preached to all the world as a witness. I think that the present state of civilization is ample testimony to this completely lost and incurable state of civilization. Never has the world been in a more unstable condition. If the lessons of the past are ignored, war of terrible proportions is ahead of our much-vaunted and self-satisfied civilization.

This picture I have drawn seems pessimistic. Many would hold me up as an enemy of peace because I don't agree with their method of gaining it. However, there is a way of gaining peace.

The Bible clearly describes an earthly condition when the desert shall blossom as a rose, when the lion and other animals shall not kill, when the lion shall eat grass like the ox, when venomous serpents will not kill, when there shall be no war, and when men shall learn war no more. It tells us of a time when there shall be no harm done in all the earth because it will be filled with the knowledge of the Lord.

It says also that a King shall reign in righteousness and that He shall judge in equity for the meek of the earth and take care of the poor, and that the law shall go forth from Jerusalem. Many teachers have sought to avoid the plain, obvious meaning of these passages, but if I made a business of construing my orders that way, I would long since have ceased my connection with the Army.

I think it should be perfectly obvious that man is utterly unable to save himself. His civilization is only an expression of himself. He cannot save it. But God has promised that the Lord Jesus Christ Himself will come again, that He will establish a Kingdom on earth by His own power, unaided by insignificant man.

We should preach the gospel of individual salvation in order that such as believe may be translated into His Kingdom, and we should constantly watch for His coming.[814]

This displays the exact contentions from Part 1 and the reductionist mindset argued prior. He justifies human violence under the belief that all humans are guilty because of sinfulness and thus they should be all judged negatively simply for being human, he doesn't delve into causes and consequences of what norms or activities of failed social systems cause violence, and holds a misanthropic view of humanity based on his belief in sinfulness to comfort himself for the violence that he contributes to being a cause of. Not only does he ignore his own self-contradiction of using Jesus Christ's teachings in support of human warfare to spread human violence, but then goes on to claim the gospel will make people more peaceful. If a Christian can use Jesus Christ's teachings to motivate, justify, and promote human violence and if such a belief is justifiable within a Biblical context, then how can the teachings of the gospel spread peace? It would result in the exact opposite, even among intra-Christian affairs, because Jesus's teachings would be giving them justifications for warfare. The final part is wishful thinking for a perfect world over the real world and does little more than show that this man has given-up on ever finding real solutions to ongoing problems that humans face in real life. The Bible has given him a convenient coping mechanism to justify not helping others after contributing to the spread of human violence. In the end, he's using the Bible as a self-righteous excuse to feel good about doing nothing to help others.[815] Preaching a worship of death referred to as the afterlife and perpetual impotence to await Jesus's Second Coming.[816]

Christian Fundamentalism

Evangelical Fundamentalist Christianity remains one of the most misunderstood religious faiths in the United States and across the world. Its powerbase is mainly in the US so it's critical to discuss what effects Evangelical Fundamentalism had from the standpoint of the US. Many of the Evangelical Fundamentalists are self-motivated by an intrinsic desire to correct what they view as the flaws of the world. They view the current state of the US as a state of godlessness and feel they must take part in the political process to realign the country with God's will. They view non-Christians as either deceivers or lost without the knowledge of Jesus Christ and seek to preach Jesus to the world. They join missionary groups, many Evangelical Fundamentalists work for weapons and oil corporations, they're funded by evangelical CEOs in the oil or weapons industries, they believe Islam is an evil religion, and that they must war endlessly to defeat it.[817][818][819] While some Evangelical Fundamentalists

---

16. [814] Harrison, William K. "May A Christian Serve in the Military?" *Officers' Christian Fellowship*, 27 June 2018, www.ocfusa.org/2009/06/christian-serve-military-2/.
17. [815] Nietzsche, Friedrich Wilhelm. *On the genealogy of morals: a polemical tract*. Translated by Ian Johnston, PDF, Richer Resources Publications, 2014.
18. [816] Nietzsche, Friedrich Wilhelm. *THE ANTICHRIST*. Translated by H. L. Mencken, The Project Gutenberg, 2006.
19. [817] Montgomery, Peter. "Meet the Billionaire Brothers You Never Heard of Who Fund the Religious

acknowledge global warming is a problem, the majority see it as the Second Coming of Jesus Christ and feel intense pleasure from the idea of the genocide of Jews in Israel for the Second Coming of Christ.[820][821] Even for the Fundamentalists who don't believe that Jews will be sent to hell after Israel is attacked by a demonic force, they still believe that Jewish people must convert or they will die in a mass genocide with the rest of the non-Christians.[822] It is an explicit belief in a genocide that would be larger in magnitude than the Holocaust.[823][824] This is not a strawman of Evangelical Fundamentalist beliefs; they explicitly and repeatedly state that they believe the Jews will be slaughtered for the Coming of Jesus, they repeatedly and explicitly say they want endless war with Islam, they are among the highest percentage of voters and the US continues to have wars in the Middle East, George W. Bush – the President they helped elect through the persona of a man of faith – explicitly said that God wanted him to attack Iraq and he remained highly favored among Evangelical Fundamentalists even at the end of his presidency.[825][826]

In the documentary film, "*Waiting for Armageddon*" they outright state they're awaiting the end of the world, take pleasure in the suffering and death of innocents in the Middle East, and celebrate the death of Jews when Palestinian terrorists kill them because Fundamentalists feel it brings the world closer to Jesus's Second Coming.[827] Evangelical Fundamentalists are primarily responsible for trying to put creationism into public schools and for advocating politicians to fund creationist schools with public taxes, Evangelical Fundamentalists see natural disasters and people suffering in wars as positive signs because they believe it means that Jesus will return, they go to the holy land to "walk where Jesus has walked" to feel closer

---

Right." *The American Prospect*, prospect.org/article/meet-billionaire-brothers-you-never-heard-who-fund-religious-right.
20. [818] Vogel, Kenneth P., and Tarini Parti. "How Rand Paul Bombed at Koch Brothers Gathering." *POLITICO*, 3 Feb. 2015, www.politico.com/story/2015/02/rand-was-a-dud-at-the-koch-brothers-conference-114853.
21. [819] Rhee, Joseph, et al. "U.S. Military Weapons Inscribed With Secret 'Jesus' Bible Codes." *ABC News*, ABC News Network, 18 Jan. 2010, abcnews.go.com/Blotter/us-military-weapons-inscribed-secret-jesus-bible-codes/story?id=9575794.
22. [820] *YouTube*, Q-Ball Productions Inc, 2010, www.youtube.com/watch?v=nNvtA_q0e20.
23. [821] Heilbroner, David. "Evangelicals, Israel, and the End of the World." *The Huffington Post*, TheHuffingtonPost.com, 25 May 2011, www.huffingtonpost.com/david-heilbroner/evangelicals-israel-and-t_b_391351.html.
24. [822] *YouTube*, Q-Ball Productions Inc, 2010, www.youtube.com/watch?v=nNvtA_q0e20.
25. [823] Heilbroner, David. "Evangelicals, Israel, and the End of the World." *The Huffington Post*, TheHuffingtonPost.com, 25 May 2011, www.huffingtonpost.com/david-heilbroner/evangelicals-israel-and-t_b_391351.html.
26. [824] *YouTube*, Q-Ball Productions Inc, 2010, www.youtube.com/watch?v=nNvtA_q0e20.
27. [825] *YouTube*, Q-Ball Productions Inc, 2010, www.youtube.com/watch?v=nNvtA_q0e20.
75. [826] "American Evangelicalism: New Leaders, New Faces, New Issues." Edited by Cheryl Jackson, *Pew Research Center's Religion & Public Life Project*, 6 May 2008, www.pewforum.org/2008/05/06/american-evangelicalism-new-leaders-new-faces-new-issues/.
28. [827] *YouTube*, Q-Ball Productions Inc, 2010, www.youtube.com/watch?v=nNvtA_q0e20.

to Jesus, and they have repeatedly made the explicit claim that they want the end of the world to happen so that Jesus will return.[828][829][830][831]

Do you believe that what I'm pointing out is too extreme or perhaps entirely facetious? Then please read and watch their material. Watch "*Waiting for Armageddon*", the self-made evangelical fundamentalist documentary in which they praise the idea of Jews being slaughtered, watch as they openly and repeatedly say they want endless war with Islam, watch their personal satisfaction with the prospect of Israelis and Palestinians killing each other because they believe it's a necessary step toward Jesus Christ's Second Coming; they believe any longstanding peace agreement with Israel and Palestine is the sign of the Anti-Christ and US politicians acquiesce to stopping any meaningful peace to appease the Evangelicals.[832][833] In the documentary, watch as they feel blissful at the idea of natural disasters killing innocents and wars causing mass slaughter for the sake of the Second Coming of Jesus.[834] You don't have to believe me; just read and watch their content as they openly say such statements, they celebrate the idea of mass death, and they have full conviction that what they cause is for the sake of Jesus Christ.[835] Read their tweets about the April 2015 earthquake in Nepal saying it happened because they didn't repent to Jesus.[836] Listen to prominent Evangelical pastors blaming the earthquake devastation of Haiti in 2010 on absurd beliefs in the Christian devil.[837] They continue to make documentaries about how evolution is false and how people need to return to the teachings of Jesus Christ.[838] They have active campaigns throughout the world spreading homophobia, transphobia, anti-condom use, anti-women's rights, and preach that all non-Christians will die once Jesus comes down from heaven.[839][840][841] They've openly supported

---

29. [828] "Prager 'University': How Billionaires Proselytize Rightwing Ignorance to Children." *Daily Kos*, www.dailykos.com/stories/2017/2/19/1635270/-Prager-University-How-Billionaires-Proselytize-Rightwing-Ignorance-to-Children.
30. [829] *YouTube*, Q-Ball Productions Inc, 2010, www.youtube.com/watch?v=nNvtA_q0e20.
31. [830] Heilbroner, David. "Evangelicals, Israel, and the End of the World." *The Huffington Post*, TheHuffingtonPost.com, 25 May 2011, www.huffingtonpost.com/david-heilbroner/evangelicals-israel-and-t_b_391351.html.
32. [831] Montgomery, Peter. "Meet the Billionaire Brothers You Never Heard of Who Fund the Religious Right." *The American Prospect*, prospect.org/article/meet-billionaire-brothers-you-never-heard-who-fund-religious-right.
33. [832] *YouTube*, Q-Ball Productions Inc, 2010, www.youtube.com/watch?v=nNvtA_q0e20.
34. [833] Heilbroner, David. "Evangelicals, Israel, and the End of the World." *The Huffington Post*, TheHuffingtonPost.com, 25 May 2011, www.huffingtonpost.com/david-heilbroner/evangelicals-israel-and-t_b_391351.html.
35. [834] *YouTube*, Q-Ball Productions Inc, 2010, www.youtube.com/watch?v=nNvtA_q0e20.
36. [835] *YouTube*, Q-Ball Productions Inc, 2010, www.youtube.com/watch?v=nNvtA_q0e20.
37. [836] "When Nepal Was Groaning in Earthquake, Christian Missionaries Were Shamelessly Selling Jesus - Opindia News." *OpIndia*, 4 May 2015, www.opindia.com/2015/04/when-nepal-was-groaning-in-earthquake-christian-missionaries-were-shamelessly-selling-jesus/.
38. [837] "Pat Robertson Says Haiti Paying for 'Pact to the Devil'." *CNN*, Cable News Network, 13 Jan. 2010, www.cnn.com/2010/US/01/13/haiti.pat.robertson/.
39. [838] Montgomery, Peter. "Meet the Billionaire Brothers You Never Heard of Who Fund the Religious Right." *The American Prospect*, prospect.org/article/meet-billionaire-brothers-you-never-heard-who-fund-religious-right.
40. [839] Montgomery, Peter. "Meet the Billionaire Brothers You Never Heard of Who Fund the Religious

Donald Trump's discrimination against women in the United States and were a major voting bloc that propelled Trump to the office of President. They're sometimes the only interaction that foreigners have with US citizens and as a result spread anti-Americanism abroad with their condemnations of the local populations by preaching they'll go to hell without Christ.[842][843][844] Billionaires fund their enterprise to preach how everyone will go to hell if they don't convert to Christianity.[845]

One final point of contention before moving onto the next section. All the while they celebrated the conflict between Israel and Palestine, the US public and perhaps the West in general continues to stifle any criticism of these horrible people due to the norm of religious tolerance even as they seek the end of the world for their own egos as per the teachings of their narcissistic God.[846] Just remember: if you supported silencing any criticism of them despite knowing what they happily preached, you also ended-up supporting their wholesale violence between Israel and Palestine including any Israeli or Palestinian child killed in that ongoing conflict. Do you think that's an illogical leap? If you supported religious tolerance as they supported political activism that promoted and happily celebrated the deaths of children on both sides, if you silenced criticism of the religious aspect of the conflict even as they protested against any peace measures to keep the conflict going, made documentaries saying they were absolutely satisfied with the violence and deaths for the Second Coming of Jesus; why is it wrong to say you're also part of the problem that contributes to this ongoing human violence? The Christian Fundamentalists of the US openly support violence in the Israeli-Palestine conflict with the full knowledge that children are being killed and they have such confidence that their views are the truth beyond doubt that they happily say they want more violence to

---

41. [840] Solomon, Brian. "Meet David Green: Hobby Lobby's Biblical Billionaire." *Forbes*, Forbes Magazine, 2 Nov. 2015, www.forbes.com/sites/briansolomon/2012/09/18/david-green-the-biblical-billionaire-backing-the-evangelical-movement/#5cb389335807.
42. [841] Shea, Brie. "Fracking Titans Spend Millions Proselytizing School Children." *Rewire.News*, Rewire.News, 1 May 2015, rewire.news/article/2015/04/30/conservatives-spend-millions-proselytizing-school-children/.
43. [842] "Pat Robertson Says Haiti Paying for 'Pact to the Devil'." *CNN*, Cable News Network, 13 Jan. 2010, www.cnn.com/2010/US/01/13/haiti.pat.robertson/.
44. [843] Neelakandan, Aravindan. "Why No Outrage over Conversion of Tsunami Victims?" *Swarajya Read India Right ATOM*, 29 Dec. 2014, swarajyamag.com/politics/why-no-outrage-over-conversion-of-tsunami-victims.
45. [844] "When Nepal Was Groaning in Earthquake, Christian Missionaries Were Shamelessly Selling Jesus - Opindia News." *OpIndia*, 4 May 2015, www.opindia.com/2015/04/when-nepal-was-groaning-in-earthquake-christian-missionaries-were-shamelessly-selling-jesus/.
46. [845] Solomon, Brian. "Meet David Green: Hobby Lobby's Biblical Billionaire." *Forbes*, Forbes Magazine, 2 Nov. 2015, www.forbes.com/sites/briansolomon/2012/09/18/david-green-the-biblical-billionaire-backing-the-evangelical-movement/#5cb389335807.
47. [846] Montgomery, Peter. "Meet the Billionaire Brothers You Never Heard of Who Fund the Religious Right." *The American Prospect*, prospect.org/article/meet-billionaire-brothers-you-never-heard-who-fund-religious-right.

bring about the Second Coming of Jesus Christ.[847] Christian religious apologists, especially in the US, act as if they're protecting "innocent" beliefs, even as the Evangelical Fundamentalists promote war knowing that it'll increase the deaths of children.[848] It is because nobody challenged their beliefs through free inquiry in order for their faith to be put in doubt.[849] If their beliefs were criticized openly, then Evangelical Fundamentalists wouldn't have such confidence to support the most brutal policy measures unchallenged. They act on such horrific aims with faith beyond doubt in the Second Coming of Jesus Christ because they believe they have the absolute truth. Silencing any criticism that others have of them only emboldens their misguided belief that nobody can deny the truth claims of their faith. That is why it is vital to put their faith in doubt, similar to what Ex-Muslims promote in an attempt to have dialogue with Muslims about bad beliefs.[850]

Psychopathy under the veneer of Christianity

There is an aspect of all religious traditions but particularly evident in extremist versions of the Abrahamic faith, especially Fundamentalist Christianity, that is utterly self-serving and the epitome of narcissism. There seems to be an intense degree of cognitive dissonance on the part of religious believers who refuse to acknowledge anything beyond their personal experience as a guidepost towards truth-seeking.

It is in this paradox: true believers see themselves as the true version of their religious faith, they view their group as the chosen people apart from a largely godless and self-indulgent herd, and view the concessions of their group as a sign of their humility in the service of God. Yet, they don't see the total self-contradiction in their thinking. They believe themselves to be humble and self-sacrificing but believe they're God's chosen above the rest of the human species; they believe themselves to be noble and good, but despise the rest of their own country, despise the various denominations of their own religion as falling under falsehoods, and despise the rest of the world as ignorant devil worshippers or the "lost" as some call them.[851][852] They don't seem to recognize the similarities in their puritanical thinking and those of other religious groups such as Wahhabi Islam, extreme subsets of Orthodox Judaism, Buddhist extremism, or Hindu nationalist extremists who deny science. They view no

---

48. [847] *YouTube*, Q-Ball Productions Inc, 2010, www.youtube.com/watch?v=nNvtA_q0e20.
49. [848] Vogel, Kenneth P., and Tarini Parti. "How Rand Paul Bombed at Koch Brothers Gathering." *POLITICO*, 3 Feb. 2015, www.politico.com/story/2015/02/rand-was-a-dud-at-the-koch-brothers-conference-114853.
50. [849] Jefferson, Thomas. "QUERY XVII The Different Religions Received into That State?" *Thomas Jefferson, Notes on the State of Virginia: Ch. 17*, University of Virginia, xroads.virginia.edu/~hyper/jefferson/ch17.html.
51. [850] Navabi, Armin. "Attacking Islam as an Act of Compassion - Armin Navabi." *YouTube*, Ex-Muslims of North America, 4 Dec. 2017, www.youtube.com/watch?v=9m7IaAlnkgo.
52. [851] Montgomery, Peter. "Meet the Billionaire Brothers You Never Heard of Who Fund the Religious Right." *The American Prospect*, prospect.org/article/meet-billionaire-brothers-you-never-heard-who-fund-religious-right.
53. [852] *YouTube*, Q-Ball Productions Inc, 2010, www.youtube.com/watch?v=nNvtA_q0e20.

inherent contradiction in indulging in the same devices as the complacent majority; the internet, cars, phones, music, and life saving medical facilities. However, they usually view such uses as sinful and would be inclined to subject themselves to needing constant forgiveness from God for using such luxuries. Moreover, on their pulpits, they continue to preach for the "salvation" of their God; the desire for the end of the world so that God can descend and save the chosen people.[853] They seem to realize that doing this would mean a mass genocide of all the Jews to an extent greater than the Nazi Holocaust and the genocide of the entire world; even if they don't believe the Jews will be slaughtered in the holy land – which contradicts their extensive documentary in which they explain that at least 50 million Fundamentalist Christians in the United States look forward to the mass genocide of all the Jews of Israel so that Jesus Christ will have a Second Coming – they would still believe in the end of the world which would lead to the same consequence of a mass genocide of Jewish people.[854] The Christian legacy of anti-Semitism and Hitler's legacy for a final solution lives on through the ideals of Evangelical Fundamentalist Christianity.[855][856] The desire for mass world genocide of the non-chosen, including any and all Jewish people, is a psychotic and patently anti-Semitic belief system. The belief in the end of the world is why the Evangelical Fundamentalists feverishly use billions upon billions in US dollars to convert people and even use coercive and abusive tactics of conversion upon innocent people including children.[857][858][859][860][861] They believe it will save billions of people from mass worldwide genocide.[862][863] They believe that

---

54. [853] Montgomery, Peter. "Meet the Billionaire Brothers You Never Heard of Who Fund the Religious Right." *The American Prospect*, prospect.org/article/meet-billionaire-brothers-you-never-heard-who-fund-religious-right.
55. [854] *YouTube*, Q-Ball Productions Inc, 2010, www.youtube.com/watch?v=nNvtA_q0e20.
56. [855] Tix, Andrew. "The Failure of Christian Love in the Holocaust." *Biola University Center for Christian Thought / The Table*, 6 July 2017, cct.biola.edu/failure-christian-love-holocaust/.
57. [856] *YouTube*, Q-Ball Productions Inc, 2010, www.youtube.com/watch?v=nNvtA_q0e20.
58. [857] Montgomery, Peter. "Meet the Billionaire Brothers You Never Heard of Who Fund the Religious Right." *The American Prospect*, prospect.org/article/meet-billionaire-brothers-you-never-heard-who-fund-religious-right.
59. [858] Neelakandan, Aravindan. "Why No Outrage over Conversion of Tsunami Victims?" *Swarajya Read India Right ATOM*, 29 Dec. 2014, swarajyamag.com/politics/why-no-outrage-over-conversion-of-tsunami-victims.
60. [859] Solomon, Brian. "Meet David Green: Hobby Lobby's Biblical Billionaire." *Forbes*, Forbes Magazine, 2 Nov. 2015, www.forbes.com/sites/briansolomon/2012/09/18/david-green-the-biblical-billionaire-backing-the-evangelical-movement/#5cb389335807.
61. [860] Neary, Sarah. "Forced to Convert: How American Missionaries Really Treat Indigenous Akha Children." *Intercontinental Cry*, IC, 23 Apr. 2013, intercontinentalcry.org/forced-to-convert-how-american-missionaries-really-treat-indigenous-akha-children/.
62. [861] Goldberg, Philip. "Missionaries in India: Conversion or Coercion?" *The Huffington Post*, TheHuffingtonPost.com, 19 Feb. 2014, www.huffingtonpost.com/philip-goldberg/missionaries-in-india_b_4470448.html.
63. [862] "Joshua Project - Ideas for Church Involvment with Unreached Peoples." *Joshua Project*, legacy.joshuaproject.net/mission-ideas-for-churches.php.
64. [863] "Joshua Project - Unreached Peoples of the World." *Joshua Project*, legacy.joshuaproject.net/index.php.

all non-Christians will die; in their self-delusional pity for others, they seek to convert people to "save them" from their own apocalyptic end of the world prophecy.[864]

There is a lack of acknowledgement of what these extremists are willing to do and there is scorn towards people who point out the issues of these 50 million people; all of whom are consistent voters in the US[865], who proudly espouse that global warming and evolution are hoaxes and make documentaries to argue such positions[866][867], who have proudly made documentaries in which they celebrate the idea of Israel being attacked by evil forces across the world[868], who go on extensive trips across the world to forcibly convert non-Christian children through coercive practices like child rape[869], and who have sermons celebrating the idea of the end of the world and endless war with Islam.[870] These people aren't just average citizens; they consist of the CEOs of oil companies who repeatedly disperse propaganda about how climate change is a hoax under the belief that the Bible is inerrant[871][872], they consist of CEOs in war corporations who sell weapons to organizations and countries that sell them to terrorists for the sake of having evangelical soldiers go into endless war with Islam[873], they are Senators like Billy Graham or Mike Huckabee and many more who vote on policies that seek to engage in constant warfare in the Middle East[874], they have extensive lobbying firms to promote anti-climate change propaganda and seek out constant hypocrisy towards anyone who disagrees with them about anything.[875][876] They have been largely successful in influencing US

---

65. [864] Montgomery, Peter. "Meet the Billionaire Brothers You Never Heard of Who Fund the Religious Right." *The American Prospect*, prospect.org/article/meet-billionaire-brothers-you-never-heard-who-fund-religious-right.
66. [865] "American Evangelicalism: New Leaders, New Faces, New Issues." Edited by Cheryl Jackson, *Pew Research Center's Religion & Public Life Project*, 6 May 2008, www.pewforum.org/2008/05/06/american-evangelicalism-new-leaders-new-faces-new-issues/.
67. [866] Montgomery, Peter. "Meet the Billionaire Brothers You Never Heard of Who Fund the Religious Right." *The American Prospect*, prospect.org/article/meet-billionaire-brothers-you-never-heard-who-fund-religious-right.
68. [867] Shea, Brie. "Fracking Titans Spend Millions Proselytizing School Children." *Rewire.News*, Rewire.News, 1 May 2015, rewire.news/article/2015/04/30/conservatives-spend-millions-proselytizing-school-children/.
69. [868] *YouTube*, Q-Ball Productions Inc, 2010, www.youtube.com/watch?v=nNvtA_q0e20.
70. [869] "Jury Finds Missionary Guilty of Abusing Cambodian Orphans." *New York Post*, New York Post, 17 May 2018, nypost.com/2018/05/17/jury-finds-missionary-guilty-of-abusing-cambodian-orphans/amp/.
71. [870] *YouTube*, Q-Ball Productions Inc, 2010, www.youtube.com/watch?v=nNvtA_q0e20.
72. [871] Montgomery, Peter. "Meet the Billionaire Brothers You Never Heard of Who Fund the Religious Right." *The American Prospect*, prospect.org/article/meet-billionaire-brothers-you-never-heard-who-fund-religious-right.
73. [872] Bowyer, Jerry. "Does God Belong In The Boardroom? 1,800 CEOs Say Yes." *GenTwenty*, The Mercury News, 12 Aug. 2016,
74. [873] Rhee, Joseph, et al. "U.S. Military Weapons Inscribed With Secret 'Jesus' Bible Codes." *ABC News*, ABC News Network, 18 Jan. 2010, abcnews.go.com/Blotter/us-military-weapons-inscribed-secret-jesus-bible-codes/story?id=9575794.
75. [874] "American Evangelicalism: New Leaders, New Faces, New Issues." Edited by Cheryl Jackson, *Pew Research Center's Religion & Public Life Project*, 6 May 2008, www.pewforum.org/2008/05/06/american-evangelicalism-new-leaders-new-faces-new-issues/.
76. [875] Hacker, Jacob S., and Paul Pierson. *Winner-Take-All Politics How Washington Made the Rich Richer - and Turned Its Back on the Middle Class*. Simon & Schuster, 2011.

policies in the Middle East; they work under security companies, they hold positions in the NSA, and they make up the majority of the US army with Evangelical churches in 80% of the US bases across the world. What motivates them is the fundamental belief that the world is broken and they need to fix it to make way for the Coming of Jesus Christ.[877] To correct the world, the Evangelical Fundamentalist Christians seek endless war with Islam[878], forced conversions of Asia[879][880][881][882], genocide denial of the Native Americans[883], and the total annihilation of Judaism either through conversions or awaiting a mass holocaust for the sake of Jesus returning.[884][885] They are an anti-Semitic hate group with too much power and willing to destroy all human life for their convictions to Jesus Christ.[886][887][888]

They need to place Jesus's image everywhere in order to feel consistent with their beliefs because the Bible has been rendered untenable in many aspects. By placing Jesus's image on everything and everywhere, they feel consistent with their beliefs and the world they're living in.[889] They question less and can comfortably try to find hypocrisies in their adversaries to demonize them. They're largely seen by the public as non-threatening in their beliefs with the assumption that they cannot do much. This is a largely false assumption and

---

77. [876] Montgomery, Peter. "Meet the Billionaire Brothers You Never Heard of Who Fund the Religious Right." *The American Prospect*, prospect.org/article/meet-billionaire-brothers-you-never-heard-who-fund-religious-right.
78. [877] "American Evangelicalism: New Leaders, New Faces, New Issues." Edited by Cheryl Jackson, *Pew Research Center's Religion & Public Life Project*, 6 May 2008, www.pewforum.org/2008/05/06/american-evangelicalism-new-leaders-new-faces-new-issues/.
79. [878] *YouTube*, Q-Ball Productions Inc, 2010, www.youtube.com/watch?v=nNvtA_q0e20.
80. [879] Gittleson, Wendy. "Christian 'Soul Vultures' Are Exploiting The Nepal Earthquake 'For Christ' (VIDEO)." *AddictingInfo*, 27 Apr. 2015, addictinginfo.com/2015/04/27/christian-soul-vultures-are-exploiting-the-nepal-earthquake-for-christ-video/.
81. [880] Neelakandan, Aravindan. "Why No Outrage over Conversion of Tsunami Victims?" *Swarajya Read India Right ATOM*, 29 Dec. 2014, swarajyamag.com/politics/why-no-outrage-over-conversion-of-tsunami-victims.
82. [881] "Jury Finds Missionary Guilty of Abusing Cambodian Orphans." *New York Post*, New York Post, 17 May 2018, nypost.com/2018/05/17/jury-finds-missionary-guilty-of-abusing-cambodian-orphans/amp/.
83. [882] Neary, Sarah. "Forced to Convert: How American Missionaries Really Treat Indigenous Akha Children." *Intercontinental Cry*, IC, 23 Apr. 2013, intercontinentalcry.org/forced-to-convert-how-american-missionaries-really-treat-indigenous-akha-children/.
84. [883] Hayes, Leonard L. "American Indian and Alaskan Native Historical Trauma and an Adlerian Perspective." *Alfredadler.edu*, The Faculty of the Adler Graduate School, Sept. 2010, alfredadler.edu/sites/default/files/Hayes MP 2010.pdf.
85. [884] *YouTube*, Q-Ball Productions Inc, 2010, www.youtube.com/watch?v=nNvtA_q0e20.
86. [885] Heilbroner, David. "Evangelicals, Israel, and the End of the World." *The Huffington Post*, TheHuffingtonPost.com, 25 May 2011, www.huffingtonpost.com/david-heilbroner/evangelicals-israel-and-t_b_391351.html.
87. [886] Montgomery, Peter. "Meet the Billionaire Brothers You Never Heard of Who Fund the Religious Right." *The American Prospect*, prospect.org/article/meet-billionaire-brothers-you-never-heard-who-fund-religious-right.
88. [887] *YouTube*, Q-Ball Productions Inc, 2010, www.youtube.com/watch?v=nNvtA_q0e20.
89. [888] Heilbroner, David. "Evangelicals, Israel, and the End of the World." *The Huffington Post*, TheHuffingtonPost.com, 25 May 2011, www.huffingtonpost.com/david-heilbroner/evangelicals-israel-and-t_b_391351.html.
90. [889] Kahneman, Daniel. *Thinking, fast and slow*. Farrar, Straus and Giroux, 2015.

the news media takes particular care to ignore these people's actions but emphasize the abuses of non-Christian extremists. The success of the Evangelical movement is largely ignored. Evangelical Fundamentalist Christians have been repeatedly successful in gaining their endless wars with various Middle Eastern countries, President Bush openly said that he went to war because God told him to do it and so thousands of US soldiers are now dead or permanently disabled because apparently God told Bush to go to war, Evangelical CEOs have largely profiteered from the war campaign at the expense of the lives of average Americans[890], and they feel pleasure from being persecuted because they truly believe that they're the chosen people of God and that what they're doing is morally righteous. They will always garner sympathy from biased US news organizations that don't speak of their forced conversions and other coercive practices; including rape scandals upon local foreign populations.[891] They have openly stated that they wish for the end of the world for the sake of Jesus's return. The majority of Evangelical Fundamentalists don't believe that global warming is real and believe that the natural disasters and deaths are merely signs of Christ's oncoming return.[892] They don't question the oil oligarchs who fund their missionary activities across the world[893][894], they're also the only interaction that many foreigners have with Americans and so foreigners who are unfamiliar with the US will make negative judgments based upon their interactions with only Evangelicals because Evangelicals may be the only Americans they meet in their lifetime.[895]

It is quite tiring to see this vicious and powerful hate group continue to have a foothold in US politics. Why should their beliefs, which are causing mass death and continued anti-American sentiments abroad, be ignored when they have such a horrible impact upon the lives of everyday Americans and foreigners? Whether these people acknowledge it or not, they're leading the world into a state of constant warfare and seek mass genocide. Their disinformation propaganda about climate change will lead to irreversible damage to the biodiversity and ecosystem of the planet; climate change will cause more droughts, hurricanes, and earthquakes throughout the US and other parts of the world. It won't just be earthquakes and hurricanes in foreign countries, as some US citizens ignorantly believe, it'll mean more earthquakes and hurricanes throughout the United States itself. Evangelical Fundamentalist Christians find this

91. [890] Rhee, Joseph, et al. "U.S. Military Weapons Inscribed With Secret 'Jesus' Bible Codes." *ABC News*, ABC News Network, 18 Jan. 2010, abcnews.go.com/Blotter/us-military-weapons-inscribed-secret-jesus-bible-codes/story?id=9575794.
92. [891] "Jury Finds Missionary Guilty of Abusing Cambodian Orphans." *New York Post*, New York Post, 17 May 2018, nypost.com/2018/05/17/jury-finds-missionary-guilty-of-abusing-cambodian-orphans/amp/.
93. [892] *YouTube*, Q-Ball Productions Inc, 2010, www.youtube.com/watch?v=nNvtA_q0e20.
94. [893] Montgomery, Peter. "Meet the Billionaire Brothers You Never Heard of Who Fund the Religious Right." *The American Prospect*, prospect.org/article/meet-billionaire-brothers-you-never-heard-who-fund-religious-right.
95. [894] Solomon, Brian. "Meet David Green: Hobby Lobby's Biblical Billionaire." *Forbes*, Forbes Magazine, 2 Nov. 2015, www.forbes.com/sites/briansolomon/2012/09/18/david-green-the-biblical-billionaire-backing-the-evangelical-movement/#5cb389335807.
96. [895] Cialdini, Robert B. "Chapter 1: Weapons of Influence (1-16)" *Influence: Science and practice*. 4th ed., 21st Century Bks, 2002.

belief to be immensely pleasurable and attempt forced conversions on children in places like Nepal, Syria, and Haiti in order to use their pain as a means of manipulating them into conversion.[896][897] Evangelical Christians, in 2004, after a particularly devastating earthquake in India came with a bus full of food and medical items.[898] They told the local population they could only have the food and medicine if they converted to Christianity.[899] They withheld food and drove off with supplies for the local population that was affected by the natural disaster when the Indians refused to convert to Christianity.[900] Evangelical Fundamentalists aren't helping anyone but themselves. They enjoy inflicting the worst cruelties upon the general American public and innocent people in third world countries to coerce them into conversion and they forgive themselves through the belief that Jesus will forgive all of their sins. Evangelicals, who only answer to Jesus, don't care at all about the suffering of others and see it as a prime opportunity for forced conversions.[901] These are the only people that foreigners are familiar with when they think of US citizens. They are the primary reason that there is anti-American sentiment abroad and that is including the activities of the politicians that they strongly favor.[902]

To leave those who suffered from natural disasters starving and without medical attention shows the level of psychopathy in the Evangelical mindset. To constantly attempt forced conversions upon refugees, people who endured natural disasters, and to use coercive practices upon innocent children shows the depth of their willingness to go into criminal behavior. They have constantly and repeatedly conducted these practices across the world and on a multitude of occasions. These people are obviously not of sound mind and shouldn't be treated as if they're capable of being of sound mind and health. It seems clear that they need to be placed into mental healthcare facilities for their own safety and especially for the general public's safety. To ignore their explicit desires for the end of the world, for their desires for a Holocaust larger than what the Nazis did to the innocent Jews, for their constant disinformation

97. [896] François, France. "Haiti Doesn't Have a Vodou Problem, It Has a Christianity Problem." *EBONY*, EBONY, 16 July 2014, www.ebony.com/news-views/haiti-doesnt-have-a-vodou-problem-043.
98. [897] Gittleson, Wendy. "Christian 'Soul Vultures' Are Exploiting The Nepal Earthquake 'For Christ' (VIDEO)." *AddictingInfo*, 27 Apr. 2015, addictinginfo.com/2015/04/27/christian-soul-vultures-are-exploiting-the-nepal-earthquake-for-christ-video/.
99. [898] Neelakandan, Aravindan. "Why No Outrage over Conversion of Tsunami Victims?" *Swarajya Read India Right ATOM*, 29 Dec. 2014, swarajyamag.com/politics/why-no-outrage-over-conversion-of-tsunami-victims.
100. [899] Neelakandan, Aravindan. "Why No Outrage over Conversion of Tsunami Victims?" *Swarajya Read India Right ATOM*, 29 Dec. 2014, swarajyamag.com/politics/why-no-outrage-over-conversion-of-tsunami-victims.
101. [900] Neelakandan, Aravindan. "Why No Outrage over Conversion of Tsunami Victims?" *Swarajya Read India Right ATOM*, 29 Dec. 2014, swarajyamag.com/politics/why-no-outrage-over-conversion-of-tsunami-victims.
102. [901] Gittleson, Wendy. "Christian 'Soul Vultures' Are Exploiting The Nepal Earthquake 'For Christ' (VIDEO)." *AddictingInfo*, 27 Apr. 2015, addictinginfo.com/2015/04/27/christian-soul-vultures-are-exploiting-the-nepal-earthquake-for-christ-video/.
103. [902] "American Evangelicalism: New Leaders, New Faces, New Issues." Edited by Cheryl Jackson, *Pew Research Center's Religion & Public Life Project*, 6 May 2008,

campaigns on climate change, for their selling of weapons to organizations that sell them to terrorist groups, and to ignore their constant abuse towards people who suffer from trauma after natural disasters or war trauma would be an unconscionable act of apathy towards the constant harm they do upon everyone in the world. We cannot pretend that these active, openly coercive groups don't have a negative impact upon the US or the world at large. They're the Christian version of ISIS and al Qaeda when it comes to women's rights, not in terms of violence but in their coercive and prejudiced practices and they encourage selling weapons to organizations that sell to those terrorists regardless via the euphemism foreign intervention.[903] The Fundamentalists have inflicted a horrific degree of mental torture, coercive practices, and depravity upon the rest of the world and continue to actively conduct a horrific level of coercive practices across the world. They constantly lie and celebrate charity work to the general public while withholding food from starving people and forcibly converting children. Why shouldn't foreigners be angry when Corporate America's vast wealth goes into funding these practices? Why should US citizens ignore the overwhelmingly negative impact that these people have had upon US government policies and the lives of Americans which have been lost as a result of them? Why do we continue to ignore the starkly clear anti-Semitism within their belief system? What will our excuses be when they irreversibly destroy the biodiversity of the planet and cause the extinction of the human species? Should we continue to parrot that they have a right to never be challenged on their beliefs when they cause so much suffering upon everyone else through violence? How are we to effectively combat their violent proclivities? The Evangelical fundamentalists are the mentally unsound and it is time that we treat them as such for the safety of our species and the world. The consequences of their beliefs are very real and they've largely held the most power in US politics since the rise of the Religious Right under President Ronald Reagan.[904][905]

104.[903] Vogel, Kenneth P., and Tarini Parti. "How Rand Paul Bombed at Koch Brothers Gathering." *POLITICO*, 3 Feb. 2015, www.politico.com/story/2015/02/rand-was-a-dud-at-the-koch-brothers-conference-114853.
105.[904] Hacker, Jacob S., and Paul Pierson. *Winner-Take-All Politics How Washington Made the Rich Richer - and Turned Its Back on the Middle Class*. Simon & Schuster, 2011.
106.[905] Frank, Robert. "Which Religion Holds the Largest Share of Wealth?" *CNBC*, CNBC, 14 Jan. 2015, www.cnbc.com/2015/01/14/the-religion-of-millionaires-.html.

Chapter 17: Ignorance Within Bliss

Christianity and the teachings of Jesus Christ are morally bankrupt and don't hold any value in modernity. It is precisely because Christianity tries to find simplistic answers to complex questions that it leads to championing anti-intellectualism.[906] The worship of innocence and simplicity towards finding solutions to complex problems is simply the worship of ignorance and never wanting to be held accountable for your wrongdoings to the public at large.[907] It is worshipping an ideal that extricates itself from reality and thus selfishly ignores the consequences of religious belief in Jesus Christ.[908]

This is why Christian missionaries can forcibly and coercively convert non-Christians with threats of perdition, threats of physical violence, bribery, withholding food from starving people who survived a natural disaster and choosing to let them all die because they didn't convert, and threats of child rape in order to convert them for the sake of saving their "soul" to send it to heaven without remorse or viewing any of their actions as problematic[909][910][911]; no different than how Christian nuns and priests physically beat, raped, and even killed young Native children from the 1870s to the 1960s in both Canada and the US for the sake of imparting to them the salvation of Jesus Christ.[912][913][914] A Christian missionary categorically sees any physical or sexual abuse as unimportant and normalizes their actions under the standards of sinfulness and repentance, while doing everything in their power to keep to the faith to send eternal souls into heaven to avoid perdition. They don't perceive human wrongdoing as anything but the norm, because no standard of violence is too egregious for Jesus Christ's forgiveness. Christian missionaries strive to be so "innocent" that they don't even consider these questions of human violence or how to stop them. While many may work to

---

1. [906] Nietzsche, Friedrich Wilhelm. *THE ANTICHRIST*. Translated by H. L. Mencken, The Project Gutenberg, 2006.
2. [907] Nietzsche, Friedrich Wilhelm. *THE ANTICHRIST*. Translated by H. L. Mencken, The Project Gutenberg, 2006.
3. [908] Nietzsche, Friedrich Wilhelm. *THE ANTICHRIST*. Translated by H. L. Mencken, The Project Gutenberg, 2006.
4. [909] Goldberg, Philip. "Missionaries in India: Conversion or Coercion?" *The Huffington Post*, TheHuffingtonPost.com, 19 Feb. 2014, www.huffingtonpost.com/philip-goldberg/missionaries-in-india_b_4470448.html.
5. [910] "Jury Finds Missionary Guilty of Abusing Cambodian Orphans." *New York Post*, New York Post, 17 May 2018, nypost.com/2018/05/17/jury-finds-missionary-guilty-of-abusing-cambodian-orphans/amp/.
6. [911] Neelakandan, Aravindan. "Why No Outrage over Conversion of Tsunami Victims?" *Swarajya Read India Right ATOM*, 29 Dec. 2014, swarajyamag.com/politics/why-no-outrage-over-conversion-of-tsunami-victims.
7. [912] Bear, Charla. "American Indian Boarding Schools Haunt Many." *NPR*. NPR, 12 May 2008. Web. 2 Nov. 2015, https://www.npr.org/templates/story/story.php?storyId=16516865?storyId=16516865.
8. [913] Paquin, Mali Ilse. "Canada Confronts Its Dark History of Abuse in Residential Schools." *The Guardian*, Guardian News and Media, 6 June 2015, www.theguardian.com/world/2015/jun/06/canada-dark-of-history-residential-schools.
9. [914] Hayes, Leonard L. "American Indian and Alaskan Native Historical Trauma and an Adlerian Perspective." *Alfredadler.edu*, The Faculty of the Adler Graduate School, Sept. 2010, alfredadler.edu/sites/default/files/Hayes MP 2010.pdf.

expose abuses, such as male cases of war rape[915], they don't perceive the physical violence as too egregious to not have warlords convert to Christianity, to then continue the violence with a clear conscience from the self-forgiveness system of Christianity. They act "innocent" of their own wrongdoing to the point that the theology essentially functions as a self-forgiveness system through Jesus Christ's doctrine of forgiveness.

The anti-intellectual belief in purity and innocence above learning is why Christian missionaries can violently and coercively threaten non-Christians to change their so-called sinful ways of independent thought in order to repent by accepting Jesus Christ, while paradoxically ignoring Christian CEOs and board of directors who hold offices within or hold vast shares of stock in companies involved in contracting the building and selling of weapons. To be a Christian weapons contractor is easy, you simply acknowledge you're a sinful human being and seek Jesus's forgiveness for your sinfulness. To a Christian missionary, they would be thought of as more idealistically Christian and keeping faith to Jesus Christ's teachings than any non-Christian who advocates for non-violence, but rejects Jesus Christ and his message. Jesus Christ's message was about his own narcissism and not peace. As an example, both Gandhi and Martin Luther King Jr. studied with Jain philosophers to learn non-violent teachings[916], but US Christians attempt to argue that both were peaceful because of Jesus's teachings; in Gandhi's case, they attempt to argue that he was deluded and denied Jesus after reading the Bible, even though it's well-established that Gandhi studied with a Jain teacher recommended by his mother and used the Jain philosophical concept of *Ahimsa* for his non-violent teachings. Yet, on the presupposition and basis for their religion, Christian missionaries and other devout Christians cannot conceive of a morality outside of Jesus's teachings and refuse to regard that idea with any degree of seriousness so they attempt to place the Jesus label on Gandhi too. Consequently, even if modern Christians reject the argument that Christian weapons contractors are really Christian and accept the argument that Gandhi used a mix of Hindu and Jain theology for his teachings, they would still have to accept the fact that the Christian weapons contractor would be going to heaven after knowingly selling millions of weapons, assisting in the worsening conditions of hundreds of thousands of children who were slaughtered or raped by terrorists that got their hands on such weapons, and profiting off the massive and purposeful mass slaughter that the Christian weapons contractor helped to perpetuate and increase in the severity of lives lost. Jesus Christ's doctrine of forgiveness is absolute; therefore, the weapons contractor will be going to heaven. This would be the case, even if they were to only repent on their deathbed despite all the harm done to others. Meanwhile, Gandhi will be going to hell for the crime of not accepting Jesus Christ; despite advocating strongly for non-violence, respecting the Christian faith as peaceful, seeing no ills in Christianity to have caused the organized subjugation and violence known as imperialism, and practicing teachings of kindness and respect.

---

10. [915] Storr, Will. "The rape of men: the darkest secret of war." *The Observer*, Guardian News and Media, 16 July 2011, www.theguardian.com/society/2011/jul/17/the-rape-of-men.
11. [916] Harris, Sam. *Letter to a Christian Nation*. Random House, 2008.

Christianity perpetuates itself by devaluing human life as sinful and uses human imperfection as an excuse to propagate human violence and nihilism towards the physical world.[917] People wonder why so many con artists exist in branching denominations of the Christian faith, but the reason is clear when looking at Jesus's teachings. The Christian con artist is the closest in likeness to Jesus Christ; harboring an exaggerated sense of self-importance, a cult of followers who thoughtlessly obey, and believe the cult leader is something more than human with features rising above mundane forms of human excellence.[918] Any detractors are seen as delusional or woefully misinformed about the cult leader; who the worshippers view as very honest, pious, and compassionate due to anecdotes of his or her personal life.[919] Likewise, the con doesn't work for those most familiar with the con artist, such as when Jesus Christ evidently couldn't do miracles in his home village.[920] His home village was rife with people who knew him growing up and were closer than any of his followers to understanding what he was like. His followers worshipped him in admiration and modern Christians today have widely deviating views on what Jesus Christ was actually like as a person. People of his home village knew of him based on forming an understanding of him and his personality as he grew up without the belief they needed to worship him based on his claims. Evidently, according to the Bible, this so-called God couldn't convince his own home village and his supposed miracles didn't work there. Why did this all-powerful God fail at convincing his hometown? Why did the so-called miracles that he performed fail to convince them, even when healing a sick person? Why did Jesus Christ's own family reject his divinity and message?

Mark 6 King James Version (KJV)

6 And he went out from thence, and came into his own country; and his disciples follow him.

2 And when the sabbath day was come, he began to teach in the synagogue: and many hearing him were astonished, saying, From whence hath this man these things? and what wisdom is this which is given unto him, that even such mighty works are wrought by his hands?

3 Is not this the carpenter, the son of Mary, the brother of James, and Joses, and of Juda, and Simon? and are not his sisters here with us? And they were offended at him.

4 But Jesus, said unto them, A prophet is not without honour, but in his own country, and among his own kin, and in his own house.

5 And he could there do no mighty work, save that he laid his hands upon a few sick folk, and healed them.

---

12. [917] Nietzsche, Friedrich Wilhelm. *On the genealogy of morals: a polemical tract*. Translated by Ian Johnston, PDF, Richer Resources Publications, 2014.
13. [918] Konnikova, Maria. *The Confidence Game: the Psychology of the Con and Why We Fall for It Every Time*. Canongate, 2017.
14. [919] Konnikova, Maria. *The Confidence Game: the Psychology of the Con and Why We Fall for It Every Time*. Canongate, 2017.
15. [920] Konnikova, Maria. *The Confidence Game: the Psychology of the Con and Why We Fall for It Every Time*. Canongate, 2017.

6 And he marvelled because of their unbelief. And he went round about the villages, teaching.[921]

Why were his family and hometown not among the first of his followers? Were the villagers "deceived" despite having known him for his entire youthful life, or is it instead possible that they were right about him being insane? To borrow and add on to a jest from Christopher Hitchens, which is more likely; all physical laws in the universe were suspended for the virgin birth of one person in the most uneducated area of bronze age Palestine or one Jewish woman, during a time where adultery could get her stoned to death, told a lie to keep herself and her child safe from violence?

What about Jesus Christ's moments before his death on the cross? I recall a cartoon show on a Christian channel where Jesus Christ is depicted to request his father to forgive the Roman soldiers for putting him to the cross before some dramatic earthquake erupted killing the soldiers and unintentionally implying the Abrahamic God was too hateful to listen to Jesus Christ's request to forgive them. Fortunately, the Bible doesn't depict this narrative, as no one gets killed when the earthquakes occur; instead, a bunch of saints are purported to rise out of their coffins after Jesus Christ's resurrection and this is something that Christians are expected to believe happened. The saints evidently rose from the dead from their own coffins (Matthew 27:52-53) and went to cities to preach the gospel of Jesus according to the Bible.

If you believe in Jesus Christ's resurrection, then why isn't this also something that you believe?

Matthew 27:52-53 King James Version (KJV)
52 And the graves were opened; and many bodies of the saints which slept arose,

53 And came out of the graves after his resurrection, and went into the holy city, and appeared unto many.[922]

If you do believe it, then what do you believe their second life upon being resurrected entailed? Where's the historical records for them; such as their own written accounts upon their resurrection? Why didn't these resurrected saints add their testimonies to the Bible in celebration of the truth of the gospel, Jesus Christ's divinity, and to prove Christianity was the only true religion for followers and potential converts? If you believe these so-called saints came out of their graves, then how is Jesus Christ resurrecting from the dead a unique event when they did it too? Why should the resurrection of Jesus Christ matter if the saints also resurrected?

---

16. [921] "BibleGateway." *Bible Gateway*, Bible Gateway Blog, www.biblegateway.com/passage/?search=Mark 6&version=KJV.
17. [922] "BibleGateway." *Bible Gateway*, Bible Gateway Blog, www.biblegateway.com/passage/?search=Matthew 27:52-53&version=KJV.

Of interest to this discussion is Christianity's theological arguments of becoming more like Jesus Christ, who is perceived to be sinless and perfect according to Christianity. What about the Bible's story of what he purportedly said when he was on the cross at his most excruciating moments? What was the lesson he conveyed for those people at their most agonizing moments in life when compared to his own life, which Christians are to perceive as far more important in magnitude?

Matthew 27:46 King James Version (KJV)
46 And about the ninth hour Jesus cried with a loud voice, saying, Eli, Eli, lama sabachthani? that is to say, My God, my God, why hast thou forsaken me?[923]

It would seem that, if Jesus Christ was indeed everything Christianity claims him to be, then he didn't believe it himself at his most vulnerable moments. When being wracked with pain upon the cross and capable of showing either his true strength of character or the splendor of his compassion for humanity, he didn't even believe that he was the Son of God or God himself when suffering from the pain that he supposedly knew was going to come to him. According to his own words, Jesus Christ wholly believed that the Abrahamic God had abandoned him to face a punishment. He didn't know why he was being stabbed on the cross and never indicated any confidence in a plan by the Abrahamic God or any display of absolute forgiveness for human folly. Therefore, if it is indeed true that Jesus Christ is sinless and perfect, that Christians should strive to be more like him, and that the Abrahamic God's plan was to sacrifice his only son to free humanity of sin; then all Jesus Christ did when speaking those words was lower the standard of the entire religion of Christianity. If his purpose was to die for humanity's sins and be a redeemer for sinfulness, then why did he cry out and question why God was forsaking him? If it was a moment of weakness, and this man is supposedly perfection itself and sinless, then people being more in his likeness are expected to completely fail at their most grueling moments in life and even question why the Abrahamic God is abandoning them instead of keeping a strong faith? To be more like Jesus Christ, is to cry out in shame, self-revulsion, question the Abrahamic God's motives, and accuse the Abrahamic God of abandoning you. If it were not so, then why did he cry out that the Abrahamic God had forsaken him? Even if it was simply the pressure bearing down upon him for his task, then that would mean that he wasn't up to the task before him and he genuinely didn't believe in it. If you grant the possibility that what he went through to die for humanity's sins and be a redeemer overwhelmed him, then was this failure to keep faith in his own apparent father suppose to make us feel pity for him? Are you, as a Christian, suppose to feel pity for Jesus Christ for being unable to keep his faith in the Abrahamic God and himself? Is being more like Jesus Christ suppose to mean abandoning faith in God and questioning why God is forsaking you when you're pushed unto your most painful struggles?

---

18. [923] "BibleGateway." *Matthew 27:46 KJV - - Bible Gateway*, www.biblegateway.com/passage/?search=Matthew 27:46&version=KJV.

According to the Bible, it was the claims of illiterate, likely impressionable, and ignorant women who preached that Jesus had risen again based on the hearsay claims of a stranger after the body of Jesus had been removed from the tomb on Easter morning. Their education level was abysmal under the misogynistic rule of the peasant villages of their time period and obviously they were nothing like educated women in modern times. If you remove the fantastical portions about angels flying down after dead saints rise out of their coffins to preach the gospel in cities, this is all the claims amount to as far as any real life people making truth claims.

According to Professor James Tabor, the professor of Christian origins and ancient Judaism for the department of religious studies at the University of North Carolina, the gospel of Mark is the closest to the time that Jesus Christ supposedly walked the earth. It makes no mention whatsoever of Jesus being cited to have resurrected in any of the passages. 16:9 and onward have been found to be complete forgeries according to the consensus of modern academia. Therefore, there were no accounts of anyone seeing Jesus Christ after his death upon the cross and such stories were added later on from the other gospels that were never close to the source material like the gospel of Mark. The other gospels often added the parts of Jesus Christ being seen after those supposedly closest to Jesus had already died so they wouldn't have been able to verify the accuracy of any information written about Jesus Christ's sightings. The letters by Peter make no mention of sighting Jesus Christ beyond having visions of him, which corroborates how the gospel of Mark portrays the resurrection of Jesus.

Dr. Tabor's detailed information in the *Biblicalarchaeology.org* website:

Most general Bible readers have the mistaken impression that Matthew, the opening book of the New Testament, must be our first and earliest Gospel, with Mark, Luke and John following. The assumption is that this order of the Gospels is a chronological one, when in fact it is a *theological* one. Scholars and historians are almost universally agreed that Mark is our *earliest* Gospel–by several decades, and this insight turns out to have *profound* implications for our understanding of the "Jesus story" and how it was passed down to us in our New Testament Gospel traditions.

The problem with the Gospel of Mark for the final editors of the New Testament was that it was grossly deficient. First it is significantly shorter than the other Gospels–with only 16 chapters compared to Matthew (28), Luke (24) and John (21). But more important is how Mark begins his Gospel and how he ends it.

He has *no account of the virgin birth* of Jesus–or for that matter, any birth of Jesus at all. In fact, Joseph, husband of Mary, is never named in Mark's Gospel at all–and Jesus is called a "son of Mary," see my previous post on this here. But even *more significant* is Mark's strange ending. He has *no appearances of Jesus* following the visit of the women on Easter morning to the empty tomb!

Like the other three Gospels Mark recounts the visit of Mary Magdalene and her companions to the tomb of Jesus early Sunday morning. Upon arriving they find the blocking stone at the entrance of the tomb removed and a young man–notice–*not an angel*–tells them:

"Do not be alarmed. You seek Jesus of Nazareth, who was crucified. He has risen; he is not here. See the place where they laid him. But go, tell his disciples and Peter that he is going before you to Galilee. There you will see him, just as he told you." And they went out and fled from the tomb, for trembling and astonishment had seized them, and they said nothing (Mark 16:6-8)

And there the Gospel simply ends!

Mark gives *no accounts of anyone seeing Jesus* as Matthew, Luke, and John later report. In fact, according to Mark, any future epiphanies or "sightings" of Jesus will be in the north, in Galilee, not in Jerusalem.

This original ending of Mark was viewed by later Christians as so deficient that not only was Mark placed second in order in the New Testament, but various endings were *added* by editors and copyists in some manuscripts to try to remedy things. The longest concocted ending, which became Mark 16:9-19, became so treasured that it was included in the King James Version of the Bible, favored for the past 500 years by Protestants, as well as translations of the Latin Vulgate, used by Catholics. This meant that for countless millions of Christians it *became* sacred scripture–but it is patently *bogus*. You might check whatever Bible you use and see if the following verses are included–the chances are good they they will be, since the Church, by and large, found Mark's original ending so lacking. Here is that forged ending of Mark:

"Now when he rose early on the first day of the week, he appeared first to Mary Magdalene, from whom he had cast out seven demons. She went and told those who had been with him, as they mourned and wept. But when they heard that he was alive and had been seen by her, they would not believe it. After these things he appeared in another form to two of them, as they were walking into the country. And they went back and told the rest, but they did not believe them. Afterward he appeared to the eleven themselves as they were reclining at table, and he rebuked them for their unbelief and hardness of heart, because they had not believed those who saw him after he had risen. And he said to them, "Go into all the world and proclaim the gospel to the whole creation. Whoever believes and is baptized will be saved, but whoever does not believe will be condemned. And these signs will accompany those who believe: in my name they will cast out demons; they will speak in new tongues; they will pick up serpents with their hands; and if they drink any deadly poison, it will not hurt them; they will lay their hands on the sick, and they will recover. So then the Lord Jesus, after he had spoken to them, was taken up into heaven and sat down at the right hand of God. And they went out and preached everywhere, while the Lord worked with them and confirmed the message by accompanying signs."

Even though this ending is patently false, people loved it, and to this day conservative Christians regularly denounce "liberal" scholars who point out this forgery, claiming that they are trying to destroy "God's word."

The evidence is clear. This ending is not found in our earliest and most reliable Greek copies of Mark. In *A Textual Commentary on the Greek New Testament*, Bruce Metzger writes: "Clement of Alexandria and Origen [early third century] show no knowledge of the existence of these verses; furthermore Eusebius and Jerome attest that the passage was absent from almost all Greek copies of Mark known to them."[1] The language and style of the Greek is clearly *not Markan*, and it is pretty evident that what the forger did was take sections of the endings of Matthew, Luke and John (marked respectively in red, blue, and purple above) and simply *create* a "proper" ending.

Even though this longer ending became the preferred one, there are two other endings, one short and the second an expansion of the longer ending, that also show up in various manuscripts:

"[I] But they reported briefly to Peter and those with him all that they had been told. And after these things Jesus himself sent out through them, from east to west, the sacred and imperishable proclamation of eternal salvation.
[II] This age of lawlessness and unbelief is under Satan, who does not allow the truth and power of God to prevail over the unclean things of the spirits [or, does not allow what lies under the unclean spirits to understand the truth and power of God]. Therefore reveal your righteousness now' – thus they spoke to Christ. And Christ replied to them, 'The term of years of Satan's power has been fulfilled, but other terrible things draw near. And for those who have sinned I was handed over to death, that they may return to the truth and sin no more, in order that they may inherit the spiritual and incorruptible glory of righteousness that is in heaven."

I trust that the self-evident spuriousness of these additions is obvious to even the most pious readers. One might in fact hope that Christians who are zealous for the "inspired Word of God" would insist that *all three of these bogus endings* be recognized for what they are–*forgeries*.

That said, what about the original ending of Mark? Its implications are rather astounding for Christian origins. I have dealt with this issue more generally in my post, "What Really Happened on Easter Morning," that sets the stage for the following implications.

1. Since Mark is our earliest Gospel, written according to most scholars around the time of the destruction of Jerusalem by the Romans in 70 CE, or perhaps in the decade before, we have strong textual evidence that the *first generation of Jesus followers* were perfectly fine with a Gospel account that recounted *no appearances of Jesus*. We have to assume that the author of Mark's Gospel did not consider his account deficient in the least and he was either passing on, or faithfully promoting, what he considered to be the authentic Gospel. What most Christians do when they think about Easter is ignore Mark. Since Mark knows nothing of any appearances of Jesus as a resuscitated corpse in Jerusalem, walking about, eating and showing his wounds, as recounted by Matthew, Luke and John, those stories are simply allowed to "fill in" for his assumed deficiency. In other words, *no one allows Mark to have a voice*. What he lacks, ironically, serves to marginalize and mute him!

2. Alternatively, if we decide to *listen* to Mark, who is our first gospel witness, what we learn is rather amazing. In Mark, on the last night of Jesus' life, he told his intimate followers following their meal, "But after I am *raised up*, I will go before you to Galilee" (Mark 14:28). What Mark believes is that Jesus has been "lifted up" or "raised up" to the right hand of God and that the disciples would "see" him in Galilee. Mark knows of no accounts of people encountering the revived corpse of Jesus, wounds and all, walking around Jerusalem. His tradition is that the disciples experienced their epiphanies of Jesus

once they returned to Galilee after the eight-day Passover festival and had returned to their fishing in despair. This is precisely what we find in the *Gospel of Peter*, where Peter says:

"Now it was the final day of the Unleavened Bread; and many went out returning to their home since the feast was over. But we twelve disciples of the Lord were weeping and sorrowful; and each one, sorrowful because of what had come to pass, departed to his home. But I, Simon Peter, and my brother Andrew, having taken our nets, went off to the sea. And there was with us Levi of Alphaeus whom the Lord ..."

You can read more about this fascinating "lost" Gospel of Peter here, but this ending, where the text happens to break off, is most revealing. What we see here is *precisely parallel* to Mark. The disciples *returned to their homes in Galilee in despair*, resuming their occupations, and *only then did they experience "sightings" of Jesus*. Strangely, this tradition shows up in an appended ending to the Gospel of John–chapter 21, where a group of disciples are back to their fishing, and Matthew knows the tradition of a strange encounter on a designated *mountain* in Galilee, where some of the eleven apostles even *doubt* what they are seeing (Matthew 28:16-17).

The faith that Mark reflects, namely that Jesus has been "raised up" or lifted up to heaven, is precisely parallel to that of Paul–who is the earliest witness to this understanding of Jesus' resurrection. Paul notably parallels his own *visionary* experience to that of Peter, James, and the rest of the apostles. What this means is that when Paul wrote, in the 50s CE, *this was the resurrection faith of the early followers of Jesus*! Since Matthew, Luke, and John come so much later, and clearly reflect the period after 70 CE when *all* of the first witnesses were dead–including Peter, Paul, and James the brother of Jesus, they are clearly 2nd generation traditions and should not be given priority.

"Mark begins his account with the line "The Gospel of Jesus Christ the Son of God" (Mark 1:1). Clearly for him, what he subsequently writes is that "Gospel," not a deficient version that needs to be supplemented or "fixed" with later alternative traditions about Jesus appearing in a resuscitated body Easter weekend in Jerusalem."

Finally, what we recently discovered in the Talpiot tomb under the condominium building, not 200 feet from the "Jesus family" tomb, offers a powerful testimony to this same kind of early Christian faith in Jesus' resurrection. On one of the ossuaries, or bone boxes in this tomb, is a four-line Greek inscription which I have translated as: *I Wondrous Yehovah lift up–lift up!* And this is next to a second ossuary representing the "sign of Jonah" with a large fish expelling the head of a human stick figure, recalling the story of Jonah. In that text Jonah sees himself as having passed into the gates of *Sheol* or death, from which he utters a prayer of salvation from the belly of the fish: "O Yehovah my God, you *lifted up* my life from the Pit!" (Jonah 2:6). It is a rare thing when our textual evidence seems to either reflect or correspond to the material evidence and I believe in the case of the two Talpiot tombs, and the early resurrection faith reflected in Paul and Mark, that is precisely what we have.[2] That this latest archaeological evidence corresponds so closely to Mark and Paul, our first witnesses to the earliest Christian understanding of Jesus' resurrection, I find to be most striking.[924]

On that note, I'll be citing the concise and thorough propositions by an ex-Christian who jotted down what he felt were the core problems of relying on the New Testament as a historical record. The following is from Mike Doolittle, he is an avid blogger and ex-Evangelical Christian and proposed a series of contentions about the New Testament that should hopefully provide thoughtful contemplation on the historicity and truth claims of the Bible.

By Mike Doolittle from *Aunicornist.com*:

- Christians claim the gospels are based on eye-witness testimony. This is dubious, because Jesus is often documented as going off to be alone, and yet somehow we are privy to the exact words he spoke (most famously, the temptation in the desert – where he was purportedly alone for 40 days – and the prayers in Gethsamane while the disciples were asleep). This means that, at best, the gospels are a combination of eye-witness testimony and hearsay.
- Even if the gospels were based on eye-witness testimony, such testimony is notoriously unreliable, as a litany of modern research reveals.
- Christian subsequently claim that these stories were passed on through meticulous oral traditions. However, such "meticulous" oral traditions among the Jews had been reserved for Rabbis, and even then they were not obsessed with historical details [link]. There's no evidence that the illiterate peasants who supposedly witnessed these events had any kind of reliable oral tradition.
- We don't have the original manuscripts, but copies of copies of copies, which are frequently littered with contradictions, omissions, additions, and errors.
- This culminates in the four books we now have, which are themselves filled with internal contradictions. When presented with these contradictions, Christians claim that the disagreement is to be expected. Of course, they propose no independent criteria to establish an acceptable amount of contradiction. What is the correct amount? Why, the amount in the Bible, of course! This is retroactive rationalization.
- The gospels make unsubstantiated historical claims, including the census and slaughter of the firstborns commanded by Herod.
- The gospels make *supernatural* claims, which demands more evidence than mundane historical claims. Christians typically invoke special pleading to rationalize their dismissal of the historicity of other cultures' supernatural claims.[925]

---

19. [924] Tabor, James. "The 'Strange' Ending of the Gospel of Mark and Why It Makes All the Difference." *Biblical Archaeology Society*, Biblical Archaeology Society, 4 May 2018, www.biblicalarchaeology.org/daily/biblical-topics/new-testament/the-strange-ending-of-the-gospel-of-mark-and-why-it-makes-all-the-difference/.
20. [925] D, Mike. "The Bible Is a Worthless Historical Document." *The Kalam Cosmological Argument: the Complete Rebuttal*, Blogger, 1 Feb. 2011, www.theaunicornist.com/2011/01/bible-is-worthless-historical-document.html.

Chapter 18: Biblical Contradictions Versus Jesus Christ

Dr. William S. Abruzzi, a former Professor for the Department of Sociology and Anthropology at Muhlenberg College in the US State of Pennsylvania has done extensive research into the Bible's accounts and historical authenticity. He has examined the research of the four Gospel writers compared to each other and compared it to the archeological findings of Early Christianity. He and other researchers have looked into the contemporary Bible's accounts compared to the survived documents of the Christian gospels that had been thrown out and declared blasphemous during the formation of the Catholic Church. Dr. Abruzzi compiled a research paper detailing his examination of the literature compared to the archaeological evidence and presented his findings on his blog to be made publicly available for anyone interested in examining and further researching the history of Christianity.

The historical research that he has compiled and presented are on his personal website "*drabruzzi.com*." He provides a thorough account of his research findings on Biblical contradictions and Jesus Christ's history in his 2015 article "*The Birth of Jesus: The Evolution of Jesus in the Infancy Narratives*" presented below. I feel it is best for you to simply read and absorb this research. After that, I'll be giving a set of questions for you to consider:

The Gospels

To understand the birth stories of Jesus, we need to understand the gospels in which they are included; and to understand the gospels, we need to examine the authors who wrote them, as well as the audiences to whom they were directed. Without going into a detailed discussion of the theologies and other characteristics that are known about the purported authors (Mark, Matthew, Luke and John), one thing is clear: they were not eyewitnesses to the events they describe. Current biblical scholarship dates the gospel attributed to Mark (generally accepted as the earliest of the canonical gospels) to around 70 CE (Common Era, formerly A.D.). The gospels attributed to Matthew and Luke are generally dated between 80-90 CE, while the gospel attributed to John is thought to have been written between 90-100 CE. Clearly, given these dates, it is highly improbable that any of the gospel writers were themselves eyewitnesses to specific events in Jesus' life. They most certainly were not present at Jesus' birth or, for that matter, at the Sanhedrin meetings where plans were made to arrest Jesus, at Jesus' trial before the Sanhedrin or his trial by Roman authorities, none of which would have been public affairs. They were also not present to take notes when Jesus was telling the various parables contained in the first three gospels or making the long speeches presented in the fourth gospel.[1] The gospels were based on stories handed down for some 2-3 generations and contain all the problems of accuracy and validity associated with such stories. (For a good example of how quickly stories can become distorted and mythologized, even in a literate and educated society, see Abruzzi *The Myth of Chief Seattle*.) In a court of law, most of what is contained in the gospels would be classified as "hearsay."

Evidence also exists which clearly suggests that the authors of the four gospels were not native to Palestine. Mark's description of the land descending into the Sea of Galilee and his story of Jesus walking 70 rather than 40 miles from Tyre to the Sea of Galilee following a route through Sidon the region of the Decapolis (Mark 7:31) demonstrate an ignorance of Palestinian geography. Similarly, Mark (10:11-13) displays ignorance of Jewish customs when he has Jesus telling a parable involving a woman who divorces her husband, a behavior that would have been impossible among the Jews of Palestine at that time. Luke (1:59-61) also demonstrates an ignorance of Jewish customs when he claims that the baby John the Baptist was to be named Zechariah after his father until Elizabeth, his mother, obeying the instructions of the angel, objected, saying, *"No, he is to be called John."* This deviation from tradition, according to Luke, generated critical comments among their neighbors. However, Jews did not traditionally name a son after the father. In fact, according to Asimov (1969: 922), there is not a single case in the Old Testament of a son being named for a living father, and "is still not done by pious Jews today." Similarly, Luke (2:22) claims that Joseph and Mary brought Jesus to the temple following his birth because *"the time came for their purification."* However, the law in *Leviticus* (12:1-5) requires only the mother to be purified after giving birth, not the father.

Purification of Women after Childbirth

The Lord said to Moses, "Say to the people of Israel, If a woman conceives, and bears a male child, then she shall be unclean seven days; as at the time of her menstruation, she shall be unclean. And on the eighth day the flesh of his foreskin shall be circumcised. Then she shall continue for thirty-three days in the blood of her purifying; she shall not touch any hallowed thing, nor come into the sanctuary, until the days of her purifying are completed. But if she bears a female child, then she shall be unclean two weeks, as in her menstruation; and she shall continue in the blood of her purifying for sixty-six days.

Several researchers (cf. Dibelius 1956; Goulder 1957; Oliver 1964; Minear 1966; Haenchen 1966; Brown 1977; Fitzmyer 1981; Goulder 1989; Freed 2001) have provided ample evidence that illustrates Luke's unreliability as a historian. In a statement that would be seconded by many scholars, Haenchen (1966:260) concludes that the evangelist "is not so much a historian in our sense of the word as he is a fascinating narrator." (see Abruzzi *When Was Jesus Born?*)

Finally, the gospels lack the elements usually found in eyewitness accounts. They rarely include the kind of details and information one would expect from first-hand descriptions of events. None of the gospel writers, for example, includes themselves in any of the events that took place, as would be expected had they actually witnessed the events they describe. Furthermore, Luke (1:1-3) begins his gospel with the following words,

Inasmuch as many have undertaken to compile a narrative of the things which have been accomplished among us, just as they were delivered to us by those who from the beginning were eyewitnesses and ministers of the word, it seemed good to me also, having followed all things closely for some time past, to write an orderly account for you, most excellent Theoph'ilus.[2]

Luke's introduction indicates rather clearly that he was not an eyewitness and, in fact, based his account on others who were the original *"eyewitnesses and ministers of the word."* Along the same lines, if Matthew and Luke were eyewitnesses to the events they describe, Matthew would not have depended on Mark for nearly two-thirds of his stories; nor would Luke have depended on Mark for nearly half of his stories. Indeed, with the exception of about 40 verses, the whole of Mark's gospel is reproduced nearly word-for-word in Matthew. If Matthew had actually witnessed the events he described, he clearly would have had his own stories to tell, and he would have told them in his own words.

Who are the authors of the four canonical gospels? While Christians have universally accepted that individuals named Matthew, Mark, Luke and John composed the four gospels, and while these four individuals have all been canonized as Christian saints, the reality is that no one knows who wrote the four canonical gospels, or if they were even written by specific individuals. Authorship of these gospels was not attributed to the four currently named individuals until 175 CE by Irenaeus, the bishop of Lyon (Ehrman 1997:79). There was, in fact, intense disagreement regarding which gospels should be considered canonical throughout the first four centuries of the Christian era. While there were dozens of Christian gospels in existence (see Hedrick 2002), including such well-known Gnostic gospels as the *Gospel of Thomas*, the *Gospel of Philip*, and the *Gospel of Mary* (see Pagels 1979) and the *Gospel of the Hebrews*, the *Gospel of the Nazaraeans* and the *Gospel of the Ebionites*, generally attributed to early Jewish Christians in Palestine (see Munck 1960), Irenaeus was insistent that there were only four legitimate gospels, the current four canonical gospels, which he named. Irenaeus' reasoning for the existence of only four canonical gospels would hardly survive scrutiny today.

The Gospels could not possibly be either more or less in number than they are. Since there are four zones of the world in which we live, and four principal winds, while the Church is spread over all the earth, and the pillar and foundation of the Church is the gospel, and the Spirit of life, it fittingly has four pillars, everywhere breathing out incorruption and revivifying men. From this it is clear that the Word, the artificer of all things, being manifested to men gave us the gospel, fourfold in form but held together by one Spirit. As David said, when asking for his coming, 'O sitter upon the cherubim, show yourself '. For the cherubim have four faces, and their faces are images of the activity of the Son of God. For the first living creature, it says, was like a lion, signifying his active and princely and royal character; the second was like an ox, showing his sacrificial and priestly order; the third had the face of a man, indicating very clearly his coming in human guise; and the fourth was like a flying eagle, making plain the giving of the Spirit who broods over the Church. Now the Gospels, in which Christ is enthroned, are like these. (Against Heresies 3.11.8) (quoted in Stanton 1989:134)

The Synoptic Gospels

As already indicated, the general consensus among biblical scholars is that Mark is the earliest of the gospels. In addition, Mark, Matthew and Luke are classified together as the *Synoptic Gospels* (synoptic = "to see with one eye") owing to the similarity of their stories about Jesus, which is to be expected given that the stories in Matthew and Luke largely derived from those in Mark. Indeed, fully 80% of Mark's gospel is reproduced by Matthew, while about 65% is reproduced by Luke (Ehrman 1997). In addition, Matthew and Luke agree in sequence "only to the degree that they both agree with Mark" (Fitzmyer 1970: 136). Luke rarely changed the order of Mark's stories, while Matthew changed it only 7 times (Stanton 1989: 35). Only once (Luke 22:59) does Luke include a chronological reference that is not already present in Mark (Stanton 1989:84). In addition, "Matthew and Luke never agree with one another against Mark in regard to the order of episodes" (Fitzmyer 1970: 136). Matthew and Luke, however, routinely modified and added to (i.e., *redacted*) Mark's account in order to adapt Mark's stories to fit their own theologies. In Matthew, many of Mark's stories were modified to accommodate an Old Testament prophecy that Matthew wanted to attribute to Jesus. Luke, on the other hand, frequently altered Mark's account in order to make Jesus more sympathetic and amenable to Gentiles (non-Jews).

While some might want to argue that Mark borrowed from Matthew and Luke, or that Mark, Matthew and Luke all borrowed from each other or from another earlier source, Fitzmyer (1970: 134-147) details the reasons why scholars nearly universally accept the priority of Mark among the Synoptic Gospels. The priority of Mark clearly emerges when examining individual texts contained in the three gospels. One obvious question, for example, is why would Mark (the shortest of the gospels) have abbreviated and conflated the more elaborate versions of the same stories contained in Matthew and Luke. Indeed, the normal direction of the subsequent retelling of stories is an increase --not a decrease-- in the elaboration of story details (see Funk, Hoover *et. al.* 1993: Chapter 1). Why also would Mark have omitted such important and popular stories as the Sermon on the Mount from Matthew and the Good Samaritan in Luke? Similarly, why would Mark have eliminated all traces of both Matthew's and Luke's infancy narratives? Given Mathew's and Luke's more elaborate resurrection narratives, Mark's almost non-existent resurrection narrative makes no sense, if Mark borrowed from them rather than they from him. Throughout the gospel, the Christology presented by Mark is substantially less developed than that presented in the other gospels, and reflects an earlier and theologically less developed conceptualization of Jesus and his mission. Thus, "given Mark, it is easy to see why Matthew and Luke were written; but given Matthew and Luke, it is hard to see why Mark was needed in the early Church." (Fitzmyer 1970: 135).

It is also difficult to explain why, having Matthew's gospel in hand, Luke should only follow Matthew's order when it agrees with Mark. If Luke borrowed equally from Matthew and Mark, or if Matthew borrowed equally from Luke and Mark, or if all the three evangelists borrowed equally from an earlier source, there should be numerous agreements in order between Matthew and Luke against Mark; but "there are next to none." (Fitzmyer 1970: 138). Bart Ehrman (1997: Chapters 5-10) presents a detailed analysis of the four canonical gospels, which similarly demonstrates the primacy of Mark among the Synoptic Gospels and which illustrates the manner in which Matthew and Luke both redacted Mark's material to accommodate their own theologies. Given such extensive interdependency among the various gospels, they cannot be considered multiple and independent affirmations of Christian beliefs about Jesus. The fact that a particular story exists in more than one gospel may simply indicate that one or more later writers borrowed the story from an earlier gospel. What is more significant is the way in which the different gospel authors modified those stories to support their own theologies..

Meanwhile, Luke and Matthew share some 230 verses that are not contained in Mark (Stanton 1989:86). Textual analysis of these verses over the past century has led scholars to conclude that Matthew and Luke borrowed the stories contained in these verses from a common source other than Mark, just as they borrowed the bulk of their stories from Mark. This other source, which is yet to be discovered, is referred to as *"Q"* [short for *Quelle*, which means "Source" in German]. There are several reasons for this consensus. Stanton (1989: 86-87) points out some of them:

1. A very close verbal agreement exists between Matthew and Luke extending over several verses. (e.g., Matt 3:7-10 = Luke 3:7-9; Matt 11:4-11, 16-19 = Luke 7:22-28, 31-350).

2. Striking agreements exist in the order in which the non-Marcan traditions are found in both Matthew and Luke.

3. Both Matthew and Luke contain several "doublet" passages in which the two authors use the Marcan form of the story at one point in their gospel and the Q version of the same story elsewhere (e.g., *"He who has, to him will more be given"* Mk 4:25 = Matt 13:12 = Luke 8:18. A similar saying is found at Matt 25:29 and Luke 19:26).

Such similarities are highly unlikely to have occurred by chance.

The Synoptic Gospels vs. the "Signs" Gospel of John

As Aviezer Tucker (2016: 137) so eloquently notes, "The problem with the Synoptic Gospels as evidence for a historical Jesus . . . is that the evidence that coheres does not seem to be independent, whereas the evidence that is independent does not seem to cohere." With the addition of the Gospel of John, a distinctly independent source, gospel coherence completely disappears. To begin with, in the Synoptic Gospels Jesus is more human; in John he is more divine. Indeed, in John, the very first verse of the gospel proclaims, *"In the beginning was the Word, and the Word was with God, and the Word was God."* (John 1:1) In other words, Jesus is one with God (which he is not in any of the Synoptics) and has always existed. He simply becomes human through an undefined process: *"And the Word became flesh and dwelt among us."* (John 1:14) There is, therefore, no birth story in John because, as God, Jesus clearly pre-existed Joseph and Mary. This stands in sharp contrast to the Synoptics where Jesus is born [in Matthew and Luke] through a very human process, experiences very human travails, and becomes God's messenger at different times during his life (at his birth, his baptism, or his resurrection). In fact, it is not clear when (or even if) Jesus becomes divine in Mark. The most that can be said is that he becomes a messenger of God at his baptism.

In those days Jesus came from Nazareth of Galilee and was baptized by John in the Jordan. And when he came up out of the water, immediately he saw the heavens opened and the Spirit descending upon him like a dove; and a voice came from heaven, "Thou art my beloved Son; with thee I am well pleased." (Mark 1:9-11)

Matthew reproduces Mark's description of Jesus' baptism almost exactly, but changes God's words (*"this"* replaces *"thou"*) in order to have God address the entire crowd present at the baptism rather than Jesus alone, as in Mark.

And when Jesus was baptized, he went up immediately from the water, and behold, the heavens were opened and he saw the Spirit of God descending like a dove, and alighting on him; and lo, a voice from heaven, saying, "This is my beloved Son, with whom I am well pleased." (Matt 3: 16-17)

Whereas in the Synoptics Jesus suffers and frequently displays his humanity, in John Jesus is more fully divine and in control of all events, including his own trial, where he tells Pilate, *"You would have no power over me unless it had been given you from above"* (John 19:10). In the Synoptic Gospels, Jesus even questions his mission and requests that he not have to suffer crucifixion (Mark 13:36; Matthew 26:39; Luke 22:42). No such doubt exists in Jesus' mind in John, and, consequently, no agony in the Garden of Gethsemane takes place in John. In the Synoptics, Jesus recruits his apostles; in John, they come to him. None of the spectacular miracles in John, such as the raising of Lazarus from the dead, are mentioned in the Synoptic Gospels. Conversely, Jesus performs no exorcisms and tells no parables in John's gospel, whereas exorcisms and parables permeate and even define Jesus' teaching in the Synoptic Gospels. In John, Jesus talks not in parables, but in long monologues. In fact, not a single statement made by Jesus in John is contained in any of the three Synoptic gospels. The repetition of long monologues and the complete lack of overlap with the words and deeds of Jesus in the Synoptic Gospels are two of the reasons why not a single quote in the entire Gospel of John was considered authentic by the 76 scholars of the *Jesus Seminar* (1993). Furthermore, Jesus' miracles are repeatedly performed in John as "signs" of his divinity, which they never are in any of the Synoptics. In fact, in Mark (8:11-13) and Matthew (12:38-39; 16:1-4) Jesus explicitly rejects all requests that he provide a sign of his divinity.

The Pharisees came and began to argue with him, seeking from him a sign from heaven, to test him. And he sighed deeply in his spirit, and said, "Why does this generation seek a sign? Truly, I say to you, no sign shall be given to this generation." And he left them, and getting into the boat again he departed to the other side. (Mark 8:11-13)

And the Pharisees and Sadducees came, and to test him they asked him to show them a sign from heaven. He answered them, "When it is evening, you say, 'It will be fair weather; for the sky is red.' And in the morning, 'It will be stormy today, for the sky is red and threatening.' You know how to interpret the appearance of the sky, but you cannot interpret the signs of the times. An evil and adulterous generation seeks for a sign, but no sign shall be given to it except the sign of Jonah." So he left them and departed. (Matt 16:1-4)

Jesus is also much more explicit and forthcoming about who he is in John's gospel. There are, for example, 46 *"I am"* statements in John where Jesus proclaims who he is openly for all to hear, compared to only 2, 5 & 2 respectively in Mark, Matthew & Luke. In fact, in Mark Jesus repeatedly tells those that he has cured or who have witnessed his miracles not to tell anyone. (Mark 1:44; 3:12; 5:43; 7:36; 8:30). Examples of *"I am"* statements made by Jesus in John, but not presented in any of the other gospels, include:

Jesus said to them, "I am the bread of life. Whoever comes to me will never be hungry, and whoever believes in me will never be thirsty. (6:35)

Again Jesus spoke to them, saying, "I am the light of the world. Whoever follows me will never walk in darkness but will have the light of life." (8:12)

He said to them, "You are from below, I am from above; you are of this world, I am not of this world. (8:23)

Jesus said to them, "Very truly, I tell you, before Abraham was, I am." (8:58)

The Father and I are one." (10:30) [the verb form is different here because the subject is plural]

Jesus said to her, "I am the resurrection and the life. Those who believe in me, even though they die, will live. (11:25)

Jesus said to him, "I am the way, and the truth, and the life. No one comes to the Father except through me. (14:6)

Finally, whereas Jesus is largely misunderstood in the Synoptics, especially in Mark, he is immediately recognized for who he is in John. This contrast is especially stark when comparing Mark (the earliest of the canonical gospel) to John (the latest). In Mark, at one point Jesus' family thinks he is crazy and tries to stop him from preaching: *"and when his friends heard of it, they went out to lay hold on him: for they said, He is beside himself."* (Mark 3:21) In addition, his own apostles did not understand who he is, even though they were specially chosen by him (Mark 3:13-19) and received instruction from him (Mark 4:10-20). When Jesus calmed a violent storm, they asked, *"Who then is this, that even the wind and sea obey him?"* (Mark 4:41) When they saw Jesus walking on the water, they still did not understand (Mark 6:49-52). Indeed, Jesus expressed frustration at their lack of understanding: *"Do you not yet understand?"* (Mark 8:21). By contrast, in John people recognize who Jesus is from the start. As indicated previously, he did not recruit his apostles in John; they came to him. Furthermore, following Jesus' first miracle in the fourth gospel, that of turning water into wine, the evangelist states, *"This, the first of his signs, Jesus did at Cana in Galilee, and manifested his glory; and his disciples believed in him"* (John 2:11), a direct contradiction to the statements in Mark. Also, in John (4:9-10, 22-23), Jesus shares a cup of water with a Samaritan woman and tells her that she will be with him in heaven. Later, when the woman tells other Samaritans about Jesus, they invite Jesus to stay in their village, which (in direct contradiction to Mark and Matthew) he does for two days. They also immediately believe in Jesus as the messiah, so charismatic is his presence (John 4:39-40), again in direct contrast to Mark and Matthew where Jesus' message is rejected by his contemporaries, Jew and Samaritan alike. Indeed, in Matthew (10:5-6), Jesus explicitly instructs his apostles to stay away from the Samaritans.

These twelve Jesus sent out, charging them, "Go nowhere among the Gentiles, and enter no town of the Samaritans, but go rather to the lost sheep of the house of Israel.

While many Christians want to explain away the contradictions as simply the result of individual authors presenting different interpretations of the events they witnessed, the gospels differ sharply on concrete empirical details, such as the year Jesus was born, who his ancestors were, the date on which the Last Supper took place, words spoken at Jesus' trial, the number and names of those who visited his tomb on Easter morning, and where and to whom Jesus made his post-resurrection appearances. Mark, for example, begins his gospel with Jesus' baptism by John the Baptist and says nothing about a virgin birth in Bethlehem or about any of the other marvels and miracles surrounding Jesus' birth that were later added to the "Jesus Story" by Matthew and Luke. Paul, the earliest Christian writer, also mentions none of these events. Similarly, while Mark makes no mention of Jesus' ancestry, Matthew (1:1-17) introduces a genealogy that traces Jesus' ancestry through Joseph all the way back to King David and to Abraham, the founding patriarch of the Israelites. Luke (3:23-38) provides an equally inventive genealogy [which includes no names contained in Matthew's genealogy] that traces Jesus' ancestry clear back to Adam. Luke even adds Zechariah and Elizabeth to Jesus' family tree as his maternal uncle and aunt and John the Baptist as his first cousin (Luke 1:36-45). Similarly, each gospel names distinct individuals who went to Jesus' tomb on Easter morning: *"Mary Magdalene, and Mary the mother of James, and Salome,"* (Mark 16:1); *"Mary Magdalene and the other Mary."* (Matt 28:1); *"Mary Magdalene and Joanna and Mary the mother of James and the other women."* (Luke 24:8-10); and first *"Mary Magdalene"* and then *"Simon Peter and the other disciple, the one whom Jesus loved"* (John 20:1-2). In addition, while Mark (16:9-18), Luke (24:1-53) and John (20:11-29) all have Jesus' post-resurrection appearances take place in and around Jerusalem, Matthew (29:16-17) describes only one appearance, which takes place in Galilee.

The Evolution of the Jesus Story

Contradictions within and between the gospels result from their being composed, either in whole or in part, at different times and places where various local traditions, together with the different theologies of each evangelist, resulted in the emergence of distinct stories and beliefs about Jesus. As traditions about Jesus were passed down, new stories were added and existing stories became modified and more elaborated. As a result, the Jesus Story became increasingly mythologized in conformity with the evolving theology of the Christian community.[3]

With regard to the birthplace of Jesus, for example, Mark repeats the phrase *"Jesus of Nazareth"* throughout his gospel (cf. 1:9; 1:24; 6:1; 10:47; 16:6), giving no indication that Jesus was born or lived anywhere but Nazareth. Mark contains none of what Asimov (1969: 903) refers to as Matthew's "Old Testament pedantry," i.e., his tendentious application of Old Testament prophecy to significant events in Jesus' life, including his birth. Nor do we see in Mark any of the angelic visitations presented in Luke. Since there is no birth story in Mark, there are no star, magi or shepherds in the fields, no slaughter of innocent children, and no flight to Egypt by Jesus' family. Nor are there any post-resurrection appearances by Jesus to his apostles. Mark's gospel ends with the two Marys (Mary Magdalene and Mary the mother of James and Salome), fleeing the tomb and telling no one what they saw (Mark 16:8).[4] Indeed, if one were to read only Mark, he or she would have no indication that Jesus lived or was born anywhere but Nazareth, or that he was anything but a noteworthy Galilean preacher whose ministry was cut short by Roman authorities who executed him in the prime of his life, as they did many other messianic pretenders (see Horsley and Hanson 1985). Furthermore, Jesus is presented twice in the gospel of John (7:41-42, 52) with a challenge to his being the Messiah based on the belief that the Messiah was to come from Bethlehem, not Galilee. This would have been a perfect opportunity for Jesus to mention his birth in Bethlehem, had it been true. However, Jesus says nothing to rebut his critics. Nor is Jesus' birth in Bethlehem mentioned anywhere else in the entire New Testament. Indeed, Jesus' birth in Bethlehem, as well as all the other features of the two infancy narratives, are not mentioned even once outside those narratives in the very gospels in which they appear. This has led some scholars to argue that the infancy narratives were later additions to Matthew's and Luke's gospels, just as Chapter 1: 1-18 (the *Prologue*) and the entirety of Chapter 21 are widely accepted as later additions to the gospel of John.[5][926]

---

1. [926] Abruzzi, William S. "THE BIRTH OF JESUS: The Evolution of the Jesus in the Infancy Narratives." *Doc A's Webpage: On the Importance of Writing Research Papers*, Dr. William S. Abruzzi, 2015, www.drabruzzi.com/birth_of_jesus.htm.

Further along this extensive research analysis, he goes on further explaining the Bible's self-contradictions among the four Canon Gospels and the violent divisions during the burgeoning years of Christianity:

Contradictions Among the Gospels

Obvious contradictions would be expected to result from the fact that the four gospels, representing four distinct theologies, present different versions of John and of his relation to Jesus, The first and most obvious is the fact that, despite John's explicit statement regarding his subordination to Jesus, whom he claimed in the fourth gospel was the true messiah, John never became a follower of Jesus, but rather, as just indicated, maintained his separate mission until he was executed by Herod Antipas (c. 29 CE). In addition, whereas the author of the gospel of John (1:27-36, see above) presents John the Baptist as absolutely understanding who Jesus was and explicitly acknowledging his own subordinate role to Jesus, in both Matthew (11:2-6) and Luke (7;19-23) [in passages likely borrowed from Q], while in prison the Baptist sends emissaries to Jesus to ask him, *"Are you he who is to come, or shall we look for another?"* Similarly, as already mentioned, whereas Jesus recruits his apostles in the three Synoptic Gospels (Mark 1:16-20; Matt 4:18-22; Luke 6:12-16), they seek him in the fourth gospel (John 1:40-42). Likewise, in Mark's (1:9-11) version of Jesus' baptism by John, the Baptist gives no indication that he knew who Jesus was. Even in the fourth gospel (John 1:32-34), John explicitly claims not to know who Jesus was, being simply instructed by the Holy Spirit to baptize him. Yet, as already mentioned, John is introduced near the beginning of Luke's Gospel (1:36-42) as Jesus' first cousin. This level of contradiction is multiplied many times over when comparing all the stories contained in more than one gospel.

Also, when reading and interpreting New Testament texts, it is necessary to recognize that those biblical documents that have survived and that are used by millions of Christians today are but a small fragment of the totality of early Christian writings that have been produced. Numerous writings, referred to collectively as Christian *Apocrypha* and *Pseudoepigrapha* exist that did not become incorporated into the New Testament. These non-canonical writings include more than two dozen gospels, as well as numerous epistles, acts of various apostles, apocalypses and homilies written in the early years of the church (see Davies 1983; Barnstone 1984; Robinson 1984; Hone, Jones & Wake 1979; Cartlidge 1997; Hedrick 2002; Ehrman 2003a, 2006b; 2013). These various documents were used among a variety of Christian communities before there was an official New Testament. Some of these writings have survived and some have been rediscovered (such as the remarkable discoveries of the Nag Hammadi Scrolls in 1945 and the Dead Sea Scrolls in 1947). However, many of these documents were destroyed by the Roman Church as it consolidated its power within the empire, or have been otherwise lost, and are known to us only through references to them by numerous early Christian writers, such as Tertullian, Irenaeus and Origen. These diverse writings contain a host of stories about Jesus, Mary, Joseph, Mary's parents, Mary Magdalene, the activities of most of the apostles, and many other topics. The New Testament writings, most notably the gospels, were also preceded not only by oral traditions, but also by other earlier as yet undiscovered documents, such as Q and possibly pre-Marcan, pre-Matthean and, pre-Lucan writings, as well as an earlier "signs" document preceding the Gospel of John (see Winter 1954a, 1954b, 1955, 1956; Koester 1968, 1980; Davis 1971; Cartlidge 1997; Bovon 1988; Burkett 2004).

When evaluating stories about the birth and childhood of Jesus (or any other stories about the life of Jesus), it is important to understand that oral traditions --and even written documents-- change over time (see Ehrman 1993, 2003a, 2003b, 2005; 2013). Inasmuch as traditions about Jesus were adapted and used in the life of early Christian communities, both before and after the canonical gospels were written, existing stories evolved and new stories emerged in response to the needs and changing theology of those communities. This process has continued down to the present, illustrated, for example, by the widespread belief in a militant Jesus during the Crusades of the Middle Ages and a Pacifist Jesus concerned with the rights of all humans in modern industrial societies (see Pelikan 1965; Robinson 1982; Prothero 2005). Luke Timothy Johnson (2004), for example, notes that most books based on the New Testament and sold in the U.S. today focus on the Gospel of Luke, which, more than any of the other gospels, presents a pacifist, universalist Jesus concerned with justice and with the poor.

In other words, both oral and written traditions tell us more about Christianity and about evolving Christian communities at the time they existed than they do about Jesus himself. Consequently, rather than viewing Christian *apocrypha* and *pseudepigrapha* as somehow less correct than the surviving canonical texts, it is more useful from a historical perspective to view all early Christian writings along a *spatio-temporal continuum* informing us about: (1) the evolution and diversity of early Christianity as a belief system; (2) competing Christian theologies and communities; (3) the theological and political factors involved in the canonization of some texts and the rejection of others; and (4) the politics of heresy declaration. Indeed, both the letters of Paul, especially *Galatians*, and the *Acts of the Apostles* (as well as many other early Christian writings) demonstrate that intense conflict emerged among Christians very shortly after Jesus' death and that this conflict revolved around the very question of who Jesus was and what message he taught.

The diversity of early Christian writings stems from the fact that Christians very quickly divided into a number of separate communities professing distinct and often competing theologies and Christologies (see Bauer 1934; Pagels 1979; Beskow 1983; Ehrman 2003b; Jenkins 2008; MacCulloch 2009). Many of the beliefs common among these various Christian communities exceeded the range of beliefs that prevail among modern Christians, contradicting the notion that there was a much greater sense of communion among early Christians than there is today. Intense conflict existed among these competing Christianities, which increased during the first four centuries (see Bauer 1934; Betz 1965; Pagels 1979; Jenkins 2008; Ehrman 1993, 2003). The consolidation of beliefs was largely the result of the eventual dominance of what has become known as the "Orthodox" faction within the early Church, centered in Rome, supported by Roman Emperors and ultimately becoming the official religion of the Roman Empire. With the consolidation of Orthodox dominance, most of the competing forms of Christianity were declared heretical, with their books burned and their adherents persecuted (see Bauer 1934; Pagels 1979; Ehrman 2003b; Jenkins 2008, 2010; MacCulloch 2009).

A few of the more notable variations in early Christianity, included:

Adoptionism: the belief that Jesus was not born divine but was chosen by God as a result of his sinless devotion to the will of God, for example, at his baptism.

Ebionites: a sect that regarded Jesus as a mortal human messianic prophet but not as divine. They insisted on the necessity of following Jewish religious laws and rituals. They also revered Jesus' brother James as the head of the Jerusalem Church (rather than Peter) and rejected Paul of Tarsus as an "apostate of the Law." The Ebionites also rejected the pre-existence, divinity, virgin birth, atoning death and physical resurrection of Jesus.

Nazarenes: The Nazarenes were an early Jewish Christian sect similar to the Ebionites in that they maintained their adherence to the Torah, but, unlike the Ebionites, they accepted the virgin birth and the divinity of Jesus. The Nazarenes were followers of John the Baptist and then James the Just, the brother of Jesus.

Gnosticism: Gnosticism was one of the most widespread forms of early Christian belief. It included a variety of religious teachings in which humans were viewed as divine souls trapped in a material world by an imperfect (sometimes evil) spirit known as the *demiurge*, generally identified as Yahweh, the god of the Old Testament. The demiurge exists alongside another more remote and unknowable supreme being who is both good and the ultimate creator of the world. According to Gnostics, the only way to escape the inferior material world is to gain spiritual knowledge (*gnosis*), which is only available to a learned elite. Gnostic Christians viewed Jesus as the embodiment of the Supreme Being who became incarnate in order to bring gnosis to the Earth. Gnostics rejected Orthodox views of the virgin birth and the physical resurrection of Jesus. These were symbolic representations of Jesus, and were not to be taken literally.

Docetism: Docetists believed that Christ was not a real human being and did not have a real human body. He only seemed to be human. In other words, there was only Christ, not Jesus.

Marcionism: Marcion proposed the first canon of Christian texts. His proposed canon consisted of the Gospel of Luke and several of Paul's epistles. However, Marcion deleted any references in these documents that showed any approval of the Old Testament or the God of the Jews.

The early Church was also racked by a continuing controversy between *Monophysites* and *Miaphysites* (or *Dyophysites*.) Monophysites claimed that following the union of the divine and the human in his *Incarnation*, Jesus Christ had only a single "nature" which was either divine or a synthesis of the divine and the human. Miaphysites, on the other hand, claimed that Jesus Christ retained two distinct natures after his Incarnation: one divine and one human. This conflict raged over several centuries resulting in the death of tens of thousands of Christians on both sides of the controversy. According to Jenkins (2010: xii),

The intra-Christian violence of the fifth- and sixth-century debates was on a far larger and more systematic scale than anything produced by the Inquisition.

The Monophysite-Miaphysite controversy produced several Ecumenical Councils during the fifth and sixth centuries through which the competing factions promoted their respective theologies (see Grant 1975; Jenkins 2010). It was not until the Council of Chalcedon in 451 CE that the Church formulated the statement that eventually became the official theology of the Roman Empire --that Christ had two natures joined into one person.

The Chalcedon Council did not end the controversy, however. Monophysites were still numerous and influential in the Church and dominated much of the Christian world and the Roman Empire long after Chalcedon. They were ultimately defeated only after decades of bloody struggle, such as occurred in the following two incidents:

Jerusalem was occupied by an army of [Monophysite] monks; in the name of the one incarnate Nature, they pillaged, they burnt, they murdered; the sepulchre of Christ was defiled with blood ... On the third day before the festival of Easter, the [Alexandrian] patriarch was besieged in the cathedral, and murdered in the baptistery. The remains of his mangled corpse were delivered to the flames, and his ashes to the wind; and the deed was inspired by the vision of a pretended angel. This deadly superstition was inflamed, on either side, by the principle and the practice of retaliation: in the pursuit of a metaphysical quarrel, many thousands were slain. (Gibbon 1854, 5:235; quoted in Jenkins 2010: xii).

Chalcedonians behaved at least as badly in their campaigns to enforce their particular orthodoxy. In the eastern city of Amida, a Chalcedonian bishop dragooned dissidents, to the point of burning them alive. His most diabolical scheme involving taking lepers, "hands festering and dripping with blood and pus," and billeting them on the Monophysite faithful until they saw reason. (Jenkins 2010: xii),

Indeed, centuries after Chalcedon, Monophysites continued to prevail in the eastern regions of the Empire, such as Syria, Palestine, and Egypt (see Jones 1963:17; Jenkins 2008; MacCulloch

2009). As heirs of the very oldest churches, the ones with the most direct and authentic ties to the apostolic age, they eventually found their interpretation of Christ ruled as heretical (Jenkins 2010:xi), as did many other varieties of Christianity, including those such as the Ebionites and Nazarenes, both of whom revered James (Jesus' brother) and claimed a direct connection to Jesus and his apostles.[10] The Monophysite/Miaphysite controversy never completely ended and eventually underlay the "Great Schism" in 1054 that divided Christianity into competing Eastern Orthodox and Roman Catholic Churches.

To complicate matters, a variety of 1st Century biblical manuscripts have survived, including a standardized Hebrew *Masoretic Text* (MT), an official Greek *Septuagint* (LXX) text, other variant Hebrew texts, *Aramaic targums* (ancient Aramaic interpretations of the Hebrew Bible), and several Greek translations of the Bible, some of which conformed more closely to the MT than does the LXX (see Brown 1977: 103). Finally, numerous changes were made to the various canonical texts over time (see Koester 1980; Bovon 1988; Ehrman 1993, 2005; Globe 1980; Holmes 2001). In 1707 John Mill, an English clergyman and theologian concluded 30 years of research by publishing his *Novum Testamentum*, which he offered as an authoritative version of the New Testament based on the examination of some 100 New Testament Greek manuscripts. In the process, however, Mill discovered 30,000 textual variations among those 100 manuscripts, much to the consternation of his contemporaries (see Ehrman 2006: 2). Given that the number of known [complete and partial] New Testament manuscripts today is closer to 25,000 --over 5,000 Greek manuscripts, some 10,000 Latin manuscripts, plus more than 9,000 manuscripts in various other ancient languages, including Syriac, Coptic, Slavic, Ethiopic and Armenian-- the number of textual variations among extant New Testament manuscripts far exceeds the 30,000 discovered by Mill. Furthermore, as demonstrated by Ehrman (1993), there is a consistent pattern in the changes that occurred in early New Testament texts; the texts changed in the direction of more clearly supporting Orthodox (Roman) interpretations of Jesus over those of the other competing Christian faiths that prevailed during the first several centuries (see also Bovon 1988: 25-27). One example demonstrates how significant many of those textual changes can be. Surviving manuscripts of the Gospel of Mark contain multiple, distinct endings, with the earliest manuscripts ending at verse 16:8 in which the two Marys flee the tomb and tell no one what they had seen (Holmes 2001).

But when they looked up, they saw that the stone, which was very large, had been rolled away. As they entered the tomb, they saw a young man dressed in a white robe sitting on the right side, and they were alarmed.

"Don't be alarmed," he said. "You are looking for Jesus the Nazarene, who was crucified. He has risen! He is not here. See the place where they laid him. But go, tell his disciples and Peter, 'He is going ahead of you into Galilee. There you will see him, just as he told you.'"

Trembling and bewildered, the women went out and fled from the tomb. They said nothing to anyone, because they were afraid. (Mark 16: 4-8)

These earliest manuscripts, therefore, contain none of the post-resurrection appearances and instruction by Jesus that are presented in verses 16: 9-20, even though they are considered authentic by most Christians.[927]

---

2. [927] Abruzzi, William S. "THE BIRTH OF JESUS: The Evolution of the Jesus in the Infancy Narratives." *Doc A's Webpage: On the Importance of Writing Research Papers*, Dr. William S. Abruzzi, 2015, www.drabruzzi.com/birth_of_jesus.htm.

Finally, after extensively detailing the contentious issues of Early Christianity, he closes with what the evidence shows to be Apostle Paul's true impact on Christianity:

10. Christianity is Jewish in origin and was originally centered in the Temple in Jerusalem under the leadership of James, the brother of Jesus, a fact acknowledged more than once by both Paul (Galatians 1: 19; 2: 9; 2: 12) and the author of Acts (12: 17; 15: 13; 21: 18). Paul even singles James out for special consideration, referring to him as *"the Lord's brother"* (Galatians 1: 19). Similarly, when Paul designates *"James and Cephas and John"* as the *"pillars"* of the Church (Galatians 2: 9), he lists James first, even before Peter. The supremacy of the Jerusalem Church was also promulgated in the creedal passage in I Corinthians (15: 3-7), which declared the unique status of Cephas and James as Resurrection witnesses. And when criticizing Peter for not eating with Gentiles --the so-called *Antioch Incident*-- Paul made it very clear that Peter's removal from the scene was in response to a directive from James.

For before certain men came from James, he ate with the Gentiles; but when they came he drew back and separated himself, fearing the circumcision party. (Galatians 2: 12)

Acts also acknowledges James' leadership role in the Jerusalem Church. When leaving to go to *"another place"* after escaping capture by Herod, Peter directs Mary, the mother of John Mark, to *"Tell this to James and to the brethren."* (Acts 12: 17). Similarly, in its description of the "The Council at Jerusalem," James is clearly presented as the leader of the assembly, who makes the final determination regarding Paul's mission to the Gentiles (Acts 15: 13-21). In addition, when describing one of Paul's visits to Jerusalem, Acts (21:18) states, *"On the following day Paul went in with us to James; and all the elders were present."* Paul, thus, went to Jerusalem specifically to see James; the other elders of the Church were merely present at their meeting.

Acts (2: 41, 47; 4: 4; 6: 1, 7; 9: 31; 21: 20) clearly indicates that a sizeable number of Jewish Christians existed in Palestine. It also discloses the continuing Jewish orthodoxy of those Christians and their expectation that Paul demonstrate his commitment to Mosaic Law.

1. The Temple continued to be their place of worship (Acts 2: 46; 3: 1; 5: 12, 42; 21: 23, 24, 26; Luke 24: 53).

2. They remained true to Jewish laws of ritual purity (Acts 10: 14; 11: 2, 3; 15: 1; 21: 21-24).

3. Their numbers included many priests and Pharisees (Acts 6: 7; 15: 5).

4. They are referred to as *"zealous for the law"*. (Acts 21: 20).

5. Ritual acts of supererogatory character were practiced by them (Acts 21: 23, 24).

6. Church leaders demanded that Paul demonstrate his Jewish orthodoxy in order to be accepted into their community, and that he repudiate claims that he had betrayed the essential customs of Judaism in his teaching (see Acts 21: 20-24).

The earliest preaching by Jesus and his immediate followers was to Jews only. According to Matthew (10: 5-6), Jesus commanded his 12 apostles to *"Go nowhere among the Gentiles, and enter no town of the Samaritans, but go rather to the lost sheep of the house of Israel."* In the two earliest gospels, Jesus even initially refuses to heal a Syrophoenician (Canaanite) woman's daughter because the woman was not Jewish (see Mark 7: 24-30; Matthew 15: 21-28).

. . . a woman whose little daughter was possessed by an impure spirit came and fell at his feet. The woman was a Greek, born in Syrian Phoenicia. She begged Jesus to

drive the demon out of her daughter. "First let the children eat all they want," he told her, "for it is not right to take the children's bread and toss it to the dogs." (Mark 7: 25-27)

A Canaanite woman from that vicinity came to him, crying out, "Lord, Son of David, have mercy on me! My daughter is demon-possessed and suffering terribly." Jesus did not answer a word. So his disciples came to him and urged him, "Send her away, for she keeps crying out after us." He answered, "I was sent only to the lost sheep of Israel." The woman came and knelt before him. "Lord, help me!" she said. He replied, "It is not right to take the children's bread and toss it to the dogs." (Matthew 15:22-26)

The word "dog" was a derogatory term used frequently in the Hebrew Bible to refer to contemptible or inferior individuals (cf. Job 30: 1; Deuteronomy 23: 18; 1 Samuel 17: 43; 2 Samuel 3: 8, 9:8, 16:9; 2 Kings 8: 13; Psalm 22: 16; 59: 6, 14; Isaiah 56: 10).

"In the biblical world dogs are not pets as they are today. It is a dirty animal, a scavenger that marauds cities around garbage dumpsters; dogs are a symbol of impurity. If Jews considered gentiles as dogs it was because they did not live according to the Torah and its laws of purity" (Acosta 2009: 323).

Reviewing Old and New Testament texts, Nanos (2009) challenges the claim that the term dog was used by Jews as an epithet for Gentiles and argues instead that this characterization of Jews was introduced later by Christians. Nevertheless, in the earliest gospels Jesus directs several derogatory comments towards Gentiles.

"Behold, we are going up to Jerusalem; and the Son of man will be delivered to the chief priests and the scribes, and they will condemn him to death, and deliver him to the Gentiles; and they will mock him, and spit upon him, and scourge him, and kill him; and after three days he will rise." (Mark 10: 33-34; see also Matthew 20: 18-19; Luke 18: 32-33)

And Jesus called them to him and said to them, "You know that those who are supposed to rule over the Gentiles lord it over them, and their great men exercise over them. But it shall not be so among you; but whoever would be great among you must be your servant, and whoever would be first among you must be slave of all. (Mark 10: 42-44; see also Matthew 20: 25-27)

"And in praying do not heap up empty phrases as the Gentiles do; for they think that they will be heard for their many words." (Matthew 6: 7).

Therefore do not be anxious, saying, 'What shall we eat?' or 'What shall we drink?' or 'What shall we wear?' For the Gentiles seek all these things; and your heavenly Father knows that you need them all. But seek first his kingdom and his righteousness, and all these things shall be yours as well. (Matthew 6: 31-33)

Beware of men; for they will deliver you up to councils, and flog you in their synagogues, and you will be dragged before governors and kings for my sake, to bear testimony before them and the Gentiles (Matthew 10: 17-18)

If he refuses to listen to them, tell it to the church; and if he refuses to listen even to the church, let him be to you as a Gentile and a tax collector. (Matthew 18: 17)

Over time, however, Christian missionary activity became extended to non-Jews (mostly by non-Jewish missionaries). Beginning with the conversion of Samaritans, each new extension of Christian teaching to non-Jews prompted the leadership in Jerusalem to determine the validity of what was being taught, as well as what was expected of converts. This included Paul's mission to Gentiles.

1. A special apostolic commission was sent by the leaders of the Jerusalem Church to respond to the situation caused by the evangelization of Samaritans (Acts 8: 14 ff.) [As just indicated, according to Matthew (10:5), Jesus had specifically commanded his apostles to *"enter no town of the Samaritans."*]

2. Receiving criticism for extending the gospel to Gentiles at Caesarea, Peter was forced to explain himself to Church leaders in Jerusalem. (Acts 11: 1-18)

3. A commission was also sent by Church leaders in Jerusalem to evaluate the evangelization of the Gentiles in Antioch. (Acts 11: 19-25)

4. According to Acts (15: 1-29), a formal council was held in Jerusalem to determine the conditions required for Gentiles to be admitted into the Church. It was at this council, specifically called to pass judgment on the mission of Paul, that the issue of circumcision and Jewish dietary regulations were discussed and resolved as criteria for membership in the Church.

5. Paul visits Jerusalem more than once in order to have his mission to the Gentiles validated by the Church leadership. (Galatians 1: 18-19; Acts 15: 1-29; 21: 17-20)

While Acts emphasized Christian unity and played down internecine conflicts within the early Christian movement, Paul shows that there was, in fact, considerable dissention within the early Church. Indeed, a prominent feature of Paul's writings consists of him berating different Christian communities for accepting missionaries who preached *"another Jesus"* or a *"different Spirit"* (cf. 2 Corinthians 11: 4). Paul expressed undisguised hostility towards those who taught a version of Jesus that differed from what he taught (2 Corinthians 11: 12-14). Indeed, Paul was quite intolerant of alternate versions of Jesus and railed against those missionaries and their teaching, proclaiming his version of Jesus as the only true gospel. He even went so far as to claim that those preaching a different gospel from his should be cursed.

For if some one comes and preaches another Jesus than the one we preached, or if you receive a different spirit from the one you received, or if you accept a different gospel from the one you accepted, you submit to it readily enough. I think that I am not in the least inferior to these superlative apostles. Even if I am unskilled in speaking, I am not in knowledge; in every way we have made this plain to you in all things. (2 Corinthians 11: 4-6)

I am astonished that you are so quickly deserting him who called you in the grace of Christ and turning to a different gospel not that there is another gospel, but there are some who trouble you and want to pervert the gospel of Christ. But even if we, or an angel from heaven, should preach to you a gospel contrary to that which we preached to you, let him be accursed. As we have said before, so now I say again, If any one is preaching to you a gospel contrary to that which you received, let him be accursed. (Galatians 1: 6-9)

Much of Paul's anger was directed against James and the Jerusalem Church, who he referred to as the *"circumcision party"* (Galatians 2: 12; Timothy 1: 10; see also Acts 11:2) and the *"superlative apostles"* (2 Corinthians 11:5). He also used the term *"Jews"* to refer to the followers of the Jerusalem Church, who today would be classified as "Jewish Christians" based on the Christology they taught.

But when Cephas came to Antioch I opposed him to his face, because he stood condemned. For before certain men came from James, he ate with the Gentiles; but when they came he drew back and separated himself, fearing the circumcision party. And with him the rest of the Jews acted insincerely, so that even Barnabas was carried away by their insincerity. (Galatians 2: 11-13)

. . . (a bishop) . . . must hold firm to the sure word as taught, so that he may be able to give instruction in sound doctrine and also to confute those who contradict it. For there are many insubordinate men, empty talkers and deceivers, especially the circumcision party. (Titus 1: 8-10)

Now the apostles and the brethren who were in Judea heard that the Gentiles also had received the word of God. So when Peter went up to Jerusalem, the circumcision party criticized him, saying, "Why did you go to uncircumcised men and eat with them?" (Acts 11:1-3)

Paul was frequently at odds with James, Peter and the other leaders of the Church in Jerusalem and was, according to Acts (15: 1-19), summoned by them to account for his actions. Leadership in the Church lay with Jesus' immediate followers. James, Cephas, John and the other members of the Jerusalem Church, are presented by Paul as supreme authorities in matters affecting Christian faith and practice. As a result, despite his open conflict with the leadership in Jerusalem, Paul was eager to obtain whatever degree of recognition they accorded him and his work, including enthusiastically undertaking a collection among his followers for the poor within the Jerusalem Church (2 Corinthians 9: 1-15).

Then after fourteen years I went up again to Jerusalem with Barnabas, taking Titus along with me. I went up by revelation; and I laid before them (but privately before those who were of repute) the gospel which I preach among the Gentiles, lest somehow I should be running or had run in vain. (Galatians 2: 2)

and when they perceived the grace that was given to me, James and Cephas and John, who were reputed to be pillars, gave to me and Barnabas the right hand of fellowship, that we should go to the Gentiles and they to the circumcised (Galatians 2: 9)

However, while Paul accepted the spiritual authority of the Jerusalem Church and sought its approval, he also complained bitterly about the Church and its leaders, and frequently proclaimed the independence and superiority of his mission. Even though he referred to the members of the Jerusalem community as *"them which were apostles before me."* (Galatians 1: 17), he repeatedly claimed that his mission superseded theirs because he received it directly from God.

For I would have you know, brethren, that the gospel which was preached by me is not man's gospel. For I did not receive it from man, nor was I taught it, but it came through a revelation of Jesus Christ. . . . when he who had set me apart before I was born, and had called me through his grace, was pleased to reveal his Son to me, in order that I might preach him among the Gentiles, I did not confer with flesh and blood, nor did I go up to Jerusalem to those who were apostles before me, but I went away into Arabia; and again I returned to Damascus. (Galatians 1: 11-17)

Am I not free? Am I not an apostle? Have I not seen Jesus our Lord? Are not you my workmanship in the Lord? If to others I am not an apostle, at least I am to you;

for you are the seal of my apostleship in the Lord. This is my defense to those who would examine me. (1 Corinthians 9:1-4)

Paul was extremely defensive of his preaching and of the legitimacy of his mission (cf. 1 Corinthian 9: 1-2; 10: 1-18; 11: 1-6). He never knew Jesus while Jesus was alive and was not one of Jesus' original apostles, as were the leaders of the Jerusalem Church. Paul was, therefore, considered an outsider with questionable legitimacy by Church leaders. He preached primarily to Gentile audiences living in a Hellenistic world removed from the Jewish Palestine where Jesus and his followers preached. Not only did he have little or no contact with Jesus' apostles or with the leaders of the Jerusalem Church, he was also by his own words unknown among the churches in Judea (Galatians 1: 22). He was, in fact, perceived as misrepresenting Jesus and his mission by the very apostles who knew Jesus and who were personally chosen by Jesus to spread his word. Paul's retort was that it was the other missionaries who taught a false gospel about Jesus and that his was the true gospel, because it came straight from Jesus and not through other men. His assertion of authority to preach about Jesus, however, was based solely on his claim (for which there are no eyewitness accounts) that Jesus appeared to him (see Galatians 1: 11-16; 1 Corinthians 15: 3-8). Paul does not describe what actually happened during that appearance; a description of the incident is contained only in Acts (9:3-6; 22:6-11; 26:12-18). However, Acts cannot be considered a reliable source of what happened, as it presents three contradictory accounts of the event.

No original documents survive that can be traced to the Jerusalem Church or its leaders. Thus, scholars have no first-hand documents describing what actually occurred at the Jerusalem Council, or during any of the other interactions between Paul and the leaders of the Church, except what is contained in Paul's letters, which of course reflect Paul's view of those events. Acts' descriptions of these events cannot be taken at face value, as Acts puts a "spin" on stories that downplays early Church opposition to Paul in order to champion Pauline Christianity. Acts' descriptions of the deliberations at the *"Jerusalem Council"* (Acts 15: 1-21) and of the *"Letter to the Gentiles"* (Acts 15: 22-29) that purportedly came out of that Council are unreliable. They were written decades after the fact by a writer who: (1) was a follower of Paul; (2) consistently promoted a Pauline (Hellenistic) version of Christianity; and (3) repeatedly played down conflicts within the early Church. There is also reason to believe that such a council never took place. Nowhere in any of Paul's writings is the existence of a council or a letter resulting from that council ever mentioned, even though the outcome presented in Acts would clearly have enhanced the legitimacy of Paul's mission. Such a positive outcome is also contradicted by the incident at Antioch (Galatians 2: 11-14), by Paul's estrangement from James and Peter and by Barnabas' abandonment of Paul's mission in favor of the Jerusalem Church (2: 13)

It is highly unlikely that the leaders of the Jerusalem Church would have countenanced much of what Paul taught about Jesus. Whereas Jesus' immediate followers focused on the life and teaching of Jesus, Paul completely ignored the living Jesus. To Paul, Jesus' life and teaching were irrelevant. All that mattered to Paul was Jesus' death and resurrection, which he viewed not in its historical context, but rather as a cosmic event. Jesus' immediate followers, who became the leaders of the original Church, would not have viewed Jesus as divine, as that would have contradicted the fundamental monotheism of Judaism, which they continued to practice. As Brandon (1951: 81-82) notes,

Monotheists by instinct and upbringing and resident at the very centre of their nation's monotheistic faith, it was logically impossible for them ever consciously to regard their master in any way which annihilated the absolute gulf between the human and divine. Consequently, although they believed that God had raised up Jesus from the dead to be the Messiah and although they found it congenial to think of him at his hoped-for Parousia in terms of the mysterious and supernatural figure of Daniel's Son of Man, to them, he remained essentially distinct from the deity. (see

Brandon 1951: Chapter 5 and Longenecker 1970 for discussions of the Christology of early Jewish Christians.)

Had the leaders of the Church promulgated the divinity of Jesus, they certainly would not have been allowed to continue worship in the Temple; nor would they have had Pharisees and those *"zealous of the law"* counted among their adherents. They would instead have been stoned for blasphemy. Their rejection of the divinity of Jesus would also explain why, when the persecution of Christians occurred following the stoning of Stephen (Acts 7: 54-60), no violence was directed at the leaders of the Jerusalem Church (Acts 8: 1).

For Paul, ignoring Jesus' life and emphasizing exclusively his death and resurrection also removed the central fact that undermined Paul's credibility compared to the leaders of the Church. They knew Jesus, and he did not. They could, thus, refute any outrageous claim he made about the living Jesus. By focusing primarily on Christ, rather than on Jesus (Paul uses the term "Christ" far more frequently than "Jesus," which is just the opposite of that found in the Gospels), however, Paul could develop an elaborate (Hellenistic) sotérioogical interpretation of Jesus that could not be contradicted as easily by those who knew Jesus best. Such a message would also find favor in a Hellenistic world where stories of divine beings serving as saviors of humanity were quite common. Judaism, on the other hand, had no history of such a belief.

The vindication of Paul and his teaching by the leaders of the Jerusalem Church, thus, likely never occurred. It is also highly unlikely that the language contained in the *Letter to the Gentiles* (Acts 15: 22-29) derives from the leaders of the Jerusalem Church, as it reflects a later Hellenistic (Pauline) Christology. Acts was first composed some 40 years after the authentic Pauline Epistles and underwent considerable revision until it was accepted into the canon in 180 CE (see Dibelius 1956:148, note 25; for a larger discussion of the alteration of early Christian texts over time, see Ehrman 1993, 2005, 2013). The much later composition of Acts, combined with situations in which it frequently disagrees with Paul's own account of events, makes it a less credible source. Its direct conflict with Paul's own testimony, among other considerations, also makes it unlikely that Luke (the purported author of Acts) was a traveling companion of Paul (see Brown 1977: 236; Ehrman 2013: 265-282). Since no documents from the Jerusalem Church have survived to contradict what Paul and the author of Acts have written, their words became canonized as the historical truth. Significantly, the Nazarenes and Ebionites, who traced their origin to James and the Jerusalem Church, rejected Paul's writings as heretical and viewed Paul as an apostate. They ironically were later to be declared as heretics by the Orthodox (Roman) Church, which eventually won the struggle to dominate Christian belief.

Both Paul (1 Corinthians 1:12; 3: 4-6, 22; 16:12; Titus 3:13) and the author of Acts (18: 24; 19:1) refer to a man named *Apollos*, who Acts (18: 24) describes as a Jewish Christian from Alexandria. According to Acts,

He was an eloquent man, well versed in the scriptures. He had been instructed in the way of the Lord; and being fervent in spirit, he spoke and taught accurately the things concerning Jesus, though he knew only the baptism of John. (Acts 18:24-25)

While Acts (18:24) states that Paul first encountered Apollos at Ephesus, most of Paul's comments regarding Apollos appear in his first letter to the Corinthians, where he complains of individuals in that congregation being allied to Apollos (and others to Cephas) rather than to him. Apollos is presented as the leader of a faction in Corinth that was in theological conflict with Paul. Indeed, Paul's comments suggest that the followers of Apollos may have been numerous enough to constitute a major party in opposition to him.

For it has been reported to me by Chloe's people that there is quarreling among you, my brethren. What I mean is that each one of you says, "I belong to Paul," or "I

belong to Apollos," or "I belong to Cephas," or II belong to Christ." Is Christ divided? Was Paul crucified for you? Or were you baptized in the name of Paul? (1 Corinthians 1: 11-13)

It is significant that a man such as Apollos could be described as "*well versed in the scriptures*" and "*fervent in spirit*" who "*spoke and taught accurately the things concerning Jesus*" and yet know only the baptism of John. The prevalence of Apollos' version of Christianity is indicated by the situation presented in Acts (19: 1-7) in which Paul encounters 12 disciples at Ephesus who also had never heard of the Holy Spirit and who had been baptized "*into Johns baptism,*" not into the baptism of Jesus. They were similarly unaware of Luke's (3: 15-16) portrayal of John's baptism of repentance as but a forerunner to the baptism in the Holy Spirit presented by Jesus.

As the people were in expectation, and all men questioned in their hearts concerning John, whether perhaps he were the Christ, 16 John answered them all, "I baptize you with water; but he who is mightier than I is coming, the thong of whose sandals I am not worthy to untie; he will baptize you with the Holy Spirit and with fire." (Luke 3:16)

Apollos evidently taught a different gospel about Jesus than that taught by Paul. He also apparently had a substantial following in Corinth and Ephesus (and perhaps elsewhere), and may even have represented a distinct regional Church. Brandon (1951: 24-26) suggests that the difference between Paul and Apollos may reflect broader differences between Alexandrian and Pauline (Hellenistic) forms of Christianity. It is also likely that, given its strong Jewish character, Alexandrian Christianity more closely resembled the Christianity of the Jerusalem Church than did the Christianity of Paul.

The main thrust of Christian history as presented in Acts is that the faith spread northwards and westwards out of Palestine. Acts focuses almost exclusively on its spread first northward into Asia Minor (modern-day Turkey), and then westward into Greece and Rome. Nowhere in Acts is there any mention of Christianity's spread southward into Egypt or eastward into Eurasia.

There exists an extraordinary silence both in Paul's writings and in the Acts with regard to the origin or the existence of Christianity in the regions to the south of Palestine, and especially in the great city of Alexandria. (Brandon 1951: 17)

While Pauline Christianity came to dominate Christian belief in the Hellenized world to the northwest of Palestine, significantly different forms of Christian belief spread to the south and east of Palestine (as well as to the north), whose history and theology were ignored by Acts and mainstream Pauline Christianity (see Ehrman 2003b; Jenkins 2008; MacCulloch 2009). Pauline Christianity thus represents only a fraction of the Christianity that spread out from Jerusalem; however, it became the version of Christianity adopted by the (Orthodox) Church in Rome, and subsequently became the official religion of the Roman and Byzantine Empires and of Medieval Europe. Roman Christianity was a later form of Christianity, centered in the capitol of the Roman Empire, which became the predominant form of Christianity when it aligned itself with the empire. In his *Orthodoxy & Heresy in Earliest Christianity*, Walter Bauer (1934) surveyed the various regions to which Christianity had spread and showed that alternate forms of Christianity prevailed in each of those regions before they became subordinated into the Roman Church. Following the Roman (Orthodox) Church's political ascendancy within the empire, alternative Christian faiths were declared heretical. Many of their sacred books were destroyed, and local clergy were replaced by those aligned with the Roman Church. Bart Ehrman summarizes what happened.

The standard view, held for many many centuries, goes back to the Church History of the fourth-century church father Eusebius, who argued that orthodoxy represented the original views of Jesus and his disciples, and heresies were corruptions of that truth by willful, mean-spirited, wicked, and demon inspired teachers who wanted to lead others astray.

In 1934 Walter Bauer challenged that view in his book Orthodoxy and Heresy in Earliest Christianity. Bauer argued that in many regions of the church, the earliest known form of Christianity was one that later came to be declared a heresy. Heresies were not, therefore, necessarily later corruptions of an original truth. In many instances they were the oldest known kind of Christianity, in one place or another. The form of Christianity that became dominant by the end of the third century or so was the only known particularly in Rome. Once this Roman form of Christianity had more or less swept aside its opponents, it then rewrote the history of the engagement, so that later Christians all came to think that it had always been the majority view among Christians, going back to the days of Jesus himself. (The Bart Ehrman Blog: Evaluating the Views of Walter Bauer; see Ehrman, 2003b: 170-179 for a more extensive discussion of Bauer's thesis).

In the end, then, we learn little from Paul or from Acts about the original Church in Jerusalem, except for its conflict with Paul, and know only the Pauline version of that conflict. We learn even less from subsequent Christian documents, In essence, the Jerusalem Church disappears from Christian history. Thus, of the very Church established by Jesus' own apostles and most intimate followers and that. therefore, most accurately promoted his teaching, "nothing is heard, either in reference to the present or in reminiscence of the past; it is as though a curtain of complete oblivion had descended to obliterate the former order" (Brandon 1951:183). We also learn nothing from Paul or from Acts regarding the spread of Christianity outside the Gentile Hellenistic world. We particularly learn nothing about the spread of Christianity to Egypt or about the large Christian community in Alexandria: (1) which likely derived from missionary activity directed by the Jerusalem Church itself; (2) whose beliefs about Jesus differed sharply from those of Paul; and (3) where many Jewish Christian refugees likely settled following Roman destruction of Jerusalem in 70 CE. (see Brandon 1951: 177-178),

What has survived as modern Christianity in the West, to the extent that it is dependent upon the teachings of Paul, not only does not represent the teachings of those most closely associated with Jesus; it does not even represent the majority of early Christian beliefs. Rather, it represents a minority view that was criticized by Jesus' closest followers. Alexandrian Christianity may have been connected to the original Church in Jerusalem in a way that Paul never was, and may, therefore, have taught a version of Jesus' teachings that was more compatible with that taught by his original disciples. Like the Nazarenes and the Ebionites, who were later to be declared heretical by the Imperial Roman Church, the Alexandrian (Coptic) Church was for centuries at odds with the dogma perpetuated by the Roman Church. It is significant that the conflict between Hellenistic and Alexandrian Christianity persisted into the Byzantine period and beyond (cf. Baynes 1926; Hardy 1946; Downey 1958; Frend 1972; Grant 1975; Gregory 1979; Haas 1991; Jenkins 2008, 2011; MacCulloch 2009), with the modern Coptic Church having its origins in Egypt during the first century. Similarly, the Monophysite-Miaphysite controversy and the calling of repeated Ecumenical Councils issuing opposing theological proclamations during the 4th and 5th centuries (see Grant 1975; Gregory 1979; Jenkins 2011) was largely centered on the competition between Alexandria and Constantinople for control of the Church and its theology. This competition eventually produced a major schism within Christianity following the Council in Chalcedon in 451 (Baynes 1926; Hardy 1946), which persists to this day.[928]

---

3. [928] Abruzzi, William S. "THE BIRTH OF JESUS: The Evolution of the Jesus in the Infancy Narratives." *Doc A's Webpage: On the Importance of Writing Research Papers*, Dr. William S. Abruzzi, 2015, www.drabruzzi.com/birth_of_jesus.htm.

Given this research, I'd like to summarize a set of questions objecting to Pauline Christianity and Paul himself as a so-called Apostle of Jesus: How can Protestants and Catholics argue that their message is about knowing Jesus Christ when it is based upon the visions of Paul, a man who didn't know Jesus at all? How can he claim to be following Jesus's word, when the original Church didn't want to spread the message to non-Jews (gentiles) and was against seeing Jesus as the Son of God - even calling such a belief espoused by Paul to be blasphemy against Jesus? Did Paul have a "revelation" or did he make-up his own fictional version of Jesus Christ? Paul never knew Jesus in person as the Original Church of James did, and the Original Church was headed by Jesus's own brother according to the research. The Original Church that James ran was the one that Jesus gave ministry to and James was opposed Paul's actions on the basis of Jesus's guidelines according to the evidence, so why shouldn't that mean following Protestantism and Catholicism is blasphemy against Jesus? How can either Catholicism or Protestantism be following the teachings of Jesus Christ, when Paul himself didn't care for the teachings of Jesus? Are the entire histories of Catholicism and Protestantism the true message of Jesus, revealed to Paul in a "vision" or are they just the lies of Paul so that he could make his own fictional version of a purportedly real life person from Nazareth? Even if you argued Jesus's message was still important, that would only validate Coptic Christianity since it follows most closely to the teachings of the original Church according to the research. The entire history of Protestantism and Catholicism is thereby meaningless and Coptic Christianity itself has had scandals similar to the Catholic Church so it doesn't seem to have morally superior values.[929][930] Are Jesus's teachings truly useful and divine, or do they lead to horrible consequences that should be avoided in our modern times? If they were so peaceful, then why were there immediate and bloody uprisings of intra-Christian massacres that Biblical scholars say were more violent than the Spanish Inquisition? Did the so-called teachings of Jesus actually come from Jesus Christ, when the disciples of his Church had their message ruthlessly purged by Pauline Christianity, or were they simply the psychotic ravings of Paul because he wanted Jesus as his personal divine daddy? Even if Paul genuinely believed in Jesus as God, why would that make his claims more valid when he never knew Jesus as a person and was contemptuous of anyone who believed in another version of Jesus? If Jesus's teachings bring peace, why was Paul and every other alternative Christian sect so filled with anger, rage, and loathing for each other over the correct version of Jesus? If Jesus's teachings bring peace, why did they immediately bring about violence amongst Christians who pitted themselves against each other over the so-called correct understanding of Jesus for hundreds of years? And if they don't bring peace, then what value do the teachings of Jesus have for anybody? Is it to fear the make-believe idea of hell so that you're compelled to believe in Jesus? If you've read all this and understand this is Christianity's historical record, and you have knowledge of Christianity's other violent histories throughout the centuries and even

---

4. [929] "Coptic Church Rocked By Scandals." *Den Katolske Kirke*, www.katolsk.no/nyheter/2001/06/26-0009
5. [930] Khalil, Ashraf. "Paper's Sex Expose Stirs Egypt Furor." *Chicagotribune.com*, 28 Aug. 2018, www.chicagotribune.com/news/ct-xpm-2001-06-20-0106200212-story.html.

contemporary to your lifetime, then why bother believing in Christianity? If the faith Paul had in Jesus was little more than celebrating his own megalomania by creating a fictitious version of a person that he never met, why believe his claims of having the revealed wisdom of Jesus just because his teachings triumphed over other Christian traditions through mass bloodshed?

In my own personal opinion, I think that this so-called "Apostle" Paul just wanted Jesus Christ to be his father. Perhaps he felt unloved in life, or perhaps he was trying to make sense of whatever mental illness may have made him psychotic. I cannot help but recall Friedrich Nietzsche's accusations in his book, *The Anti-Christ*. Nietzsche argued that Jesus Christ was a peaceful teacher, but that Apostle Paul had desecrated Jesus's teachings of peace by not only spreading violence in Jesus's name, but also coming up with crazy beliefs like the Resurrection and Judgment Day.[931] He argued that such beliefs only proved Apostle Paul was insane and that Paul had misappropriated Jesus's message of peace.[932] Essentially, Nietzsche argued that Apostle Paul was the Anti-Christ; not in the sense of miracles and cosmic wars, but in the context of a man who used violence and insane ravings to tarnish a peaceful man's teachings. To me, the most surprising part of this research is that what seemed like a censure from Nietzsche can only be seen as mild criticism given the overwhelming evidence of Paul's deception and insanity. Sadly, I suspect that this research will simply be dismissed by the majority of people and that some form of hindsight bias and post hoc justification will be made which ignores the historic persecution of Jews, Native Americans, and historic violence in Asia by Pauline Christianity in order to form some trite and banal message of "peace" that ignores the human rights crimes in favor of self-celebratory praise of how good someone feels when following Jesus as per the narcissism that is embedded in Christian theology.

In *The Anti-Christ*, Nietzsche argued that the Christian gospels aren't anything other than absurd ravings and the proof is that if you apply reality to any portion of the Gospels, then the entire theology falls apart.[933] He argued that proclamations of serving people for the afterlife are an attack upon logic itself and a hatred for all worldly knowledge, which is refuted as unimportant and loathsome for the sake of worshiping death by revering it with terms like "the Light", "God", "Eternity", "Heaven", and other nonsensical terms that really don't mean anything.[934] He brazenly accuses priests of only serving themselves and using their supposedly humble reverence of theological terms to revere themselves under the concept of prostrating themselves for a God; Nietzsche dismisses the argument that they're taking the Abrahamic God's name in vain and instead argues that the very framework of such terms and the use of conditions like "sin" were made to manipulate people by teaching psychotic ravings that have

---

6. [931] Nietzsche, Friedrich Wilhelm. *THE ANTICHRIST*. Translated by H. L. Mencken, The Project Gutenberg, 2006.
7. [932] Nietzsche, Friedrich Wilhelm. *THE ANTICHRIST*. Translated by H. L. Mencken, The Project Gutenberg, 2006.
8. [933] Nietzsche, Friedrich Wilhelm. *THE ANTICHRIST*. Translated by H. L. Mencken, The Project Gutenberg, 2006.
9. [934] Nietzsche, Friedrich Wilhelm. *THE ANTICHRIST*. Translated by H. L. Mencken, The Project Gutenberg, 2006.

no coherence to them.[935] In short, the priests are a class who inculcate and espouse contempt for life itself and the so-called holiness is a shield so they can continue raving absurdities upon absurdities about the conditions of life, distorting historical truths with lunacy like resurrections from the dead, weaving narratives about how everything in the cosmos was set-up for the worship of an absurd story, and that at the core of it all - even as priests espouse humbleness and put their lives in danger for their absurdities - is narcissism and the aphrodisiac of holding power over others through these psychotic ravings.[936] From the perspective Nietzsche shows readers, the priests praising God and praising Jesus Christ as a God is not humble, but rather they're praising their own narcissism and their power over their so-called flocks of people who give them money and attention every week.[937] They can denounce all worldly achievements and hard work itself by simply being pious and worshipping a God. To that effect, the priests can ignore or feel superior to people who have striven for hard work and dedicated their lives for greater knowledge, learning about the material world through science, and even those who have studied various forms of human ecology.[938] The desire for "equality" isn't equality among people, but actually a selfish attempt at ignoring differences in the gradations of knowledge and an attempt to feel superior to people who simply work harder and follow their personal dreams.[939] The priest wants to feel superior and hold ultimate authority over others; it isn't compassion, peace, or good morals that they hold above others.[940] They're just espousing crazy fantasy stories and using that to revere themselves above others by serving some nonsensical "divine" being.[941] Nietzsche argues Christian theology is meaningless death worship, the gospels are the ravings of the insane, and that is why Christianity should just be ignored and why people should instead focus only on loving their own bodies and the physical world.[942] According to Nietzsche, Christian theology doesn't have logic or reasoning to it; Christianity demands people ignore the physical world and reality itself.[943] To deflect from self-questioning or any sort of meaningful criticism beyond calling others hypocrites, Christian priests accuse other religious faiths of either moral wrongdoing or blasphemy in order to lull their Christian followers into annihilating foreign cultures and then guilt their flock into

10. [935] Nietzsche, Friedrich Wilhelm. *THE ANTICHRIST*. Translated by H. L. Mencken, The Project Gutenberg, 2006.
11. [936] Nietzsche, Friedrich Wilhelm. *THE ANTICHRIST*. Translated by H. L. Mencken, The Project Gutenberg, 2006.
12. [937] Nietzsche, Friedrich Wilhelm. *THE ANTICHRIST*. Translated by H. L. Mencken, The Project Gutenberg, 2006.
13. [938] Nietzsche, Friedrich Wilhelm. *THE ANTICHRIST*. Translated by H. L. Mencken, The Project Gutenberg, 2006.
14. [939] Nietzsche, Friedrich Wilhelm. *THE ANTICHRIST*. Translated by H. L. Mencken, The Project Gutenberg, 2006.
15. [940] Nietzsche, Friedrich Wilhelm. *THE ANTICHRIST*. Translated by H. L. Mencken, The Project Gutenberg, 2006.
16. [941] Nietzsche, Friedrich Wilhelm. *THE ANTICHRIST*. Translated by H. L. Mencken, The Project Gutenberg, 2006.
17. [942] Nietzsche, Friedrich Wilhelm. *THE ANTICHRIST*. Translated by H. L. Mencken, The Project Gutenberg, 2006.
18. [943] Nietzsche, Friedrich Wilhelm. *THE ANTICHRIST*. Translated by H. L. Mencken, The Project Gutenberg, 2006.

seeking forgiveness after committing the annihilation. Christianity makes people feel *ressentiment* and then preaches destruction of others as a moral good because it is perceived as defending Christian morals.[944] Nietzsche points to the historic persecution of the Jews as a prime example, but it can also be applied to the Native Americans, the hatred for women, and historic colonialism by Christian majority countries upon non-Christian countries in general.

Nietzsche's judgments about Christianity may seem harsh, but it was his conclusions after a lifelong study of the Bible throughout his boyhood and gaining perfect marks on his school tests in understanding the Bible. He never once in his writings blamed any of the violence from Christians on Jesus Christ. He seemed to make excruciating effort in tacitly arguing that Jesus Christ should be blameless of the legacy of violence in Christianity and he placed the blame squarely on the mad ravings of the self-proclaimed Apostle, Paul.[945] However, it is interesting to see just how many Christian apologists attempt to argue that Nietzsche hated Jesus Christ or that he spoke poorly of Jesus Christ. If anyone arguing against Nietzsche claim such, then you can be rest assured that they're intellectually dishonest and never read anything from Nietzsche as they claim. That's just a fact about Nietzsche's written works; he kept ruthlessly arguing, perhaps to convince himself, that Jesus Christ was peaceful and simply misunderstood. He seemed to take this reverence of his idea of Jesus Christ to an extreme and followed-up by arguing that it didn't matter if he himself was ever misunderstood or never read by anyone because he believed that someday in the future that his books could change the world for the better. He replaced Paul's fictional character of Jesus Christ with his own version so that he could hold onto some level of respect when all the logical arguments that he provided against Christianity showed a horrifying picture of systemic malice and hate.[946] Given how studious he was, I suspect that what drove Nietzsche away from Christianity is what drives every person with full faith in Jesus Christ to change and regard faith in Jesus Christ as empty and meaningless: I think that he read the entire Bible and realized that it didn't make any sense. As cited in this chapter from avid researchers of Biblical history and literature, the Bible has far too many internal inconsistencies to make coherent sense.

It was genuinely surprising for me to learn that few, if any, people who claim to hold a personal relationship with their so-called lord and savior have ever once tried to read the entire Bible. If you're a Christian, I'd like for you to consider something: You'll revere the Bible as divine, you will praise Jesus Christ as your savior, you will talk lovingly of the Bible's contents, you will try to live out the supposed ideals of being a good Christian, you will allow the Bible to determine what is morally good and justifiable as actions you must take for your

---

19. [944] Nietzsche, Friedrich Wilhelm. *THE ANTICHRIST*. Translated by H. L. Mencken, The Project Gutenberg, 2006.
20. [945] Nietzsche, Friedrich Wilhelm. *THE ANTICHRIST*. Translated by H. L. Mencken, The Project Gutenberg, 2006.
21. [946] Nietzsche, Friedrich Wilhelm. Chapter LXVIII. THE VOLUNTARY BEGGAR (240-244). *Thus spake Zarathustra: a book for all and none*. Translated by Thomas Common, PDF ed., T. Common, 1908.

entire life, and you'll even be willing to die for it; yet, you don't ever take the time to read the entire book? This is a book you're allowing to define who you are as a person and which you hold to be of sacred importance, but you don't read the entire book to make a personal determination on whether you should live by it or not? If you really believe that spreading the so-called Word of God is morally good and people becoming more Biblically literate is good, then shouldn't you be willing to read the entirety of the Bible's contents for yourself? Please consider doing the following: Read the entire Bible; take an hour a day of your time to read all of it. Don't look up what your local clergy's interpretations are, don't look online for interpretations, and don't read abbreviated samples or abridged versions. Just read the Bible on your own for yourself; not for your family, your community, or even your country. You're choosing to let this book define your entire life. Spend an hour a day reading it from start to finish, and then choose for yourself whether you should believe in it or not.

If you're willing to believe that spreading the gospels can only be morally good or that more people reading the Bible can only lead to people with better morals, then start with yourself and read the entire Bible. If you can't even do this or are unwilling to do this, then why bother being a Christian? If you are still unwilling, then keep in mind that people who read more into the Bible typically gave up on remaining Christian and generally became atheists or agnostics because their strong faith in Jesus Christ led them to conclude that he wasn't a God and that the Bible is a book of violent fables. If you don't understand how that is possible and want to know why, then I ask that take this challenge that was first recommended by the atheist Penn Jillette and read the entire Bible with all due haste. If you think this is facetious, then I must ask: if you cannot even take your own holy book seriously enough to read the entirety of it, then why bother believing it is the Word of God, why be a Christian, and why bother telling others that it is a book full of wisdom that is worthy of being followed? If you think reading the entirety of the Bible is a waste of your time, why bother being a Christian and telling others to waste their time with a book that you aren't seriously following? Why bother believing being a Christian makes you a good moral person, when you probably have met non-Christians who are just as ethical and who didn't need the Bible to follow an ethical lifestyle? Do you think they follow the Bible more closely than your fellow Christians? If so, then why not also consider the possibility that those non-Christian anecdotal examples of yours behave more morally because they don't follow the Bible? At best, you've established that the Bible is irrelevant to good moral behavior when you recognize "hypocrisy" in your fellow Christians and recognize good morals in non-Christians; at worst, you should consider the possibility that it is evidence the Bible doesn't teach good morals. Good moral behavior doesn't come from imitating or being a Christian, the very essence of that argument presupposes that only Christians can ever be good moral people. That is simply narcissism. *In other words, a collective sense of in-group narcissism is intrinsic to Christian theology.*

Christian readers may find such an argument contemptuous, but assessing Christianity by the self-contradictions of its own claims should hopefully clarify this point: Christians believe that all people are equal under the eyes of God, but that Christians themselves are Chosen People elevated above sinners who don't repent to God. So first, the claim is that every human being is equal under God, but then the claim shifts to mean that the Christian identity makes you special because you recognize everyone else outside of your Christian in-group is deluded or deceived because they don't obey the same divine moral authority that you follow. Moreover, those who don't accept the moral authority that you obey are heavily implied to be living in unrestrained selfishness and doing harm while you congratulate yourselves on being good and upstanding people for doing nothing under the identity of being a Christian. Christianity purportedly teaches to not judge others according to Jesus Christ's teachings, but then calls people hypocrites and casts judgment upon those who don't "repent" to Jesus Christ. Not only are all those contradictions in terms, they are thinly veiled forms of narcissism. Christianity posits that you are special for being part of the Christian in-group and everyone who has a different opinion is deluded for not being part of your group. The obvious aspersions about every group outside of your in-group as being selfish or possibly harming others is based upon pure speculation because they don't agree with your particular group's beliefs. Thus, it is further indication of in-group narcissism. Why is this, which is a consequence of the theological underpinnings of Christianity, not recognized as cultish behavior? It is worth noting that this supposed all-accepting message has historically not been accepting of the LGBT people and even in the West at the moment of this writing, it isn't accepting of Transgender people; even as Transgender people are being hunted down and killed throughout the US.[947] As a comparison, Transgender people don't face such threats of violence in Hindu majority India so there is evidence that Christian religiosity plays a factor in violence against Transgender people.[948] Please note, I haven't even brushed upon how contradictory it is for Christianity to claim to be about equality when the sexism towards women has existed since its inception and still exists in many Christian communities throughout the world. Moreover, Christian cults of personality, which are often argued to be deviating from the message of Jesus Christ and his teachings, may actually be the logical consequence of them. The Biblical story of Jesus Christ is one of the most thinly veiled stories of a con artist and Christian preachers who become rich and famous from deceiving gullible people are the closest to following the Christian tradition. If you doubt this, please consider the following: what could be a more simple trick for a con artist of the ancient world than saying that you should believe he is a God or you will be sent to hell for eternity? All that changes in modern times is the Christian con artist can feign humbleness better because they can argue that they are serving Jesus Christ instead of simply proclaiming themselves to be divine like Jesus Christ. While they would be more focused on material wealth, is it truly so different than the Biblical account of a man who claimed

---

22. [947] "Violence Against the Transgender Community in 2018." *Human Rights Campaign*, www.hrc.org/resources/violence-against-the-transgender-community-in-2018.
23. [948] Sampath, Rajesh. "India Has Outlawed Homosexuality. But It's Better to Be Transgender There than in the U.S." *The Washington Post*, WP Company, 29 Jan. 2015, www.washingtonpost.com/posteverything/wp/2015/01/29/india-has-outlawed-homosexuality-but-its-better-to-be-transgender-there-than-in-the-u-s/.

dominion over the whole world? What could be more selfish and narcissistic than demanding everyone repent before you by recognizing your godhood with the addendum of being sent to hell for not accepting your godhood? Have you considered the possibility that believing that you need to be more like Jesus Christ is to emulate being more like a narcissist with a God complex and that those Christian preachers who form cults of personality and gain material wealth from preaching the Bible really are the logical consequence of emulating Jesus Christ's teachings?

What If I'm Wrong?

At this point, I'm sure that some Christian readers may be interested to know what I would do if, despite all of this overwhelming evidence against Christianity and my own arguments against it, I was wrong and Christianity was somehow found to be true. What would I do then? I think there is a certain amount of gleeful revenge that some Christians attempt to impose upon others because of the contradistinction of heaven and hell in their minds. Heaven and hell are obviously concepts that belong in fantasy novels, but there is a very real sense of gleeful revenge from those who believe they're the Chosen people who will be sent to heaven under the pretense of claiming to be about equality. I doubt that any Christian reading this will understand because from the Christian perspective this will sound like a lie or a joke, but I want to be clear that I honestly mean this and to also thank you for taking an interest in my book. If Christianity were proven true, whether it was while I was alive or upon my death, then I would wholeheartedly accept going to hell. I would embrace hell willingly for a variety of reasons. If hell is the modern Christian understanding of the term which purportedly means "absence of God" then I would be genuinely happy going to hell since I would never have to be near the Abrahamic God or Jesus Christ and I can't think of a better eternal reward than that under the circumstances of Christianity being true. To better understand this, consider the story of Jean-Paul Sartre's novel *No Exit* where three people are trapped in a room together for eternity, I had only learned of the novel from watching the 1962 US film that was based upon it. The hell each of them go through is the forced interactions since they grow to detest each other the more they get to know each other and find irreconcilable differences in their beliefs and attitudes. I think that, given the teachings of Christianity, being eternally around people who believe in Jesus's teachings and submit to Jesus Christ in unquestioned obedience would be the worst hell that I could ever experience to the point that even suffering eternal torment would be more pleasurable since I would be eternally tortured for who I am instead of being told to change my beliefs and submit to Jesus Christ. The only worse torture would be Islam's heaven since Jesus Christ and the Abrahamic God would also be there, but with the horrible addition of Mohammad. Since Christianity being true would establish good and evil as being true to reality, I couldn't think of a worse evil than the Abrahamic God if I tried considering all the child rape, genocide, and discrimination imposed upon billions of people just to be a test of faith for the chosen few to enjoy heaven. Even if the majority of the world at my time of death were Christians being raptured to heaven, it still wouldn't justify the horrible human rights abuses that the Abrahamic God allowed as a test of faith throughout the entirety of human history or the plethora of species that went extinct as a test from the Abrahamic God. Essentially, I would not find either the Abrahamic God or Jesus Christ to be worthy of my worship by my own personal moral standards. As such, I would be eternally happier in hell so that I never have to be near the evil that is Jesus Christ and the Abrahamic God; I know that sounds ridiculous, but it is the truth. If the Biblical accounts were real, and therefore good and evil were real, then I'd argue that their so-called good should be considered pure evil as I find the destruction and suffering of billions of lives just to test the faith of a few to be morally unconscionable.

There are other reasons for the decision of embracing hell. When I joined a Christian club in college to learn more about Christianity to better understand why Christians believed what they did so that I would have better material for this book and possibly make a few friends whom I fundamentally disagreed with, I listened to people's personal accounts and realized much of the criticisms laid upon Christianity by Nietzsche were correct. I used my experience with the club as a baseline and became curious about the Sermon on the Mount that was probably mentioned at some point. I had known of the Sermon on the Mount before, but the club helped to highlight it. I think that I had the expectation of something that was at least as intelligent as ancient Greek philosophy that preceded the Sermon on the Mount by centuries, but all I found was something that contradicted itself. Christians seem to believe that the self-contradictions make the Sermon "difficult" and therefore "profound" but there's simply no logic behind the teachings; when following one set of instructions, you're violating another set of instructions. I honestly struggle to understand how people can read that entire Sermon and still take Christianity with any degree of seriousness. It seems to me that in order to rationalize the obvious self-contradictions, some Christians have resorted to using semantics as some kind of meaningful response when the semantics don't actually answer any of the self-contradictions. Many don't seem to recognize that rephrasing statements provide no meaningful point that counters the self-contradictory failures of Christian theology and seem to confuse rephrasing words for the so-called profoundness. It seems to be a begging the question fallacy; that is, it presupposes the truth claim in the initial premise of an argument.[949] It shows how vacuous the teachings of Christianity really are. There are sometimes attempts by some Christians to assert that criticizing a religion at length somehow implies that you secretly want to be part of that religion, but this only further displays the in-group narcissism of Christianity; if, for example, a Christian were to criticize the religion of Islam, then does that mean the Christian wants to convert and become a Muslim? If a Jew criticizes anti-Semitism in Christianity or Islam, does that imply the Jewish person wants to convert to both religious faiths at the same time? The motivation behind the argument that any criticism by an outsider belies an interest in joining a group seems to just be an attempt to further reinforce in-group

---

24. [949] "Begging the Question." *Https://Www.logicallyfallacious.com*, www.logicallyfallacious.com/tools/lp/Bo/LogicalFallacies/53/Begging-the-Question.

narcissism. To be fair, I've seen Muslims use this argument more than Christians whenever a non-Muslim criticizes Islam. It isn't exclusive to Christianity.

To conclude this portion, I'd like to be clear that my views on Jesus Christ didn't come from Friedrich Nietzsche; Nietzsche himself viewed Jesus Christ as a peaceful preacher who argued for extreme non-violence, I don't agree with him on that at all.[950] I don't believe that Jesus Christ was a peaceful teacher of any sort. Nietzsche was also under the laughable misconception that Jesus Christ was making a Buddhist peace movement that was misconstrued by his followers after his death upon the Cross.[951] While there are accounts of Buddhists in the neighboring country of the Sassanid Empire, there seems to be no evidence of Buddhists influencing credulous and illiterate Roman people who were easily swindled by messianic stories that any con artist could make-up during the time period of what seems to be the historical Jesus. To me, when I first heard of the Biblical Jesus Christ's story when I was a kid, all it sounded like to me was the story of an ancient con artist. I had assumed the man had an overinflated ego from how Christians described him, but it wasn't until listening to the debates by Christopher Hitchens during my high school years that I developed better counter arguments due to his inspiration. As a kid, I thought there was something truly hateful about teaching others to obey you as a God or you go to hell, but it wasn't until I became older that I began to recognize that the story and teachings of Jesus Christ were ridiculous to me because it was so inculcated in abject narcissism. If he really did preach that he was a God, then I honestly believe that he was just a psychotic narcissist and nothing else. If you're concerned about my "eternal soul" and believe I'm going to hell, I'll just borrow Sam Harris's argument in saying that I lose no sleep over the prospect of going to hell for not believing in Jesus Christ just as Christians lose no sleep over the Quran's claims that anyone who does believe Jesus Christ is God will be going to hell.[952] Just as Christians view the Quran as untrue, I and many others who aren't Christian or Muslim view the claims by both Islam and Christianity, the only two major religions that recognize Jesus Christ as the Messiah, as patently false due to lack of evidence for any of their claims.[953]

---

25. [950] Nietzsche, Friedrich Wilhelm. *THE ANTICHRIST*. Translated by H. L. Mencken, The Project Gutenberg, 2006.
26. [951] Nietzsche, Friedrich Wilhelm. Aphorism 42. *THE ANTICHRIST*. Translated by H. L. Mencken, The Project Gutenberg, 2006.
27. [952] Harris, Sam. *Letter to a Christian Nation*. Random House, 2008.
28. [953] Harris, Sam. *Letter to a Christian Nation*. Random House, 2008.

Chapter 19: The Misogyny of Christ

> 1 Timothy 2 King James Version (KJV)
> *2 I exhort therefore, that, first of all, supplications, prayers, intercessions, and giving of thanks, be made for all men;*
>
> *2 For kings, and for all that are in authority; that we may lead a quiet and peaceable life in all godliness and honesty.*
>
> *3 For this is good and acceptable in the sight of God our Saviour;*
>
> *4 Who will have all men to be saved, and to come unto the knowledge of the truth.*
>
> *5 For there is one God, and one mediator between God and men, the man Christ Jesus;*
>
> *6 Who gave himself a ransom for all, to be testified in due time.*
>
> *7 Whereunto I am ordained a preacher, and an apostle, (I speak the truth in Christ, and lie not;) a teacher of the Gentiles in faith and verity.*
>
> *8 I will therefore that men pray every where, lifting up holy hands, without wrath and doubting.*
>
> *9 In like manner also, that women adorn themselves in modest apparel, with shamefacedness and sobriety; not with broided hair, or gold, or pearls, or costly array;*
>
> *10 But (which becometh women professing godliness) with good works.*
>
> *11 Let the woman learn in silence with all subjection.*
>
> *12 But I suffer not a woman to teach, nor to usurp authority over the man, but to be in silence.*
>
> *13 For Adam was first formed, then Eve.*
>
> *14 And Adam was not deceived, but the woman being deceived was in the transgression.*
>
> *15 Notwithstanding she shall be saved in childbearing, if they continue in faith and charity and holiness with sobriety.*[954]

The following passages from the Bible are regarded by modern standards as unchristian, distortions of the faith, only meant in the context of their time period, or wrongfully interpreted; despite the explicit words demanding female subjugation to the authority of men (1 Timothy 2:11-12) and firmly stating that subjugation is the only good and acceptable path for Christian women to properly revere Jesus Christ. (1 Timothy 2: 3-12) A chief problem with arguing that these passages can be openly interpreted is that the more conservative Christian churches can and will interpret the passages in the exact phrases given in the Bible. Even if we concede that the majority of conservative Christians don't treat women in subjugated positions under male authority, the fact remains that a great multitude of varying denominations across the world do take the teachings in a more literal context and will act on them. Many act on such beliefs through social support mechanisms, threats of excommunication, and passing laws in deference to the Bible's teachings of keeping women under the subjugation of men. Conservative Christian men who grow up in conservative societies believe that women being silent and obedient to male authority is a woman's duty as a

---

1. [954] "BibleGateway." *Bible Gateway*, Bible Gateway Blog, www.biblegateway.com/passage/?search=1 Timothy 2&version=KJV.

Christian and an innate moral good. Irrespective of other religious faiths also harming women, conservative Christian beliefs share in the culpability and therefore must also be held accountable. Even within just the United States, there are attempts to espouse the purity and moral goodness of keeping women silent in Churches and to solely obey male authority from the father to the husband under the belief that properly worshipping Jesus Christ is acknowledging women are the property of men.[955] Many espouse these misogynistic Christian beliefs through equivocation; such as, preaching to women that they must "respect" the husband under the supposition that "respecting the husband" means being strictly obedient to the husband. Another example would be a daughter taking a vow of chastity for their father in a bizarre belief that vowing to one's father is an act of purity, especially if made public through daddy-daughter purity balls to their local communities.[956][957] It is particularly perturbing when the purity ball rituals come with the teaching that a daughter must recognize that she is married to the Abrahamic God and that her own father as her boyfriend.[958] In addition, some purity balls also contain visits from Police who teach young girls that having premarital sex means they'll eventually become rape victims, become prostitutes, join gangs, and become addicted to drugs.[959]

Some conservative Christian groups, such as the 7th Day Assembly of Yahweh proselytized by the billionaire oil tycoons popularly known as the Wilks Brothers, make it an explicit doctrinal requirement to keep women silent in Church by citing the Bible's explicit teachings to subjugate women. Below as Figure 1 and Figure 2 are two images taken from their doctrinal teachings that were shared online on their behalf to spread their particular Christian denomination. Oddly, I wasn't able to copy and paste them in plain text from the pdf file, even upon downloading it in order to cite them, so I elected to cut and paste the images and let their teachings speak for itself.

The 7th Day Assembly of Yahweh's Doctrinal teachings:

---

2. [955] "Static.reuters.com." *Reuters*, Reuters, static.reuters.com/resources/media/editorial/20150910/WilksDoctrinalPoints.pdf.
3. [956] Valenti, Jessica. "Purity Balls, Plan B and Bad Sex Policy: inside America's Virginity Obsession | Jessica Valenti." *The Guardian*, Guardian News and Media, 5 May 2014, www.theguardian.com/commentisfree/2014/may/05/purity-balls-america-virginity-obsession.
4. [957] Frank, Priscilla. "Welcome To The Bizarre And Beautiful World Of Purity Balls." *The Huffington Post*, TheHuffingtonPost.com, 7 Dec. 2017, www.huffingtonpost.com/2014/05/05/purity-ball-photos_n_5255904.html.
5. [958] Valenti, Jessica. "Purity Balls, Plan B and Bad Sex Policy: inside America's Virginity Obsession | Jessica Valenti." *The Guardian*, Guardian News and Media, 5 May 2014, www.theguardian.com/commentisfree/2014/may/05/purity-balls-america-virginity-obsession.
6. [959] Valenti, Jessica. "Purity Balls, Plan B and Bad Sex Policy: inside America's Virginity Obsession | Jessica Valenti." *The Guardian*, Guardian News and Media, 5 May 2014, www.theguardian.com/commentisfree/2014/may/05/purity-balls-america-virginity-obsession.

- That men have the obligation to conduct the worship, as Scriptures direct:

  "As in all the assemblies of the saints, the women should keep silence in the assemblies. For they are not permitted to speak, but should be subordinate, as even the law says. ... For it is shameful for a woman to speak in the assembly. ... If any one thinks he is a prophet, or spiritual, he should acknowledge that what I am writing to you is a command of Yahweh" (1 Cor. 14:33-37 RSV; 1 Tim. 2:11, 14).

Figure 1. Wilks brothers religious beliefs shared by Reuters. "Static.reuters.com." *Reuters*, Reuters, static.reuters.com/resources/media/editorial/20150910/WilksDoctrinalPoints.pdf.

Even worse than that is their arguments regarding abortion and homosexuality:

- That willful abortion is a serious crime. It is murder (Ex. 20:13; Mt. 19:18). This includes pregnancies resulting from rape and incest.

- That homosexuality is a serious crime – a very grievous sin (Rom. 1:26, 27; 1 Tim. 1:10; 1 Cor. 6:9).

Figure 2. Wilks brothers religious beliefs shared by Reuters. "Static.reuters.com." *Reuters*, Reuters, static.reuters.com/resources/media/editorial/20150910/WilksDoctrinalPoints.pdf.

Now, the initial and preferred reaction would be to vehemently argue that all of these conservative Christian people, Churches, and organizations are fake Christians and distorted the Christian faith with viewpoints that aren't true interpretations of the religious faith. This harkens back to Part 1 in Chapter 4, in which I elaborated upon the failings and circular reasoning of believing in open interpretation and a true interpretation of the religious faith. However, there is another issue yet to be addressed and persists as a glaring flaw of differing Christian denominations. How can ancient Christians, who lived much closer to the time of Jesus Christ, be wrong about the subjugation of women being the proper way to be a Christian? How can the extensive details they wrote in the Bible about a Christian woman's proper behavior be utterly wrong, when they are closer to the time of Jesus Christ than anyone living now?

Put it this way: *Do you as a Christian truly believe that for nineteen hundred years, the subjugation of women was a wrong teaching espoused by Christianity?*

If you believe that the subjugation of women is conducted by false Christians and are distortions of the faith, then consider this thought experiment I made thanks to the influence of *Letter to a Christian Nation* by Sam Harris:

Do you, as a Christian, believe that every prior generation of Christians were distorting Christianity and weren't true Christians?[960] If so, are they in hell or do they still go to heaven? If they're in hell, then does that mean the entirety of self-proclaimed Christians for 1900 years are in hell for purportedly distorting the religious faith? Are your ancestors also in hell for distorting the Christian faith? If the prior generations go to heaven, then why does it theologically matter if they distorted the faith and discriminated against women? If it only

---

7. [960] Harris, Sam. *Letter to a Christian Nation*. Random House, 2008.

matters individually based upon personal ethics, then why should anyone follow your specific denomination of Christianity or any denomination of Christianity?

Finally, it must be noted that the paradoxical teachings of open interpretation within Christianity really does have horrifying consequences. Both within the United States and outside of it; young Christian girls from conservative Christian households are being forced to marry their rapists[961], teaching young girls to silence themselves in conservative Churches helps proliferate systemic rapes by priests because they're indoctrinated to view speaking out as morally wrong, within some Evangelical Christian communities domestic violence persists as a norm based upon Christian theology that supports patriarchal standards[962][963], Christian women outside the West still face brutal forms of domestic violence by their husbands[964], Christian women in some conservative households within the US are still taught to accept beatings by their husbands based on the teachings of their faith[965], and some conservative Christian families indoctrinate their daughters into believing they must marry and take care of children in the household as their sole purpose in life instead of gaining an education.[966] I don't want to present a disingenuous picture; in the US, and likely in much of the world now, the percentage of these occurrences are a minority within conservative communities, but these horrific tragedies still happen and the laws don't protect these women and young girls as effectively as they should. Detailed in the next book will be the multifarious problems that open interpretation implicitly permits. It is imperative to understand that beliefs truly do matter in forming positive and negative outcomes for those helpless to defend themselves. I must reiterate because it is pertinent to note that the self-forgiveness system through Jesus Christ only creates apathy, indifference, and a patronizing superiority even when a person is actively harming others and act as the primary cause of violent atrocities towards innocent people. In

---

8. [961] Kristof, Nicholas. "11 Years Old, a Mom, and Pushed to Marry Her Rapist in Florida." *The New York Times*, The New York Times, 26 May 2017, www.nytimes.com/2017/05/26/opinion/sunday/it-was-forced-on-me-child-marriage-in-the-us.html?mc=adglobal&mcid=facebook&subid1=sectiondiversitytest&ad-keywords=auddevgate&mccr=opinionopinion.
9. [962] "Till death do us part: A Post and Courier Special Report." *Post and Courier*, 19 Aug. 2014, www.postandcourier.com/app/till-death/partone.html.
10. [963] Baird, Julia, et al. "'Submit to Your Husbands': Women Told to Endure Domestic Violence in the Name of God." *ABC News*, Australian Broadcasting Corporation, 23 Jan. 2018, www.abc.net.au/news/2017-07-18/domestic-violence-church-submit-to-husbands/8652028.
11. [964] Kyama, Reuben. "Infertile Man Accused of Cutting off Wife's Hands as Punishment for Not Bearing Him Children." *Los Angeles Times*, Los Angeles Times, 15 Aug. 2016, www.latimes.com/world/africa/la-fg-kenya-domesticviolence-amputation-20160815-snap-story.html.
12. [965] "Till death do us part: A Post and Courier Special Report." *Post and Courier*, 19 Aug. 2014, www.postandcourier.com/app/till-death/partthree.html.
13. [966] Kristof, Nicholas. "11 Years Old, a Mom, and Pushed to Marry Her Rapist in Florida." *The New York Times*, The New York Times, 26 May 2017, www.nytimes.com/2017/05/26/opinion/sunday/it-was-forced-on-me-child-marriage-in-the-us.html?mc=adglobal&mcid=facebook&subid1=sectiondiversitytest&ad-keywords=auddevgate&mccr=opinionopinion.

Part III, I intend to go into more detail on the historic impacts of Christianity's self-forgiveness system and why Christianity's history is proof that it was never peaceful.

Luke 14:26-33 King James Version (KJV)

If any man come to me, and hate not his father, and mother, and wife, and children, and brethren, and sisters, yea, and his own life also, he cannot be my disciple.
And whosoever doth not bear his cross, and come after me, cannot be my disciple.
For which of you, intending to build a tower, sitteth not down first, and counteth the cost, whether he have sufficient to finish it?
Lest haply, after he hath laid the foundation, and is not able to finish it, all that behold it begin to mock him,
Saying, This man began to build, and was not able to finish.
Or what king, going to make war against another king, sitteth not down first, and consulteth whether he be able with ten thousand to meet him that cometh against him with twenty thousand?
Or else, while the other is yet a great way off, he sendeth an ambassage, and desireth conditions of peace.
So likewise, whosoever he be of you that forsaketh not all that he hath, he cannot be my disciple.[967]

2 Thessalonians 1:8-10 King James Version (KJV)

[8] *In flaming fire taking vengeance on them that know not God, and that obey not the gospel of our Lord Jesus Christ:*
[9] *Who shall be punished with everlasting destruction from the presence of the Lord, and from the glory of his power;*
[10] *When he shall come to be glorified in his saints, and to be admired in all them that believe (because our testimony among you was believed) in that day.*[968]

---

14. [967] "BibleGateway." *Bible Gateway*, Bible Gateway Blog, www.biblegateway.com/passage/?search=Luke 14:25-33&version=KJV.
15. [968] "BibleGateway." *2 Thessalonians 1 KJV - - Bible Gateway*, www.biblegateway.com/passage/?search=2 Thessalonians 1&version=KJV.

John 8:21-44 King James Version (KJV)

²¹ *Then said Jesus again unto them, I go my way, and ye shall seek me, and shall die in your sins: whither I go, ye cannot come.*

²² *Then said the Jews, Will he kill himself? because he saith, Whither I go, ye cannot come.*

²³ *And he said unto them, Ye are from beneath; I am from above: ye are of this world; I am not of this world.*

²⁴ *I said therefore unto you, that ye shall die in your sins: for if ye believe not that I am he, ye shall die in your sins.*

²⁵ *Then said they unto him, Who art thou? And Jesus saith unto them, Even the same that I said unto you from the beginning.*

²⁶ *I have many things to say and to judge of you: but he that sent me is true; and I speak to the world those things which I have heard of him.*

²⁷ *They understood not that he spake to them of the Father.*

²⁸ *Then said Jesus unto them, When ye have lifted up the Son of man, then shall ye know that I am he, and that I do nothing of myself; but as my Father hath taught me, I speak these things.*

²⁹ *And he that sent me is with me: the Father hath not left me alone; for I do always those things that please him.*

³⁰ *As he spake these words, many believed on him.*

³¹ *Then said Jesus to those Jews which believed on him, If ye continue in my word, then are ye my disciples indeed;*

³² *And ye shall know the truth, and the truth shall make you free.*

³³ *They answered him, We be Abraham's seed, and were never in bondage to any man: how sayest thou, Ye shall be made free?*

³⁴ *Jesus answered them, Verily, verily, I say unto you, Whosoever committeth sin is the servant of sin.*

³⁵ *And the servant abideth not in the house for ever: but the Son abideth ever.*

³⁶ *If the Son therefore shall make you free, ye shall be free indeed.*

³⁷ *I know that ye are Abraham's seed; but ye seek to kill me, because my word hath no place in you.*

³⁸ *I speak that which I have seen with my Father: and ye do that which ye have seen with your father.*

³⁹ *They answered and said unto him, Abraham is our father. Jesus saith unto them, If ye were Abraham's children, ye would do the works of Abraham.*

⁴⁰ *But now ye seek to kill me, a man that hath told you the truth, which I have heard of God: this did not Abraham.*

⁴¹ *Ye do the deeds of your father. Then said they to him, We be not born of fornication; we have one Father, even God.*

⁴² *Jesus said unto them, If God were your Father, ye would love me: for I proceeded forth and came from God; neither came I of myself, but he sent me.*

⁴³ *Why do ye not understand my speech? even because ye cannot hear my word.*

⁴⁴ *Ye are of your father the devil, and the lusts of your father ye will do. He was a murderer from the beginning, and abode not in the truth, because there is no truth in him. When he speaketh a lie, he speaketh of his own: for he is a liar, and the father of it.*[969]

---

16. [969] "BibleGateway." *Bible Gateway*, Bible Gateway Blog, www.biblegateway.com/passage/?search=John 8:21-44&version=KJV.

Chapter 20: Islam

Islam is among the most notoriously mischaracterized religious faiths of this time period. Westerners, especially in the United States, do a terrible disservice by trying to equate their own religious right movements to the Islamic faith. They attempt to use terminology of which they misappropriate and ignore the religious definitions thereof within their own religious traditions to apply to Islam. Even worse, and far more notorious throughout Western history, is the laughable attempt at creating parallels between Jesus Christ and the Prophet Mohammad to argue that Jesus Christ was a superior teacher and moral guide. The thoroughgoing ignorance of Islam by Christianity in the West, despite their tenacious history and cultural connections, is proof of how faulty and violent both Christianity and Islam are both historically and in contemporary times. By ignoring specific terminology, many detractors instead try to equate versions of extremism within their own religious faith to the extremism they see in other religions and broadcast their own ignorance about the historicity and contexts of the terms. As a result, people of the Muslim faith and even deeply theological Christians would reject any and all criticisms being laid upon Islam by people who are misattributing words because they never bothered to read deeply into another religion's theology and therefore aren't assessing the pros and cons of Islam's actual theology. Even more damning, when questioning people who use these misattributed terms, Muslims and Christian apologists are proven correct; critiques by average Westerners don't bother to learn the theological specifics and contexts of specific terms on how they apply. This is a severe detriment to any serious discussion on the possible problems of a theology. To put it bluntly, within the context of Western culture, the so-called apologetic left-leaning groups aren't taking it seriously because conservative groups are providing no actual legitimate discussion or plausible reasoning to the discourse. While Ex-Muslims often misuse the terminology too, it seems that they do so to try to relate their experiences better with uninformed left-leaning individuals and have been acting in response to a largely ignorant populous.

As an example, examine this term: Islamic fundamentalism. This may make sense for the average person to mean extremist forms of Islam. However, to the average Muslim, to the fundamentalist Christian, and to the extremist Muslims that are being referred to; the wording of "Islamic fundamentalism" makes absolutely no sense. Everyone understands that it is meant to signify Muslim extremists, but the term is equating Christian extremism with Islamic extremism. Furthermore, what's made implicitly clear by those who read deeply into theology is that the person arguing against Islam by using such a term has likely never read deeply into Islamic or Christian theology and therefore the arguments aren't going to have much sway on changing views because of the lack of credibility. To be fair, Ex-Muslims tend to utilize this term, but it seems due to having a more relatable public discourse instead of accurate terminology with the Western audience that uses such terms loosely. The detractor will already seem profoundly ignorant about both theologies; religious people, who study the theology, have no reason to take such detractors seriously on such matters because the detractors seem pretentious. Fundamentalism is unique to Christianity and refers to Christians who are Biblical literalists who worship the Abrahamic God through acknowledging Jesus Christ in a far more austere interpretation that takes everything, except Jesus advocating the gouging of the eye and cutting off of the right hand and positions like slavery, in the literal sense. Fundamentalism is not Wahhabism or Islamism and has nothing to do with those Islamic movements in either history or theological context. It's both unconvincing, insulting to those who are educated about their histories or who practice them, and a disservice to debating these issues to not understand the terms. Comparatively, to say Islamic fundamentalism is the equivalent of saying Christian Wahhabism. It's conflating terminologies that have nothing to do with each other and are implicitly distinct. It becomes readily apparent to the learned religious scholars that people who use terms in such a way usually don't understand what they're talking about and are generalizing out of their own ignorance. For those who learn more about the Islamic faith, the correct generalized terminology for Muslim extremists would be puritanical Muslims or puritanical Islam within English terminology because it's taking a strict observance of the religious faith through the notion that a Muslim is remaining pure by keeping faith in Islam despite the sinfulness in the world.

    However, while it is important to critique theology based on its own terms, it is just as imperative to critique it based on foundations outside of the theology. A critique should use the correct definitions whenever possible, but a critique shouldn't be dismissed simply because it is the viewpoint of someone who doesn't believe in a particular faith as religious adherents commonly try to denounce. Far too often, religious believers of the Abrahamic faiths and their atheist apologists use reductionist arguments and narrowly focused generalizations to ignore any outside criticism of a religious faith. For example, the martyrdom of an Islamic suicide bomber and viewing a martyr as mentally healthy instead of merely suicidal. While puritanical Muslims who support jihad might like to believe in the convenient fiction that Islamic suicide bombers aren't suicidal, the argument is one of semantics. They are knowingly and purposefully committing suicide and many are found to have had deep psychological problems. Moreover, both the terrorist organizations that recruit them and their own families have theological reasons to argue the pointless semantics of martyrdom versus suicide because suicide is a sin that casts a Muslim into hell for eternity in Islamic theology. Martyrdom is instead seen as a morally significant act of accepting persecution for the sake of glorifying the Abrahamic God. However, death isn't proof of the truth claims of a religious faith and dying for a religious faith doesn't preclude a person from wanting to commit suicide. It makes more rational sense to accept that martyrdom is a desire to be killed and a form of acceptable suicide that celebrates death as a merciful reward within religious theology. To that end, Islamic suicide bombers try to hide their antipathy to life and commit suicide by attributing it to a form of blessed death that is really just semantics out of their own convenience. They and their families are merely trying to rationalize a suicide and the terrorist recruiters, that celebrate it in terms of defense, just want more recruits.

The following will chiefly be critiques from an outsider perspective and I will attempt to balance proper definitions to apply to my contentions with the Islamic faith from an outside viewpoint. Much of the critique and arguments are formed from viewing the Ex-Muslims of North America Panel; an Ex-Muslim atheist group that seeks to give social support to ex-Muslims who have chosen not to make their lack of religious faith public out of fear of ex-communication from their families. They seek to challenge what they see as a religion that makes kind, loving people behave in terrible ways to commit to hateful ideologies. They implore people to attack and challenge the religious dogma and theology of Islam and not to persecute or commit acts of racially motivated aggression upon Muslims as a people. *Criticize the ideas, don't persecute the people.* Persecution leads to empathy, apologetics, more support from the outside, and conversions to Islam. Criticizing ideas leads to questioning assumptions, looking into the pitfalls of a religious faith, listening to those voices who have been harmed by a religion, and having a respect for others human rights.

This critique was difficult because in the process of my research, I discovered how ignorant I truly was about the negative aspects of Islam. I had thought the portrayal from right-wing groups in the West and South Asia was far too dehumanizing to be true, and many extrapolated their points with racism against Arabs and ignorance of the financial and historic reasons for the ongoing conflict in the Arab Spring. It wasn't until the work of Ex-Muslims of North America actively arguing for further criticism and going into meaningful details on the failings of Islam that I realized that critiques by the late Christopher Hitchens had been sharp and on the mark. Looking back and comparing older New Atheist critiques with the critiques of Ghada Ibrahim, Sarah Haider, Imtiaz Shams, Muhammad Syed, Hiba Krisht, Stephanie Tessier, Armin Navabi, and Maryam Namazie; I realized how on point Christopher Hitchens was and how thoroughly ignorant Sam Harris was. By comparing and contrasting, Hitchens seemingly abrasive demeanor was one of unfettered compassion for the plight of Muslim women, but Harris peddles fear and advocated for racial profiling while depicting Muslims as some homogenized death cult without clearly articulating what was wrong with the theology. At best, Sam Harris gave a few buzzwords like martyrdom and jihad. Harris went so far as to argue that Western culture was the most humane, argued in favor of a moral landscape that touted some cultures as superior, and then advocated in favor of torture. Moreover, when there was religious persecution and mass violence against religious minorities; whether Jewish, Christian, or Muslim; Hitchens never hesitated to condemn and defended pious human rights leaders in repressive, despotic regimes with vigor. By direct contrast to Sam Harris, Christopher Hitchens put himself through waterboarding to assist in his claims against the US continuing policies of torture against the worst of criminals. Nevertheless, in fairness to Sam Harris, he has changed his mind over the course of his critique and listens to his close friend Maajid Nawaz, who is a Muslim reformer, in discussing the problems of Islam. Ex-Muslims of

North America has largely followed this tradition of defending human rights, but their critiques are more on point about the theological failings of Islam and detail how Islam destroys lives. They risk their own personal safety to publicly critique due to the penalty of apostasy in Islam. Ex-Muslims of North America vehemently argue to attack the theology and *not* the people. It is important to remember that, even in the most difficult of times.

To keep it in proportion and because I feel it is a horrible disservice for the US government to continue ignoring the real reasons for its War on Terror, I've added the economic and socio-political reasons that overlap and do have a defining impact on the ongoing cultural schism between Islam and the West. The main focus has been reserved to the current political conflict because of its importance, I recognize that the Middle East isn't where the majority of Muslims live and that most Muslims are obviously not terrorists. However, I feel it is just as important to understand the global policymaking that continues to create endless wars. Articulating the faults of just Islam felt like a disservice and a welcome to scathing criticisms on a broad political spectrum, so I've included my critique of that and the scope in which Islam and US foreign policy overlap in creating these conflicts. This chapter overlaps explanation, examination, and criticism of Islam itself because people should critique the values actually instilled in Islam and not merely compare and contrast with other theologies in ignorance of what Islam actually teaches, which would only reinforce faith in Islam by Muslims everywhere. From herein is my own small contribution in critiquing Islam.

Abrahamic Perfectionism

The chief problem with Islam is that it is predicated upon uncorrupting and correcting the Jewish and Christian faiths to form self-contained consistency. For all intents and purposes, while Islam rose in prominence through warring desert tribes, a major factor of its appeal was likely that it attempted to be the most consistent of the Abrahamic faiths during a time period that lacked any sort of education comparable to modern times. It strives to eliminate all forms of theological self-contradictions, hypocrisies, egregious pitfalls, and outright theological failings so that the Prophet Mohammad, Jesus Christ, Moses, Daniel, and Abraham are all purported to be equally revered under subservience to the Abrahamic God. While Christianity portrays perfection as teaching Christians to be more like Jesus Christ, Islam's view of perfection is far more holistic in its theological underpinnings because it goes through great effort in forming jurisprudence that requires blind faith in the Quran, the Hadiths that have "credible" chains of narration, and the Sunnah and going so far as to require understanding of the original language of which the Quran was formed to then give interpretations of Islamic laws.[970][971] Islam teaches that the Abrahamic God forgave Adam and Eve for their

---

1. [970] "Tafseer on the Basis of Narrated Texts and Tafseer on the Basis of Individual Understanding - Islam Question & Answer." *Islamqa.info*, Islam Question and Answer, 11 Mar. 2015, islamqa.info/en/answers/205290/tafseer-on-the-basis-of-narrated-texts-and-tafseer-on-the-basis-of-individual-understanding.
2. [971] Ibrahim, Abu. "Shariah And Fiqh. Do You Know The Difference?" *Islamic Learning Materials*, 5

transgressions and that every baby is born pure and sinless, but come into sinfulness due to the carnal world.[972] The Quran, Hadith, and the Sunnah encompass what Islam refers to as the Sharia which exists as the divine law of the Abrahamic God for Muslims to live by.[973][974] Sharia itself means divine law and Muslims praise the Torah of Moses, the Psalms of Daniel, and the so-called lost gospels of Jesus Christ as part of the Sharia.[975][976] Muslims view Abraham, Moses, Daniel, and Jesus as prophets of the Abrahamic God and believe that Jesus Christ, being celebrated as Islam's only Messiah, will come down during the day of judgment to fight against the anti-Messiah with the help of the Al-Mahdi (Guiding One) who will have the same first name as the Islamic Prophet Mohammad.

Islamic jurisprudence attempts to act as authoritative law for Muslims under the predicate that the Sharia is unquestionable. In brief, *Faqihs* are Muslim scholars learned in Islam and who have fulfilled the prerequisites to give an interpretation on how Muslims should behave in society and towards new forms of modernity.[977] *Fiqhs* are non-binding rulings and judgments for Muslims based on a Faqih's interpretation of Sharia; they are primarily used as interpretations for how Muslims should behave towards modern issues that the Sharia either doesn't address or the fiqh provides an interpretation of how Muslims should understand Sharia in a modern context.[978][979] A *fatwa* is how the fiqh is administered. If the fatwa doesn't break new ground, then it's inferred to be a ruling, but if it provides a new context towards an issue then it is considered a nonbinding but authoritative legal opinion on an issue. Many Muslims internally criticize their own system, because anyone considered a qualified scholar can technically make-up any fatwa they want for any opinion. Nevertheless, this is indicative of the Prophet Mohammad and his followers having created an incredibly thorough legal system to take on the challenges of modernity, specifically to keep Islam relevant throughout the future

---

3. [972] Castor, Trevor. "Sin According to Islam." *Zwemer Center*, www.zwemercenter.com/guide/sin-according-to-muslims/.
4. [973] Ibrahim, Abu. "Shariah And Fiqh. Do You Know The Difference?" *Islamic Learning Materials*, 5 Mar. 2012, islamiclearningmaterials.com/shariah-fiqh/.
5. [974] "Tafseer on the Basis of Narrated Texts and Tafseer on the Basis of Individual Understanding - Islam Question & Answer." *Islamqa.info*, Islam Question and Answer, 11 Mar. 2015, islamqa.info/en/answers/205290/tafseer-on-the-basis-of-narrated-texts-and-tafseer-on-the-basis-of-individual-understanding.
6. [975] Elias, Abu Amina. "Sharia, Fiqh, and Islamic Law Explained." *Faith in Allah* ☐☐☐☐ ☐ ☐ ☐ ☐ ☐, 21 Mar. 2018, abuaminaelias.com/is-the-sharia-a-single-code-of-law-an-explanation-of-sharia-fiqh-and-islamic-law/.
7. [976] "Al-Qur'an Al-Kareem - قرآن ال م كري ال." *Surah Al-Ma'idah [5:32-52]*, quran.com/5/32-52.
8. [977] "Who Is a Scholar ('Aalim)? - Islam Question & Answer." *Islamqa.info*, Islam Question and Answer, 18 July 2011, islamqa.info/en/answers/145071/who-is-a-scholar-aalim.
9. [978] Ibrahim, Abu. "Shariah And Fiqh. Do You Know The Difference?" *Islamic Learning Materials*, 5 Mar. 2012, islamiclearningmaterials.com/shariah-fiqh/.
10. [979] Elias, Abu Amina. "Sharia, Fiqh, and Islamic Law Explained." *Faith in Allah* ☐☐☐☐ ☐ ☐ ☐ ☐ ☐, 21 Mar. 2018, abuaminaelias.com/is-the-sharia-a-single-code-of-law-an-explanation-of-sharia-fiqh-and-islamic-law/.

ages. However, this thorough and complex quasi-legal, quasi-social support system has dire effects on Islam's ability to grapple with modernity.

It is because the Faqihs (Muslim Scholars) are legitimized as the qualified scholars to hand fiqhs on how Sharia is applied that significant problems arise in Islam. The problems aren't the self-contained consistency that Muslims fear are lost because of how the fatwa system is distributed, but rather the thoroughness of the consistency that is the crucial problem. The implication that the sacred texts are unquestionably perfect is already believed to be a given by Muslims under Islamic jurisprudence.[980] The socio-legal system of Islam is geared toward perfecting the Abrahamic religions and doesn't allow for as much cognitive dissonance or haphazard convenience through selectively choosing which parts of the holy books to live by; instead everything is conferred as unquestionable truth. Now, it is generally true that just as many Muslims doubt their faith as any believer in any other religion does, but the problem is that Islam has a collectivist social support system to thoroughly malign and even kill people who doubt the religious faith.[981][982] Christianity and Judaism admit that their holy texts aren't perfect and allow for haphazard belief systems to flourish through cognitive dissonance. The haphazard belief systems can be damaging in Christianity and Judaism, but there is always some concession involved to secularism whether implicit or explicit because their holy books are poorly written self-contradictions, incoherent (such as with Christianity's revelations), or dangerously violent like the Old Testament campaigns. This allows for sufficient cognitive dissonance that permits or concedes to secularism. While there is sliding towards conservative or religious social values, the haphazardness of the holy books and cognitive dissonance of the believers allow for secularization to spread when the holy books fail to be useful in modern situations. By direct contrast, Islam's prophet Mohammad and his subsequent followers really did make an efficient socio-legal support system that readily addresses oncoming problems of how Muslims should behave under the explicit assumption that Islam's holy books are perfect, infallible, and beyond dispute for discussion.[983] Even more importantly, the prophet Mohammad created this system by legitimizing and celebrating the Torah of Moses, the Psalms of Daniel, and the so-called "original" gospel of Jesus as the precursor revelations of the Abrahamic God.[984] Why is that important? *It means any attempt to criticize Islam by comparing it to Christianity and Judaism will only reaffirm a Muslim's faith in their religion.* Islam predicates itself on uncorrupting Jews and Christians from defective versions of worshipping the Abrahamic God; therefore, any comparison between Jews and Muslims or

---

11. [980] Elias, Abu Amina. "Sharia, Fiqh, and Islamic Law Explained." *Faith in Allah* □□□□ □□ □ □□□, 21 Mar. 2018, abuaminaelias.com/is-the-sharia-a-single-code-of-law-an-explanation-of-sharia-fiqh-and-islamic-law/.
12. [981] *The Quranic Arabic Corpus - Translation*, corpus.quran.com/translation.jsp?chapter=4&verse=89.
13. [982] Namazie, Maryam, et al. "Equality, Islam and Human Rights." *YouTube*, Ex-Muslims of North America, 26 Mar. 2018, www.youtube.com/watch?v=2W0w9ufJOh0.
14. [983] Ibrahim, Abu. "Shariah And Fiqh. Do You Know The Difference?" *Islamic Learning Materials*, 5 Mar. 2012, islamiclearningmaterials.com/shariah-fiqh/.
15. [984] *The Quranic Arabic Corpus - Translation*, corpus.quran.com/translation.jsp?chapter=4&verse=89.

especially Jesus Christ and the Islamic prophet Mohammad will only reinforce and strengthen the notion that Christians and Jews are merely ignorant of the true religion of the Abrahamic God. The fact many Jews and Christians refuse to even acknowledge the fact that Allah is just the Arabic translation of the word God, and that Islam also worships the Abrahamic God, helps to reinforce the notion that Jews and Christians are ignorant of Islam.

The implicit problem in Islam is that any outsider who does dispute the Quran, Hadith, or Sunnah is implied to be ignorant because they're not a "Islamic scholar", therefore they're not worth listening to because they're not considered an expert in Islamic jurisprudence.[985][986] While that is internally consistent and makes Muslims feel rational about their belief system because of the thorough legal support system and moderately difficult requirements to become a recognized Islamic scholar, it prevents outside voices from being perceived as legitimate or worthy of notice. What is vitally important to recognize is that Muslims are genuinely led to believe that this isn't intolerant because of how Islamic jurisprudence functions. For instance, through the *reciprocity principle* of modern psychology, they would believe that critics who aren't Islamic scholars aren't being fair and would likely make comparisons to other disciplines to drive their point across.[987] Muslims would likely equate Islamic scholarship as the same as learned scholars in specific subjects of science who can give expert opinions on the natural sciences. Similar to how only a geologist can give an expert opinion on geology or a neurologist on neurology, a devout Muslim would feel it is only fair that an Islamic scholar give opinions on matters pertaining to Islam. To an outsider, this is correctly perceived as counterproductive to discourse, potentially destructive, and an utterly insular theological system that rejects outside logic and reasoning. But to the average Muslim? This seems both reasonable and a rational course of action to take; this is not exclusively because of bigotry, but rather the internally consistent theology instills a fixed mindset that implicitly resists outside reasoning when not acknowledged by Islamic jurisprudence.[988] Most Muslims are genuinely not trying to seem bigoted or hateful, they've simply grown up in this theological bubble and observe it as entirely fair in their own subjective experience. Thus, because the average Muslim is likely to believe that only those who are Faqihs can give an honest and reasonable opinion on any theological problems within Islam. What does that mean? The average Muslim will only accept an opinion from someone who believes the Quran is the unquestionable word of the Abrahamic God, who believes the Hadith is largely the word of the Abrahamic God with some minuet corruption, that a person must strive to live like the Abrahamic prophets such as

---

16. [985] "Who Is a Scholar ('Aalim)? - Islam Question & Answer." *Islamqa.info*, Islam Question and Answer, 18 July 2011, islamqa.info/en/answers/145071/who-is-a-scholar-aalim.
17. [986] "Tafseer on the Basis of Narrated Texts and Tafseer on the Basis of Individual Understanding - Islam Question & Answer." *Islamqa.info*, Islam Question and Answer, 11 Mar. 2015, islamqa.info/en/answers/205290/tafseer-on-the-basis-of-narrated-texts-and-tafseer-on-the-basis-of-individual-understanding.
18. [987] Cialdini, Robert B. Chapter 2: Reciprocation (19-50). *Influence: Science and practice*. 4th ed., 21st Century Bks, 2002.
19. [988] Dweck, Carol S. *Mindset: How You Can Fulfill Your Potential*. Random House, 2012.

the Islamic Prophet Mohammad as per an Islamic consensus, and must be fluent in the Arabic language to have any opinion of value to Muslims on the problems of Islam.[989]

The theology of Islam is perfectionist; it is always trying to correct behavior so that Muslims fulfill their blind submission to the Abrahamic God with every thought, word, and deed; that consistency is systematized to the point it forms socio-legal backgrounds for the individual, the peoples, and an entire nation-state for the sake of glorifying the Abrahamic God. It is predicated upon the belief that all the Abrahamic prophets, all of the miracles and supernatural events stated to have occurred in parts of the Bible that Islam affirms as truth, the teachings of Jesus Christ, the teachings of Mohammad, and the existence of the Abrahamic God can never be questioned or considered wrong. Islamic jurisprudence is the celebration and proof of its internal consistency under Sharia. A question you may have is: if it is so internally consistent, how can there be so much divergence and disagreement? First, the criteria is actually incredibly low on who can have an authoritative legal opinion on matters in Islam. Technically speaking, any Faqih can make any fatwa they want without any real need of a legal consensus. Muslims have often pointed to this specific issue as a problem of internal consistency that creates Islamic violence. Secondly, I am of the opinion that they're merely deluding themselves with this contention towards their own religion. As I mentioned, the problem is not that Islam lacks consistency in some crucial aspect of its theology, but rather that it strove to be an effective, internally consistent, and stabilized religious faith. Islam has largely succeeded in this effort, but utterly destroys modernity because it is based upon the rigid belief that Sharia is unquestionable and unchangeable. Islam is one of the most thoroughgoing attempts at consistency in religion and the only one still around in modern times that has internal coherence.

The Sharia inculcates a fixed mindset about Islam's teachings to Muslims that parades itself as systematized towards being close to perfection in worshipping the Abrahamic God.[990] That is, it teaches that people must submit to the Abrahamic God in order to remain pure in this perfectionist mindset which conflates submission to the Abrahamic God with a person's moral worth[991], but that any deviation from Islam will lead to damnation in eternal hellfire. By striving to be consistent with the teachings of a violent desert tribe, it ignores a fundamental facet of human nature and how beliefs work; belief systems are always in transmission.[992] In the book *Stumbling Upon Happiness* by Daniel Gilbert, he addresses the issue of why bad beliefs sometimes take hold over civil societies. Through effective communication, new beliefs

---

20. [989] "Who Is a Scholar ('Aalim)? - Islam Question & Answer." *Islamqa.info*, Islam Question and Answer, 18 July 2011, islamqa.info/en/answers/145071/who-is-a-scholar-aalim.
21. [990] Dweck, Carol S. *Mindset: How You Can Fulfill Your Potential*. Random House, 2012.
22. [991] Dweck, Carol S. *Mindset: How You Can Fulfill Your Potential*. Random House, 2012.
23. [992] Gilbert, Daniel. Chapter 11: Reporting Live For Tomorrow (212-233). *Stumbling on Happiness*. Random House, 2006

become self-sustaining because they bring better stability and potential for personal growth.[993] Although that seems like circular reasoning, this is how beliefs including bad beliefs often grow strong and prosper.[994] That is, they reinforce their own merits by creating a strong in-group compulsion that satisfies a desire for stability and consistency.[995] Islam implicitly tries to war against new beliefs in transmission because it reinforced consistency and stability in a self-affirming feedback loop based on jurisprudence and collectivism. My utmost apologies if that statement seems bigoted, I am simply trying to assess beliefs and this is what I find from observing the holistic system of Islam. For instance, since usury is stated to be sinful and impermissible, a large swathe of Muslims refuse to go into finance or live with borrowing or paying interest payments. The changes to modernity don't matter, the teachings of the Sharia and the subservience to the Abrahamic God take paramount importance above any form of usury (or *riba* in Arabic terminology).

Islamiclearningcenter.com, a website dedicated for Muslims to remember and celebrate Islamic culture, expresses just this issue of the self-reinforcing feedback loop that denies new ideas and new forms of actions. As shown below:

> But in Islamic terms, the Shariah is made up of three things:
> - The laws dictated in the QUran.
> - The laws revealed to Prophet Mohammed (pbuh).
> - The laws that are taken from the lifestyle (Sunnah) of Prophet Muhammad (pbuh).
>
> As you can see, the Shariah comes strictly from the Quran and Sunnah. That is, it comes from Allah and His Messenger (pbuh). Therefore, it is illogical to think a devout Muslim can leave these laws behind.
>
> And just like the Quran and Sunnah does not change, the Shariah does not change. Whatever Alland and His Messenger have made permissible according to the Shariah will always be permissible. And whatever they have made forbidden will always be forbidden.
>
> Allah has made polygamy and acceptable form of marriage in Islam. So it will always be permissible and no one can change that. For anyone to say we must forbid polygamy because it is outdated and abuses women is wrong. And any Muslim who espouses this view is being sinful.
>
> Conversely, Allah has made Riba (interest) forbidden. So it will always be forbidden and no one can change that. For anyone to make it permissible because it is accepted in modern finance is wrong. And any Muslim who espouses this view is being sinful.[996]

The obvious drawback is that Islam is less able to deal with modernity because it attempts to be so holistic in its self-contained consistency. Islam is intrinsically collectivist

---

24. [993] Gilbert, Daniel. Chapter 11: Reporting Live For Tomorrow (212-233). *Stumbling on Happiness*. Random House, 2006
25. [994] Gilbert, Daniel. Chapter 11: Reporting Live For Tomorrow (212-233). *Stumbling on Happiness*. Random House, 2006
26. [995] Ispas, Alexa. *Psychology and politics: a social identity perspective*. Psychology Press, 2014.
27. [996] Ibrahim, Abu. "Shariah And Fiqh. Do You Know The Difference?" *Islamic Learning Materials*, 5 Mar. 2012, islamiclearningmaterials.com/shariah-fiqh/.

under Sharia. A pernicious and far more dangerous drawback is that, due to being so enclosed in a self-affirming loop that is spread out across the world, it would be theologically consistent for Muslims to believe that terrorism is supported by Islam and theologically consistent for Muslims to believe that terrorism is not supported by Islam at the same time. Due to Islam's jurisprudence essentially being a strange hybrid of Catholicism and Protestantism's theological framework, in which entire systems of jurisprudence are spread out across vast areas of the world, Islam lacks having a central authority like the Catholic Church and lacks the ability to assert that significant portions of its holy scriptures is entirely wrong for secularism to take a foothold like in Protestantism. While Catholicism has its highest hierarchal authority grounded solely in one location and Protestantism allows for many denominations that question the holy book itself; Islam, with its perfectionist emphasis and rigidity of Sharia being beyond argument, essentially has the defects of both religions because the central authority figure differs from nation-state to nation-state or region to region. In Britain or the United States, the central authority could be seen as one's local mosque or the most prominent and respected Islamic theologian in the respective country. In the Middle East, it could be the despotic regime or the local Imam at a local mosque who isn't educated at all outside of Islam, or even the terrorist group that has its own Islamic scholars. The Western ones could preach against violence in the name of the faith, the despotic regime could preach for violence only when serving the regime, and the terrorist organization could preach death to infidels and every single one of them would be considered correct or misconstruing Islam. All of them would be both right and wrong, because the ultimate authority of Islamic jurisprudence is the Sharia itself and not technically any of the people making fatwas. In all cases, everyone would be correct and incorrect in Islam because Islamic jurisprudence was foolishly set-up in a way that the Islamic framers believed the Sharia would be eternal. Due to this implicit assumption in its socio-legal system, it is unable to deal with the real fact of life that beliefs are diverse, spread around region to region, and different areas affirm and follow a different set of customs either due to their regional situations or modernized schools of thought overtaking a culture through their usefulness to society as a whole. Islam will modify itself to a point through fiqhs, but it refuses to engage in the idea that more than a miniscule portion of the contents of its holy teachings are falsehoods and explicitly refuses to believe the Quran is wrong about anything. When new belief systems propagate and form new styles of internal consistency that disproves or diminishes Islam, Islam has no ability for openness to allow the secularization to take hold and to dismiss more than small portions as being wrong.

I must reiterate; this is not because Islam lacks internal consistency, it suffers from far too much self-contained consistency that it refuses to deal with changes in reality and requires Muslims to hold firmly to beliefs that must remain unquestioned as divine law from the Abrahamic God. It leads to a debilitating regress in women's rights, a profound ignorance towards acknowledging scientific facts, and an intolerance towards opposing belief systems. Similar to Christianity, it has the good and evil paradigm of reductionist morality mixed with fighting sin; a pernicious suspicion is levied upon anyone who has any criticism of Islam under the assumption they're behaving to deceive.[997] In the end, this means less cognitive dissonance is possible for Muslims because there is no admittance that the holy book could be flawed and have secularization fill the gaps when people utilize interpretation.[998] Interpretation in Islam is only allowed from the qualified Islamic scholars and only of how Muslims must behave, there is no questioning the veracity of the Quran or the Sharia.[999][1000][1001][1002] The Hadith is more akin to open interpretation similar to modern Christians interpreting the Bible, but that can only go so far before cultural recidivism takes precedent to keep Muslims faithful.[1003] Thus, a lie like the 72 virgins in heaven being a wrongful translation and the actual line being raisins would seem plausible to some Muslims who wish to dismiss the idea of sexual slavery of young women in the Abrahamic heaven. The line being raisins would rationalize a more socially educated Muslim's belief in Islam being perfect. Yet, at the same time, such an argument would seem like an affront to many other Muslims who view Islam as perfect already and who would view such changes as an act of blasphemy. What's far more problematic is that Islam itself inculcates Muslims to believe everything in the Sharia is beyond question and can't be debated against at all. Thus, there's far less room for open interpretations and for secularism to sublimate Islam into modernization.

Tafsir versus Free Speech

If that isn't convoluted enough, the process described above is part of the opinions of the so-called Islamic scholars and there is a process that they must perform before administering a *fiqh*. I thought it best to make this a separate section to decrease any possible confusion. Please just keep in mind that the *Tafsir* process comes before making *fiqhs*. Interpretation, known as *Tafsir* in Arabic, is one of the most ridiculous methods of reasoning I have ever read about. It bases an entire legal system on the meaning of verses in a religious text through a literary understanding of the text. It would be the equivalent of basing a country's entire legal system on the personal views of characters in a fantasy novel or non-fiction story. In fact, the mix of fictional stories like flying horses, being a God's prophet, and non-fiction stories of the Islamic Prophet Mohammad slaughtering entire villages combined together is

28. [997] "Greater and Lesser Jihaad." Translated by Muhammed Salih Al-Munajjid, *Islam Question And Answer*, islamqa.info/en/10455.
29. [998] Kahneman, Daniel. *Thinking, fast and slow*. Farrar, Straus and Giroux, 2015.
30. [999] Ibrahim, Abu. "Shariah And Fiqh. Do You Know The Difference?" *Islamic Learning Materials*, 5 Mar. 2012, islamiclearningmaterials.com/shariah-fiqh/.
31. [1000] Elias, Abu Amina. "Sharia, Fiqh, and Islamic Law Explained." *Faith in Allah* ☐☐☐☐ ☐ ☐ ☐ ☐ ☐, 21 Mar. 2018, abuaminaelias.com/is-the-sharia-a-single-code-of-law-an-explanation-of-sharia-fiqh-and-islamic-law/.
32. [1001] "Who Is a Scholar ('Aalim)? - Islam Question & Answer." *Islamqa.info*, Islam Question and Answer, 18 July 2011, islamqa.info/en/answers/145071/who-is-a-scholar-aalim.
33. [1002] "Tafseer on the Basis of Narrated Texts and Tafseer on the Basis of Individual Understanding - Islam Question & Answer." *Islamqa.info*, Islam Question and Answer, 11 Mar. 2015, islamqa.info/en/answers/205290/tafseer-on-the-basis-of-narrated-texts-and-tafseer-on-the-basis-of-individual-understanding.
34. [1003] Tessier, Stephanie, and Muhammad Syed. "Islam: Pull and Peril." *YouTube*, Ex-Muslims of North America, 22 Apr. 2018, www.youtube.com/watch?v=jt1rWgap41g.

how predominately Islamic countries are operating when using this method for its legal systems. I think the primary value in discussing the *Tafsir* in particular is that we can better observe and understand the inherent dangers of unifying religious institutions with the national governance. Separation of Church and State is a precious societal norm and it must be protected.

I am honestly trying my best to respond in a reasonable manner to this method, but I believe it must be said: Islamic law, Islam's jurisprudence system, and the theology of Islam lack any sort of critical thinking skills. The entire epistemology of the *Tafsir* prove this to be the case. In researching this religion, just when I believed I had arrived at the nadir of sheer stupidity, Islam kept surprising me with the egregious level of stupidity the deeper I delved into learning about this religion. A clear example of this is the concept of *Fitra* (alternatively spelled *fitrah*) which posits that all human beings are born Muslim and thus pure in their natural state upon birth but are deceived away from Islam.[1004][1005] Thus, child marriages, Islamic practices of kidnapping and raping children to then marry them as a conversion to Islam in countries like Pakistan[1006], and violence upon non-Muslims are justified because of the belief the non-Muslims have deceived themselves away from Islam at birth.[1007] In fact, conversion to Islam is considered "reverting" back to the Islamic faith; it is seen as becoming pure again like analogous to birth.[1008] My research into this religion has left me repeatedly surprised at how low a society can go into the most egregious forms of stupidity. To any Western conservatives who are frustrated with trying to get Liberals to understand the dangers of Islam, I would recommend to first emphasize human rights and to follow up by explaining how the theology of the religion actually functions before getting into critiques. There are several factors for why Liberals throughout Western culture don't want to engage in a discussion about criticizing Islam and it isn't solely due to protecting Islam. I'll go through reasons that are to the best of my knowledge, but if you find more compelling arguments with strong evidence then feel free to ignore this criticism of contemporary liberal politics. A possible reason Liberals throughout the West have difficulty understanding the dangers of Islam is because there is a certain criterion of reasonableness that Liberals may believe that all people of all different religious backgrounds share. Western societies largely viewed all other faiths besides Christianity in the most negative of terms and often lied to audiences about what certain faith practices were for centuries. As such, a lot of the criticism about Islam sounds like either complete conspiratorial nonsense and is confused with bigotry towards Muslims or

---

35. [1004] Castor, Trevor. "Sin According to Islam." *Zwemer Center*, www.zwemercenter.com/guide/sin-according-to-muslims/.
36. [1005] Tessier, Stephanie, and Muhammad Syed. "Islam: Pull and Peril." *YouTube*, Ex-Muslims of North America, 22 Apr. 2018, www.youtube.com/watch?v=jt1rWgap41g.
37. [1006] "Pakistani Hindus Complain of Forced Conversion of Teenage Girls." *YouTube*, VOA News, 18 Mar. 2016, youtu.be/-i24jg4mJ4I.
38. [1007] Castor, Trevor. "Sin According to Islam." *Zwemer Center*, www.zwemercenter.com/guide/sin-according-to-muslims/.
39. [1008] Tessier, Stephanie, and Muhammad Syed. "Islam: Pull and Peril." *YouTube*, Ex-Muslims of North America, 22 Apr. 2018, www.youtube.com/watch?v=jt1rWgap41g.

Liberals may believe certain practices represent outliers and not the vast majority of Muslims. Understanding the dangers takes time because of this argument from ignorance that Muslims must have better reasons to believe what they do. More importantly, and consequently what Conservatives don't realize, is that many religious Liberals don't want to open the door to criticizing religion because it means they'll have to be fair to all religions and thereby put their own beliefs on the line to be criticized in the interest of fairness. Shouting down any criticism of Islam as offensive thereby protects their own beliefs from any scrutiny through the *reciprocity principle* of human psychology by having reciprocal concessions on what can't be discussed.[1009] By shouting down criticism of Islam as bigotry, they shut the door to their own religious beliefs being open to criticism and ridicule. Conservatives may want special exemption to criticize Islam, but once that door is open, it's not only going to be Islam that is ruthlessly criticized. Christianity, Judaism, Hinduism, Buddhism, and so forth will all be thoroughly mocked and criticized. No special privileges for exemptions will be granted. Protecting Islam from scrutiny also protects Liberal Christians from having to think about and face criticism for their own beliefs. Religious tolerance to protect Islam is a matter of self-preservation to protect their Christian beliefs because once Islam is open to criticism, then all doors are open to criticize all sacred beliefs.

A much stronger component of all of this has little to do with academia, mainstream Western journalism, or even Liberals who defend Islam on the basis of religious tolerance. This component is not new, it isn't related to postmodernism, Marxism, or academia, and in fact is the oldest and strongest cultural influence for making excuses about why Islam should be exempt from criticism. What Conservatives, Ex-Muslims, Atheists, Liberals critical of Islam, and religious groups who want to criticize Islam are actually up against is the 1400 years of Islamic culture vehemently shutting down all debate under the strong religious belief that non-Muslims have no right to an opinion on Islam.[1010][1011] That is the basis of the *Tafsir*. Regardless of what Muslim extremists do to harm us, regardless of how Muslim extremists behave around us, and regardless of how even moderate Muslims impose their views on our culture; Islam mandates that nobody but Muslims have a right to an opinion on any criticism of Islam. Even Ex-Muslims, whose lives depend on criticizing Islam, are forbidden to criticize Islam. This is fundamentally an ideological battle between Enlightenment values of Free Speech and Free Expression against Islam's *Sharia* and *Tafsir*. Therefore, Christianity is less than worthless for this discussion because of the Golden Rule. The Golden Rule is just the human norm of the reciprocity principle and thus all Christianity does is reinforce religious

---

40. [1009] Cialdini, Robert B. Chapter 2: Reciprocation (19-50), *Influence: Science and practice*. 4th ed., 21st Century Bks, 2002.
41. [1010] "Tafseer on the Basis of Narrated Texts and Tafseer on the Basis of Individual Understanding - Islam Question & Answer." *Islamqa.info*, Islam Question and Answer, 11 Mar. 2015, islamqa.info/en/answers/205290/tafseer-on-the-basis-of-narrated-texts-and-tafseer-on-the-basis-of-individual-understanding.
42. [1011] Al-Halawani, Ali. "Inimitability of Quran: Meanings and Types." *About Islam*, About Islam, 12 Apr. 2018, aboutislam.net/shariah/quran/quranic-miracles/inimitability-of-quran-meanings-types/#_ftn4

tolerance to protect itself from criticism by making concessions that all religious communities in the West implicitly share.[1012] The only way to end an ideological battle is through criticism of harmful ideologies; violence only strengthens the ideology of Islam through sympathy for a narrative of oppressed minorities that comes about from natural human empathy. As it should, as the aim is to rid the world of harmful and hateful beliefs and not to discriminate against Muslims as people. Therefore, the freedom to offend is of paramount importance and should be seen as non-violent protest. I would argue such an interpretation on non-violent resistance being Free Speech is accurate. It is the freedom to speak our minds in a non-violent action. Shutting down so-called harmful beliefs doesn't stop people from believing them. People not being able to speak their minds means that you can never know how a person thinks or feels and whether your own safety is in jeopardy or not around certain people who may mean you harm. Is it not better to recognize someone is full of horrible beliefs than to silence them and let their views fester before they seek a violent outlet because they haven't been allowed to speak their minds? Is it not safer for people to recognize what other people's views are and to judge them accordingly based on those views instead of silencing them and allowing them to hide harmful beliefs? For example, would it be better if a woman was told sexist speech by a coworker at their job or would it be better to silence that coworker, allow the coworker to gain the woman's trust, and potentially allow that coworker to harm that woman after gaining her trust?[1013] Shutting down speech doesn't preclude horrible events or the beliefs that motivate those horrible actions. Only criticizing horrible beliefs can change minds and thus, change behaviors in a society. Defending Freedom of Speech is maddeningly difficult oftentimes, you interact with the most irritating and bigoted people, and you are constantly given debunked nonsense that you must continue debunking repeatedly, but such a standard is worth suffering for because you can pursue your own goals and be free to speak your own beliefs to contend others beliefs on an equal playing field. *Free inquiry is the antidote to fighting hatred and stupidity.*[1014]

The *Tafsir* is under the guideline of *Sharia*. As such, the *Tafsir* operates under the context of the Quran being the perfect book to solve all of humanity's problems for all-time. It presumes the Quran is the perfect book of the Abrahamic God and that the Abrahamic God has the Quran in heaven in a golden tablet form. The Quran is held as the sacred teachings of the Abrahamic God that have been finalized and corrected from corruption by the Islamic Prophet Mohammad. The designation of physical evidence isn't even considered in this theology, but rather the Islamic Prophet's Quranic verses conflate the belief in miraculous signs with physical evidence (referred to as *ayahs/ayats* in Arabic) and are accepted as both due to the

---

43. [1012] Cialdini, Robert B. Chapter 2: Reciprocation (19-50), *Influence: Science and practice*. 4th ed., 21st Century Bks, 2002.
44. [1013] Hitchens, Christopher, et al. "Christopher Hitchens - Freedom of Expression Must Include the License to Offend [2006]." *YouTube*, Intelligence Squared, 25 July 2012, youtu.be/7oCmhZ-1gGc.
45. [1014] Jefferson, Thomas. "QUERY XVII The Different Religions Received into That State?" *Thomas Jefferson, Notes on the State of Virginia: Ch. 17*, University of Virginia, xroads.virginia.edu/~hyper/jefferson/ch17.html.

theology of unquestionable obedience to the Prophet Mohammad's teachings.[1015][1016][1017] There's no sense of allegory or fictional ideas from this literary interpretation, the Quran must simply be accepted as unquestionable fact even when it is being literary and using literary mechanisms.[1018] This method of epistemology sounds like nonsense to anyone who utilizes critical thinking and bases their beliefs on physical evidence, but that is the danger of following faith-based ideology when imposed upon government laws and society. Instead of facts based on testable physical evidence to correct bad beliefs, it relies upon fanciful beliefs that can't be questioned that tries to stay consistent with beliefs through how stories seem either correct via meaningless patterns or how they personally feel to religious believers.[1019]

The process of the *Tafsir* to have an answer on any particular issue in Islamic law is as follows: the first method is to find what the Quran says about a particular issue, if there is anything from a Quranic verse that can be applied to any particular issue from a so-called "scholarly commentator" who authors a *Tafsir*. The "scholarly commentator" is an author for a *Tafsir* known as a *mufassir* and is interchangeable with the term *Faqih* depending on the Islamic country.[1020] If the so-called Islamic scholar finds that there is a verse that addresses a particular issue then Muslims must simply accept it as per the unquestionable divine law of the Abrahamic God, which is referred to as the *Sharia*.[1021][1022] The so-called Islamic scholar may use a method in which a Quranic verse explains another Quranic verse in a later chapter in order to form a ruling on an issue.[1023] If that isn't possible, the next method is to look for what the Islamic Prophet Mohammad himself interpreted or explained a verse to mean from the

---

46. [1015] "Miraculous Aspects of the Holy Qur'an - Islam Question & Answer." *Islamqa.info*, Islam Question and Answer, 5 Oct. 2016, islamqa.info/en/answers/245475/miraculous-aspects-of-the-holy-quran.
47. [1016] "Tafseer on the Basis of Narrated Texts and Tafseer on the Basis of Individual Understanding - Islam Question & Answer." *Islamqa.info*, Islam Question and Answer, 11 Mar. 2015, islamqa.info/en/answers/205290/tafseer-on-the-basis-of-narrated-texts-and-tafseer-on-the-basis-of-individual-understanding.
48. [1017] Al-Halawani, Ali. "Inimitability of Quran: Meanings and Types." *About Islam*, About Islam, 12 Apr. 2018, aboutislam.net/shariah/quran/quranic-miracles/inimitability-of-quran-meanings-types/#_ftn4.
49. [1018] "Tafseer on the Basis of Narrated Texts and Tafseer on the Basis of Individual Understanding - Islam Question & Answer." *Islamqa.info*, Islam Question and Answer, 11 Mar. 2015, islamqa.info/en/answers/205290/tafseer-on-the-basis-of-narrated-texts-and-tafseer-on-the-basis-of-individual-understanding.
50. [1019] Kahneman, Daniel. *Thinking, fast and slow*. Farrar, Straus and Giroux, 2015.
51. [1020] "Who Is a Scholar ('Aalim)? - Islam Question & Answer." *Islamqa.info*, Islam Question and Answer, 18 July 2011, islamqa.info/en/answers/145071/who-is-a-scholar-aalim.
52. [1021] "Tafseer on the Basis of Narrated Texts and Tafseer on the Basis of Individual Understanding - Islam Question & Answer." *Islamqa.info*, Islam Question and Answer, 11 Mar. 2015, islamqa.info/en/answers/205290/tafseer-on-the-basis-of-narrated-texts-and-tafseer-on-the-basis-of-individual-understanding.
53. [1022] Elias, Abu Amina. "Sharia, Fiqh, and Islamic Law Explained." *Faith in Allah* □□□□ □ □ □□□□ , 21 Mar. 2018, abuaminaelias.com/is-the-sharia-a-single-code-of-law-an-explanation-of-sharia-fiqh-and-islamic-law/.
54. [1023] "Tafseer on the Basis of Narrated Texts and Tafseer on the Basis of Individual Understanding - Islam Question & Answer." *Islamqa.info*, Islam Question and Answer, 11 Mar. 2015, islamqa.info/en/answers/205290/tafseer-on-the-basis-of-narrated-texts-and-tafseer-on-the-basis-of-individual-understanding.

sunnah which comprises of the Hadiths, books related to the life of the Islamic Prophet Mohammad, from words or actions that the Prophet Mohammad said or did during his lifetime, and depending on the country may also contain local traditions of a community from their ancient history during the Prophet Mohammad's lifetime.[1024] If he explicitly commented on a verse, then it must be accepted as unquestioned fact otherwise the other portions of the *sunnah* are looked over for an answer.[1025] After that, if there is still no satisfactory answer, then a *Mufassir* must look into the consensus and explanations of the *Sahaabah*, the companions of the Islamic Prophet Mohammad.[1026] The *Sahaabah's* interpretations take precedence over other interpretations because Muslims and their so-called "scholars" believe that the *Sahaabah* learned what they did from the Islamic Prophet Mohammad.[1027] Additionally, their views are held to a higher degree of importance just below the Prophet Mohammad's own views and actions because Muslims believe that they witnessed the so-called "miracles" and "signs" of the Prophet Mohammad.[1028] Their simplistic views and interpretations (their own *Tafsirs*) of the world are seen as more pure and uncorrupted than modern materialist culture so they're held as paragons in Islamic law.[1029] After that, if there still isn't a good explanation, then the Islamic "scholar" (the *Mufassir*) must look to what the *Taabi'een,* the Muslim followers who learned from and followed the companions of the Prophet Mohammad, have to say on particular issues because they are second-hand accounts to the Prophet Mohammad's views.[1030] If the *Taabi'een* had unanimous views, then Muslims must follow it; if they had disagreements on a particular

---

55. [1024] "Tafseer on the Basis of Narrated Texts and Tafseer on the Basis of Individual Understanding - Islam Question & Answer." *Islamqa.info*, Islam Question and Answer, 11 Mar. 2015, islamqa.info/en/answers/205290/tafseer-on-the-basis-of-narrated-texts-and-tafseer-on-the-basis-of-individual-understanding.
56. [1025] "Tafseer on the Basis of Narrated Texts and Tafseer on the Basis of Individual Understanding - Islam Question & Answer." *Islamqa.info*, Islam Question and Answer, 11 Mar. 2015, islamqa.info/en/answers/205290/tafseer-on-the-basis-of-narrated-texts-and-tafseer-on-the-basis-of-individual-understanding.
57. [1026] "Tafseer on the Basis of Narrated Texts and Tafseer on the Basis of Individual Understanding - Islam Question & Answer." *Islamqa.info*, Islam Question and Answer, 11 Mar. 2015, islamqa.info/en/answers/205290/tafseer-on-the-basis-of-narrated-texts-and-tafseer-on-the-basis-of-individual-understanding.
58. [1027] "Tafseer on the Basis of Narrated Texts and Tafseer on the Basis of Individual Understanding - Islam Question & Answer." *Islamqa.info*, Islam Question and Answer, 11 Mar. 2015, islamqa.info/en/answers/205290/tafseer-on-the-basis-of-narrated-texts-and-tafseer-on-the-basis-of-individual-understanding.
59. [1028] "Tafseer on the Basis of Narrated Texts and Tafseer on the Basis of Individual Understanding - Islam Question & Answer." *Islamqa.info*, Islam Question and Answer, 11 Mar. 2015, islamqa.info/en/answers/205290/tafseer-on-the-basis-of-narrated-texts-and-tafseer-on-the-basis-of-individual-understanding.
60. [1029] "Tafseer on the Basis of Narrated Texts and Tafseer on the Basis of Individual Understanding - Islam Question & Answer." *Islamqa.info*, Islam Question and Answer, 11 Mar. 2015, islamqa.info/en/answers/205290/tafseer-on-the-basis-of-narrated-texts-and-tafseer-on-the-basis-of-individual-understanding.
61. [1030] "Tafseer on the Basis of Narrated Texts and Tafseer on the Basis of Individual Understanding - Islam Question & Answer." *Islamqa.info*, Islam Question and Answer, 11 Mar. 2015, islamqa.info/en/answers/205290/tafseer-on-the-basis-of-narrated-texts-and-tafseer-on-the-basis-of-individual-understanding.

issue then a non-binding opinion is given by the Islamic "scholar" on the matter and based on who among the *Taabi'een* individuals is considered closer to the Islamic Prophet Mohammad.[1031] After that, the Islamic "scholar" is allowed to give an *ijtihaad* provided it follows the *Tafsir* guidelines I've just explained. While *ijtihaad* means independent reasoning, it is only in the context of all the factors I just mentioned; an average Muslim isn't allowed to independently have an opinion on any Quranic verse or Islamic ruling as it is considered *bidah /bid'a* which means "invention" or "innovation" in a religion that refers to inventing new practices to change the religion and is forbidden in Islam.[1032][1033] In effect, Islam categorically rejects all outside reasoning and logic as a result of this process.

As of now, you may be in a state of disbelief, confusion, or feel a strong urge to laugh at the ridiculousness of the Islamic belief system. The fact of the matter is that it tries to be the total and complete solution to all human problems and entire Islamic societies actually believe that one book can solve all of their problems because it is divinely mandated by the Abrahamic God. While readers outside of Islamic countries may be prompted to view that notion with justified scorn, derision, and mockery; it would be wrong to argue that evaluating the framework of political Islam has no value to outside societies. We can, and should, do our best to understand why Islamic societies are total failures so that we don't fall for their mistakes. What makes these societies such thoroughgoing failures is that there is no separation of Church and State. Islam is the religion, the political parties, the public majority, and the nation-state itself; that is the political philosophy of Islam. Even more importantly, when you factor how Islamic politics and theology have historically functioned for 1400 years to the present, it should be made clear: *Islam really is the most comprehensive, honest, and thoroughgoing application of Divine Command Theory upon human behavior.* For all the Western religious apologists who argue that morality from religious values make a society behave well, Islam put that belief into practice for 1400 years and is based upon the same Abrahamic God as Christianity and Judaism. Arguably, Islam shares more similarities to either of those two religions than they do to each other. The prayer habits and Oneness of God is shared among Jews and Muslims and the belief that Jesus Christ is the Messiah who will come down during the Day of Judgment is shared among Muslims and Christians. Why aren't predominately Islamic civilizations the most moral then? Why hasn't their absolute faith in the Abrahamic God, with no secularism whatsoever, led them to unprecedented prosperity? Why do Islamic countries offer only the worst conditions for people in their penal code and culture? If

---

62. [1031] "Tafseer on the Basis of Narrated Texts and Tafseer on the Basis of Individual Understanding - Islam Question & Answer." *Islamqa.info*, Islam Question and Answer, 11 Mar. 2015, islamqa.info/en/answers/205290/tafseer-on-the-basis-of-narrated-texts-and-tafseer-on-the-basis-of-individual-understanding.
63. [1032] "Tafseer on the Basis of Narrated Texts and Tafseer on the Basis of Individual Understanding - Islam Question & Answer." *Islamqa.info*, Islam Question and Answer, 11 Mar. 2015, islamqa.info/en/answers/205290/tafseer-on-the-basis-of-narrated-texts-and-tafseer-on-the-basis-of-individual-understanding.
64. [1033] "As Eid Al Adha Approaches..." *Questions on Islam*, questionsonislam.com/content/eid-al-adha-approaches....

anything, the entire historical record of Islam, despite its oil wealth within places such as the Gulf region in more modern times, has given an incredible wealth of evidence that separation of religion and the State is vital for the prosperity of any modern society and that economic resources are important but not the sole qualifier for a thriving nation-state.

Apart from all of that, Islam seems to operate based on the critiques shared in Part I. Despite the thoroughness and a cultural strive to inculcate Divine Command Theory into every facet of human behavior in Islamic societies, Islam operates on more banal structures and is quite honestly the least interesting religion I've ever had the displeasure of researching. Islamic culture is only a culture insofar at its attempt to be so completely opposed to artistic exploits: music, poetry, art, and forming your own opinion are opposed by the religion and Muslims who take part in such activities do so in opposition to the religion. Much of an average Muslim's defense for their religion can be seen through the lens of the most basic understanding of logical fallacies along with social and cognitive psychology. For instance, the constant recital of 1.2 or 1.5 or more recently, 1.8 billion Muslims in any discussion on Free Speech having offended feelings of Muslims is an appeal to popularity fallacy to give a strong affirmation that their own faith is legitimate because of how many other people around the world also believe in it.[1034] The belief that actions involving prayer five times a day are likely due to social proof. Seeing others pray five times and building an automatic habit helps to inculcate a strong subservient piety based on that habit instead of on thinking over the theology.[1035] As such, they can clear away doubts through five times of prayer by self-interpreting their own actions as significant and important to their faith instead of thinking about the lack of physical evidence for a God's existence, the lack of evidence for Moses and Abraham's existence, and the violent texts in the Quran.[1036][1037] The pilgrimage to Hajj helps the commitment effect by having people undergo the religious journey to feel closer to the Abrahamic God by being near the *Kaaba*; the Hajj is an initiation process that is likely formed by an inner responsibility to accept the behavior as of their own volition in the absence of strong outside pressure, an important component to the Muslim identity, and done through a great effort depending upon how far away a Muslim is from Saudi Arabia and Mecca.[1038] These three factors help to strengthen the identity so long as other factors like peer pressure or family pressure aren't stronger influences on a Muslim individual because that would make them feel forced to undergo the Islamic rite of passage. Above all, the strong in-group identity on the basis of fear of hell and contempt for out-groups permeates throughout this religion and

---

65. [1034] Walton, D. N. "Appeal to Popularity." *Https://Www.logicallyfallacious.com*, www.logicallyfallacious.com/tools/lp/Bo/LogicalFallacies/40/Appeal-to-Popularity.
66. [1035] Cialdini, Robert B. "Chapter 4: Social Proof (98-140)" *Influence: Science and practice*. 4th ed., 21st Century Bks, 2002.
67. [1036] Kahneman, Daniel. *Thinking, fast and slow*. Farrar, Straus and Giroux, 2015.
68. [1037] Nietzsche, Friedrich Wilhelm. Aphorism 49. *THE ANTICHRIST*. Translated by H. L. Mencken, The Project Gutenberg, 2006.
69. [1038] Cialdini, Robert B. Chapter 3: Commitment and Consistency (52-95). *Influence: Science and practice*. 4th ed., 21st Century Bks, 2002.

is more cultish in behavior because of the theology's animosity towards non-Muslims for simply existing.[1039] Similar to Christianity but even more pronounced, Islam defines itself through hatred of out-groups as deluded, foolish, and only worthy of destruction for not following the "correct" version of the Abrahamic God; a clear example of this would be the entirety of Chapter 9 of the Quran.

To conclude this segment, I'd like to share one final argument of contention toward the virulent stupidity of believing one "sacred" book can solve all of humanity's problems for all of time: when such a belief inevitably fails, the blame will always be on placed upon out-groups. Instead of self-reflection, the process involving the painful admission of their failure, and assessing strengths and weaknesses of certain beliefs to learn from their mistakes; a society that believes one book is truly sacred, beyond questioning, and perfect for solving all solutions to ongoing human problems will blame every outside group as conspiring against them as a way to rationalize their own failure so as not to blame their "perfect" holy book. Ex-Muslims have mentioned that Muslims have a higher degree of certainty about their beliefs than most of other religious groups and that is a dangerous problem.[1040] *Most Muslims likely want to prevent the criticism of Islam to keep it as a faith beyond doubt for their own personal comfort.* To believe in a faith beyond doubt means you never have to second-guess what you're doing, you can give yourself completely to the faith, and feel absolute certainty and righteousness for your beliefs without ever reflecting upon or questioning them. Large groups in Pakistan will always try to war with and blame India for their problems, even as they commit genocide upon religious minorities like their fellow Muslims.[1041] Palestine will always blame Israel because of a faith beyond doubt inculcated from their hatemongering madrasses which preach that Jews are to blame for all their problems. Muslims in the West and in the Middle East will blame paranoid conspiracy theories about the West and anti-Semitism far too often to rationalize why their societies are failures or to justify imposing Sharia on Western societies. Without fail, Muslims will be blaming Israel, India, the Western countries, and perhaps even corrupt institutions for their violence against each other and upon out-groups because it is an attempt to rationalize why the so-called perfect and sacred holy book isn't delivering on its laughable claims of forming the perfect society. More importantly, Muslim majority countries likely won't believe women are poorly treated or suffer notorious accounts of rape in their own societies. Muslim men will likely go so far as to hide it or impose harsh penalties on raped women for "cheating" because of the faith beyond doubt that Muslims have in the Quran being the perfect book to solve all human problems for all-time. The sexism and intimidation of Muslim women and non-Muslim women by Muslim men in Europe likely occurs because of

---

70. [1039] Ispas, Alexa. "Chapter 1: Psychology and the Social Identity Perspective (1-24)" *Psychology and politics: a social identity perspective.* Psychology Press, 2014.
71. [1040] Ibrahim, Ghada, et al. "Can Islam Be Apolitical? - Armin Navabi, Ghada Ibrahim & Sarah Haider." *YouTube*, Ex-Muslims of North America, 6 Dec. 2018, www.youtube.com/watch?v=QGX0VqsiAMo.
72. [1041] Raja, Raza Habib. "The Trivialization of the Ongoing Shiite Genocide in Pakistan." *HuffPost*, HuffPost, 2 June 2017, www.huffpost.com/entry/the-trivialization-of-the-ongoing-shiite-genocide-in_b_592ece56e4b00afe556b09ea.

this issue.[1042] Thus, it is all the more reason to criticize this faith beyond doubt so that doubt can change their hateful beliefs. Otherwise, they will continue to behave in manners that only increase the suffering of others and of their own communities because they haven't been given alternatives to consider. *The absolute certainty they have in their religious convictions must be changed so that their faith is put in doubt.* According to Ex-Muslims, that is the necessary first step to change a Muslim's mind about their convictions.[1043] *Free Speech is the antidote to Divine Command Theory.*

Naskh

Abrogation, known as *Naskh* in Arabic, has often been hailed as an important domain of knowledge in Islamic theology and it also precludes non-Muslims from being allowed an opinion on Islam. It is quite honestly the most nonsensical belief and should have been sufficient proof that the Islamic Prophet Mohammad was lying to everyone. The reason being the obvious: abrogation is a self-contradiction. The fact so-called Islamic scholars require abrogation to even make sense of the Quran is evidence that their claims about the Quran's perfection is false. If you believe the Islamic Prophet Mohammad's proof of his claims to be a Prophet of the Abrahamic God is that he gave *ayats* (miraculous signs taken as physical evidence) then the fact that he substituted them or upgraded them means that he was conducting *bid'ah* on his own religion. In fact, if you apply Islamic standards of being a good Muslim person on the Islamic Prophet Mohammad, then he fails to live up to them. Why is there no contradiction in terms when Muslims argue that the Quran has to be followed as unquestioned fact, but the Islamic Prophet Mohammad's example is one to live by? For example, how can the life of this man be useful for being a good Muslim when he told Muslim men to have 2 or 4 wives, but had more than that himself? If he was really a perfect human being and his teachings were to be followed as unquestioned fact, why isn't his behavior consistent with his teachings in the Quran? If you grant that circumstances involving marriages and tribal politics influenced his decision-making, then that means that his divine authority as the final prophet of the Abrahamic God was weaker than the human behavior of those around him and that the ancient Arabs around him were more powerful than the Abrahamic God.[1044] Consequently, his divine authority only became stronger when he was ruling an empire and not beforehand which means his divine authority existed only for the sake of his own convenience in the context of human affairs. Why were the conditions of his divine authority dependent on the context of human behavior and governance around him? Furthermore, if following him closely to be a perfect human being is the ideal then why did he contradict his own teachings

---

73. [1042] "Focus: Women Made to Keep Low Profile in Some French Suburbs." *YouTube*, France 24 English, 19 Dec. 2016, www.youtube.com/watch?v=6gZFGpNdH1A.
74. [1043] Ibrahim, Ghada, et al. "Can Islam Be Apolitical? - Armin Navabi, Ghada Ibrahim & Sarah Haider." *YouTube*, Ex-Muslims of North America, 6 Dec. 2018, www.youtube.com/watch?v=QGX0VqsiAMo.
75. [1044] "The Wisdom behind the Prophet's Marrying More than Four Wives - Islam Question & Answer." *Islamqa.info*, Islam Question and Answer, 14 May 2013, islamqa.info/en/answers/127066/the-wisdom-behind-the-prophets-marrying-more-than-four-wives.

that are in the Quran and supposedly written in golden tablets within heaven? He didn't live by the words revealed to him which formed the Quran and was therefore a hypocrite by the standards of the Islamic community itself when you factor the concept of jihad against hypocrisy (*Jihad al-munaafiqeen*) and the Jihad against self (*Jihad al-nafs*).[1045] If the lived example of the Islamic Prophet Mohammad fails to follow the teachings of Islam, then why believe that he is a perfect person and why follow the teachings of Islam at all? Why isn't the Islamic Prophet Mohammad's example in life proof that Islam is false? After all, how can Muslims live by his example, when he tells them to follow teachings different from his own behavior? How does Islamic law and Islamic jurisprudence make sense in this context when there is a clear numerical contradiction in the number of women that he married compared to the number of women that Muslim men are allowed to marry?

The issues only get worse. Islam's abrogation system's failing is that it attempts to be true no matter what the conditions. Muslims argue that the Quranic verses are substituted by later verses, but that these verses aren't in contradiction. Thus, Muslims can argue that Islam respects the previous revelations of the Torah, the Psalms of Daniel, the "lost" Gospel of Jesus, and the Quran equally but also argue that the Quran, being the final revelation that corrects any "corruption" of the previous revelations of the Abrahamic God, can therefore abrogate those previous revelations and not follow them at all.[1046][1047] Many Muslims will persist in arguing that none of these are contradictions because they have deep faith in it.[1048] This is not answering the question of abrogation showing clear contradictions in the Quran, but rather a mental substitution of difficult questions involving the Quran's authenticity by instead answering an easier question that isn't relevant to what is being challenged about the Quran.[1049] When challenging whether the system of abrogation is a self-contradiction, nobody is asking whether Muslims have deep faith in the Quran or not. To divert the criticism to a deep faith argument is willful ignorance combined with an inability to accept any criticism while making large claims about the so-called truth of the Quran.[1050] What Muslims are employing is the Divine Fallacy. The Divine fallacy is a form of personal incredulity; that is, the belief that a holy book is divine because a religious believer can't imagine that their holy book isn't divine.[1051] Muslims asserting that the Quran is divine because they can't imagine otherwise isn't evidence that the Quran is a holy book from the Abrahamic God. As a comparison example, some Christians argue the Bible is divine because the Abrahamic God says so in the Bible.

---

76. [1045] "Greater and Lesser Jihaad." Translated by Muhammed Salih Al-Munajjid, *Islam Question And Answer*, islamqa.info/en/10455.
77. [1046] *THE THEORY OF ABROGATION*, www.islamawareness.net/FAQ/Logic/faq105.html.
78. [1047] "Al-Qur'an Al-Kareem - قرآن ال م كريم الـ." *Surah Al-Ma'idah [5:32-42]*, quran.com/5/32-42.
79. [1048] *THE THEORY OF ABROGATION*, www.islamawareness.net/FAQ/Logic/faq105.html.
80. [1049] Kahneman, Daniel. Chapter 9: Answering an Easier Question (97-107). *Thinking, fast and slow*. Farrar, Straus and Giroux, 2015.
81. [1050] "Willed Ignorance." *Https://Www.logicallyfallacious.com*, www.logicallyfallacious.com/tools/lp/Bo/LogicalFallacies/182/Willed-Ignorance
82. [1051] "Divine Fallacy." *Wikipedia*, Wikimedia Foundation, 22 Mar. 2019, en.wikipedia.org/wiki/Divine_fallacy.

Without outside evidence from the holy books, how can a Christian assert that their own holy book is divine? Their only method is the circular reasoning that the Bible is divine because the Bible says so. How can Muslims assert that the Bible has been corrupted and that the Quran is perfect? Is it because the Quran says that the Bible is corrupted and that the Quran is perfect? Both would need evidence outside of their holy books, and in the case of Islam outside of the Quran, Hadiths and Sunnah, to verify their claims.

This topic of abrogation cannot be taken lightly because of its consequences, please look at the example below from *Quran chapter 2, verse 256 l-baqarah (The Cow)* of the *Sahih International* translation:

> SAHIH INTERNATIONAL
> There shall be no compulsion in [acceptance of] the religion. The right course has become clear from the wrong. So whoever disbelieves in Taghut and believes in Allah has grasped the most trustworthy handhold with no break in it. And Allah is Hearing and Knowing.[1052]

The above verse is abrogated by later verses such as this one from *Quran chapter 9, verse 73 At-Tawbah (The Repentance)* of the *Sahih International* translation:

> SAHIH INTERNATIONAL
> O Prophet, fight against the disbelievers and the hypocrites and be harsh upon them. And their refuge is Hell, and wretched is the destination.[1053]

Furthermore, the belief in abrogation vindicates *Euthyphro's Dilemma* about Divine Command Theory and possibly damages the Christian defense for Divine Command Theory too. Below is a short formulization of *Euthyphro's Dilemma* from the website *philosophyofreligion.info* which reads as follows:

> The Euthyphro Dilemma
> (1) If divine command theory is true then either (i) morally good acts are willed by God because they are morally good, or (ii) morally good acts are morally good because they are willed by God.
> (2) If (i) morally good acts are willed by God because they are morally good, then they are morally good independent of God's will.
> (3) It is not the case that morally good acts are morally good independent of God's will.
> Therefore:
> (4) It is not the case that (i) morally good acts are willed by God because they are morally good.
> (5) If (ii) morally good acts are morally good because they are willed by God, then there is no reason either to care about God's moral goodness or to worship him.
> (6) There are reasons both to care about God's moral goodness and to worship

---

83. [1052] *The Quranic Arabic Corpus - Translation*, corpus.quran.com/translation.jsp?chapter=2&verse=256.
84. [1053] "Al-Qur'an Al-Kareem - ال كريم ال قرآن." *Surah At-Tawbah [9:73]*, quran.com/9/73.

him.
Therefore:
(7) It is not the case that (ii) morally good acts are morally good because they are willed by God.
Therefore:
(8) Divine command theory is false.[1054]

Many Christians attempt to counter this argument by stating God's behavior and moral goodness are the exact same with no differences of any sort, but does that work? Many Christians simply don't want to believe that the Abrahamic God's morality is arbitrary so they choose willful ignorance and substitute the dilemma for an easier question so they don't have to ponder over the dilemma.[1055][1056][1057] In Sunni Islamic theology, it is even worse since apart from the Mu'tazili which apparently died out in the 15th century, the answer to questions similar to the *Euthyphro's Dilemma* is that they refuse to think at all and simply follow the Abrahamic God's commands.[1058] I've found no evidence that Shia Islam even attempts to address the dilemma. A possible reason for the lack of a meaningful answer is that Islam makes no attempt to distinguish the Islamic Law from human intellect as the theology presupposes that Islamic Law is the pinnacle of human intellect. This is probably why many Muslims make patently absurd claims about the Quran referencing scientific miracles before they were discovered in more modern times. In effect, it means the modern Muslim is reducing their own behavior and thinking abilities to be as consistent as possible to a 7th century pedophilic and illiterate warlord who paraded himself as a Prophet. The defense by Islamic apologists to the *Euthyphro Dilemma*, even including the possibility that they adapted the Christian defense for the dilemma, would be dangerous as it would mean that the Islamic version of Divine Command Theory would be allowed to marry and then have sexual relations with female children as young as nine because it would be following the Islamic Prophet Mohammad's example, killing apostates would be justified by Sharia (the Divine Law of the Abrahamic God), violence against non-Muslims would be justified, and procedures like female genital mutilation would be justified. From the point of view of the reciprocity principle of human behavior, this would be against the self-preservation of non-Muslim communities and against an innate human norm for non-Muslim communities. Under Divine Command Theory, and a possibility of in-group and out-group tolerance for Divine Command Theory to be imposed

---

85. [1054] "Philosophy of Religion." *Philosophy of Religion The Euthyphro Dilemma Comments*, www.philosophyofreligion.info/christian-ethics/divine-command-theory/the-euthyphro-dilemma/.
86. [1055] GotQuestions.org. "What Is Euthyphro's Dilemma?" *GotQuestions.org*, 3 May 2008, www.gotquestions.org/Euthyphro-Dilemma.html.
87. [1056] "Willed Ignorance." *Https://Www.logicallyfallacious.com*, www.logicallyfallacious.com/tools/lp/Bo/LogicalFallacies/182/Willed-Ignorance
88. [1057] Kahneman, Daniel. Chapter 9: Answering an Easier Question (97-107). *Thinking, fast and slow*. Farrar, Straus and Giroux, 2015.
89. [1058] Rabbani, Faraz. "Are Good and Evil Determined by the Human Intellect or by Revelation?" *SeekersGuidance*, Sufyan Http://Www.seekersguidance.org/Wp-Content/Uploads/2019/02/Nlogo-Main.png, 18 Apr. 2011, www.seekersguidance.org/answers/islamic-belief/are-good-and-evil-determined-by-the-human-intellect-or-by-revelation/.

solely on Muslim communities so long as non-Muslim communities aren't harmed, it would be considered morally justifiable.[1059] Therefore, from the perspective of human rights, Divine Command Theory doesn't work and should be considered indefensible when Islamic communities attempt to impose it upon Muslim or non-Muslim communities due to the high possibility of human rights crimes.

I'jaz al-Quran

I'jaz al-Quran refers to the concept of inimitability of the Quran as the so-called proof of its perfection and miraculous nature. This argument comes from the point of view of the Quran's supposed "uniqueness" and argues that the Arabs during the Islamic Prophet Mohammad's time period couldn't form a book like the Quran.[1060] Therefore, the Quran is considered a miracle by Muslims. Unfortunately, the argument purports that the Quran is a miracle because Arab tribes couldn't make even a chapter that was similar to the Quran.[1061] This argument doesn't actually mean anything. The essential argument is that because the Quran's syntax, word choices, sentence structure, and the information conveyed in the wording were not exactly like any other book then it is somehow proof that the Quran is a miracle.[1062][1063] What the people who proposed this argument were asking was for Arabs, who hadn't heard of the Quran, to make a Quran chapter that was written exactly the same as the Quran in both syntax and wording to disprove the Quran. The implicit assumption of the inimitability argument being that the Quran was already "miraculous" and that the only way to disprove the miracle was for other people to make another Quran. Thus, the implications of this argument are that only another Quran could disprove the Quran. This is a clear failure in logical thinking skills and the fact modern Muslims praise this argument is worrisome as it indicates a complete inability of using critical thinking faculties. If the argument is to prove that the Quran is true to non-Muslims, then what should be the argument is what the contents of the Quran provide as evidence for its claims and what evidence outside the contents of the Quran have to support the so-called miraculous claims of Islam. To argue a bunch of people from the 7th century were astounded by the Quran or to argue the Quran is "unique" isn't proof that the Quran is a miracle from any higher spiritual being. For those who are confused, here is a hypothetical example of why: if there was a cult of self-identified Pastafarians that had faith in the Flying Spaghetti Monster and argued that their holy book was true because it was unique since no other religion believed in a Flying Spaghetti Monster or had written about a Flying

---

90. [1059] Cialdini, Robert B. " Chapter 6: Authority (178-200)." *Influence: Science and practice*. 4th ed., 21st Century Bks, 2002.
91. [1060] Al-Halawani, Ali. "Inimitability of Quran: Meanings and Types." *About Islam*, About Islam, 12 Apr. 2018, aboutislam.net/shariah/quran/quranic-miracles/inimitability-of-quran-meanings-types/#_ftn4.
92. [1061] "Miraculous Aspects of the Holy Qur'an - Islam Question & Answer." *Islamqa.info*, Islam Question and Answer, 5 Oct. 2016, islamqa.info/en/answers/245475/miraculous-aspects-of-the-holy-quran.
93. [1062] "Miraculous Aspects of the Holy Qur'an - Islam Question & Answer." *Islamqa.info*, Islam Question and Answer, 5 Oct. 2016, islamqa.info/en/answers/245475/miraculous-aspects-of-the-holy-quran.
94. [1063] Al-Halawani, Ali. "Inimitability of Quran: Meanings and Types." *About Islam*, About Islam, 12 Apr. 2018, aboutislam.net/shariah/quran/quranic-miracles/inimitability-of-quran-meanings-types/#_ftn4.

Spaghetti Monster in exactly the same details as their cult, would that prove the Pastafarian religious book to be a miracle? Would it prove that their God was real or that their religion was true? Of course not, you need physical evidence that is demonstrable to ascertain the validity of a truth claim. The argument that a bunch of people in the 7th century, who may have been illiterate, couldn't produce a book similar to it isn't evidence that the Quran is a miracle. Moreover, there's another problem that should be noted. Consider this: if two groups of geologists were to write separate books about the same topics of geology, then their books would have obvious differences in syntax, wording, word structure, and analogies used to explain geological concepts. Both books would be similar, but would also be unique from each other in a great many respects when evaluating their wording, paragraphs, chapter arrangements, and syntax. In fact, for a real life example, I have two textbooks on Statistics and while both cover largely the exact same topics, their wording is entirely different. The second Statistics textbook I acquired uses copious examples and analogies while the first one that I had purchased just muddles onward with no concrete examples and doesn't explain the terminology in nearly enough depth before using examples for the concepts that it tries to explain. Despite being the same topic and covering the same concepts, the books are entirely different and *unique* from each other. They're both unique from every other book ever written too. A book being unique from every other book is actually a meaningless argument and it is a complete non-sequitur on a book's claims of being a miracle bestowed by a God.

As for the final component of the argument about the inimitability of the Quran; which argues that the inimitability can't be denied and doesn't need any proof to be confirmed.[1064] To that I utilize Hitchen's Razor as a dismissal. To paraphrase, Hitchen's razor is the following: "*What can be asserted without evidence can also be dismissed without evidence.*"[1065] Therefore, the inimitability of the Quran as proof that it is a miracle is rejected.

---

95. [1064] Al-Halawani, Ali. "Inimitability of Quran: Meanings and Types." *About Islam*, About Islam, 12 Apr. 2018, aboutislam.net/shariah/quran/quranic-miracles/inimitability-of-quran-meanings-types/#_ftn4.
96. [1065] Hitchens, Christopher. Chapter 10: The Tawdriness of the Miraculous an the Decline of Hell (Pg. 258). *God Is Not Great: How Religion Poisons Everything*. Hachette Book Group, 2007.

Chapter 21: Isa

Christianity itself helps perpetuate these thoroughgoing problems. Accusing the Islamic Prophet Mohammad of various crimes like pedophilia means nothing because Islam is systematized to treat all of its prophets equally. Most Muslims are likely going to reject such insults and insinuations about their Prophet from perceived arrogant outsiders. As mentioned prior, Muslims will likely feel that their beliefs are being confirmed when Christians begin comparing Mohammad to Jesus as they inevitably always do. If a Muslim is amused when the two are compared, it wouldn't be surprising to learn that; after all, Mohammad's tribal wars and conquests were for the sake of exalting Jesus Christ's return as the Messiah. It is Jesus Christ that is the Messiah of Islam; his name in the Arabic translation is *Isa*. Muslims believe in the virgin birth of Jesus Christ, Muslims believe Jesus Christ was sinless, Muslims believe in the teachings of the Sermon on the Mount, and in Jesus Christ's miracles.[1066][1067][1068][1069] They just don't believe that Jesus was crucified or that he was the Son of God.[1070][1071][1072][1073] They believe the Abrahamic God saved Jesus from being crucified and would never allow the crucifixion of one of his messengers.[1074][1075] Muslims believe that Jesus was the Abrahamic God's messiah who will return during the Islamic End of Times to stop the false Messiah.[1076][1077] Any comparison between Jesus Christ and Mohammad confirms to a Muslim that they're correct about the ignorance of outsiders; Mohammad himself taught that Jesus Christ is a Messiah, the Messiah is not himself or any of the other prophets. Therefore, all of Mohammad's conquests and his entire legacy of Islam is predicated upon exalting Jesus Christ as the savior of the world. If anything, Mohammad's portrayal of Jesus Christ is a more humble portrayal and more consistent with Jesus fulfilling Jewish prophecies than any of Christianity's own claims; the

---

1. [1066] "Questions from a Confused Christian." Translated by Muhammad Salih Al-Munajjid, *Islam Question And Answer*, islamqa.info/en/10469.
2. [1067] Ally, Shabir. "The Messiah: Jesus, Son of Mary." *Facts about the Muslims & the Religion of Islam*, Whyislam.org, www.whyislam.org/comparative-religion-2/the-messiah-jesus-son-of-mary/.
3. [1068] Farina, Marianne. "What Do Muslims Think of Jesus?" *USCatholic.org*, 19 Sept. 2016, www.uscatholic.org/articles/201609/what-do-muslims-think-jesus-30772.
4. [1069] "What Do Muslims Believe about Jesus?" *Islam Guide: Life After Death*, www.islam-guide.com/ch3-10.htm.
5. [1070] Ally, Shabir. "The Messiah: Jesus, Son of Mary." *Facts about the Muslims & the Religion of Islam*, Whyislam.org, www.whyislam.org/comparative-religion-2/the-messiah-jesus-son-of-mary/.
6. [1071] Farina, Marianne. "What Do Muslims Think of Jesus?" *USCatholic.org*, 19 Sept. 2016, www.uscatholic.org/articles/201609/what-do-muslims-think-jesus-30772.
7. [1072] "Questions from a Confused Christian." Translated by Muhammad Salih Al-Munajjid, *Islam Question And Answer*, islamqa.info/en/10469.
8. [1073] "What Do Muslims Believe about Jesus?" *Islam Guide: Life After Death*, www.islam-guide.com/ch3-10.htm.
9. [1074] Ally, Shabir. "The Messiah: Jesus, Son of Mary." *Facts about the Muslims & the Religion of Islam*, Whyislam.org, www.whyislam.org/comparative-religion-2/the-messiah-jesus-son-of-mary/.
10. [1075] "What Do Muslims Believe about Jesus?" *Islam Guide: Life After Death*, www.islam-guide.com/ch3-10.htm.
11. [1076] Ally, Shabir. "The Messiah: Jesus, Son of Mary." *Facts about the Muslims & the Religion of Islam*, Whyislam.org, www.whyislam.org/comparative-religion-2/the-messiah-jesus-son-of-mary/.
12. [1077] "What Do Muslims Believe about Jesus?" *Islam Guide: Life After Death*, www.islam-guide.com/ch3-10.htm.

narcissistic aspects of Jesus's personality are removed in Islam, Mohammad's version of events was to make Jesus more consistent with Jewish prophecies, and everything about the prophets is humbled to extol the Abrahamic God as solely the one deserving of glorification. The word Islam translates to submission; it is indeed perfected Abrahamicism in every categorical sense due to the internal consistency of the religious faith. While Islam has its issues with dealing with modernity and reality, and surely has consistency issues such as Aisha's age being different in the Quran and hadith, it's only to be expected that continuity and translation errors exist for any religion that claims to be divinely mandated truth. Perfectionism is an ideal that constantly fails to take into account changes in human interaction; whether politics, culture, innovation, or education. Religious perfectionism cannot deal with any of these and constantly has to make concessions to them eventually. Muslims may acknowledge themselves as imperfect, but fail to acknowledge the Sharia as imperfect to their own detriment.

One of the focal reasons for this detriment is the teachings of Jesus Christ. While the prophet Mohammad may have done his best to form a basis of consistency between Judaism and Christianity to make Jesus's teachings consistent with the Jewish prophecies, ultimately his attempt at consistency was useless. Different subsets within Islam have disagreements on the utility of the New Testament in Christianity, some rightly point out the glaring contradictions among the four gospels and then use them as proof that Islam is correct about needing to uncorrupt Christianity. However, among the subset that believe the Gospel of Jesus is merely lost and would like to use that idea to dismiss the following criticisms, it should be noted that such a claim is an argument from ignorance since it is an assertion about a gospel supposedly lost in history that there is no evidence of. Even more problematic is the implications of this supposed lost gospel; even if such a gospel was uncovered, how would Muslims go about evaluating whether it was the lost gospel of Jesus? What criteria would be used to determine the gospel had been found? If you're the subset that believes it can never be found, then what exactly within the New Testament of Christianity can be used to give a good guide on what Jesus was teaching followers of Islam? As mentioned in the prior section when detailing the failings of Christianity, Jesus Christ's teachings are utterly worthless because they're self-contradictory. You can add a parable and a contradictory parable to just about everything the man supposedly taught. Jesus's only consistency was being a narcissist who tried to glorify himself as a god on earth and taught that anyone who didn't believe in him would go to hell. Mohammad seemed keen on trying to bridge the gap by correcting the imperfections, but Jesus Christ's teachings are far too woefully inept and worthless to have any degree of value in modern times. If you're a Muslim who believes the teachings of Jesus are somehow accurate in what the Abrahamic God wants Muslims to follow, then it's asinine to believe that the Sharia is perfect and therefore Jesus Christ's teachings are perfect on purely theological grounds, when Jesus Christ repeatedly contradicts himself in the Sermon on the Mount and allows for no ability for consistency at all. If you have only begun this book by reading this chapter, then please see the previous chapters about Judaism and Christianity. In the chapter on Judaism, I delve into the lack of evidence for the entirety of the Exodus story, and in the chapter on

Christianity, in which I delve into the failings of Jesus Christ's teachings. Jesus Christ's failure at developing a coherent moral framework is pivotal for understanding the failure of Islam as a religion. Everything applicable to Christianity about the failure of Jesus's teachings and the failed dualities of God versus Satan or Heaven versus Hell is applicable to Islam too. It is simply impossible to have correct moral guidance from Jesus Christ or to view Jesus's teachings as perfect because they are self-contradictory. He has no doctrines other than his narcissistic ramblings about wanting to be worshipped. If you believe the true gospel is lost, then that's further credence that Jesus Christ's teachings are valueless. If nobody knows what he taught, then how can he be a valid guide for understanding the Abrahamic God?

Mohammad's belief that the Abrahamic God spoke to him and his belief in Jesus Christ being the messiah prove that he was crazy, since everything he tried to affirm were mere falsehoods or by Islam's own admission, completely unknowable. His visions reaffirmed events that never happened like Exodus and Jesus's miracles. Mohammad carved out an empire through the slaughter of non-Muslims for the sake of some Judgment Day so that Jesus Christ, as the messiah of the Abrahamic God, would save the Muslims. The Christian End of Times and the Muslim End of Times is only different in semantics. In Christianity, it's a fight of Christ versus Anti-Christ. That is, Messiah versus the Anti-Messiah. In Islam, it's simply referred to in more explicit terms as the Messiah battling the Anti-Messiah. This crazed belief by Muslims and Christians that the end of the world will come to fruition and Jesus will come down to save them is therefore only different in semantics but both groups keep killing each other over the semantics. If conversion is key to salvation, and this salvation will be brought about by the end of the world prophecies that both adhere to as the reason for conversion, then Christianity and Islam are only different in semantics with respect to belief in the Abrahamic God and Jesus Christ. Their violent history against each other act as a bizarre quasi-symbiotic, quasi-parasitic relationship that has ruthlessly imposed mass violence wherever the two religions fought against each other. The in-group versus out-group social dynamics exert control on their populations where any violence upon non-Abrahamics or upon Jewish people is seen as less worse than the other religion committing the very same acts of violence upon other religious faiths or upon their own religion. In all cases, violence against each other merely reaffirms their own faiths. From the Medieval period to the still ongoing conflicts in the Middle East now, Abrahamics have a legacy of celebrating bloodshed against each other and rejecting all attempts at social reform by stating the other side conducts more egregious actions than their own violence. As a fictional example, would it come as any surprise if Palestinian Muslims stated there violence against Jewish people was justified because it was less worse than the German Christians committing the Holocaust? Does that sound stupid? It's as stupid as the very real indictment by United States citizens saying their bombings of Iraq was less worse than what al Qaeda did to the US. Iraq had nothing to do with September 11th, but the US government decided to accuse them of Weapons of Mass Destruction to justify keeping the US financial system intact. How did they convince US citizens to bomb a country that had nothing to do with terrorism at the time? A few videos by Christian preachers about how Iraq had

Christian property in it, racist generalizations of Iraqis, and false reports based on bad British intelligence to bellow paranoia about WMDs was all it took to begin a war with a country that had absolutely nothing to do with terrorism against the US and was later blamed for being "savage" by the US media simply because they were a Muslim majority country. It serves as a contemporary example of Abrahamic violence committed for no reason and promptly self-forgiven by the perpetrators of the conflict such as forgiving themselves for the Haditha killings by pretending the failure of the US justice system was working correctly when exonerating soldiers for the murders of children and the handicap.[1078] The in-group narcissism of nationalistic self-worship took precedent over the human rights of innocent children and the handicap.[1079]

What is particularly notorious is that the closer the faith, the lengthier and bloodier the historic legacy of violence has existed between these two religions. Islam and Christianity are the only religions that advocate Jesus Christ's so-called teachings of peace, they advocate him as the savior of the world, they view him as sinless and virgin born, and believe his miracles were real without question as ordained from the Abrahamic God. This is fairly paradoxical compared to psychological findings in other settings; the more similar ones values and experiences are to someone else's then the closer they usually become.[1080] However, in the instance of Islam and Christianity, it has been nothing but violence in the name of the Abrahamic God and for the sake of the messianic return of Jesus Christ. If Jesus's teachings were misinterpreted as Christians argue to comfort themselves, then does that mean every Christian and Muslim throughout the entire history of both religions has misinterpreted Jesus's teachings? Or, if we utilize Occam's razor, why is it not more likely the case that Jesus Christ's teachings don't preach peace, but rather the opposite given the history of violence between Islam and Christianity? If the two major religions recognizing him as the savior are notorious for the most bloodiest and violent clashes in human history against each other, then why bother believing that Jesus Christ's teachings are peaceful? Why not believe the opposite as the evidence shows? The Islamic prophet Mohammad committed mass violence to celebrate Jesus as the Messiah and to celebrate his return to save Muslims from the anti-Messiah. Muslims and Christians have committed violence against each other for centuries for the exact same reason and belief system of salvation with little to no meaningful differences beyond semantics. Given this history, why believe that Jesus Christ's teachings were peaceful? There's no historic or cultural basis for it since its inception when it destroyed foreign religions in Rome and referred to them as Pagan. Jesus Christ was merely a narcissist with a god complex shouting anyone who didn't submit to him was going to hell. That is why Christians and Muslims are so violent

---

13. [1078] Joyner, James. "Why We Should Be Glad the Haditha Massacre Marine Got No Jail Time." *The Atlantic*, Atlantic Media Company, 3 Feb. 2012, www.theatlantic.com/international/archive/2012/01/why-we-should-be-glad-the-haditha-massacre-marine-got-no-jail-time/251993/.
14. [1079] Ispas, Alexa. *Psychology and politics: a social identity perspective*. Psychology Press, 2014.
15. [1080] Cialdini, Robert B. "Chapter 5: Liking (143-177)" *Influence: Science and practice*. 4th ed., 21st Century Bks, 2002.

against each other. The belief in hell and the belief that the other either doesn't believe in Jesus Christ or that they have distorted his teachings.

However, a pernicious aspect of all this must be stated: *Christianity and Islam constantly use each other as scapegoats to justify violence and destruction upon Jews, non-Abrahamic religions, and secular values*. When attempting to point out the violent atrocities of their own historical record or in contemporary times, the two use each other as convenient propaganda tools to argue their side is less worse to shut down any attempt at arguing against the violence within their own religious framework. Christians, in particular, lie the most about their violent history; they attempt to argue the Spanish inquisition as the last Christian atrocity and ignore the Holocaust, the genocide of the Native Americans (from Columbus's lifetime to the modern-day USA), the Atlantic slave trade, the destruction of the Native Hawaiians, the genocide of India, the war rape upon civilians during the Boxer Rebellion, the genocide of Tasmania, the genocide of Ireland, the genocide of the Congo, and systematic rape of innocent children in modern times by different branches of Christian theology. It is absolutely true that Islam has committed unspeakable atrocities; the war rape of women and children, the purging of Zoroastrianists, the genocide of Armenian Christians, the current genocides of religious minorities under ISIS, their slave trade which had a scope and scale much larger than the Atlantic slave trade, and much more. Yet, much of that history in Islam is simply used as an excuse to ignore Christian genocides and the violent aspects of Christianity; most Christians don't care what their ancestors have done, but demand everyone be persecuted and blamed for the death of some megalomaniac on a cross in the 1st century. Christians and Muslims only use each other's history as excuses to continue holy wars against each other over differences in semantics. The reason is that the salvation both religions propose is a zero-sum theology that demands submission with the threat of persecution and eternal damnation. The assumption that any denial of their religious teachings is a sign of hate and deceit from both theologies helps to propel an endless war campaign against each other. Anything else is considered a deception and distraction from both seeing the conflict as an impetus of good versus evil, but from opposing sides. Vast majorities of Christians refuse to even acknowledge the fact that Muslims regard Jesus as the messiah who will save the world or that Muslims believe in the Abrahamic God. They make binary "Us Versus Them" and "good versus evil" scenarios for what is seen as a zero-sum belief system based on salvation; some Christians preach that Islam doesn't even believe in the Abrahamic God which is a false claim unsubstantiated by the theological teachings of Islam. Salvation forms a hideous all-or-nothing mindset and the blasphemy with saying or writing something that is "idolatry" results in warring desert tribalism where ignorance of believing in the same God and conviction to keep faith against the other tribe's denomination of your God results in constant mass killings and warfare for the same God. *Bloodshed for Yahweh by another faith is always used to justify that your version of the Yahweh faith is less worse.*

Wars between Christianity and Islam help only to rationalize the belief that Christianity is a corrupted version of Islam as Muslims are specifically led to believe in their faith, or that Westerners are godless and not Christian at all as many Muslims in the Arab Spring may believe in their perception of Europe and the US when trying to respect Christian beliefs. Muslims may point to the 33,000 denominations of Christianity as proof of its failings to be consistent and could argue they're correct about Islam being the perfected form of the Abrahamic faiths, but this less fractured theology of Islam fails to compromise with secularism.[1081] While regressive religious politics and cultural recidivism are constantly combating the push to secularism in Christian majority countries, it is done so by slowly ignoring, reinterpreting, or rationalizing parts of the Christian Bible through cognitive dissonance or complete rejection to pave the way for modernity and secular values. Islam may concede whenever questions are left blank on modern issues that come forth if there is no authoritative opinion from a so-called Islamic scholar, but the Sharia is mandated as perfect and beyond argument which results in a total dismissal of secularism. There is no filling in the void or for cognitive dissonance to flourish for a time to make significant cultural or technological progress. Even when progress is made, there is a call to revert back to old ways because Islam is suppose to be the endpoint of Abrahamic civilization.

Lastly, due specifically to the teachings of Jesus Christ, both Christianity and Islam threaten non-adherents with fear of an eternal hell as a consideration for why people must convert. Christians threaten non-Christians with hell for not accepting Jesus Christ as their lord and savior. Mohammad managed to outfox Christians by using this very idiotic belief system against them for his own desire for Abrahamic consistency. Islam preaches that anyone who believes Jesus Christ is a God and was crucified will go to hell for eternity. Islam believes that Jesus was simply the Messiah and that the Abrahamic God sent him to heaven. This was clearly made to force the conversions of Christians just as Christians attempted to forcibly convert non-Christians before Islam's creation. To be clear, the threat of eternal damnation in hell is one of the most laughably asinine beliefs and only proves how woefully inept Christianity and Islam are with addressing reality and reasonable contentions to their religious faiths. The belief in eternal hell is proof that neither faith could ever truly deal with skeptical inquiry or the most miniscule criticisms of their theologies. It is a baleful reaction of paranoia, fear, and intimidation against rationality, inquiry, and reason. However, the fact the Islamic prophet added eternal hellfire for anyone believing that Jesus Christ was a God and required even stricter religious submission is actually quite funny, because now there are two major religions; one states that the belief in Jesus Christ as the Son of the Abrahamic God will prevent eternal damnation, while the other states that believing in Jesus Christ as the Son of God will lead to eternal damnation. Therefore, we now live in a world where eternal damnation

---

16. [1081] Alt, Scott Eric. "We Need to Stop Saying That There Are 33,000 Protestant Denominations." *National Catholic Register*, Global Catholic Television Network (EWTN), www.ncregister.com/blog/scottericalt/we-need-to-stop-saying-that-there-are-33000-protestant-denominations.

is all but guaranteed by some subset of Abrahamic theology. It is to be expected from a theology of violent tribes killing each other in the desert and parading themselves as chosen people or children of their narcissistic God, Yahweh.

Chapter 22: Holistic Purity

Islam purports that all are born Muslim and lose their way into sin by denying Islam.[1082] By being born pure and Islamic, they're considered to have consented to fall prey to sinfulness in the world.[1083] Conversions to Islam are considered returning to the worship of the Abrahamic God instead of merely accepting a new religious faith.[1084] As a theological background, it seems to try to merge the Old and New Testament versions of the Abrahamic God; which is why Adam and Eve are thought to be forgiven for their transgressions in Islam, whereas it is not the case in the other Abrahamic faiths.[1085] Islam attempts to simplify and make consistent the three-god in one theology of Christianity by recognizing Jesus Christ as a prophet and Messiah, but not the Son of the Abrahamic God. Islam's emphasis on purity, the multidimensional aspects of having a jurisprudence system, and statecraft to implement country-wide systems management to be attuned to the Sharia has effectively broadcast that Islam is far more devout of a faith than Christianity ever was or could be. Whereas Christianity attempts to place Jesus paraphernalia and ignorantly attributing everything from secular institutions to Western philosophy as somehow oriented towards Christianity to thoroughly deceive themselves in believing they're being consistent with Jesus's teachings[1086]; Islam teaches Muslims to be pious by the mere act of being a Muslim. The Western societies have largely broken down in religious worship of Christianity, not because of the fear of Islam, since the divide between the two major denominations of the Abrahamic religions has only created a resurgence of faith through mutual hate and violence, but rather because Islam is a convenient scapegoat to the true destroyer of Christianity - Western philosophy itself. It was the arguments of David Hume, Friedrich Nietzsche, John Stuart Mill, Thomas Paine, Thomas Jefferson, Albert Camus, and likely many other Western philosophers that heaped criticism of Christianity, the plausibility of its contents, and the disavowal that has flourished in modern times. By contrast Islam's ancient critics like Abu al-Ala' al-Ma' arri have far less influence than religious revivalist movements like the Wahhabi founder, Muhammad ibn Abd-al-Wahhab. While Christianity's failed holy book allowed for the haphazard advent of atheist thought; Islam's strive to perfection to worship the Abrahamic God destroyed and killed off the rationalists of the Middle East as traitors of Islam under the penalty of apostasy. It invokes murderers to feel morally good about killing them for the crime of independent thought.[1087] Muslims within the faith can continue to boast the No True Scotsman fallacy of the person who has left not being a true Muslim because of erroneous beliefs such as that no one who truly

---

1. [1082] Castor, Trevor. "Sin According to Islam." *Zwemer Center*, www.zwemercenter.com/guide/sin-according-to-muslims/.
2. [1083] Castor, Trevor. "Sin According to Islam." *Zwemer Center*, www.zwemercenter.com/guide/sin-according-to-muslims/.
3. [1084] Tessier, Stephanie, and Muhammad Syed. "Islam: Pull and Peril." *YouTube*, Ex-Muslims of North America, 22 Apr. 2018, www.youtube.com/watch?v=jt1rWgap41g.
4. [1085] Castor, Trevor. "Sin According to Islam." *Zwemer Center*, www.zwemercenter.com/guide/sin-according-to-muslims/.
5. [1086] Kahneman, Daniel. *Thinking, fast and slow*. Farrar, Straus and Giroux, 2015.
6. [1087] *The Quranic Arabic Corpus - Translation*, corpus.quran.com/translation.jsp?chapter=4&verse=89.

believed in the message of the Islamic Prophet Mohammad would leave the religion of Islam.[1088] This is all done to celebrate the in-group narcissism of being a chosen people.[1089] The belief they weren't really Muslim helps to reassure Muslims of the innate purity of the religious faith and systematically makes it harder for outside logic to penetrate the understanding that the dead person was indeed a Muslim before leaving the faith.

To simply be a devout Muslim is arguably more pious than being a Christian because of what is required in the teachings. Muslims are suppose to pray five times a day, they're taught to praise the majority of the Abrahamic holy books, they fast during the celebration of Ramadan in devotion to the Abrahamic God, and it is Jesus Christ whom they await at Judgment Day in Islam's nonsensical end of the world prophecy. It's no wonder then that Christians never meaningfully challenge the theology of Islam; apart from ignorantly arguing Jesus is a better moral guide, Christians largely ignore Islam's actual theology. Many would take umbrage with the idea that Jesus's teachings are in Islam and that Islam awaits for Jesus as its Messiah; nevertheless, it must be reiterated that is what the theology of Islam teaches. It should come as no surprise; Christianity claims to be consistent, but thoroughly fractured itself into multifarious denominations within the Protestant branch. Christianity's only claim to consistency is the claim that the Abrahamic God made the Bible inerrant. By contrast, Islam has a few small sects that veered off, but largely remain consistent with either Sunni or Shia as the theology because they largely demonstrate their piety in jurisprudence systems, removing all forms of secularized culture, conducting daily rituals of prayer as proof of worship, and destroying all people who would wish to move the Islamic countries far ahead than what they currently live with. Islam is more dangerous because it is by all measures the superior religion to Christianity in the context of piety. Even the most basic argument by Islam, that Christians have become misguided because the Holy Trinity is explicitly against the proper monotheistic aspect of believing only in the one God, the Abrahamic God, is an argument that Christianity fails to have any meaningful response to challenge. Whether in the Middle East, Brunei, or Indonesia; Islam's theology is a contributing factor to anti-intellectual efforts and the worst form of it is the death penalty for apostasy for falling into unfettered sin. Islam's very word means submission to the Abrahamic God. Anything less is considered corruptive and must be cleansed to maintain purity in the sight of the Abrahamic God.

Within Islam lies the essence and fluidity of unquestioned obedience to the Abrahamic God, the simplistic paradigm of good versus evil, the war of purity against all impurities, and the self-sacrificing nature of worship to the Abrahamic God. The only implicit divide between Christianity and Islam is that Christianity attempts to forgive itself for all its wrongdoings through using the Abrahamic God as a convenient moral tool instead of asking the victims for forgiveness; Islam boasts that no forgiveness is needed because Muslims are doing the

---

7. [1088] "Your Logical Fallacy Is No True Scotsman." *Thou Shalt Not Commit Logical Fallacies*, yourlogicalfallacyis.com/no-true-scotsman.
8. [1089] Ispas, Alexa. *Psychology and politics: a social identity perspective*. Psychology Press, 2014.

Abrahamic God's work by remaining pure to properly glorify the Abrahamic God.[1090] Islam is a long series of arguments from ignorance and appeals to purity working in tandem to celebrate the annihilation of others and of itself. When the Abrahamic God orders something heinous like a mass murder or war rape to be done, such as what Moses ordered his men to do upon winning tribal wars, then it is considered morally righteous regardless of anything else in Islam. While Christianity forever lives with the inconsistencies and attempts to mitigate the glaring differences between the Old and New Testament versions of the Abrahamic God with passive responses about how the Abrahamic God doesn't authorize murder and rape anymore; Islam openly boasts that such actions were morally right because the Abrahamic God says they were morally right. They'll be morally wrong later on when others do it, but only if the Abrahamic God doesn't approve of the violence. The Sharia makes sure to keep the inconsistency beyond question through an argument from ignorance, appeal to authority, and appeal to purity. Whereas Christianity gives muted or passive answers to the subjugation of women by trying to argue other places like the Middle East are worse in order to slowly chip away at the progress of women's rights; Islam forthrightly exclaims that a husband beating a wife is an unquestionably good moral act because the Abrahamic God says it is an unquestionably good moral act through the Quran.[1091] While Christianity tries to argue its form of slavery was appropriate for its time; Islam attempts to mitigate slavery, but doesn't openly state it is morally wrong because the Abrahamic God allows slavery.[1092][1093] Whereas Judaism and Christianity attempt to ignore the negative portions and slowly allow the book to join the massive grave called mythology in successive bursts throughout history, Islam ratifies all of the vast majority of Abrahamic texts as morally good because the word of the Abrahamic God is considered inerrant. While Christianity tries to swindle and threaten people on their deathbed with threats of hellfire or a bleak absence of eternity if they don't submit to the Abrahamic God, Islam maintains the purity of the faith by killing apostates so that the apostates don't spread sin in order to make sure more Muslims aren't susceptible to spend eternity in hell.[1094][1095] Islam purports to preserve purity and innate goodness regardless of the sacrifices whether upon Muslims or non-Muslims to glorify the Abrahamic God. *Christianity claims to be the most faithful in reverence to the Abrahamic God while slowly ceding untenable parts of the Bible to secularism; Islam actually proves itself to be the most reverential to the Abrahamic*

9. [1090] Castor, Trevor. "Sin According to Islam." *Zwemer Center*, www.zwemercenter.com/guide/sin-according-to-muslims/.
10. [1091] "The Quranic Arabic Corpus - Word by Word Grammar, Syntax and Morphology of the Holy Quran." *The Quranic Arabic Corpus - Translation*, http://corpus.quran.com/translation.jsp?chapter=4&verse=34
11. [1092] "The Quranic Arabic Corpus - Word by Word Grammar, Syntax and Morphology of the Holy Quran." *The Quranic Arabic Corpus - Translation*, http://corpus.quran.com/translation.jsp?chapter=4&verse=24
12. [1093] Shams, Imtiaz, and Nourhan. "What Does Islam Say about Slavery in Its THEOLOGY?" *YouTube*, Salsalah, 14 Nov. 2016, www.youtube.com/watch?v=rHm9F1G5IRE.
13. [1094] Namazie, Maryam, et al. "Equality, Islam and Human Rights." *YouTube*, Ex-Muslims of North America, 26 Mar. 2018, www.youtube.com/watch?v=2W0w9ufJOh0.
14. [1095] *The Quranic Arabic Corpus - Translation*, corpus.quran.com/translation.jsp?chapter=4&verse=89.

God because Muslims follow their version of the the Abrahamic holy book the most thoroughly and most Muslims are unafraid to annihilate the cultural progress of their own societies to worship the Abrahamic God without hypocrisy.[1096] Self-annihilation of modernity to preclude hypocrisy is more important to devout Muslims than cultural or technological progress. *In short, Islam is the embodiment of all forms of Abrahamic asceticism and is therefore a culture of death.*[1097]

At various points in a culture's time, there is this belief in a benign form of yesteryears before the social changes made life radically different; the simplistic living that removed all the social responsibilities and complexities of modernized living feels like a heaven by comparison. Within this belief is the prevailing notion of removing the greed of consumer culture, denigrating wanting more in life as mere selfishness, and that such modernization comes with sexual exploitation, street violence, rabid crackdowns of protests, and rapid spikes in crime for the community. All such beliefs are merely a maligned view that confuses technology improving with human suffering. Technological improvement brings rapid reporting of such events with increasing propensity; the availability to document such tragedies begins to confuse cause and effect for the uneducated.[1098] The events were already happening, technology just became better at reporting on horrible events.[1099] While many Christians and Hindus fantasize about such faux-benign past times; Islam actually pursues it wholeheartedly. While Hindus and Christians lambast Islamic nation-states for being backwards hovels with no ability to move past the 7th century, this obscures the reason why; while Christians and Hindutva right-wing groups complain about progress and act as "hypocrites" with respect to technological progress, Islam removes all forms of hypocrisy in accordance to reverence to the Abrahamic God by destroying their own civilizations to properly glorify the Abrahamic God or - if that is impossible - then Islam pursues the least amount of hypocrisy possible by ignoring women's rights to stay committed to the Abrahamic God. The bellow of "God is Great" is not merely for show by Islamic extremists; Islam teaches people to live by such words and all their negative consequences wholeheartedly. *For 1400 years, Islamic theology has been resistant to change because of the pernicious theological framework of anti-materialism.* Often it cloaks these anti-materialist proclivities as a rejection of idolatry and non-Muslims who examine how the theology manifests upon predominately Islamic countries can see just how damaging a culture of thought crimes towards superstitious fears can be for an entire society. Similar to other religions conflating the attainment of material wealth with selfishness, gratuitous sex, and narcissism; Islam posits that any deviation from its teachings leads to selfishness, gratuitous sex, and narcissism but with the additional theological imposition of removing any amount of hypocrisy to have complete submission to the Abrahamic God and rejecting any change in the

---

15. [1096] Nietzsche, Friedrich Wilhelm. *On the genealogy of morals: a polemical tract*. Translated by Ian Johnston, PDF, Richer Resources Publications, 2014.
16. [1097] Nietzsche, Friedrich Wilhelm. *On the genealogy of morals: a polemical tract*. Translated by Ian Johnston, PDF, Richer Resources Publications, 2014.
17. [1098] Rosling, Hans. *Factfulness*. Macmillan, 2018.
18. [1099] Rosling, Hans. *Factfulness*. Macmillan, 2018.

practices of the religion.[1100][1101] This is likely why Muslim families often cluster and form their own subculture societies separate from others in places where they are the minority, this is likely why they advocate for Sharia court systems in non-Islamic countries, and why many Muslims often follow anti-intellectual practices despite the scientific evidence against such harmful practices. Islam's ascetic practices are more sharply focused on habitual worship as a daily activity. They're often more clear and simplified in instruction than other religious practices with an appeal to popularity as a feedback loop to assuage Muslims that their faith is correct. This naturally leads into unquestioned obedience due to the effort put into daily exertions which would feel profoundly meaningful to a Muslim's personal experience. Some Muslims may believe the daily commitments are proof of their faith being the truth because no other religion has such daily practices in reverence to the Abrahamic God; but this would confuse commitment and strong effort towards their religious faith with truth claims about reality.[1102][1103] Having a strong commitment towards religious practices and even dying for your faith doesn't prove that it is the truth.[1104] After all, millions devote themselves to a faith that is different from your own and may even die for it, so then have they died for a lie? If so, why do you believe that people who died for your religion are exempt from possibly dying for a lie too?

When viewing Islam more holistically, an outside observer can see the utter failure in not questioning just what it is that some Muslims are dying for. There is a crucial and dangerous problem with Islamic theology that Muslims ignore by solely focusing on their subjective experience with their religious faith. Westerners often ignore this failing by insisting on focusing only on anecdotal accounts of personal experience and the emotional wellbeing of Muslims that they may know. Islam is a political philosophy and a societal project with its own set of assumptions on what makes a positive functioning nation-state and government; this issue is not some trite philosophical abstraction that can simply be ignored. When Muslims commit to ritualistic prayers, fasting, giving to charity, and dying for their faith; they are also committing to and dying for this specific worldview that many Muslims want to bring to fruition. The purpose of the religion of Islam is to bring forth a supposedly perfect society that comprises of a unification of the Islamic religion with the institution of government, an emphasis on a ruler who effectively functions as a King supported by the legitimacy and power

---

19. [1100] "Greater and Lesser Jihaad." Translated by Muhammed Salih Al-Munajjid, *Islam Question And Answer*, islamqa.info/en/10455.
20. [1101] "Tafseer on the Basis of Narrated Texts and Tafseer on the Basis of Individual Understanding - Islam Question & Answer." *Islamqa.info*, Islam Question and Answer, 11 Mar. 2015, islamqa.info/en/answers/205290/tafseer-on-the-basis-of-narrated-texts-and-tafseer-on-the-basis-of-individual-understanding.
21. [1102] Cialdini, Robert B. "Chapter 3: Commitment and Consistency (52-95)" *Influence: Science and practice*. 4th ed., 21st Century Bks, 2002.
22. [1103] Kahneman, Daniel. *Thinking, fast and slow*. Farrar, Straus and Giroux, 2015.
23. [1104] Nietzsche, Friedrich Wilhelm. Aphorism 53. *THE ANTICHRIST*. Translated by H. L. Mencken, The Project Gutenberg, 2006.

of Islamic theocrats, and it is set this way in order to await the Al-Mahdi. In fact, we have a real world example of this with the current theocratic regime in Iran as awaiting the Al-Mahdi's appearance when the world is in turmoil is their basis for legitimacy in ruling Iran. Many other despotic Islamic regimes are based upon a ruling monarchy working in tandem with Islamic theologians to justify their rule and this is not something in the distant past, but rather theological justifications made in modern times even in 2019 to defend these forms of government throughout the Middle East. Countries like Tunisia are not the majority, don't have any historical precedent, and even they seem to be tenuous in holding onto any credible form of democracy as of now; I would love to be proven wrong about this and I hope that I am, but Islam is thorough in influencing and then supplanting non-Islamic institutions. Islam is a theocratic nation-state as much as it is a religion since it has never historically operated with a separation of religious institutions from the governance of the nation-state when it held power, even a supposed Islamic Republic like Pakistan have Pakistani Muslim citizens ignore their own laws that require marriages to be 18 years of age or older in order to defend Muslim men kidnapping Hindu female children as young as nine-years of age to rape them and forcibly convert them to Islam on the basis that it is consistent with Islamic theology.[1105] Countries like Indonesia and Malaysia have female genital mutilation and blasphemy laws on the basis of defending Islam.[1106][1107][1108][1109] Thus, even when secularism is attempted in a Muslim-majority country, it is often repudiated internally in a country's affairs with a secular veneer on the outset to pretend that Islam can be consistent with secular morality and a secular legal code.

    Why does this continue to happen in Muslim-majority countries? A gaggle of think tanks, Western journalists, Western politicians, University Professors, and Islamic theologians would have people believe that it is due to some socio-economic reasons, non-Islamic cultural practices, political upheavals, and especially the ignorance of non-Muslims in not understanding some deep and meaningful aspect of Islam that causes cultural insensitivity and horrible ramifications. This repeated charade was my own understanding, which I wrongfully believed to be a fuller perspective on socio-political conflicts pertaining to the Islamic world, until I decided to delve more deeply into understanding the theology of Islam for research purposes. In this particular context, the unambiguous and harsh truth is far more simple and readily easy to understand when a person takes the time to learn more about how Islamic

---

24. [1105] "Pakistani Hindus Complain of Forced Conversion of Teenage Girls." *YouTube*, VOA News, 18 Mar. 2016, youtu.be/-i24jg4mJ4I.
25. [1106] Budiharsana, Meiwita. "Female Genital Cutting Common in Indonesia, Offered as Part of Child Delivery by Birth Clinics." *The Conversation*, 10 Mar. 2019, theconversation.com/female-genital-cutting-common-in-indonesia-offered-as-part-of-child-delivery-by-birth-clinics-54379.
26. [1107] Renaldi, Erwin. "Female Circumcision: Culture and Religion in Malaysia See Millions of Girls Undergo Cut." *ABC News*, 13 Nov. 2018, www.abc.net.au/news/2018-11-13/female-circumcision-is-still-happening-in-malaysia/10473640.
27. [1108] "Indonesia Blasphemy Case: Emotional Scenes as Ahok Trial Begins." *BBC News*, BBC, 13 Dec. 2016, www.bbc.com/news/world-asia-38285515.
28. [1109] Sidhu, Sandi. "Malaysian Man Gets 10 Years in Prison for Insulting Islam on Facebook." *CNN*, Cable News Network, 9 Mar. 2019, www.cnn.com/2019/03/09/asia/malaysia-man-prison-insulting-islam-intl/.

theology functions and the impact that Islamic theology has upon Muslim-majority countries. The mundane fact of the matter is that Islam seeks to make a caliphate, which is essentially just a 7th century theocratic kingdom, because of the belief that forming a civilization on the basis of the Sharia and the example of the Islamic Prophet Mohammad, who is regarded as a perfect human being to follow the example of, is the only way to create a perfect civilization.[1110][1111] To any outside observer, this belief is absurd and asinine, but this is what most Muslims believe to be the divinely revealed truth of the Abrahamic God. As such, it is thereby consistent for Islamic armies to plunder the riches of foreign cultures, to abduct and rape non-Muslim women as sex slaves[1112][1113], to enforce a theocratic State that functions via social stratification with a royal family holding all the power under the support of Islamic theologians[1114], and then to destroy all the accumulated wealth, force non-slave women into more sexist and patriarchal societal conditions with intimidation, to impose child marriages for female children as young as nine years of age[1115], and forcibly convert non-Muslim minorities through rape and torture.[1116] The whole point is to emulate the 7th century under the Islamic Prophet Mohammad as closely as possible in order to await the Al-Mahdi and the Islamic Judgment Day.[1117] Both the Quran and the example of the life of the Islamic Prophet Mohammad affirm this behavior. In modern times and throughout Islamic history, it leads to the theft of foreign wealth, violence against non-Muslims, and then the cultural genocide of non-Islamic cultures from Iran, to the Greco-Buddhist kingdom that make-up what is modern Afghanistan and Pakistan, and even in recent times in Maldives.[1118][1119] Scholars who ignore

29. [1110] Ibrahim, Ghada, et al. "Can Islam Be Apolitical? - Armin Navabi, Ghada Ibrahim & Sarah Haider." *YouTube*, Ex-Muslims of North America, 6 Dec. 2018, www.youtube.com/watch?v=QGX0VqsiAMo.
30. [1111] Shams, Imtiaz, et al. "Fighting Allah, Defending Muslims - Armin Navabi, Imtiaz Shams, Muhammad Syed." *YouTube*, Ex-Muslims of North America, 5 Jan. 2018, www.youtube.com/watch?v=KwnHreJNavE.
31. [1112] "The Quranic Arabic Corpus - Word by Word Grammar, Syntax and Morphology of the Holy Quran." *The Quranic Arabic Corpus - Translation*, http://corpus.quran.com/translation.jsp?chapter=4&verse=24
32. [1113] "Ruling on Having Intercourse with a Slave Woman When One Has a Wife - Islamqa.info." Translated by Muhammad Salih Al-Munajjid, *Wayback Machine*, Fox News, web.archive.org/web/20160106101656/http://islamqa.info/en/10382.
33. [1114] "The Quranic Arabic Corpus - Word by Word Grammar, Syntax and Morphology of the Holy Quran." *The Quranic Arabic Corpus - Translation*, http://corpus.quran.com/translation.jsp?chapter=16&verse=71
34. [1115] "Age of the Mother of the Believers 'Aa'ishah (May Allah Be Pleased with Her) When the Prophet (Blessings and Peace of Allah Be upon Him) Married Her - Islam Question & Answer." *Islamqa.info*, Islam Question and Answer, 30 Dec. 2013, islamqa.info/en/answers/124483/age-of-the-mother-of-the-believers-aaishah-may-allah-be-pleased-with-her-when-the-prophet-blessings-and-peace-of-allah-be-upon-him-married-her.
35. [1116] "Pakistani Hindus Complain of Forced Conversion of Teenage Girls." *YouTube*, VOA News, 18 Mar. 2016, youtu.be/-i24jg4mJ4I.
36. [1117] Shams, Imtiaz, et al. "Fighting Allah, Defending Muslims - Armin Navabi, Imtiaz Shams, Muhammad Syed." *YouTube*, Ex-Muslims of North America, 5 Jan. 2018, www.youtube.com/watch?v=KwnHreJNavE.
37. [1118] Bajaj, Vikas. "Vandalism at Maldives Museum Stirs Fears of Extremism." *The New York Times*, The New York Times, 13 Feb. 2012, www.nytimes.com/2012/02/14/world/asia/political-turmoil-threatens-archaeological-treasures-in-maldives.html.

this powerful aspect of Islam only repudiate their own credibility in the eyes of the public which has grown more aware of these problems from the Islamic faith. *After all, to say that forming a caliphate as a theological basis has nothing to do with Islam is to argue that 1400 years of Islamic history has nothing to do with Islam.* If academia, journalists, business organizations, and think tanks - whether in the West or Asia - wish to regain the trust of the public, they should be honest about these religiously motivated issues caused by Islamic groups wishing to impose their religious values upon non-Islamic societies and these Islamic groups must be firmly rebuked on the basis of Free Speech and Free Expression above the hurt feelings of a religious group.

As will be shown in this chapter and the following chapters, there is nothing meaningful or profound in Islamic theology, it is just an anti-intellectual ideology that a significant population of the planet believes to be the sacred truth of the Abrahamic God. *Islam uses an illogical fear of idolatry to conduct a thoroughgoing campaign of anti-materialism.* For all the religious babble about the evils of materialism in the West and Asian countries, Islam's 1400 years of history provides religious people with the effects of a culture that strove towards removing materialism from its society and embracing collectivist social norms to properly revere the Abrahamic God. Islam is thoroughly grounded in celebrating the piety of Muslims regarding charity, prayer practices, Quranic verse chanting practices in Islamic schools, and most Muslims have a faith beyond doubt in submission to the Abrahamic God. This had the opposite effect of leading to a better society in terms of human rights and especially the wellbeing of minority groups. As two examples for this portion on the anti-intellectual dangers of Islam and its possible detrimental effects being carried over to non-Islamic societies, consider the fact that Christianity eventually had to modify to allow Christians to utilize interest rates which were considered usury and against the teachings of Christianity for hundreds of years, but Islam never modified to allow Muslims to use interest rates in over 1400 years. Christianity was able to change thanks to allowing hypocrisy to flourish through various reformations and dividing denominations; although it required pointless self-contempt, Christians were nevertheless able to change in order to improve their lives and their societies over many hundreds of years. Islam rejected any change on the basis that it was against the Sharia; that is, against the divine law of the Abrahamic God.[1120] This simple devotion by pious Muslims only hurts them in modern times and could have negative economic consequences for non-Islamic societies with more Muslims entering their countries who refuse to change their beliefs about this particular topic on the basis of religion. A dangerous health-risk problem, related to health problems in the Middle East even in modern

---

38. [1119] Wilson, Antonia. "Maldives Marine Artwork Destroyed for Being a 'Threat to Islamic Unity'." *The Guardian*, Guardian News and Media, 24 Sept. 2018, www.theguardian.com/travel/2018/sep/24/maldives-authorities-destroy-marine-artwork-for-being-un-islamic?CMP=share_btn_fb.
39. [1120] Elias, Abu Amina. "Sharia, Fiqh, and Islamic Law Explained." *Faith in Allah* ☐☐☐☐ ☐☐ ☐ ☐ ☐☐☐, 21 Mar. 2018, abuaminaelias.com/is-the-sharia-a-single-code-of-law-an-explanation-of-sharia-fiqh-and-islamic-law/.

times, is that the Islamic Prophet Mohammad celebrated drinking camel piss to cure health-related ailments and Muslims throughout the Middle East unquestionably have faith in his teachings.[1121] The so-called Islamic scholars argue that drinking camel piss cures ringworm infections, body sores, hepatitis, the swelling of the liver, cancer, poor digestive systems, blood clots, and help to invigorate the hair to make it more lustrous.[1122] The World Health Organization (WHO) soundly rejects all such claims and repeatedly has had to point out to Middle Eastern countries that are drinking camel piss only leads to MERS (Middle East Respiratory Syndrome Coronavirus) which is an acute respiratory infection that has confirmed cases of causing death.[1123][1124] Muslim-majority countries still don't acknowledge the truth because it would mean accepting the fact that the Islamic Prophet Mohammad was entirely wrong. These horrible and avoidable health-related tragedies that lead to people dying happen because of the same piety and profound personal experience that Muslims devote their lives towards. Focusing only on the hurt feelings of Muslims and anecdotal personal accounts of Muslims you may know is willful ignorance and it doesn't change the harmful effects of bad beliefs. People don't need to personally be a Muslim to understand that some beliefs have negative consequences that can harm others and if a person truly cares for their Muslim friend or Muslim family, then they should criticize harmful religious beliefs because they care about Muslims as people instead of being a bigot that holds Muslims to a lower intellectual standard.[1125]

Jihad

Jihad can be a confusing topic as different sides argue by providing completely opposing definitions and understandings. In Political Science classes, I was taught the lie that jihad means "exerted effort" or "to struggle" in the definition of the terminology when translated to English. The lie was explained as a specific form of jihad that promulgates violence within the Islamic faith and it was classified as *militant* jihad in modern American academia. I was told that Westerners commonly confuse militant jihad with the more broad theological framework that isn't encapsulated by the violent variations of the Islamic faith regarding so-called "Greater" and "Lesser" forms of Jihad. It was only much later that I recognized how utterly false this all was since the Greater and Lesser hadith isn't considered

---

40. [1121] "The Benefits of Drinking Camel Urine - Islam Question & Answer." *Islamqa.info*, Islam Question and Answer, 27 Mar. 2006, islamqa.info/en/answers/83423/the-benefits-of-drinking-camel-urine.
41. [1122] "The Benefits of Drinking Camel Urine - Islam Question & Answer." *Islamqa.info*, Islam Question and Answer, 27 Mar. 2006, islamqa.info/en/answers/83423/the-benefits-of-drinking-camel-urine.
42. [1123] Boyer, Lauren. "Stop Drinking Camel Urine, World Health Organization Says." *U.S. News & World Report*, U.S. News & World Report, www.usnews.com/news/articles/2015/06/10/stop-drinking-camel-urine-world-health-organization-says.
43. [1124] "Middle East Respiratory Syndrome Coronavirus (MERS-CoV) – Republic of Korea." *World Health Organization*, World Health Organization, 9 June 2015, www.who.int/csr/don/09-june-2015-mers-korea/en/.
44. [1125] Haider, Sarah. "Sarah Haider: Islam and the Necessity of Liberal Critique (AHA Conference 2015)." *YouTube*, American Humanist Association, 28 May 2015, www.youtube.com/watch?v=0plC24YuoJk.

authentic in Islamic theology.[1126] In fairness to the professor of the class, I was also taught at least one truthful aspect that it occupies a very deep theological and cultural sense of undertaking the struggles of life to properly revere the Abrahamic God according to Muslims. To the best of my knowledge, it would be accurate to say that Muslims see themselves as enduring the hardships of life for the sake of pursuing faith and finding truth in the Abrahamic God. Nevertheless, most of what I was taught I had to unlearn because even in academia, there is a strong culture of religious tolerance that is of tacit importance. I suspect the fear is that if religious beliefs aren't respected, then people would just go to other universities or colleges where they feel more comfortable and may feel their money is better spent. However, I think they do a disservice to their students with this sort of thinking as many college students are compassionate, open to inquiry, and willing to challenge their beliefs in riveting class discussions. To have more precise and effective critiques, we must be willing to see how the parts of a theology operate and what specific aspects engender violence. To that end, we must acknowledge the context of theology within its appropriate definition and not misattribute or take it out of context. Many Islamic apologists will probably attempt to argue the word itself just means "to strive" but that's using a reductionist argument that ignores the deep theological and historical concept that the term is rooted in. Those who argue it is just a word that means "to strive" are using the equivocation fallacy to downplay or ignore any criticism of the theological concept of *Jihad* in Islam.[1127] In brief, the equivocation fallacy is using two separate definitions of the same word to distort and confuse the meaning of the two distinct definitions through ambiguous language.[1128] Appropriate context is essential for any honest quality critique.

Jihad is a unique Islamic theological concept that has a broad array of mandates for Muslims to follow. On a personal and social level, jihad helps to reinforce both an ascetic mindset and ascetic cultural fixations that are incorporated habitually in reverence to the Abrahamic God. Cleanliness, prayer five times a day, and submission to a purely Islamic jurisprudence system as the most definitive authority that is legitimized as representing the Abrahamic God's intentions. Islam emphasizes an austere and ascetic lifestyle that is recognized by nearly all cultures as deeply pious because of the requirements. Muslims conduct such behavior in order to maintain reverence to the Abrahamic God under the belief they're obviating impurities from contaminating them. Jihad helps to reaffirm the purity of Islam from a personalized context. It is concomitant to a socio-political consensus and enforcement under Islamic jurisprudence. The personal, individualized context acts as one

---

45. [1126] "Greater and Lesser Jihaad." Translated by Muhammed Salih Al-Munajjid, *Islam Question And Answer*, islamqa.info/en/10455.
46. [1127] "Equivocation." *Https://Www.logicallyfallacious.com*, www.logicallyfallacious.com/tools/lp/Bo/LogicalFallacies/81/Equivocation.
47. [1128] "Equivocation." *Https://Www.logicallyfallacious.com*, www.logicallyfallacious.com/tools/lp/Bo/LogicalFallacies/81/Equivocation.

speck that is part of a greater whole to reinforce a collectivist approach to a society and maintain the holistic purity of Islam.

Muhammad Shaleh al-Munajjid, a prominent Islamic scholar in the Arab Spring who is part of the Salafi movement and founder of the website islamqa.info lists the different Jihad mandates that Muslims are expected to follow:

> "Undoubtedly jihaad against the self comes before jihaad against the kuffaar, because one cannot strive against the kuffaar until after one has striven against one's own self, because fighting is something which the self dislikes. Allaah says (interpretation of the meaning):
>
> *"Jihaad (holy fighting in Allaah's Cause) is ordained for you (Muslims) though you dislike it, and it may be that you dislike a thing which is good for you and that you like a thing which is bad for you. Allaah knows but you do not know"*[al-Baqarah 2:216]
>
> The point is that jihaad against the enemy cannot take place until one strives and forces oneself to do it, until one's self submits and accepts that.
>
> *Fataawa Manaar al-Islam* by Shaykh Ibn 'Uthaymeen (may Allaah have mercy on him), 2/421
>
> Ibn al-Qayyim said: "Jihaad is of four stages: *jihaad al-nafs* (striving against the self), *jihaad al-shayaateen* (striving against the shayaateen or devils), *jihaad al-kuffaar* (striving against the disbelievers) and *jihaad al-munaafiqeen* (striving against the hypocrites).
>
> *Jihaad al-nafs* means striving to make oneself learn true guidance, and to follow it after coming to know it, calling others to it, and bearing with patience the difficulties of calling others to Allaah. *Jihaad al-Shaytaan* means striving against him and warding off the doubts and desires that he throws at a person, and the doubts that undermine faith, and striving against the corrupt desires that he tries to inspire in a person. Jihaad against the kuffaar and munaafiqeen is done in the heart and on the tongue, with one's

> wealth and oneself. Jihaad against the kuffaar mostly takes the form of physical action, and jihaad against the munaafiqeen mostly takes the form of words... The most perfect of people are those who have completed all the stages of jihaad. People vary in their status before Allaah according to their status in jihaad."(*Zaad al-Ma'aad* 3/9-12)
>
> And Allaah knows best."[1129]

Jihad is not merely self-war for the sake of commitment to beliefs or anything similar to the Buddhist concepts of self-renunciation, but rather an authoritative mandate by the Abrahamic God to keep Muslims pure and to argue and commit violence to protect the purity of Muslims in order to properly glorify the Abrahamic God. Jihad is both a reaffirmation of purity and a holy war to maintain purity against anything non-Islamic that acts to deceive. In combination with the Islamic jurisprudence system, it allows the rationalization for barbaric practices through violence under the belief that the Abrahamic God ordered it and whatever the Abrahamic God says is morally good must be morally good. What Islam tries to preclude is the contamination of purity by violently warring and destroying all forms of "evil" that is considered outside Islam to protect the innate "moral good" of Muslims themselves. Islam's good versus evil dichotomy is personally and socially reinforced through the mandate of jihad and followed through by Islamic jurisprudence.

The prominent and well-established US think tank, The Brookings Institute, offers a general explanation for socio-political movements in Islamic scholarship that propose how to defend the purity of Islam within the context of modernizing or warring against modernity. Many of these are the definitions of Islamic revivalist movements that attempt to bridge the gap between maintaining Islamic purity and living in a modernized world. Senior fellow, Shadi Hamid, and research assistant, Rashid Dar detail the general ideas of each socio-political Islamic theory and movement:

> **Islamism:** Islamism as a phenomenon incorporates a wide spectrum of behavior and belief. In the broadest sense, Islamist groups believe Islamic law or Islamic values should play a central role in public life. They feel Islam has things to say about how politics should be conducted, how the law should be applied, and how other people—not just themselves—should conduct themselves morally.
>
> To be or become an Islamist, however, is a conscious act of political affirmation. As the Princeton historian Michael Cook writes, Islamists are "at pains to construe their politics out of their Islamic heritage." This also explains, in part, why Islamism isn't just a reaction to modernity, but a product of it. In the pre-modern era, Islam imbued every aspect of public life, providing an overarching religious, legal, and moral culture. It went without saying, so it wasn't said. With the advent of modernity, Islam, for the first time, became a distinct political project.

---

48. [1129] "Greater and Lesser Jihaad." Translated by Muhammed Salih Al-Munajjid, *Islam Question And Answer*, islamqa.info/en/10455.

But why not treat Islamists as we would treat any other ideology or political platform? For starters, modern liberal sensibilities shy away from enshrining a privileged position to any one religion, out of fear of placing constraints on individual freedom—yet the point of Islamism is to advocate for a privileged social and political role for Islamic belief. How each Islamist group goes about promoting Islam and Islamic values differs widely from group to group given their local circumstances.

The definition above is broad enough to capture Islamism's basic impulse, but this broadness also means that the category includes both extremist groups like ISIS that use violence and terror and mainstream parties like Tunisia's Ennahda (which is one reason Ennahda has recently distanced itself from the term). This diversity in the Islamist experience is why it's important—and, from a national security standpoint, perhaps more important ever—to make careful distinctions between Islamists. While extremists may garner the most attention, the vast majority of Islamists are not, in fact, violent.

Mainstream Islamism: Mainstream Islamist groups primarily consist of Muslim Brotherhood and Brotherhood-inspired movements. Their distinguishing features are their gradualism (historically eschewing revolution), an embrace of parliamentary politics, and a willingness to work within existing state structures, even secular ones. As Hamid discusses in his new book, *Islamic Exceptionalism: How the Struggle Over Islam is Reshaping the World*, mainstream Islamists, contrary to popular imagination, do not harken back to seventh century Arabia.

The basic project of mainstream Islamism, if it can be summed up in a sentence, is to reconcile pre-modern Islamic law with the modern nation-state. In many ways—and perhaps the most important ways—the state has gotten the better end of the deal. The very process of modern state-building—and the state-centric international environment which facilitated that process—has had an inherently secularizing effect on social and political institutions. This places pressure on Islamists to limit their religiously-motivated ambitions to a degree that would be unthinkable in the pre-modern past, introducing a substantial degree of tension within Muslim-majority societies that are still largely religious and conservative. What, then, does an Islamist future look like? What exactly are they fighting for? That answer, too, can differ widely depending on which Islamists you talk to.

Salafism: Salafism is the idea that the most authentic and true Islam is found in the lived example of the early, righteous generations of Muslims, known as the *Salaf*, who were closest in both time and proximity to the Prophet Muhammad. Salafis—often described as "ultraconservatives"—believe not just in the "spirit" but in the "letter" of the law, which is what sets them apart from their mainstream counterparts. In the Arab world today, Salafis are known for trying to imitate the particular habits of the first Muslims, such as dressing like the Prophet (by cuffing their trousers at ankle-length) or brushing their teeth like the
Prophet (with a natural teeth cleaning twig called a *miswak*).

Broadly-speaking, Salafists are less inclined towards active political engagement à la mainstream Islamists, preferring instead a "quietist" approach of preaching, religious education, and avoiding confrontation with state authorities. Some Salafis (in Kuwait and Egypt in particular) have engaged in electoral politics and even formed political parties, although they tend to focus on lobbying for specific *shariah*-based policies, rather than building big-tent, mass parties seeking executive power. A minority of Salafis are Salafi-jihadists (see below).

Jihadism: Jihadism is driven by the idea that jihad (religiously-sanctioned warfare) is an individual obligation (*fard 'ayn*) incumbent upon all Muslims, rather than a collective obligation carried out by legitimate representatives of the Muslim community (*fard kifaya*), as it was traditionally understood in the pre-modern era. They are able to do this by arguing that Muslim leaders today are illegitimate and do not command the authority to ordain justified violence. In the absence of such authority, they argue, every able-bodied Muslim should take up the mantle of jihad. Contrast this state of affairs with World War I, when the Kaiser himself had to sweet talk the Ottoman caliphate into declaring jihad against the Allied Powers.

Furthermore, the vast majority of Islamic scholars acknowledge that the Quranic verses dealing with violence and the use of force were tied to a specific set of circumstances, and it was the task of clerics to consider when war was or wasn't justified and how it should be waged. This is the jurisprudence of jihad. Freed from context and the classical rules of warfare, modern jihadist groups generally aim to incite their coreligionists to rise up and fight the enemy en masse, wherever they happen to be and by any means necessary. Theologically, Muslims of various persuasions have engaged in jihad—not just ultraconservative Salafis, but mystical Sufis as well.

Salafi-Jihadism: This is an approach to jihadism that is coupled with an adherence to Salafism. Salafi-jihadists tend to emphasize the military exploits of the *Salaf* (the early generations of Muslims) to give their violence an even more immediate divine imperative. Most jihadist groups today can be classified as Salafi-jihadists, including al-Qaida and ISIS. Given their exclusivist view that their approach to Islam is the only authentic one, Salafi-jihadists often justify violence against other Muslims, including non-combatants, by recourse to *takfir*, or the excommunication of fellow Muslims. For these groups, if Muslims have been deemed to be apostates, then violence against them is licit.[1130]

While presented in refined commentary; the ultimate purpose of jihad is defending and abiding by the standards of a warring desert tribe. Any attempt at a so-called consensus is ridiculous for the aforementioned reasons earlier in this chapter. In the end, the Islamic heritage is merely an appeal to purity and an appeal to keeping a society ignorant up to a certain amount of cultural and technological standards set by Islam itself. Jihad, as an appeal to purity, assures that it isn't merely confined to spiritual purposes but instead a multidimensional erasure of other cultures, of modernity, and of equal rights for minorities and women under the belief that the glorification of the Abrahamic God takes priority over everything else. Therefore, jihad exists specifically to assure the erasure, prejudice, and loathing for all outside logic and culture is maintained under the same dichotomy as the Christian context of the Abrahamic God facing against Satan, but with a mandate that thoroughly demands that people follow through with an additional command by the Abrahamic God in maintaining a traditional Abrahamic society to remain pure and innocent from sin so that Muslims spend eternity in heaven.[1131] It is the logical consequence of the ascetic ideal warned by Friedrich Nietzsche. It is a real life example of what it means for a cultural movement to loathe and destroy both capitalist consumer culture and far more importantly, the social justice rights of women.

Historicity

One argument by ardent ex-Muslims and other critics of Islam is the lack of scientific credibility in Islam. While they're completely correct in their arguments; it's possible that this approach would only pique the curiosity and interest of particular groups of Muslims who wish to synthesize scientific research such as studies in college with their Islamic teachings. Many Muslims may simply be incurious about the disconnect between science and Islam similar to

---

49. [1130] Hamid, Shadi, and Rashid Dar. "Islamism, Salafism, and Jihadism: A Primer." *Brookings*, Brookings Institution, 29 July 2016, www.brookings.edu/blog/markaz/2016/07/15/islamism-salafism-and-jihadism-a-primer/.
50. [1131] Nietzsche, Friedrich Wilhelm. *On the genealogy of morals: a polemical tract*. Translated by Ian Johnston, PDF, Richer Resources Publications, 2014.

Christians and the Bible. Many could attribute it to miracles, a test from the Abrahamic God, or of total irrelevance to their faith. What approach could then work against such specific groups who may be interested in questioning the faith, but are unconvinced by scientific arguments? Moreover, how can such an approach be possible, when the Sharia and Sunnah mitigate such possibilities so thoroughly to keep Islam relevant? It is far more difficult due to the Sunnah and the framework of Sharia itself.

How can one effectively criticize Islam when so much of it is motivated and reinforced by an anti-intellectual jurisprudence system and culture? Raising the living standards could be one way for some Islamic countries, but it runs the risk of cultural recidivism and an outright self-annihilation for the glorification of the Abrahamic God.[1132] Any attempt at Christian or Jewish triumphalism will only continue a long, bloody legacy of negative interdependence in which a resurgence of Islamic revivalism, cultural erasure, and hatred for infidels will surely become more rigid and continue to increase the extremism.[1133] The only accomplishment of triumphalism of warring Abrahamicism has been protracted wars in both the past and contemporary times. Most importantly, on the basis of both the history of Abrahamic wars and modern human psychology, the only accomplishment will be lengthier and bloodier conflicts repeated without any clear indication of a conclusion or what a peaceful conclusion would even look like. The surest way is to fundamentally attack the assumptions and criticize what Islam is predicated upon as a religion and an ideology. Self-righteous triumphalism on the part of Islam's critics will only have the opposite effect of ending Islam; so will mitigating the horrific contributions of Christianity and Zionism in the historical and modern conflicts that Islam is a part of. The former because of the negative interdependent reciprocity within the context of these religions intermingling; the latter because Muslims and Muslim apologists won't perceive any criticism as honest. To look to Christianity and Judaism as the answer to ending Islam at this point requires a severe amount of cognitive dissonance, ignorance of Islamic theology itself, and ignorance of the history of religious wars among the Abrahamic faiths. Christians overwhelmingly refuse to engage with the fact that Islam reveres Jesus as the Messiah of the Abrahamic God.[1134] Right-wing Israelis refuse to ever engage with their side having ever done anything wrong; even as Israeli military explosives are blowing up Palestinian homes[1135], Palestinian children as systematically shut out from having an education outside of learning the Quran in Madrassas by the IDF[1136], and the IDF torture of Palestinian

---

51. [1132] Nietzsche, Friedrich Wilhelm. *On the genealogy of morals: a polemical tract*. Translated by Ian Johnston, PDF, Richer Resources Publications, 2014.
52. [1133] Cialdini, Robert B. Chapter 2: Reciprocation (19-50). *Influence: Science and practice*. 4th ed., 21st Century Bks, 2002.
53. [1134] Ally, Shabir. "The Messiah: Jesus, Son of Mary." *Facts about the Muslims & the Religion of Islam*, Whyislam.org, www.whyislam.org/comparative-religion-2/the-messiah-jesus-son-of-mary/.
54. [1135] "Israel: Serious Violations in West Bank Operations." *Human Rights Watch*, 17 Apr. 2015, www.hrw.org/news/2014/07/03/israel-serious-violations-west-bank-operations.
55. [1136] LAZAROFF, TOVAH. "IDF Destroys Two Illegal EU-Funded Palestinian Schools." *The Jerusalem Post | JPost.com*, 24 Aug. 2017, www.jpost.com/Arab-Israeli-Conflict/IDF-destroys-two-illegal-EU-funded-Palestinian-schools-503252.

children as young as twelve years of age.[1137][1138] To vindicate Christianity and Judaism of their culpability in protracted conflicts is simply dishonest and significantly contributes to the continued thriving of Islamism.

What is the answer then? What could truly end Islam? To start, the critiques must focus on the assumptions of the Sharia; the very theological basis that Muslims adamantly argue must remain unquestioned. The Sharia is comprised of the Torah, the Old Testament Bible, Psalms of Daniel, the supposed lost Gospels of Jesus Christ, and the Quran being held as beyond questioning with the Hadiths being openly interpretative.[1139][1140] Therefore, to end Islam directly would be to challenge the Sharia with skeptical inquiry in order to destroy the assumptions of its theological framework. Wars and massacres only lead to more religiously motivated violence and extremism; to kill an idea, people must challenge the idea. First by examining it truthfully instead of the nonsensical dispositions that Christians and Zionists often take to indemnify their in-groups of any responsibility. Liberals of all kinds are far better at diagnosing the problem and coming up with solutions because it isn't mere triumphalism on their part, but rather more focus on an honest assessment of pros and cons in theology. Second, by thoroughly criticizing the precedents that Islam is founded upon to utterly discredit its coherence. In order to accomplish this, Ex-Muslims, Jewish Atheists, Ex-Christians, and other critics must be willing to speak honestly about the theological framework of Islam to thoroughly end it. Secularism and secular thought is the antidote when Muslims are willing to engage in discourse.

Therefore, attacking the basis of Sharia is required; that is, the Jewish prophecies within the Jewish holy texts of the Torah and the Old Testament, the Psalms of Daniel, and the gospels of Jesus Christ for the Muslims who believe in parts of the New Testament, and the Quran. Criticizing them would be the best way because a critic would be attacking the underlying assumptions of Islam. If you are a Muslim reading this, I highly encourage you to read the criticisms of Judaism and Christianity in the previous chapters because there is obvious overlap since all three are Abrahamic faiths that pray to the same deity, the Abrahamic God. The criticism of the Exodus, heaven and hell, God and Satan, and the teachings of Jesus all apply as criticisms of Islam too. If you're a critic of Islam who wants to assist in de-conversions of the faith, then the best way is to first help Ex-Muslims feel welcome and then to learn how to criticize Judaism and Christianity. The holy books of the other Abrahamic faiths are the predicates of Islam that Islamic theology itself tries to perfect under the assumption that parts of their holy texts are the perfect and unquestionable word of the Abrahamic God.

---

56. [1137] "UN: Palestinian Children Tortured, Used as Human Shields by Israel." *Haaretz.com*, Haaretz Com, 10 Jan. 2018, www.haaretz.com/.premium-israel-tortured-palestinian-children-1.5283333.
57. [1138] Maltz, Judy. "Israel Tortures Palestinian Children, Amnesty Report Says." *Haaretz.com*, Haaretz Com, 24 Apr. 2018, www.haaretz.com/israel-news/.premium-israel-tortures-palestinian-children-amnesty-report-says-1.5440012.
58. [1139] "Al-Qur'an Al-Kareem - ال كري م ال قرآن." *Surah Al-Ma'idah [5:32-52]*, quran.com/5/32-52.
59. [1140] Tessier, Stephanie, and Muhammad Syed. "Islam: Pull and Peril." *YouTube*, Ex-Muslims of North America, 22 Apr. 2018, www.youtube.com/watch?v=jt1rWgap41g.

Triumphalism of Christianity or Zionism merely confirms to the Muslim mind that Christians and Right-wing Jews are worshiping a corrupt version of their own faith. Targeted systematic extinction campaigns would be purposeful acts of genocide and prove that no Abrahamic faith is peaceful to both the Western and non-Western cultures. Moreover, the Abrahamic faiths primarily developed and still maintain their cultural history of warring desert tribes regardless of how much any of them modernize. Islam, Judaism, and Christianity - despite all their faults - are most certainly proficient at maintaining their unique cultural history of mass murder legitimized through a confluence of nationalism and religion. Islam's revivalist movements of al Qaeda, ISIS's attempt at their own nation-state under theological grounds, and Hamas's strict social control of Gaza despite any and all attempts to sabotage them by Israel show sufficient evidence that Islamic theology can endure and thrive despite the lengthy onslaught of powerful Western military campaigns. The protracted wars of Afghanistan, Iraq, and the United States drone bombings of seven different countries with little to no genuine effort at oversight against civilian deaths all prove as much. In all cases, Abrahamics will always endure and fight each other in endless, bloody warfare to prove their version of faith in the Abrahamic God is the true one. Abrahamics will be Abrahamics and there is no changing any of them through military might. The Abrahamics will never evolve in their thinking from their fixed belief of celebrating violent conflict because of their theology of unquestioned obedience to a hateful, warring God of the desert. Don't pretend these death worshippers didn't have at least 1400 years to change their ways; it's long past the point of pretending they'll ever stop justifying their violence when they keep blaming others, who believe in the same God, as conducting worse than their violence. All so they can continue to act with impunity and self-justify it as morally righteous war from past history to the present.

While modern science will certainly contribute to de-conversions of Muslim people who are science-focused; there is two persistent issues that come into play that preclude that for a larger swathe of Muslims in secular societies. The first is the sense of fear for having betrayed the family in tandem with the fear that their families will violently or psychologically hurt them. The second is the fear that the wider society will treat their personal stories as justification to violently attack, injure, discriminate, and murder Muslims and thereby placing their own families in severe danger within the wider public sphere. Right-wing factions within the contemporary Western world have long stopped treating Muslims as human beings capable of rational thought and instead treat them as homogenized invading monsters. Fear for their families may be part of it, but fear of what the wider public would do to their loved ones is a very real danger. What, for instance, can an Ex-Muslim do to argue against Islam, if they learn some family member was attacked by a violent right-wing leaning person who shouted racist expletives while severely injuring the family member? The Ex-Muslim family member, even in the instance of a secular-minded Muslim household, would face accusations of abetting hate and violence upon their family member. It's primarily the reason Ex-Muslims of North America don't even bother appealing to the right-wing and focus solely on liberals in North America to convince them to take a more secular approach to challenging Islamic theology through debate under heightened security.[1141] They acknowledge the faults of Islam, but still ask liberals for help since left-wing leaning people are on average considered more compassionate and intelligent than most right-wing leaning people. Liberals are capable of seeing Muslims as human beings, act with authentic curiosity and try to understand the other perspectives needs and fears, and try to ameliorate problems that contribute to worsening the social welfare of all people. At the moment, right-wing leaning people only justify their own hate towards others. That is how both a large portion of minorities and the liberal-leaning individuals have come to understand the right-wing through direct experience and survey responses of a large swathe of questions about the polarization within the US by Pew and Gallup polls.[1142][1143] Fortunately, despite the justified fears of violence that US Muslims may feel due to increased reports on social media of neo-Nazi and White Nationalist violence aimed exclusively at them, far-right neo-Nazi and White Nationalist political activists have produced the opposite effect of their political aims throughout the United States. In a 2017 Pew survey, people of all religious affiliations and both major political parties from Evangelical Fundamentalist Christians to self-identified Atheists have reported a major increase in warmer feelings towards all other religious groups including Muslims.[1144] It seems to imply that, despite the culture of social media outrage, the vast majority of people in the United States - regardless of whether they support or oppose President Donald Trump - firmly understand that US Muslims are people just like them who deserve the same civil liberties and human rights that they have.[1145]

60. [1141] Namazie, Maryam, et al. "Equality, Islam and Human Rights." *YouTube*, Ex-Muslims of North America, 26 Mar. 2018, www.youtube.com/watch?v=2W0w9ufJOh0.
61. [1142] Doherty, Carroll. "Key Takeaways on Americans' Growing Partisan Divide over Political Values." *Pew Research Center*, Pew Research Center, 5 Oct. 2017, www.pewresearch.org/fact-tank/2017/10/05/takeaways-on-americans-growing-partisan-divide-over-political-values/.
62. [1143] Dugan, Andrew, and Frank Newport. "Partisan Differences Growing on a Number of Issues." *Gallup.com*, 3 Aug. 2017, news.gallup.com/opinion/polling-matters/215210/partisan-differences-growing-number-issues.aspx?g_source=link_newsv9&g_campaign=item_236315&g_medium=copy.
63. [1144] Mitchell, Travis. "How Americans Feel About Different Religious Groups." *Pew Research Center's Religion & Public Life Project*, Pew Research Center's Religion & Public Life Project, 14 Dec. 2017, www.pewforum.org/2017/02/15/americans-express-increasingly-warm-feelings-toward-religious-groups/.
64. [1145] Mitchell, Travis. "How Americans Feel About Different Religious Groups." *Pew Research Center's Religion & Public Life Project*, Pew Research Center's Religion & Public Life Project, 14 Dec. 2017, www.pewforum.org/2017/02/15/americans-express-increasingly-warm-feelings-toward-religious-groups/.

Chapter 23: A Tool of Anti-Intellectualism

This portion will largely comprise of political commentary and significant quotations of political articles due to the broad range of topics that this subject encompasses. It is simply unavoidable and these articles are not to garner favor for a political objective, but rather to provide a better understanding of what the threat of Islamic terrorism, particularly in the United States and Europe, is partly about and why it is happening. Contentious topics are unavoidable. This portion is not to separate the religious element from the terrorist threat, but to give a clearer picture so that those who aren't aware will finally be given the tools necessary to understand why Islamic terrorism is happening. While Islam is utilized as a political tool to legitimize warfare and other forms of violence, it is also a component of a stronger economic dynamic. This is not to mitigate or ignore Islam's own culpability, but instead to give a better understanding than the mainstream narrative or the political soundbites given through public relations.

Western powers and Islamic monarchies have been able to repeatedly exploit the anti-intellectual elements of Islam to keep denigrating and causing an erasure to all forms of secular progress within predominately Islamic countries. Sometimes even using it as war propaganda; such as when the CIA assisted in the funding of weapons to puritanical Islamic extremists that formed the mujahideen of Afghanistan to fight against the Soviet Union. The US had strongly encouraged Saudi Arabia to spend money in which various Muslims from throughout the Middle East were indoctrinated into a puritanical version of the Islamic faith and called upon to holy war against the "godless" Soviets within Saudi operated schools; these men became so extreme that Islamic countries banned them from re-entry out of fear. The mujahideen, stuck in Afghanistan after the war, then promised revenge upon their erstwhile countries and the United States. US officials largely guffawed at the idea that people inhabiting a remote, desolate area like Afghanistan could ever be a credible threat to the power of the United States; the analogy of a flea attacking an elephant was amply used to joke about the Afghan terrorist threat. It wasn't until President Bill Clinton's time in office that the threat began to be recognized as credible. During the Presidency of Ronald Reagan, the United States funded puritanical Islamic textbooks to teach Afghan school children as young as six to hate and kill Westerners as a duty to Islam. Later on, both President George H.W. Bush and President Clinton continued to use US taxpayer money to fund a USAID endeavor to teach six-year old Afghan children to hate and kill Westerners as a duty to Islam.

The Washington Post's in-depth enterprise reporter Joe Stephens, winner of three George Polk awards, and David B. Ottaway, winner of the Pulitzer Prize for investigative reporting, detail the history and purpose of the Afghan schoolbooks in the article *"From US, the ABC's of Jihad"*:

> In the twilight of the Cold War, the United States spent millions of dollars to supply Afghan schoolchildren with textbooks filled with violent images and militant Islamic teachings, part of covert attempts to spur resistance to the Soviet occupation.

The primers, which were filled with talk of jihad and featured drawings of guns, bullets, soldiers and mines, have served since then as the Afghan school system's core curriculum. Even the Taliban used the American-produced books, though the radical movement scratched out human faces in keeping with its strict fundamentalist code.[1146]

Further along the article, they enumerate in greater detail:

Published in the dominant Afghan languages of Dari and Pashtu, the textbooks were developed in the early 1980s under an AID grant to the University of Nebraska-Omaha and its Center for Afghanistan Studies. The agency spent $51 million on the university's education programs in Afghanistan from 1984 to 1994.

During that time of Soviet occupation, regional military leaders in Afghanistan helped the U.S. smuggle books into the country. They demanded that the primers contain anti-Soviet passages. Children were taught to count with illustrations showing tanks, missiles and land mines, agency officials said. They acknowledged that at the time it also suited U.S. interests to stoke hatred of foreign invaders.

"I think we were perfectly happy to see these books trashing the Soviet Union," said Chris Brown, head of book revision for AID's Central Asia Task Force.

AID dropped funding of Afghan programs in 1994. But the textbooks continued to circulate in various versions, even after the Taliban seized power in 1996.

Officials said private humanitarian groups paid for continued reprintings during the Taliban years. Today, the books remain widely available in schools and shops, to the chagrin of international aid workers.

"The pictures [in] the texts are horrendous to school students, but the texts are even much worse," said Ahmad Fahim Hakim, an Afghan educator who is a program coordinator for Cooperation for Peace and Unity, a Pakistan-based nonprofit.

An aid worker in the region reviewed an unrevised 100-page book and counted 43 pages containing violent images or passages.

The military content was included to "stimulate resistance against invasion," explained Yaquib Roshan of Nebraska's Afghanistan center. "Even in January, the books were absolutely the same . . . pictures of bullets and Kalashnikovs and you name it."

During the Taliban era, censors purged human images from the books. One page from the texts of that period shows a resistance fighter with a bandolier and a Kalashnikov slung from his shoulder. The soldier's head is missing.

Above the soldier is a verse from the Koran. Below is a Pashtu tribute to the mujaheddin, who are described as obedient to Allah. Such men will sacrifice their wealth and life itself to impose Islamic law on the government, the text says.

"We were quite shocked," said Doug Pritchard, who reviewed the primers in December while visiting Pakistan on behalf of a Canada-based Christian nonprofit group. "The constant image of Afghans being natural warriors is wrong. Warriors are created. If you want a different kind of society, you have to create it."[1147]

---

1. [1146] Stephens, Joe, and David B. Ottaway. "From U.S., the ABC's of Jihad." *The Washington Post*, WP Company, 23 Mar. 2002, www.washingtonpost.com/archive/politics/2002/03/23/from-us-the-abcs-of-jihad/d079075a-3ed3-4030-9a96-0d48f6355e54/?utm_term=.cbb9b6b8a59a.
2. [1147] Stephens, Joe, and David B. Ottaway. "From U.S., the ABC's of Jihad." *The Washington Post*, WP

An Al Jazeera America article titled: *"Infidels are our enemy: Afghan fighters cherish old American schoolbooks"* written by freelance journalist, Rob Crilly, details more of the content of these US taxpayer funded schoolbooks and the purpose of their teachings on how Afghan school kids were taught to hate and kill Westerners as a duty to Islam:

"Promoting violence — in the form of jihad against the Soviet invaders and their local proxies — was the goal of the U.S.-funded education effort in the 1980s and early '90s. Textbooks such as "The Alphabet of Jihad Literacy," funded by the U.S. and published by the University of Nebraska at Omaha, came out at a time when the CIA was channeling hundreds of millions of dollars to mujahedeen fighters to resist the Soviet occupation.

USAID funded textbooks for distribution at refugee camps in Pakistan, with content written by mujahedeen groups with the support of Pakistan's Inter-Services Intelligence agency and the CIA.

Burde said the rationale of this indoctrination in the ideas of warfare as religious duty rested on the assumption of the "importance of starting early." While the U.S. program ended with the collapse of Afghanistan's communist government, its textbooks have spawned dozens of copies and revised editions, she said.

She managed to find several old copies of the Pashto-language books and a 2011 edition on sale in the Pakistani city of Peshawar as recently as last year. The Taliban, she said, continues to recommend these books for children.

The majority of the book's 41 lessons glorify violence in the name of religion. "My uncle has a gun," reads the entry for the letter T, using the Pashto word for "gun," "topak." "He does jihad with the gun."

And while some details have changed, references to Soviets and communists remain. More alarmingly for U.S. and international forces still in the country, the textbooks describe all nonbelievers as the enemy.

"Our religion is Islam. Muhammad is our leader. All the Russians and infidels are our enemy."

"Kabul is the capital of our dear country," reads the entry for the letter K. "No one can invade our country. Only Muslim Afghans can rule over this country."

Burde says the anti-infidel message in the U.S.-funded textbook of yore is easily repurposed for those seeking to indoctrinate young Afghans today to support the fight against NATO forces. She discovered in the course of her research that the Taliban today insists the books are used in schools in areas under its control.

Company, 23 Mar. 2002, www.washingtonpost.com/archive/politics/2002/03/23/from-us-the-abcs-of-jihad/d079075a-3ed3-4030-9a96-0d48f6355e54/?utm_term=.cbb9b6b8a59a.

> The failure to defeat the Taliban by the U.S.-led combat mission, which technically concludes at the end of 2014, leaves education statistics as a commonly cited indicator for those seeking to claim success for the longest war in U.S. history.
>
> During its reign, the Taliban banned girls' education. Only about 3 percent of girls were enrolled at school in 2001, according to the World Bank; today that figure is about 36 percent. USAID has spent more than $880 million on education since the fall of the Taliban."[1148]

Islam's legacy and theological underpinnings help utilize it as a tool of manipulation by Western powers for both Western and Western-backed interests. The problem is that the theology of Islam is based on warring desert tribes that is then promoted as the 7th century being the true form of civilization. Therefore, it can be utilized as a tool of both warfare and the destruction of modernity which benefits Western hegemony in the region. Any appreciation and cultural progress can be thoroughly eliminated. Hatred for progress can be amply legitimized as following a more pious version of Islamic theology whenever the West decides to manipulate a Muslim majority society to overthrow leaders that don't kowtow to Western interests.

The US installed nearly all the dictators that make-up OPEC through covert CIA operations. One of the lesser Islamist examples of which would be the Baath party in Iraq. While elements of it could be argued to be secular, Baathism is a political ideology that prided itself through racial supremacy of Arabs under Arab nationalism in conjunction with celebrating Islam as a revolutionary movement. The founder, a Christian by the name of Michel Aflaq, encouraged Arabs to follow an Islamic character because he believed that Islam was proof of Arab wisdom; his ideology was anti-atheist and against Islamic extremism. Baathism was essentially an attempt at combining a secular society with Islamic cultural traditions and Arab supremacy.

The historic transition of Saddam Hussein from a Baathist politician, to a cult-of-personality leader of Iraq that was propped up for US interests, to pushing for an Islamic revivalist movement in response to US sanctions, and then being disposed of once he continued to disobey US interests is of relevance. The effects Saddam's transition had on the Iraqi people is of vital importance in our contemporary time in understanding the wars in the Arab spring. In the initial stages of the Baathist takeover after the Ramadan Revolution in February 1963, the CIA assisted them in targeted assassinations of civilians by compiling a death list of people for the Baathist secret services to assassinate in order for them to consolidate power in Iraq after the successful coup. Killings that Saddam is said to have personally participated in. The targets were mainly doctors and lawyers for the crime of protesting against Baathist rule. The

---

3. [1148] Crilly, Rob. "'Infidels Are Our Enemy': Afghan Fighters Cherish Old American Schoolbooks." *Al Jazeera America*, Al Jazeera America, america.aljazeera.com/articles/2014/12/7/afghan-fighters-americantextbooks.html.

CIA killed any attempt at internal democratic reform and revolution by helping to eliminate the most educated people in Iraq for the crime of democratic dissent in the service of US interests.

As Roger Morris; a historian, foreign policy analyst, and journalist aptly explains in *A Tyrant 40 Years in the Making* in a NY Times article:

> As its instrument the C.I.A. had chosen the authoritarian and anti-Communist Baath Party, in 1963 still a relatively small political faction influential in the Iraqi Army. According to the former Baathist leader Hani Fkaiki, among party members colluding with the C.I.A. in 1962 and 1963 was Saddam Hussein, then a 25-year-old who had fled to Cairo after taking part in a failed assassination of Kassem in 1958.
>
> According to Western scholars, as well as Iraqi refugees and a British human rights organization, the 1963 coup was accompanied by a bloodbath. Using lists of suspected Communists and other leftists provided by the C.I.A., the Baathists systematically murdered untold numbers of Iraq's educated elite -- killings in which Saddam Hussein himself is said to have participated. No one knows the exact toll, but accounts agree that the victims included hundreds of doctors, teachers, technicians, lawyers and other professionals as well as military and political figures.
>
> The United States also sent arms to the new regime, weapons later used against the same Kurdish insurgents the United States had backed against Kassem and then abandoned. Soon, Western corporations like Mobil, Bechtel and British Petroleum were doing business with Baghdad -- for American firms, their first major involvement in Iraq.
>
> But it wasn't long before there was infighting among Iraq's new rulers. In 1968, after yet another coup, the Baathist general Ahmed Hassan al-Bakr seized control, bringing to the threshold of power his kinsman, Saddam Hussein. Again, this coup, amid more factional violence, came with C.I.A. backing. Serving on the staff of the National Security Council under Lyndon Johnson and Richard Nixon in the late 1960's, I often heard C.I.A. officers -- including Archibald Roosevelt, grandson of Theodore Roosevelt and a ranking C.I.A. official for the Near East and Africa at the time -- speak openly about their close relations with the Iraqi Baathists.
>
> This history is known to many in the Middle East and Europe, though few Americans are acquainted with it, much less understand it. Yet these interventions help explain why United States policy is viewed with some cynicism abroad. George W. Bush is not the first American president to seek regime change in Iraq. Mr. Bush and his advisers are following a familiar pattern.[1149]

Before Saddam's blunders with Kuwait and during his rule of secret police, normalization of torture, and penalization for anyone questioning the Baath party's legitimacy; he did institute reforms to improve literacy and make his schools the envy of the Arab world.[1150] According to the federal research division of the Library of Congress in the US, his healthcare was the best in Arab world.[1151] He added free healthcare services that were up to

---

4. [1149] Morris, Roger. "A Tyrant 40 Years in the Making." *The New York Times*, The New York Times, 14 Mar. 2003, www.nytimes.com/2003/03/14/opinion/a-tyrant-40-years-in-the-making.html.
5. [1150] Gause, F. Gregory. "Getting It Backward on Iraq." *Foreign Affairs*, Foreign Affairs, 28 Jan. 2009, www.foreignaffairs.com/articles/iraq/1999-05-01/getting-it-backward-iraq.
6. [1151] "Country Profile: Iraq - Library of Congress." *Library of Congress*, US Government, www.loc.gov/rr/frd/cs/profiles/Iraq.pdf.

Western sophistication in care.[1152] As history later showed, the rule of Saddam Hussein became a grave threat to US interests when Saddam attacked Kuwait which prompted George H.W. Bush to respond with military force. The US ambassador of Iraq had foolishly claimed the US wouldn't interfere with Intra-Arab affairs. President Clinton later followed up George H.W. Bush's sanctions with a policy of Dual Containment that was enthusiastically framed and argued for by Martin Indyk, Assistant Secretary of State for Near East Affairs. The sanctions had devastating effects on the quality of life for Iraqis and led to an infanticide of 500,000 children that the US tried to pass off as Saddam's fault despite the main cause being the Dual Containment policy, which was a unilateral US policy.

F. Gregory Gause III in *Foreign Affairs* article titled "*Getting it Backward on Iraq*" details the devastating effects:

> The latest twist in the Clinton administration's Iraq policy is an attempt to ratchet up military and political pressure on Saddam Hussein. The brief but intensive air campaign of December 1998 -- Operation Desert Fox -- was followed by an expansion of the rules of engagement for American and British pilots patrolling the no-fly zones in northern and southern Iraq. Iraqi provocations and subsequent allied reprisals against Iraqi military targets now occur almost daily.
>
> The administration has also appointed a special coordinator for Iraq, Frank Ricciardone, to oversee implementation of the Iraq Liberation Act and help coordinate efforts by Iraqi opposition groups to overthrow Saddam. Both Ricciardone and Assistant Secretary of State for Near East Affairs Martin Indyk have held public consultations with opposition figures, including representatives of the largest Iraqi Shiite organization, the Supreme Assembly of the Islamic Revolution in Iraq (SAIRI) -- a group the administration had previously avoided because of its close connections to Iran. A serious debate is now underway between those who advocate a greater commitment of American force to topple Saddam and those who argue that containment of Iraq is the only feasible U.S. goal.
>
> This new level of activity and debate, however, has obscured the immediate crisis that U.S. Iraq policy faces. On the ground in Iraq, there is currently no monitoring or inspection of Iraq's capacity to develop and deliver weapons of mass destruction (WMD). The United Nations Special Commission for the disarmament of Iraq (UNSCOM) has effectively ceased to function; its inspectors have been withdrawn and its long-term monitoring systems abandoned.
>
> The United States, meanwhile, continues to support crippling economic sanctions on Iraq that have neither weakened Saddam's hold on power nor prevented him from pursuing his WMD programs. They have, however, reduced the Iraqi people to penury. Iraqi society, once relatively prosperous and solidly middle class, is now mired in a daily struggle for survival. Most people live hand to mouth, relying on

---

7. [1152] "Country Profile: Iraq - Library of Congress." *Library of Congress*, US Government, www.loc.gov/rr/frd/cs/profiles/Iraq.pdf.

inadequate rations provided by the U.N. "oil for food" program. Iraq's medical and educational systems, once the envy of the Arab world, are in disarray. The social disintegration brought on by sanctions is not only a tragedy in its own right, but also diminishes the already slim chance that internal Iraqi discontent could be converted into sustained popular rebellion: people consumed with finding their next meal do not have time to overthrow dictators.[1153]

He continued in a later passage on thorough details of what the sanctions actually did to quell Saddam's ambitions for nuclear weapons and the effects on the innocent Iraqi civilians:

> Economic sanctions undoubtedly limit Saddam's ability to develop and obtain weapons of mass destruction. They restrict the amount of money Baghdad can obtain from oil sales and place the disbursement of those funds under U.N. supervision. But the more relevant question is not whether the sanctions impede Iraqi WMD plans, but rather to what extent. The evidence gathered by UNSCOM indicates that the answer is "not very much." As of October 1998, UNSCOM could not verify Iraq's contentions that it had destroyed critical components of its missile program, 550 mustard-gas shells, 500 chemical and biological bombs, and substantial amounts of biological and chemical weapons materiel. A good-sized WMD program, that is, still probably exists inside Iraq.
>
> What progress there has been in degrading Iraq's unconventional weapons capabilities, moreover, has come through UNSCOM and not the sanctions. President Clinton has famously and correctly said that UNSCOM destroyed more Iraqi WMD resources than did the Gulf War air campaigns. Since 1991, UNSCOM has demolished 48 Scud missiles, 30 chemical and biological missile warheads, 60 missile launch pads, nearly 40,000 chemical bombs and shells in various stages of production, 690 tons of chemical weapons agent, 3 million tons of chemical weapons precursor materials, and the entire al-Hakam biological weapons production facility. Furthermore, UNSCOM's very presence diverted Iraqi resources from developing more WMD to hiding what they already have. International monitoring and inspections are hardly foolproof means of disarming Iraq. But if the major threat to American interests from Iraq is WMD development, then it is much better to have UNSCOM (or something like it) without sanctions than sanctions without UNSCOM.
>
> Sanctions have also been unable to achieve their other goal, the removal of Saddam Hussein from power. He has simply passed on the costs of sanctions to his people while continuing to build palaces and coddle the military and police apparatus that maintains his regime. It might have been reasonable in 1990 or even in 1995 to think that sanctions could bring him down, but it is not reasonable to think so now. If anything, UNSCOM presents more of a threat to Saddam's regime than sanctions do. The tangible limitation of Iraqi sovereignty presented by UNSCOM and the no-fly zones, together with the military actions taken to support them, do far more to weaken Saddam in the eyes of his security and intelligence services than do the sanctions. Moreover, although UNSCOM was hardly a CIA front, as some of the

---

8. [1153] Gause, F. Gregory. "Getting It Backward on Iraq." *Foreign Affairs*, Foreign Affairs, 28 Jan. 2009, www.foreignaffairs.com/articles/iraq/1999-05-01/getting-it-backward-iraq.

more sensational recent reporting has implied, it was indeed one of the few means of gathering intelligence inside Iraq. As with the control of Iraqi WMD programs, if the chief American concern is getting rid of Saddam, then Washington should prefer UNSCOM without sanctions to sanctions without UNSCOM.

The costs of sanctions, meanwhile, have been vividly described by Denis Halliday, the U.N. official who coordinated the "oil for food" program in Baghdad before resigning in protest in August 1998. Halliday contends that the program "remains a largely ineffective response to the humanitarian crisis in the country and has not begun to tackle the underlying infrastructural causes of continuing child mortality and malnutrition." He attributes the death of 500,000 Iraqi children directly to the sanctions. Health services are unable to handle the most basic preventable diseases, like polio and diarrhea, or curtail their spread to epidemic proportions. Thousands of teachers in the Iraqi primary and secondary education systems have simply left their posts, and student dropout rates have reached 30 percent, in a country previously famous in the Arab world for the quality of its education. All this has led to the breakdown of the Iraqi family structure, with high levels of divorce and a growth in single-parent families and prostitution. It is common now to see children begging on the street, an unimaginable sight in Iraq before the 1990s.

The United States and other international actors had the best intentions in building humanitarian exceptions into the original sanctions regime and devising the "oil for food" program. And Saddam certainly bears primary responsibility for the suffering of the Iraqi people. His regime refused to accept "oil for food" aid until 1996, has obstructed its implementation since then, and has refused to disarm as required by the post-Gulf War U.N. Security Council resolutions that established the sanctions in the first place.

But acknowledging Saddam's guilt does not mean exculpating the United States and the rest of the international community, because the hardships in Iraq are predictable and would not be occurring without the sanctions. It is morally obtuse to dismiss the issue by saying, as Secretary of State Madeleine K. Albright did in May 1998, "the fact that Iraqi children are dying is not the fault of the United States, but of Saddam Hussein. . . . [I]t is ridiculous for the United States to be blamed for the dictatorial and cruel, barbaric ways that Saddam Hussein treats his people." Even with the February 1998 expansion of the amount of oil Iraq was permitted to sell under "oil for food," after all, the program remains underfunded. The drop in world oil prices last year drastically reduced the revenue available to the program. And since 40 percent of that revenue is set aside -- three-quarters for contributions to the U.N. Gulf War compensation fund, one-quarter for the operating expenses of U.N. programs in Iraq -- even a perfectly implemented "oil for food" program would not substantially improve the lot of average Iraqis.

The terrible human costs of the sanctions program might be justified if sanctions could be expected to bring down Saddam's regime in the foreseeable future or if they could prevent him from maintaining and expanding his WMD programs. Since they can do neither, it is time to propose trading them away for something else.[1154]

For this specific paragraph only, I feel I must digress to speak as a US citizen and give my personal opinion on this matter: Attempts to exonerate the US from our actions by blaming Saddam is illogical, since the US undertook unilateral sanctions on both Iran and Iraq. That decision was done following the policy that the United States developed and implemented. It was in response to Saddam, but we cannot say on one hand that Saddam is responsible and on the other hand say that Saddam is a crazy person. If he's so psychotic as to not understand reality, and we knew this and then expected rational thought from him after implementing the sanctions, then it is still obviously our fault because our leaders were the responsible party. Moreover, our leaders looked the other way when he may have either ignored when his party committed horrific acts of violence or he participated in some of the most disgusting acts of mass murder and our leaders capitalized in an opportunistic fashion as per the neorealist theory of International Relations.[1155][1156] I'm sorry, but I see no logical reason for this apart from the typical Christian ethics that blames everyone else for its own violent tendencies and apathy after orchestrating violent situations like coups. Our leaders under President Bill Clinton's administration are responsible for the genocide of 500,000 Iraqi children. Our leaders under President George W. Bush are responsible for the death toll that followed the 2003 War in Iraq. President Barack H. Obama's administration is responsible for financing corruption and the deplorably psychotic and illogical policy of "surgical strikes" that resulted in an unaccounted number of mass death upon innocent civilians and children which haven't been properly accounted for because the military treats any sixteen-year old, and sometimes younger people, as a potential insurgent under the policy they're within the vicinity of the blast radius; it is a pathetic joke of an accounting system and shows the inability of the US to handle its own power responsibly.[1157][1158] It shows people utilizing Christian ethics have too much firepower and too little in logical reasoning as per the Christian Standard of reductionist morality. To give credence to this argument, Obama cited Thomas Aquinas Saint Augustine's Just War

---

9. [1154] Gause, F. Gregory. "Getting It Backward on Iraq." *Foreign Affairs*, Foreign Affairs, 28 Jan. 2009, www.foreignaffairs.com/articles/iraq/1999-05-01/getting-it-backward-iraq.
10. [1155] Jentleson, Bruce W. *American foreign policy: the dynamics of choice in the 21st century*. 4th ed., Norton, 2010.
11. [1156] Viotti, Paul R., and Mark V. Kauppi. *International relations theory: realism, pluralism, globalism*. 3rd ed., Macmillan, 1998. For reference, Chapter 2: Realism: The State, Power, and the Balance of Power (55-197).
12. [1157] Becker, Jo, and Scott Shane. "Secret 'Kill List' Proves a Test of Obama's Principles and Will." *The New York Times*, The New York Times, 29 May 2012, www.nytimes.com/2012/05/29/world/obamas-leadership-in-war-on-al-qaeda.html.
13. [1158] Theintercept. "The U.S. Media and the 13-Year-Old Yemeni Boy Burned to Death Last Month by a U.S. Drone." *The Intercept*, 10 Feb. 2015, theintercept.com/2015/02/10/u-s-media-13-year-old-yemeni-boy-killed-u-s-drone/.

Theory as an influence for the legal justification of drone bombings.[1159] In other words, Christian values and ethics motivated the proper engagement of drone strikes. If you believe me to be facetious or disingenuous because you perceive that connection to be tenuous, then explain why Saint Augustine's ethics was one of the justifications cited. If that's going to be his cited defense, then that's justification enough to criticize him for it in any free and open society. If it's part of the general norm of US legal code and has been used as a justification or mandate for war, then it invites Christian theology to be adapted into US law through obfuscation tactics and must be removed. Please see the prior section in which I explain why Christianity has no morality. As for the conditions that led to Saddam's rise in Iraq, attempts by apologists to argue the CIA had nothing to do with the killings of Leftist educators in Iraq should be held with skepticism, since they judge that based on CIA internal reports and the CIA's supposed government watchdog, the Inspector General, is so woefully incompetent that they have been known to "accidentally" delete sensitive CIA files related to heinous human rights crimes of torture in 2016.[1160] If that is the level of oversight to be expected, then why bother trusting the CIA's official statements? They've destroyed their own credibility. In addition, there have been attempts made in more recent times in the duration of writing this book to vindicate the United States of any culpability in the death of hundreds of thousands of Iraqi children. A report by Tim Dyson and Valeria Cetorelli titled: *Changing Views on Child Mortality and Economic Sanctions In Iraq: a history of lies, damned lies, and statistics*" concludes that there was no major rise or decline in child mortality during the sanctions or afterwards during the Iraq war.[1161] This flatly contradicts the material that they cite as evidence; in fact, two of the cited pieces of evidence flatly contradict each other. For example, they quote as follows to explain how the Oil-for-Food Programme has surely declined child mortality:

> Meanwhile there was mounting debate in international circles as to who was responsible for the misery in Iraq. Some commentators blamed the government of Saddam Hussein. However, other observers attributed responsibility to countries like the USA and the UK which most supported maintaining the economic sanctions. One result of the debate was that in April 1995 the UN Security Council passed the first of several resolutions aimed at improving conditions in Iraq by permitting the sale of oil so that food and medicine could be imported. This became known as the Oil-for-Food Programme (OFFP). But the negotiations with Saddam Hussein's government to implement the OFFP were very slow. Eventually, however, one close observer of the situation was able to comment that '[s]ince March 1998 the oil for food programme has greatly increased access to essential supplies and the mortality rate [of children under 5] has surely declined.'[1162]

14. [1159] Becker, Jo, and Scott Shane. "Secret 'Kill List' Proves a Test of Obama's Principles and Will." *The New York Times*, The New York Times, 29 May 2012, www.nytimes.com/2012/05/29/world/obamas-leadership-in-war-on-al-qaeda.html.
15. [1160] Hattem, Julian. "CIA Watchdog 'Accidentally Destroyed' Copy of 'Torture Report'." TheHill, The Hill, 17 May 2016, thehill.com/policy/national-security/280002-cia-watchdog-accidentally-destroyed-only-copy-of-torture-report.
16. [1161] Dyson, Tim, and Valeria Cetorelli. "Changing Views on Child Mortality and Economic Sanctions in Iraq: a History of Lies, Damned Lies and Statistics." *BMJ Global Health*, BMJ Specialist Journals, 1 July 2017, gh.bmj.com/content/2/2/e000311#ref-8.
17. [1162] Dyson, Tim, and Valeria Cetorelli. "Changing Views on Child Mortality and Economic Sanctions in Iraq: a History of Lies, Damned Lies and Statistics." *BMJ Global Health*, BMJ Specialist Journals, 1 July

The cited material is "*Morbidity and Mortality among Iraqi Children from 1990 through 1998*" by Richard Garfield. Garfield's General Findings portion explain that the report's methods are using the most accurate estimates by utilizing a logistic regression model from a multiple imputation procedure which successfully predicted prior child mortality rates in Iraq.[1163] The report estimates eighty deaths per a thousand births of Iraqi children five years of age or younger.[1164] Garfield goes onto explain that this likely means between August 1991 and March 1998, the model predicts a minimum approximation of 100,000 excess deaths of children five years of age or younger and the far more likely estimation of approximately 227,000 children five years of age or younger that died.[1165] These premature deaths are mainly due to respiratory illness or diarrhea.[1166] About a quarter of the estimated deaths are related to the Gulf war, but the rest are attributed to the US sanctions.[1167] Garfield explains the excess deaths occur mainly in the Southern administrative areas of the country among the less-educated rural areas.[1168] After explaining this information, Garfield further elaborates that the excess deaths are mainly attributed to contaminated water, lack of quality food for children to eat, inadequate breastfeeding, poor weaning practices, and of course, inadequate supplies from the healthcare system.[1169] After that, the material cited by Dyson and Cetorelli is stated. Here is the full context of the quote being cited as evidence from the General Findings of Garfield's report, it is in the second paragraph:

> Given the most likely estimate of 227,000, there were an average of about 60 excess deaths each day. These child deaths far outnumber all deaths on all sides, among combatants and civilians, during the Gulf war. It exceeds the number of deaths known to result from any of the bombing raids in Iraq even on the days of the bombings. It exceeds each week the number of deaths that occurred in the tragic bombing of the 2 Al Furdos bomb shelter during the Gulf war. That incident caused an international uproar, an apology from the Joint Military Command, and a revision in the procedures for selecting targets.

2017, gh.bmj.com/content/2/2/e000311#ref-8.
18. [1163] "Morbidity and Mortality Among Iraqi Children from 1990 Through 1998: Assessing the Impact of the Gulf War and Economic Sanctions." *Morbidity and Mortality Among Iraqi Children*, reliefweb.int/sites/reliefweb.int/files/resources/A2E2603E5DC88A4685256825005F211D-garfie17.pdf.
19. [1164] "Morbidity and Mortality Among Iraqi Children from 1990 Through 1998: Assessing the Impact of the Gulf War and Economic Sanctions." *Morbidity and Mortality Among Iraqi Children*, reliefweb.int/sites/reliefweb.int/files/resources/A2E2603E5DC88A4685256825005F211D-garfie17.pdf.
20. [1165] "Morbidity and Mortality Among Iraqi Children from 1990 Through 1998: Assessing the Impact of the Gulf War and Economic Sanctions." *Morbidity and Mortality Among Iraqi Children*, reliefweb.int/sites/reliefweb.int/files/resources/A2E2603E5DC88A4685256825005F211D-garfie17.pdf.
21. [1166] "Morbidity and Mortality Among Iraqi Children from 1990 Through 1998: Assessing the Impact of the Gulf War and Economic Sanctions." *Morbidity and Mortality Among Iraqi Children*, reliefweb.int/sites/reliefweb.int/files/resources/A2E2603E5DC88A4685256825005F211D-garfie17.pdf.
22. [1167] "Morbidity and Mortality Among Iraqi Children from 1990 Through 1998: Assessing the Impact of the Gulf War and Economic Sanctions." *Morbidity and Mortality Among Iraqi Children*, reliefweb.int/sites/reliefweb.int/files/resources/A2E2603E5DC88A4685256825005F211D-garfie17.pdf.
23. [1168] "Morbidity and Mortality Among Iraqi Children from 1990 Through 1998: Assessing the Impact of the Gulf War and Economic Sanctions." *Morbidity and Mortality Among Iraqi Children*, reliefweb.int/sites/reliefweb.int/files/resources/A2E2603E5DC88A4685256825005F211D-garfie17.pdf.
24. [1169] "Morbidity and Mortality Among Iraqi Children from 1990 Through 1998: Assessing the Impact of the Gulf War and Economic Sanctions." *Morbidity and Mortality Among Iraqi Children*, reliefweb.int/sites/reliefweb.int/files/resources/A2E2603E5DC88A4685256825005F211D-garfie17.pdf.

> Reaction to the much greater number of child deaths associated with sanctions has been far more muted. Confusion over the number of deaths and rhetorical argument over which side is responsible for those deaths has prevented the international community from focusing more effectively on how to prevent their continued occurrence.
>
> Studies from 1996 onward suggest that there was little decline in mortality rates at that time. Since March 1998 the oil for food program has greatly increased access to essential supplies and the mortality rate has surely declined, but data are not yet available to estimate the magnitude of that decline. Indeed, the failure to institute stepped-up monitoring when sanctions were initiated in 1990 continues to limit the capacity to carry out timely and reliable assessments of humanitarian conditions in Iraq. Despite a steep rise in mortality rates, most Iraqi children survive under the social, economic, and political crises of the 1990s in Iraq but experience profound limitations on their health and well being. Far more attention needs to be devoted to identifying and minimizing the humanitarian damage to the Iraqis alive today, in preparation for an eventual shift from relief to reconstruction and development in the years ahead.[1170]

The other cited material which contradicts them is their fifth citation. The citation is of Michael Spagat's work *"Truth and Death in Iraq Under Sanctions"* which argues in its concluding remarks that the new information, which cites the same examination of the four surveys of Iraq that Dyson and Cetorelli use, would tragically mean that President George W. Bush's 2003 Invasion of Iraq most likely resulted in more child deaths and not a reduction of it as Prime Minister Tony Blair argued in the Chilcot Inquiry.[1171] As such, I don't find the conclusion of Dyson and Cetorelli's report convincing given the evidence that they have cited. However, I would be happy to be proven wrong about this and if I have ignored a critical piece of information, then I shall change my views and update this material accordingly in a subsequent edition. Furthermore, I profusely apologize for any potential insensitivity on this highly politicized topic to any of the Iraqi families impacted as I am not attempting to dehumanize the loss of innocent children. At the moment and given the evidence, I do believe that I have an obligation as a US citizen to speak out and say that the United States government is either equally to blame as Saddam Hussein or both Democrat and Republican administrations and the US Congresses that presided over those time periods are most responsible for the death of however many hundreds of thousands of Iraqi children that died as a result of the US sanctions. Human rights means nothing if we trivialize the deaths of the most vulnerable. If they conducted actions that resulted in those hundreds of thousands of deaths and made no effort to change the situation to relieve innocent children of their suffering, then why should they not be forced to recognize the consequences of their decisions and accept responsibility? Likewise, I praise them for humanitarian efforts that often go far too unnoticed like Operation Provide Comfort and Operation Provide Comfort II to the Kurds who fled their homes in northern Iraq and were subsequently given humanitarian aid by the US, UK, France, and Turkey.[1172] Finally, please understand that this argument is not due to any acrimony, but

---

25. [1170] "Morbidity and Mortality Among Iraqi Children from 1990 Through 1998: Assessing the Impact of the Gulf War and Economic Sanctions." *Morbidity and Mortality Among Iraqi Children*, reliefweb.int/sites/reliefweb.int/files/resources/A2E2603E5DC88A4685256825005F211D-garfie17.pdf.
26. [1171] Spagat, Michael. *Truth and Death in Iraq under Sanctions*. rss.onlinelibrary.wiley.com/doi/pdf/10.1111/j.1740-9713.2010.00437.x.
27. [1172] "Operation Provide Comfort." *Wikipedia*, Wikimedia Foundation, 26 May 2019, en.wikipedia.org/wiki/Operation_Provide_Comfort.

rather my own personal understanding that the religious belief in an afterlife is just a coping mechanism that people use to justify barbarity; if you believe that children who die prematurely get an automatic ticket to heaven, then consider the idea that you are rationalizing their deaths out of your own selfish convenience and not being empathetic to the victims' families. Speaking as a US citizen, I believe that it is simply a willful self-delusion to ignore the consequences of the US government's actions; a yearning to ignore the harsh reality of children being killed by the people that we in the US largely voted into power so that we don't have to look at the facts, accept what has happened, and honestly self-reflect.

Saddam's "Return to Faith" movement seems to be in response to the initial sanctions by the US, it helped solidify the rise in Islamism as a direct result of Indyk's genocide under the Dual Containment policy. UNSCOM did more to stop Saddam's program than the Dual Containment policy and for that matter, Saddam wouldn't have risen to power had the US not helped thoroughly kill off the opposition. The Iraqi people wouldn't have fallen into Islamic extremism without the sanctions that resulted in such widespread death of children as young as five-years of age.

Beirut Bureau chief of the Washington Post, Liz Sly, in the article "*The Hidden Hand Behind Islamic State Militant's? Saddam Hussein's*" reports on the "Return to Faith" movement:

> At first glance, the secularist dogma of Hussein's tyrannical Baath Party seems at odds with the Islamic State's harsh interpretation of the Islamic laws it purports to uphold.
>
> But the two creeds broadly overlap in several regards, especially their reliance on fear to secure the submission of the people under the group's rule. Two decades ago, the elaborate and cruel forms of torture perpetrated by Hussein dominated the discourse about Iraq, much as the Islamic State's harsh punishments do today.
>
> Like the Islamic State, Hussein's Baath Party also regarded itself as a transnational movement, forming branches in countries across the Middle East and running training camps for foreign volunteers from across the Arab world.
>
> By the time U.S. troops invaded in 2003, Hussein had begun to tilt toward a more religious approach to governance, making the transition from Baathist to Islamist ideology less improbable for some of the disenfranchised Iraqi officers, said Ahmed S. Hashim, a professor who is researching the ties at Singapore's Nanyang Technological University.
>
> With the launch of the Iraqi dictator's Faith Campaign in 1994, strict Islamic precepts were introduced. The words "God is Great" were inscribed on the Iraqi flag. Amputations were decreed for theft. Former Baathist officers recall friends who suddenly stopped drinking, started praying and embraced the deeply conservative form of Islam known as Salafism in the years preceding the U.S. invasion.
>
> In the last two years of Hussein's rule, a campaign of beheadings, mainly targeting women suspected of prostitution and carried out by his elite Fedayeen unit, killed more than 200 people, human rights groups reported at the time.[1173]

---

28. [1173] Sly, Liz. "The Hidden Hand behind the Islamic State Militants? Saddam Hussein's." *The Washington*

Sadly, the suffering of Iraqi civilians continues even as of writing this. The US continued following the neo-realist theory of International Relations and kept cutting and diving Iraq until it collapsed on itself due to the increased hatred between Sunni-Shia as a direct result of US policy, in which President Obama supported an Iranian puppet for President and helped shut out the Sunnis from democratic legislature.[1174][1175] Around this time, Western media saw fit to portray Iraqis as too stupid for democracy and at sole fault for all the suffering the US imposed upon them. Any and all peaceful protests by Sunnis were met with thorough disdain and ignored until they rose to violence; only then did Western media begin reporting in again on the situation in Iraq. To portray not an angry people that were shut out of the democratic process they wanted to be part of or the systematic shut out of healthcare and jobs that was encouraged by the US to further divide Iraq, but rather just scary religious fanatics to stoke more fear and hate to continue war upon war in endless succession.

One may be prompted to ask: why does the US do this? How does the US benefit from such suffering? What purpose does it serve US interests?

One may be prompted to continue blaming Iraqis for the suffering the US imposed. After all, what about ISIS's genocide of Iraqi Christians and other minority groups? Sadly, people must realize that violence itself is a social contagion. Similar to how one is prompted to laugh when they see someone laugh for no explicable reason, violence gains social acceptance and becomes normalized during times of grave suffering with no explicable cause. The geopolitical reasons wouldn't really be understood by the majority, and even if it was, the sensory experience of seeing children drop dead from curable diseases, the deterioration of quality care hospitals, and the Return to Faith horrors that Saddam contributed to the suffering imposed by the US would only prompt normal denizens of Iraq to blame their neighbors and see it as some reckoning of the Abrahamic God in punishing them for going against their Islamic faith. Conditions of immense suffering and mass death tolls only ever prompt widespread religious fanaticism because it provides a sense of meaning and illusion of control so that people can believe that their suffering can be changed.[1176][1177] It's fundamentally irrational, but it helps people cope and adapt to unmitigated death and devastation around them.[1178] The Western media and US government know this, and they know how to continue exploiting the suffering and mental lassitude of the Iraqis for their own self-interests.

Post, WP Company, 4 Apr. 2015, www.washingtonpost.com/world/middle_east/the-hidden-hand-behind-the-islamic-state-militants-saddam-husseins/2015/04/04/aa97676c-cc32-11e4-8730-4f473416e759_story.html?utm_term=.ef5d225bf17b.

29. [1174] Al-Ali, Zaid. "How Maliki Ruined Iraq." *Foreign Policy*, Foreign Policy, 19 June 2014, foreignpolicy.com/2014/06/19/how-maliki-ruined-iraq/.
30. [1175] Jentleson, Bruce W. *American foreign policy: the dynamics of choice in the 21st century*. 4th ed., Norton, 2010.
31. [1176] Kahneman, Daniel. *Thinking, fast and slow*. Farrar, Straus and Giroux, 2015.
32. [1177] Hedges, Chris. *War Is a Force That Gives Us Meaning*. PublicAffairs, 2002.
33. [1178] Hedges, Chris. *War Is a Force That Gives Us Meaning*. PublicAffairs, 2002.

So then, what did the US gain from creating this horrific death toll under Indyk's Dual Containment policy? What did US policymakers consider worth the lives of 500,000 people - most of them five-year old children dying of curable diseases? People may immediately attribute it to the defense of Israel or the prevention of Saddam becoming worse than what he was. But in reality, it was to maintain deals with OPEC and keep the US financial system intact. It is chiefly the agreement with Saudi Arabia and other Gulf allies that motives US foreign policy in the Middle East. The Gulf allies are our closest allies in the region; Israel is chiefly protected to legitimize Christians in the US for signing up to go to war, to test sophisticated weaponry on Palestinians to then sell to the Arab dictatorships, and to form negative interdependence so that the US can continue holding a monopoly on weapons sales to keep the US economy the strongest in the world. Despite all the special privileges that Israel is presumed to have, they're given special treatment because they are the US's pawn to manipulate and use to further US self-interests. Saddam Hussein had sought to change his oil currency to the Euro and that prompted the US to invade Iraq. The reason is that the US arranged dealings with OPEC. That is, an agreement largely with the dictators that the US itself installed; to protect their borders from invasion, fight their wars, and keep the geopolitical structure of the Middle East intact with a balance of power in the region. All the Islamic dictators and other members of OPEC had to do was peg oil on the US dollar. The US would keep its world reserve currency status, which was necessary in the struggle against the Soviet Union, and oil would be interlocked with the supply and demand of the US dollar to ensure US hegemony. The region of the Gulf is largely broken-up into different Arab countries in order to prevent any united Arab or Islamic empire from rising, such as what ISIS attempted to do with a united Sunni caliphate across the territories of Iraq and Syria. The broken-up nation-states is how the US prefers their economic and political order in the region to manage its own grip on the world. Without the demand for the US dollar, or a disruption in which oil was no longer pegged on the US dollar, the US economy would crumble because it would become a worthless international currency and there would be no interest in pursuing investments in the US itself with no demand for the currency.

In the article, *Non-Dollar Trading Is Killing the Petrodollar - and the Foundation of US-Saudi Policy in the Middle East,* by British diplomat Alastair Crooke, Mr. Crooke details a brief history of the US-Saudi policy:

THE RISE OF THE PETRODOLLAR

The dollar's role as the world's reserve currency was first established in 1944 with the Bretton Woods agreement. The U.S. was able assume this role by virtue of it then having the largest gold reserves in the world. The dollar was pegged at $35 an ounce — and freely exchangeable into gold at that rate. But by 1971, convertibility into gold was no longer viable as America's gold resources drained away. Instead, the dollar became a pure fiat currency (decoupled from any physical store of value), until the petrodollar agreement was concluded by President Nixon in 1973.

The essence of the deal was that the U.S. would agree to military sales and defense of Saudi Arabia in return for all oil trade being denominated in U.S. dollars.

As a result of this agreement, the dollar then became the only medium in which energy exchange could be transacted. This underpinned its reserve currency status through the need for foreign governments to hold dollars; recirculated the dollar costs of oil back into the U.S. financial system and — crucially — made the dollar effectively convertible into barrels of oil. The dollar was moved from a gold standard onto a crude oil standard.

U.S. interest rates were then managed so that oil exporters (who formerly looked to gold as the basis of their reserves) would be indifferent to whether they stored their currency reserves, earned from oil exports, in U.S. treasuries, or in gold. The value was equivalent.

According to *Sprott Global*, a specialist U.S. energy consultancy:

"The Fed consistently managed Fed funds rates to keep oil prices steady, even when it required mid-teens interest rates and back-to-back recessions in 1980-1982. Since U.S. Fed funds rates were managed to preserve U.S. creditors' and oil exporters' purchasing power in oil terms, the system proved acceptable to most nations.

While the petrodollar arrangement worked well for nearly 30 years, the arrangement began to wobble around 2002-2004. . . Oil prices began steadily rising in 2002 and 2003 while Fed funds rates remained low to mitigate the fallout from the 2001 U.S. recession/tech bubble.

As a result, the number of barrels of oil that could be purchased for a face value U.S. Treasury bond declined sharply. . . After maintaining a range of 55-60 barrels of oil per U.S. Treasury from 1986-1999, a $1,000 face value U.S. Treasury went from buying 60 barrels of oil in 1999 to under 30 by early 2004."

TOO MANY DOLLARS

But what may ultimately be seen to have proved fateful to the petrodollar system has been the policy of zero interest rate policy and "quantitative easing" pursued so unrestrainedly since 2008. Effectively, energy producers saw that the U.S. economy had now become so dependent on low interest rates that it could never again manage to keep oil prices steady relative to U.S. treasuries without blowing up the global financial system.[1179]

Dr. Ibrahim M. Oweiss, an Egyptian-born American, international economic advisor, and professor of economics at Georgetown University provides a detailed explanation of the US petrodollar system in "*Petrodollar: Problems and Prospects*."[1180] These details require an advanced understanding of economics, but they're of prominent importance in understand the relationship between the US and the Middle East. I'll summarize the gist of the information at

---

34. [1179] Crooke, Alastair. "Non-Dollar Trading Is Killing the Petrodollar -- And the Foundation of U.S.-Saudi Policy in the Middle East." *HuffPost*, HuffPost, 1 Feb. 2015, www.huffpost.com/entry/petrodollar-us-saudi-policy_b_6245914.
35. [1180] Oweiss, Ibrahim M. "Economics of Petrodollars." *Http://Faculty.georgetown.edu*, The Committee for Monetary Research and Education, faculty.georgetown.edu/imo3/petrod/petro2.htm.

the end. However, a brief summary wouldn't be a true understanding of this complex financial system. As such, I encourage you, the reader, to take the time to look-up the definitions when need be to gain a proper understanding of this complex, multi-faceted, and powerful system that has shaped the lives of both US citizens and the people of the Arab Spring.

Definition of Petrodollars

Petrodollars may be defined as the U.S. dollar earned front the sale of oil, or they may be simply defined as oil revenues denominated in U.S. dollars. Petrodollars accrued to oil-exporting nations depend on the sale price of oil as well as the volume being sold abroad, which is in turn dependent on oil production. The overall world supply of oil, on the one hand, and the world demand, on the other hand, determine sooner or later an actual market price for oil regardless of any administered pricing system. A price determined by OPEC can be maintained only so long as there is sufficient demand to absorb the amount being supplied in world markets. If demand exceeds supply, oil will be sold at an even higher price than that determined by OPEC. The opposite holds true when an oil glut occurs. This is reflected in a drop in the price after a certain time lag regardless of the price dictated by OPEC. The experience of the seventies and the eighties is no more than art application of microeconomic tools to the pricing of oil in world markets.

Petrodollar surpluses may also be defined as the net U.S. dollars earned from the sale of oil that are in excess of internal development needs. Petrodollar surpluses, accrued in the process of converting subsoil wealth into an internal income-generating capital stock, refers to oil production that exceeds such needs but is transformed into monetary units.

Since petrodollars and petrodollar surpluses are by definition denominated in U.S. dollars, then purchasing power is dependent on the U.S. rate of inflation and the rate at which the U.S. dollar is exchanged (whenever there is need for convertibility) by other currencies in international money markets. It follows that whenever economic or other factors affect the U.S. dollar, petrodollars will be affected to the same magnitude. The link, therefore, between the U.S. dollar and petrodollar surpluses, in particular, has significant economic, political, and other implications.

First, the placement of petrodollar surpluses of the Arab oil exporting nations in the United States may be regarded politically as *hostage capital*. In the event of a major political conflict between the United States and an Arab oil-exporting nation, the former with all its military power can confiscate or freeze these assets or otherwise limit their use. It can impose special regulations or at least use regulations for a time, in order to attain certain political, economic, or other goals. It may be argued that such actions are un-American, since they are a direct violation of the sacred principles of capitalism and economic freedom. Nevertheless, the U.S. government resorted to such weapons twice in the 1980s against Iranian and Libyan assets. It follows, therefore, that governments placing their petrodollar surpluses in the United States may lose part of their economic and political independence. Consequently, the more petrodollar surpluses are placed in the United States by a certain oil-exporting nation, the less independent such a nation becomes.

Second, an oil-exporting country can have petrodollar surpluses only if its absorptive capacity is less than its earnings from the sale of oil for any particular period of time. It follows, therefore, that petrodollar surpluses depend on oil prices, quantities exported, and the nation's absorptive capacity.

Third, petrodollar surpluses do not represent *real wealth* but rather are a vehicle by which the latter can be acquired. If kept in liquid form such as paper dollars, their purchasing power will gradually be eroded by inflation and adverse foreign exchange rates. Both are affected in the United States by a host of variables, for example, money supply, interest rates, marginal productivity, stage of a business cycle, and balance-of-payments deficit. Also a factor is U.S. monetary and fiscal policy which in turn affects some of these variables. Furthermore, changes in the U.S. laws and regulations have an impact on the economic variables, which may affect inflation rates and foreign exchange rates. Thus, the purchasing power of liquid petrodollar surpluses belonging, for example, to Arab oil-exporting nations is determined by a complicated set of variables whose trends and quantities are a function of factors that are not in the control of these countries.

Fourth, efficient allocation of petrodollars for internal investments could increase the productive capacity of an oil-exporting nation and may work to its relative advantage. However, dependency on imported consumer goods, including luxury and rare collector's items, promotes the export of limited resources that could have been otherwise used for internal capital development.

Fifth, the economic development of an oil-exporting nation is based on the conversion of its subsoil resources into other assets such as industrial plants, equipment, education, technology, infrastructure, and other forms of real wealth, that is, real capital stock. Obviously the conversion process can be carried on at different rates. An optimum rate is achieved when oil is pumped at a level that can maximize the present discounted value of the income created in the conversation process. By pumping oil in excess of an optimum production rate, countries such as Saudi Arabia, Kuwait, Qatar, the United Arab Emirates, and others accumulated petrodollar surpluses until 1981. It is worth noting that the difference between the volume of oil actually supplied and the volume that should have been supplied in observance of standard microeconomic theory is in fact *a subsidy granted, in real terms,* to oil-importing nations such as the United States, Germany, France, and Japan.[1181]

Allocation of Petrodollar Surpluses

The bulk of petrodollar surpluses is held either in U.S. treasury bills and other short-term instruments or in American and Western European banks. An examination of balance sheets of banks operating in Saudi Arabia, Kuwait, Qatar, Bahrain, the United Arab Emirates, and Oman reveals that most of their monetary assets are deposited in foreign banks in Europe and the United States. Petrodollar surpluses have also been used to increase the official reserves of the oil-exporting countries at both the International Monetary Fund and the International Bank for Reconstruction and Development.[2]

Petrodollar surpluses have been recycled by commercial banks in the United States and other industrialized nations as well as by international institutions. By drawing against petrodollar surpluses as deposits or certificates of deposits, banks were able to expand their volume of lending. For bankers the most obvious clients were the developing countries, mainly in Latin America, such as Mexico, Brazil, and Argentina.

The process of petrodollar recycling makes it possible for commercial banks of industrialized nations, international lending institutions, and Arab banking consortia to provide financial assistance to less-developed countries (LDCs). Western Europe, Japan, and the United States buy oil from oil-exporting countries (OECs). LDCs pay for oil imports and other foreign goods and services with money borrowed front Western commercial banks. The process of recycling is complete when those commercial banks and institutions obtain cash and investments from OECs.

Petrodollar surpluses have also contributed to the growth of the Euromoney market, which was treated by the Soviet Union in the fifties, when it opened a dollar account in London. Its purpose was to protect the Soviets from a U.S. freeze on their deposits, which could happen if such deposits were placed in the United States. Prior to the first oil shock of 1973, the main source of Eurodollars was the U.S. balance-of-payments deficits; these grew from $17 billion in 1964 to $96 billion in 1970. Additionally, several regulations set by the Department of the Treasury discouraged American multinational corporations from repatriating profits from overseas operations; thus, these deposits remained in Europe and served as a source of international finance. In 1971 U.S. balance-of-payments deficits suddenly tripled, thus

---

36. [1181] Oweiss, Ibrahim M. "Definition of Petrodollars." *Http://Faculty.georgetown.edu*, The Committee for Monetary Research and Education, faculty.georgetown.edu/imo3/petrod/define.htm.

precipitating a huge leap in dollar holdings in foreign banks that led to a massive expansion of money supplies in member countries of the Organization of Economic Cooperation and Development (OECD). In my opinion this was one of the main causes of the leap in the rate of inflation and the economic disequilibrium that came long before the rise in the price of oil at the end of 1973.

Another major use of petrodollars has been for foreign aid. Since 1973 Arab oil-exporting countries have been among the ranks of the major donors of the world. Basically, Arab states distribute aid in five ways, through (1) bilateral agreements; (2) multilateral arrangements; (3) official development assistance (ODA) flows; (4) various Arab funds established specifically to extend loans for development projects in foreign countries; and (5) the International Monetary Fund as well as the International Bank for Reconstruction and Development, by providing them with loans that are recycled to other countries in need to finance balance of payments deficits or development projects. It should be noted that Arab oil-exporting countries had extended a total of approximately $44 billion in foreign aid between 1973 and 1980. It is also important to point out that the ODA flows as a percentage of gross national product were the highest in Arab oil exporting nations, as compared with the United States and all other countries.[3] Indeed, even after the substantial decline in oil revenues, Arab funds for economic development are still active in their lending policy.

At any rate, Petrodollar surpluses accumulated after the oil shocks of 1973 arid 1979 became the second major source of outside funds, after the U.S. balance-of-payments deficits, feeding into the Euromoney market. Such surpluses whetted the appetite of Western banks, which had eagerly sought borrowers for the new Euromarket deposits.

From 1974 to the end of 1981 total current account petrodollar surpluses were approximately $450.5 billion for all members of OPEC.[4] It should be noted ill this regard that prior to 1979 Iran had accumulated some petrodollar surpluses, although the Arab OECs had acquired over 90 percent of OPEC's investable surpluses. Since 1979 OPEC's surplus has been generated mainly by the Arab Gulf countries and Libya. Since tile beginning of the 1980s Saudi Arabia alone has accounted for 42 percent of the amount of the surplus, followed by Kuwait (18 percent), Iraq (17 percent), the United Arab Emirates (11 percent), Libya (8 percent), and Qatar (3 percent).

According to the U.S. Treasury information petrodollar surpluses have turned into deficits since 1982. In my opinion there are three main reasons for this turn of events: increase in imports by oil-exporting nations; reduction in the demand for oil, particularly from OPEC; and the oil glut. which led to a reduction in its price.[1182]

Increase in Imports

Since 1974 oil-exporting nations have substantially increased their imports in order to finance development plans and to pay for highly technical military training, equipment, and sophisticated defense systems such as the airborne warning and control system, AWACS. From 1972 to 1983, OPECs imports increased approximately sevenfold. Furthermore, exports to OPEC from OECD as a percentage of the latter's total exports increased from 4.1 percent in 1972-73 to 8.8 percent in 1975-82, then to 8.4 percent in 1983; and it dropped to 7.1 percent in 1984. In spite of the absolute and relative increase in OPEC's imports from OECD, the latter had had a deficit in its balance of trade with the former as a result of the increase in the oil bill. However, this situation has been reversed since 1982.

The United States, for example, as a major trading nation with oil-exporting countries, had had a deficit in its balance of trade with Saudi Arabia in the period 1974-81. Since 1982 the U.S. balance of trade with Saudi Arabia showed an ever-increasing surplus; at the same time the overall U.S. balance of trade showed ever-increasing deficits.[5]

---

37. [1182] Oweiss, Ibrahim M. "Allocation of Petrodollar Surpluses." *Http://Faculty.georgetown.edu*, The Committee for Monetary Research and Education, faculty.georgetown.edu/imo3/petrod/allocate.htm.

There are several explanations for the reversal of the OECD's trade deficit with OPEC to a surplus. First, the substantial increase in expenditures for developmental programs in OPEC had necessitated the importation of heavy equipment and technical know-how, mainly front OECD. Second, with an unprecedented increase in per capita income, demand for luxury and consumer goods imported from OECD increased substantially. Income elasticity and the concomitant demand for such imported items showed that the relative increase in the quantity of these imports was even greater than the relative change in the per capita income in Saudi Arabia, Kuwait, Qatar, the United Arab Emirates, Oman, and Libya during the period 1974-81. Third, stimulated by the sudden upward leap in the price of oil in 1979 the OECD attempted to reduce demand for imported oil through an expansion of their internal supplies whenever possible; in addition the overall demand for oil was reduced through conservation and substitution effects. Fourth, with reduced capacity utilization of industry in the OECD as a result of the 1980 recession, demand for energy and oil was further curtailed. Fifth, OPEC members with major petrodollar surpluses had substantially increased their demand for imported weapons and military hardware in addition to unprecedented training programs carried out by Western experts either for defense purposes or for the needs of wars, such as, since September 1980, the protracted fight between Iraq and Iran.

Furthermore, oil-exporting nations, particularly the Gulf Arab countries and more specifically Saudi Arabia, had embarked on ambitious development programs since the early seventies. Having the largest dollar volume program of any other oil-exporting country, Saudi Arabia introduced to the field of economic development a unique and impressive model. Over the course of' twelve years, a modern and extensive infrastructure, including six-lane highways with overpasses and cloverleaf intersections, huge airports, several new ports, immense university buildings, housing, hospitals, communications, and public utilities, was completed, using the most sophisticated modern technology. In addition, Saudi Arabia expanded its agricultural production to tile extent that it has become a net exporter of wheat. Industrialization was also emphasized as the country built the two industrial cities of Jubail and Yanbu. The mammoth site of Jubail alone is the largest civil engineering work in history. The construction of the city in the desert necessitated moving about 370 million cubic meters of earth--enough to build a road nine meters wide and one meter deep around the equator. Jubail's industrial park of 1,100 hectares is the largest in the world. It includes 125 petroindustries and the secondary and supporting industries, in addition to a highly technical center with an ampitheater and educational facilities for training and retraining. It should be noted that major recipients of contracts in Saudi Arabia were American companies, in particular the Bechtel Corporation located in San Francisco.

Out of its sales of 35 billion barrels of crude oil during the first three development plans, in 1970-85, Saudi Arabia spent approximately $550 billion on development programs. It expects to spend another $275 billion on the current, fourth development plan, 1985-90.[6]

The economies of industrialized nations, in particular the United States, benefited significantly from the export of capital goods and services as well its consulate goods to meet the needs of such unprecedented development programs, with their massive expenditures. The gain that accrued to the industrialized nations was not restricted to the companies directly involved in business with the oil-exporting nations; it also affected all the other, related industries and economic activities through the multiplier effect of jobs created, incomes generated, and taxes collected.

In addition to their huge development programs, oil-exporting nations also significantly increased their purchase of military hardware. From 1979, after the second oil-price leap, to 1980 Bahrain, Kuwait, Oman, and Qatar increased their military purchases tenfold while tile United Arab Emirates increased them by more than six times. And Saudi Arabia's figures rose from $3.5 billion to $8 billion in one year.[7] It should be noted, however, that while actual delivery of weapons increased greatly after the 1979 oil shock, it tapered off for most of the countries in the following years as petrodollar surpluses were drying up.

The Iran-Iraq war since September 1980 drained petrodollar earnings substantially over the course of six years. Arab oil-exporting nations extended well over $30 billion to finance the Iraqi war efforts. This figure does not include the billions of dollars Baghdad spent to maintain its armed forces nor the amounts it lost in oil revenues as a result of decreased oil production. My estimate of the cost of the war from September 1980 to April 1986 is in the neighborhood of $70 billion. The futility of the war is aptly illustrated by the failure of both sides to achieve their objectives. Though bitter fighting was characteristic of this war, there seemed to be no end to hostilities. The cost of the war was a real drain on the resources of all the surrounding Gulf countries.[1183]

In summa, despite what Western movies have people believe, the one that largely holds control to set the price for US oil is the Federal Reserve, but even their grip is second only to the market forces of supply and demand that determine oil prices.[1184] The Islamic dictatorships and other members of OPEC are largely subservient to US control of pricing oil with less independence to act for their own interests because the oil pricing is determined by the internal US economics. The US can place sanctions by holding onto the money of any country that doesn't obey its policy directives when there is a major schism of interests - which can and does have dire consequences for the quality of life of average citizens of a country the US sanctions. The US and other countries that have their currency pegged on the US dollar get to import oil at a discount from its actual worth. The consequences of what this required is also clear; Saudi Arabia for instance is an absolute monarchy, they have beheadings for the crime of witchcraft, largely torture their own people with secret police killings, public opinion is considered a punishable crime, and other extrajudicial punishments like flogging or whipping happen to anyone protesting peacefully for a more democratic rule. As is known, the US has given and continues to give billions in weapons technology to Saudi Arabia and how Saudi Arabia uses such weapons is abundantly clear in its war in Yemen that the US has carefully aided in since many US-made weapons end-up in the hands of terrorists who wish to harm the West and other non-Islamic countries.[1185]

Keep in mind, even when utilized by the allies that are lawfully sold weapons by the United States, the consequences are still devastating. Journalist Samuel Oakford reported on *Vice* in the article *"All We Could Find were Body Parts: America's Role in Yemen's civilian carnage"*:

> On the morning of September 28, two families gathered in the southwestern Yemeni village of Wahija for the wedding of a young couple.

---

38. [1183] Oweiss, Ibrahim M. "Increase in Imports." *Http://Faculty.georgetown.edu*, The Committee for Monetary Research and Education, faculty.georgetown.edu/imo3/petrod/increase.htm.
39. [1184] Oweiss, Ibrahim M. "Demand for Oil and Excess Supply Since 1980." *Http://Faculty.georgetown.edu*, The Committee for Monetary Research and Education, faculty.georgetown.edu/imo3/petrod/since.htm.
40. [1185] Browne, Ryan, and Oscar Featherstone. "US Arms Sold to Saudi Arabia and UAE End up in Wrong Hands." *CNN*, Cable News Network, www.cnn.com/interactive/2019/02/middleeast/yemen-lost-us-arms/.

Dozens of women were inside a large wooden structure owned by the family of the groom, Merssal Mosaibas, helping to prepare for the festivities. A few male relatives and guests, both men and boys, were outside.

At about 9:30am, the familiar roar of Saudi-led coalition jets was heard overhead. Some people fled as the planes approached, fearing an attack, but many women and children remained inside. Bombs started falling shortly after 10am, the first striking near where the men had gathered. The structure, held up by tree branches and covered with a tarp, was obliterated minutes later. Mosaibas was nearby, but survived the attack; his bride, Hanen Makhrama, had not arrived yet from her nearby village.

The women and children inside the structure, however, were killed.

Wedding guest Shadi Taha told VICE News over the phone that the attack turned what had been a scene of joy and celebration into one of horror. Body parts were scattered all over, tree branches flecked with pieces of skin.

"There were only small, small pieces," he recalled. "People were small, small pieces of meat."

Among the dead were a mother and her five children. The body of an elderly woman who lived nearby was found on her bloodstained mattress. She had been resting when shrapnel tore through her home.

"It cut her into two or three parts," Taha said. "We had to carry her out in a carton."

The jets circled for half an hour, leaving residents fearful to help victims.

"Later, when we did try to rescue them, we could find [only] a single person alive," a local community leader told United Nations investigators as part of their monitoring of abuses in

Yemen. The UN's Office for the High Commissioner for Human Rights provided VICE News with his testimony and other witness accounts.

Initial reports put the death toll as high as 130, citing local health officials. Human rights workers and locals later clarified that at least several dozen people died, most likely between 30 and 50 people. Many of the bodies were too badly burned or mangled to identify immediately or at all. Because a large number of the wedding guests came from outside the town and others fled before and after the attack, those who survived did not know how many people were present when the bombs exploded.

Another woman told UN investigators that she called her 21-year-old daughter upon hearing planes nearby, urging her to leave. But the daughter stayed and was killed.

"Once we reached the site of the airstrike, all we could find were body parts," the mother said. "We could not find part of her dress or clothing so that we could identify our daughter."

After more than six months of Saudi-led airstrikes targeting Houthi rebels and their allies in Yemen, incidents like this have become grimly familiar. According to UN figures, more than 2,355 civilians have been killed since the hostilities began in late March.

The Houthis and allied forces loyal to former President Ali Abdullah Saleh have been implicated in the deaths of hundreds of non-combatants, often killed by indiscriminate and retaliatory shelling or mines left behind as the Houthis retreat. But the UN says that airstrikes have killed the majority of civilians. The United States military has assisted this Saudi-led campaign with logistical support and billions of dollars in equipment and weaponry.

The Houthis, who hail from a northern Zaydi Shia community, control Wahija and the area around it. One resident said the groom's uncle was associated with the Houthis, but there was no indication that the wedding in any way amounted to a military target.

Human rights monitors and the UN have heavily criticized the massive civilian toll from such strikes and the US military's supporting role. They have also raised questions about Washington's potential complicity in war crimes and violations of international law. UN Secretary-General Ban Ki-moon has said that the campaign must stop.

* * *

Last week, in its latest condemnation of the Saudi-led coalition and its backers, Amnesty International outlined what it called likely war crimes committed by the coalition in the northeast province of Sadaa, a Houthi stronghold. It called for a suspension of all arms transfers to the coalition by its backers, including the United States and United Kingdom.

Since October 2010, the US has sold Saudi Arabia more than $90 billion in aircraft, defense systems, bombs, missiles, and other weapons. When war broke out in Yemen, it began to expedite shipments. American arms manufacturers have also sold billions of dollars' worth of material to other Gulf coalition members, including the United Arab Emirates and Qatar. Both the Saudis and UAE have purchased controversial cluster munitions — banned by more than 100 countries — that have been used in the current conflict.

Since the airstrikes started on March 25, the US has provided the coalition with vital air-refueling sorties, search-and-rescue support, and help with logistics and intelligence — the centerpiece of which is a Saudi-based "Joint Combined Planning Cell" staffed with American personnel who interact daily with the Saudi military. This support involves what the US military's Central Command (CENTCOM) terms "targeting assistance."

"The Saudi-led coalition is equipped with state-of-the-art weapons and targeting technology, yet airstrikes have caused a tremendous number of civilian casualties," said Claire Talon, Middle East and North Africa director at the International Federation for Human Rights. "It is clear that states providing intelligence and assistance to the coalition, including the US, may be accused of complicity in war crimes."

But proving that the US has abetted war crimes or violations of international humanitarian law — or even obtaining the information to make a judgment about potential American responsibility — is difficult. From the start, the US has insulated itself from the fallout of a bloody intervention that it has helped sustain. Behind the scenes and in select public statements, American officials have urged the Saudis to be more careful, but there is no indication that the Obama administration has in any way adjusted its assistance in light of the continuing civilian toll.

On October 2, alluding to the Wahija wedding strike, the White House's National Security Council said that the administration was "deeply concerned" about civilian casualties and called on "all sides of the conflict in Yemen to do their utmost to avoid harm to civilians."

"We call for an investigation into these reported civilian casualties and for the findings to be reported publicly," said NSC spokesman Ned Price, though he emphasized that the US "has no role in targeting decisions made by the coalition in Yemen."

But the language used in that statement is potentially misleading according to Sarah Knuckey, director of Columbia University Law School's Human Rights Clinic.

"When I saw the statement, it struck me as carefully crafted but opaque," she said. "When you first read it, it seems to say that the US is not involved in strikes — and that's how some people interpreted it — but reading it as a lawyer the statement is actually quite ambiguous. It leaves open that the US could be providing intelligence, even if it's not 'deciding' on targets."[1186]

To get a better understanding of the lengths US policymakers will go to keep their grip on US hegemony over the world and the extent of sales to its Gulf allies; the Director of the Arms and Security Project, William D. Hartung, reports on *Foreign Policy* in the article *"It's not Diplomacy, It's an Arms Fair."* details on the extent and historical reason for the US's sale of arms under the Obama administration:

---

41. [1186] Oakford, Samuel. "'All We Could Find Were Body Parts': America's Role in Yemen's Civilian Carnage." *VICE News*, News, 17 Oct. 2015, news.vice.com/article/all-we-could-find-were-body-parts-americas-role-in-yemens-civilian-carnage.

The summit between President Barack Obama and representatives from the Persian Gulf countries that kicked off today at Camp David is meant to reassure Washington's Arab allies. "Don't worry about the nuclear deal with Iran," Obama will say. "We've got your back."

And what's the best way to show your friends that you've got their back? Sell them billions of dollars worth of advanced weapons. In fact, it seems like arms sales are the Obama administration's tool of choice these days for dealing with everything from counterterrorism to a lagging economy. And the consequences, unsurprisingly, are bloody.

In its first five years in office, the Obama administration entered into formal agreements to transfer over $64 billion in arms and defense services to Gulf Cooperation Council (GCC) member states, with about three-quarters of that total going to Saudi Arabia. And new offers worth nearly $15 billion have been made to Riyadh in 2014 and 2015. Items on offer to GCC states have included fighter aircraft, attack helicopters, radar planes, refueling aircraft, air-to-air missiles, armored vehicles, artillery, small arms and ammunition, cluster bombs, and missile defense systems.

Sales to GCC members have been the most important component of the record-level U.S. arms deals concluded during Obama's term. The Obama figures for sales worldwide even edge out levels reached during the Nixon administration, when the end of the Vietnam War and the rising purchasing power of members of the OPEC oil cartel spurred the United States' first major arms export boom.

The surge in arms sales under Obama is rooted in two factors, one political and one economic. The political aspect of the Obama approach mirrors the path pursued by President Richard Nixon in response to the unpopularity of the Vietnam War. In 1969, Nixon announced that henceforth the United States would supply generous quantities of military assistance to allied regimes, in an effort to "avoid another war like Vietnam anywhere in the world." And in a 1967 article in *Foreign Affairs*, Nixon referenced the political roots of his emerging policy, noting that Vietnam had sown "bitter dissension" domestically, producing a "deep reluctance to become involved once again in a similar intervention on a similar basis."

Substitute Obama for Nixon and Iraq for Vietnam, and you have a latter-day version of the Nixon Doctrine of arms sales promotion. Obama wants to be seen as a president who ended large-scale wars, not a president who started new ones. And, as he has made clear time and again, he is particularly reluctant to put large numbers of U.S. "boots on the ground," as the Bush administration did in both Iraq and Afghanistan. Given these restrictions, the Obama administration has developed an approach to warfare designed to limit U.S. casualties. This has relied largely on drone strikes and the extensive use of Special Forces; but boosting arms sales advances is also a part of this hands-off approach, giving allies the equipment and training to fight terrorism on their own. (Let's forget for the moment the fact that Obama's approach may spawn more terrorists than it kills by generating anti-U.S. sentiment.)

But it might be the legacy of the 2008 economic crisis, as much as the 2003 Iraq disaster that drives this White House's arms sales. The Obama administration clearly wants to create jobs in the defense industry and boost the bottom lines of major defense contractors. The Pentagon's 2010 announcements of offers involving tens of billions of dollars' worth of F-15 fighter planes, Apache attack helicopters, armored vehicles, and other equipment to Saudi Arabia listed the prime beneficiaries as Boeing, Lockheed Martin, Raytheon, General Electric, the Sikorsky Helicopter unit of United Technologies, and ITT Aerospace. But these are just the major contractors; thousands of subcontractors across the United States will get a piece of the action as well. For example, in announcing the deal for selling 84 Boeing F-15s to the Saudis, Assistant Secretary of State for Political-Military Affairs Andrew Shapiro proudly asserted that the deal would create 50,000 jobs in 44 states, most notably in St. Louis, the site of the main assembly plant for the plane.

Foreign sales are particularly critical for keeping alive weapons production lines that are about to be closed down as the Pentagon moves towards buying next-generation systems. Absent new domestic orders, Boeing's F-18 production line will have to close in early 2017. But last week's report that Kuwait intends to buy 40 F-18s for $3 billion holds out hope that the line will stay open for another year or more, during which time the company can seek more foreign sales to prolong the life of the program even further. Similarly, the General Dynamics M-1 tank, a program which the Army started winding down in 2012, has been surviving based on yearly add-ons to Pentagon budget requests spearheaded by the Ohio and Michigan delegations, whose states host the main production sites for the vehicles. These efforts have been supplemented by a deal to upgrade 84 M-1s for Saudi Arabia.

The Obama arms sales boom has bolstered the bottom lines of companies like Boeing, Lockheed Martin, and Raytheon. Each firm has been the lead contractor one or more mega-deals like the $29 billion offer of 84 Boeing F-15 fighter jets and related equipment to Saudi Arabia, a $6.5 billion sale of Lockheed Martin's THAAD missile defense system to Qatar, and the proposed transfer of the Lockheed Martin/Raytheon produced Patriot Air and Missile Defense System to Saudi Arabia for $1.8 billion. The payoff won't come all at once, but as these deals work their way through the pipeline, they will generate substantial profits for each of these firms for years to come.

As Pentagon procurement spending has dipped slightly due to the caps on the agency's budget established in the Budget Control Act of 2011, arms industry executives are looking to promote overseas sales even more aggressively — and the Middle East market will be central to these efforts. Lockheed Martin has set a goal of increasing exports to 25 percent of total sales over the next few years. In a conference call with investors in late January, Lockheed Martin CEO Marillyn Hewson suggested that continued "volatility" in the Middle East and Asia make them "growth areas" for the firm.

And a few years ago, Boeing launched an effort to get export sales in its defense division up to 25 to 30 percent, from just 7 percent in 2005. Dennis Muilenburg, a company vice president who formerly ran Boeing's defense segment, has suggested that if the F-15 deal with Saudi Arabia stays on track, the company will be "well on our way" to its goal.

The Obama administration is clearly on board with the industry's agenda. The lengths to which U.S. officials will go to help secure an arms sale for a U.S. company were revealed at a House Foreign Affairs Committee in April 2013. Asked whether the administration was doing enough to advocate for U.S. arms exports, Tom Kelly, principal deputy assistant secretary of the State Department's bureau of political-military affairs, said that, "it is an issue that has the attention of every top-level official who's working on foreign policy throughout the government, including the top officials at the State Department ... in advocating on behalf of our companies and doing everything we can to make sure that these sales go through." Just to make himself perfectly clear, Kelly went on to say that [arms sales promotion] "is something that we're doing every day, basically [on] every continent in the world, and we take it very, very seriously and we're constantly thinking of how we can do better."[1187]

Tragically, even if US citizens were to have widespread protests over weapons sales that killed innocent children in foreign countries, all that would change is the US not being the primary profiteer of weapons sales across the world. Another country would simply take its place to gain from weapons sales. If the US isn't selling them, then various European countries, China, Russia, or even Israel would happily oblige in taking over the market share to gain

---

42. [1187] Hartung, William D. "It's Not Diplomacy, It's an Arms Fair." *Foreign Policy*, Foreign Policy, 14 May 2015, foreignpolicy.com/2015/05/14/obama-arms-fair-camp-david-weapons-sales-gcc/.

wealth from the sales. This is not to vindicate the US or any other country from culpability; if the US government and US war corporations sells weapons to dictators who knowingly use them on civilians, then the US government and corporations are absolutely to blame. The same is true for Russia, the UK, China, and any other country that profits from weapons sales. For those who truly believe in human rights, this may seem like one of the most painful and cruelest lessons to learn; that no matter what, some side will profit off of innocent victims, including helpless children that had nothing to do with the conflicts that plague the world and whose only crime is being born on the wrong plot of land.

What can be done? Is it simply a bleak fatalism and nihilism that can't be changed? Not quite; there are meaningful steps that can be made to change and mitigate harrowing situations that do matter and will determine the long-term impact of how conflicts are resolved. First, for those who support allowing refugee resettlement in their own countries, this can absolutely save innocent lives and make a major difference.[1188][1189] The majority of people aren't terrorists and don't advocate for terror; in fact, it is estimated that about 10 percent of al Qaeda terrorists converted to Islam and aren't born or raised in the Islamic faith which shows a significant overrepresentation of converts in terrorist activities and leads credence to Islamic theology being the problem.[1190] Second, even if you don't support refugee resettlement, it is absolutely asinine to ask them to return to a homeland in which they watched their families or friends brutally killed. Irrespective of if the advocate is a former President or a human rights worker, to demand people return to a place where they tragically lost their loved ones as if a war never happened is one of the worst acts of human cruelty and mental torture. Just imagine, after a ten-year war, a twenty year old woman is asked to return to her "homeland" in which she witnessed her mother raped and murdered, her brother killed by bullet fire after being tortured, and her father beaten to death. Notwithstanding whatever traumatic rape or physical torture that she may have witnessed or been subjected to herself. Imagine a democratic people so ill-informed they demand she return their because of her ethnicity or religion as if that codifies her into some homogenized group that she was born into and has no say in. To advocate people return to a place in which they witnessed such forms of human cruelty is a form of disdain and apathy for their experiences that I would argue it shows anyone forming activism for this specific policy doesn't really care for victims and isn't basing such policy on anything realistic because they don't view refugees as people who underwent lived experiences, but rather as homogenized groups whose voices don't matter. Such policies are the very essence of viewing

43. [1188] Stanton, Brandon. "Humans of New York Refugee Stories – Brandon Stanton – Medium." *Medium*, Augmenting Humanity, 19 Nov. 2015, medium.com/@humansofnewyork/humans-of-new-york-refugee-stories-243336f4adeb.
44. [1189] Eleftheriou-Smith, Loulla-Mae. "Syrian Refugees Get Housed in the Same Hotel as a Furry Conventio - and the Kids Loved It." *The Independent*, Independent Digital News and Media, 11 Mar. 2016, www.independent.co.uk/news/world/americas/syrian-refugees-in-canada-got-housed-in-same-hotel-as-vancoufur-furry-convention-and-the-children-a6921341.html.
45. [1190] Benjamin, Daniel. "The Convert's Zeal: Why Are So Many Jihadists Converts to Islam?" *Brookings*, Brookings, 28 July 2016, www.brookings.edu/articles/the-converts-zeal-why-are-so-many-jihadists-converts-to-islam/.

stereotype over reality. Third, if you would prefer to avoid such a divisive real world consequence of ongoing warfare and refugee resettlement, then it is best to spend however much you can on charities that do the legwork to alleviate suffering for people.[1191] People must do their research and make sure that their assistance is going to charities that actually help people who are suffering. When a refugee in a state of unmitigated suffering; with gunfire damaging local areas, constant fear of attack pervading everyday life, and the threat of death everywhere from massive bomb blasts destroying hospitals and schools; the flight response to save their loved ones is entirely understandable. Giving aid, even the tiniest bit of food for a day, can go a long way to establish a sense of stability and hope for people suffering during warfare - they will not feel abandoned by apathy and silent contempt. Allowing makeshift school programs and community activities can help stymie boredom as they live in tents with no proper ventilation or ability to relieve themselves in a modern standard.[1192] In such conditions, any good news can feel like a miracle. Some Syrians got a sense of hope when resettled in other countries like Australia, Mexico, several European countries, and the US; comparatively, Iraq suffered the most egregious of wrongs and fell into puritanical Islamic belief systems because the world was apathetic to their plight. Whereas Europe and the US are known to bomb locations, but also to give aid and resettlement so Syrian refugees can live normal lives and to help show that Western culture isn't just some selfish, narcissistic hatred for Muslims as people; the Iraqi people who make-up ISIS likely grew up watching their siblings die of curable diseases, watching their mothers prostitute themselves in order to save their siblings by paying exorbitant medical expenses and then get beheaded by Iraqi police under Saddam, and they grew up only knowing some powerful, foreign country that is known be the most powerful in the world called the United States was primarily responsible for their catastrophic living conditions. Nobody came to save them; no hope or man-made miracle was conducted and instead the world completely forgot them and ignored their suffering. The only way to rationalize such unfettered suffering was becoming more extreme in Islamic theology to learn why the Abrahamic God was "punishing" them for their behavior - and then the US invaded their country, bombed homes, placed landmines in locations that resulted in young children getting blown apart to death[1193], conducted torture (Abu Ghraib) and civilian killings (the Haditha killings) with little oversight from the US government[1194][1195], and installed a

46. [1191] Sieczkowski, Cavan. "Donations Pour In After Syrian Refugee Scientist With Cancer Shares Moving Story." *The Huffington Post*, TheHuffingtonPost.com, 14 Dec. 2015, www.huffingtonpost.com/entry/edward-norton-syrian-refugee-crowdrise_us_566efebee4b0fccee16f44e5.
47. [1192] "Transforming Refugee Camps from Places of Boredom to Hubs of Innovation." *Positive News*, Positive News, 23 Oct. 2015, www.positive.news/2015/economics/18679/transforming-refugee-camps-boredom-to-hubs-of-innovation/.
48. [1193] Hedges, Chris. "War Is Betrayal." *Truthdig: Expert Reporting, Current News, Provocative Columnists*, 14 July 2012, www.truthdig.com/articles/war-is-betrayal/.
49. [1194] Pelley, Scott. "Haditha massacre defendant: We did what we had to." *CBS News*, CBS Interactive, 6 Jan. 2012, www.cbsnews.com/news/haditha-massacre-defendant-we-did-what-we-had-to/.
50. [1195] Joyner, James. "Why We Should Be Glad the Haditha Massacre Marine Got No Jail Time." *The Atlantic*, Atlantic Media Company, 3 Feb. 2012, www.theatlantic.com/international/archive/2012/01/why-we-should-be-glad-the-haditha-massacre-

puppet government that divided the country into a civil war.[1196] In the case of the Haditha killings, journalists of the US celebrated the ones responsible as family men of Christian family values[1197]; they celebrated the rulings that argued they were free from any punishment besides docked pay.[1198] The US media called it an act of modernity and complex law[1199]; not unilateral hegemony to act with impunity on a country that was invaded based on blatantly false premises of Weapons of Mass Destruction that didn't exist. Hope is long dead for Iraqis in agony; the US government, and people like James Joyner who don't recognize the human lives of innocent Iraqi children and the handicapped elderly as having value[1200], sufficiently killed it and then blamed it on the victims.[1201]

It is best to ignore religious charities, they only ever offer aid when people convert or spend money on religious texts just as much as they do actual aid like sleeping material, diapers for children, and food to prevent starvation. In some cases, such as during the aftermath of a tsunami in India in 2004, Christian groups went so far as to demand conversion of Muslims, Buddhists, and Hindus to Christianity to receive any assistance from a bus full of supplies; when that didn't happen, the so-called Christian relief workers drove off with all the supplies and let starvation and disease take more lives.[1202] Christian NGOs of all stripes throughout India from Catholic to Protestant denominations openly boasted about using the trauma of the natural disaster to convert Hindus, Sikhs, Buddhists, and Muslims to the Christian faith and often refused to give relief aid supplies if they didn't convert.[1203] Christian journalists and Christian theologians in India reported to newspapers and online that the

---

marine-got-no-jail-time/251993/.
51. [1196] Al-Ali, Zaid. "How Maliki Ruined Iraq." *Foreign Policy*, Foreign Policy, 19 June 2014, foreignpolicy.com/2014/06/19/how-maliki-ruined-iraq/.
52. [1197] CHEDEKEL, LISA , et al. "Haditha: Marine Linked To Civilian Deaths Was A Quiet Honor Student, Friends Say." *Hartford Courant*, 3 June 2006, articles.courant.com/2006-06-03/news/0606030586_1_frank-wuterich-haditha-squad-leader.
53. [1198] Joyner, James. "Why We Should Be Glad the Haditha Massacre Marine Got No Jail Time." *The Atlantic*, Atlantic Media Company, 3 Feb. 2012, www.theatlantic.com/international/archive/2012/01/why-we-should-be-glad-the-haditha-massacre-marine-got-no-jail-time/251993/.
54. [1199] Joyner, James. "Why We Should Be Glad the Haditha Massacre Marine Got No Jail Time." *The Atlantic*, Atlantic Media Company, 3 Feb. 2012, www.theatlantic.com/international/archive/2012/01/why-we-should-be-glad-the-haditha-massacre-marine-got-no-jail-time/251993/.
55. [1200] Joyner, James. "Why We Should Be Glad the Haditha Massacre Marine Got No Jail Time." *The Atlantic*, Atlantic Media Company, 3 Feb. 2012, www.theatlantic.com/international/archive/2012/01/why-we-should-be-glad-the-haditha-massacre-marine-got-no-jail-time/251993/.
56. [1201] Joyner, James. "Why We Should Be Glad the Haditha Massacre Marine Got No Jail Time." *The Atlantic*, Atlantic Media Company, 3 Feb. 2012, www.theatlantic.com/international/archive/2012/01/why-we-should-be-glad-the-haditha-massacre-marine-got-no-jail-time/251993/.
57. [1202] Neelakandan, Aravindan. "Why No Outrage over Conversion of Tsunami Victims?" *Swarajya*, 29 Dec. 2014, swarajyamag.com/politics/why-no-outrage-over-conversion-of-tsunami-victims.
58. [1203] Neelakandan, Aravindan. "Why No Outrage over Conversion of Tsunami Victims?" *Swarajya*, 29 Dec. 2014, swarajyamag.com/politics/why-no-outrage-over-conversion-of-tsunami-victims.

Tsunami victims suffering was a sign of Jesus's justice upon them and it was morally good to allow them to suffer more to convert them.[1204] It should come as no surprise to anybody that Christian relief workers happily do this; they've done it for centuries. To expect morality from a self-contradictory moral system like Christianity is absurd and is an argument from ignorance on how Christianity has conducted itself throughout history. While some religious charities may argue to be "honest" in their work, it is always best to maintain skepticism as their main effort is conversion to Christianity or Islam and not assistance.[1205] The belief in ubiquitous sin in the world may prompt theft of charity donations because of the belief it's only a test from the Abrahamic God and no human effort can change anything. One can only imagine how poorly such predatory charities would do in a country like Iraq if they were from US Christian groups, since Iraq has been given every credible reason to hate the US already, because of the deliberate policies of the US government.

A core component of keeping the US financial system intact is the legitimacy that Islamic dictators have over the Gulf nation-states. Without any credibility of rule, it'll be far more difficult to exact control over a population through the use of force than it is teaching the populous that it needs to follow a divinely mandated duty through systematically following the Sharia and interpreting the Hadiths under an imposing socio-legal system utilized by the dictators. A noticeable amount of wealthy Saudi businessmen and intellectuals have been jailed and executed for working with and financing ISIS. Their actions shouldn't come as a surprise; many may feel that ISIS is far less worse in their behavior than the Saud monarchy. Or, for the more democratic leaning, they may hope that ISIS and the Saud monarchy financially bankrupt each other through wars of attrition so that they can try to take over in the aftermath of ongoing bloodshed and depleted treasure. If such situations, and protests within other Islamic countries for more democratic rule, were to gain traction and take power; the US would utilize the CIA to do absolutely everything possible to make sure those people were killed and new Islamic dictators took the reins of those countries. It is an absolute lie that the US defends or supports democratic values. It only supports policies that promote US hegemony over the world.

Take for instance the response of the US to the peaceful, non-violent resistance of Bahrain's people against its despotic government. This revolution didn't gain as much Western mainstream media attention because the protests really made an effort to be as non-violent and peaceable as possible to gain support within Bahrain itself and to gain the respect of the Western nation-states. The Western powers almost uniformly ignored the non-violent protests and the US shed its restrictions of sales on the basis of human rights abuses to continue selling to the Bahrain monarchy to repress the democratic protesters in a violent crackdown.

---

59. [1204] Neelakandan, Aravindan. "Why No Outrage over Conversion of Tsunami Victims?" *Swarajya*, 29 Dec. 2014, swarajyamag.com/politics/why-no-outrage-over-conversion-of-tsunami-victims.
60. [1205] Neelakandan, Aravindan. "Why No Outrage over Conversion of Tsunami Victims?" *Swarajya*, 29 Dec. 2014, swarajyamag.com/politics/why-no-outrage-over-conversion-of-tsunami-victims.

To reiterate most of what I stated in Chapter 9 for any reader that went straight to this chapter: *The Intercept*, which is a online news website founded by independent journalists like Glenn Greenwald, is a journalist organization keen on highlighting the human rights abuses of the United States on both US citizens and people abroad in foreign countries. However, to digress a bit for those who feel this journalist group to be a questionable source, I agree that they're wrong about Edward Snowden; Snowden is a man who sold vital US intelligence to the highest bidder to make himself famous. While Glenn Greenwald and others in the Intercept could be argued to have contributed to Russia's apparent attack on influencing the 2016 US elections; the chief perpetrators were Cambridge Analytica. The main motives of the Intercept is to highlight when the civil liberties within the US and the human rights outside of the US are violated by the US government's implicit or explicit actions. This is because they seem to be true believers in the US Constitution and were therefore just as caught off-guard as every other US Constitutional idealist when their work was used for nefarious self-interests of foreign governments against the United States. They've largely tried to make-up for their horrifying blunder by reporting on human rights abuses both of US citizens by the US government and of people across the world who were abused by the policies of President Barack Obama and Donald Trump. They've also made an effort to criticize Russia's autocratic rule and Putin's attacks on freedom of speech in particular. That being said, they obviously can't be trusted with honest news when it comes to Islamist political groups as the Intercept put Ex-Muslim lives in danger through a doxxng campaign that shared an Ex-Muslim journalist's personal details to Islamist groups who wanted to rape and kill Ex-Muslims.[1206]

In *the Intercept* article "*US Will Resume Sending Weapons to Bahrain Despite Ongoing Repression*" by Jenna McLaughlin, she extrapolates on the sale of US weapons by the US government of President Obama to Bahrain during their repressive campaign and crackdown on non-violent democratic protests:

> The State Department announced it will lift its freeze on arms sales to the repressive government of Bahrain on Monday, despite the country's myriad human rights abuses in recent years, including arbitrary detention of children, torture, restrictions for journalists and a brutal government crackdown on peaceful protestors in 2011.
>
> "The Administration has decided to lift the holds on security assistance to the Bahrain Defense Force and National Guard that were implemented following Bahrain's crackdown on demonstrations in 2011," wrote John Kirby, a State Department spokesperson, in a press release on Monday.
>
> Human rights groups were quick to criticize the decision. "There is no way to dress this up as a good move," Brian Dooley, a program director at Human Rights First, said in a statement. "It's bad for Bahrain, bad for the region, and bad for the United States." Dooley said Obama should be "doing everything to stop sectarianism in the Middle East, rather than send more weapons to bolster a military drawn almost exclusively from Bahrain's Sunni sect."

---

61. [1206] Muthali, Aki. "Atheistophobia: It's Time to Talk about the Most Persecuted Minority in the World." *The Nation*, 27 Sept. 2015, nation.com.pk/27-Sep-2015/atheistophobia-it-s-time-to-talk-about-the-most-persecuted-minority-in-the-world.

Bahrain's Sunni government rules a country where the majority of the population is Shiite.

Just three weeks ago, the State Department condemned the Bahrainian regime for convicting a leading opposition figure, Ali Salman.

"We do not think that the human rights situation in Bahrain is adequate," the State Department said.

But some things are evidently more important: "Bahrain is an important and long-standing ally on regional security issues, working closely with us on the counter-ISIL campaign and providing logistical and operational support for countering terrorism and maintaining freedom of navigation."[1207]

Later, in March 2016, the Intercept's Murtaza Hussain detailed the US government's tacit support for the Bahraini monarchy's imprisonment of one non-violent, peaceful protestor for the crime of Free Speech and for her supporting a non-violent resistance movement that asked for the end of the monarchy's brutal rule. Her fifteen-month old baby was also sentenced for the crime by the Bahraini monarchy. The article below was aptly titled "*Imprisoned with her baby; Bahraini activist is victim of U.S. silence, sister says*":

> **LAST MONDAY**, Bahraini security forces arrested prominent human rights activist Zainab al-Khawaja and her 15-month-old son. The arrest came on the fifth anniversary of a Saudi military intervention that crushed an uprising by Bahrain's Shiite majority and marked a grim milestone in the country's crackdown on dissidents.
>
> Al-Khawaja was taken into custody to serve a prison term that could run between one and three years after being found guilty in 2014 of charges related to the uprising. The main charge against her relates to an incident in which she insulted the country's monarch by tearing up one of his ubiquitous portraits, a criminal offense in Bahrain. Her arrest this week, along with her infant son, signaled the government's intention to enforce the sentence. According to her family, her son will remain incarcerated with her until he reaches the age of 2.
>
> Al-Khawaja and her sister Maryam emerged as iconic figures of the 2011 uprising. Their father, Abdulhadi, also a high-profile human rights activist, was sentenced to life imprisonment after the revolution was quashed. Speaking to *The Intercept*, Maryam al-Khawaja says that continued U.S. silence over the regime's human rights abuses is helping to facilitate her sister's and father's continued detention. "Until there is international accountability, especially from close allies like the United States, we're never going to have local accountability in Bahrain," says al-Khawaja.
>
> At a State Department press conference the day of the arrest, officials declined to call for Zainab al-Khawaja's release, instead calling on Bahrain to "follow due process in all cases," an ironic statement in light of the fact that al-Khawaja has already been convicted of her charges. Human rights organizations have also noted that Bahrain does not have a free and fair judiciary, particularly in cases of political detention. A Human Rights Watch report issued last November also documented the ongoing torture of detainees held in Bahraini prisons.

---

62. [1207] McLaughlin, Jenna. "U.S. Will Resume Sending Weapons to Bahrain Despite Ongoing Repression." *The Intercept*, The Intercept: Unofficial Sources, 29 June 2015, theintercept.com/2015/06/29/u-s-will-resume-sending-weapons-bahrain-despite-ongoing-repression/.

> In a 2011 speech on the Arab Spring, President Obama called on Bahrain to release political prisoners and end its crackdown on dissidents. Since then, however, the U.S. government has been largely muted in its response to Bahrain's continued repression. Part of this hesitancy stems from the perceived strategic value of the relationship with Bahrain and other Gulf Arab states. Aside from economic and political ties, the island also hosts the U.S. Navy's Fifth Fleet and is viewed as an ally in the region against Iran.
>
> Like other Gulf Arab countries, Bahrain has an extensive lobbying operation in the United States to help sway policy in its favor and spin media coverage. U.S. officials have remained largely quiet in the face of increasingly outrageous instances of democratic suppression.
>
> "The truth is that Bahrain knows it can leverage its strategic relationship with Western powers to great effect, and that there will be no political cost to Zainab al-Khawaja's incarceration," says Nicholas McGeehan, a Gulf researcher at Human Rights Watch. "Her imprisonment should cause heads to hang in shame in Washington. Where the Gulf States are concerned, the U.S., the U.K., and the EU have not taken the side of brave and intelligent reformers like al-Khawaja, but with anti-democratic, rights-abusing monarchs."
>
> Maryam al-Khawaja says that U.S. silence about Bahrain's actions is viewed by the country's leaders as a green light for their behavior. "We've seen how public statements or silence from the U.S. can affect the behavior of the Bahraini government," she says. "In the cases of other dissidents who have been arrested, including myself, an indication of disapproval on the part of the U.S. government was enough to convince [Bahrain] to release them."
>
> During the Bahraini revolution, the al-Khawaja sisters and their father led protest marches and speeches at Bahrain's famous Pearl Roundabout monument. Fearful of being deposed, the government launched a brutal crackdown that culminated in a military intervention by neighboring Saudi Arabia. In the years since, thousands of Bahrainis have been arrested and rounded up into detention facilities, including Abdulhadi, who was detained, tortured, and sentenced to life imprisonment in 2011. The Pearl Roundabout, a national icon whose image appeared on Bahraini currency, was demolished that same year, when the government claimed it had been "desecrated" by the protests.
>
> Now, as this wave of repression continues, Zainab al-Khawaja faces the prospect of several years behind bars.[1208]

With the election of the Trump administration, Hussain extrapolated upon the difference in policy from President Obama. Hussain details the shift in policy under Donald Trump in *"Trump's deepening embrace of Bahrain's repressive monarchy may lead to more instability"* where the honesty of the new approach is made clear. The Trump administration has completely abandoned any veneer of support for human rights and actively supports violent crackdowns and repressions. The Trump administration has shown no qualms with selling more weapons to the Bahrani monarchy in open support of the brutalizing crackdown on non-violent protestors and contempt for democratic rights:

> The U.S. government has remained muted about this intensifying repression, while signaling its intention to work more closely with Gulf Arab countries. For their part, Bahraini leaders have expressed enthusiasm for Trump's presidency, with Foreign Minister Ahmed al-Khalifa

---

63. [1208] Hussain, Murtaza. "Imprisoned With Her Baby, Bahraini Activist Is Victim of U.S. Silence, Sister Says." *The Intercept*, The Intercept, 22 Mar. 2016, theintercept.com/2016/03/22/imprisoned-with-her-baby-bahraini-activist-is-victim-of-u-s-silence-sister-says/.

telling Reuters in an interview last week that Trump's election proves that "things are working in America."

These developments put democratic activists in Bahrain in a desperate position. With the United States and other Western countries heavily arming local security forces and dropping any pretensions of concern about human rights, some feel that they have nowhere to turn. While the United States initially expressed support for the 2011 uprising in Bahrain, there is a growing sense that it has now betrayed the same people whose aspirations it once encouraged.

"Among many Bahrainis, there is a feeling that the West has enabled and supported the government crackdown, and the United States and United Kingdom are now widely equated with the regime itself," says Maryam al-Khawaja, a prominent Bahraini activist leader, whose father is among the thousands now held in Bahraini prisons. This week her father, Abdulhadi al-Khawaja, began a hunger strike in protest of his detention, one of several that he has undertaken since being sentenced to life in prison in 2011. "After the protests started in 2011, the ruling family reached a point where they could no longer control the situation and had to choose between reform or ruling with an iron fist," she says. "Because of the support they've received, they've been able to do the latter."

Reached for comment, a State Department official said that they can not yet comment on the recent U.S. arms sales to Bahrain, but added that on a broader policy level "this Administration has made it clear that it will strengthen its partners." The official also told The Intercept that the U.S. continues to urge the Bahraini government to "promote reconciliation [and] advance reform efforts," adding that the targeting of human rights activists in the country, "run[s] counter to Bahrain's long term security and our mutual interests in regional stability."

But six years after the original 2011 uprising, many Bahrainis have become disillusioned with such assurances from the United States. al-Khawaja in particular fears that the desperation felt by many in the country could turn violent, as activists are both terrorized by the government and denied any avenue for political change. "As a non-violent activist I would never condone anyone taking up arms, but at the same time you have to understand that when people are oppressed and offered no hope, they will seek to defend themselves," she says. "The world reserves the term 'terrorist' only for people in the opposition, but it is the government here that has been inflicting more violence than anyone."

Shortly after a Saudi state visit to the United States this March, the State Department designated a number of Bahraini citizens as terrorists, accusing them of having ties to the Iranian Revolutionary Guard Corps. While there is little evidence of widespread Iranian military support for the opposition — which has mostly employed non-violence and whose religious ties are closer to Iraqi Shia groups — escalating repression could end up create an opening for Iran's involvement. A report earlier this month in the Washington Post cited U.S. intelligence officials who claimed that Iran had begun to provide sophisticated weapons and training to militants in Bahrain seeking to challenge the government.

"For Iran, Bahrain serves as a way to talk about U.S. double-standards and hypocrisy," says al-Khawaja. By embracing the regime, the Trump administration "is going to create a self-fulfilling prophecy regarding Iranian influence, because Shia communities there will feel like the only protector they have left is Iran and Hezbollah."

Bahrain is home to the U.S. Navy's Fifth Fleet, making it a key staging point for U.S. military operations in the Gulf. The United States thus has a logical interest in preventing violent unrest in Bahrain, above and beyond its stated commitment to promoting democracy in the region.

But rather than security or stability, some argue that the Trump administration's goals in the Gulf are primarily economic — and that the White House is willing to pursue short-term economic gain even at the expense of American strategic interests. The GCC states are among the biggest consumers of American arms, with Saudi Arabia alone purchasing more than $100 billion worth of arms under the Obama administration, including weaponry that has been used to commit likely war crimes in Yemen. This March, Amnesty International called on Trump to halt pending deals with Saudi Arabia and Bahrain, saying that weapons sales to these regimes "could implicate [Trump's] administration in war crimes or violations of international humanitarian law."

Husain Abdulla, executive director of the advocacy group Americans for Democracy and Human Rights in Bahrain, is among those who believe that the Trump administration is putting economic considerations above human rights, or even American strategic interests.

"The Trump's administration's position towards the Gulf is primarily that of a savvy businessperson looking to sell its products in a lucrative market. So from this perspective, it doesn't matter what bad things happen as a result of their relationships in the Gulf," he says. "If Trump cuts deals that help the American economy in the short-term, he can put himself in a position to be reelected in four years time."

Abdulla fears that the situation in the Gulf will only deteriorate. Without an avenue for democratic change, popular discontent may lead to a period of violent upheaval that threatens the stability of Bahrain, as well as the broader GCC region. In recent years, violent intolerance of political opposition by rulers in the Middle East has led to major conflicts in Libya and Syria. While Bahrain's population is smaller and easier to control, Abdulla says the regime cannot count on repression solving its problems indefinitely.

"Regime hardliners in Bahrain are already viewing Trump's moves as a green-light for repression and acting on that, but their actions are simply heightening the pressures within Bahraini society, not bringing stability," Abdulla says. "When you crush people who are simply calling for democracy and reform, you put them on the margins and embolden those who may actually be a threat."

"I fear that without a change of course, we will end up with an explosive situation in Bahrain that does not serve American interests, nor the interests of the people of the GCC," he says.[1209]

None of this should come as any sort of surprise. The US government follows the neorealist theory of international relations and will pursue its own interests at the detriment of the entire world to assure its own hegemony.[1210][1211] Do not for a moment believe the calming myth that the United States cares for or supports democracy in the Middle East or most of the other places in the world. Allowing democracy would mean potentially opening up to a European form of capitalism that more equally distributed wealth through progressive social programs or a communist system that did the same, but with the mass slaughter of the wealthy people taking hold. The price of oil would skyrocket and everyone else in the world would find oil unaffordable for basic travel expenses like gas for one's car. It would collapse the markets

---

64. [1209] Hussain, Murtaza. "Trump's Deepening Embrace of Bahrain's Repressive Monarchy May Lead to More Instability." *The Intercept*, The Intercept, 14 Apr. 2017, theintercept.com/2017/04/14/trumps-deepening-embrace-of-bahrains-repressive-monarchy-may-lead-to-more-instability/.
65. [1210] Jentleson, Bruce W. *American foreign policy: the dynamics of choice in the 21st century*. 4th ed., Norton, 2010.
66. [1211] Viotti, Paul R., and Mark V. Kauppi. *International relations theory: realism, pluralism, globalism*. 3rd ed., Macmillan, 1998.

of the West, destroy the development prospects of middle-class countries like India and China, and have devastating consequences for the US economy. Within the US, stagflation and an utter destruction of meeting basic necessities would follow upon the end of Islamic rule in the Arab Spring. The main reason is simple: with progressive policies comes better wages and to make sure a company has profits, the wages could only be paid by selling the product at a higher cost to the rest of the world. Gas could possibly go from $4 a gallon to $40 a gallon. The Federal Reserve of the United States would never be able to match those prices of supply and demand. The US monetary system would utterly collapse with all the money in international markets being returned to the US with demand becoming non-existent and creating hyperinflation where $4 candy could possibly cost $40 or $400. The US's only motivation is to keep itself in power; that is why anecdotes of violence against innocents by foreign political groups are used by the US mainstream media to justify war. It's to legitimize war efforts that are of the US's interest in keeping the US financial system intact, the US wealthy maintain their edge in world markets, and the price of oil is kept as low as possible for the US consumer so consumers continue getting imports at a discount comparative to the actual price of imports.

    The intellectual elites and policymakers of the US already understand that Islam is a tool and the US is the one that uses it as a foundation for policy to keep the Middle East as backwards and under strict control as possible through installed dictatorships. While keeping the population in the US ignorant of the financial dependence on the oil for dollar financial system and to legitimize the warfare of Christians against Muslims in negative interdependence.[1212] Essentially, the US elite tacitly acknowledges that Christianity, Islam, and possibly Judaism will never truly modernize to the point of seeking peace and prohibiting war; the entire US financial system depends upon endless violence among Abrahamic faiths. They utilize the paranoid conspiracy theories that Russia and the US itself may sometimes help spread throughout the region so that Israel is wrongfully blamed as a culprit by Arab peoples living in despotic regimes and the US can further utilize Israel as a tool to legitimize war to fight against anti-Semitism or to denigrate and shut down anti-war protests. Any calls to war on the basis of faith within the US is admittance to this incontrovertible historic fact about Abrahamic theology. It is not because of the idea, as is oft repeated, that humans will be humans; instead it should be recognized that Abrahamics will be Abrahamics. There can be no peaceful reform of the religion that worships the violent, genocidal god of warring desert tribes. Whether it is the Christian denomination, the Jewish denomination, or the Islamic denomination; they'll never reform for the sake of peace and will always, without fail, be violent by arguing they're less worse than the other denominations of their violent, genocidal god of warring desert tribes. The public intellectual and atheist Sam Harris argued in *Letter to a Christian Nation* that the violence between the Abrahamic faiths is proof they're different

---

67. [1212] Cialdini, Robert B. Chapter 2: Reciprocation (19-50). *Influence: Science and practice*. 4th ed., 21st Century Bks, 2002.

religions.[1213] I vehemently disagree; the separation, the insular belief that they're separate despite believing in the same monotheistic God of Abraham, and the fact they're all based on the Mosiac Law prove that they're all denominations of the same religion, but are so violent that they see each other as separate from each other. As proof, regardless of the extent of violence, US citizens are reminded of the roots of this hateful religion of death and genocide whenever mainstream US journalists show depictions of the utmost brutal violence inflicted upon Palestinians and continue supporting such violence in the name of their hateful, violent, and genocidal god of warring desert tribes. While talking about how peaceful the US or Israel are on the air and ignoring peaceful Palestinian protests[1214], the mainstream narrative counteract arguments against BDS or peaceful protests as proof of some terrorist conspiracy and try to support laws to penalize peaceful dissent.[1215] Only a group of deluded narcissists celebrating a violent, genocidal god of warring desert tribes would ever think showing images of children and old ladies bleeding to death by an imposing army and arguing in favor of that same imposing army would help support their cause. Furthermore, the fact that Islamic monarchies, Christian Presidents, and Jewish Prime Ministers have concocted and utilized a successful chain reaction of stoking historic hate and violence, legitimizing their respective roles within their respective countries on the basis of intra-Abrahamic hatred, celebrating paranoid conspiracies to engender the ongoing flow of arms dealings, legitimizing conquest on the basis of being Chosen People for the Abrahamic God to protect sacred Abrahamic lands, and placing such firm faith in this cycle of endless hate to the extent their financial wellbeing depends upon the historic and contemporary contempt that celebrates mass murder, war rape, and ongoing brutal repression of democratic reforms for freedom as its predicate; this is irrefutable, historic, and contemporary proof that the Abrahamic religion will never be peaceful and will always regress into despotic, violent regimes that promulgate adherents to endlessly war with other versions of their faith in the Abrahamic God in celebration of mass death. All celebrating how peaceful they are as they war endlessly in the same so-called "holy" deserts with more powerful, deadlier, and precise weaponry to kill each other more effectively and concocting redefinition after redefinition to promote behaving like violent tribes in a desert as a sacrosanct duty of faith. Their Abrahamic faiths largely supplanting and causing social erasure of civil liberties that ignore torture. Their faiths ending non-violent freedom of assembly to dismantle Western democratic freedoms under the argument they must be protected. Their justification of this reductionist morality always centering around the belief in sinfulness. Their belief in sinfulness trumped their beliefs in democracy and destroyed them to further continue the long, historic celebration of enacting and being worshippers of a violent god of warring desert tribes, the Abrahamic God Yahweh.

68. [1213] Harris, Sam. *Letter to a Christian Nation*. Vintage Books, 2008.
69. [1214] Marusek, Sarah. "West Must Recognize Peaceful Palestinian Resistance Movement." *The Christian Science Monitor*, The Christian Science Monitor, 7 June 2012, www.csmonitor.com/Commentary/Opinion/2012/0607/West-must-recognize-peaceful-Palestinian-resistance-movement.
70. [1215] Ibish, Hussein. "The Nonviolent Violence of Hamas." *Foreign Policy*, Foreign Policy, 6 Apr. 2018, foreignpolicy.com/2018/04/06/the-non-violent-violence-of-hamas/.

Chapter 24: The Follies of Islam

Can Islam be reformed? I use to believe so, I was under the impression that it was more similar to the theology of Christianity and how Christians openly interpret the Bible until I learned how wrong I was because of what the Sharia consists of, the Islamic jurisprudence system, the Islamic theological concept of *bidah*, and the theological concept of Jihad against hypocrisy; as such, I no longer believe it is possible. Even if it were able to be reformed, it wouldn't guarantee that it would mitigate or preclude the persecution and massacres of minority groups in Islamic countries. I only hold this view after listening to the Ex-Muslims of North America and realizing that "reforming" Islam is more costly in the long term than abolishing the religious faith entirely for the wellbeing of all people; whether they are the LGBT, Muslims of minority sects, the majority Muslim populations, Hindus, Buddhists, Christians, Zoroastrianists, Jews, and so forth that live under Islamic persecution whether it is Islamic despots or the discrimination from a Muslim-majority population. It just seems safer and more beneficial for the future, if Islam no longer existed. This is not meant to dehumanize Muslims as people, but rather to call for a normalization of dissent as Ex-Muslims of North America have done. For this portion, I'd like to first give the reasons for my current stance and how I formed it before going into critiques that are very likely to be perceived as insulting, but which I feel are necessary to help normalize dissent. Over the course of my research into the Islamic faith for this book, and despite accusations thrust upon me about Islamophobia which I no longer regard as legitimate as I don't believe Islamophobia is a legitimate term since it confuses anti-Muslim bigotry with criticism of the ideology of Islam, I've had so much difficulty putting this section into words because so much of what I learned made me conclude that I can't force myself to take this religion seriously. I would apologize for such a crass statement, but I have to be honest and open in this critique. Even in the context of the West, I don't believe for a moment that Islam can be reformed; Muslims would demand sexist double-standards upon Muslim women be imposed as a religious protection or hide the sexism within insulated communities. The Right-wing in the West seem keen on labeling every non-Abrahamic faith as filled with stupid beliefs, and unfortunately some theistic Eastern practitioners help confirm such views, but I think that despite their flaws, they can always be open to reform when looking specifically at their doctrinal teachings for those which have doctrines. There's a propensity for non-violence within Eastern faiths such as in Jainism, compassion and equality for transgenders in Hinduism, and acceptance of atheists within both Hinduism and Buddhism in Eastern philosophical traditions. Islam has none of these qualities. It has all of the negatives of Christianity and Judaism wrapped into a death cult that seeks world domination to bring the world back to the 7th century as the endpoint of civilization. All because the theology is predicated upon the Islamic Prophet Mohammad being a perfect human being; modeling society on the time of his life and his rule is perceived quite honestly as bringing society to perfection by many Muslims across the world.

I know that sounds narrow-minded, discriminatory and ignorant, but please understand that I didn't hold these views until looking more deeply in my research for the Islamic faith. I wanted to separate the positives from the negatives for all of these religious beliefs, but the more deeply I delved, I understood more clearly that I was under a misapprehension about the dangers of Islam. My reference point was originally Western Muslims, my early childhood friendships with a Muslim family before most of them moved away, my personal disgust at my own family's bigoted views towards Muslims due to the history of the Hindu-Muslim divide that seemed to impact my own family, the imperialistic legacy of the West, and the corrosive impact of the US mainstream media on accurate depictions of other cultures and people. I think my distrust of the US mainstream media is what propelled me the most towards thinking people could ever have a phobia for Islam, but over the course of my research, I kept seeing problems that I seemed to always have good reasons to dismiss analytically, because the Right-wing helped drown out genuine criticism by being explicitly discriminatory and fused criticism of Islam with bigotry towards Muslims; even worse and more damning than that, the US mainstream media always tried to ignore or blame the victims of US human rights crimes. It was mainly because the US mainstream media and the Right-wing elements of US society ignored human rights crimes by the US government upon Muslim civilians in Obama's drone bombing campaigns that I couldn't take the criticism of Islam seriously for so long. In fact, I was so depressed by Obama's drone program and its consequences on innocent lives in the Arab Spring and other Muslim majority countries, I couldn't motivate myself to do anything for a whole year outside of my usual habit of going to college when I was age 23; I was just too disturbed and disgusted with the US government's actions upon innocent civilians in foreign countries and sending an email to my Senate representative only seemed to result in there no longer being a method to track the amount of civilians killed from drone bombings. I didn't believe, and still don't believe, that my email had any effect on that decision. Even if it did, the only result was less public transparency, the very opposite of what I had hoped and asked to happen. I wanted the bomb droppings to stop and for the US government to try to act more compassionately or carefully, but it's only got worse since then under the current Presidential administration of Donald Trump. I often wonder how Obama can argue in his final speech about the public being able to make a change, yet have coordinated attacks on public protests like Occupy Wall Street or militaristic assaults on places like Ferguson, Missouri or Baltimore, Maryland. It seemed to me like the only way to protest the US mainstream media and the US government's successful destruction of First Amendment rights was highlighting the human rights abuses by the US government through social media and usually from independent US journalism or foreign journalism that was more honest than the US mainstream media which stuck to a narrative of the US government never being at fault for any of its heinous crimes against humanity.

That being said, I was wrong to give Islam a pass from criticism and maybe I'm wrong here too, but I have to judge by the evidence. My reference point now has added Ex-Muslims and Ex-Muslim activists who speak from their own experiences about what they have gone through. They do a better job than the older New Atheist movement of the US in explaining why Islam is dangerous and wrong. I feel that listening and watching their panels has really helped affirm my own beliefs in secularism and secular values; before listening to their panels, I had never truly felt that Free Speech was a real concept in the US. Free Speech just seemed to mean bigots and racists get to say what they want; while the US news media, the police, and the FBI physically assaults, sexually abuses, and gets rid of the Freedom of Assembly for Millennial Liberals and depicts Tea party protesters as racists. I had never experienced any freedom of speech in high school, instead the opposite, I was told to be quiet and obey in a very authoritarian mindset and I was under the belief from age 15 to fairly recently that democratic values didn't mean anything at all. After all, George W. Bush allowed torture despite the 8th amendment so that made the 8th amendment effectively dead, the NSA can wiretap anyone they like and George W. Bush and Obama established that they could do it without a warrant so the 4th amendment was and still is dead, and Obama made a kill list and can kill any US citizen without need of any legal justification so habeas corpus was circumvented. All we're told is that behind closed doors, everyone in power somehow has it handled without any publically transparent judicial oversight. Moreover, any criticism of Israel seemed to be labeled anti-Semitic by the US mainstream media with character assassination after character assassination given to ridicule anyone who disagreed with Israel's war crimes upon Gaza. As such, it seemed that morality also didn't matter, the US public doesn't even seem to be allowed to talk about the free aid that US taxpayers give to Israel in either public discourse or US academia because of the powerful AIPAC lobby assaulting US free speech rights. Placing it all together, I had stopped believing in democratic rights based on the evidence alone. The politicians of both major political parties in office would pay lip service to democracy and then use the police and courts to destroy the US Constitutional rights of the public. That was my understanding of how the "reality" of life in the US existed and it was not because of any Liberal or Conservative bias, I just looked at the evidence with a sense of detachment that soon grew into apathy.

    Being born and raised in the US, I slowly accepted and internalized the belief that democratic rights was just some form of sophistry that people pretended were real, but wasn't actually true about life in the United States. It wasn't until going to college that I felt the taboos finally lifted, but it was a very slow process. I feared talking in defense of gays who were persecuted by Nazis, only for professors who I had considered stubborn to bring up that history and allow open discussion about it with no ridicule. It wasn't like high school where you were told to shut up, implicitly inculcate that your rights were not of any value while learning to praise the country as benign, and then being given tests after memorizing nonsense that you would forget within the week; in college, you could just be yourself and talk about how a particular subject of discussion is relevant to you. The only time I felt maligned, by fellow students and not Professors who tried their best to stick to values of free speech, was when I challenged religion. Even criticizing Israel was allowed within classrooms and I couldn't help but criticize Obama's permissive behavior towards Israel's human rights crimes in Gaza from my own experiences. It was only through college that I learned democratic rights and norms actually were valuable and worthy of defending, but it took a long time for me to remove the brainwash from US high school. To me, it always felt like free speech was defined by limits of taboo in the US public, it felt like a joke before I learned to exercise it in college. A core component of this was my own parents, judging from my own experience, people who immigrate to the US generally feel that it's morally wrong to question the US government because of this belief that doing so means you're ungrateful for the freedom, health benefits, and peace that living in the US grants you. There's a very real mentality, at least among Indians in my family who emigrate from India, that they, the perceived foreigner, should keep their heads down and just obey whoever is in power within the US government to show their gratitude for the honor of getting a green card and then citizenship. Moreover, the belief that we should work hard is at least partially motivated by the idea of gratitude and giving back to a country that provides for us. Perhaps, I should consider the effects of this mentality within my own family more than the high school I went to, but the high school was largely run by incompetent people who did nothing as I was accused of being Muslim or Hispanic (depending on which issue was the political hot topic at the time) and bullied under these assumptions by high school peers, even though I'm a US-born Hindu Indian. It got stupid enough that a fellow Hindu Indian wouldn't be friends with me so that he could be perceived as insulting the perceived Muslim, because of the hateful mentality that permeated after the tragedy of September 11th, 2001.

    For all these reasons and more, I had sympathy for Muslims throughout my college years. To be clear, I knew I would never be a member of any of the Abrahamic faiths. Logic and rationality from as young as age 14 in which I questioned religious assumptions by comparing Hinduism and Christianity and then Hinduism with all other religions had assured that I would never believe in the supernatural, but I had sympathy. Although I disagreed with it, I couldn't help but defend Muslims in what I perceived to be Islamophobia from the far-right. I think the reason I had, for a lengthy amount of time, defended Islam from what I perceived to be bigotry was because I thought it was more similar to Protestant Christianity than it really was. I thought the text of the Quran could be interpreted metaphorically instead of literally, but the system of Islamic jurisprudence shapes it into a communalized Catholicism that is categorically against new ideas. I think, to a certain extent, I put too much trust in cognitive dissonance about beliefs than what was actually an accurate representation of Islamic theology and how Muslims truly live in the world. We all have anecdotes of Liberal Muslims, such as my childhood neighbors, but we don't understand or see how the majority of Muslim families really live; both overseas and somewhat in the US. We think certain facets we hear are eccentricities and not internalized beliefs. Worse than that, and what took me the longest to take any criticism of Islam seriously, was that the far-right conflates the two nearly all the time. Thus, it becomes easier to believe that the problems are eccentricities and not legitimate criticism of internalized beliefs. The far-right of US politics mixes racism, xenophobia, and their hateful beliefs with the genuine criticism so it becomes impossible to distinguish. For me, it was not the Left crying Islamophobia, but more so the far-right saying I was a brown monkey that had no right to an opinion and a Satanist for coming from a Hindu family, while screaming how "rapefugees" from the Middle East and Mexico all needed to die. Moreover, the vicious attacks and murders of Sikhs, people of Indian descent, and Muslims made me stop listening to anything the Right-wing of politics had to say, because the fact is that whenever I bring that up, they accuse me of "being political" and say I have no right to an opinion. The Right-wing of the US simply doesn't care if South Asians of different religious backgrounds are murdered, because it doesn't fit their narrative of wanting to righteously kill Muslims. They're just as indifferent to the targeted murders of Transgenders. I've never once seen anyone from the Right-wing of US Politics condemn them; whether they be public intellectuals, Federal politicians, or Free Speech advocates outside of the Atheist community. At best, one Republican Governor from Texas saying he won't pass laws discriminating against Transgenders because of his concern that he's condemning youth to see suicide as a favorable option over life. Why should I listen to people who don't care if my family or I end-up dead because a random stranger decides they want to kill us? I had thought the US public was smarter than this, but I no longer hold any such confidence because I never see any condemnation like I do with the so-called "whiny" SJW Left. This apathy for human rights crimes is even worse towards Black Americans; there was simply no justification for the death of Tamir Rice, but they swept it under the rug and protected the police officer who murdered a young boy. George Zimmerman is a man with a history of domestic violence, but the US mainstream media would sooner listen to Zimmerman's father's account and the US public seemed too dumb to understand the fact nothing they said could be argued against because Trayvon Martin was dead. All such stories, in conjunction with Obama's drone bombings, led me to conclude that democratic rights were a form of sophistry and that nobody really believed in them outside of US academia. Freedom of Speech was used to defend bigotry, but not democratic protests and nobody seemed to question the fact the need for a permit means that the government has the right to control public protests through police violence instead of them being a fundamental Constitutional right for all citizens of the United States of America.

    I still had some sense of faith in the US system after college, despite the fact Princeton University ran a study in 2014 that confirmed the US was now an Oligarchy and not a Republic anymore. That was because corporations used special interest groups to run monopolistic policies and politicians spent more time catering to the monopolies that continued to grow stronger at the expense of the democratic process and the rights of US citizens. However, after the election of Donald Trump, I gained a confirmation for what I suspected; I had overshot the intelligence level of the US Congress, both major US political parties, and the US public. The Democratic party was more to blame because the Hillary Clinton group continued to vilify and instigate conspiratorial policies against the Bernie Sanders campaign that they never apologized for, her statement after her loss only confirmed to me that this woman was just as unfit as a clown like Donald Trump to be President. Incompetence was the norm on both political isles within US politics, I had been coming up with excuses for what I had thought was people presumably being smarter than the evidence indicated. Perhaps, on some level, I confused wealth and success with intelligence in regards to modern US politics. The rising movement of Neo-Nazi terrorists who gain sympathy and support from US police forces across the country only solidified how wrong I was about the intelligence level of the US public, certain US governors and lawyers, and the intelligence level of the US police force in certain US States.

    Nevertheless, despite these dangerous and pervasive flaws within US society and its existence in other Western societies, Islam's teachings and violent nature were of a magnitude that is far worse than what I had initially believed it to be. Three key problems that prevented me from recognizing the dangers of Islam were the following. The first issue was that genuine criticism was being conflated with the Far-right bigots and racists like the neo-Nazis who would co-opt such arguments and then make addendums in favor of their own racist bigotry, which is what Liberal and mainstream news sources would then make news articles about. These news articles or the twitter postings by neo-Nazis on social media are where many Liberals would first become aware of these accusations and thereby reduce their credibility. The second issue is that even the more nuanced critics of Islam like Sam Harris haven't done their research on different religious groups and their cultures, he and some others painted a broad brush of racial stereotypes and generalizations early on in his criticism of Islam such as in his infamous defense of racial profiling which showed that he had no meaningful understanding of distinguishing culture and religion. For example, his argument on profiling would have led to the unnecessary "racial" profiling of men of the Sikh faith since guards at US checkpoints obviously don't know much about cultural differences of the Sikh turban; he failed to do his research into how the 9/11 hijackers were dressed when they entered the country as they had shaved their beards and worn Western style clothing to appear anonymous according to the 9/11 Commission Report, and he failed to factor in the violence that such an argument could help justify among neo-Nazis and their ilk. Moreover, the term regressive Left seemed like a childish insult that served as confirmation bias to me that no legitimate argument was available from Sam Harris or his fans. The third and final issue that prevented me from seeing the dangers was that some of the criticisms seemed so bizarre and out of the norm of what I would expect from a religion existing in the 21st century. I had thought there must have been some degree of political or social reform throughout Islamic majority countries outside of the Arab Spring, but instead I found that Islam had been far more resistant to change than I had ever given it credit for and that such conservatism came with asinine beliefs among the more popularized harmful beliefs. For those Liberals in the US who are concerned about trying to explain to fellow Liberals about the dangers of Islam, please try to be patient and understand that the third reason, the nonsensical beliefs of Islam, are the most difficult to grasp for Liberals and moderates because the immediate reaction is to believe that there simply must be something more reasonable that has replaced the issue that you have brought up. The idea that the practices listed below still continue really is hard to fathom; it isn't always denial or giving Islam special privileges, it's more the case that it is truly difficult to fathom that a religion's practices haven't changed or reformed to the degree that the other religious faiths have. The idea that such a faith could still maintain such a massive following across the world seems absurd to people unfamiliar with it.

Please try to understand that this isn't an attempt at a dehumanization campaign towards Muslims, I am forced to, due to my commitment to honesty and academic integrity, to call out what are clearly harmful beliefs that no rational person should regard as praiseworthy or respectable. The term Islamophobia is useless and harmful because it purposefully conflates and tries to confuse a religious faith with the people of that faith. I'm following the recommendations of Ex-Muslims of North America from their public panels which distinguishes criticism of a religion, Islam, from bigotry and discrimination towards Muslims as a people, which would be anti-Muslim bigotry. Criticizing harmful beliefs are an act of compassion and that is what I am attempting to do. To be blunt, Islam just has a plethora of violent and stupid ideas. The following are just some of the absurd and dangerous beliefs:

War Mandates

Islam requires Muslims to come to the defense of any Mosque in danger of being destroyed; there is a persistent belief, mandated by a supposed divine call, that Muslims everywhere must journey to defend a Mosque from being destroyed. For all intents and purposes, this is a war mandate as it requires that nothing ever be changed for what is seen as a house of worship once it is established in a foreign country. In fact, Iran's leader Rouhini used the mosques as justification to enter the war against ISIS to fight them. The religion of Islam thereby helps to legitimize warfare. Of course, this isn't a new concept and it isn't technically unique to Islam, but it is important to note that this is a mandatory theological belief, even if most Muslims don't follow it. What's important to note is that fighting over the mosque is interpreted as a form of self-defense within Islam and all foreigners of the religion are simply expected to respect them and leave the Islamic holy sites unchanged with the threat of force, if necessary. While I doubt there is much to fear from this within the West, this seems to set in trepidations for those in Islamic countries with Sunni-Shia divides that create continued discord and violence between the two major sects of Islam. It is worse for religious minorities that live in perpetual persecution in places like Pakistan, Iran, and Bangladesh that are treated with merciless contempt and dehumanization. This is in accordance with the Sharia and the rise in women wearing *hijabs* and *burqas* is something to be concerned about according to some Ex-Muslims.[1216][1217] Islam is rooted in the mission of converting the whole world to the Sharia, so Right-wing political advocacy groups aren't just being filled with irrational fears. There is a legitimate concern, but banning the clothing will only legitimize a Muslim woman's faith by creating a useful excuse that they're protesting a undemocratic law. The best way to assure

---

1. [1216] Namazie, Maryam, et al. "Equality, Islam and Human Rights." *YouTube*, Ex-Muslims of North America, 26 Mar. 2018, www.youtube.com/watch?v=2W0w9ufJOh0.
2. [1217] Haider, Sarah, et al. "Islam, Modesty and Feminism." *YouTube*, Ex-Muslims of North America, 12 Oct. 2017, www.youtube.com/watch?v=QToH2x8njJM.

social change is to criticize the religious faith of Islam through Free Speech. That may sound asinine, but questioning the religious faith means creating a space where Muslims are free to question their own assumptions about their lives, the religious teachings, the religious history, and the ultimate purpose of it all.

As mentioned prior in Chapter 20, the Sharia which comprises of the entire Quran must be accepted as unquestionable fact and the abrogation methodology of Islam mandates that latter verses abrogate earlier verses of the Quran. Therefore, any peaceful verse in the Quran's Chapter 2 "The Cow" (sūrat l-baqarah) is abrogated by the violent verses in Chapter 9 "The Repentance" (sūrat l-tawbah) and almost the entirety of the Quran's Chapter 9 is filled with violent teachings. I would recommend any Muslim and non-Muslim who doesn't believe this to simply read the entirety of Chapter 9 of the Quran for themselves to verify. The following are two verses from Chapter 9, one that deals with teachings on behavior towards polytheists which is what most Muslims regard Hindus to be and then the teaching towards any person who doesn't believe in Islam but the Quranic verse itself highlights that this is the behavior that is to be imposed by Muslims upon Jews and Christians too:

Quran chapter 9 "The Repentance" (sūrat l-tawbah), verse 5 teaching on interactions with polytheists:

> **Sahih International**: And when the sacred months have passed, then kill the polytheists wherever you find them and capture them and besiege them and sit in wait for them at every place of ambush. But if they should repent, establish prayer, and give zakah, let them [go] on their way. Indeed, Allah is Forgiving and Merciful.[1218]

Quran chapter 9 "The Repentance" (sūrat l-tawbah), verse 29 teaching on interactions with any non-Muslims, including Jews and Christians:

> **Mohsin Khan**: Fight against those who (1) believe not in Allah, (2) nor in the Last Day, (3) nor forbid that which has been forbidden by Allah and His Messenger (4) and those who acknowledge not the religion of truth (i.e. Islam) among the people of the Scripture (Jews and Christians), until they pay the Jizyah with willing submission, and feel themselves subdued.[1219]

Contempt for Dogs

Islam's contempt for dogs is one of the most illogical beliefs I've ever come across when researching this religious faith. Some Muslims and Islamic apologists may wish to argue that it was normal for the time period in which these beliefs materialized due to rabid dogs or

---

3. [1218] "The Quranic Arabic Corpus - Word by Word Grammar, Syntax and Morphology of the Holy Quran." *The Quranic Arabic Corpus - Translation*, http://corpus.quran.com/translation.jsp?chapter=9&verse=5
4. [1219] "The Quranic Arabic Corpus - Word by Word Grammar, Syntax and Morphology of the Holy Quran." *The Quranic Arabic Corpus - Translation*, http://corpus.quran.com/translation.jsp?chapter=9&verse=29

some other excuse. However, framing this debate as a quirk of ancient culture would be false because Zoroastrianists in Iran during the ancient era during the Islamic conquest of the Sassanid empire were reportedly compassionate and loving towards dogs, while the conquering Muslims were not and treated them horribly.

The arguments against dogs in Islam is frivolous. It's an appeal to purity that doesn't distinguish between unclean homeless dogs and well-groomed household dogs, but rather appeals to this notion that dogs are always impure. These negative beliefs come from the teachings of the Islamic Prophet Mohammad, who encourages violence on black dogs in particular. *Professor Ahmad Hassan* of *International Islamic University Malaysia* translates the following from the Hadith *Book 10: Kitab Al-Said* :

Game (Kitab Al-Said)
Chapter 1050: To have a dog for hunting and some other purposes

Book 10, Number 2839:
Narrated Abdullah ibn Mughaffal:
The Prophet (peace_be_upon_him) said: Were dogs not a species of creature I should command that they all be killed; but kill every pure black one.[1220]

Book 10, Number 2840:
Narrated Jabir ibn Abdullah:
The Prophet of Allah (peace_be_upon_him) ordered to kill dogs, and we were even killing a dog which a woman brought with her from the desert. Afterwards he forbade to kill them, saying: Confine yourselves to the type which is black.[1221]

This violence against dogs, especially black dogs, in Islamic countries is happening due to the unquestioned obedience to the Prophet Mohammad. To the best of my knowledge, this violence is generally more pronounced in the Arab Spring, but the fact such a stupid and unnecessary form of violence is happening at all, because some man proclaiming to be a Prophet of a God said so, speaks volumes on why Islam can't change and therefore cannot reform. The enmity towards dogs in Islam gets even more stupid than that. From the website titled *Hadith Collection, Book 24 Sahih Muslim* translates verse 5246 as follows:

Sahih Muslim Book 024, Hadith Number 5246.

Chapter : Angels do not enter a house in which there is a dog or a picture.

'Aisha reported that Gabriel (peace be upon him) made a promise with Allah's Messenger (may peace be upon him) to come at a definite hour; that hour came but he did not visit him. And there was in his hand (in the hand of Allah's Apostle) a staff. He threw it from his hand and said: Never has Allah or His messengers (angels) ever broken their promise. Then he cast a glance (and by chance) found a puppy under his cot and said: 'Aisha, when did this dog enter here? She said: BY Allah, I don't know He then

---

5. [1220] Hasan, Ahmad. "Game (Kitab Al-Said)." *Family Life in Islam*, International Islamic University Malaysia, www.iium.edu.my/deed/hadith/abudawood/010_sat.html.
6. [1221] Hasan, Ahmad. "Game (Kitab Al-Said)." *Family Life in Islam*, International Islamic University Malaysia, www.iium.edu.my/deed/hadith/abudawood/010_sat.html.

commanded and it was turned out. Then Gabriel came and Allah's Messenger (may peace be upon him) said to him: You promised me and I waited for you, but you did not come, whereupon he said: It was the dog in your house which prevented me (to come), for we (angels) do not enter a house in which there is a dog or a picture.[1222]

Evidently, an angel which is supposedly a powerful messenger from the almighty Abrahamic God can't enter a home or a tent of any person because a dog happens to be there. You're expected to believe that an angel, with the supposed blessings of an all-powerful cosmic deity, apparently has a weakness where any random dog can prevent them from entering for some unspecified reason. Think about that assertion for a moment. An angel that is harboring the blessings of the same Abrahamic God which people are taught created the entire universe, the earth itself, and who grants miracles to his apostles and his supposed Messiah Jesus, cannot even have his messenger enter a domain so long as a dog is there. How does that make any sense? How can anyone honestly believe that the supposed all-powerful Abrahamic God can't manage to send an angel to a house with a dog or a picture? Perhaps you may accuse me of the fallacy of incredulity, but I'm basing this argument off of the assumption that this all-powerful God is what he claims to be. Do dogs have a special, powerful quality that even the Abrahamic God cannot overcome? If you would like to make the argument that this was clearly a mistranslated or corrupted Hadith, unfortunately the following verse 5248 from the *Hadith Collections* gives further credence to this irrational contempt. It reads as follows:

Sahih Muslim Book 024, Hadith Number 5248.

Chapter : Angels do not enter a house in which there is a dog or a picture.

Maimuna reported that one morning Allah's Messenger (may peace be upon him) was silent with grief. Maimuna said: Allah's Messenger, I find a change in your mood today. Allah's Messenger (may peace be upon him) said: Gabriel had promised me that he would meet me tonight, but he did not meet me. By Allah, he never broke his promises, and Allah's Messenger (may peace be upon him) spent the day in this sad (mood). Then it occurred to him that there had been a puppy under their cot. He commanded and it was turned out. He then took some water in his hand and sprinkled it at that place. When it was evening Gabriel met him and he said to him: you promised me that you would meet me the previous night. He said: Yes, but we do not enter a house in which there is a dog or a picture. Then on that very morning he commanded the killing of the dogs until he announced that the dog kept for the orchards should also be killed, but he spared the dog meant for the protection of extensive fields (or big gardens).[1223]

It seems that the Abrahamic God, the Archangel Gabriel, and the Abrahamic God's Prophet Mohammad couldn't find a more peaceful way other than to slaughter the vast majority of dogs in their abode. This nearly indiscriminate mass slaughter of dogs was because the

---

7. [1222] "Sahih Muslim Book 024, Hadith Number 5246." *Hadith Collection*, hadithcollection.com/sahihmuslim/152-Sahih Muslim Book 24. Clothes and Decorations/13592-sahih-muslim-book-024-hadith-number-5246.html.
8. [1223] "Sahih Muslim Book 024, Hadith Number 5248." *Hadith Collection*, hadithcollection.com/sahihmuslim/152-Sahih Muslim Book 24. Clothes and Decorations/13590-sahih-muslim-book-024-hadith-number-5248.html.

Islamic Prophet wanted to talk to his angel friend. The ongoing ruthless treatment of dogs in the Arab Spring is because of the teachings of the Prophet Mohammad. The Abrahamic God, in his infinite wisdom, couldn't have Gabriel give the Prophet Mohammad a better solution and the Prophet Mohammad, an apparently sinless prophet just like the prophets before him, couldn't come-up with a better solution than killing the majority of dogs. Which is more likely: that the Abrahamic God exists and Mohammad is his Prophet, or Mohammad was a psychotic warlord that found excuses for his violent tendencies? Needless to say, this proves that Islam is not a religion of peace for dogs.

Animal Sacrifice

"Even as a child, this Eid was horrifying."[1224] wrote Sarah Haider, prominent Ex-Muslim activist and Co-Founder of Ex-Muslims of North America, on her twitter page explaining her experience with the annual Islamic celebration of Eid. *"I remember witnessing a sacrifice of a cow with my family, I remember the blood gushing from its throat and running through the street. The story of Abraham which it commemorates is another horror. I'll save my Mubaraks for the other Eid."*[1225]

She follows up her tweet by politely requesting for people to respect her wishes and to not respond with gruesome pictures. Another Ex-Muslim chimes in with his recollection of remembering the wrath on the slaughterer's visage and how he felt disturbed by what he experienced from the festival.[1226] Haider responds by mentioning that she remembered the son of a butcher innocently playing in the blood of the dead animal.[1227] The same Ex-Muslim male explains a quip about how fasting before the ritualized animal sacrifice was to avoid throwing up, and then goes onto mention how fortunate he is that he could leave the Islamic world before becoming desensitized to such barbarity.[1228]

I stared at my computer screen reading her tweet attempting to comprehend it. I knew Sarah Haider to be a reliable and intelligent person; her and other Ex-Muslim panels from her

---

9. [1224] Haider, Sarah. "Even as a Child, This Eid Was Horrifying. I Remember Witnessing a Sacrifice of a Cow with My Family, I Remember the Blood Gushing from Its Throat and Running through the Street. The Story of Abraham Which It Commemorates Is Another Horror. I'll Save My Mubaraks for the Other Eid." *Twitter*, Twitter, 21 Aug. 2018, twitter.com/SarahTheHaider/status/1031995695652384769.
10. [1225] Haider, Sarah. "Even as a Child, This Eid Was Horrifying. I Remember Witnessing a Sacrifice of a Cow with My Family, I Remember the Blood Gushing from Its Throat and Running through the Street. The Story of Abraham Which It Commemorates Is Another Horror. I'll Save My Mubaraks for the Other Eid." *Twitter*, Twitter, 21 Aug. 2018, twitter.com/SarahTheHaider/status/1031995695652384769.
11. [1226] Mo, Bilaal. "I Remember the Wrath on the Slaughterer's Faces Too, and Blood Stained Hands and Kurta's Afterwards. The Whole Thing Was Creepy." *Twitter*, Twitter, 21 Aug. 2018, twitter.com/takebeerism/status/1031996242685906945.
12. [1227] Haider, Sarah. "I Remember the Son of the Butcher We Hired Playing in the Blood, like a Rain Puddle." *Twitter*, Twitter, 21 Aug. 2018, twitter.com/SarahTheHaider/status/1031996570470940673.
13. [1228] Mo, Bilaal. "We Used to Joke around That the Reason We Fasted the Day or Two before This Eid Was to Avoid Throwing up. Fortunately i Wasn't in That World Long Enough to Become Desensitised to It." *Twitter*, Twitter, 21 Aug. 2018, twitter.com/takebeerism/status/1031997399969947649.

organization did much to explain the problems and dangers of Islam that I hadn't been aware of. What I had struggle internalizing for a few minutes was that this annual festival of animal sacrifice was true and not some crackpot conspiracy theory made-up by far-right organizations to dehumanize Muslims. I made a quick response explaining I was left speechless and dumbfounded by learning that such a stupid event was actually real. It confirmed in my mind what I had suspected; Islam was just the babbling insanity of a 7th century illiterate warlord who formed an imperialistic project. I searched online for more information and was shocked by the details. Islamic theology was rife with debates on the importance of sacrificing an animal with special pleading arguments. At that moment, I couldn't fathom how anybody could take Islam seriously. Snapshots of Muslims smiling in congregations to the snapshots of bloody images of dead animals as proof of their devotion to the Abrahamic God.[1229] The most immediate issue that struck me, and which convinced me that Islam could never be reformed, was that Muslims across the world hadn't even attempted to change this ritual to be more cosmetic to keep the supposed meaning without the need to slaughter helpless animals. It was because of their deep faith in the Abrahamic God as thoroughly explained in Islamic theology, the meaning was to sacrifice for the Abrahamic God as Abraham was fully willing to sacrifice his son.[1230]

For those who don't know, the celebration of Eid al-Fitr to Eid al-Adha (the latter of which translates to Festival of Sacrifice) is an annual and mandatory celebration within the Islamic faith after Ramadan.[1231] Judging from what I have read, it seems the shortened name for these two conjoined holidays is Eid. The slaughter of an animal specified as acceptable to kill is celebrated as proof of piety within Islam.[1232][1233] The reason it hasn't changed is because Islam forbids "*bid'a*" (or in other translations "bidah"[1234]) which roughly means "*innovation in religion*" as a translation according to the website *Questions on Islam* which explains the practice.[1235] When researching this Islamic holiday, I recall a joke during my high school years in which an online penpal and I mused that at least religions weren't sacrificing animals anymore. Lo and behold, how wrong I was about this notion and that Islam remains consistent

---

14. [1229] Sommerlad, Joe. "Why Do Muslims Sacrifice Animals during Eid?" *The Independent*, Independent Digital News and Media, 21 Aug. 2018, www.independent.co.uk/news/world/middle-east/eid-al-adha-animal-sacrifice-abraham-islam-muslims-goats-sheep-animal-rights-a8500556.html.
15. [1230] "As Eid Al Adha Approaches..." *Questions on Islam*, questionsonislam.com/content/eid-al-adha-approaches...
16. [1231] "The Udhiyah (the Sacrificial Animal) and Its Rulings." *Islamway*, Islamway, 29 Nov. 2012, en.islamway.net/article/12915/the-udhiyah-the-sacrificial-animal-and-its-rulings.
17. [1232] "As Eid Al Adha Approaches..." *Questions on Islam*, questionsonislam.com/content/eid-al-adha-approaches...
18. [1233] "The Udhiyah (the Sacrificial Animal) and Its Rulings." *Islamway*, Islamway, 29 Nov. 2012, en.islamway.net/article/12915/the-udhiyah-the-sacrificial-animal-and-its-rulings.
19. [1234] "Tafseer on the Basis of Narrated Texts and Tafseer on the Basis of Individual Understanding - Islam Question & Answer." *Islamqa.info*, Islam Question and Answer, 11 Mar. 2015, islamqa.info/en/answers/205290/tafseer-on-the-basis-of-narrated-texts-and-tafseer-on-the-basis-of-individual-understanding.
20. [1235] "As Eid Al Adha Approaches..." *Questions on Islam*, questionsonislam.com/content/eid-al-adha-approaches...

with this belief too, even after 1400 years. News articles attempting to be "respectful" and maintain "civil discourse" about this idiotic religious practice show the depth of how useless political correctness is.[1236] Attempting to humanize animal slaughter by depicting it as a pious social event instead of a psychotic and meaningless slaughter of animals do a grave injustice to both animal rights and the horrors in which young Muslim children are forced to witness, but it may also delegitimize the Western mainstream media in the eyes of the non-Muslim public as a whole. The reason this portion was so difficult to write is because I kept thinking: *'Do I really need to make an effort to argue why religiously sanctioned animal slaughter is wrong? Have we not moved past even this point as a species?'* but of course, people on Sarah Haider's twitter began commenting about the similarities to factories in which animals are slaughtered as an attempt to justify this idiotic practice.

Nevertheless, for the sake of my commitment to academic integrity, I will attempt to give a serious response to this asinine religious practice. However, I feel that I should mention how absurd I find the notion that I must actually argue against animal sacrifices in the 21st century and I feel I should reiterate how ridiculous I find attempts by any online media to humanize this disgusting, violent ritualized form of animal cruelty. My personal disgust with this topic due to my bias of Western moral sensibilities and Hindu religious sensibilities (which I'm sure that Buddhists, Sikhs, and Jains likely share) is what makes this entire Islamic celebration utterly stupid and vomit-inducing; after learning about this ritual and the dehumanization of women, I can no longer see anything about the Islamic religious tradition as deserving of any respect. I honestly tried to be reasonable and separate the positives from the negatives when researching Islam, but everything about this religion leads me to conclude that it is nothing more than a violent, hateful imperialist project of the 7th century. The only positive it has over Scientology is that it can make its barbarous history look exotic and mysterious because it is so old and can more successfully make an appeal to population fallacy which coincides with an appeal to tradition fallacy. Islam's faults aren't limited to just this issue and the problems only worsen as I will be elaborating further on. I honestly have to wonder how many Muslims actually tried to use logic and reason on their own religious faith, because I am genuinely bewildered that just animal sacrifice itself didn't get mocked out of the religious tradition and I can only infer that fear and intimidation within Islamic societies is far deeper than people recognize. The fact Muslims still sacrifice animals goes against the very ideas of logic and reason that practically every other culture feels accustomed to at this point and time in history. For all the arguments on the supposed backwardness of religious traditions indigenous to Asia, the vast majority are clearly superior to Islam. I'm sure many Muslims and Westerners can point to some bizarre subset of a small population within South or East Asia, but the vast majority of the religious traditions don't do animal sacrifices, eat brains, or other nonsense. Perhaps there are people in the most remote or ignored locations sacrificing animals,

---

21. [1236] Sommerlad, Joe. "Why Do Muslims Sacrifice Animals during Eid?" *The Independent*, Independent Digital News and Media, 21 Aug. 2018, www.independent.co.uk/news/world/middle-east/eid-al-adha-animal-sacrifice-abraham-islam-muslims-goats-sheep-animal-rights-a8500556.html.

but you would think that after a certain degree of educational attainment, they would stop and realize it is a stupid practice. I don't care how bigoted or stupid you find this comment, because I have to be blunt here: I doubt I will ever see a Muslim as capable or as intelligent as a non-Muslim ever again. I think I was wrong to ever believe that Muslims were equal in intelligence to any non-Muslim or that they could ever reform and change the terrible rituals that they practice. I apologize if that seems dehumanizing, but I can't hold back my utter disgust for this religious ceremony that people practice. The only reform possible for Muslims is becoming Ex-Muslims.

To set aside my personal disgust and focus on the purposes of critiquing animal sacrifice. First, the intentions of slaughtering an animal for the Abrahamic God and slaughtering an animal to eat it are as far removed in intent as possible; one requires the murder of an animal because the Abrahamic God commands that you show him deference, the other is to feed whole populations to keep a country healthy and any waste of food can be ameliorated through reform in a society that mass produces food in abundance. By contrast, Islam requires adherents to physically slit the throat of an animal and appreciate as it chokes to death in order for Muslims to prove their love and devotion to the Abrahamic God.[1237] Animals in production factories are generally in sterile conditions where people can make sure that the meat isn't diseased. Even in cases of corporations not following through with keeping conditions sterile, it's safer for there to be a factory keeping the diseased meat isolated. In the context of the ritualized murder of helpless animals by Islamic doctrine, the meat has a higher chance of being diseased and potentially causing food poisoning or worse for a Muslim family. Second, it leaves horrible mental images in children's minds that has shown to live with them for a lifetime and makes it a requirement for them to become desensitized to brutal violence against animals every year. Some may argue that I am attempting to infer an objective morality to this equation against Islam, but this horrific celebration is defended in reverence to the Abrahamic God on the basis of Islam's objective morality.[1238] The sacrifice of an animal is embedded as a annual religious holiday in Islam and is a form of Divine Command Theory. Therefore, as a third point of contention, Islam's *Eid al-Adha* (Festival of Sacrifice) is an annual real world example of the utter flaws of Divine Command Theory. Muslims actively butcher animals mercilessly every year to express their honest love and devotion to the Abrahamic God.[1239] Finally, due to Islam being a faith that seeks converts, it creates a pointless demand for the oversupply of animals so that 1.6 billion or more can kill an animal and divvy them up among seven people at most to eat.[1240] Even granting that millions of animals are slaughtered each

---

22. [1237] "As Eid Al Adha Approaches..." *Questions on Islam*, questionsonislam.com/content/eid-al-adha-approaches...
23. [1238] "As Eid Al Adha Approaches..." *Questions on Islam*, questionsonislam.com/content/eid-al-adha-approaches...
24. [1239] "As Eid Al Adha Approaches..." *Questions on Islam*, questionsonislam.com/content/eid-al-adha-approaches...
25. [1240] "As Eid Al Adha Approaches..." *Questions on Islam*, questionsonislam.com/content/eid-al-adha-approaches...

day, this ritualized religious practice still increases the slaughter of animals by approximately the hundreds of millions or possibly around 200 million even if you divide by seven family members sharing a portion of the meat. The more this religion spreads, the worse it will be for the sustainability of the environment, and that is even granting that it is a drop in the puddle of bloodshed for daily animal slaughter. This needless slaughter of animals is further credence that Islam isn't a religion of peace for animals in general. Islamic teachings are against changing this practice and therefore against making it more ceremonial.[1241] If Islam had been a religion of peace or capable of adapting with modernity, it would have changed the very real annual slaughter of animals to something else entirely. Perhaps having kids have fun striking a piñata to make this religious celebration more akin to a modernized ceremonial form of worship. It doesn't have to be precisely that, but at least something equivalent to striking a piñata. It is clear that Islam wouldn't have religious values declaring that it can't be changed, if it was actually a peaceful religion that could modernize.

Bestiality

Footage of Afghan Muslims committing bestiality outside their homes, such as atop their small rooftops have been filmed by US troops and leaked unto *liveleaks.com* for worldwide viewing.[1242] Muslim men are seen penetrating the backside or mouth of goats and other animals from thermal vision.[1243][1244] The problem has been stated to exist in other predominately Islamic countries too and isn't limited to just Afghanistan. Social critiques have been offered such as pointing out the impoverished and rural living conditions along with extreme sexual repression within the Islamic faith as explanations for these acts of bestiality in an effort to understand why this bizarre phenomena is happening. The internet term "*goatfucker*" by the internet hacktivist group Anon and other self-stylized "trolls" (trolls being an English-language colloquial term for people who intentionally seek to cause offense to others for their own fun) similar to 4Chan have been used as slang identification for these Muslims and certain prominent Islamic groups. Spy equipment has found that even Islamic terrorists commit these acts of bestiality; it is likely much to the chagrin or amusement for the soldiers who are checking the spying equipment.[1245]

Many Muslim apologists may try to use this as proof that terrorist organizations and the general public of the majority Islamic countries aren't acting in accordance with Islamic teachings. They may be quick to point to Hadiths that condemn bestiality, such as the Hadith

---

26. [1241] "As Eid Al Adha Approaches..." *Questions on Islam*, questionsonislam.com/content/eid-al-adha-approaches...
27. [1242] "Poor Goat." *LiveLeak.com - Redefining the Media*, www.liveleak.com/view?i=008_1443844876.
28. [1243] "Two Pai Taliban Jihadi Mujahideen Caught Sexing A Donkey By US Forces." *LiveLeak.com - Redefining the Media*, www.liveleak.com/view?i=825_1315923588.
29. [1244] "US ARMY Camera Catches Afghans Gangbanging a Goat." *LiveLeak.com - Redefining the Media*, www.liveleak.com/view?i=93d_1384239379.
30. [1245] "Two Pai Taliban Jihadi Mujahideen Caught Sexing A Donkey By US Forces." *LiveLeak.com - Redefining the Media*, www.liveleak.com/view?i=825_1315923588.

that equates homosexuality with bestiality and commands Muslims to kill both homosexuals and those who commit fornication with animals. From *Sunnah.com,* the Hadith from Book 10 verse 1255 in the English version and 1216 in the Arabic version states as follows:

> Ibn 'Abbas (RAA) narrated that the Messenger of Allah (ﷺ) said:
> "Whoever you find doing as the people of Lot did (i.e. homosexuality), kill the one who does it and the one to whom it is done, and if you find anyone having sexual intercourse with animal, kill him and kill the animal." Related by Ahmad and the four Imams with a trustworthy chain of narrators.[1246]

However, there are other Hadiths that are completely in line with what these Afghan men and some terrorists are doing by raping the animals. From the *Hadith Collection,* Book 33 verse 4450 says the following:

> Abu Dawud Book 033, Hadith Number 4450.
>
> Chapter : Not known.
>
> Narated By Abdullah ibn Abbas : There is no prescribed punishment for one who has sexual intercourse with an animal.[1247]

As such, bestiality is an open question in Islamic societies. How can this be a religion of peace when it is okay with raping animals? Does that seem incredibly stupid to ask? Unfortunately, Islam allows it to be an open question within its theology, so bestiality has to be questioned and repudiated from an outsider perspective too.

Incest

Consanguine marriages pervade in disproportionately high rates within predominately Islamic countries and communities. *Dr. S. Shamshad* from the women's college in Kurnool, India provides a review titled *"Prevalence of Consanguinity in Muslim Community"* which details the percentages of consanguine marriages within the Islamic faith tradition. It is important to note that this research is not meant to shame Muslims as people, Dr. S. Shamshad notes that consanguine marriages are prevalent within Mormon communities in the US too. Her main concern, and the concern of the academic research, is on the long-term health effects of children being born in these societies:

> Abstract: Consanguinity ("blood relation", from the Latin consanguinitas) is the property of being from the same kinship as another person. In that aspect, consanguinity is the quality of being descended from the same ancestor as another person. Consanguineous marriage is frequent in many populations. In fact,

---

31. [1246] "Hadith - Hudud - Bulugh Al-Maram - Sunnah.com - Sayings and Teachings of Prophet Muhammad (صلى الله عليه وسلم)." *Search Results - Fitra (Page 1) - Sunnah.com - Sayings and Teachings of Prophet Muhammad (□□□ □□ □□ □□□),* sunnah.com/urn/2015030.
32. [1247] "Abu Dawud Book 033, Hadith Number 4450." *Hadith Collection,* hadithcollection.com/abudawud/265-Abu Dawud Book 33. Prescribed Punishments/18224-abu-dawud-book-033-hadith-number-4450.html.

it has been recently estimated that consanguineous couples and their progeny suppose about 10.4 % of the 6.7 billion global population of the world. First-cousin marriage and other types of consanguineous unions are frequent in a number of current populations from different parts of the world. Consanguinity is most common among muslim population. Consanguinity rates, coupled by the large family size in some communities, could induce the expression of autosomal recessive diseases, including very rare or new syndromes. The most thoroughly investigated are sickle cell disease, haemoglobinopathies, and enzymopathies (glucose-6-phosphate dehydrogenase deficiency). It is the duty of the public health professionals to ensure accessibility to counseling services and to periodically evaluate the knowledge and awareness of the health consequences of consanguineous marriages on offspring health so as to reduce this kind of marriages. And creating awareness among the people may lessen the chance of consanguinity.

1. Introduction

Consanguinity refers to the marriage of parents with a recent common ancestor. In humans, consanguineous marriage is frequent in many populations. In fact, it has been recently estimated that consanguineous couples and their progeny suppose about 10.4 % of the 6.7 billion global population of the world [1]. First-cousin marriage and other types of consanguineous unions are frequent in a number of current populations from different parts of the world. Consanguinity is common in several populations of the world though the consanguinity rates vary from one population to another. Furthermore, there is variability between different tribes, communities, and ethnic groups within the same country. Worldwide, wide variations in the consanguinity rates among various ethnic groups have been reported. In European populations the rates are generally less than 0 5%, while in North Africa and southern and western Asian populations 22 to 55% of all unions are consanguineous. In the majority of the US States cousin marriages are illegal under the statutes passed in the 19th and 20th centuries. The practice of consanguineous marriage, or marriage between close biological relatives, shows significant heterogeneity across the world [2], [3]. While such marriages are legal in the Middle East, Africa, the UK and Australia, they are prohibited by law in China, some parts of Europe, and the United States. Prohibitions also vary by religion. While consanguineous marriages are permitted within Islam, Buddhism and Zoroastrianism, they are forbidden by Christian Orthodox churches and require special permission for members of the Roman Catholic Church. The variations in legislative and religious rules are also reflected in the prevalence of consanguineous marriage across regions. In the western world, consanguineous marriages currently constitute less than 1% of total marriages, but this practice remains widely prevalent in many other places. Estimates range from 30—50% in Middle Eastern countries, 20-40% in North Africa, and 10— 20% in South Asia [4], [5], [6], [7], [8], [9].There is also significant variation within countries. The National Family Health Survey 1992- 93 [10] reveals that 16% of marriages are consanguineous in India, but this varies from 6% in the north to 36% in the south [11]. Some new research also suggests that the practice is growing in popularity in Western countries, particularly in migrant communities [8].

2. Prevalence of consanguinity:

Consanguineous marriage remains common in many parts of the world and has been reported in various communities such as the Mormons [12], [13]. It is especially common in most of the Middle-Eastern countries where the custom in considered socially acceptable [14], [15], [16], [17], [18], [19], [20], [21], [22], [23], [24], [25]. The same applies to other Muslim countries and regions such as India [26], Pakistan [27], [28], [29], [30], [31] and Uzbekistan [32]. This practice continued in some of the communities who settled the West such as the Pakistani community in the UK [14], [33], [34]. In the

Arab countries, consanguinity has been reported with the highest frequency in Saudi Arabia [24], where it reaches 80% of marriages in certain parts of the Kingdom. From the available data, the consanguinity rate for other countries in the Middle East ranges between 59% among the Iraqis [18], 40% among the Palestinians [21], 44% among the Yemenis in Sanaa [17] 49-58% among the Jordanians [35], [15], [16] and 40-54% in the UAE [36]. In Kuwait [37] high rates of consanguineous marriages within the particular Arab communities but low frequency of intermarriage between them, and also the presence of genetic isolates and semiisolates in some extended families and Bedouin tribes have been described. Consanguinity is less common in North African Arab countries where it was reported to be 29% in Egypt; [23] however, in another study on the Nubian population in southern Egypt the figures ranged between 41.5-45.5% [19]. The highest rates of such marriages have been reported in rural areas, among individuals with low educational levels, and among the poorest. In Morocco [38], with its contact with the outside world, a marked decrease in consanguineous unions is reported; consanguinity is disappearing and does not present a preoccupying problem for public health. However, this cannot be used as a generalization as the trend has increased in younger generations in other Arab countries such as the UAE where the rate of consanguinity has risen from 39% in the parent generations to 50.5% in the current generation [36].[1248]

A separate study in 2000 on India's regional and State levels of Muslim populations found no significant changes in the rates of Consanguine marriages from the study's beginning period of 1950 to its completion in 1990.[1249] Such research shows the shocking level of cultural commitment to what scientific research and consensus has already thoroughly debunked.[1250] The pervasive commitment to consanguine marriages has reared itself in the West by the migrating population of Muslims. In the United Kingdom, the brave Baroness Shreela Flather; a cross-bench peer that has highlighted the oft-forgotten contribution of 5 million volunteers from India, Africa, and the Caribbean to Great Britain's campaigns in World Wars 1 and 2[1251]; has highlighted the plight of children being born with horrifying birth defects in Pakistani immigrant communities.[1252] Disabled children are being born within Pakistani communities because of the strong cultural and social commitment to Islam.[1253] After all, Pakistanis were

---

33. [1248] Shamshad, S. "Prevalence of Consanguinity in Muslim Community - A Review." *Pdfs.semanticscholar.org*, International Journal of Science and Research (IJSR) , pdfs.semanticscholar.org/f3db/08faf43477ce7c34146aa4b8db0769661efa.pdf.
34. [1249] Bittles, A H, and R Hussain. "An Analysis of Consanguineous Marriage in the Muslim Population of India at Regional and State Levels." *Current Neurology and Neuroscience Reports.*, U.S. National Library of Medicine, www.ncbi.nlm.nih.gov/pubmed/10768421.
35. [1250] Bittles, A H, and R Hussain. "An Analysis of Consanguineous Marriage in the Muslim Population of India at Regional and State Levels." *Current Neurology and Neuroscience Reports.*, U.S. National Library of Medicine, www.ncbi.nlm.nih.gov/pubmed/10768421.
36. [1251] "Shreela Flather." *Wikipedia*, Wikimedia Foundation, 9 July 2018, en.wikipedia.org/wiki/Shreela_Flather.
37. [1252] Swinford, Steven. "First Cousin Marriages in Pakistani Communities Leading to 'Appalling' Disabilities among Children." *The Telegraph*, Telegraph Media Group, 7 July 2015, www.telegraph.co.uk/news/health/children/11723308/First-cousin-marriages-in-Pakistani-communities-leading-to-appalling-disabilities-among-children.html.
38. [1253] Swinford, Steven. "First Cousin Marriages in Pakistani Communities Leading to 'Appalling' Disabilities among Children." *The Telegraph*, Telegraph Media Group, 7 July 2015, www.telegraph.co.uk/news/health/children/11723308/First-cousin-marriages-in-Pakistani-communities-leading-to-appalling-disabilities-among-children.html.

originally Indian and people among non-Muslim Indian communities don't have a disproportionately high level of consanguine marriages. This is not a Western versus Arab Spring cultural argument, this is about scientific evidence and the growing number of problems from this commitment to the Islamic religious tradition. Others within the British parliamentary system seem more keen on not being labeled racist and instead looking politically correct while Baroness Flather has bravely spoken out due to heartfelt concern for the damage the social practice of consanguine marriages has on children.[1254]

Physical disabilities and deformities aren't the only problem with consanguine marriages. A pilot study in Southern Israel's Arab Bedouin population has found overwhelming evidence that consanguine marriages within Islamic communities located in Negev.[1255] The consanguine marriages are forming mild to severe cognitive impairment for children born in Islamic communities.[1256] Intellectual and development disability (IDD) is rampant throughout consanguine marriages in Israel with over 60% of children suffering from some form of IDD coming from such marriages.[1257] Another study noted that a horrifying 43% of all infant deaths of Bedouin children, from either physical deformities within their bodies or hereditary diseases, is attributed to the prevalence of consanguine marriages.[1258]

Female Slaves in Heaven

Another one of Islam's numerous defects is the Hadiths related to the sexual slavery of women and the descriptions of exotic supernatural women whose sole purpose is the sexual pleasure of Muslim men.[1259] There are thorough details about how these women won't ever exhibit the so-called "impurities" of normal women on earth when faithful Muslim men go to heaven with full erections to have sex with them.[1260] This very issue shows the massive failings

---

39. [1254] Swinford, Steven. "First Cousin Marriages in Pakistani Communities Leading to 'Appalling' Disabilities among Children." *The Telegraph*, Telegraph Media Group, 7 July 2015, www.telegraph.co.uk/news/health/children/11723308/First-cousin-marriages-in-Pakistani-communities-leading-to-appalling-disabilities-among-children.html.
40. [1255] Saad, Hassan Abu, et al. "Consanguineous Marriage and Intellectual and Developmental Disabilities among Arab Bedouins Children of the Negev Region in Southern Israel: A Pilot Study." *Current Neurology and Neuroscience Reports.*, U.S. National Library of Medicine, 2014, www.ncbi.nlm.nih.gov/pmc/articles/PMC3904202/.
41. [1256] Saad, Hassan Abu, et al. "Consanguineous Marriage and Intellectual and Developmental Disabilities among Arab Bedouins Children of the Negev Region in Southern Israel: A Pilot Study." *Current Neurology and Neuroscience Reports.*, U.S. National Library of Medicine, 2014, www.ncbi.nlm.nih.gov/pmc/articles/PMC3904202/.
42. [1257] Saad, Hassan Abu, et al. "Consanguineous Marriage and Intellectual and Developmental Disabilities among Arab Bedouins Children of the Negev Region in Southern Israel: A Pilot Study." *Current Neurology and Neuroscience Reports.*, U.S. National Library of Medicine, 2014, www.ncbi.nlm.nih.gov/pmc/articles/PMC3904202/.
43. [1258] Na'amnih, Wasef, et al. "Prevalence of Consanguineous Marriages and Associated Factors among Israeli Bedouins." *Current Neurology and Neuroscience Reports.*, U.S. National Library of Medicine, Oct. 2014, www.ncbi.nlm.nih.gov/pmc/articles/PMC4159474/.
44. [1259] Al-Munajjid, Muhammed Salih. "Will Men in Paradise Have Intercourse with Al-Hoor Aliyn?" *Islamqa.info*, Islam Question and Answer, islamqa.info/en/10053.
45. [1260] Al-Munajjid, Muhammed Salih. "Will Men in Paradise Have Intercourse with Al-Hoor Aliyn?"

of making a religion's afterlife more concrete in conceptualization and the ignorance of the Islamic Prophet and his followers. Muslim apologists may be quick to argue those Hadiths have no bearing on the Quran and are inauthentic, but the Quran itself has a verse mentioning pure virgin women in Chapter 56 "The Event" (sūrat l-wāqiʿah) on verses 35 through 38.[1261] Chapter 78 "The Tidings" ("An-Naba") verses 31 through 40 also affirms the existence of female slaves in heaven created specifically for men who enter heaven.[1262]

    These teachings help to perpetuate the dehumanization of women as sex objects without any personality of their own and could credibly be argued as an ancient form of "women as reward" - a term popularly coined by sex-negative feminist and video game critic Anita Sarkeesian.[1263] Despite whatever objections people may have, the similarities of seeing women as a reward are certainly there; it is the idea that after arduous tribulations, men will be rewarded with the sexual reward of women's bodies that they will fornicate with at the man's leisure.[1264][1265] To be clear, I am not denigrating any man or woman who has such sexual fantasies or who would want to partake in such ideas among consenting adults, but this "reward" being part of a religion that largely discourages a follower to pursue a healthy sexual experience is quite jarring and based upon owning women as property of men. Moreover, the description of this Islamic afterlife doesn't devalue the argument about Islam internalizing and protecting a concept of purity, because the description of these otherworldly female slaves are celebrated in terms of purity and virginity being synonymous.[1266] It comes attached to some vague idea of heavenly radiance that seems to further symbolize otherworldly purity.[1267] As a fictional concept, this idea is fine, but people who honestly believe this is what happens after they either suicide bomb, or are martyred in some other way, do present a danger to innocent civilians everywhere. The "women as reward" functions as coping mechanism to commit horrific atrocities and feel both blessed and sexually gratified for causing violence upon others in the form of martyrdom. It is not inconsistent with Islamic doctrines, but rather exists because of Islamic doctrines.

    Here are two Hadiths from *Sunnah.com* that express women as reward for Muslim men, which could be a credible reason, or at least a partial reason, for their motives when inculcated

---

    Islamqa.info, Islam Question and Answer, islamqa.info/en/10053.

46. [1261] "Al-Qur'an Al-Kareem - ال كريم ال قرآن." *Surah Al-Waqi'ah [56:35-38]*, quran.com/56/35-38.

47. [1262] "Al-Qur'an Al-Kareem - ال كريم ال قرآن." *Surah An-Naba [78:31-40]*, quran.com/78/31-40.

48. [1263] Sarkeesian, Anita. "Women as Reward - Tropes vs Women in Video Games." *YouTube*, Feminist Frequency, 31 Aug. 2015, www.youtube.com/watch?v=QC6oxBLXtkU.

49. [1264] Al-Munajjid, Muhammed Salih. "Will Men in Paradise Have Intercourse with Al-Hoor Aliyn?" *Islamqa.info*, Islam Question and Answer, islamqa.info/en/10053.

50. [1265] Sarkeesian, Anita. "Women as Reward - Tropes vs Women in Video Games." *YouTube*, Feminist Frequency, 31 Aug. 2015, www.youtube.com/watch?v=QC6oxBLXtkU.

51. [1266] Al-Munajjid, Muhammed Salih. "Will Men in Paradise Have Intercourse with Al-Hoor Aliyn?" *Islamqa.info*, Islam Question and Answer, islamqa.info/en/10053.

52. [1267] Al-Munajjid, Muhammed Salih. "Will Men in Paradise Have Intercourse with Al-Hoor Aliyn?" *Islamqa.info*, Islam Question and Answer, islamqa.info/en/10053.

into Islamic Jihad in the face of socio-economic hardships or because of identity solidarity with Muslim terrorists:

> **Abu Sa'eed Al-Khudri narrated that the Messenger of Allah (s.a.w) said:**
> "The least of the people of Paradise in position is the one with eighty thousand servants and seventy-two wives. He shall have a tent of pearl, peridot, and corundum set up for him,(the size of which is) like that which is between Al-Jabiyyah and Sana'a."And with this chain, it is narrated from the Prophet (s.a.w) that he said: "Whoever of the people of (destined to enter) Paradise dies, young or old, they shall be brought back in Paradise thirty years old, they will not increase in that ever, and likewise the people of the Fire." And with this chain, it is narrated from the Prophet (s.a.w) that he said: "There are upon them crowns, the least of its pearls would illuminate what is between the East and the West."[1268]
>
> Grade : Da'if (Darussalam)
> English reference : Vol. 4, Book 12, Hadith 2562
> Arabic reference : Book 38, Hadith 2760[1269]
>
> **It was narrated from Abu Umamah that the Messenger of Allah said:**
> "There is no one whom Allah will admit to Paradise but Allah will marry him to seventy-two wives, two from houris and seventy from his inheritance from the people of Hell, all of whom will have desirable front passages and he will have a male member that never becomes flaccid (i.e., soft and limp).'"[1270]
>
> Grade : Da'if (Darussalam)
> English reference : Vol. 5, Book 37, Hadith 4337
> Arabic reference : Book 37, Hadith 4481[1271]

This is part of the reason I doubt Islam can ever be reformed. How do you even pursue a serious conversation about this? What reform is possible with such ideas? It is key to note that these are blatantly sexist beliefs about women's bodies that are followed by unquestioned obedience to the Abrahamic God. Everyone in the world is safer when we can freely denigrate such ridiculous views without the threat of violence from Islamic groups and the drowning out of controversial statements for questioning the supposed sacredness of religious beliefs.

Fear of Satan

This specific list was compiled and shared in a humorous video criticizing Islam by the Turkish Ex-Muslim activist Ridvan Aydemir.[1272] I've only edited it slightly and cannot claim

---

53. [1268] "Hadith - Chapters on the Description of Paradise - Jami` at-Tirmidhi - Sunnah.com - Sayings and Teachings of Prophet Muhammad (صلى الله عليه وسلم)." *Riyad as-Salihin - Sunnah.com - Sayings and Teachings of Prophet Muhammad (□□□ □□□□□□ □□□□)*, www.sunnah.com/urn/678680.
54. [1269] "Hadith - Chapters on the Description of Paradise - Jami` at-Tirmidhi - Sunnah.com - Sayings and Teachings of Prophet Muhammad (صلى الله عليه وسلم)." *Riyad as-Salihin - Sunnah.com - Sayings and Teachings of Prophet Muhammad (□□□ □□□□□□ □□□□)*, www.sunnah.com/urn/678680.
55. [1270] "Hadith - Zuhd - Sunan Ibn Majah - Sunnah.com - Sayings and Teachings of Prophet Muhammad (صلى الله عليه وسلم)." *Sahih Muslim - Sunnah.com - Sayings and Teachings of Prophet Muhammad (□□□ □□□□□□ □□□□)*, sunnah.com/urn/1294400.
56. [1271] "Hadith - Zuhd - Sunan Ibn Majah - Sunnah.com - Sayings and Teachings of Prophet Muhammad (صلى الله عليه وسلم)." *Sahih Muslim - Sunnah.com - Sayings and Teachings of Prophet Muhammad (□□□ □□□□□□ □□□□)*, sunnah.com/urn/1294400.
57. [1272] Aydemir, Ridvan. "All The Things That Satan Does (Ridiculous Islamic Teachings)." *YouTube*,

any credit on its compilation. Ridvan Aydemir left Islam several years ago while keeping silent about it in Turkey and moved to the United States where he produces video content criticizing Islam based upon Islamic sources from its own sacred books. He uses the pseudonym "Apostate Prophet" on Youtube and produces videos criticizing Islam to warn people of the dangers of Islam. He doesn't share in the disdain for all religions as some other Ex-Muslim activists do and argues in defense of other religions like Christianity, Judaism, Hinduism, Sikhism, and Buddhism as being inherently peaceful religions that don't need to be criticized. He argues that Liberals are largely naive about the dangers of Islam and they need to be more critical of it in defense of their values whether in the democratic countries of the West or in other democratic countries like India. He shares his criticisms freely on Youtube and encourages people to share and become more informed about the dangers of the Islamic faith.[1273] He is an incredible inspiration and holds an amazing wealth of knowledge about Islam. I would be remiss if I didn't acknowledge his important contributions to the dialogue of criticizing Islam and I highly encourage everyone to give his videos on Youtube a chance.[1274] Similar to Ex-Muslims of North America, I've amended and added several more points of contention to my critiques thanks to his wealth of knowledge from his video content on Youtube.[1275] Ex-Muslims like him live in fear of being killed for wanting freedom to think for themselves. They are continuing to have their voices shut down by social media companies in deference to Islamic despots, their voices are being shut down by Liberals who ignore their human rights by claiming the Free Speech rights of Ex-Muslims to criticize Islam for wanting them to be killed is offensive to Muslims, and as such Ex-Muslims have every right to be angry at Liberals who ignore the plight of their human rights in favor of the meaningless and idealistic view of tolerance.[1276] As of now, the current identity politics of many Liberal voices that argue this erroneous notion that nobody can understand or empathize with the experiences of specific groups without being part of that group is not only damaging, but actively dangerous for the human rights of Ex-Muslims. As such, I am endeavoring to promote their Free Speech and human rights as much as I can. I sincerely apologize to Ridvan Aydemir and any other Ex-Muslim, if it seems as if my support is misconstruing or somehow harming their cause in some unintentional manner. I have credited their contributions as much as I can and don't wish to claim their hard work as my own. I simply wish to make it clear that their human rights and Free Speech need to be protected and that religious tolerance can endanger their lives.

---

58. [1273] Aydemir, Ridvan. *YouTube*, Apostate Prophet, www.youtube.com/channel/UCzREuchzOqiawpEpvEM0Tyg/videos.
59. [1274] Aydemir, Ridvan. "All The Things That Satan Does (Ridiculous Islamic Teachings)." *YouTube*, Apostate Prophet, 28 Dec. 2018, www.youtube.com/watch?v=Ko2lttV8i2M&feature=youtu.be.
60. [1275] Aydemir, Ridvan. *YouTube*, Apostate Prophet, www.youtube.com/channel/UCzREuchzOqiawpEpvEM0Tyg/videos.
61. [1276] Aydemir, Ridvan. "Cowards in Control." *YouTube*, Apostate Prophet, 25 May 2019, www.youtube.com/watch?v=3Q5ZKANKaMQ.

Islam serves as an example of how ridiculous and idiotic the belief and fear of Satan is. It is not only paranoia, but the conspiratorial nature of faith-based thinking that is demonstrated with this irrational fear and lack of evidence-based critical thinking skills. The following aims to show copious amounts of evidence of that. The following was also written in a more jovial manner with the defense of Free Speech and especially the freedom to offend as the motivation.

Evidently, the Abrahamic God enjoys when Muslims sneeze and hates when Muslims yawn because yawns are caused by Satan. Satan apparently laughs at Muslims who yawn:

Collection
Sahih Bukhari

Dar-us-Salam reference
Hadith 6223

In-book reference
Book 78, Hadith 247

USC-MSA web (English) reference
Volume 8, Book 73, Hadith 242

Narrated Abu Huraira:
The Prophet (ﷺ) said, "Allah likes sneezing and dislikes yawning, so if someone sneezes and then praises Allah, then it is obligatory on every Muslim who heard him, to say: May Allah be merciful to you (Yar-hamuka-l-lah). But as regards yawning, it is from Satan, so one must try one's best to stop it, if one says 'Ha' when yawning, Satan will laugh at him."[1277]

Good dreams are apparently from the Abrahamic God and bad dreams are from Satan, the Prophet Mohammad instructed Muslims that they should spit three times over their left shoulder and seek the way of Islam's version of the Abrahamic God so that Satan's dream won't harm Muslims:

Sahih al-Bukhari Book 87 Hadith 124

Narrated Abu Qatada:

The Prophet said, "A good dream is from Allah, and a bad dream is from Satan. So whoever has seen (in a dream) something he dislike, then he should spit without saliva, thrice on his left and seek refuge with Allah from Satan, for it will not harm him, and Satan cannot appear in my shape."[1278]

The pedophile Prophet of Islam was so wise and so far ahead of his time that he warned us all that bells are the musical instrument of Satan. Truly, criticizing such astonishing wisdom is deeply offensive to Muslim sensibilities for good reason:

---

62. [1277] "QuranX.com The Most Complete Quran / Hadith / Tafsir Collection Available!" *Sahih Bukhari Hadiths*, quranx.com/Hadith/Bukhari/USC-MSA/Volume-8/Book-73/Hadith-242/.
63. [1278] "Sahih Al-Bukhari Book Number 87 Hadith Number 124." *Muflihun*, muflihun.com/bukhari/87/124.

37 The Book of Clothes and Adornment
(27) Chapter: It Is Disliked To Take Dogs And Bells On A Journey

Abu Huraira reported Allah's Messenger (ﷺ) as saying:
The bell is the musical instrument of the Satan.[1279]

In his Abrahamic God-given wisdom, the pedophile Prophet of Islam explained that babies cry when they're born because Satan touches them:

Sahih al-Bukhari Book 55 Hadith 641

Narrated Said bin Al-Musaiyab:

Abu Huraira said, "I heard Allah's Apostle saying, 'There is none born among the off-spring of Adam, but Satan touches it. A child therefore, cries loudly at the time of birth because of the touch of Satan, except Mary and her child." Then Abu Huraira recited: "And I seek refuge with You for her and for her offspring from the outcast Satan" (3.36)[1280]

According to the pedophile prophet of Islam, the crowing of roosters is a sign that roosters have seen an angel and the braying of donkeys is a sign that donkeys have seen Satan:

Collection
Sahih Bukhari

Dar-us-Salam reference
Hadith 3303

In-book reference
Book 59, Hadith 111

USC-MSA web (English) reference
Volume 4, Book 54, Hadith 522

Narrated Abu Huraira:
The Prophet (ﷺ) said, "When you hear the crowing of cocks, ask for Allah's Blessings for (their crowing indicates that) they have seen an angel. And when you hear the braying of donkeys, seek Refuge with Allah from Satan for (their braying indicates) that they have seen a Satan."[1281]

In accordance with the wise words of the illiterate and pedophilic Prophet of Islam, you should eat food you dropped from the ground because otherwise Satan will eat it and be sure to lick your fingers so the food is more likely to bless you:

Collection

---

64. [1279] *Hadith - The Book of Clothes and Adornment - Sahih Muslim - Sunnah.com - Sayings and Teachings of Prophet Muhammad (□□□ □□□ □ □□□ □ □□)*, sunnah.com/muslim/37/159.
65. [1280] "Sahih Al-Bukhari Book Number 55 Hadith Number 641." *Muflihun*, muflihun.com/bukhari/55/641.
66. [1281] "QuranX.com The Most Complete Quran / Hadith / Tafsir Collection Available!" *Sahih Bukhari Hadiths*, quranx.com/Hadith/Bukhari/USC-MSA/Volume-4/Book-54/Hadith-522/.

Sahih Muslim

In-book reference
Book 36, Hadith 177

Reference
Hadith 2033d

USC-MSA web (English) reference
Book 23, Hadith 5046

Jabir reported:
I heard Allah's Apostle (ﷺ) as saying: The Satan is present with any one of you in everything he does; he is present even when he eats food; so if any one of you drops a mouthful he should remove away anything filthy on it and eat it and not leave for the devil; and when he finishes (food) he should lick his fingers, for he does not know in what portion of his food the blessing lies.[1282]

For those of you who may be adamant to argue that I am creating a strawman of Islam or that I am unfairly implying that Muslims are somehow intellectually inferior to the practitioners of all other religions on average, I want it to be clear that I am mocking Islam as a belief system. The reason it is so illogical is precisely because it is a faith-based system that orients itself towards enforcing Divine Command Theory upon real life. Divine Command Theory is often opposed because it is authoritarian, but that shouldn't obscure its other crucial issue. Divine Command Theory is fundamentally irrational and creates so many silly suppositions and practices that cause needless mental consternation, contempt, self-loathing, and can lead to horrific outcomes. As much as you may find this mockery offensive, I would argue to allow a set of idiotic practices without any criticism is even more offensive, especially when it can and does lead to human rights crimes. The first Hadith is a chain of narration, the second portion below it is an explanation by an "Islamic Scholar" and the sheer idiocy of what you're about to read should speak for itself. However, for the select few that may find this portion to be a facile criticism, it should be noted that the dexterity of your hands is developed in the womb from the development of your spine.[1283] Therefore, what the Islamic Prophet Mohammad asked of some of his followers on what could be argued to be a innocuous demand wasn't possible because of how their motor cortex from their brains was transmitting electrical impulses with the spine.[1284] Notwithstanding, the pedophile Prophet Mohammad's ignorance and the stupidity of the hadiths chain of narration system as shown below:

Collection
Muwatta Malik

---

67. [1282] "QuranX.com The Most Complete Quran / Hadith / Tafsir Collection Available!" *Sahih Muslim Hadiths*, quranx.com/Hadith/Muslim/USC-MSA/Book-23/Hadith-5046/.
68. [1283] Andrews, Robin. "We Finally Know Why People Are Left- Or Right-Handed." *IFLScience*, IFLScience, 23 Jan. 2019, www.iflscience.com/brain/finally-know-people-left-righthanded/.
69. [1284] Andrews, Robin. "We Finally Know Why People Are Left- Or Right-Handed." *IFLScience*, IFLScience, 23 Jan. 2019, www.iflscience.com/brain/finally-know-people-left-righthanded/.

Arabic reference
Book 49, Hadith 1679

USC-MSA web (English) reference
Book 49, Hadith 6

Yahya related to me from Malik from Ibn Shihab from Abu Bakr ibn Ubaydullah ibn Abdullah ibn Umar from Abdullah ibn Umar that the Messenger of Allah, may Allah bless him and grant him peace, said, "When you eat, eat with your right hand and drink with your right hand. Shaytan eats with his left hand and drinks with his left hand."[1285]

The reason why the right hand is preferred over the left

Publication : 02-03-2007
Views : 182985
Question
Why is the right hand preferred over the left hand when greeting, eating and in other cases? What is wrong with using the left hand for these purposes?.

Answer
Praise be to Allaah.

It is part of Allaah's complete blessing upon us and the perfection of this great religion, that Islam organizes all aspects of our lives. There is nothing good but it has shown it to us, and there is nothing bad but it has warned us against it. As well as beliefs, acts of worship, interactions with others and morals and manners, that also includes our private affairs in which Islam shows us the way that is befitting to man's noble status and the way in which Allaah has honoured him. That includes the way the Muslim eats and drinks, and so on.

This is an established principle in sharee'ah: that which has to do with honour and nobility, such as putting on one's garment and pants and shoes, entering the mosque, using the siwaak, putting on kohl, clipping the nails, trimming the moustache, combing the hair, plucking the armpit hair, shaving the head, saying salaam at the end of prayer, washing the limbs when purifying oneself, exiting the toilet, eating and drinking, shaking hands, touching the Black Stone, etc are all things which it is mustahabb to start on the right or use the right hand. As for things which are the opposite, such as entering the toilet, exiting the mosque, blowing one's nose, cleaning oneself after using the toilet, taking off one's garment, pants and shoes, and so on, it is mustahabb to start on the left or use the left hand. All of that is because the right hand is more noble and honoured. This was stated by al-Nawawi in Sharh Saheeh Muslim. There is a great deal of evidence to support this principle, such as the following:

In al-Saheehayn it is narrated that 'Umar ibn Salamah (may Allaah be pleased with him) said: The Messenger of Allaah (peace and blessings of Allaah be upon him) said: "O young boy, say the name of Allaah and eat with your right hand, and eat from what is nearest to you." Narrated by al-Bukhaari (5376) and Muslim (2022).

In Saheeh Muslim (2021) it is narrated that a man ate with his left hand in the presence of the Messenger of Allaah (S). He said: "Eat with your right hand." He said: I cannot. He said: "May you never be able to," for nothing was preventing him from doing so but arrogance. And he never raised it to his mouth again.

---

70. [1285] "QuranX.com The Most Complete Quran / Hadith / Tafsir Collection Available!" *Muwatta Malik Hadiths*, quranx.com/Hadith/Malik/USC-MSA/Book-49/Hadith-6/.

The Prophet (peace and blessings of Allaah be upon him) prayed against him so that what he claimed of not being able to do it would come true, because he was too arrogant to follow the truth and he did not observe proper etiquette with the Prophet (peace and blessings of Allaah be upon him), and his excuse was a lie, and lying to the Prophet (peace and blessings of Allaah be upon him) is not like lying to anyone else.

In Sunan Abi Dawood (33) it is narrated that 'Aa'ishah (may Allaah be pleased with her) said: The right hand of the Messenger of Allaah (peace and blessings of Allaah be upon him) was for his purification and food, and his left hand was for using the toilet and anything that was dirty. Classed as saheeh by al-Albaani in Saheeh Abi Dawood.

Muslim (262) narrated that Salmaan (may Allaah be pleased with him) said: He (meaning the Prophet (peace and blessings of Allaah be upon him)) forbade any one of us to clean himself with his right hand.

And Muslim (2020) narrated from Ibn 'Umar (may Allaah be pleased with him) that the Messenger of Allaah (peace and blessings of Allaah be upon him) said: "No one among you should eat with his left hand or drink with it, for the shaytaan eats with his left hand and drinks with it."

Allaah has warned us against disobeying the commands of the Messenger of Allaah (peace and blessings of Allaah be upon him), as He says (interpretation of the meaning):

"And let those who oppose the Messenger's (Muhammad's) commandment (i.e. his Sunnah _ legal ways, orders, acts of worship, statements) (among the sects) beware, lest some Fitnah (disbelief, trials, afflictions, earthquakes, killing, overpowered by a tyrant) should befall them or a painful torment be inflicted on them"

[al-Noor 24:63]

This applies if one is able to eat with the right hand. But if one is unable to do so, there is no sin in that. Al-Nawawi said in Sharh Muslim (13/191): The objection to eating and drinking with the left hand applies so long as there is no excuse. If there is an excuse which prevents one from eating and drinking with the right hand because of sickness, injury etc, then it is not makrooh. End quote.

Al-Ghazaali said in al-Ihya' (4/93): Then the One Who gave you two hands to do things with, some of which are noble, such as picking up the Mus-haf, and some are ignoble, such as removing impurities. So if you pick up the Mus-haf with your left hand, and you remove impurities with your right hand, then you have used that which is noble to do something ignoble, and you have neglected its rights and wronged it, and turned away from what is proper. End quote.

To sum up what the scholars have said about the reasons why the right hand is preferred for things that are noble:

1-That is differing from the shaytaan, as in the case of eating and drinking.

2-It is honouring the right hand over the left.

3-It is using proper etiquette with people, so that one does not shake hands with them, take things from them or give things to them with the hand with which one removes impurities.

4-It is a sign of hope that Allaah will make us among those who are on the right hand (ahl al-yameen).

And Allaah knows best.[1286]

---

71. [1286] "The Reason Why the Right Hand Is Preferred over the Left - Islam Question & Answer." *Islamqa.info*, Islam Question and Answer, 2 Mar. 2007, islamqa.info/en/answers/82120/the-reason-why-

Satan apparently steals your food and when you catch him stealing your food, he'll teach you some crazy nonsense to recite so that the Abrahamic God will appoint someone to guard you from Satan and also Satan apparently stole food at night. Additionally, according to the pedophile Prophet Mohammad himself, Satan told the truth and is also an absolute liar:

Sahih al-Bukhari Book 38 Hadith 505

Narrated Abu Huraira:

Allah's Apostle deputed me to keep Sadaqat (al-Fitr) of Ramadan. A comer came and started taking handfuls of the foodstuff (of the Sadaqa) (stealthily). I took hold of him and said, "By Allah, I will take you to Allah's Apostle ." He said, "I am needy and have many dependents, and I am in great need." I released him, and in the morning Allah's Apostle asked me, "What did your prisoner do yesterday?" I said, "O Allah's Apostle! The person complained of being needy and of having many dependents, so, I pitied him and let him go." Allah's Apostle said, "Indeed, he told you a lie and he will be coming again." I believed that he would show up again as Allah's Apostle had told me that he would return. So, I waited for him watchfully. When he (showed up and) started stealing handfuls of foodstuff, I caught hold of him again and said, "I will definitely take you to Allah's Apostle. He said, "Leave me, for I am very needy and have many dependents. I promise I will not come back again." I pitied him and let him go. In the morning Allah's Apostle asked me, "What did your prisoner do." I replied, "O Allah's Apostle! He complained of his great need and of too many dependents, so I took pity on him and set him free." Allah's Apostle said, "Verily, he told you a lie and he will return." I waited for him attentively for the third time, and when he (came and) started stealing handfuls of the foodstuff, I caught hold of him and said, "I will surely take you to Allah's Apostle as it is the third time you promise not to return, yet you break your promise and come." He said, "(Forgive me and) I will teach you some words with which Allah will benefit you." I asked, "What are they?" He replied, "Whenever you go to bed, recite "Ayat-al-Kursi"-- 'Allahu la ilaha illa huwa-l-Haiy-ul Qaiyum' till you finish the whole verse. (If you do so), Allah will appoint a guard for you who will stay with you and no satan will come near you till morning. " So, I released him. In the morning, Allah's Apostle asked, "What did your prisoner do yesterday?" I replied, "He claimed that he would teach me some words by which Allah will benefit me, so I let him go." Allah's Apostle asked, "What are they?" I replied, "He said to me, 'Whenever you go to bed, recite Ayat-al-Kursi from the beginning to the end ---- Allahu la ilaha illa huwa-lHaiy-ul-Qaiyum----.' He further said to me, '(If you do so), Allah will appoint a guard for you who will stay with you, and no satan will come near you till morning.' (Abu Huraira or another sub-narrator) added that they (the companions) were very keen to do good deeds. The Prophet said, "He really spoke the truth, although he is an absolute liar. Do you know whom you were talking to, these three nights, O Abu Huraira?" Abu Huraira said, "No." He said, "It was Satan."[1287]

Satan's time of leisure is spending every night tying your hair into knots before untying them while you are asleep. Truly, the pedophile Prophet of Islam was a visionary of the unique variety:

Collection
Sahih Bukhari

Dar-us-Salam reference

---

the-right-hand-is-preferred-over-the-left.
72. [1287] "Sahih Al-Bukhari Book Number 38 Hadith Number 505." *Muflihun*, muflihun.com/bukhari/38/505.

Hadith 3269

In-book reference
Book 59, Hadith 79

USC-MSA web (English) reference
Volume 4, Book 54, Hadith 491

Narrated Abu Huraira:
Allah's Messenger (☪) said, "During your sleep, Satan knots three knots at the back of the head of each of you, and he breathes the following words at each knot, 'The night is, long, so keep on sleeping,' If that person wakes up and celebrates the praises of Allah, then one knot is undone, and when he performs ablution the second knot is undone, and when he prays, all the knots are undone, and he gets up in the morning lively and in good spirits, otherwise he gets up in low spirits and lethargic."[1288]

According to the wisdom of Prophet Mohammad, Satan apparently urinates in people's ears while they're asleep:

Collection
Sahih Bukhari

Dar-us-Salam reference
Hadith 1144

In-book reference
Book 19, Hadith 25

USC-MSA web (English) reference
Volume 2, Book 21, Hadith 245

Narrated `Abdullah:
A person was mentioned before the Prophet (p.b.u.h) and he was told that he had kept on sleeping till morning and had not got up for the prayer. The Prophet (☪) said, "Satan urinated in his ears."[1289]

When Satan isn't doing any of that, beware that Satan could be hiding in your nose according to the pedophile Prophet Mohammad himself:

Collection
Sahih Muslim

In-book reference
Book 2, Hadith 31

Reference
Hadith 238

USC-MSA web (English) reference

---

73. [1288] "QuranX.com The Most Complete Quran / Hadith / Tafsir Collection Available!" *Sahih Bukhari Hadiths*, quranx.com/Hadith/Bukhari/USC-MSA/Volume-4/Book-54/Hadith-491/.
74. [1289] "QuranX.com The Most Complete Quran / Hadith / Tafsir Collection Available!" *Sahih Bukhari Hadiths*, quranx.com/Hadith/Bukhari/USC-MSA/Volume-2/Book-21/Hadith-245/.

Book 2, Hadith 462
Abu Huraira reported:
The Apostle of Allah (ﷺ) said. When any one of you awakes up from sleep and performs ablution, he must clean his nose three times, for the devil spends the night in the interior of his nose.[1290]

Men should pray to the Abrahamic God while having sexual intercourse with their wives otherwise Satan will harm the child that is conceived from their sexual relations. It is also implied that Satan watches Muslims while they have sex in this hadith:

Collection
Sahih Bukhari

Dar-us-Salam reference
Hadith 3271

In-book reference
Book 59, Hadith 81

USC-MSA web (English) reference
Volume 4, Book 54, Hadith 493

Narrated Ibn `Abbas:
The Prophet (ﷺ) said, "If anyone of you, when having sexual relation with his wife, say: 'In the name of Allah. O Allah! Protect us from Satan and prevent Satan from approaching our offspring you are going to give us,' and if he begets a child (as a result of that relation) Satan will not harm it."[1291]

Satan comes in the shape of a woman and so Muslim men should go to their wives immediately to have sexual relations with them in order to relieve their sexual urges to avoid being tempted by Satan:

Collection
Sahih Muslim

In-book reference
Book 16, Hadith 10

Reference
Hadith 1403a

USC-MSA web (English) reference
Book 8, Hadith 3240

Jabir reported that Allah's Messenger (ﷺ) saw a woman, and so he came to his wife, Zainab, as she was tanning a leather and had sexual intercourse with her. He then went to his Companions and told them: The woman advances and retires in the shape of a devil, so when one of you sees a woman, he should come to his wife, for that will repel what he feels in his heart.[1292]

---

75. [1290] "QuranX.com The Most Complete Quran / Hadith / Tafsir Collection Available!" *Sahih Muslim Hadiths*, quranx.com/Hadith/Muslim/USC-MSA/Book-2/Hadith-462/.
76. [1291] "QuranX.com The Most Complete Quran / Hadith / Tafsir Collection Available!" *Sahih Bukhari Hadiths*, quranx.com/Hadith/Bukhari/USC-MSA/Volume-4/Book-54/Hadith-493/.

Satan intensifies the pain of menstrual bleeding according to the pedophile Prophet Mohammad:

1 The Book of Purification
(10) Chapter: Menstruation

Narrated Hamnah bint Jahsh:
'I had a very strong prolonged flow of blood. I went to the Prophet (Peace be upon him) to ask him about it. He said, "This is a strike from Satan. So observe your menses for six or seven days, then perform Ghusl until you see that you are clean. Pray for twenty-four or twenty-three nights and days and fast, and that will suffice you. Do so every month just as the other women menstruate (and are purified). But if you are strong enough to delay the Dhuhr prayer and advance the Asr prayer, then make Ghusl when your purified and combine the Dhuhr and the Asr prayers together; then delay the Maghrib prayer and advance the Isha prayer, and perform Ghusl and combine the two prayers, do so. Do so, and then wash at dawn and pray Fajr. This is how you may pray and fast if you have the ability to do so." And he said, "That is the more preferable way to me." [Reported by the five imams except An- Nasa'i, At-Tirmidhi graded it Sahih (sound)][1293]

Muslims must sit close together in prayer to avoid Satan entering through an opening during prayer. He watches and roams about Muslims while they pray:

Anas (May Allah be pleased with him) reported:
The Messenger of Allah (ﷺ) said, "Stand close together in your rows, keep nearer to one another, and put your necks in line, for by Him in Whose Hands my soul is, I see the Satan entering through the opening in the row like Al- hadhaf (i.e., a type of small black sheep found in Yemen)."
[Abu Dawud].[1294]

The pedophile prophet Mohammad sought refuge from Satan's poetry in a prayer to the Abrahamic God, so apparently poetry itself is from Satan:

It was narrated from Ibn Jubair bin Mut'im that his father said:
"I saw the Messenger of Allah (ﷺ) when he started the prayer. He said: 'Allahu Akbaru kabiran, Allahu Akbaru kabiran (Allah is the Most Great indeed),' three times; 'Al-hamdu Lillahi kathiran, al-hamdu Lillahi kathiran (Much praise is to Allah),' three times; 'Subhan Allahi bukratan wa asilan (Glory is to Allah morning and evening),' three times; 'Allahumma inni a'udhu bika minash-Shaitanir-rajim, min hamzihi wa nafkhihi wa nafthihi (O Allah, I seek refuge in You from the accursed Satan, from his madness, his poetry, and his pride)."[1295]

---

77. [1292] "QuranX.com The Most Complete Quran / Hadith / Tafsir Collection Available!" *Sahih Muslim Hadiths*, quranx.com/Hadith/Muslim/USC-MSA/Book-8/Hadith-3240/.
78. [1293] *Hadith - The Book of Purification - Bulugh Al-Maram - Sunnah.com - Sayings and Teachings of Prophet Muhammad (□□□ □□□□ □□ □□□)*, sunnah.com/bulugh/1/169.
79. [1294] *Hadith - The Book of Virtues - Riyad as-Salihin - Sunnah.com - Sayings and Teachings of Prophet Muhammad (□□□ □□□□ □□ □□□)*, sunnah.com/riyadussaliheen/9/102.
80. [1295] *Hadith - Establishing the Prayer and the Sunnah Regarding Them - Sunan Ibn Majah - Sunnah.com - Sayings and Teachings of Prophet Muhammad (□□□ □□□□ □□ □□□)*, sunnah.com/urn/1281560.

Satan is responsible for making people forget things:

(27) Chapter: The story of Al-Khidr with Musa (Moses) alayhis-salam
Narrated Ibn `Abbas:
That he differed with Al-Hur bin Qais Al-Fazari regarding the companion of Moses. Ibn `Abbas said that he was Al-Khadir. Meanwhile Ubai bin Ka`b passed by them and Ibn `Abbas called him saying, "My friend and I have differed regarding Moses' companion whom Moses asked the way to meet. Have you heard Allah's Messenger (ﷺ) mentioning something about him?" He said, "Yes, I heard Allah's Apostle saying, 'While Moses was sitting in the company of some Israelites, a man came and asked (him), 'Do you know anyone who is more learned than you?' Moses replied, 'No.' So, Allah sent the Divine Inspiration to Moses: 'Yes, Our slave, Khadir (is more learned than you).' Moses asked how to meet him (i.e. Khadir). So, the fish, was made, as a sign for him, and he was told that when the fish was lost, he should return and there he would meet him. So, Moses went on looking for the sign of the fish in the sea. The servant boy of Moses said to him, 'Do you know that when we were sitting by the side of the rock, I forgot the fish, and t was only Satan who made me forget to tell (you) about it.' Moses said, That was what we were seeking after,' and both of them returned, following their footmarks and found Khadir; and what happened further to them, is mentioned in Allah's Book."[1296]

Not only does he make you forget, he'll make you forget how long you pray and he'll fart when you're praying:

Sahih al-Bukhari Book 11 Hadith 582

Narrated Abu Huraira:

Allah's Apostle said, "When the Adhan is pronounced Satan takes to his heels and passes wind with noise during his flight in order not to hear the Adhan. When the Adhan is completed he comes back and again takes to his heels when the Iqama is pronounced and after its completion he returns again till he whispers into the heart of the person (to divert his attention from his prayer) and makes him remember things which he does not recall to his mind before the prayer and that causes him to forget how much he has prayed."[1297]

But worst of all, Satan might try to influence you to question religious assumptions and to think for yourself instead of being blindly dependent upon the Abrahamic God to do your thinking for you as per the pedophile Prophet Mohammad's instructions:

Sahih Muslim Book 1 Hadith 244
It is narrated on the authority of Abu Huraira that the Messenger of Allah may peace be upon him) observed: The Satan comes to everyone. of you and says: Who created this and that? till he questions: Who created your Lord? When he comes to that, one should seek refuge in Allah and keep away (from such idle thoughts).[1298]

1 The Book of Faith

---

81. [1296] *Hadith - Book of Prophets - Sahih Al-Bukhari - Sunnah.com - Sayings and Teachings of Prophet Muhammad (☐☐☐ ☐☐ ☐☐ ☐☐ ☐☐☐)*, sunnah.com/bukhari/60/73.
82. [1297] "Sahih Al-Bukhari Book Number 11 Hadith Number 582." *Muflihun*, muflihun.com/bukhari/11/582.
83. [1298] "Sahih Muslim Book Number 1 Hadith Number 244." *Muflihun*, muflihun.com/muslim/1/244.

(60) Chapter: Clarifying the Waswasah (Whispers, Bad Thoughts) with regard to faith, and what the one who experiences that should say

This hadith is transmitted by Urwa b. Zubair on the authority of Abu Huraira (and the words are):
The Satan comes to the bondsman (of Allah) and says: Who created this and that? The remaining part of the hadith is the same.[1299]

Support for Slavery

While the fears of Satan and belief in female slaves in heaven may garner some amusement and some would argue that such beliefs are harmless, the fact remains that these are deeply held religious beliefs and they are accepted as unquestioned fact because the Islamic Prophet Mohammad taught them to Muslims. In Islam, the Prophet Mohammad is seen as the perfect human being whose example is one to live by, so that means when he took sex slaves and raped them then it is morally justified for Muslim men to kidnap women and rape them as per religious instruction.[1300] When the Prophet Mohammad approves of rape, then that means Muslims have a religious right to rape their sex slaves. Most Muslim men in the West wouldn't do this because they follow secular morals and they're capable of their own reasoning faculties thanks to secular education, but this does happen in Muslim majority countries and has been spilling over to target non-Muslim women in Western countries from immigrants who originate from countries like Pakistan. The majority of Muslim men from Islamic countries are apathetic to the kidnapping and rape of girls as young as nine years of age who are then forced to marry their rapists and then are told to be obedient to their rapist.[1301] The rapist tells them to publically support what was done to them through coercion or they'll suffer worse as per Islamic teachings that instruct to beat disobedient wives.[1302] This is ingrained in Islamic teachings because the Islamic Prophet Mohammad had sex slaves; he approved the capture, enslavement, and sexual slavery of women. Moreover, because he married Aisha when she was 6-years old and had sexual intercourse with her when she was 9-years of age, it means that Muslim men are allowed to have sexual intercourse with children they kidnap when they're 9-years old.[1303] I wouldn't have taken such an issue as a serious concern in the West, but when

---

84. [1299] *Hadith - The Book of Faith - Sahih Muslim - Sunnah.com - Sayings and Teachings of Prophet Muhammad (☐☐ ☐☐☐☐ ☐☐ ☐☐☐)*, sunnah.com/muslim/1/253.
85. [1300] "The Quranic Arabic Corpus - Word by Word Grammar, Syntax and Morphology of the Holy Quran." *The Quranic Arabic Corpus - Translation*, http://corpus.quran.com/translation.jsp?chapter=4&verse=24
86. [1301] "Pakistani Hindus Complain of Forced Conversion of Teenage Girls." *YouTube*, VOA News, 18 Mar. 2016, youtu.be/-i24jg4mJ4I.
87. [1302] "The Quranic Arabic Corpus - Word by Word Grammar, Syntax and Morphology of the Holy Quran." *The Quranic Arabic Corpus - Translation*, http://corpus.quran.com/translation.jsp?chapter=4&verse=34
88. [1303] "Age of the Mother of the Believers 'Aa'ishah (May Allah Be Pleased with Her) When the Prophet (Blessings and Peace of Allah Be upon Him) Married Her - Islam Question & Answer." *Islamqa.info*, Islam Question and Answer, 30 Dec. 2013, islamqa.info/en/answers/124483/age-of-the-mother-of-the-believers-aaishah-may-allah-be-pleased-with-her-when-the-prophet-blessings-and-peace-of-allah-be-

you have grooming gangs in Britain targeting young women to rape or sexually enslave[1304][1305][1306] and Harvard Divinity Graduates of Islam in the United States advocating for sex with 9-year olds, then we have a serious problem.[1307] Additionally, it must be made explicitly clear that Islam is a racially diverse religious faith in the United States and far too often, racially motivated attacks occur upon Sikhs and ethnic minorities such as Indians under the belief they're Muslim.[1308] Regardless of the reasons, all racially motivated and religiously motivated forms of persecution and violence should be condemned. The only way to end the danger of Islam is by criticizing the beliefs, which is what I aim to do in this book. I condemn all forms of anti-Muslim bigotry, most Muslims are better than Islam. I condemn Islam just as I condemn violence against Muslims.

This portion of the critique will focus on the subject matter of particular hadiths and may not strictly focus on numerical order. This particular set of hadiths concerning sexual slavery was shared online in various comments sections with short comments concerning each one. I was doubtful that they referred to actual hadiths until I became curious enough to search the listed hadiths for myself. To my shock and disgust, this commentator was being completely honest and there are hadiths that justify sexual slavery and thereby legitimize sexual slavery, war rape, and other horrific actions conducted by groups like ISIS and targeting children for gang rapes and sexual slavery by grooming gangs of Muslim men in the West. Muslims may be keen on arguing that the hadiths aren't "authentic" but all any Islamic organization needs is an Imam of their own saying that the hadiths are authentic to legitimize them so it is a moot point. These teachings must be recognized as harmful and criticized; they must also be recognized as coming from the Islamic faith as they are explicit instructions by the pedophile Prophet Mohammad.

The Islamic Prophet Mohammad stopped the emancipation of six slaves, kept four of the slaves for himself, and cast lots to decide which two would be freed:

Sahih Muslim Book 15 Hadith 4112

'Imran b. Husain reported that a person who had no other property emancipated six slaves of his at the time of his death. Allah's Messenger (Peace be upon him) called for them and divided them into three

---

upon-him-married-her.
89. [1304] "Bradford Grooming: Nine Jailed for Abusing Girls." *BBC News*, BBC, 27 Feb. 2019, www.bbc.com/news/uk-england-leeds-47388060.
90. [1305] Chhabhadiya, Neelam. "Sexual Grooming amongst Hindu Girls." *National Hindu Students' Forum (UK)*, 5 Nov. 2017, www.nhsf.org.uk/2017/11/sexual-grooming-amongst-hindu-girls/.
91. [1306] Evans, Martin. "Newcastle Grooming Gangs Were Allowed to Abuse 700 Girls Because Police Blamed the Victims, Review Finds." *The Telegraph*, Telegraph Media Group, 23 Feb. 2018, www.telegraph.co.uk/news/2018/02/23/newcastle-grooming-gangs-acted-arrogant-persistence-serious/.
92. [1307] Navabi, Armin. "Muslim Defends Muhammad Having Sex with Aisha When She Was Nine!" *YouTube*, Atheist Republic, 3 Jan. 2019, youtu.be/yKExtzI68jM.
93. [1308] Greenwood, Shannon. "Demographic Portrait of Muslim Americans." *Pew Research Center's Religion & Public Life Project*, Pew Research Center's Religion & Public Life Project, 9 Nov. 2017, www.pewforum.org/2017/07/26/demographic-portrait-of-muslim-americans/.

sections, cast lots amongst them, and set two free and kept four in slavery; and he (the Holy Prophet) spoke severely of him.[1309]

The Prophet Mohammad sold a slave and therefore selling slaves is moral in Islam since the so-called perfect human being did it:

Sahih al-Bukhari Book 34 Hadith 351

Narrated Jabir bin Abdullah:

A man decided that a slave of his would be manumitted after his death and later on he was in need of money, so the Prophet took the slave and said, "Who will buy this slave from me?" Nu'aim bin 'Abdullah bought him for such and such price and the Prophet gave him the slave.[1310]

Manumission refers to releasing a person from slavery, please keep that in mind. This is another reference to the Islamic Prophet Mohammad cancelling the emancipation of a slave in order to sell the slave:

Sahih al-Bukhari Book 41 Hadith 598

Narrated Jabir: A man manumitted a slave and he had no other property than that, so the Prophet cancelled the manumission (and sold the slave for him). No'aim bin Al-Nahham bought the slave from him.[1311]

The Islamic Prophet Mohammad chastised a woman for releasing her slave girl from slavery and instructed that the Muslim woman would have gained a greater reward in heaven if she had sold her slave to a maternal uncle:

Sahih al-Bukhari Book 47 Hadith 765

Narrated Kurib:

the freed slave of Ibn 'Abbas, that Maimuna bint Al-Harith told him that she manumitted a slave-girl without taking the permission of the Prophet. On the day when it was her turn to be with the Prophet, she said, "Do you know, O Allah's Apostle, that I have manumitted my slave-girl?" He said, "Have you really?" She replied in the affirmative. He said, "You would have got more reward if you had given her (i.e. the slave-girl) to one of your maternal uncles."[1312]

In this hadith, the Islamic Prophet Mohammad instructs that a Muslim man who takes a slave girl to teach her the ways of Islam without "violence" and then marries her gets a double-reward in heaven. Be aware that Quran verse 4:24 makes it clear that raping slave girls is permitted by the Abrahamic God and because it is in the Quran, it must be considered

---

94. [1309] "Sahih Muslim Book Number 15 Hadith Number 4112." *Muflihun*, muflihun.com/muslim/15/4112.
95. [1310] "Sahih Al-Bukhari Book Number 34 Hadith Number 351." *Muflihun*, muflihun.com/bukhari/34/351.
96. [1311] "Sahih Al-Bukhari Book Number 41 Hadith Number 598." *Muflihun*, muflihun.com/bukhari/41/598.
97. [1312] "Sahih Al-Bukhari Book Number 47 Hadith Number 765." *Muflihun*, muflihun.com/bukhari/47/765.

unquestioned fact that nobody who is a non-Muslim is allowed to criticize.[1313] Upon marriage, Quran verse 4:34 makes it clear that beating a disobedient wife is allowed.[1314] We see the harmful effects of these Quranic teachings from grooming gangs in the West and the targeting and rape of children in Islamic majority countries like Pakistan. Moreover, according to this hadith, if Muslim men have done this with full faith in the teachings of the Islamic Prophet Mohammad, then they're awarded doubly so on top of that. Keeping slaves obedient to their Masters is also encouraged to be a moral act; so beatings, raping, and coercing women into these patriarchal norms and standards is seen as good moral behavior in the context of Islam:

Sahih al-Bukhari Book 52 Hadith 255

Narrated Abu Burda's father:

The Prophet said, "Three persons will get their reward twice. (One is) a person who has a slave girl and he educates her properly and teaches her good manners properly (without violence) and then manumits and marries her. Such a person will get a double reward. (Another is) a believer from the people of the scriptures who has been a true believer and then he believes in the Prophet (Muhammad). Such a person will get a double reward. (The third is) a slave who observes Allah's Rights and Obligations and is sincere to his master."[1315]

If all that hasn't horrified and disgusted readers enough, here are two hadiths in which the Islamic Prophet Mohammad says not to do coitus interruptus. For those who don't know what that term means, coitus interruptus is the technical term for a man pulling out his penis before ejaculating. In these specific hadiths, Muslim men who had taken slave girl captives from conquered territories are asked by the Prophet Mohammad whether they really pulled their penises out when they raped their slave girls. The conversation is in the context of questioning whether or not pulling out before ejaculating harms the price that the slave girls are sold for. The wording may seem confusing at first, but in their ancient context, people believed that souls were real. The Islamic Prophet Mohammad assures his male Muslim followers who take slave girls and rape them that ejaculating their cum into a slave girl won't impregnate them unless the Abrahamic God wills it. Therefore, due to the belief in the soul and the belief that the Abrahamic God determines the so-called miracle of childbirth, the Islamic Prophet Mohammad encouraged Muslim men to ejaculate inside their slave girls when they rape them because they believed the slave girls wouldn't become pregnant unless the Abrahamic God willed it. If that isn't horrifying enough, just imagine what members of the terrorist group ISIS does to Yazidi and Christian captives and what Pakistani and Afghan Muslims do to Hindu,

---

98. [1313] "The Quranic Arabic Corpus - Word by Word Grammar, Syntax and Morphology of the Holy Quran." *The Quranic Arabic Corpus - Translation*, http://corpus.quran.com/translation.jsp?chapter=4&verse=24
99. [1314] "The Quranic Arabic Corpus - Word by Word Grammar, Syntax and Morphology of the Holy Quran." *The Quranic Arabic Corpus - Translation*, http://corpus.quran.com/translation.jsp?chapter=4&verse=34
100. [1315] "Sahih Al-Bukhari Book Number 52 Hadith Number 255." *Muflihun*, muflihun.com/bukhari/52/255.

Sikh, Buddhist, and Christian minorities in Islamic countries when they target female children. I must reiterate that these are teachings that must be criticized:

Sahih al-Bukhari Book 34 Hadith 432

Narrated Abu Said Al-Khudri:

that while he was sitting with Allah's Apostle he said, "O Allah's Apostle! We get female captives as our share of booty, and we are interested in their prices, what is your opinion about coitus interrupt us?" The Prophet said, "Do you really do that? It is better for you not to do it. No soul that which Allah has destined to exist, but will surely come into existence.[1316]

Sahih al-Bukhari Book 62 Hadith 137

Narrated Abu Said Al-Khudri:

We got female captives in the war booty and we used to do coitus interruptus with them. So we asked Allah's Apostle about it and he said, "Do you really do that?" repeating the question thrice, "There is no soul that is destined to exist but will come into existence, till the Day of Resurrection."[1317]

Please consider comparing the so-called wisdom of the Islamic Prophet Mohammad with people from the past who you personally like or celebrate the philosophies of. Even if some of those people did benefit from or supported slavery, and they should be rightfully condemned for having done so, they aren't celebrated as being beyond the ability to criticize and we can evaluate them from their positives and negatives. This is not allowed in Islam; everything the Islamic Prophet Mohammad does and advocates for has to be regarded as the actions of a perfect human being for Muslims and they believe nobody has the right to criticize their Prophet. To Muslims, does this teaching of the Islamic Prophet Mohammad sound like emancipation to you? Islam is a religion of submission and as such, all it can do is harm people:

Sahih al-Bukhari Book 80 Hadith 753

Narrated Anas bin Malik:

The Prophet said, "The freed slave belongs to the people who have freed him," or said something similar.[1318]

The Islamic Prophet Mohammad's own religious pulpit was built by slave labor:

Sahih al-Bukhari Book 47 Hadith 743

Narrated Sahl:

The Prophet sent for a woman from the emigrants and she had a slave who was a carpenter. The Prophet said to her "Order your slave to prepare the wood (pieces) for the pulpit." So, she ordered her slave who

---

101.[1316] "Sahih Al-Bukhari Book Number 34 Hadith Number 432." *Muflihun*, muflihun.com/bukhari/34/432.
102.[1317] "Sahih Al-Bukhari Book Number 62 Hadith Number 137." *Muflihun*, muflihun.com/bukhari/62/137.
103.[1318] "Sahih Al-Bukhari Book Number 80 Hadith Number 753." *Muflihun*, muflihun.com/bukhari/80/753.

went and cut the wood from the tamarisk and prepared the pulpit, for the Prophet. When he finished the pulpit, the woman informed the Prophet that it had been finished. The Prophet asked her to send that pulpit to him, so they brought it. The Prophet lifted it and placed it at the place in which you see now."[1319]

Finally, please read these three hadiths which are accounts of the Islamic Prophet Mohammad's destruction of a Jewish tribe and the subsequent enslavement and then forced marriage of a Jewish woman, Safiya bin Huyai. In these accounts, Safiya is taken to the illiterate and pedophilic warlord, the Prophet Mohammad, because of her beauty. The accounts explain that the Prophet Mohammad's army slaughtered her entire tribe, killed all the men who surrendered, took the adult women and young female children as sex slaves, and the Prophet Mohammad had Safiya's "release from slavery" be a coerced marriage to him and that was only after he was finished pondering whether to make her into one of his personal sex slaves or into one of his wives. This pedophilic, illiterate warlord is who Muslims must strive to emulate and revere as the perfect human being:

Collection
Sahih Bukhari

Dar-us-Salam reference
Hadith 2235

In-book reference
Book 34, Hadith 181

USC-MSA web (English) reference
Volume 3, Book 34, Hadith 437

Related Qur'an verses
2.234, 4.24, 33.21, 33.52

Narrated Anas bin Malik:
The Prophet (ﷺ) came to Khaibar and when Allah made him victorious and he conquered the town by breaking the enemy's defense, the beauty of Safiya bint Huyai bin Akhtab was mentioned to him and her husband had been killed while she was a bride. Allah's Messenger (ﷺ) selected her for himself and he set out in her company till he reached Sadd-ar-Rawha' where her menses were over and he married her. Then Hais (a kind of meal) was prepared and served on a small leather sheet (used for serving meals). Allah's Messenger (ﷺ) then said to me, "Inform those who are around you (about the wedding banquet)." So that was the marriage banquet given by Allah's Messenger (ﷺ) for (his marriage with) Safiya. After that we proceeded to Medina and I saw that Allah's Messenger (ﷺ) was covering her with a cloak while she was behind him. Then he would sit beside his camel and let Safiya put her feet on his knees to ride (the camel).[1320]

Collection
Sahih Bukhari

104.[1319] "Sahih Al-Bukhari Book Number 47 Hadith Number 743." *Muflihun*, muflihun.com/bukhari/47/743.
105.[1320] "QuranX.com The Most Complete Quran / Hadith / Tafsir Collection Available!" *Sahih Bukhari Hadiths*, quranx.com/Hadith/Bukhari/USC-MSA/Volume-3/Book-34/Hadith-437/.

Dar-us-Salam reference
Hadith 4200

In-book reference
Book 64, Hadith 240

USC-MSA web (English) reference
Volume 5, Book 59, Hadith 512

Related Qur'an verses
2.234, 4.24

Narrated Anas:
The Prophet (☪) offered the Fajr Prayer near Khaibar when it was still dark and then said, "Allahu-Akbar! Khaibar is destroyed, for whenever we approach a (hostile) nation (to fight), then evil will be the morning for those who have been warned." Then the inhabitants of Khaibar came out running on the roads. The Prophet (☪) had their warriors killed, their offspring and woman taken as captives. Safiya was amongst the captives, She first came in the share of Dahya Alkali but later on she belonged to the Prophet. The Prophet (☪) made her manumission as her 'Mahr'.[1321]

Collection
Sahih Bukhari

Dar-us-Salam reference
Hadith 4213

In-book reference
Book 64, Hadith 253

USC-MSA web (English) reference
Volume 5, Book 59, Hadith 524

Related Qur'an verses
2.234, 4.24

Narrated Anas:
The Prophet (☪) stayed for three rights between Khaibar and Medina and was married to Safiya. I invited the Muslim to h s marriage banquet and there wa neither meat nor bread in that banquet but the Prophet ordered Bilal to spread the leather mats on which dates, dried yogurt and butter were put. The Muslims said amongst themselves, "Will she (i.e. Safiya) be one of the mothers of the believers, (i.e. one of the wives of the Prophet (☪)) or just (a lady captive) of what his right-hand possesses" Some of them said, "If the Prophet (☪) makes her observe the veil, then she will be one of the mothers of the believers (i.e. one of the Prophet's wives), and if he does not make her observe the veil, then she will be his lady slave." So when he departed, he made a place for her behind him (on his and made her observe the veil.[1322]

Islamic Theology and Female Genital Mutilation

In Islam, most Islamic schools of thought consider the matter of Female Genital Mutilation (FGM) to be an honor that women can choose to undertake. However, in the Shafi'i

---

106.[1321] "QuranX.com The Most Complete Quran / Hadith / Tafsir Collection Available!" *Sahih Bukhari Hadiths*, quranx.com/Hadith/Bukhari/USC-MSA/Volume-5/Book-59/Hadith-512/.
107.[1322] "QuranX.com The Most Complete Quran / Hadith / Tafsir Collection Available!" *Sahih Bukhari Hadiths*, quranx.com/Hadith/Bukhari/USC-MSA/Volume-5/Book-59/Hadith-524/.

school of Islam, it is considered mandatory to impose FGM upon young girls and they often undergo this horrific procedure in their infancy. If you don't believe that the Shafi'i school of Islam makes FGM mandatory, here is the evidence from a Shafi'i cleric who justifies the procedure in terms of a commitment to the purity of Islam and obedience to the Abrahamic God:

> *Rulings from your site regarding female circumcision appear to have been taken down. Is there is a change in opinion concerning female circumcision from a Shafii point of view? What do you say about issuing a fatwa on this issue which prohibits the practice?*

In Maratib al-Ijma' p. 157, Ibn Hazm cited that there is an established consensus (ar: ijma') that circumcision for women is permissible. This ijma' is related by other scholars too. In the Sacred Law, ijma' is a binding proof, and it is not permissible for any scholar to go against it.

In Nihayah 8/35, after mentioning the official position of the Shafi'i School, that circumcision is obligatory for both men and women, Ramli defines what it means for a woman. He says that it is the removal of some skin from the clitoral prepuce. This is also mentioned by Ibn Hajar in Tuhfah 9/198.

In these passages, the word "bazr" is mentioned. Sahib al-Misbah al-Munir mentions that the "bazr" in circumcision is the prepuce. Thus, what is intended is a part of the prepuce surrounding the clitoris and not the clitoris itself.

In Sunan Abi Dawud and Tabarani's al-Mu'jam al-Kabir, it is related that the Prophet Muhammad (upon him be peace) said,

لِلْبَعْلِ وَأَحَبُّ لِلْمَرْأَةِ أَحْظَى ذَلِكَ فَإِنَّ تُنْهِكِي لَا أَشِمِّي

"Leave it bulging, do not exaggerate in cutting. Indeed, that is more enjoyable for the woman, and the husband will like it better."

Some have declared Tabarani's chain to be authentic. While others criticized the authenticity of this narration. Here, it is not being cited to establish a basis for a practice in the Sacred Law, the aforementioned ijma' establishes that. The narration describes the manner in which the practice is to be performed. It clarifies that the procedure is minor and the reduction is slight; in fact, the verbs used are commands, which indicate obligation. Meaning, to go beyond this contravenes what the Prophet (upon him be peace) commanded.

What we have mentioned above is not FGM. In Arabic, the practice we are talking about is called "khafd," meaning, a reduction i.e. of the clitoral hood. This is actually, according to many health experts, an accepted medical procedure; something that when done properly, women are satisfied with.

Some individuals or organizations in Europe and other places argue that circumcision/unhooding is genital mutilation. The corollary of this line of argument is generally that it should be banned. This is obviously something that Muslims disagree with.

Allah commanded the Prophet Abraham (upon him be peace) to circumcise, and Allah says in the Qur'an, "Follow the way of Abraham, as a pure monotheist." (Surah al-Nahl 123) And circumcision is part of his way; it is a ritual of obedience to God first performed by the father of the monotheistic faiths.

Also, it was practiced and advised in the time of the Prophet Muhammad (upon him be peace), for both men and women.

The official position of the Shafi'i School is that it is obligatory for a woman. There is also a weaker opinion that Imam Nawawi relates in Rawdah 10/180 that it is recommended. This is the opinion maintained by other scholars who considered that it is recommended or simply a noble deed, like Imam Abu Hanifah and Imam Malik. A woman following the Shafi'i School could make taqlid of these opinions. She would thereby be omitting a meritorious act, but not an obligation.

For a Muslim scholar to issue a fatwa against it, that violates the aforementioned consensus, and to violate consensus is impermissible. Such a fatwa would also disregard many experts from the medical community who have expressed the benefits that such procedures have for women.

And Allah knows best.

Answered by: Shaykh Yaqub Abdurrahman[1323]

For any potential Muslim readers from the Shafi'i school of Islam who believe FGM is morally obligatory or who are indifferent to the procedure, please be advised that FGM does have irreversible and life-threatening health impacts for your daughters and that no qualified medical experts should be endorsing such a procedure as it has severe health risks with no benefits at all. Below is a short compilation provided by the World Health Organization (WHO) that details FGM's short-term and permanent long-term damage to the health and welfare of female children. In my honest opinion, if you pursue FGM for your children or any of your family members knowing the consequences then you obviously don't love them:

> **Health risks of female genital mutilation (FGM)**
>
> Women and girls living with FGM have experienced a harmful practice. Experience of FGM increases the short and long term health risks to women and girls and is unacceptable from a human rights and health perspective. While in general there is an increased risk of adverse health outcomes with increased severity of FGM, WHO is opposed to all forms of FGM and is emphatically against the practice being carried out by health care providers (medicalization).
>
> Short-term health risks of FGM
>
> **Severe pain**: cutting the nerve ends and sensitive genital tissue causes extreme pain. Proper anaesthesia is rarely used and, when used, is not always effective. The healing period is also painful. Type III FGM is a more extensive procedure of longer duration, hence the intensity and duration of pain may be more severe. The healing period is also prolonged and intensified accordingly.
> **Excessive bleeding**: (haemorrhage) can result if the clitoral artery or other blood vessel is cut during the procedure.
> **Shock**: can be caused by pain, infection and/or haemorrhage.
> **Genital tissue swelling**: due to inflammatory response or local infection.

---

108. [1323] "Rulings from Your Site Regarding Female Circumcision Appear to Have Been Taken down. Is There Is a Change in Opinion Concerning Female Circumcision from a Shafii Point of View? What Do You Say about Issuing a Fatwa on This Issue Which Prohibits the Practice?" Translated by Yaqub Abdurrahman, *Shafii Fiqh*, shafiifiqh.com/question-details.aspx?qstID=173.

Infections: may spread after the use of contaminated instruments (e.g. use of same instruments in multiple genital mutilation operations), and during the healing period.

Human immunodeficiency virus (HIV): the direct association between FGM and HIV remains unconfirmed, although the cutting of genital tissues with the same surgical instrument without sterilization could increase the risk for transmission of HIV between girls who undergo female genital mutilation together.

Urination problems: these may include urinary retention and pain passing urine. This may be due to tissue swelling, pain or injury to the urethra.

Impaired wound healing: can lead to pain, infections and abnormal scarring

Death: can be caused by infections, including tetanus and haemorrhage that can lead to shock.

Psychological consequences: the pain, shock and the use of physical force by those performing the procedure are mentioned as reasons why many women describe FGM as a traumatic event.

Long-term health risks from Types I, II and III (occurring at any time during life)

Pain: due to tissue damage and scarring that may result in trapped or unprotected nerve endings.

Infections:
- **Chronic genital infections**: with consequent chronic pain, and vaginal discharge and itching. Cysts, abscesses and genital ulcers may also appear.
- **Chronic reproductive tract infections**: May cause chronic back and pelvic pain.
- **Urinary tract infections**: If not treated, such infections can ascend to the kidneys, potentially resulting in renal failure, septicaemia and death. An increased risk for repeated urinary tract infections is well documented in both girls and adult women.

Painful urination: due to obstruction of the urethra and recurrent urinary tract infections.

Menstrual problems: result from the obstruction of the vaginal opening. This may lead to painful menstruation (dysmenorrhea), irregular menses and difficulty in passing menstrual blood, particularly among women with Type III FGM.

Keloids: there have been reports of excessive scar tissue formation at the site of the cutting.

Human immunodeficiency virus (HIV): given that the transmission of HIV is facilitated through trauma of the vaginal epithelium which allows the direct introduction of the virus, it is reasonable to presume that the risk of HIV transmission may be increased due to increased risk for bleeding during intercourse, as a result of FGM.

Female sexual health: removal of, or damage to highly sensitive genital tissue, especially the clitoris, may affect sexual sensitivity and lead to sexual problems, such as decreased sexual desire and pleasure, pain during sex, difficulty during penetration, decreased lubrication during intercourse, reduced frequency or absence of orgasm (anorgasmia). Scar formation, pain and traumatic memories associated with the procedure can also lead to such problems.

Obstetric complications: FGM is associated with an increased risk of Caesarean section, post-partum haemorrhage, recourse to episiotomy, difficult labour, obstetric tears/lacerations, instrumental delivery, prolonged labour, and extended maternal hospital stay. The risks increase with the severity of FGM.

Obstetric fistula: a direct association between FGM and obstetric fistula has not been established. However, given the causal relationship between prolonged and obstructed labour and fistula, and the fact that FGM is also associated with prolonged and obstructed labour it is reasonable to presume that both conditions could be linked in women living with FGM.

Perinatal risks: obstetric complications can result in a higher incidence of infant resuscitation at delivery and intrapartum stillbirth and neonatal death.

Psychological consequences: some studies have shown an increased likelihood of post-traumatic stress disorder (PTSD), anxiety disorders and depression. The cultural significance of FGM might not protect against psychological complications.[1324]

It should be clearly stated: any Islamic apologist, whether Muslim or non-Muslim, who continues to spread the lie that Islam has nothing to do with female genital mutilation is not

---

109. [1324] "Health Risks of Female Genital Mutilation (FGM)." *World Health Organization*, World Health Organization, 1 Feb. 2017, www.who.int/reproductivehealth/topics/fgm/health_consequences_fgm/en/.

morally different from people promoting anti-vaxxer campaigns that spread disinformation about vaccines. The only reason an apologist for FGM would believe that it is not morally equivalent, to lying about vaccines causing autism, is the idea of protecting sacred beliefs. The human rights - the health and welfare of young female children - should take top priority above any idiotic religious beliefs that permanently harm them. I would say the same if it were any other religion including my family background of Hinduism. People like myself who criticize these horrific practices aren't doing so because we hate Muslims, we do it because we care about the welfare of Muslims. Our criticisms and Free Speech are an act of compassion. I say the same for Hindus, Buddhists, Jains, Sikhs, Christians, and Jews who follow any barbaric practices that hurt their own communities. I will criticize them all the same because I care about them. If you're spreading disinformation and attempting to shield Muslims from criticism of these practices, then you don't give a damn about the wellbeing of Muslims and you're partly to blame for the continuation of harm imposed upon Muslim children.[1325] You are just being a bigot because a bigot is someone who holds two different sets of standards for different groups of people; it is an obvious lower standard towards Muslims as people.[1326]

The Killing of Apostates

This is perhaps the most notorious teaching of Islam. Before reading onward, please take a moment to think about everything I've just shared at this point about the fears of Satan, the practice of incest, the FGM, and being taught to live by the Islamic Prophet Mohammad's example. Imagine living in that kind of culture and worldview; imagine wanting to be free of it and yet you could be killed for leaving in an Islamic majority country or effectively thrown out of your community in a Western country. What kind of life is it to be hunted down and killed for not wanting to be part of this belief system? And yet, despite this incontrovertible fact about Islamic theology, people still defend or spread disinformation about it and effectively put Ex-Muslim lives in danger. The fact people's families would be willing to kill them for leaving the religion and the fact Ex-Muslims are forced to live in fear because of it is inexcusable. If there was any single teaching or practice that warranted the criticism that a religion isn't worth defending or reforming, this horrific practice should be it. To shield Islam from criticism is to put the lives of Ex-Muslims throughout the world in real danger. Religious tolerance is no justification for ignoring the plight of people's human rights. The obscurantism over this issue is deliberately putting people's lives in danger throughout the world. The Quran advocates for the killing of Apostates, here is verse 4:84 of the chapter "The Women" (known as chapter *sūrat l-nisāa* in Arabic) from several English translations of the Quran:

> **Sahih International**: They wish you would disbelieve as they disbelieved so you would be alike. So do not take from among them allies until they emigrate for the cause of Allah. But if they turn away, then seize them and kill them wherever you find them and take not from among them any ally or helper.

110.[1325] Saleem, Mya, et al. "Examining Honor Culture and Violence in Islam (AHA Conference 2016)." *YouTube*, American Humanist Association, 30 June 2016, www.youtube.com/watch?v=DhwrOJvPfBw.
111.[1326] Haider, Sarah. "Sarah Haider: Islam and the Necessity of Liberal Critique (AHA Conference 2015)." *YouTube*, American Humanist Association, 28 May 2015, www.youtube.com/watch?v=0plC24YuoJk.

Pickthall: They long that ye should disbelieve even as they disbelieve, that ye may be upon a level (with them). So choose not friends from them till they forsake their homes in the way of Allah; if they turn back (to enmity) then take them and kill them wherever ye find them, and choose no friend nor helper from among them,

Yusuf Ali: They but wish that ye should reject Faith, as they do, and thus be on the same footing (as they): But take not friends from their ranks until they flee in the way of Allah (From what is forbidden). But if they turn renegades, seize them and slay them wherever ye find them; and (in any case) take no friends or helpers from their ranks;-

Shakir: They desire that you should disbelieve as they have disbelieved, so that you might be (all) alike; therefore take not from among them friends until they fly (their homes) in Allah's way; but if they turn back, then seize them and kill them wherever you find them, and take not from among them a friend or a helper.

Muhammad Sarwar: They wish you to become unbelievers as they themselves are. Do not establish friendship with them until they have abandoned their homes for the cause of God. If they betray you, seize them and slay them wherever you find them. Do not establish friendship with them or seek their help

Mohsin Khan: They wish that you reject Faith, as they have rejected (Faith), and thus that you all become equal (like one another). So take not Auliya' (protectors or friends) from them, till they emigrate in the Way of Allah (to Muhammad SAW). But if they turn back (from Islam), take (hold) of them and kill them wherever you find them, and take neither Auliya' (protectors or friends) nor helpers from them.

Arberry: They wish that you should disbelieve as they disbelieve, and then you would be equal; therefore take not to yourselves friends of them, until they emigrate in the way of God; then, if they turn their backs, take them, and slay them wherever you find them; take not to yourselves any one of them as friend or helper[1327]

The Arabic version will undoubtedly verify the same instruction. If that is not enough, here are the Hadiths that certify that Muslims are instructed to kill any person who leaves the Islamic faith:

Sahih al-Bukhari Book 52 Hadith 260

Narrated Ikrima:

Ali burnt some people and this news reached Ibn 'Abbas, who said, "Had I been in his place I would not have burnt them, as the Prophet said, 'Don't punish (anybody) with Allah's Punishment.' No doubt, I would have killed them, for the Prophet said, 'If somebody (a Muslim) discards his religion, kill him.'"[1328]

Sahih al-Bukhari Book 84 Hadith 57

Narrated 'Ikrima:

Some Zanadiqa (atheists) were brought to 'Ali and he burnt them. The news of this event, reached Ibn

---

112. [1327] "The Quranic Arabic Corpus - Word by Word Grammar, Syntax and Morphology of the Holy Quran." *The Quranic Arabic Corpus - Translation*, corpus.quran.com/translation.jsp?chapter=4&verse=89.
113. [1328] "Sahih Al-Bukhari Book Number 52 Hadith Number 260." Muflihun, muflihun.com/bukhari/52/260.

'Abbas who said, "If I had been in his place, I would not have burnt them, as Allah's Apostle forbade it, saying, 'Do not punish anybody with Allah's punishment (fire).' I would have killed them according to the statement of Allah's Apostle, 'Whoever changed his Islamic religion, then kill him.'"[1329]

Sahih al-Bukhari Book 84 Hadith 58

Narrated Abu Burda:

Abu Musa said, "I came to the Prophet along with two men (from the tribe) of Ash'ariyin, one on my right and the other on my left, while Allah's Apostle was brushing his teeth (with a Siwak), and both men asked him for some employment. The Prophet said, 'O Abu Musa (O 'Abdullah bin Qais!).' I said, 'By Him Who sent you with the Truth, these two men did not tell me what was in their hearts and I did not feel (realize) that they were seeking employment.' As if I were looking now at his Siwak being drawn to a corner under his lips, and he said, 'We never (or, we do not) appoint for our affairs anyone who seeks to be employed. But O Abu Musa! (or 'Abdullah bin Qais!) Go to Yemen.'" The Prophet then sent Mu'adh bin Jabal after him and when Mu'adh reached him, he spread out a cushion for him and requested him to get down (and sit on the cushion). Behold: There was a fettered man beside Abu Muisa. Mu'adh asked, "Who is this (man)?" Abu Muisa said, "He was a Jew and became a Muslim and then reverted back to Judaism." Then Abu Muisa requested Mu'adh to sit down but Mu'adh said, "I will not sit down till he has been killed. This is the judgment of Allah and His Apostle (for such cases) and repeated it thrice. Then Abu Musa ordered that the man be killed, and he was killed. Abu Musa added, "Then we discussed the night prayers and one of us said, 'I pray and sleep, and I hope that Allah will reward me for my sleep as well as for my prayers.'"[1330]

Sahih al-Bukhari Book 84 Hadith 64

Narrated 'Ali:

Whenever I tell you a narration from Allah's Apostle, by Allah, I would rather fall down from the sky than ascribe a false statement to him, but if I tell you something between me and you (not a Hadith) then it was indeed a trick (i.e., I may say things just to cheat my enemy). No doubt I heard Allah's Apostle saying, "During the last days there will appear some young foolish people who will say the best words but their faith will not go beyond their throats (i.e. they will have no faith) and will go out from (leave) their religion as an arrow goes out of the game. So, where-ever you find them, kill them, for who-ever kills them shall have reward on the Day of Resurrection."[1331]

I would again like to thank Ridvan Aydemir, known as the Youtuber Apostate Prophet, for one of his videos which briefly references these Hadiths. He has been a wonderful resource with his public channel in which he freely disseminates the dangers of Islam. I cannot recommend his Youtube channel enough.[1332] Furthermore, I'd like to thank Ex-Muslims of North America again for helping me recognize the dangers of Islam. I'm disgusted by the level of sophistry that goes into protecting an empty, violent, and hate-filled ideology simply because it attains the sacred designation of religion to protect itself from any scrutiny. I care more about the human rights of Ex-Muslims than I do about offending the cultural sensibilities of Muslims. I criticize partly for those who cannot and because I'm deeply concerned for their human rights. If you really care about the lives of the most vulnerable people, then so should

---

114.[1329] "Sahih Al-Bukhari Book Number 84 Hadith Number 57." Muflihun, muflihun.com/bukhari/84/57.
115.[1330] "Sahih Al-Bukhari Book Number 84 Hadith Number 58." Muflihun, muflihun.com/bukhari/84/58.
116.[1331] "Sahih Al-Bukhari Book Number 84 Hadith Number 64." Muflihun, muflihun.com/bukhari/84/64.
117.[1332] Aydemir, Ridvan. *YouTube*, Apostate Prophet, www.youtube.com/channel/UCzREuchzOqiawpEpvEM0Tyg/videos.

you. We can criticize a hateful ideology, Islam, without falling into anti-Muslim bigotry and the lives of Ex-Muslims across the world and the ex-communicated Ex-Muslims in the West should take precedent over hurt feelings about Islam. To shut down Ex-Muslims critical of Islam is to partly aid in silencing and killing them. They must absolutely be allowed to speak their minds and be able to criticize as should we all for those who cannot. If Free Speech is ever to challenge the culture of submission and silence in Islam, then letting Ex-Muslims talk about their human rights and their issues with Islam is vital.

Reform versus Consistency

I feel I must reiterate to stress this point: I am not attempting to dehumanize Muslims as people and I am not calling for any laws banning Muslims or discriminating against Muslims. While I may have said something offensive about the intellect of people who follow Islam due to my disgust with Eid on a personal level, I must stress that I am against banning the hijab or the burqa because in the long-term, it allows for a shielding of criticism in which Muslims can argue that they're expressing their religious rights and defending their civil liberties instead of taking an honest self-reflection and internally deciding the hijab, burqa, niqab, and other equivalents are based on bad beliefs or make no sense from a logical point of view.

I must also stress that I am not saying that reform isn't possible because of Muslims lacking any intellectual qualities as people. I am saying that it is impossible because Islam itself is filled too much with stupid ideas that cause intelligent and otherwise compassionate people to do horrific atrocities. I fear that, if any "reform" was attempted, it would only lead into problems of political correctness from the standpoint of being a reformer and require policing Muslims into learning only certain portions of the Quran or Hadiths while vilifying other portions. Such "reform" could cause a yearning for the forbidden or "true" Islam within future Muslim generations because some Hadiths and Quranic verses were labeled as forbidden or taken out. How would such a system even work with abrogating verses in certain systems of Islamic jurisprudence? Moreover, Muslims would still be taught unquestioned obedience to the Abrahamic God and that the Prophet Mohammad was perfect and sinless despite the historical record of his actions. The Jihad against hypocrisy, on a fundamental level, seems to be a doctrine that precludes changing the faith and to stay consistent with the teachings and example of the Islamic Prophet Mohammad. The closer one lives by his example, the closer one becomes to a warlord that takes female sex slaves, rapes children via a so-called marriage, and murders people to form a 7th century caliphate. How can anyone reform that? Moreover, if Islam gets rid of the Prophet Mohammad's example, then what's the point of being a Muslim? I would like to be wrong about this, and perhaps I'm making a false dilemma fallacy, but I doubt it. This is where I must admit my limits of understanding this topic as of now. I don't think it is useful or healthy to reform Islam when so much of the content is clearly against any type of reform; I think the branching Islamic theologies that exist at the moment are attempts at keeping Islam aligned to a real world context where it doesn't fit. What would be the point of keeping it around?

Logically speaking, I honestly don't see how any reform could work. It would be better off, and everyone in the world would be safer, if Islam was rejected as the mythology that non-Muslims know it to be. Equally as important, since Christianity and Judaism are closely linked, they too would need to be rejected in order to prevent any literalist perspectives into slowly seeing Islam as the perfect correction to the contradictions they may feel about interpreting the Bible. So long as Christianity and theistic Judaism exist, there can always be converts to Islam, seeing it as the perfect answer to the question of Jewish prophecies and other nonsensical beliefs. The sacred reciprocal norm of religious tolerance should be removed and we should all be free to criticize all religious beliefs regardless of how painful it is to read or hear such criticism. Human rights should take precedent over religious social norms.[1333]

118.[1333] Haider, Sarah. "Sarah Haider: Islam and the Necessity of Liberal Critique (AHA Conference 2015)." *YouTube*, American Humanist Association, 28 May 2015, www.youtube.com/watch?v=0plC24YuoJk.

Chapter 25: Intersectional Feminism versus Islam's Patriarchy

"Before her death earlier this year, American hostage Kayla Mueller was repeatedly raped by the top leader of ISIS, Abu Bakr al-Baghdadi, according to counterterrorism officials.

Mueller's family confirmed to ABC News that government officials have told them that their daughter, who would have turned 27 today, was the victim of repeated sexual assaults by al-Baghdadi.

"We were told Kayla was tortured, that she was the property of al-Baghdadi. We were told that in June by the government," her parents, Carl and Marsha Mueller, told ABC News today.

Al-Baghdadi, an Iraqi who calls himself the caliph, or ruler, of the Islamic State, personally took the enslaved 26-year-old humanitarian aid worker to be imprisoned inside the home of Abu Sayyaf, a Tunisian in charge of oil and gas revenue for the group, counterterrorism officials told ABC News over the past several months.

"Baghdadi was at the house of Sayyaf. He delivered Kayla Mueller, live and in person," one of several counterterrorism officials briefed on the case told ABC News.

The terrorist leader later regularly visited the compound to meet with Abu Sayyaf and repeatedly sexually assault Mueller, officials said.

In early February ISIS claimed Mueller had been killed in a coalition bombardment in Syria. Three months later, on May 16, the U.S. Army's elite hostage-rescue and counterterrorism unit known as Delta Force conducted a ground raid to capture Abu Sayyaf but was forced to kill him when he raised a weapon, officials said.

The new revelations about Mueller's long ordeal — which involved torture since the beginning of her 1 1/2 years of captivity, her family has been told by the FBI — shatter rumors spread by some officials that she had cooperated or was a willing spouse, which has deeply upset her family and many involved with her case.

Some speculation was based on a smuggled letter released by her family in which the captive Mueller wrote, about a year into her captivity, that she was "completely unharmed + healthy (put on weight in fact); I have been treated w/ the utmost respect + kindness."

The information about al-Baghdadi's extraordinary direct role in the captivity and physical abuse of Mueller was drawn from, among many sources, the U.S. debriefings of at least least two Yazidi girls, ages 16 and 18, held as sex slaves in the Abu Sayyaf compound as well as from the interrogation of his wife Umm Sayyaf, who was captured in the raid, the officials told ABC News.

Officials stressed that all of what transpired with many girls kept as sex slaves in the Abu Sayyaf household hasn't been reconstructed completely and is still is in the process of being verified, though al-Baghdadi's role in abusing Mueller is certain.

At least two Yazidi teens escaped last year and another girl was rescued by the American ground assault force in Syria in May, which the White House announced at the time.

Last fall the U.S. Joint Special Operations Command in Irbil, Iraq, located one girl who had escaped Abu Sayyaf's clutches, and investigators learned the whereabouts of the last American known to be in ISIS hands, officials said. American journalists James Foley and Steven Sotloff, along with aid worker Peter "Abdul-Rahman" Kassig and two British aid workers, had been brutally beheaded in ISIS execution videos by then.

By January, U.S. special operations senior commanders were aggressively attempting to find and track Abu Sayyaf, a "top tier leader" responsible for funding the ISIS war machine, in order to plan a possible rescue of Mueller and to bring her intelligence-rich captor to justice in a U.S. courtroom, several officials said.

After enforcing a media blackout on names of hostages demanded by ISIS in private emails to their families for months, White House chief of staff Dennis McDonough inadvertently blurted out Mueller's first name on ABC News' "This Week" on Jan. 25 as he explained efforts to find her. "Kayla's family knows how strongly the president feels about this, and we will continue to work this," he said then.

Asked about Mueller on NBC on Feb. 1, President Obama said, "Well, what we can say is that, as has been true of all the hostages, that we are deploying all the assets that we can working with all the coalition allies that we can to identify her location. And we are in very close contact with the family trying to keep them updated."

But days later, Mueller was dead. ISIS said in a statement that she was killed in an airstrike by Jordanian aircraft on a building in Syria. Though U.S. officials somehow quickly confirmed her death, they have since disputed ISIS' claim of how she perished. How she died isn't known, officials told ABC News.

From that point forward, the military's Joint Special Operations Command zeroed in on Abu Sayyaf. It tracked him to a location in Syria by early March and awaited optimal conditions to launch a rare ground raid. A Delta Force ground assault team on May 16 swiftly overwhelmed Abu Sayyaf's guards — some of whom, realizing the compound was under attack, attempted unsuccessfully to hide from the U.S. operators, an official said.

It was initially suspected by U.S. officials that Mueller had been forced into a marriage to Abu Sayyaf. But after Delta Force killed him, newer intelligence pointed firmly to al-Baghdadi as Mueller's primary victimizer. The Yazidi teens and others provided the U.S. with a wealth of information used to interrogate Umm Sayyaf, who "spilled everything," including details about various ISIS leaders' "locations and patterns of life," a counterterrorism official told ABC News.

Eventually the girls who survived captivity with the Sayyafs were allowed to leave the protection of the U.S. military in Irbil and return to normal civilian lives, though occasionally shadowed by special operators worried for their safety in public places."[1334] - US journalist James Gordon Meek, "*ISIS Leader Abu Bakr al-Baghdadi Sexually Abused American Hostage Kayla Mueller, Officials Say*" from *ABC News*.

---

1. [1334] Meek, James Gordon. "ISIS Leader Abu Bakr Al-Baghdadi Sexually Abused American Hostage Kayla Mueller, Officials Say." *ABC News*, ABC News Network, 14 Aug. 2015, abcnews.go.com/International/isis-leader-abu-bakr-al-baghdadi-sexually-abused/story?id=33085923.

Islam celebrates treating women as the property of men as a mandate by the Abrahamic God.[1335] Ex-Muslims of North America provides a wealth of critique on the issues of Islamic violence against women and the micromanaged oppression of women. What Ex-Muslim women who've lived and left these societies proclaim in their protestations is that women growing up in traditional, collectivist societies often bear the burden of family honor.[1336] Their conduct and their virginity determines the social standing of their fathers and brothers to make any sort of decent financial standard of living.[1337] Islam treats little girls as young as nine as sexual objects prone to promiscuity if they don't learn to obey their parents.[1338][1339] Within many Islamic families and especially throughout the Middle East, protecting purity and the family controlling everything about the daughter from their purchasing power to their social life continue even after a daughter gains adulthood; this behavior by the family is done in order to protect the purity and honor of the family among the Islamic community that they live in.[1340] Even educated women face this issue or live by it; women who have completed postgraduate studies and are well over the age of eighteen must live under the control of their parents.[1341] It is part of Islamic culture to determine a good marriage, to have a good family social standing, and so the fathers and brothers get good jobs or are well-respected within Islamic communities.[1342] Whereas democratic reform through political pressure from Feminist movements and Enlightenment values has forced Western Christianity to abhor, argue against, and socially rebel against the sexualization and dehumanization of women as property of men; Islam's faith in the Abrahamic God as inerrant is a pure, distilled form of religion treating women as property of men by a collectivist social standard imposed upon women.[1343] What a woman does, how long she is out, and how she dresses determines the family honor of the entire family unit and can be met with beatings by fathers as punishment, if disobeyed.[1344] *The hajib symbolizes that women are property of men and the hijab is a celebration of women*

---

2. [1335] "The Quranic Arabic Corpus - Word by Word Grammar, Syntax and Morphology of the Holy Quran." *The Quranic Arabic Corpus - Translation*, http://corpus.quran.com/translation.jsp?chapter=4&verse=34
3. [1336] Haider, Sarah, et al. "Islam, Modesty and Feminism." *YouTube*, Ex-Muslims of North America, 12 Oct. 2017, www.youtube.com/watch?v=QToH2x8njJM.
4. [1337] Haider, Sarah, et al. "Islam, Modesty and Feminism." *YouTube*, Ex-Muslims of North America, 12 Oct. 2017, www.youtube.com/watch?v=QToII2x8njJM.
5. [1338] Namazie, Maryam, et al. "Equality, Islam and Human Rights." *YouTube*, Ex-Muslims of North America, 26 Mar. 2018, www.youtube.com/watch?v=2W0w9ufJOh0.
6. [1339] Haider, Sarah, et al. "Islam, Modesty and Feminism." *YouTube*, Ex-Muslims of North America, 12 Oct. 2017, www.youtube.com/watch?v=QToH2x8njJM.
7. [1340] Haider, Sarah, et al. "Islam, Modesty and Feminism." *YouTube*, Ex-Muslims of North America, 12 Oct. 2017, www.youtube.com/watch?v=QToH2x8njJM.
8. [1341] Haider, Sarah, et al. "Islam, Modesty and Feminism." *YouTube*, Ex-Muslims of North America, 12 Oct. 2017, www.youtube.com/watch?v=QToH2x8njJM.
9. [1342] Haider, Sarah, et al. "Islam, Modesty and Feminism." *YouTube*, Ex-Muslims of North America, 12 Oct. 2017, www.youtube.com/watch?v=QToH2x8njJM.
10. [1343] Haider, Sarah, et al. "Islam, Modesty and Feminism." *YouTube*, Ex-Muslims of North America, 12 Oct. 2017, www.youtube.com/watch?v=QToH2x8njJM.
11. [1344] Haider, Sarah, et al. "Islam, Modesty and Feminism." *YouTube*, Ex-Muslims of North America, 12 Oct. 2017, www.youtube.com/watch?v=QToH2x8njJM.

being imposed with less rights based upon their gender by the Abrahamic God.[1345] *The hijab itself is support for rape culture.* According to Ex-Muslim women, collectivist societies that control women reinforce the concept of conditional love and propagates narcissistic behavior on the part of parents and siblings upon their daughters and sisters.[1346] Young women who disagree with Islamic tenants or who think of leaving the faith often reflect on what impact their behavior will have on their parents.[1347] There is a genuine fear of community reprisal that motivates them to remain silent of such sexist double-standards and even physical abuse.[1348] Islam's message of holistic purity exerts itself to control and dictate Islamic children with negative reprisals. Families, even extended families, call and harass Muslim families who have a member that has abandoned Islam and escaped the penalty of apostasy.[1349] Within the confines of Islamic culture, a girl who steps out of "modesty" culture is one that is "ruined" and has no future in the community; no ability to find a husband, no acceptance from the broader Islamic community, no safety net to fall back on, no possibility of a prosperous job because there is no husband or father to give their consent to the woman working, and their family will often completely abandon them.[1350] If an Ex-Muslim woman escapes the micromanaging of their life; they will forever be demonized as nefarious, promiscuous, and evil for giving into outside logic and independent thought.[1351]

In Christian fundamentalist societies and cultures, it is often argued that the interaction of men and women cause sexual promiscuity so they must be separate and that women must cover themselves so men won't rape them. Islamic culture puts such sexism into a thoroughgoing practice. Islamic culture does absolutely everything to separate men and women; different classes, curtains between men and women in lecture halls of Muslim majority country colleges when reluctantly placed in the same classes, women forced to cover from head to toe with mothers punishing daughters for even showing their wrists because of the belief that a 9 year-old is inviting sexual promiscuity for simply showing their wrists, and no real laws to protect women from sexual assault, rape, and gang rape.[1352][1353] Men who

---

12. [1345] Haider, Sarah, et al. "Islam, Modesty and Feminism." *YouTube*, Ex-Muslims of North America, 12 Oct. 2017, www.youtube.com/watch?v=QToH2x8njJM.
13. [1346] Haider, Sarah, et al. "Islam, Modesty and Feminism." *YouTube*, Ex-Muslims of North America, 12 Oct. 2017, www.youtube.com/watch?v=QToH2x8njJM.
14. [1347] Haider, Sarah, et al. "Islam, Modesty and Feminism." *YouTube*, Ex-Muslims of North America, 12 Oct. 2017, www.youtube.com/watch?v=QToH2x8njJM.
15. [1348] Haider, Sarah, et al. "Islam, Modesty and Feminism." *YouTube*, Ex-Muslims of North America, 12 Oct. 2017, www.youtube.com/watch?v=QToH2x8njJM.
16. [1349] Haider, Sarah, et al. "Islam, Modesty and Feminism." *YouTube*, Ex-Muslims of North America, 12 Oct. 2017, www.youtube.com/watch?v=QToH2x8njJM.
17. [1350] Haider, Sarah, et al. "Islam, Modesty and Feminism." *YouTube*, Ex-Muslims of North America, 12 Oct. 2017, www.youtube.com/watch?v=QToH2x8njJM.
18. [1351] Haider, Sarah, et al. "Islam, Modesty and Feminism." *YouTube*, Ex-Muslims of North America, 12 Oct. 2017, www.youtube.com/watch?v=QToH2x8njJM.
19. [1352] Haider, Sarah, et al. "Islam, Modesty and Feminism." *YouTube*, Ex-Muslims of North America, 12 Oct. 2017, www.youtube.com/watch?v=QToH2x8njJM.

sexually assault women get a free pass to continue sexual assaults under the belief that it's what men do; women are subjected to sexual assault with Islamic justifications that they didn't have the hajib headdress on or that it was placed atop a girl's head incorrectly and that's why the men raped her.[1354]

The central reason for these ongoing forms of sexual violence is because Islam, unlike every other religious faith, recognizes what modesty and purity culture really are in their most distilled and unvarnished form: *women treated as spoils of war for men*.[1355][1356] As mentioned in part I and in Chapter 6, this discrimination against women is a cultural aftermath of primitive nation-states treating women as property to be owned and used by male soldiers.[1357][1358] This eventually became sanctified under religion as women being the property of men.[1359][1360] It is because Islam takes strides to worship every aspect and deed of the Abrahamic God that it inculcates this prevailing gender violence upon women; it uncritically celebrates the barbarism of ancient Israelis, Christians, and Muslims as a call from the Abrahamic God under Sharia.[1361][1362] The tragic story of Kayla Mueller and the sexual slavery of the 18 and 16-year old Yazidi children are some of the most contemporary examples and speak to a broader problem within Islamic culture that Ex-Muslim women have highlighted from their own personal experiences. That is, the normalization of gender disparities; the celebration of purity, modesty, and keeping women shackled to cages of "innocence" to "protect" them as the collectivist property of the family instead of seeing them as human beings worthy of unconditional love and acceptance.[1363][1364] For example, to love a child who is a

---

20. [1353] Haddad, Mais. "Victims of Rape and Law: How the Laws of the Arab World Protect Rapists, Not Victims." *Jurist*, Jurist, www.jurist.org/commentary/2017/05/mais-haddad-arab-world-laws-protect-the-rapist-not-the-victim/.
21. [1354] Haider, Sarah, et al. "Islam, Modesty and Feminism." *YouTube*, Ex-Muslims of North America, 12 Oct. 2017, www.youtube.com/watch?v=QToH2x8njJM.
22. [1355] "BibleGateway." *Numbers 31:7-18 KJV - - Bible Gateway*, www.biblegateway.com/passage/?search=Numbers 31:7-18&version=KJV.
23. [1356] "The Quranic Arabic Corpus - Word by Word Grammar, Syntax and Morphology of the Holy Quran." *The Quranic Arabic Corpus - Translation*, http://corpus.quran.com/translation.jsp?chapter=4&verse=24
24. [1357] "BibleGateway." *Numbers 31:7-18 KJV - - Bible Gateway*, www.biblegateway.com/passage/?search=Numbers 31:7-18&version=KJV.
25. [1358] "The Quranic Arabic Corpus - Word by Word Grammar, Syntax and Morphology of the Holy Quran." *The Quranic Arabic Corpus - Translation*, http://corpus.quran.com/translation.jsp?chapter=4&verse=24
26. [1359] "BibleGateway." *Bible Gateway*, Bible Gateway Blog, www.biblegateway.com/passage/?search=1 Timothy 2&version=KJV.
27. [1360] "The Quranic Arabic Corpus - Word by Word Grammar, Syntax and Morphology of the Holy Quran." *The Quranic Arabic Corpus - Translation*, http://corpus.quran.com/translation.jsp?chapter=4&verse=34
27. [1361] Castor, Trevor. "Sin According to Islam." *Zwemer Center*, www.zwemercenter.com/guide/sin-according-to-muslims/.
28. [1362] "Greater and Lesser Jihaad." Translated by Muhammed Salih Al-Munajjid, *Islam Question And Answer*, islamqa.info/en/10455.
29. [1363] Namazie, Maryam, et al. "Equality, Islam and Human Rights." *YouTube*, Ex-Muslims of North America, 26 Mar. 2018, www.youtube.com/watch?v=2W0w9ufJOh0.

homosexual would be to criticize and repudiate Islamic morality, which sees everything as a binary of good versus evil; that which is the Abrahamic God's is good, that which isn't is evil.[1365][1366] No outside logic is allowed to refute this in Islamic culture; it's the very foundation of Sharia.[1367] Simplicity, innocence, and modesty are the most dangerous weapons utilized to justify mental brutality, physical beatings. murder, rape, and the torture of women.[1368] It is why honor killings exist in Islamic culture; it is meant to maintain the "purity" of the family values and it is conditioned by treating the daughters as property of the household instead of as people.[1369]

The sexual slavery of women is still normalized in several Islamic Gulf countries that have strong bilateral ties to the US government. An article on the website *TheDailyBeast* by journalist's Asra Q. Nomani and Hala Arafa highlight in their article "*Inside the World of Gulf State Slavery*" the normalized sexual exploitation of women in Gulf countries:

> "*La, Baba,*" a young woman, pleads in Arabic, as she stands in a tidy kitchen trying to escape the attention of her cajoling Saudi boss, seconds before he gropes and sexually molests her. "No, father. It is nothing."
>
> The heart-breaking scene, filmed secretly as part of a grainy half-minute clip, shot around the world this week after a courageous—and angry—wife apparently posted it to the Internet from Saudi Arabia, shocking viewers and inspiring a social media campaign, #SaudiWomanCatchesHusbandCheating. The case, which the government of Indonesia says it is investigating and trying to confirm, became even more outrageous when media accounts reported the wife faces jail time for allegedly "defaming her husband in line with the law on information technology crimes."
>
> But the clip of the Saudi man stalking and sexually harassing his family's "maid servant" is more than just an Internet meme. It is emblematic of the de facto slave subculture that thrives in modern day Saudi Arabia, supported by fatwas from Saudi clerics from the country's

---

30. [1364] Haider, Sarah, et al. "Islam, Modesty and Feminism." *YouTube*, Ex-Muslims of North America, 12 Oct. 2017, www.youtube.com/watch?v=QToH2x8njJM.
31. [1365] Castor, Trevor. "Sin According to Islam." *Zwemer Center*, www.zwemercenter.com/guide/sin-according-to-muslims/.
32. [1366] "Greater and Lesser Jihaad." Translated by Muhammed Salih Al-Munajjid, *Islam Question And Answer*, islamqa.info/en/10455.
33. [1367] "Tafseer on the Basis of Narrated Texts and Tafseer on the Basis of Individual Understanding - Islam Question & Answer." *Islamqa.info*, Islam Question and Answer, 11 Mar. 2015, islamqa.info/en/answers/205290/tafseer-on-the-basis-of-narrated-texts-and-tafseer-on-the-basis-of-individual-understanding.
34. [1368] Haddad, Mais. "Victims of Rape and Law: How the Laws of the Arab World Protect Rapists, Not Victims." *Jurist*, Jurist, www.jurist.org/commentary/2017/05/mais-haddad-arab-world-laws-protect-the-rapist-not-the-victim/.
35. [1369] Haider, Sarah, et al. "Islam, Modesty and Feminism." *YouTube*, Ex-Muslims of North America, 12 Oct. 2017, www.youtube.com/watch?v=QToH2x8njJM.

dogmatic Wahhabi and Salafi schools of Islam, which argue that the Quran gives owners—most usually men—rights over "those whom your right hand possess," or, in Arabic, "*mā malakat aymānukum*" (4:3, 4:24, 4:24, 16:71, 23:5-6, 24:33, 24:58, 33:50).

One verse reads: "And if you fear that you will not be fair to the orphans, then marry whomever you like from the women, two or three, or four but if you fear that you won't be fair to them, then marry only one or the slaves that your right hands possess. That is the closest way to prevent injustice." (Quran, Surat Al-Nisa, "The Women," 4:3)

For sure, abuse of power is global and universal. But to progressive Muslim thinkers, the notion of power over "those whom your right hand possess" is the theological underpinning of a cultural mindset that sanctions acts of brutality, like the media reports this week of a Saudi employer in New Delhi raping two "maids" from Nepal and, then, an employer in Saudi Arabia cutting off the arm of a woman worker from India, after she filed a complaint of torture. The government of Saudi Arabia did not return a request for comment.[1370]

Later in the article, they detail abuses of women who come to be sponsored in order to make a decent income for a better life for their families:

> The leaders of the Islamic State, or ISIS, exploit the Quranic language of "whom the right hand possess" to justify their brutal sexual captivity of women, including hostages from the Yazidi ethnicity, prompting honest headlines, like "ISIS enshrines a theology of rape," by *New York Times* journalist Rukmini Callimachi.
>
> On popular modern-day websites, written like "Dear Abby" advice columns, scholars of the Wahhabi and Salafi schools of Islam use the language of "whom the right hand possess," or a "slave woman," to divinely bless sexual concubines in the 21st century. On IslamQA.info, Muhammad Al-Munajjid, a revered Saudi-educated Salafi scholar who has been the imam of a mosque in Saudi Arabia, writes, "Praise be to Allah, Islam allows a man to have intercourse with his slave woman, whether he has a wife or wives or if he is not married. A slave woman with whom a man has intercourse is known as a *sariyyah* (concubine) from the word *sir*, which means marriage."
>
> According to this scholar's playbook, it is blasphemy for anyone, like us, to declare sexual concubines *haram*, or illegal. "The scholars are unanimously agreed on that and it is not permissible for anyone to regard it as haraam or to forbid it. Whoever regards that as haraam is

---

36. [1370] Nomani, Asra Q., and Hala Arafa. "Inside the World of Gulf State Slavery." *The Daily Beast*, The Daily Beast Company, 11 Oct. 2015, www.thedailybeast.com/inside-the-world-of-gulf-state-slavery.

a sinner who is going against the consensus of the scholars." Al-Munajjid didn't respond to a request for comment.

The Salafi scholar cites as a precedent the story of Abraham, or Ibrahim in Islam, who had sex with Hagar, or Hajar, who then gave birth to baby Ishmael. They also cite the *sunnah*, or tradition, of the prophet Muhammad, who had sex with women who "the right hand possess."

On the grainy half-minute clip that went around the world, the wife wrote as a caption: "the minimum punishment for this husband is to scandalize him."

In the film, the stocky middle-aged man stands in the kitchen, in a long white thawb, or gown, dragging onto the floor, and a red-tinged keffiyeh, or headdress, flowing over his shoulders. He seems to be kissing the young woman, who wears a dark headscarf over a long tunic and loose pants, both colored a matching lavender. She pulls away and scurries to a counter, swathed in a flood of sunlight streaming into the room through a large window.

The man follows her, almost waddling, suddenly behind her, the sound of a loud smacking kiss breaking the quiet, as the woman protests. She tries to go about her business, picking something up.

And then another clips begins, the man studying the woman's hand, as she readies to take a serving plate of food out of the kitchen, and he asks: "What is this?"

"*La, Baba*," she says. "No, father. It is nothing."

He follows her and says, "No. It's not nothing. It looks like blood."

Trying to shake him off, she insists. "No. It is nothing, *ya baba*." Referring to the serving plate, she says, "I'll take it."

He hands her the plate, turns away, but then in a split second returns and gropes her in either the rear or the genital area and says. "Go on, take it there."

She yelps. And then exclaims, "*Wadhee!*" "Let me take it!

He feigns her yelp.

As he continues to finger her, her knees seem to buckle slightly.

He draws closer to her, his hand dropping to between her legs, groping her, as she doubles over slightly, squirming, saying, "La! La!" "No! No!" She lets out a muffled groan, moving into a fetal position, turning away from him, her back arched, as he finally pulls away, saying "*Yallah. Wadhee! Wadhee!*"

"OK. Take it there! Take it there!"

As we watched this film, we were left with one thought: Yes, "Baba," this *is* something. It is despicable. It is disgusting. And it is, criminally, all too common.

The kind of predatory behavior revealed by the video speaks to a universal and timeless piranha mindset that makes some people dehumanize others to the point of horrifying exploitation and degradation. It challenges all of us, no matter what culture, or faith we are born into, to contemplate and meditate deeply upon treating others with humility, compassion and respect.

The video is shocking and repulsive, in part, because the film captures the ugly manifestation of sex, power and entitlement in ordinary life. Turning the tables on the wife—making her the shameful criminal instead of her husband—is a reflection of the twisted expression of human rights, honor, and face-saving that has been exercised for far too long in traditional societies, where patriarchy, sexism, and entitlement make cultures more like men's club, where the working-class "poor" have little *wasta*, the Arabic word for "connections" and "clout." This is particularly damning in the *kafala*, or "sponsorship" industry in Saudi Arabia, in which foreigners are so often bought, sold, and traded.

What's happened in recent years is that, just as phone videos have been used in the U.S. to capture controversial police arrests and shootings, phone videos are being used today in a sort of *wasta* revolution, in which witnesses are shooting secret footage of abuse of power over maids, "servants," children, and ordinary folks.

The *wasta* revolution flips the traditional notion of honor and frames behavior, like the Saudi man's sexual harassment, as dishonorable and, in the courtroom of public opinion, it is the oppressed who have *wasta*, not the oppressor.

In Pakistan, someone shared a video last month of a family dining out with their "servant" girl, sitting at the same table, but not allowed to eat. Another clip, shared not long ago, showed another family dining out with their servants told to sit with their backs to the table. This past December, the video of a Filipino "household maid" in distress went viral. "Please help us," she said. "I beg you."

Men are very often not the only aggressors, either, and abuse exists beyond the boundaries of Saudi Arabia. Born in India and Egypt, we both grew up witnessing shockingly brutal violence against "servants" by women for whom dominance over "servants" was one of their few expressions of "power." Such social abuse has become so normative that, very often, we look at such infractions through a lens of moral and cultural relativism, but doing so fails humanity.

Human Rights Watch estimates tens of millions of women and girls are employed as household "domestic workers," and it estimates that millions of poor women from countries, including Bangladesh, the Philippines, India, Sri Lanka, and Nepal, work as "household maids" in the six countries of the Gulf Cooperation Council, Saudi Arabia, Bahrain, Kuwait, Oman, Qatar, and the United Arab Emirates. Men and boys are hired too for menial tasks too often exploited inhumanely.

Years ago, the *Economist* outlined the injustices workers face, challenging governments of the workers to protect their citizens, in a piece, headlined, "Beheading the Golden Goose," after Saudi Arabia beheaded an Indonesian "household maid."

Human Rights Watch has documented the abuses against "domestic workers" in in Saudi Arabia and the Gulf in reports titled "I Already Bought You" and "As If I Am Not Human," noting "sexual violence" against workers, including "male employers" and their "teenage or adult sons" engaging in "inappropriate touching, hugging, and kissing" and "repeated rape."

In a report in *Der Spiegel*, the investigative German magazine, two German ambulance workers who worked in Riyadh, Saudi Arabia, testified to the abuses they had seen, chronicling one raped maid who was almost unable to walk due to the pain and others who get pregnant, babies usually abandoned, including at a local garbage dump.

The issue of the treatment and conduct of "domestic workers" in Saudi Arabia has led to heated diplomatic exchanges with countries from Ethiopia to Sri Lanka and the Philippines.

Two years ago, Annette Vlieger, a researcher who went undercover in South Asia and the Gulf to investigate the issue, published a book, *Domestic Workers in Saudi Arabia and the Emirates: A Socio-Legal Study on Conflict*, telling Voice of America that "people are aware that the sexual abuse of domestic workers in the Middle East is pretty bad." When she posed as a potential employer in the Middle East, she said, "…I was very much in shock—mostly in Saudi Arabia, where they simply told me, 'She will be your slave for two years.'"

Workdays are ones of drudgery up to 20 hours, she said, and many were "abused, either physically or mentally" and "many women" were sexually abused as well.

Just like the young woman chronicled in the video, dodging the man's groping but acquiescing to his presence, the researcher noted, "The women themselves simply believe in fate." She said that poor rural families will often send one daughter to the Middle East "sort of like a sacrifice." "Very often, girls know that that is their reason for existing," she said.

A few years ago, the *Saudi Gazette* reported that "expat women commit suicide," chronicling an "Indonesian housemaid" who hanged herself in her sponsor's home in the city of eastern Asi, and an "Ethiopian housemaid" in her 20s who committed suicide inside "her sponsor's home" in the holy city of Mecca. When she didn't open her door, the story said, the family broke the door down and found "her body hanging from the ceiling."

In 1962, the leader of Saudi Arabia, "King" Faisal, abolished slavery in Saudi Arabia by royal decree. But he largely neglected to amend Saudi labor laws to provide protection for workers in the kingdom because the culture of servitude is very intricately woven into its national fabric. The Saudi version of *Romeo and Juliet* is *Qays Wa Layla*, about the impossible love between the daughter of a high-born Saudi and her cousin, born to a slave mother.

The attitude of servitude extends toward "housemaids" in the modern day. In a book, *Saudi Arabia Exposed*, John R. Bradley, a British journalist who lived and worked in Saudi Arabia for many years, detailed how these maids make between $150 and $200 a month, working around the clock without any benefits or medical insurance. Bradley explains how these maids are seen as lesser humans who should be grateful for the opportunity to serve. They are cut off from contact with their communities and kept as prisoners in the house.

This past March, Saudi Arabia executed two "household maids," accused of killing family members from the family of their "sponsor," amid protests from human rights groups, including Amnesty International.

Outside Saudi Arabia, we've seen glimpses of this abuse. In December 2001, a Saudi princess was arrested at a luxury Orlando resort, charged with beating her Indonesian servant and pushing her down a flight of stairs.

In July 2013, a Kenyan woman working for a Saudi princess escaped in Irvine, California, and complained that she and four other Filipino women were held against their will and mistreated.

Just weeks ago, a member of the Saudi ruling family was arrested in Los Angeles for allegedly forcing women workers to give him oral sex in his palatial Los Angeles mansion, with one woman attempting to scale a fence to escape the "prince," traumatized and bloodied.

With sexual assault on campuses a universal problem, the issue got a cultural dimension last week with the arrest of four Saudi national students at Johnson & Wales University in Providence, Rhode Island, for the alleged rape and sexual assault of two 18-year-old freshman women.

This week's viral video emerged at a time of backlash to the Saudi regime for the tragedy of deaths at the hajj pilgrimage, its assaults in Syria and Yemen, and its export of the Wahhabi and Salafi ideology that fuels militant groups like the Islamic State.[1371]

The pouring outcry for human rights these horrific atrocities have brought about and the activism being done to combat these forms of Islamic sexual slavery:

Fortunately, from the Philippines to Nepal, citizens are rallying to protect their own against the tyranny of abuse of power. Last year, a new Facebook page, called "Filipino Domestic Worker Abuse in Saudi Arabia," was created to facilitate a sort of "underground railroad" to help women from the Philippines escape servitude and abuse in Saudi Arabia, posting the email addresses and phone numbers for Philippines Embassy officials, as well as horror stories of the "OFW," or "Overseas Filipino Worker."

"…help is just a Text away," read an early message.

The administrator of the website is a northern California former accountant, Karl Anderson, who became an accidental activist when a Facebook friend from the Philippines asked for help. Today, he helps about 10 women a month escape abuse to go to one of the little-discussed shelters in Saudi Arabia established for "household maids."

"It is slavery," Anderson tells us. "Every day, I see the face of slavery."

"There is a woman who was forced to eat a child's feces out of a diaper because she didn't clean the diaper soon enough," he says. "Women are raped, tortured, denied food, denied water, made to work 20 hours a day, seven days a week. One woman was only allowed to eat the food that her sponsor family left on their plates. They are treated like dogs."

We as, a global society, need to answer the cry of some of the world's most vulnerable, sanction the governments of Saudi Arabia and other countries that allow the abuse of "housemaids," and promote a theology of Islam and global ethics that affirms that "the right hand" does not "possess" anyone and ordains us, based on a humanist ethos, to coexist with a sense of respect, compassion and dignity for all.[1372]

The journalists who reported on this informative article are attempting to promote a boycott of Saudi Arabia that will never happen because of how central the US-Saudi

---

37. [1371] Nomani, Asra Q., and Hala Arafa. "Inside the World of Gulf State Slavery." *The Daily Beast*, The Daily Beast Company, 11 Oct. 2015, www.thedailybeast.com/inside-the-world-of-gulf-state-slavery.
38. [1372] Nomani, Asra Q., and Hala Arafa. "Inside the World of Gulf State Slavery." *The Daily Beast*, The Daily Beast Company, 11 Oct. 2015, www.thedailybeast.com/inside-the-world-of-gulf-state-slavery.

partnership is to the financial wellbeing of the US itself.[1373] Moreover, it would likely worsen the conditions of the maid servants regardless since Saudi officials might make more thorough attempts to cover it up. Women don't endure such despicable conditions if they had options to leave for a better quality of life elsewhere. While legal entrapment could credibly play a role, the fact is they went to Gulf nation-states because there is no better life available to them and suffered as a result of dehumanizing Islamic laws that allow for sexual slavery[1374], wife beatings[1375], and cultural shame upon women who speak out.[1376] For any potential readers from middle-class or lower countries, I would honestly recommend working on trying to build a better life for your daughters within your own countries and forgo any of your children being sent to Saudi Arabia assuming you care about their lives and love them.

Islam allows for marital rape to go unpunished and is one of the motivating reasons why India won't adapt laws against it because the Islamic male community demands respect for their religious traditions through respect for the Sharia. In fact, Islamic organizations that are part of government bodies such as in Egypt openly show support for marital rape on their websites as official government policy based solely upon Islamic theology.[1377] Muslim men are allowed to beat their wives without any repercussions as mandated by the Islamic faith for the sake of manly honor and female modesty.[1378][1379] Islam allows for Muslim men to marry two to four wives so long as they are Abrahamic which is referred to as "People of the Book" - that is, Christian, Jewish, and Muslim women.[1380][1381] Islam allows men to have as many female slaves as they want.[1382] However, true to its roots of treating women as property to be owned by men, Muslim women can only marry a Muslim man.[1383] A woman who is non-Abrahamic must

39. [1373] Oweiss, Ibrahim M. "Conclusion/Notes." *Http://Faculty.georgetown.edu*, The Committee for Monetary Research and Education, faculty.georgetown.edu/imo3/petrod/conclude.htm.
40. [1374] "Ruling on Having Intercourse with a Slave Woman When One Has a Wife - Islamqa.info." Translated by Muhammad Salih Al-Munajjid, *Wayback Machine*, Fox News, web.archive.org/web/20160106101656/http://islamqa.info/en/10382.
41. [1375] "The Quranic Arabic Corpus - Word by Word Grammar, Syntax and Morphology of the Holy Quran." *The Quranic Arabic Corpus - Translation*, http://corpus.quran.com/translation.jsp?chapter=4&verse=34
42. [1376] Haider, Sarah, et al. "Islam, Modesty and Feminism." *YouTube*, Ex-Muslims of North America, 12 Oct. 2017, www.youtube.com/watch?v=QToH2x8njJM.
43. [1377] "Fatawa - Does Marital Rape Exist in Islam?" *Dar Al-Ifta Al Misriyyah*, www.dar-alifta.org/Foreign/ViewFatwa.aspx?ID=6033.
44. [1378] Haider, Sarah, et al. "Islam, Modesty and Feminism." *YouTube*, Ex-Muslims of North America, 12 Oct. 2017, www.youtube.com/watch?v=QToH2x8njJM.
45. [1379] Namazie, Maryam, et al. "Equality, Islam and Human Rights." *YouTube*, Ex-Muslims of North America, 26 Mar. 2018, www.youtube.com/watch?v=2W0w9ufJOh0.
46. [1380] Nomani, Asra Q., and Hala Arafa. "Inside the World of Gulf State Slavery." *The Daily Beast*, The Daily Beast Company, 11 Oct. 2015, www.thedailybeast.com/inside-the-world-of-gulf-state-slavery.
47. [1381] "Prohibition of Interfaith Marriage." *Prohibtion of Interfaith Marriage*, Global Legal Research Directorate, 1 Sept. 2016, www.loc.gov/law/help/marriage/interfaith-prohibition.php.
48. [1382] "Ruling on Having Intercourse with a Slave Woman When One Has a Wife - Islamqa.info." Translated by Muhammad Salih Al-Munajjid, *Wayback Machine*, Fox News, web.archive.org/web/20160106101656/http://islamqa.info/en/10382.
49. [1383] Nomani, Asra Q., and Hala Arafa. "Inside the World of Gulf State Slavery." *The Daily Beast*, The Daily Beast Company, 11 Oct. 2015, www.thedailybeast.com/inside-the-world-of-gulf-state-slavery.

convert to be part of the Muslim community.[1384] Although there is collectivist support and almost universal praise for any woman who converts to Islam, it is through a cultish collectivist mindset that seeks to control women and treat them as property of men through the holistic purity of the religion.[1385] *Muslim women are dehumanized as spoils of war in Islamic theology through the Sharia, Islamic jurisprudence system, and the implicit religious assumptions of its female specific dress code.*

If you feel that such a statement is too extreme, inaccurate, or a form of discrimination despite the aforementioned evidence presented then consider what US taxpayer money helped to fund under President George H.W. Bush. This is the real world consequences of the CIA and US presidents from Reagan, to Bush, and then to Clinton following the Realist and Neorealist theories of international relations; specifically, what President Ronald Reagan and President George H.W. Bush used US taxpayer monies to fund by giving weapons aid to the mujahideen to fight the Soviet Union. I only point that out because I believe that it is vitally important that US taxpayers understand exactly what US Presidents and the US Congress helped allow with their tax monies in fighting enemies abroad. Too many US taxpayers misunderstand that spending millions or billions on wars to finance destruction and death is not the same as giving aid to charities that run food programs or get rid of diseases that kill children. If not, then perhaps people in other countries can at least vicariously learn from the failings of US foreign policy to make the world a better place. On *The Guardian*, the 2011 article titled "*The 1980s mujahideen, the Taliban and the Shifting idea of jihad*" explains the horrific abuses caused by the mujahideen. The UCLA lecturor, Afghan cultural critic, and journalist *Nushin Arbabzadah* elaborates on the thoroughgoing brutality upon Afghan women by the mujahideen that the US Presidents helped weaponize through the CIA. Arbabzadah places sole emphasis on the mujahideen's beliefs and conduct; she had lived in Afghanistan before her family fled to Germany where she grew up with a European educational background gaining degrees from Hamburg and Cambridge universities.[1386] From her article, she explains what the mujahideen did when they were following the traditional teachings of Islam; please keep in mind the vast majority of the women in Afghanistan were Muslim women with a minority of them being part of Sikh, Christian, or Hindu religious backgrounds. I hope Arbabzadah's article helps to question what it is that US Presidents actually do in their dealings with foreign countries; from weapons aid for the mujahideen, to the effects of US Presidents using US taxpayer monies to finance USAID Afghan schoolbooks preaching hatred for non-Muslims.[1387] Most of all, to help

---

50. [1384] Tessier, Stephanie, and Muhammad Syed. "Islam: Pull and Peril." *YouTube*, Ex-Muslims of North America, 22 Apr. 2018, www.youtube.com/watch?v=jt1rWgap41g.
51. [1385] Tessier, Stephanie, and Muhammad Syed. "Islam: Pull and Peril." *YouTube*, Ex-Muslims of North America, 22 Apr. 2018, www.youtube.com/watch?v=jt1rWgap41g.
52. [1386] "Nushin Arbabzadah." *International.ucla.edu*, UCLA, www.international.ucla.edu/cisa/person/786.
53. [1387] Stephens, Joe, and David B. Ottaway. "From U.S., the ABC's of Jihad." *The Washington Post*, WP Company, 23 Mar. 2002, www.washingtonpost.com/archive/politics/2002/03/23/from-us-the-abcs-of-jihad/d079075a-3ed3-4030-9a96-0d48f6355e54/?utm_term=.cbb9b6b8a59a.

explain why feminism with secular values is essential to human rights in order to rectify, learn from, and move beyond this barbarism:

> Crucially, in a traditional jihad, the victorious party has an unspoken right to pillage, rape and loot the conquered population. This is because militia fighters are not paid soldiers in a regular army and hence looting is the material reward they receive for fighting. The original mujahideen followed this traditional pattern of jihad upon coming to power in 1992. Since competition over resources rather than ideology is key to traditional jihad, the mujahideen's war focused on Kabul where the nation's wealth and the foreign embassies, another potential source of funding, were to be found.
>
> Judging by a historical account from the 1920s, back then the women and girls of the conquered populations also belonged to the pillage package offered to militia jihadis. Hence, in the diaries of court chronicler Katib Hazara on the siege of Kabul in 1929, we read that the victorious mujahideen of the time had demanded to see the list of girls registered at a Kabul school so as to allocate female students to militia fighters.
>
> Katib's account might be exaggerated, but the story still reveals that there was an unspoken rule that women and girls were part of the conquest package. As such, the mujahideen's struggle over Kabul was a continuation of traditional jihad complete with internal rivalries, pillage and looting. The mujahideen were part of the realm of traditional politics in which a conquered region is a turf that can be exploited by strongmen, who call themselves mujahideen so as to appear respectable.
>
> The Taliban's conquest of Afghanistan in 1996, by contrast, strayed from the path of tradition. In a striking breach of precedence, the Taliban militia did not make use of their unspoken right to pillage and loot. They searched the conquered populations' homes, but only to confiscate weapons and so ensure a monopoly of violence for their state.
>
> In a comical incident that features in Sabour Bradley's documentary series The Extreme Tourist, the Taliban saw a poster of Rambo with a machine-gun in the home of an Afghan bodybuilder fan of the Hollywood star Sylvester Stallone. Ignorant of the world beyond the sharia law, the Taliban assumed that Rambo was a family member and told the bodybuilder: "Tell your cousin that he must hand over his machine gun to us." The bodybuilder's protestation that the poster depicted a fictional Hollywood hero fell flat with the Taliban, who subsequently imprisoned the man.
>
> The Taliban were exceedingly ignorant – which made them cruel – but there's no doubt that they saw jihad as a means to establish a state rather than legitimacy to pillage a conquered territory. Building a state was of utmost importance to the Taliban because without it the sharia law could not be enforced. If the mujahideen struggled over resources, the Taliban were concerned with religiosity.[1388]

The Abrahamic God versus The Information Age of Reason

In summa for this chapter, Islam's appeal to purity and appeal to tradition in a holistic sense, its repeated attempts for simplicity and insular theology that proclaims the Abrahamic God is unquestionably good, and its willingness to show that it indeed practices what it preaches to the point of annihilating its own cultures and other cultures with erasure of anything un-Islamic makes it the most dangerous religion of them all. There is no ability to criticize or argue against the theology from within because of the framework of the theology

---

54. [1388] Arbabzadah, Nushin. "The 1980s Mujahideen, the Taliban and the Shifting Idea of Jihad | Nushin Arbabzadah." *The Guardian*, Guardian News and Media, 28 Apr. 2011, www.theguardian.com/commentisfree/2011/apr/28/afghanistan-mujahideen-taliban.

itself.[1389] The reason Christianity and Judaism don't argue on the basis of comparing Islam's actual theology is because they stand no chance of proving that they're more pious than Muslims. Islam sacrifices everything for purity, innocence, and submission to the Abrahamic God. To compare Jesus Christ to Mohammad is to fundamentally misunderstand Islam; Islam celebrates Jesus as the Messiah of the Abrahamic God and any comparison will reaffirm that Muslims are correct about non-believers having no credible understanding of the basics of Islamic theology. Islam, in its war mandate of defending holy sites to await Jesus's return, prove that it is far more pious in worship of Jesus Christ than Christianity could ever hope to be. Islam commits violence to protect the purity, innocence, and perceived moral goodness in awaiting Jesus Christ on Judgment Day to save the Muslims from the Anti-Messiah. Whereas Christianity openly interprets, Islam puts belief into practice for the sake of celebrating their Messiah of the Abrahamic God, Jesus Christ, whom they believe fulfilled the Mosiac prophecies. Therefore, to truly end Islam permanently, all three major denominations of the Abrahamic faiths must be repudiated through debate and skeptical inquiry to truly end the religion of Islam. Its overarching practices, norms, and beliefs are propagated and normalized through Jewish and Christian theology with real world consequences. Therefore, as some members of Ex-Muslims of North America argue, don't just try to make a "middle-ground" of moderation that argues for reform in a patronizing manner, but convince Muslims themselves to take an honest look at their faith and at the teachings written in the Quran.[1390] Attack the ideals constructively through skeptical inquiry, don't martyr the believer by using violence. To kill and martyr the believer is to celebrate Islam, to attack the foundations of the faith through constructive criticism is to destroy Islam. Support non-violent free speech to prove our democratic ideals aren't foolish, don't take part in or celebrate the history of warring desert tribes of Yahweh. Whether the Abrahamic God goes by Yahweh, Allah, or his various other names such as in the Old Testament Bible like Elohim and El Shaddai[1391]; it is still the God of Abraham with just variations on the stories of Adam, Abraham, Daniel, Moses, and in both Islam and Christianity's case, Jesus as the Messiah. Criticize the teachings of all schools of thought worshipping the Abrahamic God and send him to the massive grave called mythology.

Take a moment to think about the fact that there's entire Islamic societies formed around nonsensical, superstitious beliefs like those mentioned in this section who think they're being as intelligent as scientists when following Islamic rules about regulations regarding their hands and who have such strong confidence in their beliefs that they wish to impose it upon outside cultures because they sincerely believe it'll lead to a perfect society because that's what

---

55. [1389] "Tafseer on the Basis of Narrated Texts and Tafseer on the Basis of Individual Understanding - Islam Question & Answer." *Islamqa.info*, Islam Question and Answer, 11 Mar. 2015, islamqa.info/en/answers/205290/tafseer-on-the-basis-of-narrated-texts-and-tafseer-on-the-basis-of-individual-understanding.
56. [1390] Namazie, Maryam, et al. "Equality, Islam and Human Rights." *YouTube*, Ex-Muslims of North America, 26 Mar. 2018, www.youtube.com/watch?v=2W0w9ufJOh0.
57. [1391] "Names of God in Judaism." *Wikipedia*, Wikimedia Foundation, 23 May 2019, en.wikipedia.org/wiki/Names_of_God_in_Judaism.

their Islamic schooling has taught them all their lives.[1392] Despite all compelling evidence to the opposite about Islamic civilizations, they believe Islam is some deep and profound wisdom that they must share with non-Islamic civilizations whether in the West or Asia and use billions in funding construction projects in Asia or tens of millions towards Think Tanks in the West to push forth the Islamization of all cultures that they deem blasphemous.[1393][1394][1395] This influence prompts people who wish to support "religious tolerance" in non-Islamic societies to lie or be willfully ignorant about the dangers of this religion, to label criticism of Islam as "Islamophobia" so they can control the narrative to make a good versus evil binary based upon confusing racial identity with religious identity to label any criticism as racist, to label any criticism of Islam as far-right extremism that supports violence against Muslims, and worst of all, to ignore the human rights of Ex-Muslims and to further ignore when social media companies have Ex-Muslim voices being shut out because they're inconvenient to the good versus evil narrative by the Left-leaning media in many countries.[1396][1397] There are tens of millions spent from Islamic countries to cajole people from supposedly respectable media establishments to support a religion that really is just a thoroughgoing anti-intellectual social movement that supports itself through intimidation and violence in Islamic majority countries.[1398][1399] This isn't even highlighting the Islamic wars still raging to this day such as the horrible humanitarian catastrophe in Yemen still going on as of this writing, but just the horrible social conditions within their own societies. I can't possibly know the mainstream Western media's views when the dangers of Islam must be obvious to them when they report on human rights abuses in the news from Islamic majority countries, but it is clear that they don't really care about violence upon minorities and Muslim women in Islamic majority countries when their funding could be influenced. They seek to blame explicitly horrific issues that come from the teachings of Islam upon the culture of the native populations as if it is a widespread social issue that has ambiguous reasons instead of explicitly Islamic doctrines

---

58. [1392] "The Reason Why the Right Hand Is Preferred over the Left - Islam Question & Answer." *Islamqa.info*, Islam Question and Answer, 2 Mar. 2007, islamqa.info/en/answers/82120/the-reason-why-the-right-hand-is-preferred-over-the-left.
59. [1393] Handjani, Amir. "Saudi Arabia Has Big Plans in India." *Foreign Policy*, Foreign Policy, 10 May 2019, foreignpolicy.com/2019/05/10/saudi-arabia-has-big-plans-in-india/.
60. [1394] Freeman, Ben. "US Foreign Policy Is for Sale." *The Nation*, 21 Feb. 2019, www.thenation.com/article/us-foreign-policy-sale-think-tanks/.
61. [1395] Miglani, Sanjeev. "Saudi Prince Expects Investment Worth More than $100 Billion in India." *Reuters*, Thomson Reuters, 20 Feb. 2019, www.reuters.com/article/us-asia-saudi-india/saudi-prince-expects-investment-worth-more-than-100-billion-in-india-idUSKCN1Q90M9.
62. [1396] "Zara Kay Was Banned for Posting This.... - Ex-Muslims of North America." *Https://Www.facebook.com/ExMuslimsOrg*, Ex-Muslims of North America, www.facebook.com/ExMuslimsOrg/photos/a.167221723467566/989587027897694/?type=3&theater.
63. [1397] Aydemir, Ridvan. "Cowards in Control." *YouTube*, Apostate Prophet, 25 May 2019, www.youtube.com/watch?v=3Q5ZKANKaMQ.
64. [1398] Freeman, Ben. "US Foreign Policy Is for Sale." *The Nation*, 21 Feb. 2019, www.thenation.com/article/us-foreign-policy-sale-think-tanks/.
65. [1399] Haddad, Mais. "Victims of Rape and Law: How the Laws of the Arab World Protect Rapists, Not Victims." *Jurist*, Jurist, www.jurist.org/commentary/2017/05/mais-haddad-arab-world-laws-protect-the-rapist-not-the-victim/.

influencing a culture's decision-making.[1400] For example, a few years ago I remember reading a CNN news article about how marital rape wasn't a crime in India and at no point did the article mention that this stems from Muslim political pressure since marital rape isn't considered a crime in Islam.[1401] It'll potentially only become more dangerous since the Indian National Congress Party (INC) is now openly advocating for "Shariat" court systems and accuse anyone who doesn't support them of "Sharia-phobia" with an explicit disinformation campaign on how such systems would impact the wellbeing of Muslim women, Muslim children, Ex-Muslims, and potentially even non-Muslim children in India who will likely suffer physical violence, rape, and torture once "Shariat" court systems begin to operate in India.[1402] The Bharatiya Janata Party (BJP), translated as the Indian People's Party, advocates for a uniform civil code and the Prime Minister Narendra Modi, in support of the HeForShe UN campaign since 2014, has made a Feminist campaign push towards women's rights throughout India in support of all Indian women's human rights.[1403][1404] The Western mainstream media will accuse India of backwardness, but ignore the reasons why and refuse to even engage in the problems of Islamic jurisprudence systems despite the overwhelming evidence that Sharia court systems support protecting the rapists over the human rights of their victims throughout the Middle East and often force victims to marry their rapists so that shame isn't brought to a woman's family due to honor culture.[1405] Given the fact that Islam doesn't recognize marital rape as a crime[1406], what do you think happens to those women throughout the Middle East? How do you think they live their lives? And this is all tacitly supported by the resounding silence of the Western mainstream media, particularly the US media whether Conservative or Liberal, who take tens of millions from Islamic despots to write favorable columns about their countries.[1407] Will they be arguing for "cultural sensitivity" and accuse people of "Islamophobia" on topics of child rape in Islamic majority countries? Will they continue to do so when successful ground is gained by Islamists within Western societies as a result of their complicity? Nothing should indemnify the Western mainstream media of their culpability in tacit support for the Islamist

66. [1400] Renaldi, Erwin. "Female Circumcision: Culture and Religion in Malaysia See Millions of Girls Undergo Cut." *ABC News*, 13 Nov. 2018, www.abc.net.au/news/2018-11-13/female-circumcision-is-still-happening-in-malaysia/10473640.
67. [1401] "Fatawa - Does Marital Rape Exist in Islam?" *Dar Al-Ifta Al Misriyyah*, www.dar-alifta.org/Foreign/ViewFatwa.aspx?ID=6033.
68. [1402] Patel, Anand, and Nikhil Dawar. "Fact File: Sharia Courts Decoded." *India Today*, 17 Sept. 2018, www.indiatoday.in/fact-check/story/fact-file-sharia-courts-decoded-1285236-2018-07-13.
69. [1403] Fishwick, Carmen. "India's BJP Manifesto Pledges Uniform Civil Code: What Do You Think of the Legislation?" *The Guardian*, Guardian News and Media, 7 Apr. 2014, www.theguardian.com/world/2014/apr/07/india-bjp-election-manifesto-uniform-civil-code-legislation.
70. [1404] Solnit, Rebecca. "Why Feminism Needs Men." *The Nation*, 8 July 2015, www.thenation.com/article/why-feminism-needs-men/.
71. [1405] Haddad, Mais. "Victims of Rape and Law: How the Laws of the Arab World Protect Rapists, Not Victims." *Jurist*, Jurist, www.jurist.org/commentary/2017/05/mais-haddad-arab-world-laws-protect-the-rapist-not-the-victim/.
72. [1406] "Fatawa - Does Marital Rape Exist in Islam?" *Dar Al-Ifta Al Misriyyah*, www.dar-alifta.org/Foreign/ViewFatwa.aspx?ID=6033.
73. [1407] Freeman, Ben. "US Foreign Policy Is for Sale." *The Nation*, 21 Feb. 2019, www.thenation.com/article/us-foreign-policy-sale-think-tanks/.

narrative and the scrubbing of Islam's impact upon human rights issues that occur because of explicitly Islamic teachings.[1408] Their stalwart defense of religious tolerance is contributing to the destruction of their own credibility and I have only opted to utilize them in more recent times out of reluctance because of a lack of options on finding other avenues of meaningful investigative journalism and not because of any confidence I have in them. Every news article that scrubs the harmful impact that Islam has upon human rights abuses in foreign countries or tries to dissuade any notion that Islam influences horrible behavior like FGM is just another blow to their credibility to me.[1409] I would love for a more accurate and useful news organization that doesn't let religious sensibilities sway its motivations and reporting to someday exist, but until such a time I'll reluctantly use what we currently have to work with at the moment.

As of this writing in 2019, Islam remains the most dangerous religious ideology that continues to produce more terrorist groups across the world, continues committing terrorism on a scope and scale that goes beyond any other group in modern times, has rampant discrimination towards fellow Muslims within Muslim-majority countries whether it is blatant patriarchal violence against Muslim women or discrimination against Muslims of other religious sects, Islam commits atrocities upon religious minorities in Islamic majority countries, and continues to spread its transnational influence into non-Islamic countries. To paraphrase what Ex-Muslim Anti-theist and activist Armin Navabi once said: *it is not the West versus Islam, but rather the world versus Islam*. Democratic governments from Europe, to the US, and to India should work together as a coalition to combat Islamic groups that seek to spread their influence outwards by supporting Free Speech and especially Free Inquiry to question, challenge, and debate the views of Islam instead of supporting blasphemy laws, safe spaces that are shielded from criticism, trigger warnings, or religious tolerance because they get financial support from Islamic despots. It can and will have severe detrimental consequences because of how dangerous Islam is and so they should allow Free Speech throughout their societies as a vanguard against harmful beliefs. *Free Speech and Free Inquiry are often acts of non-violent resistance. The belief you need to be a certain sexual orientation, ethnicity, or gender to truly understand another person is to presuppose that your reasoning faculties are limited to only your background and that you're not capable of understanding another person's perspective by using logical thinking, evidence, and facts. The belief that we can't have a right to an opinion if we are not of a certain group is nothing more than a delusion of willful ignorance. Trigger warnings are harmful attempts at policing speech to prevent you from having your beliefs challenged. How can you know that your beliefs are beneficial for you or others, if they aren't tested and challenged? Free Speech means nothing if*

---

74. [1408] Renaldi, Erwin. "Female Circumcision: Culture and Religion in Malaysia See Millions of Girls Undergo Cut." *ABC News*, 13 Nov. 2018, www.abc.net.au/news/2018-11-13/female-circumcision-is-still-happening-in-malaysia/10473640.
75. [1409] Renaldi, Erwin. "Female Circumcision: Culture and Religion in Malaysia See Millions of Girls Undergo Cut." *ABC News*, 13 Nov. 2018, www.abc.net.au/news/2018-11-13/female-circumcision-is-still-happening-in-malaysia/10473640.

people aren't free to piss you off by offensively inquiring into your beliefs regardless of your hurt feelings, speaking out against you in debates, and that they be allowed to give criticism layered upon you in the public space such as during your events pertaining to such topics. You have the Free Speech to criticize right back at them. Religious tolerance is the insipid poison of all cultures that prevents humanity from criticizing bad beliefs because they're enshrined as sacred as a reciprocal concession.[1410]

Free Speech and Free Inquiry provide another pleasure that most people probably don't realize or acknowledge; the pleasure of being wrong. The pleasure of uncertainty; of being able to change your mind based upon new information and to recognize that the people who you believed to be bigots because the Western mainstream media made character assassinations of them were actually justified in their criticism. I am dismayed to admit that I fell for the character assassinations lodged against the Atheist author, Neuroscientist, Philosopher and public intellectual Sam Harris and his cohorts, evolutionary biologist Richard Dawkins, Philosopher and Professor Daniel Dennett, and the late and great Christopher Hitchens because I had a strong level of trust in Chris Hedges and The Intercept's understanding of foreign policy since they had been active investigative journalists who had worked with and interviewed people in conflict zones. Both Hedges and the news organization, The Intercept, seemed to be emphasizing human rights or so I was led to believe and that was something I had deeply respected about them. I had thought of them as being more fact-based and less biased in their views about international politics in relation to Islamic terrorism and that the New Atheists had been extreme and bigoted, despite perhaps being well-intentioned. I was even under the false belief that Sam Harris was hiding his actual views of bigotry because I had believed that Chris Hedges criticism of him was accurate for a long time. I suppose the blog post on racial profiling and much later on the Charles Murray controversy seemed to serve as confirmation bias for me. It wasn't until listening to Ex-Muslims of North America's panels on normalizing dissent in Islamic communities that I recognized how woefully misinformed I was and it came as such a horrifying shock to me, it completely flipped my perspective on so much of what I had believed to be accurate information on world politics, religion, modern-day journalism, and the criticisms thereof. I had been so desperate for several years to place hope in religious tolerance, believing that the critics of the New Atheists were correct, and that religion was simply neutral except for what people put into it after gaining some criticism on their beliefs. My understanding of Islam had been completely wrong because I was led to believe it was openly interpretative like Christianity and I was directly misled by the expertise that I had trusted for why that was. After listening to almost all of the EX-MNA panels on the Ex-Muslims of North America Youtube channel, I began to reassess everything I had learned about Islam and from what sources I had learned of such compelling disinformation. I recalled an old HuffingtonPost article about Pew Research that I realized had completely lied to me about what the Sharia really was as a theological concept because it had stated that Sharia was

---

76. [1410] Cialdini, Robert B. Chapter 2: Reciprocation (19-50). *Influence: Science and practice*. 4th ed., 21st Century Bks, 2002.

just a code of ethics that Muslims could optionally follow. I recalled the news articles throughout my time reading about Muslims suffering from FGM which claimed, and still claim[1411], the explicit lie that FGM had nothing to do with Islam. I remember thinking that Reza Aslan was simply clarifying misconceptions about patterns of behavior in Africa about FGM before listening to Ex-Muslim Atheist and Co-founder of Ex-MNA Sarah Haider completely smash apart that narrative in her interview with David Pakman which I had found shortly after listening to the Ex-MNA Youtube content that she participated in.[1412] Most painfully of all, the understanding that a graduate course on Defense Policy for my Masters degree in Political Science had lied about the theological concept of Jihad and what it entailed. The concept of Greater and Lesser Jihad was explicitly deemed as part of a hadith that wasn't considered authentic in the chain of narration system of Islamic theology and it has no relevance for how Muslims conceptualize the religious meaning of Jihad.[1413] I was forced to accept the fact that I had been living in a bubble and it was a bubble purposefully pushed forth by the Western mainstream media, the broader public not wanting to discuss the topic of religion due to reciprocal concessions on what is sacred[1414], and the Western academia that I cherished so much was also part of the half-truths that were in favor of religious tolerance over human rights.

Reflecting on the past videos and the present conditions in Iran of public protests by Iranian women against the hijab, which they rightfully viewed as a symbol of patriarchal oppression, it became clear that when Christopher Hitchens argued against a Middle Eastern family about the violence against women in Iran, he had been entirely correct and he was passionately defending the human rights of women in Iran who suffered from patriarchal oppression of physical abuse and rape for removing their headscarves.[1415][1416] The mother of the family had been lying about the violence against women in Iran.[1417][1418] Hypothetically, just imagine what would have happened with the current social justice narrative permeating through Western society; Social justice keyboard warriors would have simply labeled Christopher Hitchens a bigot and many would have taken to social media to defend the woman

---

77. [1411] Renaldi, Erwin. "Female Circumcision: Culture and Religion in Malaysia See Millions of Girls Undergo Cut." *ABC News*, 13 Nov. 2018, www.abc.net.au/news/2018-11-13/female-circumcision-is-still-happening-in-malaysia/10473640.
78. [1412] Haider, Sarah, and David Pakman. "Ex-Muslim Drops Hammer on Reza Aslan, Conservatives, Liberals." *YouTube*, David Pakman Show, 16 Dec. 2015, www.youtube.com/watch?v=ayQ-j8lJmwE.
79. [1413] "Greater and Lesser Jihaad." Translated by Muhammed Salih Al-Munajjid, *Islam Question And Answer*, islamqa.info/en/10455.
80. [1414] Cialdini, Robert B. Chapter 2: Reciprocation (19-50). *Influence: Science and practice*. 4th ed., 21st Century Bks, 2002.
81. [1415] Hitchens, Christopher, and Tony Jones. "God, Sodomy and the Lash." *Q&A*, Australian Broadcasting Corporation, 21 Dec. 2018, www.abc.net.au/qanda/god-sodomy-and-the-lash/10663024.
82. [1416] Hitchens, Christopher. "Christopher Hitchens on Australia's Q & A - Women in Iran." *YouTube*, blob4000, 7 Oct. 2009, www.youtube.com/watch?v=YXjm31Bvomo.
83. [1417] Hitchens, Christopher, and Tony Jones. "God, Sodomy and the Lash." *Q&A*, Australian Broadcasting Corporation, 21 Dec. 2018, www.abc.net.au/qanda/god-sodomy-and-the-lash/10663024.
84. [1418] Hitchens, Christopher. "Christopher Hitchens on Australia's Q & A - Women in Iran." *YouTube*, blob4000, 7 Oct. 2009, www.youtube.com/watch?v=YXjm31Bvomo.

on the basis of her arguing against so-called "white male privilege" since Hitchens didn't have the "experience" of a Iranian woman so he would have been argued to have no right to talk about their social issues. This would have been despite all the facts being firmly on Christopher Hitchens side about the physical violence that Iranian women endure which has only become more publicized since the feminist protests against the hijab in Iran[1419][1420]; Hitchens would have been told that regardless of his fact-based research, he couldn't talk about or show concern for such issues and to instead focus on his "white male issues" instead of the human rights issues that he was passionate about. The social justice keyboard warriors would have felt smug satisfaction in "defending" Iranian women by telling Christopher Hitchens that he shouldn't care about their human rights when the Iranian police and possibly their male family members physically beat or possibly rape them for not wearing the hijab. Does that sound absolutely ridiculous? That is the discourse of modern Western politics as of this writing in 2019. Back when Christopher Hitchens was alive, he would have been celebrated for defending human rights from misinformation, but in this modern political climate, people would probably be defending a woman lying about human rights abuses instead of the person pointing out the facts simply because of both of their respective genders and their skin pigmentation.

Needless to say, my personal views of both The Intercept and Chris Hedges have radically shifted. I was astonished and horrified to learn that The Intercept had gone so far as to defend Islamist groups to the extent that they had publically revealed the private information of an atheist journalist who was critical of Islam.[1421] The woman, Aki Muthali, subsequently endured rape and death threats in Canada alongside her mother from Islamist groups, anti-Feminist groups, and Neo-Nazi groups with serious safety issues for their wellbeing because of The Intercept's actions which they doubled-down on.[1422][1423] The article she wrote was a severe blow to my confidence and respect for what they were doing as a news organization. I still try to look at the pros and cons and share information that I think is important, but I will never again trust The Intercept's arguments about Islam based on the current evidence I've accumulated from my own research into the topic. I had lost confidence in Chris Hedges

85. [1419] Kenyon, Peter. "In Iran Protests, Women Stand Up, Lift Their Hijab, For Their Rights." *NPR*, NPR, 3 Aug. 2018, www.npr.org/2018/08/03/631784518/in-iran-protests-women-stand-up-lift-their-hijab-for-their-rights.
86. [1420] Wither, Emily. "I Did It for My Daughter, Says Woman Arrested for Headscarf Protest..." *Reuters*, Thomson Reuters, 6 Mar. 2019, www.reuters.com/article/us-iran-protest-hijab/i-did-it-for-my-daughter-says-woman-arrested-for-headscarf-protest-in-iran-idUSKCN1Q30Q7.
87. [1421] Muthali, Aki. "Atheistophobia: It's Time to Talk about the Most Persecuted Minority in the World." *The Nation*, 27 Sept. 2015, nation.com.pk/27-Sep-2015/atheistophobia-it-s-time-to-talk-about-the-most-persecuted-minority-in-the-world.
88. [1422] Muthali, Aki. "Atheistophobia: It's Time to Talk about the Most Persecuted Minority in the World." *The Nation*, 27 Sept. 2015, nation.com.pk/27-Sep-2015/atheistophobia-it-s-time-to-talk-about-the-most-persecuted-minority-in-the-world.
89. [1423] Muthali, Aki. "I Wasn't in Sri Lanka in 2015. Lived in Canada for 25 Years. The Doxxing Did Cause Serious Safety Issues as the Info the Muslim Extremist Posted, Was Used by Many People, Including Nazis and Anti-Feminists Who, along with the Islamists, Sent Death and Rape Threats to Me & My Mom." *Twitter*, Crotchety Misanthrope, 15 May 2019, twitter.com/akimuthali/status/1128508967561437185.

rapidly over reading and listening to his material since he seemed to just be advocating an impotent nihilism towards politics and nothing else. To be clear, I still think that his seminal work, *War is a Force That Gives Us Meaning*, is an excellent book regardless of how anyone feels about his personal politics and I highly recommend it to anyone who wants a better understanding on the ramifications of war. I think he's prescient in some of his political observations, but its drowned in far too much cynicism and nihilism towards life and he seems to exemplify the failings of the belief in Original Sin that I critiqued in chapters 6 and 7. However, the worst sense of betrayal for me was recognizing that both Hedges and The Intercept must have heard of the murder of LGBT people and Ex-Muslims during their travels and research in Islamic majority countries at some point; moreover, they must have seen the sexist discrimination and violence against women firsthand during their many years of investigative travels. Christopher Hitchens had spoken up and acknowledged violence of all sorts within the Islamic world and he had made sure to mention the patriarchal aspects of religion that lead to violence against women. Why hadn't The Intercept or Chris Hedges spoken of how normalized it was in the social context of Islamic majority countries which they surely must have seen with their own eyes? Why did they not acknowledge it, but instead try to downplay the Islamic patriarchy and all its social ills? After revisiting their content, I concluded it was because of religious tolerance. Chris Hedges attempts to conflate criticism of Islam with racism and The Intercept publishes articles endlessly about Islamophobia which effectively perpetuates the same ambiguity in order to defend religious tolerance. It felt like another betrayal because they willingly sacrifice human rights at the altar of the sacred and that the New Atheist criticisms were entirely justified. They argue for so-called cultural sensitivity above the human rights of Ex-Muslims, religious minorities, the LGBT, and Muslim women. What I had thought was a melodramatic diatribe by Sam Harris about the "end of Liberalism" if they didn't criticize Islam, which was implied to be because of some deep sense of animosity towards Muslims as people by Hedges and The Intercept, turned out to be wholly accurate and justified criticism.[1424] For all his faults, such as the fallout of the Charles Murray podcast over race and IQ, his woefully inept argument about racial profiling since the hijackers had made sure not to wear traditionally Islamic clothing, and his friendly association with Right-wing bigots; Sam Harris was the one who was most sincere about defending the human rights of Muslims and Ex-Muslims. As of now, he doesn't even advocate for the annihilation of Islam through criticism, but rather he has argued for reform to modernize Islam by taking his good friend Maajid Nawaz's lead on criticizing Islam in order to reform it. All the animosity thrown towards Sam Harris, Richard Dawkins, and onto the late and great Christopher Hitchens only proves that all these men were fallible human beings. Just like The Intercept, Chris Hedges, myself, you, and everyone else; we are all just fallible human beings and we will always be fallible human beings due to our biases. Nevertheless, when the human rights of Ex-Muslims, Muslim women, and the LGBT are at stake; it wasn't The Intercept, Chris Hedges, or the

---

90. [1424] Harris, Sam. "The End of Liberalism? - Samharris.org." *The End of Liberalism? : : Sam Harris*, www.samharris.org/site/full_text/the-end-of-liberalism/. Accessed 15 Feb. 2015.

Western mainstream media that came to defend their human rights once it meant honestly criticizing religiously motivated atrocities. Those groups simply behave by reacting to Islamic atrocities, but not by actively criticizing the beliefs that motivate those human rights crimes and terrorism. They continue to be silent about oppression in Islamic countries that are caused directly by the beliefs in Islam. In the end, The New Atheist Movement was vindicated by Ex-Muslims who argue simply for the right to exist and to be heard. Many Ex-Muslims who champion Western values of the Enlightenment are also foreign-born from places like Pakistan and the Middle East, so their existence becomes even more inconvenient to the good versus evil identitarian worldview and binary narrative.

Islam is a global threat, Wahhabism is rapidly spreading across the world thanks chiefly to Saudi Arabia's influence, and the only way to stop it is by supporting those who speak out against it. We must be willing to question and criticize Islam instead of running in fear from it. The assumptions of the Islamic faith is what we must destroy to pave the way for changing the attitudes of Muslims. Islam thrives from narratives of Muslims being oppressed to garner empathy, but it falls apart when criticizing the religious beliefs because Islam has nothing to offer modern society; some Islamist activists in the West currently argue against the victories of Second-Wave Feminism. Second-Wave Feminism spread throughout the West to support women's suffrage, property rights for women, and criticized issues of domestic violence and marital rape. Islamist activists seek to undo the victories Second-Wave Feminism because it is against the Sharia.[1425] I fear that supporting religious tolerance and anti-Feminist hate will allow them to persevere in their goals unchallenged. Therefore, they must be exposed and ruthlessly criticized through Free Speech and Free Inquiry. Unfortunately, the current discourse in the West has worked to shield Muslims from being exposed to any criticism of Islam thanks to the West's religious tolerance. While the Social Justice movement has been chiefly responsible for shielding Islam from criticism in recent times, it is not the origin or the main factor; the pernicious social pressure holding back the West from criticizing Islam, far more than attempts to confuse criticism of Islam with racial discrimination, is the social taboo of religious tolerance that pervades Western societies. To list a few recent examples of the perturbing trends that persist; when President Obama tried to get assistance from social media companies to remove Islamic jihadist propaganda in 2015, they refused the President's request on the grounds of Free Speech.[1426] Twitter eventually changed course by deleting ISIS content, but has also behaved neutrally to the targeted harassment of Arab atheists throughout the Middle East by Islamist groups.[1427][1428] Twitter has shifted focus to assisting Islamic majority

---

91. [1425] Hijab, Mohammed. "The Fundamental Flaws in Feminism." *YouTube*, YouTube, 29 Aug. 2017, www.youtube.com/watch?v=IKhIeCF1kPY.
92. [1426] Scola, Nancy. "Obama's Anti-ISIL Push Falls Flat on Social Media." *POLITICO*, 12 Aug. 2015, www.politico.com/story/2015/08/obamas-anti-isil-push-falls-flat-on-social-media-121301.
93. [1427] "Twitter Says It Is Weeding Out More Users Promoting Terrorism and Violence." *Fortune*, fortune.com/2017/09/19/twitter-accounts-terrorism-hate-speech/.
94. [1428] Fenton, Siobhan. "Twitter Trolls Are Reporting Muslim Girls for Being Atheist in Countries That Carry the Death Penalty." *The Independent*, Independent Digital News and Media, 22 June 2016,

countries like Pakistan to threaten and intimidate US, Canadian, and Australian residents with violating Pakistan's blasphemy laws despite Pakistan having no legal jurisdiction in the United States, Canada, or Australia.[1429] Twitter seems to be holding Pakistan's laws as more important than Western values. Twitter says these forms of intimidation won't have any meaningful legal impacts and claims to be balancing spreading their online audience to countries like Pakistan, but they seem to be naively serving as a useful test case by Pakistani Prime Minister Imran Khan to push for an international blasphemy law and could be used to push for a de facto international blasphemy law if current trends continue.[1430][1431] Pakistani Prime Minister Imran Khan hopes to appease the domestic Islamists in his country.[1432] To appease Islamists throughout the globe, companies like Twitter have created arbitrary and often one-sided enforcement of rules imposed mostly upon critics of Islam which coincide with changes in rules ever since a Saudi prince took ownership of more shares of Twitter than its current CEO Jack Dorsey.[1433] Therefore, Twitter seems willing to enforce impositions towards Free Speech content ever since gaining investment from Saudi money, but seems to ignore content supporting marital rape on the basis of religious sensitivity. On March 2019, Ex-Muslim Anti-Theist and Founder of Faithless Hijabi, Zara Kay dealt with arbitrary Twitter suspensions for criticizing Islam while facing a plethora of misogynistic harassment by Muslims on Twitter.[1434] Fortunately, her Twitter handle was restored thanks to a criticism from Ex-Muslims and Muslim reformers and remains active as of this writing.[1435] However, Twitter has become more harsh over the months in 2019 by outright banning Turkish American and Ex-Muslim Atheist Ridvan Aydemir - known on Youtube as Apostate Prophet - for his criticisms of Islam, ignoring his appeals, and giving no justification for "indefinite suspensions" that are really

---

www.independent.co.uk/life-style/gadgets-and-tech/twitter-trolls-are-reporting-muslim-girls-to-the-police-for-posting-blasphemous-messages-online-a7096191.html.

95. [1429] Furey, Anthony. "FUREY: The Pakistan Government Is Accusing Me of a Crime – and Twitter Is Acting as Its Messenger." *Toronto Sun*, 10 Dec. 2018, torontosun.com/opinion/columnists/furey-the-pakistan-government-doesnt-like-one-of-my-old-tweets-and-twitter-passed-along-the-message.
96. [1430] "Dangerous: Imran Khan to Campaign for New Blasphemy Laws around the World." *Humanists UK*, humanism.org.uk/2018/08/30/new-pakistani-pm-imran-khan-pledges-to-revive-un-campaign-for-global-blasphemy-laws/.
97. [1431] Furey, Anthony. "FUREY: The Pakistan Government Is Accusing Me of a Crime and Twitter Is Acting as Its Messenger." *Toronto Sun*, 10 Dec. 2018, torontosun.com/opinion/columnists/furey-the-pakistan-government-doesnt-like-one-of-my-old-tweets-and-twitter-passed-along-the-message.
98. [1432] "Dangerous: Imran Khan to Campaign for New Blasphemy Laws around the World." *Humanists UK*, humanism.org.uk/2018/08/30/new-pakistani-pm-imran-khan-pledges-to-revive-un-campaign-for-global-blasphemy-laws/.
99. [1433] Truong, Alice. "This Saudi Prince Now Owns More of Twitter than Jack Dorsey Does." *Quartz*, Quartz, 16 Dec. 2015, qz.com/519388/this-saudi-prince-now-owns-more-of-twitter-than-jack-dorsey-does/.
100. [1434] "Zara Kay Was Banned for Posting This.... - Ex-Muslims of North America." *Https://Www.facebook.com/ExMuslimsOrg*, Ex-Muslims of North America, www.facebook.com/ExMuslimsOrg/photos/a.167221723467566/989587027897694/?type=3&theater.
101. [1435] "Zara Kay Was Banned for Posting This.... - Ex-Muslims of North America." *Https://Www.facebook.com/ExMuslimsOrg*, Ex-Muslims of North America, www.facebook.com/ExMuslimsOrg/photos/a.167221723467566/989587027897694/?type=3&theater.

outright bans to silence his criticism of rape culture in Islam.[1436] In fact, as I was in the process of writing this, yet another Ex-Muslim is being targeted but in more pernicious ways for denouncing Islamist extremism and far-right politics. Rayhana Sultan, founder of Empower Muslims and Ex-Muslims (emexs.org), has been targeted with what is colloquially called a "shadow ban" in which she is unable to be searched on Twitter and limited in her account activities.[1437] Please consider this: Twitter's new policy says it won't allow hate speech against groups of people, but allows a Sheikh by the name of Assim Al-Hakeem, who according to his own website is accredited in Islamic studies and has attained a university degree in Islamic theology within Saudi Arabia[1438], to tweet that "*There Is No Such Thing as Marital Rape. As Long as She Is Married, This Is Not Rape!*"[1439] without being taken down for violating their rules (unless they no longer believe women count as a group of people). Yet, Twitter bans Ridvan Aydemir for criticizing rape culture in Islam which he witnessed firsthand during his life in Turkey before moving to the US and for posting lengthy videos detailing the Islamic culture, Quranic verses, and other related teachings in Islam that promote violence against women throughout the Middle East. This thoughtless double-standard by Twitter has been denounced throughout social media from Ex-Muslim Anti-Theist Armin Navabi to Christian Apologist David Wood. After several lengthy denouncements by Ex-Muslims and supporters of Ex-Muslims, it has slowly changed for the better, but the situation seems to be becoming more dire for Ex-Muslims who are already risking their very lives to speak out simply to have the right to independent thought, to have their voices be heard, and to enjoy the same civil liberties that everyone else in the West already has without the threat of violence. While Ridvan Aydemir and others were eventually restored after harsh public outcry, Twitter wasn't even following its own guidelines in these arbitrary suspensions of Ex-Muslims and people have grown confused about its policies; Facebook has slowly become the same too. The reason why this is happening and could potentially worsen for Ex-Muslims on social media is because of religious tolerance. We are coming to a point in history where we have to choose between defending the human rights and civil liberties of all people or we defend religious toleration with trigger warnings, arguments about privilege, and how people of different backgrounds are too distinct for empathy to foster between us to potentially pave the way for a situation like Lebanon where people must live within specific communities with little to no interaction

---

102. [1436] Aydemir, Ridvan. "Cowards in Control." *YouTube*, Apostate Prophet, 25 May 2019, www.youtube.com/watch?v=3Q5ZKANKaMQ.
103. [1437] Sultan, Rayhana. "Hi @Twittersecurity @Policy @TwitterSupport, It Looks like I Am Being Made Invisible on Twitter (Shadowbanned, Friend/Followers Removed). Much of My Writings Focus on Denouncing Islamist Extremism, and Anti-Muslim, Far-Right Extremism. Could This Be a Reason?Who Can Help Me? Pic.twitter.com/Sy3K5V5SYm." *Twitter*, @Rayhana, 2 June 2019, twitter.com/rayhana/status/1135286904004534275.
104. [1438] ALHAKEEM, ASSIM. "ABOUT US - SHEIKH ASSIM ALHAKEEM." *Http://Www.assimalhakeem.net*, Assimalhakeem.net/about/, www.assimalhakeem.net/about/.
105. [1439] Alhakeem, Assim. "There Is No Such Thing as Marital Rape. As Long as She Is Married, This Is Not Rape! It Is Domestic Violence, It Is Physical Abuse or Any Other Form of Aggression. Https://T.co/7leRTCdzVn." *Twitter*, Twitter, 11 Nov. 2017, twitter.com/Assimalhakeem/status/929295190648553472.

because we pretend we're too different to understand each other as human beings. Religious tolerance really is putting these people's lives in danger and it is absolutely unjustified to argue that Ex-Muslims should have no opinion to speak on a religion that actively seeks to kill them for leaving it. At this point, religious tolerance means they must live in fear of being killed even in the West. Islam must be criticized for the sake of the lives of Ex-Muslims in the West who speak out at risk of their own personal safety and arguably even more so for the Ex-Muslims in the Islamic world who must remain silent under the threat of torture, rape, and death.

In order to succeed, and if you're interested in taking part even a little to help defend the human rights of Ex-Muslims, I think the best approach would be to try learning sharper criticisms of Islam and to stick to the topic of Islamic theology whenever debates about Islam arise on social media. While I don't have any personal affiliation with Ex-Muslims of North America, I have donated to their cause multiple times in support of their work of making safe living places for Ex-Muslims in North America but I obviously can't be soliciting for them. I would recommend checking out their work to learn more about them and if you're in Europe to check their list of partners at "exmuslims.org/partners" if you're an Ex-Muslim looking for support in Europe. If you like watching Youtube videos with wry humor and useful knowledge in criticism Islam, I recommend the Apostate Prophet Youtube Channel, but if you prefer watching something more academic, then I recommend the *Ex-Muslims of North America* panel discussions. I learned so much from both Youtube channels and they're an invaluable wealth of knowledge in critiquing and criticizing the doctrines of Islam. The Ex-Muslims of North America panels were particularly good to listen to in order to gain a foothold in understanding Islam and plunging into research by knowing what to look for. As an example, I learned what to look for in Islam's theological influence in FGM from Imtiaz Shams brief mention of Shafi'i Islam's influence on the practice during his excellent panel discussion along with the intellectual juggernaut Muhammad Syed.[1440] If you'd like to learn more on the problems of Islam, but not have the topic solely focused on Islam due to boredom, then I recommend Armin Navabi and Ali Rizvi's podcast *Secular Jihadists* which interviews a variety of people for a multitude of topics from Islam to more interesting topics pertaining to history and science. *To defeat Islam, we must normalize a culture of dissent against Islam's pernicious tendencies.* For that matter, I would like to give a sincere thank you to every member of Ex-MNA and their speakers in the Normalizing Dissent Tour for their tireless work and effort in trying to make the world a better place. In the off-chance this book is ever read by a Ex-MNA member, I hope that your organization doesn't mind my use of your wealth of knowledge and experience shared in panel discussions to critique Islamic theology and I certainly hope I haven't misused it in any possible form as that wasn't my intention. If so, my sincerest apologies, but I would like you to know that I would never have finished writing this book if

---

106.[1440] Syed, Muhammad, and Imtiaz Shams. "Leaving Islam, Normalizing Dissent - Imtiaz Shams & Muhammad Syed." *YouTube*, Ex-Muslims of North America, 10 Oct. 2018, www.youtube.com/watch?v=reQmi-lAxLw.

not for your panel discussions because I seriously worried it could lead to anti-Muslim bigotry and violence so I considered deleting it all. I had fully embraced The Intercept's Islamophobia narrative at the time and it had me worried that speaking out would perpetuate violence. It wasn't until listening to your panel discussions that I recognized how idiotic my actions and beliefs had been. Funnily enough, I found one of the panel videos shared on the sidebar of a random blog post while browsing search pages in an effort to find out more nuanced views about Islamic theology to better critique it and that random video on the sidebar is how I first became aware of your organization and I watched all your videos from then on. While I loved every panel discussion, I'd say my personal favorite speakers were Sarah Haider, Armin Navabi the Founder of Atheist Republic, Ex-MNA President and Co-Founder Muhammad Syed, Human rights activist Ghada Ibrahim, and exquisite writer Hiba Krisht chiefly because they hammer the point that Islam is false but the "Pull and Peril" panel discussion with Muhammad Syed and Stephanie Tessier, which was the second one that I watched, really hit home that it's the Islamic teachings making otherwise morally upstanding people conduct such unbelievably absurd and dangerous actions. It was like listening to a visceral representation of everything Christopher Hitchens, Richard Dawkins, and Sam Harris had warned the West about since 2006. Speaking more generally, I honestly find it surreal that there are still people in the 21st century that will kill people over cartoons and for leaving a religion; I had thought that killing apostates was some fringe activity in the Islamic world because that's what the Western mainstream media, liberal bloggers, and organizations like the Intercept led me to believe but the research I conducted for this book shattered that illusion thanks to it having led me to your Ex-MNA Youtube channel. I sincerely wish you all the best of luck, the utmost safety, and I wish to convey to you all my sincerest compassion and respect for all of your efforts. I wrote this book in an effort to assist in my own small contribution in defense of your human rights and I hope that I have helped in some meaningful way.

Finally, and speaking more generally to all potential readers, it must be said that we, as a global community, really do have a pressing issue in our midst with Saudi Arabia and Iran both looking to gain nuclear technology, we could potentially have a nuclear arms race in the Middle East and once countries following a 7th century warlord's morality attain nuclear capabilities, and then there will be no ability for the global community to pressure the Middle East into stopping any nuclear war. Worst of all, Saudi Arabia will likely share information and possibly nuclear technology with Islamic terrorist groups and that could open the door to nuclear-armed terrorism upon Israel, India, Europe, or the US. I doubt a regime like Saudi Arabia will act rationally, because the Sunni-Shia divide is a real life example of the simplistic Good versus Evil morality mentioned in Part I. The appeal to purity within Islamic theology causes any deviation from what is considered fulfilling purity and sacred perfection as falling for the deceptions of Satan. Thereby, both Sunni and Shia would see themselves as pure against sin and would see the other side as irredeemably deceiving themselves away from the Abrahamic God's teachings despite being close to the purity. The intent perceived of the opposition is seen as willfully falling for Satan after having heard the Abrahamic God and rejecting him for Satan. Therefore, the opposite Islamic denomination is considered irredeemable and must be eradicated to protect purity and the moral good of the community from being contaminated by the evil of Satan from those who rejected the Abrahamic God, as taught in the Quran and the superstitious teaching of Jihad al-Shayten to strive against various threats from Satan.[1441] Needless to say, anyone without doubts on their religious convictions could cause a massive death toll because they're convinced that they're protecting purity, moral goodness, and following the Divine Command of the Abrahamic God. Criticizing the assumptions of the Islamic faith may be necessary for a stable and healthy future for all of humanity. *Human rights must be held above the sacredness of religion.*[1442]

"*God has made some of you richer than others. The rich ones do not have to give away their property to their slaves to make them equally rich. Do they reject the bounties of God?*"[1443] - 71st verse of chapter 16 (*sūrat l-naḥl*). Muhammad Sarwar translation.

"*And they who guard their private parts. Except from their wives or those their right hands possess, for indeed, they will not be blamed - But whoever seeks beyond that, then those are the transgressors - And they who are to their trusts and their promises attentive. And they who carefully maintain their prayers - Those are the inheritors. Who will inherit al-Firdaus. They will abide therein eternally.*"[1444][1445][1446][1447][1448][1449][1450] - the 5th through 11th verses of chapter 23 (*sūrat l-mu'minūn*). Sahih International.

---

107. [1441] "Greater and Lesser Jihaad." Translated by Muhammed Salih Al-Munajjid, *Islam Question And Answer*, islamqa.info/en/10455.
108. [1442] Haider, Sarah. "Sarah Haider: Islam and the Necessity of Liberal Critique (AHA Conference 2015)." *YouTube*, American Humanist Association, 28 May 2015, www.youtube.com/watch?v=0plC24YuoJk.
109. [1443] "The Quranic Arabic Corpus - Word by Word Grammar, Syntax and Morphology of the Holy Quran." *The Quranic Arabic Corpus - Translation*, http://corpus.quran.com/translation.jsp?chapter=16&verse=71
110. [1444] "The Quranic Arabic Corpus - Word by Word Grammar, Syntax and Morphology of the Holy Quran." *The Quranic Arabic Corpus - Translation*, http://corpus.quran.com/translation.jsp?chapter=23&verse=5
111. [1445] "The Quranic Arabic Corpus - Word by Word Grammar, Syntax and Morphology of the Holy Quran." *The Quranic Arabic Corpus - Translation*, http://corpus.quran.com/translation.jsp?chapter=23&verse=6
112. [1446] "The Quranic Arabic Corpus - Word by Word Grammar, Syntax and Morphology of the Holy Quran." *The Quranic Arabic Corpus - Translation*, http://corpus.quran.com/translation.jsp?chapter=23&verse=7
113. [1447] "The Quranic Arabic Corpus - Word by Word Grammar, Syntax and Morphology of the Holy Quran." *The Quranic Arabic Corpus - Translation*, http://corpus.quran.com/translation.jsp?chapter=23&verse=8
114. [1448] "The Quranic Arabic Corpus - Word by Word Grammar, Syntax and Morphology of the Holy Quran." *The Quranic Arabic Corpus - Translation*, http://corpus.quran.com/translation.jsp?chapter=23&verse=9
115. [1449] "The Quranic Arabic Corpus - Word by Word Grammar, Syntax and Morphology of the Holy Quran." *The Quranic Arabic Corpus - Translation*, http://corpus.quran.com/translation.jsp?chapter=23&verse=10
116. [1450] "The Quranic Arabic Corpus - Word by Word Grammar, Syntax and Morphology of the Holy Quran." *The Quranic Arabic Corpus - Translation*, http://corpus.quran.com/translation.jsp?chapter=23&verse=11

"*Let those who find not the wherewithal for marriage keep themselves chaste, until Allah gives them means out of His grace. And if any of your slaves ask for a deed in writing (to enable them to earn their freedom for a certain sum), give them such a deed if ye know any good in them: yea, give them something yourselves out of the means which Allah has given to you. But force not your maids to prostitution when they desire chastity, in order that ye may make a gain in the goods of this life. But if anyone compels them, yet, after such compulsion, is Allah, Oft-Forgiving, Most Merciful (to them),*"[1451] - 33rd verse of chapter 24 (*sūrat l-nūr*). Yusuf Ali translation.

"*O you who believe! let those whom your right hands possess and those of you who have not attained to puberty ask permission of you three times; before the morning prayer, and when you put off your clothes at midday in summer, and after the prayer of the nightfall; these are three times of privacy for you; neither is it a sin for you nor for them besides these, some of you must go round about (waiting) upon others; thus does Allah make clear to you the communications, and Allah is Knowing, Wise.*"[1452] - 58th verse of chapter 24 (*sūrat l-nūr*). Shakir translation.

"*Also (forbidden are) women already married, except those (captives and slaves) whom your right hands possess. Thus has Allah ordained for you. All others are lawful, provided you seek (them in marriage) with Mahr (bridal money given by the husband to his wife at the time of marriage) from your property, desiring chastity, not committing illegal sexual intercourse, so with those of whom you have enjoyed sexual relations, give them their Mahr as prescribed; but if after a Mahr is prescribed, you agree mutually (to give more), there is no sin on you. Surely, Allah is Ever AllKnowing, AllWise.*"[1453] - 24th verse of Chapter 4 (sūrat l-nisāa). Mohsin Khan translation.

"*Men are in charge of women, because Allah hath made the one of them to excel the other, and because they spend of their property (for the support of women). So good women are the obedient, guarding in secret that which Allah hath guarded. As for those from whom ye fear rebellion, admonish them and banish them to beds apart, and scourge them. Then if they obey you, seek not a way against them. Lo! Allah is ever High, Exalted, Great.*"[1454] - 34th verse of Chapter 4 (sūrat l-nisāa). Pickthall translation.

---

117. [1451] "The Quranic Arabic Corpus - Word by Word Grammar, Syntax and Morphology of the Holy Quran." *The Quranic Arabic Corpus - Translation*, http://corpus.quran.com/translation.jsp?chapter=24&verse=33
118. [1452] "The Quranic Arabic Corpus - Word by Word Grammar, Syntax and Morphology of the Holy Quran." *The Quranic Arabic Corpus - Translation*, http://corpus.quran.com/translation.jsp?chapter=24&verse=58
119. [1453] "The Quranic Arabic Corpus - Word by Word Grammar, Syntax and Morphology of the Holy Quran." *The Quranic Arabic Corpus - Translation*, http://corpus.quran.com/translation.jsp?chapter=4&verse=24
120. [1454] "The Quranic Arabic Corpus - Word by Word Grammar, Syntax and Morphology of the Holy Quran." *The Quranic Arabic Corpus - Translation*, http://corpus.quran.com/translation.jsp?chapter=4&verse=34

Chapter 26: Buddhism

"The Four Aryan (or Noble) Truths are perhaps the most basic formulation of the Buddha's teaching. They are expressed as follows:

1. All existence is dukkha. *The word dukkha has been variously translated as 'suffering', 'anguish', 'pain', or 'unsatisfactoriness'. The Buddha's insight was that our lives are a struggle, and we do not find ultimate happiness or satisfaction in anything we experience. This is the problem of existence.*

2. The cause of dukkha is craving. *The natural human tendency is to blame our difficulties on things outside ourselves. But the Buddha says that their actual root is to be found in the mind itself. In particular our tendency to grasp at things (or alternatively to push them away) places us fundamentally at odds with the way life really is.*

3. The cessation of dukkha comes with the cessation of craving. *As we are the ultimate cause of our difficulties, we are also the solution. We cannot change the things that happen to us, but we can change our responses.*

4. There is a path that leads from dukkha. *Although the Buddha throws responsibility back on to the individual he also taught methods through which we can change ourselves, for example the Noble Eightfold Path."* - The Buddhist Centre, *The Four Noble Truths*. From: *https://thebuddhistcentre.com/text/four-noble-truths.*[1455]

The Eightfold Path

"The Buddha laid down the eightfold path for his followers and enunciated that by following this path, they could put an end to their suffering.

Directly related to the Four Noble Truths, *the eightfold path, as laid down by Buddha, helps an individual attain the state of Nirvana by freeing him from attachments and delusions and thereby helping him understand the innate truth of all things. This path, therefore, helps a person with his ethical and mental growth and development.*

Buddha laid great emphasis on implementing the teachings since a higher level or existence can be attained only by putting translating thoughts into actions.

The eightfold path suggested by Buddha involves adherence to:

*1. **The Right View***

---

1. [1455] "Four Noble Truths." *The Buddhist Centre*, thebuddhistcentre.com/text/four-noble-truths.

By right view, Buddha means seeing things in the right perspective. Seeing things as they really are, without any false illusions or pretenses. He wanted his followers to see and to understand the transient nature of worldly ideas and possessions and to understand that they can attain salvation only if they practiced the right karma.

2. The Right Thought

Buddha says that we are what we are because of what we think. What goes on inside our minds (our thought process) determines our course of action. It is, therefore, necessary to follow the path of Right thought or Right Intention. To have the Right Intention or the Right Thought, a person should be aware of his purpose or role in life and is studying the teachings of Buddha.

3. The Right Speech

Buddha asks his followers to speak truth, to avoid slander and malicious gossip and to refrain from abusive language. Harsh words that can cause distress or offend others should also be avoided while also staying clear of mindless idle chatter which lacks any depth.

4. The Right Action

Behaving peacefully and harmoniously; Right action, according to Buddha, lies in adherence to the following guidelines:

- *Staying in harmony with fellow human beings*
- *Behaving peacefully*
- *Not stealing*
- *Not killing anyone*
- *Avoiding overindulgence in sensual pleasure*
- *Abstaining from sexual misconduct*
- *Not indulging in fraudulent practices, deceitfulness and robbery*

5. The Right Livelihood

By laying down this guideline, Buddha advises his followers to earn their bread and butter righteously, without resorting to illegal and nefarious activities. He does not expect his followers to exploit other human beings or animals or to trade in weapons or intoxicants.

6. The Right Effort

Buddha believed that human nature imposes undue restrictions on the mind at times, causing a person to harbor ill thoughts. So we have to train our mind to think in the right direction if we wish to become better human beings. Once we gain control over our thoughts and replace the unpleasant ones with positive ones, we shall be moving in the right direction.

7. The Right Mindfulness

The Right Mindfulness, together with the Right Concentration, forms the basis of Buddhist meditation. By proposing this, Buddha suggests his followers to focus mentally on their emotions, mental faculties, and capabilities while staying away from worldly desires and other distractions. It refers to the ability of the mind to see things as they are without being led astray by greed, avarice, anger and ignorance.

8. The Right Concentration

This eighth principle laid down by Buddha is fundamental for proper meditation. . . . Needless to add, this is the most vital of all the aspects stated in the Noble Eightfold path since, without proper meditation, an individual cannot move on to a higher level of well-being."[1456] *- Zen-Buddhism.net, The Eightfold path, From: http://www.zen-buddhism.net/buddhist-principles/eightfold-path.html.*

This chapter will primarily focus upon critiquing the core teachings of Gautama Buddha, the four noble truths and the eightfold path. This is to make the critique as widely applicable to the two major branches of Buddhism. The above are the general teachings of Buddhism followed by the majority of Buddhists, for the purposes of this general overview I've had to ignore the quote on a specific Zen meditation practice from quotations on the Eightfold path provided by the Zen website. It is not my intention to distort Zen practices, but rather to focus on the general tenants of Buddhism before going into further details.

Buddhism has had a monumental historic impact where it has spread and it would be beyond the scope of this chapter to go in-depth about each Asian country's unique Buddhist history. Within the West, Buddhist translations in the 1800s likely had an enormous impact upon Western philosophy and Buddhism influences spiritual shifts within the West even to this day. Schopenhauer and Nietzsche were both influenced by Buddhist tenants and critiques, and followers of these two philosophers may have utilized such analyses of Buddhism. The attempts to co-opt Buddhism into a Christian practice have historically failed in Sri Lanka, India, and other Asian countries.[1457]

---

2. [1456] "The Eightfold Path." *ZEN BUDDHISM | What Is Zen? What Is Buddhism?*, Www.zen-Buddhism.net, www.zen-buddhism.net/buddhist-principles/eightfold-path.html.
3. [1457] Son, Bo Kyung. "WHKMLA : The History of Persecution of the Buddhist Faith." *WHKMLA :*

Christianity has slowly been losing ground within the West to Buddhist schools of thought that show more compassion and humility than Christianity could ever claim in its history. While some Indologists and Christian missionaries attempt to harp about India somehow having an inferiority complex to the Christian religion, it's clear that they only argue such bizarre arguments due to Buddhism being a genuine attempt at a peaceful religion that destroys Christianity without expending any effort to proselytize. Unlike the psychotic ravings of a narcissist with a God complex who demanded blind worship with a threat of eternal damnation lauded in the Christian tradition, the Buddha was actually a peaceful teacher who explicitly taught people to be non-violent.[1458] The Buddha, like Mahavira and some Hindu schools of thought, explicitly made a call to non-violence as a practice.[1459] However, what truly made Gautama Buddha's teachings so revered was that he cut across the nonsensical beliefs of religion and focused on the core issue of why religion exists and what its purpose has been: to understand human suffering and to provide a way to ameliorate it.[1460][1461] There were no rationalizations of diseases as a God's will or fantastical prophecies celebrating the end of the world in psychotic ravings like the Abrahamic traditions. Buddhism focused on suffering and provided a way to address the problem of human suffering.[1462] To speak frankly in colloquial terms, it cut across the bullshit and got to the point. This single fact was too much for Abrahamics to handle; steeped in self-deceptions of misanthropy referred to as sinfulness, the Abrahamic traditions had no genuine answer to such a critique.[1463] Even the argument of freewill fell apart, because Buddhism argued a cessation from self-will to preclude and avoid human violence.[1464] The entire Abrahamic tradition proved its inferiority by being unable to counter such a simple argument. Now, the arguments from Western philosophy are certainly noteworthy contentions, but those came from outside the Abrahamic traditions. Imperialist campaigns by Christians to force conversion of Hindus and Buddhists repeatedly failed throughout Asia. Only through cultural genocide, such as the ongoing one in Tibet by Christians capitalizing on China's horrific human rights abuses to further aid China in cultural erasure upon Tibetan children, is massive conversion possible from people who are predominately Buddhist.[1465][1466]

Nihilism in Russia, www.zum.de/whkmla/sp/1112/sbk/sbk2.html#iii23.
4. [1458] Buddha, Gautama. *The Dhammapada* (pgs. 3, 6, 7, 8, 12, 18. 20. 22. 24, 26, 27, 28, 31, 32, and 33). Start Publishing LLC. Kindle Edition.
5. [1459] Buddha, Gautama. *The Dhammapada* (pgs. 3, 6, 7, 8, 12, 18. 20. 22. 24, 26, 27, 28, 31, 32, and 33). Start Publishing LLC. Kindle Edition.
6. [1460] Buddha, Gautama. *The Dhammapada* (pgs. 3, 6, 7, 8, 12, 18. 20. 22. 24, 26, 27, 28, 31, 32, and 33). Start Publishing LLC. Kindle Edition.
7. [1461] "Four Noble Truths." *The Buddhist Centre*, thebuddhistcentre.com/text/four-noble-truths.
8. [1462] Buddha, Gautama. *The Dhammapada* (pgs. 3, 6, 7, 8, 12, 18. 20. 22. 24, 26, 27, 28, 31, 32, and 33). Start Publishing LLC. Kindle Edition.
9. [1463] Nietzsche, Friedrich Wilhelm. *THE ANTICHRIST*. Translated by H. L. Mencken, The Project Gutenberg, 2006.
10. [1464] "Four Noble Truths." *The Buddhist Centre*, thebuddhistcentre.com/text/four-noble-truths.
11. [1465] "Q&A: China and the Tibetans." *BBC News*, BBC, 15 Aug. 2011, www.bbc.com/news/world-asia-pacific-14533879.
12. [1466] Barnett, Robert. "Saving Tibet from Satan's Grip: Present-Day Missionary Activity in Tibet." *Saving Tibet from Satan's Grip: Present-Day Missionary Activity in Tibet by Robert Barnett*, info-

As a result of the historical failings of Christianity, and since it no longer has the privileged position of utilizing physical violence to force conversions in Western countries such as the brutalization of Native Americans throughout their history and Black Americans during the era of slavery, its tactics have changed to wrongfully labeling Buddhism as somehow an atheistic religion. This comes as no surprise, Christians have always attempted to distort other peoples beliefs with lies because the Christian Standard is one of having no actual moral beliefs, but rather distorting others beliefs to make their in-group feel a sense of superiority. Alternatively, some Western atheists, inoculated in their culturally narcissistic society that sees the West as the endpoint of progress and civilization, see it their self-given duty to separate the bad theological elements of Buddhism with the psychological and philosophical aspects; they base this not on the philosophical underpinnings of Buddhism, but rather on anecdotes of the extreme aspects of Mahayana Buddhist meditation practices and rituals. When reading Western op-eds on these matters from both the predominate Christians and the avid atheists, one can see a complete refusal to engage in honest intellectual discourse about Buddhism's actual belief systems or its two primary diverging schools of thought. It has never even occurred to many people that Buddhism is simply accepting of both atheists and theists; it tries its utmost to reject a set of dogmas for most of its schools of thought. Moreover, at this point and time, Westerners remain largely unaware that Hindus have atheistic schools of thought that likely precede Buddhism within South Asian philosophical traditions. It's clear why Westerners don't bother; many are taught schoolbooks that only explain how their civilizations were the epicenters of the world. Any belief that forces them to acknowledge that they aren't ahead in cultural and intellectual hegemony compared to less developed middle class and poorer countries and therefore aren't able to ascertain some great truths from the privileged position of colonialists civilizing savages causes them pause, because it would mean recognizing their histories as having distortions about how the world actually is compared to what they've been inculcated to believe is reality. Consequently, this is a problem that emerges from older Westerners than it does the youth, who have largely been bombarded with facts and evidence about historical distortions through the internet and therefore learn a healthy dose of skepticism.

A clear contradiction emerges from the spurious Western narrative and contributes to the belief that mainstream news sources are largely untrustworthy and remain as dubious as any paranoid conspiracy theorist blog. Buddhism is treated with disdain based on incoherent arguments about how Buddhist practitioners are somehow hypocrites for using modern toilet systems while following a supposed nihilistic cult of death. Meanwhile, Christian groups unabashedly label Buddhism as atheistic and therefore a deceptive evil in their psychotic worldview. Even some atheist blogs try to label Buddhism as something "New Age" - a colloquial US term used to denigrate foreign religions which are much older and to conflate them with paranoid conspiracy theories, pagan religious worship, witchcraft, Wiccanism, and other religious practices that Christians are inculcated to hate and commit violence upon for the sake of their worship of a psychotic narcissist with a God complex; some Western atheists do this as vanguards of defense for their erstwhile Christian faith. In both

---

buddhism.com/Present-day-Missionary-Activity-in-Tibet_Barnett.html.

cases, neither the Christians or the atheists bother with a simple examination of Buddhist schools of thought to learn of the two major schools of thought that have diverging views on Buddhism. This is not for a lack of information either; the internet provides abundant sources, these hostile groups are simply too lazy and stupid to bother putting any real work in their criticisms. They would much rather appease their own egos in believing a psychotic narcissist with a God complex is somehow the more logical religion when such a belief lacks in so many critical thinking faculties from prophecies, to virgin births, to the psychotic narcissist's rambling self-contradictions that have no intrinsic value, and to an end of the world prophecy in veneration of the psychotic narcissist, Jesus Christ. By contrast, Buddhism simply points out the problem of suffering and provides instructions on how to mitigate it. Only one religion looked abysmally stupid in any logical comparison and it wasn't Buddhism. Both Western groups lie because they refuse to engage with the fact that Buddhism is equally accepting of both atheists and theists and embracing them with compassion. In fact, there is compelling evidence that Pyrrho, the founder of the Greek school of Skepticism, was influenced by Buddhists that he met in India during his journey with Alexander the Great into India; he may have also utilized the Buddhist teaching of the Three Marks of Existence to shape the philosophy of skepticism since his teachings could be seen as paraphrasing or even translating the Three Marks of Existence into a different language.[1467] Further credence of his use of Buddhist practices comes from independent anecdotal accounts of his life by people who knew him, descriptions of his lifestyle are strikingly similar to early Buddhist practices of solitude and renunciation.[1468]

However, all of this shouldn't be misconstrued to mean that Buddhism doesn't have genuine faults within its religious axioms or that it is somehow too perfect to criticize. There are several problems with the Buddhist style of belief that cause violence, corruption, and a general culture of impassivity to improving social conditions. Irrespective of if other religions are worse in tackling these issues, it doesn't vindicate Buddhism from its own contributions to such problems and its failings on correcting such events when they happen or especially when Buddhism is a contributing factor to such events.

Theravada and Mahayana

Theravada and Mahayana are the two major schools of thought where Buddhism splits. It's most effective to evaluate the major split in Buddhism by acknowledging the differences and then evaluating each of the Mahayana school's drawbacks separately from each other. This serves two purposes; the first is to give a clearer distinction to practitioners of Buddhism and aspiring Buddhists about each denomination's faults for those who don't know about the different schools of thought; second, to give a brief examination of the history before going into the critiques for those who are

---

13. [1467] Beckwith, Christopher I. *Greek Buddha: Pyrrhos Encounter with Early Buddhism in Central Asia*. PDF ed., Princeton University Press, 2017. *Princeton University Press*, assets.press.princeton.edu/chapters/s10500.pdf.
14. [1468] Beckwith, Christopher I. *Greek Buddha: Pyrrhos Encounter with Early Buddhism in Central Asia*. PDF ed., Princeton University Press, 2017. *Princeton University Press*, assets.press.princeton.edu/chapters/s10500.pdf.

entirely unfamiliar with Buddhism and who make spurious generalizations without any understanding of the two major schools of thought.

The website *Buddhanet.net*, a Buddhist educational website, gives a concise history on the two branching schools and the differences among the subsets of Mahayana Buddhism:

The two major schools of Buddhism, Theravada and the Mahayana, are to be understood as different expressions of the same teaching of the historical Buddha. Because, in fact, they agree upon and practice the core teachings of the Buddha's Dharma. And while there was a schism after the first council on the death of the Buddha, it was largely over the monastic rules and academic points such as whether an enlightened person could lapse or not. Time, culture and customs in the countries in Asia which adopted the Buddha-dharma have more to do with the apparent differences, as you will not find any animosity between the two major schools, other than that created by healthy debate on the expression of and the implementation of the Buddha's Teachings.

Theravada (The Teachings of the Elders)

In the Buddhist countries of southern Asia, there never arose any serious differences on the fundamentals of Buddhism. All these countries - Sri Lanka, Cambodia, Laos, Burma, Thailand, have accepted the principles of the Theravada school and any differences there might be between the various schools is restricted to minor matters.

The earliest available teachings of the Buddha are to be found in Pali literature and belongs to the school of the Theravadins, who may be called the most orthodox school of Buddhism. This school admits the human characteristics of the Buddha, and is characterised by a psychological understanding of human nature; and emphasises a meditative approach to the transformation of consciousness.

The teaching of the Buddha according to this school is very plain. He asks us to 'abstain from all kinds of evil, to accumulate all that is good and to purify our mind'. These can be accomplished by The Three Trainings: the development of ethical conduct, meditation and insight-wisdom.

The philosophy of this school is straight forward. All worldly phenomena are subject to three characteristics - they are impermanent and transient; unsatisfactory and that there is nothing in them which can be called one's own, nothing substantial, nothing permanent. All compounded things are made up of two elements - the non-material part, the material part. They are further described as consisting of nothing but five constituent groups, namely the material quality, and the four non-material qualities - sensations, perception, mental formatives and lastly consciousness.

When an individual thus understands the true nature of things, she/he finds nothing substantial in the world. Through this understanding, there is neither indulgence in the pleasures of senses or self-mortification, following the Middle Path the practitioner lives according to the Noble Eightfold Path which consist of Right View, Right Resolve, Right Speech, Right Actions, Right Occupation, Right Effort, Right Mindfulness and Right Concentration. She/he realises that all worldly suffering is caused by craving and that it is possible to bring suffering to an end by following the Noble Eight Fold Path. When that perfected state of insight is reached, i.e.Nibanna, that person is a 'worthy person' an Arhat. The life of the Arhat is the ideal of the followers of this school, 'a life where all (future) birth is at an end, where the holy life is fully achieved, where all that has to be done has been done, and there is no more returning to the worldly life'.

Mahayana (The Great Vehicle)

The Mahayana is more of an umbrella body for a great variety of schools, from the Tantra school (the secret teaching of Yoga) well represented in Tibet and Nepal to the Pure Land sect, whose essential teaching is that salvation can be attained only through absolute trust in the saving power of Amitabha, longing to be reborn in his paradise through his grace, which are found in China, Korea and Japan. Ch'an and Zen Buddhism, of China and Japan, are meditation schools. According to these schools, to look inward and not to look outwards is the only way to achieve enlightenment, which to the human mind is ultimately the same as Buddhahood. In this system, the emphasis is upon 'intuition', its peculiarity being that it has no words in which to express itself at all, so it does this in symbols and images. In the course of time this system developed its philosophy of intuition to such a degree that it remains unique to this day.

It is generally accepted, that what we know today as the Mahayana arose from the Mahasanghikas sect who were the earliest seceders, and the forerunners of the Mahayana. They took up the cause of their new sect with zeal and enthusiasm and in a few decades grew remarkably in power and popularity. They adapted the existing monastic rules and thus revolutionised the Buddhist Order of Monks. Moreover, they made alterations in the arrangements and interpretation of the Sutra (Discourses) and the Vinaya (Rules) texts. And they rejected certain portions of the canon which had been accepted in the First Council.

According to it, the Buddhas are lokottara (supramundane) and are connected only externally with the worldly life. This conception of the Buddha contributed much to the growth of the Mahayana philosophy.

Mahayana Buddhism is divided into two systems of thought: the Madhyamika and the Yogacara. The Madhyamikas were so called on account of the emphasis they laid on the middle view. Here, the middle path, stands for the non-acceptance of the two views concerning existence and nonexistence, eternity and non eternity, self and non-self. In short, it advocates neither the theory of reality nor that of the unreality of the world, but merely of relativity. It is, however, to be noted that the Middle Path propounded at Sarnath by the Buddha had an ethical meaning, while that of the Madhyamikas is a metaphysical concept.

The Yogacara School is another important branch of the Mahayana. It was so called because it emphasised the practice of yoga (meditation) as the most effective method for the attainment of the highest truth (Bodhi). All the ten stages of spiritual progress of Bodhisattvahood have to be passed through before Bodhi can be attained. The ideal of the Mahayana school, therefore, is that of the Bodhisattva, a person who delays his or her own enlightenment in order to compassionately assist all other beings and ultimately attains to the highest Bodhi.[1469]

As Theravada comprises of the main teachings of Buddhism and Mahayana comprises either the Theravada teachings with additions in supernatural belief systems or a new interpretation of the Theravada teachings that is formulated into new supernatural belief systems of Buddhism, the first critique will focus on the Mahayana school and each denominations' specific drawbacks. After that, there'll be more focus on Theravada and my main contentions to Buddhism.

Drawbacks of Mahayana

---

15. [1469] "The Buddhist Schools: Theravada and Mahayana." *Do Buddhist Believe in God?*, www.buddhanet.net/e-learning/buddhistworld/schools1.htm.

Nichiren Buddhism

This form of Buddhism can be the most readily dismissed based on its hateful teachings. The founder of this subset of Buddhism essentially tried to manipulate the peaceful teachings of Gautama Buddha by explicitly teaching his followers to be violent and intolerant towards so-called "false" religions such as Christianity.[1470] The founder, Nichiren Daishonin, while proclaiming violence on all other variations of Buddhism to be good, also went out of his way to preach intolerance and hate towards Christians.[1471] Even worse, while repudiating Christianity, he attempted to steal the most psychotic parts and apply it to himself.[1472] Nichiren Buddhism itself underwent a split between two major factions. The main differences between the two forms of Nichiren Buddhism are as follows: Perceiving Buddha as a type of godhood, the Nichiren Shousou followers argue that he was somehow a reincarnation of Gautama Buddha and that he is the "real" Buddha.[1473] The Nichiren Shu followers simply argue that he was a priest.[1474] In either case, they attempt to mitigate his intolerance and calls for violence upon other religious faiths, upon Christians in particular, and calls for violence towards other Buddhists.[1475] His preaching of violence is clearly an attempt to assimilate Jesus Christ's hateful and psychopathic teachings about the end of the world and his intolerance towards others into a Buddhist variation. It lacks the teaching of *Ahimsa (non-violence)* and instead promotes violence upon others. In his lifetime, Nichiren preached that others would go to hell if they didn't follow his particular form of Buddhism.[1476][1477] Now, hell meant a state of despair in his teachings, but the fact he taught all who didn't follow his Lotus Sutra were wrong shows an asinine level of intolerance towards others.[1478][1479] Despite the moral veneer, he clearly wanted people to only follow his own teachings and nothing else. Therefore, Nichiren was little more than a violent preacher, a man who attempted theft of peaceful Buddhist practices for his own hateful delusions of wanting to kill foreigners, and - if he truly believed what he taught - a psychopath of the highest order. Nichiren Buddhists who attempt to mitigate the more hateful aspects are no different than Muslims who try to ignore the clear acts of pedophilia and murder by their Prophet Mohammad in Islam or Jesus Christ's psychopathic narcissism in both Christianity and Islam. If the argument by practitioners' is that I've

---

16. [1470] Weldon, John. "Nichiren Shoshu Buddhism." *Christian Research Institute*, www.equip.org/article/nichiren-shoshu-buddhism/.
17. [1471] Weldon, John. "Nichiren Shoshu Buddhism." *Christian Research Institute*, www.equip.org/article/nichiren-shoshu-buddhism/.
18. [1472] Weldon, John. "Nichiren Shoshu Buddhism." *Christian Research Institute*, www.equip.org/article/nichiren-shoshu-buddhism/.
19. [1473] "Religions - Buddhism: Nichiren Buddhism." *BBC*, BBC, 13 July 2005, www.bbc.co.uk/religion/religions/buddhism/subdivisions/nichiren_1.shtml.
20. [1474] "Religions - Buddhism: Nichiren Buddhism." *BBC*, BBC, 13 July 2005, www.bbc.co.uk/religion/religions/buddhism/subdivisions/nichiren_1.shtml.
21. [1475] "Christianity and SGI Nichiren Buddhism." *What Is 'Divine' in Buddhism?*, www.sokahumanism.com/nichiren-buddhism/Christianity_and_SGI_Nichiren_Buddhism.html.
22. [1476] "Nichiren Facts." *YourDictionary*, biography.yourdictionary.com/nichiren.
23. [1477] "Religions - Buddhism: Nichiren Buddhism." *BBC*, BBC, 13 July 2005, www.bbc.co.uk/religion/religions/buddhism/subdivisions/nichiren_1.shtml.
24. [1478] "Religions - Buddhism: Nichiren Buddhism." *BBC*, BBC, 13 July 2005, www.bbc.co.uk/religion/religions/buddhism/subdivisions/nichiren_1.shtml.
25. [1479] "Nichiren Facts." *YourDictionary*, biography.yourdictionary.com/nichiren.

somehow dishonored Nichiren Buddhism, then this would simply be an appeal to tradition fallacy and be against open and free skeptical debate about the religious values of Nichiren Buddhism.[1480] Moreover, it's still no different than practitioners of the Abrahamic faiths trying to mitigate the even worse offenses of Mohammad, Jesus, or Moses by intolerantly declaring any outsider opinion isn't valid simply because it's from an outsider. It's a way of ignoring criticism by declaring the teachings to be too above mere human opinion to criticize. Furthermore, irrespective of the veracity of his criticisms, the fact this man purposefully chose to preach intolerance and violence means his teachings are no different than the intolerance and violence that he purportedly tried to stop from Christianity and other forms of Buddhism. Violence reciprocates violence in a social system of negative interdependence and this man, for all his so-called greatness, didn't repudiate violence and instead encouraged it upon those that he perceived to be foreign.[1481] Therefore, it falls into the same intolerant practices of the Abrahamic traditions of blasphemy and their failings. To be clear, his actual criticisms of other religions are sharp and could have been interesting, but his ultimate solution was committing violence against them while attempting to co-opt peaceful religious teachings to proclaim as his own. Thus, he should be adamantly dismissed because his answers were to simply to satisfy his own narcissism and he advocated for violence upon innocent people for thought crimes.

Tibetan Buddhism

Tibetan Buddhism is a form of Buddhism that has largely overlapped and combined itself with the ancient Tibetan religion called *Bon* in ritualized practices and syncretistic beliefs.[1482][1483][1484] It harbors beliefs in spirits and various benevolent and wrathful deities as real and apparent.[1485][1486][1487] Tibetan Buddhism, like the historical Catholic Church, is strictly against homosexuality and has not made reforms to be more inclusive of homosexuality, unlike the slow progress of the current Catholic Church.[1488] It holds contradictory views towards women; rejecting their ability to move up in teaching within their monastic systems whilst praising the meditation and wisdom goddess, Tara and its manifold forms representing multi-faceted aspects of Tibetan Buddhist

---

26. [1480] "Appeal to Tradition." *Https://Www.logicallyfallacious.com*, www.logicallyfallacious.com/tools/lp/Bo/LogicalFallacies/44/Appeal-to-Tradition.
27. [1481] Cialdini, Robert B. Chapter 2: Reciprocation (19-50). *Influence: Science and practice*. 4th ed., 21st Century Bks, 2002.
28. [1482] "Bön, Tibet's Indigenous Belief System." *Khan Academy*, Khan Academy, www.khanacademy.org/humanities/art-asia/himalayas/tibet/a/bn-tibets-indigenous-belief-system.
29. [1483] "Religions - Buddhism: Tibetan Buddhism." *BBC*, BBC, 14 Jan. 2004, www.bbc.co.uk/religion/religions/buddhism/subdivisions/tibetan_1.shtml.
30. [1484] Hays, Jeffrey. "TIBETAN BUDDHIST GODS, BODHISATTVAS AND BUDDHAS." *Facts and Details*, factsanddetails.com/china/cat6/sub34/entry-4428.html.
31. [1485] "Religions - Buddhism: Tibetan Buddhism." *BBC*, BBC, 14 Jan. 2004, www.bbc.co.uk/religion/religions/buddhism/subdivisions/tibetan_1.shtml.
32. [1486] "Bön, Tibet's Indigenous Belief System." *Khan Academy*, Khan Academy, www.khanacademy.org/humanities/art-asia/himalayas/tibet/a/bn-tibets-indigenous-belief-system.
33. [1487] Hays, Jeffrey. "TIBETAN BUDDHIST GODS, BODHISATTVAS AND BUDDHAS." *Facts and Details*, factsanddetails.com/china/cat6/sub34/entry-4428.html.
34. [1488] Bixby, Scott. "Dalai Lama OK with Gay Marriage." *The Daily Beast*, The Daily Beast Company, 8 Mar. 2014, www.thedailybeast.com/dalai-lama-ok-with-gay-marriage.

piety, meditation, and spiritual resonance within the subjective experience of Buddhist Monks.[1489][1490] Beneficial spirits such as the fiercely protective Simhavaktra Dakini work in service of the Glorious Goddess, Panden Lhamo, who is seen as the protector of Tibetan Dharma and Tibet itself.[1491] Thus, within Tibetan Buddhist theology, goddess's are both protectors of people and proffers of wisdom.[1492] Despite this surprisingly progressive theology for an institutional religious system, the Dalai Lama has only made lip service to women's empowerment and the Monastic institutions of Tibetan Buddhism aren't keen on allowing lay women to learn more and become higher ranks within the religion.[1493] The patriarchal norms and values of Catholicism find a shared pastime with modern Tibetan Buddhist hierarchical systems. While less misogynistic in its theological underpinnings, it's no less misogynistic than Catholicism in its actual behavior. While the patriarchal norms and discrimination of women in Catholicism is predicated upon actual theology, there is still misogyny within Tibetan Buddhism due to the patriarchal system the defines women as unable to join as a result of technicalities of the lineage of Female Monks being broken long ago and therefore there being no Female Monk to ordain other Female Monks.[1494][1495] This is a thinly veiled form of misogyny and laziness wrapped into one deplorable system that's simply awaiting its own annihilation from either modernity or foreign religious conversions. I can't help but personally give my lamentations that a rich, diverse cultural heritage of Tibetan literature, art, and music - which has the foremost historical progress in depictions of divine feminine art far beyond any of the Abrahamic traditions - could be so bigoted and self-destructive that they don't empower their heritage further by reinstating a powerful religious and cultural tradition that could potentially demolish and shock both the secular world and the Abrahamic world into acknowledging their wrongful notions of religious superiority. However, I can't help but feel disdain for what seems to be an asinine and facile reason to

---

35. [1489] Holmes-Tagchungdarpa, Amy. "Can Women Become Leaders in the Buddhist Tradition?" *Georgetown University*, berkleycenter.georgetown.edu/forum/can-women-become-leaders-in-the-buddhist-tradition.
36. [1490] "Limitless Tara, Beyond the Green: Buddha, Bodhisattva, Savior, Mother of All the Buddhas, Hindu Maa Tara, Goddess of Many Colors, Consort of Buddhas, Wisdom Mother, Action Hero…" *Buddha Weekly: Buddhist Practices, Mindfulness, Meditation*, 26 Dec. 2017, buddhaweekly.com/limitless-tara-beyond-green-buddha-bodhisattva-savior-mother-buddhas-hindu-maa-tara-goddess-many-colors-consort-buddhas-wisdom-mother-action-hero/.
37. [1491] "The Buddhist Deity Simhavaktra Dakini." *Khan Academy*, Khan Academy, www.khanacademy.org/humanities/art-asia/himalayas/tibet/v/simhavaktra-dakini.
38. [1492] "Limitless Tara, Beyond the Green: Buddha, Bodhisattva, Savior, Mother of All the Buddhas, Hindu Maa Tara, Goddess of Many Colors, Consort of Buddhas, Wisdom Mother, Action Hero…" *Buddha Weekly: Buddhist Practices, Mindfulness, Meditation*, 26 Dec. 2017, buddhaweekly.com/limitless-tara-beyond-green-buddha-bodhisattva-savior-mother-buddhas-hindu-maa-tara-goddess-many-colors-consort-buddhas-wisdom-mother-action-hero/.
39. [1493] "Interview with the Dalai Lama about the Full Ordination of Women." *The Ever-Changing Forms of Buddhism by James Blumenthal*, info-buddhism.com/Interview_Dalai_Lama_about_the_Full_Ordination_of_Women.html.
40. [1494] "Interview with the Dalai Lama about the Full Ordination of Women." *The Ever-Changing Forms of Buddhism by James Blumenthal*, info-buddhism.com/Interview_Dalai_Lama_about_the_Full_Ordination_of_Women.html.
41. [1495] Holmes-Tagchungdarpa, Amy. "Can Women Become Leaders in the Buddhist Tradition?" *Georgetown University*, berkleycenter.georgetown.edu/forum/can-women-become-leaders-in-the-buddhist-tradition.

not allow women full ordination into Tibetan Buddhist hierarchical structures. Many Tibetan women seek support networks and are earnest in attempts to express their Buddhist faith but have only been ignored by the very people who should be supporting them.[1496] The fact that the Lamas (known as teachers of the Tibetan Buddhist tradition) don't aid them is evidence that Tibetan Buddhism is causing its own demise; there is nothing positive that can be said here, it may just be stupidity and sexism on the part of a patriarchal religious order that should have worked to build stronger community foundations since they were already refugees from their homeland.[1497] By building a firmer community by including Buddhist women, they may not have been dwindling in numbers within their community as they are now.

Death worship is of paramount importance in Tibetan Buddhism. Tibetan Buddhism attempts to frame the belief as an awareness of death through acknowledging the impermanence of life.[1498] As a result of this, Tibetan Buddhists pursue spiritual techniques of meditation and spiritual rituals because the spiritual is perceived to have lasting value. Concentrated meditation practices put emphasis on imagining death and preparing for the intermediary realm between death and rebirth called *bardo*.[1499] It is unambiguous that these ritualized spiritual practices and emphasis on death constitute a theology that is explicitly about death worship.[1500][1501] Asceticism takes on a ritualized form and it is encouraged through deep meditative practices to visualize bardo.[1502] Impotence is celebrated as of vital importance because the material world is seen as impermanent and full of decaying life forms.[1503][1504] That is, it is strict ritualized meditative practices that essentially celebrate doing nothing in life, except to prepare for death as some elusive journey.[1505][1506] It blends death worship and a will to nothingness into one theology. Analogies like cell death and the eventuality of life ending in death are used as reasons to accept preparation for the journey of the intermediary

---

42. [1496] "Women in Tibetan Buddhism." *Shambhala*, 29 Mar. 2017, www.shambhala.com/snowlion_articles/women-in-tibetan-buddhism/.
43. [1497] Holmes-Tagchungdarpa, Amy. "Can Women Become Leaders in the Buddhist Tradition?" *Georgetown University*, berkleycenter.georgetown.edu/forum/can-women-become-leaders-in-the-buddhist-tradition.
44. [1498] "Religions - Buddhism: Tibetan Buddhism." *BBC*, BBC, 14 Jan. 2004, www.bbc.co.uk/religion/religions/buddhism/subdivisions/tibetan_1.shtml.
45. [1499] "Religions - Buddhism: Tibetan Buddhism." *BBC*, BBC, 14 Jan. 2004, www.bbc.co.uk/religion/religions/buddhism/subdivisions/tibetan_1.shtml.
46. [1500] "Religions - Buddhism: Tibetan Buddhism." *BBC*, BBC, 14 Jan. 2004, www.bbc.co.uk/religion/religions/buddhism/subdivisions/tibetan_1.shtml.
47. [1501] Nietzsche, Friedrich Wilhelm. *Thus spake Zarathustra: a book for all and none*. Translated by Thomas Common, PDF ed., T. Common, 1908.
48. [1502] "Religions - Buddhism: Tibetan Buddhism." *BBC*, BBC, 14 Jan. 2004, www.bbc.co.uk/religion/religions/buddhism/subdivisions/tibetan_1.shtml.
49. [1503] "Religions - Buddhism: Tibetan Buddhism." *BBC*, BBC, 14 Jan. 2004, www.bbc.co.uk/religion/religions/buddhism/subdivisions/tibetan_1.shtml.
50. [1504] Nietzsche, Friedrich Wilhelm. *On the genealogy of morals: a polemical tract*. Translated by Ian Johnston, PDF, Richer Resources Publications, 2014.
51. [1505] "Religions - Buddhism: Tibetan Buddhism." *BBC*, BBC, 14 Jan. 2004, www.bbc.co.uk/religion/religions/buddhism/subdivisions/tibetan_1.shtml.
52. [1506] Nietzsche, Friedrich Wilhelm. *On the genealogy of morals: a polemical tract*. Translated by Ian Johnston, PDF, Richer Resources Publications, 2014.

world of Bardo; in essence, wasting away one's life by creating an imaginary realm to visualize and prepare for death.[1507][1508] Therefore, although it has a wonderful culture of the arts (paintings, music, literature, and so forth) that rightly deserves celebration, Tibetan Buddhism is ultimately a meaningless and impotent religion that makes a thoroughgoing attempt at visualizing death as blessed, morally good, and sees such systematic impotence as divine.[1509][1510]

One final note of political importance concerning current affairs: This critique is not and should never be construed as an endorsement of China's ethnic and cultural genocide of Tibetan peoples. Tibetans have suffered a barbarous campaign of genocide; including forced sterilizations, mass murders, rape campaigns, and the burning down of their monasteries and cultural heritage by the Maoist and subsequent Communist governments of China in what should be recognized as one of China's shameful legacies of intolerance, hate, and persecution towards a people they claim to be fellow Chinese people.[1511] If the claim that Tibetans are Chinese is true, then the Chinese government can't claim to have ever cared about its citizens wellbeing since the Tibetans were treated with a hostile takeover and persecution that involved forced sterilization campaigns, rape, the destruction of living quarters, and the systematic and purposeful mass murder of people they claim to be their own citizens.[1512]

A message to Tibetans, if any Tibetan has been marginalized or dehumanized as a result of this critique, then I duly apologize to them or you. I am not trying to dehumanize you or mock your religious practices. I am simply trying to make a critique of religious faiths through rigorous examination. I am not trying to justify or legitimize any violence against you. I want nothing more than for you to feel valued and respected as a human being and for you to be protected from persecution. For any Tibetan readers in India, I can't know how it is to feel from the decades of lengthy controversy and refugee status, or how you feel about the decision by India to offer citizenship.[1513] It may feel like a complete loss and acknowledgement of defeat of Tibetans with a

53. [1507] "Religions - Buddhism: Tibetan Buddhism." *BBC*, BBC, 14 Jan. 2004, www.bbc.co.uk/religion/religions/buddhism/subdivisions/tibetan_1.shtml.
54. [1508] Nietzsche, Friedrich Wilhelm. *On the genealogy of morals: a polemical tract*. Translated by Ian Johnston, PDF, Richer Resources Publications, 2014.
55. [1509] "Introduction to Tibetan Buddhism." *Khan Academy*, Khan Academy, www.khanacademy.org/humanities/art-asia/himalayas/tibet/a/introduction-to-tibetan-buddhism.
56. [1510] Nietzsche, Friedrich Wilhelm. *On the genealogy of morals: a polemical tract*. Translated by Ian Johnston, PDF, Richer Resources Publications, 2014.
57. [1511] Doshi, Vidhi. "After Nearly Six Decades of Exile, Some Tibetans in India Are Slowly Letting Go of the Past." *The Washington Post*, WP Company, 9 Oct. 2017, www.washingtonpost.com/world/asia_pacific/after-nearly-six-decades-of-exile-some-tibetans-in-india-are-slowly-letting-go-of-the-past/2017/10/07/c00325b0-a2da-11e7-b573-8ec86cdfe1ed_story.html?utm_term=.b4e28775e88f.
58. [1512] Doshi, Vidhi. "After Nearly Six Decades of Exile, Some Tibetans in India Are Slowly Letting Go of the Past." *The Washington Post*, WP Company, 9 Oct. 2017, www.washingtonpost.com/world/asia_pacific/after-nearly-six-decades-of-exile-some-tibetans-in-india-are-slowly-letting-go-of-the-past/2017/10/07/c00325b0-a2da-11e7-b573-8ec86cdfe1ed_story.html?utm_term=.b4e28775e88f.
59. [1513] Madhukar, Abhishek. "Sixty Years after Fleeing Tibet, Refugees in India Get Passports,..." *Reuters*, Thomson Reuters, 22 June 2017, www.reuters.com/article/us-india-refugees-tibet/sixty-years-after-

Chinese victory. The strategy of the Central Tibetan Administration (CTA) has not yielded any results when begging Western powers like the United States of America or Europe to intervene to help their plight.[1514] The harsh fact is that there was nothing of value for the United States or Europe to gain from any military or economic intervention and it would have undermined their economic policy towards China. It is not considered within their rational self-interest within the Realist Theory of International Relations and would upset the geopolitical balance of power for no discernible value at the end of such political action. The sad reality is that an autonomous Tibet is impossible due to the lack of military power in the Tibetan region and any Western willingness to create a counterweight could have dire consequences; such actions could unfortunately cause a spillover of warfare or political violence to other regions outside of Tibet from Chinese resistance and neighboring regions attempting to capitalize on any weakening borders. What would be needed is a strong, disciplined military force to counterweight China's hegemony in the region and that would open the door on any possible nuclear or gas attack by China, upon whichever country would invade Tibet, to keep control of the region. However, it isn't all negative news; I don't want to leave you with feelings of hopelessness over this precarious situation. I can only suggest the actions that I believe would be the most effective in obtaining your interests in reclaiming your homeland. Being Stateless accomplishes nothing and is only likely to induce a sense of helplessness that doesn't help in motivating change. The first step would be to accept the Indian passports and become citizens of India; work in improving the local areas and in lobbying for Tibetan schools and healthcare to remain intact as part of the multicultural Indian tradition. Emphasize the appreciation for the diversity of languages and the compassion of fellow Indian people for your plight. I'd recommend the BJP over the current Congress party at this time, since the BJP is actually working to make reforms and the Congress party has largely spat on its old legacy and fallen into worsening degrees of political corruption than the BJP party. The BJP party is largely the only one motivated to help improve the country, while the Congress party does little more than complain at the moment of this writing. I'd recommend working to improve the country's military technology, encouraging recruitment and participating in recruitment, and genuinely holding allegiance to India. Once military improvements are made; perhaps from increasing the commerce within India internally and with the United States externally to obtain up-to-date military weaponry for India, or if the US is hesitant then with Israel, to gain an advantage. However, of crucial importance throughout this step is social reforms and condemnations for any sexual assaults and especially rapes by anyone in the Indian military; it is an important step, because while it'll come with slurs and insults, reforming the military's conduct would yield a superior fighting force that has stronger moral conviction in its actions and it can then push a more humanitarian message to counter the anti-India message of the West and other areas of the world. After that, any altercation with China could build-up to defending the rights of Tibetans under Chinese rule and your plight could be made useful to legitimize India's takeover of Tibet from brutal Chinese rule. Political legitimacy is an important component of all military takeovers, the only

---

fleeing-tibet-refugees-in-india-get-passports-not-property-idUSKBN19D019.
60. [1514] Madhukar, Abhishek. "Sixty Years after Fleeing Tibet, Refugees in India Get Passports,..." *Reuters*, Thomson Reuters, 22 June 2017, www.reuters.com/article/us-india-refugees-tibet/sixty-years-after-fleeing-tibet-refugees-in-india-get-passports-not-property-idUSKBN19D019.

country too dumb to understand this is the United States of America, whose Joint Chiefs largely see an inherent right in conquering whichever part of the world that they please due to feelings of being chosen people of Jesus Christ; it's why so much emphasis is always on a particular Middle Eastern country being a holy Christian land of some sort by right-wing televangelists.[1515] Those right-wing Christian televangelists wouldn't be so successful throughout US history if Christianity wasn't successfully legitimizing war in the name of Jesus Christ.[1516] In the case of more intelligent countries with political savvy, Iran holds an embassy for Palestine, doesn't recognize Israel, and supports the rights of Palestinians. Why? So that, in times of war or if ever a war against Israel should break out, Iranians will rally around the Palestinian cause and justify warfare against Israel by presenting itself as defending the human rights of Palestinians. Thus, political legitimacy will be established within their own country by even the most Western supportive Iranians. By having your thoughts and feelings expressed on live television in India or through Indian social media, a sense of legitimacy for the war and for your plight will take hold. Unfortunately, there's no possibility of Tibet ever being autonomous, but under Indian rule and being legitimized as an Indian State, it could gain freedom of religion and end the persecution of Tibetans.[1517] At the very least, it would be under a democratic rule and you would be able to freely practice Tibetan Buddhism within Tibet once again.

Zen Buddhism

Zen Buddhism sets itself against all forms of dogma and belief.[1518][1519] Formed from the intermixing of Mahayana Buddhism and Daoism (or Taoism, in some translations), it sets itself apart by repudiating any form of doctrines or even definitions for itself.[1520][1521] At best, its philosophical side is the belief that everything is interconnected; Zen re-contextualizes Karma as simply the universe reflecting back on what deeds you do, such as violence begetting violence and good begetting good.[1522] Furthermore, Zen re-contextualizes reincarnation (Samsara) as simply emptiness by recognizing that all substances are interdependent of each other and therefore empty of its own solitary and permanent existence.[1523] The concept of Zanshin asserts to be vigilant against attachment

---

61. [1515] Phillips, Kevin P. *American Theocracy: the Peril and Politics of Radical Religion, Oil, and Borrowed Money in the 21st Century*. Penguin Books, 2007.
62. [1516] Phillips, Kevin P. *American Theocracy: the Peril and Politics of Radical Religion, Oil, and Borrowed Money in the 21st Century*. Penguin Books, 2007.
63. [1517] "Q&A: China and the Tibetans." *BBC News*, BBC, 15 Aug. 2011, www.bbc.com/news/world-asia-pacific-14533879.
64. [1518] www.zen-buddhism.net. "What Is Zen?" *ZEN BUDDHISM | What Is Zen? What Is Buddhism?*, www.zen-buddhism.net/.
65. [1519] www.zen-Buddhism.net. "Beliefs & Dogmas." *Buddhist Beliefs | ZEN BUDDHISM*, www.zen-buddhism.net/beliefs/beliefs-and-dogmas.html.
66. [1520] "Religions - Buddhism: Zen Buddhism." *BBC*, BBC, 2 Oct. 2002, www.bbc.co.uk/religion/religions/buddhism/subdivisions/zen_1.shtml.
67. [1521] www.zen-buddhism.net. "What Is Zen?" *ZEN BUDDHISM | What Is Zen? What Is Buddhism?*, www.zen-buddhism.net/.
68. [1522] www.zen-buddhism.net. "What Is Karma?" *ZEN BUDDHISM | What Is Zen? What Is Buddhism?*, www.zen-buddhism.net/beliefs/karma.html.
69. [1523] www.zen-buddhism.net. "What Is Samsara or Rebirth?" *ZEN BUDDHISM | What Is Zen? What Is Buddhism?*, www.zen-buddhism.net/beliefs/samsara.html.

and to be present in every moment of existence; tautologies about eating and fighting while fully engaged abound in the explanation of its concept.[1524] Zen insists that questions like the existence of a deity and the afterlife are unimportant and impossible to answer because of our limited subjective experience.[1525] Zen prefers to remain silent about these questions and instead to focus on the present moment.[1526] Zen forms of enlightenment, like Mushin and Satori, are insisted to be lacking any categorical definitions and are presented as experiences that a person must undergo to form any true understanding.[1527][1528]

At a cursory glance, Zen Buddhism's attempts to remain neutral to questions about deities and the afterlife may seem valiant and open-minded, but upon deeper inspection, it could be considered a fear of judgment by others. Pervading throughout its concepts, which are repeatedly contrived as forms of experience and not forms of viewpoints, is the fear of needing to defend one's views from the judgment of others. It could be argued that this is simply a fear of having any self-confidence in one's beliefs. Thereby, Zen strives to be a concept in which nobody can be allowed to make an opinion on. It has a peculiar agnostic focus on questions of the existence of a Goddess or God and on the existence of an afterlife after death. It tries to re-contextualize Samsara and Karma into vague generalities that seem to harbor a thinly veiled nihilism towards anything having inherent meaning to it.[1529] Zashin seems to be a concept that attempts to give underserved, grandiose meaning to subsistence living and daily routine based on vague tautologies and possibly circular reasoning.

There is pernicious component to all of Zen Buddhism as a result of this broad rejection of any definition, category, and axiom. It is predicated upon and celebrates being anti-intellectual. It is possibly the most thoroughgoing anti-intellectual religious concept because it refuses to establish what it is from what it isn't, for people to make sense of it. It argues an experiential basis, but without any reason or meaning for why. In fact, their revision of Samsara refers to it as emptiness which derives no meaning from anything due to their interdependence. Thus, the concept lacks having any sense of meaning or greater purpose in Zen.[1530] Compounding this issue is that it has an acute version of asceticism that is far more stagnating and damaging to any sense of effort focused activity on personal goals than any other theology.[1531][1532] Whilst Islam's form of asceticism is worse in the

---

70. [1524] www.zen-buddhism.net. "Zanshin." *ZEN BUDDHISM | What Is Zen? What Is Buddhism?*, www.zen-buddhism.net/zen-concepts/zanshin.html.
71. [1525] www.zen-Buddhism.net. "Beliefs & Dogmas." *Buddhist Beliefs | ZEN BUDDHISM*, www.zen-buddhism.net/beliefs/beliefs-and-dogmas.html.
72. [1526] www.zen-buddhism.net. "How to Practice Meditation?" *ZEN BUDDHISM | What Is Zen? What Is Buddhism?*, www.zen-buddhism.net/practice/zen-meditation.html.
73. [1527] www.zen-Buddhism.net. "Mushin." *Mushin | ZEN BUDDHISM*, www.zen-buddhism.net/zen-concepts/mushin.html.
74. [1528] www.zen-Buddhism.net. "Satori or Buddhist Enlightenment." *Satori or Buddhist Enlightenment | ZEN BUDDHISM*, www.zen-buddhism.net/zen-concepts/satori.html.
75. [1529] Nietzsche, Friedrich Wilhelm. *On the genealogy of morals: a polemical tract*. Translated by Ian Johnston, PDF, Richer Resources Publications, 2014.
76. [1530] www.zen-buddhism.net. "The Three Jewels." *ZEN BUDDHISM | What Is Zen? What Is Buddhism?*, www.zen-buddhism.net/buddhist-principles/three-jewels.html.
77. [1531] www.zen-buddhism.net. "The Three Jewels." *ZEN BUDDHISM | What Is Zen? What Is Buddhism?*, www.zen-buddhism.net/buddhist-principles/three-jewels.html.

context of propagating violence upon others for different beliefs; Zen's acute ascetic style is about doing nothing of any significance at all. It is the ultimate form of a will to nothingness and celebrates Zashin with an overemphasis on daily activities and subsistence living, because it willfully accomplishes nothing of value.[1533][1534][1535] There is no seeking an outward goal, no sense of personal satisfaction in goal-oriented behavior that isn't about experiential methods related to meditation, and a strict focus on Zen opposes the very idea of attaining goals outside of meditation practices. Zen's meditation practices are known to be the obscene and extreme forms of Zen meditation are popularly mocked by the general public for going on for such extensive lengths that moss grows on people's legs from such intense and self-motivated concentration. Some Zen practitioners may argue that the general public doesn't really understand Zen. Yet, what value do such meditation practices really have when conducted for several hours? It is concentrated effort on having no thoughts and doing nothing of any worth.[1536] Ultimately, Zen is a do-nothing, think-nothing, and valueless religious faith.

Pure Land Buddhism

Pure Land Buddhism is an interesting denomination of Buddhism that largely reconfigures the Buddha's teachings to form a belief system that comprises of multiple deities and the belief of becoming reborn in the Pure Land (alternatively known as Western Paradise) by chanting to the Amitabha Buddha in order to then reach Enlightenment.[1537][1538] That is, a believer of Pure Land must chant and find oneness with Amitabha Buddha to be reborn in the Pure Land and then journey to reach Enlightenment for the purpose of liberation.[1539] Religious piety is done by chanting and feeling grateful to Amitabha Buddha, accepting a personal relationship with Amitabha Buddha, and feel gratitude for having faith in Amitabha Buddha.[1540] A sinner who has true faith is more likely to be

---

78. [1532] Nietzsche, Friedrich Wilhelm. *On the genealogy of morals: a polemical tract*. Translated by Ian Johnston, PDF, Richer Resources Publications, 2014.
79. [1533] www.zen-buddhism.net. "The Three Jewels." *ZEN BUDDHISM | What Is Zen? What Is Buddhism?*, www.zen-buddhism.net/buddhist-principles/three-jewels.html.
80. [1534] www.zen-Buddhism.net. "Mushin." *Mushin | ZEN BUDDHISM*, www.zen-buddhism.net/zen-concepts/mushin.html.
81. [1535] www.zen-Buddhism.net. "Satori or Buddhist Enlightenment." *Satori or Buddhist Enlightenment | ZEN BUDDHISM*, www.zen-buddhism.net/zen-concepts/satori.html.
82. [1536] Nietzsche, Friedrich Wilhelm. *On the genealogy of morals: a polemical tract*. Translated by Ian Johnston, PDF, Richer Resources Publications, 2014.
83. [1537] "Religions - Buddhism: Pure Land Buddhism." *BBC*, BBC, 2 Oct. 2002, www.bbc.co.uk/religion/religions/buddhism/subdivisions/pureland_1.shtml.
84. [1538] Cornick, Jenny. "Key Differences between Pure Land Buddhism and Zen Buddhism." *Academia.edu*, www.academia.edu/34413183/Key_Differences_between_Pure_Land_Buddhism_and_Zen_Buddhism.
85. [1539] "Religions - Buddhism: Pure Land Buddhism." *BBC*, BBC, 2 Oct. 2002, www.bbc.co.uk/religion/religions/buddhism/subdivisions/pureland_1.shtml.
86. [1540] "Religions - Buddhism: Pure Land Buddhism." *BBC*, BBC, 2 Oct. 2002, www.bbc.co.uk/religion/religions/buddhism/subdivisions/pureland_1.shtml.

accepted than a good person who merely chants so long as they accept Amitabha Buddha and feel grateful to him.[1541]

The failures of Pure Land Buddhism is clear. It has similar failings to Zen, in that its little more than a do-nothing religion that teaches its followers to chant for no real purpose.[1542][1543] Pure land Buddhism uses ascetic ideals and practices in service to little more than an imaginary world in which death is given the human characteristics of a paradise.[1544] It is quintessential death worship and its requirement to have utterances of the chant prior to death gives credence to this notion.[1545] The artistic and textual details in celebration of Western Paradises and other deified Buddhas serve to confirm this worship of death by giving it allusions to purity and a new life.[1546] Buddhas with terms of infinite life and infinite light further reinforce the sanitizing of death as something to have blissful feelings for and to worship as the ultimate good.[1547] The implications of disdain for the life a Pure Land Buddhist is living here and now is made evident from texts and teachings viewing the material world and ego as full of selfishness and portrayed as fetters away from the true purpose of the Pure Land.[1548] It could be argued to portray human life in misanthropic terms similar to Original Sin, although perhaps less extreme in contempt for the human body. It can be argued to be anti-intellectual, but far less so than Zen. Arguably, a Zen mix-up of the two denominations would have the same anti-intellectual axioms as Zen though. Overall, Pure Land Buddhism wastes time and energy on meaningless chanting that it doesn't even guarantee within its own theology that a person will be granted rebirth into Pure Land.[1549][1550]

What's peculiar to me, however, is the lack of any historical records on whether Pure Land was influential to the West of India; there's plenty of documentation for East Asia, which purportedly spread around 2 CE, but little to no evidence of whether the Greco-Buddhist empire, cultural links between the Greek peoples and India, and the trade routes thereof ever spread Pure Land Buddhism

---

87. [1541] "Religions - Buddhism: Pure Land Buddhism." *BBC*, BBC, 2 Oct. 2002, www.bbc.co.uk/religion/religions/buddhism/subdivisions/pureland_1.shtml.
88. [1542] Nietzsche, Friedrich Wilhelm. *On the genealogy of morals: a polemical tract*. Translated by Ian Johnston, PDF, Richer Resources Publications, 2014.
89. [1543] "Religions - Buddhism: Pure Land Buddhism." *BBC*, BBC, 2 Oct. 2002, www.bbc.co.uk/religion/religions/buddhism/subdivisions/pureland_1.shtml.
90. [1544] Nietzsche, Friedrich Wilhelm. *On the genealogy of morals: a polemical tract*. Translated by Ian Johnston, PDF, Richer Resources Publications, 2014.
91. [1545] Nietzsche, Friedrich Wilhelm. Chapter IX: Preachers of Death (50-52). *Thus spake Zarathustra: a book for all and none*. Translated by Thomas Common, PDF ed., T. Common, 1908.
92. [1546] Nietzsche, Friedrich Wilhelm. Chapter IX: Preachers of Death (50-52). *Thus spake Zarathustra: a book for all and none*. Translated by Thomas Common, PDF ed., T. Common, 1908.
93. [1547] Nietzsche, Friedrich Wilhelm. *On the genealogy of morals: a polemical tract*. Translated by Ian Johnston, PDF, Richer Resources Publications, 2014.
94. [1548] Nietzsche, Friedrich Wilhelm. *On the genealogy of morals: a polemical tract*. Translated by Ian Johnston, PDF, Richer Resources Publications, 2014.
95. [1549] Nietzsche, Friedrich Wilhelm. *On the genealogy of morals: a polemical tract*. Translated by Ian Johnston, PDF, Richer Resources Publications, 2014.
96. [1550] "Religions - Buddhism: Pure Land Buddhism." *BBC*, BBC, 2 Oct. 2002, www.bbc.co.uk/religion/religions/buddhism/subdivisions/pureland_1.shtml.

to the Middle East.[1551][1552][1553] It's odd to me, because there's extensive historical information on the influence in China, but not the West.[1554] Pure Land itself celebrates the idea of a Western Paradise, and if it was disseminated to illiterate laypeople, then why didn't it move further westward beyond the outer regions of India and into the Middle East? How can there be no records of any possible movement westward? It's known that the Seleucid and Ptolemaic dynasties traded from far-off places such as Arabia, to sub-Saharan Africa, and to India.[1555] Indo-Greek kingdoms are known to have achieved a level of unity and syncretism that is unparallel in history.[1556] Beliefs like Manichaeism combined beliefs about Jesus Christ and other Messianic figures with the Buddha and rivaled Christianity from the 3rd to the 5th AD before being persecuted out of existence.[1557] How did the belief system of Pure Land Buddhism not reach the Middle East then, if it propagated so thoroughly well into China and Japan?[1558][1559] It's already well-known that Zoroastrianism had cultural impact in both Northern India and the Middle East. This lack of cultural exposure of Pure Land Buddhism seems at odds with the known history between the periods of Alexander the Great's failed conquest of India and Mahmud of Ghazni's butchering and plunder of India.[1560]

Cessation of Dukkha

The overarching failure of Buddhism is the overemphasis on detachment from suffering. It finds no suffering to be meaningful and renounces all forms of pleasure, desire, and egoism for the purpose of avoiding suffering. It doesn't provide a response that tackles suffering to mitigate its

---

97. [1551] de Lubac, Henry. "History of Pure Land Buddhism - Chapter 4." Translated by Amita Bhaka, *World Fellowship of Buddhists Second Two-Year Plan (B.E. 2544-2*, www.bdcu.org.au/bddronline/bddr12no6/pureland4.html.
98. [1552] Ghose, Sanujit. "Cultural Links between India & the Greco-Roman World." *Ancient History Encyclopedia*, Ancient History Encyclopedia, 30 Apr. 2019, www.ancient.eu/article/208/cultural-links-between-india--the-greco-roman-worl/.
99. [1553] "Religions - Buddhism: Pure Land Buddhism." *BBC*, BBC, 2 Oct. 2002, www.bbc.co.uk/religion/religions/buddhism/subdivisions/pureland_1.shtml.
100. [1554] de Lubac, Henry. "History of Pure Land Buddhism - Chapter 4." Translated by Amita Bhaka, *World Fellowship of Buddhists Second Two-Year Plan (B.E. 2544-2*, www.bdcu.org.au/bddronline/bddr12no6/pureland4.html.
101. [1555] Ghose, Sanujit. "Cultural Links between India & the Greco-Roman World." *Ancient History Encyclopedia*, Ancient History Encyclopedia, 30 Apr. 2019, www.ancient.eu/article/208/cultural-links-between-india--the-greco-roman-worl/.
102. [1556] Ghose, Sanujit. "Cultural Links between India & the Greco-Roman World." *Ancient History Encyclopedia*, Ancient History Encyclopedia, 30 Apr. 2019, www.ancient.eu/article/208/cultural-links-between-india--the-greco-roman-worl/.
103. [1557] "Manichaeism." *Wikipedia*, Wikimedia Foundation, 4 May 2019, en.wikipedia.org/wiki/Manichaeism#Spread.
104. [1558] de Lubac, Henry. "History of Pure Land Buddhism - Chapter 4." Translated by Amita Bhaka, *World Fellowship of Buddhists Second Two-Year Plan (B.E. 2544-2*, www.bdcu.org.au/bddronline/bddr12no6/pureland4.html.
105. [1559] "Religions - Buddhism: Pure Land Buddhism." *BBC*, BBC, 2 Oct. 2002, www.bbc.co.uk/religion/religions/buddhism/subdivisions/pureland_1.shtml.
106. [1560] Ghose, Sanujit. "Cultural Links between India & the Greco-Roman World." *Ancient History Encyclopedia*, Ancient History Encyclopedia, 30 Apr. 2019, www.ancient.eu/article/208/cultural-links-between-india--the-greco-roman-worl/.

negative repercussions; it simply generalizes the personal confluence of pleasure and suffering and then asks us to detach from them. This form of withdrawal from desires is actually pernicious and leads to dangerous consequences. The Buddha asks us to be a non-entity and act as non-human as possible. That is, the Buddha teaches us to pursue inner peace and live with a sense of tranquility, but this avoidance of suffering leads to infantile responses and makes us woefully inept to grapple with circumstances that inevitably cause us emotional pain. The Buddha's teachings are correct insofar as analyzing suffering as a the main cause of our life's woes, but his response of the Eightfold path is too extreme and discourages us from dealing with our emotions in a rational and responsible manner. The Eightfold path generalizes emotions, especially desire, as a poison.

The beginning of the Dhammapada expresses this flaw; aphorisms three and four asks us to simply change our perception of a wrongful act inflicted upon us, but that isn't the same as reducing or stopping the violent offender from continuing their wrongful acts upon you and others.[1561] This passive submission fails to set boundaries that others should respect and fails to motivate people to change situations of social injustice. The Eightfold path encourages a perpetual state of detachment to abstain from negative thoughts from seeing suffering, including the suffering of others, in order to meditate to keep oneself centered towards inner peace.[1562][1563] First, this form of sharp focus on negative thoughts fails to account for intrusive thoughts which are normal and aren't personal desires of any sort.[1564] Second, meditation as the only response is too extreme; whilst detaching from emotional rage would be beneficial, the Eightfold path teaches that this is the only action that needs to be done.[1565][1566] Meditation can't be the sole solution. The renunciation of desire as the only response is neither rational nor tenable to human experience. It instills within us a repeated pattern of behavior in which we refuse to deal with real life discrimination including acts of violence inflicted upon us and others.

The emphasis on detaching from personal desires and focusing only on clearing our perception to negative stimuli embodies the failings of asceticism. It proposes a do nothing attitude and venerates impotence as the highest form of human willpower and wisdom.[1567] While it doesn't necessarily teach us to hate humanity like original sin in the Abrahamic traditions, it does teach us that dismissing life as unimportant is virtuous.[1568] Detachment from suffering and a sense of

---

107.[1561] Buddha, Gautama. *The Dhammapada* (pgs. 3, 6, 7, 8, 12, 18. 20. 22. 24, 26, 27, 28, 31, 32, and 33). Start Publishing LLC.
108.[1562] Buddha, Gautama. *The Dhammapada* (pgs. 3, 6, 7, 8, 12, 18. 20. 22. 24, 26, 27, 28, 31, 32, and 33). Start Publishing LLC.
109.[1563] Kornfield, Jack, and Gil Fronsdal, editors. *Teachings of the Buddha*. Shambhala, 2012.
110.[1564] Reese, Hannah. "Intrusive Thoughts: Normal or Not?" Psychology Today, Sussex Publishers, www.psychologytoday.com/us/blog/am-i-normal/201110/intrusive-thoughts-normal-or-not.
111.[1565] Kornfield, Jack, and Gil Fronsdal, editors. *Teachings of the Buddha*. Shambhala, 2012.
112.[1566] Buddha, Gautama. *The Dhammapada* (pgs. 3, 6, 7, 8, 12, 18. 20. 22. 24, 26, 27, 28, 31, 32, and 33). Start Publishing LLC.
113.[1567] Nietzsche, Friedrich Wilhelm. *On the genealogy of morals: a polemical tract*. Translated by Ian Johnston, PDF, Richer Resources Publications, 2014.
114.[1568] Nietzsche, Friedrich Wilhelm. Chapter IX: Preachers of Death (50-52). *Thus spake Zarathustra: a book for all and none*. Translated by Thomas Common, PDF ed., T. Common, 1908.

tranquility is certainly valuable in proper contexts when faced with emotional turmoil, but it being the sole response leads to logical absurdities in which life is viewed with complete indifference. Furthermore, the feelings of tranquility and inner peace cannot be viewed as the highest response or repeated ad infinitum when it fails to help ease our emotional anguish or ire. I can see the value when it is set in appropriate context to refocus our personal commitments, but detaching from all forms of emotions is asinine and this method is unfit as a ubiquitous response to all emotions, especially in the context of negative emotions. The ire will only grow and we will not form constructive outlets for such rising anger to be dealt with in a peaceful manner.

Therefore, while Buddhism certainly has great insights and the teachings of the Buddha and other South Asian philosophers were sharp and prescient in their overarching value to the extent they can be utilized and compared to scientific findings in modern times regarding human wellbeing; it is best to modify our understanding of the Buddha's teachings so that his views aren't overshot in its application to modern life. They're indeed useful and worthy of praise, the Buddha was far more compassionate and intelligent than anything the Abrahamic faiths ever taught from the warring psychopaths and child rape practitioners like Moses and Mohammad to the incoherence and psychopathic narcissism of Jesus Christ. Nevertheless, while his teachings go beyond Abrahamic barbarism, so too do the philosophies of the Ancient Greeks which were also older than the violent Abrahamic cultures. It is probably best to see the Buddha within the same context where we take what we determine to be valuable insights from his teachings and expand upon them wherever applicable in the Humanities, Social Sciences, and Natural Sciences just as Ancient Greek teachings were expanded upon.

Eightfold Path Drawbacks

The core failing of the Eightfold Path is that it teaches Buddhists to annihilate their own self-will in order to behave as a non-entity.[1569][1570] Detaching from emotions is an attempt to detach from being human. Buddhism makes spurious analogies of human emotions, essentially likening them to intoxicants and other poisons but coming from within the body.[1571][1572] It preaches for people to follow an untenable position of not acting like a human being at all in order to avoid hatred, suffering, and committing violence. It lacks an overarching goal beyond personal fulfillment of certain people's wishes to abandon desire altogether to avoid violence and hate.[1573][1574] Nevertheless, the disdain for

---
115.[1569] Kornfield, Jack, and Gil Fronsdal, editors. *Teachings of the Buddha*. Shambhala, 2012.
116.[1570] Buddha, Gautama. *The Dhammapada* (pgs. 3, 6, 7, 8, 12, 18. 20. 22. 24, 26, 27, 28, 31, 32, and 33). Start Publishing LLC.
117.[1571] Buddha, Gautama. *The Dhammapada* (pgs. 3, 6, 7, 8, 12, 18. 20. 22. 24, 26, 27, 28, 31, 32, and 33). Start Publishing LLC.
118.[1572] Kornfield, Jack, and Gil Fronsdal, editors. *Teachings of the Buddha*. Shambhala, 2012.
119.[1573] Kornfield, Jack, and Gil Fronsdal, editors. *Teachings of the Buddha*. Shambhala, 2012.
120.[1574] Buddha, Gautama. *The Dhammapada* (pgs. 3, 6, 7, 8, 12, 18. 20. 22. 24, 26, 27, 28, 31, 32, and 33). Start Publishing LLC.

desires doesn't actually preclude one from committing violence and hate upon others. It merely generalizes desires as always wrong.[1575][1576]

The Eightfold Path discourages us from doing better for ourselves: it discourages us from challenging social injustice, it disincentivizes us from believing that any social change can be meaningful and positively impact others, it's detached state of being precludes us from bettering ourselves as people to correct ourselves in our relations to understanding and helping others who are more disadvantaged than us. The Buddha's chief aim was to end suffering by preventing ourselves from committing to selfishness, so that we may find inner peace to stop our feelings of instant gratification or short-sighted selfishness from taking control of us.[1577][1578] This is a very good teaching and message, but it needs to be placed in proper categorization and the Eightfold Path is simply too extreme because it generalizes too much that we shouldn't detach from in the long-term. The Buddha was right in that detachment from feelings of hate, outrage, and indignation; even at the plight of others whom we identify with; can be beneficial and morally good.[1579] However, it is only beneficial insofar as it stops us from committing to violence and hate out of empathy with certain groups[1580]; but afterwards, it's important to take peacefully corrective steps to stop the harm being done to victims. To simply detach is not possible, not beneficial or conducive to correcting any ongoing social injustices, and not intrinsically desirable from the standpoint of our *selfless desires* of compassion for others.[1581] In effect, Buddhism seeks a detached form of instant gratification to replace selfish instant gratification. This detached form of instant gratification is one in which people pay attention to the present moment because it feels easier than understanding the past, learning the facts, and placing hopes on the future.[1582][1583] *Finally, instead of working towards a meaningful goal in life simply because a person must endure suffering, Buddhism teaches an apathy and indifference to our desires in order to strictly focus on detachment in the present moment.*[1584][1585]

Buddhism versus Social Justice

Buddhism is a hindrance to Social Justice activism. Buddhism promotes inner peace and personal fulfillment through detachment from desires. By direct contrast, social justice is about

---

121.[1575] Buddha, Gautama. *The Dhammapada* (pgs. 3, 6, 7, 8, 12, 18. 20. 22. 24, 26, 27, 28, 31, 32, and 33). Start Publishing LLC.
122.[1576] Kornfield, Jack, and Gil Fronsdal, editors. *Teachings of the Buddha*. Shambhala, 2012.
123.[1577] Kornfield, Jack, and Gil Fronsdal, editors. *Teachings of the Buddha*. Shambhala, 2012.
124.[1578] Buddha, Gautama. *The Dhammapada* (pgs. 3, 6, 7, 8, 12, 18. 20. 22. 24, 26, 27, 28, 31, 32, and 33). Start Publishing LLC.
125.[1579] Bloom, Paul. *Against Empathy: the Case for Rational Compassion*. The Bodley Head Ltd, 2016.
126.[1580] Bloom, Paul. *Against Empathy: the Case for Rational Compassion*. The Bodley Head Ltd, 2016.
127.[1581] Bloom, Paul. *Against Empathy: the Case for Rational Compassion*. The Bodley Head Ltd, 2016.
128.[1582] Buddha, Gautama. *The Dhammapada* (pgs. 3, 6, 7, 8, 12, 18. 20. 22. 24, 26, 27, 28, 31, 32, and 33). Start Publishing LLC.
129.[1583] Kornfield, Jack, and Gil Fronsdal, editors. *Teachings of the Buddha*. Shambhala, 2012.
130.[1584] Buddha, Gautama. *The Dhammapada* (pgs. 3, 6, 7, 8, 12, 18. 20. 22. 24, 26, 27, 28, 31, 32, and 33). Start Publishing LLC.
131.[1585] Kornfield, Jack, and Gil Fronsdal, editors. *Teachings of the Buddha*. Shambhala, 2012.

promoting compassion and equality for all through vigorous protests and strong demands for immediate change. Central to this contradistinction is how Buddhism and Social Justice activism view the problem of suffering. Buddhist teachings inculcate people to detach themselves and to devalue our wants because they instill us with suffering. Social Justice activism calls upon people to recognize their suffering and the suffering of others to create a more equal and egalitarian world; that is, Buddhism detaches from wants to avoid suffering, while Social Justice activism endures suffering for the sake of positive changes in service to others.

Buddhism strives for freedom from opinion; that is, the freedom from believing any opinion is greater or lesser than each other and seeks to cleanse the mind from forming any opinion at all.[1586] Social Justice activism is about attacking ignorant assumptions, falsehoods and distortions of evidence, and basing judgments on either compassion with middle-ground fallacies from the less educated or statistical analysis, facts, and compassion from the more educated. Buddhism seeks to detach and ignore suffering for the sake of inner peace and personal fulfillment; Social Justice activism is predicated on tackling, arguing against, and destroying ignorance and intolerance for the sake of equality for all based on fact-finding research. Buddhism seeks to be a non-entity as a sublime standard; seeking no opinions and thus no differentiation from a racist, sexist, or homophobic bigot against the victim of such bigotry; to Buddhism, all is equal as far as human opinion.[1587][1588] For Social Justice activists, it matters that a minority is being treated with intolerance and that they're not getting full respect as a human due to discrimination of their identity. A Social Justice activist vicariously feels the pain of those who suffer from reading, learning, witnessing, and attaining better understanding of the situations of others. While the freedom from opinion mindset in Buddhism asserts an origin point for the human mind being unbiased and in some pure state to allow for meditation and the rejection of suffering[1589][1590][1591], modern psychological studies have found through repeated testing that forming group orientations happen instantaneously and subconsciously within the human mind.[1592] It's part of how humans build a coherent framework for the mind and make sense of the subjective experience of the world around them.[1593] Within the studies of cognitive neuroscience, it's been found that our thoughts are a statistical distribution and that we must first learn the problems with our beliefs before ascertaining new knowledge that is radically alien to what we

---

132.[1586] Kornfield, Jack, and Gil Fronsdal, editors. *Teachings of the Buddha*. Shambhala, 2012.
133.[1587] Kornfield, Jack, and Gil Fronsdal, editors. *Teachings of the Buddha*. Shambhala, 2012.
134.[1588] Buddha, Gautama. *The Dhammapada* (pgs. 3, 6, 7, 8, 12, 18. 20. 22. 24, 26, 27, 28, 31, 32, and 33). Start Publishing LLC.
135.[1589] Kornfield, Jack, and Gil Fronsdal, editors. *Teachings of the Buddha*. Shambhala, 2012.
136.[1590] Buddha, Gautama. *The Dhammapada* (pgs. 3, 6, 7, 8, 12, 18. 20. 22. 24, 26, 27, 28, 31, 32, and 33). Start Publishing LLC.
137.[1591] "Three Jewels." *The Buddhist Centre*, thebuddhistcentre.com/text/three-jewels.
138.[1592] Ispas, Alexa. "Chapter 1: Psychology and the Social Identity Perspective (1-24)" *Psychology and politics: a social identity perspective*. Psychology Press, 2014.
139.[1593] Kahneman, Daniel. *Thinking, fast and slow*. Farrar, Straus and Giroux, 2015.

feel to be normative in our subjective experience.[1594][1595] That is, we must first unlearn our biases to learn new information that is based on statistical data or other fact-finding research by learning the building blocks of new knowledge.[1596] The reason for that is because we often feel our own personal perception of the world is how reality actually functions as far as our opinion on broad social dynamics within our societies and historical or technological information that we know about.[1597] Our personal views can also be misguided because we often fail to take into account events that don't happen and the statistical significance regarding their lack of happening when forming judgments about causal factors.[1598] Therefore, the belief in some origin point of the mind and the meditation practices argued in favor towards such beliefs seem to lack corroboration from modern psychology and modern cognitive neuroscience. We instantly form new understandings of the world around us to form a coherent framework of our world and the personal meaning that we ascribe to it.[1599]

Buddhism strives to be free from suffering with a goal of personal fulfillment in detaching from situations and especially contentious scenarios under the belief that a Buddhist shouldn't have desire.[1600][1601] Social Justice activism strives to have others free from suffering with the goal of mitigating and expelling all forms of human rights violations under the belief that other people shouldn't be harmed or discriminated against. Buddhism detaches from scenarios for the sake of personal fulfillment; in some cases, enduring discrimination for personal fulfillment but not actively challenging corruption.[1602] Social Justice activism protests and tackles active agents of corruption and institutional discrimination to demand social improvements for all people through vigorous protests. Often, enduring police blockades, false allegations, police beatings, discrimination, derogatory insults, smear campaigns by the news media, and violent attacks so that others don't suffer; Social Justice activists aren't afraid to shout and demand a peaceful resolution for the sake of equality for all people. Buddhism does nothing and strives for ascetic personal fulfillment; to glorify detachment and act as a non-entity leaving it structurally ill-equipped and socially inept to change anything in its world for the better and has no goal or purpose to make any changes to the world around it.[1603][1604] A Buddhist strives to only be mindful of the present moment with no attention to the past or the future, but rather just awareness of one's existence of the subjective self in its current form.[1605][1606] Social

---

140. [1594] Kahneman, Daniel. Chapter 7: A Machine for Jumping to Conclusions (79-88). *Thinking, fast and slow*. Farrar, Straus and Giroux, 2015.
141. [1595] Lotto, Beau. Chapter 5: The Frog Who Dreamed of Being a Prince (1356 - 1670). *Deviate: the Science of Seeing Differently*. Hachette Books, 2017.
142. [1596] Lotto, Beau. Chapter 5: The Frog Who Dreamed of Being a Prince (1356 - 1670). *Deviate: the Science of Seeing Differently*. Hachette Books, 2017.
143. [1597] Gilbert, Daniel. *Stumbling on Happiness*. Random House, 2006.
144. [1598] Gilbert, Daniel. *Stumbling on Happiness*. Random House, 2006.
145. [1599] Kahneman, Daniel. *Thinking, fast and slow*. Farrar, Straus and Giroux, 2015.
146. [1600] Kornfield, Jack, and Gil Fronsdal, editors. *Teachings of the Buddha*. Shambhala, 2012.
147. [1601] Buddha, Gautama. *The Dhammapada* (pgs. 3, 6, 7, 8, 12, 18. 20. 22. 24, 26, 27, 28, 31, 32, and 33). Start Publishing LLC.
148. [1602] Kornfield, Jack, and Gil Fronsdal, editors. *Teachings of the Buddha*. Shambhala, 2012.
149. [1603] Buddha, Gautama. *The Dhammapada* (pgs. 3, 6, 7, 8, 12, 18. 20. 22. 24, 26, 27, 28, 31, 32, and 33). Start Publishing LLC.
150. [1604] Kornfield, Jack, and Gil Fronsdal, editors. *Teachings of the Buddha*. Shambhala, 2012.

Justice activists pay keen attention to the horrific past, they place their hopes on a brighter future for all people, and seek to change the social standards of the current state of affairs in order to bring about social progress so that suffering is mitigated for the present and future generations. Social Justice activism exhausts itself with feelings of despair, anger, hate, and guilt for the sake of empathizing with others whom they identify with and protest loudly to demand social change so that more victims aren't killed, physically or mentally scarred, or suffer lifelong injuries from the status quo of institutional discrimination and oppression. A Buddha seeks to be free from suffering by not dealing with negative emotions and thus seeks to close themselves from all viewpoints through detachment; their goal being harmony with all and inner tranquility within one's mind.[1607][1608] A Social Justice activist seeks to fight institutional corruption, human exploitation, and discrimination; they potentially risk and endure arrests, potential physical injuries, organized rape, torture, and possible death so that the activist comes as close as possible to suffering in the place of the disadvantaged group so that the disadvantaged group won't ever have to suffer in the future. In short, a Social Justice activist seeks to take the suffering away from the disadvantaged group by suffering in their place to the extent that such is possible. A Buddha simply detaches from suffering for their own peace of mind and possibly their ego.

Self-Reflection versus Self-Will

Currently in Myanmar, Rohingya Muslims are facing some of the most egregious forms of persecution; the burning down and bulldozing of their property, the theft of their homes, physical violence, mass rapes of Rohingya women, and mass slaughter by the Buddhist majority due to the religious faith of the Rohingya.[1609][1610] All of this constitutes genocide. Furthermore, Myanmar is run by the country's military who often have deep levels of corruption in the form of nepotism.[1611] In Sri Lanka, squads of soldiers have been known to slaughter Tamil civilians en masse by the Buddhist majority during their civil war.[1612] Acts of genocide by the Buddhist majority upon the Hindu minority haven't yet been ruled out in some of the violence in Sri Lanka.[1613] These are some of the

---

151.[1605] Buddha, Gautama. *The Dhammapada* (pgs. 3, 6, 7, 8, 12, 18. 20. 22. 24, 26, 27, 28, 31, 32, and 33). Start Publishing LLC.
152.[1606] Kornfield, Jack, and Gil Fronsdal, editors. *Teachings of the Buddha*. Shambhala, 2012.
153.[1607] Kornfield, Jack, and Gil Fronsdal, editors. *Teachings of the Buddha*. Shambhala, 2012.
154.[1608] Buddha, Gautama. *The Dhammapada* (pgs. 3, 6, 7, 8, 12, 18. 20. 22. 24, 26, 27, 28, 31, 32, and 33). Start Publishing LLC.
155.[1609] Kantar, Sally. "The Myanmar Military's Legacy of Impunity." *Foreign Affairs*, Foreign Affairs, 14 Dec. 2017, www.foreignaffairs.com/articles/burma-myanmar/2017-12-14/myanmar-militarys-legacy-impunity.
156.[1610] Gelineau, Kristen. "Rohingya Women Methodically Raped by Myanmar's Armed Forces." *Chicagotribune.com*, 11 Dec. 2017, www.chicagotribune.com/news/nationworld/ct-rohingya-women-rape-myanmar-20171211-story.html.
157.[1611] Barany, Zoltan. "Where Myanmar Went Wrong." *Foreign Affairs*, Foreign Affairs Magazine, 6 Mar. 2019, www.foreignaffairs.com/articles/burma-myanmar/2018-04-16/where-myanmar-went-wrong.
158.[1612] Pararajasingham, Ana. "Why Is Sri Lanka Defying the United Nations?" *The Diplomat*, The Diplomat, 22 Dec. 2017, thediplomat.com/2017/12/why-is-sri-lanka-defying-the-united-nations/.
159.[1613] Pararajasingham, Ana. "Why Is Sri Lanka Defying the United Nations?" *The Diplomat*, The Diplomat, 22 Dec. 2017, thediplomat.com/2017/12/why-is-sri-lanka-defying-the-united-nations/.

most horror-stricken stories that seriously challenge our perceptions of Buddhism, Buddhism's supposed peaceful nature, and the corrupt elements of governments like Myanmar that conduct these horrific affairs challenge the very notion of any religion ever being peaceful. Many people who saw Buddhism as a peaceful alternative to the more violent Abrahamic traditions have shifted their stances back to believing that some deep evil or sinfulness is within all human beings. Generalizing it as simply an abstract evil without trying to understand it.

    Consider this question, which form of Buddhism does most of Sri Lanka and Myanmar believe in? Is it Theraveda, the Buddhist school that accepts both atheists and theists while not requiring any belief in a deity or rituals beyond meditation, or is it Mahayana, which has a more explicit calls to theistic ritualistic practices and beliefs about death? Which Buddhist school is widespread in those countries and failed to prevent calls of violence within both majority Buddhist countries? The answer is Theravada Buddhism. The teachings closest to the Buddha failed to preclude violence while the more theistic forms of Buddhism of Mahayana with their rituals to spirits and Gods have largely precluded violence even when being slaughtered, forcibly sterilized, and having their property destroyed.[1614][1615] Objections such as Zen Buddhism having a history of kamikaze pilots during World War 2 wouldn't dissuade this point since Zen remains largely indifferent - arguably agnostic - to belief in the supernatural and Zen practitioners don't even need to learn Buddhist tenants since it claims to be an experiential practice. The difference between Theravada's inability to maintain peaceful coexistence and the more religious Mahayana's ability to maintain peaceful coexistence can't be understated. Take the example of Tibetan Buddhist displacement, persecution, and genocide. While violent elements exist in situations like Tibet, it's in reaction to brutal Chinese Communist oppression and they're actively living as persecuted peoples in their own country or have fled to neighboring countries.[1616] For decades, Tibetans have peacefully asked the West for assistance and the West has promptly ignored them like always when it's economic interests are at stake.[1617] Western journalists have dutifully provided articles of character assassination, mockery, and contempt towards the Dalai Lama as he's kept peacefully requesting assistance from the West because of his appreciation and respect for Western values; Western journalists have capitalized on his peaceful approach by portraying him as a bigot for his stance on LGBTQ rights and neglecting to mention he and around a hundred thousand other Tibetans live in

---

160. [1614] Doshi, Vidhi. "After Nearly Six Decades of Exile, Some Tibetans in India Are Slowly Letting Go of the Past." *The Washington Post*, WP Company, 9 Oct. 2017, www.washingtonpost.com/world/asia_pacific/after-nearly-six-decades-of-exile-some-tibetans-in-india-are-slowly-letting-go-of-the-past/2017/10/07/c00325b0-a2da-11e7-b573-
161. [1615] "Q&A: China and the Tibetans." *BBC News*, BBC, 15 Aug. 2011, www.bbc.com/news/world-asia-pacific-14533879.
162. [1616] "Q&A: China and the Tibetans." *BBC News*, BBC, 15 Aug. 2011, www.bbc.com/news/world-asia-pacific-14533879.
163. [1617] Doshi, Vidhi. "After Nearly Six Decades of Exile, Some Tibetans in India Are Slowly Letting Go of the Past." *The Washington Post*, WP Company, 9 Oct. 2017, www.washingtonpost.com/world/asia_pacific/after-nearly-six-decades-of-exile-some-tibetans-in-india-are-slowly-letting-go-of-the-past/2017/10/07/c00325b0-a2da-11e7-b573-

exile and that he's pleading the West for help to protect his persecuted people.[1618][1619] In India, he's only ever called upon Indians to remember their culture of peace and tolerance towards all religions and spoken out against violence and persecution against Muslim Indians that occur in reaction to Islamic terrorism in India; the Dalai Lama has held religious panels to call upon people to remember the peace and tolerant nature of India's cultural diversity. He has not spoken out or demeaned LGBTQ rights being pushed into India's laws thanks to progressive LGBTQ activism to protect LGBTQ people in India. The only time he's ever spoken out is in favor of peace and tolerance among all religious faiths in India. Still, the Western journalists have never stopped with the character assassinations and attempts to denigrate his religious beliefs as crazy or nonsensical compared to Christianity. Instead of having his pleas heard, he's become a pop media icon for public consumption thanks to Western journalists dismissal of his peaceful approach and pleas for help by smugly characterizing the Dalai Lama as a bigot while he's pleading to help people suffering torture, forced sterilization, and cultural and physical genocide.[1620][1621] Despite all this, the Dalai Lama and Tibetans earnestly tried for decades to conduct peaceful pleas for the sake of Tibetans still suffering.

The reason for Mahayana being more peaceful isn't Theravada's open-minded approach in the acceptance of theists and atheists. It is not due to the ritualistic practices and doctrinal beliefs of theistic Mahayana sects. The failure lies in Buddhism's response to human suffering. Buddhism doesn't tackle it at all, but instead denies human suffering having an external source of any kind including in instances when violence is inflicted upon us.[1622] It is fully ego-centric in the sense of making reactive responses to suffering instead of proactive actions to mitigate our suffering.[1623] As a result, it fails to look externally at all to find constructive methods to express our emotions. Theravada zealously tries to keep the mind towards having no opinion on anything and thus, doesn't seek value in life itself but rather focuses on passivity and neutrality towards seeking meaning in life.[1624] Instead of tackling pain, anger, resentment, or loss directly, Buddhism detaches itself from the scenario through deep meditative reflection, but doesn't do anything else.[1625][1626] In the end,

---

164.[1618] Bixby, Scott. "Dalai Lama OK with Gay Marriage." *The Daily Beast*, The Daily Beast Company, 8 Mar. 2014, www.thedailybeast.com/dalai-lama-ok-with-gay-marriage.

165.[1619] Doshi, Vidhi. "After Nearly Six Decades of Exile, Some Tibetans in India Are Slowly Letting Go of the Past." *The Washington Post*, WP Company, 9 Oct. 2017, www.washingtonpost.com/world/asia_pacific/after-nearly-six-decades-of-exile-some-tibetans-in-india-are-slowly-letting-go-of-the-past/2017/10/07/c00325b0-a2da-11e7-b573-

166.[1620] "Q&A: China and the Tibetans." *BBC News*, BBC, 15 Aug. 2011, www.bbc.com/news/world-asia-pacific-14533879.

167.[1621] Doshi, Vidhi. "After Nearly Six Decades of Exile, Some Tibetans in India Are Slowly Letting Go of the Past." *The Washington Post*, WP Company, 9 Oct. 2017, www.washingtonpost.com/world/asia_pacific/after-nearly-six-decades-of-exile-some-tibetans-in-india-are-slowly-letting-go-of-the-past/2017/10/07/c00325b0-a2da-11e7-b573-

168.[1622] Buddha, Gautama. *The Dhammapada* (pgs. 3, 6, 7, 8, 12, 18. 20. 22. 24, 26, 27, 28, 31, 32, and 33). Start Publishing LLC.

169.[1623] Buddha, Gautama. *The Dhammapada* (pgs. 3, 6, 7, 8, 12, 18. 20. 22. 24, 26, 27, 28, 31, 32, and 33). Start Publishing LLC.

170.[1624] Kornfield, Jack, and Gil Fronsdal, editors. *Teachings of the Buddha*. Shambhala, 2012.

171.[1625] Kornfield, Jack, and Gil Fronsdal, editors. *Teachings of the Buddha*. Shambhala, 2012.

people have no meaningful outlet in Theravada to deal with their emotions constructively and detaching from them to such an extent may not be emotionally healthy in the long term. By contrast, the theistic branches of Mahayana Buddhism provide constructive meaning through multifarious forms of self-expression; therapeutic forms of painting art[1627][1628][1629], listening to or making music, dancing, making videos, writing poems or books[1630][1631], and rallying for peaceful activism. Artistic depictions of Gods and Goddesses, spirits, and ritualized age ceremonies may seem backwards or counterproductive, but they provide a sense of control and greater purpose to individuals within a religious faith.[1632] This illusion of control helps give people comfort. It helps us give meaning to loss, hate, grief, pain, and so many other emotions in a positive and constructive manner. It gives us catharsis to our sense of self, our purpose in life, our self-image, and our self-will. Theravada Buddhism utterly fails at accomplishing this important component of human experience and does everything to ignore it through the Eightfold path.

Buddhism and Christianity

One note of clarification before proceeding any further, this shouldn't be an endorsement to support the Abrahamic traditions above Buddhism or to view psychotic religions like Christianity or Islam as somehow superior to Buddhism in doctrinal beliefs, teachings, or practices. Both Christianity and Islam go on repeated justifications of revealed wisdoms of mass murderers like Moses and Mohammad or the psychotic ramblings and self-contradictions of Jesus Christ. Throughout these psychotic actions and ramblings, the Abrahamic traditions failed to get the problem of suffering in human experience as the central issue to human existence. The Buddha set his beliefs on the problem of suffering and how our desires cause our suffering.

The inability of Abrahamic traditions to contend with such a simple concept in an Eastern tradition should be of no surprise. The Abrahamic traditions' answer to suffering is misanthropy for the human race under a sanctified veneer and the psychotic ramblings called prophecies.[1633] The only way for Abrahamics to fight Buddhism, in typical Abrahamic style, are attempts at forcible conversions, mass genocides, and attempting to frighten peaceful people with psychotic ravings about a Judgment day or End of Times to justify their uniquely violent religious traditions of warring

---

172.[1626] Buddha, Gautama. *The Dhammapada* (pgs. 3, 6, 7, 8, 12, 18. 20. 22. 24, 26, 27, 28, 31, 32, and 33). Start Publishing LLC.
173.[1627] "Mahayana Buddhism and Tradition | Buddha Blog." *Celebrated in Different Buddhist Countries*, www.burmese-art.com/blog/mahayana-buddhism.
174.[1628] "The Bodhisattva Avalokiteshvara." *Khan Academy*, Khan Academy, www.khanacademy.org/humanities/art-asia/himalayas/tibet/a/the-bodhisattva-avalokiteshvara.
175.[1629] India, Mystery Of. "A Peep Into Hindu & Buddhist Past of Afghanistan." *Mystery of India*, 1 Feb. 2016, www.mysteryofindia.com/2015/11/a-peep-into-hindu-buddhist-past-of-afghanistan.html.
176.[1630] "Popular Deities of Chinese Buddhism." *Http://Www.buddhanet.net/*, Buddha Dharma Education Association Inc., www.buddhanet.net/pdf_file/ancientsgrfx.pdf.
177.[1631] Müller F. Max. *The Way of the Buddha: the Illustrated Dhammapada*. Abrams, 2008.
178.[1632] Kahneman, Daniel. *Thinking, fast and slow*. Farrar, Straus and Giroux, 2015.
179.[1633] Nietzsche, Friedrich Wilhelm. *THE ANTICHRIST*. Translated by H. L. Mencken, The Project Gutenberg, 2006.

desert tribes to themselves. The pervasive psychotic ramblings of the West were unable to change the minds of the Eastern traditions despite hundreds of years of imperialism and they successively failed in their attempts at religious conversion in those lengthy periods of time. A typical Abrahamic follower may argue its due to sinfulness, or freewill, or some other psychotic rambling about Jesus, Mohammad, or Yahweh. In truth, it's because Islam and Christianity have a symbiotic relationship of endless violence that helps each other to gain conviction and converts to keep killing each other as a duty to Yahweh. When faced with religions with peaceful doctrines that are allowed to express themselves in free and open debate, Christianity and Islam fall apart completely, because they rely on violence and without imperialistic violence, there is no longer a societal imbalance to force control upon others.[1634] The Abrahamic faiths are inferior religions of warring desert tribes based on barbaric practices justifying the mass murder of children, war rape, a cultish in-group narcissism, and hatred for others. The Abrahamic traditions slaughter more peaceful civilizations, burn other peoples religious and cultural relics through cultural erasure by accusing them of idol worship as if that's wrong, steal whatever they can to co-opt it into Christianity or totally destroy it in Islam, and then write history books pointing to one or two horrid practices of an indigenous group to justify the collective war rape, mass murder of children, mass torture, and endless campaigns of violence; at the end of their bloodletting, they celebrate how peaceful and compassionate they are after their successful mass murder campaigns that have destroyed the foreign population's tradition or successfully wiped them out. This has happened like clockwork throughout the Abrahamic traditions: Tasmania, the Native Americans from Canada to the USA to South America, Islam's conquest of Iran, modern-day Afghanistan and Pakistan, throughout Africa, and ancient Europe. Elaborations on this point of contention will be explored further in Part III.

    As a result of Asia's proven cultural supremacy in refusing conversion when fraught with imperialistic violence such as man-made famines, pogroms that spread diseases and killed millions, and war rape campaigns on women and children by the Western Christians; Christian missionaries were forced to change tactics when forcible conversions failed to deliver results of a Christian harvest that would be ripe with new converts to worship their deluded narcissist with a god complex, Jesus Christ. As Buddhism didn't separate through hate and violence like the Abrahamic religion of warring desert tribes, they're deserving of this critique. The critiques are made more possible because the Mahayana's branching divisions isn't an absurd amount like the 33,000 various Christian sects and Mahayana has more distinct traditions than the so-called "parables" of Jesus Christ, which is just a euphemism for his psychopathic and narcissistic ravings.[1635] Buddhism is based on actual teachings and so the divisions aren't merely superstitious semantics like in the Abrahamic traditions. It is indeed amusing to witness the lunacy of 33,000 denominations all claiming to be the true word of Jesus,

---

180.[1634] Nietzsche, Friedrich Wilhelm. *THE ANTICHRIST*. Translated by H. L. Mencken, The Project Gutenberg, 2006.

181.[1635] Alt, Scott Eric. "We Need to Stop Saying That There Are 33,000 Protestant Denominations." *National Catholic Register*, Global Catholic Television Network (EWTN), www.ncregister.com/blog/scottericalt/we-need-to-stop-saying-that-there-are-33000-protestant-denominations.

only to then proclaim nobody knows what Jesus really said besides proclaiming himself a god based on unsubstantiated claims.[1636]

It's clear that Jesus Christ's psychotic ramblings were as incoherent and idiotic as any other psychopath with delusions of grandeur. Philosophers like Bertrand Russell attempt to create some sort of unity with idiotic thought experiments that try to depict Buddhism and Christianity as the same peaceful teachings such as his Nietzsche versus Buddha thought experiment.[1637] However, for the same reason the British were unable to understand Gandhi's teachings of peace during Gandhi's lifetime, people like Russell attempted to selfishly conflate actual peaceful teachings in Dharmic religious traditions with the psychopathic and incoherent teachings of Jesus Christ in order to make themselves feel superior and claim a culture that was superior to theirs somehow belonged to them.[1638] The teachings of Jesus Christ and Gautama Buddha are nothing alike. The Buddha looked at the problem of human suffering and gave us a valuable answer: at the very least, a good starting point on how to create a meaningful life for ourselves.[1639] Jesus Christ paraded himself as a god, based his self-contradictory teachings on fulfilling or abolishing the Mosiac Law which - in either case of the term since it has no meaning - can be interpreted as no longer needing to follow Thou Shalt Not Kill since Christians are no longer bound to the Mosiac law, and said anyone who didn't believe in him wouldn't go to heaven while also being sent to hell for not accepting him. As surprising as this may seem to some Christians, Jesus Christ didn't teach non-violence as is wrongly believed; he taught reciprocity and reciprocity is an innate animal norm that humans are born with.[1640] That is, the teaching of the so-called golden rule doesn't prevent violence, but rather reciprocates anything negative or positive that someone else does to you.[1641] That isn't a teaching of non-violence, in which any wrong committed must be responded to with constructive and positive actions, but rather a call to reciprocate any wrongful act inflicted upon you with a wrongful act inflicted back upon the other person. By direct contrast, the Buddha taught *ahimsa* which means *non-violence* and made it a clear point in the beginning of the Dhammapada that this non-violence extended to anyone who physically harmed you in aphorisms three and four.[1642] Further credence is lent to this since Jainism has explicit teachings of non-violence and so does some teachings within

---

182. [1636] Alt, Scott Eric. "We Need to Stop Saying That There Are 33,000 Protestant Denominations." *National Catholic Register*, Global Catholic Television Network (EWTN), www.ncregister.com/blog/scottericalt/we-need-to-stop-saying-that-there-are-33000-protestant-denominations.
183. [1637] Russel, Bertrand. "The Buddha and Nietzsche." *YouTube*, Psychosophy, 14 July 2012, www.youtube.com/watch?v=B6WPFH4KPCc.
184. [1638] Russel, Bertrand. "The Buddha and Nietzsche." *YouTube*, Psychosophy, 14 July 2012, www.youtube.com/watch?v=B6WPFH4KPCc.
185. [1639] Nietzsche, Friedrich Wilhelm. *THE ANTICHRIST*. Translated by H. L. Mencken, The Project Gutenberg, 2006.
186. [1640] Cialdini, Robert B. Chapter 2: Reciprocation (19-50). *Influence: Science and practice*. 4th ed., 21st Century Bks, 2002.
187. [1641] Cialdini, Robert B. Chapter 2: Reciprocation (19-50). *Influence: Science and practice*. 4th ed., 21st Century Bks, 2002.
188. [1642] Buddha, Gautama. *The Dhammapada* (pgs. 3, 6, 7, 8, 12, 18. 20. 22. 24, 26, 27, 28, 31, 32, and 33). Start Publishing LLC. Kindle Edition.

Hinduism. Thereby, the Buddha and other Dharmic philosophers and theologians were superior to Jesus Christ and their superior teachings preceded him by centuries.

In fact, this superiority can be seen by the Buddha's thoughts on purifying oneself of their wrongful actions, as he provides a far more honest and articulate response in one aphorism than Jesus Christ did in the entirety of the Bible:

> *165. By oneself the evil is done, by oneself one suffers; by oneself evil is left undone, by oneself one is purified. Purity and impurity belong to oneself, no one can purify another.*"[1643]

The Buddha was about taking responsibility for ourselves; Christianity's entire theology is predicated on forgiving oneself of all responsibility by using Jesus Christ as a convenient scapegoat to continue atrocities like murder, torture, rape, and genocide under the belief that accepting Jesus Christ into your heart and never feeling responsible for your actions will lead you to heaven. In sharp contrast, the Buddha provided a superior teaching of holding ourselves accountable and accepting when we're at fault for horrible atrocities or when we've committed terrible actions.[1644][1645]

Many Christians may use the appeal to population fallacy as proof that their religious teachings are superior while ignoring that the poor have more children and women generally have less access to safe forms of birth control that Christianity itself actively discourages to the detriment of women everywhere in the world. However, there is a goal-oriented element to this notion. Christianity, despite its cultish loathing for anything that doesn't agree with Jesus Christ and its propensity for violence, has the goal of obliterating free speech, skeptical inquiry, and rationality for the sake of being chosen people to be whisked away from the physical world into an eternal paradise. It has a psychotic goal as the basis for conversion to the religious faith and sees anything that doesn't agree with Jesus as sinful by the reductionist Christian Standard mentioned prior in the section on Christianity. By contrast, Buddhism simply does nothing due to a strict asceticism and refrains from challenging any issue or forming an opinion on any issue thereby failing to preclude harmful effects.[1646] Theravada and many sects of Mahayana simply don't have any goal or long-term purpose within the religion and it's a detriment to Buddhism.

Bodhisattva versus Übermensch

XXXVII. IMMACULATE PERCEPTION

"WHEN YESTER-EVE the moon arose, then did I fancy it about to bear a sun: so broad and teeming did it lie on the horizon.
But it was a liar with its pregnancy; and sooner will I believe in the man in the moon than in the woman.

---

189. [1643] Buddha, Gautama. *The Dhammapada* (pgs. 3, 6, 7, 8, 12, 18. 20. 22. 24, 26, 27, 28, 31, 32, and 33). Start Publishing LLC. Kindle Edition.
190. [1644] Nietzsche, Friedrich Wilhelm. *THE ANTICHRIST*. Translated by H. L. Mencken, The Project Gutenberg, 2006.
191. [1645] Buddha, Gautama. *The Dhammapada* (pgs. 3, 6, 7, 8, 12, 18. 20. 22. 24, 26, 27, 28, 31, 32, and 33). Start Publishing LLC. Kindle Edition.
192. [1646] Nietzsche, Friedrich Wilhelm. *On the genealogy of morals: a polemical tract*. Translated by Ian Johnston, PDF, Richer Resources Publications, 2014.

To be sure, little of a man is he also, that timid nightreveller. Verily, with a bad conscience doth he stalk over the roofs.

For he is covetous and jealous, the monk in the moon; covetous of the earth, and all the joys of lovers.

Nay, I like him not, that tom-cat on the roofs! Hateful unto me are all that slink around half-closed windows!

Piously and silently doth he stalk along on the starcarpets:—but I like no light-treading human feet, on which not even a spur jingleth. Every honest one's step speaketh; the cat however, stealeth along over the ground. Lo! cat-like doth the *moon come along, and dishonestly.— This parable speak I unto you sentimental dissemblers, unto you, the "pure discerners!" You do I call—covetous ones!*

Also ye love the earth, and the earthly: I have divined you well!—but shame is in your love, and a bad conscience—ye are like the moon!

To despise the earthly hath your spirit been persuaded, but not your bowels: these, however, are the strongest in you! And now is your spirit ashamed to be at the service of your bowels, and goeth by-ways and lying ways to escape its own shame.

"That would be the highest thing for me"—so saith your lying spirit unto itself—"to gaze upon life without desire, and not like the dog, with hanging-out tongue: To be happy in gazing: with dead will, free from the grip and greed of selfishness—cold and ashy-grey all over, but with intoxicated moon-eyes!

That would be the dearest thing to me"—thus doth the seduced one seduce himself,—"to love the earth as the moon loveth it, and with the eye only to feel its beauty.

And this do I call immaculate perception of all things: to want nothing else from them, but to be allowed to lie before them as a mirror with a hundred facets."— Oh, ye sentimental dissemblers, ye covetous ones! Ye lack innocence in your desire: and now do ye defame desiring on that account!

Verily, not as creators, as procreators, or as jubilators do ye love the earth!

Where is innocence? Where there is will to procreation. And he who seeketh to create beyond himself, hath for me the purest will.

Where is beauty? Where I must will with my whole Will; where I will love and perish, that an image may not remain merely an image.

Loving and perishing: these have rhymed from eternity.

Will to love: that is to be ready also for death. Thus do I speak unto you cowards!

But now doth your emasculated ogling profess to be "contemplation!" And that which can be examined with cowardly eyes is to be christened "beautiful!" Oh, ye violators of noble names!

But it shall be your curse, ye immaculate ones, ye pure discerners, that ye shall never bring forth, even though ye lie broad and teeming on the horizon!

Verily, ye fill your mouth with noble words: and we are to believe that your heart overfloweth, ye cozeners? But my words are poor, contemptible, stammering words: gladly do I pick up what falleth from the table at your repasts.

Yet still can I say therewith the truth—to dissemblers! Yea, my fish-bones, shells, and prickly leaves shall—tickle the noses of dissemblers!

Bad air is always about you and your repasts: your lascivious thoughts, your lies, and secrets are indeed in the air!

Dare only to believe in yourselves—in yourselves and in your inward parts! He who doth not believe in himself always lieth.

A God's mask have ye hung in front of you, ye "pure ones": into a God's mask hath your execrable coiling snake crawled.

Verily ye deceive, ye "contemplative ones!" Even Zarathustra was once the dupe of your godlike exterior; he did not divine the serpent's coil with which it was stuffed.

A God's soul, I once thought I saw playing in your games, ye pure discerners! No better arts did I once dream of than your arts!

Serpents' filth and evil odour, the distance concealed from me: and that a lizard's craft prowled thereabouts lasciviously.

But I came nigh unto you: then came to me the day,— and now cometh it to you,—at an end is the moon's love affair!
See there! Surprised and pale doth it stand—before the rosy dawn!
For already she cometh, the glowing one,—her love to the earth cometh! Innocence and creative desire, is all solar love!
See there, how she cometh impatiently over the sea! Do ye not feel the thirst and the hot breath of her love?
At the sea would she suck, and drink its depths to her height: now riseth the desire of the sea with its thousand breasts.
Kissed and sucked would it be by the thirst of the sun; vapour would it become, and height, and path of light, and light itself!
Verily, like the sun do I love life, and all deep seas. And this meaneth to me knowledge: all that is deep shall ascend—to my height!—"[1647] - Friedrich Nietzsche, *Thus; spake Zarathustra*, Chapter: *Immaculate Perception*, pgs 116 - 119. Thomas Common translation.

An uncanny and articulate contention to Buddhism came from Friedrich Nietzsche's philosophical novel, *Thus Spake Zarathustra,* in which Nietzsche's fictitious depiction of Zarathustra explains his contentions against Buddhism's Eightfold Path of correct perceptions. This has wrongly been attributed to a criticism of academia by ignorant, racist people who had an anti-Jewish agenda. In fact, Nietzsche was describing his qualms with Buddhism in the aforementioned passage. To contend against the Buddha's ideals about detachment from life, Nietzsche proposed life-affirmation: that is, to find meaning in suffering in order to find fulfillment in one's subjective experience in life. To pursue self-satisfaction over wretched self-complacency by striving for our personal ambitions and carrying the burdens in life that we choose to carry instead of merely detaching ourselves from our own life.[1648]

Buddhism is adept at clearing the mind in order to refocus our intentions. It temporarily precludes our emotions from disrupting our personal life goals through detachment, but it teaches us to abandon goals entirely to flee from suffering.[1649][1650] It fails to give a meaningful purpose in life. Buddhism's ubiquitous detachment from life results in corruptive practices due to an inability to mitigate emotional outbursts in a constructive manner for the long-term. Buddhism's extreme focus on its form of personal fulfillment leads to emotionally stultified people who do nothing but look away from their own suffering and the suffering of others. Even if one were to valiantly advocate for human rights against horrible crimes like the sexual exploitation of children, Buddhism's Eightfold Path teaches us to simply detach because of the suffering it instills upon us and unintentionally denigrates our selfless desires to keep children unharmed. Instead, it teaches us to do nothing in response to suffering.[1651] Mahayana's ability to mitigate negative emotions through positive and

---

193.[1647] Nietzsche, Friedrich Wilhelm. Chapter XXXVII: Immaculate Perception (116-119). *Thus spake Zarathustra: a book for all and none*. Translated by Thomas Common, PDF ed., T. Common, 1908.
194.[1648] Nietzsche, Friedrich Wilhelm. *Thus spake Zarathustra: a book for all and none*. Translated by Thomas Common, PDF ed., T. Common, 1908.
195.[1649] Buddha, Gautama. *The Dhammapada* (pgs. 3, 6, 7, 8, 12, 18. 20. 22. 24, 26, 27, 28, 31, 32, and 33). Start Publishing LLC. Kindle Edition.
196.[1650] Kornfield, Jack, and Gil Fronsdal, editors. *Teachings of the Buddha*. Shambhala, 2012.
197.[1651] Nietzsche, Friedrich Wilhelm. *On the genealogy of morals: a polemical tract*. Translated by Ian Johnston, PDF, Richer Resources Publications, 2014.

socially constructive methods of utilizing various forms of art produces better results in precluding violence instead of simply detaching from our own life.

By direct contrast and in direct refutation of being a Bodhisattva, Nietzsche's Ubermensch philosophy teaches people to carry their self-given burdens of suffering in order to pursue a higher goal in life.[1652] Nietzsche generally meant to pursue art such as theater, music, and painting during his time but it can be more broadly applied to our current technological advancements and Nietzsche did want his philosophy to be open-ended on what people decide fulfilled them in life so long as it was pursuing a tangible goal. Nietzsche's version of personal fulfillment was active in contrast to the Buddha's passive form of personal fulfillment. Thereby, whether it be drawing art, writing literature or music, creating a video game, running a business, dancing, participating in sports, or advocating for human rights; what matters is carrying the burdens of such priorities and working towards them for the goal of surpassing ourselves and to provide our interests and insights to others to encourage those who want to pursue their own goals.[1653] The goals would obviously be different for each; a writer wants to become a published author, a CEO wants their business to be a success, and human rights advocates wants laws changed so that victims get the protection that they deserve. What matters is putting our beliefs towards actions that we care about.[1654]

Nietzsche was about pursuing our desires to achieve our dream goals. The Buddha was about utilizing self-restraint to stop ourselves from doing anything. Nietzsche was about self-empowerment of the individual in times of crisis, the Buddha taught us to be analogous to a rock and live in austere self-regulation in order to ignore the world around us. Nietzsche taught us to embrace our suffering to carry our self-given burdens in order to pursue our goals; the Buddha taught us to not suffer at all and to instead view emotions as a poison. Both philosophers looked at the central problem of the human condition: "*Why do we suffer?*" and came to opposite conclusions on what to do about our suffering in order to find meaning in life.

Blooming Buddhism

The teachings of the Buddha were indeed prescient and provide much value for people in terms of a living by a useful life philosophy[1655], but it's best to place the Buddha within the proper context of the past and work to improve on modern Buddhism as it exists now. Paul Bloom, a professor of psychology and cognitive science at Yale University, authored a book that I'd argue helps tackle this failing in Buddhism. In his polemic book, *Against Empathy: A Case for Rational Compassion*, It would be beyond the scope of this chapter to detail everything noted by Bloom, so I will briefly summarize his book; however, for those curious, I strongly encourage reading his book as

---

198.[1652] Nietzsche, Friedrich Wilhelm. *Thus spake Zarathustra: a book for all and none.* Translated by Thomas Common, PDF ed., T. Common, 1908.
199.[1653] Nietzsche, Friedrich Wilhelm. *Thus spake Zarathustra: a book for all and none.* Translated by Thomas Common, PDF ed., T. Common, 1908.
200.[1654] Nietzsche, Friedrich Wilhelm. *Thus spake Zarathustra: a book for all and none.* Translated by Thomas Common, PDF ed., T. Common, 1908.
201.[1655] "Three Jewels." *The Buddhist Centre*, thebuddhistcentre.com/text/three-jewels.

it's an informative polemic on the failings of empathy. Empathy is defined in his book as feeling other people's pain.[1656] Bloom notably sought the opinions of Buddhist practitioners who agreed with the overarching message of his book. That is, empathy is found to cause the most egregious forms of human violence; from torture, rape, murder, and so forth because empathy has a spotlight effect in which we only empathize with people we consider undeserving of suffering (usually people most similar to us) and feel anger towards the out-group perceived to be the cause of the suffering.[1657] Thereby, empathy - feeling the other person's pain vicariously - influences us to commit horrible atrocities in defense of others.[1658] We also see our actions as more to do with our social conditions instead of our personal desires and see the horrible actions of others as their personal desire to commit wrongdoing instead of their social conditions.[1659] Moreover, it's been found that nurses who empathize with patients in the worst physical conditions typically collapse or are unable to do the job because they feel the patient's pain.[1660] By contrast, nurses who detach from the patient's suffering, focus on alleviating any further suffering from a patient instead of focusing on the patient's current state of suffering, and respond with a clear focus on helping the patient instead of echoing the patient's emotional turmoil are found to be more productive and latched onto for support far more often because they focus on what actions need to be taken to alleviate further suffering.[1661] They represent the opposite and not the echo of suffering.[1662]

What I propose is to utilize detachment, the cessation of craving, when we feel other people's pain, and perhaps meditation can also be useful for this purpose. Nevertheless, with respect to meditation, it should be more limited than what Zen and Tibetan Buddhism propose in the length of time suggested for any such meditation. However, I understand that such a prospect is arbitrary and would likely depend on the individual's personal preference. It's beyond the scope of this chapter to go into full length details about the pros and cons of Buddhist meditation and yogi practices, particularly since I have no experience with them at the moment and my primary focus is to critique the teachings, so it should be up to the preference of the individual. However, I must caution the idea of going above a whole day's worth of meditation, if meditation is indeed something you do for a great length of time.

The primary purpose of this is not merely to prevent violence, but to prevent ourselves from feeling a perpetual state of helplessness; in which frustration, anger, and contempt for the world or ourselves or another group of people blind our rational judgment. Empathy, like detachment, has its time and place and sometimes we need to detach so we don't fall into a constant circle of outrage culture and reactionary anger to every piece of bad news that we learn about. Being detached to refocus our efforts on positive and constructive actions doesn't mean that you care less about others or

---

202.[1656] Bloom, Paul. *Against Empathy: the Case for Rational Compassion*. The Bodley Head Ltd, 2016.
203.[1657] Bloom, Paul. *Against Empathy: the Case for Rational Compassion*. The Bodley Head Ltd, 2016.
204.[1658] Bloom, Paul. *Against Empathy: the Case for Rational Compassion*. The Bodley Head Ltd, 2016.
205.[1659] Bloom, Paul. *Against Empathy: the Case for Rational Compassion*. The Bodley Head Ltd, 2016.
206.[1660] Bloom, Paul. *Against Empathy: the Case for Rational Compassion*. The Bodley Head Ltd, 2016.
207.[1661] Bloom, Paul. *Against Empathy: the Case for Rational Compassion*. The Bodley Head Ltd, 2016.
208.[1662] Bloom, Paul. *Against Empathy: the Case for Rational Compassion*. The Bodley Head Ltd, 2016.

your own goals, it just means that you need to recharge and refocus so that the emotional turmoil doesn't poison you from within. In conjunction to Buddhist detachment from empathy when it elicits negative and violent emotions within us, we should have a Ubermensch style of acting on our beliefs as proposed by Friedrich Nietzsche. That is, we should find positive, constructive actions for our selfless desires in order to best meet our motives and we're willing to carry the burdens of what those actions entail.[1663] What we prioritize is the life goal that we've set for ourselves. For example, a human rights advocate would detach from seeing further extrajudicial killings of their fellow citizens or minority group and then refocus efforts on protesting for remedial litigation or the banishment of some terrible practice or organization that is not conducive to resolving an ongoing social or political conflict. To keep focused on helping others, the human rights advocate should rejuvenate through detachment to refocus themselves when they feel hopelessness. After that, the human rights advocate can go back to letting out their emotions and demanding change for continued human rights crimes conducted upon their fellow citizens. The goal of changing the laws or abolishing horrible practices present in their minds with a razor focus on what concrete steps are needed to bring about meaningful social change. If, however, hopelessness feels particularly overwhelming, I recommend writing down your feelings on a Word document or a piece of paper, jotting down all your feelings of loathing or self-loathing, and then attacking each one with a point-by-point comparison on why its false or - if it is true - what positive, constructive steps you can take to change that situation.[1664] Writing down your personal values and jotting down why you honestly feel it is important can also help.[1665] *To properly focus on helping others without feeling overwhelmed; one must detach from empathy in imagining other people's pain and focus on the present moment of what actionable steps you can take after a tragic event towards easing other people's suffering as best as possible for the other people's best interests. It is the most effective method because it focuses on the efficacy of how to best help everyone you care about. Do something positive with your emotional outcry in a measured and controlled way, instead of just detaching from consequences or being outraged.*[1666]

For the purposes of more artistic exploits like writing a book, creating music, creating video games, and so forth; I would recommend the above steps when it comes to your self-doubt. When self-doubt feels overwhelming, write down a list of steps in either why it's not true[1667] or what steps you can take to positively change the circumstances if you feel it is true.[1668] Generally, you should focus on detaching from feelings of impotence to refocus on your goals and carry the burden of what

---

209.[1663] Nietzsche, Friedrich Wilhelm. *Thus spake Zarathustra: a book for all and none.* Translated by Thomas Common, PDF ed., T. Common, 1908.
210.[1664] Dryden, Windy. *Overcoming Procrastination.* Sheldon, 2000.
211.[1665] McGonigal, Kelly. *The Willpower Instinct: How Self-Control Works, Why It Matters, and What You Can Do to Get More of It.* Avery, 2013.
212.[1666] Bloom, Paul. *Against Empathy: the Case for Rational Compassion.* The Bodley Head Ltd, 2016.

213.[1667] Dryden, Windy. *Overcoming Procrastination.* Sheldon, 2000.

214.[1668] Halvorson, Heidi Grant. *Succeed: How We Can Reach Our Goals.* Plume, 2012.

it takes to achieve your desires to achieve self-satisfaction with your own life.[1669][1670] If you hit a roadblock, focus on what you could be doing to change that and remember why it's important to you.[1671] Detach from self-doubt and focus on your intrinsic desires to achieve your life goal. The point is to keep focused on what is important to you and to not let self-doubt, hopelessness, or indifference to overrun your desires in order for you to create something that you sorely wish to make a reality. To achieve catharsis in letting out your inner feelings in an artistic or constructive manner can be a wonderful experience; you form an idea that you, perhaps along with others, mold into reality.

Outline of Blooming Buddhism

- Detach from vicarious suffering (Empathy) to focus on your goal of alleviating the victim's suffering. Caring isn't just about feeling bad for others, which is simply a form of pity. It is about doing what's in the best interest of the people that you care about. Detaching and focusing on the goal of ameliorating their suffering is what's best for them. You're detaching *because* you care.
- Let your intrinsic desires for positive change focus your attention on your goals. Protests, making artistic works that point out human rights abuses by the perpetrators, changing litigation, and other possibilities. It must be positive, constructive, and non-violent (ahimsa) since the point is peaceful social change. For the purposes of artistic exploits, make outlines and follow through with them. Remember you're doing this for your own self-satisfaction to do what makes your life meaningful.
- Accept setbacks and carry your burdens. Don't let setbacks define you or your project. Everyone has setbacks, nobody is ever going to make a truly perfect project. Don't try to be a perfectionist, instead focus on what you really want to convey from your outline or, in the case of making social change, learn the interests of others and try to cajole them into supporting your interests by unifying it with either their interests or maintain a positive feedback loop with a politician or businessperson favorable to your views in which you're both gaining from the relationship. If you gain nothing from such a relationship, find someone else and let go of placing hopes on an individual who fails to further your interests in helping people that you care about. If there is nobody else, try to build rapport with people who influence the individual in charge to change their position to be more favorable to your views. Think about or preferably thoroughly analyze the pros and cons of supporting a particular group before making a decision. If not that, then try to learn how to professionally document abuses and investigate crimes in order so that those who suffer have their voices

---

215. [1669] Buddha, Gautama. *The Dhammapada* (pgs. 3, 6, 7, 8, 12, 18. 20. 22. 24, 26, 27, 28, 31, 32, and 33). Start Publishing LLC. Kindle Edition.

216. [1670] Nietzsche, Friedrich Wilhelm. *Thus spake Zarathustra: a book for all and none*. Translated by Thomas Common, PDF ed., T. Common, 1908.

217. [1671] Halvorson, Heidi Grant. *Succeed: How We Can Reach Our Goals*. Plume, 2012.

heard. Always remember, for most people, just being there and listening to them can help in their recovery from traumatic experiences.
- When self-doubt or feelings of powerlessness overwhelm you: first practice meditation or the Buddha's teachings of detachment, and then jot down a list of issues that are bothering you and then attack those issues by pointing out either their falsities or, if they're true, write what positive, constructive steps you can take to change the social situation. *If you believe you can't accomplish your goals, you're lying to yourself.*
- Utilize constructive outlets such as making, viewing, or participating in making art, drawing or listening to music, dancing, movies, video games, or writing to constructively release your emotions. The focal purpose is to constructively release your emotions towards doing something positive. Meditation and breathing exercises can help to detach, but consider participating in activities that release pent-up negative emotions in a positive, peaceful, and emotionally gratifying way.
- Self-overcoming. Continue to try to improve your behavior and actions to meet your goals. Strive either to selflessly serve your community or to focus your talents on your dream goals by acknowledging when you've made missteps, focused on how to correct them, implemented corrections, and keep on pursuing your intrinsic desire of meeting your life goal through rigorous effort.

Blooming Buddhism is analogous to a lotus flower that is perpetually blooming. Three of the Four Noble Truths are indeed useful in proper contexts, but the Eightfold path should be discarded and replaced by Blooming Buddhism's precepts. What matters is either your intrinsic desire to help others or your dream goals; in either case, I think this reformulation of the current Theravada Buddhism into a Mahayana School of Blooming Buddhism is for the best to rectify the pitfalls of Buddhism. I'd like to restate that the Buddha's teachings were prescient for his time and that I find he truly was a peaceful, compassionate teacher; but in our modern times, we need to revise some of his teachings in order to pursue our best interests. I apologize to any Buddhist if this suggestion has offended and to Paul Bloom, whom I have nothing but great respect for. It is not my intention to offend, I just see certain problems that I believe can be ameliorated with the current understanding of psychology and neuroscience in order to reshape Buddhism into a modern practice that continues to help people.

Sariputta's Lion's Roar

16. Then the Venerable Sariputta went to the Blessed One, respectfully greeted him, sat down at one side, and spoke thus to him:

"This faith, Lord, I have in the Blessed One, that there has not been, there will not be, nor is there now, another recluse or brahman more exalted in Enlightenment than the Blessed One."

"Lofty indeed is this speech of yours, Sariputta, and lordly! A bold utterance, a veritable sounding of the lion's roar! But how is this, Sariputta? Those Arahants, Fully Enlightened Ones of the past — do you have direct personal knowledge of all those Blessed Ones, as to their virtue, their meditation, their wisdom, their abiding, and their emancipation?"

"Not so, Lord."

"Then how is this, Sariputta? Those Arahants, Fully Enlightened Ones of the future — do you have direct personal knowledge of all those Blessed Ones, as to their virtue, their meditation, their wisdom, their abiding, and their emancipation?"

"Not so, Lord."

"Then how is this, Sariputta? Of me, who am at present the Arahant, the Fully Enlightened One, do you have direct personal knowledge as to my virtue, my meditation, my wisdom, my abiding, and my emancipation?"

"Not so, Lord."

"Then it is clear, Sariputta, that you have no such direct personal knowledge of the Arahats, the Fully Enlightened Ones of the past, the future, and the present. How then dare you set forth a speech so lofty and lordly, an utterance so bold, a veritable sounding of the lion's roar, saying: 'This faith, Lord, I have in the Blessed One, that there has not been, there will not be, nor is there now another recluse or brahman more exalted in Enlightenment than the Blessed One'?"[1672]

[1672] Wolf, Hannelore, and Francis Story. "Maha-Parinibbana Sutta: Last Days of the Buddha." *Maha-Parinibbana Sutta: Last Days of the Buddha*, www.accesstoinsight.org/tipitaka/dn/dn.16.1-6.vaji.html#fn-11.

Chapter 27: Sanatana Dharma

The topic of Hinduism has probably been the most difficult topic to research and effectively put into words. Learning about all the ongoing controversies about Hinduism's past while in the process of research has given me pause because I became genuinely concerned that whatever I said would be seen as either being an apologist or an attack depending on where I stood in my critique. This has bothered me so much that I considered just omitting Hinduism from a critique by stating that as a Hindu I would be too biased to make any fair critique on a religion that I grew-up in and still identify with. However, that could conceivably constitute its own bias since I made a wealth of critiques against all other major religions except the one that I identify with. The political controversies over this topic makes me believe that no matter what I do, I'll be judged unfavorably and I was chiefly concerned that getting involved in these controversies by giving my own views could negatively impact or overtake focus from the other critiques that I made on the other religions. At this time in history, criticizing Islam is by far the most important topic and I really am concerned about the lives of Ex-Muslims who undoubtedly suffer to a point that I may never truly understand within Islamic communities and especially in Islamic majority countries. I didn't want involvement in what I found to be a largely petty squabble among what seems to be sycophants pitted against the gullible to overtake focus on the human rights issues of critical importance. Also, I wondered if I was just being biased myself and whether I was being as objective about the facts as possible in my views on these contemporary issues regarding Hinduism. My concern was because my views had radically shifted upon purchasing and reading books from prominent members of US Indology. While I didn't find what I expected when purchasing them and reading them, I hope that they have refined my critique by some measure. I considered simply ignoring the political controversies and just providing my own critique, but the contemporary controversy between certain groups in India and US Indology over Hinduism is such that if I did that, I would simply be opening the door for accusations of being ignorant, biased, and would probably be accused of not having researched or read much of the contemporary consensus by Indology itself. Moreover, US Indology does seem to have some measure of influence on public assumptions made about Hinduism for anyone curious enough to try to read more deeply into the topic and has an oversized influence in contemporary political discourse in India. I had really wanted to just pursue my own critiques freely when writing this book without getting into this contemporary controversy. Yet, as with almost all destructive ideas and beliefs, it simply tries to gain more power through coercive ends and there are accusations that it is trying to legitimize itself by co-opting the research of geneticists ignorant of these controversies for their own nefarious political purposes.[1673] That act of brazen

---

1. [1673] Talageri, Shrikant, et al. "Panel Discussion on the Current State of Aryan Theories." Moderated by Rajiv Malhotra, *YouTube*, Swadeshi Indology, 24 Mar. 2018, www.youtube.com/watch?v=KmeVR8sqSd4.

disregard for logical reasoning and fact-finding research shocked me and it seems geneticists don't know that by referencing these people that they're just legitimizing utterly vacuous arguments that don't use any evidence from either qualified historians or modern archaeologists.

Debunking US Indology

I want to be clear that I honestly didn't hold these views until after reading into the arguments by Indology in more depth. I was firmly on the side of US Indology because I expected to find credible and logical arguments for their assertions about Hinduism not being a unified religion. I expected fact-finding research like the contemporary Religious Studies department arguments on Christianity, but instead all I found was dubious claims, an ignorance of contemporary archaeological findings, and an ignorance within Western Indology's scholarship on Islam's entry into India. Western Indology has a lack of apparent knowledge of one of the most well-respected historians from the US who is known throughout world history, Will Durant. Even worse than this, there are largely pretentious claims about the impact of British imperialism upon modern India. I expected strong fact-finding research based on a fusion of archaeology, history, and perhaps different subjective viewpoints about culture based on factual evidence when I began researching Indology, but I learned soon after from friends who studied history and philosophy in Western academia that Indology, as a part of Religious Studies, are the least credible sources of information in Western academia because they don't do any research into topics like archaeology and history. This was surprising to me because what I had thought was rigorous research into India's religious history, comparable to studies on Christianity among Religious Studies scholars, was actually just a bunch of people making up their own personal views on a religion and claiming to have more authority than actual hard evidence from archaeology, history, and genetic research showed. These Indologists behave as if they have special knowledge or a better understanding of a deeper meaning, but they don't do any real research. To my surprise, they instead make-up their own beliefs and have been using their influence to assert their personal beliefs about Hinduism as equivalent to hard evidence from archaeology. When confronted with hard evidence from archaeologists from India, excerpts from US historians like Will Durant, and criticisms of their approach from Indians of India; they have almost collectively dismissed any and all controversy by depicting criticisms against them as rabid, hostile, and made in bad faith instead of critiquing or responding to the arguments themselves. I personally contacted Indologist Andrew J. Nicholson by email and he never responded; months later, I noticed that his twitter account had vanished. From what I've observed of the more notorious incidents, it seems bizarre to me that this would be their approach to controversy since they should be able to satisfy any criticisms by showing research and evidence, but have instead behaved in an overly sensitive manner by depicting all criticism as beneath their notice while making spurious accusations on the character of the people criticizing them. However, what really caused me to doubt the approaches by US Indologists was their attempts to paint all criticisms of them by people in India or of Indian descent as a monolith of rabid hostility and their explicit refusal to engage in any of it on that basis. As you'll probably be able to tell if you notice my real name which is on the copyright of this book, I am of Indian descent. It is because I am of Indian descent criticizing them that I fear retribution and slander because of how I've observed people in US Indology departments behave. Judging from the evidence, it seems their aim is to silence any criticism from people of India or of Indian descent outside of these Indology departments who criticize the consensus of US Indology departments. I don't know the extent of this issue for other Western Indology departments, but I'll be critiquing some of them too.

The Oxford Handbook of Indian Philosophy

I'll begin my critique with *The Oxford Handbook of Indian Philosophy* of 2017, which was reprinted in 2018, and since I can't make lengthy quotes of any portion of the book without the express permission of Oxford University Press, I'll have to lay out in explicit terms what I find problematic with these Indologist critiques and may sometimes list both the chapters and pages of those chapters when necessary. While my primary aim is criticizing US Indology, I've chosen to critique others in Western Indology insofar as they show the same failings of US Indology and sustain arguments based on either insufficient or bad evidence. Usually it is a complete lack of evidence on their part. Essentially, the underlying assumptions should be highlighted and then critiqued in order to expose the failings of what may well be this entire department on a global scale throughout the West, if the most current version of *The Oxford Handbook of Indian Philosophy* as of 2019 serves as an indication. As it would be beyond the scope of this book to give a general review of the entirety of its contents, I've narrowed the focus to pertinent specifics that I'll be addressing, I've settled for critiquing the Introduction and the four chapters of *Part 1: Methods, Literatures, and Histories* of *The Oxford Handbook of Indian Philosophy* which exists as the main thesis of the textbook; it is geared to explain to an audience of upcoming Indologists about what to expect in the academic discipline. I've chosen this method due to constraints, as I'm of the opinion that the entirety of the text is problematic due to ample evidence from the textbook itself and the chapters I've read outside of Part 1.

I'll begin with the introductory chapter, "*Introduction: Why Indian Philosophy? Why Now?*" by the editor of the textbook, Jonardon Ganeri, who is listed as a Global Network Professor of Philosophy, Faculty of Arts and Science at New York University and a visiting Professor at King's College.[1674] His chapter shows no evidence that he has any awareness or knowledge of the mass genocides of the Indian population during the Islamic conquests of India[1675]; on page 4, he refers to the purported Aryan settlers that Indian archaeologists have

---

2. [1674] Kapstein, Matthew T., et al. Contributors (IX - XVII). *The Oxford Handbook of Indian Philosophy*. Edited by Jonardon Ganeri, Oxford University Press, 2018.
3. [1675] Kapstein, Matthew T., et al. Introduction: Why Indian Philosophy? Why now? by Jordan Ganeri (1-14). *The Oxford Handbook of Indian Philosophy*. Edited by Jonardon Ganeri, Oxford University Press, 2018.

shown to be a falsehood with extensive evidence that'll be detailed in another section below and the introductory page itself mentions the so-called impact of British colonialism but never mentions the Islamic colonialism prior to that.[1676] On page 8, he briefly touches upon so-called Mughal patronage but fails to mention the massacres and colossal death toll of Islam's ravaging, plundering, and enslavement of Indians throughout the entirety of the Indian subcontinent.[1677] This has been copiously documented by legendary historian, Will Durant. In volume 1 of his series *The Story of Civilization: Our Oriental Heritage*, Will Durant details the mass genocides perpetuated by Islamic invaders in Chapter 16 from subsection "*VI. The Moslem Conquest*" to the very end of Chapter 16 of *The Story of Civilization: Our Oriental Heritage*.[1678] Will Durant himself refers to it as "probably the bloodiest story in history" before going into the grizzly details.[1679] At no point does Jonardon Ganeri show any indication that he is knowledgeable about this history at all throughout the Introduction of *The Oxford Handbook of Indian Philosophy* and seems to depict interactions between Indians and the Islamic invaders as congenial when the only time period that could credibly be argued would be under Akbar the Great after he had de-converted from Islam, ordered the shut down of the mosques throughout India, and forbade the teachings of the Quran.[1680][1681] However, before and after Akbar under more pious Islamic rulers, the story is an unambiguous bloodbath and Will Durant doesn't mince words or soften the details of the horror that Islam brought upon India.[1682] If you doubt this, feel free to read Chapter 16, subsection VI all the way to the end of Chapter 16 of *The Story of Civilization: Our Oriental Heritage*.[1683] The only time the practitioners of Sanatana Dharma - be it Hindu, or Buddhist, or Jain, or later on the Sikhs - ever lived in any

4. [1676] Kapstein, Matthew T., et al. Introduction: Why Indian Philosophy? Why now? by Jordan Ganeri (Pg.4). *The Oxford Handbook of Indian Philosophy*. Edited by Jonardon Ganeri, Oxford University Press, 2018.
5. [1677] Kapstein, Matthew T., et al. Introduction: Why Indian Philosophy? Why now? by Jordan Ganeri (Pg. 8). *The Oxford Handbook of Indian Philosophy*. Edited by Jonardon Ganeri, Oxford University Press, 2018.
6. [1678] Durant, Will. Chapter XVI: From Alexander to Aurangzeb (10072 - 10817). *Our Oriental Heritage: Being a History of Civilization in Egypt and the Near East to the Death of Alexander, and in India, China and Japan from the Beginning to Our Own Day*. Simon and Schuster, 1935.
7. [1679] Durant, Will. Chapter XVI: From Alexander to Aurangzeb: VI. The Moslem Conquest (Pgs. 10447-10448). *Our Oriental Heritage: Being a History of Civilization in Egypt and the Near East to the Death of Alexander, and in India, China and Japan from the Beginning to Our Own Day*. Simon and Schuster, 1935.
8. [1680] Kapstein, Matthew T., et al. Introduction: Why Indian Philosophy? Why now? by Jordan Ganeri (1-14). *The Oxford Handbook of Indian Philosophy*. Edited by Jonardon Ganeri, Oxford University Press, 2018.
9. [1681] Durant, Will. Chapter XVI: From Alexander to Aurangzeb: VII. Akbar The Great (Pgs. 10520 - 10691). *Our Oriental Heritage: Being a History of Civilization in Egypt and the Near East to the Death of Alexander, and in India, China and Japan from the Beginning to Our Own Day*. Simon and Schuster, 1935.
10. [1682] Durant, Will. Chapter XVI: From Alexander to Aurangzeb (10072 - 10817). *Our Oriental Heritage: Being a History of Civilization in Egypt and the Near East to the Death of Alexander, and in India, China and Japan from the Beginning to Our Own Day*. Simon and Schuster, 1935.
11. [1683] Durant, Will. Chapter XVI: From Alexander to Aurangzeb (10072 - 10817). *Our Oriental Heritage: Being a History of Civilization in Egypt and the Near East to the Death of Alexander, and in India, China and Japan from the Beginning to Our Own Day*. Simon and Schuster, 1935.

peace during Islamic rule was when a Islamic ruler de-converted from Islam and rejected the Islamic religion. At no point does Jonardon Ganeri put this in proper context and doesn't even seem to be aware of this history in his introductory chapter.[1684]

The next chapter was what made me lose confidence in Western Indology and gradually caused me to change my views on this entire enterprise called Indology within the US, but this view may be applicable throughout the West too. I had assumed that they based their views on hard evidence, but "*Chapter 1: Interpreting Indian Philosophy Three Parables*" by Matthew T. Kapstein, a Professor at the University of Chicago who purportedly specializes in Tibetan Buddhism, makes it clear that this isn't true.[1685] Kapstein explains without any ambiguity on pages 15-16 of the book that Western Indologists have absolutely no criteria for determining what interpretations are valid and what aren't valid.[1686] They don't base their understanding from any deep understanding of the ancient Sanatana Dharma theology and they hold no special knowledge or criterion of procedures for how to develop an understanding of Indian philosophies.[1687] In short, they haven't developed any method at all that can make accurate and reliable judgments on the theology of Hinduism.[1688] In fact, Kapstein outright explains on page 16 that hermeneutics, with the exclusion of legal hermeneutics, offers absolutely nothing as a guideline to demarcate valid and honest interpretations from dishonest or unreliable interpretations.[1689] This means that they have no method at all for separating their own make-believe with any potentially credible scholarship. Kapstein claims that Indology attempts to utilize archaeology, but this is plainly proven false since they never accepted information from Indian archaeologists who reliably and credibly debunked the Aryan Race Conspiracy Theory with scientific and historical evidence.[1690] The Aryan Race theory was supported by Nazism and Adolf Hitler. Western Indologists have held onto those Nazi viewpoints which pervades the entirety of *The Oxford Handbook of Indian Philosophy* of

12. [1684] Kapstein, Matthew T., et al. Introduction: Why Indian Philosophy? Why now? by Jordan Ganeri (1-14). *The Oxford Handbook of Indian Philosophy*. Edited by Jonardon Ganeri, Oxford University Press, 2018.
13. [1685] Kapstein, Matthew T., et al. Contributors (IX - XVII). *The Oxford Handbook of Indian Philosophy*. Edited by Jonardon Ganeri, Oxford University Press, 2018.
14. [1686] Kapstein, Matthew T., et al. Chapter 1: Interpreting Indian Philosophy Three Parables by Matthew Kapstein (15-16). *The Oxford Handbook of Indian Philosophy*. Edited by Jonardon Ganeri, Oxford University Press, 2018.
15. [1687] Kapstein, Matthew T., et al. Chapter 1: Interpreting Indian Philosophy Three Parables by Matthew Kapstein (15-31). *The Oxford Handbook of Indian Philosophy*. Edited by Jonardon Ganeri, Oxford University Press, 2018.
16. [1688] Kapstein, Matthew T., et al. Chapter 1: Interpreting Indian Philosophy Three Parables by Matthew Kapstein (15-31). *The Oxford Handbook of Indian Philosophy*. Edited by Jonardon Ganeri, Oxford University Press, 2018.
17. [1689] Kapstein, Matthew T., et al. Chapter 1: Interpreting Indian Philosophy Three Parables by Matthew Kapstein (Pg. 16). *The Oxford Handbook of Indian Philosophy*. Edited by Jonardon Ganeri, Oxford University Press, 2018.
18. [1690] Kapstein, Matthew T., et al. Chapter 1: Interpreting Indian Philosophy Three Parables by Matthew Kapstein (15-31). *The Oxford Handbook of Indian Philosophy*. Edited by Jonardon Ganeri, Oxford University Press, 2018.

2017-2018 despite the Aryan Race theory having been debunked in 2014-2015 by Indian archaeologists through empirical and scientific evidence.[1691][1692][1693] For whatever reason, Western Indologists have since tried to push these Nazi theories that they've held as sacrosanct into the work of modern Western geneticists, possibly without the awareness of the broader scientific community that the methods of Indology are arbitrary, unreliable, and seem to be pure guesswork without any basis on historic evidence. One must question why these Western Indologists hold onto these Nazi theories so strongly and dismiss any criticism from outside as not part of their arbitrary consensus that isn't based on empirical evidence. And, if the scientific community doesn't know about how unreliable their methods are, then why weren't Western scientists duly informed and instead have had their meaningful scientific work, their trust, and goodwill co-opted by Western Indologists? Further along in Chapter 1, on pages 20 - 23 in the subsection titled "*The Meaning of Moksa*" in the book, Kapstein cherry-picks three philosophers - Rousseau, Locke, and Hobbes - in order to ignorantly assert that Western philosophy's entire body of work on the terminology of the word freedom is based upon civic governments and political participation.[1694] He demonstrates no understanding of Dharmic teachings of *Moksha* being an existential philosophical disposition and he shows no indication that existential philosophers of so-called Anglophone and continental philosophy such as Schopenhauer was influenced by the Upanishads[1695]; Nietzsche was profoundly influenced and impressed by Buddhism even declaring it, and the intellectual capacity of the Brahmins of Sanatana Dharma, as entirely superior to Christianity in *The Anti-Christ*.[1696][1697] How did Kapstein miss not only the basic usage of Moksha's terminology of freedom, but also two of the most famous Western philosophers who were influenced by Dharmic views on freedom? Why did he use a reductionist argument on the various philosophical dispositions of Western Philosophy's views on freedom? Even from his chosen selection, he doesn't seem to be aware of the extent Rousseau praised and had his philosophy influenced by Islamic theology.

---

19. [1691] Kapstein, Matthew T., et al. *The Oxford Handbook of Indian Philosophy*. Edited by Jonardon Ganeri, Oxford University Press, 2018.
20. [1692] Sridhar, Nithin. "No Evidence for Warfare or Invasion; Aryan Migration Too Is a Myth: B B Lal." *NewsGram*, 30 Nov. 2015, www.newsgram.com/no-evidence-for-warfare-or-invasion-aryan-migration-too-is-a-myth-b-b-lal
21. [1693] Sridhar, Nithin. "Vedic and Harappan Are Respectively Literary and Material Facets of Same Civilization: B. B. Lal." *NewsGram*, 2 Dec. 2015, www.newsgram.com/vedic-and-harappan-are-respectively-literary-and-material-facets-of-same-civilization-b-b-lal
22. [1694] Kapstein, Matthew T., et al. Chapter 1: Interpreting Indian Philosophy Three Parables by Matthew Kapstein (Pg. 20-23). *The Oxford Handbook of Indian Philosophy*. Edited by Jonardon Ganeri, Oxford University Press, 2018.
23. [1695] Durant, Will. Chapter XIV: The Foundations of India: VII. The Philosophy of the Upanishads (9463 - 9469). *Our Oriental Heritage: Being a History of Civilization in Egypt and the Near East to the Death of Alexander, and in India, China and Japan from the Beginning to Our Own Day*. Simon and Schuster, 1935.
24. [1696] Nietzsche, Friedrich Wilhelm. Aphorism 23. *THE ANTICHRIST*. Translated by H. L. Mencken, The Project Gutenberg, 2006.
25. [1697] Kapstein, Matthew T., et al. Chapter 1: Interpreting Indian Philosophy Three Parables by Matthew Kapstein (15-31). *The Oxford Handbook of Indian Philosophy*. Edited by Jonardon Ganeri, Oxford University Press, 2018.

However, another equally compelling issue must be asked: how can any so-called "consensus" within the sphere of Western Indology be allowed to dismiss empirical scientific evidence by Indian archaeologists?[1698,1699] Moreover, on what grounds can Western Indology claim any special privilege on knowledge of Hinduism over any random Hindu individual when they have no methods and their so-called research is the equivalent of any random person making a blind guess?[1700] How can they dismiss Rajiv Malhotra or any other Hindu who has criticism on the basis of consensus, when their consensus is pure blind guessing with no real methodology, they have no recognition of Hindu practices like Yogi, and there is no evidence from their behavior of any interest in archaeology that disproves Nazi theories that they harbor? To my surprise, throughout *The Oxford Handbook of Indian Philosophy*, Western Indologists demonstrate no awareness of the mass genocide by Islamic conquests elaborated by historian Will Durant in *The Story of Civilization: Our Oriental Heritage* and the subsequent mass starvation policies which may also credibly constitute genocide caused by British colonialism as copiously documented by historian and Marxist Mike Davis in his work, *Late Victorian Holocausts: El Nino Famines and the Making of the Third World* in which he collected and referenced numerous documented accounts by mostly US Christian missionaries and US journalists who spoke out against the British policies in defense of the human rights of the people of India.[1701,1702] How can they claim to be searching for proper context and a better understanding of India's changing philosophies throughout the history of the subcontinent, if they categorically ignore the most notorious impacts of Islamic and British imperialism?[1703,1704,1705] Judging from their lack of methodology, I don't quite understand why Indians of the Dharmic faiths within India even bother protesting or view anything Western Indologists say as credible when any random opinion that they have on their own religion is actually more valid than the so-called hermeneutic methodology which is quite honestly just

---

26. [1698] Sridhar, Nithin. "No Evidence for Warfare or Invasion; Aryan Migration Too Is a Myth: B B Lal." *NewsGram*, 30 Nov. 2015, www.newsgram.com/no-evidence-for-warfare-or-invasion-aryan-migration-too-is-a-myth-b-b-lal
27. [1699] Sridhar, Nithin. "Vedic and Harappan Are Respectively Literary and Material Facets of Same Civilization: B. B. Lal." *NewsGram*, 2 Dec. 2015, www.newsgram.com/vedic-and-harappan-are-respectively-literary-and-material-facets-of-same-civilization-b-b-lal
28. [1700] Kapstein, Matthew T., et al. Chapter 1: Interpreting Indian Philosophy Three Parables by Matthew Kapstein (15-31). *The Oxford Handbook of Indian Philosophy*. Edited by Jonardon Ganeri, Oxford University Press, 2018.
29. [1701] Durant, Will. Chapter XVI: From Alexander to Aurangzeb (10072 - 10817). *Our Oriental Heritage: Being a History of Civilization in Egypt and the Near East to the Death of Alexander, and in India, China and Japan from the Beginning to Our Own Day*. Simon and Schuster, 1935.
30. [1702] Davis, Mike. *Late Victorian Holocausts: El Nino Famines and the Making of the Third World*. Penguin Random House Publisher Services, 2001.
31. [1703] Kapstein, Matthew T., et al. Chapter 1: Interpreting Indian Philosophy Three Parables by Matthew Kapstein (15-31). *The Oxford Handbook of Indian Philosophy*. Edited by Jonardon Ganeri, Oxford University Press, 2018.
32. [1704] Durant, Will. Chapter XVI: From Alexander to Aurangzeb (10072 - 10817). *Our Oriental Heritage: Being a History of Civilization in Egypt and the Near East to the Death of Alexander, and in India, China and Japan from the Beginning to Our Own Day*. Simon and Schuster, 1935.
33. [1705] Davis, Mike. *Late Victorian Holocausts: El Nino Famines and the Making of the Third World*. Penguin Random House Publisher Services, 2001.

pure, blind guesswork on the part of these so-called scholars in the West.[1706] It's a methodology that claims to have no methodology and just makes random guesses with the hopes that others who are equally as uninformed about Hinduism agree with them. This insularity can be comparable with the *Tafsir* of Islam, but with the clear difference that they claim nobody outside their insular community has any right to an opinion on a religion that isn't even theirs. Kapstein ends the chapter by emphasizing that Western Indologists have no conceptual framework except for hypothetical ideas that they critique each other with and it is thus a reaffirmation that they have no knowledge beyond pure, blind guesswork.[1707]

Chapter 2 "*History and Doxography of the Philosophical Schools*" by Ashok Aklujkar, a Sanskritist and Indologist working at the University of British Columbia[1708], falsely assumes an isolated distinction between Western Philosophy and Sanatana Dharma on page 32 since it isn't as clearly demarcated as he assumed and will be explained further below.[1709] He asserts that proper guidance is required (assuming Western Indologists) but fails to detail specific procedures since Western Indology has none according to the chapter prior to his chapter.[1710][1711] Finally, he contradicts himself on page 35 and continuing on to page 36 by first correctly asserting that Indian Philosophy isn't irrational and then using the very stereotype that he just stated was wrong by demarcating philosophy as purely rational and then implying religion that isn't based on rational arguments should have its definition broadened as somehow conforming to rationality.[1712] This is simply a self-contradiction that is trying to re-contextualize words by redefining illogical beliefs within Hinduism as somehow rational, but refusing to simply use actual rational arguments within Hinduism itself. Chapter 3 "*Philosophy As A Distinct Cultural Practice*" by Justin E. H. Smith, listed as a Professor of History and Philosophy of Science at the Universite Paris Diderot (Paris 7)[1713], explicitly begins on page 56

---

34. [1706] Kapstein, Matthew T., et al. Chapter 1: Interpreting Indian Philosophy Three Parables by Matthew Kapstein (15-31). *The Oxford Handbook of Indian Philosophy*. Edited by Jonardon Ganeri, Oxford University Press, 2018.
35. [1707] Kapstein, Matthew T., et al. Chapter 1: Interpreting Indian Philosophy Three Parables by Matthew Kapstein (15-31). *The Oxford Handbook of Indian Philosophy*. Edited by Jonardon Ganeri, Oxford University Press, 2018.
36. [1708] Kapstein, Matthew T., et al. Contributors (IX - XVII). *The Oxford Handbook of Indian Philosophy*. Edited by Jonardon Ganeri, Oxford University Press, 2018.
37. [1709] Kapstein, Matthew T., et al. Chapter 2: History and Doxography of the Philosophical Schools by Ashok Aklujkar (Pg. 32). *The Oxford Handbook of Indian Philosophy*. Edited by Jonardon Ganeri, Oxford University Press, 2018.
38. [1710] Kapstein, Matthew T., et al. Chapter 1: Interpreting Indian Philosophy Three Parables by Matthew Kapstein (15-31). *The Oxford Handbook of Indian Philosophy*. Edited by Jonardon Ganeri, Oxford University Press, 2018.
39. [1711] Kapstein, Matthew T., et al. Chapter 2: History and Doxography of the Philosophical Schools by Ashok Aklujkar (32-55). *The Oxford Handbook of Indian Philosophy*. Edited by Jonardon Ganeri, Oxford University Press, 2018.
40. [1712] Kapstein, Matthew T., et al. Chapter 2: History and Doxography of the Philosophical Schools by Ashok Aklujkar (32-55). *The Oxford Handbook of Indian Philosophy*. Edited by Jonardon Ganeri, Oxford University Press, 2018.
41. [1713] Kapstein, Matthew T., et al. Contributors (IX - XVII). *The Oxford Handbook of Indian Philosophy*. Edited by Jonardon Ganeri, Oxford University Press, 2018.

by asserting the audience of Indology is for people of "European" or "Western" backgrounds and then goes onto explain that comparative studies should never include comparing philosophies of two distinct cultural backgrounds.[1714] On page 57, he asserts that Greece and India only had significant contact in geography and astronomy, he explains how the philosophical exchange that created Pyrrhonian skepticism by Christopher Beckworth has been dismissed without any explanation why, and goes onto explain that there seems to be no evidence of a philosophical exchange between Greece and India because there is no "smoking gun" at all.[1715] Evidently, Smith is either utterly ignorant of or entirely dismissive of the period of Hellenization of India that occurred shortly after the defeat of Alexander the Great[1716]; many Greek people migrated in droves.[1717] The cities and military colonies of Alexander the Great were expanded by the Greek migration from approximately 70 to an additional 250 and eventually, the Greco-Bactarian kingdom was formed by King Demetrius I of Bactria from his successful invasion of Northern India in which there is evidence to indicate that he effectively ruled over it.[1718] A cultural syncretism that is unparallel in history proceeded for almost 200 years from 180 BCE to 10 CE.[1719] This astonishing level of peaceful intermingling of what is known as the Indo-Greek kingdoms is shown from several compelling pieces of evidence. The Greek and Indian languages and symbols fused within the coinage such as the Greek language in the front and the Pali language in the back.[1720] Archaeological evidence shows the blending of Ancient Greek and Ancient Sanatana Dharma practices; statues of the Buddha protected by the Greek God Herakles/Heracles, statues of Mahayana Buddhist deities, and Greco-Buddhist statues of the Buddha in general.[1721] Given all of this fascinating history, which Smith doesn't

---

42. [1714] Kapstein, Matthew T., et al. Chapter 3: Philosophy as a Distinct Cultural Practice: The Transregional Context by Justin E.H. Smith (Pg. 56). *The Oxford Handbook of Indian Philosophy*. Edited by Jonardon Ganeri, Oxford University Press, 2018.
43. [1715] Kapstein, Matthew T., et al. Chapter 3: Philosophy as a Distinct Cultural Practice: The Transregional Context by Justin E.H. Smith (Pg. 57). *The Oxford Handbook of Indian Philosophy*. Edited by Jonardon Ganeri, Oxford University Press, 2018.
44. [1716] Kapstein, Matthew T., et al. Chapter 3: Philosophy as a Distinct Cultural Practice: The Transregional Context by Justin E.H. Smith (56-74). *The Oxford Handbook of Indian Philosophy*. Edited by Jonardon Ganeri, Oxford University Press, 2018.
45. [1717] Ghose, Sanujit. "Cultural Links between India & the Greco-Roman World." *Ancient History Encyclopedia*, Ancient History Encyclopedia, 30 Apr. 2019, www.ancient.eu/article/208/cultural-links-between-india--the-greco-roman-worl/.
46. [1718] Ghose, Sanujit. "Cultural Links between India & the Greco-Roman World." *Ancient History Encyclopedia*, Ancient History Encyclopedia, 30 Apr. 2019, www.ancient.eu/article/208/cultural-links-between-india--the-greco-roman-worl/.
47. [1719] Ghose, Sanujit. "Cultural Links between India & the Greco-Roman World." *Ancient History Encyclopedia*, Ancient History Encyclopedia, 30 Apr. 2019, www.ancient.eu/article/208/cultural-links-between-india--the-greco-roman-worl/.
48. [1720] Ghose, Sanujit. "Cultural Links between India & the Greco-Roman World." *Ancient History Encyclopedia*, Ancient History Encyclopedia, 30 Apr. 2019, www.ancient.eu/article/208/cultural-links-between-india--the-greco-roman-worl/.
49. [1721] Ghose, Sanujit. "Cultural Links between India & the Greco-Roman World." *Ancient History Encyclopedia*, Ancient History Encyclopedia, 30 Apr. 2019, www.ancient.eu/article/208/cultural-links-between-india--the-greco-roman-worl/.

demonstrate to have any knowledge of in Chapter 3[1722], is it reasonable to believe that there was no cultural exchange of philosophical viewpoints or a shared philosophy? There is ample, compelling evidence that indicates Buddhism flourished as a result of this cultural exchange which may have conceivably helped spread Buddhism to East Asia.[1723] Yet, despite this astonishing history, Western Indologists expect people to believe that there was no philosophical exchange or perhaps that this almost 200 years of history doesn't count as a significant and compelling wealth of evidence of such exchange?[1724][1725] Does that honestly make sense? Further along on pages 58-59, Justin E. H. Smith demonstrates no understanding that Adivasi is a term coined in the 1930s for people in India who didn't own land and doesn't mean that they were the original inhabitants as he heavily implies since all Indians are the original inhabitants of India.[1726] On page 59, he wrongfully presumes that the debunked Nazi Aryan Race theory is true by claiming that Adivasi traditions show evidence of pre-Aryan origins.[1727] He can only claim that it is pre-Aryan, if he assumes the Nazi conspiracy theory is true.[1728] He goes on in page 59 to argue the dubious claim that all philosophical positions have anthropological roots which implies that people throughout history can't have used their reasoning faculties or imagination.[1729] Finally, the only useful content that can be gleaned on page 70 is that a Mughal leader attempted to fuse the psychotic teachings of the book, the Quran, as being somehow proved true by the mostly more intellectual and interesting Upanishads; Smith demonstrates no knowledge as to how utterly absurd such a task is, but instead Smith discusses some insane translator by the name of Francois Bernier who cut open animals in front of a Hindu pandit to teach the pandit philosophy and Smith acts as if this was a failure of cultural exchange instead of the act itself being entirely insane on the part of Bernier

---

50. [1722] Kapstein, Matthew T., et al. Chapter 3: Philosophy as a Distinct Cultural Practice: The Transregional Context by Justin E.H. Smith (56-74). *The Oxford Handbook of Indian Philosophy*. Edited by Jonardon Ganeri, Oxford University Press, 2018.
51. [1723] Ghose, Sanujit. "Cultural Links between India & the Greco-Roman World." *Ancient History Encyclopedia*, Ancient History Encyclopedia, 30 Apr. 2019, www.ancient.eu/article/208/cultural-links-between-india--the-greco-roman-worl/.
52. [1724] Kapstein, Matthew T., et al. Chapter 3: Philosophy as a Distinct Cultural Practice: The Transregional Context by Justin E.H. Smith (56-74). *The Oxford Handbook of Indian Philosophy*. Edited by Jonardon Ganeri, Oxford University Press, 2018.
53. [1725] Ghose, Sanujit. "Cultural Links between India & the Greco-Roman World." *Ancient History Encyclopedia*, Ancient History Encyclopedia, 30 Apr. 2019, www.ancient.eu/article/208/cultural-links-between-india--the-greco-roman-worl/.
54. [1726] Kapstein, Matthew T., et al. Chapter 3: Philosophy as a Distinct Cultural Practice: The Transregional Context by Justin E.H. Smith (Pg. 58-59). *The Oxford Handbook of Indian Philosophy*. Edited by Jonardon Ganeri, Oxford University Press, 2018.
55. [1727] Kapstein, Matthew T., et al. Chapter 3: Philosophy as a Distinct Cultural Practice: The Transregional Context by Justin E.H. Smith (Pg. 59). *The Oxford Handbook of Indian Philosophy*. Edited by Jonardon Ganeri, Oxford University Press, 2018.
56. [1728] Kapstein, Matthew T., et al. Chapter 3: Philosophy as a Distinct Cultural Practice: The Transregional Context by Justin E.H. Smith (Pg. 59). *The Oxford Handbook of Indian Philosophy*. Edited by Jonardon Ganeri, Oxford University Press, 2018.
57. [1729] Kapstein, Matthew T., et al. Chapter 3: Philosophy as a Distinct Cultural Practice: The Transregional Context by Justin E.H. Smith (Pg. 59). *The Oxford Handbook of Indian Philosophy*. Edited by Jonardon Ganeri, Oxford University Press, 2018.

as it is doubtful most people in the West would begin a cultural exchange by butchering a living animal (in this case, a goat) in front of non-Westerners.[1730] Finally, there isn't much to be said about Chapter 4, "*Comparison or Confluence of Philosophy*" by Mark Siderits, a retired Analytical Asian Philosophy Professor from Seoul National University[1731]. The entirety of the chapter reaffirms comparative philosophy being unwilling to mix philosophies with the pretense that they're isolated and then he mentions fusion philosophy, but then warns that it could be a form of cultural appropriation and mangling an Indian philosophical school's ideas.[1732] One wonders why on earth a person couldn't simply reference where they got an idea and then explain how their new idea departs from it before exploring their own philosophical inquiry.

Gerald J. Larson, Andrew J. Nicholson, and Sheldon Pollock

Gerald J. Larson is a Religious Studies Professor at Indiana University and he has focused his work on India.[1733] Gerald J. Larson's book, *India's Agony Over Religion,* began with one of the most astonishing premises that I had ever read from a supposed scholar. He has conducted no formal study in Political Science and yet presumed to have knowledge about it and had the confidence to make one of the most shoddy pieces of scholarship ever written. I had to stop reading due to the thoroughgoing anti-intellectual joke of a premise and I honestly can't believe that this was accepted by any university. The initial premise is that India has been influenced by the outside world and there is no distinct Hindu or Indian thought in the secular and modern government of India. Not only does he imply that India's intellectual history is wholly borrowed and heavily alludes that this fact is shameful (within the title, no less), but he credits the Western world for the accomplishments of the Indian people in forming a secular Republic because the initial ideas were from the Western world.[1734] I decided not to read further partly because the premise is utterly faulty and mostly because I needed to conserve spending since the original plan was to make a Three-part book; I had already bought the main textbook and Andrew J. Nicholson's works so I really needed to conserve spending. Nevertheless, to further the point and to better understand why it is absurd: *Can anyone name a modern country in the world that has ideas wholly distinct and isolated from all influences by other countries either in its governance or its views on religion?* The premise was an absurd one. Larson failed to explain what an isolated Hindu or Indian thought would even be. If you

---

58. [1730] Kapstein, Matthew T., et al. Chapter 3: Philosophy as a Distinct Cultural Practice: The Transregional Context by Justin E.H. Smith (56-74). *The Oxford Handbook of Indian Philosophy*. Edited by Jonardon Ganeri, Oxford University Press, 2018.
59. [1731] Kapstein, Matthew T., et al. Contributors (IX - XVII). *The Oxford Handbook of Indian Philosophy*. Edited by Jonardon Ganeri, Oxford University Press, 2018.
60. [1732] Kapstein, Matthew T., et al. Chapter 4: Comparison or Confluence in Philosophy? by Mark Siderits (75-92). *The Oxford Handbook of Indian Philosophy*. Edited by Jonardon Ganeri, Oxford University Press, 2018.
61. [1733] "Gerald J. Larson." *Gerald J. Larson - Department of Religious Studies*, indiana.edu/~relstud/people/profiles/larson_gerald.
62. [1734] Larson, Gerald James. "India's Agony Over Religion (SUNY Series in Religious Studies)." *Amazon*, Amazon, 16 Feb. 1995, www.amazon.com/Indias-Agony-Religion-Religious-Studies/dp/079142412X.

wish me to further explain, then please consider what this premise would mean if regarded with any degree of seriousness. If we take Larson's absurd premise to its logical conclusion, then Cyrus the Great should be credited for any Western abolitionist movement because he was the originator of the idea of banning slavery, India should be credited for the care for animals in all countries because of how it was the first to treat animals well and codify it into a set of rules throughout a government, and - if we're crediting the Western world for the actions of other people - then the Western world would have to collectively be blamed for Mao Zedong's Great Leap Forward which killed tens of millions of Chinese civilians due to his following the ideals of Marxism which were developed in the West. Larson's asinine claims fail to explore the category of human psychology and the transmission of beliefs from one culture to another, which he clearly didn't even think about when writing his book. Finally, his other book *Classical Samkhya: an Interpretation of its History and Meaning*, which I did read two chapters of, showcases the blind guesswork of hermeneutics and affirms that there is no credible reason for Indology to have any internal consensus since he critiques people who aren't even Indologists and takes their ignorant views seriously with the objections being his own ignorant assertions.[1735] Why, then, does Western Indology disqualify the views of so many Hindus in India who have criticisms? Their consensus has no criteria at all, so on what intellectual grounds can Indology departments refuse the views of anyone with an opinion on Indian intellectual traditions?

In a June 2018 interview with *The Indian Express*, Indologist Professor from Columbia University, Sheldon Pollock claimed that he looked at the ugly in Indian history[1736], but it would seem that he turned a blind eye to the ugliness that Islam brought upon India and the mass death toll in its wake.[1737] Pollock depicts his detractors in a very one-sided view and seems to present himself as above the supposed hate, while refusing to honestly engage with them in dialogue.[1738] He seems to be blissfully unaware of the Hindutva side of the conflict in Kashmir before signing his name in opposition to it.[1739] He has shown no knowledge of the Kashmiri Hindus who were driven out via mass violence by terrorist groups and mobs of

63. [1735] Larson, Gerald James. "Classical Sāṃkhya: An Interpretation of Its History and Meaning." *Google Books*, books.google.com/books?id=Ih2aGLp4d1gC&pg=PR7&source=gbs_selected_pages&cad=3#v=onepage&q&f=false.
64. [1736] Ghosh, Tanushree. "I'm a Target Because I'm an Outsider: Sanskrit Scholar Sheldon Pollock." *The Indian Express*, 4 June 2018, indianexpress.com/article/express-sunday-eye/im-a-target-because-im-an-outsider-sanskrit-scholar-sheldon-pollock-5191995/.
65. [1737] Durant, Will. Chapter XVI: From Alexander to Aurangzeb (10072 - 10817). *Our Oriental Heritage: Being a History of Civilization in Egypt and the Near East to the Death of Alexander, and in India, China and Japan from the Beginning to Our Own Day*. Simon and Schuster, 1935.
66. [1738] Ghosh, Tanushree. "I'm a Target Because I'm an Outsider: Sanskrit Scholar Sheldon Pollock." *The Indian Express*, 4 June 2018, indianexpress.com/article/express-sunday-eye/im-a-target-because-im-an-outsider-sanskrit-scholar-sheldon-pollock-5191995/.
67. [1739] Ramakrishnan, Ganesh. "Removal of Sheldon Pollock as Mentor and Chief Editor of Murty Classical Library." *Change.org*, www.change.org/p/mr-n-r-narayana-murthy-and-mr-rohan-narayan-murty-removal-of-prof-sheldon-pollock-as-mentor-and-chief-editor-of-murty-classical-library.

Kashmiri Muslims or the cluster of Islamic terrorist groups that Kashmir has affiliated itself with from Pakistan over the years which includes al Qaeda-linked groups.[1740][1741] If his 1985 essay and details about his other works from Nicholson's book are any indication, it seems that he may not have any knowledge of the genocidal history of the Islamic conquests in India either or the fact that - as utterly awful as Casteism is - it was the horror of the Islamic conquests that caused untouchables to flee India in droves in a mass exodus from which they eventually became identified as the Romani people.[1742][1743][1744][1745] Oh, and the fact they had common Sanskrit words in their language casts doubt on arguments that it was an exclusive language of the upper-caste in ancient India.[1746] He neither seems aware or interested in learning of the political issues in contemporary India that he knowingly and willingly involves himself with. It seems to me that his entire career has been made by categorically denying genocides of Hindus from both his writings and his political participation. Whether its ancient history like the Islamic conquests or contemporary history like the Kashmiri Hindu Pandits who were driven out of Kashmir.[1747] If he was simply ignorant of the political issue of Kashmir, then why did he choose to knowingly get himself involved? If he pleads ignorance to the history of Islamic invasion in India despite attaining his Ph.D. in 1975 on Indian studies, then what kind of scholar does that make him, if he's purportedly trying to bring an improved context on Indian history as an Indologist throughout his career?

Andrew J. Nicholson's books were of interest to me because, before I had acquired and read *The Oxford Handbook of Indian Philosophy* and bore witness to his lack of understanding of the basics of the burden of proof in analytical philosophy along with his thesis advisor

---

68. [1740] Ahmed, Zubair. "Kashmiri Hindus: Driven out and Insignificant." *BBC News*, BBC, 6 Apr. 2016, www.bbc.com/news/world-asia-india-35923237.
69. [1741] Wani, Riyaz. "How Al-Qaeda Came to Kashmir." *The Diplomat*, The Diplomat, 20 Dec. 2017, thediplomat.com/2017/12/how-al-qaeda-came-to-kashmir/.
70. [1742] Pollock, Sheldon. "Is There an Indian Intellectual History? Introduction to ''Theory and Method in Indian Intellectual History.''" *Http://Www.columbia.edu*, Columbia University, www.columbia.edu/cu/mesaas/faculty/directory/pollock_pub/indian_intellectual_history.pdf.
71. [1743] Durant, Will. Chapter XVI: From Alexander to Aurangzeb (10072 - 10817). *Our Oriental Heritage: Being a History of Civilization in Egypt and the Near East to the Death of Alexander, and in India, China and Japan from the Beginning to Our Own Day*. Simon and Schuster, 1935.
72. [1744] Nicholson, Andrew J. Chapter 10: Hindu Unity And The Non-Hindu Other (4806-5293). *Unifying Hinduism: Philosophy and Identity in Indian Intellectual History (South Asia Across the Disciplines)*. Columbia University Press, 2010.
73. [1745] Nelson, Dean. "European Roma Descended from Indian 'Untouchables', Genetic Study Shows." *The Telegraph*, Telegraph Media Group, 3 Dec. 2012, www.telegraph.co.uk/news/worldnews/europe/9719058/European-Roma-descended-from-Indian-untouchables-genetic-study-shows.html.
74. [1746] Nelson, Dean. "European Roma Descended from Indian 'Untouchables', Genetic Study Shows." *The Telegraph*, Telegraph Media Group, 3 Dec. 2012, www.telegraph.co.uk/news/worldnews/europe/9719058/European-Roma-descended-from-Indian-untouchables-genetic-study-shows.html.
75. [1747] Ahmed, Zubair. "Kashmiri Hindus: Driven out and Insignificant." *BBC News*, BBC, 6 Apr. 2016, www.bbc.com/news/world-asia-india-35923237.

Sheldon Pollock[1748], I had assumed that he had knowledge about Samkhya philosophical thought and I had been eager to read more in order to learn more of the historical development of my own religion and perhaps to better critique it with an outsider view. However, I kept spotting logical fallacies and errors in his book, *Unifying Hinduism*, from the beginning. I was astonished to find that the entire premise, and apparently a large portion of Western Indologist scholarship, has been solely devoted to one-word as the disputed reason why Hinduism is supposedly a modern invention, which is the word Hinduism itself.[1749] Nicholson's book was an attempt at a middle-ground approach; yet, he never seems to question the fact that his entire book is premised upon an argument of semantics.[1750] It is a false premise. I actually couldn't believe that this was the controversy and that the bold claim that Hinduism was never a religion was based upon nothing more than semantics.[1751] Quite honestly, I wonder how can people from India get so riled-up and angry over this shoddy scholarship which seems to be the norm of Western Indology. Even more astonishing, I found it difficult to process the idea that many decades worth of so-called scholarship by Western Indology to make bold arguments was based upon semantics and almost nothing else as evidence.[1752][1753] Every other religious group would have probably laughed at this premise as what matters are the definition and the self-identification of the religious practitioners; the Abrahamic faiths themselves aren't based on a solid grounding of history. The core of Sanatana Dharma has always been that we are part of the same Oneness and that we have our own interpretations about that oneness; reading portions of the *Mahabharata*, *The Upanishads*, the *Devi Gita*, the *Bhagavad Gita*, and even Andrew J. Nicholson's own translation of the *Siva Gita*, which I bought and read before *Unifying Hinduism*, led me to that understanding and affirmed that understanding when I delved more deeply into Sanatana Dharma religious texts. That's the core of Hinduism, Buddhism, Jainism, and Sikhism. We're all the same religion, but we each have our own denomination based upon interpreting our Oneness. Many atheists and others curious enough to look into Hinduism have also accepted this as the main thesis of Sanatana Dharma; yet, Western Indology seems incapable of understanding this basic premise.

---

76. [1748] Nicholson, Andrew J., et al. "Andrew Nicholson on 'Anti-Theistic Arguments in Sāṃkhya and Vedānta Philosophy." *YouTube*, 2 Apr. 2018, youtu.be/myjdOsKu8iY?t=2890. For reference: Timestamp of 48:10 - 48:23. Nicholson, Pollock, and Raghunathan show no understanding of Analytical Philosophy's Burden of Proof.
77. [1749] Nicholson, Andrew J. *Unifying Hinduism: Philosophy and Identity in Indian Intellectual History (South Asia Across the Disciplines)*. Columbia University Press, 2010.
78. [1750] Nicholson, Andrew J. Chapter 1: Introduction (181-715). *Unifying Hinduism: Philosophy and Identity in Indian Intellectual History (South Asia Across the Disciplines)*. Columbia University Press, 2010.
79. [1751] Nicholson, Andrew J. Chapter 1: Introduction (181-715). *Unifying Hinduism: Philosophy and Identity in Indian Intellectual History (South Asia Across the Disciplines)*. Columbia University Press, 2010.
80. [1752] Nicholson, Andrew J. Chapter 1: Introduction (181-715). *Unifying Hinduism: Philosophy and Identity in Indian Intellectual History (South Asia Across the Disciplines)*. Columbia University Press, 2010.
81. [1753] Nicholson, Andrew J. Chapter 10: Hindu Unity And The Non-Hindu Other (4806-5293). *Unifying Hinduism: Philosophy and Identity in Indian Intellectual History (South Asia Across the Disciplines)*. Columbia University Press, 2010.

Nonetheless, there's deeper problems with the behavior of Western Indology, and possibly the entirety of Indology. These Indologists, especially Western Indologists, don't seem to be aware of the fact that there is no evidence that the Exodus of Moses or the slavery of the Israelites in Egypt ever happened.[1754] Therefore, any historical comparison between the Abrahamic faiths and Hinduism is based upon falsehoods about the history of the Abrahamic faiths. That means Judaism, Christianity, and Islam are all founded upon a falsification of history; moreover, Islam itself claims that Judaism and Christianity are falsehoods and that the prophets were all Muslim since the beginning of time. Andrew Nicholson never attempts to address this issue when mentioning the Abrahamic faiths as a comparison and it seems that he doesn't know judging from the book itself.[1755] Moreover, judging from actual Christian history, if we were to take the various Christian sects at their word, then they've never been unified; for example, many Protestants consider both Mormonism and Catholicism as aberrations that aren't part of Christianity. Jews, Muslims, and Christians all have varied sects which entirely disagree and the latter two go so far as to argue that other practitioners of their faith aren't legitimate Muslims and Christians respectively. Comparatively, some Hindus consider each other as part of the same Oneness and are willing to include Zoroastrians, Christians, and Jews if they are comfortable with it; this is under the presumption that Buddhism, Jainism, and Sikhism are already part of Sanatana Dharma. Nicholson never once bothers to consider why it is that Christians, Jews, and Zoroastrians lived in peace and harmony with practitioners of Sanatana Dharma for many hundreds of years while the Islamic conquests brought upon an immediate massacre after an already bloody history of Islam's massacres of Jews, Christians, and Zoroastrians throughout its history in the Middle East. While European imperialism brought upon its own sordid affairs like the Goa Inquisition in which Catholic Portuguese, upon first contact in India in their "civilizing mission" on behalf of the Catholic Church, decided to immediately burn down Indian Jewish synagogues and forcibly amputate Hindus and Jews in front of their families to bring about forced conversions to the Catholic faith[1756][1757]; I haven't found evidence of persecutions or violence by Indian Christians upon other Indians before the European conquests, but if I am mistaken then I'll adjust accordingly upon obtaining valid historical information.

The most problematic view is in Nicholson's tenth chapter. If his references to other Indologists are to be believed, then Sheldon Pollock, Romila Thapor, Cynthia Talbot, and the so-called anonymous number of historians are all entirely ignorant of the mass genocides

---

82. [1754] "Archeology of the Hebrew Bible." *PBS*, Public Broadcasting Service, 18 Nov. 2008, www.pbs.org/wgbh/nova/ancient/archeology-hebrew-bible.html.
83. [1755] Nicholson, Andrew J. Chapter 10: Hindu Unity And The Non-Hindu Other (4806-5293). *Unifying Hinduism: Philosophy and Identity in Indian Intellectual History (South Asia Across the Disciplines)*. Columbia University Press, 2010.
84. [1756] Weiss, Gary. "India's Jews." *Forbes*, Forbes Magazine, 17 July 2012, www.forbes.com/2007/08/05/india-jews-antisemitism-oped-cx_gw_0813jews.html#4d526e5f3d45.
85. [1757] de Souza, Teotónio Rosário. "The Goa Inquisition." *Goa Inquisition*, vgweb.org/unethicalconversion/GoaInquisition.htm.

perpetuated by Islamic invaders and subsequent rulers on the Indian subcontinent[1758]; for all the arguments about proper context, none of them seem to be aware of one of the bloodiest tragedies in India's history which was solely the act of Islamic invaders and rulers.[1759] I suspect that I will be vilified by these so-called scholars and have ad hominem attacks thrust at me for arguing this point due to my religious and ethnic background, so here is a snippet from Will Durant's *The Story of Civilization: Our Oriental Heritage* from subsection *VI. The Moslem Conquest*:

> Each winter Mahmud descended into India, filled his treasure chest with spoils, and amused his men with full freedom to pillage and kill; each spring he returned to his capital richer than before. At Mathura (on the Jumna) he took from the temple its statues of gold encrusted with precious stones, and emptied its coffers of a vast quantity of gold, silver and jewelry; he expressed his admiration for the architecture of the great shrine, judged that its duplication would cost one hundred million dinars and the labor of two hundred years, and then ordered it to be soaked with naphtha and burnt to the ground.73 Six years later he sacked another opulent city of northern India, Somnath, killed all its fifty thousand inhabitants, and dragged its wealth to Ghazni. In the end he became, perhaps, the richest king that history has ever known. Sometimes he spared the population of the ravaged cities, and took them home to be sold as slaves; but so great was the number of such captives that after some years no one could be found to offer more than a few shillings for a slave. Before every important engagement Mahmud knelt in prayer, and asked the blessing of God upon his arms. He reigned for a third of a century; and when he died, full of years and honors, Moslem historians ranked him as the greatest monarch of his time, and one of the greatest sovereigns of any age.74
>
> Seeing the canonization that success had brought to this magnificent thief, other Moslem rulers profited by his example, though none succeeded in bettering his instruction. In 1186 the Ghuri, a Turkish tribe of Afghanistan, invaded India, captured the city of Delhi, destroyed its temples, confiscated its wealth, and settled down in its palaces to establish the Sultanate of Delhi—an alien despotism fastened upon northern India for three centuries, and checked only by assassination and revolt. The first of these bloody sultans, Kutb-d Din Aibak, was a normal specimen of his kind—fanatical, ferocious and merciless. His gifts, as the Mohammedan historian tells us, "were bestowed by hundreds of thousands, and his slaughters likewise were by hundreds of thousands." In one victory of this warrior (who had been purchased as a slave), "fifty thousand men came under the collar of slavery, and the plain became black as pitch with Hindus."75 Another sultan, Balban, punished rebels and brigands by casting them under the feet of elephants, or removing their skins, stuffing these with straw, and hanging them from the gates of Delhi. When some Mongol inhabitants who had settled in Delhi, and had been converted to Islam, attempted a rising, Sultan Alau-d-din (the conquerer of Chitor) had all the males—from fifteen to thirty thousand of them—slaughtered in one day. Sultan Muhammad bin Tughlak acquired the throne by murdering his father, became a great scholar and an elegant writer, dabbled in mathematics, physics and Greek philosophy, surpassed his predecessors in bloodshed and brutality, fed the flesh of a rebel nephew to the rebel's wife and children, ruined the country with reckless inflation, and laid it waste with pillage and murder till the inhabitants fled to the jungle. He killed so many Hindus that, in the words of a Moslem historian, "there was constantly in front of his royal pavilion and his Civil Court a mound of dead bodies

---

86. [1758] Durant, Will. Chapter XVI: From Alexander to Aurangzeb (10072 - 10817). *Our Oriental Heritage: Being a History of Civilization in Egypt and the Near East to the Death of Alexander, and in India, China and Japan from the Beginning to Our Own Day*. Simon and Schuster, 1935.
87. [1759] Nicholson, Andrew J. Chapter 10: Hindu Unity And The Non-Hindu Other (4806-5293). *Unifying Hinduism: Philosophy and Identity in Indian Intellectual History (South Asia Across the Disciplines)*. Columbia University Press, 2010.

and a heap of corpses, while the sweepers and executioners were wearied out by their work of dragging" the victims "and putting them to death in crowds."[1760]

This history was entirely available to them in world-renown historian Will Durant's book, *The Story of Civilization: Our Oriental Heritage*, which was published in 1935. They repeatedly argue in a collective, one-sided view of vilification and yet none of these so-called scholars seem to be aware of the catastrophes that Islam wrought upon India. Nicholson suggests the peaceful and tolerant Akbar the Great, but asserts that he is a Muslim and makes no mention of the fact that Akbar abandoned the Muslim faith to set-up his own religion; if anything, Akbar was the first and probably only *Ex-Muslim* King.[1761] Even worse, Nicholson's assertions and references to other so-called scholars only casts further doubt on their credibility because the lack of textual information on Hindu-Muslim encounters that Nicholson mentions in his book are likely due to the way Islamic countries set-up their societies.[1762] Islam traditionally, and even today throughout multiple Islamic countries like Lebanon and Syria before the Civil War, follow a process of religious apartheid which includes enforcing societal customs of gender apartheid.[1763][1764] Blasphemy is an offense that would get people killed even back then since they would be under strict Sharia observance and Muslims essentially live with special privileges in Islamic societies when they are the ruling power. What can explain these supposedly high-profile Western Indologist scholars sheer ignorance of these facts about Islam and Nicholson's own ignorance in which he states that Hindu intellectuals are arguing a myth while he himself shows no awareness of the historic context of Islamic invasions?[1765] Is it laziness? Is it political correctness? Unfortunately, the problem seems to be much worse than that. The study of hermeneutics, lacking any basis in guidelines or any procedures, repeatedly

---

88. [1760] Durant, Will. Chapter XVI: From Alexander to Aurangzeb: VI. The Moslem Conquest (Pgs. 10447-10520). *Our Oriental Heritage: Being a History of Civilization in Egypt and the Near East to the Death of Alexander, and in India, China and Japan from the Beginning to Our Own Day*. Simon and Schuster, 1935.
89. [1761] Durant, Will. Chapter XVI: From Alexander to Aurangzeb: VII. Akbar The Great (Pgs. 10520 - 10691). *Our Oriental Heritage: Being a History of Civilization in Egypt and the Near East to the Death of Alexander, and in India, China and Japan from the Beginning to Our Own Day*. Simon and Schuster, 1935.
90. [1762] Nicholson, Andrew J. Chapter 10: Hindu Unity And The Non-Hindu Other (4806-5293). *Unifying Hinduism: Philosophy and Identity in Indian Intellectual History (South Asia Across the Disciplines)*. Columbia University Press, 2010.
91. [1763] Shams, Imtiaz, et al. "Fighting Allah, Defending Muslims - Armin Navabi, Imtiaz Shams, Muhammad Syed." *YouTube*, Ex-Muslims of North America, 5 Jan. 2018, www.youtube.com/watch?v=KwnHreJNavE. For reference: Timestamp 55:17 - 1:00:58. Imtiaz Shams explains that the Pact of Umar is an apartheid document and its relevance in Islamic dominated civilizations. He, Armin Navabi, and Muhammad Syed then discuss contemporary Ex-Muslim human rights issues.
92. [1764] Haider, Sarah, et al. "Islam, Modesty and Feminism." *YouTube*, Ex-Muslims of North America, 12 Oct. 2017, www.youtube.com/watch?v=QToH2x8njJM.
93. [1765] Nicholson, Andrew J. Chapter 10: Hindu Unity And The Non-Hindu Other (4806-5293). *Unifying Hinduism: Philosophy and Identity in Indian Intellectual History (South Asia Across the Disciplines)*. Columbia University Press, 2010.

fails to put important events in historic context because it is just the practice of make-believe. Beyond using Western academia as a shield from criticism, it builds a capricious consensus on the basis of personal whims within an insular community and pretends to be a scholarly endeavor because of its setting. Western Indology isn't a legitimate academic discipline and it probably doesn't deserve to waste anymore University grant money when much more intellectual scholarly work in STEM departments or social science work such as Political Science, Ethics Philosophy of AI, and Business are much more important and accurate. *In effect, US Indology is intrinsically worthless.*

Debunking The Aryan Invasion/Immigration Theory

Due to this being a hotly contested political issue, I've decided to simply share the full two-part interview by journalist Nithin Sridhar who works for a US-based non-profit independent media organization, NewsGram.[1766] In his interview with an accredited Indian archaeologist whose research is based upon the scientific method and empirical evidence. From the November 30th, 2015 article "*No Evidence for warfare or invasion; Aryan migration too is a myth: B. B. Lal*" by Nithin Sridhar is as follows:

> **Aryan Question: Part 1**
>
> Recently, Congress Parliamentary Party (CPP) leader Mallikarjuna Kharge raked up a controversy in the Parliament by saying: "Ambedkar and we are from this country. Aryans came from outside. We are the original inhabitants of this land."
>
> His statements have again shed light on the Aryan question that continues to remain unresolved and controversial. The issue of Aryans first arose during the colonial period when the European scholars conceived of two different races- Aryan and Dravidian. They further propounded that Aryans invaded India and destroyed the native culture, forcing Dravidians to move south-words.
>
> Later, the racial connotations were removed and replaced by linguistic divisions between speakers of the Aryan group of languages and the Dravidian group of languages. But, even today this the racial division continues to be harbored in Indian politics, especially in Dravidian politics and in certain Dalit groups.
>
> In the last few decades, the proposition of military invasion has also been largely rejected and replaced by the proposition of immigration of Aryan speakers into India. Further, many Indologists have raised serious questions regarding this proposed migration as well, and they have propounded a non-migration scenario. Some have also proposed a possible westward migration of people from India. The issue is further complicated by the fact that it is multi-dimensional and requires investigation from diverse fields ranging from Archaeology and Linguistics to Genetics and Hydrology. Thus, the Aryan issue is mired in confusion and controversy.
>
> In order to highlight few salient features of the Aryan issue and assess the current position regarding various questions like identification of the Aryans, their homeland, their dating, their connection with Indus-Valley civilization, etc. NewsGram decided to interview various Indologists, academicians, and Independent scholars who have worked for decades on various aspects of this issue.
>
> In this first interview for the 'Aryan Question' series, NewsGram spoke to Brij Basi Lal, popularly known as B. B. Lal, regarding Aryan people, their movement, and their relationship with Harappan civilization.

---

94. [1766] "About NewsGram." *NewsGram*, www.newsgram.com/about-newsgram/.

B. B. Lal is a renowned archeologist and former Director General of the Archaeological Survey of India (ASI) who has written many books and papers on the Aryan issue including his 2015 book- 'The Rigvedic People: Invaders?/ Immigrants? Or Indigenous?' Here is the first installment of the interview–

Interview with B. B. Lal-1

Nithin Sridhar: How deep are the roots of the most ancient civilization of the Indian subcontinent, known as the Harappan Civilization, and through what stages did it develop?

B. Lal: The Harappan Civilization (also called the Indus Civilization or Indus-Sarasvati Civilization), which reached its peak in the 3rd millennium BCE, grew up on the Indian soil itself. While there are likely to have been earlier stages, the earliest one so far identified is at Bhirrana, a site in the upper reaches of the Sarasvati valley, in Haryana. This is the stage when the people dwelt in pits and used incised and appliqué pottery called the Hakra Ware. According to Carbon-14 dates, it is ascribable to the 6th -5th millennium BCE. I call it Stage I.

In Stage II, identified at a nearby site called Kunal, the people gave up pit-dwellings and built houses on the land-surface, used copper and silver artifacts and a special kind of pottery which was red in color and painted with designs in black outline, the inner space being filled with white color. This Stage may be assigned to the 4th millennium BCE.

In Stage III, beginning around 3,000 BCE, a new feature came up, namely the construction of a peripheral (fortification?) wall around the settlement, which has been noted at Kalibangan, located on the left bank of the Sarasvati in Hanumangarh District of Rajasthan. Another important feature that can be noted here is an agricultural field, marked by a criss-cross pattern of furrows. It may incidentally be mentioned that this the earliest agricultural field ever discovered anywhere in the world in an excavation. An earthquake, occurring around 2,700 BCE, brought about the end of Stage III at Kalibangan. This is the earliest evidence of earthquake ever recorded in an archeological excavation.

However, after about a century or so the people returned to Kalibangan, but with a bang. This is Stage IV. They now had two parts of the settlement, a 'Citadel' on the west and a 'Lower Town' on the east. Both were fortified. In the Lower Town there lived agriculturalists and merchants, while the Citadel was the seat of priests and elites. In the southern part of the Citadel, there were many high, mud-brick platforms on which there stood specialized structures, including fire-altars and sacrificial pits. There is ample evidence of writing, seals, weights, measures, objects of art in this Stage, assignable to circa 2600 to 2000 BCE. The peak had been reached.

Citadel, Middle Town, and Lower Town were also features of other sites of Indus-Sarasvati civilization.

For various reasons, including sharp climatic changes, the drying up of the Sarasvati, and steep fall in trade, the big cities disappeared and there was a reversal to the rural scenario. Some people migrated from the Sarasvati valley into the upper Ganga-Yamuna terrain, as indicated by sites like Hulas and Alamgirpur. The curtain was drawn on a mighty Indian civilization.

NS: Many people hold that there was an 'Aryan Invasion' which destroyed the Harappan Civilization. How far is this true?

Lal: Let us first go to the background against which the 'Aryan Invasion' theory emerged. In the 19th century, Max Muller, a German Indologist, dated the Vedas to 1200 BCE. Accepting that the Sutras existed around 600 BCE and assigning 200 years to each of the preceding stages, namely those of the Aranyakas, Brahmanas, and Vedas, he arrived at the magic figure of 1,200 BCE.

There were serious objections to such ad-hocism by contemporary scholars, like Goldstucker, Whitney, and Wilson. Thus cornered, Max Muller finally surrendered by stating: "Whether the Vedic hymns were composed in 1000 or 1500 or 2000 or 3000 BC, no power on earth will ever determine." But the great pity is that some scholars even today cling to 1200 BCE and dare not cross this *Lakshamana Rekha!*

In the 1920s, the Harappan Civilization was discovered and dated to 3rd millennium BCE on the basis of its contacts with West Asian civilizations. Since the Vedas had already been dated, be it wrongly, to 1200 BCE, the Harappan Civilization was declared to be Non-Vedic. And since the only other major language group in India was the Dravidian, it was readily assumed that the Harappans was a Dravidian-speaking people.

In 1946, Wheeler discovered a fort at Harappa; and since the Aryan god Indra has been mentioned in the Rigveda as puramdara, i.e. 'destroyer of forts', he lost no time in declaring that Aryan Invaders destroyed the Harappan Civilization.

In the excavations at Mohenjo-Daro, some human skeletons had been found. In support of his 'Invasion' theory, Wheeler stated that these were the people who had been massacred by the invaders. However, since the skeletons had been found at different stratigraphic levels and could not, therefore, be related to a single event, much less to an invasion, Wheeler's theory was prima facie wrong. Dales, an American archeologist, has rightly dubbed it as a 'mythical massacre'.

Indeed, there is no evidence whatsoever of an invasion at any of the hundreds of Harappan sites. On the other hand, there is ample evidence of continuity of habitation, though marked by gradual cultural devolution. A detailed study of human skeletal remains from various sites by Hemphill and his colleagues has established that no new people at all entered India between 4500 and 800 BCE. Thus, if there is no evidence of warfare or of entry of an alien people where is the case for any 'invasion', much less by Aryans?

NS: In the last few decades, many scholars have taken recourse to the theory of 'Aryan Migration' from Central Asia. How far does this new theory stand scrutiny?

Lal: The ghost of 'Invasion' has re-appeared in a new avatāra (incarnation), namely that of 'Immigration'. Romila Thapar says: "If the invasion is discarded, then the mechanism of migration and occasional contacts come into sharper focus. These migrations appear to have been of pastoral cattle breeders who are prominent in the Avesta and Rigveda." Faithfully following her, R. S. Sharma adds: "The pastoralists who moved to the Indian borderland came from Bactria-Margiana Archaeological Complex or BMAC which saw the genesis of the culture of the Rigveda."

Contrary to what has been stated by Thapar and Sharma, the BMAC is not a pastoral culture, but a highly developed urban one. The settlements are marked not only by well-planned houses but also by distinctive public buildings like temples, e.g. those at Dashly-3 and Toglok-21 sites. Then there were Citadel complexes like that at Gonur. The antiquities found at BMAC sites also speak volumes about the high caliber of this civilization. In the face of such a rich heritage of the BMAC, would you like to deduce that the BMAC people were nomads – whom Thapar and Sharma would like to push into India as progenitors of the Rigvedic people? I am sure, you wouldn't.

But much more important is the fact that no BMAC element, whether seals or bronze axes or sculptures or pot-forms or even the style of architecture ever reached east of the Indus, which was the area occupied by the Vedic Aryans as evidenced by the famous Nadi-stuti hymn (RV 10.75.5-6). Hence, there is no question of the BMAC people having at all entered the Vedic region. Thus, the theory of 'Aryan Migration' too is a myth.

NS: Some people hold that the Rigvedic flora and fauna pertain to a cold climate and hence the Rigvedic people must have come from a cold region. What do you think of this view?

Lal: If the attempt at bringing the Vedic Aryans into India from the BMAC has failed, why not try other means? In this category falls the attempt by certain scholars who hold that that Vedic flora pertains to a cold climate and, therefore, the Ṛigvedic people must have come from a cold region and cannot be indigenous. In this context, they refer to species such as birch, Scotch pine, linden, alder, and oak. But, let us examine Rigveda.

In the Rigveda the following trees are mentioned: Aśvattha (Ficus religiosa L.); Kiṁśuka (Butea monosperma [Lamk.]; Khadira (Acacia catechu Wild.); Nyagrodha (Ficus benghalensis L); Vibhīdaka/Vibhītaka (Terminalia Billerica Roxb.); Śālmali (Bombax Ceiba L. Syn. Salmalia malabarica [DC.] Schott); Śiṁsipā (Dalbergia sisso Roxb,). The main regions of the occurrence the foregoing trees are – India, Pakistan, Afghanistan, Sri Lanka, and Myanmar.

In fact, what is true in the case of the flora is equally true in the case of the fauna as well. Some of the animals mentioned in the Ṛigveda include Vṛiṣabha (Bos Indicus); Siṁha (Lion, Panthera leo L.); Hastin/Vaaaraṇa (Elephas maximus L. and Loxodonta africana), which all typically occur in a tropical climate.

Moreover, even the birds testify to the fact that Ṛigveda have been composed in a tropical climate. In this context, two typical birds may be cited: Mayūra (Pavo cristatus L.) and Chakravāka (Anus Casarca).

From what has been stated in the preceding paragraphs, it must have become abundantly clear that the flora, as well as fauna mentioned in the Ṛigveda, are typically tropical. Further, no cold-climate flora and fauna find a place in this text. Thus, there is no case to hold that the authors of the Ṛigveda belonged to a cold climate.[1767]

The second part of the NewsGram interview, from the December 1st, 2015 article *"Vedic and Harrapan are respectively literally and materially facets of the same civilization: B. B. Lal"* by Nithin Sridhar with Indian archaeologist Brij Basi Lal is as follows:

Interview with B. B. Lal-2

Nithin Sridhar: If the Aryans were neither 'Invaders' nor 'Immigrants', were they 'Indigenous'?

B.B. Lal: To answer this question, we must first settle the date of the Rigveda since the entire mess has been created by wrongly dating the Vedas to 1200 BCE. In this context, the history of the River Sarasvati plays a very vital role. In the Rigveda, it has been referred to as a mighty river, originating in the Himalayas and flowing all the way down to the ocean (RV 7.95.2). But by the time of the Panchavimsha Brahmana (XXV.10.16) it had dried up.

Against this literary background, let us see what archaeology and other sciences have to say in the matter. Along the bank of the Sarasvati (now called the Ghaggar) is located Kalibangan, a site of the Harappan Civilization. It had to be abandoned while it was still in a mature stage, owing to the drying up of the adjacent river. According to the radiocarbon dates, this abandonment took place around 2000. Since, as already stated, during the Rigvedic times the Sarasvati was a mighty flowing river and it dried up around 2,000 BCE, the Rigveda has got to be earlier than 2000 BCE. How much earlier is anybody's guess; but at least a 3rd millennium BCE horizon is indicated. Further, Rigveda X.75.5-6 very clearly defines the area occupied by Rigvedic people, in the 3rd millennium BCE, as follows:

imam me Gaṅge Yamune Sarasvati Śutudri stotam sachatā Paruṣṇyā / Asiknyā Marudvṛidhe Vitastayā Ārjīkīye śriṇuhya- Suṣomayā // 5 //

Triṣṭāmayā prathamam yātave sajūḥ.Susartvā Rasayā Śvetyā tyā / Tvam Sindho Kubhayā Gomatīm Krumum Mehatnvā saratham yābhiṛiyase // 6 //

Which means the area occupied by Rigvedic people was from the upper reaches of the Ganga-Yamuna on the east to the Indus and its western tributaries on the west. Now, if a simple question is asked, viz. archaeologically, which culture occupied this very area during the Rigvedic times, i.e. in the 3rd millennium BCE, the inescapable answer shall have to be: 'The Harappan Civilization'. Thus, it is amply clear that the Harappan Civilization and the Vedas are but two faces of the same coin. Further, as already stated earlier, the Harappans were the sons of Indian soil. Hence, the Vedic people who themselves were the Harappans were indigenous.

NS: But, materially, many objections has been raised against the Vedic = Harappan equation. How do you reconcile them?

Lal: Yes, I am aware that against such a chronological-cum-spatial Vedic = Harappan equation, many objections have been raised. Notably, three important objections have been raised, namely: (1) Whereas the Vedic people were nomads, the Harappans were urbanites; (2) The Vedic people knew the horse while the Harappans did not; and (3) The Vedic people used spoked wheels, but the Harappans had no knowledge of such wheels.

Let us take up the first question. The Vedic people were not nomads wandering from place to place, but had regular settlements, some of which were even fortified. In RV 10.101.8 the prayer is: "stitch ye [oh

---

95. [1767] Sridhar, Nithin. "No Evidence for Warfare or Invasion; Aryan Migration Too Is a Myth: B B Lal." *NewsGram*, 30 Nov. 2015, www.newsgram.com/no-evidence-for-warfare-or-invasion-aryan-migration-too-is-a-myth-b-b-lal

gods] the coats of armour, wide and many; make metal forts secure from all assailants." RV 7.15.14 runs as follows: "And, irresistible, be thou a mighty metal fort to us, with hundred walls for man's defense." Even on the economic front, the Vedic people were highly advanced. Trade was carried on even on the seas. Says RV 9.33.6: "O Soma, pour thou forth four seas filled with a thousand-fold riches." The ships had sometimes as many as 'a hundred oars (sataritra)'. Politically, the Vedic people had sabhas and samitis and even a hierarchy of rulers: Samrat, Rajan and Rajakas (RV 6.27.8 & 8.21.8). That these gradations were real and not imaginary is confirmed by the Satapatha Brahmana (V.1.1.12-13): "By offering Rajasuya he becomes Raja and by Vajapeya, Samrat; the office of Raja is lower and of Samrat, higher." In the face of the foregoing evidence, can we still call the Rigvedic people 'Nomads'?

Now coming to the horse, in his Mohenjo-daro Report, Mackay states: "Perhaps the most interesting of the model animals is the one that I personally take to represent a horse." Wheeler confirmed the above view of Mackay, adding that "a jawbone of a horse is also recorded from the same site." Now a lot of new material has come to light: from Lothal, Surkotada, Kalibangan, etc. Lothal has yielded a terracotta figure as well as the faunal remains of the horse. Reporting on the faunal remains from Surkotada, the renowned international authority on horse-bones, Sandor Bokonyi of Hungary, emphasized: "The occurrence of true horse (Equus Caballus L.) was evidenced by the enamel pattern of the upper and lower cheek and teeth and by the size and form of the incisors and phalanges (toe bones)."

Now lastly, the spoked wheel. Though the hot and humid climate of India does not let wooden specimens survive, there are enough terracotta models of spoked wheels, e.g. from Kalibangan, Rakhigarhi, Banawali, etc. Thus, all the objections against the Vedic=Harappan equation are baseless. The two are respectively the literary and material facets of the same civilization.

NS: Some proponents of the 'Aryan Invasion' or 'Aryan Migration' theory hold that the Harappans was a Dravidian-speaking people. What do you think of that?

Lal: According to the 'Aryan Invasion' thesis, the Invading Aryans drove away the supposed Dravidian-speaking Harappans to South India. If there was any truth in it, one would find settlements of Harappan refugees in South India, but there is not even a single Harappan or even Harappa-related settlement in any of the Dravidian-speaking States, be it Tamil Nadu, Andhra Pradesh, Karnataka or Kerala! Further, it is seen that even when new people occupy a land, the names of at least some places and rivers given by earlier people do continue. For example, in USA names of rivers like Missouri and Mississippi or of places like Chicago and Massachusetts, given by earlier inhabitants, do continue even after the European occupation. But there is no Dravidian river/place-name in the entire area once occupied by the Harappans, viz. from the Indus to upper reaches of the Yamuna. All told, therefore, there is no evidence whatsoever for holding that the Harappans was a Dravidian-speaking people.

NS: Some scholars have stated that Vedic Aryans migrated from India towards the West. Did some Vedic people really emigrate to the West?

Lal: The answer is in the affirmative and the evidence is as follows: Inscribed clay tablets discovered at Bogazkoy in Turkey record a treaty between a Mitanni king named Matiwaza and a Hittite king, Suppilulima. It is dated to 1380 BCE. In it the two kings invoke, as witnesses, the Vedic gods Indra, Mitra, Nasatya and Varuna. Commenting on this treaty, the renowned Indologist T. Burrow observes: "Aryans appear in Mitanni as the ruling dynasty, which means that they must have entered the country as conquerors." 'Conquerors from where?' may not one ask? At that point of time (1380 BCE) there was no other country in the world except India where these gods were worshipped. Thus, the Aryans must have gone from India.

This emigration from India is duly confirmed by what is recorded in the Baudhayana Srautasutra.

"Pranayuh pravavraja.Tasyaite Kuru-Panchalah Kasi-Videha ityetad Ayavam pravrajam Pratyan Amavasus * Tasyaite Gandharayas Parsvo Aratta ityetad Amavasavam."

The verb used in the first part is pravavraja. Thus, as per rules of grammar, the unstated verb in the second part * should also be 'pravavraja'. The correct translation of the second part would, therefore, be: "Amavasu migrated westwards. His (people) are the Gandhari, Parsu and Aratta."

Thus, the Baudhayana Srautasutra does in fact narrate the story of a section of the Vedic Aryans, namely the descendants of Amavasu, having migrated westwards, via Kandahar (Gandhara of the text) in

Afghanistan to Persia (Parsu) and Ararat (Aratta) in Armenia. From there they went to Turkey, where the Bogazkoy tablets of the 14th century BCE, as already stated, refer to the Vedic gods Indra, Mitra, Varuna and Nasatyas. Indeed, there is enough archaeological, epigraphic, and literary evidence from Iran, Iraq and Turkey, which duly establishes this westward migration of the Vedic people in the 2nd -3rd millennium BCE.

NS: There is a clear linguistic relationship between various languages in the Indo-European family. How is this explained if there was no invasion/migration of the Aryans into India?

Lal: No doubt similarity of language between any two areas does envisage a movement of some people from one to the other. But why must it be presumed that in the case under consideration, it must necessarily be from west to east? A movement of people from east to west would also lead to the same result? Isn't it? There is plenty of archaeological evidence that the Harappans, who were none other than the Vedic people (as I mentioned before), spread outside India into Afghanistan, Central Asia, Iran, and Iraq. In Afghanistan, there was a full-fledged settlement of the Harappans, at Shortughai. In Central Asia, sites like Namazga Tepe have yielded a great deal of Harappan material. At the southern end of the Persian Gulf, there was a colony of the Harappans in Oman. In Bahrain a seal bearing Harappan script and the Indian national bird, the peacock, stand as indisputable testimony to the presence of the Harappans in that island. In fact, king Sargon of Akkad hailed Harappan boats berthed in the quay of his capital. All these movements of the Harappans are assignable the 3rd millennium BCE.

In answer to the previous question, I had mentioned that there was an unquestionable presence of the Vedic people in the region now known as Turkey, in the second millennium BCE. From Turkey to Greece it is a stone-throw distance and from there Italy is just next door. The entire foregoing evidence would squarely explain the similarity between Sanskrit, Greek, and Latin. For this, one need not conjure up an 'Aryan Invasion' of India!

NS: It has been held by some scholars that the Harappan Civilization became extinct, leaving no vestiges behind. How far is this true?

Lal: Because of various reasons, such as break up in external trade, drastic climatic changes, the drying up of the Sarasvati and so on, the Harappan urbanization had a major setback: cities gradually vanished, but villages continued. There was no extinction of the people who carried on their day-to-day life, though in a humble way than before. Thus, we find many of the Harappan traits in vogue even today. For example, the application by married Hindu women of vermilion (sindūra) in the partition line of the hair on the head, the wearing of multiple bangles on the arms and of pāyala around the ankles; practice of yogic exercises; worshipping Lord Shiva, even in the form of liṅga-cum-yoni; performing rituals using fire-altars, using sacred symbols like the svastika; and so on. Indeed, be not surprised if I told you that the way you greet each other with namaste goes back to the Harappan times. Above all, even some of the folk tales, like those of 'A Thirsty Crow' or 'The Cunning Fox', which grandmothers narrate to the children while putting them to sleep originated in the Harappan times. Tradition dies hard![1768]

There have been accusations that some Western Indologists, instead of accepting and adapting to new information, fraudulently began adding their unsubstantiated suppositions to the work of US geneticists; if this is so, then it must be ascertained how thoroughly they've committed these fraudulent activities as that would mean that they lied to the US scientific community by arguing their make-believe assumptions held the same standing as empirical facts.[1769] The archeological investigations by Indian archaeologists were never added to *The Oxford Handbook of Indian Philosophy* and multiple Western Indologists display no awareness

---

96. [1768] Sridhar, Nithin. "Vedic and Harappan Are Respectively Literary and Material Facets of Same Civilization: B. B. Lal." *NewsGram*, 2 Dec. 2015, www.newsgram.com/vedic-and-harappan-are-respectively-literary-and-material-facets-of-same-civilization-b-b-lal
97. [1769] Talageri, Shrikant, et al. "Panel Discussion on the Current State of Aryan Theories." Moderated by Rajiv Malhotra, *YouTube*, Swadeshi Indology, 24 Mar. 2018, www.youtube.com/watch?v=KmeVR8sqSd4.

of them. Controversy over so-called genetics in the male line of Indian genealogy arose to argue in defense of the debunked Aryan Race Theory and it became a topic of further controversy within the country of India until finally the study's much anticipated conclusions were released. On *Outline.com*, in the article "*Harrapan Site of Rakhigarhi: DNA study finds no Central Asian trace, junks Aryan invasion theory*" by journalist Anubhuti Vishnoi in which she concisely details as follows:

> The much-awaited DNA study of the skeletal remains found at the Harappan site of Rakhigarhi, Haryana, shows no Central Asian trace, indicating the Aryan invasion theory was flawed and Vedic evolution was through indigenous people.
>
> The lead researchers of this soon-tobe published study — Vasant Shinde and Neeraj Rai — told ET that this establishes the knowledge ecosystem in the Vedic era was guided by "fully indigenous" people with limited "external contact".
>
> "The Rakhigarhi human DNA clearly shows a predominant local element — the mitochondrial DNA is very strong in it. There is some minor foreign element which shows some mixing up with a foreign population, but the DNA is clearly local," Shinde told ET. He went on to add: "This indicates quite clearly, through archeological data, that the Vedic era that followed was a fully indigenous period with some external contact."
>
> According to Shinde's findings, the manner of burial is quite similar to the early Vedic period, also known as the Rigvedic Era. The pottery, the brick type used for construction and the general 'good health' of the people ascertained through the skeletal remains in Rakhigarhi, he said, pointed to a well-developed knowledge system that evolved further into the Vedic era. The study has, in fact, noted that some burial rituals observed in the Rakhigarhi necropolis prevail even now in some communities, showing a remarkable continuity over thousands of years.
>
> Shinde, who is the vice-chancellor of the Deccan College, Pune, was the lead archaeologist in the study while Rai, who is the head of the ancient DNA laboratory at Lucknow's Birbal Sahni Institute of Palaeosciences, did the DNA study.
>
> **MINOR TRACES OF IRANIAN STRAINS**
> According to Rai, the evidence points to a predominantly indigenous culture that voluntarily spread across other areas, not displaced or overrun by an Aryan invasion. "The condition of the human skeletons, the burial...all show absence of palaeo-pathology symptoms which could indicate ailments due to lack of medical care. The persons here were healthy; denture morphology showed teeth free of any infection; bones are healthy, as is the cranium," Rai told ET.
>
> He also discounted the notion of any violent conflict. "There are no cuts and marks which would be associated with a population subjected to warfare. All this indicates that the people were receiving well-developed healthcare and had full-fledged knowledge systems." The excavations in Rigvedic phase, he said, corroborate this. "This points to greater continuity rather than to a new Aryan race descending and bringing superior knowledge systems to the region," Rai said.
>
> The Rakhigarhi study, he said, while showing absence of any Central Asian/Steppe element in the genetic make-up of the Harappan people, does indicate minor traces of Iranian strains which may point to contact, not invasion.
>
> The Aryan invasion theory holds forth that a set of migrants came from Central Asia armed with superior knowledge and arms and invaded the existing settlements to establish a more sophisticated civilisation in India and pushed the original inhabitants down south. Rakhigarhi is one of the biggest Harappan civilisation sites spread across 300 hectares in Hisar, Haryana. It's estimated to be 6,000 years old and was part of the mature phase of the Harappan period.
>
> Rai disclosed that 148 independent skeletal elements from Rakhigarhi were screened for the presence of DNA molecules at the Centre for Cellular and Molecular Biology in Hyderabad. Of the 148 skeletal remains, only two samples yielded any relevant DNA material.

Meanwhile, hectic last-minute efforts are on to get additional genetic details of the DNA material. One of the DNA samples recently faced contamination in a Seoul laboratory and efforts are on to segregate it. Samples were sent to laboratories in Seoul and Harvard for establishing accuracy. The contamination, Rai said, is unlikely to have any major bearing on the study's primary findings.[1770]

Western Academia versus Western Indology

I don't know to what extent this critique will even be useful or effective. I had wanted cogent and intellectual critiques of Hinduism, so I had naturally looked more into Western Indology in the hopes of gaining an outsider view of my own religious background. A year ago, I had a negative disposition of the BJP because I had trusted that the Western mainstream media was reporting honestly about the situation in India. Although they may detest me for writing this, Ex-Muslims of North America's critiques on Islam is what made me re-evaluate everything that I had learned and implicitly trusted as reliable, particularly Muhammad Syed's criticism of the Islamic slave trade being far worse in terms of impact on the lives of African civilians than the Atlantic slave trade (both were equally reprehensible in terms of human rights) and Sarah Haider's arguments about Islam's propensity for cultural genocide.[1771][1772] Arguments from individuals like Koenraad Elst, which I had believed to be insane and hateful due to mainstream Western Indologists portrayal of his work, turned out to be true once I internalized the Ex-MNA critiques and began to factually re-evaluate everything. What horrified me the most was that the first time I had learned of the genocide of India by Islam, it had been from a far-right British political organization whose stated goal was ethnocentrism in Great Britain. I had naturally believed that these were abhorrent lies about the history of Islam, or perhaps exaggerated details about the historical record which ignored whatever it was that Hindus did at the very least. I anonymously asked Indians from India online and they had never heard of such massacres; I had believed that surely they would have heard of such events if they were so detrimental and important in understanding India's history. Yet, a Sikh website also shared similar info and cited similar historians and journalists; I quickly assumed that it was all some harebrained conspiracy theory because why did Western Indology seem so ignorant of such tragic events? Surely, they've looked over this information? I had read Andrew J. Nicholson's *Unifying Hinduism* and at no point does he seem aware of this history, nor does anyone else in Western Indology that he cites.[1773] He even cited Romila Thapar who argues that Muslims and Hindus weren't aware of any distinction in period of Islam's entrance

---

98. [1770] VISHNOI, ANUBHUTI. "Read & Annotate without Distractions." *Outline*, The Economic Times, outline.com/8eLEVN.
99. [1771] Tessier, Stephanie, and Muhammad Syed. "Islam: Pull and Peril." *YouTube*, Ex-Muslims of North America, 22 Apr. 2018, www.youtube.com/watch?v=jt1rWgap41g.
100. [1772] Haider, Sarah, and Gad Saad. "Islam's ERASURE of Distinct Cultures & Histories - Sarah Haider (with Gad Saad)." *YouTube*, Gravitahn, 15 Feb. 2017, www.youtube.com/watch?v=XrvVqi5dOxk.
101. [1773] Nicholson, Andrew J. Chapter 10: Hindu Unity And The Non-Hindu Other (4806-5293). *Unifying Hinduism: Philosophy and Identity in Indian Intellectual History (South Asia Across the Disciplines)*. Columbia University Press, 2010.

into India.[1774] That was why I had thought it was either an exaggeration or lies. After listening to Ex-MNA, I had looked through several Islamic sources online and began to realize the horrible truth when I reflected on what I thought I knew was credible information from Western Indology and compared it to the internal beliefs of Islamic teachings. To my personal horror, Elst's claim about approximately 80 million deaths seemed to gain significant ground when reading Islam's own history before it entered India. Several months worth of research on Hinduism from Western Indology turned out to be complete garbage after I looked at the supposed far-right sources and picked the most reliable one to read; Will Durant's *The Story of Civilization: Our Oriental Heritage*. Durant had visited India to conduct thorough research, he had briefly paused to write *The Case For India* in defense of Indian liberty against British imperialism after being aghast at the mass starvation under British policies, and Durant largely cites Muslim historians when copiously detailing the horrific bloodbath that Islamic conquests caused in India upon practitioners of Sanatana Dharma. Will Durant's work has largely stood the test of time and the only portion he seems to be wrong about regarding India would be the Indo-Aryan conquest; in that specific chapter, he mainly focuses on the amazing technological developments and he was working with what was believed to be reliable information. Durant focuses on accuracy and the fact the Indo-Aryan invasion has proven to be a myth doesn't discount his other historical writings which are more on point. Dismissing his entire work because one portion, during a time when it seemed to be the most reliable information, would be a fallacy of composition; the fallacy essentially means that because something is true for one component of a particular thing then it must be true for all of it. He even adds a caveat before the chapters on India's history in his book about specific dates in Indian time periods before the 1600s being speculation based on the best information available, but the events themselves did happen from what can be gleaned from the sources. Unlike contemporary Christian missionaries in India who shout about how Hindus are all devil worshippers while proselytizing and goading impoverished people into forced conversions, Will Durant seems to have cared out of genuine concern for his fellow human beings when he was in India and in my personal opinion, his return to Catholicism in his later years is incidental to his legacy. I think his work largely withstood the test of time because he was aiming for accuracy to the best of his abilities when he published *Our Oriental Heritage* in 1935.

The information in Will Durant's book was wholly available to Western Indology for several decades, but it seems that none of them are aware of it since none of them mention the Islamic conquests. Moreover, the theses of the Western Indologists that I looked into seem to be hasty generalizations; a hasty generalization is a rushed conclusion without looking at all the factors. Larson isn't qualified to make his argument as he has never studied Political Science, Psychology, or Sociology. Romila Thapar's conclusion about supposed pastoral migration of Indo-Aryans contradicts the facts and her arguments about Muslims and Hindus

---

102.[1774] Nicholson, Andrew J. Chapter 10: Hindu Unity And The Non-Hindu Other (4806-5293). *Unifying Hinduism: Philosophy and Identity in Indian Intellectual History (South Asia Across the Disciplines)*. Columbia University Press, 2010.

not being aware of each other contradict both the historical record and psychological studies of human behavior regarding how different social groups interact upon contact.[1775][1776] Neither Sheldon Pollock nor Andrew J. Nicholson show any awareness of the brutal massacres by Islamic invaders in the writings of theirs that I've read.[1777][1778] Some readers may reasonably conclude that this is due to ignorance of Islam and a result of special privilege being granted to Islam in Western academia, but there's a more pernicious aspect to all of this when *The Oxford Handbook of Indian Philosophy* is also added into this issue for evaluation. The supposed "research" of Western Indology seems to be categorically wrong; at no point is any shred of information that they're arguing actually the truth because they don't base it upon empirical evidence from what I've read. As two examples, Justin E. H. Smith shows no knowledge that the Adivasi term was coined in the 1930s and doesn't refer to any original inhabitants of India.[1779] Romila Thapar claimed that the term Hindu was formed in the 14th Century CE according to Nicholson's book and shows no knowledge of the fact that Hindu was derived from an Old Persian inscription on Darius The Great I's grave made in 490 BCE which describes the people of India as the "Hindush" when *Hidush* is translated into another language since the n is silent.[1780] These are basic elements of information that Western Indology has uniformly failed in acknowledging throughout the West. The problem runs deeper still; if they weren't aware of these basic facts, then they are incompetent, but if they were aware yet never posed any response with factual evidence to back them up to counter these arguments, then they're deliberately lying and distorting history for whatever reasons they have. Regardless of either scenario, to the best of my knowledge with the information given to me, Western Indology is proving to be an anti-intellectual, insular community that is thoroughly destroying the credibility of Western academia from within and it remains unchallenged. Any opposing view is seen as beneath them or it is argued to be conspiratorial without evidence despite the fact that all they have to show is hermeneutics, which is just their own personal views which they're trying to push into the scientific domain to claim more credibility than what they actually have to offer. For my part, I fear that regardless of what I've written here, I'll just be lumped as a hateful bigot or a conspiracy theorist and be forced to watch as Western academia - a community that I both admire and of which I am a proud product of - becomes beleaguered

---

103. [1775] Durant, Will. Chapter XVI: From Alexander to Aurangzeb: VI. The Moslem Conquest (Pgs. 10447-10448). *Our Oriental Heritage: Being a History of Civilization in Egypt and the Near East to the Death of Alexander, and in India, China and Japan from the Beginning to Our Own Day*. Simon and Schuster, 1935.
104. [1776] Ispas, Alexa. *Psychology and politics: a social identity perspective*. Psychology Press, 2014.
105. [1777] Nicholson, Andrew J. Chapter 10: Hindu Unity And The Non-Hindu Other (4806-5293). *Unifying Hinduism: Philosophy and Identity in Indian Intellectual History (South Asia Across the Disciplines)*. Columbia University Press, 2010.
106. [1778] Pollock, Sheldon. "Is There an Indian Intellectual History? Introduction to ''Theory and Method in Indian Intellectual History.'''" *Http://Www.columbia.edu*, Columbia University, www.columbia.edu/cu/mesaas/faculty/directory/pollock_pub/indian_intellectual_history.pdf.
107. [1779] Kapstein, Matthew T., et al. Chapter 3: Philosophy as a Distinct Cultural Practice: The Transregional Context by Justin E.H. Smith (Pg. 56). *The Oxford Handbook of Indian Philosophy*. Edited by Jonardon Ganeri, Oxford University Press, 2018.
108. [1780] "Hindush." *Wikipedia*, Wikimedia Foundation, 24 Mar. 2019, en.wikipedia.org/wiki/Hindush.

with these falsehoods while all I can do is watch from afar. At the very least, the experience of this research was what slowly began my appreciation for Free Speech and Free Inquiry after my early life throughout grade school and bearing witness to the US Federal government's actions had almost thoroughly destroyed my confidence in the US Constitution.

Chapter 28: Casteism versus Truthseeking

If there was historically a theological conflict ingrained within Sanatana Dharma comparable to Catholic-Protestant, Sunni-Shia, Reform-Conservative/Ultra Orthodox divides within the major branching denominations of the Abrahamic religion into their large subgroups; it would be Casteism versus Truthseeking and the history that has survived seems to largely indicate such a theological divide. However, I'd like to be clear by pointing out that practitioners don't consider each other members of different religions and that there doesn't seem to be much in the case of historic violence or oppression on this basis unlike with Caste itself. Any social conflict that undoubtedly occurred seems to always have been resolved either through religious texts or philosophical disputation with little historical violence. I don't want to suggest or downplay the misogynistic aspects or to implicitly suggest that the horrors of Casteism weren't harmful elements or that they somehow have no relation to Sanatana Dharma. Despite what some of you may think of me for what I wrote in the previous chapter, I felt that I had to write it because it honestly seems to me like Western Indologists are trying to ignore the history of Islam's genocide of India and they seem to be trying to dehumanize the Dalits of India in a subtle way. To argue that Hinduism was never a religion until modern times means that nobody is responsible for the dehumanization of the Dalits throughout India's history; to argue India was never a nation equivalent to Europe until recently may only further cement that claim. Even if you hate Hinduism, you must surely see the logical contradiction of first arguing that Hinduism was never a religion and then arguing that Hinduism oppressed Dalits for thousands of years.[1781] That is a self-evident contradiction in logic, especially in the Western domain of philosophical inquiry because their argument about Hinduism and Caste violates the Law of non-contradiction. These Western Indologists clearly don't seem to understand Western philosophy, except superficially from what I've read into their arguments. Moreover, they don't seem to have any coherent arguments about either Western or Eastern philosophy at all. Western Indologists only seem to be making the Casteism of Hinduism stronger because their arguments honestly make no logical sense at all. I am not trying to dehumanize Dalits and I am not denying the patriarchal aspects that marginalized women throughout Hinduism's history, but what I am saying is that Western Indology is not being honest, they aren't making any coherent arguments when examined with more scrutiny, and they clearly aren't allies in the efforts to decrease misogyny and Casteism throughout India because their arguments seem to just be lies that only embolden the Brahaminical aspects of Hinduism. How can Hinduism's misogynistic or Casteist power structures exist, if Hinduism never existed until modern times?[1782] How can they argue that Hinduism has no internal theological underpinning, but then argue that Casteism is the fault of Hinduism?[1783] These are fundamental contradictions

---

1. [1781] "Inconsistency." *Https://Www.logicallyfallacious.com*, www.logicallyfallacious.com/tools/lp/Bo/LogicalFallacies/112/Inconsistency.
2. [1782] "Inconsistency." *Https://Www.logicallyfallacious.com*, www.logicallyfallacious.com/tools/lp/Bo/LogicalFallacies/112/Inconsistency.
3. [1783] "Inconsistency." *Https://Www.logicallyfallacious.com*,

that take little effort to dismiss. Western Indologists aren't intellectually honest, they're echo-chambers that use the respect afforded from the beneficial and rigorous aspects that exist outside their field of study in Western academia to spew falsehoods and distortions of history; dishonesty doesn't benefit anyone and it will eventually bring harm by not challenging them. I learned that the hard way by thinking that speaking out was a negative action and then living with the horrible ramifications.

    That being said, I can't discount the possibility of motivated reasoning for what I write. I'm a fallible human being, so I can't be sure to what extent that I'm being biased in favor of a religion that I grew-up with and still identify with on a cultural level. If it helps, this self-identification is pretty fragile as I find the Casteism and sexism to be incredibly abhorrent and if they can't reform then I would only be able to view it as just a more distant cultural background of mine. Moreover, with all topics related to religion, life has taught me to expect egregious human stupidity as the only response to any mild criticism and so I have chosen to simply be more blunt and outspoken as a more honest approach. You can slander me all you like for such an approach, but don't doubt that I speak from a place of honest inquiry and compassion in service of human rights for all. If there should be accusations that I'm somehow affiliated with a different religion than Sanatana Dharma, despite copiously detailing my criticisms of each of the Abrahamic religions and affirming that Sanatana Dharma (Hinduism, Buddhism, Jainism, and Sikhism) are all one religion but with multiple denominations based upon interpreting our Oneness, then I'd like to firmly state that such accusations are false. Some may point to me joining a Christian club in college, but it was my understanding that Hinduism has nothing against exploring concepts or getting a better understanding unlike religions that impose blasphemy, which is just an imposition of thought crimes. Indeed, this remains a truism of Sanatana Dharma which is referred to as *Purva paksha*; which means gaining a deep insight into an opposing view before criticizing it.[1784] Joining that Christian club helped me know what to look for to better write my critiques in the section on Christianity. That was the motivation and purpose of doing it, so I don't see why that isn't consistent with *Purva Paksha*. I like exploring, evaluating, and critiquing theological concepts without having to listen to others cry foul about how my perspective and criticisms are offensive to their personal feelings. It is something that always struck my curiosity since late middle-school to early high school and was only broadened further when listening to the New Atheist critiques of such concepts in live debates. For all those reasons, and perhaps similar to my fellow American the late and great Christopher Hitchens before me, it seems the United States is the only country where I would have the right to simply exist as even Canada and European countries impose blasphemy laws by making people pay fines on the grounds of so-called human rights being violated when criticizing a religion.

---

    www.logicallyfallacious.com/tools/lp/Bo/LogicalFallacies/112/Inconsistency.
4.   [1784] Malhotra, Rajiv. Purva Paksha: Reversing The Gaze (835-929). *Being Different: an Indian Challenge to Western Universalism*. HarperCollins Publishers India, 2018.

I've probably done more research on my own religion to critique it than any other, but it probably isn't reflected because I had learned that so much of what I had read from Western Indology was patently false and therefore unusable. I feel irritated for having ever taken Western Indology seriously and even on this point, I wonder if I'm just inviting hostility for speaking honestly about how utterly vacuous Western Indology is when I closely examined it. In addition, the other source I relied upon, Eknath Easwaran's translations, had omitted crucial aspects that distorted the failings of the Upanishads and Bhagavad Gita. I wonder if I can even do this chapter the justice that it deserves because I had to discard so much that I had assumed was true because of the association with Western academia, but which turned out to be blatantly false information and even the other source was a failure in certain respects. In the end, I think this'll just be assumed to be lies by others or a point of cuddling my own religious background from real scrutiny, even though I consider Buddhism to be part of my religion but as a different denomination. I'll try to do this chapter the justice it deserves, but if it seems to reflect a bias or weak arguments on my part, then I sincerely apologize. For those who are curious of just what someone should search for to gain the most accurate information about Sanatana Dharma, then I would highly recommend the *Carvaka Podcast* by *Kushal Mehra* as he seems to be the most informed and astute person when it comes to the topic of Sanatana Dharma. He self-identifies as a Dharmic Skeptic and many of his livestream videos are about explaining the different schools of Hindu thought and he's made helpful book recommendations in his Youtube livestreams to assist others to gain accurate knowledge about Sanatana Dharma. He is the most informed and articulate person on these topics from what I've observed. I would have added Rajiv Malhotra too, but certain criticisms have been raised about him trying to re-contextualize the Dharmic tradition into more Abrahamic terms such as vilifying atheism within Sanatana Dharma which I can't agree with, if such accusations are true. I don't know what to think of the organization that he's part of, the Srijan Foundation, and its Youtube channel, SrijanTalks. I'll withhold any firm opinion until learning more about it as I'm skeptical about their comparison of the Indian Constitution and the US Constitution. Since 2014, the US has been classified as an oligarchy and not a democratic form of government because of how the US government operates according to a Princeton research study.[1785] While there has been criticism of that study, the increasing concern for the longevity of democratic institutions and freedoms throughout US intelligentsia seem to both vindicate the study and delve into deeper failings with US democratic institutions.[1786] I'll endeavor to give a general summary of my opinion the US government based on my own fallible personal views in the conclusion of this book and I hope people of the Republic of India who desire to change the Indian Constitution take notice.

A Brief Overview of India's Religious History

---

5. [1785] "Study: US Is an Oligarchy, Not a Democracy." *BBC News*, BBC, 17 Apr. 2014, www.bbc.com/news/blogs-echochambers-27074746.
6. [1786] Rose, Gideon. "What Happened to the American Century?" *Foreign Affairs*, 30 July 2019, www.foreignaffairs.com/articles/2019-06-11/what-happened-american-century.

I believe this portion is necessary simply because there seems to be so much disinformation about India's religious and ethnic history. However, I want to make it completely clear that I am not a historian, I don't claim to be a historian, and that this is simply my own layperson attempt at making a brief overview of over 3000 years of Indian history. It'll likely have errors, but I'll try my best with what I find to be credible information. Much of the timeframe for events is unfortunately speculation because of both the lack of survived texts as a result of the materials used in ancient India being more fragile than what ancient China had and possibly the Islamic invasions committing cultural genocide like in almost every other country that Islam currently holds a majority population within. As is probably clear from the prior chapter, I don't find Western Indology credible and I have no reason to trust any historical accounts that they give, especially if it is predicated upon the farcical narrative of a 1200 BCE invasion that has no evidence of being true from what I've researched. Credible archaeological evidence by Indian archaeologists were available to Western Indology departments since 2015 and yet they still chose to push a perpetual falsehood in their so-called academic books in 2017 and reprinted that same falsehood in 2018. Such a checkered history, along with everything else mentioned in the previous chapter, leads me to doubt their veracity and their commitment to evidence-based methods of research. In my personal view, Western Indology as a whole can't be deemed as a credible academic discipline at all. I'll mainly rely upon Will Durant's work of *The Story of Civilization: Our Oriental Heritage* for this portion because Durant shows an honest effort for accuracy. I must point out that he mentions that the dates before 1600 AD are uncertain and dates before 329 B.C. are speculative in a citation before giving the chronology.[1787] While I would have liked to use Western Indology's information since I had hoped it would be more up to date, it is clear that Western Indology is too unreliable and there is no reason for any serious researcher to trust anything that they say or write since their failures on basic information runs deeply throughout different Western countries where the so-called academic discipline of Western Indology is conducted. All it has to offer is overglorified make-believe with almost no fact-based evidence whatsoever. As such, I'll use Will Durant exclusively for this section since he seems to remain the only trustworthy source of information that I've found in my own research on this topic. I must also emphasize that as a layperson, there'll hopefully be better and credible historians in the future and not those so-called historians of Western Indology like Romila Thapar who propagate falsehoods and don't assess information using fact-based research as seems to be the case with the purported 1200 BCE invasion that has no evidence of happening to claims of pastoral migrations that have no evidence to support her claims.

As cited in the previous chapter, the Rigveda seems to have been formed approximately before 2000 BCE, possibly even in the 3000 BCE era since the specific date can't be ascertained as of yet and may not ever be. From the best available evidence, the period of 2000

---

7. [1787] Durant, Will. "Chronological Table Of Indian History (Pg. 9109). *Our Oriental Heritage: Being a History of Civilization in Egypt and the Near East to the Death of Alexander, and in India, China and Japan from the Beginning to Our Own Day.* Simon and Schuster, 1935.

BCE all the way to the 800 BCE time period largely seemed to be composed of what the most popular and superficial notions of modern Hinduism continue to be for most people across the world. Beliefs in polytheistic superstitions to make snap judgments in order to explain various weather patterns, natural disasters, famines, diseases, and forms of ritualized sacrifices including human sacrifices due to lack of understanding of cause and effect for why such disastrous events occurred.[1788] Ridiculous rituals in order to supposedly ward off demons, spirits, and disaster under the control of the Brahmins of the Caste system through beliefs in a cosmic version of Karma and Samsara (reincarnation/rebirth).[1789] During this time period there was the typical histories of polygamy with one husband and two wives or more for those highly valued in society, misogyny existed since women and children were considered a man's property that could be thrown out whenever he wanted, and there were nonsensical rituals affirming the Caste system as the moral order of the world that they thought that they knew.[1790] This theological denomination of Hinduism has come to be known as the tradition of Brahminism as the priestly class, the Brahmins, held the reins of power over religious tradition while the Kshatriyas (the social class that rules as Princes/Kings) ruled the domain through either joint control with other Kshatriyas or through absolute monarchy depending on the relative power and stability of their domain.[1791] Brahmins held religious control throughout societies, but Kshatriyas eventually grew rebellious and began their own counterculture movements to reform the Vedic traditions in order to wrest control from the Brahmins.[1792] These were often done by undergoing their own spiritual journeys, gaining followers for their philosophical views, and engaging in philosophical disputations with others over their views.[1793] These movements starting from 800 BCE and ending approximately around 500 BCE came to be known as the Sramana movements; Sramana has a general meaning of "one

---

8. [1788] Durant, Will. Chapter XIV: The Foundations of India: V. The Religion of the Vedas (9307-9384). *Our Oriental Heritage: Being a History of Civilization in Egypt and the Near East to the Death of Alexander, and in India, China and Japan from the Beginning to Our Own Day*. Simon and Schuster, 1935.
9. [1789] Durant, Will. Chapter XIV: The Foundations of India: V. The Religion of the Vedas (9307-9384). *Our Oriental Heritage: Being a History of Civilization in Egypt and the Near East to the Death of Alexander, and in India, China and Japan from the Beginning to Our Own Day*. Simon and Schuster, 1935.
10. [1790] Durant, Will. Chapter XIV: The Foundations of India: IV. Indo-Aryan Society (9254-9307). *Our Oriental Heritage: Being a History of Civilization in Egypt and the Near East to the Death of Alexander, and in India, China and Japan from the Beginning to Our Own Day*. Simon and Schuster, 1935.
11. [1791] Durant, Will. Chapter XIV: The Foundations of India: V. The Religion of the Vedas (9307-9384). *Our Oriental Heritage: Being a History of Civilization in Egypt and the Near East to the Death of Alexander, and in India, China and Japan from the Beginning to Our Own Day*. Simon and Schuster, 1935.
12. [1792] Durant, Will. Chapter XIV: The Foundations of India: V. The Religion of the Vedas (9307-9384). *Our Oriental Heritage: Being a History of Civilization in Egypt and the Near East to the Death of Alexander, and in India, China and Japan from the Beginning to Our Own Day*. Simon and Schuster, 1935.
13. [1793] Durant, Will. Chapter XIV: The Foundations of India: VII. The Philosophy of the Upanishads (9463 - 9469). *Our Oriental Heritage: Being a History of Civilization in Egypt and the Near East to the Death of Alexander, and in India, China and Japan from the Beginning to Our Own Day*. Simon and Schuster, 1935.

who toils, labors, or exerts themselves for a higher purpose" in terms of translation.[1794] These counterculture movements don't show evidence of violence; they don't seem to be similar to Protestant-Catholic or Sunni-Shia bloodbaths. Most were individuals espousing new philosophical outlooks about the Vedic traditions and attempting to reform it and it was likely an attempt at diminishing the power of the Brahmins and not so much about genuinely reforming the Caste system from the best available evidence.[1795] They went on journeys across India, disputed philosophy and theology, and gained converts to their cause.[1796][1797] The Sramana movements likely began the theological concept of what modern Hindus refer to as *Truthseeking* within the theology of Hinduism; the belief that followers of Sanatana Dharma are all one, but have their own personal opinion on what that truth is as the grounding of the theology. Moreover, the earlier Sramana movements were different in intention and overall impact from the latter and it might be better to demarcate them on that basis since they differed in results. The theological and philosophical disputations that created major changes for Hinduism also impacted the religion differently. I would argue that the earlier movements should be classified as the Upanishadic movements in which the theistic branches of Hinduism became what it is today. The collection of various theological critiques and arguments essentially argued for a pantheistic deity; their textual teachings also varied considerably in terms of the treatment of women, such as the Brihadarankya Upanishads teachings having some of the most deplorably violent behavior against women while the Chandogya Upanishads treated women equally to men in philosophical disputations. The Upanishads came to be known as the end of the Vedas and was eventually subsumed into the previously polytheistic Vedic tradition of the Brahmins.[1798] I would argue that this began what is the theistic branch of modern Hinduism today, Hinduism and concepts like Atman and Brahman are an emphasis on pantheism. The theological underpinning of all practitioners of Sanatana Dharma being one but with their own subjective interpretations on that Oneness, the Truthseeking aspect to explore to one's own contentment of finding a meaning in a higher power, and the idea of Brahman being both part of our inner selves (Atman) and the spiritual reality of the world around us was firmly established as part of the Vedic traditions once the Brahmin priests affirmed the Upanishads as

---

14. [1794] "Śramaṇa." *Wikipedia*, Wikimedia Foundation, 18 July 2019, en.wikipedia.org/wiki/Śramaṇa.
15. [1795] Durant, Will. Chapter XIV: The Foundations of India: VII. The Philosophy of the Upanishads (9463 - 9469). *Our Oriental Heritage: Being a History of Civilization in Egypt and the Near East to the Death of Alexander, and in India, China and Japan from the Beginning to Our Own Day*. Simon and Schuster, 1935.
16. [1796] Durant, Will. Chapter XIV: The Foundations of India: VII. The Philosophy of the Upanishads (9463 - 9469). *Our Oriental Heritage: Being a History of Civilization in Egypt and the Near East to the Death of Alexander, and in India, China and Japan from the Beginning to Our Own Day*. Simon and Schuster, 1935.
17. [1797] Durant, Will. Chapter XV: The Buddha (9581 - 10035). *Our Oriental Heritage: Being a History of Civilization in Egypt and the Near East to the Death of Alexander, and in India, China and Japan from the Beginning to Our Own Day*. Simon and Schuster, 1935.
18. [1798] Durant, Will. Chapter XIV: The Foundations of India: VII. The Philosophy of the Upanishads (9463 - 9469). *Our Oriental Heritage: Being a History of Civilization in Egypt and the Near East to the Death of Alexander, and in India, China and Japan from the Beginning to Our Own Day*. Simon and Schuster, 1935.

the end of the Vedas.[1799][1800] Obviously, it didn't end there. A new counterculture aim of the Sramana movements began and the clues were in the textual arguments critical of religious dogma in the Upanishads themselves.[1801][1802]

The earlier Upanishadic movement had been subsumed and hadn't changed the power dynamics of the Brahmin priests or the abhorrent Caste system that they affirmed which maintained ancient Vedic societies through what was quite clearly an institution of slavery of the Dalit Caste. Thus, began a portion of the Sramana movements that has been downplayed and mostly de-emphasized by Hindus of the 1800s and some of the modern Hindus of today who are ashamed of it due to Abrahamic criticism and due to the later popularity of Buddhism and Jainism which eventually overcame this movement to become more widely renown throughout the world. It is quite the tragedy, because this middle period of the Sramana movements is my favorite social movement in all of the ancient history that I've researched thus far. Sometime after the Upanishads were adapted as the last of the Vedas and presumably before the Buddha was born or became an adult, the Sramana movements were overcome by Kshatriya mendicants who advocated for a thoroughgoing atheism.[1803] Movements of rationalism, skeptical inquiry, even a movement arguing in favor of materialism being regarded more highly than spirituality, and argumentations about cause-and-effect on the veracity of truth claims to dismiss superstitious claims about ritual sacrifices swept throughout northern India like a tidal wave that redefined just how open Hinduism remains and formed yet another denomination which became the *atheistic* branch of Hinduism.[1804] Truthseeking and philosophical inquiry in favor of Hindu Pantheism eventually gave rise to movement of skepticism and the first recorded atheists in human history, this may have been even earlier than the Ancient Greek playwright Diagoras of Melos and unlike Ancient Greece, the reception that these mostly ascetic atheists brought was overwhelmingly positive to their general audiences.[1805]

---

19. [1799] Eknath, Easwaran, translator. *The Upanishads*. Nilgiri Press, 2007.
20. [1800] Durant, Will. Chapter XIV: The Foundations of India: VII. The Philosophy of the Upanishads (9463 - 9469). *Our Oriental Heritage: Being a History of Civilization in Egypt and the Near East to the Death of Alexander, and in India, China and Japan from the Beginning to Our Own Day*. Simon and Schuster, 1935.
21. [1801] Eknath, Easwaran, translator. *The Upanishads*. Nilgiri Press, 2007.
22. [1802] Durant, Will. Chapter XV: The Buddha (9581 - 10035). *Our Oriental Heritage: Being a History of Civilization in Egypt and the Near East to the Death of Alexander, and in India, China and Japan from the Beginning to Our Own Day*. Simon and Schuster, 1935.
23. [1803] Durant, Will. Chapter XV: The Buddha: I. The Heretics (9581 - 9656). *Our Oriental Heritage: Being a History of Civilization in Egypt and the Near East to the Death of Alexander, and in India, China and Japan from the Beginning to Our Own Day*. Simon and Schuster, 1935.
24. [1804] Durant, Will. Chapter XV: The Buddha: I. The Heretics (9581 - 9656). *Our Oriental Heritage: Being a History of Civilization in Egypt and the Near East to the Death of Alexander, and in India, China and Japan from the Beginning to Our Own Day*. Simon and Schuster, 1935.
25. [1805] Durant, Will. Chapter XV: The Buddha: I. The Heretics (9581 - 9656). *Our Oriental Heritage: Being a History of Civilization in Egypt and the Near East to the Death of Alexander, and in India, China and Japan from the Beginning to Our Own Day*. Simon and Schuster, 1935.

As I'm sure that people will doubt this completely, some readers may think I'm deluding myself that ancient people known for superstitions could have possibly produced skeptics who challenged religious orthodoxy through an avid call for atheism, and possibly even wrongfully argue that atheism and agnosticism have no place in Sanatana Dharma, I find it best to share Will Durant's research and explanation of the middle portion of the Sramana movements in a pre-emptive response to such possible accusations. Will Durant paints a picture of the culture within ancient India that the Buddha likely grew up in. From Will Durant's *The Story of Civilization: Our Oriental Heritage*:

> "Indeed, as scholarship unearths some of the less respectable figures in Indian philosophy before Buddha, a picture takes form in which, along with saints meditating on Brahman, we find a variety of persons who despised all priests, doubted all gods, and bore without trepidation the name of Nastiks, No-sayers, Nihilists. Sangaya, the agnostic, would neither admit nor deny life after death; he questioned the possibility of knowledge, and limited philosophy to the pursuit of peace. Purana Kashyapa refused to accept moral distinctions, and taught that the soul is a passive slave to chance. Maskarin Gosala held that fate determines everything, regardless of the merits of men. Ajita Kasakambalin reduced man to earth, water, fire and wind, and said: "Fools and wise alike, on the dissolution of the body, are cut off, annihilated, and after death they are not."4 The author of the Ramayana draws a typical sceptic in Jabali, who ridicules Rama for rejecting a kingdom in order to keep a vow."[1806]

And further on:

> "When Buddha grew to manhood he found the halls, the streets, the very woods of northern India ringing with philosophic disputation, mostly of an atheistic and materialistic trend. The later Upanishads and the oldest Buddhist books are full of references to these heretics.6 A large class of traveling Sophists—the Paribbajaka, or Wanderers—spent the better part of every year in passing from locality to locality, seeking pupils, or antagonists, in philosophy. Some of them taught logic as the art of proving anything, and earned for themselves the titles of "Hair-splitters" and "Eelwrigglers"; others demonstrated the non-existence of God, and the inexpediency of virtue. Large audiences gathered to hear such lectures and debates; great halls were built to accommodate them; and sometimes princes offered rewards for those who should emerge victorious from these intellectual jousts.7 It was an age of amazingly free thought, and of a thousand experiments in philosophy. Not much has come down to us from these sceptics, and their memory has been preserved almost exclusively through the diatribes of their enemies.8 The oldest name among them is Brihaspati, but his nihilistic Sutras have perished, and all that remains of him is a poem denouncing the priests in language free from all metaphysical obscurity:
>
>> No heaven exists, no final liberation,
>> No soul, no other world, no rites of caste. . . .
>> The triple Veda, triple self-command,
>> And all the dust and ashes of repentance—
>> These yield a means of livelihood for men
>> Devoid of intellect and manliness. . . .
>> How can this body when reduced to dust
>> Revisit earth?
>> And if a ghost can pass
>> To other worlds, why does not strong affection

---

26. [1806] Durant, Will. Chapter XV: The Buddha: I. The Heretics (9581 - 9656). *Our Oriental Heritage: Being a History of Civilization in Egypt and the Near East to the Death of Alexander, and in India, China and Japan from the Beginning to Our Own Day*. Simon and Schuster, 1935.

> *For those he leaves behind attract him back?*
> *The costly rites enjoined for those who die*
> *Are but a means of livelihood devised*
> *By sacerdotal cunning—nothing more. . . .*
> *While life endures let life be spent in ease*
> *And merriment; let a man borrow money*
> *From all his friends, and feast on melted butter.9*

> "Out of the aphorisms of Brihaspati came a whole school of Hindu materialists, named, after one of them, Charvakas. They laughed at the notion that the Vedas were divinely revealed truth; truth, they argued, can never be known, except through the senses. Even reason is not to be trusted, for every inference depends for its validity not only upon accurate observation and correct reasoning, but also upon the assumption that the future will behave like the past; and of this, as Hume was to say, there can be no certainty.10 What is not perceived by the senses, said the Charvakas, does not exist; therefore the soul is a delusion, and Atman is humbug. We do not observe, in experience or history, any interposition of supernatural forces in the world. All phenomena are natural; only simpletons trace them to demons or gods.11 Matter is the one reality; the body is a combination of atoms;12 the mind is merely matter thinking; the body, not the soul, feels, sees, hears, thinks.13 "Who has seen the soul existing in a state separate from the body?" There is no immortality, no rebirth. Religion is an aberration, a disease, or a chicanery; the hypothesis of a god is useless for explaining or understanding the world. Men think religion necessary only because, being accustomed to it, they feel a sense of loss, and an uncomfortable void, when the growth of knowledge destroys this faith.14 Morality, too, is natural; it is a social convention and convenience, not a divine command. Nature is indifferent to good and bad, virtue and vice, and lets the sun shine indiscriminately upon knaves and saints; if nature has any ethical quality at all it is that of transcendent immorality. There is no need to control instinct and passion, for these are the instructions of nature to men. Virtue is a mistake; the purpose of life is living, and the only wisdom is happiness.15 This revolutionary philosophy of the Charvakas put an end to the age of the Vedas and the Upanishads. It weakened the hold of the Brahmans on the mind of India, and left in Hindu society a vacuum which almost compelled the growth of a new religion. But the materialists had done their work so thoroughly that both of the new religions which arose to replace the old Vedic faith were, anomalous though it may sound, atheistic religions, devotions without a god. Both belonged to the Nastika or Nihilistic movement; and both were originated not by the Brahman priests but by members of the Kshatriya warrior caste, in a reaction against sacerdotal ceremonialism and theology. With the coming of Jainism and Buddhism a new epoch began in the history of India.[1807]"

Given Will Durant's explanation, it seems that whatever comparisons are made about the atheistic traditions and whatever insults bestowed upon them by other denominations of Sanatana Dharma, they were nevertheless highly respected by the wider society, by Brahmins (some of these philosophers were probably Brahmins themselves), and by Kshatriyas who gave them patronage as grand audiences came to listen to their philosophical debates about the nature of human existence and of questions relating to the existence of a God. This was not the same cultural norms of animosity shown in Ancient Greece and latter Western societies up to certain places in the modern-day West. Ancient Indian atheists were highly respected members of society whose philosophical arguments were accepted and venerated by the wider Dharmic

---

27. [1807] Durant, Will. Chapter XV: The Buddha: I. The Heretics (9581 - 9656). *Our Oriental Heritage: Being a History of Civilization in Egypt and the Near East to the Death of Alexander, and in India, China and Japan from the Beginning to Our Own Day*. Simon and Schuster, 1935.

culture and society; moreover, there seems to be no evidence of Brahmins or anyone else casting them out as non-believers or as heretics. At worst, they seemed to have been insulted as extremely annoying and at best, they dazzled large audiences who were enthralled with their debates about human existence and the possible non-existence of a God. Despite what contemporary Indian Atheists from organizations like the grassroots Indian Freethinkers group, *Nirmukta*, would like to believe and argue in their articles from their organization's website. Their portrayal of this ancient period of atheist philosophers as a marginalized outside group that was supposedly vilified by the wider Hindu population who they repeatedly portray as superstitious and gullible seems to be contrary to the evidence of how ancient Dharmic societies grew to value and adapt their practices. The historic evidence from Will Durant's research shows that these atheist philosophers were highly respected throughout northern India and seen as simply another denomination of Sanatana Dharma that was no different than the theistic branch. The supposedly superstitious and gullible ancient Hindus marveled and appreciated the atheistic arguments. Judging from the best available evidence the broader public, Kshatriya rulers, and the Brahmins all seemed to view atheism as simply another viewpoint of Oneness from Truthseeking in Sanatana Dharma and readily adapted it as part of Sanatana Dharma in both its Astika tradition, the tradition that states the Vedas are either a valid moral guide (in part or in whole) or a valid authority on discerning reality and the Nastika tradition, the tradition that denies the Vedas as a valid authority. Thus, most of what we now call modern Hinduism with both its theistic and atheistic views was likely established approximately around the 500 BCE period and the only other component of what makes-up modern Hinduism that was yet to be created around this approximate time period was Advaita Vedanta. Furthermore, to better understand the impact of the Charvakas essentially dominating Sanatana Dharma's philosophical thought, consider the fact that Buddhism, Jainism, and the Vedic traditions all adapted their arguments into their own philosophies. For example, the atheistic influence in Mahavira's Jain philosophy which came after atheism swept over the majority of Ancient India:

> *"Gradually this sect developed one of the strangest bodies of doctrine in all the history of religion. They began with a realistic logic, in which knowledge was described as confined to the relative and temporal. Nothing is true, they taught, except from one point of view; from other points of view it would probably be false. They were fond of quoting the story of the six blind men who laid hands on different parts of an elephant; he who held the ear thought that the elephant was a great winnowing fan; he who held the leg said the animal was a big, round pillar.17 All judgments, therefore, are limited and conditional; absolute truth comes only to the periodic Redeemers or Jinas. Nor can the Vedas help; they are not inspired by God, if only for the reason that there is no God. It is not necessary, said the Jains, to assume a Creator or First Cause; any child can refute that assumption by showing that an uncreated Creator, or a causeless Cause, is just as hard to understand as an uncaused or uncreated world. It is more logical to believe that the universe has existed from all eternity, and that its infinite changes and revolutions are due to the inherent powers of nature rather than to the intervention of a deity.18"*[1808]

---

28. [1808] Durant, Will. Chapter XV: The Buddha: II. Mahavira and the Jains (9656 - 9707). *Our Oriental Heritage: Being a History of Civilization in Egypt and the Near East to the Death of Alexander, and in*

Even if some contemporary Hindus were to argue that only the Astika tradition is Hinduism since it more clearly embodies the Vedic traditions, the Samkhya (Enumeration) school of thought accepts both theism and atheism as a valid viewpoint that an individual can take, so distinguishing between Astika and Nastika seems moot as the philosophies and teachings have always been happily shared. This goes so far that Buddhists, Sikhs, Hindus, and Jains interchangeably pray in each other's temples because the underlying philosophy of Sanatana Dharma has always been that we are all one, but with our own personal interpretation on our Oneness. That is a very positive and wonderful cultural tradition to have within the theology of Sanatana Dharma, because it means that so long as we celebrate and acknowledge it, we will never have the horrific bloodbaths so common over the most miniscule disputes in the Abrahamic religious traditions to the point that subgroups of each branching denomination hate each other and view each other as devil worshippers while claiming to all be part of one of their major denominations. Yet, even among their major denominations, they claim to be separate religions as a result of historical bloodshed. Practitioners of Sanatana Dharma can be proud of a history of philosophical inquiry and equality among branching denominations that are more diverse than the Abrahamic traditions whilst the Abrahamic traditions literally kill each other in massacres over the most trite arguments as shown in the previous sections on Christianity's history and examining the structure of Islamic theology. While I arranged a comprehensive set of arguments as a refutation for them, it was clear the underlying failure runs deeper for both Islam and Christianity and it'll be explained in the conclusion chapter of this book. For Dalits or any others who are seriously considering the Abrahamic faiths, please read those chapters first before you make any deeply personal and life-changing decisions. Those chapters are only a few hours of your time, but a change in religion could impact your entire life and not necessarily for the better. Buddhism, Jainism, Sikhism or the new section in the Indian government's consensus forms of exclusively atheism with no relation to any religion would probably be better options, especially if Hinduism continues to fail Dalits in its historic and barbaric discrimination of Dalits.

While I and possibly many others would like to think the atheistic philosophies could have helped decrease the impact of the Caste system to some degree, such a belief would be spurious even with the knowledge that the teachings of atheist philosophers had an impact on the culture of India and theology of Sanatana Dharma. There have been some arguments that the Ajivikas fatalistic philosophy was meant for the ancient Dalits, but we probably will never know and can only speculate as of now. The Caste was a social norm that probably was considered no different than breathing air; the cruelty of it was something that probably didn't even register in their conscious awareness of ancient people. For instance, the Charvaka quote above that pertains to Caste could be interpreted as arguing for social justice against Caste discrimination or it may have just been limited to a strict criticism of the Brahmins privileges in ancient India and not about helping Dalits at all. To what extent and purpose the Charvakas

---

India, China and Japan from the Beginning to Our Own Day. Simon and Schuster, 1935.

meant to take their criticism about Caste is unknown and may always remain a mystery at this point. The Charvaka group's overall philosophy, from what little remains of their texts, seemed to be a neophyte version of the Pleasure-Pain principle similar to John Stuart Mill's philosophy. The obvious drawbacks and limitations of that model of belief and from their ancient time period would likely influence their societies; the Pleasure-Pain principle ignores the desire for a purpose in life and the reaction to the Charvakas brief period of dominance was the teachings of Jainism and Buddhism. We don't know to what extent the Charvakas dominated ancient India during the Sramana movements; it could have been anywhere from as little as fifty years to as long as a hundred or two hundred years. One important aspect to note is that Buddhism was seen as a cultural reversion back to the Vedic tradition and not a social reform movement like the atheists arguing against Brahminism prior to the Buddha despite what more contemporary Indian intellectuals and the broader public within both India and the West would like to believe about Buddhism's history.[1809] As for the atheist philosophers; at best, there is weak circumstantial evidence that the atheists were social reformers in any meaningful sense since they argued on the grounds of the intellectual likelihood of the belief in a God being true or false and not specifically that it was immoral for the Caste system to exist.

    I don't mean to vilify Buddhism in favor of Hinduism or some such nonsense since it is obvious that Hinduism deserves blame for the Caste system's treatment of the Dalits. I consider Buddhism a different and equally respectable denomination of my own religion of Sanatana Dharma. There was social reform to a certain degree, but it wasn't to the extent that people would like to believe. Buddhist monasteries had equality among different Castes within the monasteries themselves, but I haven't found any information indicating that it was pushed as social change for the wider Indian culture and societies.[1810] I would welcome being corrected with credible evidence on that, if I am wrong about that. Will Durant explains that once the Buddha had abandoned his family to go on a spiritual journey and formed the precepts of Buddhism that we know of today; Buddhism eventually swept across India over the years after his death.[1811] It dominated the void left by the atheistic philosophers of the middle of the Sramana movement that preceded the Buddha's movement.[1812] Jainism and Buddhism culminated as the final portion of what is known today as the independent Sramana movements. Jainism gained a respectable following and Buddhism eventually dominated the majority of India making the Vedic traditions of Hinduism a large minority for hundreds of

---

29. [1809] Elst, Koenraad. "Gautam Buddha Was Every Inch a Hindu - Koenraad Elst." *YouTube*, Upword, 24 Feb. 2019, www.youtube.com/watch?v=i9TEslTqc-s.
30. [1810] Durant, Will. Chapter XV: The Buddha (9581 - 10035). *Our Oriental Heritage: Being a History of Civilization in Egypt and the Near East to the Death of Alexander, and in India, China and Japan from the Beginning to Our Own Day*. Simon and Schuster, 1935.
31. [1811] Durant, Will. Chapter XV: The Buddha (9581 - 10035). *Our Oriental Heritage: Being a History of Civilization in Egypt and the Near East to the Death of Alexander, and in India, China and Japan from the Beginning to Our Own Day*. Simon and Schuster, 1935.
32. [1812] Durant, Will. Chapter XV: The Buddha (9581 - 10035). *Our Oriental Heritage: Being a History of Civilization in Egypt and the Near East to the Death of Alexander, and in India, China and Japan from the Beginning to Our Own Day*. Simon and Schuster, 1935.

years.[1813] I'd like to again emphasize that there wasn't rivalry or antagonism over this, Will Durant depicts Hindu and Buddhist Kshatriya rulers as practically interchangeable during the Maurya Empire for example.[1814] In the context of the ancient world, the Maurya Empire was a golden age of philosophy, art, culture, and it had a strict absolute monarchy that ruled from parts of Afghanistan and Pakistan all the way to near the southern tip of the Indian subcontinent during the height of its power.[1815] Durant explains that its governance was more skillful and controlled than even the Ex-Muslim ruler Akbar the Great and they were effective in avoiding famine throughout the subcontinent.[1816]

Incidentally, avoiding famine is something the British government during its rule of India pretended it was incapable of doing because they didn't concern themselves with what seems to be the purposeful starvation of the subcontinent through their own policies of Malthusian economics.[1817] After all, how could the ancient empire of the Maurya's avoid famine, but the British government couldn't on four separate occasions? More about this issue will be discussed with the details that it deserves in Part III which will be the next book, but for those curious I recommend reading *Late Victorian Holocausts* by Mike Davis. He makes it quite clear that the British policies were most likely purposeful starvation because the point of imperialism was to make as much profit off of cheaply acquired resources and nothing else. Numerous accounts by US and other non-British missionaries along with US journalists documented the barbarity of British colonial rule of India with its mass starvation policies; sadly, the current crop of US missionaries seem entirely ignorant of this remarkable history and don't seem to know of their own cultural heritage opposing British policies instead of idolizing the barbarity of British imperialism which is not morally different than contemporary Muslims idolizing the barbarity of Islamic imperialism.[1818] There seems to be little moral difference with the two approaches between the active destruction of Islamic imperialism and the more passive destruction of British imperialism in their end-results for the Indian subcontinent; neither can claim to be about any sort of progress towards the subjective standard of human rights since illiteracy, poverty, and death were always the conclusion for the majority of the

---

33. [1813] Durant, Will. Chapter XV: The Buddha (9581 - 10035). *Our Oriental Heritage: Being a History of Civilization in Egypt and the Near East to the Death of Alexander, and in India, China and Japan from the Beginning to Our Own Day*. Simon and Schuster, 1935.
34. [1814] Durant, Will. Chapter XVI: From Alexander to Aurangzeb (10072 - 10817). *Our Oriental Heritage: Being a History of Civilization in Egypt and the Near East to the Death of Alexander, and in India, China and Japan from the Beginning to Our Own Day*. Simon and Schuster, 1935.
35. [1815] Durant, Will. Chapter XVI: From Alexander to Aurangzeb (10072 - 10817). *Our Oriental Heritage: Being a History of Civilization in Egypt and the Near East to the Death of Alexander, and in India, China and Japan from the Beginning to Our Own Day*. Simon and Schuster, 1935.
36. [1816] Durant, Will. Chapter XVI: From Alexander to Aurangzeb (10072 - 10817). *Our Oriental Heritage: Being a History of Civilization in Egypt and the Near East to the Death of Alexander, and in India, China and Japan from the Beginning to Our Own Day*. Simon and Schuster, 1935.
37. [1817] Davis, Mike. *Late Victorian Holocausts: El Nino Famines and the Making of the Third World*. Penguin Random House Publisher Services, 2001.
38. [1818] Davis, Mike. *Late Victorian Holocausts: El Nino Famines and the Making of the Third World*. Penguin Random House Publisher Services, 2001.

subcontinent. For all the laughable claims that the British brought democratic freedoms to India, this is contradicted by the fact that the British imposed a blasphemy law that is still in effect in the country of India today and which Muslims from Pakistan likely adapted into their own laws which create the horrible human rights abuses seen in modern Pakistan.[1819] In fact, the blasphemy law in India, section 295A of the Indian Penal Code, was formed in 1927 by the British government to protect the hurt feelings of the Muslim community in the Indian subcontinent after a Hindu group wrote a book mocking the Islamic Prophet Mohammad's sex life in response to an book written by Muslims depicting the Goddess Sita as a prostitute.[1820] The publisher of the book, Mahashe Rajpal, was assassinated in court by a Muslim agitator Ilm Deen just after being acquitted since the British had no law against mocking religion at the time.[1821] After the shameful attack that killed a man for exercising his Free Speech to publish a book, the British responded with drafting and passing section 295A at the behest of the Muslim community to defend the religion of Islam and in direct opposition to the ideology of Free Speech.[1822] Therefore, along with British soldiers hunting down and jailing Transgender people throughout their entire rule of the Indian subcontinent dehumanizing them for the crime of simply existing[1823], the legacy of British culture and history across the world has stood firmly in opposition to the ideology of Free Speech, Free Inquiry, and thus, in opposition to freedom of thought.

Moving along, prior to great empires like the Maurya which began in 322 BCE approximately 200 years after the Buddha's time which is said to be around the 500 BCE time period, Will Durant explains how the Buddha's death brought a resurgence of beliefs in deities and how some of his followers immediately began to venerate him as a God because his teachings were so highly valued among his adherents during his lifetime and onward.[1824] Durant explains that the Buddha had been strictly neutral on the question of a God which brought in adherents who were both atheist and theist alike.[1825] Many of the tall tales of the Buddha traveling in heaven or being surrounded by gods were not part of his original teachings and seem to have grown thanks to the popularity of the Mahayana branches. Accusations by atheists that Buddhism is filled with absurdities and accusations by Christian apologists that

---

39. [1819] Sorabjee, Soli J. "Insult to Religion - Indian Express." *Archive*, archive.indianexpress.com/news/insult-to-religion-/7214/.
40. [1820] Sorabjee, Soli J. "Insult to Religion - Indian Express." *Archive*, archive.indianexpress.com/news/insult-to-religion-/7214/.
41. [1821] Sorabjee, Soli J. "Insult to Religion - Indian Express." *Archive*, archive.indianexpress.com/news/insult-to-religion-/7214/.
42. [1822] Sorabjee, Soli J. "Insult to Religion - Indian Express." *Archive*, archive.indianexpress.com/news/insult-to-religion-/7214/.
43. [1823] "History." *Transindia Film*, www.transindiafilm.co.uk/?page_id=16.
44. [1824] Durant, Will. Chapter XV: The Buddha (9581 - 10035). *Our Oriental Heritage: Being a History of Civilization in Egypt and the Near East to the Death of Alexander, and in India, China and Japan from the Beginning to Our Own Day*. Simon and Schuster, 1935.
45. [1825] Durant, Will. Chapter XV: The Buddha (9581 - 10035). *Our Oriental Heritage: Being a History of Civilization in Egypt and the Near East to the Death of Alexander, and in India, China and Japan from the Beginning to Our Own Day*. Simon and Schuster, 1935.

Buddhism is an atheistic religion are both wrong in terms of the original teachings from how Durant describes it. The original Buddhist teachings of Theravada are strictly neutral on the question of deities, but it didn't stop the expansion of the Mahayana sects which eventually jettisoned Buddhism in popularity. There is some speculation that it was actually the Greek migrants of the Greco-Bactarian empire who had expanded and popularized Mahayana Buddhism throughout both India and the East into countries like China, Tibet, and Japan because there statues depict the Buddha being protected by the God Herakles and their emphasis on a unified Greco-Buddhist architecture leads some credence to such speculation.[1826] Regardless, the atheistic push by the prior Sramana movements of atheistic philosophers were mostly undone as more people accepted Buddhism. Some readers who are inclined towards scientific progress may question how it was possible that such an occurrence could happen; the answer may lay in the limitations of the time period.

First, despite having philosophies which can arguably compete with contemporary philosophical thought, there was no way of ascertaining truth claims since they had no tools to explore scientific evidence unlike centuries later in the West. It was most likely far more difficult to tackle absurd claims when only philosophical positions existed without scientific tools to convince a greater majority of people. Without the filter of scientific evidence, beliefs in atoms and their relation to the world around them would have equal weight to more simplistic beliefs like a local god being responsible for some event. The atheist philosophers of ancient India are staunchly in the realm of philosophy despite postulating the existence of atoms similar to the Ancient Greeks. Second, while the majority of people who listened in rapt attention to the philosophical debates of ancient atheists were eventually convinced that God didn't exist, there is circumstantial evidence from stories of the Buddha's musings that the belief in Karma and Samsara (reincarnation) were still largely believed in despite the Charvakas best efforts.[1827] It may seem delusional in modern times, but reincarnation and karma were inculcated social norms that went so far as to influence the economic structure of ancient India under the Caste system. As mentioned before, just like Caste, Karma and Samsara were probably no different than breathing in terms of the awareness of the majority population in those ancient times. Moreover, since there were no scientific methods to filter or disprove wacky snap judgments about life from rational beliefs made from careful consideration, it is possible that Karma and Samsara were compared to stages of plant life or weather patterns but with these beliefs used on relation to their own physical bodies and the concept of human souls as a way of rationalizing such strongly held cultural beliefs. Despite what contemporary philosophers may want to hear, the history of ancient India could arguably be a case for the scientific method being far more important than philosophical concepts as

---

46. [1826] Ghose, Sanujit. "Cultural Links between India & the Greco-Roman World." *Ancient History Encyclopedia*, Ancient History Encyclopedia, 30 Apr. 2019, www.ancient.eu/article/208/cultural-links-between-india--the-greco-roman-worl/.
47. [1827] Durant, Will. Chapter XV: The Buddha (9581 - 10035). *Our Oriental Heritage: Being a History of Civilization in Egypt and the Near East to the Death of Alexander, and in India, China and Japan from the Beginning to Our Own Day*. Simon and Schuster, 1935.

crucial for convincing a large swathe of people to have a more rational worldview. The idea that philosophy and science are separate spheres may need to be reassessed when we observe histories of cultures that didn't have the scientific method, but had very powerful philosophical ideas and arguments. In ancient India, some of the very best ideas in philosophy weren't enough to stop ridiculous beliefs from re-emerging. Compare that with the scientific method and all the progress made in the West thanks exclusively to science and it has slowly been kept in check over the course of many years despite religious counterculture movements that attempt to destroy the social order with anti-intellectual and rabid beliefs in traditionalism and patriarchy.

Second, and crucially after the time period of the Sramana movements, the precariousness of absolute monarchies almost certainly contributed in negatively impacting and eroding the strong gains in philosophical inquiry for the wider public. While intellectual strides from philosophical debates under benevolent leaders helped to spur intellectual growth, the cultures and societies likely stalled or fell apart upon a complete lack of physical security when incompetent or vicious rulers took the place of benevolent ones or when kingdoms eventually fell apart due to internal political strife. Absolute monarchies can arguably be considered better than a democratic form of governance when a sophisticated, intelligent, and benign dictator rules the country, but that falls apart when a weak or vicious ruler takes the reins of empire and causes disaster to happen or - as is more often the case in history - fails to avoid an impending disaster from happening. Governments without checks and balances included with strong security for the wider public don't have much longevity compared to democratic forms of governance with checks and balances. To be sure, democratic governance may fail too, but they fail less often and make enough great strides when functioning well that a system with checks and balances are mostly better than one ruler holding complete political power. For every great Xi Jinping in history, there'll probably eventually be a Suddam Hussein to ruin it in countries with various forms of dictatorship. Likewise, for every horrible Donald Trump, George W. Bush, or Hillary Clinton placed into public office within a democratic government, there could be a Thomas Jefferson, Margaret Thatcher, or Narendra Modi waiting around the corner to move the nation-state forward toward a brighter future. A country without a proper and legitimate checks and balances system will eventually, and possibly rapidly, fall apart which is precisely why they're the most important component to maintain in any democratic form of governance. Without a checks and balances system, only the arbitrary whims of political groups - usually the ones with the most power - remain and it is most likely that a rising tide of agitation and violence will follow when other groups needs, from basic necessities like food to livable wages for a consistent but adjustable living standard, aren't met for the broader public's satisfaction.

Finally, and arguably the worst and most lasting failure of all in ancient India which negatively impacted India thereafter, the social ill of misogyny that followed after the time period of the Sramana movements. While many modern Hindus, Indian atheists, and others credibly blame the disgusting misogyny of Adi Shankara when he eventually displaced Buddhism with Hinduism's Advaita Vedanta (Non-Dualism) philosophy[1828], which was a return to the Upanishadic beliefs in Hindu Pantheism with an emphasis on there being no duality between the physical world and spiritual beliefs. The initial seeds of misogyny regrettably began nearly one thousand years prior to Shankara's lifetime of approximately 788-820 AD due to the Buddha himself in his lifetime which was approximately in the 500 BCE time period. Historic accounts of the Buddha view him to have disdained the idea of women joining the Buddhist monasteries, he eventually allowed it but it seems to have been out of reluctance and only on condition that the lowest male monk held rank over the highest female monk.[1829][1830] He reportedly spoke of how it would doom Buddhism by allowing women to join.[1831] This is rather saddening, but in fairness to the Buddha, the most credible historic accounts show that he never wanted to be venerated as any sort of God.[1832] As cited in the final quote of the chapter on Buddhism's theology, and much like Friedrich Nietzsche several centuries after him, the historical Buddha wanted his followers to be open to questioning his teachings and challenging them with their own beliefs should they find his teachings lacking. I would personally argue that there was one such contender who showed superior insight to the Buddha in his own lifetime, if the historic accounts of this person are accurate, but she was unfortunately not given much attention in the historical record likely due to sexism. Who was this person and what did she do? Her name was Yasodhara and she is most famously known as the wife of Siddhartha Gautama before he became renown as Gautama Buddha. If Will Durant's cited Buddhist texts are accurate, then Yasodhara should be known as having surpassed her husband's teachings in their lifetime. According to Durant's brief explanation of the historical record of Yasodhara, after Siddhartha left on his journey, Yasodhara had sent her helpers from the kingdom to look for him to make sure that he was safe from harm.[1833] They related the Buddha's teachings to her after confirming that nothing horrible had happened to him. From then on, Yasodhara adapted her husband's teachings while he was away; she learned of his proper meditation practices which she practiced regularly, she followed suit in adapting

---

48. [1828] Anamika. "'The Scholarship of the Daughter Is Regarding Domestic Affairs Only, for She Is Not Entitled to Read the Vedas."~Adi Shankara, That Renowned 9th Century Indian Sage of Advaita Vedanta, in His Bhāṣya on the Ancient Upanishads (Sacred Shruti Literature)." *Twitter*, Twitter, 3 Apr. 2018, twitter.com/AnaMyID/status/981146807433510914.
49. [1829] Durant, Will. Chapter XV: The Buddha (9581 - 10035). *Our Oriental Heritage: Being a History of Civilization in Egypt and the Near East to the Death of Alexander, and in India, China and Japan from the Beginning to Our Own Day*. Simon and Schuster, 1935.
50. [1830] Elst, Koenraad. "Gautam Buddha Was Every Inch a Hindu - Koenraad Elst." *YouTube*, Upword, 24 Feb. 2019, www.youtube.com/watch?v=i9TEslTqc-s.
51. [1831] Durant, Will. Chapter XV: The Buddha (9581 - 10035). *Our Oriental Heritage: Being a History of Civilization in Egypt and the Near East to the Death of Alexander, and in India, China and Japan from the Beginning to Our Own Day*. Simon and Schuster, 1935.
52. [1832] Durant, Will. Chapter XV: The Buddha (9581 - 10035). *Our Oriental Heritage: Being a History of Civilization in Egypt and the Near East to the Death of Alexander, and in India, China and Japan from the Beginning to Our Own Day*. Simon and Schuster, 1935.
53. [1833] Durant, Will. Chapter XV: The Buddha (9581 - 10035). *Our Oriental Heritage: Being a History of Civilization in Egypt and the Near East to the Death of Alexander, and in India, China and Japan from the Beginning to Our Own Day*. Simon and Schuster, 1935.

her husband's dietary habits as per his teachings, there is no evidence that Yasodhara was ever unfaithful to her husband throughout her entire life, and all that time, Yasodhara raised their only son.[1834] It is possible that she had the help of whatever attendants that she had in her kingdom under her father, the King. I find it rather remarkable that Rahula, the Buddha and Yasodhara's son, displays no evidence of having resented his father and seemed to think highly of him almost immediately when he first truly met his father from what the stories relate.[1835] While we may never know for sure, given all that Yasodhara did during the Buddha's absence, it doesn't seem to be a stretch to speculate that it was her influence on Rahula that impacted Rahula's positive disposition towards his father. When the Buddha and her finally reunited upon his return home, Rahula evidently prostrated herself before him after it was explained what she had been up to in his absence and all he did was give her a typical blessing before moving on his way.[1836] The Buddha's life story is one of a deeply profound philosophy of detachment from desires that still has relevance in modern times, but Yasodhara's life story is of following the philosophy of her husband through her attachment to him along with an unfailing love for both her son and husband. I'd argue that, despite the Buddha being the initiator of the philosophy, Yasodhara's lived example and nuanced expression of his philosophy is a more beneficial lesson for modern times.

Approximately a thousand years later, Adi Shankara's philosophy and commentaries, likely influenced from the more misogynistic aspects of the Upanishads and potentially influenced by sexism within Buddhist teachings and social norms, took an even more disgustingly misogynistic view when he argued that women being educated was morally wrong.[1837] Equally as repugnant, while claiming to be against Caste, Adi Shankara claimed that knowledge of the Vedas should be restricted to the three higher Castes and shouldn't be imparted to the lower Castes. His beliefs and teachings was a tightening of the Caste system. Even worse, he was claiming the upper echelons of Hindu society shouldn't follow Caste while benefiting from its privileges. Shankara was less a philosopher and more a charlatan; he seemed to be a talented musician and poet, but his philosophy was equally about hiding his own privilege to benefit from slavery and misogyny as much as it was about Truthseeking for a pantheistic worldview influenced by the Upanishads. Yet, for all his strides in truthseeking, I would argue that Adi Shankara was not a Truthseeker, but rather a return to Brahminism

---

54. [1834] Durant, Will. Chapter XV: The Buddha (9581 - 10035). *Our Oriental Heritage: Being a History of Civilization in Egypt and the Near East to the Death of Alexander, and in India, China and Japan from the Beginning to Our Own Day*. Simon and Schuster, 1935.
55. [1835] Durant, Will. Chapter XV: The Buddha (9581 - 10035). *Our Oriental Heritage: Being a History of Civilization in Egypt and the Near East to the Death of Alexander, and in India, China and Japan from the Beginning to Our Own Day*. Simon and Schuster, 1935.
56. [1836] Durant, Will. Chapter XV: The Buddha (9581 - 10035). *Our Oriental Heritage: Being a History of Civilization in Egypt and the Near East to the Death of Alexander, and in India, China and Japan from the Beginning to Our Own Day*. Simon and Schuster, 1935.
57. [1837] Anamika. "'The Scholarship of the Daughter Is Regarding Domestic Affairs Only, for She Is Not Entitled to Read the Vedas."~Adi Shankara, That Renowned 9th Century Indian Sage of Advaita Vedanta, in His Bhāṣya on the Ancient Upanishads (Sacred Shruti Literature)." *Twitter*, Twitter, 3 Apr. 2018, twitter.com/AnaMyID/status/981146807433510914.

dominating India through some Upanishadic influence. The reason I say that is because he quite clearly didn't respect any possibility of lower Castes and women being allowed to have their own personal journeys in Truthseeking much unlike many of the Sramana Upanishads which held women more favorably in social status. His commentaries shouldn't be taken as anything other than his opinion in terms of the foundational philosophy of Sanatana Dharma; that we are all one, but with our own interpretations. It is clear that - beyond the Pantheistic philosophy which shows some merit - Adi Shankara didn't understand or didn't attempt to understand anything else in the Upanishads or other works beyond inculcating misogyny and Caste discrimination. He attempted to reinterpret all of it as either part of his philosophy or his own narrow-minded misogynistic and Casteist viewpoints. This is unlike the Buddha who allowed lower Castes to join his monasteries and for all his faults, he did allow a monastery for female Monks. Moreover, the Sramana movements touting atheism show no evidence of having supported explicit sexism against women like Adi Shankara's teachings. While Adi Shankara was most certainly free to hold his disgusting views, and he is obviously a member of the Vedic tradition of Hinduism and part of Sanatana Dharma, I'd personally hold Adi Shankara as little more than a misogynistic charlatan who didn't contribute anything of value beyond music and poetry to Sanatana Dharma since I hold very little regard for his Advaita Vedanta philosophy which I found to be nonsensical until I learned something that is personally infuriating to me about his philosophy that'll be explored further in the next chapter.

After the time period of Adi Shankara, the Islamic conquests began approximately three hundred years later, then the European squabble for India much later, and then the British colonial period. roughly 900 years of Abrahamic barbarism, discrimination, stupidity, and cruelty was imposed and impoverished India from then onward until it gained independence and founded its own secular Republic after Islam and British policies tore it apart and left mass death tolls in their wake. The blood, sweat, and tears of the Indian population eventually pulled through for the relatively stable secular democratic country that exists today that all Indians of India can be proud of.

Examination of the Gitas

For this portion, I'll be reviewing the most noteworthy Gitas of Hinduism. The Gitas are essentially poem-format teachings with several chapters imparting the wisdom of each specific deity onto their followers in the stories that the Gitas lay out. This'll be a short critique of each of the ones that have been translated to English that I've had the pleasure of reading. I'll outline the pros and cons of each of the Gitas.

The Bhagavad Gita[1838][1839]

---

58. [1838] Eknath, Easwaran, translator. *The Bhagavad Gita*. Nilgiri Press, 2007.
59. [1839] "Bhagavadgita: 1. The Yoga of Arjuna's Sorrow." Translated by Jayaram V, *Bhagavadgita: The Yoga of Arjuna's Sorrow*, www.hinduwebsite.com/gita1.asp.

The first and my favorite one among the three that I've read is the Bhagavad Gita (Song of God) which is about Sri Krishna. In this book, Krishna taking the form of a chariot driver, imparts knowledge to the Prince Arjuna on why he should fight in a civil war instead of immediately surrendering. For my part, I was pleasantly surprised by Arjuna's questions about the bloody effects of war and how slaying kinsmen only leads to worse problems in the future. It seemed to take such questions responsibly, even if the teachings on that specific context of fighting a war can become problematic.

Pros: The Bhagavad Gita has probably one of the best philosophical arguments that I've seen and I'm surprised that such an old story could have such a universal argument. The entire basis of the philosophy of Krishna is selfless service without the sake of a reward. Utter selfless devotion to the community at large or to one's personal goals so long as they are about selflessly helping others that you love and care about. Krishna points out that seeking rewards for work selfishly can be very exhausting for an individual and that is why selflessly helping others without any desire for a reward is what is best at maintaining a strong society and community. In fact, this lesson echoes modern psychological studies that show intrinsic motivation and not inducements like money are what help to foster growth in modern corporations.[1840] So long as workers have their monetary needs met, they don't need any further inducements to push a company forward and help it prosper with teamwork and creative ideas so long as they have an intrinsic interest in helping the company succeed by exploring their own creativity.[1841] Another interesting tidbit is that when Krishna speaks of inaction, he's referring to meditation practices as a positive form of inaction, but expressly mentions that action is more important because you carry on selfless work for the wellbeing of others.

However, the most positive argument in terms of theology is that Krishna explicitly tells Arjuna that nobody who doesn't believe in him is damned at all. The only requirement for going to any positive afterlife according to Krishna is being a good moral person and not any belief in him specifically. Please keep in mind that the Bhagavad Gita was made centuries before the Bible and the Quran. Krishna mentions the idea that all ways are valid as he explicitly states that people who don't believe in him aren't doomed.

Cons: Despite these positives, the text shows its age in numerous ways. Misogyny and Casteism are explicit in the beginning of the text itself by blaming women for disharmony in society and explicitly arguing against different Castes mixing to have progeny with each other. The idea of manly Ascetic honor is implicit in the text. Worst of all, this text is clearly a war mandate to cajole people into a civil war. It is surprisingly less violent than most chapters of the Quran or Bible, but it emphasizes the necessity of going to war as part of selfless service without the desire for victory in a war. This displays similar problematic themes to the Abrahamic texts in unquestioned obedience to a God's authority. Moreover, there seems to an

---

60. [1840] Pink, Daniel H. *Drive: the Surprising Truth about What Motivates Us*. Canongate Books, 2018.
61. [1841] Pink, Daniel H. *Drive: the Surprising Truth about What Motivates Us*. Canongate Books, 2018.

underlying philosophical proposition of determinism as a justification for why people shouldn't care whether there is bloodshed on their side or the opposing side of a war and to simply focus on doing one's duty for the sake of protecting their community regardless of the consequences. Krishna is also arguably patronizing throughout the text in his attitude too. Needless to say, this is not a text that inspires philosophical inquiry to question a God's motives as just or unjust. While it is remarkable for its time period and I would even argue that it is certainly superior to the Bible and Quran, it has its own historic defects calling for barbarous actions which mustn't be ignored or downplayed.

The Isvara Gita[1842]

This particular Gita translation that I read is purportedly by Andrew J. Nicholson and I really did like reading it, but I was left confused when reading Nicholson's other book, *Unifying Hinduism*. I am honestly bewildered that anybody who has read the *Isvara Gita* from start to finish could say with any degree of honesty that it disputes any unity in Sanatana Dharma. I want to be careful here, I'm sure Nicholson is the translator of this piece and I have no reason to expect otherwise, but I honestly am perplexed how anyone could read this to completion and conclude Hinduism was never unified. Such a conclusion doesn't just make me doubt the credibility of Western Indology, it makes me question if they ever had honest intentions as this is already on top of what seems to be a categorical attempt at genocide denial of the Islamic conquest of India. Nevertheless, I've said everything I intended to in the previous chapter so I'll focus on giving a critique of the contents of the *Isvara Gita* itself from Nicholson's translation of the work.

The Isvara Gita is Shiva imparting wisdom about all the deities and Brahman to followers of Vishnu and Shiva who seem to be on opposing sides.

Pros: The entire story is quite clearly an argument in support of the Vedic tradition being a unified religion. That's what the whole story of this book is about and it is quite unambiguous in this argument. Shiva speaks of the Upanishads, being part of Brahman, and the entirety of two chapters is devoted to listing every popular God and Goddess, whether the *Devas* and *Devis* (benevolent and holy deities) or *Asuras* (Demonic Gods and Goddesses) to explain how they're all part of Shiva who is One with everything.[1843] The end of the story solidifies his message of the unified Vedic tradition with Vishnu, who has largely remained silent during Shiva's teachings as he sat next to him, to return within Shiva as proof that they're the same deity. Therefore, the entire story is about the Vedic traditions all being the same religion in the most explicit terms. How anyone could think this was disunity or interpret it as

---

62. [1842] Nicholson, Andrew J., translator. *Lord Siva's Song: The Isvara Gita*. State Univ Of New York Pr, 2015.
63. [1843] Nicholson, Andrew J., translator. Chapter 6: The Glory of Lord Siva (1135-1213) and Chapter 7: The Master of Beasts (1214-1268). *Lord Siva's Song: The Isvara Gita*. State Univ Of New York Pr, 2015.

the Vedic traditions not being unified is almost certainly being disingenuous and can't be trusted with intellectual honesty.

Cons: Similar to the *Bhagavad Gita*, the *Isvara Gita* depicts Shiva as very patronizing, except it is far worse. It is drowning out the opinions of others and even goes so far as to threaten seven hells of torment for anyone who disagrees with the view that the religion is unified. It has the same defects as the Abrahamic traditions and its contrary to the *Bhagavad Gita*'s philosophical disposition that everyone goes to a positive afterlife by just being a good person. The *Isvara Gita* doesn't really impart any moral teachings like the *Bhagavad Gita* but seems explicitly designed to demand people accept a unified Vedic tradition under the threat of seven hells. Also, the references to magical power are just comical and has no evidence of being true.

Devi Gita[1844]

The Devi Gita is a story about the ultimate and most powerful manifestation of the Goddesses of the Vedic traditions appearing to help weakened Gods who were being soundly defeated by Asuras prior to the beginning of the story. The Gods then prayed and did sacrifices to summon the most powerful form of the Goddess, who emerges to assure her devotees and the Gods that she'll save them by making an incarnation of herself as a daughter to one of her devotees before imparting her lessons.

Pros: It uses the Upanishads, Vedas, the concept of Brahman, and other deities like Sita, Vishnu, and Shiva as its predicate for establishing how the Vedic tradition is a unified religion just like the *Isvara Gita*. It teaches that followers can pray anywhere they want. It mentions that yogi practices are a form of veneration and prayer, thereby debunking all of Western Indology's claims that yogi and meditation practices don't matter as part of the Hindu faith tradition. Best of all to me, when it mentions the Goddess's breasts, at no point does it say that they're covered by the red cloth that adorns her body. Therefore, she is implied to be topless when preaching and being revered; as a sex-positive feminist, I find this admiration for female sexuality to be an abject positive for Hindu theology.

Cons: The worst aspect of her teachings is assuredly that, just like the *Ishvara Gita*, she threatens to send people to seven hells for not believing in the Vedic tradition. The second worst, and most embarrassing, portion is Chapter 2 since it is an incoherent mess that reads as some ancient writer having no knowledge of mathematics and trying to sound clever by shoehorning their ideas into the Goddess that they're venerating. Moreover, it is clearly biased towards the Brahminism denomination since it tries to treat ritual sacrifices as important symbolism pertaining to Brahman.

---

64. [1844] Brown, Cheever Mackenzie, translator. *The Song of the Goddess the Devī Gītā: Spiritual Counsel of the Great Goddess*. State University of New York Press, 2002.

Fatalistic Determinism

When reading the *Mahabharata*, I didn't find much value within most of it. It was mostly an annoying chore to read because it primarily consisted of characters relating stories of other characters with run-on sentences, excessive venerated phrasings of different names for the same character, and the information seemed to just be self-contained to an ancient culture that didn't have much of any value to offer as wisdom or even as ancient wisdom. It was a poorly explained and haphazard collection of jumbled stories without much interesting content; the only positive I found was that the translation seemed mostly good. Indeed, if the Quran or Bible is hard for an average person to read, then the Mahabharata is entirely unreadable since it doesn't even follow a specific train of thought in its stories. The supposed writer, Veda Vyasa, which was most likely a title granted to various people who performed some unknown qualification and not a name of any sort, had writings that were downright incoherent. It isn't even a stream of consciousness narrative, but rather a random assortment of things documented whether it be events with an emphasis on flowery long-winded venerations that are so annoying to read and they are stupidly placed. I say this while emphasizing that I actually enjoy reading the Vedas poems, the Bhagavad Gita, most of the Upanishads with atheistic views, and the philosophical disputes and propositions in the theology of Sanatana Dharma. I enjoy most of the modernized forms of Dharmic music and even some old versions of songs. However, I have to be honest, while there are one or two segments of the Mahabharata that I enjoyed, the entire book is largely an incoherent mess of stupid that is almost as bad as the Bible and the Quran.

As I continued reading to see if anything valuable could be gleaned, you can imagine my reaction at finding a rather astonishing passage that seemed to be arguing in favor of the philosophical position of hard determinism as the correct way of viewing life albeit in a more fatalistic perspective than in modern contexts. The passage I had read surprised me since before I had read it, I had seen inclinations of a implicit deterministic bias when reading the *Bhagavad Gita's* arguments in favor of selfless work without a reward, some of the *Upanishads* arguments with regards to Samsara, and it was much more explicit as a teaching in the *Isvara Gita* and they always seemed to be in relation to a theological concept. Whether it was Karma (*Bhagavad Gita*), Samsara (*the Upanishads*), or framing everything in unambiguously as Oneness (*Isvara Gita*). The *Devi Gita* echoed the same sentiments as the *Isvara Gita* but emphasized Vedic rituals, prayer sites, and prayer itself as part of the importance. Nevertheless, these seemed to be heavily implied, but it wasn't until reading the passage in the Mahabharata that I recognized there was a deep philosophical social norm that existed in ancient India that had been ignored due to the utter incompetence of Western Indology. After reading the passage, I had delved to search online to see if Western Indology had any say at all since at the time I had still held a positive view of them. When I recognized they had no knowledge or understanding and didn't even seem to be intellectually capable of placing anything in proper socio-political context of ancient times, that was where my initial distrust of their viewpoints began. In fact, Sheldon Pollock's arguably incompetent 1985 article claiming that context was a Eurocentric concept, which explicitly ignored psychological studies that existed since the 1950s and 1960s which gave significant credence to humans distinguishing each other into differing groups instantaneously, expressed this quite well when I compared the nonsensical conclusions of Western Indology to psychological studies still relevant in modern psychology which still dominate due to repeated testing having verified them.[1845] When I looked-up ancient Indian games and reassessed the Caste system based on how Vedic tradition justified it in theological terms, I began to see compelling pieces of evidence that began to unravel my trust in Western Indology. I had seen the pieces before, but it wasn't until reading that passage that I felt there was credence to my line of reasoning since I hadn't seen any mention in Western Indology which I wrongfully believed to be a trustworthy and credible academic discipline. After all, how was it that I was putting these pieces together based upon evidence and this entire so-called academic discipline was incapable of doing the same for several decades? It made me question if they ever had honest intentions.

Appropriate context is required before sharing the passage. As with much of the *Mahabharata*, it is a story within a story; the story begins with a soldier being briefly mentioned to have performed Vedic rituals before coming to his Prince and explaining how he laments in participating in the bloodshed of what seems to be a civil war and how his grief for his actions consume him. The Prince responds with the story of a old woman having lost her infant son to a snake. A Fowler, having caught the snake, brings it to the old woman to ask how she wants it killed in return for killing the infant. In the story, the snake speaks in its own defense about why it can't be blamed. Soon enough, both Mrityu (an incarnation of Death) and Kala (an incarnation of Time) appear and speak stating they can't be blamed for what happened to the dead infant either. The concepts "*Sattva*" (Goodness), "*Rajas*" (Passion), and "*Tattvas*" (Inertia) in the passage refer to the three Gunas of Hinduism; they're a metaphysical concept in certain schools of thought within the Vedic traditions that conflate a person's ability and virtues with analogies of a string or a thread. In the context of the passage below, it provides further credence for a metaphysical viewpoint that favors determinism since even activities involving inertia, and therefore disorder and chaos in the Vedic tradition, are argued to be predetermined. The discussion throughout the piece seems to be an argument in defense of the philosophical disposition of hard determinism.

From the *Anusasana Parva* (Book of Instructions), Section I, Part I of the *Mahabharata*:

> """Bhishma replied, "Why, O fortunate one, dost thou consider thy soul, which is dependent (on God and Destiny and Time) to be the cause of thy actions? The manifestation of its inaction is subtle and imperceptible to the senses. In this connection is cited the ancient story of the conversation between Mrityu and Gautami with Kala and the Fowler and the serpent. There was, O son of Kunti, an old lady of the name of Gautami, who was possessed of great patience and tranquillity of mind. One day she found her son dead in consequence of having been bitten by a serpent. An angry fowler, by name Arjunaka,

---

65. [1845] Ispas, Alexa. *Psychology and politics: a social identity perspective*. Psychology Press, 2014.

bound the serpent with a string and brought it before Gautami. He then said to her,—'This wretched serpent has been the cause of thy son's death, O blessed lady. Tell me quickly how this wretch is to be destroyed. Shall I throw it into the fire or shall I hack it into pieces? This infamous destroyer of a child does not deserve to live longer.'

"'"Gautami replied, 'Do thou, O Arjunaka of little understanding, release this serpent. It doth not deserve death at thy hands. Who is so foolish as to disregard the inevitable lot that awaits him and burdening himself with such folly sink into sin? Those that have made themselves light by the practice of virtuous deeds, manage to cross the sea of the world even as a ship crosses the ocean. But those that have made themselves heavy with sin sink into the bottom, even as an arrow thrown into the water. By killing the serpent, this my boy will not be restored to life, and by letting it live, no harm will be caused to thee. Who would go to the interminable regions of Death by slaying this living creature?'

"'"The fowler said, 'I know, O lady that knowest the difference between right and wrong, that the great are afflicted at the afflictions of all creatures. But these words which thou hast spoken are fraught with instruction for only a self-contained person (and not for one plunged in sorrow). Therefore, I must kill this serpent. Those who value peace of mind, assign everything to the course of Time as the cause, but practical men soon assuage their grief (by revenge). People through constant delusion, fear loss of beatitude (in the next world for acts like these). Therefore, O lady, assuage thy grief by having this serpent destroyed (by me).'

"'"Gautami replied, 'People like us are never afflicted by (such misfortune). Good men have their souls always intent on virtue. The death of the boy was predestined: therefore, I am unable to approve of the destruction of this serpent. Brahmanas do not harbour resentment, because resentment leads to pain. Do thou, O good man, forgive and release this serpent out of compassion.'

"'"The fowler replied, 'Let us earn great and inexhaustible merit hereafter by killing (this creature), even as a man acquires great merit, and confers it on his victim sacrificed as well, by sacrifice upon the altar. Merit is acquired by killing an enemy: by killing this despicable creature, thou shalt acquire great and true merit hereafter.'

"'"Gautami replied, 'What good is there in tormenting and killing an enemy, and what good is won by not releasing an enemy in our power? Therefore, O thou of benign countenance, why should we not forgive this serpent and try to earn merit by releasing it?'

"'"The fowler replied, 'A great number (of creatures) ought to be protected from (the wickedness of) this one, instead of this single creature being protected (in preference to many). Virtuous men abandon the vicious (to their doom): do thou, therefore, kill this wicked creature.'

"'"Gautami replied, 'By killing this serpent, O fowler, my son will not be restored to life, nor do I see that any other end will be attained by its death: therefore, do thou, O fowler, release this living creature of a serpent.'"

"'"'The fowler said, 'By killing Vritra, Indra secured the best portion (of sacrificial offerings), and by destroying a sacrifice Mahadeva secured his share of sacrificial offerings: do thou, therefore, destroy this serpent immediately without any misgivings in thy mind!'"

"'Bhishma continued, "The high-souled Gautami, although repeatedly incited by the fowler for the destruction of the serpent did not bend her mind to that sinful act. The serpent, painfully bound with the cord, sighing a little and maintaining its composure with great difficulty, then uttered these words slowly, in a human voice.

"'"The serpent said, 'O foolish Arjunaka, what fault is there of mine? I have no will of my own, and am not independent. Mrityu sent me on this errand. By his direction have I bitten this child, and not out of any anger or choice on my part. Therefore, if there be any sin in this, O fowler, the sin is his.'

"'"The fowler said, 'If thou hast done this evil, led thereto by another, the sin is thine also as thou art an instrument in the act. As in the making of an earthen vessel the potter's wheel and rod and other things are all regarded as causes, so art thou, O serpent, (cause in the production of this effect). He that is guilty deserves death at my hands. Thou, O serpent, art guilty. Indeed, thou confessest thyself so in this matter!'

"'"The serpent said, 'As all these, viz., the potter's wheel, rod, and other things, are not independent causes, even so I am not an independent cause. Therefore, this is no fault of mine, as thou shouldst grant. Shouldst thou think otherwise, then these are to be considered as causes working in unison with one another. For thus working with one other, a doubt arises regarding their relation as cause and effect. Such being the case, it is no fault of mine, nor do I deserve death on this account, nor am I guilty of any sin. Or, if thou thinkest that there is sin (in even such causation), the sin lies in the aggregate of causes.'

"'"The fowler said, 'If thou art neither the prime cause nor the agent in this matter, thou art still the cause of the death (of this child). Therefore, thou dost deserve death in my opinion. If, O serpent, thou thinkest that when an evil act is done, the doer is not implicated therein, then there can be no cause in this matter; but having done this, verily thou deservest death. What more dost thou think?'

"'"The serpent said, 'Whether any cause exists or not,[1] no effect is produced without an (intermediate) act. Therefore, causation being of no moment in either case, my agency only as the cause (in this matter) ought to be considered in its proper bearings. If, O fowler, thou thinkest me to be the cause in truth, then the guilt of this act of killing a living being rests on the shoulders of another who incited me to this end.'[2]

"'"The fowler said, 'Not deserving of life, O foolish one, why dost thou bandy so many words, O wretch of a serpent? Thou deservest death at my hands. Thou hast done an atrocious act by killing this infant.'

"'"The serpent said, 'O fowler, as the officiating priests at a sacrifice do not acquire the merit of the act by offering oblations of clarified butter to the fire, even so should I be regarded with respect as to the result in this connection.'"

"'Bhishma continued, "The serpent directed by Mrityu having said this, Mrityu himself appeared there and addressing the serpent spoke thus.

"'"Mrityu said, 'Guided by Kala, I, O serpent, sent thee on this errand, and neither art thou nor am I the cause of this child's death. Even as the clouds are tossed hither and thither by the wind, I am like the clouds, O serpent, influenced by Kala. All attitudes appertaining to Sattwa or Rajas, or Tamas, are provoked by Kala, and operate in all creatures. All creatures, mobile and immobile, in heaven, or earth, are influenced by Kala. The whole universe, O serpent, is imbued with this same influence of Kala. All acts in this world and all abstentions, as also all their modifications, are said to be influenced by Kala. Surya, Soma, Vishnu, Water, Wind, the deity of a hundred sacrifices, Fire, Sky, Earth, Mitra and Parjanya, Aditi, and the Vasus, Rivers and Oceans, all existent and non-existent objects, are created and destroyed by Kala. Knowing this, why dost thou, O serpent, consider me to be guilty? If any fault attaches to me in this, thou also wouldst be to blame.'

"'"The serpent said, 'I do not, O Mrityu, blame thee, nor do I absolve thee from all blame. I only aver that I am directed and influenced (in my actions) by thee. If any blame attaches to Kala, or, if it be not desirable to attach any blame to him, it is not for me to scan the fault. We have no right to do so. As it is incumbent on me to absolve myself from this blame, so it is my duty to see that no blame attaches to Mrityu.'"

"'Bhishma continued, "Then the serpent, addressing Arjunaka, said—'Thou hast listened to what Mrityu has said. Therefore, it is not proper for thee to torment me, who am guiltless, by tying me with this cord.'

"'"The fowler said, 'I have listened to thee, O serpent, as well as to the words of Mrityu, but these, O serpent, do not absolve thee from all blame. Mrityu and thyself are the causes of the child's death. I consider both of you to be the cause and I do not call that to be the cause which is not truly so. Accursed be the wicked and vengeful Mrityu that causes affliction to the good. Thee too I shall kill that art sinful and engaged in sinful acts!'

"'"Mrityu said, 'We both are not free agents, but are dependent on Kala, and ordained to do our appointed work. Thou shouldst not find fault with us if thou dost consider this matter thoroughly.'

"'"The fowler said, 'If ye both, O serpent and Mrityu, be dependent on Kala, I am curious to know how pleasure (arising from doing good) and anger (arising from doing evil) are caused.'

"'"Mrityu said, 'Whatever is done is done under the influence of Kala. I have said it before, O fowler, that Kala is the cause of all and that for this reason we both, acting under the inspiration of Kala, do our appointed work and therefore, O fowler, we two do not deserve censure from thee in any way!'"

"'Bhishma continued, "Then Kala arrived at that scene of disputation on this point of morality, and spoke thus to the serpent and Mrityu and the fowler Arjunaka assembled together.

"'"Kala said, 'Neither Mrityu, nor this serpent, nor I, O fowler, am guilty of the death of any creature. We are merely the immediate exciting causes of the event. O Arjunaka, the Karma of this child formed the exciting cause of our action in this matter. There was no other cause by which this child came by its death. It was killed as a result of its own Karma. It has met with death as the result of its Karma in the past. Its Karma has been the cause of its destruction. We all are subject to the influence of our respective Karma. Karma is an aid to salvation even as sons are, and Karma also is an indicator of virtue and vice in man. We urge one another even as acts urge one another. As men make from a lump of clay whatever they wish to make, even so do men attain to various results determined by Karma. As light and shadow are related to each other, so are men related to Karma through their own actions. Therefore, neither art thou, nor am I, nor Mrityu, nor the serpent, nor this old Brahmana lady, is the cause of this child's death. He himself is the cause here.' Upon Kala, O king, expounding the matter in this way, Gautami, convinced in her mind that men suffer according to their actions, spoke thus to Arjunaka.

"'"Gautami said, 'Neither Kala, nor Mrityu, nor the serpent, is the cause in this matter. This child has met with death as the result of its own Karma. I too so acted (in the past) that my son has died (as its consequence). Let now Kala and Mrityu retire from this place, and do thou too, O Arjunaka, release this serpent."'

"'Bhishma continued, "Then Kala and Mrityu and the serpent went back to their respective destinations, and Gautami became consoled in mind as also the fowler. Having heard all this, O king, do thou forego all grief, and attain to peace of mind. Men attain to heaven or hell as the result of their own Karma. This evil has neither been of thy own creation, nor of Duryodhana's. Know this that these lords of Earth have all been slain (in this war) as a result of acts of Kala."'

"Vaisampayana said, 'Having heard all this, the powerful and virtuous Yudhishthira became consoled in mind, and again enquired as follows.""[1846]

When reading this passage, I was struck by the similarity to New Atheist Philosopher and neuroscientist Sam Harris's arguments about free will in his lengthy video explaining why Free Will is unlikely to exist.[1847] Moreover, when I later read the opening of his book *Free Will* I was again struck by the similarity of the comparison between the Mahabharata passage and Sam Harris's book.[1848] Of course, it is entirely possible that he had read the Mahabharata passage at some point and was inspired by the idea; it is also far more likely that I am just allowing a personal bias for Sanatana Dharma to influence me when making this comparison since this coincidence is entirely possible even without him having read it. I can't be sure though. Nevertheless, the passage itself is a strong philosophical argument for a society that holds a view of hard determinism as the social norm, albeit with a nihilistic fatalism. Holding

---

66. [1846] Ganguli, Kisari Mohan, translator. *Mahabharata of Krishna-Dwaipayana Vyasa, Volume 4 Books 13, 14, 15, 16, 17 and 18*. Vol. 4, Project Gutenberg.
67. [1847] Harris, Sam. "Sam Harris on 'Free Will.'" *YouTube*, Skeptic, 27 Mar. 2012, www.youtube.com/watch?v=pCofmZlC72g.
68. [1848] Harris, Sam. *Free Will*. Free Press, 2012.

no one accountable due to prior causes influencing everything from their emotions, to their premeditated and conscious act of murder, along with teaching people not to feel guilty for murdering others can have disastrous results for a society from the perspective of Consequentialist ethics and our own biological desire for survival. The story most likely existed to assuage guilt for acts of violence on behalf of absolute monarchies in ancient India, which is probably why a Prince is reciting the tale, and for ancient Indian philosophers to debate the idea of cause-and-effect of actions and explaining why they viewed hard determinism as truth with an emotive fictional story to generate interest in the debate. The concept of *Karma,* with its various definitions from action to its relation to the soul and to *Samsara* (reincarnation/rebirth), was explicitly mentioned to have been predicated upon hard determinism in the passage. This would explain the multiple definitions from various denominations of Sanatana Dharma like the differences in the Buddhist sect. Karma seems to have been a multidimensional concept within ancient India as a mental shortcut for individuals to understand their lives in relation to hard determinism for most denominations of Sanatana Dharma.[1849] To further clarify; for the less educated in ancient India, fanciful ideas like Shiva controlling everything assuaged any rivalry such as in the *Isvara Gita,* for others who were more educated, it was more interesting to study the complex ideas about consciousness and it's relation to the physical body like in the *Samkhya Karika* which argues that consciousness isn't the doer of a person's actions but rather a viewer of them.[1850] The reason the definitions changed fluidly may have to do with the religious concept of the *Gunas* making cultural connotations of one's work ethic being the same as a thread or a string.[1851] The connotation, affirmed by Karma in the above passage, is that their life is inevitably following a predestined path that they understood to largely have no control over. In fact, the more evidence I examined, the more confidence I gained for this conclusion of ancient Indian society. Passages such as Krishna's argument for why he must do selfless work or the society would fall apart, the Great Goddess being the ruler of everything and fulfilling predestined prophecies in the *Devi Gita,* and the ubiquity of the belief in Karma and Samsara even as some of the most powerful criticisms of the existence of God temporarily killed the belief in a God throughout the majority of Northern Indian society until approximately after the Buddha's death all lead significant credence to this argument of mine. The implicit assumption of ancient Sanatana Dharma practitioners was most likely hard determinism similar to the Abrahamic faiths beginning with the uncritical assumption that free will exists.

Perhaps this argument about hard determinism being the cultural norm of ancient India will garner staunch dismissal and refutations by modern Hindus and especially by Western

---

69. [1849] Cialdini, Robert B. "Chapter 1: Weapons of Influence (1-16)" *Influence: Science and practice.* 4th ed., 21st Century Bks, 2002.
70. [1850] Bawra, Brahmrishi Vishvatma, translator. Samkhya Aphorisms: VI, VIII, XI, XIII and Karika Aphorisms: LXII, LXIV, LXV, LXVI, LXVII *Sāmkhya Kārikā With Gaudapādācarya Bhāsya.* Brahmrishi Yoga Publications, 2012.
71. [1851] Bawra, Brahmrishi Vishvatma, translator. *Sāmkhya Kārikā With Gaudapādācarya Bhāsya.* Brahmrishi Yoga Publications, 2012.

Indologists since it would mean that the entire body of work for several decades across several Western countries would need to be dismissed as worthless since Western Indologists failed to do even the most basic research. An important context to note is that a cursory examination of the ancient board games that the multitude of civilizations played from ancient Egypt, to ancient Greece, and ancient India reveal that their ancient games were predicated on the randomness of dice throws which were often viewed as signs of a person's fate or a imparting a teaching about the lack of free will in any individual action.[1852] Makeshift dice from cowry shells in ancient India, animal bones in other ancient parts of the world, and so forth were used to play these games of chance and these games often involved imparting the religious teachings of their respective cultures through the gameplay itself as a metaphor.[1853] The belief in a predestined event and that deities predetermined one's life was a norm across most of the ancient world as can be demonstrated by their board games which took on religious qualities throughout their histories.[1854] Therefore, ancient India having such conditions in its ancient board games would actually be the norm similar to almost all ancient societies and not an aberration from the norm. Crucially, this social norm of hard determinism seems to exist in all ancient Indian board games as either an implicit or explicit lesson to be inculcated by its players.[1855] Over the course of history in ancient India, the teaching of accepting one's fate as predetermined was made as a metaphor from the mechanics of board games like Leela, which seems to be the earliest version of ancient Indian board games where the rolling of cowry shells as dice was first implemented as part of its rules, to the more advanced forms of these fate-based board games that took Leela as the template.[1856][1857] Pachisi and Chaupar have strong implications of hard determinism as a metaphor in the instructions of their teachings through dice rolls.[1858][1859] In particular, Pachisi seems to be a board game designed to indoctrinate youth in understanding the religious concepts of the Karmic cycle of Samsara (rebirth), Moksha (Self-liberation), and the Caste system itself.[1860][1861][1862] The dice rolls imply hard determinism,

---

72. [1852] Meadows, Andre. "Ancient Games: Crash Course Games #2." *YouTube*, CrashCourse, 8 Apr. 2016, www.youtube.com/watch?v=H1lv3cOmlzM.
73. [1853] Meadows, Andre. "Ancient Games: Crash Course Games #2." *YouTube*, CrashCourse, 8 Apr. 2016, www.youtube.com/watch?v=H1lv3cOmlzM.
74. [1854] Meadows, Andre. "Ancient Games: Crash Course Games #2." *YouTube*, CrashCourse, 8 Apr. 2016, www.youtube.com/watch?v=H1lv3cOmlzM.
75. [1855] Floyd, Daniel. "Snakes and Ladders - How the Meaning of an Ancient Children's Game Adapted Over Time - Extra Credits." *YouTube*, Extra Credits, 24 Dec. 2014, www.youtube.com/watch?v=PzLYKY1nPsY.
76. [1856] Floyd, Daniel. "Snakes and Ladders - How the Meaning of an Ancient Children's Game Adapted Over Time - Extra Credits." *YouTube*, Extra Credits, 24 Dec. 2014, www.youtube.com/watch?v=PzLYKY1nPsY.
77. [1857] "Leela (Game)." *Wikipedia*, Wikimedia Foundation, 19 Dec. 2017, en.wikipedia.org/wiki/Leela_(game).
78. [1858] Floyd, Daniel. "Snakes and Ladders - How the Meaning of an Ancient Children's Game Adapted Over Time - Extra Credits." *YouTube*, Extra Credits, 24 Dec. 2014, www.youtube.com/watch?v=PzLYKY1nPsY.
79. [1859] "Pachisi." *Wikipedia*, Wikimedia Foundation, 15 June 2019, en.wikipedia.org/wiki/Pachisi.
80. [1860] "Pachisi." *Wikipedia*, Wikimedia Foundation, 15 June 2019, en.wikipedia.org/wiki/Pachisi.
81. [1861] Floyd, Daniel. "Snakes and Ladders - How the Meaning of an Ancient Children's Game Adapted

the four different color schemes available seem to indicate the upper four Castes since the Caste system's oldest terminology denoted color albeit the game seems to imply it is about the color of one's soul (to what extent there is a racial connotation, I can't say and I would welcome empirical evidence on the issue for further clarification), and certain rules within the game of Pachisi such as two pieces of the same color being able to block another piece of a different color from moving further in the board within certain spaces of the game seem to be pertaining to teachings of Caste differences and its relation to Samsara.[1863][1864] The ultimate goal of Pachisi is the attainment of Moksha (self-liberation) for the soul once all four pieces of a player's color scheme have got to the finishing goal through dice rolls.[1865][1866] Pachisi was later adapted in the modern West as the games *Ludo, Trouble.* and *Sorry!* along with specific French and German variants like *Jeu dets petits Chevaux* (Game of Little Horses) and *Mensch Agere Dich Nicht* (Do Not Get Angry, Man).[1867] Chaupar is a game very similar to Pachisi, but seems to have been modified within ancient India to eventually become Gyan Chaupar with distinct moral teachings based on Hindu or Jain moral principles.[1868][1869][1870] Gyan Chaupar was eventually adapted to the West with its more popularly known name as *Snakes and Ladders* in Great Britain and *Chutes and Ladders* in the United States which modified the game to have the exact same number of virtues and vices unlike the Indian versions.[1871][1872] As with the other ancient Indian games that included dice rolls in board games, the mechanics as metaphor of Gyan Chaupar was to inculcate children with the teaching of hard determinism as they attempt to get to the finish line of Moksha through dice rolls but have no control over the movements of their representative piece.[1873][1874]

---

82. [1862] Korea(Jolie), Vakko. "Ravensburger Pachisi - by Vakko Korea(Jolie)." *YouTube*, 라벤스부르거바코, 13 Aug. 2011, www.youtube.com/watch?v=2w8-pZlNdrY.
83. [1863] Korea(Jolie), Vakko. "Ravensburger Pachisi - by Vakko Korea(Jolie)." *YouTube*, 라벤스부르거바코, 13 Aug. 2011, www.youtube.com/watch?v=2w8-pZlNdrY.
84. [1864] "Pachisi." *Wikipedia*, Wikimedia Foundation, 15 June 2019, en.wikipedia.org/wiki/Pachisi.
85. [1865] "Pachisi." *Wikipedia*, Wikimedia Foundation, 15 June 2019, en.wikipedia.org/wiki/Pachisi.
86. [1866] Korea(Jolie), Vakko. "Ravensburger Pachisi - by Vakko Korea(Jolie)." *YouTube*, 라벤스부르거바코, 13 Aug. 2011, www.youtube.com/watch?v=2w8-pZlNdrY.
87. [1867] "Pachisi." *Wikipedia*, Wikimedia Foundation, 15 June 2019, en.wikipedia.org/wiki/Pachisi.
88. [1868] "Chaupar." *Wikipedia*, Wikimedia Foundation, 7 July 2019, en.wikipedia.org/wiki/Chaupar.
89. [1869] Floyd, Daniel. "Snakes and Ladders - How the Meaning of an Ancient Children's Game Adapted Over Time - Extra Credits." *YouTube*, Extra Credits, 24 Dec. 2014, www.youtube.com/watch?v=PzLYKY1nPsY.
90. [1870] "Gyan Chauper." *Wikipedia*, Wikimedia Foundation, 1 Aug. 2018, en.wikipedia.org/wiki/Gyan_chauper.
91. [1871] Floyd, Daniel. "Snakes and Ladders - How the Meaning of an Ancient Children's Game Adapted Over Time - Extra Credits." *YouTube*, Extra Credits, 24 Dec. 2014, www.youtube.com/watch?v=PzLYKY1nPsY.
92. [1872] "Snakes and Ladders." *Wikipedia*, Wikimedia Foundation, 23 July 2019, en.wikipedia.org/wiki/Snakes_and_Ladders.
93. [1873] "Gyan Chauper." *Wikipedia*, Wikimedia Foundation, 1 Aug. 2018, en.wikipedia.org/wiki/Gyan_chauper.

The Caste system is a more obvious usage of hard determinism as a social system within Hindu theology. Everything about a person's Caste is predicated upon their previous life resulting in the social status that they're born into. While it could be argued that their behavior would garner a better life upon reincarnation, this doesn't dispute that Caste is predetermined both theologically and in the real world context of discrimination against Dalits. Moreover, within the context of Hindu theology, any behavior that could change their rebirth to something like Moksha (self-liberation) to avoid reincarnation would be an argument for compatibilism. Compatibilism is essentially the argument that the universe and life in general is largely predetermined with the past determining the future, but that some human actions are free.[1875] Compatibilism has many varieties that emphasize either a soft determinism or relative free will after a predetermined beginning in one's life depending upon the specifics of each compatibilist argument.[1876] In this case, it would be a compatibilism with an emphasis on soft determinism above free will since the only reason a person of lower Caste would be conducting such behavior would be to avoid rebirth and because they were already dealt an unfair hand at birth in the lower Caste life that they have. The Brahmins zealously maintaining the Caste system despite refutations from the Sramana movements from the Upanishads to the atheists may have largely been due to a steadfast belief in hard determinism with a fear that not doing so would collapse societies and bring ruination. This particular belief seems to be mentioned in the Bhagavad Gita with an emphasis on misogyny to use women as scapegoats for why collapse happens.[1877]

Finally, I'd like to indulge in a form of pure speculation on my part. If this speculation of mine should prove bemusing in its ignorance, then feel free to dismiss it as I have dismissed Western Indology as worthless. When reading Will Durant's *Our Oriental Heritage* and online searches on the history of India, I am struck by the peculiarity of how these ancient civilizations - largely composed of absolute monarchies - had a constant cycle of overwhelming the subcontinent and retracting into collapse throughout various periods of Indian history.[1878] Moreover, it struck me as rather odd that there didn't seem to be any meaningful defense from a constant surge of foreign invasions that came about from the Ancient Greeks onward until Islam's horrific massacres and then Western imperialism. When I considered the deterministic beliefs of ancient Sanatana Dharma practitioners and the adaption

---

94. [1874] Floyd, Daniel. "Snakes and Ladders - How the Meaning of an Ancient Children's Game Adapted Over Time - Extra Credits." *YouTube*, Extra Credits, 24 Dec. 2014, www.youtube.com/watch?v=PzLYKY1nPsY.
95. [1875] Green, Hank. "Compatibilism: Crash Course Philosophy #25." *YouTube*, Crash Course / PBS Digital Studios, 22 Aug. 2016, www.youtube.com/watch?v=KETTtiprINU.
96. [1876] Green, Hank. "Compatibilism: Crash Course Philosophy #25." *YouTube*, Crash Course / PBS Digital Studios, 22 Aug. 2016, www.youtube.com/watch?v=KETTtiprINU.
97. [1877] "Bhagavadgita: 1. The Yoga of Arjuna's Sorrow." Translated by Jayaram V, *Bhagavadgita: The Yoga of Arjuna's Sorrow*, www.hinduwebsite.com/gita1.asp.
98. [1878] Durant, Will. *Our Oriental Heritage: Being a History of Civilization in Egypt and the Near East to the Death of Alexander, and in India, China and Japan from the Beginning to Our Own Day*. Simon and Schuster, 1935.

of practices like *Purdoh* and *Sita* from foreign cultures that assimilated shortly before the Islamic conquests to begin intra-subcontinent wars, a possibility entered my mind.[1879] I reiterate that this is pure speculation on my part and it'll probably be disproven and wholly dismissed rather quickly. What if the belief in Samsara (reincarnation) applied to civilizations too? What if the constant disintegration and re-emergence of new civilizations within the subcontinent before Western imperialism wasn't a defect, but a natural feature of ancient India?[1880] Perhaps analogies were made from individual rebirth to societal rebirth which was why war, bloodshed, and lack of resistance to foreign invasions up until the Islamic despotism was a bizarre standard in ancient India? In effect, they wouldn't see their societies as a precious good like in the modern context of the Republic of India, but rather as a societal system constantly in flux with a predetermined path of success or failure. If the society was filled with a *fatalistic* sense of hard determinism, then why wouldn't this be the case on a societal level? Many Kshatriya rulers abandoned their posts to go on spiritual journeys or otherwise retired to a religious monastery that they identified with upon their retirement. Also, there remains a possibility that many ancient Indians, whether educated or not, may have expected a cosmic rebirth as per the belief in Kali Yuga with the remaking of the universe itself and that this process of disintegration and reformation of societies was an anticipated occurrence for such a ridiculous belief similar to the Abrahamic faiths own ridiculous beliefs in a last judgment before the so-called end of the world. Perhaps I am jumping to far-reaching conclusions without significant enough evidence, but what struck me to pose these questions was the question of how different ancient Indian civilization must've been on a societal basis compared to a civilization where personal liberty is the social norm. What sort of consequences does such a society create and how can we learn from their failings so we don't repeat their history? If ancient India's beliefs were closer to hard determinism, and all credible evidence seems to indicate such, then what can we learn from their ancient civilization as modern science shows that the ancient Indians and other ancient civilizations may have been correct about hard determinism despite whatever superstitions attached to the belief?

A Culture of Self-Negation

To preemptively dismantle any potential future accusations foisted upon me, I am not attempting to mitigate or ignore the harm of Casteism in the theology of Hinduism. Casteism is arguably the most vapid, worthless, and pernicious theological teaching in all of human history. It quite clearly guarantees a brain drain in modern India in which many Dalits suffering from persecution will inevitably attempt to leave for a better life in places like the Western societies. They could even remain Hindu, but feel that Indian society hates them and

---

99. [1879] Durant, Will. Chapter XVI: From Alexander to Aurangzeb (10072 - 10817). *Our Oriental Heritage: Being a History of Civilization in Egypt and the Near East to the Death of Alexander, and in India, China and Japan from the Beginning to Our Own Day*. Simon and Schuster, 1935.
100. [1880] Durant, Will. Chapter XVI: From Alexander to Aurangzeb (10072 - 10817). *Our Oriental Heritage: Being a History of Civilization in Egypt and the Near East to the Death of Alexander, and in India, China and Japan from the Beginning to Our Own Day*. Simon and Schuster, 1935.

that they have no future in India. Despite the negative outlook of the Western mainstream media upon India, US far-right extremism leading to the killings of Indians, and especially the persecution of Sikhs on the fatuous basis that they're related to the Islamic faith in the US; for the most part, Sanatana Dharma practitioners of Indian descent who are living in the West are highly respected within Western societies by the vast majority within the West and that includes the United States. Of course, that means Hindus are highly respected within the West and specifically within the US too. Hindus in the West don't care about Caste differences. Hindus flourish when they live in societies that support Free Speech and leave behind Casteism as a relic of ancient times. Why is it that Hindus can so easily leave behind Caste when emigrating to the West? Because of Hindu theology teaching us to modernize with the social norms of the nation-state that we come to respect as our home. To give an example of the success of Hindus who abandon Caste entirely within my own country which I was born and raised in, the United States of America, we US Hindus have the highest academic achievement of any religious group and we have the second highest income level as a religious demographic which is second only to members of the Jewish faith.[1881][1882] Some might claim that this is due to selective immigration of highly-educated Hindus to the United States and not related to any qualities within Hinduism itself. However, when examining the success of American people who are of the Indian ethnic background of which approximately fifty-eight percent are part of Sanatana Dharma (that is, approximately fifty-one percent Hindu, around five percent Sikh, and around two percent Jain), approximately ten percent are unaffiliated, and around twenty-eight percent belong to an Abrahamic faith tradition; the picture of Indian Americans seems to skew favorably towards Hindu culture playing an important factor in achievement.[1883] To lead further credence to this argument since many Hindus remain unconvinced when I've explained this in online discussions; among Indians who are 25 years of age or older, approximately seventy-two percent of foreign-born Indians hold a Bachelors or Postgraduate degree, but approximately seventy-four percent of US-born Indians hold a Bachelors or Postgraduate degree.[1884] Therefore, if it was solely selective immigration policies, then why does it seem that US-born and raised Hindus succeed slightly better than foreign-born Hindus since approximately fifty-one percent of Indian Americans are Hindus and fifty-eight percent follow Sanatana Dharma?[1885] It is possible that this particular aspect of my argument could be wrong

---

101. [1881] Murphy, Caryle. "The Most and Least Educated U.S. Religious Groups." *Pew Research Center*, Pew Research Center, 4 Nov. 2016, www.pewresearch.org/fact-tank/2016/11/04/the-most-and-least-educated-u-s-religious-groups/.
102. [1882] Masci, David. "How Income Varies among U.S. Religious Groups." *Pew Research Center*, Pew Research Center, 11 Oct. 2016, www.pewresearch.org/fact-tank/2016/10/11/how-income-varies-among-u-s-religious-groups/.
103. [1883] DeSilver, Drew. "5 Facts about Indian Americans." *Pew Research Center*, Pew Research Center, 30 Sept. 2014, www.pewresearch.org/fact-tank/2014/09/30/5-facts-about-indian-americans/.
104. [1884] "Indians: Data on Asian Americans." *Pew Research Center's Social & Demographic Trends Project*, Pew Research Center's Social & Demographic Trends Project, 8 Sept. 2017, www.pewsocialtrends.org/fact-sheet/asian-americans-indians-in-the-u-s/.
105. [1885] DeSilver, Drew. "5 Facts about Indian Americans." *Pew Research Center*, Pew Research Center, 30 Sept. 2014, www.pewresearch.org/fact-tank/2014/09/30/5-facts-about-indian-americans/.

since I couldn't find a specific examination comparing US-born and foreign-born Hindu education attainment, but since the Indian American demographic is fifty-one percent Hindu then this should be strong evidence for it. The lack of Casteism seems to be either an equal or more important factor for the economic and educational success of Hindus in the West. *Nevertheless, regardless of that specific issue, it is a well-established and demonstrable fact that Hindus thrive in societies without Caste and that is precisely why they decide to leave India in order to settle in them.*

As I fear this still isn't sufficient evidence in convincing Hindus within India, please consider what Casteism essentially means for a Hindu person's dream goals in India. While other religious faiths entirely separate from Hinduism and other denominations of Sanatana Dharma can choose their occupations, Hindus are restricted in terms of government employment within India to specific scheduled Caste occupations. Due to the outsized impact of government-related jobs in India, such government guidelines could prevent a person of a specific Caste from working towards their life goals since a Hindu person can't even apply to a job that they have an intrinsic interest in. Despite what most people in any country think or believe about job prospects, the most satisfying experience in daily life is working towards a life goal through finding a selection of jobs that move them towards that life goal.[1886][1887] In order to do that, a person has to work towards entry level and mid-level job prospects before going towards the goals that they want to achieve, but if there are impermeable barriers of entry to fulfilling a person's intrinsic motivations of working to build the life and career that they want then what happens? They will work hard to go elsewhere towards a country that values their hard work, treats them with human dignity, and where they can fulfill their lifelong prospects of building the life and career that they want. It is true for uneducated immigrants, it is true for Saudi women fleeing the misogynistic barriers within Saudi Arabia, and it is true for the highly educated Hindus who migrate to the West. Keep in mind, it may not necessarily be Dalits, but members of other Castes who simply want a better life without Caste-specific career restrictions preventing them from gaining the life they want to live. Most people in any society may not think much of career prospects, but the hard working people who become highly talented in their fields of interest matter in every single society and those highly talented people will always seek a better life. If you're a Hindu from India, do you despise them for it? For being an "NRI" (Non-resident Indian) and leaving their birthplace instead of working to build India towards a better future for all those living in India? They *deserve* to seek such a life where they can attain what they want and they probably tried in India before giving up to look elsewhere. *If you want India as a civilization to thrive like the West, China, Japan, and to be closer to the educated Hindus who live in the West, then you must rid India of the Caste system entirely.* I don't mean that Hindus of India should stop talking about Caste and especially not Caste-specific discrimination. *When I say that the Caste system must be destroyed, I mean that Hindus of India must internalize the fact that the Caste system is false and immoral on the*

---

106. [1886] Pink, Daniel H. *Drive: the Surprising Truth about What Motivates Us*. Canongate Books, 2018.
107. [1887] Duckworth, Angela. *Grit: the Power of Passion and Perseverance*. Scribner, 2016.

basis of human rights and that it is just superstitious nonsense with no basis in reality. Far too often, people supportive of BJP policies simply don't want to discuss it and that disposition is the reverse of what it takes to ameliorate social ills like the Caste system. You don't end a tyrannical system of oppression by ignoring the issue; that only festers and grows the issue unchallenged.

Due to some subsets of contemporary Left-leaning politics in the US arguing the nonsensical notion that we as human beings can't understand or empathize with a different social background because it is not part of our lived experience, I'd like to share what seems to me to be the emotional anguish of the founder of the Indian Republic, Bhimrao Ramji Ambedkar (popularly titled by many Indians as *Dr. Babasaheb Ambedkar* as a note of respect for his legacy of activism), who was a Dalit himself and whom the BJP-leaning political groups in India argue to be the true founder of the Indian Republic instead of Mohandis Gandhi and Jawaharlal Nehru. I'd like to make note that I find such arguments to be silly as all three probably deserve to be known as the Founding Fathers of the Republic of India along with Savarkar who has a more checkered past. I find it amusing that among them only Gandhi believed in a higher power; Ambedkar should probably be considered a Buddhist Atheist, Savarkar - the founder of the Hindutva movement - was a Hindu Atheist, and Nehru was apparently an Atheist too. Nevertheless, if the people of India who lean towards the BJP party wish to truly carry the legacy of Ambedkar, they can only claim such a legacy by annihilating the Caste system out of existence as he so wished. Ambedkar's entire legacy is proof that Casteism is false and immoral. Imagine for a moment how many more people like him could exist to help further progress India, if Casteism was eliminated.

The following is from Bhimrao Ramji Ambedkar's *Essays on Untouchables and Untouchability*. I edited the spacing slightly because certain portions had periods and question-marks in a separate space when copied from the Kindle version, but everything written is from Ambedkar himself and I didn't modify anything else. This specific portion is framed as Ambedkar specifying what the Dalits can ask other Hindus who are in Castes above them. The material that he wrote suggests this was possibly his own emotional turmoil over his treatment as a Dalit in India:

> "Does Hinduism recognize their worth as human beings? Does it stand for their equality? Does it extend to them the benefit of liberty? Does it at least help to forge the bond of fraternity between them and the Hindus? Does it teach the Hindus that the Untouchables are their kindred? Does it say to the Hindus it is a sin to treat the Untouchables as being neither man nor beast? Does it tell the Hindus to be righteous to the Untouchables? Does it preach to the Hindus to be just and humane to them? Does it inculcate upon the Hindus the virtue of being friendly to them ? Does it tell the Hindus to love them, to respect them and to do them no wrong. In fine, does Hinduism universalize the value of life without distinction?
>
> No Hindu can dare to give an affirmative answer to any of these questions? On the contrary the wrongs to which the Untouchables are subjected by the Hindus are acts which are sanctioned by the Hindu religion. They are done in the name of Hinduism and are justified in the name of Hinduism. The spirit and tradition which makes lawful the lawlessness of the Hindus towards the Untouchables is founded and supported by the teachings of Hinduism. How can the Hindus ask the Untouchables accept Hinduism and stay in Hinduism? Why should the Untouchables adhere to Hinduism which is solely

responsible for their degradation? How can the Untouchables stay in Hinduism? Untouchability is the lowest depth to which the degradation of a human being can be carried. To be poor is bad but not so bad as to be an Untouchable. The poor can be proud. The Untouchable cannot be. To be reckoned low is bad but it is not so bad as to be an Untouchable. The low can rise above his status. An Untouchable cannot. To be suffering is bad but not so bad as to be an Untouchable. They shall some day be comforted. An Untouchable cannot hope for this. To have to be meek is bad but it is not so bad as to be an Untouchable. The meek if they do not inherit the earth may at least be strong. The Untouchables cannot hope for that.

In Hinduism there is no hope for the Untouchables."[1888]

A bit further on in the essay, Bhimrao Ramji Ambedkar states the following in his justification of the Dalits of Hinduism converting to another religious faith or another denomination of Sanatana Dharma:

"That Hinduism is inconsistent with the self-respect and honour of the Untouchables is the strongest ground which justifies the conversion of the Untouchables to another and nobler faith.

The opponents of conversion are determined not to be satisfied even if the logic of conversion was irrefutable. They will insist upon asking further questions. There is one question which they are always eager to ask largely because they think it is formidable and unanswerable; what will the Untouchables gain materially by changing their faith? The question is not at all formidable. It is simple to answer. It is not the intention of the Untouchables to make conversion an opportunity for economic gain. The Untouchables it is true will not gain wealth by conversion. This is however no loss because while they remain as Hindus they are doomed to be poor. Politically the Untouchables will lose the political rights that are given to the Untouchables. This is, however, no real loss. Because they will be entitled to the benefit of the political rights reserved for the community which they would join through conversion. Politically there is neither gain nor loss. Socially, the Untouchables will gain absolutely and immensely because by conversion the Untouchables will be members of a community whose religion has universalized and equalized all values of life. Such a blessing is unthinkable for them while they are in the Hindu fold.

The answer is complete. But by reason of its brevity it is not likely to give satisfaction to the opponents of conversion. The Untouchables need three things. First thing they need is to end their social isolation. The second thing they need is to end their inferiority complex. Will conversion meet their needs? The opponents of conversion have a feeling that the supporters of conversion have no case. That is why they keep on raising questions. The case in favour of conversion is stronger than the strongest case. Only one does wish to spend long arguments to prove what is so obvious. But since it is necessary to put an end to all doubt, I am prepared to pursue the matter. Let me take each point separately.

How can they end their social isolation? The one and the only way to end their social isolation is for the Untouchables to establish kinship with and get themselves incorporated into another community which is free from the spirit of caste. The answer is quite simple and yet not many will readily accept its validity. The reason is, very few people realize the value and significance of kinship.

Nevertheless its value and significance are very great."[1889]

To my surprise, Ambedkar seemed to change his views somewhat later in life. It should be noted that Ambedkar, despite the horrors that he undoubtedly personally experienced as a

---

108. [1888] Ambedkar, Bhimrao Ramji. *Essays on Untouchables and Untouchability*. Kindle ed., Amazon Digital Services LLC, 2017.
109. [1889] Ambedkar, Bhimrao Ramji. *Essays on Untouchables and Untouchability*. Kindle ed., Amazon Digital Services LLC, 2017.

Dalit and all the issues that he explained, eventually concluded that Islam was far worse than Casteism in Hinduism.[1890] I was astonished that such a well-respected social reformer and person who undoubtedly suffered under Casteism would vehemently such a position in his writings as I assumed that Casteism had to be the worst and most disgusting form of dehumanization imaginable. Yet, to my surprise, Ambedkar's writings reveal that he believed Islam was worse than Casteism.[1891] This was specifically because Muslims in India during his time refused to engage in any social change to alleviate the wrongdoings of misogyny against Muslim women, violence against non-Muslims such as in the Moplah rebellion were not condemned but rather hailed as heroic despite credible accounts of rape and massacre upon non-Muslims, and hatred for non-Muslims using gangsterism as a tactic specifically to create violent conflict with Hindus was a notorious form of Islamic political activity that was repeatedly conducted according to Ambedkar's writings.[1892] Ambedkar explained that, despite all the horrific faults of Hinduism, there were a tiny minority of socially conscious Hindus seeking to ameliorate the historic wrongdoings against Dalits while Muslims steadfastly refused to make any concessions or changes towards Muslim women within their own communities and mostly treated non-Muslims with unvarnished and unrepentant hatred solely for being non-Muslim.[1893] What astonished me even more was that Ambedkar actually argued that Hindu gangsterism was a form of self-defense against Islamic gangsterism which was done purely out of malice against Hindus; yet, Ambedkar notes that such violent conflicts from both groups would inevitably lead to riots and the disintegration of India despite arguing that it was primarily Islamic groups who were culpable.[1894] Nevertheless, despite such acknowledgements, it cannot be used to ignore the historic and brutal discrimination of Casteism which must be ameliorated for Hinduism to have a chance at overcoming the threats of Islamism in India.

As mentioned in Part I, the recognition of social identity differences among groups of people occur instantaneously according to the lengthy history of repeated studies within modern psychological research.[1895] The Caste system is an instantaneous categorical form of

---

110. [1890] Banerjee, Abhishek. "10 Things Ambedkar Said That Indian Secularists Wouldn't Bear to Hear - OpIndia News." *OpIndia*, 12 Nov. 2018, www.opindia.com/2018/04/10-things-ambedkar-said-that-indian-secularists-wouldnt-bear-to-hear/.
111. [1891] Banerjee, Abhishek. "10 Things Ambedkar Said That Indian Secularists Wouldn't Bear to Hear - OpIndia News." *OpIndia*, 12 Nov. 2018, www.opindia.com/2018/04/10-things-ambedkar-said-that-indian-secularists-wouldnt-bear-to-hear/.
112. [1892] Banerjee, Abhishek. "10 Things Ambedkar Said That Indian Secularists Wouldn't Bear to Hear - OpIndia News." *OpIndia*, 12 Nov. 2018, www.opindia.com/2018/04/10-things-ambedkar-said-that-indian-secularists-wouldnt-bear-to-hear/.
113. [1893] Banerjee, Abhishek. "10 Things Ambedkar Said That Indian Secularists Wouldn't Bear to Hear - OpIndia News." *OpIndia*, 12 Nov. 2018, www.opindia.com/2018/04/10-things-ambedkar-said-that-indian-secularists-wouldnt-bear-to-hear/.
114. [1894] Banerjee, Abhishek. "10 Things Ambedkar Said That Indian Secularists Wouldn't Bear to Hear - OpIndia News." *OpIndia*, 12 Nov. 2018, www.opindia.com/2018/04/10-things-ambedkar-said-that-indian-secularists-wouldnt-bear-to-hear/.
115. [1895] Ispas, Alexa. *Psychology and politics: a social identity perspective*. Psychology Press, 2014.

differences in social status of different Caste identities and tribal identities, the social proof within Indian society makes it an impermeable component of India's social self-conceptions and Hindu culture, and the worst aspect of Casteism is that it is impermeable with no hope for the different Castes to change such a status which leads to discrimination against Dalits.[1896][1897] Casteism is internalized and inculcated by the fatuous assumption that Dalits are born guilty of supposed wrongdoings in a previous life and Samsara (rebirth/reincarnation) acts as a system that thoroughly devalues human life; Moksha (self-liberaton) in the theistic context can be seen as an aversion to life and desire for death as a release.[1898] People are assumed to be cogs in a spiritual wheel that rationalizes seeing fellow human beings as non-entities incapable of changing some intrinsic defect that they're born with and can't control. It is fixed within the Hindu conceptualization of souls and no matter how much a Dalit shows respect to fellow Hindus, loves fellow Hindus, and wishes to celebrate Hindu culture; they are mistreated for simply being born. They internalize the shame of simply being born. Hinduism is to blame for this social discrimination and Hinduism must work to rectify it because otherwise Hinduism itself will perish. If I'm being honest, Hinduism would deserve to perish for the historic and cruel discrimination of the Dalits, but Hinduism claims to be about inclusiveness and truthseeking so perhaps Hinduism can end its own insipid poison and support the human rights of Dalits? Discrimination of Dalits can only come by recognizing the historic abuses and not by ignoring them; it can only come by treating Dalits as fellow human beings and not as impure filth that is beneath the notice of upper Castes. The discrimination of Dalits must be overcome by thoroughly repudiating, speaking out, and criticizing discrimination against Dalits and the only way to do that is Free Speech. *Hindu theological justifications for the historic abuse of Dalits must be recognized and internalized as wrong, mocked as wrong, and repudiated on both the basis of human rights and on Samsara and cosmic views of Karma being falsehoods with no credible evidence to their veracity.* Creating social barriers of different Castes refusing to intermingle only leads to intra-Hindu hatred and violence such as misogynistic crimes like killing daughters for marrying out of Caste or promoting gangsterism which disproportionately harms Dalits. Free Speech will undoubtedly open the doors to deplorable comments of Casteism, but that simply means that the problem will be more noticeable and much easier to counteract in order to make meaningful social change for their human rights. India has made strides, but to paraphrase Kushal Mehra of *The Carvaka Podcast*, it's only at sixty percent improvement at best in contemporary Indian society and not the ninety-nine percent that India should aim for. I say ninety-nine percent, because one-hundred percent is probably too absurd when recognizing the ubiquity of human ignorance, cruelty, and stupidity. However, major social changes to ameliorate historic discrimination can be done to help the vast majority of Dalits and I don't mean government social programs; I mean treating

---

116.[1896] Cialdini, Robert B. "Chapter 4: Social Proof (98-140)" *Influence: Science and practice*. 4th ed., 21st Century Bks, 2002.
117.[1897] Ispas, Alexa. *Psychology and politics: a social identity perspective*. Psychology Press, 2014.
118.[1898] Nietzsche, Friedrich Wilhelm. *On the genealogy of morals: a polemical tract*. Translated by Ian Johnston, PDF, Richer Resources Publications, 2014.

Dalits as human beings instead of different Castes choosing to self-segregate into Caste-specific social norms on making friends and selectively choosing only a specific Caste to have romantic relationships with to prevent inter-Caste marriages. The quality of the person should matter and not their Caste, but these pervasive social norms embedded within Hindu culture prevent that on the basis of theology.

Let me be clear and outspoken about this so there is no misunderstanding; the protection, defense for, and the passive lack of action in repudiating the Caste system is the death of Hinduism. Perhaps not the death of Sanatana Dharma, but it is assuredly the death of the Vedic denominations of Sanatana Dharma that is called Hinduism. Perhaps you will find this argument mindboggling, but if you are a Hindu then it is incumbent upon you to understand this pernicious issue on a systemic level. *To protect and defend the Caste system is to hate and destroy Hinduism. To be passive towards repudiating the Caste system is to bring certain death to Hinduism.* Why? Because the religious theology behind why Dalits are so mistreated, which is a disgusting and shameful stupidity that should be repudiated, is the closest theological concept to Original Sin from the Abrahamic faith traditions and ultimately rationalizes conversion out of Hinduism to an Abrahamic faith of either Christianity or Islam. After all, if a Dalit is taught their very existence is filthy, disgusting, and that they deserve abuse for the crime of being born then a theological teaching that preaches humans are born sinful, that they must seek forgiveness for their sins, and that all humans are sinners for not accepting Jesus Christ as their lord and savior is effectively rationalized as morally and socially correct to a person suffering the social stigma of being a Dalit. Conversely, a Dalit being taught everyone who is Muslim is pure, but that non-Muslims are all kaffirs who work together to hurt, oppress, and destroy Islamic societies can also be rationalized for a Dalit who is suffering legitimate social discrimination under Hindu culture. *Simply being a Dalit is an open-door invitation for conversion to an Abrahamic faith tradition and it is entirely the fault of the theology of Hinduism.* To be clear, if you're a Hindu reader eager to help ameliorate this issue, you must understand that a Dalit surely knows when you're being sincere and insincere in ending Casteism; they are not stupid people, they live with the discrimination every day and can tell when someone shows genuine concern for their wellbeing or not. *If you wish to protect and defend Hinduism, you must have an intrinsic and genuine concern for the human rights of Dalits and not simply act out of fear for the future of India from the prospect of no longer living in a Hindu majority country.* To mistreat Dalits is to mistreat Hinduism because you devalue your fellow Hindus for intra-Hindu bigotry instead of caring about them as fellow human beings.

Sadly, I understand that this'll simply be seen as a "naive plea" and not as a rational assessment because of the pervasive culture of Abrahamicism that teaches violence is rational via derivatives of the concepts of Original Sin and the so-called Golden Rule, which is just the reciprocity principle that is a fundamental human norm, intermixing to spread hatred for the human race.[1899] That is, Original Sin and the Golden Rule in tandem teach that violence is rational and are not morally different than Islam's teaching of Qisas ("Eye for an Eye / Retaliation in kind") because when harm is done to you, then you feel the urge to reciprocate the violence and this is easily done when you believe that the other person is filled with sin and then seek forgiveness from Jesus Christ for any violence you inflicted on them; to Christianity's credit, it has a teaching of turning the other cheek but all a Christian has to do is openly interpret their actions which effectively makes the verse of "turning the other cheek" moot and Jesus's forgiveness for all sins makes it entirely moot far more than open interpretation does.[1900][1901] Victorian British culture did little more than worsen the pre-existing conditions in India because of their steadfast use of the Realist Theory of International Relations for its own economic interests. Regardless of those reasons, it is incumbent upon Hindus of India in contemporary times to work toward fixing this shameful social stigma against Dalits, it cannot be used to make excuses for not changing now nor on being the first to make such social changes against stigmas in general whether it is the Intra-Hindu bigotry of Caste, homophobia, transphobia, Anti-Muslim bigotry, racism, Anti-Christian bigotry, misogyny, or other forms of bigotry. I despise making this argument, but for those Hindus who are narrow-minded and focused more on self-interests which they wrongfully assume means empowering themselves in a zero-sum game; consider that there is no hope of building a stronger India in order to build a stronger defense against foreign threats like Pakistan, Bangladesh, and possibly China if the people of India are too preoccupied in shutting down and oppressing fellow Indian people for wanting to be treated with human dignity as part of the social fabric of India. Casteism then inspires insurrection movements that seek to break India into smaller and separate States whether by Islamist groups spreading terrorism throughout India or the Christian-Marxist coalitions doing the same. Further consider that Hindus in societies without Caste seem to guarantee diverse intellectual pursuits in STEM fields, IT technologies, business, the medical fields, and space research and think about how all of that intellectual clout is being lost by India to the Western societies mainly because of Casteism. Think of all the damage even simple forms of Caste discrimination like a barbershop refusing to serve Dalits does for a local economy in India. In short, to bestow India a true rebirth in which it'll become one of the greatest civilizations again similar to the Maurya empire instead of being broken into pieces by malevolent foreign influences like the British empire, it must obliterate the Caste system. *There is no rational basis for supporting Casteism. In order to defend and empower India morally, philosophically, intellectually, and with national pride for the culture of Sanatana Dharma as a diverse civilization becoming a robust civilization in its diversity; Casteism must be destroyed.*

119.[1899] Cialdini, Robert B. Chapter 2: Reciprocation (19-50). *Influence: Science and practice*. 4th ed., 21st Century Bks, 2002.

120.[1900] "Qisas." *Wikipedia*, Wikimedia Foundation, 9 Sept. 2018, en.wikipedia.org/wiki/Qisas.

121.[1901] Cialdini, Robert B. Chapter 2: Reciprocation (19-50). *Influence: Science and practice*. 4th ed., 21st Century Bks, 2002.

There is a fundamental self-contradiction within Hindu theology, which I would argue is the true problem within the Vedic tradition. *How can a Hindu person be a Truthseeker and yet forced by Hindu theology to be a specific Caste?* Casteism instantly codifies people into particular occupations and perpetuates a self-defeating social norm that treats Caste as if that is their essence as a human being, but if a Hindu of any Caste has a desire for an occupation that doesn't belong to their specific Caste but rather another Caste, then how can they be allowed to fulfill their personal desire to be part of that occupation which may have come about from their Truthseeking to discover their own personal desire? No matter what a person from a specific Caste finds to be their truth through toiling and contemplation, they would be marginalized to live only within the specific norms of their particular Caste regardless due to discrimination from Hindu theology. If their Truthseeking led them to the love for a particular occupation, but Caste prevented them from attaining such employment, then the Caste system would prevent them from fulfilling their personal interest as a Truthseeker. The specific job could even be something selfless within the mind of a Hindu Truthseeker for Indian society at large but because of Casteism, they wouldn't be able to achieve their lifelong goal which Indian society could benefit from. This doesn't just impair them, it impairs the loyalty towards and protection of Hindu culture and a society where Sanatana Dharma remains the majority. *Casteism is the ultimate barrier of Truthseeking.* Even for Hindus who reconverted to Hinduism, the question of Caste remains a barrier that is simply destroying Hinduism. What about arguments that without Caste, then Hinduism has no core and thus no longer makes any internal sense? I hope that I've sufficiently demonstrated via the evidence of ancient practices and board games of Sanatana Dharma that it was the philosophical proposition of hard determinism that was the binding cultural norm of nearly all of Sanatana Dharma and not Casteism specifically, even if Casteism was unfortunately included in that due to the ubiquity of the belief in Samsara in ancient India. Yet, there is another core from the Upanishads onwards and it follows along the foundation of all of us being One but with our own interpretations; how does a Truthseeker verify their truth claims? How can they know that their beliefs have justifiable merit? Quite simply from the true core of Sanatana Dharma from 800 BCE onwards until Islamic imperialism and the later European squabble and subsequent British imperialism tried to shut down this core component of all of Sanatana Dharma. *The other core of Sanatana Dharma, including the Vedic tradition of Hinduism, is debate.* From the Sramana movements Upanishadic cultural movement, to the Atheistic cultural movement after that, and then to the Jain and Buddhism cultural movement after the success of the Astika and Nastika traditions of atheism dominating ancient India; *the core of Truthseeking in all of Sanatana Dharma is debate.* Don't believe me? Explain the many Darshanas (Schools) of the Vedic tradition of Sanatana Dharma eagerly engaged in debates over truth claims about the universe throughout their entire ancient history, explain why the *Tarka-Shastra* even exists as a general concept, and explain why Purva Paksha was always used as a teaching specifically for Truthseeking. *The core of the Truthseeking denominations of Sanatana Dharma is debate and for the human rights of Dalits who suffer so horribly under Casteism, Truthseeking must defeat Casteism!*

The key to doing that is allowing India to have a constitutional right to Free Speech with no blasphemy laws restricting it in India. Some Hindus may complain that this'll open the floodgates to complaints against Hindus, but that is already happening while Islam - a pedophilic warlord's cult of personality - remains exempt from criticism due to blasphemy laws left over by British imperialism.[1902] British imperialism supported the barbaric and backwards culture of Victorian values; they are especially barbaric when compared to the perspective of the superior Enlightenment values of the United States. The barbaric British eventually learned to civilize themselves after forcibly raping nearly the entire world of resources because they unfortunately had more military power than intelligence during the era of British imperialism which is likely why they lost such power. The superior and humanitarian American empire and US public, which historically has shown more of a commitment to Enlightenment values and compassion for human rights, from the stunning history of US Christian missionaries and US journalists of the 1800s standing firmly opposed to British imperial rule by copiously documenting the horrors of British policy in India in defense of the human rights of all Indians regardless of their religious background[1903], to the programs like FERPA in Sub-Saharan Africa to save the lives of an innumerable number of innocent African children, and to the wonderful American business leaders like Warren Buffett along with the Bill and Melinda Gates foundation tirelessly working to absolve the levels of absolute poverty left by the legacy of European imperialism. People of the US have helped to clean up much of the mess from the filthy legacy of British barbarism which should never be forgotten as it is the moral equivalent of the Holocaust and the Armenian genocide from the perspective of Enlightenment values because Enlightenment values teaches that human rights should be equal for all people and the British brought a mass death toll wherever it ruled for the purpose of their own national interests as per the Realist Theory of International Relations. British Victorian imperialism is therefore not morally different than Islamic imperialism, Stalin's brutal oppression of his own people, or the policy of the Great Leap Forward under Mao Zedong unless the argument is that human rights doesn't matter if a Western country abuses other countries for their own national interests. To be clear, defending the British isn't defending Secular Republics because the British has never been a Secular Republic and arguably still doesn't have a democracy since it is officially a Constitutional Monarchy. As of this writing in 2019, Great Britain's legal model for government is more similar to Saudi Arabia than it is to Secular Republics like India and the United States because Great Britain is still a monarchy with a unified Church and State along with no physically written constitution of its own. This legal model is fundamentally opposed to the US model for a Secular Republic. Meanwhile, India is a Secular Republic with a written constitution and all that is required now is separating Hindu temples from the State and allowing Free Speech for the purpose of further revenge against the British empire in favor of Enlightenment values similar to the United States of America. The US and India can then

---

122.[1902] Sorabjee, Soli J. "Insult to Religion - Indian Express." *Archive*, archive.indianexpress.com/news/insult-to-religion-/7214/.
123.[1903] Davis, Mike. *Late Victorian Holocausts: El Nino Famines and the Making of the Third World*. Penguin Random House Publisher Services, 2001.

share in their revenge against the British as they both grew into power by opposing British rule. What revenge am I speaking of? The best type of revenge, of course! The revenge that exists with no violence or ill will towards today's British people who aren't to blame for their barbarian ancestors of the past while documenting their shameful, barbaric Victorian legacy. *The best revenge is living well.*

To the best of my knowledge, from listening to the *Carvaka Podcast* by Kushal Mehra in one of his segments where he explained contemporary Indian politics, many Indians argue that a better police force is necessary before Free Speech can be allowed that there must be a larger police force to deal with any rise in crime over Islamists attacking and possibly preventing Islamists from killing people for criticizing Islam in India. However, Islamist violence has already been happening for years, I recall the most famous member of the Indian National Congress party, Shashi Tharoor, opposing Free Speech in a debate with Christopher Hitchens on the basis of Muslim mobs in India attacking and destroying a Bangalore newspaper company's workplace over their offended feelings in a Sunday article titled "*Mohammad the Idiot*" which was about the discrimination of a mentally disabled boy; this was misunderstood by Muslims who carried out the violence to be an insult to the pedophile Prophet of Islam.[1904] Hitchens had promptly repudiated Tharoor for his argument and pointed out that civilization is a real, precious thing that must be protected and that it is absurd to capitulate to people who physically harm and even kill others on the arbitrary basis of how offended they are and just as absurd to blame those who supposedly "started" controversies by writing books or publishing cartoons since it is conceding to people committing mass violence and letting Muslim mobs rule the social norms through threats of mass violence. The Islamist violence has only risen in the Jammu-Kashmir region and throughout India from Islamic terror attacks which the Western mainstream media don't focus on while disproportionately focusing on mob violence by Hindus.[1905] Likewise, Hindu gangsterism in response to Islamic gangsterism has risen and the targets are often innocent Muslim civilians or sometimes alleged criminals whom the mobs physically beat or kill.[1906] Needless to say, mob justice of any kind cannot be the rule of law. Politicians of both major parties in India have ties to organized crime, many are pending legal trials, and some elected officials in India openly have connections to organized crime.[1907] The assassinations of journalists and politicians occur from both sides of India but aren't denounced by either of the major parties at all. Some of the reason Kashmiri Muslims resist India could be based on the utter falsehood perpetuated by

---

124. [1904] Hitchens, Christopher, and Shashi Tharoor. "Christopher Hitchens vs. Shashi Tharoor FREEDOM OF SPEECH." *YouTube*, ChristopherHitchslap, 30 Dec. 2011, www.youtube.com/watch?v=jw3dDbc1BHE. For reference: The 2007 debate between Hitchens and Tharoor.
125. [1905] "India 2017/2018." *Amnesty International*, www.amnesty.org/en/countries/asia-and-the-pacific/india/report-india/.
126. [1906] "India 2017/2018." *Amnesty International*, www.amnesty.org/en/countries/asia-and-the-pacific/india/report-india/.
127. [1907] Sharma, Ashok. "Dozens of New Indian Parliamentarians Face Criminal Charges." *AP NEWS*, Associated Press, 17 June 2019, www.apnews.com/1678c2a6c0004b799a34cb0ff9434a90.

contemporary Christian missionary teachers who purposefully lie to Kashmiris about being one of the lost tribes of Israel when the tribe are a complete fiction with no evidence that any lost tribes ever existed in real life and all DNA tests of Kashmiris show them to be indigenous to India which disproves both the Abrahamic claims of lost tribes since no such thing ever existed.[1908] In short, the lack of Free Speech leads to so many consequences of negative reciprocal interdependence in a society instead of a more positive reciprocal interdependence that slowly improves society.[1909] I would argue that rather than be a powder keg that unleashes more violence by introducing Free Speech as a constitutionally protected law in Indian society, Free Speech instead should be conceptualized on how it has empirically functioned in all societies that have it.[1910] Free Speech is a failsafe that deters violence; I would even go further and argue that Free Speech is the modern form of *Ahimsa* (non-violence) and that Indian society could more peacefully and gradually put an end to Islamic violence and many other issues by allowing everyone to be able to speak their minds about any topic. It'll unleash the floodgates of intolerance on social media.[1911] Racism, sexism, and many other forms of bigotry will undoubtedly be unleashed . . . and the first step to changing a society peacefully is recognizing the people who hold those views in order to challenge and speak out against them. India can't fight against Islamism by military or police force alone, that is essentially fighting a violent ideology through force while hugging and shielding the teachings that constantly promote such violence. As further proof, despite Islamist regimes in Qatar, Saudi Arabia, the United Arab Emirates, and many others pumping huge sums of money into US national news media[1912], the election campaigns of US politicians[1913], at one point a hundred million directly to the US government before talks regarding the then disappearance of journalist Jamal Khashoggi began[1914], and US universities like Harvard which now offer degrees and treat men who support having sex with 9-year olds as a respected religious position on the basis of

---

128. [1908] Downie, Jonathan M, et al. "A Genome-Wide Search for Greek and Jewish Admixture in the Kashmiri Population." *PloS One*, Public Library of Science, 4 Aug. 2016, www.ncbi.nlm.nih.gov/pmc/articles/PMC4973929/.
129. [1909] Cialdini, Robert B. Chapter 2: Reciprocation (19-50). *Influence: Science and practice*. 4th ed., 21st Century Bks, 2002.
130. [1910] "Free Expression in Practice." *Big Think*, Charles Koch Foundation, 1 Dec. 2018, bigthink.com/Charles-Koch-Foundation/forced-examination-how-the-free-speech-of-others-benefits-us-all?rebelltitem=2#rebelltitem2.
131. [1911] "Free Expression in Practice." *Big Think*, Charles Koch Foundation, 1 Dec. 2018, bigthink.com/Charles-Koch-Foundation/forced-examination-how-the-free-speech-of-others-benefits-us-all?rebelltitem=2#rebelltitem2.
132. [1912] Wintour, Patrick. "Saudis Demanded Good Publicity over Yemen Aid, Leaked UN Document Shows." *The Guardian*, Guardian News and Media, 30 Oct. 2018, www.theguardian.com/global-development/2018/oct/30/saudis-demanded-good-publicity-over-yemen-aid-leaked-un-document-shows?CMP=share_btn_tw.
133. [1913] Massoglia, Anna. "Saudi Foreign Agents' Political Donations Top $1.6 Million in 2018 Elections." *OpenSecrets News*, Center for Responsive Politics, 24 Oct. 2018, www.opensecrets.org/news/2018/10/saudi-foreign-agents-donations-top-1point6-mill/.
134. [1914] Burke, Michael. "$100M In Saudi Money Lands in US Accounts as Pompeo Landed in Riyadh: Report." *TheHill*, 17 Oct. 2018, thehill.com/policy/international/411802-100m-in-saudi-money-lands-in-us-accounts-as-pompeo-landed-in-riyadh.

Religious Tolerance[1915][1916]; Islam hasn't grown in any percentage within the US because approximately 24 percent of people who come from a Muslim background leave Islam every year while there is a similar percentage of conversions to Islam every year.[1917] At best, Islam keeps itself from utterly collapsing in the US from the millions spent on trying to hoodwink Westerners about it. Yet, it hasn't remotely grown at all. All that's left is to try to increase the de-conversion rate, or decrease the rate of those who convert to Islam, or preferably both by challenging it on its harmful beliefs more openly. Ultimately, Free Speech is a great benefit for all societies, India would only be strengthened internally by making it a constitutional right, and killings across India should ultimately decrease in the long-term because Free Speech does have psychological benefits of putting repressed feelings into either thoughtful or callous words to let out one's personal feelings on a matter that they believe to be important.[1918] Society is thereby better informed on what needs to change. Finally, think about it from the perspective of International Relations. While China is imposing concentration camps upon Uyghur Muslims disproportionately blaming an entire population for terrorist groups in the Uyghur community due to terrorism linked to al Qaeda attempting to hijack a Chinese airliner to crash into a trade center in China to make another 9/11 style event happen and Pakistan is imposing blasphemy laws and jailing people indefinitely or killing people in their own streets for blaspheming against the Islamic Prophet Mohammad; India, the only Secular Republic among the three major powers of South Asia, could become a shining beacon of democratic norms and freedoms which would bolster India's appeal in the international community and would garner additional acclaim due to the psychological contrast principle since the other major powers to compare would be Pakistan and China.[1919] Of course, such change would have to be legitimate and no exemption for Islam or Hinduism should be made; I find the trend to borrow concepts from Islamist groups like Islamophobia into Hinduphobia to be disturbing as it seems that without Free Speech, Hindus play by Islam's political rulebook and it softens the way for Islamism to thrive in India. Hindus claim that there is no blasphemy in Hinduism, but then the killing of Narendra Dabholkar, an Indian Atheist and founder of *Maharashtra Andhashraddha Nirmoolan Samiti* (Committee for Eradication of Blind Faith), for supporting activism in which he wanted people to stop using Hinduism to justify criminal offense like sexual violence and monetary fraud on low-educated people by charlatans pretending to be

---

135. [1915] Sokolove, Michael. "Why Is There So Much Saudi Money in American Universities?" *The New York Times*, The New York Times, 3 July 2019, www.nytimes.com/2019/07/03/magazine/saudi-arabia-american-universities.html
136. [1916] Navabi, Armin. "Muslim Defends Muhammad Having Sex with Aisha When She Was Nine!" *YouTube*, Atheist Republic, 3 Jan. 2019, youtu.be/yKExtzI68jM.
137. [1917] Mohamed, Besheer, and Elizabeth Podrebarac Sciupac. "Islam Gains about as Many Converts as It Loses in U.S." *Pew Research Center*, Pew Research Center, 26 Jan. 2018, www.pewresearch.org/fact-tank/2018/01/26/the-share-of-americans-who-leave-islam-is-offset-by-those-who-become-muslim/.
138. [1918] "Free Expression in Practice." *Big Think*, Charles Koch Foundation, 1 Dec. 2018, bigthink.com/Charles-Koch-Foundation/forced-examination-how-the-free-speech-of-others-benefits-us-all?rebelltitem=2#rebelltitem2.
139. [1919] Cialdini, Robert B. "Chapter 1: Weapons of Influence (1-16)" *Influence: Science and practice*. 4th ed., 21st Century Bks, 2002.

reborn forms of deceased loved ones within his State.[1920][1921][1922] This was misunderstood to be an attack on the Hindu faith by those opposing his political activism and two assassins killed him for it in 2013 with only one of the alleged assailants having been found as recently as 2018.[1923] Immediately after his death, many Indians across the country protested the government after his horrific death demanding justice with all political parties condemning his murder.[1924] The bill he supported was passed into law the very next year.[1925] I am honestly of the opinion that an India without Free Speech not only prevents Hindus from truly practicing their faith, but also morphs Hinduism into a slow Islamization and Christianization because Hindus aren't allowed to debate such as utilizing some of the *Tarka Sastras* to argue their positions and seek truth by challenging one's own beliefs through intellectual rigor. Moreover, the lack of Free Speech really damages *Ahimsa* (non-violence) as a core practice of Hinduism because Hindus aren't allowed to speak out against Christian missionaries abetting Marxist terrorism in India or Islamic terrorism in general.[1926][1927] Thus, without Free Speech, the Hindu response is only gangsterism similar to Islamist tactics. The trend is both unconscionable and can lead to the further break-up of the nation-state of India; that is why Free Speech must be allowed. Free Speech is a moral necessity from a human rights standpoint, it is therapeutic for anyone who wishes to vent their frustrations, it helps to free people's minds into free inquiry towards any topic that they have a personal interest in, and it is a societal failsafe that prevents violence which makes it the ultimate form of *Ahimsa* (non-violence).[1928]

Misogyny of Brahminism

---

140. [1920] Phadke, Anant. "The Murder of Dr Narendra Dabholkar: a Fascist Attack on Rationalism: Indian Journal of Medical Ethics." *The Murder of Dr Narendra Dabholkar: a Fascist Attack on Rationalism | Indian Journal of Medical Ethics*, ijme.in/articles/the-murder-of-dr-narendra-dabholkar-a-fascist-attack-on-rationalism/?galley=html.
141. [1921] "Narendra Dabholkar." *Wikipedia*, Wikimedia Foundation, 20 July 2019, en.wikipedia.org/wiki/Narendra_Dabholkar.
142. [1922] "Dr.Narendra Dabholkar – A Tribute." *Nirmukta*, 23 Aug. 2013, nirmukta.com/2013/08/22/dr-narendra-dabholkar-a-tribute/.
143. [1923] "Narendra Dabholkar." *Wikipedia*, Wikimedia Foundation, 20 July 2019, en.wikipedia.org/wiki/Narendra_Dabholkar.
144. [1924] Phadke, Anant. "The Murder of Dr Narendra Dabholkar: a Fascist Attack on Rationalism: Indian Journal of Medical Ethics." *The Murder of Dr Narendra Dabholkar: a Fascist Attack on Rationalism | Indian Journal of Medical Ethics*, ijme.in/articles/the-murder-of-dr-narendra-dabholkar-a-fascist-attack-on-rationalism/?galley=html.
145. [1925] "Narendra Dabholkar." *Wikipedia*, Wikimedia Foundation, 20 July 2019, en.wikipedia.org/wiki/Narendra_Dabholkar#Legacy.
146. [1926] Dash, Jatindra. "Indian Maoists Kill Hindus over Christian Conversions." *Reuters*, Thomson Reuters, 24 Aug. 2008, www.reuters.com/article/us-india-religion/indian-maoists-kill-hindus-over-christian-conversions-idUSBOM35357220080824.
147. [1927] "India 2017/2018." *Amnesty International*, www.amnesty.org/en/countries/asia-and-the-pacific/india/report-india/.
148. [1928] "Free Expression in Practice." *Big Think*, Charles Koch Foundation, 1 Dec. 2018, bigthink.com/Charles-Koch-Foundation/forced-examination-how-the-free-speech-of-others-benefits-us-all?rebelltitem=2#rebelltitem2.

Misogyny is entrenched within Sanatana Dharma, since before the Upanishadic counterculture movement to the varied treatment of women depending upon which Upanishadic Truthseeker was giving the teachings, to the Buddha's misogynistic disposition (although, to his credit, he did allow women to set-up their own forms of worship even if reluctantly and under the misogynistic condition that the lowest male monk had authority over the highest female monk), and to the misogynistic bigot who also privileged himself using Casteism, Adi Shankara, who almost single-handedly used his influence to impose a harsher level of misogyny than the Buddha ever did. While the Upanishadic counterculture movement has a checkered past with misogyny and while there were practitioners who supported the positive treatment of women, it would only be by ancient standards of being the most progressive amongst the ancient world and only selectively depending upon the Truthseeker espousing their philosophy. The freedom women enjoyed in ancient India before Adi Shankara's time obviously doesn't compare to modern standards. However, one curious facet about the ancient history of Sanatana Dharma to note, which honestly might be due to the lack of records left so please keep that in mind, is that there doesn't seem to be any evidence that the atheistic branch of Sanatana Dharma led to a greater level of misogyny against women despite the Carvaka's philosophy of a neophyte Pleasure-Pain principle having dominated ancient India for a brief period of time. In fact, a small level of misogyny seems to have risen after the Buddha's teachings dominated and then it overran India more than a thousand years later from the teachings of Adi Shankara. There's no historic evidence that the atheist denominations of Hinduism treated women with less value and women seemed to retain greater rights than they did years later under Sanatana Dharma's Buddhist and Advaita Vedanta denominations. Is there possibly something more to this? We may never know due to the lack of records.

For their time approximately in the 800 - 500 BCE era, the Upanishads provides progressive depictions of a wife asking her husband philosophical questions in the *Chandogya Upanishad* (transliterated as "Uprising of Great Song" - End of Vedas).[1929][1930] Within the context of the Upanishads in general, the people asking questions are usually either eager students or respected Kings, so the addition of a wife asking philosophical questions may indicate a respected status for some women in the context of ancient India in the approximate time period of 800 BCE - 500 BCE. The *Chandogya Upanishad* is notorious for its implications of being open to the possibility of atheism, but the other most notorious Upanishad open to the possibility of atheism, the *Brihadaranyaka Upanishad* (transliterated as "Of the Great Forests" - End of Vedas), has the most sexist and violent passages against women. I had discovered this disappointing fact only after reading Will Durant and then searching online to find *Nirumukta* (Freethinker group comprised of Indian atheists within

---

149. [1929] Durant, Will. Chapter XIV: The Foundations of India: VII. The Philosophy of the Upanishads (9113-9576). *Our Oriental Heritage: Being a History of Civilization in Egypt and the Near East to the Death of Alexander, and in India, China and Japan from the Beginning to Our Own Day*. Simon and Schuster, 1935.
150. [1930] Eknath, Easwaran, translator. *The Upanishads*. Nilgiri Press, 2007.

India) referencing the barbaric and misogynistic passage supporting spousal rape.[1931][1932] I had believed Eknath Easwaran to be reliable in his translations only to discover that he had purposefully taken chapter 6 of the *Brihadaranyaka Upanishad* out of his translation entirely and so I was forced to accept the fact that both Western Indology and some Western Hindu translators were perpetuating falsehoods and distortions.[1933] I had previously enjoyed his translations under the wrong belief that they were honest and not whitewashing anything about ancient religious teachings; I had even recommended them to friends so this was a painful shock that I had to accept for intellectual honesty and to maintain accuracy in my views.

The sexist passages and support for spousal rape should be highlighted because they're a problematic component that mustn't ever return from ancient India's times with any possible religious movement that seeks a return to the ancient religious culture represented in the Vedas. From the *Brihadaranyaka Upanishad's* Chapter/Part Six within subsection Four, translated honestly by Dinesh Chandra Gas Gupta, or as he was more known for his religious name in the Ramakrishna Monastic Order, Swami Nikhilananda:

> 6 Now, if a man sees himself (his reflection) in water, he should recite the following mantra: "May the gods bestow on me vigour, manhood, fame, wealth and merit." In praise of the wife who will bear him a son: She (his wife) has put on the soiled clothes of impurity; she is, verily, loveliness among women. Therefore when she has removed the clothes of impurity and appears beautiful, he should approach her and speak to her.
> 7 If she does not willingly yield her body to him, he should buy her with presents. If she is still unyielding, he should strike her with a stick or with his hand and overcome her, repeating the following mantra: "With power and glory I take away your glory." Thus she becomes discredited.
> 8 If she grants his desire, he should repeat the following mantra: "With power and glory I give you glory." Thus they both become glorious.
> 9 If a man desires his wife with the thought: "May she enjoy love with me," then, after inserting the member in her, joining mouth to mouth and stroking her organ, he should utter the following mantra: "O semen, you have been produced from my every limb, especially from my heart through the essence of food you are the essence of the limbs. Bring this woman under my control, like a deer pierced by a poisoned arrow."
> 10 Now, the wife whom he desires with the thought: "May she not conceive"—after inserting the member in her and joining mouth to mouth, he should inhale and then exhale, repeating the following mantra: "With power, with semen, I reclaim the semen from you." Thus she comes to be without semen.
> 11 Now, the wife whom he desires with the thought: "May she conceive"—after inserting the member in her and joining mouth to mouth, he should inhale and then exhale, repeating the following mantra: "With power, with semen, I deposit semen in you." Thus she verily becomes pregnant.[1934]

151.[1931] Durant, Will. Chapter XIV: The Foundations of India: VII. The Philosophy of the Upanishads (9113-9576). *Our Oriental Heritage: Being a History of Civilization in Egypt and the Near East to the Death of Alexander, and in India, China and Japan from the Beginning to Our Own Day*. Simon and Schuster, 1935.
152.[1932] Anamika. "'The Scholarship of the Daughter Is Regarding Domestic Affairs Only, for She Is Not Entitled to Read the Vedas."~Adi Shankara, That Renowned 9th Century Indian Sage of Advaita Vedanta, in His Bhāṣya on the Ancient Upanishads (Sacred Shruti Literature)." *Twitter*, Twitter, 3 Apr. 2018, twitter.com/AnaMyID/status/981146807433510914.
153.[1933] Eknath, Easwaran, translator. *The Upanishads*. Nilgiri Press, 2007.
154.[1934] Nikhilananda, Swami, translator. *English Tanslation of Brihadaranyaka Upanishad*. PDF ed., Www.ishwar.com, Www.ishwar.com.

On the non-profit organization Srijan Foundation's Youtube page, SrijanTalks, a Hindu woman following the Shiva branch of the Vedic traditions, Arti Agarwal (not to be confused with the actress of the same name), lectured a class on the ancient Shiva traditions of the Vedas and the differences in levels of importance of Vedic texts.[1935] Now, I appreciate her enthusiasm for religious theology, religious history, and her earnestness in reviving and celebrating ancient cultural aspects of Sanatana Dharma by having them translated into digital platforms for everyone to read.[1936] I have no problems with any of that at all. Insofar as the practices don't harm human rights, it is simply people wanting to recover their roots, learn more about ancient India, and practice their culture. Nonetheless, dangers exist in all cultures and societies that believe that ancient books have all of the solutions to all of life's problems. Perhaps there is important philosophical teachings that can be gleaned or ceremonial practices that feel personally meaningful to a Hindu's subjective experience, but there are obvious dangers in treating ancient books as the infallible revealed wisdom of a God or placing faith without any evidence in the claims of rituals that purport to cure diseases. I've given copious examples of the failings of the Abrahamic faiths and I'd like for Hindus to consider the following as I'm not sure people from Abrahamic backgrounds will take this argument seriously despite Islam remaining a clear example of this: The West is often stunned by the fast-paced rise of East Asia into modernity as many experts believed it would take much longer, even factoring that much of the innovation for modernity was already made. Many often argue there's a unique quality to East Asian culture that makes them so successful at such an unprecedented pace, but what if the reverse is true? What if, for 500 years, the West had been unnecessarily slow because of an internal defect in their culture? What if Christianity had held the West back from an even greater unprecedented prosperity during the 500 years of the West's rise to power? It would essentially be similar to the Casteism harming the Indian economy and the Abrahamic faiths holding back India from meaningful progress to a better future with a more robust economy, but less transparent than the Caste system. Far too often, Christians conflate the Enlightenment of the West, which was quite clearly a rejection of traditional Christian values, for Christian values themselves. Essentially, the teachings of revealed wisdom would be a defect holding back the progress of human rights under Enlightenment values. Similarly, a desire for a return to ancient social norms could honestly just bring a resurgence of Casteism and misogyny in the name of reviving an ancient culture. I have no problems with modeling houses based on ancient architecture or finding a way to unify (artistically or otherwise in a safe manner) ancient architectural work with modern innovations like solar panels when building new homes. I have no issues with reviving ancient cultural texts to read them for pleasure in the context of reading religious history. However, modeling one's life on the basis of the idea that the revealed wisdom of a God can solve all of your problems always fails and will always result in blaming others for one's own problems. That's why Palestine and the Islamic world

---

155. [1935] Agarwal, Arti. "Shiva Agamas | Arti Agarwal | Who Is Shiva | Paramahamsa Nithyananda Disciple." *YouTube*, SrijanTalks, 19 Nov. 2018, www.youtube.com/watch?v=-GUgBvBMuOw.
156. [1936] Agarwal, Arti. "Shiva Agamas | Arti Agarwal | Who Is Shiva | Paramahamsa Nithyananda Disciple." *YouTube*, SrijanTalks, 19 Nov. 2018, www.youtube.com/watch?v=-GUgBvBMuOw.

always blame Israel, it is why Islamic countries surrounding India blame each other or India, it is why many Islamic terrorist groups blame the US or the West in general, and it is why Bangladesh, Pakistan, and Afghanistan routinely fall apart nearing failed state statuses. *Put simply and bluntly, a civilization that believes in revealed wisdom of an ancient book or even several ancient books as infallible teachings that can cure all your problems is a civilization without any real future for their people.* Pakistan, Afghanistan, and Bangladesh don't progress because they gaze backward and idolize a time period that never was; India, being a Secular Republic that could very well become the most powerful Secular Republic within fifty years time if they continue to progress forward, should stop idolizing the ancient past and instead push forward for a better future for all Indians. I don't mean to say that you cannot be proud of ancient history or use teachings from the ancient time period of the Sramana movements, but you must understand that those ancient Sanatana Dharma philosophers are India's intellectual equivalence to the Ancient Greeks. We can be happy about our history and the sharp wit of those ancient philosophers. However, it would make no sense to build a civilization of the future from the teachings of Aristotle (who had deplorable views on women) just as it would make no sense to build a civilization from the teachings of the Upanishdic philosophers or even the atheistic branch of Sanatana Dharma. Instead, we should borrow what we say as interesting and agreeable and fuse those teachings with more modern beliefs, social norms, philosophical ideals, and so forth. As for any fatuous claims that I'm discriminating against Dharmic or Indian culture, allow me to provide a counter narrative that many Western Political Science experts from Samuel P. Huntington onwards have touted and which has only been vindicated as Islam has grown in number and as the West has irrevocably fallen as Huntington's infamous book, *The Clash of Civilizations*, predicted: *In the context of implementing government institutions and reforms, it doesn't matter if the West was the origin of Enlightenment values, democracy, or human rights. The only important fact that matters for setting up government institutions that help people is who implemented those ideologies in other countries and how effective they function in those societies. In other words, the effort and efficacy are all that matters and not the origin point of the idea and that is how Political Science assesses different governments.* Origins of ideas like cultural customs should be acknowledged so that there is no discriminatory cultural theft or cultural genocide, but it becomes an absurd argument in terms of implementing government institutions, reforms, or political policies and I've seen no evidence throughout my years of study in Political Science within Western academia that such arguments would ever be taken seriously. To put it bluntly, when Western Indologists like Gerald Larson, Sheldan Pollock, and Andrew J. Nicholson made their books and arguments with such absurd claims, they would have been seen as spreading their own racism in the lens of real academia like Political Science and that could be why they only shared it in their arbitrary "consensus" of anti-intellectual fakery called Western Indology. Their claims are an insult to Foreign policy, to US Think Tanks, and to Social Science departments; linguists have no right to make their bold claims when they hold no degrees or classes to show having taken any serious study of such Social Science issues which may indicate the entire department within the US deserves to be scrapped because they are not behaving as a credible academic discipline. To better understand why such claims are absurd, consider applying their inept arguments to Communism and Marxism. Karl Marx was the origin of Marxism and Communism; should Belgium, Germany, and Great Britain be blamed for China's Great Leap Forward and Stalin's horrific abuses because Karl Marx happened to reside in those countries at some point during his life time and was influenced by their culture in formulating his ideas? Of course not, because the belief that the idea's origins matter for government institutions that enact policies is absurd and what really matters was the implementation and the theory behind it which is then sufficiently established to have a causal factor for the consequences of the implementation. Political analysts try to be careful about these issues and to have such ignoramuses in Western Indology profiteer from their own racism against Indian people is absolutely infuriating because it diminishes the credibility of Western academia. The same careful consideration of Political analysis is true for the implementation of democratic social norms and setting up a government that is a Secular Republic. Hypothetically, if in the future Europe became majority Islamic and no longer followed democratic social norms but the Islamic Sharia instead, then how and why would Europe's past being the origin of democratic social values be relevant at all? For those still unsure about this, I highly recommend obtaining and reading *The Clash of Civilizations* by Samuel P. Huntington. His predictions seem to be the most accurate at this point and his chief arguments were about the West's precipitous decline, the rise of Islam as the largest religion in terms of population size, and the re-emergence of China and India as the dominant world powers with the West's history having been a mere 500-year speck to the millennia of power, prestige, and greatness of China and India which will go back to being the dominant powers of the world as Islam conquers the West and rends it asunder.[1937] The only real difference is that Brazil may also become a great emerging power.[1938] Please seriously consider it, because it is an excellent book. I'd like to believe that the majority of Western academia doesn't vilify Indian culture or Sanatana Dharma, but I judge by the evidence.

Female Foeticide

This specific topic made me so furious that I seriously considered abandoning Hinduism and Sanatana Dharma entirely because it is an issue that should never have existed. I feel nothing but disgust and hatred for anyone foolish enough to ignore this issue. Far more than Islamic terrorism, forced conversions by contemporary Christians, and perhaps even Casteism; the main issue leading to the death of Hindu culture is misogyny. On this issue, the Western mainstream media, Qatar-backed Al Jazeera, and fierce critics of Sanatana Dharma are all correct and have all the facts to back them up; the only real difference is that the amount

---

157.[1937] Huntington, Samuel P. *The Clash of Civilizations and the Remarking of World Order*. Simon and Schuster, 2003.
158.[1938] Huntington, Samuel P. *The Clash of Civilizations and the Remarking of World Order*. Simon and Schuster, 2003.

of selective abortions is approximately 12 million according to the accredited British medical journal, Lancet.[1939] This issue is so serious that it must be highlighted. Hindu patriarchy and the tradition of Brahaminism must perish because it is nothing more than a death cult and shows the absolute worst of any religion in its failures via the social norms that it expresses.[1940] I have nothing but contempt for my fellow Hindus who do this and to my shock, it disproportionately happens in educated areas so evidently uneducated Hindus have more intelligence than upper-caste educated Hindus who are so idiotic that they decide their ignorant, illiterate parents, with a mother who probably has an internalized misogyny from the social conditions of her patriarchal culture, should get to decide if a young couple should have a daughter.[1941] This is the death of Hinduism and it is entirely the fault of Hindus. While they're selectively aborting females, Islam is breeding as quickly as possible. To blame young Hindu women for this trend is ridiculous, it is entirely the fault of Hindu men and illiterate Hindu men and women of elderly age, the culture of death known as Hindu patriarchy, and the narcissism so prevalent in communal cultures that don't put more of an emphasis on personal liberty. If the culture taught that the young couple or just the woman who is carrying should decide to keep the baby and that men along with older women who are the in-laws or mothers should stay out of it, then this would never have happened. Feminist values supporting personal autonomy for young adults are the key to ending this abhorrent patriarchal social custom.

The following is a July 6th, 2015 *Al Jazeera* article from Sanjay Pandey titled "*Female Foeticide, India's Ticking Bomb*" where he explains the horrifying situation and the Modi government's valiant Pro-Feminist steps to stop this barbaric, misogynistic practice:

> **Bibipur, India -** The jubilant young man's arrival brought an abrupt halt to the card game contested by the turbaned group sitting under the tree.
> He thought he had good news for them: "I've been blessed with a baby girl!" he announced proudly.
> The response was not what he expected - the group's shock quickly turned to ridicule.
> "Why didn't you get her killed in the womb?" came the collective cry. "Did you not get a gender determination test done on the foetus?"
> Such a test is illegal in India, but this reaction - discovered during an undercover investigation by Al Jazeera in the village of Bibipur - is a reflection of prevailing male-chauvinistic attitudes in the country.
> **Cycle of imbalance**
> The deep-seated cultural preference for sons has skewed India's 1.2 billion population's gender demographic, particularly in the western states of Haryana, Rajasthan, and Punjab.
>
> In Haryana's Jind district, where Bibipur is located, the sex ratio is 871 females per 1,000 males, compared with the national average of 940, according to the 2011 census.

---

159. [1939] "Millions of Female Foetuses Aborted in India." *The Telegraph*, Telegraph Media Group, 24 May 2011, www.telegraph.co.uk/news/worldnews/asia/india/8532190/Millions-of-female-foetuses-aborted-in-India.html.
160. [1940] Nietzsche, Friedrich Wilhelm. *On the genealogy of morals: a polemical tract*. Translated by Ian Johnston, PDF, Richer Resources Publications, 2014.
161. [1941] "Millions of Female Foetuses Aborted in India." *The Telegraph*, Telegraph Media Group, 24 May 2011, www.telegraph.co.uk/news/worldnews/asia/india/8532190/Millions-of-female-foetuses-aborted-in-India.html.

It has prompted men from these areas to hunt for brides in impoverished regions such as West Bengal and Bihar, and even as far away as Kerala in the south.

But it hasn't changed their attitudes: Even the brides brought in are forced to abort their baby girls, thus perpetuating the cycle of imbalance - as in Bibipur.

One of the cardplayers - whose own conservative family had broken strict social norms and bought him a teenage bride from West Bengal due to the scarcity of girls in Haryana - was quick to boast about his experience with female foeticide.

"My wife was already three months pregnant when we got to know about it," said the 40-year-old, who asked not to be named for fear of reprisals.

"We immediately got an ultrasonography test done on her. Reports suggested that it was a baby girl, but the doctor refused to abort the baby, saying that it could endanger the life of both the mother and the baby," the cardplayer said.

Undeterred, the man's family and friends gave him "a list of doctors and clinics in Haryana and Rajasthan where hassle-free abortions are done".

The next stage involved fooling the 19-year-old wife into thinking she was going to a distant relative's wedding in Jaipur.

People start planning their family in a rather regressive way - instead of counting their numbers, they start counting the children's sex.
 Minister Maneka Gandhi, Women and Child Welfare

"We took her to a predesignated clinic in the city," explained the husband.

"Since it was not possible to abort the baby, the doctors put a pill in her genitals. In the morning, the game was over as my visibly shaken wife confirmed the news that the 'bits of the baby's body parts came out while passing urine'," the man said.

'Wives are like slaves'

In a 2011 study, British medical journal Lancet found that up to 12 million Indian female foetuses had been aborted in the previous three decades.

Last year, the United Nations said the dwindling number of Indian girls had reached "emergency proportions" and was contributing to crimes against women.

The imported brides, known as "paros", are treated like domestic slaves who have little or no inheritance rights on the family property, according to Smita Khanijow of anti-poverty agency ActionAid India.

"Women are not a commodity which can be traded as 'brides' on demand of the market," she told Al Jazeera.

"We need to treat women as equal human beings to men, and give them dignity and rights."

But in many parts of India, the list of unmarried males older than 40 is growing longer - and more desperate for a wife.

During last year's general elections, Bibipur - which means "Village of Brides" - hit the headlines when a local organisation called Kunwara Union - or "Bachelors' Union" - told candidates: "Give us brides and win our votes!"

India's Minister of Women and Child Welfare Maneka Gandhi says sex-selective abortion is a "problem of affluence".

"Every day around 2,000 girls are killed in the womb or immediately after birth in India," she told Al Jazeera - though a UN report says the daily number is around 7,000.

"People start planning their family in a rather regressive way - instead of counting their numbers, they start counting the children's sex. What they want, they want. Anything else becomes collateral damage."

'Shame the families'

It is not just poor women who are forced to fight to save their baby girls. Doctor Mitu Khurana, a Delhi-based paediatrician, is hoping to set a legal precedent after taking her husband and in-laws to court for "conspiring to kill her twin daughters in the womb".

Khurana said her in-laws sedated her and illegally procured a gender test during her pregnancy, and then pressured her to abort the babies.

She defied them, and returned to her family's home to give birth in 2005.

"When I returned at my in-laws' house with the babies, my mother-in-law pushed one of the infants down the stairs. Fortunately, I arrived in time and rescued my baby," Khurana told Al Jazeera.

As well as being an issue of cultural preference, female foeticide is also an economic issue for families.

Although the long-standing tradition of dowry - a payment to the groom's family - has been illegal since 1961, it is still practised in many communities.

"We are poor people, somehow making ends meet," said a three-wheel rickshaw driver in Jaipur, Rajasthan - another state where the sex ratio is under the national average, according to the 2011 census. "I got my second daughter aborted for fear of paying dowry for her marriage when she grows up," the 30-year-old told Al Jazeera, under the condition of anonymity. "As it is, I am finding it difficult to save enough money for the dowry of my first daughter."

Khurana said India needs to change its attitude towards dowry in order to save the lives of female children.

"Dowry is already illegal, but it has to be made shameful," she said. "You have to shame the families giving and taking dowry."

State intervention

Gandhi said the government is making progress, through Prime Minister Narendra Modi's Beti Bacho, Beti Padho- the "Save daughters, educate daughters" programme.

It has targeted 100 gender-critical districts, where those who give and accept dowries have been publicly shamed, and informants have been rewarded.

The programme also focuses on influencing the mother-in-law of a family, who usually decides whether the baby lives or not.

"Women in the house will have to be trained as much as the men," said Gandhi.

Government reports show that in these 100 districts the number of female children in Palnas, state-run orphanages - has gone up by hundreds.

"In Amritsar alone, there were 89 girls given to Palnas in a month. Then we found the same thing in Mohali and Tamil Nadu," said Gandhi.

"These are the girls who would otherwise be killed in the womb or immediately after birth," Gandhi said. There is evidence of change even in Biwipur, where this month the village held a "selfie with your daughter" photo contest in order to raise awareness of the issue. The winner, out of 800 submissions, received a prize of 2,100 rupees ($316).

But the bigger battle is yet to be won, said Khurana, who has filed a suit against her inlaws and the clinic involved for carrying out a gender-selective test, which is a crime, on her foetus without her consent. Khurana claims the presiding judge, a woman, called her "a prostitute in the open court" for standing up against her husband.

Her case, which was filed in 2008, is still ongoing. If found guilty all the accused parties will face jail time and a significant monetary fine.

"Forget about the common people - when the judges try to convince us that there is nothing wrong in seeking a male child and eliminating a female one, only God can help us! We are sitting on a ticking bomb!"[1942]

Alka Gupta, a communications specialist for UNICEF India, submitted a press release article on the dire situation of sex-selective abortions titled "*Female Foeticide in India*" on behalf of UNICEF India:

> Eligible Jat boys from Haryana travel 3,000 km across the country to find themselves a bride. With increasingly fewer girls in Haryana, they are seeking brides from as far away as Kerala as the only way to change their single status.
>
> The girls have not vanished overnight. Decades of sex determination tests and female foeticide that has acquired genocide proportions are finally catching up with states in India.
>
> This is only the tip of the demographic and social problems confronting India in the coming years. Skewed sex ratios have moved beyond the states of Punjab, Haryana, Delhi, Gujarat and Himachal

---

162. [1942] Pandey, Sanjay. "Female Foeticide, India's 'Ticking Bomb'." *Asia | Al Jazeera*, Al Jazeera, 6 July 2015, www.aljazeera.com/indepth/features/2015/06/female-foeticide-india-ticking-bomb-150629090758927.html.

Pradesh. With news of increasing number of female foetuses being aborted from Orissa to Bangalore there is ample evidence to suggest that the next census will reveal a further fall in child sex ratios throughout the country.

The decline in child sex ratio in India is evident by comparing the census figures. In 1991, the figure was 947 girls to 1000 boys. Ten years later it had fallen to 927 girls for 1000 boys.

Since 1991, 80% of districts in India have recorded a declining sex ratio with the state of Punjab being the worst.

States like Maharashtra, Gujarat, Punjab, Himachal Pradesh and Haryana have recorded a more than 50 point decline in the child sex ratio in this period.

Despite these horrific numbers, foetal sex determination and sex selective abortion by unethical medical professionals has today grown into a Rs. 1,000 crore industry (US$ 244 million). Social discrimination against women, already entrenched in Indian society, has been spurred on by technological developments that today allow mobile sex selection clinics to drive into almost any village or neighbourhood unchecked.

The PCPNDT Act 1994 (Preconception and Prenatal Diagnostic Techniques Act) was modified in 2003 to target the medical profession - the 'supply side' of the practice of sex selection. However non implementation of the Act has been the biggest failing of the campaign against sex selection

According to the latest data available till May 2006, as many as 22 out of 35 states in India had not reported a single case of violation of the act since it came into force. Delhi reported the largest number of violations – 76 out of which 69 were cases of non registration of birth! Punjab had 67 cases and Gujarat 57 cases.

But the battle rages on.

In a recent landmark judgment the Mumbai High Court upheld an amendment to the PCPNDT Act banning sex selection treatment. The Court pronounced that pre natal sex determination would be as good as female foeticide. Pre-conception sex determination violated a woman's right to live and was against the Constitution, it said.

While the boys from Haryana may have found a temporary solution to the problem of missing brides, experts warn that the demographic crisis will lead to increasing sexual violence and abuse against women and female children, trafficking, increasing number of child marriages, increasing maternal deaths due to abortions and early marriages and increase in practices like polyandry.

There have been only two convictions -- a fine of 300 rupees ($7) and another fine of 4,000 rupees ($98) -- from over 400 cases lodged under the Pre-conception and Pre-natal Diagnostic Techniques Act.

Bringing about changes in the demand for sex determination is a long process and has to be tackled through women's education and empowerment including the right to property and land rights. States in the North East and in Kerala where women have these rights show a comparatively better sex ratio.

The battle against sex selection has proved to be long drawn out. But some signs are visible that demonstrate that the fight can be won.

Lakhanpal, a small village in Punjab has turned the tide of male births for the first time. In a state that has the lowest sex ratio in the country, the village boasts of 1,400 girls for every 1000 boys.

Arvind Kumar, the collector of Hyderabad district has illustrated the power of the Act. Hyderabad had the lowest child sex ratio (0-6 years) in Andhra Pradesh. After taking over in 2004 he tracked down all 389 diagnostic clinics in the city and took action. 361 ultrasound scan centres were issued notices for non compliance with the PNDT Act.

Licenses of 91 centres were cancelled. 83 machines were seized and 71 released after an undertaking and fine. Three suppliers were prosecuted for supplying machines to clinics with no registration licenses.[1943]

163.[1943] Gupta, Alka. "Female Foeticide in India." *UNICEF*, unicef.in/PressReleases/227/Female-foeticide-

As of March 2017, *Reuters* journalist, Roli Srivastava, reported on the continued problem of illegal female foeticide rackets in the article titled "*India police find 19 fetuses dumped in plastic bags, suspect female feticide racket*" which explains as follows:

> MUMBAI (Thomson Reuters Foundation) - Indian police found 19 aborted fetuses dumped in plastic bags in the western state of Maharashtra while they investigated a woman's death after an abortion - uncovering what officials suspect is an inter-state female feticide racket.
>
> Police said on Monday they had teamed up with health officials to launch a major investigation into the case in a village in Sangli district near the border with Karnataka state.
>
> A homeopathic doctor, suspected of performing illegal sex-selective abortions in the basement of his dispensary in the village, was on the run, police said.
>
> Indian laws ban doctors and health workers from sharing an unborn child's sex with the parents, or carrying out tests to determine the child's gender. Only registered medical practitioners are allowed to perform abortions.
>
> Nevertheless, female feticide continues in parts of India, where a preference for sons runs deep.
>
> Indian wedding customs mean girls are often seen as a huge cost with very little returns, partly because the practice of demanding dowries remains the norm, despite being illegal.
>
> Sons, on the other hand, can inherit property, continue the family line, and play a vital role in important Hindu rituals.
>
> Police were alerted by villagers after a 26-year-old woman died after undergoing an abortion at the clinic of the homoeopathist, who was not licensed to terminate pregnancies.
>
> Their investigation led them to the fetuses in a sewer near the clinic, local media reported.
>
> "We our presuming these could be female fetuses and our investigation is on this line," Satish Pawar, director of health services in Maharashtra told the Thomson Reuters Foundation.
>
> The recovered fetuses have been sent for DNA testing to determine their sex.
>
> "We suspect radiologists in major cities would determine sex of the baby and direct cases to this doctor," Pawar said.
>
> India's child sex ratio is 919 females per 1,000 males, according to government statistics. A 2001 government study had shown that Pakistan and Bangladesh had a better sex ratio than India.
>
> Dwindling numbers of Indian girls, caused by the illegal abortion of millions of babies, has reached "emergency proportions", fuelling an increase in crimes such as kidnapping and trafficking, the United Nations has said.
>
> A Maharashtra minister announced he would work with the Karnataka government to crack down on a trend of women seeking sex-selective abortions in border towns of the two states.
>
> Investigation teams reached the village on Monday to seek out families who may have used abortion services at the dispensary and could direct them to ultrasound clinics they visited for sex determination.
>
> Maharashtra officials said all health facilities in rural areas in the state would now be surveyed.[1944]

---

in-India.

164. [1944] Srivastava, Roli. "India Police Find 19 Fetuses Dumped in Plastic Bags, Suspect Female..." *Reuters*, Thomson Reuters, 6 Mar. 2017, www.reuters.com/article/us-india-abortion-foeticide/india-police-find-19-fetuses-dumped-in-plastic-bags-suspect-female-feticide-racket-idUSKBN16D1NF.

Brahminism produces a death cult of female foeticide on the basis of communal culture imposing patriarchal norms and values upon Hindu women instead of allowing personal liberty with the Hindu woman or just the young couple deciding together without any outside influence if they wish to keep the potential baby or not. *Therefore, Hindu patriarchy and specifically Brahminism is the death of Hindu civilization.*

Brahminical Misogyny in the Public of India

The people of India should have the right of Free Speech and Free Inquiry, they should have the right to criticize the barbaric teachings of Islam, Christianity, and the barbaric patriarchal social norms of Hinduism and inquire into their faith traditions. A citizen of India should have the right to say that they hate all religions and that includes Sanatana Dharma. *Likewise, a person from India who takes umbrage with such insults should have the right to harshly criticize back and insult the other person's beliefs in turn.* I respect anyone's Free Speech rights for their misogynistic views, but I reserve the right to criticize back on such views that I find hateful when they are espoused.[1945] There is a mutual understanding that no violence will come between us for holding views that we believe are important to us nor will violence come to the other person whose beliefs we find to be idiotic and repugnant.[1946] That is the reciprocal norm of a society with Free Speech and Free Inquiry, it is the greatest test of non-violence within a civilization and it must become part of India's legal code and cultural norms to save India itself.[1947]

One such repugnant view that I find made by Hindus of India is the phrasing of discrimination against women. Comments such as "misbehaves with women" when discussing the rape of women by men or fictional stories about life lessons depicting a wife leaving a man who is downtrodden and filled with bad luck are quite honestly just misogynistic rhetoric that supports an entrenched social norm of treating women like the property of men and not as independent human beings who were wronged by society or hurt by others as individuals valued as their own person. Such rhetoric only serves to dehumanize Hindu women as objects instead of seeing them as individuals with the right of personal liberty and autonomy from men. Even more disturbing, just as with the nonsensical act of adapting and enforcing Islamic taboos such as Islamophobia into Hinduism with terms like Hinduphobia, Hindu men now speak of Hindu Goddesses as if they were the Islamic Prophet Mohammad. It's the exact same rhetoric and it is disturbing trend in Indian culture even if there is no evidence any deity exists. Comparisons to Hindu Goddesses with comparisons to why it is wrong to insult another person's mother is the exact same argument that Islamists use to defend Islamophobia in an

---

165.[1945] Cialdini, Robert B. Chapter 2: Reciprocation (19-50). *Influence: Science and practice*. 4th ed., 21st Century Bks, 2002.

166.[1946] Cialdini, Robert B. Chapter 2: Reciprocation (19-50). *Influence: Science and practice*. 4th ed., 21st Century Bks, 2002.

167.[1947] Cialdini, Robert B. Chapter 2: Reciprocation (19-50). *Influence: Science and practice*. 4th ed., 21st Century Bks, 2002.

attempt to forbid others from insulting the Prophet Mohammad; they compare insulting the pedophile Prophet of Islam to the equivalent of insulting their mothers. Moreover, this is worse because Hindu men are treating Hindu women as extensions of Hindu men by arguing such blatantly misogynistic rhetoric instead of treating them like their individual selves. *Hindu men are embarrassed by depictions of Hindu Goddesses in the nude, or for slaying demons, or for behaving as independent, fierce, and brave instead of as property subservient to the whims of Hindu Gods. Instead Hindu men seem to want Hindu Goddesses to be similar to the Islamic Prophet Mohammad's wives (Mother of Believers) being subservient to him or depictions of Jesus Christ's Mother's role of motherhood as being the only appropriate role for a woman.* Hindu men are embarrassed when Hindu Goddesses aren't depicted as meek, weak, submissive, and obedient to men instead of being brave, fierce, threatening wrongdoers with their power, and happily glorifying their own female sexuality as independent women instead of being extensions of men whom they must sexually please. Hindu women, just as the Hindu Goddesses, aren't allowed to express the fullness of their personal depth as human beings with real experiences and they are being reduced to misogynistic social norms even worse than before because of the influence of the Abrahamic faiths destroying the most feminist aspects of Hinduism which supported female sexuality, depicted Hindu Goddesses as complex and independent in mythological stories, venerated Transgenderism and homosexuality as a path that Hindus are free to choose in religious texts, and often depicted Hindu Goddesses in the same reverence as Hindu Gods. *In short, Hindu men are embarrassed and ashamed of Hinduism and are conforming to the social norms of the Abrahamic faith traditions to dictate their own religious beliefs by adapting the Abrahamic traditions misogynistic practices of treating women as property instead of as independent people capable of their own reasoning and valued for their own self-worth without the approval of men.*

Finally, I'd like for readers from India to consider the problems of contemporary forms of misogyny in India and the disastrous consequences of not changing the culture to oppose misogyny. To be sure, great strides have been made under the Modi government where women can speak out and finally be heard thanks to many of Prime Minister Modi's feminist initiatives but the culture of India must internalize the changes all the more quickly to strengthen the Republic of India. I have no patience for misogyny and I will explain bluntly to drive the point forward why misogyny must be countered in any society because I genuinely care about the safety of people. Take for example the potentially disastrous consequences of what seems to be a fairly innocuous practice of misogyny in contemporary India; many Indian families refuse to give their daughters cell phones under the misogynistic assumption that they'll use it for some nefarious purpose and become "impure" or some such poor reasoning by ignorant parents. Instead of Indian parents trusting their daughters or taking the time to have a conversation on what parents find appropriate or objectionable for daughters to use cell phones for, they decide to not trust their daughters at all. Meanwhile, many Indian families give their sons cell phones with no such issues regarding trust. If you're an Indian parent who does this in India, you've probably made it more likely for your daughter to be targeted, beaten, raped, and killed and you only have yourself to blame for your misogynistic behavior that could lead to such a horrific conclusion for your daughter's life. You might be thinking something along the lines of "what on earth am I talking about" and "how dare I make such rude remarks", right? Allow me to explain how your misogyny could lead to your daughter's death and why it'll be all your fault. UNICEF Global Goodwill Ambassador, Professional Youtube Comedian, and Sikh Canadian Lilly Singh took the time to make a video on Youtube in support of the Modi government's #ENDviolence campaign to spread the message throughout India's social media that the people of India can now utilize a quick number available 24/7 for a confidential conversation to alert authorities of any dangers they see or to call for help if they are in danger themselves; this was specifically done to curb violence against children.[1948] The number available to all Indians is 1098 and the hope is that people who see violence or are in danger of violence can quickly call the number because of the prevalence of cell phones across India due to their affordability.[1949] Here's the obvious problem that any parent living in India should have realized if they used two seconds of critical thinking in concern for the safety of their daughters: *how can female Indian children utilize this wonderful government resource when they are in life-threatening danger without having a cell phone?* They can't and they could end-up beaten, raped, or killed because of their parents stupidity. If you are a parent in India, what happens if someone with nefarious intent manages to isolate your daughter through either kidnapping or coercion and intends to do harm to them? If they have a cell phone, they can call the number for help immediately so that the authorities respond as quickly as possible, but if they don't have cell phones then they will be beaten, tortured, raped, and/or killed with no ability to seek help because you were too stupid to give them a mobile phone which could have saved their lives. And should such a horrible tragedy happen, what are you going to think after the event? To Indian parents within India, you're going to probably regret, for the rest of your life, not having given your daughter a cell phone and you will know at her funeral or when her ashes are scattered that it was all your fault. I write this in harsh words because I want to make it clear how dangerous an entrenched culture of misogyny is out of genuine concern for the human rights of the Indian people and making the consequences of misogyny clear so that Indian parents don't have to regret a potentially avoidable tragedy while their daughters suffer the worst from misogyny. Sadly, not all tragedies can be avoided, but responsive parenting of listening to their daughters concerns and providing them with a mobile phone with explicit instructions to call 1098 if they feel they're in life-threatening danger could potentially save their lives from people who wish to harm them. You cannot end violence without placing trust in your daughters, educating them on the dangers, and informing them of what they should do when they feel their life is in danger.

Extricating Islamic Imperialist Misogyny from Sanatana Dharma

---

168.[1948] Singh, Lilly. "Will You Help Me End Violence?" *YouTube*, IISuperwomanII, 23 May 2018, www.youtube.com/watch?v=3y-jH6XuVt8.

169.[1949] Singh, Lilly. "Will You Help Me End Violence?" *YouTube*, IISuperwomanII, 23 May 2018, www.youtube.com/watch?v=3y-jH6XuVt8.

For this portion, I'd like for readers from India to consider where some social norms in contemporary India possibly originated from historically. During the course of my research, I noticed a troubling trend within news stories in which Hindus and Buddhists seemed to be following explicitly Islamic practices under the basis that they're somehow traditionally Dharmic practices in India. Having researched Islam more in-depth, I'm under the impression that contemporary Hindus and Buddhists of India mistakenly believe that they're protecting Sanatana Dharma when all they're actually doing is normalizing the culture of Islamism within India through their rampant misogyny against young Indian couples. The main example of this is Buddhists and Hindus ridiculing, punishing, or preventing young couples from holding hands, kissing in public, or showing any sort of affection. One may assume it is part of ascetic beliefs in Sanatana Dharma, but this practice largely pervades in Islamic societies by enforcement of Sharia Police. In other words, Buddhists and Hindus who punish or mock any young couple for kissing in public, holding hands, hugging, or other forms of public affection are acting as de facto Sharia police in support of normalizing the social values of Islamism and not Sanatana Dharma. Implicit within the behavior of shunning or stopping physical affection between young couples is a hatred for all forms of physical and sexual intimacy and a hatred for the human body as per Islamic values.[1950] This behavior is most likely a holdover from Islamic imperialism as such social customs were undoubtedly demanded by Islamist rulers upon practitioners of Sanatana Dharma. Buddhists and Hindus who stop young couples from expressing affection like kissing, holding hands, hugging, or holding each other closely are supporting the Islamization of India and not defending Sanatana Dharma. While Sanatana Dharma's ascetic practices are just as deplorable and express a hatred for a healthy sexual love life, it was not to the extent of crushing all public displays of romantic affection. The statues of Hindu deities engaged in physical intimacy and the thought-provoking theological book of *Kama Sutra,* which should remain as a venerated religious text, are proof that sex-positivity was celebrated in Sanatana Dharma even if unfortunately patriarchal in social norms. Hindus should be honored to have a religious text celebrating sex-positivity and can still practice some of the techniques among consenting adults. If any practitioner of Sanatana Dharma wishes to reclaim the lost heritage of body-positivity and sex-positivity, I have added a useful book and suggested Youtube videos in the Further Reading section in order to help better inform readers who have such an interest. Body-positivity was celebrated in ancient India when considering the religious respect of Devadasis before Islamic imperialism destroyed their wonderful religious position and when considering the usefulness of saris to make women feel confident with their own bodies, especially if they feel obese or face other forms of body shaming since it is difficult for onlookers to tell a woman's physical attributes when gazing at a woman in a sari.

The misogynistic culture of *Purdah* and *Sati* most likely expanded across all of India due to Islamic imperialism; Muslim men were allowed to take women as sex slaves as per their

---

170.[1950] Nietzsche, Friedrich Wilhelm. *On the genealogy of morals: a polemical tract*. Translated by Ian Johnston, PDF, Richer Resources Publications, 2014.

barbaric holy teachings mentioned in the earlier section on Islam and this increased the practice of Sati from women who didn't want to be a Muslim rapist's plaything since it was considered more honorable to burn themselves than submit to Islamic tyranny under the conditions they suffered due to Islamic rule.[1951] Prior to that, Will Durant seems to indicate that the practice of Sati was limited to the families of Rajput warriors and Durant explains that women in India began to find it more honorable than to be forced into lifelong sexual slavery under the barbarity of Muslim men.[1952] He explains that child marriage became widespread among practitioners of Sanatana Dharma throughout medieval India as a life and death defense because Muslim men of the medieval period preferred enslaving and raping non-married women throughout India due to Muslim men's deep faith in Islam.[1953] Purdah obviously follows Islamic culture even in contemporary times; separating men and women is a holdover of Islamic imperialism because such gender division was massively increased by the people of India being imposed upon by Sharia under Islamic despots. While Purdah certainly existed in ancient India prior to Islam, it was enforced by the outdated rules of the *Manusmriti* and other legal documents like the *Arthashastra* under the context of women being beholden to their husbands which are only about enforcing rules within a specific time period of Indian civilization; The Arthashastra's in particular are about upholding the legal structures of monarchy and have no relevance to the Republic of India. The Manusmriti gets burned annually in India as a triumphant revolt from Dalits like Ambedkar protesting its barbarity since December 25th, 1927 and the religious denomination of Brahminism that created it. Neither the misogyny of the Arthashastra or the Manusmriti are part of the social norms of the Secular Republic of India. Given that Purdah is pervasive and has had a more damaging effect against women due to Islamic theology still being respected in India, it might be time for practitioners of Sanatana Dharma to burn the Quran along with the Manusmriti as a Free Speech protest against misogyny in India and the threat of violence as a hold that Islam still has over modern Indian society. Does that suggestion sound insane or terrifying? It is because the people of India are allowing the threat of violence and intimidation from Islamists determine what they can or cannot say; the Indian Penal Code's 295A law by the British imperialists was imposed to protect the "hurt feelings" of the Muslim community in India that protested for protecting their feelings after an Islamist murdered the Hindu publisher in court. The British imperialists made that rule as part of the IPC (Indian Penal Code) because they valued the feelings of Muslims above the human rights and life of a Hindu. The British imperialists made

---

171. [1951] Durant, Will. Chapter XVI: From Alexander to Aurangzeb: IV. Annals of Rajputana (10356-10387). *Our Oriental Heritage: Being a History of Civilization in Egypt and the Near East to the Death of Alexander, and in India, China and Japan from the Beginning to Our Own Day*. Simon and Schuster, 1935.
172. [1952] Durant, Will. Chapter XVI: From Alexander to Aurangzeb: IV. Annals of Rajputana (10356-10387). *Our Oriental Heritage: Being a History of Civilization in Egypt and the Near East to the Death of Alexander, and in India, China and Japan from the Beginning to Our Own Day*. Simon and Schuster, 1935.
173. [1953] Durant, Will. Chapter XVII The Life of People: III. Morals and Marriage (11052-11088). *Our Oriental Heritage: Being a History of Civilization in Egypt and the Near East to the Death of Alexander, and in India, China and Japan from the Beginning to Our Own Day*. Simon and Schuster, 1935.

that law for the sole purpose of shackling the Indian mind to the fear of violence and intimidation of Islamism and to rob practitioners of Sanatana Dharma of the peaceful solution of Free Speech and Free Inquiry to challenge the threat of Islamism. People in the Republic of India are being mentally shackled, having their religious rights stamped upon, and being forbidden to peacefully challenge Islamism. Do you wish to overthrow the yoke of the colonial mindset imposed by Great Britain? Do you wish to challenge Islamism via *ahimsa* (non-violence)? Burn the Quran as protest and demand that Free Speech and Free Inquiry - including the ability to speak against and question Islam - is part of a Constitutional amendment in the Indian constitution. *The Republic of India must stand against Islamism, violent and coercive Christian conversions, Casteism, and all forms of misogyny and the way to do that peacefully is by allowing Free Speech and Free Inquiry.*

Alas, I suspect that this will simply engender ire, fear, and accusations of bigotry as a suggestion despite the fact that Indian people are living in fear of being killed by Islamists for speaking out of turn; along with the Indian government taking the side of Islamic mobs who threaten violence when anything doesn't go their way and which the Western mainstream media makes sure to categorically ignore or otherwise de-emphasize in their selective news coverage across the Western world to depict practitioners of Sanatana Dharma as solely responsible while catering to the petulant attitude of Saudi Arabia.[1954][1955] As such, consider these two so-called cultural traditions that followers of Sanatana Dharma probably wrongfully believe to be part of their culture and which were most likely imposed by Islamic imperialism in India. First the seemingly innocuous one, the culture of the left-hand being bad luck in certain poverty-stricken locations of India which are majority Hindu is probably derived from Islamic theology's censure of it due to the teachings of the pedophile Prophet of Islam.[1956][1957] As mentioned in the section on Islam, this seemingly innocuous Islamic rule has pointlessly negative consequences for people who honestly cannot use the right hand for certain tasks due to their growth in their mother's wombs determining how their motor cortex sends signals from their brain through the spine.[1958] In other words, there is nothing wrong or evil about it, it is completely natural for some people to be left-handed. The second is child marriages; I want to

---

174. [1954] Malik, Nesrine. "The Bizarre Spat with Canada Shows Mohammed Bin Salman's True Colours | Nesrine Malik." *The Guardian*, Guardian News and Media, 12 Aug. 2018, www.theguardian.com/commentisfree/2018/aug/12/saudi-arabia-spat-canada-mohammed-bin-salman-true-colours.
175. [1955] "Hindu Boy's Family Forced out of Village for Marrying Muslim Girl, Police Advices Boy to Convert as Villagers Threaten to Kill - Opindia News." *OpIndia*, 19 July 2019, www.opindia.com/2019/07/hindu-boys-family-forced-out-of-village-for-marrying-muslim-girl-police-advices-boy-to-convert-as-villagers-threaten-to-kill/.
176. [1956] "QuranX.com The Most Complete Quran / Hadith / Tafsir Collection Available!" *Muwatta Malik Hadiths*, quranx.com/Hadith/Malik/USC-MSA/Book-49/Hadith-6/.
177. [1957] "The Reason Why the Right Hand Is Preferred over the Left - Islam Question & Answer." *Islamqa.info*, Islam Question and Answer, 2 Mar. 2007, islamqa.info/en/answers/82120/the-reason-why-the-right-hand-is-preferred-over-the-left.
178. [1958] Andrews, Robin. "We Finally Know Why People Are Left- Or Right-Handed." *IFLScience*, IFLScience, 23 Jan. 2019, www.iflscience.com/brain/finally-know-people-left-righthanded/.

be careful and explain that I don't mean that Islam brought child marriages to India, but rather that Islam worsened an already terrible social standard. There are degrees of worsening conditions that we can analyze by modern standards of human rights on even this issue. The *Arthashastra,* a legal document with a codification of laws set forth by the absolute monarchy of the Maurya empire which existed approximately between 322 BCE-185 BCE and which Will Durant states ruled effectively[1959], states in *Section III. Concerning Laws* in the subsection*: Chapter III. The Duty of a Wife; Maintenance of a Woman; Cruelty to Woman; Enmity Between Husband and Wife; Her Kindness to Another; And Forbidden Transactions* that women attain the age of maturity at age 12 and men at age 16 in the context of marriage.[1960] So what, it is still barbaric, right? By our subjective modern standards in defense of human rights, of course it is. However, please note a significant fact, the Arthashastra was more socially progressive by our modern standards in the approximate 322-185 BCE era than the teachings of Islam in the 7th Century AD, and even if a critic were to argue that the Arthashastra being referenced may have only been completed in the 3rd CE time period then that still means that the culture of Sanatana Dharma was more socially progressive approximately 400 years prior to Islam's existence. Under Islamic imperialism, the age of child marriages seemed to change throughout India from age twelve for girls and age sixteen for boys from what the Arthashastra shows into ages six and nine for acceptable child marriages.[1961] Perhaps not so coincidentally, these ages six and nine are the age of marriage and sexual intercourse of the pedophile Prophet's child bride, Aisha.[1962] The facts are that the age of marriage and what was considered maturity changed from ages twelve for girls and sixteen for boys under the culture of Sanatana Dharma into ages six and nine for both genders after the period of Islamic imperialism when the West began squabbling to conquer India. Therefore, child marriage happening in contemporary India is most likely the result of Islamic imperialism.

I do believe criticizing the issue of misogyny and its roots is an important step to end the misogyny in India as it honestly hurts me to read news articles of what some women in India suffer due to blatant patriarchal misogyny. I'd like to offer my own small contribution in fixing such gender inequalities as a positive contribution instead of just stereotyping India as backwards or vilifying an entire culture for the actions of some violent people, but the

---

179.[1959] Durant, Will. Chapter XVI: From Alexander to Aurangzeb (10072 - 10817). *Our Oriental Heritage: Being a History of Civilization in Egypt and the Near East to the Death of Alexander, and in India, China and Japan from the Beginning to Our Own Day*. Simon and Schuster, 1935.
180.[1960] Shamasastry, Rudrapatna, translator. *Kautilya's ARTHASHASTRA*. PDF ed., Bangalore: Government Press, 1915.
181.[1961] Shamasastry, Rudrapatna, translator. *Kautilya's ARTHASHASTRA*. PDF ed., Bangalore: Government Press, 1915.
182.[1962] "Age of the Mother of the Believers 'Aa'ishah (May Allah Be Pleased with Her) When the Prophet (Blessings and Peace of Allah Be upon Him) Married Her - Islam Question & Answer." *Islamqa.info*, Islam Question and Answer, 30 Dec. 2013, islamqa.info/en/answers/124483/age-of-the-mother-of-the-believers-aaishah-may-allah-be-pleased-with-her-when-the-prophet-blessings-and-peace-of-allah-be-upon-him-married-her.

patriarchal culture within India is what disproportionately creates such violence in the first place and it must be ruthlessly criticized. I was stunned to find the Modi government was doing everything it could to end misogyny, but the Indian people have a duty to themselves, their friends and family, and their society to work towards changing their own internal views too. It isn't easy, but nothing worthwhile ever is. I am honestly of the opinion that if India really tried to end Casteism, misogyny, and work towards building a better future with social norms similar to the West, then India would amaze and possibly outpace the West in scientific innovation, social equality for LGBT people, and be able to more effectively respond to Islamic terrorism with harsh critiques of the dangers and failings of Islamic societies from the Middle East to those that neighbor India and which provide a wealth of information already useful in proving Islam is false and immoral. Enlightenment values were not the values that the British imposed upon India, but rather barbaric Victorian values from Anglican Christianity are what was imposed. The US Christians who were missionaries, journalists, and aid workers who copiously documented the thoroughgoing human rights abuses of the British empire were following Enlightenment values more closely and those Enlightenment values were in the defense of the human rights of all people in India regardless of religious background. Enlightenment values shared the facts and the narrative of the horrific atrocities that the Indian people suffered and was leveraged as an argument for Indian independence during the time of British colonial rule over India. It is the values of Free Speech, Free Inquiry, and the Freedom of Thought that spoke in defense of the human rights of the Indian people under the despotic and barbaric rule of the British which tried to stifle Free Speech and peaceful protests. It doesn't matter where they originated from; what matters is what those values help people achieve. Free Speech, Free Inquiry, and Freedom of Thought are the values that helped to prove the tragedies that Indian people suffered and which valued the human rights of all Indian people. The most effective way to make peaceful change to end Casteism, misogyny, violent and coercive Christian conversions, Islamic terrorism, Marxist terrorism, and likely many other problems is through Free Speech, Free Inquiry, and Freedom of Thought. The Republic of India deserves to free its citizens by unshackling it from a barbaric British colonial law of 295A in the IPC that is no different than Saudi Arabia's laws against public opinion. *The Republic of India should bestow a Constitutional amendment that allows for Free Speech, Free Inquiry, and Freedom of Thought on all topics including those pertaining to all religions for the human rights of all people in India.*

Chapter 29: The Insights of Sanatana Dharma

This chapter has been one of the most difficult for me to write for reasons that'll be made clear. I seriously considered scrapping this chapter entirely out of fear, but such an act wouldn't be one of integrity or honesty. I'm partly afraid of looking like some sort of biased religious fanatic due to how bonkers some of this information seems, I wonder whether I'm discounting any possible motivated reasoning or personal bias, and I'm terrified that this'll just unravel all the work I've striven towards with this book. My initial outline for this chapter was suppose to show evidence for how Sanatana Dharma can be seen as a primitive study of consciousness, but as I researched . . . I found out that it was being appropriated for modern scientific studies of consciousness. I was stunned by this finding and delved more deeply to understand why this wasn't more well-known. I discovered that some Western "intellectuals" have been reading the material, changing the names, and profiteering from the religion of Sanatana Dharma via copyrighting it as their original work with no actual changes to the material itself. The Western mainstream media has dutifully lied to the US public about "changes" to the material that is being profiteered from. Some academics in the West have simply been pilfering and quite honestly committing cultural genocide while the Western mainstream media supported their activities unconditionally and don't concern themselves with the religious bigotry of their actions.

I realize the charge of cultural genocide is a heavy claim and perhaps open to abuse or misuse of language. Therefore, I'll share an enlightening explanation from David Nersessian of Babson college in his April, 22 2005 article on *Carnegie Council for Ethics in International Affairs* titled: "*Rethinking Cultural Genocide Under International Law*"; I've added quote marks and italicized the section in which he cites Raphael Lemkin to avoid confusion for readers. Nersessian's article reads as follows:

> "Genocide" is an amalgam of the Greek genos (race or tribe) and the Latin cide (killing), speaking literally to the destruction of a group. The term was conceived in 1944 by Raphael Lemkin, a Polish law professor who narrowly escaped the Nazi occupation of his homeland. In *Axis Rule in Occupied Europe*, a seminal text on Nazi race policy, Lemkin noted that genocide signifies:
>
> *"a coordinated plan of different actions aiming at the destruction of essential foundations of the life of national groups, with the aim of annihilating the groups themselves. The objectives of such a plan would be disintegration of the political and social institutions, of culture, language, national feelings, religion, and the economic existence of national groups, and the destruction of the personal security, liberty, health, dignity, and even the lives of the individuals belonging to such groups. Genocide is directed against the national group as an entity, and the actions involved are directed against individuals, not in their individual capacity, but as members of the national group."*
>
> Lemkin described eight dimensions of genocide—political, social, cultural, economic, biological, physical, religious, and moral—each targeting a different aspect of a group's existence. Of these, the most commonly recognized are physical, biological, and cultural. Physical genocide is the tangible annihilation of the group by killing and maiming its members, either directly or through what the International Criminal Tribunal for Rwanda recognized as "slow death" techniques such as concentration camps. Biological genocide consists of imposing measures calculated to decrease the reproductive capacity of the group, such as involuntary sterilization or forced segregation of the sexes.

Cultural genocide extends beyond attacks upon the physical and/or biological elements of a group and seeks to eliminate its wider institutions. This is done in a variety of ways, and often includes the abolition of a group's language, restrictions upon its traditional practices and ways, the destruction of religious institutions and objects, the persecution of clergy members, and attacks on academics and intellectuals. Elements of cultural genocide are manifested when artistic, literary, and cultural activities are restricted or outlawed and when national treasures, libraries, archives, museums, artifacts, and art galleries are destroyed or confiscated.

The 1948 Convention on the Prevention and Punishment of the Crime of Genocide prohibits physical and biological genocide but makes no mention of cultural genocide. This omission was deliberate. Early drafts of the Genocide Convention directly prohibited cultural genocide. As the treaty was finalized, however, a debate emerged over its proper scope. Many state representatives drafting the treaty understood cultural genocide to be analytically distinct, with one arguing forcefully that it defied both logic and proportion "to include in the same convention both mass murders in gas chambers and the closing of libraries." Others agreed with Lemkin's broader initial conception that a group could be effectively destroyed by an attack on its cultural institutions, even without the physical/biological obliteration of its members.

Cultural genocide ultimately was excluded from the final Convention, except for a limited prohibition on the forcible transfer of a group's children. The drafters acknowledged that the removal of children was physically and biologically destructive but further recognized that indoctrinating children into the customs, language, and values of a foreign group was "tantamount to the destruction of the [child's] group, whose future depended on that next generation."

Despite the limited definition of the offense itself, broader cultural considerations do still play two important roles in prosecuting genocide under the Convention. First, acts of cultural genocide—conduct violating what the International Criminal Tribunal for the Former Yugoslavia (ICTY) referred to as the "very foundation of the group"—tend to establish the genocidist's specific intent to destroy the protected group. The ICTY, for example, held that Serbian destruction of Muslim libraries and mosques and attacks on cultural leaders established genocidal intent against Muslims in the former Yugoslavia.

Second, cultural characteristics are used to help define the contours of the protected groups enumerated in the Convention. Since there are no universally accepted definitions of racial, ethnic, religious, or national groups, each must be assessed on a case-by-case basis in light of unique historical and contextual considerations. Cultural concerns, such as a group's social, historical, and linguistic characteristics, help to determine whether a given group of people is protected under the Convention.

Cultural genocide thus plays a subsidiary role in our present understanding of genocide and group destruction. But this is a product of the political realities of treaty negotiation between states rather than any limitation inherent in the concept. The Convention's drafters acknowledged the legitimacy of cultural genocide, and indicated that it might be addressed through other international instruments. Indeed, an individual right to cultural existence was recognized in the 1948 Universal Declaration of Human Rights and subsequently affirmed in the International Covenant on Economic, Social and Cultural Rights. And to accommodate the erosion of traditional geographic and economic boundaries, more recent treaties such as the Charter of the European Union and the Council of Europe's Framework Convention for the Protection of National Minorities contain anti-assimilation language and create express obligations to respect cultural diversity. Culture also is protected through such specific-purpose instruments as the European Cultural Convention and the Convention for the Protection of Cultural Property in the Event of Armed Conflict.

Without denigrating the importance of such developments, it nevertheless is important to recognize their limitations. Human rights treaties (and their concomitant compliance and adjudicatory mechanisms) depend upon the voluntary and good faith participation of states party to the instruments themselves. Adjudicated violations (including those amounting to cultural genocide) create at most an obligation to desist from the offending practice and to pay compensation. The responsible parties are states, and there is no recognition of individual civil or criminal responsibility for the conduct at issue. Those most likely to commit cultural genocide are least likely to participate in any voluntary human rights scheme.

Human rights jurisprudence lacks sufficient flexibility to properly redress cultural genocide, which differs from other infringements upon cultural rights in both scope and substance. The existing human rights scheme redresses the intentional and systematic eradication of a group's cultural existence (for example, destroying original historical texts or prohibiting all use of a language) with the same mechanisms as it would consider the redaction of an art textbook. But cultural genocide is far more sinister. In such cases, fundamental aspects of a group's unique cultural existence are attacked with the aim of destroying the group, thereby rendering the group itself (apart from its members) an equal object and victim of the attack. The existing rubric of human rights law fails to recognize and account for these important differences.

Collective identity is not self-evident but derives from the numerous, inter-dependent aspects of a group's existence. Lemkin's original conception of genocide expressly recognized that a group could be destroyed by attacking any of these unique aspects. By limiting genocide to its physical and biological manifestations, a group can be kept physically and biologically intact even as its collective identity suffers in a fundamental and irremediable manner. Put another way, the present understanding of genocide preserves the body of the group but allows its very soul to be destroyed.

This is hardly a satisfactory situation, and it is time to revisit the issue put aside by the Convention's drafters through a new treaty dealing specifically with cultural genocide. These efforts should be preceded by a comprehensive analysis of state practice and *opinio juris* to ascertain the current status of cultural genocide under customary international law. The need is patent. Cultural genocide is a unique wrong that should be recognized independently and that rises to the level of meriting individual criminal responsibility. After all, if indeed the highest values of a society are expressed through its criminal laws, what message is being conveyed by not labeling acts of cultural genocide as criminal? Perhaps a message better left unsent.[1963]

The Cultural Genocide of Sanatana Dharma by the West

The following is from *Wikipedia* and the only alterations made were removing the "edit" signs from the information being quoted and skipping the awards and works section. I was so dismayed to learn this information and I honestly wonder why the West seems to have malevolent hatred of followers of Sanatana Dharma to the point they would condone and support erasing our identity and culture while stealing from our religious traditions and history in order to personally profiteer from it and then depict us as savages in the Western mainstream media. Most of the information cited below is from page 35 of author Jeff Wilson's book *Mindful America* which tries to portray Mindfulness as simply another extension of how Buddhism was adapted into new countries according to its own summary, but in all honesty that doesn't make any sense if all references to Buddhism is erased while pilfering from its intellectual tradition.[1964] Onto the Wikipedia article about Jon Kabat-Zinn, the creator of mindfulness-based stress reduction program (MBSR):

---

1. [1963] Nersessian, David. "Rethinking Cultural Genocide Under International Law." *Carnegie Council for Ethics in International Affairs*, www.carnegiecouncil.org/publications/archive/dialogue/2_12/section_1/5139.
2. [1964] Wilson, Jeff. "Mindful America: The Mutual Transformation of Buddhist Meditation and American Culture - Kindle Edition by Jeff Wilson. Religion & Spirituality Kindle EBooks @ Amazon.com." *Amazon*, Amazon, smile.amazon.com/Mindful-America-Transformation-Buddhist-Meditation-ebook/dp/B00LNE8Q6C/ref=tmm_kin_swatch_0?_encoding=UTF8&qid=&sr=.

Jon Kabat-Zinn (born **Jon Kabat**, June 5, 1944) is an American professor emeritus of medicine and the creator of the Stress Reduction Clinic and the Center for Mindfulness in Medicine, Health Care, and Society at the University of Massachusetts Medical School. Kabat-Zinn was a student of Zen Buddhist teachers such as Philip Kapleau, Thich Nhat Hanh and Seung Sahn and a founding member of Cambridge Zen Center. His practice of yoga and studies with Buddhist teachers led him to integrate their teachings with scientific findings. He teaches mindfulness, which he says can help people cope with stress, anxiety, pain, and illness. The stress reduction program created by Kabat-Zinn, mindfulness-based stress reduction (MBSR), is offered by medical centers, hospitals, and health maintenance organizations.[1]

Life and work

Kabat-Zinn was born in New York City in 1944 as the youngest of nine children to Elvin Kabat, a biomedical scientist, and Sally Kabat, a painter. He graduated from Haverford College in 1964 and went on to earn a Ph.D. in molecular biology in 1971 from MIT, where he studied under Salvador Luria, Nobel Laureate in medicine.

While at MIT, Kabat-Zinn was a leading campaigner against military research at the university as well as a campaigner against the Vietnam war.[2] During this time, he pondered his life's purpose, which he called his "karmic assignment."[3]

Career

Kabat-Zinn was first introduced to meditation by Philip Kapleau, a Zen missionary who came to speak at MIT where Kabat-Zinn was a student. Kabat-Zinn went on to study meditation with other Buddhist teachers such as Thích Nhất Hạnh and Seungsahn.[4] He also studied at the Insight Meditation Society and eventually taught there.[4] In 1979 he founded the Stress Reduction Clinic at the University of Massachusetts Medical School, where he adapted the Buddhist teachings on mindfulness and developed the Stress Reduction and Relaxation Program. He subsequently renamed the structured eight-week course Mindfulness-Based Stress Reduction (MBSR). He removed the Buddhist framework and any connection between mindfulness and Buddhism, instead putting MBSR in a scientific context.[4] He subsequently also founded the Center for Mindfulness in Medicine, Health Care, and Society at the University of Massachusetts Medical School. His secular technique of Mindful Yoga, which combines meditation and Hatha yoga, has since spread worldwide.[4] The course aims to help patients cope with stress, pain, and illness by using what is called "moment-to-moment awareness."[5][6]

Kabat-Zinn's MBSR began to get increasing notice with the publication of his first book, *Full Catastrophe Living: Using the Wisdom of Your Body and Mind to Face Stress, Pain, and Illness* (Delta, 1991), which gave detailed instructions for the practice. Then, in 1993, his work in the Stress Reduction Clinic was featured in Bill Moyers's PBS special *Healing and the Mind*, spurring wide interest in MBSR and helping to make Kabat-Zinn nationally famous.[4] In 1994 Kabat-Zinn's second book, titled *Wherever You Go, There You Are*, became a national bestseller.[7] In the latter part of the 1990s, many MBSR clinics were opened, either as standalone centers or as part of a hospital's holistic medicine program.[4]

Research by Kabat-Zinn includes the effect of MBSR on psoriasis, pain, anxiety, brain function, and immune function.[8]

He is a board member of the Mind and Life Institute, a group that organizes dialogues between the Dalai Lama and Western scientists.[9]

MBSR has been adapted for use by the US military to improve combatants' "operational effectiveness," apparently with Kabat-Zinn's approval, which has provoked some controversy among mindfulness practitioners.[10][11][12]

Discussing the integration of narratives into mindfulness practice, Kabat-Zinn has said, "*the map... can occlude... the territory.'* [3][*further explanation needed*]

Kabat-Zinn is Professor of Medicine Emeritus at the University of Massachusetts Medical School.[13]

Personal life

Kabat-Zinn is married to Myla Zinn, the daughter of Roslyn and Howard Zinn. They have three grown children.[14]

Kabat-Zinn grew up in a non-practicing Jewish family.[15] He has stated that his beliefs growing up were a fusion of science and art.[13] Although he has been "trained in Buddhism and espouses its principles", he rejects the label of "Buddhist",[7] preferring to "apply mindfulness within a scientific rather than a religious frame".[4]

References

1. ^ Horstman, Judith (2010). *The Scientific American Brave New Brain*. San Francisco, Calif.: John Wiley & Sons. p. 33. ISBN 0470376244.
2. ^ *The Tech*, 7/10/69 p2-3 and 5/11/69 p1,3,4 and 7/11/69 p1,3,5 and 17/3/70 p1 and 5/5/70 p6 and 6/5/70 p1; *MIT Review Panel on Special Laboratories Final Report*; J. Kabat-Zinn, *Coming to Our Senses* p556-9.
3. ^ Jump up to:$^{a\ b}$ https://www.umassmed.edu/uploadedFiles/cfm2/training/JKZ_paper_Contemporary_Buddhism_2011.pdf
4. ^ Jump up to:$^{a\ b\ c\ d\ e\ f\ g}$ Wilson, Jeff (2014). *Mindful America: The Mutual Transformation of Buddhist Meditation and American Culture*. Oxford University Press. p. 35.
5. ^ "What is the Mindfulness-Based Stress Reduction Course?". Center for Mindfulness in Medicine, Health Care, and Society. Retrieved August 4, 2014.
6. ^ Thompson, Sylvia (10 April 2012). "The Father of Mindfulness". *The Irish Times*.
7. ^ Jump up to:$^{a\ b}$ Boyce, Barry (May 2005). "Jon Kabat-Zinn: The Man Who Prescribes the Medicine of the Moment". *Shambhala Sun*. Retrieved March 27, 2017.
8. ^ "Jon Kabat-Zinn: Selected Publications". UMass Profiles. Retrieved August 22, 2014.
9. ^ "Jon Kabat-Zinn bio". Mind and Life Institute. Archived from the original on 2010-12-27.
10. ^ Christopher Titmuss, 'Are Buddhist Mindfulness Practices used to support International War Crimes?'
11. ^ Ronald Purser, 'The Militarization of Mindfulness', *Inquiring Mind*, Spring 2014
12. ^ 'Dr. Kabat-Zinn talks about Mindfulness Program in Camp Zama'.
13. ^ Jump up to:$^{a\ b}$ Cochran, Tracy (December 6, 2004). "Mindful Writing: Jon Kabat-Zinn asks us to come to our senses". Retrieved August 4,2014.
14. ^ *Gesund durch Meditation* p330 and 331 the German translation of *Full Catastrophe Living: Using the Wisdom of Your Body and Mind to Face Stress, Pain and Illness*
15. ^ Booth, Robert (22 October 2017). "Master of mindfulness, Jon Kabat-Zinn: 'People are losing their minds. That is what we need to wake up to'". *The Guardian*. Retrieved 23 October 2017.
16. ^ Kabat-Zinn, Jon (2012). *Mindfulness for Beginners: reclaiming the present moment--and your life*. Boulder, Colorado: Sounds True, Inc. p. 165. ISBN 978-1-60407-658-5. OCLC 747533622.[1965]

Kabat-Zinn learned from Buddhist monks, identifies with the principles of Buddhism, and yet removed all references of Buddhism and profiteered from using Buddhist meditation and Dharmic yoga by categorically erasing the history and context to personally enrich himself. Even more ridiculous, he used science as a self-justification for his bigotry against the Dharmic religious tradition. I've often heard from scientists in debates, in speaking tours, and in a multitude of science promoting videos on Youtube that science is universal for all humans . . . so why is Kabat-Zinn arbitrarily using science as a justification for his profiteering from and cultural genocide of Sanatana Dharma? Keep in mind, he didn't actually add anything new, the "technique" that he supposedly created is the norm of all practitioners of Sanatana Dharma because Hindus, Buddhists, Jains, and Sikhs overlap and exchange beliefs, yoga practices, and

---

3. [1965] "Jon Kabat-Zinn." *Wikipedia*, Wikimedia Foundation, 22 July 2019, en.wikipedia.org/wiki/Jon_Kabat-Zinn.

meditation practices with no hostility because the core principle of Sanatana Dharma is that we're all One and have our own interpretation to our Oneness. People have used his so-called "technique" before under its religious terminology. All that Kabat-Zinn did was erase all mentions of Buddhism and Hinduism to profiteer from an ancient religious tradition. Why did the Western mainstream media not bother to fact-check his obvious lies? Why do they suddenly not care when a non-Islamic minority group's cultural identity is being erased? This is not just bigotry against Buddhism or Hinduism, it is bigotry against Sanatana Dharma itself. Why did White Liberals of the US ignore this act of cultural genocide, anti-Dharmic bigotry, and blatant erasure of a cultural identity of a religious minority group in the US? Why do they instead practice and support this act of cultural genocide? *Make no mistake, to support Mindfulness Meditation is to support cultural genocide.* It is the religion of Sanatana Dharma that you are practicing when you learn our Dharmic principles, Dharmic concepts of self and the world, Dharmic breathing techniques, Yoga techniques which is to practice our religion of Sanatana Dharma, Dharmic dietary techniques, Dharmic sex techniques, Dharmic stress relief, and Dharmic parenting techniques. *To espouse otherwise is to purposefully claim willful ignorance of the history of where your "Mindfulness" techniques come from and to support the cultural genocide of the religious history of Sanatana Dharma. If you follow any of the teachings, meditation techniques, breathing techniques, dietary techniques, and so forth that are the religion of Sanatana Dharma, then you are practicing the religion of Sanatana Dharma.*

    I am almost certain that this'll change no views because privileged Western White Liberals personally enrich themselves by passing off a minority group's religious history as their own techniques and achievements. I can just imagine the slew of articles calling me a bigot for arguing in defense of my religious and cultural tradition while privileged Western White, upper-class Liberals who benefit the most from this pilfering and cultural genocide by their fellow White, upper-class Liberals make arbitrary reasons to ignore a cultural genocide that they benefit from. When it comes to benefitting for their own selfish indulgences, I doubt that they'll care about erasing a minority group's religious history and traditions; I suspect they'll accuse me of bigotry by saying I'm somehow "discriminating" against another minority group without proof to justify their own deeds or perhaps they'll resort to Tokenism by using someone of the same skin pigmentation as I to justify cultural genocide. Perhaps some will even take advantage of Buddhism's principle of detachment as a way of satisfying their narcissism over the issue. If White, upper-class Liberals were to make such arguments then that would mean that an entire culture's religious history, intellectual traditions, and our personal identity can't be valid unless we have the approval of White, upper-class Liberals. The White, upper-class Liberals would thereby justify cultural genocide by their own arbitrary whims and ignore their own bigotry towards a minority group's religious faith which they benefit from. *If you call it Mindfulness and don't recognize it as part of Sanatana Dharma, then you are practicing and preaching cultural genocide of Sanatana Dharma.* It isn't Sanatana Dharma's fault that its religious techniques are being proven effective by modern science and that acknowledging such scientific facts hurts the feelings of people who follow other religions which have no basis in scientific evidence and aren't intellectually equal to Sanatana Dharma. If science is suppose to be for everyone regardless of cultural norms and based solely on facts, then the way to acknowledge that is not by erasing the cultural history of a religion whose techniques are proven effective by modern science. *Is science for everyone as scientists so claim, or are the xenophobes who classify it as "Western Science" justified in claiming it is bigotry against their religious views? Will such xenophobes in other cultures and countries be proven correct because of this horrendous act of cultural genocide being perpetuated by bigots like Kabat-Zinn in the West which continues to go unchallenged?* If Max Strom, a businessman who has made a fortune by removing Dharmic terms and renaming Yoga techniques as "Inner Axis" with his justification of Sanskrit being a dead language, can become a success by utilizing cultural genocide then the implication is that he changed the names because of Western White upper-class Liberals lack of comfort with Hindu terminology in Yoga and their unvarnished hatred for Sanatana Dharma, while practicing its religious techniques to the point they've made a billion-dollar Yoga industry.[1966][1967] Judging from the evidence, it seems that Western White upper-class Liberals fulfill their own narcissistic proclivities while self-righteously claiming to be selfless, compassionate, and not supportive of a consumer culture while participating in that very same consumer culture which has become more popular because of their own support for cultural genocide exclusively for the sake of their own personal comfort.

Prana

The Science Director of the Center for Compassion and Altruism Research and Education of Stanford University and author of *The Happiness Track*, Emma Seppala has promoted and supported the breathing technique of *Sudershan Kriya Yoga* in a December 2nd, 2014 interview that is on her official Youtube page which she only referred to as Sky Yoga as a breathing technique.[1968] Two years later on April 14th, 2016, she explained in a TEDxSacramento speech posted on the *TEDx Talks* Youtube page that clinical trials and reports from US veterans of Iraq and Afghanistan who distrust pharmaceutical companies and didn't want to take therapy have reported vast improvements in their daily life dealing with stress even a year later after using *Sudershan Kriya Yoga*.[1969] In the Ted talk, she referred to

---

4. [1966] "Max Strom Is a Teacher, Speaker, Author, and Creator of Inner Axis." *Max Strom*, maxstrom.com/about/.
5. [1967] "Going Deep and Wide with Max Strom." *Yogamatters Blog*, Yogamatters, 26 Feb. 2018, www.yogamatters.com/blog/going-deep-with-max-strom/. For reference: "Sanskrit is a dead language that is only spoken in one tiny corner of the world. It's like Latin. And yet we expect people to be OK with attending a movement class that includes words from this language and some allusions to Hindu spirituality. And some people are really put off by this. I think the Vinyasa Flow yoga world is not serving the majority of people any more." - Max Strom
6. [1968] Seppälä, Emma. "Interview on Emma's Research of Yoga-Breathing for Veterans with PTSD." *YouTube*, YouTube, 2 Dec. 2014, www.youtube.com/watch?v=c6_k1QfPYq4.
7. [1969] Seppälä, Emma. "Breathing Happiness | Emma Seppälä | TEDxSacramento." *YouTube*, TEDx Talks, 14 Apr. 2016, www.youtube.com/watch?v=Uvli7NBUfY4.

the breathing technique by its real name and many Veteran's families in the comments sections vouching for her work and praising *Sudershan Kriya Yoga's* benefits on improving the lives of US veterans of Iraq and Afghanistan.[1970] A month later, on May 19th, 2016, on a Big Think Youtube page titled "*Stressed? Use this Breathing Technique to Improve Your Attention and Memory, with Emma Seppala*" she explained a breathing technique in which she alternated breathing from the nostrils after explaining the technique's success in clinical trials, she didn't mention that this was the Dharmic breathing technique called *Nadishodhana* also known more popularly as *Anuloma Viloma Pranayama* and was lambasted in the comments for not mentioning the religious history of the technique.[1971][1972] Nadishodhana/Anuloma Viloma Pranayama was featured on Prime Minister Narendra Modi's verified Youtube channel a year before the Big Think video on June 17th, 2015 as part of the celebration of Yoga day.[1973] This is consistent with the BJP's agitation with Western patent claims attempting to pilfer religious techniques and practices for personal gain of Western businesspeople to the point that the Indian government has resorted to building a database featuring 1500 different Yoga poses to thwart those attempted patent claims by Western businesses on Dharmic religious practices.[1974]

To be clear so that I am not misunderstood on this point, **I'm *not* criticizing her for the excellent work that she's done in helping US servicemen and servicewomen who have returned from Afghanistan and Iraq and who prefer using Dharmic breathing techniques, I feel nothing but happiness that techniques from my religious background of Sanatana Dharma can help US military personnel and their families with effectively working through the harrowing traumas of war**. *I feel both pride and happiness that techniques from my religious background can aid the US military and their families, I have absolutely nothing against that.* The *only* component that I am criticizing is specifically when people who promote Dharmic techniques of breathing, meditation, diet, and so forth erase all mentions of the specific religious history when sharing the techniques because that is a form of cultural genocide. I can't know what researchers and practitioners like the three aforementioned are thinking when they erase all mentions of the religious history and context, but it seems to me that this is a cultural problem in the West with Religious Tolerance. Simply adding a few short comments about its religious history would alleviate this, but instead it is a major turn-off for Western audiences who do want to use Dharmic religious techniques, but also want to whitewash the history because they can't stand the idea that science is proving another religious traditions techniques to be effective while the history of their Abrahamic religion has been

---

8. [1970] Seppälä, Emma. "Breathing Happiness | Emma Seppälä | TEDxSacramento." *YouTube*, TEDx Talks, 14 Apr. 2016, www.youtube.com/watch?v=Uvli7NBUfY4.
9. [1971] Seppälä, Emma. "Stressed? Use This Breathing Technique to Improve Your Attention and Memory, with Emma Seppälä." *YouTube*, Big Think, 19 May 2016, www.youtube.com/watch?v=NrJZu6bGyHg.
10. [1972] "Why Do Pranayama?" *Kripalu*, 15 July 2019, kripalu.org/resources/why-do-pranayama.
11. [1973] Modi, Narendra. "Nadishodhana / Anuloma Viloma Pranayama." *YouTube*, YouTube, 17 June 2015, www.youtube.com/watch?v=AV_WDQ740Yk.
12. [1974] "India Creates Database of 1,500 Yoga Poses to Thwart Western Patent Claims." *RT International*, www.rt.com/news/312015-india-yoga-asanas-patent/.

debunked. Perhaps acknowledging the religious history, and technically the religion's teachings being proven effective by modern scientific consensus, would be painful to acknowledge for people of other religious faiths, but if such acknowledgement is a barrier for people then the response shouldn't be cultural genocide because it proves that the so-called melting pot analogy of US culture is false and that the US isn't comfortable to be open to another culture having effective methods that help people. This is the barrier of Religious Tolerance in concomitant with the predominance of Christian culture teaching that other religions are devil worship or misleading because they don't follow the teachings of Jesus Christ. I suspect many US readers will be confused because Dharmic teachings were portrayed as nonsensical spiritual-speaking garbage with no value in science, but that is actually the fault of Westerners in the 1800s who sought mysticism and mystery with "alternative medicine" as a way of rationalizing Christianity with science in the 1800s which they referred to as Christian Science.[1975] When "Christian Science" and its claims of prayer healing, magic stones, magic oils, and many other occultist ideas failed; it splintered into more ridiculous nonsense.[1976] Several examples of Christian Science practitioners making up nonsense are Ouija board and Tarot occultism[1977], an American religious movement in the 1870s to early 1900s called Theosophy which borrowed terminology from Sanatana Dharma in order to try to argue their own Last Judgment prophecies by stating all major world religions had prophets and that they all taught the same thing with a "Jesus-Maitreya" as a savior[1978,1979,1980,1981], and many specifically Christian organizations throughout the late 1800s to modern times borrow whatever terms sound "exotic" to create their own liberal and esoteric versions of Christianity in order to try to be more open in hopes of converting non-Christians.[1982] In a very real way, Westerners only ever wanted to see mystery, occultism, exoticism, and other anti-intellectual aspects from Sanatana Dharma because it helped them feel like their religion of Christianity is somehow more rational by contrast. I'm sure this'll prompt many to point out mythical stories or some obscure teaching for Western Christians and some Western atheists to rationalize Christianity as more "intelligent" by comparison to Sanatana Dharma, but this obfuscates the point being made. *Why is it that when Sanatana Dharma's teachings prove to have value by modern scientific consensus, Westerners suddenly opt to categorically erase all references to my religion while*

---

13. [1975] "Christian Science." *Wikipedia*, Wikimedia Foundation, 1 Aug. 2019, en.wikipedia.org/wiki/Christian_Science.
14. [1976] "Christian Science." *Wikipedia*, Wikimedia Foundation, 1 Aug. 2019, en.wikipedia.org/wiki/Christian_Science.
15. [1977] "Ouija." *Wikipedia*, Wikimedia Foundation, 18 July 2019, en.wikipedia.org/wiki/Ouija.
16. [1978] "Theosophy (Blavatskian)." *Wikipedia*, Wikimedia Foundation, 4 Aug. 2019, en.wikipedia.org/wiki/Theosophy_(Blavatskian)#Influence_on_other_religious_and_esoteric_groups.
17. [1979] "Original Theosophy and Later Versions." *T H E O S O P H Y*, 15 Apr. 2019, blavatskytheosophy.com/original-theosophy-and-later-versions/.
18. [1980] "Maitreya in the Light of Real Theosophy." *T H E O S O P H Y*, 15 Apr. 2019, blavatskytheosophy.com/maitreya-in-the-light-of-real-theosophy/.
19. [1981] "Maitreya." *IPS-Eye-White*, www.inplainsite.org/html/maitreya.html#BCM1.
20. [1982] "Liberal Catholic Church." *Wikipedia*, Wikimedia Foundation, 12 June 2019, en.wikipedia.org/wiki/Liberal_Catholic_Church.

using its teachings? If that isn't bigotry and cultural genocide against my religion, then what is it? Why do Westerners only feel comfortable when calling something a religious practice from my religion of Sanatana Dharma when they feel confident enough to mock it, but when it benefits their health and livelihood then they want to erase all references to my religion? I suspect that it is the bigotry of Religious Tolerance because the unintentional assumption is that all religions are somehow equal, so when that is disproven by modern scientific evidence, the response is to erase all mentions of religion for the comfort of those who follow the Abrahamic faiths and who still wish to believe they're true with the paradoxical belief of open interpretation. Open interpretation seems to have created a bizarre societal standard whereby not following the teachings of the Abrahamic faiths because they're barbaric while following and practicing the teachings of Sanatana Dharma because they provide health benefits can be called consistent with following the Abrahamic faiths. Thereby, the West is normalizing bigotry against Sanatana Dharma while practicing its teachings.

For those skeptical of the value that modern science places on Sanatana Dharma's breathing techniques, here is the conclusion portion of a 2013 article by Sameer A. Zope and Rakesh A. Zope titled "*Sudarshan kriya yoga: Breathing for health*" from the *International Journal of Yoga* and presented online on the *National Center for Biotechnology Information* (NCBI)'s website which is a subsidiary of the *US National Library of Medicine* (NLM):

> CONCLUSION
> The ancient yogic science of breath is the science that deals with body, breath, mind, soul, and ultimately, the universe itself. Just as a thread links the kite-flier to his kite, breath is said to link the mind with the universal force. Medical science is currently rediscovering and validating many of the ancient health practices from traditional cultures worldwide. SKY is one novel practice that is undergoing extensive research to show it as an evidence-based treatment. SKY has been reported to be effective not only for treating stress and anxiety, but also for PTSD, depression, stress-related medical illness, and substance abuse, and for rehabilitation of criminal offenders.
> SKY practices are cost-effective, well-tolerated tools that can be easily integrated into diverse community care models. SKY relieves stress and develops an individual's mind–body–spirit so that they can be happier, healthier, and possibly even longer lived. In the competitive modern world, in which stress and anxiety are part of everyday life, adding a time-honored, evidence-based breathing program like SKY may facilitate a healthy life.
> Further studies are needed to assess the therpeutic potential of SKY in the treatment of bipolar disorder, dissociative disorders, or schizophrenic spectrum illnesses and various stress-induced illnesses.[1983]

Lastly, I'd like to clarify that I have no problems with any Western White person promoting, using, or celebrating the techniques or teachings of Sanatana Dharma. My ire is strictly about how Western culture is erasing all mentions of Sanatana Dharma while using its meditation exercises, dietary recommendations, breathing techniques, religious teachings, and so forth without acknowledging them; I don't care that White scholars or White businesspeople make money from promoting it as I find that to be perfectly reasonable and a wonderful form

---

21. [1983] Zope, Sameer A, and Rakesh A Zope. "Sudarshan Kriya Yoga: Breathing for Health." *International Journal of Yoga*, Medknow Publications & Media Pvt Ltd, Jan. 2013, www.ncbi.nlm.nih.gov/pmc/articles/PMC3573542/.

of capitalism that is helping large swathes of people by providing goods and services that can provide health benefits and perhaps personal meaning. They're putting the work in and serving others; I have no problems with White Westerners wanting to take part in my culture or my religious culture at all. Although, as a capitalist, I personally find it amusing that people are making a multi-billion dollar industry from Sanatana Dharma while claiming to be escaping consumerism; I think the real problem is this ridiculous derivative of Original Sin from Abrahamic culture that teaches Western people to hate the material world. Aspects of this exist in Sanatana Dharma too, but I don't find it to be as potent and prevalent. However, I hope that I've made my point unambiguously clear, my only contentions are that they're categorically erasing the religious history, attempting to claim they've invented these practices when they're religious practices that are part of the religion of Sanatana Dharma and not something they can use patents on, and that is why it is cultural genocide. Otherwise, I wouldn't have any issues whatsoever and would probably support their efforts. Sharing a culture is fine, but erasing and then claiming ownership of someone else's culture is a form of cultural genocide. Sadly, I don't expect this to change any minds or have any impact in dissuading the negative reciprocal trajectory that the West and India have over this contentious issue. Keep in mind, the blame for this negative trajectory is entirely the fault of the West in this specific context.

The Cultural Appreciation of Sanatana Dharma by the West

"In the whole world, there is no study so beneficial and so elevating as that of the Upanishads. It has been the solace of my life - it will be the solace of my death."[1984] - Arthur Schopenhauer

If there is one aspect of the culture derived from Sanatana Dharma that is highly respected throughout India and the West, it is the culture that encourages Indians to join the medical profession and serve as doctors and nurses for the various medical departments related to patient care. This is a aspect of Sanatana Dharma and Indian culture in general that almost certainly has no drawbacks for anyone. What is probably one of the least surprising aspects of ancient Indian culture and history is the emphasis on medicine and the high ethical standards of ancient Indian physicians in their conduct with helping their patients.[1985] The medical profession of ancient India changed from hokey nonsense that one can imagine from stereotyping an ancient civilization with beliefs in casting out demons and providing blessings for sick people to transforming its medical profession into one of strict, objective standards that sought to help sick patients with a holistic approach of checking their temperament, food habits, age, and so forth under the medical profession of *Ayurveda*.[1986] Ayurveda emerged

---

22. [1984] Durant, Will. Chapter XIV: The Foundations of India: VII. The Philosophy of the Upanishads (9463 - 9469). *Our Oriental Heritage: Being a History of Civilization in Egypt and the Near East to the Death of Alexander, and in India, China and Japan from the Beginning to Our Own Day*. Simon and Schuster, 1935.
23. [1985] Saini, Anu. "Physicians of Ancient India." *Journal of Family Medicine and Primary Care*, Medknow Publications & Media Pvt Ltd, 2016, www.ncbi.nlm.nih.gov/pmc/articles/PMC5084543/.
24. [1986] Saini, Anu. "Physicians of Ancient India." *Journal of Family Medicine and Primary Care*, Medknow Publications & Media Pvt Ltd, 2016, www.ncbi.nlm.nih.gov/pmc/articles/PMC5084543/.

approximately around 600 BCE in the middle of the approximate period of the Sramana movements; they had a wide-range of knowledge on drugs and focused on health benefits and disease prevention for their patients.[1987] *Vaidyaas*, the medical profession's term in ancient times, were highly respected and during ancient times it was the one profession where multiple Castes could join, they were held to a high ethical conduct with strict penalties from the government for any malpractice, they were highly respected among all of the four upper-castes, and there is much evidence to suggest they were paid well for their profession.[1988] Of course, due to the entrenched misogyny during the ancient time period, there's little evidence to suggest Indian women could participate in the profession, but thankfully Indian women have made headway in the participation of their own culture in modern times. In chapter eight of his book, *The Argumentative Indian*, Amartya Sen's explanation of Chinese visitors accounts of the ancient Indian medical system, from the 3rd and 6th centuries respectively, depicted the visitors as being too polite and aggrandizing of ancient India's medical facilities and techniques after quoting their overwhelmingly positive views of India's medical system and the Vaidyaas methods.[1989] However, there's ample evidence that this wasn't mere flattery. In the educational Youtube video created by the organization *CrashCourse* and hosted by one of the Vlogbrothers Hank Green, "*India: Crash Course History of Science #4*", he explains that Ayurvedic texts like the *Charaka Samhita* listed 300 bones, 500 muscles, 210 joints, and 70 vessels within the human body; he further explains it was written sometime before 200 CE.[1990] As such, Hank Green explains that this provides significant credence that ancient India's medical and surgical procedures was highly likely to be the most advanced of any of its contemporary ancient civilizations during its time period.[1991] Tragically, the Islamic massacres almost certainly destroyed whatever advantage that India had.

Flow and Moksha

"*Buddhism, I repeat, is a hundred times more austere, more honest, more objective. It no longer has to justify its pains, its susceptibility to suffering, by interpreting these things in terms of sin—it simply says, as it simply thinks, "I suffer." To the barbarian, however, suffering in itself is scarcely understandable: what he needs, first of all, is an explanation as to why he suffers. (His mere instinct prompts him to deny his suffering altogether, or to endure it in silence.) Here the word "devil" was a blessing: man had to have an omnipotent and terrible enemy—there was no need to be ashamed of suffering at the hands of such an enemy.—*

At the bottom of Christianity there are several subtleties that belong to the Orient. In the first place, it knows that it is of very little consequence whether a thing be true or not, so long as it is believed to be true. Truth and faith: here we have two wholly distinct worlds of ideas, almost two diametrically opposite worlds—the road to the one and the road to the other lie miles apart. To understand that fact thoroughly—this is almost enough, in

---

25. [1987] Saini, Anu. "Physicians of Ancient India." *Journal of Family Medicine and Primary Care*, Medknow Publications & Media Pvt Ltd, 2016, www.ncbi.nlm.nih.gov/pmc/articles/PMC5084543/.
26. [1988] Saini, Anu. "Physicians of Ancient India." *Journal of Family Medicine and Primary Care*, Medknow Publications & Media Pvt Ltd, 2016, www.ncbi.nlm.nih.gov/pmc/articles/PMC5084543/.
27. [1989] Sen, Amartya. Chapter 8. China and India (2879-3351). *The Argumentative Indian: Writings on Indian History, Culture and Identity*. Macmillan, 2005.
28. [1990] Green, Hank. "India: Crash Course History of Science #4." *YouTube*, CrashCourse, 25 Apr. 2018, www.youtube.com/watch?v=bDQkpNbsly4.
29. [1991] Green, Hank. "India: Crash Course History of Science #4." *YouTube*, CrashCourse, 25 Apr. 2018, www.youtube.com/watch?v=bDQkpNbsly4.

the Orient, to make one a sage. The Brahmins knew it, Plato knew it, every student of the esoteric knows it. When, for example, a man gets any pleasure out of the notion that he has been saved from sin, it is not necessary for him to be actually sinful, but merely to feel sinful. But when faith is thus exalted above everything else, it necessarily follows that reason, knowledge and patient inquiry have to be discredited: the road to the truth becomes a forbidden road.—Hope, in its stronger forms, is a great deal more powerful stimulans to life than any sort of realized joy can ever be. Man must be sustained in suffering by a hope so high that no conflict with actuality can dash it—so high, indeed, that no fulfilment can satisfy it: a hope reaching out beyond this world. (Precisely because of this power that hope has of making the suffering hold out, the Greeks regarded it as the evil of evils, as the most malign of evils; it remained behind at the source of all evil.)—In order that love may be possible, God must become a person; in order that the lower instincts may take a hand in the matter God must be young. To satisfy the ardor of the woman a beautiful saint must appear on the scene, and to satisfy that of the men there must be a virgin. These things are necessary if Christianity is to assume lordship over a soil on which some aphrodisiacal or Adonis cult has already established a notion as to what a cult ought to be. To insist upon chastity greatly strengthens the vehemence and subjectivity of the religious instinct—it makes the cult warmer, more enthusiastic, more soulful.—Love is the state in which man sees things most decidedly as they are not. The force of illusion reaches its highest here, and so does the capacity for sweetening, for transfiguring. When a man is in love he endures more than at any other time; he submits to anything. The problem was to devise a religion which would allow one to love: by this means the worst that life has to offer is overcome—it is scarcely even noticed.—So much for the three Christian virtues: faith, hope and charity: I call them the three Christian ingenuities.—Buddhism is in too late a stage of development, too full of positivism, to be shrewd in any such way.—"[1992] - Friedrich Nietzsche, *Aphorism 23* of *The Anti-Christ*. Translated by H. L. Mencken.

In his seminal book, *Flow: The Psychology of Optimal Experience*, author and Hungarian-American psychology Mihaly Csikszentmihalyi explains the ubiquitous ways in which the psychological state of Flow can be utilized in a multifarious range of activities from viewing a painting, to Yoga, to working at a satisfying job, to thinking deeply about an issue, to amorous activities like sex, and much more.[1993] The state of Flow requires attention to an activity with deep concentration, finding the activity intrinsically pleasurable for its own sake with extrinsic rewards being irrelevant, the subjective feeling that the activity is controllable for the person doing the activity, and it is often associated with a subjective sense of eternity or timelessness whereby a person is entirely absorbed in the activity without any distractions and usually doesn't pay attention to the time spent on the activity at all.[1994] Csikszentmihalyi references the Brahmins of India and the religious system of the Brahmins as an example of a society's religious beliefs producing the state of Flow among its inhabitants.[1995] Further on, he explains how Yoga practices could utilize Flow too with people's intense concentration to the experience of Yoga, but he admits that this viewpoint of his may not be valid because some people have pointed out to him that the Buddhist teaching postulates that the self is an illusion and so Csikszentmihalyi's argument of Flow reclaiming the inner self or having a goal can't be applied in this context.[1996] The meditation and Yoga within a Buddhist context doesn't

---

30. [1992] Nietzsche, Friedrich Wilhelm. Aphorism 23. *THE ANTICHRIST*. Translated by H. L. Mencken, The Project Gutenberg, 2006.
31. [1993] Csikszentmihalyi, Mihaly. *Flow: the Psychology of Optimal Experience*. 1st ed., Harper Perennial, 2008.
32. [1994] Csikszentmihalyi, Mihaly. *Flow: the Psychology of Optimal Experience*. 1st ed., Harper Perennial, 2008.
33. [1995] Csikszentmihalyi, Mihaly. Chapter 4 (71-93). *Flow: the Psychology of Optimal Experience*. 1st ed., Harper Perennial, 2008.
34. [1996] Csikszentmihalyi, Mihaly. Chapter 5 (94-116). *Flow: the Psychology of Optimal Experience*. 1st ed.,

internalize pleasure, but rather detachment from personal wants. However, what about the context of the other denominations of Sanatana Dharma? While Hinduism contains teachings of detaching from the Self in the *Upanishads*, there is also the teaching of working to attain the supreme form of the Self as a goal and acknowledging the duality that it is the Brahman within and the Brahman that is part of the universe itself.[1997] These other teachings and the *Bhagavad Gita* contain explanations of meditation and normal activities that are clearly within the parameters of what constitutes the Flow State.[1998] While this was in the context of recognizing one's unity with the pantheistic deity of *Brahman*, it could be possible that feeling the intense concentration of the Flow State was what was being referred to as the Self while perhaps wrongfully interpreting the Flow State as proof of the pantheistic deity *Brahman*. When the *Bhagavad Gita* and the *Upanishads* speak of understanding the Self as a goal to strive towards with adamant recommendations of focusing upon it as the goal in life and for the *Bhagavad Gita* the other optional goal being selfless service without a desire for a reward, it seems highly plausible given the descriptions that the entirety of Sanatana Dharma was focused on studying the Flow State which was perceived in ancient times as a higher form of consciousness that connected people to the divinity of *Brahman*.[1999][2000] The points of difference concerning *no-Self* and acknowledging the *Self* were accepted within the *Bhagavad Gita* as two different aspects of following Krishna's teachings.[2001] Krishna refers to renouncing action as a path, but the active commitment of selfless service as the preferred path.[2002] Sanatana Dharma's religious teachings focusing on the Flow State could possibly explain why the Hindu denomination of Sanatana Dharma demarcated itself into Castes in the first place since Caste may have more easily brought about the Flow State due to societal activities being restricted. Within human psychology, constraint is found to help keep focus, so the existence of Caste could have emerged because a stricter focus on the Flow State was misunderstood to be a closer way for Hindu society to be collectively pleasing their imaginary Gods by achieving a perceived "higher consciousness" and the belief in a fatalistic form of determinism kept the Brahmins adamant about preserving Castes throughout society. To lend credence to this, the *Bhagavad Gita* itself claims that forms of chaos would take hold by not following one's duty and fulfilling their Caste obligations as per selfless service without any desire for a reward.[2003]

---

35. [1997] Eknath, Easwaran, translator. Taittiriya: Ascent to Joy (3236-3637). *The Upanishads*. Nilgiri Press, 2007.
36. [1998] Eknath, Easwaran, translator. Chapter 5: Renounce and Rejoice (115-123) and Chapter 6: The Practice of Meditation (124-136). *The Bhagavad Gita*. Nilgiri Press, 2007.
37. [1999] Eknath, Easwaran, translator. Chapter 5: Renounce and Rejoice (115-123) and Chapter 6: The Practice of Meditation (124-136). *The Bhagavad Gita*. Nilgiri Press, 2007.
38. [2000] Eknath, Easwaran, translator. Taittiriya: Ascent to Joy (3236-3637). *The Upanishads*. Nilgiri Press, 2007.
39. [2001] Eknath, Easwaran, translator. *The Bhagavad Gita*. Nilgiri Press, 2007.
40. [2002] Eknath, Easwaran, translator. *The Bhagavad Gita*. Nilgiri Press, 2007.
41. [2003] Eknath, Easwaran, translator. *The Bhagavad Gita*. Nilgiri Press, 2007.

At a cursory glance, the context of *Moksha* (Self-liberation) is seen as the supreme goal to go beyond *Samsara* (rebirth/reincarnation), but Moksha has more open-ended interpretations which are exclusively in the context of the physical world; this has baffled Indologists and some Hindus who try to understand or interpret it. Why would random activities pertaining to hobbies and jobs that people are doing qualify as *Moksha* like in meditation? Well, what if *Moksha* (Self-liberation) in the context of the physical world was referring to the Flow State as I just described? It may have been an open-ended usage for when a person was in intense concentration on a pleasurable activity they did for the sake of doing it; the sense of eternity and timelessness when committing to the activity may have been misunderstood as reaching a higher consciousness towards *Brahman*. This would be consistent with the teachings of the *Bhagavad Gita*. Ancient Vedic society misinterpreting the Flow State in conjunction with the belief in a fatalistic form of determinism may have been the reason and *Moksha* in the context of when it was used for activities in the physical world could have been their word for the Flow State.

Csikszentmihalyi mentions the *Kama Sutra* in the chapter on utilizing the Flow State with sex.[2004] While this may cause discomfort due to the prudish nature of modern Indian society as a result of the influence of the Abrahamic faiths, I'd like to point out that it is a complete self-contradiction for the Right-leaning Hindus of India to argue that they must de-colonize the Indian mind, but abruptly behave obsequiously to the morality of the Abrahamic God as Christian missionaries and pious Muslims demand when the subjects of sex, masturbation, and female sexuality become the topic of discussion. If Right-leaning Hindus are honest about their desire to de-colonize themselves, then why do they disparage the *Kama Sutra* at the behest of the Abrahamic morality that they've inculcated from the culture of Islam and subsequently British Victorian culture? Why do they not instead act in firm deviance of Abrahamic morality and state clearly that they're proud of the *Kama Sutra* being part of Sanatana Dharma? Sex is an integral part of the human condition and life satisfaction. If Right-leaning Hindus are truly serious about de-colonizing the Indian mind, then they should work towards building better sex education for late-teens to young adults in their society instead of bowing to the morality of the Abrahamic God. As shown in the previous sections, the worthless morality of Christianity and Islam sees sex as dirty due to the misogyny within the Abrahamic faiths and because the concept of Original Sin inculcates people to hate their own human existence. By contrast, sex education teaches responsibility, decreases teen pregnancies at a higher rate than teaching people to follow Abrahamic morality, and masturbation is entirely healthy for people and not something to be ashamed of. This'll probably cause even more ire and repudiation than what I just mentioned, but I think that the Devadasi system should return for consenting adults of both genders; both adult men and women who aren't under any coercive impositions should freely be allowed to practice this ancient tradition. The ridicule of it being prostitution and contempt towards women who participated in the

---

42. [2004] Csikszentmihalyi, Mihaly. Chapter 5 (94-116). *Flow: the Psychology of Optimal Experience*. 1st ed., Harper Perennial, 2008.

profession during British colonialism is quite clearly a victory of British colonization and Abrahamic morality above the more sex-positive views of Sanatana Dharma. Before Islamic and British imperialism, Devadasi men and women were respected members of the community and female Devadasis often had more freedom in ancient India to learn and participate in conversations about theology than married women.[2005] It didn't have the cultic obsession with virginity required in Christian organizations like the Catholic Church, US Southern Baptists, and Jehovah's Witnesses which have all resulted in widespread child rape cases.[2006][2007][2008] The cultic obsession with virginity, misogyny, and hatred of sex almost certainly directly impacted their behavior towards children meanwhile the sex-positive Devadasi system was vilified by people who hold the cultic obsession with virginity and anti-sex views as morally righteous when they simply spread lies about sexual pleasure, sexual health like masturbation, and they ignore that safe sex is possible with government support for testing for any possible diseases, condom usage being a possibility now to prevent pregnancies, and authorities being responsive with treating Devadasis as any other typical person in the community with respect instead of viewing them as less respectable for their profession.

Vedic Influence on Cosmology

"I am convinced that everything has come down to us from the banks of the Ganges, – astronomy, astrology, metempsychosis, etc... It is very important to note that some 2,500 years ago at the least Pythagoras went from Samos to the Ganges to learn geometry...But he would certainly not have undertaken such a strange journey had the reputation of the Indians' science not been long established in Europe."[2009] - Voltaire, from *Lettres sur l'origine des sciences et sur celle des peuples de l'Asie (first published Paris, 1777).*

Perhaps the most difficult history to accept is that Hindu theology helped to conceptualize the groundbreaking discoveries recognized in modern cosmology. People may have an immediate impulse to reject this claim as crackpot theories related to spiritual beliefs, but it was the cosmologists themselves who formed the theories that stated the Vedic texts of Hinduism helped them to better accept and conceptualize their own scientific theories. From Gaurav Sharma's May, 12th 2015 article titled "*How scientists like Niels Bohr, Schrodinger,*

---

43. [2005] Durant, Will. Chapter XVII The Life of People: III. Morals and Marriage (11052-11088). *Our Oriental Heritage: Being a History of Civilization in Egypt and the Near East to the Death of Alexander, and in India, China and Japan from the Beginning to Our Own Day*. Simon and Schuster, 1935.
44. [2006] Park, Madison. "Timeline: A Look at the Catholic Church's Sex Abuse Scandals." *CNN*, Cable News Network, 29 June 2017, www.cnn.com/2017/06/29/world/timeline-catholic-church-sexual-abuse-scandals/index.html.
45. [2007] Bundy, Trey. "Jehovah's Witnesses Sued in Canada over History of Sex Abuse Cover-Up." *Reveal*, 30 Jan. 2018, www.revealnews.org/blog/jehovahs-witnesses-sued-in-canda-for-history-of-sex-abuse-cover-up/?utm_source=Reveal&utm_medium=social_media&utm_campaign=facebook.
46. [2008] Downen, Robert, et al. "20 Years, 700 Victims: Southern Baptist Sexual Abuse Spreads as Leaders Resist Reforms." *Houston Chronicle*, Houston Chronicle, 6 June 2019, www.houstonchronicle.com/news/investigations/article/Southern-Baptist-sexual-abuse-spreads-as-leaders-13588038.php.
47. [2009] "Indomania." *Wikipedia*, Wikimedia Foundation, 13 June 2019, en.wikipedia.org/wiki/Indomania#18th_and_19th_centuries.

Nikola Tesla, and Albert Einstein found the true meaning of Physics in Vedas" which is as follows:

At first glance, the subjects of science and metaphysics seem to be polar opposites of each other. The pioneers of Quantum Mechanics, however, believed it to be otherwise. In fact, the founding fathers of Quantum Physics, while formulating their groundbreaking theories, sumptuously dug into annals of Vedic philosophy and found their experiments to be consistent with the knowledge expounded in Vedas. Danish physicist and Nobel laureate Niels Bohr was fascinated with Vedas. His remark, "I go to the Upanishad to ask questions," reveals a lot about his respect for the ancient wisdom of India. Erwin Schrodinger, an Austrian-Irish physicist who also won the Nobel Prize for his famous wave equation, was also a keen proponent of the Vedic thought. In his book Meine Weltansicht, Schrodinger says, "This life of yours which you are living is not merely a piece of this entire existence, but in a certain sense the whole; only this whole is not so constituted that it can be surveyed in one single glance. This, as we know, is that sacred, mystic formula which is yet really so simple and so clear; tat tvam asi, this is you. Or, again, in such words as "I am in the east and the west, I am above and below, I am this entire world." This is nothing but a Mundaka Upanishad mantra which proposes the connectivity of all living beings. "The unity and continuity of Vedanta are reflected in the unity and continuity of wave mechanics. This is entirely consistent with the Vedanta concept of All in One", Schrodinger said while referring to each particle in the universe as a wave function.

WERNER HEISENBERG'S UNCERTAINTY PRINCIPLE, WHICH STATES THAT WE CANNOT MEASURE BOTH THE POSITION AND MOMENTUM OF A PARTICLE AT THE SAME TIME, IS ALSO A REFLECTION OF THE ADVAITIC APHORISM OF ROPE AND SNAKE;" WHEN A SNAKE IS SEEN IN THE PLACE OF A ROPE, ONLY THE SNAKE IS SEEN AS REAL. BUT IS IT INDEPENDENTLY REAL?"

But perhaps the greatest example of how modern-science viz quantum physics is inextricably intertwined with the spiritual concepts of the ancient world, comes through the works and words of Nikola Tesla. The mastermind scientist and inventor, apart from knowing complex mathematical formulas possessed the subtle knowledge of the working of the universe. In his seminal book Man's Greatest Achievement, Tesla says, "All perceptible matter comes from a primary substance, or tenuity beyond conception, filling all space, the akasha or luminiferous ether, which is acted upon by the life giving Prana or creative force, calling into existence, in never-ending cycles all things and phenomena." The usage of words such as Prana and Akasha clearly show that the father of electricity was well-versed in the teachings of the Vedic worldview. The relationship Tesla shared with Swami Vivekananda, a great Hindu reformist is also quite well-known. Vivekananda in one of his works states: "Mr Tesla was charmed to hear about the Vedantic Prana and Akasha and Kalpas, which according to him are the only theories modern science can entertain. Now both Akasha and Prana are produced from the Mahat or the Universal Mind. Mr. Tesla thinks he can demonstrate mathematically that force and matter are reducible to potential energy. In that case the Vedantic cosmology will be placed on the surest of foundations. I am working a good deal now upon the cosmology and eschatology of the Vedanta. I clearly see their perfect union with modern science, and the elucidation of the one will be followed by that of the other." Tesla revolutionized science with the concepts of "Free energy", also known as "Zero-point energy". Unfortunately, the theories could never actualized, as his funding and grants were constantly revoked by those running the economy, such as JP Morgan, Westinghouse etc. Albert Einstein, the father of the Theory of Relativity and developer of Quantum Mechanics also believed in the unity of the universe. "There is no spooky action at a distance", he is known to have said. In his book, The World as I See It, Einstein says "I maintain that the cosmic religious feeling is the strongest and noblest motive for scientific research". This clearly elucidates the fact that science cannot function in isolation with nature. And therefore, the current scientific view of extracting energy for the sole purpose of economic development is farcical. Modern science can and should build on the work of previous western scientists, many of whom drew significant inspiration from the Vedas and Upanishad.[2010]

---

48. [2010] Sharma, Gaurav. "How Scientists like Niels Bohr, Schrodinger, Nikola Tesla and Albert Einstein Found the True Meaning of Physics in Vedas." *NewsGram*, 12 May 2015, www.newsgram.com/how-

Conscious Awareness and so-called "Western" Science

"As mentioned, the typical notion of "self," along with other misperceptions of everyday experiences, can be overcome through meditation training, which is also now better understood at the level of the brain. For thousands of years, Eastern contemplative traditions have used meditation as an experimental basis for studying the nature of consciousness, and although Western science is a relative latecomer to these methods of introspection, research is now being conducted by neuroscientists on the specific effects of meditation on the mind and brain. This research will hopefully lead to new discoveries about how training our attention in systematic ways can provide a better understanding of consciousness and human psychology. At the very least, it confirms that valuable insights can be had through first-person tools of investigation. The Buddhist scholar Andrew Olendzki describes the illusory nature of self that can be revealed through meditation: Like the flatness of the earth or the solidity of the table, it [the notion of self] has utility at a certain level of scale—socially, linguistically, legally—but thoroughly breaks down when examined with closer scrutiny.9"[2011] — Annaka Harris, from "Conscious: A Brief Guide to the Fundamental Mystery of the Mind"

Notions of a division between science and Sanatana Dharma seem to have become thinner these several decades as neuroscientists, cosmologists, and psychologists of the West utilize the religious concepts and teachings of Sanatana Dharma to further progress modern scientific discoveries. To the infamy of Westerners who sought only spiritual mystery, people within India who hold their own xenophobic views trying to portray science as a strictly Western phenomena, and to some Western practitioners who want to erase the culture and religious history of Sanatana Dharma while committing their life to its teachings; the idea that science has validated Sanatana Dharma comes as an uncomfortable shock. This shouldn't be so surprising, Sanatana Dharma is not about unquestioned obedience to a God. Apart from the abhorrent Caste system in some denominations, the central foundations of Sanatana Dharma is truthseeking and debate. Despite the theistic denominations with hokey beliefs in an elephant God, as I am so reminded by people who don't know much about Sanatana Dharma but want to mock it, that is simply part of the theistic denomination of multiple denominations which involve different forms of theism within a pantheistic context. Atheism is another denomination since the whole point is *truthseeking* under the basis that we are all One but have our own personal, subjective interpretations to our Oneness.

According to Annaka Harris's splendid book, *Consciousness: A Brief Guide to the Fundamental Mystery of the Mind*, neuroscience has confirmed that Sanatana Dharma's teachings on how the internal identity of the self functions in the human body is a truism about human existence:

> *"As we go about our daily lives, we experience what appears to be a continuous stream of present-moment events, yet we actually become conscious of physical events in the world slightly after they have occurred. In fact, one of the most startling findings in neuroscience has been that consciousness is often "the last to know." Visual, auditory, and other kinds of sensory information move*

---

scientists-niels-bohr-schrodinger-nikola-tesla-albert-einstein-true-meaning-physics-vedas.

49. [2011] Harris, Annaka. Chapter 5: Who Are We? *Conscious: a Brief Guide to the Fundamental Mystery of the Mind*. Harper, an Imprint of HarperCollinsPublishers, 2019.

through the world (and our nervous system) at different rates. The light waves and sound waves emitted the moment the tennis ball makes contact with your racket, for example, do not arrive at your eyes and ears at the same time, and the impact felt by your hand holding the racket occurs at yet another interval. To complicate matters further, the signals perceived by your hands, eyes, and ears travel different distances through your nervous system to reach your brain (your hands are a lot farther away from your brain than your ears are). Only after all the relevant input has been received by the brain do the signals get synchronized and enter your conscious experience through a process called "binding"—whereby you see, hear, and feel the ball hit the racket all in the same instant. As the neuroscientist David Eagleman puts it:

'Your perception of reality is the end result of fancy editing tricks: the brain hides the difference in arrival times. How? What it serves up as reality is actually a delayed version. Your brain collects up all the information from the senses before it decides upon a story of what happens. . . . The strange consequence of all this is that you live in the past. By the time you think the moment occurs, it's already long gone. To synchronize the incoming information from the senses, the cost is that our conscious awareness lags behind the physical world.1'"[2012]

For those who don't know, here are the teachings of Sanatana Dharma that modern neuroscience has found to be true about how human consciousness operates within us. First, from the *Bhagavad Gita* translated by Eknath Easwaran:

"27 All actions are performed by the gunas of prakriti. Deluded by identification with the ego, a person thinks, "I am the doer." 28 But the illumined man or woman understands the domain of the gunas and is not attached. Such people know that the gunas interact with each other; they do not claim to be the doer."[2013]

"Those who know this truth, whose consciousness is unified, think always, "I am not the doer." While seeing or hearing, touching or smelling; eating, moving about, or sleeping; breathing 9 or speaking, letting go or holding on, even opening or closing the eyes, they understand that these are only the movements of the senses among sense objects."[2014]

Further evidence of such teachings can be found within the *Brihadaranyaka*, *Chandogya*, and *Prashna Upanishads*. I've used the Eknath Easwaran translation. Arguably, this could be considered flimsy evidence in this specific instance but neuroscience is already validating and looking deeper into Sanatana Dharma's religious teachings despite trying to phrase it as "Eastern contemplative traditions" while synonymously acknowledging the Buddhist denomination.[2015] Therefore, these and possibly similar verses may have been an influence for modern neuroscience and the next section pertaining to the *Samkhya-Karika* :

Brihadaranyaka:

---

50. [2012] Harris, Annaka. Chapter 3: Is Consciousness Free? *Conscious: a Brief Guide to the Fundamental Mystery of the Mind*. Harper, an Imprint of HarperCollinsPublishers, 2019.
51. [2013] Eknath, Easwaran, translator. Chapter 3: Selfless Service (93-103). *The Bhagavad Gita*. Nilgiri Press, 2007.
52. [2014] Eknath, Easwaran, translator. Chapter 5: Renounce and Rejoice (115-123). *The Bhagavad Gita*. Nilgiri Press, 2007.
53. [2015] Harris, Annaka. Chapter 5: Who Are We? *Conscious: a Brief Guide to the Fundamental Mystery of the Mind*. Harper, an Imprint of HarperCollinsPublishers, 2019.

This Self has to be realized. Hear about this Self and meditate upon him, Maitreyi. When you hear about the Self, meditate upon the Self, and finally realize the Self, you come to understand everything in life. 4.6 For brahmins confuse those who regard them as separate from the Self. Kshatriyas confuse those who regard them as separate from the Self. The universe confuses those who regard it as separate from the Self. Gods and creatures confuse those who regard them as separate from the Self. Everything confuses those who regard things as separate from the Self. Brahmins, kshatriyas, creatures, the universe, the gods, everything: these are the Self. 4.7 No one can understand the sounds of a drum without understanding both drum and drummer; 4.8 nor the sounds of a conch without understanding both the conch and its blower; 4.9 nor the sounds of a vina without understanding both vina and musician. 4.10 As clouds of smoke arise from a fire laid with damp fuel, even so from the Supreme have issued forth all the Vedas, history, arts, sciences, poetry, aphorisms, and commentaries. All these are the breath of the Supreme. 4.11 As there can be no water without the sea, no touch without the skin, no smell without the nose, no taste without the tongue, no form without the eye, no sound without the ear, no thought without the mind, no wisdom without the heart, no work without hands, no walking without feet, no scriptures without the word, so there can be nothing without the Self. 4.12 As a lump of salt thrown in water dissolves and cannot be taken out again, though wherever we taste the water it is salty, even so, beloved, the separate self dissolves in the sea of pure consciousness, infinite and immortal. Separateness arises from identifying the Self with the body, which is made up of the elements; when this physical identification dissolves, there can be no more separate self. This is what I want to tell you, beloved."[2016]

5 The Self is indeed Brahman, but through ignorance people identify it with intellect, mind, senses, passions, and the elements of earth, water, air, space, and fire. This is why the Self is said to consist of this and that, and appears to be everything."[2017]

Chandogya:

"*Smaller than a grain of rice, smaller than a grain of barley, smaller than a mustard seed, smaller than a grain of millet, smaller even than the kernel of a grain of millet is the Self. This is the Self dwelling in my heart, greater than the earth, greater than the sky, greater than all the worlds. 14.4 This Self who gives rise to all works, all desires, all odors, all tastes, who pervades the universe, who is beyond words, who is joy abiding, who is ever present in my heart, is Brahman indeed. To him I shall attain when my ego dies. So said Shandilya; so said Shandilya.*[2018]

Prashna:

"*Earth, water, fire, air, space, and their subtle Elements, the eyes and what can be seen, The ears and what can be heard, the nostrils And what can be smelled, the palate and what Can be tasted, the skin and what can be touched, The tongue and what can be spoken, The hands and what can be held, the organ Of sex and its object of enjoyment, The organ of excretion and what is Excreted, the feet and what they walk on, The mind and what it thinks, the intellect And what it knows, the ego and what It grasps, the heart and what it loves, the light And what it reveals: all things in life Find their rest in the Self in dreamless sleep." 9 "It is the Self who sees, hears, smells, touches, And tastes, who thinks, acts, and is pure consciousness."*[2019]

---

54. [2016] Eknath, Easwaran, translator. Brihadaranyaka: The Forest of Wisdom (1139-1407). *The Upanishads*. Nilgiri Press, 2007.
55. [2017] Eknath, Easwaran, translator. Brihadaranyaka: The Forest of Wisdom (1139-1407). *The Upanishads*. Nilgiri Press, 2007.
56. [2018] Eknath, Easwaran, translator. Chandogya: Sacred Song (1408-1857). *The Upanishads*. Nilgiri Press, 2007.
57. [2019] Eknath, Easwaran, translator. Prashna: The Breath of Life (2900-3235). *The Upanishads*. Nilgiri Press, 2007.

The *Samkhya-Karika* is a book of aphorisms that is written in two parts. The first part, referred to as Samkhya, was written by the founder of Hinduism's Samkhya school of thought, Kapila. The second part was purportedly by a student of the Samkhya school, Ishvara Krishna.[2020] It is notorious because while Indologists argue that it is suppose to show Samkhya's methods, the truth is that nobody knows what its contents are supposed to mean or be applied to. I recall reading several pages of Western Indologist Gerald Larson's laughable commentary where he cited people making up their own guesswork because they didn't understand the text. Larson proceeded to state they were wrong in favor of his own guesswork; all of them citing no evidence whatsoever to corroborate their beliefs and simply creating their own make-believe. I decided to delve more deeply after I found a translation online by a religious leader in India by the name of Brahmrishi Vishvatma Bawra. I was struck by the emphasis on cognitive perception from the translation. I ignored most of the lengthy explanations that Bawra gave in his translation after each aphorism, the only important thing to note was that he translated "Seer" as a shorthand for conscious awareness because of the emphasis that people aren't the doer of actions.[2021] I thought that was quite clever as it helps reinforce precisely what neuroscientists try to explain about conscious awareness in their long-winded fashion; that is, instead of viewing ourselves as the doer of our actions, we should perceive ourselves as a Seer envisioning events happening while perceiving our premonition in real-time to better understand how conscious awareness operates.[2022] Samkhya presumably focuses upon perception and inference, but the translation seemed to imply a deeper probing into questioning conscious awareness itself.

Originally, I had planned to make the case that the *Samkhya-Karika* was a book of primitive science on the topic of consciousness based on my own impressions of the text. To be clear, as I don't want to be misunderstood, I say primitive science because it was obviously nowhere near the level of modern science; ancient Samkhya practitioners lacked the scientific method, they obviously didn't have any scientific tools to study these insights, they limited their content to aphorisms for any of their insights in their understanding of consciousness, and they obviously held beliefs limited to their time period such as certain aphorisms that attempt to link emotional wellbeing to conscious awareness based upon faulty premises. Nevertheless, I do believe a few of the insights are worth exploring given the fact that it later adapted atheism as an acceptable position within the Astika branch of Sanatana Dharma and more importantly, due to the apparent emphasis upon conscious awareness itself. Since modern science is looking into Dharmic religious texts, I wonder if any of these following aphorisms have either been read already or could help further modern neuroscience studies. Regardless of any of that, I do think these provide an intriguing perspective on why Sanatana Dharma's teachings seem to be

---

58. [2020] Bawra, Brahmrishi Vishvatma, translator. *Sāmkhya Kārikā With Gaudapādācarya Bhāsya*. Brahmrishi Yoga Publications, 2012.
59. [2021] Bawra, Brahmrishi Vishvatma, translator. *Sāmkhya Kārikā With Gaudapādācarya Bhāsya*. Brahmrishi Yoga Publications, 2012.
60. [2022] Bawra, Brahmrishi Vishvatma, translator. *Sāmkhya Kārikā With Gaudapādācarya Bhāsya*. Brahmrishi Yoga Publications, 2012.

disproportionately useful for furthering modern science. Also, the allusions to pottery gives further credence to the argument that they had an implicit belief in a fatalistic form of hard determinism:

Samkhya Aphorisms

VI. They who regard sentient and insentient objects to be the self, and rejoice at their prosperity believing such prosperity to be one's own, and grieve at their adversity, thinking it to be one's own, are deluded.[2023]

VIII. The Seer, which is unchangeable as well as inactive, appears as if transferred to the modifying faculty (mahat) becoming mixed up with and imitating its modifications. As the modifying medium appears endowed with consciousness, owing to association, it is thought that the Seer is indistinguishable from or identical with the modification.[2024]

XI. Knowing at last that inexplicable Self, one realizes "I am that" only.[2025]

XIII. There is no separateness or diversity in causal nature (pradhāna) as differences of specific character, form or class do not exist in it.[2026]

Karika Aphorisms

XXXV. Since the intellect, along with the internal organs, apprehends all the objects, these three [internal] organs are the gatekeepers and the rest are the gates.[2027]

XXXVII. As it is the intellect which brings about the entire enjoyment [of objects], so it is again that [very intellect] which discriminates the subtle difference between Nature and Spirit.[2028]

LXI. Nothing in my opinion is more modest than Nature who, once seen, never again exposes itself to the view of Spirit.[2029]

LXII. Therefore, not any Spirit is bound or liberated, nor does any migrate. It is Nature, abiding in manifold forms, that migrates or is bound or liberated.[2030]

LXIV. By practicing the principles thus, there arises the knowledge, 'I am not, not mine, not I', which is complete, absolute and pure because there remains no doubt.[2031]

LXV. By this knowledge, the Spirit seated composed like a spectator, perceives Nature, which has ceased to be productive and consequently, which has now reverted from seven forms.[2032]

---

61. [2023] Bawra, Brahmrishi Vishvatma, translator. Samkhya Aphorism VI. *Sāmkhya Kārikā With Gaudapādācarya Bhāsya*. Brahmrishi Yoga Publications, 2012.
62. [2024] Bawra, Brahmrishi Vishvatma, translator. Samkhya Aphorism VIII. *Sāmkhya Kārikā With Gaudapādācarya Bhasya*. Brahmrishi Yoga Publications, 2012.
63. [2025] Bawra, Brahmrishi Vishvatma, translator. Samkhya Aphorism XI. *Sāmkhya Kārikā With Gaudapādācarya Bhāsya*. Brahmrishi Yoga Publications, 2012.
64. [2026] Bawra, Brahmrishi Vishvatma, translator. Samkhya Aphorism XIII. *Sāmkhya Kārikā With Gaudapādācarya Bhāsya*. Brahmrishi Yoga Publications, 2012.
65. [2027] Bawra, Brahmrishi Vishvatma, translator. Karika Aphorism XXXV. *Sāmkhya Kārikā With Gaudapādācarya Bhāsya*. Brahmrishi Yoga Publications, 2012.
66. [2028] Bawra, Brahmrishi Vishvatma, translator. Karika Aphorism XXXVII. *Sāmkhya Kārikā With Gaudapādācarya Bhāsya*. Brahmrishi Yoga Publications, 2012.
67. [2029] Bawra, Brahmrishi Vishvatma, translator. Karika Aphorism LXI. *Sāmkhya Kārikā With Gaudapādācarya Bhāsya*. Brahmrishi Yoga Publications, 2012.
68. [2030] Bawra, Brahmrishi Vishvatma, translator. Karika Aphorism LXII. *Sāmkhya Kārikā With Gaudapādācarya Bhāsya*. Brahmrishi Yoga Publications, 2012.
69. [2031] Bawra, Brahmrishi Vishvatma, translator. Karika Aphorism LXIV. *Sāmkhya Kārikā With Gaudapādācarya Bhāsya*. Brahmrishi Yoga Publications, 2012.

LXVI. One Spirit is indifferent like a spectator at a play; one Nature desists, as it has been seen. Now in spite of their contact there is no motive for creation.[2033]

LXVII. Although by the attainment of perfect knowledge, virtue and the rest cease to be producers, yet because of past impressions Spirit remains invested with a body like a potter's wheel with a whirl.[2034]

Lastly, Annaka Harris's book covers the possibility of pan-psychism being true; pan-psychism is theory that everything that exists has consciousness.[2035] To be clear, it is not consciousness in the sense of the human mind, Harris makes it abundantly clear that everything having the equivalent of a human mind is nonsensical and that is not what the theory advocates, but rather consciousness in the sense of bacteria or a clump of cells being able to interact with its environment.[2036] There's been some controversy over this theory chiefly because of the Abrahamic culture that permeates throughout the West which seems to hold it back even now from exploring scientific evidence because it sounds ridiculous in the Abrahamic cultural context[2037], while beliefs in a resurrection and Second Coming, a devil being mysteriously responsible for evil throughout the world, and the idea of heaven and hell don't sound ridiculous to most Westerners. Nevertheless, more legitimate controversy has been created since other scientific branches have argued that pan-psychism contradicts quantum mechanics and therefore doesn't make sense when trying to combine the two.[2038] I was honestly confused by this accusation and thought to myself: *why wouldn't pan-psychism help explain the mystery in quantum physics behind why particles change behavior when we humans observe them? Why wouldn't all things being conscious help explain how the "messaging" between two portions of the same particle influence each other while being far apart?* Alas, I am not an expert on this, but a fallible human being whose only real reference is Annaka Harris's book and a few Youtube videos on quantum physics, so I don't have the ability to ask the right questions about this issue.[2039] I just thought I'd share my own perspective and personal confusion for public consumption, I'm worried I've opened the door for mockery on this issue though, but it seems that the act of mockery itself for asking dumb questions is an anti-intellectual cultural impediment to learning. For instance, I've wondered to what extent

---

70. [2032] Bawra, Brahmrishi Vishvatma, translator. Karika Aphorism LXV. *Sāmkhya Kārikā With Gaudapādācarya Bhāsya*. Brahmrishi Yoga Publications, 2012.
71. [2033] Bawra, Brahmrishi Vishvatma, translator. Karika Aphorism LXVI. *Sāmkhya Kārikā With Gaudapādācarya Bhāsya*. Brahmrishi Yoga Publications, 2012.
72. [2034] Bawra, Brahmrishi Vishvatma, translator. Karika Aphorism LXVII. *Sāmkhya Kārikā With Gaudapādācarya Bhāsya*. Brahmrishi Yoga Publications, 2012.
73. [2035] Harris, Annaka. *Conscious: a Brief Guide to the Fundamental Mystery of the Mind*. Harper, an Imprint of HarperCollinsPublishers, 2019.
74. [2036] Harris, Annaka. *Conscious: a Brief Guide to the Fundamental Mystery of the Mind*. Harper, an Imprint of HarperCollinsPublishers, 2019.
75. [2037] Harris, Annaka. *Conscious: a Brief Guide to the Fundamental Mystery of the Mind*. Harper, an Imprint of HarperCollinsPublishers, 2019.
76. [2038] Schneider, Susan. "Is Panpsychism Accurate? Modern Physics Delivers a Reality Check. | Dr. Susan Schneider." *YouTube*, Big Think, 28 July 2019, www.youtube.com/watch?v=qv1MIj0m9fY.
77. [2039] Khutoryansky, Eugene. "Quantum Mechanics: Animation Explaining Quantum Physics." *YouTube*, Physics Videos by Eugene Khutoryansky, 23 Mar. 2013, www.youtube.com/watch?v=iVpXrbZ4bnU.

pan-psychism would prove religions like Animism, Neo-Animism, and concepts like *Brahman* to be true about material reality, even if the pan-psychism would disprove their potency in impacting human existence. If pan-psychism is true, then Animism or a Neo-Animism would thereby be verified as true about reality according to modern science. Likewise, if pan-psychism means that the universe itself has consciousness, then conceptually the Hindu belief in *Brahman* is validated as true about reality by modern science because science has thereby verified the existence of a pantheistic deity. In this specific context, if pan-psychism is verified by scientific evidence and applicable to the universe itself, it would mean that Adi Shankara's *Advaita Vedanta* denomination of Hinduism is verified by science as a core feature of reality itself.

The Adaptive Truthseeking of Sanatana Dharma

I'm annoyed at the growing emergence of my fellow Dharmic followers who flippantly ignore or impulsively reject the wonderful history of the Sramana movements and the atheistic denominations of Sanatana Dharma. It seems like some Hindus, not well-versed in the theology of Sanatana Dharma, think that rejecting atheists and agnostics are needed for "respectability" in a religion and confuse Marxism with the origin of atheism, agnosticism, and anti-theism when the origins of such concepts were Sanatana Dharma itself due to the foundational principles of truthseeking and debate. I would argue that this has happened because Hindus, Buddhists, Sikhs, and Jains have not been allowed to practice the full range of their beliefs because of the culture of the Abrahamic faiths attempting to impose "harmony" via banning criticism of religion. They do this because it is the only advantage they could ever possibly have against Sanatana Dharma; if the people of India were allowed to debate and criticize all religious beliefs, then Sanatana Dharma would almost certainly win against the Abrahamic faiths. The Abrahamic faiths have been taking a consistent nosedive in adherents because of criticisms in the West. *Free Speech is absolutely vital for preserving, practicing, and progressing Sanatana Dharma.* Furthermore, I find it rather disheartening that the self-sabotaging Brahamanical traditions continue to preoccupy people's minds and are so foolishly attempting to demarcate science as a Western construct; this may indicate their inability to distinguish science from Western religions since science is consistently deposing Christianity which is why some Christians are so desperate for Christian conversions in India. Islamic de-conversions happen at a faster rate in the US than Christian de-conversions and this may lead to desperation on their part too. *All religions are dying and perhaps all of them should die, but they don't all have to die equally or lose their significance as part of a people's cultural and religious history.* If followers of Sanatana Dharma wish for it to survive the growing wave of atheism that is bringing death to all the deities in people's minds, then I'd argue that they should focus on the principles of the second-wave Sramana movement; debate with styles like Purva Paksha, free thought with full acceptance and affection towards the atheistic branches of Sanatana Dharma, and moving forward with the principle of *Truthseeking*. Such principles provide a celebration of personal liberty and freedom of thought instead of behaving like a mere Abrahamic faith by imposing a stricture that demands unquestioned obedience like the denomination of Brahmanism which supports unjustifiable beliefs like Caste and misogyny.

    As I'm sure you've noticed, I reclassified my own religious identity as a Hindu Atheist to a Hindu Anti-Theist. A Hindu Theist may argue that I'm part of the Nastika branch (rejects the Vedas) and not the Astika branch (affirms the Vedas), but one of Sanatana Dharma's most splendid differences is that it doesn't follow the Abrahamic style of branching into a voluminous amount of denominations that all oppose each other (often arguing other denominations are going to hell). Sanatana Dharma has no qualms with sharing beliefs, practices, and teachings among any voluminous amount of denominations; arguably, even the term denomination doesn't necessarily apply to Sanatana Dharma. Hindus, Sikhs, Jains, and Buddhists are all the same religion of Sanatana Dharma and can share in prayer at each other's religious temples with the people who follow the other denomination, share in teachings, share in meditation and yoga practices, and debate on religious matters as a form of *Truthseeking*. This is not encouraged or possible in most denominations of the Abrahamic religions who have historically slaughtered each other over the most miniscule of differences like whether Jesus Christ was a spirit or a God made flesh.[2040] Some may assume that I identify with the Charvaka philosophy of Sanatana Dharma, I don't identify with that because of the Pleasure-Pain principle which I repudiate as trivial.[2041] The concept of the Pleasure-Pain principle falls apart when people willingly engage in suffering to fight wars, go into hunger strikes, and many other activities; the Pleasure-Pain principle ignores the importance of intrinsic meaning in a person's life. I suppose I do follow Ajivika somewhat because I believe in hard determinism, but not in the fatalistic sense; I find it more mentally healthy to view it in the psychological and scientific sense that I've incorporated. However, if the notion of Astika-Nastika distinction is insisted upon, I'd like to point out that I find the concept of Astika-Nastika differences to just be a useful reference demarcating Vedic and non-Vedic, but never a distinction that they're different religions. I still self-identify as Hindu and the school of thought that I most identify with is Samkhya. It became open to the question of whether a God or Gods exist or not and eventually adapted those Nastika teachings as acceptable within its school of thought. *This should be less surprising once you remember that the Nastika preachers of the Sramana movements were highly respected and seen as furthering the Truthseeking of Sanatana Dharma. There was never any persecution or hatred by ancient Vedic practitioners towards them unlike their atheist equivalents in ancient Greece and throughout the history of Islam and Christianity. It is entirely fine to hold both Astika and Nastika teachings of Sanatana Dharma at the same time.* I'm not sure to what extent this'll be ridiculed, but I do feel a strong personal connection to the philosophical view of *selfless service* from the *Bhagavad Gita*, the philosophical argument in *Brihadaranyaka Upanishad* about following one's deep desire towards a goal albeit in a more

---

78. [2040] Abruzzi, William S. "THE BIRTH OF JESUS: The Evolution of the Jesus in the Infancy Narratives." *Doc A's Webpage: On the Importance of Writing Research Papers*, Dr. William S. Abruzzi, 2015, www.drabruzzi.com/birth_of_jesus.htm.
79. [2041] "Carvaka." *Carvaka*, Humanistictexts.org, www.humanistictexts.org/carvaka.htm.

secular context and not in the misogynistic one within the text, and the *Chandogya Upanishad*'s view that people can't necessarily call themselves free without self-knowledge and knowing what to strive towards. It could possibly be argued that these are just interpretations I adapted to comport with my own internalized views on Nietzschean philosophy, but Nietzsche himself favored the idea that people should take what they can from his philosophy and pursue their own goals[2042]; I don't find that to be incompatible with *Truthseeking* as a Hindu. Moreover, I obviously don't agree with all of Nietzsche's views. For just as I oppose sexist views within Sanatana Dharma, I oppose Nietzsche's support for violence against women[2043], his thoroughgoing misogyny in general[2044], and I oppose his disturbing celebration of the Manusmriti as an example of a healthy civilization.[2045] Nevertheless, I agree with his idea for a *Transvaluation of Values* which is about probing society's cultural norms to understand it's failings more clearly and then to challenge the problematic and often implicit assumptions of the society to correct the internal failings and improve society.[2046][2047] Often, Nietzsche advocated for using an outside culture and comparing the two or better still, listening to an informed critique of our own culture from an outsider's view to better understand our own internal failings without an impulsive rejection of an outsider's point of view for not being part of our in-group.[2048] Nietzsche hoped to better understand the implicit assumptions in order to directly challenge the harmful beliefs within our society. For Nietzsche it meant every part of Europe that wasn't Germany which he thought of as unsalvageable due to German Christianity's hawkish anti-Semitism during his lifetime.[2049] My attempt at a *Transvaluation of Values* is instead an emphasis on personal liberty, Free Speech, and a repudiation of Religious Tolerance within Western societies and Secular Republics like India.

My personal identity as a Hindu Anti-Theist is my attempt at an *Anti-Caste Hinduism. I believe Truthseeking must win against Casteism and I think the proper way to do that is to effectively address B. R. Ambedkar's contentions against Hinduism by reforming it into something that he would be proud of instead of spitting on his memory and keeping Caste in place. If Hinduism is truly about Truthseeking, then it must destroy the social norm of the*

---

80. [2042] Nietzsche, Friedrich Wilhelm. Chapter XXII. THE BESTOWING VIRTUE (76-80). *Thus spake Zarathustra: a book for all and none.* Translated by Thomas Common, PDF ed., T. Common, 1908.
81. [2043] Nietzsche, Friedrich Wilhelm. Chapter XVIII. OLD AND YOUNG WOMEN (68-70). *Thus spake Zarathustra: a book for all and none.* Translated by Thomas Common, PDF ed., T. Common, 1908.
82. [2044] Nietzsche, Friedrich Wilhelm. *Beyond Good and Evil.* Translated by Helen Zimmern, Word ed., Gutenberg Press, 2009.
83. [2045] Nietzsche, Friedrich. The "Improvers" of Mankind (37-41). *Twilight of the Idols.* Amazon Digital Services LLC.
84. [2046] Nietzsche, Friedrich Wilhelm. *THE ANTICHRIST.* Translated by H. L. Mencken, The Project Gutenberg, 2006.
85. [2047] Nietzsche, Friedrich. *The Dawn of Day.* Translated by J. M. Kennedy, Dover Publications, 2012.
86. [2048] Nietzsche, Friedrich Wilhelm. *THE ANTICHRIST.* Translated by H. L. Mencken, The Project Gutenberg, 2006.
87. [2049] Nietzsche, Friedrich. *Nietzsche Complete Works – World's Best Ultimate Collection - 20 Books – Incl. Zarathustra, Gay Science, Morals, Beyond Good And Evil, Birth Of Tragedy, Ecce Homo Plus Biography & Bonuses.* Translated by Anthony Ludovici, Kindle ed., Amazon Digital Services LLC, 2010.

Caste system. Also, I believe that it is vital to have a filter against nonsensical beliefs and that being open to criticizing any supernatural belief is crucial for Truthseeking and gaining knowledge. The filter of rational empiricism, skepticism, and an emphasis on scientific evidence helps to take power away from Hindu Godmen who attempt to formulate their own hierarchal cults of personality that are no different than the Abrahamic faiths by using Hinduism's Brahminical traditions in opposition to Truthseeking. This is my attempt at an adaptive Truthseeking since Hinduism has always striven towards upgrading itself based on the social norms of the community that it considers home. There is a dire drawback to the idea of upgrading with the dominant culture; Hindus could have supported LGBT rights sooner in the US, but fell in step with the dominant culture of Christianity because it was seen as "progressive" to vilify the LGBT by the majority Christian population. The only previous reference to this issue outside of the acceptance of it in Sanatana Dharma for most Hindus, especially those who go from India to the US, had been to inculcate the Victorian culture of British imperialism over India which continues to have support via Christian missionaries taking up teaching positions in India. Until LGBT rights became a social norm open to questioning in the US and resulted in most Hindus supporting LGBT rights since it was always acceptable within Hinduism, there was little to no rebuke from most of the foreign-born Hindu community out of gratitude to their new home which they didn't want to show disrespect towards. As such, Hindu Anti-Theism strives to focus on both rational empiricism as a core component of Truthseeking and human rights for all people whenever possible. Human rights in this context of Enlightenment values, which seems to have proven effective for Hindus in Western societies judging from the evidence.

An important component is moving forward with philosophical inquiry within Sanatana Dharma instead of behaving like a mere Abrahamic faith (specifically Islam and Christianity) and constantly looking backwards to infantilize the issues facing Sanatana Dharma followers in modern times. I'd like to encourage people to build upon the philosophical arguments of ancient India instead of trying to use them as a challenge by comparing them to modern scientific insights of the West as that makes no sense. It is the equivalent of using the ancient Greek philosophers to challenge modern scientific insights, the ancient world had limitations in its knowledge and we should build on what we've found to be useful or profound philosophical critiques and not foist them as some sort of opposition to modern science as that is using their insights for the purpose of justifying anti-intellectualism instead of carrying the torch to progress them. Ancient philosophers had their own failings such as misogyny and the belief in slavery, whatever profound insights they had should be furthered and not used as excuses to hate new forms of Truthseeking and building knowledge. Therefore, I'd like to present my own example of furthering the philosophy of Sanatana Dharma as a form of Truthseeking and I recommend checking a few books in the Further Reading section for avid readers to help. I recommend Annie Duke's *Thinking in Bets, Factfulness* by Hans Rosling, *Politics and Identity: A Social Identity Perspective* by Alexa Ispas, and *Thinking Fast and Slow* by Daniel Kahneman for fellow Hindus as I have no interest in behaving like some Godman; I want it to be known that I see myself as a fallible human being who makes mistakes and I try to correct my mistakes with the best effort involved. If you found anything I've said of value, I'd like it to be known that I wouldn't have got this far without my deep interest in reading.

Below I've transcribed Andrew J. Nicholson's translation of the *Samkhya Sutra on God* which is a refutation of the existence of a God (*Isvara*) due to suffering (*duhkha*), I wanted to give readers a thorough understanding for this segment so I'd like to first show the initial translation, then the Wikipedia version created by some unknown individual which cites Nicholson's translation itself, and then show my own way of furthering the philosophy of Samkhya by adding to its critique and applying it to a few thought experiments that I've made. In addition, please keep in mind that the citation from *The Oxford Handbook of Indian Philosophy* makes it abundantly clear from the quotes of the Samkhya practitioners and the people making commentaries on the Samkhya practitioners' views that they held the belief that there was no evidence for the existence of *Isvara* (God) on the basis that God's existence hasn't been proven by either inference or *prakriti* (material energy) of any kind.[2050] While I don't value the translators opinions, I do value the translation itself. Analogous to the racist bigot, Anthony Ludovici, who had good translations of Friedrich Nietzsche's works but was unable to understand nearly everything of Friedrich Nietzsche's philosophy that he translated; I find a similar issue with Western Indology, especially after listening to the entirety of one of their discussions online.[2051] Due to the bigotry permeating throughout Western Indology against people of Indian descent, **I'd like to reiterate that I am transcribing and citing Andrew J. Nicholson's work from *The Oxford Handbook of Indian Philosophy* and crediting him for the translation**:

> If Isvara were an independent creator, he would create even without karma. Now if you say that he creates with karma as an auxiliary cause, then let karma be the only cause. What need is there of Isvara? And it cannot be that the auxiliary cause obstructs the power of the primary cause, for then the primary cause would no longer be independent.[2052]
>
> Furthermore, we know from experience that all activity is either self-interested or for the sake of another. But Isvara has no self-interested motives. Suppose his activity were for the sake of others. Then it would impossible that the created world, which consists of suffering (*duhkha*), could be ascribed to him, since he is compassionate. Additionally, no activity is purely for the sake of others. Even by actions such as helping others, an agent furthers his own interests. Therefore, we must accept that karma alone is the cause of the world.[2053]

---

88. [2050] Kapstein, Matthew T., et al. Chapter 31: Hindu Disproofs of God: Refuting Vedantic Theism in the Samkhya-Sutra by Andrew J. Nicholson (598-619). *The Oxford Handbook of Indian Philosophy*. Edited by Jonardon Ganeri, Oxford University Press, 2018.
89. [2051] Nicholson, Andrew J., et al. "Andrew Nicholson on 'Anti-Theistic Arguments in Sāṃkhya and Vedānta Philosophy." *YouTube*, 2 Apr. 2018, youtu.be/myjdOsKu8iY.
90. [2052] Kapstein, Matthew T., et al. Chapter 31: Hindu Disproofs of God: Refuting Vedantic Theism in the Samkhya-Sutra by Andrew J. Nicholson (598-619). *The Oxford Handbook of Indian Philosophy*. Edited by Jonardon Ganeri, Oxford University Press, 2018.
91. [2053] Kapstein, Matthew T., et al. Chapter 31: Hindu Disproofs of God: Refuting Vedantic Theism in the Samkhya-Sutra by Andrew J. Nicholson (598-619). *The Oxford Handbook of Indian Philosophy*. Edited by Jonardon Ganeri, Oxford University Press, 2018.

The following is the Wikipedia version changed into a bullet point fashion to better articulate Samkhya's arguments against the existence of a God (*Isvara*):

> Samkhya gave the following arguments against the idea of an eternal, self-caused, creator God:
>
> If the existence of karma is assumed, the proposition of God as a moral governor of the universe is unnecessary. For, if God enforces the consequences of actions then he can do so without karma. If however, he is assumed to be within the law of karma, then karma itself would be the giver of consequences and there would be no need of a God.
>
> Even if karma is denied, God still cannot be the enforcer of consequences. Because the motives of an enforcer God would be either egoistic or altruistic. Now, God's motives cannot be assumed to be altruistic because an altruistic God would not create a world so full of suffering. If his motives are assumed to be egoistic, then God must be thought to have desire, as agency or authority cannot be established in the absence of desire. However, assuming that God has desire would contradict God's eternal freedom which necessitates no compulsion in actions. Moreover, desire, according to Samkhya, is an attribute of prakriti and cannot be thought to grow in God. The testimony of the Vedas, according to Samkhya, also confirms this notion.
>
> Despite arguments to the contrary, if God is still assumed to contain unfulfilled desires, this would cause him to suffer pain and other similar human experiences. Such a worldly God would be no better than Samkhya's notion of higher self.
>
> Furthermore, there is no proof of the existence of God. He is not the object of perception, there exists no general proposition that can prove him by inference and the testimony of the Vedas speak of prakriti as the origin of the world, not God.
>
> Therefore, Samkhya maintained that the various cosmological, ontological and teleological arguments could not prove God.[2054][2055]

Now, I am of the opinion that Andrew J. Nicholson - despite apparently being an excellent translator - somehow doesn't quite understand the philosophical depth as he compared the Samkhya sutra to the ancient Greek Problem of Evil, but they're far apart in intention and purpose since they focus on two entirely different aspects of the social issue for humans with relation to an omnipotent God. It is not merely suffering, but the more pronounced question of the intent of a supposedly omnipotent God in a world of suffering. Here is my own modernized version of this excellent critique of the Samkhya school of thought in which I focus upon aspects that can be applicable to all religions that believe in an omnipotent, infallible, and benevolent deity:

Modernized Samkhya Thought Experiment

---

92. [2054] "Atheism in Hinduism." *Wikipedia*, Wikimedia Foundation, 26 July 2019, en.wikipedia.org/wiki/Atheism_in_Hinduism#Arguments_against_existence_of_God_in_Hindu_philosophy.
93. [2055] "Atheism in Hinduism." *Atheism*, atheism.wikia.org/wiki/Atheism_in_Hinduism#.5Bedit.5DArguments_against_God.

If we assume a benevolent, infallible, and omnipotent God exists, then it doesn't follow that a world of suffering should exist because such a God should be able to end suffering entirely. If this omnipotent God doesn't want to end suffering entirely for some other purpose, then it is not benevolent because it allows suffering instead of simply ending suffering through its omnipotent power. If we assume that something prevents a benevolent and omnipotent God from following through with its compassionate desire to end suffering, then it cannot be omnipotent because it has unfulfilled desires that prevent it from ending suffering. If it truly has these unfulfilled benevolent desires, then it is not infallible or omnipotent since it suffers pain from something preventing it from fulfilling its benevolent desires. If God's own decision-making prevents it from fulfilling its desires and it suffers from this decision, then it cannot be called either infallible or omnipotent. If an omnipotent God has these unfulfilled desires, but doesn't suffer from being unable to fulfill them, then it lacks compassion for humanity and cannot be called benevolent. Finally, if you argue that we cannot know for what purpose God has planned for us, then why bother praying to God or believing that God is benevolent, infallible, and omnipotent since we humans simply don't know and can't assume to understand a God's motives at all?

I've written these three thought experiments by applying the Samkhya Sutra and my own personal variation of it onto different topics that I've thought of. I hope that you find them intriguing or they engender you to ponder more about religion and its association to your life. The next chapter will be the conclusion; I shall begin with my own critique of the problems of Religious Tolerance within my own country, the United States of America. I am proud to have been born and raised within the US and I'm deeply concerned with its current trajectory. Just as with my fellow Hindus, I'd like to share my harsh critiques with my fellow Americans because I care about my country and my fellow citizens. I want to do my part in strengthening it and preventing the social issues from worsening further throughout the US before moving onto the problems of Religious Tolerance in a general context. For now, please enjoy a Hindu critique of the flaws of Christian morality:

Hindu Anti-Theist Refutation of Christian Salvation

If the Abrahamic God could only fulfill salvation through sacrificing his son, then the Abrahamic God cannot be omnipotent because he needed to sacrifice his son as a requirement before he could bring people salvation and thus something prevented him from bringing salvation to people before this time period. Moreover, if the Abrahamic God desired to save people but couldn't before Jesus's sacrifice, then this means he had unfulfilled desires. The Abrahamic God is therefore neither omnipotent nor perfect since something prevented him from saving people beforehand and thus he was prevented from acting on his desire to save human souls. This precludes the argument of freewill, since before Jesus's birth, people had no freewill to choose salvation since the path to salvation didn't exist before Jesus came to earth. If, however, people were saved prior to Jesus's birth as part of the Abrahamic God's plan, then why make the sacrifice of Jesus a requirement for salvation at all? Why would an all-loving, all-knowing, and all-powerful Abrahamic God plan for the torture and execution of his own son only for it to increase the statistical likelihood that people would reject the Abrahamic God's word and for people to be sent to hell as part of his all-knowing plan? If the Abrahamic God truly intended to increase the likelihood that people would find salvation out of his love for humanity, then why limit it through recognizing Jesus Christ as their personal Lord and Savior instead of the prior system which saved all souls without Jesus being a factor at all? If the point was to test people's faith with the alternative being an eternity in hell, then how is the Abrahamic God all-loving and concerned with saving souls instead of just damning the majority of humans to hell for their ignorance? If the Abrahamic God is not damning souls to hell for their ignorance of Jesus being the Lord and Savior and instead allowing those who still don't know of Jesus Christ to be saved, then why must the gospel be spread throughout the entire world, if it'll result in people using freewill to reject it and causing Christians to damn more souls to hell through their actions with the Abrahamic God's plan intending for this to happen? If it isn't part of the Abrahamic God's plan for people with freewill to reject Jesus Christ as their personal Lord and Savior, then does that mean freewill is beyond the Abrahamic God's power to influence? If the Abrahamic God knows who will hear and reject the gospel of Jesus and sends them to hell as a result for not accepting Jesus Christ as their personal lord and savior, then how did those people have freewill to choose Jesus Christ?

Hindu Anti-Theist Refutation of Christian Freewill

If the Abrahamic God is perfect, all-loving, and omnipotent, then why create a world of suffering? Why create humanity to make them fulfill a test of suffering at all? If the argument is that it is for some plan or purpose, then the Abrahamic God can't be considered omnipotent because something prevents the Abrahamic God from simply changing circumstances for the positive and acting upon its altruistic intentions for humanity. If the argument for why the Abrahamic God doesn't intervene is freewill as Christianity oft argues, then the Abrahamic God must have unfulfilled desires for humanity which prevents the Abrahamic God's intended course and cannot be considered either perfect or omnipotent, since freewill can circumvent and change the Abrahamic God's plan. Freewill would also imply that humanity can surpass the Abrahamic God's plan or otherwise stop it from ever happening. If the Abrahamic God's plan for every human life is destined to happen regardless of freewill, then freewill doesn't actually exist for humanity. It's not merely an ultimatum of humanity choosing between heaven or hell, it is simply a misunderstanding to identify human action as having freewill if all choices are preordained under the Abrahamic God's plan such as the lives of innocent children who are killed in war zones. If human action cannot have any meaningful change to the Abrahamic God's plan, then why call it freewill?

Hindu Anti-Theist Refutation of the Morality of the Abrahamic God

Consider this possibility under the hypothetical assumption that a moral, omnipotent, and loving Abrahamic God bestows humanity with Freewill to choose whether to accept or reject him. The parents of two young children are shot dead by warring tribes in a local area (potentially Syria, Somalia, or the Congo) and then the older child sees the younger sibling dying slowly due to an illness. The older child can't find medicine for their younger sibling and it is too dangerous to go out because they risk being shot dead like their parents or kidnapped and used as a child soldier or sex slave with the younger sibling being left to die as a result. Where is the freewill for either of these children in such a horrifying condition? The freewill argument loses all meaning as the young child dies and the older one is left with lifelong guilt over a situation they had no control over. If a moral and omnipotent God could have saved the younger child by miraculously curing the illness, but chose to instead suffer the same pain of loss as the older child, then how can such a God be thought of as loving or moral towards humanity? A supposedly moral, loving and omnipotent God would have easily cast a miracle to save the younger child. Even if the people around them were sinners who committed heinous crimes, what sins did those two young children commit for one to die of illness and the other to live under lifelong threats of violence and then guilt over their younger sibling's death?

Finally, I'd like to mix Samkhya and Charvaka teachings to fully express my personal Anti-theistic view in the context of Sanatana Dharma and follow it up with the philosophical views that I find personally meaningful:

There is no heaven, no final liberation,
nor any soul in another world,
Nor do the actions of the four castes,
orders, or priesthoods produce any real effect.[2056]
Furthermore, there is no proof of the existence of God. He is not the object of perception, there exists no general proposition that can prove him by inference and the testimony of the Vedas speak of prakriti as the origin of the world, not God.[2057][2058]

"The Self desires only what is real, thinks nothing but what is true. Here people do what they are told, becoming dependent on their country, or their piece of land, or the desires of another, so their desires are not fulfilled and their works come to nothing, both in this world and in the next. Those who depart from this world without knowing who they are or what they truly desire have no freedom here or hereafter. But those who leave here knowing who they are and what they truly desire have freedom everywhere, both in this world and in the next."[2059] - **Chandogya Upanishad**

---

94. [2056] "Carvaka." *Carvaka*, Humanistictexts.org, www.humanistictexts.org/carvaka.htm#9 Spontaneity in Nature.
95. [2057] "Atheism in Hinduism." *Atheism*, atheism.wikia.org/wiki/Atheism_in_Hinduism#.5Bedit.5DArguments_against_God.
96. [2058] "Atheism in Hinduism." *Wikipedia*, Wikimedia Foundation, 26 July 2019, en.wikipedia.org/wiki/Atheism_in_Hinduism#Arguments_against_existence_of_God_in_Hindu_philosophy.
97. [2059] Eknath, Easwaran, translator. Chandogya: Sacred Song (1408-1857). *The Upanishads*. Nilgiri Press, 2007.

"As a person acts, so he becomes in life. Those who do good become good; those who do harm become bad. Good deeds make one pure; bad deeds make one impure. You are what your deep, driving desire is. As your desire is, so is your will. As your will is, so is your deed. As your deed is, so is your destiny."[2060] - **Brihadaranyaka Upanishad**

"Strive constantly to serve the welfare of the world; by devotion to selfless work one attains the supreme goal of life. Do your work with the welfare of others always in mind. It was by such work that Janaka attained perfection; others too have followed this path. What the outstanding person does, others will try to do. The standards such people create will be followed by the whole world. There is nothing in the three worlds for me to gain, Arjuna, nor is there anything I do not have; I continue to act, but I am not driven by any need of my own. If I ever refrained from continuous work, everyone would immediately follow my example. If I stopped working I would be the cause of cosmic chaos, and finally of the destruction of this world and these people. The ignorant work for their own profit, Arjuna; the wise work for the welfare of the world, without thought for themselves. By abstaining from work you will confuse the ignorant, who are engrossed in their actions. Perform all work carefully, guided by compassion."[2061] *- The character of Krishna, from the* **Bhagavad Gita**.

---

98. [2060] Eknath, Easwaran, translator. Brihadaranyaka: The Forest of Wisdom (1139-1407). *The Upanishads*. Nilgiri Press, 2007.
99. [2061] Eknath, Easwaran, translator. *The Bhagavad Gita*. Nilgiri Press, 2007.

Chapter 30: The Transvaluation of Values

"Religion is man-made. Even the men who made it cannot agree on what their prophets or redeemers or gurus actually said or did. Still less can they hope to tell us the "meaning" of later discoveries and developments which were, when they began, either obstructed by their religions or denounced by them. And yet—the believers still claim to know! Not just to know, but to know everything. Not just to know that god exists, and that he created and supervised the whole enterprise, but also to know what "he" demands of us—from our diet to our observances to our sexual morality."[2062] - Christopher Hitchens, *God is Not Great: How Religion Poisons Everything*. Chapter 1, Page 18.

I wish I could offer some positive solace as the conclusion, and I'll try, but I feel that it is first better to share my misgivings about the future. Please don't mistake this to mean that I wish to spread negativity, I don't want to do that but rather to explain what we can do to peacefully combat bad beliefs that cause harm for those of us who are willing and have the motivation to do so. I wanted to believe in Religious Tolerance and I really tried my utmost to defend such a worldview, but the more I researched for this book and the more conflicts I witnessed popping-up due to religiously motivated behaviors, the more I was forced to painfully conclude that human rights insofar as human wellbeing is concerned is constantly opposed by religion. The only truth that the Abrahamic faiths being the majority opinion across the world reveal is that the sexual exploitation of children, murders and rapes of children, military violence against large swathes of people, and destruction of ancient history will always be successful in changing people's beliefs to the religion of the oppressor. The fundamental belief that helps capitalize such human violence is victory and success; the religion that wins from bloodshed is seen as the truth because it succeeded where all others fell. That is, people think: "It must be the truth because so many of us believe in it and why did it succeed in our civilization if it wasn't the truth?"[2063] But truth isn't about majority opinion, it is about accumulating evidence to verify truth claims. Too often, people confuse truth with the appeal to popularity fallacy of what belief system holds majority sway. The violence of religion is thereby legitimized as morally good on false pretenses. Truth doesn't come from majority opinion, it comes from demonstrable evidence being verified. Even if hypothetically, most Christians or Muslims destroyed all historical artifacts, physically beat and raped women into submission and demanded they keep wearing conservative clothing, destroyed scientific evidence, and killed all scientists; it wouldn't suddenly mean science is false or that women's freedom didn't lead to greater economic productivity and health. Yet, I see rampant violence and destruction along with a complete antipathy towards criticizing hateful beliefs that encourage cultural and human genocide due to so-called religious sensitivity. There are

---

1. [2062] Hitchens, Christopher. *God Is Not Great: How Religion Poisons Everything*. Hachette Book Group, 2007.
2. [2063] Kahneman, Daniel. Chapter 19: The Illusion of Understanding (199-208) and Chapter 20: The Illusion of Validity (209-221). *Thinking, fast and slow*. Farrar, Straus and Giroux, 2015.

harmful beliefs, especially in the Abrahamic faiths, that don't get enough scrutiny despite their historic cases of genocide simply because of Religious Tolerance. As of now, it is getting so dangerous that the Western powers are now competing on who to give nuclear weapons to Saudi Arabia the quickest and nobody seems to be protesting this, even though all evidence shows the Saudi government will give it to Islamic terrorists who will surely use it upon either the West, Israel, or India and it will be the fault of the country that sold, built, and profiteered from the deal made with Saudi Arabia since Islam's brand of extremism makes people behave in dangerous ways without any doubt that killings of innocents are justified.

I'm tired. I'm tired of constantly needing to repeat myself and this constant need to debunk the same stupid beliefs over and over by incessant loudmouths who not only are dishonest about having dialogue, but will shut down any who disagree with their worldview; whether it's Right-wing religious utopias that a holy book is all you need or Left-leaning ideas of a multicultural utopia that only seeks to see positives in differences and not human rights abuses that often occur disproportionately in certain religious communities. It's always an oppressor versus oppressed narrative that ignores violence against women when it is inconvenient and further ignores the vapid basis for all these religious doctrines. Safe spaces are becoming nothing but a delusion of willful ignorance when people argue entire college campuses are safe spaces and trigger warnings are policing speech to prevent you from having your beliefs challenged. Even if you look at the origins of beliefs like Safe Spaces and Trigger warnings in the West, the adaption of such practices occurred because the Free Speech to criticize Israel and distinguish such criticism from anti-Semitism wasn't allowed throughout Western colleges. When Free Speech against Israel was effectively criminalized, it seems to have collapsed the entire structure for Free Inquiry and debate in colleges across the West. Free Speech means nothing if people aren't free to piss you off by offensively inquiring into your beliefs, speaking out against you in debates, and are allowed to give criticism layered upon you in the public space such as during your events pertaining to such topics. Even when religion isn't being actively violent like motivating suicide bombers, it wars against civil liberties and human rights such as abortion bans that result in rape victims being put in prison and criminalizing or vilifying any criticism of other countries who conduct human rights abuses. I wanted to believe that this could at least contribute a little in changing the trajectory of Safe Spaces, the culture of a refusal to engage and challenge bad beliefs, and shouting down "offensive" speech. But most of all, I want this book to challenge the taboo of Religious Tolerance; if nothing else than for the rights of LGBT people, women's rights, and to further highlight and defend the often ignored topic of the rights of Ex-Muslims.

I don't know what, if any, impact this book has had in changing your mind about religion. Sometimes I end-up awfulizing and think that whatever I write has absolutely no value to any discussion. Nevertheless, even if it is useless, I don't think that I could go on without having written and published this book with the hopes that it offers some value to other people. However, if the disinformation campaign against the New Atheist movement and modern-day atheism is evidence of what to anticipate, I fear that all I can expect is one or two quotes being taken out of context to vilify me as somehow genocidal, insane, or idiotic. I suspect information about my personal life will also be utilized for such a purpose and that it'll cause neutral observers to simply view me as a rabid extremist. I've noticed most journalistic reviews of books give a count of how many times a particular word is used, even though that means absolutely nothing of value since topics can be discussed without using particular words. Judging a book by specific word usage seems rather ridiculous and utterly pointless to me. I don't understand what such reviews are attempting to convey or if it even makes any point at all. It seems such tactics are used to lazily dismiss a book. If what you're seeking is harsh criticism for this book, then I'll happily oblige since I do feel acknowledging my failures is a necessary step towards improving upon any of my future life endeavors. I feel as if my major failing was the section on Judaism as it mostly consisted of collecting outside sources to make a few of my points clear, I could have chosen to write several paragraphs going into specific details but I thought it was better to provide the sources and show the archaeologists explaining in their own terms why the Exodus story is fiction, what Jewish women are going through because of the Ultra-Orthodox branch of Judaism, and the legal barriers imposed on LGBT people by the Ultra-Orthodox in Israel. Overall, I'm quite happy with the chapters on Part I, Islam, and Christianity; I suspect there'll be glaring flaws that people notice though. My ultimate failing is having forced to make this a two-part series instead of just one book because I didn't properly account for how many pages I had already written since I was having too much fun writing the psychological, philosophical, and logical fallacy portions of this book. I find writing to be cathartic; it is a peaceful way at protesting and condemning human rights abuses that always bothered me and for which I could never find a healthy way to let go otherwise.

  I was not lying or exaggerating when I previously wrote that at age 23, President Obama's drone bombing policy tormented me and led to a year-long depression. I felt like I was suffocating, since the United States touts about Free Speech, but then the public space would make so many topics taboo to the point that you were never accepted as credible or trustworthy regardless of the facts if you stepped upon certain taboos like criticizing Drone policy, criticizing Israel foreign aid, discussing the Saudi Arabia and the US partnership, the CIA's support for the mujahedeen in Afghanistan, and it was always with a ubiquitous taboo of criticizing religion in general. I felt stifled from expressing myself and so I never tried; it was because I had no faith whatsoever in Free Speech, the US Constitution, and I felt that people wouldn't find what I said to have any value at all. After all, regardless of whatever college degrees I have, I am just a single individual in the broad spectrum of the US public and why would my beliefs or ideas matter at all when we have all these experts in the Joints Chiefs of Staff, the Presidential cabinet, the US Congress, the Federal Reserve, the Think Tanks, and expert Lobbyists who project an image of knowing what they're doing? To be sure, I had seen evidence of incompetence on all levels as I grew up in the United States, but I had believed these arguments I pushed to the back of my mind to be a misapprehension due to confirmation bias and the selection bias of negative news in the media. Besides which, even if I had no faith, that didn't necessarily mean the broader public didn't since I was just one person and even if public confidence in the US government was decreasing, it might just be individuals with similar dispositions as mine being dissatisfied; part of this view of mine came from the eventual conclusion that Chris Hedges was just too nihilistic when I read his articles criticizing the US government and that I wasn't adequately being grateful for personal freedoms even if I was under the belief political freedoms in the US were rapidly dying thanks to bipartisan efforts by Republicans and Democrats. All discussion about my fears online were rebuked as arrogance on my part by fellow citizens in the US Republic for even making such a line of questioning along with accusations that I was some sort of conspiracy theorist, so I felt it was best not to say anything at all. Before the rise of Donald Trump, you suffered a penalty of being seen as crazy in US society for speaking out about those taboo political topics. While the New Atheists were seemingly speaking out on the fringes against religion, their criticism helped to normalize atheism to be more acceptable than before in society even if atheists are still despised throughout many parts of the US.

Political freedoms in the United States were something that I learned not to have any faith in from my own examination of the facts of political participation. For the longest time, I felt a sense of irrational paranoia flare-up whenever I tried broaching political topics that the norms of US society had deemed taboo. The United States projected an image of freedom that quite clearly didn't comport with the facts on the ground for the US public. For all those paying attention, it was clearly becoming a police state that was slowly imposing a soft fascism throughout US society and it was a bipartisan effort by both Republicans and Democrats. The United States claimed to be a country of freedom and political protests, but it became completely obvious that this was limited to the purpose of the protest. Protests against the US Federal Reserve by the Tea Party resulted in being labeled racists, portrayed as crazies, and a purposeful attempt by the Western mainstream media - especially CNN - to produce a disingenuous portrayal of the protest whose main grievances were about the bailout by the Federal Reserve to the largest banks in the United States.[2064] The Bush and Obama years would slowly reveal that the Western mainstream media had become a tacit agent of corporate fascism in the US. Chris Hedges had labeled the bailout as socialism for the wealthy elite while they continued to bark about Libertarianism, they touted the so-called "Free Markets" after using US tax dollars to bail themselves out, and proceeded to support policies that cut away at the US public's social safety net as thanks for their legalized theft of US public money. The takedown of Occupy Wall Street was far worse since it was shown the FBI and the police collaborated in an effort to sabotage it and therefore to purposefully and knowingly violate the First Amendment of the United States Constitution.[2065] They completely succeeded in their

---

3. [2064] "Chicago Tax Day Tea Party - What CNN Did Not Show You Behind The Scenes - Reporter Owned 4/16/09." *YouTube*, Mark ResourceU, 16 Apr. 2009, www.youtube.com/watch?v=y6xWGvdRQ9Q.
4. [2065] Wolf, Naomi. "Revealed: How the FBI Coordinated the Crackdown on Occupy | Naomi Wolf." *The Guardian*, Guardian News and Media, 29 Dec. 2012,

efforts in the interests of yet another group of wealthy elite and in direct violation of the US Constitution that they clearly don't care to uphold as shown by their actions in willfully supporting fascism.[2066] If there were any doubts about just how the First Amendment has been curtailed in favor of Corporate fascism in the United States, it happened yet again during the Dakota access pipeline protests and yet again the police acted on behalf of the wealthy elite.[2067][2068] The only time the US public wasn't physically beaten, sexually harassed, and driven off from being allowed to exercise their First Amendment rights was when Climate Change protests occurred outside Wall Street and that was only because it coincided with the concerns of many of the wealthy elite about Climate Change.[2069] In effect, the United States of America showed that so-called guaranteed US Constitutional freedoms were only in effect insofar as they aligned with the arbitrary preferences of the wealthy elite of the United States of America. If I were to take a blind guess in order to look for a positive alternative hypothesis, I'd assume that the US government simply didn't want the petrodollar system negatively impacted, but the rational course of action for that explanation would have simply been to explain what every stockbroker at Wall Street probably knows to the US public. It's not like it is a conspiracy of any sort, even *Investopedia* provides a clear explanation for anyone interested in learning more about the sophisticated US money system and the Federal Reserves' key part in maintaining it.[2070]

My analysis throughout the many years prior to the aforementioned social issues only worsened my already negative disposition, from the Bush years of warrantless wiretapping to the Obama years of expanded NSA surveillance. A clear neutering, if not outright destruction of the Fourth Amendment of the US Constitution. I understand they had sensible and logical reasons for this one, but there is no point in pretending that it isn't upsetting as a member of the nameless and faceless US public. I tried calming any paranoia that flared-up as obviously the US government needed to take at least this necessary step to protect the US public. I began to worry about the competence of the people in charge upon reading in *Good Strategy, Bad Strategy* by *Richard Rumelt* that the NSA had no formal strategy in mind on its general mission and that they have had trouble in recent decades on even formulating any sort of strategy at all.[2071] I clamped down on my concerns about their competence in running a government

---

5. [2066] Wolf, Naomi. "Revealed: How the FBI Coordinated the Crackdown on Occupy | Naomi Wolf." *The Guardian*, Guardian News and Media, 29 Dec. 2012, www.theguardian.com/commentisfree/2012/dec/29/fbi-coordinated-crackdown-occupy.
6. [2067] Brady, Jeff. "2 Years After Standing Rock Protests, Tensions Remain But Oil Business Booms." *NPR*, NPR, 29 Nov. 2018, www.npr.org/2018/11/29/671701019/2-years-after-standing-rock-protests-north-dakota-oil-business-is-booming.
7. [2068] "Standing Rock Sioux and Dakota Access Pipeline | Teacher Resource." *Standing Rock Sioux and Dakota Access Pipeline | Teacher Resource*, americanindian.si.edu/nk360/plains-treaties/dapl.
8. [2069] Restuccia, Andrew. "Greens: Climate March Breaks Record." *POLITICO*, 22 Sept. 2014, www.politico.com/story/2014/09/peoples-climate-march-nyc-111177.
9. [2070] Tun, Zaw Thiha. "How Petrodollars Affect The U.S. Dollar." *Investopedia*, Investopedia, 12 Mar. 2019, www.investopedia.com/articles/forex/072915/how-petrodollars-affect-us-dollar.asp.
10. [2071] Rumelt, Richard. *Good Strategy, Bad Strategy: the Difference and Why It Matters*. Random House

efficiently under the belief that I was just being arrogant and I needed to stop having these arrogant thoughts. There was surely reasons that I couldn't possibly know since I was just a lowly citizen on why such a situation was happening; I tried to stifle the counterargument in my mind that I was using an argument from ignorance. I was just a young person studying for his Masters degree, who was I to have such negative thoughts on the competence of the NSA? The news about a massive hack by some Chinese hackers which put 4 million US Federal employees personal information at risk only worsened my worries about US government incompetence, but again I told myself; selection bias, negative news, and so forth.[2072][2073] Besides, despite my degree, I was never selected for any federal government jobs as I'm sure there were people more qualified than I. Surely, people were aware of these issues that even I could spot from the outset and knew how to manage them from within? The cruel and unusual punishment of so-called "enhanced interrogation" techniques like waterboarding didn't leave me with much confidence and they seemed to be perfectly fine with violating the Eighth amendment of the US Constitution, but perhaps I was just being naive. Events such as the prison and torture location of Abu Ghraib was evidence that told me otherwise. Yet again, I tried to stay optimistic about the US government's competence throughout the Bush and Obama years. The shameful trial of the Haditha killings which resulted in only docked pay for the killing of innocent children and the handicapped elderly which was celebrated as a form of good legal conduct by anti-Iraqi bigots in the US mainstream media kept reminding me otherwise.

Most of all, what caused me to lose faith in the United States was learning that my high school textbooks perpetuated a complete falsehood by claiming Native Americans had superior rights thanks to treaties with the US government; only to discover that in response to Native human rights protests, the US government had purposefully made it legally possible to rape Native American women and young Native American girls by making sure they didn't have the right to sue their rapists in US courts[2074]; Tribal authorities who held "concurrent powers" with State governments often had those powers relinquished and their powers were limited to only a year's jail time for raping Native Americans or a five thousand dollar fine that rapists had to pay to get out of any possible jail time but even that was curtailed arbitrarily.[2075] The US government effectively made the Native American territories lawless on purpose; it is likely due to the Realist Theory of International Relations to further impose suffering and torture

---

LLC, 2017.
11. [2072] Zengerle, Patricia. "Millions More Americans Hit by Government Personnel Data Hack." *Reuters*, Thomson Reuters, 9 July 2015, www.reuters.com/article/us-cybersecurity-usa/millions-more-americans-hit-by-government-personnel-data-hack-idUSKCN0PJ2M420150709.
12. [2073] Sanders, Sam. "Massive Data Breach Puts 4 Million Federal Employees' Records At Risk." *NPR*, NPR, 4 June 2015, www.npr.org/sections/thetwo-way/2015/06/04/412086068/massive-data-breach-puts-4-million-federal-employees-records-at-risk.
13. [2074] "MAZE OF INJUSTICE ." *Amnesty International USA*, Amnesty International, www.amnestyusa.org/pdfs/mazeofinjustice.pdf.
14. [2075] "MAZE OF INJUSTICE ." *Amnesty International USA*, Amnesty International, www.amnestyusa.org/pdfs/mazeofinjustice.pdf.

upon Native Americans to keep them at a subsistence level. Several US States forcibly sterilized Native American women without their consent due to racist eugenics policies in the 1960s and this was after US Christian boarding schools from the 1870s to the 1960s raped, starved, tortured, and sometimes killed Native American children with the sole purpose of causing cultural genocide upon Native Americans in the US.[2076][2077] It has been noted US teachers of Native Americans still felt it was important to continue "civilizing" and essentially imposing cultural genocide upon Native Americans as per their faith in the barbaric teachings of Jesus Christ.[2078] I intend to cover more of this particular issue of Native American human rights and the horrific atrocities of Christianity upon Native Americans in Part III; needless to say, it shouldn't be considered extreme to argue that Islam's atrocities throughout the world are rivaled by Christianity's upon the Native Americans throughout the history of North, Central, and South America.

I never spoke out like Chris Hedges or Glenn Greenwald's organization *The Intercept* against this abuse of power and subtle destruction of the US Constitution. I had no power and I felt the only effect that would be produced was being seen as crazy so I kept silent and internalized the belief that democratic freedoms are believed by gullible people and aren't real within US society or its laws. More and more confirmations kept popping up such as the *Citizens United* case by the US Supreme Court. It all felt overwhelming and futile so I just stopped believing in the United States being a democratic country at all and understood that the US public didn't really have any rights - Constitutional or otherwise. What was one the impact of one voice dissenting ever going to accomplish? It all felt useless and presumably the US government was unstoppable in its destruction of Civil Liberties according to Hedges; moreover, there would always be a bunch of Conservative Christians celebrating the destruction of Civil Liberties and mouthing the trite nonsense of being free under Libertarianism and Ayn Rand Objectivism while the wealthy elite kept robbing them blind using those policies by getting government bailouts and financial support using US taxpayer money. It felt to me that Friedrich Nietzsche's argument in *Beyond Good and Evil* against all forms of democracy was true; he argued that to place your faith in change upon the herd - the broader public - is to constantly reduce yourself to abject nihilism because there will never be a day when they "wake up" to the corruption around them.[2079] It wasn't until being a witness to Donald Trump's rise to the Presidency that I understood that I had overshot the intelligence level of possibly the entire Federal government, I had most definitely overestimated the skills

---

15. [2076] Rutecki, Gregory W. "Forced Sterilization of Native Americans: Late Twentieth Century." *The Center for Bioethics & Human Dignity*, 8 Oct. 2010, cbhd.org/content/forced-sterilization-native-americans-late-twentieth-century-physician-cooperation-national-.
16. [2077] Bear, Charla. "American Indian Boarding Schools Haunt Many." *NPR*. NPR, 12 May 2008. Web. 2 Nov. 2015, https://www.npr.org/templates/story/story.php?storyId=16516865?storyId=16516865.
17. [2078] Bear, Charla. "American Indian Boarding Schools Haunt Many." *NPR*. NPR, 12 May 2008. Web. 2 Nov. 2015, https://www.npr.org/templates/story/story.php?storyId=16516865?storyId=16516865.
18. [2079] Nietzsche, Friedrich Wilhelm. *Beyond Good and Evil*. Translated by Helen Zimmern, Word ed., Gutenberg Press, 2009.

and intelligence of the Republican nominees who had thought they were contenders for the Presidency with Right-wing analysts declaring them to be an amazing crop of candidates with Jeb Bush seemingly poised for victory, I had overshot the intelligence level of the Western mainstream media since they played into Trump's hands by going into scathing news stories about him in blatant favor of Hillary Clinton after Trump won the Republican nomination, I had overshot the intelligence level of the Democratic party since they had largely ignored their populist heavyweights in order to support a candidate that they knew had the worst shot at winning the election, and I had overshot the intelligence of the US public since the older Democrats were being led by the nose in favor of the awful and incompetent Hillary Clinton. Hillary Clinton's response to her loss as Democratic Presidential nominee upon Donald Trump's victory cemented that she had no idea what she was doing, but presented the image that she did. Millennials such as myself who supported Bernie Sanders were ignored, insulted, swept under the rug, belittled as naive, and then blamed for not voting for her by the Western mainstream media. Obviously, this doesn't vindicate the Pro-Trump Republicans for any racism or sexism, but that wasn't the focal issue to begin with. The Trump voters, particularly in the South, had never recovered from the so-called Great Recession (a cute euphemism the Western mainstream media made for our generation's Depression) and had been abandoned a decade afterwards. I obviously don't support their views on religious extremism, but to argue that it was just bigotry is nonsense. Even as I write, the divide between the Left and the Right of the US has only spiraled and worsened as the Trump Administration nears its third year in the White House.

What happened? A great multitude of factors played out; many of which would require their own books, likely to have opposing perspectives, and are beyond the scope of this one to discuss in the details they require to obtain a clear picture of it all. *Foreign Affairs* magazine is already delving into many details as of this writing and there is an expectation that there will be much more discussion on such topics within the field of Political Science for decades to come. However, one variable that I'd like to place the spotlight upon, because it'll surely be ignored due to the taboo of Religious Tolerance, is the impact that the United States War on Terror had upon Muslims who were inclined to join terrorist groups whether they were al Qaeda, ISIS, or possibly others in their opposition to the West. Other places from countries like India to several countries in the continent of Africa had their own share of troubles from Islamic terror groups so the problem wasn't the West versus Islam, but the world versus Islam and continues to be so at the harrowing expense of non-Muslim and Muslim civilians who don't support terrorist organizations. Yet, too many in the West still treat it as the West versus Islam and this provincial focus can have dire consequences since Islamism is a global threat that requires a unified global response. I fear that this is due partly to incompetence within the US political class, but also a cultural unwillingness to challenge the taboo topic of religion that exist within Think Tanks, the US Congress, the Presidential administrations of either party, and which continue to be a natural reflection of the attitudes of the broader US public. The success of Donald Trump displays the incompetence of the political class quite well; they were so assured of victory and kept thinking they could sway public opinion by ignoring what the public wanted for decades. Far more than Donald Trump's influence, all notorious forms of bipartisanship before his ascendency to the US Presidency likely played more of an influence in rupturing the increasing divide amongst Liberals and Conservatives in the US that had grown for decades. The incompetence of Hillary Clinton was plain to see for anyone who wasn't beguiled by her surname, the delusions of the ruling class, and the Western mainstream media; she had no argument or public message against Donald Trump apart from not being Trump. She had nothing to offer the US public and her campaign team wasn't intelligent enough to come-up with any real strategy in opposition to Donald Trump's blistering public messages. However, her public downfall shouldn't lead to excusing or ignoring the broader incompetence of the political class; Hillary Clinton was merely a product of a much deeper problem within the culture of the political class and particularly the aging US Congress. For instance, a 2017 Vox article quotes a pharmacist who made an off-hand remark indicating that some members of the US Congress might be suffering from Alzheimer's disease and require Alzheimer's medication as the prescriptions his company must give to the US Congress.[2080] The pharmacist in question later recanted his statement to add a so-called "clarification" that he meant to general US public, but I would speculate that he most likely added this qualification because the publicity would hurt his business with the privileged and lucrative position of having a business contract to work for the US Congress.[2081] If there were any doubts about this concern on the US Congress's critical thinking faculties, the death of John McCain from natural causes while he was serving as a Arizona Senator and the bizarre lack of reaction from the US Congress, the US mainstream media, and even the US public shows a rather perturbing trend within the United States on the cultural normalization of incompetence. To be clear, I have nothing but respect for John McCain's military and political service in the United States and I sincerely apologize to anyone who knew him personally - whether family, friend, or co-worker - and this is not an attempt to vilify his service record, his lifelong hard work and dedication in service to the United States, or to insult him on a personal level. While I disagreed with him on some political issues, I have nothing but respect for him on those particular subject matter and I found it heartening that he supported defending the rights of Native American women and children suffering from rape crimes that were overwhelmingly conducted by non-Native men as a result of US laws that were enacted before he was ever part of the US Congress and which got too little scrutiny until the Amnesty International report on the horrific living conditions Native women and children endured. If this is an offensive line of questioning, I sincerely apologize, but I think it is a potentially taboo topic that must be probed because I sincerely fear the possible consequences of not doing so. It should be a self-evident

---

19. [2080] Kliff, Sarah. "A Pharmacist Says He Has Filled Alzheimer's Prescriptions for Members of Congress." *Vox*, Vox, 11 Oct. 2017, www.vox.com/policy-and-politics/2017/10/11/16458142/congress-alzheimers-pharmacist.
20. [2081] Kliff, Sarah. "A Pharmacist Says He Has Filled Alzheimer's Prescriptions for Members of Congress." *Vox*, Vox, 11 Oct. 2017, www.vox.com/policy-and-politics/2017/10/11/16458142/congress-alzheimers-pharmacist.

fact that a person suffering from an aggressive brain tumor is incapable of fulfilling their Senate duties and should have retired once learning they had such an affliction. Who exactly gets to fulfill their duties? Their team? The team wasn't elected by the US public. The special interest groups? Well then, we have a corruption problem if they're making the laws. Worse yet, and potentially putting national security interests at risk, foreign nationals or lobbyists working for the interests of foreign governments could potentially manipulate such situations for their benefit. Even situations like the Alzheimer's disease if proven credible, would mean that national security interests or economic interests were at risk because Senators were mentally unfit to carry out their duties and potentially in a credulous state of mind for the benefit of foreign nationals or lobbyists working for foreign governments to obtain or copy sensitive US government documents or other disastrous possibilities that I wouldn't - as a mere US citizen - be able to consider since I wouldn't be aware of such possibilities as I never worked for the US Congress. It's possible that targeting Senators who don't work on Intelligence committees could have dangerous consequences too. There are a plethora of situations that could open-up the possibility of unknown unknowns as it were and all because nobody is questioning sheer incompetence being defended as somehow rational or good for the US. The dangers don't necessarily have to be intentional on the part of a US Senator or member of the House of Representatives. John McCain was on his sixth term as US Senator until he died while in office; it is quite clear that a pervading culture of incompetence has been rationalized as somehow beneficial for the United States by the highest offices of the US government, the incompetent US mainstream media which at no point tried to probe deeper or even consider the dangers of normalizing people dying of natural causes while in public office, and the broader US public which didn't question this but simply fell in step with the emotional significance but didn't seem to consider questions about either their safety under such a system or how such a normalization could negatively impact the ability to pass bills beneficial for US society as a whole.

    Laughing at Congressional panels of several aging members of the US Congress not being able to understand simplistic concepts of technology and software during a hearing about Russian hacking of a US election stops being funny when you realize they're the ones writing the laws that a US citizen must obey and their ignorance could be used by special interest groups and foreign nationals to harm the US public. Moreover, and I hope this is a ridiculous belief, I fear that the Presidency of Donald Trump is an open-door invitation for any US-born person who has nefarious intent upon on any particular demographic of the US public to attain power and irrevocably harm the lives of millions within the US public. This is because it is quite clear that a US born citizen doesn't need to be among the most intelligent of people to become US President, but instead they just need to be slightly more intelligent than Donald Trump, they just need to be as skilled in his public theatrics, and I fear that is an open invitation for any person who seeks power for harmful aims. Given the utter incompetence of the current US Congress, I doubt we, the US public, can place any trust in the checks and balances system anymore so long as the US Congress is run by aging members in either of the major political parties. Regardless of what their political affiliations are, they must retire and let the younger generations be in charge of ruling the country because the current, aging members have absolutely proven themselves to be unfit to serve the US public's needs. Neither Republicans or Democrats in office seem to have any idea on how to tackle Climate Change, the threat of Islamization, the future of AI technology, the problems with the healthcare system, the growing erosion of Free Speech on social media, the human rights of Ex-Muslims and Transgender people, or . . . anything that needs addressing now. Not soon, not latter, but *now* in our contemporary time. I'm not saying that we should vote for any particular candidate or ideology, but rather that we need new people who better understand our needs because the aging, incompetent US Congress that still represents the US cannot be the ones that remain in power because they're destroying the US Republic with their inability to tackle these issues that the US public needs addressing. We'll continue to have hurdles and disagreements like the topic of Free Speech and Human Rights versus Religious Tolerance, but regardless of whichever side of the political spectrum we're on . . . we need new, younger people to take the helm because it seems gerrymandering will slowly turn the US Republic into a psychotic dictatorship at this breakneck pace of incompetence by the incumbents of the US Congress.

    Conspiracy theorists and nihilists among the US public may argue that it is all part of some plan of theirs. There is no plan, they have no plan, and nothing about their actions indicates any intelligent vision on how they want US society to prosper or what avenues to take in order to accomplish that. They don't even have a powerful message of opposition when Donald Trump has given them all the material they could ask for in a political contest. If the Republican nomination of Donald Trump against his fellow Republican nominees doesn't prove that, then nothing does. The US Congress clearly have no idea what they're doing, but think of themselves as the only ones capable of ruling when it is far past their generation's time to step down and let the new generation of Gen X and Millennials takeover to steer the country in a new era. I want to be clear that this is not an attempt to vilify the US Congress; they're fallible human beings and the US public too often doesn't take note of their more positive contributions that benefit US society. It's easy to only selectively focus on the negative aspects of politics. By and large, they are not horrible people, but rather fallible human beings and I am writing that we, as a US public, should vote them out because their negatives far outweigh their positives for far too long. They have neither ideas nor vision and the only way to send a clear message is to vote them out of power. The US public may not need vision, but if you're ruling a country then you certainly must have it because otherwise you're leaving the country directionless and vulnerable. I must stress that they're not terrible people, but have grown too myopic and ignorant to move the country forward in many ways; I'd like to highlight a positive contribution of theirs before moving on. The US Congress, both Republican and Democrat, unanimously added the protection of atheist human rights as part of the Franklin R. Wolf Religious Freedom Act which President Obama signed into law and promoted the training of US Foreign Service Officers in highlighting abuses against and advocating for the human rights of atheists being persecuted globally.[2082][2083][2084] The largely religious US Congress and a Christian President quite clearly show compassion for human rights for all people and genuine concern for atheist minorities even if they vehemently disagree with atheism due to their own personal ethics. They don't extend negative views to ignoring the human rights of the most vulnerable atheists across the world. Moreover, despite what a large percentage of the US public erroneously believe; atheism is considered a religion and protected on the basis of the First Amendment in US law since it is still a point of view on personal ethics, the existence of Gods or a God, and beliefs concerning life after death.[2085]

Nonetheless, despite the positives, it is clear that the eras of President George W. Bush and President Barack H. Obama were leading towards a world that almost nobody in the US public wanted. US Civil Liberties were slowly being withered to dust. Please consider President Obama's public message to the UN General Assembly on September 5th, 2012:

> *"The future must not belong to those who slander the prophet of Islam. But to be credible, those who condemn that slander must also condemn the hate we see in the images of Jesus Christ that are desecrated, or churches that are destroyed, or the Holocaust that is denied. (Applause.)*
>
> *Let us condemn incitement against Sufi Muslims and Shiite pilgrims. It's time to heed the words of Gandhi: "Intolerance is itself a form of violence and an obstacle to the growth of a true democratic spirit." (Applause.) Together, we must work towards a world where we are strengthened by our differences, and not defined by them. That is what America embodies, that's the vision we will support."*[2086]

I'm afraid that he couldn't have been more wrong. The future *must* belong to those who slander Islam and the pedophile Prophet Mohammad. To slander religion with words is not the moral equivalent of defacing and destroying religious property, which is an act of hate. To criticize religion is not intolerance, it is an act of compassion for those who are harmed by religion the most - the religious believers themselves. People are criticizing Islam out of compassion for the victims and the primary victims are Muslims themselves. The same for criticizing the hateful belief system of Christianity out of compassion for Christians. As can be said for the theistic aspects of Hinduism, Judaism, and Buddhism. To oppose slandering

---

21. [2082] "H.R.1150 - 114th Congress (2015-2016): Frank R. Wolf International Religious Freedom Act." *Congress.gov*, 16 Dec. 2016, www.congress.gov/bill/114th-congress/house-bill/1150.
22. [2083] Worley, Will. "Obama Just Signed a Law Protecting Atheists from Religious Persecution." *The Independent*, Independent Digital News and Media, 22 Dec. 2016, www.independent.co.uk/news/world/americas/atheists-legal-protection-us-religious-freedom-bill-signed-barack-obama-a7489641.html.
23. [2084] Johnson, Alex. "With Obama's Signature, U.S. Religious Freedom Law Now Protects Atheists." *NBCNews.com*, NBCUniversal News Group, www.nbcnews.com/news/us-news/obama-s-signature-u-s-religious-freedom-law-protects-atheists-n699356.
24. [2085] "First Amendment." *American Atheists*, www.atheists.org/legal/faq/first-amendment/.
25. [2086] Obama, Barack. "Remarks by the President to the UN General Assembly." *National Archives and Records Administration*, National Archives and Records Administration, obamawhitehouse.archives.gov/the-press-office/2012/09/25/remarks-president-un-general-assembly.

religion is to oppose Free Speech, Free Inquiry, and especially, Freedom of Thought. All of those often require the *freedom to offend*.

Please take a moment to consider what the Presidencies of the second President Bush and President Obama helped to forge: *a world that empowered a global Jihadist movement.* By cutting apart US Constitutional freedoms instead of exercising them in opposition to a pathological set of beliefs that were held as sacred, Presidents Bush and Obama shaped a world that empowered Islam by making it look infallible from the perspective of any Muslim susceptible to ISIS recruitment. Due to the asinine norm of Religious Tolerance, we actually live in a world where Foreign Policy think tanks, Foreign Policy analysts, the US Presidential administrations of Republicans and Democrats, and the Western mainstream media are baffled because they have trouble understanding why a ideology that purports an illiterate and pedophilic warlord who raped women that he took as sex slaves, raped a 9-year old that he took as a child bride, slaughtered people of other religions who didn't agree with his message, and who taught all these actions of his were infallible and that Muslims should strive to be perfect like him could create violence in modern times. They actually don't understand why something so obvious could create violence because they wish to maintain the social norm of Religious Tolerance to protect their own religious beliefs from scrutiny. All these efforts from gutting US Constitutional freedoms through NSA surveillance, waterboarding, a massive drone program that is utilized in seven foreign countries, and two major wars the US has been embroiled in has only strengthened the convictions of Islamists and those who may consider becoming Islamists. Why? From their point of view, the US simply looks desperate in trying to stop the "true message" of Islam. It emboldens this idea that they should continue to have faith beyond doubt in Islam. Whereas Free Speech and Free Inquiry would make them reflect more deeply on the glaring flaws of such an obviously barbaric ideology. *Criticizing Islam is the key to destroying it and ending Islamic terrorism.*

Finally, consider this foreign policy proposal I thought of: theoretically, it should be easy for any non-Islamic country to destroy or takeover an Islamic country in the age of drone warfare. This is because of the crucial "design flaw" in Islamic theology. Simply put a hefty amount of leaflets comprised of the most offensive images of the Islamic Prophet Mohammad and have them spread tactically around key cities for either a massive political distraction to focus on an invasion of an Islamic country or to create as much socio-economic upheaval as possible to destroy the country from inside without ever having to send even one foot soldier into the line of fire. Offensive to a religion? Who cares if it saves the lives of US soldiers and decreases the death toll of innocent civilians in the Islamic country from an outright war? Of course, we would have to work to get journalists from the West or non-Islamic countries and any civilians visiting that country out of the country to the best of our ability before using such a strategy. Here are my counterpoints to arguments about it being childish or offensive to use such a strategy: First, it would likely bring about *less* damage and violence than a drone bombing or other military equivalent that would kill a larger number of innocent people who live in a Islamic country. It would thus minimize human casualties. Second, any destruction of infrastructure or human violence would solely be seen as the culpability of the Islamic society that is burning down and destroying itself and the foreign country - whether the West or not - could credibly argue that they weren't at all culpable for the human violence being perpetuated over people killing their fellow citizens because of cartoon images being sent down from above. Lastly, if even the mostly Islamic army of the country gets offended and distracted by such images that they choose to burn their own countries down, then the risk for any invading force could conceivably lessen dramatically. Why does this policy proposal sound like childish gibberish and not something that we will credibly do despite the potential ability of saving the lives of US soldiers, coalition forces that aid the US, and even innocent civilians in foreign countries? Because we collectively value Religious Tolerance even above Human Rights. *The value of Human Rights must overcome the taboos of Religious Tolerance and misanthropic concepts like Original Sin.*

The Facts Over Feelings Bullet Points for the Abrahamic Faiths

"Doing Harm to Stupidity. It is certain that the belief in the reprehensibility of egoism, preached with such stubbornness and conviction, has on the whole done harm to egoism (in favour of the herd instinct, as I shall repeat a hundred times!), especially by depriving it of a good conscience, and by bidding us seek in it the source of all misfortune. "Your selfishness is the bane of your life " so rang the preaching for millenniums: it did harm, as we have said, to selfishness, and deprived it of much spirit, much cheerfulness, much ingenuity, and much beauty; it stultified and deformed and poisoned selfishness!

Philosophical antiquity, on the other hand, taught that there was another principal source of evil: from Socrates downwards, the thinkers were never weary of preaching that "your thoughtlessness and stupidity, your unthinking way of living according to rule, and your subjection to the opinion of your neighbour, are the reasons why you so seldom attain to happiness, we thinkers are, as thinkers, the happiest of mortals." Let us not decide here whether this preaching against stupidity was more sound than the preaching against selfishness; it is certain, however, that stupidity was thereby deprived of its good conscience: those philosophers did harm to stupidity."[2087] - Friedrich Nietzsche, The Joyful Wisdom. *Aphorism 328. Translated by Thomas Common.*

Please take the time to consider each of these statements individually and what it would mean for your personal understanding of your religion, if these statements are true. I would recommend at least ten seconds to ponder each of them, but please take as long as you wish:

- Your religious history of being persecuted by other religious faiths doesn't make your religion more truthful or real.
- The horrifying deaths of hundreds of thousands or more people in mass genocides who were persecuted for having faith in your religious beliefs doesn't make your religion more truthful or real.

---

26. [2087] Nietzsche, Friedrich. "The Joyful Wisdom, by Friedrich Nietzsche." Translated by Thomas Common, *The Joyful Wisdom, by Friedrich Nietzsche : BOOK FOURTH*, ebooks.adelaide.edu.au/n/nietzsche/friedrich/n67j/book4.html.

- There is no intrinsic meaning in the deaths of those who were massacred and their deaths don't serve as proof that your religious faith is more truthful or real.
- Facing persecution for your beliefs including physical assault, torture, and death doesn't make your religion more truthful or real.
- That asshole who you despise being part of another religion doesn't make yours more truthful or real. Every religion has its idiots and they increase the more religion decides to spread itself. Thereby, the more it spreads itself, the more likely the statistical odds that violent people will commit violence in its name.
- Your loved ones dying as a result of persecution for their religious faith doesn't prove your religion is more truthful or real.
- Your loved ones having faith and dying in protection of your country as a soldier doesn't make your religion more truthful or real.
- The reason the Abrahamic faiths are so violent is because they all preach to fulfill the psychopathic ravings of people who call themselves infallible whether as prophets or gods. In particular, Islam and Christianity are just the most popular cults of personality and Judaism's search for a Messiah is a search to become part of a cult of personality.
- The only purpose of your religious faith is a psychotic end of the world prophecy, those prophecies are the ravings of madmen who had a poor understanding of reality and called themselves prophets and gods in an era where people thought magic was real and slavery was defended on the basis of your god allowing it. The main purpose of your belief is to fulfill their insane ravings simply because you believe they're infallible because they gave themselves titles to argue they were infallible to credulous people in a time before people understood biology, cosmology, modern mathematics, or even that the world was round.
- The reason you justify violence on other Abrahamic faiths is because you believe your version of psychopathic ravings is more true than the other Abrahamic faith's psychopathic ravings.
- *Religion is the patriarchy*: The patriarchy doesn't come from being male, some absurd and unfounded idea of maleness leading to oppressing women, and pointing out beliefs that lead to misogynistic actions shouldn't be ridiculed. It's pointing out facts. Belief informs actions; the teachings of religion is what causes men to oppress women throughout world history. It must be either reformed with Sex-positive Feminist values which can hopefully be the case for the Dharmic faiths or outright destroyed in the case of Islam and Christianity since their precepts are antagonistic to change.
- The insane ravings of these psychotic people called prophets and god aren't real. Thereby, there is no reason to believe in your religious faith or for your religion to exist, because the theology is predicated on their psychopathic ravings being absolute truth.
- Some religious believers waste their lives being offended when anti-theists insult their holy teachings and when the holy books are insulted. Religious believers will try to

spread it, talk about how wise and wonderful the teachings are, and about how it is good for more people to become part of their particular religion -- yet, they never once take the opportunity to read the entire religious book themselves. How can you know that it is wise, peaceful, and good for you without having read the entire book in your own private time? Why should others believe that reading your holy book would be beneficial when most religious believers don't bother to do so? For those living in the US, why are atheists in the US the most knowledgeable about religion?[2088]

- Feelings of warmth, bliss, and love when recalling the happy times with those who passed away while in prayer doesn't make your religion more truthful or real. Everyone experiences those feelings when recalling their dead loved ones including polytheists or atheists like myself. It doesn't make your belief in god or your religious faith more truthful or real.
- Your yearning to meet your dead relatives in some afterlife doesn't make your religious faith more truthful or real. Everyone has regrets about the past. Consider the prospect that you will never meet them again after this life you have now. When they died, they were gone forever upon the decomposition of their body.
- Your feelings of antipathy towards the fact you will never see your relatives again and your strong rejection of my factual statement doesn't make your religious belief more truthful or real. Your feelings increasing your faith don't matter. Likewise, your feelings to rectify or apologize to your loved ones for your mistakes don't matter. You will never see them again.
- Your focus on dead loved one during prayer and your community telling you that they're smiling down at you in heaven or watching you with love and care in some afterlife is proof that your god is your dead loved one. You are using religion as a tool to fulfill your wish to see them again. Your selfless feelings of love for them and your grief over their death doesn't make your religion more truthful and real.
- Instead of focusing on life after death, focus on this remaining life you have. What constructive improvements can you do to either better yourself or help other people in service to your loved ones memory without the need of the superstitions of religious faith?

Finally, and this is more of a personal opinion of mine, arguing that a bunch of ignorant desert dwellers sincerely believed and died for their religious faith doesn't prove that the supernatural events ever happened; it just proves that the most illiterate, barbaric, and ignorant people during that time period were exactly what we would expect them to be. In my personal point of view, there are far more interesting histories of greater civilizations in the locations of what is modern-day Egypt, Iran, Japan, India, China, and the Native Americas who show a

---

27. [2088] "U.S. Religious Knowledge Survey." *Pew Research Center's Religion & Public Life Project*, Pew Research Center's Religion & Public Life Project, 19 Dec. 2017, www.pewforum.org/2010/09/28/u-s-religious-knowledge-survey/.

history of far more intelligence compared to a bunch of ignorant people who wrote the Bible and Quran. If you doubt this, just compare the Bible or the Quran to the teachings of Lao Tzu or the Buddha and remember that Lao Tzu and the Buddha came before the creation of the Bible or Quran by at least five hundred years. Why waste your time pondering the psychology of a bunch of illiterate, savage, and ignorant people just because they chose to die for a belief that has no evidence of being true? They died and sincerely believed in what they died for, but so what? Do Muslim suicide bombers not do the same, even if we assume they're depressed? What's the point of wasting your life by devoting the only life that you know upon people who were far dumber than probably anybody living in modern times? Think of the dumbest person you know personally and realize they were probably smarter than people who lived in the most barbaric places of the ancient world in the 1st and 7th centuries. Why allow the thinking of 1st and 7th century barbarians to influence, infect, and impose judgments on human behavior at all?

Normalizing Dissent and Self-Surpassing

"The offer of certainty, the offer of complete security, the offer of an impermeable faith that can't give way is an offer of something not worth having. I want to live my life taking the risk all the time that I don't know anything like enough yet; that I haven't understood enough, that I can't know enough, that I'm always hungrily operating on the margins of a potentially great harvest of future knowledge and wisdom. I wouldn't have it any other way and I'd urge you to look at those of you who tell you - those people who tell you at your age - that you're dead till you believe as they do. What a terrible thing to be telling to children. And that you can only live by accepting an absolute authority. Don't think of that as a gift, think of it as a poison chalice. Push it aside however tempting it is. Take the risk of thinking for yourself, much more happiness, truth, beauty, and wisdom will come to you that way."[2089,2090] - Christopher Hitchens

    By now, this may all seem overwhelming and you may even feel nihilistic about the future. I've noticed far too often that the vast majority of people prefer simplistic narratives with easy solutions to systemic social issues. In a podcast known as the *Rationally Speaking Podcast* on February 2019, two of my favorite public intellectuals who have been a personal inspiration to me got together to speak on the topic of *Dissent and Free Speech*. The Co-Founder of Ex-Muslims of North America and public speaker, Sarah Haider, was interviewed by the Co-Founder of Center for Applied Rationality (CFAR) and the host of the Rationally Speaking Podcast, Julia Galef and after discussing several variety of topics, they both mentioned that they've noticed a strange quirk of public engagement; the simpler the message

---

28. [2089] Hitchens, Christopher. "Christopher Hitchens Delivers Yet Another Masterpiece." *YouTube*, Religion, Atheism, Science, 16 Mar. 2011, www.youtube.com/watch?v=YiU5u6zAtyc.
29. [2090] Hitchens, Christopher. "Does a Good God Exist? A Debate Between Hitchens and Dembski (November 2010)." *YouTube*, ReasonPublic / Biblical Worldview Institute, 19 Apr. 2012, www.youtube.com/watch?v=ctuloBOYolE.

that they give to the public, the more widespread the message becomes.[2091] This seems to imply an inversion with complex arguments and the ability for the broader public to acknowledge, understand, and possibly accept more nuanced arguments. Oddly enough, I have experienced a bizarre form of this in which the people who did it were claiming to be conducting the opposite. On Discord servers inspired by the Nerdfighteria culture fostered by the Vlogbrothers, two Youtube content creators known as John and Hank Green, the administrators of the Discord saw fit to have my posts removed and my posting abilities silenced for "triggering" Muslims by sharing content about Ex-Muslims talking about their human rights and the human rights crimes in Muslim-majority countries in the Discord channels labeled for sharing "Controversial Political Topics" for other people in the server.[2092] While silencing me and soon kicking me out of the server, they claimed repeatedly to care about Ex-Muslim human rights but deleted all content related to it, silenced my voice in speaking on behalf of human rights, and then threw me out of the server so they didn't have to listen.[2093] The Administrator's defense was that I was freely allowed to speak but I had to understand things "complexly" or I was a troll who didn't recognize that I was trolling (trolling being a colloquial internet term for posting offensive content to insult or ridicule others).[2094] This was despite the fact I brought up serious topics of violence against women and panels of Ex-Muslims discussing the threats to their own human rights within the US. The people who did this were self-professed atheists who claimed I was making a "strawman" for sharing factual evidence and college panels about Ex-Muslim issues by Ex-Muslims themselves. I tried explaining why I felt it was important for the human rights of Ex-Muslims, but these people simply shouted me down for making "strawman" and one claimed I was a "troll" who didn't understand I was a "troll" as a response to my criticisms which were in defense of the human rights of Ex-Muslims.[2095]

Needless to say, I was shocked and disgusted; I had been under the misapprehension that people from the Nerdfighteria community (the name that Hank and John Green named their community) actually cared about human rights, but it became clear that what they really cared about is only witnessing positives in a common humanity and didn't want to include criticism of cultural practices that infringed upon human rights. To be clear, this is obviously not the fault of the framers of this community, but rather a fault that is intrinsic to the

---

30. [2091] Galef, Julia, and Sarah Haider. "Rationally Speaking | Official Podcast of New York City Skeptics - Current Episodes - RS 227 - Sarah Haider on 'Dissent and Free Speech.'" *Rationally Speaking Podcast*, New York City Skeptics, rationallyspeakingpodcast.org/show/rs-227-sarah-haider-on-dissent-and-free-speech.html.
31. [2092] "The Intolerance of Nerdfighteria: How Discussing Human Rights Gets You Muted And Banned." *Jarin Jove's Blog*, 2 Mar. 2019, jarinjove.com/2019/02/27/intolerance-of-nerdfighteria/.
32. [2093] "The Intolerance of Nerdfighteria: How Discussing Human Rights Gets You Muted And Banned." *Jarin Jove's Blog*, 2 Mar. 2019, jarinjove.com/2019/02/27/intolerance-of-nerdfighteria/.
33. [2094] "The Intolerance of Nerdfighteria: How Discussing Human Rights Gets You Muted And Banned." *Jarin Jove's Blog*, 2 Mar. 2019, jarinjove.com/2019/02/27/intolerance-of-nerdfighteria/.
34. [2095] "The Intolerance of Nerdfighteria: How Discussing Human Rights Gets You Muted And Banned." *Jarin Jove's Blog*, 2 Mar. 2019, jarinjove.com/2019/02/27/intolerance-of-nerdfighteria/.

community itself since it seeks to be "inclusive" without any real attempt at taking part in criticism of dangerous practices. Yet, by not doing so, it is at the expense of Ex-Muslim human rights; people who really do have to take precautions in order to avoid being killed in the name of Islam even in the West. While I still support their selfless work like *CrashCourse* to bring education to disadvantaged people across the world and the annual *Project For Awesome* which is a massive charity drive which provides matching donations to help third-world countries thrive under better living conditions from clean water, to education for young girls, and so forth. I still can't help but feel incredibly disappointed that an otherwise amazing organization would still skillfully avoid this issue because of Religious Tolerance. The same can be said, but even more so, for the Gates Foundation and Warren Buffett despite their clear liberal-leaning sensibilities with supporting contraceptives for women in third-world countries. I must emphasize that this isn't to malign them; Melinda and Bill Gates, the Vlogbrothers, and Warren Buffett are all amazing people who have done so much good for the world by helping people suffering from absolute poverty to live better lives. Their efforts have undoubtedly saved millions of children from what would have been certain death, if not for their selfless and tireless work. The leaders of these groups are all liberals whether Christian in John Green, and Bill and Melinda Gates's case; agnostic in Warren Buffett's case, or an atheist in Hank Green's case. They do a lot more to decrease poverty and increase human wellbeing than Conservative billionaires like the Koch Brothers who consistently spend money peddling pseudo-science like Climate Change denial or, potentially worse than them, the Wilks Brothers whose Conservative Christian faith teach them to be in opposition to abortion even in cases of incest and rape and that homosexuality is a sin.[2096] Despite that, I realize I don't belong in the community of Nerdfighteria after several years of participation since they refuse to accept listening to the human rights of Ex-Muslims, even when they're in danger of being killed. Just as I have become a reluctant Anti-Theist who grew to accept and internalize the label; I've become a reluctant Contrarian and I'll probably be reading Christopher Hitchens's *Letter To A Young Contrarian* soon after finishing this book to cope with that. Contrarian is a term I hated and rejected throughout my college years since I was always treated as an outsider no matter what I did throughout grade school. Perhaps, it was just a label that I never had a choice to be, due to social stigma within US society.

Worse than the knowledge of strangers refusing to help was learning of the duplicitous nature of fellow Liberals that I had gotten to personally meet, speak with, and share contact information (primarily just Facebook information) in order to keep in contact about political campaigns and political causes that we cared about. I spent 2017 largely feeling hopeless and shared negative news content about Donald Trump in my salty ire over my surprise at the election results. I wondered if it was also my fault for having protest voted for Third-party since I refused to vote for Hillary Clinton. In the process of what was really a year-long sharing of negative news about Trump, I didn't lose any of these contacts that I made from my

---

35. [2096] "Static.reuters.com." *Reuters*, Reuters, static.reuters.com/resources/media/editorial/20150910/WilksDoctrinalPoints.pdf.

volunteer work with the Bernie Sanders campaign. It was only when I started sharing Ex-Muslims of North America videos in which Ex-Muslims were simply talking in college panels about their human rights, the dangers they face, and the problems with Islam that I saw the truth. What I believed were supposedly open-minded and compassionate people began to gradually unfriend me for supporting their human rights. I would say around eighty to one hundred people by my count and it was most certainly the majority of the contacts I had made. In the absence of any major study on this topic, I'm forced to concede that the overwhelming cultural norm that would cause people to abandon me in such droves for speaking out on human rights is Religious Tolerance. Whenever I shared this content, with Muslim friends or non-Muslim friends, I was permanently blocked. They didn't care about the human rights issues of Ex-Muslims and my perception of them being compassionate and kind people was proven wrong. In fact, when the topic of Islam versus Muslim rights came-up on a Friend's Facebook feed and I mentioned my concerns when this friend was attempting to lecture another person in their own Facebook friend group about bigotry, they blocked me after I refuted their argument with facts and my own concerns about the human rights of Ex-Muslims. I don't believe that any personal disappointments I've dealt with could match the monumental disappointment and sadness I felt when I was forced to accept the facts and view all these people, who I had thought were wonderful and compassionate, in a new light. It was as Christopher Hitchens had always warned: *"Religion Poisons Everything"* and it further cemented that Religious Tolerance was morally unconscionable as a position for me. The only ones willing to discuss, listen to, and talk about helping Ex-Muslims with their human rights issues were Liberal Atheists and Anti-Theists who wish to push for Secular moral values and a scant few Christian apologists like David Wood who wish to push for Christian moral values. What brings such divisive groups together on the topic of Ex-Muslims? Their genuine concern for the human rights of Ex-Muslims. It's a concern that the majority on the Left and Right who value Religious Tolerance don't share judging by the best available evidence that I have accumulated in the absence of survey studies. I fear that even if such studies were conducted, they could react like the Trump election surveys with people lying about their actual behavior and so a more thorough study on actions by people who value Religious Tolerance would need to be conducted to verify their true beliefs and actions.

Those of you who are concerned about this issue and who wish to contribute in ending these dangerous beliefs may be wondering: What can be done? Is it all hopeless? Should the answer be to just give-up, ignore it, and allow Ex-Muslims to suffer by being apathetic to their plight? *Never!* And, it is not necessarily the case that all is lost or that the threat of Islamism is guaranteed to take over the West. For example, despite Islam being the fastest breeding religion, it hasn't grown at all in the United States because as many people leave Islam as much as they convert to it.[2097] However, I must emphasize, that if you are serious and willing to

---

36. [2097] "Islam Gains about as Many Converts as It Loses in U.S." *Pew Research Center*, www.pewresearch.org/fact-tank/2018/01/26/the-share-of-americans-who-leave-islam-is-offset-by-those-who-become-muslim/.

combat Islamism, then you should only proceed with these suggestions if you honestly care about the human rights of both Muslims and Ex-Muslims. Ex-Muslims want to normalize dissent because they care about victims of Islam and they believe the largest victims to be Muslims themselves; this often includes their own families. This is neither condoning violence against Muslims nor imposing bigoted laws against Muslims; Muslims are people and Islam is a dangerous ideology that poisons their minds and makes them believe absurd beliefs that lead to harmful actions. The point is to care about Muslims as fellow human beings and not to harm them. To better understand this, I'd like to share a perspective I had unlearned thanks to listening to the Ex-MNA content of Ex-Muslim Anti-theist Armin Navabi but I'll have to step back a bit to explain the significance and how one of his panel discussions significantly impacted my life for the better despite that impact having nothing to do with Islam or Muslims, per se.

Due to my curiosity about themes leading me to find a blog by someone named Sam Hatting in 2009 that explained the influence of the philosophical novel *Thus Spake Zarathustra* by Friedrich Nietzsche upon a video game that quickly became one of my all-time favorites, *Shin Megami Tensei: Nocturne,* which was made by the gaming company known as Atlus; I became interested in Friedrich Nietzsche's philosophy and plunged into reading it after multiple completed playthroughs of *Shin Megami Tensei: Nocturne.*[2098] In the course of my reading, Friedrich Nietzsche's *Beyond Good and Evil,* I read Nietzsche's detailed response to an issue I had tried to understand about myself for practically my entire life. Why did I always ask questions that made other people uncomfortable? Why did I always get so inexplicably curious only to get rebuffed for touching the taboo subject matter of religion and other political topics? Why did I enjoy discussing taboo topics from suicide, to religion, and to other subjects implicitly deemed demonic by the wider Christian society? What was the internal cause that made me behave this way towards others and for which others had told me that it was something they didn't like about me? According to Friedrich Nietzsche, who described having the same desire but in far more of a meaningful explanation than mine and which caused him to suffer animosity from the people that he cared about, he had concluded that the desire to ask about such perturbing questions was due to an innate desire for cruelty within people like himself towards other people.[2099] This answer devastated me. It felt like a heart-wrenching punch and I felt that it validated all the horrible criticisms I had endured all my early life. Nietzsche went onto explain that the cure for people like himself, whom he classified as Free Spirits in the context of the book, was to seek true freedom by simply concealing ourselves and our views so that we could hold back our cruelty towards our loved ones and speak or write about our personal views in a more private fashion among those we classified as social equals

---

37. [2098] Hatting, Sam. "Sam Hatting: 'Shin Megami Tensei III: Nocturne and Nietzsche's Übermensch.'" 女神転生・学, A Megami Tensei Study Guide, 5 Apr. 2013, megatengaku.wordpress.com/essays/sam-hatting-shin-megami-tensei-iii-nocturne-and-nietzsches-ubermensch/.
38. [2099] Nietzsche, Friedrich Wilhelm. *Beyond Good and Evil*. Translated by Helen Zimmern, Word ed., Gutenberg Press, 2009.

so as not to disturb our loved ones peace of mind.[2100] If there were no such social equals, then it was better to conceal oneself because by concealing our views, we simply agreed with others so as not to hurt their feelings and kept focused on our personal goals in private. Nietzsche made sure to explicitly explain that we must not deceive ourselves about our tendency for cruelty upon others so that we maintain ourselves as Free Spirits from the masses instead of hurting them.[2101] I took the advice to heart and it opened so many doors that I thought was impossible by simply concealing my personal views since I thought it would hurt others feelings to reveal them. In fact, it inspired me to write under the pseudonym that I chose for this book when I initially started. I did get frustrated too often to my liking since I lived in a purportedly free country but the social norms dictated not to step out of line on certain implicit taboos. I felt stifled throughout my entire life even before reading Nietzsche's books and taking Nietzsche's advice to heart because I genuinely didn't want to hurt the feelings of either my family or classmates so I kept it all to myself. I did end up slipping up many times to make arguments about human rights crimes in classes out of what was my concern for the lives of Palestinian civilians or on rare occasions question the religious taboos in society that could credibly be linked to such violence like the Israel-Palestine divide. Nevertheless, despite what I felt were personal failings, I tried to stick to it even to the point of making it obvious to my entire family by never explaining when they questioned my behavior and I kept on sticking to it because I thought telling the truth would hurt their feelings; besides which, being open and honest had never worked when I expressed myself anyway throughout my entire life with my parents or in the high school I went to. I was repeatedly called crazy in public, even before I had read Friedrich Nietzsche, so his advice on concealment did make a lot of sense to me at the time and I obtained results like being able to join clubs that would otherwise be uncomfortable for others because of my atheist views; I joined a few so that I could learn more about religion as a good baseline for writing this book. Obtaining internships, jobs, and so forth all became slightly easier so I thought it was the correct path; I shouldn't express my personal views as an atheist because they would be viewed as too radical and that it would result in a loss of job opportunities. Such was the life in a so-called free country which I had assumed was only the veneer of freedom and that I had been conditioned by society through high school to understand that it had never meant real freedoms under the US Constitution. After all, the US government was rather flippant about when it applied such as with Occupy Wall Street protests, the Dakota Access Pipeline protests, the extrajudicial killings of Black people, the rape and torture of Native American women by non-Native men that the Western mainstream media disingenuously and likely with racist motivations tried to portray as a "Native problem" to blame the rape victims and their communities[2102], the fact the US Supreme Court ruled in

---

39. [2100] Nietzsche, Friedrich Wilhelm. *Beyond Good and Evil*. Translated by Helen Zimmern, Word ed., Gutenberg Press, 2009.
40. [2101] Nietzsche, Friedrich Wilhelm. *Beyond Good and Evil*. Translated by Helen Zimmern, Word ed., Gutenberg Press, 2009.
41. [2102] Williams, Timothy. "Native Americans Struggle With High Rate of Rape." *The New York Times*, The New York Times, 22 May 2012, www.nytimes.com/2012/05/23/us/native-americans-struggle-with-high-

Castle Rock v. Gonzales that the police don't have a duty to protect US citizens which were codified as "private citizens" so the public duty doctrine didn't apply to the US public, the legalized corruption with lobbyists spending millions for their own self-interests, the possibility that legal disputes using arbitration by US corporations may eventually result in Muslim CEOs introducing Sharia Courts through arbitration by making sure not to call it Sharia Courts, and so forth. Democratic rights was just a joke that the gullible believed; having been born and raised in the US all my life, that was my understanding of the United States of America due to the social conditioning of US society up until 2018 when I began listening to the college panels of *Ex-Muslims of North America*. Although there were times where I tried to fight against such feelings as too cynical, the cynicism always seemed to be validated by the results in the news. Yet, I eventually changed my mind and it was mostly thanks to an Ex-Muslims of North America panel discussion by Armin Navabi. I had warmed up to the idea of defending Enlightenment values and democratic freedoms after listening to the safety risks that Ex-Muslims endure even in the US which should technically be the safest place on the planet for them to live their lives, but it was not ideally safe because of the very credible threat of being killed for their apostasy. That really caused me to change my outlook on the entire US conflict with the Middle East since even the Western mainstream media depicted that as extremism and not normalized up until Ex-MNA gained a larger presence online due to their campus tours which were about normalizing dissent within Muslim communities and building communities for Ex-Muslims who were ostracized and driven out by their Muslim families. I had no idea such problems even arose since I had never seen it among my Muslim friends and family whenever I had interacted with them so I wasn't even aware of these social issues. It wasn't until listening to the panel "*The Future of Islam*" with Ex-MNA Co-Founder and President Muhammad Syed, Faith to Faithless Founder Imtiaz Shams, and Armin Navabi the Founder of the Atheist Republic that I had a perspective change after having gradually shifted my views thanks to listening to some of the other videos beforehand. In the panel, Armin Navabi's main thrust in his argument was that criticizing and challenging Islam was out of compassion for the victims of Islam and that the primary victims of Islam are Muslims themselves.[2103] So, challenging the bad beliefs, and in effect hurting their feelings, was not out of spite or contempt but out of utter compassion to get them away from dangerous ideas that could lead them to horrifying actions or lead them into becoming unnecessary victims.[2104] This meant that the intrinsic desire to challenge taboo ideas that Nietzsche had portrayed as cruelty on the part of those who challenged them was thoroughly wrong. Nietzsche's views on this particular issue was shown to be a falsehood to me and it was thanks to Armin Navabi's explanation that criticizing harmful ideas didn't mean ill intent, or selfishness, or some deep animosity towards others; instead, what it truly meant was selfless compassion and concern for

---

42. [2103] Navabi, Armin. "Attacking Islam as an Act of Compassion - Armin Navabi." *YouTube*, Ex-Muslims of North America, 4 Dec. 2017, www.youtube.com/watch?v=9m7IaAlnkgo.
43. [2104] Navabi, Armin. "Attacking Islam as an Act of Compassion - Armin Navabi." *YouTube*, Ex-Muslims of North America, 4 Dec. 2017, www.youtube.com/watch?v=9m7IaAlnkgo.

their wellbeing out of love for family, friends, and perhaps even strangers. I felt relieved that I didn't have to think of myself as a monster for challenging people on taboo subjects and I honestly can't thank Armin Navabi enough for explaining it so emphatically on that panel discussion. When I think of why Friedrich Nietzsche wrote that explanation of cruelty, it seems to me that Friedrich Nietzsche had tragically internalized the bigotry thrown his way during his life and never was given a helpful hand or a compassionate opposing viewpoint so that he didn't have to think of himself as a monster. I wonder to what degree it influenced his horribly patriarchal and misogynistic polemic against equality for women and his ardent defense of traditionalist views on gender roles in the second-half of *Beyond Good and Evil*.[2105]

For those concerned about the future growth of Islam in both the West and possibly within non-Islamic countries; what needs to be done is to tip the scales on those statistics so that each successive year more people leave Islam than convert to it. If each successive study on conversion and de-conversions in each country show an increase in de-conversions and a decrease in conversions to Islam, then we'll know that it is working. This is fundamentally an ideological cold war against a culture of anti-intellectualism and the cure is to attack the religious assumptions that Islam is predicated upon along with arguments in favor of Enlightenment values, Free Speech, Free Expression, an emphasis on Human Rights, and philosophical criticisms against all forms of Islamism. In the Further Reading section, I have a Further Watching section in which I list several Ex-Muslim activists whose videos can be of monumental value in changing the conversation on Religious Tolerance. If you feel concerned about this issue, then I recommend listening to as many as you possibly can to be better informed on Ex-Muslim issues; if you're like me and prefer a more academic approach, then I recommend listening to Ex-Muslims of North America's college panels on their Youtube channel. If you find most academic settings boring and would prefer sarcastic remarks and wry humor, but with Pew polls and extensive research into Islamic theology, then I recommend the Youtube channel Apostate Prophet. If, however, you prefer listening to personal accounts and narratives by Ex-Muslims, then the other recommended Ex-Muslim videos are likely more to your personal preference. We must become better informed about the issue of Islamism ourselves by listening to Ex-Muslims to then be more sharp and powerful in our criticisms. *The more we normalize dissent on behalf of the human rights of Ex-Muslims, the safer they will be to live their lives without fear of being murdered for the crime of independent thought. The more we help them to normalize dissent on Islam, the less we will ever have to worry about the threat of Islamization of non-Muslim countries whether in the democratic countries of the West or other democratic countries like India.* To be clear about engagement, this should only be towards locations or social media groups that invite controversial political opinions with Muslims who are willing to engage. This shouldn't be misconstrued as suggesting that we run up to Muslims or perceived Muslims like men of the Sikh faith and begin barraging them with accusations of bigotry and shouting at them to change their ways as that isn't how you have a

---

44. [2105] Nietzsche, Friedrich Wilhelm. *Beyond Good and Evil*. Translated by Helen Zimmern, Word ed., Gutenberg Press, 2009.

meaningful exchange of dialogue or get people willing to change their views. Having clothing or discussions depicting horrible Islamic verses as a Free Speech protest can make changes happen. The *freedom to offend* is just as key to changing views on Islam, even if it hurts people's feelings. What it means is finding areas where people allow controversial political topics such as on Discord servers, Facebook groups, Twitter, Reddit forums, and so forth; share Ex-Muslim content that you believe is most effective to get engaging discussions going and challenge them on arguments you've read, listened to, watched, or formed on your own to challenge Islam's theology. It may not have worked for me, but my experience is an anecdote and perhaps others can think of more refined strategies to improve engagement with these taboo social issues.

What if nothing changes? What if there is no de-conversions? What if we just repeatedly get blocked or banned? First, I want to point out that given Islam probably requires a lower IQ to ever believe as truth, I find it highly unlikely that criticizing Islam won't work since many Muslims get deeply offended by stick-figures with the name "Prophet Mohammad" on them. Judging from just that evidence, I find it unlikely that they would not begin to doubt and de-convert from Islam with this approach as long as we are consistent with the message of Free Speech and Human Rights, relentless in our resolve for defending the human rights of Ex-Muslims, and above all, *honest* about our approach. Armin Navabi mentioned and argued in the discussion panel that even if Muslims never give-up on their faith in Islam, it would still be enough to bring a seed of doubt into their minds because nobody sacrifices their lives for something that they are only ninety-nine percent certain about.[2106] The offer of complete certainty, of absolute surrender of the mind to the idea of a higher being, is why many young Muslims join Jihadist groups despite living in safe and luxurious countries in the West. It isn't merely an in-group identity of the *Ummah* (the community), but also the certainty of a higher importance that guarantees ones place, even if all it amounts to in the real world is a renunciation of the life they have for the sake of death worship which they view as submission to their interpretation of the Abrahamic God. It is the belief that their God wishes them to follow a higher purpose. If you nudge that belief that many Muslims have and put their *faith in doubt*, then according to Ex-Muslims, you will not have to worry about them devoting their life and time to the possibility of Islamization of non-Islamic countries. It is because the belief that Islamization is an absolute moral good that can't be questioned because the Abrahamic God commands them to do it will itself be put into doubt and could lead to severe questioning from then onward. Violence is not the answer to the threat of Islamization, exposing Muslims to thoughts and ideas that effectively make them doubt Islam is the peaceful, effective, and the most powerful route to changing the conversation. If we care about human rights, civil liberties, and our societies wherever that we may live whether it be in the West or not, then we must be allowed to criticize, question, and challenge beliefs that are controversial and Religious Tolerance gets in the way of doing that. *Religious Tolerance prevents us from truly*

---

45. [2106] Navabi, Armin. "Doubt as an Alternative to Reform - Armin Navabi." *YouTube*, Ex-Muslims of North America, 5 Dec. 2017, www.youtube.com/watch?v=Zk70fXQgZwY.

caring about our fellow human beings and that is why I am opposed to it. People do change their minds; not immediately, but over a lengthy amount of time of self-reflection; it's long, arduous, and I have personally found myself repeatedly insulted as having deceptive motives, but change is real, it is possible, and openly expressing our values of Free Speech, Free Expression, and Free Inquiry is the most effective way of protecting our values.

What if we're not good at criticizing? What if we make the situation worse by arguing poorly and Islam ends-up looking more favorable in discussions and arguments? Before I begin, I'd like to preface that this obviously doesn't include examples where our or our loved ones personal safety would be at risk, but rather in free and open societies where such challenges are possible with safety measures against physical dangers are in place. First, it is critical to remind ourselves that we are all fallible human beings and that such situations will unfortunately happen, but what we must put focus in is the statistical percentage of Muslims who listen and de-convert as that is the chief aim. The Atheist Youtuber, Shannon Q, provided a crucial video on topics similar to this and explained her argument in favor of criticizing harmful ideas. She points out that people need exposure to different perspectives in multiple settings to become open to changing their ideas and without that exposure, it is unlikely to ever happen.[2107] We simply don't believe ourselves to be thinking incorrectly without exposure to different perspectives that challenge our beliefs.[2108] While confirmation bias does set in to prevent people from changing their mind and we all have such a bias, consistent findings of counter arguments can eventually lead to change.[2109] The more that hateful or bad beliefs proliferate and take hold of communities, major areas of a country, or an entire country; the more these harmful beliefs need to be challenged so that they don't become widespread in causing further harm and so that they are rebuked back by sharp criticisms which we proliferate to protect our values for the sake of human rights for all people. If we seek views that confirm our biases and shy away from views that could change our minds, what can we really do to change them within ourselves and others? Shannon suggests that in the context of people gullibly following a cult leader, we should seek to challenge such cult leaders in debates and counter their claims.[2110] However, a crucial rebuttal to this idea is that argument that providing odious views a platform could cause more people to convert to such deplorable viewpoints. Moreover, what if we do poorly in our criticisms or debates and are soundly refuted? Wouldn't such a failure from that engagement cause more harm? Shannon's counter is this: *"If we all relinquish the opportunity for fear that we may fail, they exist without*

---

46. [2107] Q, Shannon. "To Debate or Not to Debate? Can You Be a Responsible Platformer: w TellTale." *YouTube*, YouTube, 15 Mar. 2019, www.youtube.com/watch?v=31jFFOmMaZs.
47. [2108] Q, Shannon. "To Debate or Not to Debate? Can You Be a Responsible Platformer: w TellTale." *YouTube*, YouTube, 15 Mar. 2019, www.youtube.com/watch?v=31jFFOmMaZs.
48. [2109] Q, Shannon. "To Debate or Not to Debate? Can You Be a Responsible Platformer: w TellTale." *YouTube*, YouTube, 15 Mar. 2019, www.youtube.com/watch?v=31jFFOmMaZs.
49. [2110] Q, Shannon. "To Debate or Not to Debate? Can You Be a Responsible Platformer: w TellTale." *YouTube*, YouTube, 15 Mar. 2019, www.youtube.com/watch?v=31jFFOmMaZs.

opposition."[2111] Their views will seem unassailable and social proof may cause people to believe there is some deeper cause for why their popularity is increasing. By not challenging them, we could create a self-fulfilling prophecy in which they will rise to power and could cause dangerous consequences for the people that we are seeking to defend. How does that help the people that we care about? How does it make even our lives better? Shannon goes onto explain that if after we fail, and we could because we are all fallible human beings, then we shouldn't discourage others from making attempts to challenge the person holding repulsive views because they could be the ones that successfully help to sway people to our cause in defense of the human rights of people that we're concerned about.[2112] According to Shannon, although in the context of people who have audiences on social media, if we wish to challenge reprehensible ideologies, then our arguments must be cogent and our approach must be tactical because what we do matters more than we probably recognize because people with hateful beliefs who feel empowered to enact them would be of far worse consequences for everyone, especially if they continue having those horrible beliefs reinforced with no challenge at all.[2113] Of course, you don't necessarily need to have the same type of tools to challenge harmful beliefs; people can do so through different means from vlogs, blogs, books (such as this one), challenging a friend's views, challenging a member of your community whether in real life or social media platforms like Reddit or Discord servers, and so forth to spread *dissent* against harmful ideas. In the absence of being able to challenge the person spreading the idea directly, this is the next best option and likely the only option for most people. As Shannon explains, *"Multiple approaches are required, if our ultimate goals are the same."*[2114] If we discourage others who share our goals from trying to challenge cult leaders and their supporters with harmful ideas, we're leaving ourselves vulnerable and the people who we're fighting for will be the ones directly suffering the consequences of our incompetence. As Shannon continues on, *"If you feel that their counter was ineffective and you truly desire minds be changed; Offer an answer, offer support, engage with each other and share ideas that can improve the approach and increase the likelihood of a preferential outcome the next time. There is no one best and only way to attack the bad ideas, but there are so many ways to create factions that act as a deterrent from encouraging one another to even try."*[2115] If we care about the human rights of the LGBT community, women's rights, and the human rights of Ex-Muslims then we must engage and criticize those who hold harmful beliefs that could lead to dangerous consequences for those that we care about. To not do so is to fail them as nefarious actors seek to impose

---

50. [2111] Q, Shannon. "To Debate or Not to Debate? Can You Be a Responsible Platformer: w TellTale." *YouTube*, YouTube, 15 Mar. 2019, www.youtube.com/watch?v=31jFFOmMaZs.
51. [2112] Q, Shannon. "To Debate or Not to Debate? Can You Be a Responsible Platformer: w TellTale." *YouTube*, YouTube, 15 Mar. 2019, www.youtube.com/watch?v=31jFFOmMaZs.
52. [2113] Q, Shannon. "To Debate or Not to Debate? Can You Be a Responsible Platformer: w TellTale." *YouTube*, YouTube, 15 Mar. 2019, www.youtube.com/watch?v=31jFFOmMaZs.
53. [2114] Q, Shannon. "To Debate or Not to Debate? Can You Be a Responsible Platformer: w TellTale." *YouTube*, YouTube, 15 Mar. 2019, www.youtube.com/watch?v=31jFFOmMaZs.
54. [2115] Q, Shannon. "To Debate or Not to Debate? Can You Be a Responsible Platformer: w TellTale." *YouTube*, YouTube, 15 Mar. 2019, www.youtube.com/watch?v=31jFFOmMaZs.

harm upon them and consider this: the reason they feel emboldened, gain popularity, and eventually gain power is due to us ignoring them or vilifying them as a person instead of sharply criticizing their ideas.

It bears reminding that engaging people with harmful beliefs should exclude people who would physically seek to harm you or your loved ones. Engaging with those types of people is genuinely dangerous and most importantly, they are not seeking to engage in a dialogue. The people who should be sought out and refuted are people who are able, willing, and *honest* about engaging in a dialogue. To be clear, this is not to assume dishonesty or to accuse people of hypocrisy, those are just personal biases that we hold which we're imposing upon others. *Dishonesty in this context means people who aren't even listening to your arguments. You can't have a meaningful dialogue when people who don't listen, evaluate, and respond as you respond back to them.* So for instance, a Discord Server in which people just insult you, say that your response is too long to read or they're too bored to read, and who only engage in insults are obviously not being honest actors. As you can probably tell, I am explaining this from personal experience. People must be willing to listen to your arguments and you can reciprocate by listening to their arguments; a level of mutual respect must be maintained. This doesn't mean that you or the other person can't engage in wisecracks, but rather that you focus on the topic issue and don't devolve into personal insults. Of course, engaging in the topic of religion or other human rights issues like Transgender rights is likely to get a person banned from servers, internet web forums, perhaps even from private locations, and so forth; but even so, they react because your dissent makes them uncomfortable. Keep engaging in other places and keep at it. As a group with shared goals in human rights, we must be persistent, clear, engaged in responses to any questions, and firm on the goal of human rights for all people in our societies. We must also be willing to admit when we're wrong, understand that sometimes we'll lose debates or discussions in the process, learn more by seeking out facts and evidence to improve our positions, and re-engage in all forms of dialogue. *Most importantly, we must always remember that we're fallible human beings who can be deceived by others and admit when we've been deceived in order to spot deception more readily and correct ourselves.*[2116] We must always be willing to make incremental changes to our beliefs, think over where we learned our beliefs, and upgrade appropriately when we run into overwhelming counter-evidence by reliable experts or the factual evidence.[2117] *That is what it means to engage in self-surpassing ourselves.*[2118]

---

55. [2116] Konnikova, Maria. *The Confidence Game: the Psychology of the Con and Why We Fall for It Every Time*. Canongate, 2017.
56. [2117] Duke, Annie. *Thinking in Bets: Making Smarter Decisions When You Don't Have All the Facts.* Penguin Group (USA), 2018.
57. [2118] Nietzsche, Friedrich Wilhelm. *Thus spake Zarathustra: a book for all and none*. Translated by Thomas Common, PDF ed., T. Common, 1908.

Final Thoughts

"Now, happily most Christians and Jews now disregard the morality on offer in the Old Testament and they rationalize the barbarity we find there by saying: "Oh, this was appropriate to the time - was appropriate to the ancient world." The idea being that the Canaanites were so ill-behaved that just getting together a short list of reasons to kill your neighbor and sticking to it was a great improvement over the general barbarity of the time. No, it wasn't. It was within the moral compass of human beings then to recognize that killing somebody for adultery was evil. The Buddha managed it, Mahavira the Jain patriarch managed it, numerous Greek philosophers managed it. So, Jews and Christians are simply lying to themselves when they talk about the impediments to morality that prevailed in the fifth century BC and the other thing to notice is that rationalizing the barbarism we find in the Old Testament merely renders it irrelevant, it doesn't render these books morally-wise. It is faint praise indeed, if the best that can be said of much of Scripture is that it can now be safely ignored. Now, despite what Christians say on the subject, the New Testament isn't so good as to make the Bible a reliable basis of morality. In fact, much of the book is an embarrassment to anybody who would say that it is a moral book, much less a perfectly moral book and nowhere is this clearer than on the question of slavery. The truth is the Bible in its totality - Old Testament, New Testament - supports slavery."[2119] - Sam Harris, Aspen Ideas Festival in July 2007.

When I was young, I always had a tendency to question what was considered taboo subject matter. I didn't quite understand why that was or why other people were so disinterested in questioning different taboos of society. I was prone to thinking about societal dynamics of power and what led to people becoming world leaders versus the average people that I was amongst. When I spoke of criticizing religion or morbid topics that I was curious about like morality in war compared to societal morality, societal morality versus conditions in other countries, or the topic of suicide, I was always viewed with some form of derision and it led to allegations that I wanted to pursue violence of some kind. However, more than any of that, the topic of religion was what really caused a stir amongst people; I mostly spoke of it among my age group with classmates I had familiarized myself with in school since it was obvious that adults would simply think you were crazy for being an atheist. Why didn't anyone think about the demographics of different religions across the world and the unlikely chance of a single denomination even in a specific religion being correct like I did? It wasn't until being introduced to the Youtube video of Sam Harris at the Aspen Festival by my younger sister in 2007 that I stopped feeling like something was mentally wrong with me. Discussing the topic with classmates who were also atheist had helped too as did watching the Youtuber TJ Kirk, but they weren't anywhere near as articulate in deconstructing the problems with religion like Sam Harris. It was Sam Harris explaining and picking apart the faultiness of religion that helped me by making me stop feeling like I was somehow either crazy or that the accusations by educational institutions that I was somehow a danger to others were true. Before then, I had

---

58. [2119] Harris, Sam. "Sam Harris Aspen Ideas Festival Full Unedited Video." *YouTube*, Aspen Institute, 25 Nov. 2012, www.youtube.com/watch?v=hfgwFESH_jM.

learned to internalize that fear and keep it to myself. It was Sam Harris and later Christopher Hitchens numerous debate videos that I vociferously watched throughout my early college years that got me through feeling like others were right to judge me with disdain should I ever reveal I was an atheist. They were not only highly entertaining in debates, but invaluable in helping atheists like myself feel comfortable with who we are.

I would go so far as to argue that New Atheist criticisms of religion helped normalize it among the Millennial generation and in my personal opinion, whatever their personal foibles on social media, they deserve to be remembered as the greatest contemporary thinkers of our time for bringing about that social change. I don't believe that most people in our lives can come close to Richard Dawkins, Sam Harris, or Christopher Hitchens in terms of wit, argumentation, and especially empathy for those who suffer religious persecution or religiously sponsored discrimination. I had thought compassionate people like them to be the norm, but I was sorely mistaken. For all those impotent moralists among journalism or so-called Christian philosophers in academia, as if Christianity had anything to offer intellectually, it was not their books being illegally translated and downloaded ten million times throughout the Arab world and Iran by eager people who live under Islamic oppression but rather Richard Dawkins "*The God Delusion*" that was worth the risk to their personal safety.[2120] People are so invested in New Atheism across the world, they literally risk death to read "*The God Delusion*" and if that doesn't show the contemporary importance of the New Atheist philosophies to our cultural understanding of the globalized world, then what does?[2121] I have yet to see evidence likewise of people risking their lives to read contemporary Christian philosophers like William Lane Craig. For any of these ostentatious and insular Christian philosophers which hold influence in contemporary Western academia, whose conclusions about serving Jesus would have to be drawn before they even make their philosophies; what exactly is the point of trying to explore philosophy if you're never allowed to disagree with the conclusions that Jesus Christ teaches you about how to live life properly? What new and exciting ideas can you ever provide when shackled to the teachings of a 1st century godman who seemed to only bellow his own narcissistic ravings with the psychotic threat of hell on those who disagreed with him? Apparently, Christian philosophy's greatest achievement is Intelligent Design.[2122] It is a teaching that, for those children who leave it and learn scientific evidence to verify truth claims, often conclude that Intelligent Design is child abuse. So, the books of Richard Dawkins and possibly his cohorts helped and were eagerly devoured by people in the most despotic countries; it gave them peace of mind and valuable reading material that they were so

---

59. [2120] Ghazzali, Kacem El. "Reading 'The God Delusion' In The Arab World." *HuffPost Canada*, HuffPost Canada, 10 May 2017, www.huffingtonpost.ca/kacem-el-ghazzali/the-god-delusion_b_9867606.html.
60. [2121] Ghazzali, Kacem El. "Reading 'The God Delusion' In The Arab World." *HuffPost Canada*, HuffPost Canada, 10 May 2017, www.huffingtonpost.ca/kacem-el-ghazzali/the-god-delusion_b_9867606.html.
61. [2122] Craig, William Lane. "The Revolution in Anglo-American Philosophy | Reasonable Faith." *Philosophic Revolution | Popular Writings | Reasonable Faith*, www.reasonablefaith.org/writings/popular-writings/apologetics/the-revolution-in-anglo-american-philosophy/.

engrossed with that they risked death to read them, while people in First World countries have contemporary Christian philosophers to thank for concocting a legalized way to vandalize the minds of children with pseudo-scientific mythology they term as Intelligent Design.[2123] By the way, to be clear so there is no ambiguity, the people primarily calling it child abuse are the people who were taught Intelligent Design as children. All because Christian philosophers in the late 1900s wasted their lives to concoct psychotic beliefs about the world and tried to push it as science when it had nothing to do with science.[2124] For all the talk of New Atheism being "scientism" as an argument against it, there seems to be no criticism whatsoever of Christian philosophers peddling pseudo-scientific filth throughout the late 1900s in an attempt to bridge the gap of science and philosophy with their psychotic beliefs in the teachings of Jesus Christ.[2125] Meanwhile, New Atheists have been consistently reviled throughout the Western mainstream media for what seems to be the crime of being fallible human beings when engaging in social media. While the Western mainstream media continued to revile their views on religion as too extreme; the Catholic Church[2126], Southern Baptists[2127], and Jehovah's Witnesses[2128] were all revealed to have a decade or several decades of child rape scandals hidden from the legal authorities. In the case of the Catholic Church, it was across multiple countries. In Islamic countries, rape conversions - that is, kidnapping non-Muslim girls as young as 9 to rape them and convert them to Islam in what is a forcible rape and marriage without their consent[2129] - is the increasing social norm in countries like Pakistan, the war zone of Syria, and rape including gang rape is utilized; furthermore, rape has been a tool to silence male and female atheists in Bangladesh and Pakistan.[2130][2131] In Afghanistan, they're outright

---

62. [2123] Craig, William Lane. "The Revolution in Anglo-American Philosophy | Reasonable Faith." *Philosophic Revolution | Popular Writings | Reasonable Faith*, www.reasonablefaith.org/writings/popular-writings/apologetics/the-revolution-in-anglo-american-philosophy/.
63. [2124] Craig, William Lane. "The Revolution in Anglo-American Philosophy | Reasonable Faith." *Philosophic Revolution | Popular Writings | Reasonable Faith*, www.reasonablefaith.org/writings/popular-writings/apologetics/the-revolution-in-anglo-american-philosophy/.
64. [2125] Craig, William Lane. "The Revolution in Anglo-American Philosophy | Reasonable Faith." *Philosophic Revolution | Popular Writings | Reasonable Faith*, www.reasonablefaith.org/writings/popular-writings/apologetics/the-revolution-in-anglo-american-philosophy/.
65. [2126] Park, Madison. "Timeline: A Look at the Catholic Church's Sex Abuse Scandals." *CNN*, Cable News Network, 29 June 2017, www.cnn.com/2017/06/29/world/timeline-catholic-church-sexual-abuse-scandals/index.html.
66. [2127] Downen, Robert, et al. "20 Years, 700 Victims: Southern Baptist Sexual Abuse Spreads as Leaders Resist Reforms." *Houston Chronicle*, Houston Chronicle, 6 June 2019, www.houstonchronicle.com/news/investigations/article/Southern-Baptist-sexual-abuse-spreads-as-leaders-13588038.php.
67. [2128] Bundy, Trey. "Jehovah's Witnesses Use 1st Amendment to Hide Child Sex Abuse Claims." *Reveal*, 29 Nov. 2018, www.revealnews.org/article/jehovahs-witnesses-use-1st-amendment-to-hide-child-sex-abuse-claims/.
68. [2129] "Pakistani Hindus Complain of Forced Conversion of Teenage Girls." *YouTube*, VOA News, 18 Mar. 2016, youtu.be/-i24jg4mJ4I.
69. [2130] Hashem, Rumana. "Has Rape Become a Weapon to Silence Atheists in Bangladesh?" *OpenDemocracy*, www.opendemocracy.net/en/5050/rape-weapon-silence-atheists-bangladesh/.

killed for even the unfounded assumption of insulting the Quran.[2132] While Richard Dawkins was assisting in the promotion of *Center for Inquiry*'s mission of *Secular Rescue* to help save the lives of people being persecuted and brutally murdered in the Islamist country of Bangladesh[2133], the Western mainstream media saw fit to ignore any of his humanitarian efforts in order to repeatedly present him as a bigot suffering from myopia. They cared so little about the victims of such heinous atrocities that they don't ever bother to write about what Richard Dawkins and the *Center for Inquiry* are trying to shed light upon in any of their endless stream of articles about what he said on Twitter with their outlandish claims about how he doesn't identify or concern himself with ethnic minorities while he's doing his utmost to share awareness of the suffering of people in religiously despotic countries, speak on their human rights issues, and discuss why Free Speech is vital so that the West can better address the problems of these religiously motivated views.[2134] He personally interviewed Rana Ahmad to learn about her life in the despotic regime of Saudi Arabia, the threats to her life from her own brother who came to Germany explicitly to kill her, to share more information about her book about what she had underwent in Saudi Arabia, and even that was wholly ignored by the Western mainstream media.[2135] The New Atheists have their flaws; they will probably always be making comments on social media that belies ignorance about various subject matter, reveals the insularity of their socio-economic status, perhaps even shows situations that some women or ethnic minorities go through that they haven't fully considered, or annoying things that Millennials find about older generations in general; nevertheless, all that proves is that they're fallible human beings like our neighbors, our teachers, our parents, our siblings, our closest friends, and us. They just happen to be more famous and harshly criticize bad ideas regardless of if it smashes into the sensibilities of Religious Tolerance or not. Social media melodrama about comments that people find ridiculous or asinine shouldn't outweigh their genuine concern for people's human rights and their assistance to help save the lives of vulnerable people throughout the world or their criticism of the harmful ideas within religion. The only gap I've ever seen is the case of continued association with Michael Shermer since they're not affiliated with the problems with The Amazing Meeting (TAM), but if a rape did indeed happen then that does need to be proven in a court of law.[2136] In the vast majority of

---

70. [2131] Sultan, Harris. "Rescue an Atheist in Pakistan, Spartacus." *YouTube*, YouTube, 12 Nov. 2018, www.youtube.com/watch?v=y154jQsEkQk.
71. [2132] "Murder of Farkhunda Malikzada." *Wikipedia*, Wikimedia Foundation, 11 June 2019, en.wikipedia.org/wiki/Murder_of_Farkhunda_Malikzada.
72. [2133] De Dora, Michael. "Secular Rescue - Saving Freedom. Saving Lives." *YouTube*, Richard Dawkins Foundation for Reason & Science, 30 Sept. 2016, www.youtube.com/watch?v=xM_JCxogySM.
73. [2134] De Dora, Michael. "Secular Rescue - Saving Freedom. Saving Lives." *YouTube*, Richard Dawkins Foundation for Reason & Science, 30 Sept. 2016, www.youtube.com/watch?v=xM_JCxogySM.
74. [2135] Dawkins, Richard, and Rana Ahmad. "Richard Dawkins Interviews Saudi Arabian Atheist Author Rana Ahmad." *YouTube*, Richard Dawkins Foundation for Reason & Science, 25 Feb. 2019, www.youtube.com/watch?v=_zncB6hngZg.
75. [2136] Oppenheimer, Mark. "Will Misogyny Bring Down The Atheist Movement?" *BuzzFeed*, BuzzFeed, 12 Sept. 2014, www.buzzfeed.com/markoppenheimer/will-misogyny-bring-down-the-atheist-movement?utm_term=.gd2E4jVYd#.cbZ23Vp9A.

times, they sacrifice any positive public image for the sake of being consistent with their values in support of human wellbeing. I do think that they deserve to be considered some of the greatest contemporary philosophers of our lifetime; in fairness, it is partly because Christian philosophy is merely anti-intellectualism because it requires the conclusions to always be made before asking any questions and the conclusions come with their own teachings of hatred for the human race under the religious concept of Original Sin.

    For those tired of my gushing of New Atheism, I would like to make note of the fact that despite my admiration for them after having reassessed my information about the problems of Islam and found them to be stating the harsh truth all along; it wasn't their influence that made me enamored with exploring rationality, skepticism, and empiricism as methods of verifying truth claims and subsequently influenced me to delve more deeply into reading human psychology. Moreover, it wasn't their influence that contributed to writing this book to critique religion from the perspective of cognitive and social psychology, logical fallacies, Nietzschean philosophy, and modern skepticism. New Atheism sprouted by initial interest in rationality, but it probably would have vanished eventually since I didn't have an interest in reading more deeply into the topic until much later since I didn't know what to look for as a baseline. While the contemporary Ex-Muslim movement, especially the illuminating panel discussions by the organization *Ex-Muslims of North America,* made me regain confidence in the US Republic and convinced me not to delete what was then a three-year draft of this book; they obviously weren't the ones who influenced my deeper interest in rationality, skepticism, and empiricism. I have only been a regular follower of theirs since 2018; I was pleasantly surprised that the public intellectuals Sam Harris, Christopher Hitchens, Richard Dawkins, and Daniel Dennett gave rise to a global Ex-Muslim movement with intellectual juggernauts like Sarah Haider, Muhammad Syed, Armin Navabi, and many others speaking on behalf of secular values against the falsehoods of religious dogma. Ex-Muslim atheists and anti-theists continue advocating for criticism of the hateful ideology of Islam, due to selfless love and compassion for their families and for other people from Muslim communities, while at real risk of death for making such challenges. Sarah Haider, Muhammad Syed, and others have publicly mentioned that New Atheism had an influence on their lives and the lives of many still living in the Islamic world in their journey towards atheism. In a very real way, the global Ex-Muslim movement is the second-generation of New Atheism. Of course, New Atheism isn't limited in its impact on Ex-Muslims; it has also influenced a new generation of incredibly intelligent young people who don't come from Islamic backgrounds and who are interested in philosophy and rationality such as Alex J. O'Connor (known online by his alias "Cosmic Skeptic") and Stephen Woodford (known as "Rationality Rules"). Even more astonishing, Ex-Muslim atheists and anti-theists along with Western atheists and anti-theists from other religious backgrounds seem to be coalescing into a *non-violent social movement of Transnational Anti-Theism* in order to combat the growing Islamization of the West with Free Speech to argue against harmful ideas, Free Inquiry to question religious assumptions, their own brand of Intersectional Feminism that questions the Islamic Patriarchy, and Enlightenment values in non-violent opposition to Islamic values of the Sharia. While I am very happy to bear witness to all of these events; they're obviously not what influenced writing this book since I began this book before I had ever watched their Youtube channels or heard of any of them. There is only one person whose social media influence convinced me to write this book and who was a profound influence on my personal drive to strive towards a more rational worldview. It wasn't any of the the New Atheists, it wasn't Ex-MNA, it wasn't Ex-Muslims or other Ex-religious folk who aren't affiliated with Ex-MNA, it wasn't any of my college professors, it wasn't anything from my mostly horrible time in high school, it wasn't any of my close friends, and it certainly wasn't any member of my family. The person whose content inspired me to write this book was Host of the *Rationally Speaking Podcast* and Co-Founder of *Center for Applied Rationality*, Julia Galef. It was Julia Galef's *Straw Vulcan* Youtube video that blossomed by interest in pursuing rationality, it was Julia Galef's recommendation of Daniel Kahneman's *Thinking Fast and Slow* on her personal website that made me interested in further exploring human psychology, and it was video content on Julia Galef's personal Youtube channel that made me further think of exploring a critique of religion on the basis of human psychology and how rationality would fit in that mold. In fact, I read Eliezier Yudkowsky's Fanfiction and his books partially to fill the dismay of Julia Galef having never published any books of her own on the topic of Rationality. Julia Galef is such an intelligent and inspiring person who takes great pains to emphasize that rationality isn't devoid of human empathy. I highly recommended checking out her old Youtube content because they were so fascinating and always challenged me to think differently. The content she produces is definitely the mark of quality over quantity.

The growing *Transnational Anti-Theism* is mostly circumscribed to Western countries and mostly contains challenges to Islam through the filter of Youtube, but these criticisms are having an impact in changing the conversations, keeping regular Westerners away from the appeal of Far-right bigotry, and challenging the religious dogma of Islam that causes so much harm upon Muslims themselves. It is possible that it runs the risk of becoming an echo chamber through social media channels. They may not even want this moniker that I've given them but it is my belief they're far more competent than what seems to be a growing crop of ignorant and worthless Foreign Policy analysts among respected Foreign Policy think tanks in the specific issue of deconstructing and countering the very real threat of Islamization in the West along with other forms of religious bigotry. One of my criticisms would be that instead of just adapting a position of hopefulness in creating doubt in Islamic communities that this growing anti-theist movement should also look into making reliable statistical surveys to better assess their impact in the West and to better ascertain their strengths and weaknesses to spread doubt on Islam and religion in general. I do believe that this is the right step forward to combat Islamization, far-right Christian extremism like White Nationalism and the KKK, and other odious views that are religiously motivated. Unlike the Western mainstream media, Think Tanks, the Intercept, or Chris Hedges, this movement is genuine in its commitment to human rights for all. Perhaps I'm desperate in wanting to see it shine because I'm weary of seeing religiously motivated violence be excused or ignored on the basis of Religious Tolerance. I would argue that they fit the definition of a transnational social movement since they are trying to defend the Western world from the real ills of Islamization, Far-right Christianity, and other forms of harmful religious beliefs and practices with speaking events across the West from the US, to Canada, to Australia, and the UK. Regardless of how ridiculous it seems to others, I do believe their current activities of challenging religious dogma is a good step forward for a more peaceful future; I believe that we should further help to inspire and grow a thriving non-violent Anti-Theist social movement to protect the human rights of all people, but focusing on the West is a good first step.

    What largely prevents people from disassociating from religion is the belief that there is an inherent lack of meaning with such an existence. I would challenge this claim by arguing religious meaning is simply a glorified worship of death and delusions of personal immortality which obfuscates finding personal fulfillment in real life. You've likely heard it before: *Nobody can tell you what the meaning of your life is, you must make your life into your own meaning.* What personal aspirations of yours would be worth suffering for? What personal beliefs of yours would be worth enduring failure for? You have to take the painful step to choose that for yourself; nobody can decide your life for you. The psychotic teachings of people who made narcissistic claims about their infallibility over a thousand years ago won't be of any help. Previously, in the section on Original Sin, I mentioned that nation-states exist to manipulate and use people for their own benefit and shared Erich Fromm's excerpt which explained how primitive countries began to form because of the earliest agricultural settlements enslaving other settlements and hunter-gatherers. Humans using other humans as tools of exploitation for their own benefit. The nation-state emerged by humans using fellow humans as tools of exploitation. However, despite whatever negative parallels are foisted in the modern era from Western governments curtailing civic freedoms out of fear of terrorism to unfettered corporate power silently dismantling political freedoms, regardless of how stupid it feels and how silly it is made out to be by the corporate-owned Western mainstream media; the best way to protect Enlightenment values, Civic freedoms, and democratic political power is by continuously exercising them in opposition to such threats. *The best way to protect democracy is by exercising the rights of a democracy.* Democracies and Republics are double-edged swords, but they're much healthier, safer, and freer than any other form of governance. Nation-states began by the enslavement of humans; but the best nation-states thrive by allowing its people to explore their full potentialities through personal liberty. Obviously, most people probably won't ever be interested in exploring their full potential, but the main benefit is that people are free to choose the life they wish to live so long as it doesn't harm others. Citizens being allowed Free Speech to harshly whine about stupid melodrama and also to shed understanding towards harmful practices that a government is doing, Free Inquiry to make stupidly offensive questions on a subset of the general public but also to challenge assumptions that could continue to be a detriment to a free society, and human rights to nihilistically complain about how brutal our countries are but to also highlight human rights issues that need to be either ameliorated or eventually are ameliorated by a democratic republic acknowledging its past wrongdoings. It was a struggle for me to believe in the US Republic, but only because it was being maintained by people who were dismantling and curtailing freedoms unopposed and who seemed to project an air of invincibility only for my personal criticisms to have been vindicated by the rise of President Donald Trump. I hope that I never lose faith in the US Republic, democracies and republics in general, and my own ability to make a small but meaningful contribution to others in US society and overseas as a citizen of a free society ever again.

If, like me, you're interested in decreasing the religious violence in the world and if this book has convinced you that such a goal would be beneficial then, what we need to do is continue making our own small contributions for a more holistic *Transvaluation of Values* regarding religion in both the West and throughout the world until beliefs in the supernatural no longer infect the human mind and cause horrific human rights abuses like in the barbarous countries of Pakistan and Saudi Arabia. It may seem pointless, but all small contributions help to blossom social movements that are about changing the lives of people for the better. *A Transvaluation of Values is about challenging religious assumptions about human life and the world in order to erode religious influence in public discourse and public policies that we all must live by under the law of our countries.* Therefore, Religious Tolerance impedes human rights and too often encourages people to ignore human rights abuses out of so-called respect or "sensitivity" for the sacred. Often this "sensitivity" can include genital mutilation and obfuscates religious activities that contribute to the rape of children. We must offer a non-violent resistance to such impositions on democratic freedoms and be the change we wish to see in our societies by advancing those changes ourselves. Demagogues rise and democracies fall when we fail to exercise our freedoms. Historically, religion has been receding and should continue to be receding so that it no longer harms humanity; it certainly won't fix all problems and I don't pretend that it will, but religion is too often an aphrodisiac of violence and that is particularly evident among the Abrahamic faiths. Even in small ways like homeopathy or wasting large quantities of money on fortune telling can conceivably be harmful. Opposing such views doesn't have to be dramatic rallies in protest, although when the situation calls for it then that would be beneficial for a functioning democracy, but small contributions like challenging our loved ones on religious assumptions when the topic comes up instead of having a patronizing view that they're better off wallowing in ignorance. Perhaps sharing with them our reasons why we don't believe, if they're the type to not behave unreasonably by threatening to block out, kick out, or harm us for opposing religious views. Above all, this is not to impugn their religious beliefs by supporting policies that discriminate against religious people, but rather to support policies that prevent religion from causing human rights abuses. On his 2007 Aspen Festival discussion on religion, Sam Harris explained how the slave holders of the South were on the winning side of the theological argument of the Bible in support of slavery[2137], it took a civil war to rectify Christian dogma in support of slavery in the United

---

76. [2137] Harris, Sam. "Sam Harris Aspen Ideas Festival Full Unedited Video." *YouTube*, Aspen Institute, 25

States; from then on, religion has slowly been receding thanks to a questioning of religious assumptions in the US through Free Speech, Freedom of Assembly, and Free Inquiry. The religious assumptions of women being viewed as property and not as people was slowly reversed from a *Transvaluation of Values* regarding Women's suffrage and property rights through First-wave Feminism. The religious assumptions of men never being held accountable for marital rape, domestic violence, and women having no rights to divorce were reversed by a *Transvaluation of Values* to upend those injustices through Second-wave Feminism. In some cases, and despite religion playing a prominent role in the Civil Rights movement, even the Civil Rights movement was a *Transvaluation of Values* against religion in some areas when factoring the racist beliefs that Mormonism espoused and was only abandoned shortly before the 1964 Civil Rights Act officially ended the racial discrimination of Black people so that the US represented a legitimate equality among US citizens of all ethnic backgrounds with the regrettable exception of the Native Americans. The Gay Rights movement was most certainly a *Transvaluation of Values* in opposition to religious dogma espoused by the Abrahamic faiths. The personal liberties of Pro-choice for Women's reproductive freedom, the human rights of Ex-Muslims and Native Americans, and the human rights of Transgender people should be the next steps forward as a *Transvaluation of Values* against religious bigotry and hate, so that religion no longer harms others in our free society, particularly vulnerable Transgender people, Native Americans, and Ex-Muslims in our contemporary times. *To defend the human rights of the vulnerable is to defend their right to personal liberty in a free society.* To do that, we must also be willing to defend the rights of people that we find to hold odious views about others. For example, as a challenge to readers who may identify as social justice advocates in the US, would you defend the human rights of a Transgender person who was an ardent Trump supporter? If you wouldn't consider helping them by assisting them and giving them aid or to listen to their concerns after they may have been vilified by their own community of fellow Trump supporters, then you may honestly be pushing them towards considering suicide as a way out because you've slammed the door on their cry for help. A cry they entrusted you with. Human sympathy can't be limited to political parties for a healthy and functioning democracy. *We should strive to create a Transvaluation of Values on the basis of personal liberty for all those in a Free society.* It is the best way of advancing human rights, technological advancement, and our overall human wellbeing. This has been my own small contribution to a much larger global conversation in order to further progress our free societies towards a *Transvaluation of Values*.

Nov. 2012, www.youtube.com/watch?v=hfgwFESH_jM.

"Do not let yourself be deceived: great intellects are sceptical. Zarathustra is a sceptic. The strength, the **freedom** which proceed from intellectual power, from a superabundance of intellectual power, **manifest** themselves as scepticism.

Men of fixed convictions do not count when it comes to determining what is fundamental in values and lack of values. Men of convictions are prisoners. They do not see far enough, they do not see what is **below** them: whereas a man who would talk to any purpose about value and non-value must be able to see five hundred convictions **beneath** him— and **behind** him.... A mind that aspires to great things, and that wills the means thereto, is necessarily sceptical. Freedom from any sort of conviction **belongs** to strength, and to an independent point of view.... That grand passion which is at once the foundation and the power of a sceptic's existence, and is both more enlightened and more despotic than he is himself, drafts the whole of his intellect into its service; it makes him unscrupulous; it gives him courage to employ unholy means; under certain circumstances it does not **begrudge** him even convictions. Conviction as a means: one may achieve a good deal by means of a conviction. A grand passion makes use of and uses up convictions; it does not yield to them—it knows itself to be sovereign.—

On the contrary, the need of faith, of something unconditioned by yea or nay, of Carlylism, if I may be allowed the word, is a need of **weakness.** The man of faith, the "believer" of any sort, is necessarily a dependent man—such a man cannot posit **himself** as a goal, nor can he find goals within himself. The "believer" does not belong to himself; he can only be a means to an end; he must be **used up**; he needs someone to use him up. His instinct gives the highest honours to an ethic of self-effacement; he is prompted to embrace it by everything: his prudence, his experience, his vanity. Every sort of faith is in itself an evidence of self-effacement, of self-estrangement.... When one reflects how necessary it is to the great majority that there be regulations to restrain them from without and hold them fast, and to what extent control, or, in a higher sense, **slavery**, is the one and only condition which makes for the well-being of the weak-willed man, and especially woman, then one at once understands conviction and "faith." To the man with convictions they are his backbone. To **avoid** seeing many things, to be impartial about nothing, to be a party man through and through, to estimate all values strictly and infallibly—these are conditions necessary to the existence of such a man. But by the same token they are **antagonists** of the truthful man—of the truth....

The believer is not free to answer the question, "true" or "not true," according to the dictates of his own conscience: integrity on **this** point would work his instant downfall. The pathological limitations of his vision turn the man of convictions into a fanatic—Savonarola, Luther, Rousseau, Robespierre, Saint-Simon—these types stand in opposition to the strong, **emancipated** spirit. But the grandiose attitudes of these **sick** intellects, these intellectual epileptics, are of influence upon the great masses—fanatics are picturesque, and mankind prefers observing poses to listening to **reasons**...."[2138] - Friedrich Nietzsche, Aphorism 54 of The Anti-Christ. Translated by H. L. Mencken.

---

77. [2138] Nietzsche, Friedrich Wilhelm. Aphorism 54. *THE ANTICHRIST*. Translated by H. L. Mencken, The Project Gutenberg, 2006.

Bibliography

<u>Chapter 1</u>

1. Barker, Jeff. "Statisticians question logic of buying multiple lottery tickets as jackpot rises to $1.5 B." *Baltimoresun.com*, 13 Jan. 2016, www.baltimoresun.com/business/bs-bz-powerball-maryland-odds-20160111-story.html.
2. Boseley, Sarah. "How Bill and Melinda Gates helped save 122m lives – and what they want to solve next." *The Guardian*, Guardian News and Media, 14 Feb. 2017, www.theguardian.com/world/2017/feb/14/bill-gates-philanthropy-warren-buffett-vaccines-infant-mortality.
3. "CASTLE ROCK V. GONZALES." *Legal Information Institute*, Cornell University Law School, 21 Mar. 2005, www.law.cornell.edu/supct/html/04-278.ZS.html.
4. CHEDEKEL, LISA, et al. "Haditha: Marine Linked To Civilian Deaths Was A Quiet Honor Student, Friends Say." *Hartford Courant*, 3 June 2006, articles.courant.com/2006-06-03/news/0606030586_1_frank-wuterich-haditha-squad-leader. I had initially hoped to use a Huffington Post article that described Frank Wuterich as a family man in conjunction with this, but it seems to have been removed.
5. Cialdini, Robert B. *Influence: Science and practice*. 4th ed., 21st Century Bks, 2002. Chapter 1: Weapons of Influence (1-16), Chapter 3: Commitment and Consistency (52-95), Chapter 4: Social Proof (98-140), Chapter 6: Authority (178-200)
6. "Facts Statistics: Mortality risk." *Facts Statistics: Mortality risk | III*, www.iii.org/fact-statistic/facts-statistics-mortality-risk.
7. "Full text: bin Laden's 'letter to America'." *The Guardian*, Guardian News and Media, 24 Nov. 2002, www.theguardian.com/world/2002/nov/24/theobserver.
8. Gause, F. Gregory. "Getting It Backward on Iraq." *Foreign Affairs*, Foreign Affairs, 28 Jan. 2009, www.foreignaffairs.com/articles/iraq/1999-05-01/getting-it-backward-iraq.
9. Goldberg, Philip. "Missionaries in India: Conversion or Coercion?" *The Huffington Post*, TheHuffingtonPost.com, 19 Feb. 2014, www.huffingtonpost.com/philip-goldberg/missionaries-in-india_b_4470448.html
10. Greenhouse, Linda. "Justices Rule Police Do Not Have a Constitutional Duty to Protect Someone." *The New York Times*, The New York Times, 28 June 2005, www.nytimes.com/2005/06/28/politics/justices-rule-police-do-not-have-a-constitutional-duty-to-protect.html.
11. Hackett, Conrad, and David McClendon. "World's Largest Religion by Population Is Still Christianity." *Pew Research Center*, Pew Research Center, 5 Apr. 2017, www.pewresearch.org/fact-tank/2017/04/05/christians-remain-worlds-largest-religious-group-but-they-are-declining-in-europe/.
12. Hedges, Chris. *War Is a Force That Gives Us Meaning*. PublicAffairs, 2002.
13. Isidore, Chris. "These are your odds of winning Powerball or Mega Millions." *CNNMoney*, Cable News Network, money.cnn.com/2018/01/04/news/powerball-mega-millions-odds/index.html.
14. Ispas, Alexa. *Psychology and politics: a social identity perspective*. Psychology Press, 2014. For reference purposes: Chapter 1: Psychology and the Social Identity Perspective (1-24), Chapter 2: The Psychology of Social Influence (26-50).
15. Kahneman, Daniel. *Thinking, fast and slow*. Farrar, Straus and Giroux, 2015. For reference purposes: The Introduction (1-17), Chapter 4: The Associative Machine (50-58), Chapter 5: Cognitive Ease (59-70), Chapter 6:"Norms, Surprises, and Causes" (71-78), Chapter 7: A Machine for Jumping to Conclusions (79-88), Chapter 8: How Judgments Happen (89-96), Chapter 9: Answering an Easier Question (97-107), Chapter 11: Anchors (119-128), Chapter 12: The Science of Availability (129-136), Chapter 13: Availability, Emotion, and Risk (137-145), Chapter 19: The Illusion of Understanding (199-208), Chapter 20: The Illusion of Validity (209-221), and Chapter 28: Bad Events (300-309).
16. McDermott, Rose. *Political Psychology in International Relations*. Ann Arbor: U of Michigan, 2004. Print. For reference: Chapter 4: Cognition and Attitudes (77-117), Chapter 5: Do Actions Speak Louder Than Words? (119-152).
17. Merritt, Jonathan. "Insisting Jesus Was White Is Bad History and Bad Theology." *The Atlantic*, Atlantic Media Company, 12 Dec. 2013, www.theatlantic.com/politics/archive/2013/12/insisting-jesus-was-white-is-bad-history-and-bad-theology/282310/.
18. Morgan, Piers. *YouTube*, CNN, 7 Jan. 2013, www.youtube.com/watch?v=ror9v2LwHoY.

19. Nietzsche, Friedrich Wilhelm. *THE ANTICHRIST*. Translated by H. L. Mencken, The Project Gutenberg, 2006. For reference: Aphorism 40 and 41.
20. No. 04-278 TOWN OF CASTLE ROCK, COLORADO v. JESSICA GONZALES. https://www.justice.gov/sites/default/files/osg/briefs/2004/01/01/2004-0278.mer.ami.pdf 1-45. Supreme Court of the United States. 27 June 2005.*Justice.Gov*. United States, 27 June 2005. Web. 5 Feb. 2018. <https://www.justice.gov/sites/default/files/osg/briefs/2004/01/01/2004-0278.mer.ami.pdf>.
21. O'Brien, Matt. "Why you should never, ever play the lottery." *The Washington Post*, WP Company, 14 May 2015, www.washingtonpost.com/news/wonk/wp/2015/05/14/why-you-should-never-ever-play-the-lottery/?utm_term=.60541de1ad73.
22. Pelley, Scott. "Haditha massacre defendant: We did what we had to." *CBS News*, CBS Interactive, 6 Jan. 2012, www.cbsnews.com/news/haditha-massacre-defendant-we-did-what-we-had-to/.
23. Puente, Mark. "Sun Investigates: Undue force." *The Baltimore Sun*, 28 Sept. 2014, data.baltimoresun.com/news/police-settlements/.
24. Roser, Max. "Visual History of The Rise of Political Freedom and the Decrease in Violence." *Visual History of The Rise of Political Freedom and the Decrease in Violence*. Web. 3 Jan. 2016.
25. Rubenstein, J. "Cannibals and Crusaders." *French Historical Studies*, vol. 31, no. 4, Jan. 2008, pp. 525–552., doi:10.1215/00161071-2008-005. PDF.
26. Teitelbaum, Joel, et al. "Town Of Castle Rock, Colorado V. Gonzales: Implications for Public Health Policy and Practice." *Public Health Reports*, Association of Schools of Public Health, 2006, www.ncbi.nlm.nih.gov/pmc/articles/PMC1525280/.
27. "The Changing Global Religious Landscape." *Pew Research Center's Religion & Public Life Project*, Pew Research Center's Religion & Public Life Project, 26 July 2017, www.pewforum.org/2017/04/05/the-changing-global-religious-landscape/.
28. Walton, D. N. "Appeal to Popularity." *Https://Www.logicallyfallacious.com*, www.logicallyfallacious.com/tools/lp/Bo/LogicalFallacies/40/Appeal-to-Popularity.

Chapter 2

1. Boseley, Sarah. "How Bill and Melinda Gates helped save 122m lives – and what they want to solve next." *The Guardian*, Guardian News and Media, 14 Feb. 2017, www.theguardian.com/world/2017/feb/14/bill-gates-philanthropy-warren-buffett-vaccines-infant-mortality.
2. Camp, Jim. "Decisions Are Emotional, Not Logical: the Neuroscience behind Decision Making." *Big Think*, Big Think, 11 June 2012, bigthink.com/experts-corner/decisions-are-emotional-not-logical-the-neuroscience-behind-decision-making.
3. Cialdini, Robert B. *Influence: Science and practice*. 4th ed., 21st Century Bks, 2002. For reference: Chapter 4: Social Proof (98-140).
4. Cooper, Spring Chenoa, and Anthony J. Santellla. "Happy news! Masturbation actually has health benefits." *The Conversation*, 5 Dec. 2017, theconversation.com/happy-news-masturbation-actually-has-health-benefits-16539.
5. Freeman, Daniel, and Jason Freeman. "Why are men more likely than women to take their own lives?" *The Guardian*, Guardian News and Media, 21 Jan. 2015, www.theguardian.com/science/2015/jan/21/suicide-gender-men-women-mental-health-nick-clegg.
6. Galef, Julia. "The Straw Vulcan, Julia Galef Skepticon 4." *YouTube*, YouTube, 17 Aug. 2013, www.youtube.com/watch?v=Fv1nMc-k0N4.
7. Gates, Bill. *YouTube*, Thegatesnotes, 5 Jan. 2015, www.youtube.com/watch?v=bVzppWSIFU0.
8. Gates, Bill, and Melinda Gates. "Warren Buffett's Best Investment." *Gatesnotes.com*, Bill and Melinda Gates, 14 Feb. 2017, www.gatesnotes.com/2017-Annual-Letter.
9. Gittleson, Wendy. "Christian 'Soul Vultures' Are Exploiting The Nepal Earthquake 'For Christ' (VIDEO)." *AddictingInfo*, 27 Apr. 2015, addictinginfo.com/2015/04/27/christian-soul-vultures-are-exploiting-the-nepal-earthquake-for-christ-video/.
10. Hedges, Chris. *War Is a Force That Gives Us Meaning*. PublicAffairs, 2002.
11. Hitchens, Christopher. "Christopher Hitchens: Hell's Angel: Mother Teresa (English Subtitles)." *YouTube*, BBC News, 7 Jan. 2015, youtu.be/NK7l_IhtKNU.
12. Ispas, Alexa. *Psychology and politics: a social identity perspective*. Psychology Press, 2014.

13. Jentleson, Bruce W. *American foreign policy: the dynamics of choice in the 21st century*. 4th ed., Norton, 2010. Chapter 1: The Strategic Context: Foreign Policy Strategy and the Essence of Choice (2-26), Readings for Part 1 Power by Hans J. Morgenthau (198-201)
14. Kahneman, Daniel. *Thinking, fast and slow*. Farrar, Straus and Giroux, 2015. For reference purposes: Chapter 5: Cognitive Ease (59-70).
15. "Masturbation Side Effects and Benefits." *Healthline*, Healthline Media, www.healthline.com/health/masturbation-side-effects.
16. "Masturbation | Get the Facts About Masturbation Health." *Planned Parenthood*, Planned Parenthood, www.plannedparenthood.org/learn/sex-and-relationships/masturbation.
17. Neary, Sarah. "Forced to Convert: How American Missionaries Really Treat Indigenous Akha Children." *Intercontinental Cry*, IC, 23 Apr. 2013, intercontinentalcry.org/forced-to-convert-how-american-missionaries-really-treat-indigenous-akha-children/.
18. Neelakandan, Aravindan. "Why No Outrage over Conversion of Tsunami Victims?" *Swarajya*, 29 Dec. 2014, swarajyamag.com/politics/why-no-outrage-over-conversion-of-tsunami-victims.
19. Nietzsche, Friedrich Wilhelm. *Thus spake Zarathustra: a book for all and none*. Translated by Thomas Common, PDF ed., T. Common, 1908. Chapter IX: Preachers of Death (50-52), Chapter XXVI: THE PRIESTS (88-91)
20. Nietzsche, Friedrich Wilhelm. *THE ANTICHRIST*. Translated by H. L. Mencken, The Project Gutenberg, 2006. For reference: Aphorisms 15 and 16.
21. Nietzsche, Friedrich Wilhelm. *On the genealogy of morals: a polemical tract*. Translated by Ian Johnston, PDF, Richer Resources Publications, 2014.
22. Roser, Max. "Visual History of The Rise of Political Freedom and the Decrease in Violence." *Visual History of The Rise of Political Freedom and the Decrease in Violence*. Web. 3 Jan. 2016.
23. Viglianco-VanPelt, Michelle, and Kyla Boyse. "Masturbation." Edited by Jennifer Gold Christner, *University of Michigan Health System*, July 2009, www.med.umich.edu/yourchild/topics/masturb.htm.
24. Viotti, Paul R., and Mark V. Kauppi. *International relations theory: realism, pluralism, globalism*. 3rd ed., Macmillan, 1998. For reference, Chapter 2: Realism: The State, Power, and the Balance of Power (55-197)
25. "When Nepal Was Groaning in Earthquake, Christian Missionaries Were Shamelessly Selling Jesus." *OpIndia*, 4 May 2015, www.opindia.com/2015/04/when-nepal-was-groaning-in-earthquake-christian-missionaries-were-shamelessly-selling-jesus/.
26. Yudkowsky, Eliezer. "What Do We Mean By "Rationality"?" *Less Wrong*, 16 Mar. 2009, lesswrong.com/lw/31/what_do_we_mean_by_rationality/.

Chapter 3

1. Carr, Kelly, and Scot J. Paltrow. "Reuters Investigates - UNACCOUNTABLE: The Pentagon's bad bookkeeping." *Reuters*, Thomson Reuters, 2 July 2013, www.reuters.com/investigates/pentagon/#article/part1.
2. Carr, Kelly, and Scot J. Paltrow. "Reuters Investigates - UNACCOUNTABLE: The Pentagon's bad bookkeeping." *Reuters*, Thomson Reuters, 2 July 2013, www.reuters.com/investigates/pentagon/#article/part2.
3. Carr, Kelly, and Scot J. Paltrow. "Reuters Investigates - UNACCOUNTABLE: The Pentagon's bad bookkeeping." *Reuters*, Thomson Reuters, 2 July 2013, www.reuters.com/investigates/pentagon/#article/part3.
4. "Circular Reasoning." *Https://Www.logicallyfallacious.com*, www.logicallyfallacious.com/tools/lp/Bo/LogicalFallacies/66/Circular-Reasoning.
5. Eggen, Dan, and Scott Wilson. "Suicide Bombs Potent Tools of Terrorists." *The Washington Post*, WP Company, 17 July 2005, www.washingtonpost.com/archive/politics/2005/07/17/suicide-bombs-potent-tools-of-terrorists/e11ed483-9936-45c0-b6c6-2653d4519ff5/?utm_term=.c23458392a4a.
6. Grinnell, Renée. "Just-World Hypothesis." *Encyclopedia of Psychology*, 17 July 2016, psychcentral.com/encyclopedia/just-world-hypothesis/.
7. Hitchens, Christopher. "Christopher Hitchens: Hell's Angel: Mother Teresa (English Subtitles)." *YouTube*, BBC News, 7 Jan. 2015, youtu.be/NK7l_IhtKNU.
8. Ispas, Alexa. *Psychology and politics: a social identity perspective*. Psychology Press, 2014.

9. Kahneman, Daniel. *Thinking, fast and slow*. Farrar, Straus and Giroux, 2015. For reference purposes: The Introduction (1-17), Chapter 6: Norms, Surprises, and Causes (71-78), Chapter 8: How Judgments Happen (89-96), Chapter 9: Answering an Easier Question (97-104), Chapter 29: The Fourfold Pattern (310-321), Chapter 30: Rare Events (322-333), Chapter 31: Risk Policies (334-341), and Chapter 32: Keeping Score (342 - 352)
10. Lankford, Adam. "Martyr myth: Inside the minds of suicide bombers." *New Scientist*, 3 July 2013, www.newscientist.com/article/mg21929240-200-martyr-myth-inside-the-minds-of-suicide-bombers/.
11. Lankford, Adam. "Exposing false 'martyrs' as suicidal." *The Jerusalem Post | JPost.Com*, 17 Feb. 2013, www.jpost.com/Opinion/Op-Ed-Contributors/Exposing-false-martyrs-as-suicidal.
12. Lankford, Adam. "What You Don't Understand about Suicide Attacks." *Scientific American*, 27 July 2015, www.scientificamerican.com/article/what-you-don-t-understand-about-suicide-attacks/.
13. Lester, David. "Female Suicide Bombers: Clues from Journalists." *Suicidology Online*, Suicidology Online, 14 Nov. 2011, www.suicidology-online.com/pdf/SOL-2011-2-62-66.pdf.
14. Lowe, Josh. "How Britain's history with the IRA made it resilient to attacks." *Newsweek*, 29 Mar. 2017, www.newsweek.com/london-attack-ira-terror-threat-severe-bomb-terrorism-573629.
15. McCann, Eamonn. "Real IRA's lust for violence matters more than ideology on the streets | Eamonn McCann." *The Guardian*, Guardian News and Media, 21 Aug. 2010, www.theguardian.com/uk/2010/aug/22/northern-ireland-dissidents-peace-process.
16. McDermott, Rose. *Political Psychology in International Relations*. Ann Arbor: U of Michigan, 2004. Print. For reference: Chapter 5: Behavior (119-152).
17. McDonald, Henry. "UK agents 'did have role in IRA bomb atrocities'." *The Observer*, Guardian News and Media, 9 Sept. 2006, www.theguardian.com/politics/2006/sep/10/uk.northernireland1.
18. Nietzsche, Friedrich Wilhelm. *Thus spake Zarathustra: a book for all and none*. Translated by Thomas Common, PDF ed., T. Common, 1908. For reference: Chapter IX: Preachers of Death (50-52), Chapter XXVI: THE PRIESTS (88-91), and Chapter XXXIV: Self-Surpassing (108-111).
19. Nietzsche, Friedrich Wilhelm. *THE ANTICHRIST*. Translated by H. L. Mencken, The Project Gutenberg, 2006. For reference: Aphorisms 15, 16, 41, 43, 53, 54, and 55.
20. Nietzsche, Friedrich Wilhelm. *On the genealogy of morals: a polemical tract*. Translated by Ian Johnston, PDF, Richer Resources Publications, 2014.
21. POGATCHNIK, SHAWN. "IRA Proxy Bombings Kill 6 Troops, Civilian : Northern Ireland: The attack by the terrorist group is the deadliest against British forces in two years." *Los Angeles Times*, Los Angeles Times, 25 Oct. 1990, articles.latimes.com/1990-10-25/news/mn-4248_1_northern-ireland.
22. Webb, David. "Fritz Heider & Marianne Simmel: An Experimental Study of Apparent Behavior." *Psychology*, www.all-about-psychology.com/fritz-heider.html.

Chapter 4

1. "A Mathematical Proof That The Universe Could Have Formed Spontaneously From Nothing." *Medium*, The Physics ArXiv Blog, 11 Apr. 2014, medium.com/the-physics-arxiv-blog/a-mathematical-proof-that-the-universe-could-have-formed-spontaneously-from-nothing-ed7ed0f304a3.
2. Abels, Richard. "Crusades and early Christian attitudes toward warfare." *Academia.edu - Share research*, www.academia.edu/22844402/Crusades_and_early_Christian_attitudes_toward_warfare. For reference: the original website for this has been removed from the US Naval Academy website when I first found it. Abels, Richard. "Timeline for the Crusades and Christian Holy War." Timeline for the Crusades and Christian Holy War. 2009. Web. 2016.
   <http://www.usna.edu/Users/history/abels/hh315/crusades_timeline.htm>
3. Baird, Julia. "Doubt as a Sign of Faith." *The New York Times*, The New York Times, 25 Sept. 2014, www.nytimes.com/2014/09/26/opinion/julia-baird-doubt-as-a-sign-of-faith.html.
4. "Christopher Hitchens Debates Al Sharpton - New York Public." *YouTube*, YouTube, 6 Dec. 2011, www.youtube.com/watch?v=HPYxA8dYLBY.
5. Cialdini, Robert B. *Influence: Science and practice*. 4th ed., 21st Century Bks, 2002. Chapter 1: Weapons of Influence (1-16), Chapter 2: Reciprocation (19-50), Chapter 3: Commitment and Consistency (52-95), Chapter 4: Social Proof (98-140), Chapter 6: Authority (178-200)
6. "Circular Reasoning." *Https://Www.logicallyfallacious.com*, www.logicallyfallacious.com/tools/lp/Bo/LogicalFallacies/66/Circular-Reasoning.

7. "Full text: bin Laden's 'letter to America'." *The Guardian*, Guardian News and Media, 24 Nov. 2002, www.theguardian.com/world/2002/nov/24/theobserver.
8. Gause, F. Gregory. "Getting It Backward on Iraq." *Foreign Affairs*, Foreign Affairs, 28 Jan. 2009, www.foreignaffairs.com/articles/iraq/1999-05-01/getting-it-backward-iraq.
9. Hedges, Chris. *War Is a Force That Gives Us Meaning*. PublicAffairs, 2002.
10. Ispas, Alexa. *Psychology and politics: a social identity perspective*. Psychology Press, 2014. For reference purposes, Chapter 1: Psychology and the Social Identity Perspective (1-24), Chapter 2: The Psychology of Social Influence (26-50)
11. Kahneman, Daniel. *Thinking, fast and slow*. Farrar, Straus and Giroux, 2015. For reference purposes: The Introduction (1-17), Chapter 4: The Associative Machine (50-58), Chapter 5: Cognitive Ease (59-70), Chapter 6:"Norms, Surprises, and Causes" (71-78), Chapter 7: A Machine for Jumping to Conclusions (79-88), Chapter 9: Answering an Easier Question (97-104), and Chapter 27: The Prospect Theory (278-288).
12. Lane, Christopher. "Losing Our Religion: Why Doubt Is a Passionate Exercise." *Psychology Today*, Sussex Publishers, 20 May 2011, www.psychologytoday.com/blog/side-effects/201105/losing-our-religion-why-doubt-is-passionate-exercise.
13. McDermott, Rose. *Political Psychology in International Relations*. Ann Arbor: U of Michigan, 2004. Print. For reference: Chapter 4: Cognition and Attitudes (77-117). Chapter 5: Behavior (119-152)
14. Mill, John Stuart. *Three essays on religion*. Timeless Wisdom Collection, 2016. For reference: c. Argument For a First Cause (71-77)
15. "Moving the Goalposts." *Https://Www.logicallyfallacious.com*, www.logicallyfallacious.com/tools/lp/Bo/LogicalFallacies/129/Moving-the-Goalposts.
16. Nietzsche, Friedrich Wilhelm. *The gay science (the joyful wisdom)*. Edited by Oscar Levy. Translated by Thomas Common, #52881, Gutenberg, 2016, www.gutenberg.org/files/52881/52881-h/52881-h.htm.
17. "No True Scotsman." *Https://Www.logicallyfallacious.com*, www.logicallyfallacious.com/tools/lp/Bo/LogicalFallacies/135/No-True-Scotsman.
18. "U.S. Religious Knowledge Survey." *Pew Research Center's Religion & Public Life Project*, Pew Research Center's Religion & Public Life Project, 19 Dec. 2017, www.pewforum.org/2010/09/28/u-s-religious-knowledge-survey/.

Chapter 5

1. "About Us." *Doctors Opposing Circumcision*, www.doctorsopposingcircumcision.org/about-us/#_statement-principles.
2. "Appeal to Tradition." *Https://Www.logicallyfallacious.com*, www.logicallyfallacious.com/tools/lp/Bo/LogicalFallacies/44/Appeal-to-Tradition.
3. Batrinos, Menelaos L. "Testosterone and Aggressive Behavior in Man." *International Journal of Endocrinology and Metabolism*, NCBI, 2012, www.ncbi.nlm.nih.gov/pmc/articles/PMC3693622/.
4. BEINER, THERESA M. "SEXY DRESSING REVISITED: DOES TARGET DRESS PLAY A PART IN SEXUAL HARASSMENT CASES?." *Duke University School of Law*, Duke Journal of Gender Law & Policy, 2007, scholarship.law.duke.edu/cgi/viewcontent.cgi?&article=1109&context=djglp. III. SOCIAL SCIENCE AND DRESS (143-148), IV. IMPLICATIONS OF DRESS FOR SEXUAL HARASSMENT LAW (148-151).
5. "BibleGateway." *Numbers 31:7-18 KJV - - Bible Gateway*, www.biblegateway.com/passage/?search=Numbers 31:7-18&version=KJV.
6. Boyle, G. J. "Issues associated with the introduction of circumcision into a non-Circumcising society." *Issues associated with the introduction of circumcision into a non-Circumcising society*, THE CIRCUMCISION REFERENCE LIBRARY, Nov. 2003, www.cirp.org/library/disease/HIV/boyle-sti/.
7. Bronselaer, G A, et al. "Male circumcision decreases penile sensitivity as measured in a large cohort." *BJU international.*, U.S. National Library of Medicine, May 2013, www.ncbi.nlm.nih.gov/pubmed/23374102.
8. Cialdini, Robert B. *Influence: Science and practice*. 4th ed., 21st Century Bks, 2002. Chapter 1: Weapons of Influence (1-16), Chapter 2: Reciprocation (19-50), Chapter 3: Commitment and Consistency (52-95), Chapter 4: Social Proof (98-140), Chapter 6: Authority (178-200).
9. Dweck, Carol S. *Mindset: How You Can Fulfill Your Potential*. Random House, 2012.
10. Freeman, Daniel, and Jason Freeman. "Why are men more likely than women to take their own lives?"

The Guardian, Guardian News and Media, 21 Jan. 2015, www.theguardian.com/science/2015/jan/21/suicide-gender-men-women-mental-health-nick-clegg.

11. Freeman, David. "Circumcision Linked To Autism In Controversial New Study." *The Huffington Post*, TheHuffingtonPost.com, 20 Jan. 2015, www.huffingtonpost.com/2015/01/20/circumcision-autism-new-study_n_6503106.html.
12. Frisch, M, et al. "Male circumcision and sexual function in men and women: a survey-Based, cross-Sectional study in Denmark." *International journal of epidemiology.*, U.S. National Library of Medicine, Oct. 2011, www.ncbi.nlm.nih.gov/pubmed/21672947.
13. Frisch, Morten, and Jacob Simonsen. "Ritual circumcision and risk of autism spectrum disorder in 0- to 9-Year-Old boys: national cohort study in Denmark." *Journal of the Royal Society of Medicine*, SAGE Publications, July 2015, www.ncbi.nlm.nih.gov/pmc/articles/PMC4530408/.
14. Frisch, Morten, and Jacob Simonsen. "Ritual circumcision and risk of autism spectrum disorder in 0- to 9-Year-Old boys: national cohort study in Denmark." *Journal of the Royal Society of Medicine*, vol. 108, no. 7, Aug. 2015, pp. 266–279., doi:10.1177/0141076814565942.
15. Goldman, R. "The psychological impact of circumcision." *Circumcision Resource Center*, THE CIRCUMCISION REFERENCE LIBRARY, www.cirp.org/library/psych/goldman1/.
16. Green, Laci. "I LOVE FORESKIN (Wtf circumcision?)." *YouTube*, YouTube, 14 Aug. 2013, www.youtube.com/watch?v=JbTdkWV89Ak.
17. Green, Laci. "WHY I'M A...FEMINIST *Gasp*." *YouTube*, YouTube, 23 Apr. 2014, www.youtube.com/watch?v=UwJRFClybmk.
18. Green, Laci. "THE F-WORD." *YouTube*, YouTube, 8 July 2014, www.youtube.com/watch?v=EJPT_U97lNs.
19. Green, Laci. "TOXIC MASCULINITY!" *YouTube*, YouTube, 20 Dec. 2017, www.youtube.com/watch?v=i5juyXjDnJ0.
20. Grinnell, Renée. "Just-World Hypothesis." *Encyclopedia of Psychology*, 17 July 2016, psychcentral.com/encyclopedia/just-world-hypothesis/.
21. Healy, Melissa. "In addition to fueling aggression, testosterone can also make men more generous, study says." *Los Angeles Times*, Los Angeles Times, 26 Sept. 2016, www.latimes.com/science/sciencenow/la-sci-sn-testosterone-behavior-men-20160926-snap-story.html.
22. "Infant Responses to Circumcision." *Circumcision Resource Center*, circumcision.org/infant-responses-to-circumcision/.
23. Kahneman, Daniel. *Thinking, fast and slow*. Farrar, Straus and Giroux, 2015. For reference purposes: Chapter 6:"Norms, Surprises, and Causes" (71-78), Chapter 8: How Judgments Happen (89-96), and Chapter 9: Answering an Easier Question (97-104).
24. Konner, Melvin. "MUTILATED IN THE NAME OF TRADITION." *The New York Times*, The New York Times, 14 Apr. 1990, www.nytimes.com/1990/04/15/books/mutilated-in-the-name-of-tradition.html.
25. Kovac, Sarah. "New autism dispute: is circumcision a factor?" *Time*, Time, time.com/4314388/new-autism-dispute-is-circumcision-a-factor/.
26. Lightfoot-Klein, Hanny. *National Organization of Circumcision Resource Centers*, NOCIRC, Mar. 1994, www.nocirc.org/symposia/third/hanny3.html.
27. Mims, Christopher. "Strange but True: Testosterone Alone Does Not Cause Violence." *Scientific American*, 5 July 2007, www.scientificamerican.com/article/strange-but-true-testosterone-alone-doesnt-cause-violence/.
28. Myers, A, and J Myers. *Rolling out male circumcision as a mass HIV/AIDS intervention seems neither justified nor practicable*, www.cirp.org/library/disease/HIV/myers2008/.
29. Myers, J. "Male circumcision and HIV infection." *History of Circumcision*, Historyofcircumcision.net, www.historyofcircumcision.net/index.php?option=content&task=view&id=85.
30. Narvaez, Darcia. "More Circumcision Myths You May Believe: Hygiene and STDs." *Psychology Today*, Sussex Publishers, 13 Sept. 2011, www.psychologytoday.com/blog/moral-landscapes/201109/more-circumcision-myths-you-may-believe-hygiene-and-stds.
31. Narvaez, Darcia. "Myths about Circumcision You Likely Believe." *Psychology Today*, Sussex Publishers, 11 Sept. 2011, www.psychologytoday.com/blog/moral-landscapes/201109/myths-about-circumcision-you-likely-believe.
32. Narvaez, Darcia. "Circumcision's Psychological Damage." *Psychology Today*, Sussex Publishers, 11 Jan. 2015, www.psychologytoday.com/blog/moral-landscapes/201501/circumcision-s-psychological-damage.

33. Nietzsche, Friedrich Wilhelm. *On the genealogy of morals: a polemical tract*. Translated by Ian Johnston, PDF, Richer Resources Publications, 2014.
34. Page, Gayle Giboney. "Are There Long-Term Consequences of Pain in Newborn or Very Young Infants?" *The Journal of Perinatal Education*, U.S. National Library of Medicine, 2004, www.ncbi.nlm.nih.gov/pmc/articles/PMC1595204/.
35. Storr, Will. "The rape of men: the darkest secret of war." *The Observer*, Guardian News and Media, 16 July 2011, www.theguardian.com/society/2011/jul/17/the-rape-of-men.
36. "Till death do us part: A Post and Courier Special Report." *Post and Courier*, 19 Aug. 2014, www.postandcourier.com/app/till-death/partone.html.

a.) Original Sin

Chapter 6

1. Bazelon, Emily. "We've Been Measuring Rape All Wrong." *Slate Magazine*, Slate, 19 Nov. 2013, www.slate.com/articles/double_x/doublex/2013/11/national_crime_victimization_survey_a_new_report_finds_that_the_justice.html.
2. Berman, Mark, and Samantha Schmidt. "He Yelled 'Get out of My Country,' Witnesses Say, and Then Shot 2 Men from India, Killing One." *The Washington Post*, WP Company, 24 Feb. 2017, www.washingtonpost.com/news/morning-mix/wp/2017/02/24/get-out-of-my-country-kansan-reportedly-yelled-before-shooting-2-men-from-india-killing-one/?utm_term=.87088ce6c874.
3. "BibleGateway." *Bible Gateway*, Bible Gateway Blog, www.biblegateway.com/passage/?search=Isaiah 45:7&version=KJV.
4. "Circular Reasoning." *Https://Www.logicallyfallacious.com*, www.logicallyfallacious.com/tools/lp/Bo/LogicalFallacies/66/Circular-Reasoning.
5. Cialdini, Robert B. *Influence: Science and practice*. 4th ed., 21st Century Bks, 2002. Chapter 1: Weapons of Influence (1-16), Chapter 2: Reciprocation (19-50), and 6: Authority (178-200).
6. Davis, Mike. *Late Victorian Holocausts: El Nino Famines and the Making of the Third World*. Penguin Random House Publisher Services, 2001.
7. Dweck, Carol S. *Mindset: How You Can Fulfill Your Potential*. Random House, 2012.
8. Feaver, Peter, and Will Inboden. "We Are Witnessing the Elimination of Christian Communities in Iraq and Syria." *Foreign Policy*, Foreign Policy, 6 Sept. 2017, foreignpolicy.com/2017/09/06/we-are-witnessing-the-elimination-of-christian-communities-in-iraq-and-syria/.
9. Fromm, Erich. *The Anatomy of Human Destructiveness*. Open Road Media. Kindle Edition. For reference: Chapter 8: Anthropology (153-208).
10. Halvorson, Heidi Grant. *Succeed: How We Can Reach Our Goals*. Plume, 2012. For reference: Chapter 2: Do You Know Where Your Goals Come From? (657-952)
11. "History of Hate: Crimes Against Sikhs Since 9/11." *The Huffington Post*, TheHuffingtonPost.com, 7 Aug. 2012, www.huffingtonpost.com/2012/08/07/history-of-hate-crimes-against-sikhs-since-911_n_1751841.html.
12. "India Is Third in Rape Cases, Second in Murder in the World." *The Hindu*, The Hindu, 23 July 2014, www.thehindu.com/news/national/india-is-third-in-rape-cases-second-in-murder-in-the-world/article6242011.ece.
13. Ispas, Alexa. *Psychology and politics: a social identity perspective*. Psychology Press, 2014.
14. Jentleson, Bruce W. *American foreign policy: the dynamics of choice in the 21st century*. 4th ed., Norton, 2010. Chapter 1: The Strategic Context: Foreign Policy Strategy and the Essence of Choice (2-26), Readings for Part 1 Power by Hans J. Morgenthau (198-201)
15. Kahneman, Daniel. *Thinking, fast and slow*. Farrar, Straus and Giroux, 2015. For reference purposes: The Introduction (1-17), Chapter 4: The Associative Machine (50-58), Chapter 5: Cognitive Ease (59-70), Chapter 6:"Norms, Surprises, and Causes" (71-78), Chapter 7: A Machine for Jumping to Conclusions (79-88), Chapter 8: How Judgments Happen (89-96), Chapter 12: The Science of Availability (129-136), Chapter 13: Availability, Emotion, and Risk (137-145), Chapter 19: The Illusion of Understanding (199-208), Chapter 20: The Illusion of Validity (209-221), Chapter 22: Expert Intuition: When Can We Trust It? (234-244), and Chapter 28: Bad Events (300-309).
16. Kaplan, Sarah. "'Terrorist, Go Back to Your Country,' Attacker Yelled in Assault of Sikh Man." *The

Washington Post, WP Company, 10 Sept. 2015, www.washingtonpost.com/news/morning-mix/wp/2015/09/10/terrorist-go-back-to-your-country-attacker-yelled-in-alleged-assault-of-sikh-man/?utm_term=.a1a63bf192d7.

17. Kishi, Katayoun. "Assaults against Muslims in U.S. Surpass 2001 Level." *Pew Research Center*, Pew Research Center, 15 Nov. 2017, www.pewresearch.org/fact-tank/2017/11/15/assaults-against-muslims-in-u-s-surpass-2001-level/.
18. May, Rollo. "Madness and Powerlessness." *Power and Innocence: A Search for the Sources of Violence*. New York, NY: Norton, 1972. 19-46. Print.
19. "MAZE OF INJUSTICE ." *Amnesty International USA*, Amnesty International, www.amnestyusa.org/pdfs/mazeofinjustice.pdf.
20. Moxham, Roy. *The Theft of India: the European Conquests of India, 1498-1765*. HarperCollins, 2016. Chapter 1:Spices, Christianity and Extreme Violence (1-21), Chapter 2: Conquest, Horticulture, the Church and the Inquisition (22-43), and Chapter Five: Religious Freedom and Peaceful Trade (88-120).
21. Nietzsche, Friedrich Wilhelm. *On the genealogy of morals: a polemical tract*. Translated by Ian Johnston, PDF, Richer Resources Publications, 2014.
22. Nietzsche, Friedrich Wilhelm. *THE ANTICHRIST*. Translated by H. L. Mencken, The Project Gutenberg, 2006. For reference: Aphorisms 43, 46, 47, 48, and 49.
23. Nietzsche, Friedrich. Aphorism 148. *The Dawn of Day*. Translated by J. M. Kennedy, Dover Publications, 2012.
24. Pink, Daniel H. *Drive: the Surprising Truth about What Motivates Us*. Canongate Books, 2018.
25. Reese, Hannah. "Intrusive Thoughts: Normal or Not?" Psychology Today, Sussex Publishers, www.psychologytoday.com/us/blog/am-i-normal/201110/intrusive-thoughts-normal-or-not.
26. "Till death do us part: A Post and Courier Special Report." *Post and Courier*, 19 Aug. 2014, www.postandcourier.com/app/till-death/partone.html.
27. Viotti, Paul R., and Mark V. Kauppi. *International relations theory: realism, pluralism, globalism*. 3rd ed., Macmillan, 1998. For reference, Chapter 2: Realism: The State, Power, and the Balance of Power (55-197)
28. Woodall, Bernie. "Victim in Virginia Melee Wept for Social Justice, Her Boss Says." *Reuters*, Thomson Reuters, 14 Aug. 2017, www.reuters.com/article/us-virginia-protests-victim/victim-in-virginia-melee-wept-for-social-justice-her-boss-says-idUSKCN1AT0QR.
29. Wootson, Cleve R. "Sikh Community Asks for Hate-Crime Probe after Man Is Told 'Go Back to Your Own Country' and Shot." *The Washington Post*, WP Company, 5 Mar. 2017, www.washingtonpost.com/news/post-nation/wp/2017/03/04/go-back-to-your-own-country-sikh-man-shot-in-his-driveway-in-suspected-hate-crime/?utm_term=.cf9016ea0b1e.

Chapter 7

1. Camp, Jim. "Decisions Are Emotional, Not Logical: the Neuroscience behind Decision Making." *Big Think*, Big Think, 11 June 2012, bigthink.com/experts-corner/decisions-are-emotional-not-logical-the-neuroscience-behind-decision-making.
2. "Circular Reasoning." *Https://Www.logicallyfallacious.com*, www.logicallyfallacious.com/tools/lp/Bo/LogicalFallacies/66/Circular-Reasoning.
3. "Fewer in U.S. View Iraq, Afghanistan Wars as Mistakes." *Gallup.com*, Gallup, Inc, 12 June 2015, news.gallup.com/poll/183575/fewer-view-iraq-afghanistan-wars-mistakes.aspx.
4. Dweck, Carol S. *Mindset: How You Can Fulfill Your Potential*. Random House, 2012.
5. Frank, Priscilla. "Welcome To The Bizarre And Beautiful World Of Purity Balls." *The Huffington Post*, TheHuffingtonPost.com, 7 Dec. 2017, www.huffingtonpost.com/2014/05/05/purity-ball-photos_n_5255904.html.
6. Gannon, Megan. "Race Is a Social Construct, Scientists Argue." *Scientific American*, 5 Feb. 2016, www.scientificamerican.com/article/race-is-a-social-construct-scientists-argue/.
7. Gilbert, Daniel. *Stumbling on Happiness*. Random House, 2006. For reference: Chapter 4: In the Blind Spot of the Mind's Eye (75-95) and Chapter 11: Reporting Live For Tomorrow (212-233).
8. Green, Hank. "Compatibilism: Crash Course Philosophy #25." *YouTube*, Crash Course / PBS Digital Studios, 22 Aug. 2016, www.youtube.com/watch?v=KETTtiprINU.

9. Green, Hank. "Determinism vs Free Will: Crash Course Philosophy #24." *YouTube*, Crash Course / PBS Digital Studios, 15 Aug. 2016, www.youtube.com/watch?v=vCGtkDzELAI.
10. Haider, Sarah, et al. "Islam, Modesty and Feminism." *YouTube*, Ex-Muslims of North America, 12 Oct. 2017, www.youtube.com/watch?v=QToH2x8njJM.
11. Ispas, Alexa. *Psychology and politics: a social identity perspective*. Psychology Press, 2014.
12. Jarrett, Christian. "Neuroscience and Free Will Are Rethinking Their Divorce." *The Cut*, 3 Feb. 2016, www.thecut.com/2016/02/a-neuroscience-finding-on-free-will.html.
13. Kahneman, Daniel. *Thinking, fast and slow*. Farrar, Straus and Giroux, 2015. For reference purposes: The Introduction (1-17), Chapter 4: The Associative Machine (50-58), Chapter 5: Cognitive Ease (59-70), Chapter 6:"Norms, Surprises, and Causes" (71-78), Chapter 7: A Machine for Jumping to Conclusions (79-88), Chapter 8: How Judgments Happen (89-96), Chapter 9: Answering an Easier Question (97-107), Chapter 12: The Science of Availability (129-136), Chapter 13: Availability, Emotion, and Risk (137-145), Chapter 19: The Illusion of Understanding (199-208), Chapter 20: The Illusion of Validity (209-221), Chapter 22: Expert Intuition: When Can We Trust It? (234-244), and Chapter 38: Thinking About Life (398-407).
14. Lotto, Beau. *Deviate: the Science of Seeing Differently*. Hachette Books, 2017. For reference: Chapter 5: The Frog Who Dreamed of Being a Prince (1356 - 1670), Chapter 6: The Physiology of Assumptions (1671 - 2121), and Chapter 7: Changing the Future Past (2122 - 2429).
15. Nietzsche, Friedrich Wilhelm. *THE ANTICHRIST*. Translated by H. L. Mencken, The Project Gutenberg, 2006. For reference: Aphorisms 43, 46, 47, 48, and 49.
16. Puente, Mark. "Sun Investigates: Undue force." *The Baltimore Sun*, 28 Sept. 2014, data.baltimoresun.com/news/police-settlements/.
17. Roser, Max. "Visual History of The Rise of Political Freedom and the Decrease in Violence." *Visual History of The Rise of Political Freedom and the Decrease in Violence*. Web. 3 Jan. 2016.
18. Rosling, Hans. *Factfulness*. Macmillan, 2018.
19. Schultze-Kraft, Matthias, et al. "The Point of No Return in Vetoing Self-Initiated Movements." *PNAS*, National Academy of Sciences, 26 Jan. 2016, www.pnas.org/content/113/4/1080.
20. "Study Tackles Neuroscience Claims to Have Disproved 'Free Will'." *NC State News The Difference Between Baking Soda and Baking Powder Comments*, 12 Mar. 2018, news.ncsu.edu/2018/03/free-will-review-2018/.
21. Valenti, Jessica. "Purity Balls, Plan B and Bad Sex Policy: inside America's Virginity Obsession | Jessica Valenti." *The Guardian*, Guardian News and Media, 5 May 2014,

b.) <u>Judaism</u>

Chapter 8

1. Beinart, Peter. "American Jewish Establishment Stifles Free Speech to Silence Zionism's Critics." *Haaretz.com*, Haaretz Com, 24 Apr. 2018, www.haaretz.com/opinion/.premium-how-zionism-is-losing-the-contest-of-ideas-in-the-u-s-1.5470232.
2. "BibleGateway." *Bible Gateway*, Bible Gateway Blog, www.biblegateway.com/passage/?search=John 8:21-44&version=KJV.
3. Browne, Ryan, and Oscar Featherstone. "US Arms Sold to Saudi Arabia and UAE End up in Wrong Hands." *CNN*, Cable News Network, www.cnn.com/interactive/2019/02/middleeast/yemen-lost-us-arms/.
4. Daly, Matthew. "US Approves Deal to Share Nuclear Tech with Saudi Arabia." *The Times of Israel*, www.timesofisrael.com/us-approves-deal-to-share-nuclear-tech-with-saudi-arabia/.
5. Dorell, Oren. "U.S. $38B Military Aid Package to Israel Sends a Message." *USA Today*, Gannett Satellite Information Network, 14 Sept. 2016, www.usatoday.com/story/news/world/2016/09/14/united-states-military-aid-israel/90358564/.
6. Gouri, Daniel, et al. "Holocaust Survivors Condemn Israel for 'Gaza Massacre,' Call for Boycott." *Haaretz.com*, Haaretz Com, 10 Apr. 2018, www.haaretz.com/holocaust-survivors-condemn-israel-for-gaza-massacre-1.5260588#.VMR7SI5whq8.twitter.
7. Gross, Judah Ari. "Suicide Was Top Cause of Death for IDF Soldiers in 2016." *The Times of Israel*, www.timesofisrael.com/idf-15-soldiers-committed-suicide-in-the-past-year/.

8. Hartung, William D. "It's Not Diplomacy, It's an Arms Fair." *Foreign Policy*, Foreign Policy, 14 May 2015, foreignpolicy.com/2015/05/14/obama-arms-fair-camp-david-weapons-sales-gcc/.
9. "Israel." *U.S. Department of State*, U.S. Department of State, 14 May 2018, www.state.gov/r/pa/ei/bgn/3581.htm.
10. Johnson, Barbara C. "The Cochin Jews Of Kerala." *My Jewish Learning*, www.myjewishlearning.com/article/the-cochin-jews-of-kerala/.
11. Kennard, Matthew. "The Cruel Experiments of Israel's Arms Industry." *The Electronic Intifada*, 27 June 2017, electronicintifada.net/content/cruel-experiments-israels-arms-industry/19011.
12. Lis, Jonathan. "Israel's Contentious Nation-State Law: Everything You Need to Know." *Haaretz.com*, Haaretz Com, 19 July 2018, www.haaretz.com/israel-news/.premium-israel-s-contentious-nation-state-law-everything-you-need-to-know-1.6292733?=&ts=_1532742032458.
13. Mackey, Robert. "University of California Adopts Policy Linking Anti-Zionism to Anti-Semitism." *The Intercept*, 23 Mar. 2016, theintercept.com/2016/03/23/university-of-california-adopts-policy-linking-anti-zionism-to-anti-semitism/.
14. Moses, Nissim. "Bene Israel of India." *Avotaynu Online*, 24 Mar. 2015, www.avotaynuonline.com/2007/07/bene-israel-of-india-by-nissim-moses/.
15. Nietzsche, Friedrich Wilhelm. *THE ANTICHRIST*. Translated by H. L. Mencken, The Project Gutenberg, 2006. For reference: Aphorisms 24, 25, and 26.
16. Rosenblatt, Lauren, et al. "US Seeks to Increase Aid to Israel by $200M in 2019." *The Pittsburgh Jewish Chronicle*, jewishchronicle.timesofisrael.com/us-seeks-to-increase-aid-to-israel-by-200m-in-2019/.
17. Shalev, Chemi. "Hungary PM Orban's Upcoming Visit: A Stain on Israel's History." *Haaretz.com*, Haaretz Com, 3 July 2018, www.haaretz.com/israel-news/.premium-hungary-pm-orban-s-upcoming-visit-a-blot-on-netanyahu-s-record-and-a-stain-on-israel-s-history-1.6223675.
18. Sharp, Jeremy M. "U.S. Foreign Aid to Israel - Federation of American Scientists." *FAS.ORG*, Congressional Research Service, fas.org/sgp/crs/mideast/RL33222.pdf.
19. "Timeline of Antisemitism." *Wikipedia*, Wikimedia Foundation, 27 Mar. 2019, en.wikipedia.org/wiki/Timeline_of_antisemitism.
20. Toi. "France to Study Building Nuclear Reactors in Saudi Arabia." *The Times of Israel*, www.timesofisrael.com/france-to-study-building-nuclear-reactors-in-saudi-arabia/.
21. Toi, et al. "IDF Commander Seeks God's Help to Fight 'Blasphemous' Gazans." *The Times of Israel*, www.timesofisrael.com/idf-commander-calls-on-troops-to-fight-blasphemous-gazans/.
22. Weiss, Gary. "India's Jews." *Forbes*, Forbes Magazine, 17 July 2012, www.forbes.com/2007/08/05/india-jews-antisemitism-oped-cx_gw_0813jews.html#4d526e5f3d45.
23. *YouTube*, The Intercept, 23 Aug. 2018, www.youtube.com/watch?v=3yr0G50rL28.
24. *YouTube*, Q-Ball Productions Inc, 2010, www.youtube.com/watch?v=nNvtA_q0e20.

Chapter 9

1. Beinart, Peter. "American Jewish Establishment Stifles Free Speech to Silence Zionism's Critics." *Haaretz.com*, Haaretz Com, 24 Apr. 2018, www.haaretz.com/opinion/.premium-how-zionism-is-losing-the-contest-of-ideas-in-the-u-s-1.5470232.
2. "British Ethnologist Richard Dawkins Declares 'Jew' Is Not a Race." *Algemeiner.com*, www.algemeiner.com/2015/04/28/british-ethnologist-richard-dawkins-jew-is-not-a-race/.
3. Dorell, Oren. "U.S. $38B Military Aid Package to Israel Sends a Message." *USA Today*, Gannett Satellite Information Network, 14 Sept. 2016, www.usatoday.com/story/news/world/2016/09/14/united-states-military-aid-israel/90358564/.
4. Fang, Lee, and Zaid Jilani. "Politicians Campaign on Free Speech While Voting to Penalize Boycotts of Israel." *The Intercept*, 14 Mar. 2018, theintercept.com/2018/03/14/campus-free-speech-bds-israel-boycott
5. Glausiusz, Josie. "Blood Brothers: Palestinians and Jews Share Genetic Roots." *Haaretz.com*, 10 Apr. 2018, www.haaretz.com/science-and-health/palestinians-and-jews-share-genetic-roots-1.5411201.
6. Greenwald, Glenn. "The Greatest Threat to Campus Free Speech Is Coming From Dianne Feinstein and Her Military-Contractor Husband." *The Intercept*, 25 Sept. 2015, theintercept.com/2015/09/25/dianne-feinstein-husband-threaten-univ-calif-demanding-ban-excessive-israel-criticism/.
7. Greenwald, Glenn, and Andrew Fishman. "Greatest Threat to Free Speech in the West: Criminalizing Activism Against Israeli Occupation." *The Intercept*, 16 Feb. 2016,

theintercept.com/2016/02/16/greatest-threat-to-free-speech-in-the-west-criminalizing-activism-against-israeli-occupation/.
8. Greenwald, Glenn. "NYT's Bari Weiss Falsely Denies Her Years of Attacks on the Academic Freedom of Arab Scholars Who Criticize Israel." *The Intercept*, 8 Mar. 2018, theintercept.com/2018/03/08/the-nyts-bari-weiss-falsely-denies-her-years-of-attacks-on-the-academic-freedom-of-arab-scholars-who-criticize-israel/.
9. Hedges, Chris. "Banning Dissent in the Name of Civility." *Common Dreams*, Common Dreams, 22 Dec. 2014, www.commondreams.org/views/2014/12/22/banning-dissent-name-civility.
10. Hussain, Murtaza. "Students in California Might Face Criminal Investigation for Protesting Film on Israeli Army." *The Intercept*, 23 June 2016, theintercept.com/2016/06/23/students-in-california-might-face-criminal-investigation-for-protesting-film-on-israeli-army/.
11. Kahneman, Daniel. *Thinking, fast and slow*. Farrar, Straus and Giroux, 2015. For reference purposes: Chapter 6:"Norms, Surprises, and Causes" (71-78).
12. Lis, Jonathan. "Israel's Contentious Nation-State Law: Everything You Need to Know." *Haaretz.com*, Haaretz Com, 19 July 2018, www.haaretz.com/israel-news/.premium-israel-s-contentious-nation-state-law-everything-you-need-to-know-1.6292733?=&ts=_1532742032458.
13. Mackey, Robert. "University of California Adopts Policy Linking Anti-Zionism to Anti-Semitism." *The Intercept*, 23 Mar. 2016, theintercept.com/2016/03/23/university-of-california-adopts-policy-linking-anti-zionism-to-anti-semitism/.
14. Muthali, Aki. "Atheistophobia: It's Time to Talk about the Most Persecuted Minority in the World." *The Nation*, 27 Sept. 2015, nation.com.pk/27-Sep-2015/atheistophobia-it-s-time-to-talk-about-the-most-persecuted-minority-in-the-world.
15. Neturei Karta. "Jewish Rabbi Condemning Israeli Attack on Gaza." *YouTube*, Neturei Karta, 20 July 2014, www.youtube.com/watch?v=JaSqvutvI1k.
16. "NYCLU Defends Academic Freedom At Columbia University." *New York Civil Liberties Union*, 21 Feb. 2007, www.nyclu.org/en/press-releases/nyclu-defends-academic-freedom-columbia-university.
17. Palumbo-Liu, David. "Steven Salaita, Professor Fired for 'Uncivil' Tweets, Vindicated in Federal Court." *The Nation*, 11 Aug. 2015, www.thenation.com/article/steven-salaita-professor-fired-for-uncivil-tweets-vindicated-in-federal-court/.
18. "Protests Held In NYC Against Israeli Violence In Gaza." *ANIMAL*, 11 July 2014, animalnewyork.com/2014/protests-held-nyc-israeli-violence-gaza/.
19. Rosenblatt, Lauren, et al. "US Seeks to Increase Aid to Israel by $200M in 2019." *The Pittsburgh Jewish Chronicle*, jewishchronicle.timesofisrael.com/us-seeks-to-increase-aid-to-israel-by-200m-in-2019/.
20. Sharp, Jeremy M. "U.S. Foreign Aid to Israel - Federation of American Scientists." *FAS.ORG*, Congressional Research Service, fas.org/sgp/crs/mideast/RL33222.pdf.
21. "U.S. Foreign Aid to Israel: Total Aid." *Jewish Virtual Library*, www.jewishvirtuallibrary.org/total-u-s-foreign-aid-to-israel-1949-present.

Chapter 10

1. "Archeology of the Hebrew Bible." *PBS*, Public Broadcasting Service, 18 Nov. 2008, www.pbs.org/wgbh/nova/ancient/archeology-hebrew-bible.html.
2. David, Ariel. "How the Jews Invented God, and Made Him Great." *Haaretz.com*, Haaretz Com, 5 June 2018, www.haaretz.com/archaeology/.premium.MAGAZINE-how-the-jews-invented-god-and-made-him-great-1.5392677.
3. Deitch, Ian. "Egypt: New Find Shows Slaves Didn't Build Pyramids." *U.S. News & World Report*, U.S. News & World Report, www.usnews.com/science/articles/2010/01/12/egypt-new-find-shows-slaves-didnt-build-pyramids.
4. "Europe's Hypocritical History of Cannibalism." *Smithsonian.com*, Smithsonian Institution, 24 Apr. 2013, www.smithsonianmag.com/history/europes-hypocritical-history-of-cannibalism-42642371/.
5. Isaacs, Ronald H. "The Ten Commandments." *My Jewish Learning*, My Jewish Learning, www.myjewishlearning.com/article/the-ten-commandments/.
6. Kennard, Matthew. "The Cruel Experiments of Israel's Arms Industry." *The Electronic Intifada*, 27 June 2017, electronicintifada.net/content/cruel-experiments-israels-arms-industry/19011.
7. Mintz, Josh. "Were Jews Ever Really Slaves in Egypt, or Is Passover a Myth?" *Haaretz.com*, Haaretz Com, 10 Apr. 2018, www.haaretz.com/jewish/were-jews-ever-really-slaves-in-egypt-1.5208519.

8. Pelaia, Ariela. "What Is a Passover Seder?" *ThoughtCo*, ThoughtCo, www.thoughtco.com/what-is-a-passover-seder-2076456.
9. Rosch, Staks. "The Biblical Exodus Story Is Fiction." *The Huffington Post*, TheHuffingtonPost.com, 7 Dec. 2017, www.huffingtonpost.com/staks-rosch/the-biblical-exodus-story-is-fiction_b_1408123.html.
10. Rosenberg, Stephen Gabriel. "The Exodus: Does Archaeology Have a Say?" *The Jerusalem Post | JPost.com*, 14 Apr. 2014, www.jpost.com/Opinion/Op-Ed-Contributors/The-Exodus-Does-archaeology-have-a-say-348464.

Chapter 11

1. Abu El-Haj, Nadia. "Dr. Nadia Abu El-Haj on the Occupation's Effects on Palestinian Academia." *YouTube*, Anthropologists Boycott, 31 Mar. 2016, www.youtube.com/watch?v=3Q0w3-RtnQg.
2. "Archeology of the Hebrew Bible." *PBS*, Public Broadcasting Service, 18 Nov. 2008, www.pbs.org/wgbh/nova/ancient/archeology-hebrew-bible.html.
3. Blackler, Zoë. "Brooklyn DA Accused of Failing to Tackle Orthodox Jews' Cover-up of Sex Abuse." *The Guardian*, Guardian News and Media, 29 Mar. 2012, www.theguardian.com/world/2012/mar/29/brooklyn-da-orthodox-jews-cover-up.
4. Blackler, Zoë. "Brooklyn's Ultra-Orthodox Jews Rally behind Accused in Child Abuse Case." *The Guardian*, Guardian News and Media, 16 May 2012, www.theguardian.com/world/2012/may/16/orthodox-sex-abuse-scandal-new-york.
5. Byrne, Joe. "C4's Jewish Abuse Documentary Didn't Tell the Whole Story." *The Telegraph*, Telegraph Media Group, 18 Feb. 2013, www.telegraph.co.uk/lifestyle/9872924/C4s-Jewish-abuse-documentary-didnt-tell-the-whole-story.html.
6. "Can a Rabbi Get Married?" *Mitzvahs & Traditions*, www.chabad.org/library/article_cdo/aid/248162/jewish/Can-a-Rabbi-Get-Married.htm.
7. *Children in Israeli Military Detention ... - UNICEF*. www.unicef.org/oPt/Children_in_Israeli_Military_Detention_-_Observations_and_Recommendations_-_Bulletin_No._2_-_February_2015.pdf.
8. Davey, Melissa. "Rabbi Was Allowed to Keep Teaching after Admitting Abuse of Children, Inquiry Told." *The Guardian*, Guardian News and Media, 3 Feb. 2015, www.theguardian.com/australia-news/2015/feb/03/rabbi-was-allowed-to-keep-teaching-after-admitting-abuse-of-children-inquiry-told.
9. Davey, Melissa. "Catholic Sexual Abuse Partly Caused by Secrecy and Mandatory Celibacy, Report Finds." *The Guardian*, Guardian News and Media, 13 Sept. 2017, www.theguardian.com/australia-news/2017/sep/13/catholic-sexual-abuse-partly-caused-by-celibacy-and-secrecy-report-finds.
10. Dorell, Oren. "U.S. $38B Military Aid Package to Israel Sends a Message." *USA Today*, Gannett Satellite Information Network, 14 Sept. 2016, www.usatoday.com/story/news/world/2016/09/14/united-states-military-aid-israel/90358564/.
11. Ibish, Hussein. "The Nonviolent Violence of Hamas." *Foreign Policy*, Foreign Policy, 6 Apr. 2018, foreignpolicy.com/2018/04/06/the-non-violent-violence-of-hamas/.
12. Kahneman, Daniel. *Thinking, fast and slow*. Farrar, Straus and Giroux, 2015. For reference purposes: Chapter 31: Risk Policies (334-341) and Chapter 32: Keeping Score (342 - 352).
13. Kennard, Matthew. "The Cruel Experiments of Israel's Arms Industry." *The Electronic Intifada*, 27 June 2017, electronicintifada.net/content/cruel-experiments-israels-arms-industry/19011.
14. LAZAROFF , TOVAH. "IDF Destroys Two Illegal EU-Funded Palestinian Schools." *The Jerusalem Post | JPost.com*, 24 Aug. 2017, www.jpost.com/Arab-Israeli-Conflict/IDF-destroys-two-illegal-EU-funded-Palestinian-schools-503252.
15. Lowenstein , Nitza. "Leading Rabbi Calls on Jewish Leaders to Stand down Following Child Abuse Royal Commission." *SBS PopAsia*, SBS News, 30 Nov. 2016, www.sbs.com.au/yourlanguage/hebrew/en/article/2016/12/01/leading-rabbi-calls-jewish-leaders-stand-down-following-child-abuse-royal.
16. Maltz, Judy. "Israel Tortures Palestinian Children, Amnesty Report Says." *Haaretz.com*, Haaretz Com, 24 Apr. 2018, www.haaretz.com/israel-news/.premium-israel-tortures-palestinian-children-amnesty-report-says-1.5440012.
17. Mintz, Josh. "Were Jews Ever Really Slaves in Egypt, or Is Passover a Myth?" *Haaretz.com*, Haaretz Com, 10 Apr. 2018, www.haaretz.com/jewish/were-jews-ever-really-slaves-in-egypt-1.5208519.
18. "Moving the Goalposts." *Https://Www.logicallyfallacious.com*,

19. Nietzsche, Friedrich. *The Dawn of Day*. Translated by J. M. Kennedy, Dover Publications, 2012. For reference: Aphorisms 26, 28, 31, 32, 33, 34, 35, 36, 40, 42, 91, 93, and 95.
20. Otterman, Sharon, and Ray Rivera. "Ultra-Orthodox Shun Their Own for Reporting Child Sexual Abuse." *The New York Times*, The New York Times, 10 May 2012, www.nytimes.com/2012/05/10/nyregion/ultra-orthodox-jews-shun-their-own-for-reporting-child-sexual-abuse.html.
21. Rickman, Dan. "Does Judaism Discriminate against Women? | Dan Rickman." *The Guardian*, Guardian News and Media, 10 June 2009, www.theguardian.com/commentisfree/belief/2009/jun/10/judaism-women-feminism-orthodox.
22. Rosenblatt, Lauren, et al. "US Seeks to Increase Aid to Israel by $200M in 2019." *The Pittsburgh Jewish Chronicle*, jewishchronicle.timesofisrael.com/us-seeks-to-increase-aid-to-israel-by-200m-in-2019/.
23. Saul, Josh. "Sex Abuse Victim Shamed during Synagogue Prayers." *New York Post*, New York Post, 9 Sept. 2013, nypost.com/2013/09/09/sex-abuse-victim-shamed-during-synagogue-prayers/.
24. Septimus, Daniel. "Must a Jew Believe in God?" *My Jewish Learning*, www.myjewishlearning.com/article/must-a-jew-believe-in-god/.
25. Shalev, Chemi. "Netanyahu to American Jews: Drop Dead." *Haaretz.com*, Haaretz Com, 24 Apr. 2018, www.haaretz.com/israel-news/.premium-netanyahu-to-american-jews-drop-dead-1.5488498.
26. Sharp, Jeremy M. "U.S. Foreign Aid to Israel - Federation of American Scientists." *FAS.ORG*, Congressional Research Service, fas.org/sgp/crs/mideast/RL33222.pdf.
25. Sommer, Allison Kaplan. "Israel's Western Wall Crisis: Why Jews Are Fighting with Each Other over the Jewish Holy Site, Explained." *Haaretz.com*, Haaretz Com, 24 Apr. 2018, www.haaretz.com/israel-news/israel-s-western-wall-crisis-explained-1.5488942.
26. "UN: Palestinian Children Tortured, Used as Human Shields by Israel." *Haaretz.com*, Haaretz Com, 10 Jan. 2018, www.haaretz.com/.premium-israel-tortured-palestinian-children-1.5283333.
27. Winer, Stuart, and Toi. "Religious-Zionist Rabbis Back Decision to Block Gay Adoption." *The Times of Israel*, www.timesofisrael.com/religious-zionist-rabbis-back-decision-to-block-gay-adoption/?utm_source=dlvr.it&utm_medium=twitter.
28. "Your Logical Fallacy Is False Cause." *Thou Shalt Not Commit Logical Fallacies*, yourlogicalfallacyis.com/false-cause.
29. "Your Logical Fallacy Is Middle Ground." *Thou Shalt Not Commit Logical Fallacies*, yourlogicalfallacyis.com/middle-ground.

Chapter 12

1. "9 Young Jews Arrested at NYC Anti-Israel Protest." *The Jerusalem Post | JPost.com*, 30 July 2014, www.jpost.com/Jewish-World/Jewish-News/9-young-Jews-arrested-at-NYC-anti-Israel-protest-369365.
2. AHRONHEIM, ANNA. "Third Druze Officer Resigns from IDF in Protest of Nation-State Law." *The Jerusalem Post | JPost.com*, 2 Aug. 2018, www.jpost.com/Israel-News/Third-Druze-officer-resigns-in-protest-of-Nation-State-Law-563926.
3. "Archeology of the Hebrew Bible." *PBS*, Public Broadcasting Service, 18 Nov. 2008, www.pbs.org/wgbh/nova/ancient/archeology-hebrew-bible.html.
4. Bahar, Dany, and Natan Sachs. "How Much Does BDS Threaten Israel's Economy?" *Brookings*, Brookings, 26 Jan. 2018, www.brookings.edu/blog/order-from-chaos/2018/01/26/how-much-does-bds-threaten-israels-economy/.
5. Beinart, Peter. "American Jewish Establishment Stifles Free Speech to Silence Zionism's Critics." *Haaretz.com*, Haaretz Com, 24 Apr. 2018, www.haaretz.com/opinion/.premium-how-zionism-is-losing-the-contest-of-ideas-in-the-u-s-1.5470232.
6. "BibleGateway." *Bible Gateway*, Bible Gateway Blog, www.biblegateway.com/passage/?search=John 8:21-44&version=KJV.
7. "BibleGateway." *Bible Gateway*, Bible Gateway Blog, www.biblegateway.com/passage/?search=Matthew 5&version=KJV.
8. Blumenthal, David J. "Is Forgiveness Necessary?" *My Jewish Learning*, www.myjewishlearning.com/article/is-forgiveness-necessary/.
9. Bowyer, Jerry. "Does God Belong In The Boardroom? 1,800 CEOs Say Yes." *GenTwenty*, The Mercury News, 12 Aug. 2016,

10. Deitch, Ian. "Egypt: New Find Shows Slaves Didn't Build Pyramids." *U.S. News & World Report*, U.S. News & World Report, www.usnews.com/science/articles/2010/01/12/egypt-new-find-shows-slaves-didnt-build-pyramids.
11. Dorell, Oren. "U.S. $38B Military Aid Package to Israel Sends a Message." *USA Today*, Gannett Satellite Information Network, 14 Sept. 2016, www.usatoday.com/story/news/world/2016/09/14/united-states-military-aid-israel/90358564/.
12. "Diya (Islam)." *Wikipedia*, Wikimedia Foundation, 8 Sept. 2018, en.wikipedia.org/wiki/Diya_(Islam).
13. *Embassies.gov.il*, embassies.gov.il/delhi/NewsAndEvents/Pages/rnational day of Holocaust observed in Delhi.aspx. For reference:http://embassies.gov.il/delhi/NewsAndEvents/Pages/rnational%20day%20of%20Holocaust%20observed%20in%20Delhi.aspx
14. Fang, Lee, and Zaid Jilani. "Politicians Campaign on Free Speech While Voting to Penalize Boycotts of Israel." *The Intercept*, 14 Mar. 2018, theintercept.com/2018/03/14/campus-free-speech-bds-israel-boycott
15. Fraser, Giles. "Ultra-Orthodox Attitudes towards Gender Segregation Go to the Core of What Israel Is All about | Giles Fraser." *The Guardian*, Guardian News and Media, 4 Oct. 2013, www.theguardian.com/commentisfree/belief/2013/oct/04/ultra-orthodox-gender-segregation-core-israel.
16. "Gaza and the Propaganda Machines." *The Guardian*, Guardian News and Media, 15 Aug. 2014, www.theguardian.com/world/2014/aug/15/gaza-propaganda-machines.
17. Gouri, Daniel, et al. "Holocaust Survivors Condemn Israel for 'Gaza Massacre,' Call for Boycott." *Haaretz.com*, Haaretz Com, 10 Apr. 2018, www.haaretz.com/holocaust-survivors-condemn-israel-for-gaza-massacre-1.5260588#.VMR7SI5whq8.twitter.
18. Greenwald, Glenn. "The Greatest Threat to Campus Free Speech Is Coming From Dianne Feinstein and Her Military-Contractor Husband." *The Intercept*, 25 Sept. 2015, theintercept.com/2015/09/25/dianne-feinstein-husband-threaten-univ-calif-demanding-ban-excessive-israel-criticism/.
19. Gross, Judah Ari. "Suicide Was Top Cause of Death for IDF Soldiers in 2016." *The Times of Israel*, www.timesofisrael.com/idf-15-soldiers-committed-suicide-in-the-past-year/.
20. "Holocaust Survivors Condemn Israel´s Massacre in Gaza/End to Israeli Occupation and Colonization." *Astrid Essed*, www.astridessed.nl/holocaust-survivors-condemn-israels-massacre-in-gazaend-to-israeli-occupation-and-colonization/.
21. Hussain, Murtaza. "Students in California Might Face Criminal Investigation for Protesting Film on Israeli Army." *The Intercept*, 23 June 2016, theintercept.com/2016/06/23/students-in-california-might-face-criminal-investigation-for-protesting-film-on-israeli-army/.
22. Ispas, Alexa. *Psychology and politics: a social identity perspective*. Psychology Press, 2014.
23. Johnson, Barbara C. "The Cochin Jews Of Kerala." *My Jewish Learning*, www.myjewishlearning.com/article/the-cochin-jews-of-kerala/.
24. Lis, Jonathan. "Israel's Contentious Nation-State Law: Everything You Need to Know." *Haaretz.com*, Haaretz Com, 19 July 2018, www.haaretz.com/israel-news/.premium-israel-s-contentious-nation-state-law-everything-you-need-to-know-1.6292733?=&ts=_1532742032458.
25. Moses, Nissim. "Bene Israel of India." *Avotaynu Online*, 24 Mar. 2015, www.avotaynuonline.com/2007/07/bene-israel-of-india-by-nissim-moses/.
26. Murphy, Caryle. "The Most and Least Educated U.S. Religious Groups." *Pew Research Center*, Pew Research Center, 4 Nov. 2016, www.pewresearch.org/fact-tank/2016/11/04/the-most-and-least-educated-u-s-religious-groups/.
27. Navabi, Armin. "Attacking Islam as an Act of Compassion - Armin Navabi." *YouTube*, Ex-Muslims of North America, 4 Dec. 2017, www.youtube.com/watch?v=9m7IaAlnkgo.
28. Neturei Karta. "Jewish Rabbi Condemning Israeli Attack on Gaza." *YouTube*, Neturei Karta, 20 July 2014, www.youtube.com/watch?v=JaSqvutvI1k.
29. *News of the World*, newsoftheworldnews.wordpress.com/tag/international-jewish-anti-zionism-network/.
30. Nietzsche, Friedrich Wilhelm. *THE ANTICHRIST*. Translated by H. L. Mencken, The Project Gutenberg, 2006. For reference: Aphorisms 24, 25, and 26.
31. Nietzsche, Friedrich. *The Dawn of Day*. Translated by J. M. Kennedy, Dover Publications, 2012. For reference: Aphorisms 26, 28, 31, 32, 33, 34, 35, 36, 40, 42, 91, 93, and 95.
32. "Protests Held In NYC Against Israeli Violence In Gaza." *ANIMAL*, 11 July 2014, animalnewyork.com/2014/protests-held-nyc-israeli-violence-gaza/.
33. "Qisas." *Wikipedia*, Wikimedia Foundation, 9 Sept. 2018, en.wikipedia.org/wiki/Qisas.
30. Rosenblatt, Lauren, et al. "US Seeks to Increase Aid to Israel by $200M in 2019." *The Pittsburgh Jewish*

Chronicle, jewishchronicle.timesofisrael.com/us-seeks-to-increase-aid-to-israel-by-200m-in-2019/.

34. Rosch, Staks. "The Biblical Exodus Story Is Fiction." *The Huffington Post*, TheHuffingtonPost.com, 7 Dec. 2017, www.huffingtonpost.com/staks-rosch/the-biblical-exodus-story-is-fiction_b_1408123.html.
35. Septimus, Daniel. "Must a Jew Believe in God?" *My Jewish Learning*, www.myjewishlearning.com/article/must-a-jew-believe-in-god/.
27. Shalev, Chemi. "Hungary PM Orban's Upcoming Visit: A Stain on Israel's History." *Haaretz.com*, Haaretz Com, 3 July 2018, www.haaretz.com/israel-news/.premium-hungary-pm-orban-s-upcoming-visit-a-blot-on-netanyahu-s-record-and-a-stain-on-israel-s-history-1.6223675.
28. Sharp, Jeremy M. "U.S. Foreign Aid to Israel - Federation of American Scientists." *FAS.ORG*, Congressional Research Service, fas.org/sgp/crs/mideast/RL33222.pdf.
36. Shaw, Barry. "Unmasking BDS: A New Method to Fight the Movement Has Emerged, and It's Working." *The Jerusalem Post | JPost.com*, 15 July 2017, www.jpost.com/Jerusalem-Report/The-unmasking-of-BDS-498347.
37. "Static.reuters.com." *Reuters*, Reuters, static.reuters.com/resources/media/editorial/20150910/WilksDoctrinalPoints.pdf.
38. "Timeline of Antisemitism." *Wikipedia*, Wikimedia Foundation, 27 Mar. 2019, en.wikipedia.org/wiki/Timeline_of_antisemitism.
39. Toi, et al. "Druze-Led Rally against Nation-State Law in Tel Aviv Draws at Least 50,000." *The Times of Israel*, www.timesofisrael.com/tens-of-thousands-gather-in-tel-aviv-to-protest-controversial-nation-state-law/.
40. "U.S. Foreign Aid to Israel: Total Aid." *Jewish Virtual Library*, www.jewishvirtuallibrary.org/total-u-s-foreign-aid-to-israel-1949-present.
41. WABC. "Another Flag: Palestinian Flag Turns up on Manhattan Bridge." *ABC7 New York*, 21 Aug. 2014, abc7ny.com/news/another-flag-palestinian-flag-turns-up-on-manhattan-bridge-/273742/.
42. Weiss, Gary. "India's Jews." *Forbes*, Forbes Magazine, 17 July 2012, www.forbes.com/2007/08/05/india-jews-antisemitism-oped-cx_gw_0813jews.html#4d526e5f3d45.
43. *YouTube*, Q-Ball Productions Inc, 2010, www.youtube.com/watch?v=nNvtA_q0e20.
44. *YouTube*, The Intercept, 23 Aug. 2018, www.youtube.com/watch?v=3yr0G50rL28.

c.) <u>Christianity</u>

<u>Chapter 13</u>

1. *1 Corinthians 6 KJV*, biblehub.com/kjv/1_corinthians/6.htm.
2. "BibleGateway." *Bible Gateway*, Bible Gateway Blog, www.biblegateway.com/passage/?search=Mark 11:12-25&version=KJV.
3. "BibleGateway." *Bible Gateway*, Bible Gateway Blog, www.biblegateway.com/passage/?search=John 14:6&version=KJV. For reference:John 14:6 King James Version (KJV)6 Jesus saith unto him, I am the way, the truth, and the life: no man cometh unto the Father, but by me.
4. "BibleGateway." *Bible Gateway*, Bible Gateway Blog, www.biblegateway.com/passage/?search=1 Timothy 2&version=KJV.
5. BuffMaister. "Shin Megami Tensei 4 Apocalypse Boss Vishnu-Flynn [APOCALYPSE] [ANARCHY]." *YouTube*, YouTube, 16 Feb. 2018, www.youtube.com/watch?v=YMUk4i6h1GY&t=39s.
6. Cialdini, Robert B. *Influence: Science and practice*. 4th ed., 21st Century Bks, 2002. For reference: Chapter 1: Weapons of Influence (1-16) and Chapter 3: Commitment and Consistency (52-95).
7. Hackett, Conrad, and David McClendon. "Christians Remain World's Largest Religious Group, but They Are Declining in Europe." *Pew Research Center*, Pew Research Center, 5 Apr. 2017, www.pewresearch.org/fact-tank/2017/04/05/christians-remain-worlds-largest-religious-group-but-they-are-declining-in-europe/.
8. Kahneman, Daniel. *Thinking, fast and slow*. Farrar, Straus and Giroux, 2015. For reference purposes: The Introduction (1-17), Chapter 4: The Associative Machine (50-58), Chapter 5: Cognitive Ease (59-70), Chapter 6:"Norms, Surprises, and Causes" (71-78), Chapter 7: A Machine for Jumping to Conclusions (79-88), Chapter 8: How Judgments Happen (89-96), Chapter 12: The Science of Availability (129-136), Chapter 13: Availability, Emotion, and Risk (137-145), Chapter 19: The Illusion of Understanding (199-208), and Chapter 20: The Illusion of Validity (209-221).

9. "Moving the Goalposts." *Https://Www.logicallyfallacious.com*, www.logicallyfallacious.com/tools/lp/Bo/LogicalFallacies/129/Moving-the-Goalposts.
10. Nietzsche, Friedrich Wilhelm. *On the genealogy of morals: a polemical tract*. Translated by Ian Johnston, PDF, Richer Resources Publications, 2014.
11. Nietzsche, Friedrich Wilhelm. *THE ANTICHRIST*. Translated by H. L. Mencken, The Project Gutenberg, 2006. For reference: Aphorisms 39, 40, 41, 42, 43, 44, 45, 46, 47, 48, 49, 50, 51, 52, 53, 54, and 55.
12. Nietzsche, Friedrich Wilhelm. *Thus spake Zarathustra: a book for all and none*. Translated by Thomas Common, PDF ed., T. Common, 1908. For reference: Chapter IX: Preachers of Death (50-52) and Chapter XXVI: THE PRIESTS (88-91).
13. Nietzsche, Friedrich. *Twilight of the Idols*. Amazon Digital Services LLC. For reference: How the "True World" Finally Became a Fable. The History of an Error (19-21), Morality as Anti-Nature (21-26), and The Four Great Errors (27-37).
14. "Shin Megami Tensei IV: Apocalypse." US, Atlus, 2016. For reference: Select the Anarchy path before the penultimate dungeon boss.

Chapter 14

1. Bear, Charla. "American Indian Boarding Schools Haunt Many." *NPR*. NPR, 12 May 2008. Web. 2 Nov. 2015, https://www.npr.org/templates/story/story.php?storyId=16516865?storyId=16516865.
2. "BibleGateway." *Mark 10 KJV - - Bible Gateway*, www.biblegateway.com/passage/?search=mark 10&version=KJV.
3. "BibleGateway." *2 Thessalonians 1:8-9 KJV - - Bible Gateway*, www.biblegateway.com/passage/?search=2 Thessalonians 1:8-9&version=KJV.
4. "BibleGateway." *Bible Gateway*, Bible Gateway Blog, www.biblegateway.com/passage/?search=Matthew 10&version=KJV.
5. "BibleGateway." *Bible Gateway*, Bible Gateway Blog, www.biblegateway.com/passage/?search=Matthew 5&version=KJV.
6. Bukhari, Shujaat. "Pastor Admits to Conversion by Missionaries in Kashmir." *The Hindu*, The Hindu, 2 Aug. 2016, www.thehindu.com/news/national/pastor-admits-to-conversion-by-missionaries-in-kashmir/article2640084.ece.
7. Cialdini, Robert B. *Influence: Science and practice*. 4th ed., 21st Century Bks, 2002. For reference: Chapter 1: Weapons of Influence (1-16) and Chapter 3: Commitment and Consistency (52-95).
8. "Circular Reasoning." *Https://Www.logicallyfallacious.com*, www.logicallyfallacious.com/tools/lp/Bo/LogicalFallacies/66/Circular-Reasoning.
9. *Christian Voice - Jerry Springer the Opera*, Christian Voice, www.repentuk.com/springer.html.
10. "Goat-Headed Satanic Statue Sparks Protests in Detroit - BBC Newsbeat." *BBC*, BBC, 27 July 2015, www.bbc.co.uk/newsbeat/article/33674383/goat-headed-satanic-statue-sparks-protests-in-detroit.
11. Goldberg, Philip. "Missionaries in India: Conversion or Coercion?" *The Huffington Post*, TheHuffingtonPost.com, 19 Feb. 2014, www.huffingtonpost.com/philip-goldberg/missionaries-in-india_b_4470448.html.
12. Hayes, Leonard L. "American Indian and Alaskan Native Historical Trauma and an Adlerian Perspective." *Alfredadler.edu*, The Faculty of the Adler Graduate School, Sept. 2010, alfredadler.edu/sites/default/files/Hayes MP 2010.pdf. Sexual abuse in Christian Boarding schools that Native children were kidnapped into going into by the US government. For reference:In the eyes of American Indian and Alaskan Native families, children away atboarding schools faced risks to their health. One of the dangers was disease, especiallytrachoma, influenza, and tuberculosis. The second risk was homesickness, which deeplyaffected the children"s mind and spirit. A third risk which affected the children atboarding schools was the violence that occurred. This violence entailed physical,emotional, neglect, and sexual abuse (Archuleta, Child, Lomawaima, 2000, p. 38).Intimidation and fear were very much present in our daily lives. Forinstance, we would cower from the abusive disciplinary practices of somesuperiors, such as the one who yanked my cousin"s ear hard enough to tearit. After a nine year-old girl was raped in our dormitory bed during thenight; we girls would be so scared that we would jump into each other"sbed as soon as the lights went out. The sustained terror in our heartsfurther tested our endurance, as it was better to suffer with a full bladderand be safe than to walk through the dark, seemingly endless hallway tothe bathroom. When we were older, we girls anguished each time

weentered the classroom of a certain male teacher who stalked and molestedgirls (Archuleta, Child, Lomawaima, 2000, p. 43).In the eyes of another:It always seemed like every time I wanted to talk about this sexual abuse,it seemed like nobody wanted to listen…It hurts, it really hurts! It"s atough thing to have to live with. I want to put out in the open, to talkAmerican Indian and Alaskan Native Historical Trauma 29about it, „cause I want to deal with it, I need to deal with it…I was reallyscared to come out into this world because of the way I felt, a lot of shame(Ehattesaht, Nuu-Chah-Nulth Tribal Conference, 1996) (Archuleta, Child,& Lomawaima, 2000, p. 43).

13. Hicap Mon, Jonah. "Christian Protesters Denounce Unveiling of Huge Goat-Headed Satan Statue in Detroit." *Christian News on Christian Today*, Christian Today, 27 July 2015, www.christiantoday.com/article/christian-protesters-denounce-unveiling-of-huge-goat-headed-satan-statue-in-detroit/60228.htm.
14. Ispas, Alexa. *Psychology and politics: a social identity perspective*. Psychology Press, 2014.
15. Kahneman, Daniel. *Thinking, fast and slow*. Farrar, Straus and Giroux, 2015. For reference purposes: The Introduction (1-17), Chapter 4: The Associative Machine (50-58), Chapter 6:"Norms, Surprises, and Causes" (71-78), Chapter 7: A Machine for Jumping to Conclusions (79-88), Chapter 8: How Judgments Happen (89-96), Chapter 12: The Science of Availability (129-136), Chapter 13: Availability, Emotion, and Risk (137-145), Chapter 25: Bernoulli's Errors (269-277), and Chapter 27: Endowment Effect (289-299).
16. Kingkade, Tyler. "'Stomp On Jesus' Controversy Gets Worse." *The Huffington Post*, TheHuffingtonPost.com, 2 Apr. 2013, www.huffingtonpost.com/2013/04/01/stomp-on-jesus-professor_n_2990116.html.
17. Kingkade, Tyler. "University Decides On Prof Involved In 'Stomp On Jesus' Controversy." *The Huffington Post*, TheHuffingtonPost.com, 24 June 2013, www.huffingtonpost.com/2013/06/24/deandre-poole-fau-stomp-on-jesus_n_3490263.html.
15. Knaus, Bill. "Escape the Guilt Trap." *Psychology Today*, Sussex Publishers, www.psychologytoday.com/us/blog/science-and-sensibility/201401/escape-the-guilt-trap.
16. Lee, Kristen. "The Dangers of Perfectionism." *Psychology Today*, Sussex Publishers, www.psychologytoday.com/us/blog/rethink-your-way-the-good-life/201807/the-dangers-perfectionism.
17. Neary, Sarah. "Forced to Convert: How American Missionaries Really Treat Indigenous Akha Children." *Intercontinental Cry*, IC, 23 Apr. 2013, intercontinentalcry.org/forced-to-convert-how-american-missionaries-really-treat-indigenous-akha-children/.
18. Nietzsche, Friedrich Wilhelm. *On the genealogy of morals: a polemical tract*. Translated by Ian Johnston, PDF, Richer Resources Publications, 2014.
19. Nietzsche, Friedrich Wilhelm. *THE ANTICHRIST*. Translated by H. L. Mencken, The Project Gutenberg, 2006. For reference: Aphorisms 39, 40, 41, 42, 43, 44, 45, 46, 47, 48, 49, 50, 51, 52, 53, 54, and 55.
20. Nietzsche, Friedrich Wilhelm. *Thus spake Zarathustra: a book for all and none*. Translated by Thomas Common, PDF ed., T. Common, 1908. For reference: Chapter XXVI: THE PRIESTS (88-91).
21. Nietzsche, Friedrich. *Twilight of the Idols*. Amazon Digital Services LLC. For reference: Morality as Anti-Nature (21-26) and The Four Great Errors (27-37).
22. "No True Scotsman." *Https://Www.logicallyfallacious.com*, www.logicallyfallacious.com/tools/lp/Bo/LogicalFallacies/135/No-True-Scotsman.
23. Paquin, Mali Ilse. "Canada Confronts Its Dark History of Abuse in Residential Schools." *The Guardian*, Guardian News and Media, 6 June 2015, www.theguardian.com/world/2015/jun/06/canada-dark-of-history-residential-schools.
24. Pearce, Jonathan MS. "16 Problems with Divine Command Theory." *Faith on the Couch*, Patheos, 5 Sept. 2016, www.patheos.com/blogs/tippling/2016/09/04/16-problems-with-divine-command-theory/11/. For reference:Murder, rape, and pillage at Jabesh-gilead (Judges 21:10-24)Murder, rape and pillage of the Midianites (Numbers 31:7-18)More Murder Rape and Pillage (Deuteronomy 20:10-14)Laws of Rape (Deuteronomy 22:28-29)Death to the Rape Victim (Deuteronomy 22:23-24)David's Punishment – Polygamy, Rape, Baby Killing, and God's "Forgiveness" (2 Samuel 12:11-14)Rape of Female Captives (Deuteronomy 21:10-14)Rape and the Spoils of War (Judges 5:30)Sex Slaves (Exodus 21:7-11)God Assists Rape and Plunder (Zechariah 14:1-2)
25. Reese, Hannah. "Intrusive Thoughts: Normal or Not?" Psychology Today, Sussex Publishers, www.psychologytoday.com/us/blog/am-i-normal/201110/intrusive-thoughts-normal-or-not.
26. Reuters. "Satanists Unveil Sculpture in Detroit after Rejection at Oklahoma Capitol." *The Guardian*, Guardian News and Media, 26 July 2015, www.theguardian.com/us-news/2015/jul/26/satanic-temple-

sculpture-detroit-oklahoma.
27. "Sam Harris Aspen Ideas Festival Full Unedited Video." *YouTube*, YouTube, 25 Nov. 2012, www.youtube.com/watch?v=hfgwFESH_jM.
28. "Special Pleading." *Https://Www.logicallyfallacious.com*, www.logicallyfallacious.com/tools/lp/Bo/LogicalFallacies/163/Special-Pleading.
29. "The Facts and Stats on 33000 Denominations: World Christian Encyclopedia (2001, 2nd Edition)." *All About Horus: An Egyptian Copy of Christ? Response to Zeitgeist Movie*, www.philvaz.com/apologetics/a106.htm.
30. "What Is Biblical Repentance?" *Grace to You*, 13 July 2009, www.gty.org/library/articles/A330/what-is-biblical-repentance.
31. "What Is Repentance and Is It Necessary for Salvation?" *GotQuestions.org*, 20 June 2018, www.gotquestions.org/repentance.html.

Chapter 15

1. "BibleGateway." *Bible Gateway*, Bible Gateway Blog, www.biblegateway.com/passage/?search=Matthew 5&version=KJV
2. Cialdini, Robert B. *Influence: Science and practice*. 4th ed., 21st Century Bks, 2002. For reference: Chapter 1: Weapons of Influence (1-16) and Chapter 2: Reciprocation (19-50).
3. Cipriano, Ralph. "Catholic Church Priests Raped Children in Philadelphia, but the Wrong People Went to Jail." *Newsweek*, 15 Dec. 2017, www.newsweek.com/2017/12/08/catholic-church-priests-raped-children-philadelphia-725894.html.
4. "Circular Reasoning." *Https://Www.logicallyfallacious.com*, www.logicallyfallacious.com/tools/lp/Bo/LogicalFallacies/66/Circular-Reasoning
5. Fitz, Jennifer. "Does the Seal of Confession Help Criminals?" *National Catholic Register*, www.ncregister.com/blog/jenfitz/does-the-seal-of-confession-help-criminals.
6. Fitz, Jennifer. "What Happens If Sacramental Confession Ceases to Be Secret?" *Faith on the Couch*, Patheos, 27 Dec. 2014, www.patheos.com/blogs/jenniferfitz/2014/09/what-happens-if-sacramental-confession-ceases-to-be-secret/.
7. Halvorson, Heidi Grant. *Succeed: How We Can Reach Our Goals*. Plume, 2012. For reference: Chapter 2: Do You Know Where Your Goals Come From? (657-952) and Chapter 12: Know When To Hang On (3008 - 3192).
8. Ispas, Alexa. *Psychology and politics: a social identity perspective*. Psychology Press, 2014.
9. Kahneman, Daniel. *Thinking, fast and slow*. Farrar, Straus and Giroux, 2015. For reference purposes: The Introduction (1-17), Chapter 4: The Associative Machine (50-58), Chapter 5: Cognitive Ease (59-70), Chapter 6:"Norms, Surprises, and Causes" (71-78), Chapter 7: A Machine for Jumping to Conclusions (79-88), Chapter 8: How Judgments Happen (89-96), Chapter 12: The Science of Availability (129-136), Chapter 13: Availability, Emotion, and Risk (137-145), Chapter 19: The Illusion of Understanding (199-208), Chapter 20: The Illusion of Validity (209-221), Chapter 22: Expert Intuition: When Can We Trust It? (234-244), Chapter 25: Bernoulli's Errors (269-277), and Chapter 27: Endowment Effect (289-299).
10. McDermott, Rose. *Political Psychology in International Relations*. Ann Arbor: U of Michigan, 2004. Print. For reference: Group Processes (239-260)
11. McGonigal, Kelly. *The Willpower Instinct: How Self-Control Works, Why It Matters, and What You Can Do to Get More of It*. Avery, 2013. For reference: Chapter 4: License to Sin: Why Being Good Gives Us Permission to Be Bad (81-106)
12. Nietzsche, Friedrich Wilhelm. *On the genealogy of morals: a polemical tract*. Translated by Ian Johnston, PDF, Richer Resources Publications, 2014.
13. Nietzsche, Friedrich Wilhelm. *THE ANTICHRIST*. Translated by H. L. Mencken, The Project Gutenberg, 2006. For reference: Aphorisms 39, 40, 41, 42, 43, 44, 45, 46, 47, 49, 50, 51, 52, 53, 54, and 55.
14. Nietzsche, Friedrich Wilhelm. *Thus spake Zarathustra: a book for all and none*. Translated by Thomas Common, PDF ed., T. Common, 1908. For reference: Chapter IX: Preachers of Death (50-52) and Chapter XXVI: THE PRIESTS (88-91).
15. "No True Scotsman." *Https://Www.logicallyfallacious.com*, www.logicallyfallacious.com/tools/lp/Bo/LogicalFallacies/135/No-True-Scotsman.
16. "Priest in Nunavut Pleads Guilty to 8 Sex Charges | CBC News." *CBCnews*, CBC/Radio Canada, 18

Nov. 2013, www.cbc.ca/news/canada/north/eric-dejaeger-catholic-priest-pleads-guilty-to-sex-charges-1.2429865.

17. Ruland, Sam. "'No More Pain' Victim Wrote of Pa. Priest Sex Abuse, as He and Others Took Their Own Lives." *The York Daily Record*, York Daily Record, 21 Aug. 2018, www.ydr.com/story/news/2018/08/21/pennsylvania-priest-sex-abuse-some-took-their-own-lives-others-considered-suicide-grand-jury-report/1042459002/.
18. Silva, Christianna. "New Report Details Child Sex Abuse by More than 300 Catholic Clergy in Pennsylvania, but Most Will Go Unpunished." *VICE News*, VICE News, 14 Aug. 2018, news.vice.com/en_us/article/43p5kn/new-report-details-child-sex-abuse-by-more-than-300-catholic-clergy-in-pennsylvania-but-most-will-go-unpunished.
19. "Special Pleading." *Https://Www.logicallyfallacious.com*, www.logicallyfallacious.com/tools/lp/Bo/LogicalFallacies/163/Special-Pleading.
20. "What Is Biblical Repentance?" *Grace to You*, 13 July 2009, www.gty.org/library/articles/A330/what-is-biblical-repentance.
21. "What Is Repentance and Is It Necessary for Salvation?" *GotQuestions.org*, 20 June 2018, www.gotquestions.org/repentance.html.

Chapter 16

1. Abels, Richard. "Crusades and Early Christian Attitudes toward Warfare." *Academia.edu*, www.academia.edu/22844402/Crusades_and_early_Christian_attitudes_toward_warfare. "American Evangelicalism: New Leaders, New Faces, New Issues." Edited by Cheryl Jackson, *Pew Research Center's Religion & Public Life Project*, 6 May 2008, www.pewforum.org/2008/05/06/american-evangelicalism-new-leaders-new-faces-new-issues/.
2. "BibleGateway." *Bible Gateway*, Bible Gateway Blog, www.biblegateway.com/passage/?search=John 14:6&version=KJV. For reference:John 14:6 King James Version (KJV)6 Jesus saith unto him, I am the way, the truth, and the life: no man cometh unto the Father, but by me.
3. Bowyer, Jerry. "Does God Belong In The Boardroom? 1,800 CEOs Say Yes." *GenTwenty*, The Mercury News, 12 Aug. 2016, webcache.googleusercontent.com/search?q=cache:uTRTKmPg1sMJ:https://www.forbes.com/sites/jerrybowyer/2016/08/12/does-god-belong-in-the-boardroom-1800-ceos-say-yes/&cd=1&hl=en&ct=clnk&gl=us.
4. Cialdini, Robert B. *Influence: Science and practice*. 4th ed., 21st Century Bks, 2002. Chapter 1: Weapons of Influence (1-16), Chapter 2: Reciprocation (19-50), and Chapter 6: Authority (178-200).
5. François, France. "Haiti Doesn't Have a Vodou Problem, It Has a Christianity Problem." *EBONY*, EBONY, 16 July 2014, www.ebony.com/news-views/haiti-doesnt-have-a-vodou-problem-043.
6. Frank, Robert. "Which Religion Holds the Largest Share of Wealth?" *CNBC*, CNBC, 14 Jan. 2015, www.cnbc.com/2015/01/14/the-religion-of-millionaires-.html.
7. Gittleson, Wendy. "Christian 'Soul Vultures' Are Exploiting The Nepal Earthquake 'For Christ' (VIDEO)." *AddictingInfo*, 27 Apr. 2015, addictinginfo.com/2015/04/27/christian-soul-vultures-are-exploiting-the-nepal-earthquake-for-christ-video/.
8. Goldberg, Philip. "Missionaries in India: Conversion or Coercion?" *The Huffington Post*, TheHuffingtonPost.com, 19 Feb. 2014, www.huffingtonpost.com/philip-goldberg/missionaries-in-india_b_4470448.html.
9. Hacker, Jacob S., and Paul Pierson. *Winner-Take-All Politics How Washington Made the Rich Richer - and Turned Its Back on the Middle Class*. Simon & Schuster, 2011.
10. Harrison, William K. "May A Christian Serve in the Military?" *Officers' Christian Fellowship*, 27 June 2018, www.ocfusa.org/2009/06/christian-serve-military-2/.
11. Hayes, Leonard L. "American Indian and Alaskan Native Historical Trauma and an Adlerian Perspective." *Alfredadler.edu*, The Faculty of the Adler Graduate School, Sept. 2010, alfredadler.edu/sites/default/files/Hayes MP 2010.pdf.
12. Heilbroner, David. "Evangelicals, Israel, and the End of the World." *The Huffington Post*, TheHuffingtonPost.com, 25 May 2011, www.huffingtonpost.com/david-heilbroner/evangelicals-israel-and-t_b_391351.html.
13. Jefferson, Thomas. "QUERY XVII The Different Religions Received into That State?" *Thomas

Jefferson, Notes on the State of Virginia: Ch. 17, University of Virginia, xroads.virginia.edu/~hyper/jefferson/ch17.html.

14. "Joshua Project - Ideas for Church Involvment with Unreached Peoples." *Joshua Project*, legacy.joshuaproject.net/mission-ideas-for-churches.php.
15. "Joshua Project - Unreached Peoples of the World." *Joshua Project*, legacy.joshuaproject.net/index.php.
16. "Jury Finds Missionary Guilty of Abusing Cambodian Orphans." *New York Post*, New York Post, 17 May 2018, nypost.com/2018/05/17/jury-finds-missionary-guilty-of-abusing-cambodian-orphans/amp/.
17. Kahneman, Daniel. *Thinking, fast and slow*. Farrar, Straus and Giroux, 2015. For reference purposes: Chapter 4: The Associative Machine (50-58), Chapter 5: Cognitive Ease (59-70), Chapter 6:"Norms, Surprises, and Causes" (71-78), Chapter 7: A Machine for Jumping to Conclusions (79-88), Chapter 8: How Judgments Happen (89-96), Chapter 12: The Science of Availability (129-136), Chapter 13: Availability, Emotion, and Risk (137-145), Chapter 19: The Illusion of Understanding (199-208), Chapter 20: The Illusion of Validity (209-221), Chapter 31: Risk Policies (334-341), and Chapter 32: Keeping Score (342 - 352).
18. Montgomery, Peter. "Meet the Billionaire Brothers You Never Heard of Who Fund the Religious Right." *The American Prospect*, prospect.org/article/meet-billionaire-brothers-you-never-heard-who-fund-religious-right.
19. Navabi, Armin. "Attacking Islam as an Act of Compassion - Armin Navabi." *YouTube*, Ex-Muslims of North America, 4 Dec. 2017, www.youtube.com/watch?v=9m7IaAlnkgo.
20. Neary, Sarah. "Forced to Convert: How American Missionaries Really Treat Indigenous Akha Children." *Intercontinental Cry*, IC, 23 Apr. 2013, intercontinentalcry.org/forced-to-convert-how-american-missionaries-really-treat-indigenous-akha-children/.
21. Neelakandan, Aravindan. "Why No Outrage over Conversion of Tsunami Victims?" *Swarajya Read India Right ATOM*, 29 Dec. 2014, swarajyamag.com/politics/why-no-outrage-over-conversion-of-tsunami-victims.
22. Nietzsche, Friedrich Wilhelm. *On the genealogy of morals: a polemical tract*. Translated by Ian Johnston, PDF, Richer Resources Publications, 2014.
23. Nietzsche, Friedrich Wilhelm. *THE ANTICHRIST*. Translated by H. L. Mencken, The Project Gutenberg, 2006.   For reference: Aphorisms 39, 40, 41, 42, 43, 44, 45, 46, 47, 49, 50, 51, 52, 53, 54, and 55.
24. "Pat Robertson Says Haiti Paying for 'Pact to the Devil'." *CNN*, Cable News Network, 13 Jan. 2010, www.cnn.com/2010/US/01/13/haiti.pat.robertson/.
25. "Prager 'University': How Billionaires Proselytize Rightwing Ignorance to Children." *Daily Kos*, www.dailykos.com/stories/2017/2/19/1635270/-Prager-University-How-Billionaires-Proselytize-Rightwing-Ignorance-to-Children.
26. Rhee, Joseph, et al. "U.S. Military Weapons Inscribed With Secret 'Jesus' Bible Codes." *ABC News*, ABC News Network, 18 Jan. 2010, abcnews.go.com/Blotter/us-military-weapons-inscribed-secret-jesus-bible-codes/story?id=9575794.
27. Shea, Brie. "Fracking Titans Spend Millions Proselytizing School Children." *Rewire.News*, Rewire.News, 1 May 2015, rewire.news/article/2015/04/30/conservatives-spend-millions-proselytizing-school-children/.
28. "Shin Megami Tensei IV: Apocalypse." US, Atlus, 2016.   For reference: Select the Anarchy path before the penultimate dungeon boss.
29. Solomon, Brian. "Meet David Green: Hobby Lobby's Biblical Billionaire." *Forbes*, Forbes Magazine, 2 Nov. 2015, www.forbes.com/sites/briansolomon/2012/09/18/david-green-the-biblical-billionaire-backing-the-evangelical-movement/#5cb389335807.
30. Tix, Andrew. "The Failure of Christian Love in the Holocaust." *Biola University Center for Christian Thought / The Table*, 6 July 2017, cct.biola.edu/failure-christian-love-holocaust/.
31. Vogel, Kenneth P., and Tarini Parti. "How Rand Paul Bombed at Koch Brothers Gathering." *POLITICO*, 3 Feb. 2015, www.politico.com/story/2015/02/rand-was-a-dud-at-the-koch-brothers-conference-114853.
32. Withrow, Brandon. "Is There a Christian Double Standard on Religious Violence?" *The Daily Beast*, The Daily Beast Company, 5 Mar. 2017, www.thedailybeast.com/is-there-a-christian-double-standard-on-religious-violence.
33. "When Nepal Was Groaning in Earthquake, Christian Missionaries Were Shamelessly Selling Jesus - Opindia News." *OpIndia*, 4 May 2015, www.opindia.com/2015/04/when-nepal-was-groaning-in-earthquake-christian-missionaries-were-shamelessly-selling-jesus/.
34. *YouTube*, Q-Ball Productions Inc, 2010, www.youtube.com/watch?v=nNvtA_q0e20.

Chapter 17

1. Bear, Charla. "American Indian Boarding Schools Haunt Many." *NPR*. NPR, 12 May 2008. Web. 2 Nov. 2015, https://www.npr.org/templates/story/story.php?storyId=16516865?storyId=16516865.
2. "BibleGateway." *Bible Gateway*, Bible Gateway Blog, www.biblegateway.com/passage/?search=Mark 6&version=KJV.
3. "BibleGateway." *Matthew 27:46 KJV - - Bible Gateway*, www.biblegateway.com/passage/?search=Matthew 27:46&version=KJV.
4. "BibleGateway." *Bible Gateway*, Bible Gateway Blog, www.biblegateway.com/passage/?search=Matthew 27:52-53&version=KJV. For reference:Matthew 27:52-53 King James Version (KJV)52 And the graves were opened; and many bodies of the saints which slept arose,53 And came out of the graves after his resurrection, and went into the holy city, and appeared unto many.
5. D, Mike. "The Bible Is a Worthless Historical Document." *The Kalam Cosmological Argument: the Complete Rebuttal*, Blogger, 1 Feb. 2011, www.theaunicornist.com/2011/01/bible-is-worthless-historical-document.html.
6. Goldberg, Philip. "Missionaries in India: Conversion or Coercion?" *The Huffington Post*, TheHuffingtonPost.com, 19 Feb. 2014, www.huffingtonpost.com/philip-goldberg/missionaries-in-india_b_4470448.html.
7. Harris, Sam. *Letter to a Christian Nation*. Random House, 2008.
8. Hayes, Leonard L. "American Indian and Alaskan Native Historical Trauma and an Adlerian Perspective." *Alfredadler.edu*, The Faculty of the Adler Graduate School, Sept. 2010, alfredadler.edu/sites/default/files/Hayes MP 2010.pdf.
9. "Jury Finds Missionary Guilty of Abusing Cambodian Orphans." *New York Post*, New York Post, 17 May 2018, nypost.com/2018/05/17/jury-finds-missionary-guilty-of-abusing-cambodian-orphans/amp/.
10. Konnikova, Maria. *The Confidence Game: the Psychology of the Con and Why We Fall for It Every Time*. Canongate, 2017. Chapter 1: The Grifter and The Mark (15-52), The Put-Up (53-88), and Chapter 3: The Play (89-128).
11. Neelakandan, Aravindan. "Why No Outrage over Conversion of Tsunami Victims?" *Swarajya Read India Right ATOM*, 29 Dec. 2014, swarajyamag.com/politics/why-no-outrage-over-conversion-of-tsunami-victims.
12. Nietzsche, Friedrich Wilhelm. *On the genealogy of morals: a polemical tract*. Translated by Ian Johnston, PDF, Richer Resources Publications, 2014.
13. Nietzsche, Friedrich Wilhelm. *THE ANTICHRIST*. Translated by H. L. Mencken, The Project Gutenberg, 2006. For reference: Aphorisms 38, 39, 40, 41, 42, 43, 44, 45, 46, 47, 49, 50, 51, 52, 53, 54, and 55.
14. Paquin, Mali Ilse. "Canada Confronts Its Dark History of Abuse in Residential Schools." *The Guardian*, Guardian News and Media, 6 June 2015, www.theguardian.com/world/2015/jun/06/canada-dark-of-history-residential-schools.
15. Storr, Will. "The rape of men: the darkest secret of war." *The Observer*, Guardian News and Media, 16 July 2011, www.theguardian.com/society/2011/jul/17/the-rape-of-men.
16. Tabor, James. "The 'Strange' Ending of the Gospel of Mark and Why It Makes All the Difference." *Biblical Archaeology Society*, Biblical Archaeology Society, 4 May 2018, www.biblicalarchaeology.org/daily/biblical-topics/new-testament/the-strange-ending-of-the-gospel-of-mark-and-why-it-makes-all-the-difference/.

Chapter 18

1. Abruzzi, William S. "THE BIRTH OF JESUS: The Evolution of the Jesus in the Infancy Narratives." *Doc A's Webpage: On the Importance of Writing Research Papers*, Dr. William S. Abruzzi, 2015, www.drabruzzi.com/birth_of_jesus.htm. For reference: Copyright permission: "I have recently retired from teaching (May 2012) and am now able to spend more time doing research, working around the farm, riding my motorcycle, and being with my lovely wife, Amy. I have left the various syllabi for the courses I taught on my website, however, in case they prove useful to anyone, especially as I created

numerous web pages for each course and established links to several web pages containing information relevant to the topics covered in those courses." From: http://www.drabruzzi.com/index.html
2. "Begging the Question." *Https://Www.logicallyfallacious.com*, www.logicallyfallacious.com/tools/lp/Bo/LogicalFallacies/53/Begging-the-Question.
3. "Coptic Church Rocked By Scandals." *Den Katolske Kirke*, www.katolsk.no/nyheter/2001/06/26-0009
4. Harris, Sam. *Letter to a Christian Nation*. Random House, 2008.
5. Nietzsche, Friedrich Wilhelm. *THE ANTICHRIST*. Translated by H. L. Mencken, The Project Gutenberg, 2006. For reference: Aphorisms 39, 40, 41, 42, 43, 44, 45, 46, 47, 48, 49, 50, 51, 52, 53, 54, and 55.
6. Khalil, Ashraf. "Paper's Sex Expose Stirs Egypt Furor." *Chicagotribune.com*, 28 Aug. 2018, www.chicagotribune.com/news/ct-xpm-2001-06-20-0106200212-story.html.
7. Nietzsche, Friedrich Wilhelm. *Thus spake Zarathustra: a book for all and none*. Translated by Thomas Common, PDF ed., T. Common, 1908. For reference: Chapter LXVIII. THE VOLUNTARY BEGGAR (240-244).
8. Sampath, Rajesh. "India Has Outlawed Homosexuality. But It's Better to Be Transgender There than in the U.S." *The Washington Post*, WP Company, 29 Jan. 2015, www.washingtonpost.com/posteverything/wp/2015/01/29/india-has-outlawed-homosexuality-but-its-better-to-be-transgender-there-than-in-the-u-s/.
9. "Violence Against the Transgender Community in 2018." *Human Rights Campaign*, www.hrc.org/resources/violence-against-the-transgender-community-in-2018.

Chapter 19

1. Baird, Julia, et al. "'Submit to Your Husbands': Women Told to Endure Domestic Violence in the Name of God." *ABC News*, Australian Broadcasting Corporation, 23 Jan. 2018, www.abc.net.au/news/2017-07-18/domestic-violence-church-submit-to-husbands/8652028.
2. "BibleGateway." *2 Thessalonians 1 KJV - - Bible Gateway*, www.biblegateway.com/passage/?search=2 Thessalonians 1&version=KJV.
3. "BibleGateway." *Bible Gateway*, Bible Gateway Blog, www.biblegateway.com/passage/?search=John 8:21-44&version=KJV.
4. "BibleGateway." *Bible Gateway*, Bible Gateway Blog, www.biblegateway.com/passage/?search=1 Timothy 2&version=KJV.
5. "BibleGateway." *Bible Gateway*, Bible Gateway Blog, www.biblegateway.com/passage/?search=Luke 14:25-33&version=KJV.
6. Frank, Priscilla. "Welcome To The Bizarre And Beautiful World Of Purity Balls." *The Huffington Post*, TheHuffingtonPost.com, 7 Dec. 2017, www.huffingtonpost.com/2014/05/05/purity-ball-photos_n_5255904.html.
7. Kristof, Nicholas. "11 Years Old, a Mom, and Pushed to Marry Her Rapist in Florida." *The New York Times*, The New York Times, 26 May 2017, www.nytimes.com/2017/05/26/opinion/sunday/it-was-forced-on-me-child-marriage-in-the-us.html?mc=adglobal&mcid=facebook&subid1=sectiondiversitytest&ad-keywords=auddevgate&mccr=opinionopinion.
8. Kyama, Reuben. "Infertile Man Accused of Cutting off Wife's Hands as Punishment for Not Bearing Him Children." *Los Angeles Times*, Los Angeles Times, 15 Aug. 2016, www.latimes.com/world/africa/la-fg-kenya-domesticviolence-amputation-20160815-snap-story.html.
9. Harris, Sam. *Letter to a Christian Nation*. Random House, 2008.
10. "Static.reuters.com." *Reuters*, Reuters, static.reuters.com/resources/media/editorial/20150910/WilksDoctrinalPoints.pdf.
11. "Till death do us part: A Post and Courier Special Report." *Post and Courier*, 19 Aug. 2014, www.postandcourier.com/app/till-death/partone.html.
12. "Till death do us part: A Post and Courier Special Report." *Post and Courier*, 19 Aug. 2014, www.postandcourier.com/app/till-death/partthree.html.
13. Valenti, Jessica. "Purity Balls, Plan B and Bad Sex Policy: inside America's Virginity Obsession | Jessica Valenti." *The Guardian*, Guardian News and Media, 5 May 2014, www.theguardian.com/commentisfree/2014/may/05/purity-balls-america-virginity-obsession.

d.) Islam

Chapter 20

1. Al-Halawani, Ali. "Inimitability of Quran: Meanings and Types." *About Islam*, About Islam, 12 Apr. 2018, aboutislam.net/shariah/quran/quranic-miracles/inimitability-of-quran-meanings-types/#_ftn4.
2. "Al-Qur'an Al-Kareem - القرآن الكريم." *Surah Al-Ma'idah [5:32-42]*, quran.com/5/32-42.
3. "Al-Qur'an Al-Kareem - القرآن الكريم." *Surah Al-Ma'idah [5:32-52]*, quran.com/5/32-52.
4. "Al-Qur'an Al-Kareem - القرآن الكريم." *Surah At-Tawbah [9:73]*, quran.com/9/73.
5. Castor, Trevor. "Sin According to Islam." *Zwemer Center*, www.zwemercenter.com/guide/sin-according-to-muslims/.
6. "As Eid Al Adha Approaches..." *Questions on Islam*, questionsonislam.com/content/eid-al-adha-approaches….
7. Cialdini, Robert B. *Influence: Science and practice*. 4th ed., 21st Century Bks, 2002. For reference: Chapter 2: Reciprocation (19-50), Chapter 3: Commitment and Consistency (52-95), Chapter 4: Social Proof (98-140), and Chapter 6: Authority (178-200).
8. "Divine Fallacy." *Wikipedia*, Wikimedia Foundation, 22 Mar. 2019, en.wikipedia.org/wiki/Divine_fallacy.
9. Dweck, Carol S. *Mindset: How You Can Fulfill Your Potential*. Random House, 2012.
10. Elias, Abu Amina. "Sharia, Fiqh, and Islamic Law Explained." *Faith in Allah* ☐☐☐ ☐☐ ☐☐ ☐☐☐ , 21 Mar. 2018, abuaminaelias.com/is-the-sharia-a-single-code-of-law-an-explanation-of-sharia-fiqh-and-islamic-law/.
11. "Focus: Women Made to Keep Low Profile in Some French Suburbs." *YouTube*, France 24 English, 19 Dec. 2016, www.youtube.com/watch?v=6gZFGpNdH1A.
12. Gilbert, Daniel. *Stumbling on Happiness*. Random House, 2006. For reference: Chapter 11: Reporting Live For Tomorrow (212-233).
13. GotQuestions.org. "What Is Euthyphro's Dilemma?" *GotQuestions.org*, 3 May 2008, www.gotquestions.org/Euthyphro-Dilemma.html.
14. "Greater and Lesser Jihaad." Translated by Muhammed Salih Al-Munajjid, *Islam Question And Answer*, islamqa.info/en/10455.
15. Hitchens, Christopher. *God Is Not Great: How Religion Poisons Everything*. Hachette Book Group, 2007. For reference: Chapter 10: The Tawdriness of the Miraculous an the Decline of Hell (Pg. 258).
16. Hitchens, Christopher, et al. "Christopher Hitchens - Freedom of Expression Must Include the License to Offend [2006]." *YouTube*, Intelligence Squared, 25 July 2012, youtu.be/7oCmhZ-1gGc.
17. Ibrahim, Abu. "Shariah And Fiqh. Do You Know The Difference?" *Islamic Learning Materials*, 5 Mar. 2012, islamiclearningmaterials.com/shariah-fiqh/.
18. Ibrahim, Ghada, et al. "Can Islam Be Apolitical? - Armin Navabi, Ghada Ibrahim & Sarah Haider." *YouTube*, Ex-Muslims of North America, 6 Dec. 2018, www.youtube.com/watch?v=QGX0VqsiAMo.
19. Ispas, Alexa. *Psychology and politics: a social identity perspective*. Psychology Press, 2014.
20. Jefferson, Thomas. "QUERY XVII The Different Religions Received into That State?" *Thomas Jefferson, Notes on the State of Virginia: Ch. 17*, University of Virginia, xroads.virginia.edu/~hyper/jefferson/ch17.html.
21. Kahneman, Daniel. *Thinking, fast and slow*. Farrar, Straus and Giroux, 2015. For reference purposes: The Introduction (1-17), Chapter 4: The Associative Machine (50-58), Chapter 5: Cognitive Ease (59-70), Chapter 6:"Norms, Surprises, and Causes" (71-78), Chapter 7: A Machine for Jumping to Conclusions (79-88), Chapter 8: How Judgments Happen (89-96), Chapter 9: Answering an Easier Question (97-107), Chapter 12: The Science of Availability (129-136), Chapter 13: Availability, Emotion, and Risk (137-145), Chapter 19: The Illusion of Understanding (199-208), and Chapter 20: The Illusion of Validity (209-221).
22. "Miraculous Aspects of the Holy Qur'an - Islam Question & Answer." *Islamqa.info*, Islam Question and Answer, 5 Oct. 2016, islamqa.info/en/answers/245475/miraculous-aspects-of-the-holy-quran.
23. Namazie, Maryam, et al. "Equality, Islam and Human Rights." *YouTube*, Ex-Muslims of North America, 26 Mar. 2018, www.youtube.com/watch?v=2W0w9ufJOh0.
24. Nietzsche, Friedrich Wilhelm. *THE ANTICHRIST*. Translated by H. L. Mencken, The Project Gutenberg, 2006. For reference: Aphorism 49.
25. "Pakistani Hindus Complain of Forced Conversion of Teenage Girls." *YouTube*, VOA News, 18 Mar.

2016, youtu.be/-i24jg4mJ4I.
26. "Philosophy of Religion." *Philosophy of Religion The Euthyphro Dilemma Comments*, www.philosophyofreligion.info/christian-ethics/divine-command-theory/the-euthyphro-dilemma/. For reference: The Euthyphro Dilemma(1) If divine command theory is true then either (i) morally good acts are willed by God because they are morally good, or (ii) morally good acts are morally good because they are willed by God.(2) If (i) morally good acts are willed by God because they are morally good, then they are morally good independent of God's will.(3) It is not the case that morally good acts are morally good independent of God's will.Therefore:(4) It is not the case that (i) morally good acts are willed by God because they are morally good.(5) If (ii) morally good acts are morally good because they are willed by God, then there is no reason either to care about God's moral goodness or to worship him.(6) There are reasons both to care about God's moral goodness and to worship him.Therefore:(7) It is not the case that (ii) morally good acts are morally good because they are willed by God.Therefore:(8) Divine command theory is false.
27. Rabbani, Faraz. "Are Good and Evil Determined by the Human Intellect or by Revelation?" *SeekersGuidance*, Sufyan Http://Www.seekersguidance.org/Wp-Content/Uploads/2019/02/Nlogo-Main.png, 18 Apr. 2011, www.seekersguidance.org/answers/islamic-belief/are-good-and-evil-determined-by-the-human-intellect-or-by-revelation/.
28. Raja, Raza Habib. "The Trivialization of the Ongoing Shiite Genocide in Pakistan." *HuffPost*, HuffPost, 2 June 2017, www.huffpost.com/entry/the-trivialization-of-the-ongoing-shiite-genocide-in_b_592ece56e4b00afe556b09ea.
29. "Tafseer on the Basis of Narrated Texts and Tafseer on the Basis of Individual Understanding - Islam Question & Answer." *Islamqa.info*, Islam Question and Answer, 11 Mar. 2015, islamqa.info/en/answers/205290/tafseer-on-the-basis-of-narrated-texts-and-tafseer-on-the-basis-of-individual-understanding.
30. Tessier, Stephanie, and Muhammad Syed. "Islam: Pull and Peril." *YouTube*, Ex-Muslims of North America, 22 Apr. 2018, www.youtube.com/watch?v=jt1rWgap41g.
31. *The Quranic Arabic Corpus - Translation*, corpus.quran.com/translation.jsp?chapter=2&verse=256.
32. *The Quranic Arabic Corpus - Translation*, corpus.quran.com/translation.jsp?chapter=4&verse=89.
33. *THE THEORY OF ABROGATION*, www.islamawareness.net/FAQ/Logic/faq105.html.
34. "The Wisdom behind the Prophet's Marrying More than Four Wives - Islam Question & Answer." *Islamqa.info*, Islam Question and Answer, 14 May 2013, islamqa.info/en/answers/127066/the-wisdom-behind-the-prophets-marrying-more-than-four-wives.
35. Walton, D. N. "Appeal to Popularity." *Https://Www.logicallyfallacious.com*, www.logicallyfallacious.com/tools/lp/Bo/LogicalFallacies/40/Appeal-to-Popularity.
36. "Who Is a Scholar ('Aalim)? - Islam Question & Answer." *Islamqa.info*, Islam Question and Answer, 18 July 2011, islamqa.info/en/answers/145071/who-is-a-scholar-aalim.
37. "Willed Ignorance." *Https://Www.logicallyfallacious.com*, www.logicallyfallacious.com/tools/lp/Bo/LogicalFallacies/182/Willed-Ignorance

Chapter 21

1. Ally, Shabir. "The Messiah: Jesus, Son of Mary." *Facts about the Muslims & the Religion of Islam*, Whyislam.org, www.whyislam.org/comparative-religion-2/the-messiah-jesus-son-of-mary/.
2. Alt, Scott Eric. "We Need to Stop Saying That There Are 33,000 Protestant Denominations." *National Catholic Register*, Global Catholic Television Network (EWTN), www.ncregister.com/blog/scottericalt/we-need-to-stop-saying-that-there-are-33000-protestant-denominations. Despite trying to declare 33,000 denominations facetious, I felt the explanation only affirmed it. For reference:Thus the imme-di-ate prob-lem is that the WCE only clas-si-fies 9000 denom-i-na-tions (27% of the whole) as Protes-tant. To get to 33,000, one must add in the Inde-pen-dents, Mar-gin-als, Angli-cans, and 232 of the Ortho-dox.Among the 23,600 "Inde-pen-dents" and "Mar-gin-als" (70% of the whole) are large num-bers of groups one would have a hard time call-ing Protes-tant. They include Mor-mons (122 denom-i-na-tions), Jehovah's Wit-nesses (229 denom-i-na-tions), Masons (28 denom-i-na-tions), Chris-tadel-phi-ans (21 denom-i-na-tions) Uni-tar-i-ans (29 denom-i-na-tions), Chris-t-ian Sci-ence (59 denom-i-na-tions), Theosophists (3 more denom-i-na-tions), British Israelites (8 denom-i-na-tions), Pros-per-ity Gospel groups (27

denom-i-na-tions), One-ness Pen-te-costals (680 denom-i-na-tions), "Hid-den Bud-dhist Believ-ers in Christ" (9 denom-i-na-tions), wan-der-ing bish-ops (12 denom-i-na-tions), Inde-pen-dent Nesto-ri-ans (5 denom-i-na-tions), occultists (3 denom-i-na-tions), spiri-tists (20 denom-i-na-tions), Zion-ists (159 denom-i-na-tions), even "Arab radio/TV net-work" (19 denom-i-na-tions), "gay/homosexual tra-di-tion" (2 denom-i-na-tions), and schis-matic Catholics (435 denom-i-na-tions). It is a strange and eclec-tic list. (See here and here.)How-ever strong the temp-ta-tion some may have to char-ac-ter-ize any-thing not Catholic or Ortho-dox as "Protes-tant," you can't do that. All that tells Protes-tant apol-o-gists is that you don't know what Protes-tantism is, or what its dis-tinc-tives are—and they would be right. And why would they take any-thing you say seri-ously after that? If you don't know what Protes-tantism is, who are you to be talk-ing about its errors? Not only are Mor-mons, Jehovah's Wit-nesses, One-ness Pen-te-costals, Uni-tar-i-ans, Pros-per-ity Gospel believ-ers (included among 23,600 Inde-pen-dents and Mar-gin-als) not Protes-tant, they are not even Chris-t-ian; they adhere to a false Chris-tol-ogy. Protes-tants and Catholics are in agree-ment about who Christ is; these other groups have other ideas.

3. Cialdini, Robert B. *Influence: Science and practice*. 4th ed., 21st Century Bks, 2002. Chapter 5: Liking (143-177).
4. Farina, Marianne. "What Do Muslims Think of Jesus?" *USCatholic.org*, 19 Sept. 2016, www.uscatholic.org/articles/201609/what-do-muslims-think-jesus-30772.
5. Ispas, Alexa. *Psychology and politics: a social identity perspective*. Psychology Press, 2014.
6. Joyner, James. "Why We Should Be Glad the Haditha Massacre Marine Got No Jail Time." *The Atlantic*, Atlantic Media Company, 3 Feb. 2012, www.theatlantic.com/international/archive/2012/01/why-we-should-be-glad-the-haditha-massacre-marine-got-no-jail-time/251993/.
7. "Questions from a Confused Christian." Translated by Muhammad Salih Al-Munajjid, *Islam Question And Answer*, islamqa.info/en/10469.
8. "What Do Muslims Believe about Jesus?" *Islam Guide: Life After Death*, www.islam-guide.com/ch3-10.htm.

Chapter 22

1. "Age of the Mother of the Believers 'Aa'ishah (May Allah Be Pleased with Her) When the Prophet (Blessings and Peace of Allah Be upon Him) Married Her - Islam Question & Answer." *Islamqa.info*, Islam Question and Answer, 30 Dec. 2013, islamqa.info/en/answers/124483/age-of-the-mother-of-the-believers-aaishah-may-allah-be-pleased-with-her-when-the-prophet-blessings-and-peace-of-allah-be-upon-him-married-her.
2. "Al-Qur'an Al-Kareem - ‫القرآن الكريم‬." *Surah Al-Ma'idah [5:32-52]*, quran.com/5/32-52.
3. Ally, Shabir. "The Messiah: Jesus, Son of Mary." *Facts about the Muslims & the Religion of Islam*, Whyislam.org, www.whyislam.org/comparative-religion-2/the-messiah-jesus-son-of-mary/.
4. Bajaj, Vikas. "Vandalism at Maldives Museum Stirs Fears of Extremism." *The New York Times*, The New York Times, 13 Feb. 2012, www.nytimes.com/2012/02/14/world/asia/political-turmoil-threatens-archaeological-treasures-in-maldives.html.
5. Boyer, Lauren. "Stop Drinking Camel Urine, World Health Organization Says." *U.S. News & World Report*, U.S. News & World Report, www.usnews.com/news/articles/2015/06/10/stop-drinking-camel-urine-world-health-organization-says.
6. Budiharsana, Meiwita. "Female Genital Cutting Common in Indonesia, Offered as Part of Child Delivery by Birth Clinics." *The Conversation*, 10 Mar. 2019, theconversation.com/female-genital-cutting-common-in-indonesia-offered-as-part-of-child-delivery-by-birth-clinics-54379.
7. Castor, Trevor. "Sin According to Islam." *Zwemer Center*, www.zwemercenter.com/guide/sin-according-to-muslims/.
8. Cialdini, Robert B. *Influence: Science and practice*. 4th ed., 21st Century Bks, 2002. Chapter 2: Reciprocation (19-50) and Chapter 3: Commitment and Consistency (52-95).
9. Doherty, Carroll. "Key Takeaways on Americans' Growing Partisan Divide over Political Values." *Pew Research Center*, Pew Research Center, 5 Oct. 2017, www.pewresearch.org/fact-tank/2017/10/05/takeaways-on-americans-growing-partisan-divide-over-political-values/.
10. Dugan, Andrew, and Frank Newport. "Partisan Differences Growing on a Number of Issues." *Gallup.com*, 3 Aug. 2017, news.gallup.com/opinion/polling-matters/215210/partisan-differences-growing-number-issues.aspx?g_source=link_newsv9&g_campaign=item_236315&g_medium=copy.

11. Elias, Abu Amina. "Sharia, Fiqh, and Islamic Law Explained." *Faith in Allah* ☐☐☐☐ ☐☐ ☐☐ ☐☐, 21 Mar. 2018, abuaminaelias.com/is-the-sharia-a-single-code-of-law-an-explanation-of-sharia-fiqh-and-islamic-law/.
12. "Equivocation." *Https://Www.logicallyfallacious.com*, www.logicallyfallacious.com/tools/lp/Bo/LogicalFallacies/81/Equivocation.
13. "Greater and Lesser Jihaad." Translated by Muhammed Salih Al-Munajjid, *Islam Question And Answer*, islamqa.info/en/10455.
14. Haider, Sarah. "Sarah Haider: Islam and the Necessity of Liberal Critique (AHA Conference 2015)." *YouTube*, American Humanist Association, 28 May 2015, www.youtube.com/watch?v=0plC24YuoJk.
15. Hamid, Shadi, and Rashid Dar. "Islamism, Salafism, and Jihadism: A Primer." *Brookings*, Brookings Institution, 29 July 2016, www.brookings.edu/blog/markaz/2016/07/15/islamism-salafism-and-jihadism-a-primer/.
16. Ibrahim, Ghada, et al. "Can Islam Be Apolitical? - Armin Navabi, Ghada Ibrahim & Sarah Haider." *YouTube*, Ex-Muslims of North America, 6 Dec. 2018, www.youtube.com/watch?v=QGX0VqsiAMo.
17. "Indonesia Blasphemy Case: Emotional Scenes as Ahok Trial Begins." *BBC News*, BBC, 13 Dec. 2016, www.bbc.com/news/world-asia-38285515.
18. Ispas, Alexa. *Psychology and politics: a social identity perspective*. Psychology Press, 2014.
19. "Israel: Serious Violations in West Bank Operations." *Human Rights Watch*, 17 Apr. 2015, www.hrw.org/news/2014/07/03/israel-serious-violations-west-bank-operations.
20. Kahneman, Daniel. *Thinking, fast and slow*. Farrar, Straus and Giroux, 2015. For reference purposes: The Introduction (1-17), Chapter 4: The Associative Machine (50-58), Chapter 5: Cognitive Ease (59-70), Chapter 6:"Norms, Surprises, and Causes" (71-78), Chapter 7: A Machine for Jumping to Conclusions (79-88), Chapter 8: How Judgments Happen (89-96), Chapter 9: Answering an Easier Question (97-107), Chapter 12: The Science of Availability (129-136), Chapter 13: Availability, Emotion, and Risk (137-145), Chapter 19: The Illusion of Understanding (199-208), and Chapter 20: The Illusion of Validity (209-221).
21. LAZAROFF, TOVAH. "IDF Destroys Two Illegal EU-Funded Palestinian Schools." *The Jerusalem Post | JPost.com*, 24 Aug. 2017, www.jpost.com/Arab-Israeli-Conflict/IDF-destroys-two-illegal-EU-funded-Palestinian-schools-503252.
22. Maltz, Judy. "Israel Tortures Palestinian Children, Amnesty Report Says." *Haaretz.com*, Haaretz Com, 24 Apr. 2018, www.haaretz.com/israel-news/.premium-israel-tortures-palestinian-children-amnesty-report-says-1.5440012.
23. "Middle East Respiratory Syndrome Coronavirus (MERS-CoV) – Republic of Korea." *World Health Organization*, World Health Organization, 9 June 2015, www.who.int/csr/don/09-june-2015-mers-korea/en/.
24. Mitchell, Travis. "How Americans Feel About Different Religious Groups." *Pew Research Center's Religion & Public Life Project*, Pew Research Center's Religion & Public Life Project, 14 Dec. 2017, www.pewforum.org/2017/02/15/americans-express-increasingly-warm-feelings-toward-religious-groups/.
25. Namazie, Maryam, et al. "Equality, Islam and Human Rights." *YouTube*, Ex-Muslims of North America, 26 Mar. 2018, www.youtube.com/watch?v=2W0w9ufJOh0.
26. Nietzsche, Friedrich Wilhelm. *On the genealogy of morals: a polemical tract*. Translated by Ian Johnston, PDF, Richer Resources Publications, 2014.
27. Nietzsche, Friedrich Wilhelm. *THE ANTICHRIST*. Translated by H. L. Mencken, The Project Gutenberg, 2006. For reference: Aphorism 53.
28. "Pakistani Hindus Complain of Forced Conversion of Teenage Girls." *YouTube*, VOA News, 18 Mar. 2016, youtu.be/-i24jg4mJ4I.
29. Renaldi, Erwin. "Female Circumcision: Culture and Religion in Malaysia See Millions of Girls Undergo Cut." *ABC News*, 13 Nov. 2018, www.abc.net.au/news/2018-11-13/female-circumcision-is-still-happening-in-malaysia/10473640.
30. Rosling, Hans. *Factfulness*. Macmillan, 2018.
31. "Ruling on Having Intercourse with a Slave Woman When One Has a Wife - Islamqa.info." Translated by Muhammad Salih Al-Munajjid, *Wayback Machine*, Fox News, web.archive.org/web/20160106101656/http://islamqa.info/en/10382.
32. Sidhu, Sandi. "Malaysian Man Gets 10 Years in Prison for Insulting Islam on Facebook." *CNN*, Cable News Network, 9 Mar. 2019, www.cnn.com/2019/03/09/asia/malaysia-man-prison-insulting-islam-intl/.

33. Shams, Imtiaz, and Nourhan. "What Does Islam Say about Slavery in Its THEOLOGY?" *YouTube*, Salsalah, 14 Nov. 2016, www.youtube.com/watch?v=rHm9F1G5IRE.
34. Shams, Imtiaz, et al. "Fighting Allah, Defending Muslims - Armin Navabi, Imtiaz Shams, Muhammad Syed." *YouTube*, Ex-Muslims of North America, 5 Jan. 2018, www.youtube.com/watch?v=KwnHreJNavE.
35. "Tafseer on the Basis of Narrated Texts and Tafseer on the Basis of Individual Understanding - Islam Question & Answer." *Islamqa.info*, Islam Question and Answer, 11 Mar. 2015, islamqa.info/en/answers/205290/tafseer-on-the-basis-of-narrated-texts-and-tafseer-on-the-basis-of-individual-understanding.
36. Tessier, Stephanie, and Muhammad Syed. "Islam: Pull and Peril." *YouTube*, Ex-Muslims of North America, 22 Apr. 2018, www.youtube.com/watch?v=jt1rWgap41g.
37. "The Benefits of Drinking Camel Urine - Islam Question & Answer." *Islamqa.info*, Islam Question and Answer, 27 Mar. 2006, islamqa.info/en/answers/83423/the-benefits-of-drinking-camel-urine.
38. *The Quranic Arabic Corpus - Translation*, corpus.quran.com/translation.jsp?chapter=4&verse=89.
39. "The Quranic Arabic Corpus - Word by Word Grammar, Syntax and Morphology of the Holy Quran." *The Quranic Arabic Corpus - Translation*, corpus.quran.com/. For reference:
Chapter 4, Verse 24:
http://corpus.quran.com/translation.jsp?chapter=4&verse=24
Chapter 4, Verse 34:
http://corpus.quran.com/translation.jsp?chapter=4&verse=34
Chapter 16, Verse 71:
http://corpus.quran.com/translation.jsp?chapter=16&verse=71
40. "UN: Palestinian Children Tortured, Used as Human Shields by Israel." *Haaretz.com*, Haaretz Com, 10 Jan. 2018, www.haaretz.com/.premium-israel-tortured-palestinian-children-1.5283333.
41. Wilson, Antonia. "Maldives Marine Artwork Destroyed for Being a 'Threat to Islamic Unity'." *The Guardian*, Guardian News and Media, 24 Sept. 2018, www.theguardian.com/travel/2018/sep/24/maldives-authorities-destroy-marine-artwork-for-being-un-islamic?CMP=share_btn_fb.
42. "Your Logical Fallacy Is No True Scotsman." *Thou Shalt Not Commit Logical Fallacies*, yourlogicalfallacyis.com/no-true-scotsman.

Chapter 23

1. Al-Ali, Zaid. "How Maliki Ruined Iraq." *Foreign Policy*, Foreign Policy, 19 June 2014, foreignpolicy.com/2014/06/19/how-maliki-ruined-iraq/.
2. Becker, Jo, and Scott Shane. "Secret 'Kill List' Proves a Test of Obama's Principles and Will." *The New York Times*, The New York Times, 29 May 2012, www.nytimes.com/2012/05/29/world/obamas-leadership-in-war-on-al-qaeda.html. For reference:

Excerpt 1: The administration's failure to forge a clear detention policy has created the impression among some members of Congress of a take-no-prisoners policy. And Mr. Obama's ambassador to Pakistan, Cameron P. Munter, has complained to colleagues that the C.I.A.'s strikes drive American policy there, saying "he didn't realize his main job was to kill people," a colleague said.Beside the president at every step is his counterterrorism adviser, John O. Brennan, who is variously compared by colleagues to a dogged police detective, tracking terrorists from his cavelike office in the White House basement, or a priest whose blessing has become indispensable to Mr. Obama, echoing the president's attempt to apply the "just war" theories of Christian philosophers to a brutal modern conflict.But the strikes that have eviscerated Al Qaeda — just since April, there have been 14 in Yemen, and 6 in Pakistan — have also tested both men's commitment to the principles they have repeatedly said are necessary to defeat the enemy in the long term. Drones have replaced Guantánamo as the recruiting tool of choice for militants; in his 2010 guilty plea, Faisal Shahzad, who had tried to set off a car bomb in Times Square, justified targeting civilians by telling the judge, "When the drones hit, they don't see children."

Excerpt 2: The nominations go to the White House, where by his own insistence and guided by Mr.

Brennan, Mr. Obama must approve any name. He signs off on every strike in Yemen and Somalia and also on the more complex and risky strikes in Pakistan — about a third of the total. Aides say Mr. Obama has several reasons for becoming so immersed in lethal counterterrorism operations. A student of writings on war by Augustine and Thomas Aquinas, he believes that he should take moral responsibility for such actions. And he knows that bad strikes can tarnish America's image and derail diplomacy.

3. Benjamin, Daniel. "The Convert's Zeal: Why Are So Many Jihadists Converts to Islam?" *Brookings*, Brookings, 28 July 2016, www.brookings.edu/articles/the-converts-zeal-why-are-so-many-jihadists-converts-to-islam/.
4. Browne, Ryan, and Oscar Featherstone. "US Arms Sold to Saudi Arabia and UAE End up in Wrong Hands." *CNN*, Cable News Network, www.cnn.com/interactive/2019/02/middleeast/yemen-lost-us-arms/.
5. CHEDEKEL, LISA, et al. "Haditha: Marine Linked To Civilian Deaths Was A Quiet Honor Student, Friends Say." *Hartford Courant*, 3 June 2006, articles.courant.com/2006-06-03/news/0606030586_1_frank-wuterich-haditha-squad-leader.
6. Cialdini, Robert B. *Influence: Science and practice*. 4th ed., 21st Century Bks, 2002. Chapter 2: Reciprocation (19-50).
7. "Country Profile: Iraq - Library of Congress." *Library of Congress*, US Government, www.loc.gov/rr/frd/cs/profiles/Iraq.pdf.
8. Crilly, Rob. "'Infidels Are Our Enemy': Afghan Fighters Cherish Old American Schoolbooks." *Al Jazeera America*, Al Jazeera America, america.aljazeera.com/articles/2014/12/7/afghan-fighters-americantextbooks.html.
9. Crooke, Alastair. "Non-Dollar Trading Is Killing the Petrodollar -- And the Foundation of U.S.-Saudi Policy in the Middle East." *HuffPost*, HuffPost, 1 Feb. 2015, www.huffpost.com/entry/petrodollar-us-saudi-policy_b_6245914.
10. Dyson, Tim, and Valeria Cetorelli. "Changing Views on Child Mortality and Economic Sanctions in Iraq: a History of Lies, Damned Lies and Statistics." *BMJ Global Health*, BMJ Specialist Journals, 1 July 2017, gh.bmj.com/content/2/2/e000311#ref-8.
11. Eleftheriou-Smith, Loulla-Mae. "Syrian Refugees Get Housed in the Same Hotel as a Furry Conventio - and the Kids Loved It." *The Independent*, Independent Digital News and Media, 11 Mar. 2016, www.independent.co.uk/news/world/americas/syrian-refugees-in-canada-got-housed-in-same-hotel-as-vancoufur-furry-convention-and-the-children-a6921341.html.
12. Gause, F. Gregory. "Getting It Backward on Iraq." *Foreign Affairs*, Foreign Affairs, 28 Jan. 2009, www.foreignaffairs.com/articles/iraq/1999-05-01/getting-it-backward-iraq.
13. Harris, Sam. *Letter to a Christian Nation*. Vintage Books, 2008.
14. Hartung, William D. "It's Not Diplomacy, It's an Arms Fair." *Foreign Policy*, Foreign Policy, 14 May 2015, foreignpolicy.com/2015/05/14/obama-arms-fair-camp-david-weapons-sales-gcc/.
15. Hattem, Julian. "CIA Watchdog 'Accidentally Destroyed' Copy of 'Torture Report'." TheHill, The Hill, 17 May 2016, thehill.com/policy/national-security/280002-cia-watchdog-accidentally-destroyed-only-copy-of-torture-report.
16. Hedges, Chris. "War Is Betrayal." *Truthdig: Expert Reporting, Current News, Provocative Columnists*, 14 July 2012, www.truthdig.com/articles/war-is-betrayal
17. Hedges, Chris. *War Is a Force That Gives Us Meaning*. PublicAffairs, 2002.
18. Hussain, Murtaza. "Imprisoned With Her Baby, Bahraini Activist Is Victim of U.S. Silence, Sister Says." *The Intercept*, The Intercept, 22 Mar. 2016, theintercept.com/2016/03/22/imprisoned-with-her-baby-bahraini-activist-is-victim-of-u-s-silence-sister-says/.
19. Hussain, Murtaza. "Trump's Deepening Embrace of Bahrain's Repressive Monarchy May Lead to More Instability." *The Intercept*, The Intercept, 14 Apr. 2017, theintercept.com/2017/04/14/trumps-deepening-embrace-of-bahrains-repressive-monarchy-may-lead-to-more-instability/.
20. Ibish, Hussein. "The Nonviolent Violence of Hamas." *Foreign Policy*, Foreign Policy, 6 Apr. 2018, foreignpolicy.com/2018/04/06/the-non-violent-violence-of-hamas/.
21. Jentleson, Bruce W. *American foreign policy: the dynamics of choice in the 21st century*. 4th ed., Norton, 2010. Chapter 1: The Strategic Context: Foreign Policy Strategy and the Essence of Choice (2-26), Readings for Part 1 Power by Hans J. Morgenthau (198-201).
22. Joyner, James. "Why We Should Be Glad the Haditha Massacre Marine Got No Jail Time." *The Atlantic*, Atlantic Media Company, 3 Feb. 2012, www.theatlantic.com/international/archive/2012/01/why-we-should-be-glad-the-haditha-massacre-marine-got-no-jail-time/251993/.

23. Kahneman, Daniel. *Thinking, fast and slow*. Farrar, Straus and Giroux, 2015. For reference purposes: The Introduction (1-17), Chapter 4: The Associative Machine (50-58), Chapter 5: Cognitive Ease (59-70), Chapter 6:"Norms, Surprises, and Causes" (71-78), Chapter 7: A Machine for Jumping to Conclusions (79-88), Chapter 8: How Judgments Happen (89-96), Chapter 9: Answering an Easier Question (97-107), Chapter 12: The Science of Availability (129-136), Chapter 13: Availability, Emotion, and Risk (137-145), Chapter 19: The Illusion of Understanding (199-208), and Chapter 20: The Illusion of Validity (209-221).
24. Marusek, Sarah. "West Must Recognize Peaceful Palestinian Resistance Movement." *The Christian Science Monitor*, The Christian Science Monitor, 7 June 2012, www.csmonitor.com/Commentary/Opinion/2012/0607/West-must-recognize-peaceful-Palestinian-resistance-movement.
25. McLaughlin, Jenna. "U.S. Will Resume Sending Weapons to Bahrain Despite Ongoing Repression." *The Intercept*, The Intercept: Unofficial Sources, 29 June 2015, theintercept.com/2015/06/29/u-s-will-resume-sending-weapons-bahrain-despite-ongoing-repression/.
26. "Morbidity and Mortality Among Iraqi Children from 1990 Through 1998: Assessing the Impact of the Gulf War and Economic Sanctions." *Morbidity and Mortality Among Iraqi Children*, reliefweb.int/sites/reliefweb.int/files/resources/A2E2603E5DC88A4685256825005F211D-garfie17.pdf. For Reference: Summary of General FindingsBy Richard GarfieldSustained increases in young child mortality are extremely rare. In Iraq, there have been many reportssuggesting a rise in rates of death and disease since the Gulf war of January/February 1991 and theeconomic sanctions that followed it and continue to this day. There is no agreement, however, on themagnitude of the mortality increase, its causes, who is responsible for these deaths, or how to stop themfrom happening. Because the best data and the greatest changes in mortality occur among young children,this report focuses exclusively on deaths among children under five years of age. Information from twentytwo field studies, including data from thirty-six nutritional assessments were reviewed, along withdemographic estimates from nine sources, three Iraqi government reports, ten UN-related reports, andeighteen press and research reports.Data on the health and well being of children were drawn from four large, well designed and managedstudies examining death rates among children from 1988 through 1998; Iraqi Ministry of Health data (26,28) serve as a prewar baseline. Before the establishment of sanctions prior to the Gulf war in August 1990,for each 1000 children born, 40 died before reaching five years of age. Careful reexamination of a previousstudy showed a slight increase in mortality during sanctions prior to the Gulf war. A large rise in mortalityin the period during and eight months after the Gulf war was reported in the well publicized internationalstudy done by an international study team from Harvard University (29, 30). Data are not available fromany reliable studies on mortality since 1991. Very good data are available for the years 1996 through 1998,however, on child nutrition, water quality, adult literacy, and other social and health indicators whichinfluence child mortality.A variety of methods were used to estimate the mortality rate that is predicted by these indicators. The mostreliable estimates were derived from a logistic regression model using a multiple imputation procedure. Themodel successfully predicted both the mortality rate in 1990, under stable conditions, and in 1991,following the Gulf war. For 1996, after five years of sanctions and prior to receipt of humanitarian foodsvia the oil for food program, this model shows mortality among children under five to have reached aminimum of 80 per one thousand, a rate last experienced more than thirty years ago. This rise in themortality rate accounted for between a minimum of 100,000 and a more likely estimate of 227,000 excessdeaths among young children from August 1991 through March 1998. About one-quarter of these deathswere mainly associated with the Gulf war; most were primarily associated with sanctions. Mortality washighest in the southern governorates of the country and lowest in Baghdad. Mortality was higher in ruralareas, among the poor, and among those families with lower educational achievement. The increase inmortality was caused mainly by diarrhea and respiratory illnesses. The underlying causes of these excessdeaths include contaminated water, lack of high quality foods, inadequate breast feeding, poor weaningpractices, and inadequate supplies in the curative health care system. This was the product of both a lack ofsome essential goods, and inadequate or inefficient use of existing essential goods.Given the most likely estimate of 227,000, there were an average of about 60 excess deaths each day.These child deaths far outnumber all deaths on all sides, among combatants and civilians, during the Gulfwar. It exceeds the number of deaths known to result from any of the bombing raids in Iraq even on thedays of the bombings. It exceeds each week the number of deaths that occurred in the tragic bombing of the2Al Furdos bomb shelter during the Gulf war. That incident caused an international uproar, an apology fromthe Joint Military Command, and a revision in

the procedures for selecting targets. Reaction to the muchgreater number of child deaths associated with sanctions has been far more muted. Confusion over thenumber of deaths and rhetorical argument over which side is responsible for those deaths has prevented theinternational community from focusing more effectively on how to prevent their continued occurrence.Studies from 1996 onward suggest that there was little decline in mortality rates at that time. Since March1998 the oil for food program has greatly increased access to essential supplies and the mortality rate hassurely declined, but data are not yet available to estimate the magnitude of that decline. Indeed, the failureto institute stepped-up monitoring when sanctions were initiated in 1990 continues to limit the capacity tocarry out timely and reliable assessments of humanitarian conditions in Iraq. Despite a steep rise inmortality rates, most Iraqi children survive under the social, economic, and political crises of the 1990s inIraq but experience profound limitations on their health and well being. Far more attention needs to bedevoted to identifying and minimizing the humanitarian damage to the Iraqis alive today, in preparation foran eventual shift from relief to reconstruction and development in the years ahead.

27. Morris, Roger. "A Tyrant 40 Years in the Making." *The New York Times*, The New York Times, 14 Mar. 2003, www.nytimes.com/2003/03/14/opinion/a-tyrant-40-years-in-the-making.html.
28. Muthali, Aki. "Atheistophobia: It's Time to Talk about the Most Persecuted Minority in the World." *The Nation*, 27 Sept. 2015, nation.com.pk/27-Sep-2015/atheistophobia-it-s-time-to-talk-about-the-most-persecuted-minority-in-the-world.
29. Neelakandan, Aravindan. "Why No Outrage over Conversion of Tsunami Victims?" *Swarajya*, 29 Dec. 2014, swarajyamag.com/politics/why-no-outrage-over-conversion-of-tsunami-victims.
30. Oakford, Samuel. "'All We Could Find Were Body Parts': America's Role in Yemen's Civilian Carnage." *VICE News*, News, 17 Oct. 2015, news.vice.com/article/all-we-could-find-were-body-parts-americas-role-in-yemens-civilian-carnage. \
31. "Operation Provide Comfort." *Wikipedia*, Wikimedia Foundation, 26 May 2019, en.wikipedia.org/wiki/Operation_Provide_Comfort.
32. Oweiss, Ibrahim M. "Economics of Petrodollars." *Http://Faculty.georgetown.edu*, The Committee for Monetary Research and Education, faculty.georgetown.edu/imo3/petrod/petro2.htm.
33. Oweiss, Ibrahim M. "Definition of Petrodollars." *Http://Faculty.georgetown.edu*, The Committee for Monetary Research and Education, faculty.georgetown.edu/imo3/petrod/define.htm.
34. Oweiss, Ibrahim M. "Allocation of Petrodollar Surpluses." *Http://Faculty.georgetown.edu*, The Committee for Monetary Research and Education, faculty.georgetown.edu/imo3/petrod/allocate.htm.
35. Oweiss, Ibrahim M. "Increase in Imports." *Http://Faculty.georgetown.edu*, The Committee for Monetary Research and Education, faculty.georgetown.edu/imo3/petrod/increase.htm.
36. Oweiss, Ibrahim M. "Demand for Oil and Excess Supply Since 1980." *Http://Faculty.georgetown.edu*, The Committee for Monetary Research and Education, faculty.georgetown.edu/imo3/petrod/since.htm.
37. Pelley, Scott. "Haditha massacre defendant: We did what we had to." *CBS News*, CBS Interactive, 6 Jan. 2012, www.cbsnews.com/news/haditha-massacre-defendant-we-did-what-we-had-to/.
38. Sieczkowski, Cavan. "Donations Pour In After Syrian Refugee Scientist With Cancer Shares Moving Story." *The Huffington Post*, TheHuffingtonPost.com, 14 Dec. 2015, www.huffingtonpost.com/entry/edward-norton-syrian-refugee-crowdrise_us_566efebee4b0fccee16f44e5.
39. Sly, Liz. "The Hidden Hand behind the Islamic State Militants? Saddam Hussein's." *The Washington Post*, WP Company, 4 Apr. 2015, www.washingtonpost.com/world/middle_east/the-hidden-hand-behind-the-islamic-state-militants-saddam-husseins/2015/04/04/aa97676c-cc32-11e4-8730-4f473416e759_story.html?utm_term=.ef5d225bf17b.
40. Spagat, Michael. *Truth and Death in Iraq under Sanctions*. rss.onlinelibrary.wiley.com/doi/pdf/10.1111/j.1740-9713.2010.00437.x.
41. Stanton, Brandon. "Humans of New York Refugee Stories – Brandon Stanton – Medium." *Medium*, Augmenting Humanity, 19 Nov. 2015, medium.com/@humansofnewyork/humans-of-new-york-refugee-stories-243336f4adeb.
42. Stephens, Joe, and David B. Ottaway. "From U.S., the ABC's of Jihad." *The Washington Post*, WP Company, 23 Mar. 2002, www.washingtonpost.com/archive/politics/2002/03/23/from-us-the-abcs-of-jihad/d079075a-3ed3-4030-9a96-0d48f6355e54/?utm_term=.cbb9b6b8a59a.
43. Theintercept. "The U.S. Media and the 13-Year-Old Yemeni Boy Burned to Death Last Month by a U.S. Drone." *The Intercept*, 10 Feb. 2015, theintercept.com/2015/02/10/u-s-media-13-year-old-yemeni-boy-killed-u-s-drone/.
44. "Transforming Refugee Camps from Places of Boredom to Hubs of Innovation." *Positive News*, Positive

News, 23 Oct. 2015, www.positive.news/2015/economics/18679/transforming-refugee-camps-boredom-to-hubs-of-innovation/.
45. Viotti, Paul R., and Mark V. Kauppi. *International relations theory: realism, pluralism, globalism*. 3rd ed., Macmillan, 1998. For reference, Chapter 2: Realism: The State, Power, and the Balance of Power (55-197).

Chapter 24

1. "Abu Dawud Book 033, Hadith Number 4450." *Hadith Collection*, hadithcollection.com/abudawud/265-Abu Dawud Book 33. Prescribed Punishments/18224-abu-dawud-book-033-hadith-number-4450.html. For reference: Abu Dawud Book 033, Hadith Number 4450.Chapter : Not known.Narated By Abdullah ibn Abbas : There is no prescribed punishment for one who has sexual intercourse with an animal.
2. Al-Munajjid, Muhammed Salih. "Will Men in Paradise Have Intercourse with Al-Hoor Aliyn?" *Islamqa.info*, Islam Question and Answer, islamqa.info/en/10053.
3. "Al-Qur'an Al-Kareem - القرآن الكريم." *Surah Al-Waqi'ah [56:35-38]*, quran.com/56/35-38.
4. "Al-Qur'an Al-Kareem - القرآن الكريم." *Surah An-Naba [78:31-40]*, quran.com/78/31-40.
5. Andrews, Robin. "We Finally Know Why People Are Left- Or Right-Handed." *IFLScience*, IFLScience, 23 Jan. 2019, www.iflscience.com/brain/finally-know-people-left-righthanded/.
6. "Age of the Mother of the Believers 'Aa'ishah (May Allah Be Pleased with Her) When the Prophet (Blessings and Peace of Allah Be upon Him) Married Her - Islam Question & Answer." *Islamqa.info*, Islam Question and Answer, 30 Dec. 2013, islamqa.info/en/answers/124483/age-of-the-mother-of-the-believers-aaishah-may-allah-be-pleased-with-her-when-the-prophet-blessings-and-peace-of-allah-be-upon-him-married-her.
7. "As Eid Al Adha Approaches..." *Questions on Islam*, questionsonislam.com/content/eid-al-adha-approaches...
8. Aydemir, Ridvan. *YouTube*, Apostate Prophet, www.youtube.com/channel/UCzREuchzOqiawpEpvEM0Tyg/videos.
9. Aydemir, Ridvan. "All The Things That Satan Does (Ridiculous Islamic Teachings)." *YouTube*, Apostate Prophet, 28 Dec. 2018, www.youtube.com/watch?v=Ko2lttV8i2M&feature=youtu.be.
10. Aydemir, Ridvan. "Cowards in Control." *YouTube*, Apostate Prophet, 25 May 2019, www.youtube.com/watch?v=3Q5ZKANKaMQ.
11. Bittles, A H, and R Hussain. "An Analysis of Consanguineous Marriage in the Muslim Population of India at Regional and State Levels." *Current Neurology and Neuroscience Reports.*, U.S. National Library of Medicine, www.ncbi.nlm.nih.gov/pubmed/10768421.
12. "Bradford Grooming: Nine Jailed for Abusing Girls." *BBC News*, BBC, 27 Feb. 2019, www.bbc.com/news/uk-england-leeds-47388060.
13. Chhabhadiya, Neelam. "Sexual Grooming amongst Hindu Girls." *National Hindu Students' Forum (UK)*, 5 Nov. 2017, www.nhsf.org.uk/2017/11/sexual-grooming-amongst-hindu-girls/.
14. Evans, Martin. "Newcastle Grooming Gangs Were Allowed to Abuse 700 Girls Because Police Blamed the Victims, Review Finds." *The Telegraph*, Telegraph Media Group, 23 Feb. 2018, www.telegraph.co.uk/news/2018/02/23/newcastle-grooming-gangs-acted-arrogant-persistence-serious/.
15. Greenwood, Shannon. "Demographic Portrait of Muslim Americans." *Pew Research Center's Religion & Public Life Project*, Pew Research Center's Religion & Public Life Project, 9 Nov. 2017, www.pewforum.org/2017/07/26/demographic-portrait-of-muslim-americans/.
16. *Hadith - Book of Prophets - Sahih Al-Bukhari - Sunnah.com - Sayings and Teachings of Prophet Muhammad (☐☐☐ ☐☐☐☐ ☐☐ ☐☐ ☐☐☐☐)*, sunnah.com/bukhari/60/73.
17. "Hadith - Chapters on the Description of Paradise - Jami` at-Tirmidhi - Sunnah.com - Sayings and Teachings of Prophet Muhammad (صلى الله عليه وسلم)." *Riyad as-Salihin - Sunnah.com - Sayings and Teachings of Prophet Muhammad (☐☐☐ ☐☐☐☐ ☐☐ ☐☐ ☐☐☐☐)*, www.sunnah.com/urn/678680.
18. *Hadith - Establishing the Prayer and the Sunnah Regarding Them - Sunan Ibn Majah - Sunnah.com - Sayings and Teachings of Prophet Muhammad (☐☐☐ ☐☐☐☐ ☐☐ ☐☐ ☐☐☐☐)*, sunnah.com/urn/1281560.
19. "Hadith - Hudud - Bulugh Al-Maram - Sunnah.com - Sayings and Teachings of Prophet Muhammad (صلى الله عليه وسلم)." *Search Results - Fitra (Page 1) - Sunnah.com - Sayings and Teachings of Prophet Muhammad (☐☐☐ ☐☐☐☐ ☐☐ ☐☐ ☐☐☐☐)*, sunnah.com/urn/2015030.
20. *Hadith - The Book of Clothes and Adornment - Sahih Muslim - Sunnah.com - Sayings and Teachings of*

Prophet Muhammad (ﷺ), sunnah.com/muslim/37/159.

21. Hadith - The Book of Faith - Sahih Muslim - Sunnah.com - Sayings and Teachings of Prophet Muhammad (ﷺ), sunnah.com/muslim/1/253.
22. Hadith - The Book of Purification - Bulugh Al-Maram - Sunnah.com - Sayings and Teachings of Prophet Muhammad (ﷺ), sunnah.com/bulugh/1/169.
23. Hadith - The Book of Virtues - Riyad as-Salihin - Sunnah.com - Sayings and Teachings of Prophet Muhammad (ﷺ), sunnah.com/riyadussaliheen/9/102.
24. "Hadith - Zuhd - Sunan Ibn Majah - Sunnah.com - Sayings and Teachings of Prophet Muhammad (صلى الله عليه وسلم)." *Sahih Muslim - Sunnah.com - Sayings and Teachings of Prophet Muhammad (ﷺ)*, sunnah.com/urn/1294400.
25. Haider, Sarah. "Even as a Child, This Eid Was Horrifying. I Remember Witnessing a Sacrifice of a Cow with My Family, I Remember the Blood Gushing from Its Throat and Running through the Street. The Story of Abraham Which It Commemorates Is Another Horror. I'll Save My Mubaraks for the Other Eid." *Twitter*, Twitter, 21 Aug. 2018, twitter.com/SarahTheHaider/status/1031995695652384769.
26. Haider, Sarah. "I Remember the Son of the Butcher We Hired Playing in the Blood, like a Rain Puddle." *Twitter*, Twitter, 21 Aug. 2018, twitter.com/SarahTheHaider/status/1031996570470940673.
27. Haider, Sarah, et al. "Islam, Modesty and Feminism." *YouTube*, Ex-Muslims of North America, 12 Oct. 2017, www.youtube.com/watch?v=QToII2x8njJM.
28. Haider, Sarah. "Sarah Haider: Islam and the Necessity of Liberal Critique (AHA Conference 2015)." *YouTube*, American Humanist Association, 28 May 2015, www.youtube.com/watch?v=0plC24YuoJk.
29. Hasan, Ahmad. "Game (Kitab Al-Said)." *Family Life in Islam*, International Islamic University Malaysia, www.iium.edu.my/deed/hadith/abudawood/010_sat.html.
30. "Health Risks of Female Genital Mutilation (FGM)." *World Health Organization*, World Health Organization, 1 Feb. 2017, www.who.int/reproductivehealth/topics/fgm/health_consequences_fgm/en/.
31. Mo, Bilaal. "I Remember the Wrath on the Slaughterer's Faces Too, and Blood Stained Hands and Kurta's Afterwards. The Whole Thing Was Creepy." *Twitter*, Twitter, 21 Aug. 2018, twitter.com/takebeerism/status/1031996242685906945.
32. Mo, Bilaal. "We Used to Joke around That the Reason We Fasted the Day or Two before This Eid Was to Avoid Throwing up. Fortunately i Wasn't in That World Long Enough to Become Desensitised to It." *Twitter*, Twitter, 21 Aug. 2018, twitter.com/takebeerism/status/1031997399969947649.
33. Na'amnih, Wasef, et al. "Prevalence of Consanguineous Marriages and Associated Factors among Israeli Bedouins." *Current Neurology and Neuroscience Reports.*, U.S. National Library of Medicine, Oct. 2014, www.ncbi.nlm.nih.gov/pmc/articles/PMC4159474/.
34. Namazie, Maryam, et al. "Equality, Islam and Human Rights." *YouTube*, Ex-Muslims of North America, 26 Mar. 2018, www.youtube.com/watch?v=2W0w9ufJOh0.
35. "Pakistani Hindus Complain of Forced Conversion of Teenage Girls." *YouTube*, VOA News, 18 Mar. 2016, youtu.be/-i24jg4mJ4I.
36. Navabi, Armin. "Muslim Defends Muhammad Having Sex with Aisha When She Was Nine!" *YouTube*, Atheist Republic, 3 Jan. 2019, youtu.be/yKExtzI68jM.
37. "Poor Goat." *LiveLeak.com - Redefining the Media*, www.liveleak.com/view?i=008_1443844876.
38. "QuranX.com The Most Complete Quran / Hadith / Tafsir Collection Available!" *Sahih Muslim Hadiths*, quranx.com/Hadith/Muslim/USC-MSA/Book-2/Hadith-462/. For reference: Collection Sahih MuslimIn-book reference Book 2, Hadith 31Reference Hadith 238USC-MSA web (English) reference Book 2, Hadith 462Abu Huraira reported:The Apostle of Allah (ﷺ) said. When any one of you awakes up from sleep and performs ablution, he must clean his nose three times, for the devil spends the night in the interior of his nose.
39. "QuranX.com The Most Complete Quran / Hadith / Tafsir Collection Available!" *Sahih Muslim Hadiths*, quranx.com/Hadith/Muslim/USC-MSA/Book-8/Hadith-3240/.
40. "QuranX.com The Most Complete Quran / Hadith / Tafsir Collection Available!" *Sahih Muslim Hadiths*, quranx.com/Hadith/Muslim/USC-MSA/Book-23/Hadith-5046/.
41. "QuranX.com The Most Complete Quran / Hadith / Tafsir Collection Available!" *Muwatta Malik Hadiths*, quranx.com/Hadith/Malik/USC-MSA/Book-49/Hadith-6/.
42. "QuranX.com The Most Complete Quran / Hadith / Tafsir Collection Available!" *Sahih Bukhari Hadiths*, quranx.com/Hadith/Bukhari/USC-MSA/Volume-2/Book-21/Hadith-245/. For reference: Collection Sahih BukhariDar-us-Salam reference Hadith 1144In-book reference Book 19, Hadith 25USC-MSA web (English) reference Volume 2, Book 21, Hadith 245Narrated `Abdullah:A person was mentioned

before the Prophet (p.b.u.h) and he was told that he had kept on sleeping till morning and had not got up for the prayer. The Prophet (ﷺ) said, "Satan urinated in his ears."

43. "QuranX.com The Most Complete Quran / Hadith / Tafsir Collection Available!" *Sahih Bukhari Hadiths*, quranx.com/Hadith/Bukhari/USC-MSA/Volume-3/Book-34/Hadith-437/.
44. "QuranX.com The Most Complete Quran / Hadith / Tafsir Collection Available!" *Sahih Bukhari Hadiths*, quranx.com/Hadith/Bukhari/USC-MSA/Volume-4/Book-54/Hadith-491/.
45. "QuranX.com The Most Complete Quran / Hadith / Tafsir Collection Available!" *Sahih Bukhari Hadiths*, quranx.com/Hadith/Bukhari/USC-MSA/Volume-4/Book-54/Hadith-493/. For Reference: Collection Sahih BukhariDar-us-Salam reference Hadith 3271In-book reference Book 59, Hadith 81USC-MSA web (English) reference Volume 4, Book 54, Hadith 493Narrated Ibn `Abbas:The Prophet (ﷺ) said, "If anyone of you, when having sexual relation with his wife, say: 'In the name of Allah. O Allah! Protect us from Satan and prevent Satan from approaching our offspring you are going to give us,' and if he begets a child (as a result of that relation) Satan will not harm it."
46. "QuranX.com The Most Complete Quran / Hadith / Tafsir Collection Available!" *Sahih Bukhari Hadiths*, quranx.com/Hadith/Bukhari/USC-MSA/Volume-4/Book-54/Hadith-522/.
47. "QuranX.com The Most Complete Quran / Hadith / Tafsir Collection Available!" *Sahih Bukhari Hadiths*, quranx.com/Hadith/Bukhari/USC-MSA/Volume-5/Book-59/Hadith-512/.
48. "QuranX.com The Most Complete Quran / Hadith / Tafsir Collection Available!" *Sahih Bukhari Hadiths*, quranx.com/Hadith/Bukhari/USC-MSA/Volume-5/Book-59/Hadith-524/.
49. "QuranX.com The Most Complete Quran / Hadith / Tafsir Collection Available!" *Sahih Bukhari Hadiths*, quranx.com/Hadith/Bukhari/USC-MSA/Volume-8/Book-73/Hadith-242/. For reference: Narrated Abu Huraira:The Prophet (ﷺ) said, "Allah likes sneezing and dislikes yawning, so if someone sneezes and then praises Allah, then it is obligatory on every Muslim who heard him, to say: May Allah be merciful to you (Yar-hamuka-l-lah). But as regards yawning, it is from Satan, so one must try one's best to stop it, if one says 'Ha' when yawning, Satan will laugh at him."
50. "Rulings from Your Site Regarding Female Circumcision Appear to Have Been Taken down. Is There Is a Change in Opinion Concerning Female Circumcision from a Shafii Point of View? What Do You Say about Issuing a Fatwa on This Issue Which Prohibits the Practice?" Translated by Yaqub Abdurrahman, *Shafii Fiqh*, shafiifiqh.com/question-details.aspx?qstID=173.
51. Saad, Hassan Abu, et al. "Consanguineous Marriage and Intellectual and Developmental Disabilities among Arab Bedouins Children of the Negev Region in Southern Israel: A Pilot Study." *Current Neurology and Neuroscience Reports.*, U.S. National Library of Medicine, 2014, www.ncbi.nlm.nih.gov/pmc/articles/PMC3904202/.
52. "Sahih Al-Bukhari Book Number 11 Hadith Number 582." *Muflihun*, muflihun.com/bukhari/11/582.
53. "Sahih Al-Bukhari Book Number 34 Hadith Number 351." *Muflihun*, muflihun.com/bukhari/34/351.
54. "Sahih Al-Bukhari Book Number 34 Hadith Number 432." *Muflihun*, muflihun.com/bukhari/34/432.
55. "Sahih Al-Bukhari Book Number 38 Hadith Number 505." *Muflihun*, muflihun.com/bukhari/38/505.
56. "Sahih Al-Bukhari Book Number 41 Hadith Number 598." *Muflihun*, muflihun.com/bukhari/41/598.
57. "Sahih Al-Bukhari Book Number 47 Hadith Number 743." *Muflihun*, muflihun.com/bukhari/47/743.
58. "Sahih Al-Bukhari Book Number 47 Hadith Number 765." *Muflihun*, muflihun.com/bukhari/47/765.
59. "Sahih Al-Bukhari Book Number 52 Hadith Number 255." *Muflihun*, muflihun.com/bukhari/52/255.
60. "Sahih Al-Bukhari Book Number 52 Hadith Number 260." *Muflihun*, muflihun.com/bukhari/52/260.
61. "Sahih Al-Bukhari Book Number 55 Hadith Number 641." *Muflihun*, muflihun.com/bukhari/55/641. For reference: Sahih al-Bukhari Book 55 Hadith 641Narrated Said bin Al-Musaiyab:Abu Huraira said, "I heard Allah's Apostle saying, 'There is none born among the off-spring of Adam, but Satan touches it. A child therefore, cries loudly at the time of birth because of the touch of Satan, except Mary and her child." Then Abu Huraira recited: "And I seek refuge with You for her and for her offspring from the outcast Satan" (3.36)
62. "Sahih Al-Bukhari Book Number 62 Hadith Number 137." *Muflihun*, muflihun.com/bukhari/62/137.
63. "Sahih Al-Bukhari Book Number 80 Hadith Number 753." *Muflihun*, muflihun.com/bukhari/80/753.
64. "Sahih Al-Bukhari Book Number 84 Hadith Number 57." *Muflihun*, muflihun.com/bukhari/84/57.
65. "Sahih Al-Bukhari Book Number 84 Hadith Number 58." *Muflihun*, muflihun.com/bukhari/84/58.
66. "Sahih Al-Bukhari Book Number 84 Hadith Number 64." *Muflihun*, muflihun.com/bukhari/84/64.
67. "Sahih Al-Bukhari Book Number 87 Hadith Number 124." *Muflihun*, muflihun.com/bukhari/87/124.
68. "Sahih Muslim Book Number 1 Hadith Number 244." *Muflihun*, muflihun.com/muslim/1/244. For reference: Sahih Muslim Book 1 Hadith 244It is narrated on the authority of Abu Huraira that the

Messenger of Allah may peace be upon him) observed: The Satan comes to everyone. of you and says: Who created this and that? till he questions: Who created your Lord? When he comes to that, one should seek refuge in Allah and keep away (from such idle thoughts).

69. "Sahih Muslim Book Number 15 Hadith Number 4112." *Muflihun*, muflihun.com/muslim/15/4112.
70. "Sahih Muslim Book 024, Hadith Number 5246." *Hadith Collection*, hadithcollection.com/sahihmuslim/152-Sahih Muslim Book 24. Clothes and Decorations/13592-sahih-muslim-book-024-hadith-number-5246.html.
71. "Sahih Muslim Book 024, Hadith Number 5248." *Hadith Collection*, hadithcollection.com/sahihmuslim/152-Sahih Muslim Book 24. Clothes and Decorations/13590-sahih-muslim-book-024-hadith-number-5248.html.
72. Saleem, Mya, et al. "Examining Honor Culture and Violence in Islam (AHA Conference 2016)." *YouTube*, American Humanist Association, 30 June 2016, www.youtube.com/watch?v=DhwrOJvPfBw.
73. Shamshad, S. "Prevalence of Consanguinity in Muslim Community - A Review." *Pdfs.semanticscholar.org*, International Journal of Science and Research (IJSR), pdfs.semanticscholar.org/f3db/08faf43477ce7c34146aa4b8db0769661efa.pdf.
74. Sarkeesian, Anita. "Women as Reward - Tropes vs Women in Video Games." *YouTube*, Feminist Frequency, 31 Aug. 2015, www.youtube.com/watch?v=QC6oxBLXtkU.
75. "Shreela Flather." *Wikipedia*, Wikimedia Foundation, 9 July 2018, en.wikipedia.org/wiki/Shreela_Flather.
76. Sommerlad, Joe. "Why Do Muslims Sacrifice Animals during Eid?" *The Independent*, Independent Digital News and Media, 21 Aug. 2018, www.independent.co.uk/news/world/middle-east/eid-al-adha-animal-sacrifice-abraham-islam-muslims-goats-sheep-animal-rights-a8500556.html.
77. Swinford, Steven. "First Cousin Marriages in Pakistani Communities Leading to 'Appalling' Disabilities among Children." *The Telegraph*, Telegraph Media Group, 7 July 2015, www.telegraph.co.uk/news/health/children/11723308/First-cousin-marriages-in-Pakistani-communities-leading-to-appalling-disabilities-among-children.html.
78. "Tafseer on the Basis of Narrated Texts and Tafseer on the Basis of Individual Understanding - Islam Question & Answer." *Islamqa.info*, Islam Question and Answer, 11 Mar. 2015, islamqa.info/en/answers/205290/tafseer-on-the-basis-of-narrated-texts-and-tafseer-on-the-basis-of-individual-understanding.
79. "The Quranic Arabic Corpus - Word by Word Grammar, Syntax and Morphology of the Holy Quran." *The Quranic Arabic Corpus - Translation*, corpus.quran.com/. For reference:
Chapter 4, Verse 24:
http://corpus.quran.com/translation.jsp?chapter=4&verse=24
Chapter 4, Verse 34:
http://corpus.quran.com/translation.jsp?chapter=4&verse=34
Chapter 4, Verse 89:
corpus.quran.com/translation.jsp?chapter=4&verse=89
Chapter 9, Verse 5:
http://corpus.quran.com/translation.jsp?chapter=9&verse=5
Chapter 9, Verse 29:
http://corpus.quran.com/translation.jsp?chapter=9&verse=29
80. "The Reason Why the Right Hand Is Preferred over the Left - Islam Question & Answer." *Islamqa.info*, Islam Question and Answer, 2 Mar. 2007, islamqa.info/en/answers/82120/the-reason-why-the-right-hand-is-preferred-over-the-left.
81. "The Udhiyah (the Sacrificial Animal) and Its Rulings." *Islamway*, Islamway, 29 Nov. 2012, en.islamway.net/article/12915/the-udhiyah-the-sacrificial-animal-and-its-rulings.
82. "Two Pai Taliban Jihadi Mujahideen Caught Sexing A Donkey By US Forces." *LiveLeak.com - Redefining the Media*, www.liveleak.com/view?i=825_1315923588.
83. "US ARMY Camera Catches Afghans Gangbanging a Goat." *LiveLeak.com - Redefining the Media*, www.liveleak.com/view?i=93d_1384239379.

Chapter 25

1. ALHAKEEM, ASSIM. "ABOUT US - SHEIKH ASSIM ALHAKEEM." *Http://Www.assimalhakeem.net*, Assimalhakeem.net/about/, www.assimalhakeem.net/about/.

2. Alhakeem, Assim. "There Is No Such Thing as Marital Rape. As Long as She Is Married, This Is Not Rape! It Is Domestic Violence, It Is Physical Abuse or Any Other Form of Aggression. Https://T.co/7leRTCdzVn." *Twitter*, Twitter, 11 Nov. 2017, twitter.com/Assimalhakeem/status/929295190648553472.
3. Arbabzadah, Nushin. "The 1980s Mujahideen, the Taliban and the Shifting Idea of Jihad | Nushin Arbabzadah." *The Guardian*, Guardian News and Media, 28 Apr. 2011, www.theguardian.com/commentisfree/2011/apr/28/afghanistan-mujahideen-taliban
4. Aydemir, Ridvan. "Cowards in Control." *YouTube*, Apostate Prophet, 25 May 2019, www.youtube.com/watch?v=3Q5ZKANKaMQ.
5. "BibleGateway." *Bible Gateway*, Bible Gateway Blog, www.biblegateway.com/passage/?search=1 Timothy 2&version=KJV.
6. "BibleGateway." *Numbers 31:7-18 KJV - - Bible Gateway*, www.biblegateway.com/passage/?search=Numbers 31:7-18&version=KJV.
7. Castor, Trevor. "Sin According to Islam." *Zwemer Center*, www.zwemercenter.com/guide/sin-according-to-muslims/.
8. Cialdini, Robert B. *Influence: Science and practice*. 4th ed., 21st Century Bks, 2002. Chapter 2: Reciprocation (19-50).
9. "Dangerous: Imran Khan to Campaign for New Blasphemy Laws around the World." *Humanists UK*, humanism.org.uk/2018/08/30/new-pakistani-pm-imran-khan-pledges-to-revive-un-campaign-for-global-blasphemy-laws/.
10. "Fatawa - Does Marital Rape Exist in Islam?" *Dar Al-Ifta Al Misriyyah*, www.dar-alifta.org/Foreign/ViewFatwa.aspx?ID=6033.
11. Fenton, Siobhan. "Twitter Trolls Are Reporting Muslim Girls for Being Atheist in Countries That Carry the Death Penalty." *The Independent*, Independent Digital News and Media, 22 June 2016, www.independent.co.uk/life-style/gadgets-and-tech/twitter-trolls-are-reporting-muslim-girls-to-the-police-for-posting-blasphemous-messages-online-a7096191.html.
12. Fishwick, Carmen. "India's BJP Manifesto Pledges Uniform Civil Code: What Do You Think of the Legislation?" *The Guardian*, Guardian News and Media, 7 Apr. 2014, www.theguardian.com/world/2014/apr/07/india-bjp-election-manifesto-uniform-civil-code-legislation.
13. Freeman, Ben. "US Foreign Policy Is for Sale." *The Nation*, 21 Feb. 2019, www.thenation.com/article/us-foreign-policy-sale-think-tanks/.
14. Furey, Anthony. "FUREY: The Pakistan Government Is Accusing Me of a Crime – and Twitter Is Acting as Its Messenger." *Toronto Sun*, 10 Dec. 2018, torontosun.com/opinion/columnists/furey-the-pakistan-government-doesnt-like-one-of-my-old-tweets-and-twitter-passed-along-the-message.
15. "Greater and Lesser Jihaad." Translated by Muhammed Salih Al-Munajjid, *Islam Question And Answer*, islamqa.info/en/10455.
16. Haddad, Mais. "Victims of Rape and Law: How the Laws of the Arab World Protect Rapists, Not Victims." *Jurist*, Jurist, www.jurist.org/commentary/2017/05/mais-haddad-arab-world-laws-protect-the-rapist-not-the-victim/.
17. Haider, Sarah, and David Pakman. "Ex-Muslim Drops Hammer on Reza Aslan, Conservatives, Liberals." *YouTube*, David Pakman Show, 16 Dec. 2015, www.youtube.com/watch?v=ayQ-j8lJmwE.
18. Haider, Sarah, et al. "Islam, Modesty and Feminism." *YouTube*, Ex-Muslims of North America, 12 Oct. 2017, www.youtube.com/watch?v=QToH2x8njJM.
19. Haider, Sarah. "Sarah Haider: Islam and the Necessity of Liberal Critique (AHA Conference 2015)." *YouTube*, American Humanist Association, 28 May 2015, www.youtube.com/watch?v=0plC24YuoJk.
20. Hijab, Mohammed. "The Fundamental Flaws in Feminism." *YouTube*, YouTube, 29 Aug. 2017, www.youtube.com/watch?v=IKhIeCF1kPY.
21. Handjani, Amir. "Saudi Arabia Has Big Plans in India." *Foreign Policy*, Foreign Policy, 10 May 2019, foreignpolicy.com/2019/05/10/saudi-arabia-has-big-plans-in-india/.
22. Harris, Sam. "The End of Liberalism? - Samharris.org." *The End of Liberalism? : : Sam Harris*, www.samharris.org/site/full_text/the-end-of-liberalism/. Accessed 15 Feb. 2015.
23. Hitchens, Christopher. "Christopher Hitchens on Australia's Q & A - Women in Iran." *YouTube*, blob4000, 7 Oct. 2009, www.youtube.com/watch?v=YXjm31Bvomo.
24. Hitchens, Christopher, and Tony Jones. "God, Sodomy and the Lash." *Q&A*, Australian Broadcasting Corporation, 21 Dec. 2018, www.abc.net.au/qanda/god-sodomy-and-the-lash/10663024.
25. Kenyon, Peter. "In Iran Protests, Women Stand Up, Lift Their Hijab, For Their Rights." *NPR*, NPR, 3

Aug. 2018, www.npr.org/2018/08/03/631784518/in-iran-protests-women-stand-up-lift-their-hijab-for-their-rights.
26. Meek, James Gordon. "ISIS Leader Abu Bakr Al-Baghdadi Sexually Abused American Hostage Kayla Mueller, Officials Say." *ABC News*, ABC News Network, 14 Aug. 2015, abcnews.go.com/International/isis-leader-abu-bakr-al-baghdadi-sexually-abused/story?id=33085923.
27. Miglani, Sanjeev. "Saudi Prince Expects Investment Worth More than $100 Billion in India." *Reuters*, Thomson Reuters, 20 Feb. 2019, www.reuters.com/article/us-asia-saudi-india/saudi-prince-expects-investment-worth-more-than-100-billion-in-india-idUSKCN1Q90M9.
28. Muthali, Aki. "Atheistophobia: It's Time to Talk about the Most Persecuted Minority in the World." *The Nation*, 27 Sept. 2015, nation.com.pk/27-Sep-2015/atheistophobia-it-s-time-to-talk-about-the-most-persecuted-minority-in-the-world.
29. Muthali, Aki. "I Wasn't in Sri Lanka in 2015. Lived in Canada for 25 Years. The Doxxing Did Cause Serious Safety Issues as the Info the Muslim Extremist Posted, Was Used by Many People, Including Nazis and Anti-Feminists Who, along with the Islamists, Sent Death and Rape Threats to Me & My Mom." *Twitter*, Crotchety Misanthrope, 15 May 2019, twitter.com/akimuthali/status/1128508967561437185.
30. Namazie, Maryam, et al. "Equality, Islam and Human Rights." *YouTube*, Ex-Muslims of North America, 26 Mar. 2018, www.youtube.com/watch?v=2W0w9ufJOh0.
31. "Names of God in Judaism." *Wikipedia*, Wikimedia Foundation, 23 May 2019, en.wikipedia.org/wiki/Names_of_God_in_Judaism.
32. Nomani, Asra Q., and Hala Arafa. "Inside the World of Gulf State Slavery." *The Daily Beast*, The Daily Beast Company, 11 Oct. 2015, www.thedailybeast.com/inside-the-world-of-gulf-state-slavery.
33. "Nushin Arbabzadah." *International.ucla.edu*, UCLA, www.international.ucla.edu/cisa/person/786.
34. Oweiss, Ibrahim M. "Conclusion/Notes." *Http://Faculty.georgetown.edu*, The Committee for Monetary Research and Education, faculty.georgetown.edu/imo3/petrod/conclude.htm.
35. Patel, Anand, and Nikhil Dawar. "Fact File: Sharia Courts Decoded." *India Today*, 17 Sept. 2018, www.indiatoday.in/fact-check/story/fact-file-sharia-courts-decoded-1285236-2018-07-13.
36. "Prohibition of Interfaith Marriage." *Prohibtion of Interfaith Marriage*, Global Legal Research Directorate, 1 Sept. 2016, www.loc.gov/law/help/marriage/interfaith-prohibition.php.
37. Renaldi, Erwin. "Female Circumcision: Culture and Religion in Malaysia See Millions of Girls Undergo Cut." *ABC News*, 13 Nov. 2018, www.abc.net.au/news/2018-11-13/female-circumcision-is-still-happening-in-malaysia/10473640.
38. "Ruling on Having Intercourse with a Slave Woman When One Has a Wife - Islamqa.info." Translated by Muhammad Salih Al-Munajjid, *Wayback Machine*, Fox News, web.archive.org/web/20160106101656/http://islamqa.info/en/10382
39. Scola, Nancy. "Obama's Anti-ISIL Push Falls Flat on Social Media." *POLITICO*, 12 Aug. 2015, www.politico.com/story/2015/08/obamas-anti-isil-push-falls-flat-on-social-media-121301.
40. Solnit, Rebecca. "Why Feminism Needs Men." *The Nation*, 8 July 2015, www.thenation.com/article/why-feminism-needs-men/.
41. Stephens, Joe, and David B. Ottaway. "From U.S., the ABC's of Jihad." *The Washington Post*, WP Company, 23 Mar. 2002, www.washingtonpost.com/archive/politics/2002/03/23/from-us-the-abcs-of-jihad/d079075a-3ed3-4030-9a96-0d48f6355e54/?utm_term=.cbb9b6b8a59a.
42. Sultan, Rayhana. "Hi @Twittersecurity @Policy @TwitterSupport, It Looks like I Am Being Made Invisible on Twitter (Shadowbanned, Friend/Followers Removed). Much of My Writings Focus on Denouncing Islamist Extremism, and Anti-Muslim, Far-Right Extremism. Could This Be a Reason?Who Can Help Me? Pic.twitter.com/Sy3K5V5SYm." *Twitter*, @Rayhana, 2 June 2019, twitter.com/rayhana/status/1135286904004534275.
43. Syed, Muhammad, and Imtiaz Shams. "Leaving Islam, Normalizing Dissent - Imtiaz Shams & Muhammad Syed." *YouTube*, Ex-Muslims of North America, 10 Oct. 2018, www.youtube.com/watch?v=reQmi-lAxLw.
44. "Tafseer on the Basis of Narrated Texts and Tafseer on the Basis of Individual Understanding - Islam Question & Answer." *Islamqa.info*, Islam Question and Answer, 11 Mar. 2015, islamqa.info/en/answers/205290/tafseer-on-the-basis-of-narrated-texts-and-tafseer-on-the-basis-of-individual-understanding.
45. Tessier, Stephanie, and Muhammad Syed. "Islam: Pull and Peril." *YouTube*, Ex-Muslims of North America, 22 Apr. 2018, www.youtube.com/watch?v=jt1rWgap41g.

46. "The Quranic Arabic Corpus - Word by Word Grammar, Syntax and Morphology of the Holy Quran." *The Quranic Arabic Corpus - Translation*, corpus.quran.com/. For reference: Chapter 4:24 by Mohsin Khan, Chapter 4:34 by Pickthall, Chapter 16:71 by Muhammad Sarwar, Chapter 23:5-11 by Sahih International, Chapter 24:33 by Yusuf Ali, and Chapter 24:58 by Shakir.
    Chapter 4, Verse 24:
    http://corpus.quran.com/translation.jsp?chapter=4&verse=24
    Chapter 4, Verse 34:
    http://corpus.quran.com/translation.jsp?chapter=4&verse=34
    Chapter 16, Verse 71:
    http://corpus.quran.com/translation.jsp?chapter=16&verse=71
    Chapter 23:5-11:
    http://corpus.quran.com/translation.jsp?chapter=23&verse=5
    http://corpus.quran.com/translation.jsp?chapter=23&verse=6
    http://corpus.quran.com/translation.jsp?chapter=23&verse=7
    http://corpus.quran.com/translation.jsp?chapter=23&verse=8
    http://corpus.quran.com/translation.jsp?chapter=23&verse=9
    http://corpus.quran.com/translation.jsp?chapter=23&verse=10
    http://corpus.quran.com/translation.jsp?chapter=23&verse=11
    Chapter 24:33 and 58:
    http://corpus.quran.com/translation.jsp?chapter=24&verse=33
    http://corpus.quran.com/translation.jsp?chapter=24&verse=58
47. "The Reason Why the Right Hand Is Preferred over the Left - Islam Question & Answer." *Islamqa.info*, Islam Question and Answer, 2 Mar. 2007, islamqa.info/en/answers/82120/the-reason-why-the-right-hand-is-preferred-over-the-left.
48. Truong, Alice. "This Saudi Prince Now Owns More of Twitter than Jack Dorsey Does." *Quartz*, Quartz, 16 Dec. 2015, qz.com/519388/this-saudi-prince-now-owns-more-of-twitter-than-jack-dorsey-does/.
49. "Twitter Says It Is Weeding Out More Users Promoting Terrorism and Violence." *Fortune*, fortune.com/2017/09/19/twitter-accounts-terrorism-hate-speech/.
50. Wither, Emily. "I Did It for My Daughter, Says Woman Arrested for Headscarf Protest..." *Reuters*, Thomson Reuters, 6 Mar. 2019, www.reuters.com/article/us-iran-protest-hijab/i-did-it-for-my-daughter-says-woman-arrested-for-headscarf-protest-in-iran-idUSKCN1Q30Q7.
51. "Zara Kay Was Banned for Posting This.... - Ex-Muslims of North America." *Https://Www.facebook.com/ExMuslimsOrg*, Ex-Muslims of North America, www.facebook.com/ExMuslimsOrg/photos/a.167221723467566/989587027897694/?type=3&theater.

e.) <u>Sanatana Dharma</u>

Chapter 26

1. Alt, Scott Eric. "We Need to Stop Saying That There Are 33,000 Protestant Denominations." *National Catholic Register*, Global Catholic Television Network (EWTN), www.ncregister.com/blog/scottericalt/we-need-to-stop-saying-that-there-are-33000-protestant-denominations. Despite trying to declare 33,000 denominations facetious, I felt the explanation only affirmed it. For reference:Thus the imme-di-ate prob-lem is that the WCE only clas-si-fies 9000 denom-i-na-tions (27% of the whole) as Protes-tant. To get to 33,000, one must add in the Inde-pen-dents, Mar-gin-als, Angli-cans, and 232 of the Ortho-dox.Among the 23,600 "Inde-pen-dents" and "Mar-gin-als" (70% of the whole) are large num-bers of groups one would have a hard time call-ing Protes-tant. They include Mor-mons (122 denom-i-na-tions), Jehovah's Wit-nesses (229 denom-i-na-tions), Masons (28 denom-i-na-tions), Chris-tadel-phi-ans (21 denom-i-na-tions) Uni-tar-i-ans (29 denom-i-na-tions), Chris-t-ian Sci-ence (59 denom-i-na-tions), Theosophists (3 more denom-i-na-tions), British Israelites (8 denom-i-na-tions), Pros-per-ity Gospel groups (27 denom-i-na-tions), One-ness Pen-te-costals (680 denom-i-na-tions), "Hid-den Bud-dhist Believ-ers in Christ" (9 denom-i-na-tions), wan-der-ing bish-ops (12 denom-i-na-tions), Inde-pen-dent Nesto-ri-ans (5 denom-i-na-tions), occultists (3 denom-i-na-tions), spiri-tists (20 denom-i-na-tions), Zion-ists (159 denom-i-na-tions), even "Arab radio/TV net-work" (19 denom-i-na-tions), "gay/homosexual tra-di-tion"

(2 denominations), and schismatic Catholics (435 denominations). It is a strange and eclectic list. (See here and here.) However strong the temptation some may have to characterize anything not Catholic or Orthodox as "Protestant," you can't do that. All that tells Protestant apologists is that you don't know what Protestantism is, or what its distinctives are—and they would be right. And why would they take anything you say seriously after that? If you don't know what Protestantism is, who are you to be talking about its errors? Not only are Mormons, Jehovah's Witnesses, Oneness Pentecostals, Unitarians, Prosperity Gospel believers (included among 23,600 Independents and Marginals) not Protestant, they are not even Christian; they adhere to a false Christology. Protestants and Catholics are in agreement about who Christ is; these other groups have other ideas.

2. "Appeal to Tradition." *Https://Www.logicallyfallacious.com*, www.logicallyfallacious.com/tools/lp/Bo/LogicalFallacies/44/Appeal-to-Tradition.
3. Barany, Zoltan. "Where Myanmar Went Wrong." *Foreign Affairs*, Foreign Affairs Magazine, 6 Mar. 2019, www.foreignaffairs.com/articles/burma-myanmar/2018-04-16/where-myanmar-went-wrong.
4. Barnett, Robert. "Saving Tibet from Satan's Grip: Present-Day Missionary Activity in Tibet." *Saving Tibet from Satan's Grip: Present-Day Missionary Activity in Tibet by Robert Barnett*, info-buddhism.com/Present-day-Missionary-Activity-in-Tibet_Barnett.html.
5. Beckwith, Christopher I. *Greek Buddha: Pyrrhos Encounter with Early Buddhism in Central Asia*. PDF ed., Princeton University Press, 2017. *Princeton University Press*, assets.press.princeton.edu/chapters/s10500.pdf.
6. Bixby, Scott. "Dalai Lama OK with Gay Marriage." *The Daily Beast*, The Daily Beast Company, 8 Mar. 2014, www.thedailybeast.com/dalai-lama-ok-with-gay-marriage.
7. Bloom, Paul. *Against Empathy: the Case for Rational Compassion*. The Bodley Head Ltd, 2016.
8. "Bön, Tibet's Indigenous Belief System." *Khan Academy*, Khan Academy, www.khanacademy.org/humanities/art-asia/himalayas/tibet/a/bn-tibets-indigenous-belief-system.
9. Buddha, Gautama. *The Dhammapada* (pgs. 3, 6, 7, 8, 12, 18. 20. 22. 24, 26, 27, 28, 31, 32, and 33). Start Publishing LLC. Kindle Edition.
10. Cialdini, Robert B. *Influence: Science and practice*. 4th ed., 21st Century Bks, 2002. For reference: Chapter 2: Reciprocation (19-50).
11. "Christianity and SGI Nichiren Buddhism." *What Is 'Divine' in Buddhism?*, www.sokahumanism.com/nichiren-buddhism/Christianity_and_SGI_Nichiren_Buddhism.html.
12. Cornick, Jenny. "Key Differences between Pure Land Buddhism and Zen Buddhism." *Academia.edu*, www.academia.edu/34413183/Key_Differences_between_Pure_Land_Buddhism_and_Zen_Buddhism.
13. de Lubac, Henry. "History of Pure Land Buddhism - Chapter 4." Translated by Amita Bhaka, *World Fellowship of Buddhists Second Two-Year Plan (B.E. 2544-2*, www.bdcu.org.au/bddronline/bddr12no6/pureland4.html.
14. Doshi, Vidhi. "After Nearly Six Decades of Exile, Some Tibetans in India Are Slowly Letting Go of the Past." *The Washington Post*, WP Company, 9 Oct. 2017, www.washingtonpost.com/world/asia_pacific/after-nearly-six-decades-of-exile-some-tibetans-in-india-are-slowly-letting-go-of-the-past/2017/10/07/c00325b0-a2da-11e7-b573-8ec86cdfe1ed_story.html?utm_term=.b4e28775e88f.
15. Dryden, Windy. *Overcoming Procrastination*. Sheldon, 2000.
16. "Four Noble Truths." *The Buddhist Centre*, thebuddhistcentre.com/text/four-noble-truths.
17. Gelineau, Kristen. "Rohingya Women Methodically Raped by Myanmar's Armed Forces." *Chicagotribune.com*, 11 Dec. 2017, www.chicagotribune.com/news/nationworld/ct-rohingya-women-rape-myanmar-20171211-story.html.
18. Ghose, Sanujit. "Cultural Links between India & the Greco-Roman World." *Ancient History Encyclopedia*, Ancient History Encyclopedia, 30 Apr. 2019, www.ancient.eu/article/208/cultural-links-between-india--the-greco-roman-worl/.
19. Gilbert, Daniel. *Stumbling on Happiness*. Random House, 2006. For reference: Chapter 4: In the Blind Spot of the Mind's Eye (75-95) and Chapter 5: The Hound of Silence (96-108).
20. Halvorson, Heidi Grant. *Succeed: How We Can Reach Our Goals*. Plume, 2012.
21. Hays, Jeffrey. "TIBETAN BUDDHIST GODS, BODHISATTVAS AND BUDDHAS." *Facts and Details*, factsanddetails.com/china/cat6/sub34/entry-4428.html.
22. Holmes-Tagchungdarpa, Amy. "Can Women Become Leaders in the Buddhist Tradition?" *Georgetown University*, berkleycenter.georgetown.edu/forum/can-women-become-leaders-in-the-buddhist-tradition.
23. India, Mystery Of. "A Peep Into Hindu & Buddhist Past of Afghanistan." *Mystery of India*, 1 Feb. 2016,

www.mysteryofindia.com/2015/11/a-peep-into-hindu-buddhist-past-of-afghanistan.html.
24. "Interview with the Dalai Lama about the Full Ordination of Women." *The Ever-Changing Forms of Buddhism by James Blumenthal*, info-buddhism.com/Interview_Dalai_Lama_about_the_Full_Ordination_of_Women.html.
25. "Introduction to Tibetan Buddhism." *Khan Academy*, Khan Academy, www.khanacademy.org/humanities/art-asia/himalayas/tibet/a/introduction-to-tibetan-buddhism.
26. Ispas, Alexa. *Psychology and politics: a social identity perspective*. Psychology Press, 2014. For reference purposes: Chapter 1: Psychology and the Social Identity Perspective (1-24).
27. Kahneman, Daniel. *Thinking, fast and slow*. Farrar, Straus and Giroux, 2015. For reference purposes: The Introduction (1-17), Chapter 4: The Associative Machine (50-58), Chapter 5: Cognitive Ease (59-70), Chapter 6:"Norms, Surprises, and Causes" (71-78), Chapter 7: A Machine for Jumping to Conclusions (79-88), Chapter 8: How Judgments Happen (89-96), Chapter 19: The Illusion of Understanding (199-208), and Chapter 20: The Illusion of Validity (209-221).
28. Kantar, Sally. "The Myanmar Military's Legacy of Impunity." *Foreign Affairs*, Foreign Affairs, 14 Dec. 2017, www.foreignaffairs.com/articles/burma-myanmar/2017-12-14/myanmar-militarys-legacy-impunity.
29. McGonigal, Kelly. *The Willpower Instinct: How Self-Control Works, Why It Matters, and What You Can Do to Get More of It*. Avery, 2013.
30. Kornfield, Jack, and Gil Fronsdal, editors. *Teachings of the Buddha*. Shambhala, 2012. For reference: Master Your Senses (pg. 44), Nirvana (pg. 45-46), Master Yourself (pg. 47), The Refinement of Mind (pg. 48-51), The Heart (pg. 70), The Abandoning of Sorrow (pg. 71-76), Abandoning All Hindrances (pg. 80-81), Patience (pg. 96), Criticism and Praise (pg. 97), On Conflict and Concord (pg. 98-99), Admonishing Others (pg. 100), Conceit of Views (pg. 101), Treasure (pg. 107), Tending the Sick (pg. 110-111), Free From All Opinions (pg. 116-117), A Lamp Unto Yourselves (pg. 122), Living in the World (pg. 123), The Eye of Wisdom (pg. 132), Heart Sutra (pg. 133), Fleeting World (pg. 144), Verses On The Faith Mind (pg. 143 - 149), The Natural Abiding (pg. 159), Enlightenment Has No Form (pg. 160 - 162)
31. "Limitless Tara, Beyond the Green: Buddha, Bodhisattva, Savior, Mother of All the Buddhas, Hindu Maa Tara, Goddess of Many Colors, Consort of Buddhas, Wisdom Mother, Action Hero..." *Buddha Weekly: Buddhist Practices, Mindfulness, Meditation*, 26 Dec. 2017, buddhaweekly.com/limitless-tara-beyond-green-buddha-bodhisattva-savior-mother-buddhas-hindu-maa-tara-goddess-many-colors-consort-buddhas-wisdom-mother-action-hero/.
32. Lotto, Beau. *Deviate: the Science of Seeing Differently*. Hachette Books, 2017. For reference: Chapter 5: The Frog Who Dreamed of Being a Prince (1356 - 1670).
33. Madhukar, Abhishek. "Sixty Years after Fleeing Tibet, Refugees in India Get Passports,..." *Reuters*, Thomson Reuters, 22 June 2017, www.reuters.com/article/us-india-refugees-tibet/sixty-years-after-fleeing-tibet-refugees-in-india-get-passports-not-property-idUSKBN19D019.
34. "Mahayana Buddhism and Tradition | Buddha Blog." *Celebrated in Different Buddhist Countries*, www.burmese-art.com/blog/mahayana-buddhism.
35. Müller F. Max. *The Way of the Buddha: the Illustrated Dhammapada*. Abrams, 2008.
36. Nietzsche, Friedrich Wilhelm. *On the genealogy of morals: a polemical tract*. Translated by Ian Johnston, PDF, Richer Resources Publications, 2014.
37. Nietzsche, Friedrich Wilhelm. *THE ANTICHRIST*. Translated by H. L. Mencken, The Project Gutenberg, 2006. For reference: Aphorisms 20, 21, 22, and 23.
38. Nietzsche, Friedrich Wilhelm. *Thus spake Zarathustra: a book for all and none*. Translated by Thomas Common, PDF ed., T. Common, 1908. For reference: Zarathustra's Prologue (23-24), Chapter IX: Preachers of Death (50-52), Chapter XXXIV: Self-Surpassing (108-111). and Chapter XXXVII: Immaculate Perception (116-119).
39. "Nichiren Facts." *YourDictionary*, biography.yourdictionary.com/nichiren.
40. Pararajasingham, Ana. "Why Is Sri Lanka Defying the United Nations?" *The Diplomat*, The Diplomat, 22 Dec. 2017, thediplomat.com/2017/12/why-is-sri-lanka-defying-the-united-nations/.
41. Phillips, Kevin P. *American Theocracy: the Peril and Politics of Radical Religion, Oil, and Borrowed Money in the 21st Century*. Penguin Books, 2007.
42. "Popular Deities of Chinese Buddhism." *Http://Www.buddhanet.net/*, Buddha Dharma Education Association Inc., www.buddhanet.net/pdf_file/ancientsgrfx.pdf.
43. "Q&A: China and the Tibetans." *BBC News*, BBC, 15 Aug. 2011, www.bbc.com/news/world-asia-

pacific-14533879.
44. Reese, Hannah. "Intrusive Thoughts: Normal or Not?" Psychology Today, Sussex Publishers, www.psychologytoday.com/us/blog/am-i-normal/201110/intrusive-thoughts-normal-or-not.
45. "Religions - Buddhism: Nichiren Buddhism." *BBC*, BBC, 13 July 2005, www.bbc.co.uk/religion/religions/buddhism/subdivisions/nichiren_1.shtml.
46. "Religions - Buddhism: Pure Land Buddhism." *BBC*, BBC, 2 Oct. 2002, www.bbc.co.uk/religion/religions/buddhism/subdivisions/pureland_1.shtml.
47. "Religions - Buddhism: Tibetan Buddhism." *BBC*, BBC, 14 Jan. 2004, www.bbc.co.uk/religion/religions/buddhism/subdivisions/tibetan_1.shtml.
48. "Religions - Buddhism: Zen Buddhism." *BBC*, BBC, 2 Oct. 2002, www.bbc.co.uk/religion/religions/buddhism/subdivisions/zen_1.shtml.
49. Son, Bo Kyung. "WHKMLA : The History of Persecution of the Buddhist Faith." *WHKMLA : Nihilism in Russia*, www.zum.de/whkmla/sp/1112/sbk/sbk2.html#iii23.
50. "The Bodhisattva Avalokiteshvara." *Khan Academy*, Khan Academy, www.khanacademy.org/humanities/art-asia/himalayas/tibet/a/the-bodhisattva-avalokiteshvara.
51. "The Buddhist Deity Simhavaktra Dakini." *Khan Academy*, Khan Academy, www.khanacademy.org/humanities/art-asia/himalayas/tibet/v/simhavaktra-dakini.
52. "The Buddhist Schools: Theravada and Mahayana." *Do Buddhist Believe in God?*, www.buddhanet.net/e-learning/buddhistworld/schools1.htm.
53. Russel, Bertrand. "The Buddha and Nietzsche." *YouTube*, Psychosophy, 14 July 2012, www.youtube.com/watch?v=B6WPFH4KPCc.
54. "The Eightfold Path." *ZEN BUDDHISM | What Is Zen? What Is Buddhism?*, Www.zen-Buddhism.net, www.zen-buddhism.net/buddhist-principles/eightfold-path.html.
55. "Three Jewels." *The Buddhist Centre*, thebuddhistcentre.com/text/three-jewels.
56. Weldon, John. "Nichiren Shoshu Buddhism." *Christian Research Institute*, www.equip.org/article/nichiren-shoshu-buddhism/.
57. Wolf, Hannelore, and Francis Story. "Maha-Parinibbana Sutta: Last Days of the Buddha." *Maha-Parinibbana Sutta: Last Days of the Buddha*, www.accesstoinsight.org/tipitaka/dn/dn.16.1-6.vaji.html#fn-11.
58. "Women in Tibetan Buddhism." *Shambhala*, 29 Mar. 2017, www.shambhala.com/snowlion_articles/women-in-tibetan-buddhism/.
59. www.zen-Buddhism.net. "Beliefs & Dogmas." *Buddhist Beliefs | ZEN BUDDHISM*, www.zen-buddhism.net/beliefs/beliefs-and-dogmas.html.
60. www.zen-buddhism.net. "How to Practice Meditation?" *ZEN BUDDHISM | What Is Zen? What Is Buddhism?*, www.zen-buddhism.net/practice/zen-meditation.html.
61. www.zen-Buddhism.net. "Mushin." *Mushin | ZEN BUDDHISM*, www.zen-buddhism.net/zen-concepts/mushin.html.
62. www.zen-Buddhism.net. "Satori or Buddhist Enlightenment." *Satori or Buddhist Enlightenment | ZEN BUDDHISM*, www.zen-buddhism.net/zen-concepts/satori.html.
63. www.zen-buddhism.net. "The Three Jewels." *ZEN BUDDHISM | What Is Zen? What Is Buddhism?*, www.zen-buddhism.net/buddhist-principles/three-jewels.html.
64. www.zen-buddhism.net. "What Is Karma?" *ZEN BUDDHISM | What Is Zen? What Is Buddhism?*, www.zen-buddhism.net/beliefs/karma.html.
65. www.zen-buddhism.net. "What Is Samsara or Rebirth?" *ZEN BUDDHISM | What Is Zen? What Is Buddhism?*, www.zen-buddhism.net/beliefs/samsara.html.
66. www.zen-buddhism.net. "What Is Zen?" *ZEN BUDDHISM | What Is Zen? What Is Buddhism?*, www.zen-buddhism.net/.
67. www.zen-buddhism.net. "Zanshin." *ZEN BUDDHISM | What Is Zen? What Is Buddhism?*, www.zen-buddhism.net/zen-concepts/zanshin.html.

Chapter 27

1. "About NewsGram." *NewsGram*, www.newsgram.com/about-newsgram/.
2. Ahmed, Zubair. "Kashmiri Hindus: Driven out and Insignificant." *BBC News*, BBC, 6 Apr. 2016, www.bbc.com/news/world-asia-india-35923237.
3. "Archeology of the Hebrew Bible." *PBS*, Public Broadcasting Service, 18 Nov. 2008,

www.pbs.org/wgbh/nova/ancient/archeology-hebrew-bible.html.
4. Davis, Mike. *Late Victorian Holocausts: El Nino Famines and the Making of the Third World*. Penguin Random House Publisher Services , 2001.
5. de Souza, Teotónio Rosário. "The Goa Inquisition." *Goa Inquisition*, vgweb.org/unethicalconversion/GoaInquisition.htm.
6. Durant, Will. *Our Oriental Heritage: Being a History of Civilization in Egypt and the Near East to the Death of Alexander, and in India, China and Japan from the Beginning to Our Own Day*. Simon and Schuster, 1935. For reference: XIV: The Foundations of India: VII. The Philosophy of the Upanishads (9463 - 9469) and Chapter XVI: From Alexander to Aurangzeb (10072 - 10817).
7. "Gerald J. Larson." *Gerald J. Larson - Department of Religious Studies*, indiana.edu/~relstud/people/profiles/larson_gerald.
8. Ghose, Sanujit. "Cultural Links between India & the Greco-Roman World." *Ancient History Encyclopedia*, Ancient History Encyclopedia, 30 Apr. 2019, www.ancient.eu/article/208/cultural-links-between-india--the-greco-roman-worl/.
9. Ghosh, Tanushree. "I'm a Target Because I'm an Outsider: Sanskrit Scholar Sheldon Pollock." *The Indian Express*, 4 June 2018, indianexpress.com/article/express-sunday-eye/im-a-target-because-im-an-outsider-sanskrit-scholar-sheldon-pollock-5191995/.
10. Haider, Sarah, and Gad Saad. "Islam's ERASURE of Distinct Cultures & Histories - Sarah Haider (with Gad Saad)." *YouTube*, Gravitahn, 15 Feb. 2017, www.youtube.com/watch?v=XrvVqi5dOxk.
11. Haider, Sarah, et al. "Islam, Modesty and Feminism." *YouTube*, Ex-Muslims of North America, 12 Oct. 2017, www.youtube.com/watch?v=QToH2x8njJM.
12. "Hindush." *Wikipedia*, Wikimedia Foundation, 24 Mar. 2019, en.wikipedia.org/wiki/Hindush.
13. Kapstein, Matthew T., et al. *The Oxford Handbook of Indian Philosophy*. Edited by Jonardon Ganeri, Oxford University Press, 2018. For reference: Contributors (IX - XVII), Introduction: Why Indian Philosophy? Why now? by Jordan Ganeri (1-14), Chapter 1: Interpreting Indian Philosophy Three Parables by Matthew Kapstein (15-31), Chapter 2: History and Doxography of the Philosophical Schools by Ashok Aklujkar (32-55), Chapter 3: Philosophy as a Distinct Cultural Practice: The Transregional Context by Justin E.H. Smith (56-74), Chapter 4: Comparison or Confluence in Philosophy? by Mark Sideritis (75-92).
14. Larson, Gerald James. "Classical Sāṃkhya: An Interpretation of Its History and Meaning." *Google Books*, books.google.com/books?id=Ih2aGLp4d1gC&pg=PR7&source=gbs_selected_pages&cad=3#v=onepage&q&f=false.
15. Larson, Gerald James. "India's Agony Over Religion (SUNY Series in Religious Studies)." *Amazon*, Amazon, 16 Feb. 1995, www.amazon.com/Indias-Agony-Religion-Religious-Studies/dp/079142412X.
16. Nelson, Dean. "European Roma Descended from Indian 'Untouchables', Genetic Study Shows." *The Telegraph*, Telegraph Media Group, 3 Dec. 2012, www.telegraph.co.uk/news/worldnews/europe/9719058/European-Roma-descended-from-Indian-untouchables-genetic-study-shows.html.
17. Nicholson, Andrew J. *Unifying Hinduism: Philosophy and Identity in Indian Intellectual History (South Asia Across the Disciplines)*. Columbia University Press, 2010. For reference: Chapter 1: Introduction (181-715) and Chapter 10: Hindu Unity And The Non-Hindu Other (4806-5293).
18. Nicholson, Andrew J., et al. "Andrew Nicholson on 'Anti-Theistic Arguments in Sāṃkhya and Vedānta Philosophy." *YouTube*, 2 Apr. 2018, youtu.be/myjdOsKu8iY?t=2890. For reference: Timestamp of 48:10 - 48:23. Nicholson, Pollock, and Raghunathan show no understanding of Analytical Philosophy's Burden of Proof.
19. Nietzsche, Friedrich Wilhelm. Aphorism 23. *THE ANTICHRIST*. Translated by H. L. Mencken, The Project Gutenberg, 2006.
20. Pollock, Sheldon. "Is There an Indian Intellectual History? Introduction to ''Theory and Method in Indian Intellectual History.''" *Http://Www.columbia.edu*, Columbia University, www.columbia.edu/cu/mesaas/faculty/directory/pollock_pub/indian_intellectual_history.pdf.
21. Ramakrishnan, Ganesh. "Removal of Sheldon Pollock as Mentor and Chief Editor of Murty Classical Library." *Change.org*, www.change.org/p/mr-n-r-narayana-murthy-and-mr-rohan-narayan-murty-removal-of-prof-sheldon-pollock-as-mentor-and-chief-editor-of-murty-classical-library.
22. Shams, Imtiaz, et al. "Fighting Allah, Defending Muslims - Armin Navabi, Imtiaz Shams, Muhammad Syed." *YouTube*, Ex-Muslims of North America, 5 Jan. 2018,

www.youtube.com/watch?v=KwnHreJNavE. For reference: Timestamp 55:17 - 1:00:58. Imtiaz Shams explains that the Pact of Umar is an apartheid document and its relevance in Islamic dominated civilizations. He, Armin Navabi, and Muhammad Syed then discuss contemporary Ex-Muslim human rights issues.
23. Sridhar, Nithin. "No Evidence for Warfare or Invasion; Aryan Migration Too Is a Myth: B B Lal." *NewsGram*, 30 Nov. 2015, www.newsgram.com/no-evidence-for-warfare-or-invasion-aryan-migration-too-is-a-myth-b-b-lal.
24. Sridhar, Nithin. "Vedic and Harappan Are Respectively Literary and Material Facets of Same Civilization: B. B. Lal." *NewsGram*, 2 Dec. 2015, www.newsgram.com/vedic-and-harappan-are-respectively-literary-and-material-facets-of-same-civilization-b-b-lal.
25. Talageri, Shrikant, et al. "Panel Discussion on the Current State of Aryan Theories." Moderated by Rajiv Malhotra, *YouTube*, Swadeshi Indology, 24 Mar. 2018, www.youtube.com/watch?v=KmeVR8sqSd4.
26. Tessier, Stephanie, and Muhammad Syed. "Islam: Pull and Peril." *YouTube*, Ex-Muslims of North America, 22 Apr. 2018, www.youtube.com/watch?v=jt1rWgap41g.
27. VISHNOI, ANUBHUTI. "Read & Annotate without Distractions." *Outline*, The Economic Times, outline.com/8eLEVN.
28. Wani, Riyaz. "How Al-Qaeda Came to Kashmir." *The Diplomat*, The Diplomat, 20 Dec. 2017, thediplomat.com/2017/12/how-al-qaeda-came-to-kashmir/.
29. Weiss, Gary. "India's Jews." *Forbes*, Forbes Magazine, 17 July 2012, www.forbes.com/2007/08/05/india-jews-antisemitism-oped-cx_gw_0813jews.html#4d526e5f3d45.

Chapter 28

1. Agarwal, Arti. "Shiva Agamas | Arti Agarwal | Who Is Shiva | Paramahamsa Nithyananda Disciple." *YouTube*, SrijanTalks, 19 Nov. 2018, www.youtube.com/watch?v=-GUgBvBMuOw.
2. "Age of the Mother of the Believers 'Aa'ishah (May Allah Be Pleased with Her) When the Prophet (Blessings and Peace of Allah Be upon Him) Married Her - Islam Question & Answer." *Islamqa.info*, Islam Question and Answer, 30 Dec. 2013, islamqa.info/en/answers/124483/age-of-the-mother-of-the-believers-aaishah-may-allah-be-pleased-with-her-when-the-prophet-blessings-and-peace-of-allah-be-upon-him-married-her.
3. Ambedkar, Bhimrao Ramji. *Essays on Untouchables and Untouchability*. Kindle ed., Amazon Digital Services LLC, 2017.
4. Anamika. "'The Scholarship of the Daughter Is Regarding Domestic Affairs Only, for She Is Not Entitled to Read the Vedas."~Adi Shankara, That Renowned 9th Century Indian Sage of Advaita Vedanta, in His Bhāṣya on the Ancient Upanishads (Sacred Shruti Literature)." *Twitter*, Twitter, 3 Apr. 2018, twitter.com/AnaMyID/status/981146807433510914.
5. Andrews, Robin. "We Finally Know Why People Are Left- Or Right-Handed." *IFLScience*, IFLScience, 23 Jan. 2019, www.iflscience.com/brain/finally-know-people-left-righthanded/.
6. Banerjee, Abhishek. "10 Things Ambedkar Said That Indian Secularists Wouldn't Bear to Hear - Opindia News." *OpIndia*, 12 Nov. 2018, www.opindia.com/2018/04/10-things-ambedkar-said-that-indian-secularists-wouldnt-bear-to-hear/.
7. Bawra, Brahmrishi Vishvatma, translator. *Sāmkhya Kārikā With Gaudapādācarya Bhāsya*. Brahmrishi Yoga Publications, 2012.
8. "Bhagavadgita: 1. The Yoga of Arjuna's Sorrow." Translated by Jayaram V, *Bhagavadgita: The Yoga of Arjuna's Sorrow*, www.hinduwebsite.com/gita1.asp.
9. Brown, Cheever Mackenzie, translator. *The Song of the Goddess the Devī Gītā: Spiritual Counsel of the Great Goddess*. State University of New York Press, 2002.
10. Burke, Michael. "$100M In Saudi Money Lands in US Accounts as Pompeo Landed in Riyadh: Report." *TheHill*, 17 Oct. 2018, thehill.com/policy/international/411802-100m-in-saudi-money-lands-in-us-accounts-as-pompeo-landed-in-riyadh.
11. "Chaupar." *Wikipedia*, Wikimedia Foundation, 7 July 2019, en.wikipedia.org/wiki/Chaupar.
12. Cialdini, Robert B. *Influence: Science and practice*. 4th ed., 21st Century Bks, 2002. Chapter 1: Weapons of Influence (1-16), Chapter 2: Reciprocation (19-50), and Chapter 4: Social Proof (98-140).
13. Dash, Jatindra. "Indian Maoists Kill Hindus over Christian Conversions." *Reuters*, Thomson Reuters, 24 Aug. 2008, www.reuters.com/article/us-india-religion/indian-maoists-kill-hindus-over-christian-conversions-idUSBOM35357220080824.

14. Davis, Mike. *Late Victorian Holocausts: El Nino Famines and the Making of the Third World*. Penguin Random House Publisher Services, 2001.
15. DeSilver, Drew. "5 Facts about Indian Americans." *Pew Research Center*, Pew Research Center, 30 Sept. 2014, www.pewresearch.org/fact-tank/2014/09/30/5-facts-about-indian-americans/.
16. Downie, Jonathan M, et al. "A Genome-Wide Search for Greek and Jewish Admixture in the Kashmiri Population." *PloS One*, Public Library of Science, 4 Aug. 2016, www.ncbi.nlm.nih.gov/pmc/articles/PMC4973929/.
17. "Dr.Narendra Dabholkar – A Tribute." *Nirmukta*, 23 Aug. 2013, nirmukta.com/2013/08/22/dr-narendra-dabholkar-a-tribute/.
18. Duckworth, Angela. *Grit: the Power of Passion and Perseverance*. Scribner, 2016.
19. Durant, Will. *Our Oriental Heritage: Being a History of Civilization in Egypt and the Near East to the Death of Alexander, and in India, China and Japan from the Beginning to Our Own Day*. Simon and Schuster, 1935. For reference: Chronological Table Of Indian History (8872-9109), Chapter XIV: The Foundations of India (9113 - 9577), Chapter XV: The Buddha (9581 - 10035), Chapter XVI: From Alexander to Aurangzeb (10072 - 10817), and Chapter XVII The Life of People. (10818-11427).
20. Eknath, Easwaran, translator. *The Upanishads*. Nilgiri Press, 2007.
21. Eknath, Easwaran, translator. *The Bhagavad Gita*. Nilgiri Press, 2007.
22. Elst, Koenraad. "Gautam Buddha Was Every Inch a Hindu - Koenraad Elst." *YouTube*, Upword, 24 Feb. 2019, www.youtube.com/watch?v=i9TEslTqc-s.
23. Floyd, Daniel. "Snakes and Ladders - How the Meaning of an Ancient Children's Game Adapted Over Time - Extra Credits." *YouTube*, Extra Credits, 24 Dec. 2014, www.youtube.com/watch?v=PzLYKY1nPsY.
24. "Free Expression in Practice." *Big Think*, Charles Koch Foundation, 1 Dec. 2018, bigthink.com/Charles-Koch-Foundation/forced-examination-how-the-free-speech-of-others-benefits-us-all?rebelltitem=2#rebelltitem2.
25. Ganguli, Kisari Mohan, translator. *Mahabharata of Krishna-Dwaipayana Vyasa, Volume 4 Books 13, 14, 15, 16, 17 and 18*. Vol. 4, Project Gutenberg.
26. Ghose, Sanujit. "Cultural Links between India & the Greco-Roman World." *Ancient History Encyclopedia*, Ancient History Encyclopedia, 30 Apr. 2019, www.ancient.eu/article/208/cultural-links-between-india--the-greco-roman-worl/.
27. Green, Hank. "Compatibilism: Crash Course Philosophy #25." *YouTube*, Crash Course / PBS Digital Studios, 22 Aug. 2016, www.youtube.com/watch?v=KETTtiprINU.
28. Gupta, Alka. "Female Foeticide in India." *UNICEF*, unicef.in/PressReleases/227/Female-foeticide-in-India.
29. "Gyan Chauper." *Wikipedia*, Wikimedia Foundation, 1 Aug. 2018, en.wikipedia.org/wiki/Gyan_chauper.
30. Harris, Sam. "Sam Harris on 'Free Will.'" *YouTube*, Skeptic, 27 Mar. 2012, www.youtube.com/watch?v=pCofmZlC72g.
31. Harris, Sam. *Free Will*. Free Press, 2012.
32. "Hindu Boy's Family Forced out of Village for Marrying Muslim Girl, Police Advices Boy to Convert as Villagers Threaten to Kill - Opindia News." *OpIndia*, 19 July 2019, www.opindia.com/2019/07/hindu-boys-family-forced-out-of-village-for-marrying-muslim-girl-police-advices-boy-to-convert-as-villagers-threaten-to-kill/.
33. "History." *Transindia Film*, www.transindiafilm.co.uk/?page_id=16.
34. Hitchens, Christopher, and Shashi Tharoor. "Christopher Hitchens vs. Shashi Tharoor FREEDOM OF SPEECH." *YouTube*, ChristopherHitchslap, 30 Dec. 2011, www.youtube.com/watch?v=jw3dDbc1BHE. For reference: The 2007 debate between Hitchens and Tharoor.
35. Huntington, Samuel P. *The Clash of Civilizations and the Remarking of World Order*. Simon and Schuster, 2003.
36. "Inconsistency." *Https://Www.logicallyfallacious.com*, www.logicallyfallacious.com/tools/lp/Bo/LogicalFallacies/112/Inconsistency.
37. "India 2017/2018." *Amnesty International*, www.amnesty.org/en/countries/asia-and-the-pacific/india/report-india/.
38. "Indians: Data on Asian Americans." *Pew Research Center's Social & Demographic Trends Project*, Pew Research Center's Social & Demographic Trends Project, 8 Sept. 2017, www.pewsocialtrends.org/fact-sheet/asian-americans-indians-in-the-u-s/.

39. Ispas, Alexa. *Psychology and politics: a social identity perspective*. Psychology Press, 2014.
40. Korea(Jolie), Vakko. "Ravensburger Pachisi - by Vakko Korea(Jolie)." *YouTube*, 라벤스부르거바코, 13 Aug. 2011, www.youtube.com/watch?v=2w8-pZlNdrY.
41. "Leela (Game)." *Wikipedia*, Wikimedia Foundation, 19 Dec. 2017, en.wikipedia.org/wiki/Leela_(game).
42. Malhotra, Rajiv. *Being Different: an Indian Challenge to Western Universalism*. HarperCollins Publishers India, 2018. For Reference: Purva Paksha: Reversing The Gaze (835-929).
43. Malik, Nesrine. "The Bizarre Spat with Canada Shows Mohammed Bin Salman's True Colours | Nesrine Malik." *The Guardian*, Guardian News and Media, 12 Aug. 2018, www.theguardian.com/commentisfree/2018/aug/12/saudi-arabia-spat-canada-mohammed-bin-salman-true-colours.
44. Masci, David. "How Income Varies among U.S. Religious Groups." *Pew Research Center*, Pew Research Center, 11 Oct. 2016, www.pewresearch.org/fact-tank/2016/10/11/how-income-varies-among-u-s-religious-groups/.
45. Massoglia, Anna. "Saudi Foreign Agents' Political Donations Top $1.6 Million in 2018 Elections." *OpenSecrets News*, Center for Responsive Politics, 24 Oct. 2018, www.opensecrets.org/news/2018/10/saudi-foreign-agents-donations-top-1point6-mill/.
46. Meadows, Andre. "Ancient Games: Crash Course Games #2." *YouTube*, CrashCourse, 8 Apr. 2016, www.youtube.com/watch?v=H1lv3cOmlzM.
47. "Millions of Female Foetuses Aborted in India." *The Telegraph*, Telegraph Media Group, 24 May 2011, www.telegraph.co.uk/news/worldnews/asia/india/8532190/Millions-of-female-foetuses-aborted-in-India.html.
48. Mohamed, Besheer, and Elizabeth Podrebarac Sciupac. "Islam Gains about as Many Converts as It Loses in U.S." *Pew Research Center*, Pew Research Center, 26 Jan. 2018, www.pewresearch.org/fact-tank/2018/01/26/the-share-of-americans-who-leave-islam-is-offset-by-those-who-become-muslim/.
49. Murphy, Caryle. "The Most and Least Educated U.S. Religious Groups." *Pew Research Center*, Pew Research Center, 4 Nov. 2016, www.pewresearch.org/fact-tank/2016/11/04/the-most-and-least-educated-u-s-religious-groups/.
50. "Narendra Dabholkar." *Wikipedia*, Wikimedia Foundation, 20 July 2019, en.wikipedia.org/wiki/Narendra_Dabholkar.
51. Navabi, Armin. "Muslim Defends Muhammad Having Sex with Aisha When She Was Nine!" *YouTube*, Atheist Republic, 3 Jan. 2019, youtu.be/yKExtzI68jM.
52. Nicholson, Andrew J., translator. *Lord Siva's Song: The Isvara Gita*. State Univ Of New York Pr, 2015.
53. Nietzsche, Friedrich Wilhelm. *On the genealogy of morals: a polemical tract*. Translated by Ian Johnston, PDF, Richer Resources Publications, 2014.
54. Nikhilananda, Swami, translator. *English Tanslation of Brihadaranyaka Upanishad*. PDF ed., Www.ishwar.com, Www.ishwar.com. .
55. "Pachisi." *Wikipedia*, Wikimedia Foundation, 15 June 2019, en.wikipedia.org/wiki/Pachisi.
56. Pandey, Sanjay. "Female Foeticide, India's 'Ticking Bomb'." *Asia | Al Jazeera*, Al Jazeera, 6 July 2015, www.aljazeera.com/indepth/features/2015/06/female-foeticide-india-ticking-bomb-150629090758927.html.
57. Phadke, Anant. "The Murder of Dr Narendra Dabholkar: a Fascist Attack on Rationalism: Indian Journal of Medical Ethics." *The Murder of Dr Narendra Dabholkar: a Fascist Attack on Rationalism | Indian Journal of Medical Ethics*, ijme.in/articles/the-murder-of-dr-narendra-dabholkar-a-fascist-attack-on-rationalism/?galley=html.
58. Pink, Daniel H. *Drive: the Surprising Truth about What Motivates Us*. Canongate Books, 2018.
59. "Qisas." *Wikipedia*, Wikimedia Foundation, 9 Sept. 2018, en.wikipedia.org/wiki/Qisas.
60. "QuranX.com The Most Complete Quran / Hadith / Tafsir Collection Available!" *Muwatta Malik Hadiths*, quranx.com/Hadith/Malik/USC-MSA/Book-49/Hadith-6/.
61. Rose, Gideon. "What Happened to the American Century?" *Foreign Affairs*, 30 July 2019, www.foreignaffairs.com/articles/2019-06-11/what-happened-american-century.
62. Shamasastry, Rudrapatna, translator. *Kautilya's ARTHASHASTRA*. PDF ed., Bangalore: Government Press, 1915. For reference: CHAPTER III. THE DUTY OF A WIFE; MAINTENANCE OF A WOMAN;CRUELTY TO WOMEN; ENMITY BETWEEN HUSBAND AND WIFE; A WIFE's TRANSGRESSION; HER KINDNESS TO ANOTHER; AND FORBIDDEN TRANSACTIONS. WOMEN, when twelve years old, attain their majority (práptavyavahára) and men when sixteen years

old. If after attaining their majority, they prove disobedient to lawful authority (asusrúsháyám), women shall be fined 15 panas and men, twice the amount.

63. Sharma, Ashok. "Dozens of New Indian Parliamentarians Face Criminal Charges." *AP NEWS*, Associated Press, 17 June 2019, www.apnews.com/1678c2a6c0004b799a34cb0ff9434a90.
64. Singh, Lilly. "Will You Help Me End Violence?" *YouTube*, IISuperwomanII, 23 May 2018, www.youtube.com/watch?v=3y-jH6XuVt8.
65. "Snakes and Ladders." *Wikipedia*, Wikimedia Foundation, 23 July 2019, en.wikipedia.org/wiki/Snakes_and_Ladders.
66. Sokolove, Michael. "Why Is There So Much Saudi Money in American Universities?" *The New York Times*, The New York Times, 3 July 2019, www.nytimes.com/2019/07/03/magazine/saudi-arabia-american-universities.html.
67. Sorabjee, Soli J. "Insult to Religion - Indian Express." *Archive*, archive.indianexpress.com/news/insult-to-religion-/7214/.
68. Srivastava, Roli. "India Police Find 19 Fetuses Dumped in Plastic Bags, Suspect Female..." *Reuters*, Thomson Reuters, 6 Mar. 2017, www.reuters.com/article/us-india-abortion-foeticide/india-police-find-19-fetuses-dumped-in-plastic-bags-suspect-female-feticide-racket-idUSKBN16D1NF.
69. "Study: US Is an Oligarchy, Not a Democracy." *BBC News*, BBC, 17 Apr. 2014, www.bbc.com/news/blogs-echochambers-27074746.
70. "The Reason Why the Right Hand Is Preferred over the Left - Islam Question & Answer." *Islamqa.info*, Islam Question and Answer, 2 Mar. 2007, islamqa.info/en/answers/82120/the-reason-why-the-right-hand-is-preferred-over-the-left.
71. Wintour, Patrick. "Saudis Demanded Good Publicity over Yemen Aid, Leaked UN Document Shows." *The Guardian*, Guardian News and Media, 30 Oct. 2018, www.theguardian.com/global-development/2018/oct/30/saudis-demanded-good-publicity-over-yemen-aid-leaked-un-document-shows?CMP=share_btn_tw.
72. "Śramaṇa." *Wikipedia*, Wikimedia Foundation, 18 July 2019, en.wikipedia.org/wiki/Śramaṇa.

Chapter 29

1. Abruzzi, William S. "THE BIRTH OF JESUS: The Evolution of the Jesus in the Infancy Narratives." *Doc A's Webpage: On the Importance of Writing Research Papers*, Dr. William S. Abruzzi, 2015, www.drabruzzi.com/birth_of_jesus.htm.
2. "Atheism in Hinduism." *Atheism*, atheism.wikia.org/wiki/Atheism_in_Hinduism#.5Bedit.5DArguments_against_God.
3. "Atheism in Hinduism." *Wikipedia*, Wikimedia Foundation, 26 July 2019, en.wikipedia.org/wiki/Atheism_in_Hinduism#Arguments_against_existence_of_God_in_Hindu_philosophy.
4. Bawra, Brahmrishi Vishvatma, translator. *Sāmkhya Kārikā With Gaudapādācarya Bhāsya*. Brahmrishi Yoga Publications, 2012. For reference: Samkhya Aphorisms: VI, VIII, XI, XIII and Karika Aphorisms: XXXV, XXXVII, LXI, LXII, LXIV, LXV, LXVI, and LXVII.
5. Bundy, Trey. "Jehovah's Witnesses Sued in Canada over History of Sex Abuse Cover-Up." *Reveal*, 30 Jan. 2018, www.revealnews.org/blog/jehovahs-witnesses-sued-in-canda-for-history-of-sex-abuse-cover-up/?utm_source=Reveal&utm_medium=social_media&utm_campaign=facebook.
6. "Carvaka." *Carvaka*, Humanistictexts.org, www.humanistictexts.org/carvaka.htm#9 Spontaneity in Nature.
7. "Carvaka." *Carvaka*, Humanistictexts.org, www.humanistictexts.org/carvaka.htm.
8. "Christian Science." *Wikipedia*, Wikimedia Foundation, 1 Aug. 2019, en.wikipedia.org/wiki/Christian_Science.
9. Csikszentmihalyi, Mihaly. *Flow: the Psychology of Optimal Experience*. 1st ed., Harper Perennial, 2008.
10. Downen, Robert, et al. "20 Years, 700 Victims: Southern Baptist Sexual Abuse Spreads as Leaders Resist Reforms." *Houston Chronicle*, Houston Chronicle, 6 June 2019, www.houstonchronicle.com/news/investigations/article/Southern-Baptist-sexual-abuse-spreads-as-leaders-13588038.php.
11. Durant, Will. *Our Oriental Heritage: Being a History of Civilization in Egypt and the Near East to the Death of Alexander, and in India, China and Japan from the Beginning to Our Own Day*. Simon and Schuster, 1935. For reference: The Foundations of India: VII. The Philosophy of the Upanishads (9463 -

9469) and Chapter XVII The Life of People. (10818-11427).
12. Eknath, Easwaran, translator. *The Bhagavad Gita*. Nilgiri Press, 2007.
13. Eknath, Easwaran, translator. *The Upanishads*. Nilgiri Press, 2007.
14. "Going Deep and Wide with Max Strom." *Yogamatters Blog*, Yogamatters, 26 Feb. 2018, www.yogamatters.com/blog/going-deep-with-max-strom/. For reference: "Sanskrit is a dead language that is only spoken in one tiny corner of the world. It's like Latin. And yet we expect people to be OK with attending a movement class that includes words from this language and some allusions to Hindu spirituality. And some people are really put off by this. I think the Vinyasa Flow yoga world is not serving the majority of people any more." - Max Strom
15. Green, Hank. "India: Crash Course History of Science #4." *YouTube*, CrashCourse, 25 Apr. 2018, www.youtube.com/watch?v=bDQkpNbsly4.
16. Harris, Annaka. *Conscious: a Brief Guide to the Fundamental Mystery of the Mind*. Harper, an Imprint of HarperCollinsPublishers, 2019.
17. "India Creates Database of 1,500 Yoga Poses to Thwart Western Patent Claims." *RT International*, www.rt.com/news/312015-india-yoga-asanas-patent/.
18. "Indomania." *Wikipedia*, Wikimedia Foundation, 13 June 2019, en.wikipedia.org/wiki/Indomania#18th_and_19th_centuries.
19. "Jon Kabat-Zinn." *Wikipedia*, Wikimedia Foundation, 22 July 2019, en.wikipedia.org/wiki/Jon_Kabat-Zinn.
20. Kapstein, Matthew T., et al. Chapter 31: Hindu Disproofs of God: Refuting Vedantic Theism in the Samkhya-Sutra by Andrew J. Nicholson (598-619). *The Oxford Handbook of Indian Philosophy*. Edited by Jonardon Ganeri, Oxford University Press, 2018.
21. Khutoryansky, Eugene. "Quantum Mechanics: Animation Explaining Quantum Physics." *YouTube*, Physics Videos by Eugene Khutoryansky, 23 Mar. 2013, www.youtube.com/watch?v=iVpXrbZ4bnU.
22. "Liberal Catholic Church." *Wikipedia*, Wikimedia Foundation, 12 June 2019, en.wikipedia.org/wiki/Liberal_Catholic_Church.
23. "Maitreya." *IPS-Eye-White*, www.inplainsite.org/html/maitreya.html#BCM1.
24. "Maitreya in the Light of Real Theosophy." *T H E O S O P H Y*, 15 Apr. 2019, blavatskytheosophy.com/maitreya-in-the-light-of-real-theosophy/.
25. "Max Strom Is a Teacher, Speaker, Author, and Creator of Inner Axis." *Max Strom*, maxstrom.com/about/.
26. Modi, Narendra. "Nadishodhana / Anuloma Viloma Pranayama." *YouTube*, YouTube, 17 June 2015, www.youtube.com/watch?v=AV_WDQ740Yk.
27. Nersessian, David. "Rethinking Cultural Genocide Under International Law." *Carnegie Council for Ethics in International Affairs*, www.carnegiecouncil.org/publications/archive/dialogue/2_12/section_1/5139.
28. Nicholson, Andrew J., et al. "Andrew Nicholson on 'Anti-Theistic Arguments in Sāṃkhya and Vedānta Philosophy." *YouTube*, 2 Apr. 2018, youtu.be/myjdOsKu8iY.
29. Nietzsche, Friedrich. *Nietzsche Complete Works – World's Best Ultimate Collection - 20 Books – Incl. Zarathustra, Gay Science, Morals, Beyond Good And Evil, Birth Of Tragedy, Ecce Homo Plus Biography & Bonuses*. Translated by Anthony Ludovici, Kindle ed., Amazon Digital Services LLC, 2010.
30. Nietzsche, Friedrich. *Twilight of the Idols*. Amazon Digital Services LLC
31. Nietzsche, Friedrich Wilhelm. *Beyond Good and Evil*. Translated by Helen Zimmern, Word ed., Gutenberg Press, 2009.
32. Nietzsche, Friedrich Wilhelm. *THE ANTICHRIST*. Translated by H. L. Mencken, The Project Gutenberg, 2006.
33. Nietzsche, Friedrich. *The Dawn of Day*. Translated by J. M. Kennedy, Dover Publications, 2012.
34. Nietzsche, Friedrich Wilhelm. *Thus spake Zarathustra: a book for all and none*. Translated by Thomas Common, PDF ed., T. Common, 1908.
35. "Original Theosophy and Later Versions." *T H E O S O P H Y*, 15 Apr. 2019, blavatskytheosophy.com/original-theosophy-and-later-versions/.
36. "Ouija." *Wikipedia*, Wikimedia Foundation, 18 July 2019, en.wikipedia.org/wiki/Ouija.
37. Park, Madison. "Timeline: A Look at the Catholic Church's Sex Abuse Scandals." *CNN*, Cable News Network, 29 June 2017, www.cnn.com/2017/06/29/world/timeline-catholic-church-sexual-abuse-scandals/index.html.

38. Saini, Anu. "Physicians of Ancient India." *Journal of Family Medicine and Primary Care*, Medknow Publications & Media Pvt Ltd, 2016, www.ncbi.nlm.nih.gov/pmc/articles/PMC5084543/.
39. Schneider, Susan. "Is Panpsychism Accurate? Modern Physics Delivers a Reality Check. | Dr. Susan Schneider." *YouTube*, Big Think, 28 July 2019, www.youtube.com/watch?v=qv1MIj0m9fY.
40. Sen, Amartya. *The Argumentative Indian: Writings on Indian History, Culture and Identity*. Macmillan , 2005.
41. Seppälä, Emma. "Interview on Emma's Research of Yoga-Breathing for Veterans with PTSD." *YouTube*, YouTube, 2 Dec. 2014, www.youtube.com/watch?v=c6_k1QfPYq4.
42. Seppälä, Emma. "Breathing Happiness | Emma Seppälä | TEDxSacramento." *YouTube*, TEDx Talks, 14 Apr. 2016, www.youtube.com/watch?v=Uvli7NBUfY4.
43. Seppälä, Emma. "Stressed? Use This Breathing Technique to Improve Your Attention and Memory, with Emma Seppälä." *YouTube*, Big Think, 19 May 2016, www.youtube.com/watch?v=NrJZu6bGyHg.
44. Sharma, Gaurav. "How Scientists like Niels Bohr, Schrodinger, Nikola Tesla and Albert Einstein Found the True Meaning of Physics in Vedas." *NewsGram*, 12 May 2015, www.newsgram.com/how-scientists-niels-bohr-schrodinger-nikola-tesla-albert-einstein-true-meaning-physics-vedas.
45. "Theosophy (Blavatskian)." *Wikipedia*, Wikimedia Foundation, 4 Aug. 2019, en.wikipedia.org/wiki/Theosophy_(Blavatskian)#Influence_on_other_religious_and_esoteric_groups.
46. "Why Do Pranayama?" *Kripalu*, 15 July 2019, kripalu.org/resources/why-do-pranayama.
47. Wilson, Jeff. "Mindful America: The Mutual Transformation of Buddhist Meditation and American Culture - Kindle Edition by Jeff Wilson. Religion & Spirituality Kindle EBooks @ Amazon.com." *Amazon*, Amazon, smile.amazon.com/Mindful-America-Transformation-Buddhist-Meditation-ebook/dp/B00LNE8Q6C/ref=tmm_kin_swatch_0?_encoding=UTF8&qid=&sr=.
48. Zope, Sameer A, and Rakesh A Zope. "Sudarshan Kriya Yoga: Breathing for Health." *International Journal of Yoga*, Medknow Publications & Media Pvt Ltd, Jan. 2013, www.ncbi.nlm.nih.gov/pmc/articles/PMC3573542/.

Chapter 30

1. Bear, Charla. "American Indian Boarding Schools Haunt Many." *NPR*. NPR, 12 May 2008. Web. 2 Nov. 2015, https://www.npr.org/templates/story/story.php?storyId=16516865?storyId=16516865.
2. Brady, Jeff. "2 Years After Standing Rock Protests, Tensions Remain But Oil Business Booms." *NPR*, NPR, 29 Nov. 2018, www.npr.org/2018/11/29/671701019/2-years-after-standing-rock-protests-north-dakota-oil-business-is-booming.
3. Bundy, Trey. "Jehovah's Witnesses Use 1st Amendment to Hide Child Sex Abuse Claims." *Reveal*, 29 Nov. 2018, www.revealnews.org/article/jehovahs-witnesses-use-1st-amendment-to-hide-child-sex-abuse-claims/.
4. "Chicago Tax Day Tea Party - What CNN Did Not Show You Behind The Scenes - Reporter Owned 4/16/09." *YouTube*, Mark ResourceU, 16 Apr. 2009, www.youtube.com/watch?v=y6xWGvdRQ9Q.
5. Craig, William Lane. "The Revolution in Anglo-American Philosophy | Reasonable Faith." *Philosophic Revolution | Popular Writings | Reasonable Faith*, www.reasonablefaith.org/writings/popular-writings/apologetics/the-revolution-in-anglo-american-philosophy/.
6. Dawkins, Richard, and Rana Ahmad. "Richard Dawkins Interviews Saudi Arabian Atheist Author Rana Ahmad." *YouTube*, Richard Dawkins Foundation for Reason & Science, 25 Feb. 2019, www.youtube.com/watch?v=_zncB6hngZg.
7. De Dora, Michael. "Secular Rescue - Saving Freedom. Saving Lives." *YouTube*, Richard Dawkins Foundation for Reason & Science, 30 Sept. 2016, www.youtube.com/watch?v=xM_JCxogySM.
8. Downen, Robert, et al. "20 Years, 700 Victims: Southern Baptist Sexual Abuse Spreads as Leaders Resist Reforms." *Houston Chronicle*, Houston Chronicle, 6 June 2019, www.houstonchronicle.com/news/investigations/article/Southern-Baptist-sexual-abuse-spreads-as-leaders-13588038.php.
9. Duke, Annie. *Thinking in Bets: Making Smarter Decisions When You Don't Have All the Facts*. Penguin Group (USA), 2018.
10. "First Amendment." *American Atheists*, www.atheists.org/legal/faq/first-amendment/.
11. Galef, Julia, and Sarah Haider. "Rationally Speaking | Official Podcast of New York City Skeptics - Current Episodes - RS 227 - Sarah Haider on 'Dissent and Free Speech.'" *Rationally Speaking Podcast*, New York City Skeptics, rationallyspeakingpodcast.org/show/rs-227-sarah-haider-on-dissent-and-free-

speech.html.
12. Ghazzali, Kacem El. "Reading 'The God Delusion' In The Arab World." *HuffPost Canada*, HuffPost Canada, 10 May 2017, www.huffingtonpost.ca/kacem-el-ghazzali/the-god-delusion_b_9867606.html.
13. "H.R.1150 - 114th Congress (2015-2016): Frank R. Wolf International Religious Freedom Act." *Congress.gov*, 16 Dec. 2016, www.congress.gov/bill/114th-congress/house-bill/1150.
14. Harris, Sam. "Sam Harris Aspen Ideas Festival Full Unedited Video." *YouTube*, Aspen Institute, 25 Nov. 2012, www.youtube.com/watch?v=hfgwFESH_jM.
15. Hashem, Rumana. "Has Rape Become a Weapon to Silence Atheists in Bangladesh?" *OpenDemocracy*, www.opendemocracy.net/en/5050/rape-weapon-silence-atheists-bangladesh/.
16. Hatting, Sam. "Sam Hatting: 'Shin Megami Tensei III: Nocturne and Nietzsche's Übermensch.'" 女神転生・学, A Megami Tensei Study Guide, 5 Apr. 2013, megatengaku.wordpress.com/essays/sam-hatting-shin-megami-tensei-iii-nocturne-and-nietzsches-ubermensch/.
17. Hitchens, Christopher. "Christopher Hitchens Delivers Yet Another Masterpiece." *YouTube*, Religion, Atheism, Science, 16 Mar. 2011, www.youtube.com/watch?v=YiU5u6zAtyc.
18. Hitchens, Christopher. "Does a Good God Exist? A Debate Between Hitchens and Dembski (November 2010)." *YouTube*, ReasonPublic / Biblical Worldview Institute, 19 Apr. 2012, www.youtube.com/watch?v=ctuloBOYolE.
19. Hitchens, Christopher. *God Is Not Great: How Religion Poisons Everything*. Hachette Book Group, 2007.
20. "Islam Gains about as Many Converts as It Loses in U.S." *Pew Research Center*, www.pewresearch.org/fact-tank/2018/01/26/the-share-of-americans-who-leave-islam-is-offset-by-those-who-become-muslim/.
21. Johnson, Alex. "With Obama's Signature, U.S. Religious Freedom Law Now Protects Atheists." *NBCNews.com*, NBCUniversal News Group, www.nbcnews.com/news/us-news/obama-s-signature-u-s-religious-freedom-law-protects-atheists-n699356.
22. Kahneman, Daniel. *Thinking, fast and slow*. Farrar, Straus and Giroux, 2015. For reference purposes: Chapter 19: The Illusion of Understanding (199-208) and Chapter 20: The Illusion of Validity (209-221).
23. Kliff, Sarah. "A Pharmacist Says He Has Filled Alzheimer's Prescriptions for Members of Congress." *Vox*, Vox, 11 Oct. 2017, www.vox.com/policy-and-politics/2017/10/11/16458142/congress-alzheimers-pharmacist.
24. Konnikova, Maria. *The Confidence Game: the Psychology of the Con and Why We Fall for It Every Time*. Canongate, 2017.
25. "MAZE OF INJUSTICE ." *Amnesty International USA*, Amnesty International, www.amnestyusa.org/pdfs/mazeofinjustice.pdf.
26. "Murder of Farkhunda Malikzada." *Wikipedia*, Wikimedia Foundation, 11 June 2019, en.wikipedia.org/wiki/Murder_of_Farkhunda_Malikzada.
27. Navabi, Armin. "Attacking Islam as an Act of Compassion - Armin Navabi." *YouTube*, Ex-Muslims of North America, 4 Dec. 2017, www.youtube.com/watch?v=9m7IaAlnkgo.
28. Navabi, Armin. "Doubt as an Alternative to Reform - Armin Navabi." *YouTube*, Ex-Muslims of North America, 5 Dec. 2017, www.youtube.com/watch?v=Zk70fXQgZwY.
29. Nietzsche, Friedrich Wilhelm. "The Joyful Wisdom, by Friedrich Nietzsche." Translated by Thomas Common, *The Joyful Wisdom, by Friedrich Nietzsche : BOOK FOURTH*, ebooks.adelaide.edu.au/n/nietzsche/friedrich/n67j/book4.html.
30. Nietzsche, Friedrich Wilhelm. *Beyond Good and Evil*. Translated by Helen Zimmern, Word ed., Gutenberg Press, 2009.
31. Nietzsche, Friedrich Wilhelm. *THE ANTICHRIST*. Translated by H. L. Mencken, The Project Gutenberg, 2006. For reference: Aphorism 54.
32. Nietzsche, Friedrich Wilhelm. *Thus spake Zarathustra: a book for all and none*. Translated by Thomas Common, PDF ed., T. Common, 1908.
33. Obama, Barack. "Remarks by the President to the UN General Assembly." *National Archives and Records Administration*, National Archives and Records Administration, obamawhitehouse.archives.gov/the-press-office/2012/09/25/remarks-president-un-general-assembly.
34. Oppenheimer, Mark. "Will Misogyny Bring Down The Atheist Movement?" *BuzzFeed*, BuzzFeed, 12 Sept. 2014, www.buzzfeed.com/markoppenheimer/will-misogyny-bring-down-the-atheist-movement?utm_term=.gd2E4jVYd#.cbZ23Vp9A.

35. "Pakistani Hindus Complain of Forced Conversion of Teenage Girls." *YouTube*, VOA News, 18 Mar. 2016, youtu.be/-i24jg4mJ4I.
36. Park, Madison. "Timeline: A Look at the Catholic Church's Sex Abuse Scandals." *CNN*, Cable News Network, 29 June 2017, www.cnn.com/2017/06/29/world/timeline-catholic-church-sexual-abuse-scandals/index.html.
37. Q, Shannon. "To Debate or Not to Debate? Can You Be a Responsible Platformer: w TellTale." *YouTube*, YouTube, 15 Mar. 2019, www.youtube.com/watch?v=31jFFOmMaZs.
38. Restuccia, Andrew. "Greens: Climate March Breaks Record." *POLITICO*, 22 Sept. 2014, www.politico.com/story/2014/09/peoples-climate-march-nyc-111177.
39. Rumelt, Richard. *Good Strategy, Bad Strategy: the Difference and Why It Matters*. Random House LLC, 2017.
40. Rutecki, Gregory W. "Forced Sterilization of Native Americans: Late Twentieth Century." *The Center for Bioethics & Human Dignity*, 8 Oct. 2010, cbhd.org/content/forced-sterilization-native-americans-late-twentieth-century-physician-cooperation-national-.
41. Sanders, Sam. "Massive Data Breach Puts 4 Million Federal Employees' Records At Risk." *NPR*, NPR, 4 June 2015, www.npr.org/sections/thetwo-way/2015/06/04/412086068/massive-data-breach-puts-4-million-federal-employees-records-at-risk.
42. "Standing Rock Sioux and Dakota Access Pipeline | Teacher Resource." *Standing Rock Sioux and Dakota Access Pipeline | Teacher Resource*, americanindian.si.edu/nk360/plains-treaties/dapl.
43. "Static.reuters.com." *Reuters*, Reuters, static.reuters.com/resources/media/editorial/20150910/WilksDoctrinalPoints.pdf.
44. Sultan, Harris. "Rescue an Atheist in Pakistan, Spartacus." *YouTube*, YouTube, 12 Nov. 2018, www.youtube.com/watch?v=y154jQsEkQk.
45. "The Intolerance of Nerdfighteria: How Discussing Human Rights Gets You Muted And Banned." *Jarin Jove's Blog*, 2 Mar. 2019, jarinjove.com/2019/02/27/intolerance-of-nerdfighteria/.
46. Tun, Zaw Thiha. "How Petrodollars Affect The U.S. Dollar." *Investopedia*, Investopedia, 12 Mar. 2019, www.investopedia.com/articles/forex/072915/how-petrodollars-affect-us-dollar.asp.
47. "U.S. Religious Knowledge Survey." *Pew Research Center's Religion & Public Life Project*, Pew Research Center's Religion & Public Life Project, 19 Dec. 2017, www.pewforum.org/2010/09/28/u-s-religious-knowledge-survey/.
48. Williams, Timothy. "Native Americans Struggle With High Rate of Rape." *The New York Times*, The New York Times, 22 May 2012, www.nytimes.com/2012/05/23/us/native-americans-struggle-with-high-rate-of-rape.html?_r=0.
49. Wolf, Naomi. "Revealed: How the FBI Coordinated the Crackdown on Occupy | Naomi Wolf." *The Guardian*, Guardian News and Media, 29 Dec. 2012, www.theguardian.com/commentisfree/2012/dec/29/fbi-coordinated-crackdown-occupy.
50. Worley, Will. "Obama Just Signed a Law Protecting Atheists from Religious Persecution." *The Independent*, Independent Digital News and Media, 22 Dec. 2016, www.independent.co.uk/news/world/americas/atheists-legal-protection-us-religious-freedom-bill-signed-barack-obama-a7489641.html.
51. Zengerle, Patricia. "Millions More Americans Hit by Government Personnel Data Hack." *Reuters*, Thomson Reuters, 9 July 2015, www.reuters.com/article/us-cybersecurity-usa-millions-more-americans-hit-by-government-personnel-data-hack-idUSKCN0PJ2M420150709.

Further Reading:

Psychology:
Politics and Identity: A Social Identity Perspective by Alexa Ispas
Thinking Fast and Slow by Daniel Kahneman
Deviate by Beau Lotto
Stumbling on Happiness by Daniel Gilbert
Influence: Science and Practice by Robert Cialdini
The Confidence Game by Maria Konnikova
Mindset by Carol S. Dweck
Succeed by Heidi Grant Halvorson

Social Science:
Maze of Injustice by Amnesty International
Factfulness by Hans Rosling
The Argumentative Indian by Amartya Sen
Late Victorian Holocausts by Mike Davis
Purifying the Land of the Pure by Farahnaz Ispahani
A Problem from Hell by Samantha Power
The Graves Are Walking by John Kelly
The Famine Plot by Tim Pat Coogen
Anatomy of Human Destructiveness by Erich Fromm
Godless Americana by Sikivu Hutchinson
God is not Great by Christopher Hitchens
War is a Force That Gives Us Meaning by Chris Hedges

Religious Studies:
Letter to a Christian Nation by Sam Harris
Why There Is No God by Armin Navabi
Ebony Exodus Project by Candace R. M. Gorham

Philosophy:
On the Genealogy of Morals by Friedrich Nietzsche and translated by Ian Johnston
The Anti-Christ by Friedrich Nietzsche (Any translation that **isn't** Kaufman or Hollingdale)
Thus Spake Zarathustra by Friedrich Nietzsche and translated by Thomas Common
Thinking in Bets by Annie Duke
Rationality: From AI to Zombies by Eliezer Yudkowsky
Harry Potter and the Methods of Rationality by Eliezer Yudkowsky, a Fanfic at *HPMOR.com* that is **free** to read.

Sexual Self-Care:
Sex Plus: Learning, Loving, and Enjoying Your Body by Laci Green (For women who want to read more on having a healthy, safe sex life and to bust misogynistic myths about women's bodies).

Further Watching:
On Youtube:

On Improving Ourselves Through Rationality:
Julia Galef: Straw Vulcan video and Her Personal Channel

Secular Sex Ed:
Laci Green: A Naked Notion and Her Personal Channel
Sexplanations

Cultural Progress and History:
Vlogbrothers: Crash Course and their Personal Channel
Secular Jihadists by Ali Rizvi and Armin Navabi
Gatesnotes by Bill Gates

Exploring Various Religious Perspectives:
Ideas Unboxed by Armin Navabi

Atheist versus Theist Debates:
Christopher Hitchens and Sam Harris in Religion versus Atheism Debates.

General Atheist Criticisms Against Religion:
Rationality Rules, Genetically Modified Skeptic, CosmicSkeptic, Rachel Oates, Atheist Republic by Armin Navabi, and Shannon Q

Ex-Muslim Perspectives on Religion:
Ex-Muslims of North America; particularly the panel on Feminism.
Zara Kay and Fay, The Most Gracious
Mimzy Vidz; particularly "*Why I Left Islam*", "*ISIS & Islamic Radicalisation*", and "*I Changed My Mind On Islamic Reform*" videos
Veedu Vidz; particularly the "*Why Islam Will Never Be Better Than The West*" video and "*Mind of Veedu*" Interviews

Hindu Perspective on Hinduism, Atheism, and Indian Politics:
Carvaka Podcast by Kushal Mehra

BJP Political Perspective on Indian Politics:
The Sham Sharma Show (*Some discussions exclusively in Hindi and require subtitles for non-Hindi speakers*)

On Film:
Islam and the Future of Tolerance by Maajid Nawaz

Further Gaming:
Shin Megami Tensei IV
Shin Megami Tensei IV: Apocalypse / Shin Megami Tensei IV: Final

Author's Influences:

Demonstrable scientific evidence, JK Rowling, Alexa Ispas, Beau Lotto, Daniel Gilbert, Robert Cialdini, Laci Green, Vlogbrothers Hank and John Green, Ex-Muslims of North America, Mike Davis, Chris Hedges, Sam Harris, Christopher Hitchens, Julia Galef, Daniel Kahneman and Amos Tversky, Heidi Grant Halvorson, Melinda and Bill Gates and the Gates Foundation's selfless work and Gatesnotes, Hans Rosling, Glenn Greenwald and the Intercept, Shin Megami Tensei, Tales of the Abyss, Tales of Berseria, Erich Fromm, Amnesty International, Rollo May, Brihadaranyaka Upanishads (Except the disgusting Chapter 6), Chandogya Upanishads, Samkhya Philosophical thought, Bhagavad Gita chapters on selflessness and acceptance of all, and Friedrich Nietzsche.

About the Author

Jarin Jove is the pseudonym of Niraj Choudhary in his ill-conceived attempt at being clever by making a nickname based upon switching his first name and using the shortest name of his favorite planet in the solar system. He holds a Bachelors of Science in Political Science from the New York Institute of Technology (2012) and a Masters of Arts in Political Science from Long Island University (2016). His intersecting interests of understanding the psychology of politics, the influence of New Atheism in criticizing the human rights abuses of religion, his avid love of reading psychology books and Friedrich Nietzsche's main works, and especially, Julia Galef's activism in support of a more rational world is what inspired him to write this book in the hopes of making a small contribution to a much greater and global conversation. He is an ardent capitalist, but doesn't believe capitalism can fill the void of government services or social safety nets and is concerned about governments maintaining any legitimacy if such programs are entirely eroded.

He has a personal blog: **www.jarinjove.com**. He can be reached via email at **jovejarin@hotmail.com** and on Twitter via the handle **@NocturneDream**.

He uses another pseudonym, Jason D. Visaria, to write fantasy novels and is the author of a dark humor book called *Ku Cuck Klan: The Family Values* written in order to exercise his Free Speech rights to mock Neo-Nazis and White Nationalists.

Copyright Notice:

Copyright Niraj Choudhary, 2019. All Rights Reserved.

www.ingramcontent.com/pod-product-compliance
Lightning Source LLC
Chambersburg PA
CBHW060241240426
43673CB00048B/1934